ADVANCED MATHEMATICS

A PURE COURSE

Martin and Patricia Perkins

ADVANCED MATHEMATICS

A PURE COURSE

Martin and Patricia Perkins

Unwin Hyman

Published in 1987 by Unwin Hyman Ltd
15–17 Broadwick Street
London W1V 1FP

© Martin and Patricia Perkins 1987
First published in 1987 by Unwin Hyman Ltd
Reprinted 1988

British Library Cataloguing in Publication Data

Perkins, Martin
  Advanced mathematics: a pure course.
  1. Mathematics — 1961–
  I. Title II. Perkins, Patricia
  510   QA37.2

ISBN 0713528214

Printed in Great Britain
by Anchor Brendon Ltd

Published in 1987 by Unwin Hyman Ltd
15–17 Broadwick Street
London W1V 1FP

© Martin and Patricia Perkins 1987
First published in 1987 by Unwin Hyman Ltd
Reprinted 1990

British Library Cataloguing in Publication Data

Perkins, Martin
    Advanced mathematics: a pure course.
    1. Mathematics——1961–
    I. Title II. Perkins, Patricia
    510   QA39.2

ISBN 0 7135 2821 4

Printed in Hong Kong
by Astros Printing Ltd.

Contents

Preface

This is one of two books designed to cover most Advanced Level single subject Mathematics syllabuses. The present volume provides a complete pure course. Both books should also be suitable for subsidiary level mathematics courses of various kinds. Students in schools and colleges embarking on advanced work come from a variety of backgrounds. We have therefore tried to introduce each new topic gradually to cater for those to whom it is unfamiliar.

We believe that the split between 'modern' and 'traditional' mathematics has been damaging and consider that the subject should be seen as a whole: we have attempted in this book to use what we see as the best in these two approaches to create a coherent forward-looking course. SI units are used throughout and we assume that students will have access to an adequate 'scientific' calculator.

Topics are presented in a logical sequence, but the text is arranged in short chapters to allow individual students or teachers to vary the order of study. The chapters are divided into numbered sections each followed by an exercise. The early questions in these exercises are intended to provide plenty of routine practice in newly acquired skills, whereas the aim of later questions is to develop a greater understanding of the ideas involved. There is a selection of further questions in the miscellaneous exercise at the end of each chapter.

We are most grateful for permission to use questions from past G.C.E. Advanced Level examinations. These are acknowledged as follows:

University of London University Entrance and Schools Examination Council (L)
The Associated Examining Board (AEB)
Joint Matriculation Board (JMB)
University of Cambridge Local Examinations Syndicate (C)
Oxford and Cambridge Schools Examination Board (O & C)
Oxford Delegacy of Local Examinations (O)
Southern Universities Joint Board (SU)
Welsh Joint Education Committee (W)

Our thanks are also due to the staff of Messrs. Bell and Hyman, especially Peter Kaner and Anne Forsyth for their helpful criticism, and to many friends and colleagues for their encouragement and patience.

M.L.P.

P.P.

List of symbols

s.f.	significant figures
d.p.	decimal places
$\approx$	is approximately equal to
$\equiv$	is identically equal to
$<$	is less than
$\leqslant$	is less than or equal to
$>$	is greater than
$\geqslant$	is greater than or equal to
$\Rightarrow$	implies
$\Leftrightarrow$	is equivalent to
$\in$	is an element of
:	such that
$\subseteq$	is a subset of
$\subset$	is a proper subset of
$\varnothing$	empty set
$\mathscr{E}$	universal set
A'	complement of set A
$n(A)$	number of elements in the set A
$A \times B$	Cartesian product of sets A and B
$\mathbb{N}$	set of natural numbers $\{0,1,2,3,\ldots\}$
$\mathbb{Z}$	set of integers
$\mathbb{Z}^+$	set of positive integers
$\mathbb{Q}$	set of rational numbers
$\mathbb{R}$	set of real numbers
$\mathbb{R}^2$	set of ordered pairs of real numbers (x, y)
$\cup$	union
$\cap$	intersection
$f : x \rightarrow y$	the function f maps x to y
$f(x)$	image of x under f
f^{-1}	inverse of function f
gf	function f followed by function g

$[a, b]$	the closed interval $\{x \in \mathbb{R} : a \leqslant x \leqslant b\}$
(a, b)	the open interval $\{x \in \mathbb{R} : a < x < b\}$
$\displaystyle\lim_{x \to a} f(x)$	limit of $f(x)$ as x tends to a
∞	infinity
δ	small increment
$f'(x)$ or $\dfrac{dy}{dx}$	first derivative of $y = f(x)$
$f''(x)$ or $\dfrac{d^2y}{dx^2}$	second derivative of $y = f(x)$
$\displaystyle\int f(x)\,dx$	indefinite integral
$\displaystyle\int_a^b f(x)\,dx$	definite integral
$\left[f(x) \right]_a^b$	$f(b) - f(a)$
$\sqrt{x}$	non-negative square root of x
$|x|$	modulus (or magnitude) of x
$[x]$	integral part of x
e^x, $\exp x$	exponential function of x
$\log_a x$	logarithm to the base a of x
$\ln x$	the natural logarithm of x, $\log_e x$
$\lg x$	the common logarithm of x, $\log_{10} x$
$\sin^{-1}$	inverse function of sin with range $[-\tfrac{1}{2}\pi, \tfrac{1}{2}\pi]$
$\cos^{-1}$	inverse function of cos with range $[0, \pi]$
$\tan^{-1}$	inverse function of tan with range $(-\tfrac{1}{2}\pi, \tfrac{1}{2}\pi)$
$n!$	n factorial
$_nP_r$	number of permutations of r objects chosen from n
$_nC_r$	number of combinations of r objects chosen from n
u_n	nth term of a sequence or series
S_n	sum to n terms of a series
$\displaystyle\sum_{r=1}^{n} f(r)$	$f(1) + f(2) + \ldots + f(n)$
$\dbinom{n}{r}$	the binomial coefficient: $_nC_r = \dfrac{n!}{r!(n-r)!}$ for $n \in \mathbb{Z}^+$, $\dfrac{n(n-1)\ldots(n-r+1)}{r!}$ for $n \in \mathbb{Q}$
$\mathbf{PQ}$	vector represented by line segment $\overrightarrow{PQ}$
$|\mathbf{PQ}|$ or PQ	magnitude of vector $\mathbf{PQ}$

$|\mathbf{a}|$, a	magnitude of vector $\mathbf{a}$
$\hat{\mathbf{a}}$	unit vector in the direction of $\mathbf{a}$
$\mathbf{i}, \mathbf{j}, \mathbf{k}$	unit vectors in the directions of the x-, y- and z-axes
$\mathbf{a} . \mathbf{b}$	scalar product of $\mathbf{a}$ and $\mathbf{b}$
i	square root of -1
z	complex number, $z = x + iy = r(\cos\theta + i\sin\theta)$
$\mathrm{Re}(z)$	real part of z, $\mathrm{Re}(z) = x = r\cos\theta$
$\mathrm{Im}(z)$	imaginary part of z, $\mathrm{Im}(z) = y = r\sin\theta$
z^*	complex conjugate of z, $z^* = x - iy$
$|z|$	modulus of z, $|z| = \sqrt{(x^2 + y^2)} = r$
$\arg z$	principal argument of z, $\arg z = \theta$, where $\sin\theta = x/r$, $\cos\theta = y/r$ and $-\pi < \theta \leqslant \pi$
$\mathbb{C}$	set of complex numbers

The use of the symbols $=$ and $\approx$

In numerical work it is important to distinguish between exact values and approximate values. When giving exact answers we use the symbol $=$. For approximate results we use either the symbol $=$ (together with an appropriate phrase, such as 'by calculator', 'to 3 s.f.'), or the symbol $\approx$. The use of the symbol $\approx$ may show that a result has been obtained by an approximate method, but often indicates that a more accurate result obtained by calculator has been rounded to the given number of significant figures (or, in the case of angles, to the nearest tenth of a degree).

1 Real numbers and their properties

1.1 The language of sets

A *set* is a collection of objects. These objects are the *elements* of the set. A set may be defined either by listing the elements or by describing their properties, e.g. $A = \{2, 4, 7\}$, B is the set of all triangles, $C = \{\ldots, -5, -3, -1, 1, 3, \ldots\}$ or {odd integers}. Using the colon : to mean 'such that', we may also write $P = \{p : p$ is a prime number}, which is read 'P is the set of all elements p such that p is a prime number'. Whatever form is chosen it must always be possible to decide from the definition whether or not an object belongs to the set.

The statement $x \in S$ means 'x is an element of S' or 'x belongs to S'. Similarly $x \notin S$ means 'x is not an element of the set S'. Thus, for the sets defined above, $2 \in A$ but $2 \notin C$ and $9 \in C$ but $9 \notin P$.

Two sets are *equal* if they contain exactly the same elements, e.g. $\{16, 25, 36, 49, 64, 81\} = \{36, 81, 16, 25, 64, 49\} = $ {two digit squares}. The way in which the elements are listed or described is not important.

Sometimes all the elements of one set are contained in another. If every element of a set A also belongs to a set B, then A is a *subset* of B, written $A \subseteq B$. If A is a subset of B and there is at least one element of B which is not an element of A, then A is a *proper subset* of B and we write $A \subset B$. For instance, if $X = \{a, c\}, Y = \{a, c, e\}$ and $Z = \{a, b, c, d\}$, then $X \subset Y$ and $X \subset Z$ but $Y \not\subset Z$. We may also write $Y \supset X$ and $Z \supset X$ using the symbol $\supset$ to mean 'contains as a proper subset'.

Three important properties of the set inclusion relation follow from the definition.
(1) Any set A is a subset of itself, i.e. $A \subseteq A$.
(2) $A \subseteq B$ and $B \subseteq C \Rightarrow A \subseteq C$.
(3) $A \subseteq B$ and $B \subseteq A \Leftrightarrow A = B$.

[Note that if p and q represent statements, then $p \Rightarrow q$ means 'if p then q' or 'p implies q'. The symbol $\Leftarrow$ means 'is implied by'. We write $p \Leftrightarrow q$ meaning 'p implies and is implied by q' when the statements p and q are equivalent.]

1

All the objects under consideration in any mathematical discussion form a set called the *universal set* (or *universe of discourse*), often denoted by $\mathscr{E}$. For instance, in a geometrical problem the universal set may be a set of points, a set of lines or a set of plane figures. Once a universal set $\mathscr{E}$ has been defined any other set considered must be one of its subsets. Thus for any set A, $A \subseteq \mathscr{E}$.

The set with no elements is called the *null* or *empty set*, written $\varnothing$ or sometimes $\{\ \}$. The empty set $\varnothing$ is considered to be a subset of any set A, i.e. $\varnothing \subseteq A$.

The *complement* of a set A is the set containing all the elements of $\mathscr{E}$ which are not elements of A and is written A'. For instance, if $\mathscr{E} = \{1,2,3,4,5\}$ and $A = \{1,3,5\}$ then $A' = \{2,4\}$. It follows from the definition that for any set A, $(A')' = A$. We also find that $\varnothing' = \mathscr{E}$ and $\mathscr{E}' = \varnothing$.

Consider now two sets X and Y. If $x \in X$ and $y \in Y$, then (x,y) is called an *ordered pair*. Although the set $\{3,4\}$ is equal to the set $\{4,3\}$, the ordered pairs $(3,4)$ and $(4,3)$ are not the same. The set of all ordered pairs (x,y) where $x \in X$ and $y \in Y$ is called the *product set* or *Cartesian product* of X and Y, written $X \times Y$. For example, if $X = \{1,2,3\}$ and $Y = \{4,5\}$,

then $\quad X \times Y = \{(1,4),(1,5),(2,4),(2,5),(3,4),(3,5)\}$
and $\quad Y \times X = \{(4,1),(5,1),(4,2),(5,2),(4,3),(5,3)\}$.

This example demonstrates the fact that in general $X \times Y \neq Y \times X$.

Exercise 1.1

1. State whether the following statements are true or false:
    (a) $4 \in \{\text{even integers}\}$ (b) $\{a\} \in \{a,b,c\}$
    (c) $51 \notin \{\text{prime numbers}\}$ (d) $\varnothing \subset \{3,7,11,12\}$
    (e) $\{x,y\} = \{\{x\},\{y\}\}$ (f) $0 \subset \{0,1,2\}$
    (g) $\{p : p \text{ is prime and } p \neq 2\} \subset \{x : x \text{ is an odd integer}\}$
    (h) $\{n : n \text{ is divisible by 2, 3 and 4}\} = \{k : k \text{ is a multiple of 24}\}$.

2. Use the symbols $=$ and $\subset$ to write down any relationships between the following:
    $A = \{1,2,0\}, \quad B = \{2,1\}, \quad C = \{0,1,2\}, \quad D = \{2,3\}, \quad E = \{3\}.$

3. Use the symbols $=$, $\subset$ and $\in$ to write down any relationships between the following:
    $\varnothing, \quad X = \{0\}, \quad Y = \{0,1\}, \quad 0, \quad P = \{\{0\}\}, \quad Q = \{\varnothing\}.$

4. In each of the following cases state the connection between the statements p and q by writing $p \Leftrightarrow q$, $p \Rightarrow q$ or $p \nRightarrow q$.
    (a) $p : x \in A$ and $A \subset B$, $q : x \in B$
    (b) $p : 1 \in X$ and $2 \in X$, $q : \{1,2\} \subseteq X$
    (c) $p : a = x$ and $b = y$, $q : \{a,b\} = \{x,y\}$
    (d) $p : x \notin A$ and $x \in B$, $q : A$ is a proper subset of B.

5. Write down the connection between the sets X and Z if
    (a) $W \subset Y$, $X \subset W$ and $Y \subset Z$,   (b) $X \subseteq Y$, $Y \subseteq Z$ and $Z \subseteq X$.

6.   Find the sets A, B, C and D which are distinct subsets of the set $\{1,2,3\}$ given that:

$2 \in C$, $3 \notin D$, $A \subset B$, $B \subset C$, $B \subset D$ and $D \not\subset C$.

7.   List the elements of the following product sets, where $A = \{x\}$, $B = \{p,q\}$ and $C = \{f,g,h\}$
(a) $A \times C$,   (b) $A \times B$,   (c) $B \times A$,   (d) $A \times A$.

8.   If $A \times B = \{(1,1), (2,1), (1,2), (3,2), (3,1), (2,2)\}$, list the elements of the sets A and B.

9.   If the universal set $\mathscr{E} = \{0,1,2\}$, write down the complements of the following sets
(a) $\{1\}$,   (b) $\varnothing$,   (c) $\{0,1\}$,   (d) $\{0,1,2\}$.

10.   Discuss the following statements
(a) $x \in A' \Leftrightarrow x \notin A$
(b) $A = \{\text{even integers}\} \Leftrightarrow A' = \{\text{odd integers}\}$
(c) $A \subset B \Leftrightarrow B' \subset A'$
(d) $A \subset B$ and $B' \subset C' \Rightarrow A \not\subset C$.

1.2 Rational and irrational numbers

Most people are familiar with the counting numbers 0,1,2,3,4,... The set $\{0,1,2,3,4,...\}$ containing all such numbers is called the set of *natural numbers* $\mathbb{N}$. Any two natural numbers, a and b, may be added to produce a third, $a+b$. However, the solution of the equation $a+x = b$, where a, $b \in \mathbb{N}$, is a natural number only if $a \leqslant b$, 'a is less than or equal to b'.

To solve the equation $a+x = b$ for all elements a, $b \in \mathbb{N}$, it is necessary to extend the set of natural numbers to create a new set containing all numbers of the form $b-a$. For example, the set must include as elements $3-8$, i.e. -5, and $4-6$, i.e. -2. All such numbers form the set of *integers*, $\mathbb{Z} = \{..., -2, -1,0,1,2,...\}$. Clearly the set $\mathbb{N}$ is a subset of $\mathbb{Z}$ and we may write $\mathbb{N} \subset \mathbb{Z}$. The set of *positive integers* $\{1,2,3,4,...\}$ is denoted by $\mathbb{Z}^+$. Since the set $\mathbb{N}$ contains all non-negative integers including zero, $\mathbb{Z}^+ \subset \mathbb{N}$, i.e. $\mathbb{Z}^+$ is a proper subset of $\mathbb{N}$.

The addition, subtraction or multiplication of two integers always produces another integer. However, to solve all equations of the type $bx = a$, where a, $b \in \mathbb{Z}$ and $b \neq 0$, a further extension of the number system is needed. The enlarged set must include elements such as $3/4$, $-7/11$, $10/3$. The set containing all numbers of the form a/b, where a is any integer and b is any non-zero integer, is the set of *rational numbers* $\mathbb{Q}$. Since any integer k can be expressed in the form a/b by writing $a = k$ and $b = 1$, we may write $\mathbb{Z} \subset \mathbb{Q}$.

The natural numbers, $\mathbb{N}$, the integers, $\mathbb{Z}$, and the rationals, $\mathbb{Q}$, are all subsets of the set of *real numbers* $\mathbb{R}$. The real numbers may be represented as the points on a straight line called the *real number line*. As shown in the diagram, the integers are represented by points evenly spaced along the line. Every point on the line represents some real number.

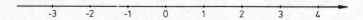

Real numbers which are not rational are called *irrational numbers*. To prove that such numbers exist, we consider $\sqrt{2}$, the positive root of the equation $x^2 = 2$. If $\sqrt{2}$ is rational, then it can be expressed as a fraction in its lowest terms i.e. as a/b, where a and b are integers with no common factor greater than 1.

$$\sqrt{2} = \frac{a}{b} \Rightarrow 2 = \frac{a^2}{b^2} \Rightarrow a^2 = 2b^2 \Rightarrow a^2 \text{ is an even number. Since no odd number has}$$

an even square, a itself must be an even number. If we let $a = 2c$, then $(2c)^2 = 2b^2$ so that $b^2 = 2c^2$. This implies that b is an even number. Thus a and b are both divisible by 2, which contradicts the assumption that a and b have no common factor greater than 1. Hence the assumption that $\sqrt{2}$ is rational must be false. We deduce that $\sqrt{2}$ is an irrational number.

All rational numbers and many irrational numbers, such as $\sqrt{2}$, which are roots of equations of the form $a_0 x^n + a_1 x^{n-1} + \ldots + a_{n-1}x + a_n = 0$, where $a_0, a_1, \ldots, a_n \in \mathbb{Z}$, are known as *algebraic numbers*. Real numbers which are not algebraic are called *transcendental numbers*, the most familiar of these being π.

We now consider the expression of rational and irrational numbers as decimals. A proper fraction a/b is converted into decimal form by the process of long division. Each division by b leaves a remainder, which may be $0, 1, 2, \ldots$, $b-2$ or $b-1$. If at any stage this remainder is zero, then the process is complete and a/b has been expressed as a finite decimal. If at every stage a non-zero remainder is obtained, then there are $(b-1)$ different possible remainders. This means that in the first b divisions at least one remainder, R, must be repeated. After the repetition of R, the sequence of remainders following R must also be repeated. Thus a recurring decimal will be produced. Hence a rational number may be expressed either as a finite decimal or as a recurring decimal.

Conversely every finite decimal represents a rational number, e.g. $0{\cdot}45 = 45/100 = 9/20$. Any recurring decimal may be written in rational form by a method similar to the following:

let	$x = 0{\cdot}\dot{4}\dot{5} = 0{\cdot}454545\ldots$
then	$100x = 45{\cdot}454545\ldots$
subtracting	$99x = 45$
giving	$x = 45/99 = 5/11.$

These results together imply that in decimal form rational numbers are either finite or recurring and irrational numbers are infinite and non-recurring.

Exercise 1.2

1. If $X = \{2, 0, -2, 0{\cdot}\dot{7}, \sqrt[3]{2}, \pi, 7{\cdot}3\}$, write down all the elements of X which are (a) integers, (b) rational, (c) irrational, (d) algebraic, (e) transcendental.

2. Repeat question 1 for $X = \{7, -1, 4/3, \ \pi + 2, 3 \cdot 142, \sqrt{\pi}, \sqrt{3} + 2\}$.

3. List the elements of the set A when (i) $x \in \mathbb{N}$, (ii) $x \in \mathbb{Z}$, (iii) $x \in \mathbb{Q}$, (iv) $x \in \mathbb{R}$, given that
(a) $A = \{x : x^2 - 3x - 4 = 0\}$ (b) $A = \{x : x^2 - 5 = 0\}$
(c) $A = \{x : 2x^2 - 3x + 1 = 0\}$ (d) $A = \{x : x^2 + 5 = 0\}$

4. State which of the following rational numbers may be expressed as a finite decimal. (You need not write the numbers in decimal form.)
$$\frac{1}{2}, \frac{1}{3}, \frac{7}{16}, \frac{4}{9}, \frac{1}{25}, \frac{8}{11}, \frac{1}{625}, \frac{5}{64}, \frac{2}{7}, \frac{4}{45}, \frac{1}{150}, \frac{51}{75}.$$

5. Express the following recurring decimals in rational form:
(a) $0 \cdot \dot{5}$, (b) $0 \cdot 4\dot{9}$, (c) $0 \cdot \dot{2}\dot{7}$, (d) $0 \cdot 0\dot{3}\dot{7}$, (e) $0 \cdot \dot{1}4285\dot{7}$.

1.3 Binary operations on real numbers

A *binary operation*, $*$, is a rule for combining two objects, a and b, to give a third object c, written $c = a * b$. In later chapters it will be shown that binary operations can be performed on objects such as vectors, functions and sets. However, we will consider here only binary operations in which two real numbers are combined to form another real number. The most important of these are addition, subtraction, multiplication and division.

When adding or multiplying two numbers the order in which the numbers are written is not important, e.g. $3 + 5 = 5 + 3$ and $4 \times 6 = 6 \times 4$. For this reason addition and multiplication are said to be *commutative*. However, $8 - 3 \neq 3 - 8$ and $15 \div 5 \neq 5 \div 15$. Thus subtraction and division are not commutative. More formally, the *commutative laws* for addition and multiplication state that

$$a + b = b + a, \quad ab = ba \quad \text{for all} \quad a, b \in \mathbb{R}.$$

We next examine the addition or multiplication of three or more real numbers. The order in which the operations are performed does not affect the result, e.g. $5 + (4 + 3) = (5 + 4) + 3$ and $5 \times (4 \times 3) = (5 \times 4) \times 3$. This property of addition and multiplication is called *associativity*. Subtraction and division are not associative, e.g. $5 - (4 - 3) = 4$ but $(5 - 4) - 3 = -2$; $24 \div (4 \div 2) = 12$ but $(24 \div 4) \div 2 = 3$. In general, the *associative laws* for addition and multiplication state that

$$a + (b + c) = (a + b) + c, \quad a(bc) = (ab)c \quad \text{for all} \quad a, b, c \in \mathbb{R}.$$

Another important property which involves both addition and multiplication is the *distributive law*. This is the rule used when 'removing brackets' or 'factorising' in elementary algebra. It states that

$$a(b+c) = ab+ac \quad \text{for all} \quad a, b, c \in \mathbb{R}.$$

Multiplication is said to be *distributive over addition*.

Within the set of real numbers there are two numbers with special properties, namely 0 and 1. We find that

$$a+0 = 0+a = a, \quad a \times 1 = 1 \times a = a \quad \text{for all} \quad a \in \mathbb{R}.$$

Both addition of 0 and multiplication by 1 leave a real number a unchanged (i.e. identical in value). Hence 0 and 1 are called *identity elements*. The number 0 is the identity for addition and 1 is the identity for multiplication.

This leads to the notion of an *inverse* under a binary operation. If an inverse exists then the combination of an element with its inverse gives the identity element. Thus, since $a+(-a) = (-a)+a = 0$, the inverse of a real number a with respect to addition is $(-a)$. Similarly, since $a \times \dfrac{1}{a} = \dfrac{1}{a} \times a = 1$ (assuming $a \neq 0$), the inverse of any non-zero real number a with respect to multiplication is $1/a$.

In further study of the structure of the real number system, it is often convenient to regard the subtraction of a number a as the addition of $(-a)$ and division by a, where $a \neq 0$, as multiplication by $1/a$.

We now consider the use made of inverses and the properties of binary operations in the solution of a simple equation.

$$
\begin{array}{lll}
& 3(x+2) = 8 & \\
\Rightarrow & 3x+6 = 8 & \text{distributive law} \\
\Rightarrow & \{3x+6\}+(-6) = 8+(-6) & \text{using the inverse of 6 for } + \\
\Rightarrow & 3x+\{6+(-6)\} = 2 & \text{associative law for } + \\
\Rightarrow & 3x+0 = 2 & \\
\Rightarrow & 3x = 2 & \text{property of 0} \\
\Rightarrow & \tfrac{1}{3} \times (3x) = \tfrac{1}{3} \times 2 & \text{using the inverse of 3 for } \times \\
\Rightarrow & (\tfrac{1}{3} \times 3)x = \tfrac{2}{3} & \text{associative law for } \times \\
\Rightarrow & 1 \times x = \tfrac{2}{3} & \\
\Rightarrow & x = \tfrac{2}{3} & \text{property of 1.}
\end{array}
$$

In work with real numbers we usually take their properties for granted. However, the terms introduced here will be useful when comparing the behaviour of real numbers with that of other mathematical objects.

Exercise 1.3

1. Write down the inverses with respect to addition of the real numbers 5, $\frac{1}{4}$, -2, k and $-n$.

2. Write down the inverses with respect to multiplication of the real numbers 2, $-\frac{1}{3}$, -1, $4/5$ and $1/x$.

3.   Given that $x * y = x^y$, where x and y are positive integers, state whether the binary operation $*$ is (a) commutative, (b) associative.

4. Repeat question 3 given that $x * y$ is defined as the highest common factor of x and y.

5.   Repeat question 3 given that $x * y = \frac{1}{2}(x+y)$.

6.   Solve the following equations, stating which properties of real numbers are used.
(a) $3x = 12$ (b) $x - 4 = 5$ (c) $2x + 5 = 9$
(d) $2x = x - 2$ (e) $3(x+2) = x$ (f) $x^2 - 2x = 0$.

1.4 Introduction to inequalities

An inequality is a statement involving one of the symbols $<$ 'is less than', $>$ 'is greater than', $\leqslant$ 'is less than or equal to', $\geqslant$ 'is greater than or equal to'. Inequalities such as $2x + 3 < 7$, can be 'solved' by methods similar to those used to solve equations.

$$2x + 3 < 7$$
Subtract 3 from both sides $2x < 4$
Divide both sides by 2 $x < 2$

The result can be represented as a set of points on the real number line. An open circle is used to indicate that $x = 2$ is not a solution of the inequality.

In general we find that when simplifying inequalities, any number may be added to or subtracted from both sides. However, when both sides are multiplied or divided by a number, the inequality remains valid only if the number is positive. If both sides of an inequality are multiplied or divided by a negative number, then the inequality sign must be reversed. For instance, $3 < 4$ but $-3 > -4$. Similarly, if $-x > 2$ then $x < -2$.

Example 1   Simplify the inequality $2x - 5 \leqslant 5x + 4$.

$$2x - 5 \leqslant 5x + 4 \Leftrightarrow \quad 2x \leqslant 5x + 9$$
$$\Leftrightarrow -3x \leqslant 9$$
$$\Leftrightarrow \quad x \geqslant -3$$

This result is illustrated in the diagram below.

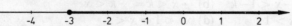

The set of numbers satisfying an equation or inequality is called the *solution set*. For instance, the solution set of the equation $2x + 3 = 7$ is the set $\{2\}$ containing one element. The solution set of the inequality $2x + 3 < 7$ is the set $\{x : x < 2\}$, which has infinitely many elements. [To avoid ambiguity we may describe this set more fully by writing $\{x \in \mathbb{R} : x < 2\}$.]

Example 2   Find, and represent on the real number line, the solution set of the inequalities $0 < 4x - 3 \leqslant 9$.

$$0 < 4x - 3 \leqslant 9 \Leftrightarrow 3 < 4x \leqslant 12$$
$$\Leftrightarrow \tfrac{3}{4} < x \leqslant 3$$
$\therefore$ the solution set is $\{x : \tfrac{3}{4} < x \leqslant 3\}$.

The *modulus* of a real number x, written $|x|$, is the magnitude of x. For instance, $|3| = 3$ and $|-5| = 5$. Using this notation inequalities such as $-2 < x < 2$ can be written in the form $|x| < 2$.

Example 3   Find the range of values of x for which $|3x| > 12$.

$$|3x| > 12 \Rightarrow 3x < -12 \quad \text{or} \quad 3x > 12$$
$$\Rightarrow x < -4 \quad \text{or} \quad x > 4.$$

Exercise 1.4

1.   Represent the following sets on the real number line
(a) $\{x : x > -1\}$ (b) $\{x : x \leqslant 4\}$ (c) $\{x : 0 < x < 3\}$
(d) $\{x : -3 \leqslant x \leqslant 1\}$ (e) $\{x : |x| \leqslant 3\}$ (f) $\{x : |x| > 2\}$.

2.   Find, and represent on the real number line, the solution sets of the following inequalities.
(a) $x + 2 < 9$ (b) $x - 4 \geqslant 1$ (c) $1 - x > 2$
(d) $2x - 5 \leqslant 3$ (e) $1 - 3x > 7$ (f) $5x + 3 < x$

3.   Find the range of values of x satisfying the following inequalities.
(a) $2x - 3 < 4 - 5x$ (b) $2x + 9 \leqslant 4x - 7$
(c) $2(x + 1) < x - 1$ (d) $\tfrac{1}{2}(3x + 1) \geqslant \tfrac{1}{3}(4x + 5)$
(e) $|2x| \geqslant 10$ (f) $|\tfrac{1}{2}x| < 3$

4.   Simplify the following inequalities.
(a) $-1 < 2x < 1$ (b) $0 \leqslant -3x \leqslant 6$
(c) $-2 < 5x - 7 < 3$ (d) $-3 \leqslant 1 - 4x < 3$
(e) $|x - 1| < 2$ (f) $|x + 3| \leqslant 7$

5.   State whether the following statements are true or false.
(a) $x < k \Rightarrow 1 - x < 1 - k$ (b) $-x < k \Rightarrow -k < x$
(c) $x^2 > 1 \Rightarrow x > 1$ (d) $x^2 < 1 \Rightarrow x < 1$
(e) $x < y \Rightarrow x^2 < y^2$ (f) $x < y < 0 \Rightarrow x^2 > y^2$
(g) $x < y \Rightarrow \dfrac{1}{x} > \dfrac{1}{y}$ (h) $0 < x < y \Rightarrow \dfrac{1}{x} > \dfrac{1}{y}$
(i) $x < y \Rightarrow |x| < |y|$ (j) $x < y < 0 \Rightarrow |y| < |x|$
Check your answers by considering some numerical examples.

1.5 Surds and indices

The reader will be familiar with the basic laws of indices which state that, for positive integers m and n,

$$a^m \times a^n = a^{m+n} \quad \text{and} \quad (a^m)^n = a^{mn}.$$

For example, $a^2 \times a^3 = (a \times a) \times (a \times a \times a) = a^5$
and $(a^2)^3 = (a \times a)^3 = (a \times a) \times (a \times a) \times (a \times a) = a^6$.

The rule for division is that, for $m > n$, $a^m \div a^n = a^{m-n}$. By assuming that this rule also holds for $m \leqslant n$, we can give meanings to the expressions a^0 and a^{-n}, (provided that $a \neq 0$).

We write $\quad a^0 \;= a^{n-n} = a^n \div a^n = 1$
and $\qquad a^{-n} = a^{0-n} = a^0 \div a^n = 1 \div a^n = 1/a^n$.

Thus it is consistent with the laws of indices to let $a^0 = 1$ and $a^{-n} = 1/a^n$.

We extend this process by assuming that the laws of indices also apply to fractional powers of positive real numbers. It then follows that $(a^{1/2})^2 = a^{1/2} \times a^{1/2} = a^1 = a$. Hence $a^{1/2}$ must be a square root of a. It is usual to take $a^{1/2}$ to be the positive square root $\sqrt{a}$. More generally, we can write

$$(a^{1/n})^n = a^{(1/n) \cdot n} = a^1 = a.$$

Hence, if n is a positive integer, $a^{1/n}$ is considered to be the positive nth root of a, written $\sqrt[n]{a}$. It follows that

$$a^{m/n} = (a^{1/n})^m = (\sqrt[n]{a})^m \quad \text{and} \quad a^{m/n} = (a^m)^{1/n} = \sqrt[n]{(a^m)},$$

where m and n are positive integers.

We can now summarise the laws of indices for rational powers of a positive real number a.

$$\boxed{\begin{array}{ll} a^m \times a^n = a^{m+n} & a^0 = 1, \quad a^{-n} = 1/a^n \\ a^m \div a^n = a^{m-n} & \\ (a^m)^n = a^{mn} & a^{m/n} = \sqrt[n]{(a^m)} = (\sqrt[n]{a})^m. \end{array}}$$

Example 1 Evaluate (a) 2^{-2} (b) $16^{1/2}$ (c) $8^{2/3}$ (d) $\left(\dfrac{4}{9}\right)^{-1/2}$

(a) $2^{-2} = \dfrac{1}{2^2} = \dfrac{1}{4}$, (b) $16^{1/2} = \sqrt{16} = 4$, (c) $8^{2/3} = (\sqrt[3]{8})^2 = 2^2 = 4$,

(d) $\left(\dfrac{4}{9}\right)^{-1/2} = \left(\dfrac{9}{4}\right)^{1/2} = 9^{1/2}/4^{1/2} = \dfrac{\sqrt{9}}{\sqrt{4}} = \dfrac{3}{2} = 1\frac{1}{2}$.

[We have not considered rational powers of negative numbers at this stage because of the difficulties which arise. One problem is that no negative number has a real nth root when n is even. In the case of odd values of n, contradictory results can be produced. For instance, $(-8)^{1/3} = \sqrt[3]{(-8)} = -2$, but $(-8)^{1/3} = (-8)^{2/6} = \sqrt[6]{\{(-8)^2\}} = \sqrt[6]{64} = 2$.]

Equations involving indices can be solved in a variety of ways.

Example 2   Solve the equation $8^x = 32$.

Expressing both sides of the equation as powers of 2,
$$8^x = 32 \Leftrightarrow (2^3)^x = 2^5 \Leftrightarrow 2^{3x} = 2^5$$
$$\therefore \quad 3x = 5, \text{ i.e. } x = 1\tfrac{2}{3}.$$

Example 3   Solve the equation $2^{2x} - 5.2^x + 4 = 0$.

Substituting $y = 2^x$,
$$
\begin{aligned}
2^{2x} - 5.2^x + 4 &= 0 \\
\Leftrightarrow \quad y^2 - 5y + 4 &= 0 \\
\Leftrightarrow (y-1)(y-4) &= 0 \\
\Leftrightarrow y = 0 \quad \text{or} \quad y &= 4 \\
\Leftrightarrow 2^x = 1 \quad \text{or} \quad 2^x &= 4 \\
\Leftrightarrow x = 0 \quad \text{or} \quad x &= 2.
\end{aligned}
$$

Example 4   Solve the equation $9^{x+1} - 3^{x+3} - 3^x + 3 = 0$.

Substituting $y = 3^x$,
$$
\begin{aligned}
9^{x+1} - 3^{x+3} - 3^x + 3 &= 0 \\
\Leftrightarrow 9.9^x - 3^3.3^x - 3^x + 3 &= 0 \\
\Leftrightarrow \quad 9y^2 - 27y - y + 3 &= 0 \\
\Leftrightarrow \quad (9y-1)(y-3) &= 0 \\
\Leftrightarrow y = 1/9 \quad \text{or} \quad y &= 3 \\
\Leftrightarrow 3^x = 1/9 \quad \text{or} \quad 3^x &= 3 \\
\Leftrightarrow x = -2 \quad \text{or} \quad x &= 1.
\end{aligned}
$$

Numbers such as $\sqrt{3}$ and $\sqrt[3]{5}$ are called *surds*. It is often helpful to simplify expressions involving surds. For instance, since $(\sqrt{2}.\sqrt{3})^2 = \sqrt{2}.\sqrt{3}.\sqrt{2}.\sqrt{3} = (\sqrt{2})^2(\sqrt{3})^2 = 2.3 = 6$, we see that $\sqrt{2}.\sqrt{3} = \sqrt{6}$. This is an illustration of the useful result $(\sqrt{a})(\sqrt{b}) = \sqrt{(ab)}$.

Example 5   Simplify (a) $\sqrt{50}$, (b) $\sqrt{18}/\sqrt{2}$, (c) $\sqrt{12} - \sqrt{27} + \sqrt{3}$.

(a) $\sqrt{50} = \sqrt{(25.2)} = \sqrt{25}.\sqrt{2} = 5\sqrt{2}$
(b) $\sqrt{18}/\sqrt{2} = \sqrt{(18/2)} = \sqrt{9} = 3$
(c) $\sqrt{12} - \sqrt{27} + \sqrt{3} = \sqrt{4}.\sqrt{3} - \sqrt{9}.\sqrt{3} + \sqrt{3} = 2\sqrt{3} - 3\sqrt{3} + \sqrt{3} = 0$.

It is usual to *rationalise* fractions which involve surds, so that the denominators are integers. For instance, $1/\sqrt{2}$ may be written $\sqrt{2}/2$. To rationalise a denominator of the form $a + \sqrt{b}$, we use the fact that $(a+\sqrt{b})(a-\sqrt{b})$ reduces to the 'difference of squares' $a^2 - (\sqrt{b})^2$, i.e. $a^2 - b$.

Example 6   Simplify $\dfrac{1+\sqrt{3}}{2+\sqrt{3}}$.

$$\frac{1+\sqrt{3}}{2+\sqrt{3}} = \frac{(1+\sqrt{3})(2-\sqrt{3})}{(2+\sqrt{3})(2-\sqrt{3})} = \frac{2-\sqrt{3}+2\sqrt{3}-3}{4-2\sqrt{3}+2\sqrt{3}-3} = \frac{-1+\sqrt{3}}{1} = -1+\sqrt{3}.$$

The remaining examples concern surds and fractional indices in algebraic expressions.

Example 7 Simplify $x\sqrt{\left(\dfrac{1}{x^2}-1\right)}$.

$$x\sqrt{\left(\frac{1}{x^2}-1\right)}=x\sqrt{\left(\frac{1-x^2}{x^2}\right)}=x\cdot\frac{\sqrt{(1-x^2)}}{\sqrt{(x^2)}}=\sqrt{(1-x^2)}.$$

Alternative method:

$$x\sqrt{\left(\frac{1}{x^2}-1\right)}=\sqrt{(x^2)}\sqrt{\left(\frac{1}{x^2}-1\right)}=\sqrt{x^2\left(\frac{1}{x^2}-1\right)}=\sqrt{(1-x^2)}.$$

Example 8 Simplify $(x+1)^{3/2}-(x+1)^{1/2}$.

$$(x+1)^{3/2}-(x+1)^{1/2}=(x+1)^{1/2}(x+1)^1-(x+1)^{1/2}$$
$$=(x+1)^{1/2}\{(x+1)-1\}=x(x+1)^{1/2}.$$

Exercise 1.5

In questions 1 to 4 simplify the given expressions.

1. (a) 7^2,   (b) 4^0,   (c) 5^{-1},   (d) $36^{1/2}$,
    (e) $8^{1/3}$,   (f) 2^{-3},   (g) $(12\tfrac{1}{4})^{1/2}$,   (h) $27^{-1/3}$.

2. (a) $16^{3/4}$,   (b) $(1\tfrac{1}{2})^{-1}$,   (c) $64^{2/3}$,   (d) $9^{-1/2}$,
    (e) $\left(\dfrac{3}{5}\right)^{-2}$,   (f) $(3\tfrac{3}{8})^{1/3}$,   (g) $\left(\dfrac{2}{5}\right)^0$,   (h) $\left(\dfrac{1}{4}\right)^{-3/2}$

3. (a) $\sqrt{54}$,   (b) $\sqrt{98}$,   (c) $\sqrt{72}$,   (d) $\sqrt{68}$,
    (e) $\sqrt{12}\times\sqrt{27}$,   (f) $\sqrt{252}\div\sqrt{63}$,   (g) $\sqrt{75}-\sqrt{48}$,   (h) $\sqrt{32}-\sqrt{18}$.

4. (a) $\sqrt{32}\times\sqrt{15}\div\sqrt{24}$,   (b) $\sqrt{80}-\sqrt{20}+\sqrt{45}$,
    (c) $\sqrt{84}\times\sqrt{140}\div\sqrt{120}$,   (d) $\sqrt{112}-\sqrt{63}-\sqrt{28}$.

5. Express as a single square root
(a) $3\sqrt{2}$,   (b) $5\sqrt{5}$,   (c) $x\sqrt{y}$,   (d) $2a^2\sqrt{b}$.

6. Rationalise the denominators of the following fractions, simplifying your answers

(a) $\dfrac{10}{\sqrt{5}}$ (b) $\dfrac{3+\sqrt{28}}{\sqrt{7}}$ (c) $\dfrac{3\sqrt{20}-\sqrt{60}}{2\sqrt{3}}$

(d) $\dfrac{\sqrt{5}+2}{\sqrt{5}-1}$ (e) $\dfrac{1+2\sqrt{2}}{5-3\sqrt{2}}$ (f) $\dfrac{\sqrt{3}+\sqrt{2}}{\sqrt{3}-\sqrt{2}}$.

In questions 7 to 9 solve the given equations.

7. (a) $9^x=27$,   (b) $4^x=128$,   (c) $5^{x+3}=1$.

8. (a) $2^{x-3}=4^{x+1}$ (b) $3^{2x}\cdot3^{x-1}=9$
    (c) $2^x\cdot5^{x+1}=\tfrac{1}{2}$ (d) $3^x\cdot2^{2x-3}=18$.

9. (a) $2^{2x} - 9 \cdot 2^x + 8 = 0$ (b) $3^{2x} - 10 \cdot 3^x + 9 = 0$

   (c) $4^x - 3 \cdot 2^{x+1} + 8 = 0$ (d) $2^{2x+1} + 4 = 2^{x+3} + 2^x$

   (e) $3^{2x-3} - 4 \cdot 3^{x-2} + 1 = 0$ (f) $16^x - 5 \cdot 2^{2x-1} + 1 = 0$.

10. Simplify the following expressions

(a) $x^2 \sqrt{\left(1 - \dfrac{1}{x^3}\right)}$ (b) $\dfrac{1}{x}\sqrt{(x^2 + x^4)}$

(c) $(x-2)^{3/2} + 2(x-2)^{1/2}$ (d) $(2x-1)^{-1/2} + (2x-1)^{1/2}$.

1.6 Logarithms

If a and x are positive real numbers and $x = a^p$, then p is the *logarithm* of x to the *base a*, written $\log_a x$.

Thus

$$\boxed{x = a^p \Leftrightarrow \log_a x = p.}$$

Any statement in index form, such as $25 = 5^2$, has an equivalent logarithmic form, $\log_5 25 = 2$. To determine the logarithm to the base a of a number x, we must find the power of a which is equal to x.

Example 1   Find the logarithms to the base 4 of (a) 16, (b) 2, (c) $\frac{1}{4}$, (d) 4, (e) 1, (f) 8.

(a) $16 = 4^2$ $\therefore \log_4 16 = 2$ (b) $2 = 4^{1/2}$ $\therefore \log_4 2 = \frac{1}{2}$

(c) $\frac{1}{4} = 4^{-1}$ $\therefore \log_4 \frac{1}{4} = -1$ (d) $4 = 4^1$ $\therefore \log_4 4 = 1$

(e) $1 = 4^0$ $\therefore \log_4 1 = 0$ (f) $8 = 4^{3/2}$ $\therefore \log_4 8 = \frac{3}{2}$.

As illustrated in this example, for any base a,

$$\boxed{\log_a a = 1 \quad \text{and} \quad \log_a 1 = 0.}$$

Because logarithms are themselves indices, the laws of logarithms are closely related to the laws of indices.

Let $x = a^p, y = a^q$ then $\log_a x = p, \log_a y = q$.

Using the laws of indices:

$xy = a^p \times a^q = a^{p+q}$ $\therefore \log_a xy = p + q = \log_a x + \log_a y$

$\dfrac{x}{y} = a^p \div a^q = a^{p-q}$ $\therefore \log_a \dfrac{x}{y} = p - q = \log_a x - \log_a y$

$x^n = (a^p)^n = a^{pn}$ $\therefore \log_a x^n = pn = n \log_a x$.

Summarising:

$$\log_a xy = \log_a x + \log_a y$$
$$\log_a \frac{x}{y} = \log_a x - \log_a y$$
$$\log_a x^n = n \log_a x.$$

Example 2 Express $\log (x^3/\sqrt{y})$ in terms of $\log x$ and $\log y$.

$\log (x^3/\sqrt{y}) = \log (x^3/y^{1/2}) = \log (x^3) - \log (y^{1/2}) = 3 \log x - \frac{1}{2} \log y.$

Example 3 Express $\frac{1}{3} \log 8 - \log \frac{2}{5}$ as a single logarithm.

$\frac{1}{3} \log 8 - \log \frac{2}{5} = \log 8^{1/3} + \log \left(\frac{2}{5}\right)^{-1} = \log 2 + \log \frac{5}{2} = \log \left(2 . \frac{5}{2}\right) = \log 5.$

Example 4 Solve the equation $\log_6 x + \log_6 (x+5) = 2$.

$\begin{aligned}
\log_6 x + \log_6 (x+5) = 2 \quad &\Rightarrow \quad \log_6 x(x+5) = \log_6 36 \\
&\Rightarrow \qquad\quad x(x+5) = 36 \\
&\Rightarrow \qquad x^2 + 5x - 36 = 0 \\
&\Rightarrow \quad (x+9)(x-4) = 0.
\end{aligned}$

Hence either $x = -9$ or $x = 4$.
However, since $\log_6 x$ and $\log_6 (x+5)$ are undefined for $x = -9$, the only valid solution of the given equation is $x = 4$.

We now establish some important relationships between logarithms to different bases.

Let $\log_a x = p$ so that $x = a^p$.

Taking logarithms to the base x,

$\log_x x = \log_x (a^p) \Leftrightarrow 1 = p \log_x a \Leftrightarrow \log_x a = 1/p$

$$\therefore \quad \log_x a = 1/\log_a x.$$

Taking logarithms to the base b,

$\log_b x = \log_b (a^p) \Leftrightarrow \log_b x = p \log_b a \Leftrightarrow p = \log_b x/\log_b a$

$$\therefore \quad \log_a x = \log_b x/\log_b a.$$

In particular, when $b = 10$, $\log_a x = \log_{10} x/\log_{10} a$.

Example 5   Given that $\log_2 N = k$, express in terms of k

(a) $\log_2 N^2$,   (b) $\log_2 2N$,   (c) $\log_8 N$,   (d) $\log_N 4$.

(a) $\log_2 N^2 = 2\log_2 N = 2k$,   (b) $\log_2 2N = \log_2 2 + \log_2 N = 1 + k$,
(c) $\log_8 N = \log_2 N/\log_2 8 = \log_2 N/\log_2 2^3 = k/3$,
(d) $\log_N 4 = \log_2 4/\log_2 N = \log_2 2^2/\log_2 N = 2/k$.

Example 6   Solve the equation $2\log_4 x + 1 - \log_x 4 = 0$.

$$\text{Substituting } \log_4 x = y, \quad 2\log_4 x + 1 - \log_x 4 = 0$$
$$\Leftrightarrow \qquad 2y + 1 - 1/y = 0$$
$$\Leftrightarrow \qquad 2y^2 + y - 1 = 0$$
$$\Leftrightarrow \qquad (2y - 1)(y + 1) = 0$$
$$\Leftrightarrow \qquad y = \tfrac{1}{2} \quad \text{or} \quad y = -1$$
$$\Leftrightarrow \log_4 x = \tfrac{1}{2} \quad \text{or} \quad \log_4 x = -1$$
$$\Leftrightarrow \qquad x = 4^{1/2} \quad \text{or} \quad x = 4^{-1}$$

Hence $x = 2$ or $x = \tfrac{1}{4}$.

For some years the main use of logarithms in elementary work was in performing calculations involving multiplication and division. However, many people now use electronic calculators for such operations in preference to slide rules and sets of mathematical tables. Nevertheless, we now review briefly the use of tables of *common logarithms*, i.e. logarithms to the base 10. We will use the notation $\lg x$ instead of the more cumbersome $\log_{10} x$.

Logarithm tables usually give $\lg x$ for values of x between 1 and 10, e.g. $\lg 5\cdot3 = 0\cdot7243$. For other values of x, $\lg x$ is found by expressing x in *standard form*, i.e. in the form $k \times 10^n$, where $1 \leqslant k < 10$ and n is an integer. For example,

$$\lg 530 = \lg (5\cdot3 \times 10^2) = \lg 5\cdot3 + \lg 10^2 = 0\cdot7243 + 2 = 2\cdot7243,$$
$$\lg 0\cdot53 = \lg (5\cdot3 \times 10^{-1}) = \lg 5\cdot3 + \lg 10^{-1} = 0\cdot7243 - 1 = -0\cdot2757,$$

which is often written as $\bar{1}\cdot7243$.

Anti-logarithm tables give values of 10^p for $0 \leqslant p < 1$. They are used to find a number given its logarithm, e.g. if $\lg x = 0\cdot78$, then $x = 10^{0\cdot78} = 6\cdot026$. For other values of p, 10^p is found by using the laws of indices.

If $\lg x = 1\cdot78$, then $x = 10^{1\cdot78} = 10^{0\cdot78} \times 10^1 = 60\cdot26$.
If $\lg x = \bar{1}\cdot78$, then $x = 10^{0\cdot78-1} = 10^{0\cdot78} \times 10^{-1} = 0\cdot6026$.
If $\lg x = -1\cdot22$, then $x = 10^{-1\cdot22} = 10^{0\cdot78} \times 10^{-2} = 0\cdot06026$.

[For further numerical work involving logarithms see §4.2.]

Exercise 1.6

1. Express the following statements in logarithmic form
(a) $16 = 2^4$ (b) $1/9 = 3^{-2}$ (c) $4 = 16^{1/2}$
2. Express the following statements in index form
(a) $\log_4 64 = 3$ (b) $\log_5 0\cdot2 = -1$ (c) $\log_9 27 = 1\cdot5$
3. Find the logarithms to the base 2 of
(a) 8   (b) $\tfrac{1}{4}$ (c) 1   (d) 2   (e) $\sqrt{2}$

4. Find the logarithms to the base 9 of
(a) 81 (b) 3 (c) 1/9 (d) 27 (e) 1
5. Find the following logarithms
(a) $\log_3 81$ (b) $\log_{27} 3$ (c) $\log_4 0 \cdot 5$ (d) $\log_{100} 10$
(e) $\log_8 0 \cdot 25$ (f) $\log_{0 \cdot 5} 8$ (g) $\log_6 6 \sqrt{6}$ (h) $\log_5 0 \cdot 04$
6. Express in terms of $\log x$ and $\log y$
(a) $\log x^2 y$ (b) $\log \sqrt{(xy)}$ (c) $\log (x^4/y^3)$
7. Express in terms of $\log A$, $\log B$ and $\log C$
(a) $\log (AB^2/C^3)$ (b) $\log (A\sqrt{B}/C^{-2})$ (c) $\log \sqrt{(A^3 B^2 C)}$
8. Express as a single logarithm
(a) $\log 14 - \log 21 + \log 6$ (b) $4 \log 2 + \frac{1}{2} \log 25$
(c) $\frac{3}{2} \log 9 - 2 \log 6$ (d) $2 \log (\frac{2}{3}) - \log (\frac{8}{9})$
9. Find the values of
(a) $\log_a 32/\log_a 2$ (b) $\log_x 125/\log_x 25$ (c) $\log_3 x/\log_9 x$
10. Given that $\log_3 2 = p$ and $\log_3 5 = q$, express in terms of p and q
(a) $\log_3 60$ (b) $\log_3 6 \cdot 4$ (c) $\log_{10} 2$.
11. Given that $\log_5 x = t$, express in terms of t
(a) $\log_5 5x^2$ (b) $\log_x 5$ (c) $\log_{25} x$ (d) $\log_x 0 \cdot 2$

In questions 12 to 14 solve the given equations.

12. (a) $\log_2 x^4 + \log_2 4x = 12$ (b) $\log_5 x + \log_5 (1/x^3) = 2$
13. (a) $\log_3 x + \log_3 (x+6) = 3$ (b) $\log_4 2x + \log_4 (x+1) = 1$
14. (a) $\log_3 x = 4 \log_x 3$ (b) $2 \log_4 x + 3 \log_x 4 = 7$
(c) $3 \log_8 x = 2 \log_x 8 + 5$ (d) $\log_5 x + \log_x 25 = 3$
15. Solve the simultaneous equations: $\log_2 x^2 + \log_2 y^3 = 1$,
$$\log_2 x - \log_2 y^2 = 4.$$

Exercise 1.7 (*miscellaneous*)

In questions 1 to 4, assuming that $A = \{x \in \mathbb{R} : x^2 < 4\}$, $B = \{x \in \mathbb{Z} : 0 \leqslant x \leqslant 2\}$ and $C = \{-2, -1, 0, 1, 2\}$, decide whether the given statements are true or false.

1. (a) $A \subset C$, (b) $B \subset C$, (c) $B \subset A$, (d) $B \subset \mathbb{Z}$.

2. (a) $2 \in A$, (b) $\sqrt{2} \in A$, (c) $2 \in B$, (d) $\sqrt{2} \in B$.

3. (a) $(-1, 1) \in A \times B$, (b) $(1, -1) \in A \times B$,
(c) $(2, 2) \in A \times C$, (d) $(0, 0) \in A \times C$.

4. (a) $n \in A$ and $n \in B \Leftrightarrow n \in \{0, 1\}$,
(b) $n \notin B$ and $n \in C \Rightarrow n \in \{-2, -1, 0\}$,
(c) $n \notin A$ and $n \in C \Rightarrow n \in B$,
(d) $n \in A$ and $n \notin C \Leftrightarrow n \notin \mathbb{Z}$.

5. If the universal set $\mathscr{E}$ is the set of real numbers $\mathbb{R}$, find the complements of the following sets
(a) {rational numbers}, (b) {negative numbers},
(c) $\{x : x \leqslant 4\}$, (d) $\{x : x < 0 \text{ or } x > 0\}$,
(e) $\{x : x^2 < 0\}$, (f) $\{x : -1 < x < 1\}$.

6.   Given that $x * y = \sqrt{(xy)}$, where x and y are real numbers, decide whether the binary operation $*$ is (a) commutative (b) associative.

7.   Use the properties of real numbers to prove that
(a) $k+x = k+y \Rightarrow x = y$,
(b) $kx = ky$ and $k \neq 0 \Rightarrow x = y$.

8. Find the range of values of x satisfying the following inequalities.
(a) $3x+1 < x-5$,   (b) $2(2x-3) \geqslant 5x+2$,
(c) $0 < 2x-1 \leqslant 3$,   (d) $x(x+2) > 2x+9$,
(e) $|x+2| < 5$,   (f) $|x-3| \geqslant 2$.

9.   Arrange the following in order of magnitude:
$$7, \quad 2\sqrt{11}, \quad 4\sqrt{3}, \quad 5\sqrt{2}, \quad 3\sqrt{5}.$$

10. Simplify the following expressions
(a) $54^{1/3} \times 2^{-4/3}$,   (b) $25^{1/6} \times 200^{1/3}$,   (c) $54^{1/3} - 16^{1/3}$.

11. Find in the form $p+q\sqrt{2}$, where p and q are integers,
(a) the reciprocal of $3-2\sqrt{2}$,   (b) the square of $3-2\sqrt{2}$,
(c) the square roots of $3-2\sqrt{2}$.

12. Solve the simultaneous equations
$$2^x + 3^y = 5, \quad 2^{x+3} - 3^{y+2} = 23.$$

13. Given that $\log_3 2 \approx 0.63$, find the values of x for which
(a) $6^x \cdot 2^{3-x} = 1$,   (b) $3^{2x} = 3^x + 2$,   (c) $2 \cdot 9^x + 3^{x-1} + 4 = 2 \cdot 3^{x+1}$.

14. Write down the value of x given that
(a) $\log_x 8 = \frac{3}{4}$,   (b) $\log_x 0.01 = \log_{0.1} 100$,
(c) $\log_9 x = -\frac{1}{2}$,   (d) $\log_3 x = \log_9 4$.

15. Simplify the following expressions
(a) $3\log_2\left(\dfrac{5}{3}\right) - 2\log_2\left(\dfrac{10}{9}\right) + \log_2\left(\dfrac{1}{30}\right)$,
(b) $\log_a \sqrt{(a^4+1)} - \frac{1}{2}\log_a\left(1 + \dfrac{1}{a^4}\right)$,
(c) $\log_4\{(a^2+1)^2 - (a^2-1)^2\} - \log_2 2a$.

16. Solve the following equations
(a) $\log_2 4x = 8\log_x 2$,   (b) $\log_9 x = \log_3 3x$.

17. Prove that, if a, b and c are positive real numbers, then
$$(\log_a b)(\log_b c) = \log_a c.$$

2 Functions and graphs

2.1 Mappings and functions

A *mapping* or *function* f is a rule which assigns to an object x an *image* y. We write $f: x \rightarrow y$ or $x \xrightarrow{f} y$ and say 'f maps x to y'. The notation $y = f(x)$ is also used.

Consider a function f which maps each day of the week onto its initial letter. This function is represented in the diagram below. If X is the set containing the days of the week and Y is the set containing all letters of the alphabet, then f can be described as a mapping from X into Y, written $f: X \rightarrow Y$. The set X is called the *domain* of f and the set Y is called the *codomain*. By definition every element in the domain of a function has one and only one image in the codomain.

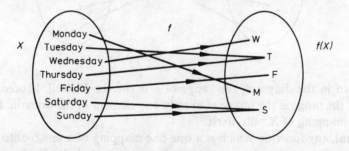

The set $\{W, T, F, M, S\}$ containing all the images under f is the *range* of the function, denoted by $f(X)$. Any element in the range is the image of one or more elements in the domain, e.g. F is the image of Friday, but T is the image of both Tuesday and Thursday. As every element of the range $f(X)$ belongs to the codomain, $f(X) \subset Y$. In this example, as there are letters of the alphabet, such as L and D, which are not images under f, the range $f(X)$ is a proper subset of the codomain Y.

We now examine some functions with special properties.

(1) Let X be the set of natural numbers $\{0,1,2,3,\dots\}$ and let Y be the set of single digits $\{0,1,2,\dots,8,9\}$. Let $f: X \rightarrow Y$ be the function which maps a natural number to its final digit.

As before X is the domain of f and Y is the codomain. However, as every element of Y is the final digit of at least one natural number, the set Y is also the range of f, i.e. $f(X) = Y$.

In general, if every element of the codomain Y of a function f is the image of at least one element of the domain X, then f is said to be a mapping of X *onto* Y. [A function which is 'onto' can also be called *surjective*.]

(2) Let g be the mapping of the set of natural numbers $\mathbb{N}$ into itself defined by $g : x \to x^2$.

In this case the set $\mathbb{N}$ is both the domain and the codomain of g, but the range of g is a proper subset of $\mathbb{N}$, $\{0, 1, 4, 9, 16, \ldots\}$. Hence g is a mapping 'into' rather than 'onto' $\mathbb{N}$. However, every element of the range is the image of only one element of the domain.

In general, if every element of the range $f(X)$ of a function f is the image of exactly one element of the domain X, then f is said to be *one-one*, sometimes written 1-1. A function which is not one-one may be described as *many-to-one*. Thus the function g defined above is one-one, but both the function f in (1) and the function defined earlier on the set of days of the week are many-to-one. [A one-one function can also be called *injective*.]

(3) Let $X = \{1, 2, 3, 4, 5\}$ and let h be a mapping from X to itself defined by $h : x \to 6 - x$.

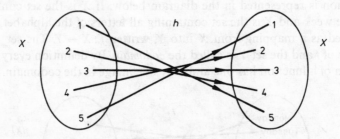

As shown in the diagram, the range of h is the set X itself. Moreover, every element of the range is the image of exactly one element of the domain. Hence h is a one-one mapping of X onto itself.

In general, any function which is a one-one mapping of a set X onto a set Y is said to form a *one-one correspondence* between X and Y. The symbol $\leftrightarrow$ is sometimes used to link object and image under a one-one correspondence. For example, under the mapping h, $1 \leftrightarrow 5$, $2 \leftrightarrow 4$, $3 \leftrightarrow 3$, $4 \leftrightarrow 2$, $5 \leftrightarrow 1$. [A function which is both one-one and 'onto' is said to be *bijective*.].

Exercise 2.1

1. Decide whether the following are valid definitions of a mapping f from the set $X = \{0, 1, 2, \ldots, 10\}$ into the set of real numbers $\mathbb{R}$.
(a) f maps any element of X onto its cube,
(b) f maps any element of X onto its square root,
(c) f maps any element of X onto its reciprocal.

2.   Decide whether the following are valid definitions of a mapping f from the set of all triangles into the set $\mathbb{R}$.
(a) f maps any triangle onto its area,
(b) f maps any triangle onto its height,
(c) f maps any triangle onto the number of vertices it has.

3.   Let f be the function defined on the set $\mathbb{Z}^+$ of positive integers which maps each integer onto the sum of its digits.
(a) Find $f(4), f(19)$ and $f(301)$.
(b) Decide whether f is one-one or many-to-one.
(c) Are there any elements of $\mathbb{Z}^+$ which do not belong to the range of f? If so, give an example.
(d) Is f a mapping from $\mathbb{Z}^+$ onto itself?

4.   Repeat question 3 for the function f from $\mathbb{Z}^+$ into itself denfined by $f: x \rightarrow 2x$.

5.   Repeat question 3 for the function f from $\mathbb{Z}^+$ into itself defined by $f: x \rightarrow x^2 - x + 1$.

6.   Repeat question 3 for the function f from $\mathbb{Z}^+$ into itself which maps a positive integer onto the sum of its factors, e.g. $f(12) = 1 + 2 + 3 + 4 + 6 + 12 = 28$.

In questions 7 to 15 a mapping f from a set X into a set Y is defined. In each case find the range of the mapping, then decide whether (a) f maps X onto Y, (b) f is one-one, (c) f is a one-one correspondence between X and Y.

7. $X = Y = \mathbb{R}, f: x \rightarrow 2x.$

8. $X = Y = \mathbb{R}, f: x \rightarrow 2.$

9. $X = Y = \mathbb{R}, f: x \rightarrow \frac{1}{2}x.$

10. $X = Y = \mathbb{R}, f: x \rightarrow x^2.$

11. $X = Y = \mathbb{Z}, f: x \rightarrow x - 1.$

12. $X = Y = \mathbb{Z}, f: x \rightarrow 1 - x.$

13. $X = \{$all polygons$\}, Y = \{x \in \mathbb{R}: x > 0\}, f$ maps a polygon onto the length of its perimeter.

14. $X = \{x \in \mathbb{R}: 0 < x < 1\}, Y = \mathbb{R}, f: x \rightarrow 1/x.$

15. $X = \{$all sets$\}, Y = \mathbb{N}, f$ maps any set onto the number of subsets it has, e.g. $f: \{a, b, c\} \rightarrow 8.$

2.2 The graph of a function

A function f from a set X to a set Y can be represented as the set of all ordered pairs (x, y) such that $f: x \rightarrow y$, i.e. as a subset of the product set $X \times Y$. By marking off the elements of X along a horizontal axis and the elements of Y along a vertical axis, the function may be represented by a set of points with coordinates (x, y). This set of points is called the *graph* of the function.

Of particular interest are functions which map the set of real numbers $\mathbb{R}$ into itself. Such functions are represented as sets of ordered pairs (x, y) which are subsets of the product set $\mathbb{R} \times \mathbb{R}$, also written $\mathbb{R}^2$. Thus the graph of any function $f : \mathbb{R} \to \mathbb{R}$ is the set of all points (x, y) in the x, y plane such that $f : x \to y$. Points are plotted using horizontal and vertical axes called the x-axis and y-axis respectively. The coordinates (x, y) are often called the *Cartesian coordinates* of the point after René Descartes† who first described the system. The number x is called the x-coordinate or *abscissa* and y the y-coordinate or *ordinate*. Since every point (x, y) on the graph of a function f satisfies the relation $y = f(x)$, this is called the *Cartesian equation* of the graph. For instance, the graph of the function $f : x \to x + 2$ has equation $y = x + 2$.

It is clearly impossible to plot all the points on the graph of a function whose domain is the set of all real numbers. However, we can draw a graph of a function defined in a given interval of the form $\{x : a \leqslant x \leqslant b\}$.

Example 1   Draw the graph of the function defined by the equation $y = 2x^2 - 5x$, taking $-1 \leqslant x \leqslant 4$.

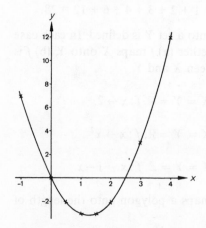

x	-1	0	1	2	3	4
y	7	0	-3	-2	3	12

To improve accuracy we consider two additional values of x.

x	$\frac{1}{2}$	$1\frac{1}{2}$
y	-2	-3

Although drawing a graph can be useful when considering a particular function, important features of the graph may lie beyond the points plotted. In later chapters we will see that there are ways of examining the general behaviour of a function. These can be used to produce a sketch indicating the form of the graph over the whole domain.

An equation $y = f(x)$ describes the relation between x and y as their values vary over the domain and range of the function f. Thus x and y are called *variables*. Since the value of x may be chosen freely from the domain of f, x is called the *independent variable*. However, the value of y depends on the value

† *Descartes, René* (1596–1650) French rationalist philosopher and mathematician. In mathematics his greatest achievements were advances in the theory of equations and the invention of coordinate geometry, as described in his essay *La Géométrie* (1637).

chosen for x, so y is called the *dependent variable*. The statement 'y is a function of x' is another way of expressing this relationship.

When defining a function on the set of real numbers, either in the form $f: x \to y$ or $y = f(x)$, the domain is usually taken to be the set of values of x for which a value of y can be determined. For instance, the domain of the function $f: x \to 1/(x-1)$ is the set containing all real numbers except 1, written $\mathbb{R} - \{1\}$. There is no value of x such that $f(x) = 0$. Hence the range of the function is the set $\mathbb{R} - \{0\}$. Since a negative number has no real square root, the domain of the function defined by $y = \sqrt{(1-x^2)}$ is the set $\{x \in \mathbb{R}: -1 \leqslant x \leqslant 1\}$. It follows that the range of the function is the set $\{y \in \mathbb{R}: 0 \leqslant y \leqslant 1\}$.

[In general an equation connecting variables x and y defines a *relation* on the set $\mathbb{R}$. Such an equation defines a function only if for every value of x in the domain there is exactly one value of y. For example, the equation $y^2 = x$ defines a relation, but not a function, because for any positive value of x there are two possible values of y.]

Exercise 2.2

In questions 1 to 6 write down the equation of the graph of the given function, then draw the graph taking values of x in the stated interval.

1. $f: x \to 2 - x$, $-1 \leqslant x \leqslant 3$.
   2. $f: x \to 2x + 1$, $-2 \leqslant x \leqslant 2$.

3. $f: x \to 4 - x^2$, $-3 \leqslant x \leqslant 1$.
   4. $f: x \to x^3 - 2x^2$, $-2 \leqslant x \leqslant 3$.

5. $f: x \to 1/x^2$, $\frac{1}{2} \leqslant x \leqslant 4$.
   6. $f: x \to 1/(1-x)$, $-5 \leqslant x \leqslant \frac{1}{2}$.

In questions 7 to 18 decide whether the given equation defines on some subset of $\mathbb{R}$ a function of the form $f: x \to y$. If so, determine the largest possible domain for f and the corresponding range, and state whether f is one-one or many-to-one.

7. $y = x + 4$.
   8. $x + y = 4$.
   9. $y = 4x + 1$.

10. $y = x^2 + 4$.
   11. $y^2 = x + 4$.
   12. $y = 1 - x^2$.

13. $y = \dfrac{1}{x^2}$.
   14. $y = \dfrac{1}{x - 1}$.
   15. $y = \dfrac{1}{4 - x}$.

16. $x^2 + y^2 = 4$.
   17. $y = \sqrt{x}$.
   18. $y^3 = x^2$.

2.3 Points, lines and curves

Any equation connecting variables x and y may be considered as the Cartesian equation of a curve or graph in the x, y plane. The curve consists of the set of points whose coordinates (x, y) satisfy the equation. It is possible to decide whether or not a point lies on a curve by substituting its coordinates into the equation.

Example 1   Which of the points $A(-1,1)$, $B(1,-2)$ and $C(-2,2)$ lie on the curve $x^2+y^2 = 5$?

At A: $x^2+y^2 = (-1)^2+1^2 = 2$ i.e. $x^2+y^2 \neq 5$
At B: $x^2+y^2 = 1^2+(-2)^2 = 5$ i.e. $x^2+y^2 = 5$
At C: $x^2+y^2 = (-2)^2+2^2 = 8$ i.e. $x^2+y^2 \neq 5$
$\therefore$ B lies on the curve $x^2+y^2 = 5$, but A and C do not.

Since the x-coordinate of any point on the y-axis is 0, points of intersection of a curve with the y-axis are found by substituting $x = 0$ in the equation. Similarly points of intersection with the x-axis are found by substituting $y = 0$. The point $(0,0)$, where the axes themselves intersect, is called the *origin*.

Example 2   Find the points of intersection of the curve $y = x^2-1$ with the coordinate axes.

$x = 0 \Rightarrow y = -1$
$\therefore$ the curve cuts the y-axis at the point $(0, -1)$.

$y = 0 \Leftrightarrow x^2-1 = 0 \Leftrightarrow (x+1)(x-1) = 0$
$\qquad\qquad \Leftrightarrow x+1 = 0 \quad$ or $\quad x-1 = 0$
$\qquad\qquad \Leftrightarrow \quad x = -1 \quad$ or $\qquad x = 1$

$\therefore$ the curve cuts the x-axis at the points $(-1,0)$ and $(1,0)$.

We now consider pairs of points in the x, y plane and the straight lines joining them.

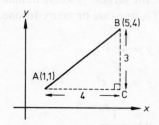

The diagram shows the points $A(1,1)$ and $B(5,4)$. In triangle ABC, AC and BC are parallel to the coordinate axes, so that $\angle ACB = 90°$.
By Pythagoras' theorem,
$$AB^2 = AC^2+BC^2$$

$$\therefore \quad AB^2 = (5-1)^2+(4-1)^2 = 4^2+3^2 = 25$$

Hence the distance between the points A and B is 5.

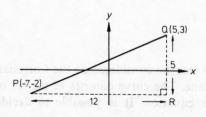

Similarly, if P and Q are the points $(-7, -2)$ and $(5,3)$ respectively,
$$PQ^2 = PR^2+QR^2$$
$$\therefore \quad PQ^2 = (5+7)^2+(3+2)^2$$
$$= 12^2+5^2 = 169$$
$$\therefore \quad PQ = 13.$$

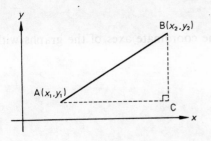

Thus, for a typical pair of points $A(x_1, y_1)$ and $B(x_2, y_2)$,
$$AC = x_2 - x_1, \quad BC = y_2 - y_1$$

$$\therefore \quad \boxed{AB = \sqrt{\{(x_2 - x_1)^2 + (y_2 - y_1)^2\}}.}$$

Example 3 Find the distance between the points $S(-1, 2)$ and $T(3, -1)$.

$$ST = \sqrt{\{(-1-3)^2 + (2-(-1))^2\}} = \sqrt{\{4^2 + 3^2\}} = \sqrt{25} = 5.$$

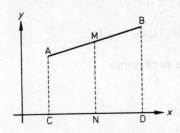

Let M be the mid-point of the line joining the points $A(x_1, y_1)$ and $B(x_2, y_2)$. If AC, MN and BD are drawn parallel to the y-axis then N is the mid-point of CD.

Since
$$CD = x_2 - x_1,$$
$$CN = \tfrac{1}{2}(x_2 - x_1)$$

$$\therefore \quad ON = OC + CN = x_1 + \tfrac{1}{2}(x_2 - x_1) = \tfrac{1}{2}(x_1 + x_2),$$

i.e. the x-coordinate of M is $\tfrac{1}{2}(x_1 + x_2)$.

By a similar argument the y-coordinate of M is $\tfrac{1}{2}(y_1 + y_2)$

$$\therefore \quad \boxed{\text{the mid-point of } AB \text{ is } (\tfrac{1}{2}\{x_1 + x_2\}, \tfrac{1}{2}\{y_1 + y_2\}).}$$

Example 4 Find the mid-points of the lines joining the points (a) $(4, -1)$ and $(0, 3)$ (b) $(-5, 1)$ and $(-2, 5)$.

(a) The mid-point is $(\tfrac{1}{2}\{4+0\}, \tfrac{1}{2}\{-1+3\})$, i.e. $(2, 1)$.
(b) The mid-point is $(\tfrac{1}{2}\{-5-2\}, \tfrac{1}{2}\{1+5\})$, i.e. $(-3\tfrac{1}{2}, 3)$.

Example 5 Given that the points $A(5, -3)$, $B(3, 6)$, $C(-1, 7)$ are the vertices of a parallelogram $ABCD$, find the coordinates of D.

Since the diagonals of a parallelogram bisect each other, the diagonals AC and BD of the parallelogram $ABCD$ have the same mid-point.
The mid-point of AC is $(\tfrac{1}{2}\{5-1\}, \tfrac{1}{2}\{-3+7\})$, i.e. $(2, 2)$.
Letting D be the point (h, k), the mid-point of BD is $(\tfrac{1}{2}\{3+h\}, \tfrac{1}{2}\{6+k\})$.
$$\therefore \quad \tfrac{1}{2}\{3+h\} = 2 \quad \text{and} \quad \tfrac{1}{2}\{6+k\} = 2 \quad \text{i.e.} \quad h = 1, k = -2.$$
Hence the coordinates of D are $(1, -2)$.

Exercise 2.3

1. Find the points of intersection with the coordinate axes of the graphs with the following equations.
(a) $y = x - 1$ (b) $y = 2x + 5$
(c) $y = x^2 + 3x$ (d) $y = 2x^2 + 3x - 2$
(e) $y = \dfrac{2}{x-2}$ (f) $y = \dfrac{x-3}{x-6}$

2. In each of the following cases determine which points lie on the given curve.
(a) $y = x^2 + x$; $(1, 3), (-2, 6), (-3, 6), (0, 2)$.
(b) $y = 1/(x - 2)$; $(0, \frac{1}{2}), (3, 1), (-1, -1), (6, \frac{1}{3})$.
(c) $y = 3x^2 - 7x + 5$; $(2, 3), (-5, 115), (-2, 29), (1, 4)$.
(d) $y = x^3 - 5x - 9$; $(-2, -7), (1, -11), (4, 35), (-1, -5)$.
(e) $4x^2 + y^2 = 20$; $(3, -4), (-2, 2), (5, 0), (-1, -4)$.
(f) $x^2 + y^2 - 8x + 4y - 5 = 0$; $(4, -2), (7, -6), (0, 1), (-1, -1)$.

3. Find the distances between the following pairs of points.
(a) $(0, 7), (12, -2)$ (b) $(-3, -5), (-7, -8)$
(c) $(-2, 14), (3, 2)$ (d) $(5, -1), (11, 7)$
(e) $(4, -10), (-4, 5)$ (f) $(-4, -4), (3, 20)$
(g) $(7, -4), (5, -1)$ (h) $(-2, 3), (1, -3)$.

4. Find the mid-points of the lines joining the points given in question 3.

5. Given that B is the mid-point of the line segment AC, find the coordinates of C when
(a) $A(1, 2), B(3, 1)$ (b) $A(6, 2), B(3, -2)$
(c) $A(-5, 4), B(-2, -1)$ (d) $A(4, -3), B(3, -1)$.

6. Find the coordinates of the vertex D of the parallelogram $ABCD$ given
(a) $A(5, 0), B(-3, 2), C(1, -6)$ (b) $A(-2, 7), B(4, 5), C(6, -1)$
(c) $A(3, -4), B(0, -7), C(2, 5)$ (d) $A(1, -5), B(-3, 7), C(-2, 8)$.

7. Determine whether the triangles with vertices given below are (i) isosceles, (ii) right-angled.
(a) $A(4, 7), B(-3, 8), C(9, 2)$ (b) $P(3, -1), Q(-4, 2), R(1, -6)$
(c) $S(-2, 5), T(4, 3), U(-5, -4)$ (d) $X(5, 9), Y(15, 3), Z(-1, -1)$.

8. Given points $P(5, 5)$, $Q(-1, -3)$ and $R(-2, 4)$, show that the mid-point M of the line PQ is the centre of the circle through P, Q and R.

9. Show that the point $P(4, 5)$ lies on the perpendicular bisector of the line joining the points $A(5, -2)$ and $B(-3, 4)$. Find the distance of P from the line AB.

10. Show that the triangle with vertices $D(2, 5)$, $E(3, -7)$ and $F(-6, 1)$ is isosceles and find its area.

11. Given that $A(0, -5)$, $B(-7, 2)$, $C(2, 11)$ are the vertices of a parallelogram $ABCD$, find the coordinates of D. Prove that $ABCD$ is a rectangle and find its area.

12. Given that $A(1, -7)$, $B(6, 1)$ and $C(1, 9)$ are the vertices of a parallelogram $ABCD$, find the coordinates of D. Prove that $ABCD$ is a rhombus and find its area.

13. The points $P(-1, -2)$, $Q(3, 4)$ and $R(11, 6)$ are the vertices of a parallelogram $PQRS$. A point T is taken on RS produced so that S is the mid-point of RT. Find the coordinates of S and T. Prove that $RP = RT$.

14. The coordinates of the points A, B, C are $(t, -1)$, $(-2, 1)$ and $(4, 3)$ respectively. Given that $AB = AC$, calculate the value of t. The line BC is produced to D so that $BC = CD$. Calculate the coordinates of D and the length of AD.

15. The vertices of a quadrilateral $ABCD$ are $A(-4, 3)$, $B(2, 1)$, $C(1, -2)$ and $D(-2, -3)$. Prove that $AB = AD$ and $BC = CD$. Find the area of the quadrilateral.

2.4 Gradient of a straight line

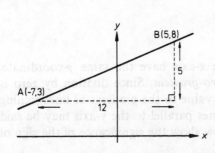

The *gradient* of a straight line is a quantity used for measuring the direction of a line in relation to the co-ordinate axes. Consider the straight line which passes through the points $A(-7, 3)$ and $B(5, 8)$. Moving from A to B results in increases of 12 in the x-coordinate and 5 in the y-coordinate. The gradient of AB is the ratio of these increases,

i.e.   gradient of $AB = \dfrac{\text{increase in } y}{\text{increase in } x} = \dfrac{5}{12}$.

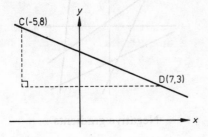

For the points $C(-5, 8)$ and $D(7, 3)$ the increase in x is 12, but there is a decrease in y of 5. This can be considered as an increase of -5

$\therefore$ gradient of $CD = -\dfrac{5}{12}$.

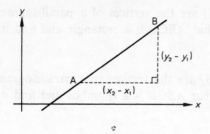

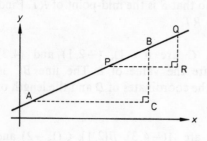

In general, for a line passing through the points $A(x_1, y_1)$ and $B(x_2, y_2)$, we have:

$$\text{gradient} = \frac{y_2 - y_1}{x_2 - x_1} \text{ or } \frac{y_1 - y_2}{x_1 - x_2}.$$

By considering similar triangles ABC and PQR, we see that $\dfrac{BC}{CA} = \dfrac{QR}{RP}$.

Thus the value of the gradient of a line does not depend on the particular points used to calculate it, but only on the angle the line makes with the x-axis. As *parallel* lines make equal angles with the x-axis, they must have equal gradients.

Example 1   Find the gradients of the lines joining
(a) $A(4, -3)$ and $B(2, 1)$ (b) $C(4, 3)$ and $D(-2, 1)$.

(a) Gradient of $AB = \dfrac{-3 - 1}{4 - 2} = \dfrac{-4}{2} = -2.$

(b) Gradient of $CD = \dfrac{3 - 1}{4 - (-2)} = \dfrac{2}{6} = \dfrac{1}{3}.$

All the points on a line parallel to the x-axis have the same y-coordinate. Hence lines parallel to the x-axis have *zero gradient*. Since division by zero is undefined, we can give no finite numerical value to the gradient of lines joining points with the same x-coordinate. Thus lines parallel to the y-axis may be said to have *infinite gradient*. The diagrams below show the significance of the sign of the gradient of a line.

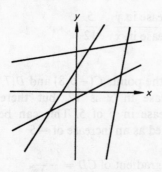

Positive gradients

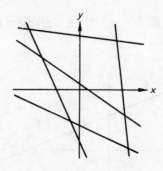

Negative gradients

To find the relationship between the gradients of *perpendicular* lines, consider a pair of perpendicular lines through the origin with gradients m_1 and m_2.

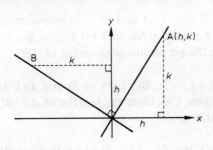

Let $A(h,k)$ be a typical point on the first line and let B be a point on the second line such that $OB = OA$. If OA is rotated anti-clockwise through $90°$, the point A moves to B. Hence the coordinates of B are $(-k, h)$. Thus,

gradient of $OA = m_1 = \dfrac{k}{h}$ and

gradient of $OB = m_2 = -\dfrac{h}{k}$

$$\therefore \quad m_1 m_2 = \frac{k}{h} \times \left(-\frac{h}{k}\right), \quad \text{i.e.} \quad m_1 m_2 = -1.$$

For any pair of perpendicular lines there is a corresponding pair through the origin, therefore the product of the gradients of perpendicular lines is -1.

Example 2 Write down the gradients of lines perpendicular to lines with gradients (a) 2, (b) $\frac{1}{2}$, (c) $-5/4$.

The gradients of the perpendicular lines are
(a) $-\frac{1}{2}$, (b) -2, (c) $4/5$.

Exercise 2.4

1. Find the gradients of the lines joining the points
(a) $(3,5)$ and $(-1,2)$ (b) $(4,6)$ and $(5,-1)$
(c) $(-2,6)$ and $(-1,4)$ (d) $(-2,-3)$ and $(-9,-6)$
(e) $(-4,0)$ and $(-3,5)$ (f) $(0,-7)$ and $(2,-5)$

2. Write down the gradients of lines perpendicular to those given in question 1.

3. By comparing the gradients of AB and BC, or otherwise, decide whether or not the points A, B and C are collinear.
(a) $A(1,-6)$, $B(3,-2)$, $C(-7,6)$ (b) $A(-2,6)$, $B(5,7)$, $C(-9,5)$
(c) $A(3,4)$, $B(-1,-8)$, $C(5,10)$ (d) $A(1,1)$, $B(6,-2)$, $C(-3,4)$.

4. Given the points $A(8,-1)$, $B(5,5)$, $C(-5,5)$ and $D(-3,1)$, show that
(a) $ABCD$ is a trapezium, (b) AB is perpendicular to BD.

5. Given the points $X(-6,-2)$, $Y(-4,3)$ and $Z(6,-1)$, show that $\angle XYZ$ is a right angle. If M and N are the mid-points of XY and YZ, verify that MN is parallel to XZ.

6. The coordinates of the points P, Q and R are $(4,-3)$, $(-1,2)$ and $(2,t)$

respectively. Calculate the values of t given that (a) P, Q and R are collinear, (b) $\angle QPR = 90°$, (c) $\angle PRQ = 90°$.

7. The coordinates of the points A and B are $(1,6)$ and $(5, -2)$ respectively. Find the coordinates of the point C on the x-axis, given that (a) C also lies on AB, (b) $\angle ABC$ is a right angle, (c) C lies on the perpendicular bisector of AB.

8. A quadrilateral $ABCD$ has vertices $A(-1, -2)$, $B(5,0)$, $C(4,3)$ and $D(1,2)$. Show that $\angle ABC$ and $\angle BCD$ are right angles. Calculate the lengths of AB, BC and CD and hence find the area of the quadrilateral.

9. Given the points $P(7, -4)$, $Q(9,8)$, $R(-3,10)$, $S(-12, -7)$, show that (a) QS is perpendicular to PR, (b) QS passes through the mid-point of PR.

10. Given that the triangle with vertices $X(1,2)$, $Y(2,a)$ and $Z(-4, -3)$ is right-angled at Y, find the two possible values of a and the area of the triangle in each case.

11. A quadrilateral $ABCD$ has vertices $A(10,5)$, $B(5, -4)$, $C(-5, -7)$ and $D(-3,6)$. Show that AC is perpendicular to BD and calculate the area of the quadrilateral.

12. Show that the points $D(5, -3)$, $E(2,6)$, $F(-1,10)$ and $G(-4,9)$ are the vertices of a trapezium. Show also that DE is perpendicular to FG and that the area of the trapezium is 30 square units.

2.5 The equation of a line

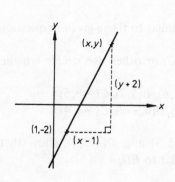

The equation of a straight line is an equation connecting the variables x and y which is satisfied by any point (x, y) on the line. The gradient is used to find a suitable equation. Consider the line with gradient 2, which passes through the point $(1, -2)$. If the point (x, y) lies on the line, then its gradient is given by $\dfrac{y+2}{x-1}$.

Hence $\dfrac{y+2}{x-1} = 2$ for any point (x, y) on the line.

Rearranging, $y+2 = 2(x-1)$,   i.e. $y+2 = 2x-2$

$\therefore$ the equation of the line is $y = 2x - 4$.

The same method can be used to find the equation of a line with gradient m passing through the point (x_1, y_1).

The gradient of the line $= \dfrac{y - y_1}{x - x_1} = m$

$\therefore$ the equation of the line is $y - y_1 = m(x - x_1)$.

Example 1   Find the equation of the line with gradient $-\frac{1}{2}$ which passes through the point $(2, -3)$.

The equation of the line is $y + 3 = -\frac{1}{2}(x - 2)$
i.e. $2(y + 3) = -(x - 2)$
$2y + 6 = -x + 2$

$\therefore$ the required equation is $x + 2y + 4 = 0$.

Example 2   Find the equation of the line which passes through the points $(2, -2)$ and $(1, 3)$.

The gradient of the line $= \dfrac{-2 - 3}{2 - 1} = -5$

$\therefore$ the equation of the line is $y + 2 = -5(x - 2)$, i.e. $5x + y - 8 = 0$.

The general form of the straight line equation emerges when we consider a line with gradient m passing through the point $(0, c)$ on the y-axis. Its equation is $y - c = m(x - 0)$, i.e. $y = mx + c$. Hence the equation $y = mx + c$ represents a straight line with gradient m, where c is the *intercept* on the y-axis. In particular, $y = mx$ is a line through the origin $(0, 0)$ and $y = c$ is a line parallel to the x-axis. Lines parallel to the y-axis have equations of the form $x = k$.

Example 3   Find the gradient of the line $3x + 4y = 8$ and the intercept on the y-axis.

The equation may be written $4y = -3x + 8$, i.e. $y = -\frac{3}{4}x + 2$

$\therefore$ the gradient of the line is $-\frac{3}{4}$ and the intercept on the y-axis is 2, i.e. the line cuts the y-axis at the point $(0, 2)$.

A straight line is usually sketched by finding its points of intersection with both x- and y-axes.

Example 4   Sketch the line $2x - 3y = 12$.

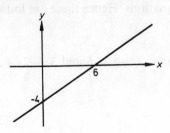

$x = 0 \Rightarrow -3y = 12 \Rightarrow y = -4$

$\therefore$ the line cuts the y-axis at $(0, -4)$.

$y = 0 \Rightarrow 2x = 12 \Rightarrow x = 6$

$\therefore$ the line cuts the x-axis at $(6, 0)$.

The general equation of a straight line can also be written $y - mx = c$. This form is sometimes used when obtaining the equation of a line with given gradient. The constant c is determined by substituting the coordinates of a point on the line.

Example 5   Find the equation of the line through $(-1, 2)$ with gradient 3.

The equation of the line is $y - 3x = 2 - 3(-1)$, i.e. $y - 3x = 5$.

The properties of the gradients of parallel and perpendicular lines are used in the next example.

Example 6   Find the equations of the lines parallel and perpendicular to the line $3x - 2y = 1$, which pass through the point $(2, 3)$.

Method 1   Rearranging the given equation, we obtain $y = \dfrac{3}{2}x - \dfrac{1}{2}$

$\therefore$ the gradient of the given line is $3/2$.
Hence the gradient of any parallel line is $3/2$.
The equation of the parallel line through $(2, 3)$ is

$$y - 3 = \frac{3}{2}(x - 2), \quad \text{i.e.} \quad 2(y - 3) = 3(x - 2)$$
$$2y - 6 = 3x - 6$$

which may be written $3x - 2y = 0$.
The gradient of any perpendicular line is $-\frac{2}{3}$.
$\therefore$ the equation of the perpendicular line through $(2, 3)$ is

$$y - 3 = -\tfrac{2}{3}(x - 2), \quad \text{i.e.} \quad 3(y - 3) = -2(x - 2)$$
$$3y - 9 = -2x + 4$$

which may be written $2x + 3y = 13$.

In time, the reader may prefer to adopt a quicker method based on the fact that any line parallel to $3x - 2y = 1$ has an equation of the form $3x - 2y = c$, and any perpendicular line the form $2x + 3y = k$.

Method 2   The equation of the required parallel line is

$$3x - 2y = 3.2 - 2.3, \quad \text{i.e.} \quad 3x - 2y = 0.$$

The equation of the required perpendicular line is

$$2x + 3y = 2.2 + 3.3, \quad \text{i.e.} \quad 2x + 3y = 13.$$

The point of intersection of two straight lines is the point which lies on both lines, therefore its coordinates must satisfy both equations. Hence these are found by solving the equations simultaneously.

Example 7   Find the point of intersection of the lines $3x + y = 5$ and $3x - 2y + 1 = 0$.

At the point of intersection $3x + y = 5$ .... (1)

   and $3x - 2y = -1$ .... (2)

Subtracting (2) from (1): $3y = 6$ $\therefore y = 2$
Substituting in (1): $3x + 2 = 5$ $\therefore x = 1$
$\therefore$ the point of intersection is $(1, 2)$.

[This method will break down if the two lines are parallel and thus have no point of intersection.]

Exercise 2.5

1.   Find the equations of the straight lines through the given points with the given gradients.
(a) $(-2, 3)$; 4   (b) $(2, -3)$; $-\frac{1}{2}$ (c) $(4, -1)$; -3
(d) $(-5, -7)$; $\frac{2}{3}$ (e) $(-12, 5)$; $-5/12$ (f) $(t^2, 2t)$; $1/t$.

2.   Find the equations of the lines joining the following points.
(a) $(0, -7)$, $(2, -5)$ (b) $(-2, 6)$, $(-1, 4)$
(c) $(4, 7)$, $(-5, 7)$ (d) $(4, 3)$, $(-4, -3)$
(e) $(-2, -3)$, $(-9, -6)$ (f) $(6, 2)$, $(6, -3)$
(g) $(p^2, 2p)$, $(q^2, 2q)$ (h) $(p, 1/p)$, $(q, 1/q)$.

3.   Find the gradients and intercepts on the y-axis of the following lines.
(a) $2y = 5x + 9$,   (b) $4y - 7x + 13 = 0$,   (c) $2x + 8y + 19 = 0$,
(d) $3x - 6y - 17 = 0$,   (e) $2y + 5 = 0$,   (f) $5x + 9y - 27 = 0$.

4.   In each of the following cases sketch the given lines and find their points of intersection, if any.
(a) $4x + 3y = 7$, $3x - 4y + 1 = 0$,   (b) $y = 4x - 10$, $4y = 11 - x$,
(c) $2x - 5y = 15$, $3x - 7y = 21$,   (d) $5y = 17 - 4x$, $8x + 10y = 19$,
(e) $8x + 7y = 23$, $8y = 7x - 6$,   (f) $5y - 2x = 3$, $2y - 5x = 4$.

5.   Decide whether the pairs of lines given in question 4 are (i) perpendicular, (ii) parallel.

6.   In each of the following cases find the equations of the lines parallel and perpendicular to the given line through the given point.
(a) $y = 2x - 3$, $(-1, 3)$ (b) $3x + 2y = 7$, $(0, 2)$
(c) $3x - 5 = 0$, $(3, -4)$ (d) $3x - 9y = 4$, $(-2, -1)$.

7.   Find the coordinates of the foot of the perpendicular from the point $(-2, 4)$ to the line $x - 2y - 5 = 0$.

8.   Find the coordinates of the foot of the perpendicular from the point $(4, 5)$ to the line $2x + 5y = 4$.

9.   Prove that the lines $3x - 2y + 7 = 0$, $5x + 4y = 3$ and $2x + 5y = 8$ are concurrent. Find the equation of the line through the point of intersection which has gradient 3.

10. Find the equation of the perpendicular bisector of the line joining the points $(-2, 3)$ and $(8, -7)$.

11. Given the points $A(9, -4)$, $B(2, 10)$ and $C(-4, 2)$, show that the perpendicular bisector of BC intersects AB on the x-axis.

12. The points $A(7, 3)$, $B(1, -4)$, $C(-5, -1)$ are three vertices of a trapezium $ABCD$. Given that $\angle BCD = 90°$, find (a) the equations of AD and CD, (b) the coordinates of D.

13. The points $P(-3, 1)$, $Q(-1, 5)$, $R(6, 4)$ are three vertices of a trapezium $PQRS$ in which PQ is parallel to SR. Given that the diagonals intersect at right angles, find the coordinates of S.

14. The point $A(7, 5)$ is one vertex of a parallelogram $ABCD$. The equations of the sides BC and CD are $3y = 2x - 9$ and $2y = 3x - 1$ respectively. Find the coordinates of B and D. Show that the diagonals cut at right angles.

15. The equations of two sides of a triangle PQR are $x + 2y + 4 = 0$ and $3x - 4y + 37 = 0$. Given that $\angle PQR = 90°$ and that P is the point $(6, -5)$, find the coordinates of Q.

16. Find the reflection of the point $P(3, 1)$ in the line l with equation $y = 2x$. Use your answer to find the reflection in l of the line $y = x - 2$.

2.6 Linear inequalities

In the previous section it was shown that the equation $y = mx + c$ represents a straight line. We now consider inequalities, such as $y > mx + c$, and the sets of points they represent in the x, y plane.

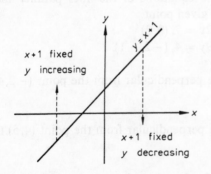

Consider the line $y = x + 1$. At any point on the line, the value of y is equal to the value of $x + 1$. If we move away from the line in a direction parallel to the y-axis, then the value of $x + 1$ remains unchanged. However, the value of y either increases or decreases as shown in the diagram. Thus, for points above the line $y > x + 1$ and for points below the line $y < x + 1$.

By a similar argument, we find that the inequality $y > mx + c$ represents the set of points above the line $y = mx + c$, and $y < mx + c$ the set of points below the line $y = mx + c$.

Example 1 Sketch the region of the x, y plane represented by the inequality $y > 2x + 3$.

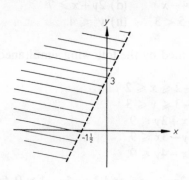

On the boundary of the region $y = 2x + 3$.

$$x = 0 \Rightarrow y = 3$$
$$y = 0 \Rightarrow 2x + 3 = 0 \Rightarrow x = -1\tfrac{1}{2}$$

∴ the boundary line cuts the axes at $(0, 3)$ and $(-1\tfrac{1}{2}, 0)$. Hence $y > 2x + 3$ represents the shaded region shown in the diagram.

[The broken line is used to indicate that points on the boundary do not belong to the region.]

An alternative approach is used in the next example.

Example 2 Sketch the region of the x, y plane represented by the inequality $x + 3y - 2 \leqslant 0$,

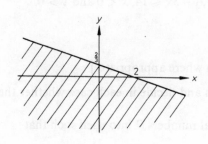

On the boundary of the region $x + 3y - 2 = 0$.

$$x = 0 \Rightarrow 3y - 2 = 0 \Rightarrow y = \tfrac{2}{3}$$
$$y = 0 \Rightarrow x - 2 = 0 \Rightarrow x = 2$$

∴ the boundary line cuts the axes at $(0, \tfrac{2}{3})$ and $(2, 0)$.
At the origin, $x + 3y - 2 = -2$
∴ the origin lies in the required region.
Hence $x + 3y - 2 \leqslant 0$ represents the set of points on and below the line $x + 3y - 2 = 0$.

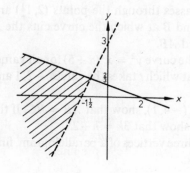

Combining the results of Examples 1 and 2, we obtain the region in which the inequalities $y > 2x + 3$ and $x + 3y - 2 \leqslant 0$ hold simultaneously.

Exercise 2.6

1. Sketch the region of the x, y plane represented by the following inequalities.
(a) $y > x+1$ (b) $y < 3x-6$ (c) $y \leqslant 4-x$ (d) $2y+x \geqslant 7$
(e) $2y < 5x$ (f) $3y-2x > 8$ (g) $2x-5 < 3$ (h) $y^2 \leqslant 4$.

2. Sketch the region of the x, y plane represented by the following simultaneous inequalities.

(a) $2y > x+5$ (b) $x < y$ (c) $-2 \leqslant x \leqslant 2$
    $x > -1$ $x+y \leqslant 8$ $-3 \leqslant y \leqslant 3$
(d) $-x < y < x$ (e) $y+2 > 0$ (f) $x+3y \leqslant 9$
    $2 < 2x+y < 4$ $y < 2x+4$ $y-3x \leqslant 9$
                    $y+3x < 6$ $3x-4y \leqslant 9$.

3. Given that x and y satisfy the inequalities $2x-y < 8$ and $3x+5y+1 > 0$, find the range of possible values for y.

4. Given that x and y satisfy the inequalities $4x+3y \leqslant 15$ and $3x-2y < 7$, find the range of possible values for x.

5. Given that $2x+y > 0$, $2y > x$ and $y < 3$, find the range of possible values of
(a) x, (b) y, (c) $x+y$.

6. Repeat question 5 given that $x+4y \leqslant 17$, $y-3x \leqslant 14$, $x < 0$ and $y > 0$.

Exercise 2.7   *(miscellaneous)*

[Leave answers in surd form where appropriate.]

1. Find the range of the following functions and decide in each case whether the function is (i) one-one, (ii) 'onto'.
(a) f is the function which maps the set of real numbers $\mathbb{R}$ into itself such that
    $f : x \rightarrow x^2-4$.
(b) g is the function which maps the set of positive integers $\mathbb{Z}^+$ into the set of rational numbers $\mathbb{Q}$ defined by $g : x \rightarrow 1/x$.
(c) h is the function from $\mathbb{R} \times \mathbb{R}$ into $\mathbb{R}$ defined by $h : (r, s) \rightarrow r+s$.
2. Draw the graph of the function f defined by $f : x \rightarrow x(x-3)$ for the domain $-2 \leqslant x \leqslant 5$. Find the range of the function corresponding to this domain. Find also the largest possible domain for which the range is $0 \leqslant f(x) \leqslant 18$.
3. Given that the curve $y = (x+a)/(x+b)$ passes through the points $(2, 1\frac{1}{2})$ and $(-1, 3)$, find the coordinates of the points A and B at which the curve cuts the x- and y-axes and calculate the length of the chord AB.
4. Show that the point (t^2-5, t^3-5t) lies on the curve $y^2 = x^2(x+5)$ for all values of t. Show also that if P, Q and R are the points at which t takes the values -2, 1 and 3 respectively, then P, Q and R are collinear.
5. Given the points $A(-3, -2)$, $B(4, 2)$ and $C(-4, 1)$, show that $AB = BC$. If the point $P(h, k)$ is also equidistant from A and C, show that $3k = h+2$.
6. If the points $(2, -1)$, $(6, 7)$ and $(-2, 7)$ are three vertices of a parallelogram, find the three possible positions of the fourth vertex.

7.   Find the equations of the following straight lines:
(a) the line through $(1, 3)$ with gradient 2,
(b) the line through the points $(3, -5)$ and $(-2, 4)$,
(c) the line through $(2, -1)$ parallel to the line $4x - 3y = 2$,
(d) the line through $(-3, 6)$ perpendicular to the line $3x - 5y = 7$.
8.   The sides AB, BC of the parallelogram $ABCD$ have equations $y + 3x = 1$ and $y = 5x - 7$ respectively. If the coordinates of D are $(5, 10)$, find the coordinates of A, B and C.
9.   A triangle has vertices $A(-3, 0)$, $B(5, 4)$, $C(7, -2)$. If D, E and F are the mid-points of BC, CA and AB respectively, find the point of intersection of the medians AD and BE. Show that this point also lies on the median CF.
10. Show that the points $(5, 3)$, $(-1, -5)$ and $(-2, 2)$ are three vertices of a square and find the coordinates of the fourth vertex. Find also the area of the square.
11. The points $(2, 4)$, $(-1, 2)$, $(2, -1)$ are the mid-points of the sides of a triangle. Find the coordinates of the vertices of the triangle.
12. The points A, B, C and D have coordinates $(3, -2)$, $(p, 3)$, $(6, 2)$ and (q, r) respectively. Given that quadrilateral $ABCD$ is a rhombus, find (a) the values of p, q and r, (b) the area of the rhombus.
13. The line $y = x + 5$ is the perpendicular bisector of the line joining the points $P(3, 10)$ and $Q(h, k)$. Find in terms of h and k (a) the coordinates of the mid-point of PQ and (b) the gradient of PQ. Deduce that $h + 3 = k$ and that $h + k = 13$.
14. The equation of the side QR of a triangle PQR is $3x - 4y = 10$, the coordinates of P are $(3, 6)$ and the gradient of PQ is 7. Given that $PQ = PR$, find (a) the coordinates of the foot of the perpendicular from P to QR, (b) the equation of the side PR.
15. Given that X, Y and Z are the feet of the perpendiculars from the origin O to the lines with equations $x = 3$, $x + y = 18$ and $8x - 6y = 25$, show that X, Y and Z lie on a straight line.
16. The line $3x + 4y = 30$ cuts the x-axis at A and the y-axis at B. Find (a) the perpendicular distance from the origin O to the line AB, (b) the equation of the perpendicular bisector of AB.
17. P is the point of intersection of the lines $3x - y = 7$ and $x + 4y + 2 = 0$. Find (a) the equation of the line parallel to $2x + 3y = 40$ which passes through P, (b) the perpendicular distance of P from the line $2x + 3y = 40$.
18. The points $A(3, -1)$, $B(-2, 4)$, $C(-1, 7)$ are three vertices of the quadrilateral $ABCD$. Given that $\triangle ADC$ is the reflection in the line AC of $\triangle ABC$, find (a) the coordinates of D, (b) the area of quadrilateral $ABCD$.
19. The points $(3, -2)$, $(4, 5)$, $(-3, 6)$ are the vertices of a triangle. Find the coordinates of the centre and the radius of the circumscribed circle.
20. Draw a diagram illustrating the region S of the x, y plane which is defined by the simultaneous inequalities $x + y \geqslant 7$, $2x + y \leqslant 13$, $2x + 3y \leqslant 19$, and give the coordinates of the vertices of S. Prove that, if the line $y = kx$ intersects S, then $1/6 \leqslant k \leqslant 2\frac{1}{2}$.

 The point P lies on $y = kx$ and is in the region S. Prove that, when $1/6 \leqslant k \leqslant 3/5$, the maximum value for the y-coordinate of P is $13k/(2 + k)$, and find the corresponding expression when $3/5 \leqslant k \leqslant 2\frac{1}{2}$.   (C)

3 Polynomials and equations

3.1 The quadratic function

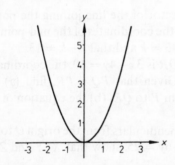

A *quadratic function* is a function of the form $f(x) = ax^2 + bx + c$, i.e. $f: x \to ax^2 + bx + c$, where $a \neq 0$. Thus the graph of a quadratic function has an equation of the form $y = ax^2 + bx + c$.

As shown in the diagram, the graph of $y = x^2$ is symmetrical about the y-axis. The lowest point of the graph, called the *minimum point*, occurs at the origin $(0, 0)$. Hence the *minimum value* of the function $f(x) = x^2$ is zero.

The graphs of some related functions are shown in the diagrams below.

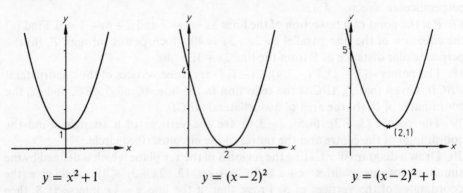

$$y = x^2 + 1 \qquad y = (x-2)^2 \qquad y = (x-2)^2 + 1$$

In each case a curve identical to the curve $y = x^2$ is produced. The term $+1$ in the equation $y = x^2 + 1$ moves the curve up 1 unit. In the graph of $y = (x-2)^2$ the original curve is moved 2 units to the right. The result of moving the curve 2 units to the right and 1 unit up is the graph with equation $y = (x-2)^2 + 1$, i.e. $y = x^2 - 4x + 5$.

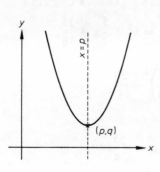

Hence the equation $y = (x-p)^2 + q$ represents a graph of the same shape as $y = x^2$, moved p units to the right and q units up. Thus it is symmetrical about the line $x = p$ and has a minimum point (p, q). This is confirmed by considering the range of the function $f(x) = (x-p)^2 + q$. Since $(x-p)^2$ is never negative, the least possible value of $f(x)$ is given by $(x-p)^2 = 0$. Hence $f(x)$ takes its minimum value q when $x = p$, and its range is the set $\{y \in \mathbb{R} : y \geqslant q\}$.

Example 1   Find the minimum value of the function $f(x) = x^2 - 2x + 5$ and sketch its graph.

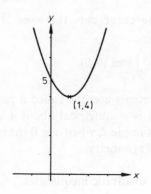

$$f(x) = x^2 - 2x + 5 = (x^2 - 2x + 1) + 4$$
$$= (x-1)^2 + 4$$

$\therefore$ $f(x)$ has a minimum value 4 given by $x = 1$.

Since $f(0) = 5$, the graph cuts the y-axis at the point $(0, 5)$.

[Note that $x^2 - 2x + 5$ is expressed as $(x-1)^2 + 4$ by 'completing the square' of the form $x^2 - 2x + \ldots$. The -1 in the bracket is half the original coefficient of x.]

We now consider the graph of $y = ax^2 + bx + c$ for values of a other than 1.

Example 2   Sketch the graph of $y = 5 - 4x - x^2$.

$y = 5 - 4x - x^2 = 5 - (x^2 + 4x) = 9 - (x^2 + 4x + 4) = 9 - (x+2)^2$

$\therefore$ y has a maximum value 9 given by $x = -2$.

$x = 0 \Rightarrow y = 5$ $\therefore$ the graph cuts the y-axis at $(0, 5)$.
$y = 0 \Leftrightarrow$ $5 - 4x - x^2 = 0$
$\Leftrightarrow (5 + x)(1 - x) = 0$
$\Leftrightarrow 5 + x = 0$ or $1 - x = 0$
$\Leftrightarrow$ $x = -5$ or $x = 1$

$\therefore$ the graph cuts the x-axis at $(-5, 0)$ and $(1, 0)$.

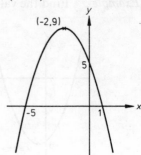

Example 3   Sketch the curve $y = 2x^2 + 5x$.

$$y = 2x^2 + 5x = 2\left\{x^2 + \frac{5}{2}x\right\}, \quad \text{but} \quad \left(x + \frac{5}{4}\right)^2 = x^2 + \frac{5}{2}x + \frac{25}{16}$$

$$\therefore \quad y = 2\left\{\left(x^2 + \frac{5}{2}x + \frac{25}{16}\right) - \frac{25}{16}\right\} = 2\left(x + \frac{5}{4}\right)^2 - \frac{25}{8}.$$

Hence y has a minimum value $-\dfrac{25}{8}$ given by $x = -\dfrac{5}{4}$.

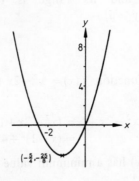

$$x = 0 \Rightarrow y = 0$$
$$y = 0 \Leftrightarrow 2x^2 + 5x = 0$$
$$\Leftrightarrow x(2x + 5) = 0$$
$$\Leftrightarrow x = 0 \quad \text{or} \quad 2x + 5 = 0$$
$$\Leftrightarrow x = 0 \quad \text{or} \quad x = -\frac{5}{2}$$

$\therefore$ the curve cuts the axes at the points

$$\left(-\frac{5}{2}, 0\right) \text{ and } (0,0).$$

In general, the equation $y = ax^2 + bx + c$ represents a curve called a *parabola*. For $a > 0$, the curve has a minimum point and is symmetrical about a vertical axis through this point. However, as shown in Example 2, when $a < 0$ the curve is inverted and has a maximum point on the axis of symmetry.

The last two examples in this section deal with quadratic inequalities.

Example 4   Prove that $2x^2 + 8x + 9 > 0$ for all real values of x.

$$2x^2 + 8x + 9 = 2(x^2 + 4x) + 9 = 2(x^2 + 4x + 4) - 8 + 9 = 2(x + 2)^2 + 1.$$

For all real values of x, $(x + 2)^2 \geqslant 0 \therefore 2x^2 + 8x + 9 > 0$.

Example 5   Find the values of x for which $x^2 - 1 < x + 5$.

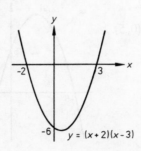

$$x^2 - 1 < x + 5$$
$$\Leftrightarrow \quad x^2 - x - 6 < 0$$
$$\Leftrightarrow (x + 2)(x - 3) < 0.$$

The sketch shows that the curve $y = (x + 2)(x - 3)$ lies below the x-axis for $-2 < x < 3$.
Hence if $x^2 - 1 < x + 5$, then $-2 < x < 3$.

Exercise 3.1

1. Find the maximum or minimum value of each of the quadratic functions given below and sketch the graph of the function.
(a) $x^2 + 4x - 5$ (b) $2x - x^2$ (c) $x^2 - 3x + 4$ (d) $x^2 + 4$
(e) $4x^2 - 12$ (f) $4x^2 - 12x + 9$ (g) $2 + x - 3x^2$ (h) $4x - 6x^2 - 9$.

2. Find the range of each of the following functions.
(a) $f: x \to x^2 - 5$ (b) $f: x \to x^2 - 6x$ (c) $f: x \to 2x^2 + 2x + 1$ (d) $f: x \to 6 - 5x - x^2$.

3. Express the function $f(x) = x^2 - 4x + 8$ in the form $(x - p)^2 + q$. Deduce that $f(x)$ is positive for all real values of x.

4. Prove that the expression $x - 2 - x^2$ is negative for all real values of x.

5. Prove that the following inequalities hold for all real values of x.
(a) $2x^2 + 5 > 4x$ (b) $2(2x - 1) < 3x^2$ (c) $9x^2 - 30x + 25 \geqslant 0$ (d) $2x < 2x^2 + 1$.

6. Find the values of x for which
(a) $x^2 - 2x < 0$ (b) $x^2 + 8 \leqslant 6x + 3$ (c) $x^2 - 4 \geqslant 0$
(d) $4x + 1 < x^2 + 4$ (e) $3x^2 + 2x < 1$ (f) $2x^2 + 7x + 3 \geqslant 0$.
[You may find sketch graphs helpful.]

7. Find the minimum value of the function $3x^2 - 12x + 5$ and sketch the curve $y = 3x^2 - 12x + 5$. Find the range of values of c for which the function $3x^2 - 12x + c$ is positive for all values of x.

8. Find the range of values of k such that $x^2 + 3x + k \geqslant 0$ for all real values of x.

9. If $y = x^2 + 2px + q$, find the values of p and q in each of the following cases.
(a) $y = 0$ when $x = 2$ and when $x = 4$,
(b) $y = 1$ when $x = 2$ and $y = 7$ when $x = -4$,
(c) y has a minimum value of 2 when $x = -1$.

10. The maximum value of the function $f(x) = ax^2 + bx + c$ is 10. Given that $f(3) = f(-1) = 2$, find $f(2)$.

3.2 Quadratic equations

An equation of the form $ax^2 + bx + c = 0$ is called a *quadratic equation*. Many such equations are solved by factorising. Others may be solved by completing the square as follows:

$$x^2 - 6x + 7 = 0 \Leftrightarrow x^2 - 6x + 9 = 2$$
$$\Leftrightarrow (x - 3)^2 = 2$$
$$\Leftrightarrow x - 3 = \pm\sqrt{2}$$
$$\Leftrightarrow x = 3 \pm \sqrt{2}.$$

Hence if $x^2 - 6x + 7 = 0$ then $x = 1 \cdot 59$ or $4 \cdot 41$ (to 2 d.p.).

However, in some cases the method breaks down.

$$x^2 - 2x + 5 = 0 \Leftrightarrow x^2 - 2x + 1 = -4$$
$$\Leftrightarrow \quad (x-1)^2 = -4$$

Since $(x-1)^2$ can never be negative, there are no real values of x which satisfy this equation.

Let us now consider the general quadratic equation.

$$ax^2 + bx + c = 0 \Leftrightarrow \quad x^2 + \frac{b}{a}x + \frac{c}{a} = 0$$

$$\Leftrightarrow x^2 + \frac{b}{a}x + \frac{b^2}{4a^2} = \frac{b^2}{4a^2} - \frac{c}{a}$$

$$\left(x + \frac{b}{2a}\right)^2 = \frac{b^2 - 4ac}{4a^2}.$$

Hence the nature of the roots of the equation $ax^2 + bx + c = 0$ depends on the sign of $b^2 - 4ac$.

(i) If $b^2 - 4ac > 0$, then $x + \dfrac{b}{2a} = \pm \dfrac{\sqrt{(b^2 - 4ac)}}{2a}$

∴   the equation has two distinct real roots given by

$$x = \frac{-b \pm \sqrt{(b^2 - 4ac)}}{2a}.$$

(ii) If $b^2 - 4ac = 0$, then $\left(x + \dfrac{b}{2a}\right)^2 = 0$

∴   the equation has two equal roots given by $x = -\dfrac{b}{2a}$.

(iii) If $b^2 - 4ac < 0$, then $\left(x + \dfrac{b}{2a}\right)^2 < 0$, which is not possible for real values of x

∴   the equation has no real roots.

The diagrams opposite show the curve $y = ax^2 + bx + c$ in these three cases, for $a > 0$. Each curve has a minimum point at $x = -\dfrac{b}{2a}$ and is symmetrical about the line $x = -\dfrac{b}{2a}$.

In case (iii) the graph shows that if $a > 0$ and $b^2 - 4ac < 0$ the function $ax^2 + bx + c$ is always positive. Similarly if $a < 0$ and $b^2 - 4ac < 0$ the function $ax^2 + bx + c$ is always negative.

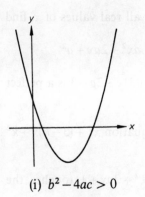 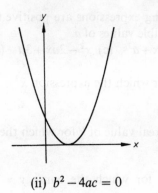 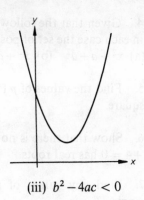

(i) $b^2 - 4ac > 0$ (ii) $b^2 - 4ac = 0$ (iii) $b^2 - 4ac < 0$

Example 1 Solve the equation $3x^2 - 4x - 2 = 0$.

$$3x^2 - 4x - 2 = 0 \Rightarrow x = \frac{-(-4) \pm \sqrt{\{(-4)^2 - 4.3.(-2)\}}}{2.3}$$

$$\Rightarrow x = \frac{4 \pm \sqrt{(16+24)}}{6}$$

$$\Rightarrow x = \frac{4 \pm \sqrt{40}}{6}$$

$\therefore$ the roots of the equation are -0.39 and 1.72 (to 2 d.p.).

Example 2 Find the range of values of p for which the equation $x^2 + px + p = 0$ has real roots.

The equation $ax^2 + bx + c = 0$ has real roots if $b^2 - 4ac \geqslant 0$
$\therefore$ the equation $x^2 + px + p = 0$ has real roots if $p^2 - 4p \geqslant 0$
    i.e.   if $p(p-4) \geqslant 0$.
Since p and $(p-4)$ are both positive when $p > 4$ and both negative when $p < 0$, the equation has real roots when $p \leqslant 0$ and when $p \geqslant 4$.

Exercise 3.2

1. Find the real roots, if any, of the following quadratic equations, giving your answers in surd form.
(a) $x^2 - 3x + 1 = 0$ (b) $2x^2 + 3x - 1 = 0$ (c) $1 - 2x - x^2 = 0$
(d) $3x^2 - 4x + 2 = 0$ (e) $4x^2 - 12x - 27 = 0$ (f) $2x^2 - 6x + 3 = 0$.

2. Find the values of k for which the following equations have equal roots.
(a) $x^2 + 2kx + k + 6 = 0$,   (b) $(x+1)(x+3) = k$.

3. Find the range of values of p for which each of the given equations has two distinct real roots.
(a) $x^2 + 2px - 5p = 0$ (b) $3x^2 + 3px + p^2 = 1$
(c) $x(x+3) = p(x-1)$ (d) $p(x^2 - 1) = 3x + 2$.

4.   Given that the following expressions are positive for all real values of x, find in each case the set of possible values of a.

(a) $x^2 + a + a^2$ (b) $x^2 + ax + a^2$ (c) $x^2 - 2ax + 3a$ (d) $ax^2 + 2ax + a^2$.

5.   Find the values of p for which the expression $x^2 + (p+3)x + 2p + 3$ is a perfect square.

6.   Show that there is no real value of k for which the equation $x^2 + (3-k)x + k^2 + 4 = 0$ has real roots.

7.   Find any values of p for which the curve $y = 3px^2 + 2px + 1$ touches the x-axis.

8.   Find the set of values of k for which the equation $kx^2 + x + k - 1 = 0$ has real roots, one positive and one negative.

9.   Find the set of values of k for which the roots of the equation $x^2 + kx - k + 3 = 0$ are real and of the same sign.

10.   Given that $y = px^2 + 2qx + r$, show that y will have the same sign for all real values of x if and only if $q^2 < pr$.

3.3 Sum and product of roots

The quadratic equation with roots α and β may be written

$$(x - \alpha)(x - \beta) = 0 \quad \text{i.e.} \quad x^2 - (\alpha + \beta)x + \alpha\beta = 0.$$

The equation $ax^2 + bx + c = 0$ may be written $x^2 + \dfrac{b}{a}x + \dfrac{c}{a} = 0$.

Hence if the equation $ax^2 + bx + c = 0$ has roots α and β,

$$\alpha + \beta = -\frac{b}{a}, \quad \alpha\beta = \frac{c}{a}.$$

Example 1   Write down the sum and product of the roots of the equation $3x^2 - 6x + 2 = 0$.

The sum of the roots $= -\dfrac{(-6)}{3} = 2$.

The product of the roots $= \dfrac{2}{3}$.

When the sum and product of the roots of a quadratic equation are known, the equation may be written down in the form

$$x^2 - (\text{sum of roots})x + (\text{product of roots}) = 0.$$

Example 2 Write down the quadratic equation, the sum and product of whose roots are $\frac{3}{4}$ and -7 respectively.

The equation is $x^2 - \frac{3}{4}x + (-7) = 0$ i.e. $4x^2 - 3x - 28 = 0$.

Example 3 Given that one root of the equation $3x^2 + 4x + k = 0$ is three times the other, find k.

Let the roots of the given equation be α and 3α.

The sum of the roots $= \alpha + 3\alpha = -\frac{4}{3}$ i.e. $4\alpha = -\frac{4}{3}$

The product of the roots $= \alpha . 3\alpha = \frac{k}{3}$ i.e. $3\alpha^2 = \frac{k}{3}$

Hence $\alpha = -\frac{1}{3}$ and $k = 1$.

If α and β are the roots of a given quadratic equation, it is usually possible to find the value of a symmetrical function of α and β by expressing it in terms of $\alpha + \beta$ and $\alpha\beta$. [A symmetrical function of α and β is one which is unaltered if α and β are interchanged.]

Example 4 If α and β âre the roots of the equation $3x^2 - 5x + 1 = 0$, find the values of (i) $\frac{1}{\alpha} + \frac{1}{\beta}$ (ii) $\alpha^2 + \beta^2$.

$$\alpha + \beta = \frac{5}{3}, \qquad \alpha\beta = \frac{1}{3}$$

(i) $\dfrac{1}{\alpha} + \dfrac{1}{\beta} = \dfrac{\alpha + \beta}{\alpha\beta} = \dfrac{5}{3} \div \dfrac{1}{3} = \dfrac{5}{3} . \dfrac{3}{1} = 5$

(ii) $\alpha^2 + \beta^2 = (\alpha + \beta)^2 - 2\alpha\beta = \dfrac{25}{9} - 2 . \dfrac{1}{3} = \dfrac{19}{9}$.

Example 5 If α and β are the roots of the equation $x^2 + 7x + 5 = 0$, find an equation whose roots are $\alpha + 1$ and $\beta + 1$.

Method 1: $\alpha + \beta = -7$, $\alpha\beta = 5$
$(\alpha + 1) + (\beta + 1) = \alpha + \beta + 2 = -7 + 2 = -5$
$(\alpha + 1)(\beta + 1) = \alpha\beta + \alpha + \beta + 1 = 5 - 7 + 1 = -1$
$\therefore$ the required equation is $x^2 - (-5)x + (-1) = 0$
i.e. $x^2 + 5x - 1 = 0$.

Method 2: For the equation with roots $x = \alpha + 1$ or $x = \beta + 1$,
either $x - 1 = \alpha$ or $x - 1 = \beta$.

Since the equation with roots α and β is $x^2 + 7x + 5 = 0$, the required equation must take the form

$$(x-1)^2 + 7(x-1) + 5 = 0$$
$$x^2 - 2x + 1 + 7x - 7 + 5 = 0$$
$$\text{i.e.} \quad x^2 + 5x - 1 = 0.$$

Exercise 3.3

1. Find the sums and products of the roots of the following equations.
(a) $2x^2 - 5x - 3 = 0$ (b) $6 + x - x^2 = 0$ (c) $3x^2 - 5 = 0$
(d) $x^2 + px - p = 0$ (e) $x(x-2) = 5(x-1)$ (f) $4x - 1/x = 3$.

2. Find equations, the sums and products of whose roots are, respectively:
(a) $3, 2$ (b) $-\frac{1}{2}, \frac{3}{4}$ (c) $0, -4$
(d) $3/7, -1/14$ (e) $p - q, p + q$ (f) $a/b, 1/ab$.

3. Given that one root of the equation $2x^2 - kx + k = 0$, where $k \neq 0$, is twice the other, find k.

4. Given that the two roots of the equation $x^2 + (7 - p)x - p = 0$ differ by 5, find the possible values of p.

5. If α and β are the roots of the equation $ax^2 + bx + c = 0$, prove that
(i) if $\beta = 4\alpha$ then $4b^2 = 25ac$,   (ii) if $\beta = \alpha + 1$ then $a^2 = b^2 - 4ac$.

6. If α and β are the roots of the equation $x^2 - 3x - 2 = 0$, find the values of
(i) $\alpha + \beta$, (ii) $\alpha\beta$, (iii) $\alpha^2 + \beta^2$, (iv) $\alpha^3 + \beta^3$.

7. If α and β, where $\alpha > \beta$, are the roots of the equation $x^2 + 2x - 5 = 0$, find the values of (i) $(\alpha + \beta)^2$, (ii) $(\alpha - \beta)^2$, (iii) $\alpha - \beta$, (iv) $\alpha^2 - \beta^2$.

8. If α and β are the roots of the equation $2x^2 - x - 4 = 0$, find the values of
(a) $\alpha^2 + \beta^2$ (b) $(\alpha - \beta)^2$ (c) $\alpha^3 + \beta^3$
(d) $\dfrac{1}{\alpha} + \dfrac{1}{\beta}$ (e) $\dfrac{1}{\alpha^2} + \dfrac{1}{\beta^2}$ (f) $\dfrac{\alpha}{\beta^2} + \dfrac{\beta}{\alpha^2}$.

9. If $p + q = 5$ and $p^2 + q^2 = 19$, find the value of pq and write down an equation in x whose roots are p and q.

10. If $a - b = 3$ and $a^2 + b^2 = 65$, write down an equation in x whose roots are a and b.

11. If α and β are the roots of the equation $x^2 - 4x + 2 = 0$, find equations whose roots are
(a) $3\alpha, 3\beta$,   (b) $\alpha + 3, \beta + 3$,   (c) $\alpha + 3\beta, \beta + 3\alpha$.

12. If α and β are the roots of the equation $x^2 + x + k = 0$, find equations whose roots are

(a) α^2, β^2,　　　(b) $-\alpha, -\beta$,　　　(c) $\alpha - 1, \beta - 1$.

13. If α and β are the roots of the equation $ax^2 + bx + c = 0$, find equations whose roots are

(a) $\dfrac{1}{\alpha}, \dfrac{1}{\beta}$,　　　(b) $\alpha - \beta, \beta - \alpha$,　　　(c) $\dfrac{\alpha}{\alpha+\beta}, \dfrac{\beta}{\alpha+\beta}$.

14. Given that the equations $x^2 - 2x + p = 0$ and $2x^2 - 5x + q = 0$ have a common root, by eliminating the terms in x^2, show that this common root is $q - 2p$. Find expressions for the other roots of the equations.

15. Given that the equations $2x^2 + 3x + k = 0$ and $3x^2 + x - 2k = 0$ have a common root, find the possible values of k.

3.4 Non-linear simultaneous equations

In this section we deal with pairs of simultaneous equations in which at least one of the equations is non-linear. It is often necessary to solve such equations when finding the points of intersection of a line and a curve.

Example 1 Find the points of intersection of the line $y = x + 1$ and the curve $2x^2 + y^2 = 6$.

At the points of intersection
$$y = x + 1$$
$$\text{and} \quad 2x^2 + y^2 = 6$$
$$\therefore \quad 2x^2 + (x+1)^2 = 6$$
$$2x^2 + x^2 + 2x + 1 = 6$$
$$3x^2 + 2x - 5 = 0$$
$$(3x+5)(x-1) = 0$$

Hence either　$3x + 5 = 0$　or　$x - 1 = 0$
$$x = -5/3 \qquad\qquad x = 1$$

$\therefore$　the points of intersection are $(-5/3, -2/3)$ and $(1, 2)$.

Example 2 Show that the line $y = 3x - 1$ does not meet the curve $y = x^2 + 3x$.

At any points of intersection　$y = 3x - 1$
$$\text{and} \quad y = x^2 + 3x$$
$$\therefore \quad x^2 + 3x = 3x - 1, \text{ i.e. } x^2 = -1.$$

Since this equation has no real roots, there are no real points of intersection between the line and the curve.

Example 3 Find the points of intersection of the line $y = -x$ and the curve $y = x^3 + 6x^2 + 8x$.

At the points of intersection $x^3 + 6x^2 + 8x = -x$
i.e. $x^3 + 6x^2 + 9x = 0$
$$x(x+3)^2 = 0$$
∴   either $x = 0, y = 0$ or $x = -3, y = 3$.
Hence the points of intersection are $(0,0)$ and $(-3,3)$.

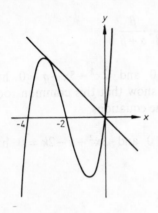

The significance of the fact that $x = -3$ appears as a repeated root in the above example is shown in this sketch graph. The line $y = -x$ is a tangent to the curve at the point $(-3,3)$.

In general, when solving simultaneous equations, one linear and the other quadratic, a method similar to the following is used.

Example 4   Solve the equations $2x - 3y = 4$ (1)
$$x^2 - 3xy + 3y^2 = 7 \qquad (2)$$

Rearranging (1) $3y = 2x - 4$
Equation (2) × 3 $3x^2 - 9xy + 9y^2 = 21$
Substituting for $3y$ $3x^2 - 3x(2x - 4) + (2x - 4)^2 = 21$
$$3x^2 - 6x^2 + 12x + 4x^2 - 16x + 16 = 21$$
$$x^2 - 4x - 5 = 0$$
$$(x - 5)(x + 1) = 0$$
∴   either $x = 5$ or $x = -1$.

Substituting in (3) to find the corresponding values of y, we obtain the solutions $x = 5$, $y = 2$ and $x = -1$, $y = -2$.

In certain cases there is an alternative to the method of Example 4.

Example 5   Solve the equations $x + 2y = 3$ (1)
$$3x^2 + 7xy + 2y^2 = 12 \qquad (2)$$

Factorising (2) $(x + 2y)(3x + y) = 12$
Dividing by (1) $3x + y = 4$
Multiplying (1) by 3 $3x + 6y = 9$.
Subtracting $5y = 5$ ∴ $y = 1$
Substituting in (1) $x + 2 = 3$ ∴ $x = 1$
Hence the equations have one soloution $x = 1$, $y = 1$.

[Note that when dealing with non-linear simultaneous equations it is always advisable to check that the solutions obtained satisfy the original equations.]

Exercise 3.4

1. Find any points of intersection between the given curves and straight lines.
(a) $y = x^2 + 1$, $y = 5x - 3$ (b) $y = 3 - x^2$, $y = 7 - 4x$
(c) $y = x - 3$, $xy + 2 = 0$ (d) $x^2 + y^2 + 4x = 1$, $y = 2 - x$
(e) $y = 2x - 7$, $2xy + 3y + 5x + 11 = 0$ (f) $4x^2 - 9y^2 = 36$, $2x + 3y + 2 = 0$.

In questions 2 to 14 solve the given pairs of simultaneous equations.

2. $x + y = 1$
    $xy = -12$.

3. $3x = 2y$
    $xy = 24$.

4. $x + y = 1$
      $x^2 - y^2 = 5$.

5. $x - 5y = 8$
    $x^2 + 9y^2 + 3x - xy = 30$.

6. $3x + y = 5$
     $5x^2 - 2xy + y^2 = 5$.

7. $3x + 2y = 10$
   $3x^2 - 2xy + 4y^2 = 25$.

8. $x - 3y = 2$
    $x^2 - 2xy - 3y^2 = 12$.

9. $x + y = -1$, $\dfrac{1}{x} + \dfrac{1}{y} = \dfrac{1}{2}$.

10. $2x + y = 1$, $\dfrac{1}{x} - \dfrac{1}{y} = 2$.

11. $x + y = 1$
    $x^3 + y^3 = 91$.

12. $2x + 3y = 3$
    $8x^3 + 27y^3 = 117$.

13. $x^2 - 2xy + 3y^2 = 3$
    $x^2 + 2xy + 3y^2 = 11$.

14. $4xy = -15$
    $4x^3 + 4y^3 = 49$.

In questions 15 to 18 solve the given pairs of simultaneous equations by eliminating either the terms in x^2 or the terms in y^2.

15. $x^2 + y^2 + 2x - 3y = 3$
    $2x^2 - y^2 + 4x + 18y = 54$.

16. $x^2 + 2y^2 + 4y = 4$
    $x^2 - y^2 + 2x - 2y = 0$.

17. $x^2 + xy + y^2 = 3$
     $x^2 - y^2 = 3$.

18. $x^2 + y^2 - 3x = 9$
    $x^2 - y^2 + x + 4y = 3$.

3.5 Products and factors

A function of the form $P(x) = a_0 x^n + a_1 x^{n-1} + \ldots + a_n$ ($a_0 \neq 0$), where n is a positive integer, is called a *polynomial* of degree n. The real numbers a_0, $a_1, \ldots$ are called the *coefficients* of x^n, $x^{n-1}, \ldots$. For instance, $x^5 - 4x^2 + 3x$ is a polynomial of degree 5. A *linear* function, such as $ax + b$, is a polynomial of degree 1. A *quadratic* function is a polynomial of degree 2. A polynomial of degree 3 is often called a *cubic*.

The product of two polynomials can be found by either of the methods illustrated overleaf.

Example 1   Multiply $2x^3 - x^2 + 3$ by $3x + 1$.

$$(3x+1)(2x^3 - x^2 + 3) = 3x(2x^3 - x^2 + 3) + 1(2x^3 - x^2 + 3)$$
$$= 6x^4 - 3x^3 + 9x + 2x^3 - x^2 + 3$$
$$= 6x^4 - x^3 - x^2 + 9x + 3.$$

OR

$$
\begin{array}{r}
2x^3 - x^2 \qquad +3 \\
3x + 1 \\
\hline
2x^3 - x^2 \qquad +3 \\
6x^4 - 3x^3 \qquad +9x \\
\hline
6x^4 - \ x^3 - x^2 + 9x + 3.
\end{array}
$$

When the complete product is not required, the coefficients of particular terms can be picked out.

Example 2   Find the coefficient of x^4 in the product of $x^3 - 3x^2 + x - 2$ and $2x^3 + x^2 - 3x + 1$.

The diagram shows the mental processes involved.

$$(x^3 - 3x^2 + x - 2)(2x^3 + x^2 - 3x + 1)$$

The coefficient of x^4 in the product

$$= 1.(-3) + (-3).1 + 1.2 = -3 - 3 + 2 = -4.$$

Sometimes it is possible to *factorise* a polynomial, i.e. express it as a product. This process is useful when simplifying fractions.

Example 3   Simplify $\dfrac{2x}{x^2 - 4} + \dfrac{7}{2x^2 + x - 6}$.

$$\frac{2x}{x^2 - 4} + \frac{7}{2x^2 + x - 6} = \frac{2x}{(x-2)(x+2)} + \frac{7}{(2x-3)(x+2)}$$

$$= \frac{2x(2x-3)}{(x-2)(x+2)(2x-3)} + \frac{7(x-2)}{(x-2)(x+2)(2x-3)}$$

$$= \frac{4x^2 - 6x + 7x - 14}{(x-2)(x+2)(2x-3)}$$

$$= \frac{4x^2 + x - 14}{(x-2)(x+2)(2x-3)}$$

$$= \frac{(4x-7)(x+2)}{(x-2)(x+2)(2x-3)}$$

$$\therefore \quad \frac{2x}{x^2-4} + \frac{7}{2x^2-x-6} = \frac{4x-7}{(x-2)(2x-3)}.$$

It is often difficult to find factors of a polynomial of degree 3 or more. Testing possible factors by long division is a cumbersome process as the next example shows.

Example 4   Divide $x^4 - 3x + 5$ by $x - 2$.

$$
\begin{array}{r}
x^3 + 2x^2 + 4x + 5 \\
x-2 \overline{\smash{\big)}\ x^4 \qquad\qquad\quad -3x + 5} \\
\underline{x^4 - 2x^3} \\
2x^3 \\
\underline{2x^3 - 4x^2} \\
4x^2 - 3x \\
\underline{4x^2 - 8x} \\
5x + 5 \\
\underline{5x - 10} \\
15
\end{array}
$$

$\therefore$ when $x^4 - 3x + 5$ is divided by $x - 2$, the quotient is $x^3 + 2x^2 + 4x + 5$ and the remainder is 15.

This result can be expressed in the form of an *identity*:

$$x^4 - 3x + 5 \equiv (x-2)(x^3 + 2x^2 + 4x + 5) + 15.$$

[The symbol $\equiv$ means 'is identically equal to', i.e. equal for all values of x.]
    More generally, we can consider the division of a polynomial $P(x)$ by $(x - a)$. If $Q(x)$ is the quotient and R the remainder, then we may write

$$P(x) \equiv (x-a)Q(x) + R.$$

Since this identity holds for all values of x, we substitute $x = a$ to obtain $P(a) = (a-a)Q(a) + R = R$. Thus, when a polynomial $P(x)$ is divided by $(x-a)$ the remainder is $P(a)$. This result is called the *remainder theorem*.

Example 5   Find the remainder when $P(x) = 2x^3 + 7x^2 - 5x - 4$ is divided by $x + 3$.

$$P(-3) = 2(-3)^3 + 7(-3)^2 - 5(-3) - 4 = -54 + 63 + 15 - 4 = 20$$

$\therefore$ the remainder when $P(x)$ is divided by $x + 3$ is 20.

If for a polynomial $P(x)$ we find that $P(a) = 0$, we deduce from the remainder theorem that there is no remainder when $P(x)$ is divided by $(x-a)$. Thus we have the *factor theorem*, which states that

$$\boxed{\text{if } P(a) = 0 \text{ then } (x-a) \text{ is a factor of } P(x).}$$

We use this result to test for linear factors of polynomials.

Example 6   Factorise $f(x) = 6x^3 + 13x^2 - 4$.
Since the constant term is -4, we first try values of x which are factors of -4, i.e. $\pm 1, \pm 2$ or ± 4.

$$f(1) = 6.1^3 + 13.1^2 - 4 = 6 + 13 - 4 \neq 0$$
$$f(-1) = 6(-1)^3 + 13(-1)^2 - 4 = -6 + 13 - 4 \neq 0$$
$$f(2) = 6.2^3 + 13.2^2 - 4 = 48 + 52 - 4 \neq 0$$
$$f(-2) = 6(-2)^3 + 13(-2)^2 - 4 = -48 + 52 - 4 = 0.$$

Hence, by the factor theorem, $x+2$ is a factor of $f(x)$. By inspection or by long division,

$$f(x) = (x+2)(6x^2 + x - 2)$$
$$\therefore \quad f(x) = (x+2)(2x-1)(3x+2).$$

Note that in some cases a cubic polynomial is the product of a linear factor and an irreducible quadratic factor. For example,

$$x^3 - a^3 = (x-a)(x^2 + ax + a^2)$$
$$x^3 + a^3 = (x+a)(x^2 - ax + a^2).$$

Exercise 3.5

1. Find the product of
(a) $2x^2 - x + 7$ and $x + 2$
(b) $3x^3 - 2x^2 + 5x - 1$ and $2x - 3$
(c) $x^2 + 3x - 2$ and $4x^2 - x + 1$
(d) $5x^3 - 2x + 3$ and $x^2 - 1$
(e) $3x^4 - 2x^3 + 6x - 4$ and $3x + 2$
(f) $x^5 - x^4 + x^3 - x^2 + x - 1$ and $x + 1$.

2. Find the coefficients of the given terms in the following products.
(a) $(2x - 5)(x^3 - x^2 + 2x - 3)$; x, x^3.
(b) $(x^2 - 2x + 3)(3x^2 + x - 2)$; x, x^2.
(c) $(x^3 - x - 1)(2x^2 + 3x - 1)$; x^2, x^4.
(d) $(3x^3 - x^2 - 2x + 5)(x^3 + 2x^2 - x - 2)$; x^3, x^5.

3. Simplify the following expressions.

(a) $\dfrac{2}{x^2 - 1} - \dfrac{7}{2x^2 - 3x - 5}$

(b) $\dfrac{1}{x+2} + \dfrac{6x}{x^3 + 8}$

(c) $\dfrac{x^4 - x}{2x - 3x^2} \times \dfrac{3x^2 + x - 2}{1 - x^2}$

(d) $\dfrac{8x^3 + 1}{4x^2 - 8x + 3} \div \left(2x - \dfrac{1}{1 - 2x}\right)$.

4.   Find the remainder when
(a) $5x^2 + 3x - 7$ is divided by $x - 2$ (b) $x^3 - 2x^2 + 8x - 3$ is divided by $x - 5$
(c) $x^4 - 3x^3 + 4x^2 - x + 6$ is divided by   (d) $x^5 + 16$ is divided by $x + 2$
     $x + 1$
(e) $3x^2 - 2ax - 4a^2$ is divided by $x + a$ (f) $a^3 - 3a^2b + 2b^3$ is divided by $a - b$.

5.   Find by long division the quotient and remainder when
(a) $3x^2 - 2x + 5$ is divided by $x + 1$
(b) $4x^3 - 4x^2 + 5x + 1$ is divided by $2x - 3$
(c) $x^3 - 3$ is divided by $x + 3$
(d) $3x^5 - x^4 - 6x^3 + 11x^2 - 1$ is divided by $3x - 1$
(e) $x^4 - 2x^3 + 6x - 5$ is divided by $x^2 - x - 1$
(f) $2x^4 - x^3 + 3x^2 - 7$ is divided by $x^2 - 2$.

6.   Factorise the following polynomials
(a) $2x^3 - 3x^2 + 1$ (b) $3x^3 - 2x^2 - 7x - 2$
(c) $x^4 - x^2 - 72$ (d) $x^5 + x^3 + x$
(e) $4x^3 - 13x + 6$ (f) $4x^4 - 4x^3 - 9x^2 + x + 2$.

7.   When the function $x^2 + ax + b$ is divided by $x - 1$ and $x + 2$, the remainders are 4 and 5 respectively. Find the values of a and b.

8.   When $x^3 + px^2 + qx + 1$ is divided by $x - 2$ the remainder is 9; when divided by $x + 3$ the remainder is 19. Find the values of p and q.

9.   Given that the expression $2x^3 + ax^2 + b$ is divisible by $x + 1$ and that there is a remainder of 16 when it is divided by $x - 3$, find the values of a and b.

10. The expression $ax^3 - 8x^2 + bx + 6$ is exactly divisible by $x^2 - 2x - 3$. Find the values of a and b.

11. The polynomials $x^3 + 4x^2 - 2x + 1$ and $x^3 + 3x^2 - x + 7$ leave the same remainder when divided by $x - p$. Find the possible values of p.

12. Given that the expressions $x^3 - 4x^2 + x + 6$ and $x^3 - 3x^2 + 2x + k$ have a common factor, find the possible values of k.

13. If $x - a$ is a factor of the expression $ax^3 - 3x^2 - 5ax - 9$, find the possible values of a and factorise the expression for each of these values.

14. Prove that when a polynomial $P(x)$ is divided by $(ax - b)$ the remainder is $P(b/a)$. Hence find the remainder when (a) $12x^2 - 4x + 9$ is divided by $2x - 1$, (b) $9x^3 - x + 5$ is divided by $3x + 2$.

15. Factorise (a) $8x^3 - 36x^2 + 46x - 15$, (b) $12x^3 + 4x^2 - 5x - 2$,
         (c) $3x^3 - x^2 + 4x + 4$.

3.6 Polynomial equations

In practice it is often difficult to solve polynomial equations. However, sometimes solutions can be found by factorisation.

Example 1   Solve the equation $2x^4 - 5x^2 - 12 = 0$.

$$2x^4 - 5x^2 - 12 = 0 \Leftrightarrow \quad (2x^2 + 3)(x^2 - 4) = 0$$
$$\Leftrightarrow (2x^2 + 3)(x - 2)(x + 2) = 0$$
$$\therefore \quad 2x^2 + 3 = 0 \quad \text{or} \quad x - 2 = 0 \quad \text{or} \quad x + 2 = 0.$$

Since $2x^2 + 3 = 0$ has no real roots, either $x = 2$ or $x = -2$.

Example 2   Solve the equation $x^3 + 3x^2 + x - 1 = 0$.

Let $f(x) = x^3 + 3x^2 + x - 1$, then
$f(1) = 1 + 3 + 1 - 1 \neq 0, \quad f(-1) = -1 + 3 - 1 - 1 = 0$
$\therefore \quad x + 1$ is a factor of $f(x)$.
By division $f(x) = (x + 1)(x^2 + 2x - 1)$.

Hence if $x^3 + 3x^2 + x - 1 = 0$,
either $x + 1 = 0$ or $x^2 + 2x - 1 = 0$

$$x = -1 \qquad\qquad x = \frac{-2 \pm \sqrt{(4 + 4)}}{2}$$
$$= -1 \pm \sqrt{2}$$

$\therefore$ the roots of the given equation are -1, $-1 - \sqrt{2}$ and $-1 + \sqrt{2}$.

Equations involving surds can sometimes be expressed in polynomial form. However, since extra roots may be introduced in this process all solutions must be tested in the original equation.

Example 3   Solve the equation $\sqrt{(3 - x)} - \sqrt{(7 + x)} = 2$.

Rearranging $\sqrt{(3 - x)} = \sqrt{(7 + x)} + 2$.
Squaring both sides $3 - x = \{\sqrt{(7 + x)} + 2\}^2$
i.e. $3 - x = (7 + x) + 4\sqrt{(7 + x)} + 4$
$\therefore$ $-2x - 8 = 4\sqrt{(7 + x)}$
$\therefore$ $-(x + 4) = 2\sqrt{(7 + x)}$.
Squaring both sides $x^2 + 8x + 16 = 4(7 + x)$
$\therefore$ $x^2 + 4x - 12 = 0$
                             $(x + 6)(x - 2) = 0$.
Hence either $x = -6$ or $x = 2$.
If $x = -6, \sqrt{(3 - x)} - \sqrt{(7 + x)} = \sqrt{9} - \sqrt{1} = 2$.
If $x = 2, \sqrt{(3 - x)} - \sqrt{(7 + x)} = \sqrt{1} - \sqrt{9} = -2$.
Thus the only root of the given equation is $x = -6$.

In Example 1 a polynomial equation of degree 4 was found to have 2 real roots, whereas the cubic equation in Example 2 had 3 real roots. In general, if $x = a$ is a root of a polynomial equation $P(x) = 0$ then $(x - a)$ is a factor of $P(x)$.

Thus, since a polynomial of degree n can have up to n factors of the form $(x-a)$, a polynomial equation of degree n can have up to n real roots.

In §3.2 it was shown that if the roots of the quadratic equation $ax^2+bx+c=0$ are α and β, then $\alpha+\beta = -b/a$ and $\alpha\beta = c/a$. Similar expressions can be obtained for equations of higher degree. For example, if the equation $ax^3+bx^2+cx+d=0$ has roots α, β and γ, then it may be written both in the form

$$x^3 + \frac{b}{a}x^2 + \frac{c}{a}x + \frac{d}{a} = 0$$

and as $$(x-\alpha)(x-\beta)(x-\gamma) = 0$$

i.e. $$x^3 - (\alpha+\beta+\gamma)x^2 + (\alpha\beta+\beta\gamma+\gamma\alpha)x - \alpha\beta\gamma = 0.$$

Hence $$\alpha+\beta+\gamma = -\frac{b}{a}, \quad \alpha\beta+\beta\gamma+\gamma\alpha = \frac{c}{a}, \quad \alpha\beta\gamma = -\frac{d}{a}.$$

Example 4 Given that 1 and -2 are two roots of the equation $3x^3 - x^2 + px + q = 0$, find the third root and the values of p and q.

Since the sum of the roots is $1/3$, the third root is

$$1/3 - \{1 + (-2)\}, \quad \text{i.e.} \quad 4/3.$$

The product of the roots $= -\dfrac{q}{3} = 1.(-2).\dfrac{4}{3} \quad \therefore \quad q = 8.$

Since $x = 1$ satisfies the equation, $3 - 1 + p + q = 0$

$$\therefore \quad p = -2 - q = -10.$$

Hence the third root is $4/3$ and the values of p and q are -10 and 8 respectively.

Exercise 3.6

In questions 1 to 14 solve the given equations.

1. $x^3 - 8x^2 + 5x + 14 = 0$.   2. $6 - x - 4x^2 - x^3 = 0$.

3. $4 + 7x + 2x^2 - x^3 = 0$.   4. $6x^3 + 31x^2 + 48x + 20 = 0$.

5. $4x^4 + 23x^2 - 6 = 0$.   6. $x^4 - 11x^2 + 18 = 0$.

7. $x^3 - 6x - 4 = 0$.   8. $x^3 - 6x^2 + 12x - 9 = 0$.

9. $2x^3 + x^2 - 6x - 3 = 0$.   10. $x^4 - 5x^3 + 4x^2 + 6x - 4 = 0$.

11. $\sqrt{(x+6)} - \sqrt{(x+1)} = 1$.   12. $\sqrt{(12+x)} - \sqrt{(13-x)} = 1$.

13. $\sqrt{(3x+1)} - \sqrt{(x-1)} = 2$.   14. $\sqrt{(9-4x)} - \sqrt{(5-x)} = 2$.

15. If $f(x) = x^3 + px + q$ is exactly divisible by $(x+2)$ and $(x-3)$, find the values of p and q. With these values of p and q, find the roots of the equation $f(x) = 0$.

16. Find the value of k if one root of the equation $12x^3 + kx^2 - 17x + 6 = 0$ is $\frac{1}{2}$. When k has this value, find the other roots of the equation.

17. Write down the sums and products of the roots of the following equations.
(a) $2x^3 + 3x^2 - 8x - 12 = 0$ (b) $2x^3 + 5x^2 - 3x = 0$
(c) $3x^3 + 4x^2 - 5x - 2 = 0$ (d) $x^3 - 11x - 6 = 0$.

18. Given that -1 and 4 are two roots of the equation $x^3 + 5x^2 + ax + b = 0$, find the third root and the values of a and b.

19. Given that 2 is a repeated root of the equation $2x^3 + px^2 + qx - 4 = 0$, find the third root and the values of p and q.

20. Write down the sums and products of the roots of the following equations.
(a) $x^4 - 6x^3 + 9x^2 - 4 = 0$ (b) $2x^4 - x^3 - 12x + 3 = 0$
(c) $x^5 - 3x^3 + 2x = 0$ (d) $2x^5 - 3x^4 - 2x^3 + 4x^2 = 1$.

21. Solve the equation $3x^4 + 4x^3 - 14x^2 + 4x + 3 = 0$ by writing it in the form $a\left(x + \dfrac{1}{x}\right)^2 + b\left(x + \dfrac{1}{x}\right) + c = 0$.

22. Solve the equation $10x^4 - 37x^3 + 50x^2 - 37x + 10 = 0$ by the method of the previous question.

Exercise 3.7 (miscellaneous)

1. Sketch the following curves, showing any maximum or minimum points.
(a) $y = x^2 + 2x$ (b) $y = 2x^2 + x - 3$
(c) $y = 3 + 4x - 4x^2$ (d) $y = x^2 - 6x + 10$.

2. Show that $x^2 - 2x + 2$ is positive for all values of x. Hence find the range of values of x for which the expression $x^3 - x^2 + 2$ is positive.

3. By means of a suitable substitution, solve the equation
$(x^2 - 3x)^2 - 9(x^2 - 3x) - 10 = 0$.

4. Find the values of k for which the equation $x^2 + 2kx + 3k = 0$ has (a) equal roots, (b) real roots which differ by 4.

5. Given that the equation $x^2 + px + q = 0$ has roots α and β, find an equation whose roots are $\alpha(\alpha - 1)$ and $\beta(\beta - 1)$.

6. If α and β are the roots of the equation $x^2 - x - 3 = 0$, show that $\alpha^3 + \beta^3 = 10$ and find a quadratic equation whose roots are α^2/β and β^2/α.

7. The function $f(x) = x^2 + px + 1$, where p is a constant, is zero when $x = \alpha$ and $x = \beta$; and the function $g(x) = x^2 - 9x + q$, where q is a constant, is zero when $x = \alpha + 2\beta$ and $x = \beta + 2\alpha$. Find p and q, and show that $f(3) = g(3)$. (JMB)

8. (a) The sum of the squares of the roots of the equation $x^2 + px + q = 0$ is 56 and the sum of the reciprocals of the roots is 2. Find the values of p and q. (b) Show that, for all real values of α, the equation $x^2 + (3\alpha - 2)x + \alpha(\alpha - 1) = 0$ has real roots for x.   (C)

9. The roots of the equation $9x^2 + 6x + 1 = 4kx$, where k is a real constant, are denoted by α and β. (a) Show that the equation whose roots are $1/\alpha$ and $1/\beta$ is $x^2 + 6x + 9 = 4kx$. (b) Find the set of values of k for which α and β are real. (c) Find also the set of values of k for which α and β are real and positive.   (L)

10. Given that a and b are non-zero constants, prove that if the equations $x^2 + ax + b = 0$ and $4x^2 - ax + 6b = 0$ have a common root then $35a^2 + 4b = 0$.

11. A straight line of gradient -2 passes through the point with x-coordinate -1 on the curve $y = 2x^2 - 3x + 8$. Find the coordinates of the point at which the line meets the curve again.

12. The line $y = 2kx$ cuts the curve $y = x^2 - 4x + 1$ at the points A and B. Without finding the coordinates of the points A and B, find the coordinates of the mid-point of the line AB in terms of k.

13. Solve the simultaneous equations $2x - y - 1 = x - 2y = 3x^2 - 8y^2$.

14. Solve the simultaneous equations $3x^2 + y^2 = 7, \quad 4x^2 - xy + y^2 = 6$.

15. If $P(x) = 2x^5 + 3x^4 - 8x^3 + px^2 + q$ has factors $(x + 1)$ and $(x - 2)$, find the values of p and q. Obtain also the remaining factors.

16. If the roots of the equation $x^3 + 5x^2 + hx + k = 0$ are α, 2α and $\alpha + 3$, find the values of α, h and k.

17. The quadratic polynomial $P(x)$ leaves a remainder of -6 on division by $(x + 1)$, a remainder of -5 on division by $(x + 2)$ and no remainder on division by $(x + 3)$. Find $P(x)$ and solve the equation $P(x) = 0$.   (O&C)

18. Factorise the expression $n^4 + 2n^3 - n^2 - 2n$. Given that n is an integer greater than 1, prove that the expression is divisible by 24.

19. The real numbers a, b, c are such that $b^2 < 4ac$ and $c > 0$. Show that $ax^2 + bx + c > 0$ for all real numbers x and, conversely, that if $ax^2 + bx + c > 0$ for all real x, then $c > 0$ and $b^2 < 4ac$.   (AEB 1978)

20. For what range of values of c does the system of equations $x^2 + xy + y^2 = 1$, $2x + y = c$ have real solutions?   (O)

21. (a) Solve the equations $xy = 4$, $x^2 + x + y = 6$. (b) Find the value of $x^6 + y^6$ in terms of a and b where $x + y = a$, $x^2 + y^2 = b^2$. Show also that these equations give real values for x and y only if $a^2 \leqslant 2b^2$.   (W)

22. If $f(x) \equiv ax^3 + (a + b)x^2 + (a + 2b)x + 1$ is exactly divisible by $(x + 1)$, express b in terms of a, and find the quotient when the division is carried out, expressing the coefficients in terms of a only. Prove that in this case the equation $f(x) = 0$ has only one real root if $a^2 - 6a + 1 < 0$. Show that this inequality implies that $3 - 2\sqrt{2} < a < 3 + 2\sqrt{2}$.

4 The calculator and numerical work

4.1 Accuracy and types of error

In problems requiring a numerical answer it is sometimes possible to give an exact result, e.g. $1 \cdot 4 \times 2 \cdot 3 = 3 \cdot 22$. In practice, it is much more likely that an approximate solution will be obtained. Such a solution may be of little value unless its degree of accuracy can be estimated. This is done by examining sources of error in the original data and in the method of calculation. In this context possible inaccuracies due to mistakes or blunders are not taken into account. The use of the word *error* is confined to inaccuracies arising in other ways.

The error in calculations based on experimental data depends mainly on the accuracy of the instruments used. If, in an experiment, estimates are made of the errors in the readings, these can be used to find the total possible error in any calculated result.

Example 1   The length and breadth of a rectangular room are $9 \cdot 7$ m and $6 \cdot 8$ m respectively. If the possible error in each of these measurements is $\pm 0 \cdot 05$ m, find the two values between which the floor area of the room must lie. Find the area and give your answer to an appropriate degree of accuracy.

Minimum area of room $= (9 \cdot 65 \times 6 \cdot 75) \, \text{m}^2 = 65 \cdot 1375 \, \text{m}^2$
Maximum area of room $= (9 \cdot 75 \times 6 \cdot 85) \, \text{m}^2 = 66 \cdot 7875 \, \text{m}^2$
$\therefore$ the area lies between $65 \cdot 1375 \, \text{m}^2$ and $66 \cdot 7875 \, \text{m}^2$.
Area of room as measured $= (9 \cdot 7 \times 6 \cdot 8) \, \text{m}^2 = 65 \cdot 96 \, \text{m}^2$.
Hence, taking possible errors into account the area of the room may be given as $66 \pm 1 \, \text{m}^2$.

In some calculations the method itself leads to inaccuracies. For instance, to convert a temperature given in a weather forecast from degrees Celsius to degrees Fahrenheit one method is to 'double and add 30'. This formula is attractive because it is easier to use than the true formula, i.e. 'multiply by 9/5 and add 32', and because for temperatures from $-5°C$ to $25°C$ the maximum error is only

$\pm 3°F$. Suppose, however, that this conversion formula were used to express an oven temperature of 200°C given in a recipe as 430°F. The error of 38°F in this result is clearly unacceptable. Thus we see that approximate methods must always be used with care, and that if such a process is used in the wrong situation the error in the result may be large.

Consider now a problem such as the division of 37 by 13. We can calculate the answer by long division, giving as many decimal places as necessary, but we cannot obtain an exact answer. For instance, working as far as the third decimal place, $37 \div 13 = 2·846\ldots$ The answer 2·846 is said to be *truncated* (i.e. cut short) to 3 decimal places. Since the true value must lie between 2·846 and 2·847, the *truncation error* lies between 0 and 0·001. The result could also be given as $37 \div 13 = 2·85$, *rounded* to 2 decimal places. This statement implies that $2·845 \leqslant 37 \div 13 < 2·855$. Hence the *rounding error* lies between $-0·005$ and $+0·005$.

To show how to estimate errors in a longer calculation, we consider the division of 37 by 13 performed using 4-figure logarithm tables.

Number	Logarithm	Possible error
37	1·5682	$\pm 5 \times 10^{-5}$
13	1·1139	$\pm 5 \times 10^{-5}$
2·846	0·4543	$\pm 1 \times 10^{-4}$

Thus the logarithm of $37 \div 13$ lies between 0·4542 and 0·4544. Allowing for rounding errors in the antilogarithm tables, both in the main table and the difference columns, we estimate that $37 \div 13 = 2·846 \pm 0·002$. Hence we may write $37 \div 13 = 2·8$ correct to 1 decimal place, but we cannot be certain that the answer 2·85 is correct to 2 decimal places.

Truncation and rounding errors also arise when working with an electronic calculator. A typical calculator, which displays 8 digits or 6 digits and a 2-digit exponent, produced the following results.

$$37 \div 13 = 2·8461538$$
$$3·7 \div 13 = 0·2846153$$
$$0·037 \div 13 = 2·84615 \times 10^{-3}.$$

We see that these values are truncated rather than rounded. Thus they are subject to a truncation error of between 0 and 1 in the final digit.

Using the same calculator the result

$$53 \div 13 = 4·076923$$

is obtained. The calculator displays 7 digits rather than 8 only because the 8th digit would be a zero. The read-out should be interpreted as 4·0769230 truncated at the final zero.

To estimate error in longer calculations it is necessary to know how numbers are stored in the working register and memory of the calculator. This can be established by tests similar to the following:

Divide 1000 by 7:   142·85714
Subtract 140:   2·8571428.

These results show that a calculator which displays 8 digits may actually work with 10 digits.

In the case of scientific functions many electronic calculators produce rounded values. For example, using a calculator which rounds to 6 significant figures and suppresses unnecessary zeros,

$$\lg 5{\cdot}3 = 0{\cdot}724276 \quad \lg 5{\cdot}2 = 0{\cdot}716003$$
$$\lg 53 = 1{\cdot}72428 \quad \lg 52 = 1{\cdot}716.$$

The maximum rounding error in these values is $\pm 0{\cdot}5$ in the 6th significant figure.

Example 2   Allowing for rounding errors, find two values between which $(\lg 7 \div \lg 3)$ must lie. Calculate $\lg 7 \div \lg 3$ and give your answer to an appropriate number of significant figures.

Taking possible rounding errors into account

$$0{\cdot}8450975 < \lg 7 < 0{\cdot}8450985$$
$$0{\cdot}4771205 < \lg 3 < 0{\cdot}4771215$$

$$\therefore \quad \text{maximum value of } \frac{\lg 7}{\lg 3} = \frac{0{\cdot}8450985}{0{\cdot}4771205} = 1{\cdot}7712475$$

$$\text{minimum value of } \frac{\lg 7}{\lg 3} = \frac{0{\cdot}8450975}{0{\cdot}4771215} = 1{\cdot}7712417.$$

By calculator, $\lg 7 \div \lg 3 = 1{\cdot}7712446$

Hence $\lg 7 \div \lg 3 = 1{\cdot}7712$ to   5 s.f.

[In a longer calculation it would probably be unrealistic to give an answer to more than 4 significant figures.]

Thus although a calculator produces more accurate results than 4-figure tables, these results do contain unavoidable rounding and truncation errors. The approximate methods used within the calculator when determining the values of scientific functions may lead to further error, especially at the extremes of the calculator's range. Clearly it is not necessary to make detailed estimates of possible error after every calculation performed. However, it is important to know what degree of accuracy can be expected from the calculating aid one is using, be it mathematical tables, slide rule or calculator. Efforts can then be made to choose methods of working which minimise error.

Exercise 4.1

In questions 1 to 4 find two values between which z must lie, then calculate z giving your answer to an appropriate degree of accuracy.

1. $z = xy$ where $x = 8{\cdot}7 \pm 0{\cdot}1$, $y = 5{\cdot}3 \pm 0{\cdot}1$.

2. $z = x^2 + y^2$ where $x = 7{\cdot}3 \pm 0{\cdot}05$, $y = 6{\cdot}4 \pm 0{\cdot}05$.

3. $z = \dfrac{1}{x} + \dfrac{1}{y}$ where $x = 4{\cdot}16 \pm 0{\cdot}01$, $y = 6{\cdot}72 \pm 0{\cdot}01$.

4. $z = \sqrt{(x-y)}$ where $x = 62 \pm 0.5$, $y = 45 \pm 0.5$.

5.   Find two values between which the product pq must lie given that $p = 4.26$, $q = 2.51$, (a) rounded to 2 decimal places, (b) truncated to 2 decimal places. In each case give the value of pq to an appropriate number of decimal places.

6.   Repeat question 5 for the quotient p/q.

7.   Use 4-figure logarithm tables to perform the following calculations. Estimate the possible errors and give your answers to an appropriate number of significant figures.
(a) 7.34×2.69 (b) $0.581 \div 8.07$
(c) $(3.3)^2 \div 0.76$ (d) $\sqrt{(4.9 \times 32.8)}$.

8.   Answer the following questions about the calculator you are using. If possible, compare its performance with that of other calculators.
(a) How many digits are displayed?
(b) Are unnecessary zeros suppressed?
(c) How many digits are stored in the working register?
(d) In basic function operations, i.e. $+$, $-$, $\times$, $\div$, are the results truncated or rounded?
(e) Are the values of scientific functions, such as $\sqrt{x}$, $\lg x$, $\sin x$, truncated or rounded, and to how many figures?
(f) What degree of accuracy for the various calculator functions is claimed by the manufacturer?

9.   Use an electronic calculator to perform the following calculations. By estimating the possible errors, give your answers to an appropriate number of significant figures.
(a) $3.6 \times 12.7 \div 6.84$ (b) $1/\sqrt{(5.13)}$
(c) $\sin 40° \times \cos 20°$ (d) $\lg 3.6 \div \lg 1.8$.
[The answers to this question will vary according to the type of calculator used.]

4.2 Some functions and their inverses

Consider a function f which is a one-one mapping of a set X onto a set Y. This means that every element of the range Y is the image of exactly one element of the domain X. Under these conditions it is possible to define an *inverse function* f^{-1} with domain Y and range X such that if $f(a) = b$ then $f^{-1}(b) = a$.

Any scientific calculator provides several examples of inverse functions. For instance, if $\lg a = b$ then $10^b = a$. Thus the function 10^x is the inverse of the function $\lg x$. It follows from this relationship that $10^{(\lg x)} = x$ and $\lg(10^x) = x$. [Discrepancies due to rounding errors may occur when testing such results. For instance, using certain calculators it is found that $10^{(\lg 9)} = 9.00001$ and $\lg(10^{0.29}) = 0.289999$.]

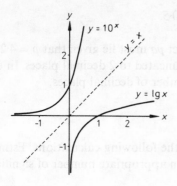

The sketch shows how the graphs $y = \lg x$ and $y = 10^x$ are related. If a point (a, b) lies on the graph $y = \lg x$, then the point (b, a) lies on the graph $y = 10^x$. Hence each graph is the reflection of the other in the line $y = x$.

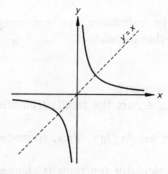

The function $1/x$ is its own inverse, since if $1/a = b$, then $1/b = a$. We find that in this case the graph of $y = 1/x$ is itself symmetrical about the line $y = x$.

The function $f: x \rightarrow x^2$ with domain the set of real numbers has no true inverse, since it is not one-one. For instance, the element 4 in the range is the image of both -2 and $+2$, so it is impossible to assign a single value to $f^{-1}(4)$. However, if the domain of the function $f: x \rightarrow x^2$ is the set of all real numbers greater than or equal to zero, every element of the range is the image of only one element of the domain. Thus we can define the inverse function as $f^{-1}: x \rightarrow \sqrt{x}$.

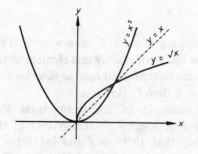

Comparing the graphs of $y = x^2$ and $y = \sqrt{x}$, we again see symmetry about the line $y = x$, but only for $x \geqslant 0$.

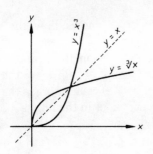

The functions x^y and $x^{1/y}$ are functions of two variables x and y, usually defined only for positive values of x. Using a constant value of y, functions such as x^3 and $\sqrt[3]{x}$ can be studied. From the symmetry of the graphs, we see that x^3 and $\sqrt[3]{x}$ are mutually inverse.

More generally, if $a^k = b$ and $a > 0$, then $b^{1/k} = \sqrt[k]{b} = a$. Hence the function $x^{1/k}$ is the inverse of the function x^k.

The following examples show some of the uses of the calculator functions discussed in this section.

Example 1   Evaluate $\left(2{\cdot}3 + \dfrac{1}{2{\cdot}3}\right)^2$.

By pressing the following keys: | 2 | $\cdot$ | 3 | + | 1/x | = | x^2 |

$\left(2{\cdot}3 + \dfrac{1}{2{\cdot}3}\right)^2 = 7{\cdot}4790359$ (truncated to 8 digits).

Example 2   Evaluate $\sqrt[5]{(5{\cdot}6 \times 10^{-4})}$.

By pressing the following keys: | .5 | $\cdot$ | 6 | EXP | 4 | +/− | $x^{1/y}$ | 5 | = |

$\sqrt[5]{(5{\cdot}6 \times 10^{-4})} = 0{\cdot}223685$ (rounded to 6 s.f.).

Example 3   Find $\log_2 3$.

Using the formula $\log_a x = \log_{10} x / \log_{10} a$ (see §1.6)

$\quad \log_2 3 = \lg 3 / \lg 2 \approx 1{\cdot}5849616$

Hence $\log_2 3 = 1{\cdot}5850$ (to 5 s.f.).

Alternative method:

$\log_2 3 = x \;\Leftrightarrow\; 2^x = 3$
$\qquad\qquad \Leftrightarrow \lg(2^x) = \lg 3$
$\qquad\qquad \Leftrightarrow x \lg 2 = \lg 3$
$\qquad\qquad \Leftrightarrow \quad x = \lg 3 / \lg 2$

$\therefore$ as before $\log_2 3 = 1{\cdot}5850$ (to 5 s.f.).

Example 4   Solve the equation $2^x . 3^{x-2} = 1$.

$$2^x . 3^{x-2} = 1 \Leftrightarrow 2^x . 3^x . 3^{-2} = 1$$
$$\Leftrightarrow \qquad (2.3)^x = 3^2$$
$$\Leftrightarrow \qquad 6^x = 9$$
$$\Leftrightarrow \qquad \lg(6^x) = \lg 9$$
$$\Leftrightarrow \qquad x \lg 6 = \lg 9$$
$$\Leftrightarrow x = \lg 9/\lg 6 \approx 1 \cdot 2262954$$

$$x = 1 \cdot 2263 \quad \text{(to 5 s.f.)}$$

Exercise 4.2

[Give numerical answers to 4 s.f.]

1.   Write down the inverses of the following functions
(a) $f : x \to 3x$ (b) $f : x \to \frac{1}{2}x$ (c) $f : x \to x - 1$
(d) $f : x \to 1 - x$ (e) $f : x \to 2x + 3$ (f) $f : x \to 4(x - 1)$

2.   Write down the equations of the reflections of the following graphs in the line $y = x$.
(a) $y = 2x$ (b) $y = 2/x$ (c) $y = 2 - x$
(d) $y = x - 2$ (e) $y = 2^x$ (f) $y = \lg(x - 2)$.

3.   Using the same pair of axes, draw accurate graphs of the functions x^y and $x^{1/y}$ for $y = 1 \cdot 5$, taking $0 \leqslant x \leqslant 4$.

4.   Evaluate the following expressions

(a) $\sqrt{\left(1 \cdot 9 - \dfrac{1}{1 \cdot 9}\right)}$ (b) $\{(0 \cdot 34)^2 + (0 \cdot 27)^2\}^{-5/2}$

(c) $1/(7 \cdot 1 \times 10^{-3})^2$ (d) $\sqrt[3]{(0 \cdot 027 \times 10^4)}$.

5.   Evaluate   (a) $\log_4 7$,   (b) $\log_3 10$,   (c) $\log_5 2$

6.   Solve the following equations
(a) $2^x = 9$,   (b) $10^{3x} = 15$,   (c) $8 \cdot 7^x = 3 \cdot 2$.

7.   Using the same pair of axes, draw accurate graphs of $y = 3^x$ for $-2 \leqslant x \leqslant 2$ and $y = \log_3 x$ for $0 \cdot 1 \leqslant x \leqslant 10$.

8.   Solve the following equations
(a) $5^{2x} . 5^{1-x} = 40$ (b) $3^x . 4^{x+1} = 100$
(c) $2^{x-1} . 3^{x-2} = 1$ (d) $12^{x-1} = 3^{x+4}$.

9. By taking logarithms of both sides solve the equations
(a) $4^{x+2} = 7^{x-1}$, (b) $3^{2x} \cdot 4^{1-x} = 13$.

10. Solve the equation $\log_3 x + \log_5 x = 1$.

4.3 Simple flow diagrams

Any mathematical calculation consists of a sequence of steps performed one after the other. A rule or systematic process for carrying out a calculation is sometimes called an *algorithm*. The list of instructions describing how to perform the calculation or algorithm can be referred to as a *program*. In a computer program each step must be within the capabilities of the computer concerned. Programs are usually simpler to follow when they are given in the form of a *flow diagram* or *flow chart*. In a flow diagram the individual steps are written in 'boxes' of various shapes and the order in which the steps are to be performed is indicated by arrows. The shapes used in simple flow diagrams are:

for START and STOP   for other instructions.

The instructions   X: = A + B   and   LET X = A + B

both mean: 'Calculate X, given that $X = A + B$'.

READ X   'Assign to X the value of x given in the data'

PRINT X   'Write down the value of X'

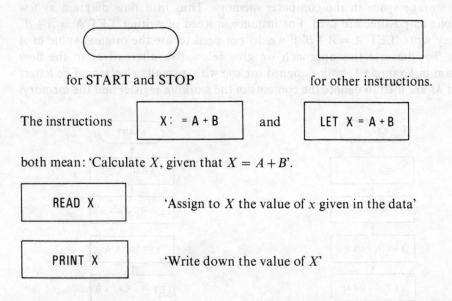

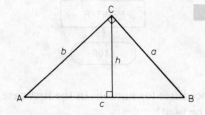

Example 1 In $\triangle ABC$, $\angle C = 90°$ and h is the height of the triangle taking AB as base. Carry out the procedure given in the flow diagram to find h given $a = 6$ and $b = 8$.

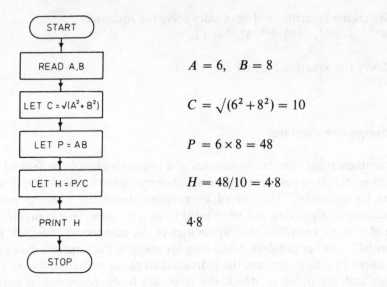

START

READ A,B $A = 6, \quad B = 8$

LET C = √(A² + B²) $C = \sqrt{(6^2 + 8^2)} = 10$

LET P = AB $P = 6 \times 8 = 48$

LET H = P/C $H = 48/10 = 4 \cdot 8$

PRINT H $4 \cdot 8$

STOP

When writing a computer program, introducing a new variable involves using extra storage space in the computer memory. Thus in a flow diagram as few variables as possible are used. For instance, instead of writing 'LET $X = A + B$', we may write 'LET $A = A + B$' if we do not need to use the original value of A again. To illustrate this approach we give below two alternatives to the flow diagram in Example 1, both designed for use with a small calculator. The letters R and M are used to denote the contents of the working register and the memory.

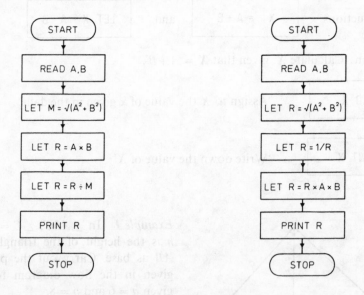

START

READ A,B

LET M = √(A² + B²)

LET R = A × B

LET R = R ÷ M

PRINT R

STOP

START

READ A,B

LET R = √(A² + B²)

LET R = 1/R

LET R = R × A × B

PRINT R

STOP

The reader is recommended to test these procedures for himself. In the first case a key sequence similar to the following would be used:

$$\boxed{6}\ \boxed{x^2}\ \boxed{+}\ \boxed{8}\ \boxed{x^2}\ \boxed{=}\ \boxed{\sqrt{x}}\ \boxed{\text{M in}}\ \boxed{6}\ \boxed{\times}\ \boxed{8}\ \boxed{\div}\ \boxed{\text{MR}}\ \boxed{=}$$

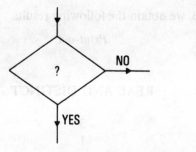

In some calculations the method used depends on the answer to various questions. In a flow diagram these questions are written in *decision boxes*, which have different exits for the answers YES and NO. The use of one of these exits will result in a *jump* to another part of the flow diagram.

Example 2   Construct a flow diagram for a procedure to determine the nature of the roots of the equation $x^2 - 2px + q = 0$ and find their values if real.

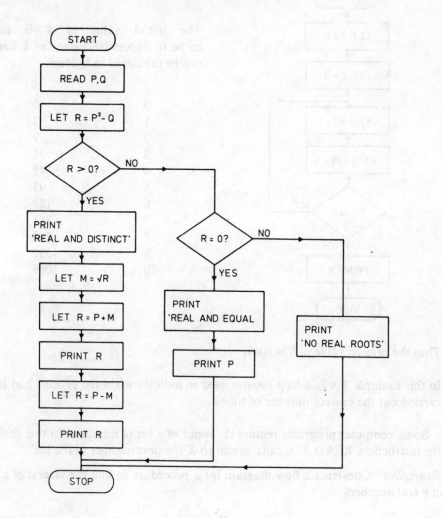

Testing the procedure for $p = 2$ and $q = 3$, we obtain the following results.

Working	Print-out
$P = 2, Q = 3$	
$R = 2^2 - 3 = 1$	
$R > 0$	REAL AND DISTINCT
$M = \sqrt{1} = 1$	
$R = 2 + 1 = 3$	3
$R = 2 - 1 = 1$	1

A flow diagram for a repetitive process may contain *loops* as shown in the next example.

Example 3   Construct a flow diagram for finding the sum to 10 terms, S_{10}, of the series $3 + 6 + 12 + 24 + \ldots$ using the relation $S_r = 2S_{r-1} + 3$.

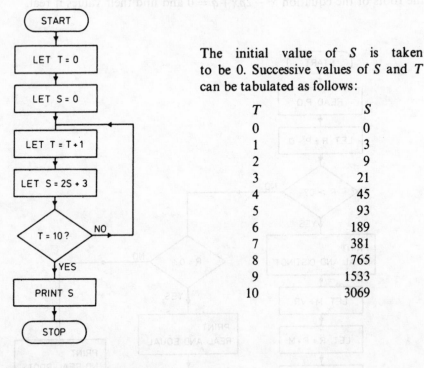

The initial value of S is taken to be 0. Successive values of S and T can be tabulated as follows:

T	S
0	0
1	3
2	9
3	21
4	45
5	93
6	189
7	381
8	765
9	1533
10	3069

Thus the printed value of S is 3069.

In this example T was a *loop counter* used to indicate when the process had been carried out the correct number of times.

Some computer programs require the input of a list of numbers. In this context the instruction 'READ X' means 'assign to X the next number of the list'.

Example 4   Construct a flow diagram for a procedure to find the largest of a set of n real numbers.

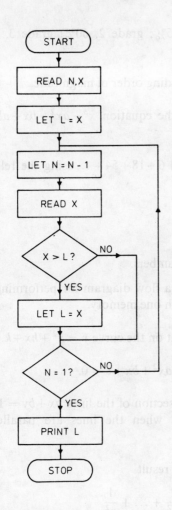

If the given set of numbers is 5, -7, 8, 12, -3, 2, then the values of N, X and L are as follows:

N	X	L
6	5	5
5	-7	5
4	8	8
3	12	12
2	-3	12
1	2	12

Thus the print-out is the number 12, the largest element of the given set.

[Note that this flow diagram contains both a jump and a loop.]

Exercise 4.3

1. Carry out the procedure given in Example 1 for
(a) $a = 2, b = 1.5$,   (b) $a = 3.5, b = 12$.

2. Carry out the procedure given in Example 2 for
(a) $p = 1, q = -15$ (b) $p = -0.5, q = 0.25$
(c) $p = 2.3, q = 5.3$ (d) $p = 3.7, q = -4.8$.

In questions 3 to 10 construct flow diagrams for carrying out the given processes.

3. Find and print out the total number of seconds in x hours, y minutes and z seconds.

4. Calculate x given that $a + b/x = c$, printing out suitable messages when $a = c$ or $b = 0$.

5. Print out the examination grade corresponding to a mark of $x\%$ given that the

lowest marks in each grade are: grade 1, 75%; grade 2, 60%; grade 3, 50%. Candidates with less than 50% fail.

6.   Arrange three real numbers a, b, c in ascending order of magnitude.

7.   Determine the number of real roots of the equation $x^3 - ax^2 - bx + ab = 0$ and print out their values.

8.   Find the sum to 8 terms of the series $2 + 6 + 18 + 54 + \ldots$ using the relation $S_r = 3S_{r-1} + 2$.

9.   Find the nth term of the Fibonacci series
$1 + 1 + 2 + 3 + 5 + 8 + 13 + \ldots$

10. Find the sum of the squares of a set of n numbers.

In each of the remaining questions construct a flow diagram for performing the given calculation using a pocket calculator with one memory.

11. Find the coordinates of the minimum point on the curve $y = x^2 + hx + k$.

12. Find the real roots, if any, of the equation $ax^2 + bx + c = 0$.

13. Find the coordinates of the point of intersection of the lines $ax + by = 1$ and $cx + dy = 1$, printing out suitable messages when the lines are parallel or coincident.

14. Find an approximate value for π using the result

$$\frac{\pi^2}{6} \approx \frac{1}{1^2} + \frac{1}{2^2} + \frac{1}{3^2} + \frac{1}{4^2} + \ldots + \frac{1}{n^2}$$

for any given value of n.

4.4 Efficient methods of calculation

When performing a numerical calculation the main aims are to
(1) avoid mistakes
(2) use as few steps as possible
(3) minimise error
[In work with a calculator effective use of the memory may help to achieve all three aims.]

To avoid mistakes numerical answers should be checked whenever possible.

Example 1   The value 1·5 has been obtained for a root of the equation $2x^3 - x^2 + 9 = 0$. Check this result.

Without detailed calculation it is clear that

$$2(1{\cdot}5)^3 - (1{\cdot}5)^2 + 9 > 0$$

∴   1·5 is not a root of the equation.
[In fact the correct value of the root is $-1{\cdot}5$.]

Example 2   A student using a calculator obtained the result $38{\cdot}76 \div 0{\cdot}2497 = 6{\cdot}4422 \times 10^{-3}$. Is this answer reasonable?

Rough check: $38{\cdot}76 \div 0{\cdot}2497 \approx 40 \div \frac{1}{4} = 160$
The answer $6{\cdot}4422 \times 10^{-3}$ must be incorrect.

[On some calculators this wrong answer is obtained by inadvertently pressing the $\div$ key twice.]

The number of steps required in a calculation will depend on the type of calculator, table book or slide rule used. However, when evaluating a polynomial the method called *nested multiplication* is often the most efficient. For instance, rearranging the polynomial $3x^3 - 2x^2 + 4x - 1$ as $\{(3x-2)x+4\}x-1$, we can quickly calculate that its value is 23 when $x = 2$.

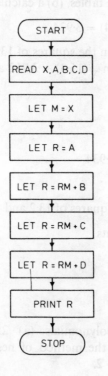

This flow diagram gives the procedure for evaluating the polynomial $ax^3 + bx^2 + cx + d$ using a calculator. In each step the same pattern of operations is repeated. Thus the method of nested multiplication can be summarised as follows:

(i)   Take the coefficient of the highest power of x.

(ii) Multiply by x and add the next coefficient.

(iii) Repeat (ii) until constant term has been added.

When accuracy is an important consideration, it may be possible to reduce error by choosing a suitable method.

Example 3   Evaluate $5\sqrt{2}$ using 4-figure tables.

$\sqrt{2} = 1\cdot414 \pm 0\cdot0005$ $\therefore$ $5\sqrt{2} = 7\cdot07 \pm 0\cdot0025$
The possible rounding error is reduced by writing
$5\sqrt{2} = \sqrt{50} = 7\cdot071 \pm 0\cdot0005$.

Example 4   Evaluate $2 \div 7 \times 32$ using a calculator.

$2 \div 7 = 0\cdot2857142$ with error between 0 and 1×10^{-7}.
Assuming that the working register carries no additional digits, $2 \div 7 \times 32$
$= 9\cdot1428544$, subject to an error between 0 and 32×10^{-7}.
Hence the maximum number of significant figures that can be given in the
answer is 5,

$$2 \div 7 \times 32 = 9\cdot1429 \quad \text{(to 5 s.f.)}$$

Accuracy may be improved by writing

$$2 \div 7 \times 32 = 2 \times 32 \div 7 = 9\cdot1428571.$$

Since the maximum possible truncation error is now 1×10^{-7}, we know that
$2 \div 7 \times 32 = 9\cdot142857$ (to 7 s.f.)

Example 5   Find $\sqrt{(13\cdot2^2 - 12\cdot6^2)}$ using (a) 4-figure tables, (b) a calculator.

(a) $\sqrt{(13\cdot2^2 - 12\cdot6^2)} = \sqrt{(174\cdot2 - 158\cdot8)} = \sqrt{(15\cdot4)} = 3\cdot924$

Allowing for possible rounding errors of $\pm 0\cdot05$ in the squares of $13\cdot2$ and $12\cdot6$,
the true value of the expression must lie between $\sqrt{(15\cdot3)} \approx 3\cdot912$ and $\sqrt{(15\cdot5)}$
$\approx 3\cdot937$.
Hence $\sqrt{(13\cdot2^2 - 12\cdot6^2)} = 3\cdot9$ (to 2 s.f.)
A more accurate result is obtained by writing

$$\sqrt{(13\cdot2^2 - 12\cdot6^2)} = \sqrt{\{(13\cdot2 + 12\cdot6)(13\cdot2 - 12\cdot6)\}}$$
$$= \sqrt{\{25\cdot8 \times 0\cdot6\}} = \sqrt{(15\cdot48)} = 3\cdot934$$

$\therefore$ $\sqrt{(13\cdot2^2 - 12\cdot6^2)} = 3\cdot93$ (to 3 s.f.)

(b) Since a calculator gives exact values for the squares of $13\cdot2$ and $12\cdot6$,

$\sqrt{(13\cdot2^2 - 12\cdot6^2)} = 3\cdot9344631$ (truncated to 8 digits)

Hence $\sqrt{(13\cdot2^2 - 12\cdot6^2)} = 3\cdot934463$ (to 7 s.f.)

Exercise 4.4

1. Draw flow diagrams for evaluating the polynomials (a) $2x^2 - 7x + 3$,
(b) $x^3 + 3x^2 - 5x - 4$ and (c) $3x^4 - x^3 - 4x + 8$, by the method of nested multiplication. Test your procedures for $x = -1$ and $x = 2$.

2. Use a calculator to evaluate the following
   (a) $3x^2 - 5x + 1$ for $x = 2 \cdot 8$ and $x = -0 \cdot 6$
   (b) $2x^3 + x^2 - 8x - 3$ for $x = -1 \cdot 3$ and $x = 2 \cdot 67$
   (c) $x^5 - 3x^3 + 10x + 5$ for $x = 1 \cdot 54$ and $x = -0 \cdot 09$
   (d) $2x^4 - x^3 - 6x^2 + 3x$ for $x = 3 \cdot 02$ and $x = -1 \cdot 4$.

In the remaining questions in the exercise, perform the given calculations by the most direct method, then decide whether there is a way of producing a more accurate result. Consider, if available, the use of 4-figure tables and various types of calculator. Illustrate your answers with flow diagrams where appropriate.

3. Evaluate (a) $3\sqrt{10}$, (b) $\frac{1}{2}\sqrt{6}$, (c) $4 \div 7 \cdot 36$.

4. Evaluate (a) $\dfrac{8 \cdot 71}{4 \cdot 03 \times 5 \cdot 64}$, (b) $\dfrac{1}{3 \cdot 61} \times \dfrac{1}{0 \cdot 52} \times 7 \cdot 3$.

5. Evaluate (a) $\sqrt{(25 \cdot 3^2 - 24 \cdot 7^2)}$, (b) $\sqrt{(25 \cdot 3^2 + 24 \cdot 7^2)}$.

6. Evaluate (a) $2 \lg 6$, (b) $(1 \cdot 76)^4$, (c) $10^{4 \lg 1 \cdot 76}$.

7. Find the sum of the first 8 terms of the series $1 + x + x^2 + x^3 + \dots$ given
   (a) $x = 2$, (b) $x = -3 \cdot 4$, (c) $x = 0 \cdot 8136$.

8. Find the sum of the series $1 + 2x + 3x^2 + \dots$ as far as the first term which is less than $0 \cdot 1$, given (a) $x = 0 \cdot 5$, (b) $x = 0 \cdot 42$, (c) $x = 0 \cdot 61$.

[As a rough guide only, answers correct to 4 s.f. are provided for this exercise.]

4.5 Reduction of laws to straight line form

In §2.5 we saw that an equation of the form $y = mx + c$ represents a straight line, where m is the gradient and c is the intercept on the y-axis. If a table of values of variables x and y leads to a straight line graph, we can use the gradient and the intercept on the y-axis to write down the law connecting x and y.

Example 1   Some values of the variables x and y are given in the table below:

x	1	2	3	4	5
y	1·2	2·0	2·8	3·6	4·4

Find a relationship between the variables, giving y in terms of x.

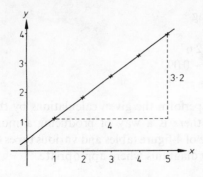

Plotting y against x, a straight line graph is obtained. Hence the relationship between x and y takes the form $y = mx + c$. The intercept on the y-axis is $0 \cdot 4$

$$\therefore \quad c = 0 \cdot 4.$$

The gradient can be found using the points $(1, 1 \cdot 2)$ and $(5, 4 \cdot 4)$

$$\therefore \quad m = \frac{4 \cdot 4 - 1 \cdot 2}{5 - 1} = \frac{3 \cdot 2}{4} = 0 \cdot 8.$$

Hence the required relationship is $y = 0 \cdot 8x + 0 \cdot 4$.

If a graph is drawn from experimental data and the points on it all lie close to a straight line, we often assume that the relationship between the variables is approximately linear. We then draw the line that best fits the data and use points on it to determine the law connecting the variables. When finding the gradient of the line, errors are minimised by choosing two points near the ends of the line whose coordinates are easily read from the graph.

Example 2   The following observations were recorded when weights were suspended at the end of a coiled spring.

Load on spring in grammes, W	20	40	60	80	100
Length of spring in cm, L	8·1	9·0	10·0	10·9	11·8

Find an expression for L in terms of W, assuming that the relationship is linear.

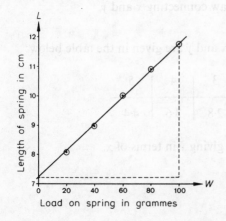

Load on spring in grammes

The points representing the observations all lie close to a straight line, which cuts the vertical axis at $L = 7 \cdot 2$. Using the points $(0, 7 \cdot 2)$ and $(100, 11 \cdot 8)$ on the line, its gradient

$$= \frac{11 \cdot 8 - 7 \cdot 2}{100 - 0}$$

$$= \frac{4 \cdot 6}{100} = 0 \cdot 046.$$

Hence the relationship between L and W is approximately

$$L = 0.046W + 7.2.$$

[When estimating error in a result of this kind, it is necessary to consider the range of possible positions of the 'best' straight line graph, allowing for experimental errors.]

When variables are connected by a non-linear law, it is sometimes possible to find related variables which obey a linear law.

Example 3   The table below gives values of the variables x and y, which are related by an equation of the form $y^2 = ax^2 + b$. Plot y^2 against x^2 and use your graph to obtain the values of a and b.

x	1	2	3	4	5
y	3·32	4·12	5·20	6·40	7·68

Let $X = x^2$ and $Y = y^2$, then working to 3 s.f. the values of X and Y are:

X	1	4	9	16	25
Y	11·0	17·0	27·0	41·0	59·0

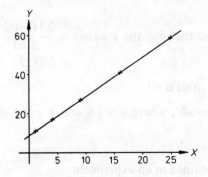

The intercept on the vertical axis is at $Y = 9$. Using the points $(1, 11)$ and $(25, 59)$ the gradient is

$$\frac{59 - 11}{25 - 1} = \frac{48}{24} = 2$$

$$\therefore \quad Y = 2X + 9.$$

Hence the variables x and y are related by the equation $y^2 = ax^2 + b$, where $a = 2$ and $b = 9$.

Logarithms are often used to express experimental laws in linear form.

Example 4   The following values of x and y are believed to obey a law of the form $y = ab^x$, where a and b are constants:

x	1	2	3	4	5
y	3·8	9·2	22·1	53·1	127·4

Show graphically that this is so and estimate the values of a and b correct to 1 decimal place.

Assuming that $y = ab^x$, then $\lg y = \lg(ab^x)$,

i.e. $\lg y = x \lg b + \lg a$.

Hence plotting $\lg y$ against x should produce a straight line graph with gradient $\lg b$ and intercept $\lg a$.

x	1	2	3	4	5
$Y = \lg y$	0·58	0·96	1·34	1·73	2·11

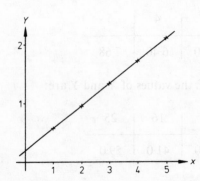

The intercept on the vertical axis is at

$$Y = 0·2$$

$$\therefore \quad \lg a \approx 0.2.$$

Hence $a = 1·6$ (to 1 d.p.)

Using the points $(1, 0·58)$ and $(5, 2·11)$ on the line, the gradient $= \dfrac{2·11 - 0·58}{5 - 1}$

$$= 0·3825$$

$\therefore$ $\lg b \approx 0·3825$ and hence $b = 2·4$ (to 1 d.p.)

$\therefore$ x and y obey a law of the form $y = ab^x$, where $a = 1·6$ and $b = 2·4$ (to 1 d.p.).

Example 5   The following readings were obtained in an experiment:

x	20	40	60	80	100
y	55	150	280	430	600

Show graphically that, allowing for small errors of observation, there is a relation between y and x of the form $y = ax^k$. Find approximate values for a and k.

Assuming that $y = ax^k$, then $\lg y = \lg(ax^k)$,

i.e. $\lg y = k \lg x + \lg a$.

Hence plotting $\lg y$ against $\lg x$ should produce a straight line graph with gradient k and intercept $\lg a$.

$X = \lg x$	1·301	1·602	1·778	1·903	2·000
$Y = \lg y$	1·740	2·176	2·447	2·633	2·778

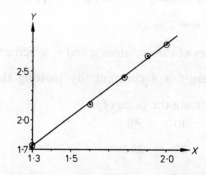

[In order to make full use of the graph paper the X-axis is marked from 1·3 to 2·0 and the Y-axis from 1·7 to 2·8. A suitable scale on both axes would then be 0·1 unit: 2 cm. This means that the true intercept on the Y-axis is not shown. Thus $\lg a$ cannot be read directly from the graph.]

The graph passes through the points $(1·3, 1·73)$ and $(2, 2·78)$

$$\therefore \quad \text{the gradient} = \frac{2·78 - 1·73}{2 - 1·3} = \frac{1·05}{0·7} = 1·5.$$

Hence X and Y obey a law of the form $Y = 1·5X + \lg a$.
Substituting $X = 2$, $Y = 2·78$, $2·78 = 3 + \lg a$

$$\therefore \quad \lg a = -0·22 \quad \text{and} \quad a \approx 0·60$$

Hence there is a relation between y and x of the form $y = ax^k$, where the approximate values of a and k are 0·60 and 1·5 respectively.

Exercise 4.5

[Give answers to 2 significant figures.]

1. By using the given table of values to draw a graph, find the relationship between the variables x and y in the form $y = mx + c$.

x	0	2	4	7	9
y	0·6	1·2	1·8	2·7	3·3

2. In an electrical experiment the following results were obtained.

V	86	80	70	60	50	40	30
R	282	267	252	231	208	176	154

Determine the law connecting R and V in the form $R = aV + b$.

3. In a test to determine the efficiency of a crane the following values were obtained for the effort E required to raise a load L. Find the law connecting E and L in the form $E = aL + b$.

L	10	20	30	40	50	60	70	80	90	100
E	1·0	1·7	2·1	2·6	3·2	3·8	4·2	4·9	5·5	6·0

4. In an experiment the following observations were recorded:

T	0	12	20	30	42	48	60
θ	7·6	3·9	1·1	−1·9	−5·7	−7·8	−11·8

Find the law connecting T and θ in the form $\theta = T_0 + kT$.

5. The table below gives experimental values of the variables u and v, which are connected by the equation $\dfrac{1}{u} + \dfrac{1}{v} = \dfrac{1}{f}$, where f is a constant. By plotting the reciprocal of v against the reciprocal of u, estimate the value of f.

u	20	25	30	40	50
v	79	45	34	27	23·5

6. The following values for x and y have been found in an experiment:

x	1	2	3	4	5
y	8.29	11·2	8·67	0·84	−12·5

By plotting y/x against x, verify that x and y are connected by a law of the form $y = ax^2 + bx$ and find approximate values for a and b.

7. Two quantities, x and y, are known to be connected by a law of the form $x^n y = k$, where n and k are constants. Using the given table of values, plot $\lg y$ against $\lg x$ and hence find approximate values for n and k.

x	2	3	4	5	6
y	3·54	1·92	1·25	0·90	0·68

8. The given values of x and y are believed to obey a law of the form $y = ab^x$, where a and b are constants. Show graphically that this is so and estimate the values of a and b.

x	1	2	3	4	5
y	0·91	1·27	1·78	2·50	3·50

9. The table below gives experimental values of x and y, which are known to be related by a law of the form $a/x + b/y = 1$. By drawing a suitable graph find approximate values for a and b.

x	1	2	3	4	5
y	−3·25	−19·1	28·8	12·7	9·7

10. The variables x and y tabulated below are believed to satisfy a relationship of the form $y = a(x+2)^n$, where a and n are constants. Show graphically that this is so and obtain approximate values for a and n.

x	0	1	2	3	4	5	
y	1·25	0·56	0·31	0·20	0·14	0·10	(AEB 1977)

Exercise 4.6   *(miscellaneous)*

1. The base and height of a triangle are measured as 16 cm and 23 cm respectively. If the possible error in these measurements is ± 0.2 cm, find two values between which the area of the triangle must lie. Find the area and give your answer to an appropriate degree of accuracy.

2. The radius of a circle is 5·95 cm rounded to 2 decimal places. Calculate the circumference by each of the methods given below. By estimating the possible error in each case give the answer to the appropriate number of significant figures.
(a) Use 4-figure tables taking $\lg \pi = 0.4971$.
(b) Take $\pi = 22/7$ and use no calculating aids.
(c) Use a calculator and its value for π.

3. Find the inverses of the following functions.
(a) $f : x \rightarrow 1 - 2x$,   (b) $g : x \rightarrow 5^x$,   (c) $h : x \rightarrow -1/x$.
4. Find $\log_7 12$.

5. Solve the equation $3^{2x} - 5 . 3^x + 4 = 0$.

6. Solve the equation $\log_3 x = \log_x 5$.

7. Suggest a relationship of the form $z = ap + 10b$, where a and b are integers, given the following experimental data.

p	145	160	170	185	195	200
z	65	170	225	300	360	410

8. Explain how a straight line graph of the form $y = mx + c$ may be drawn to represent the following relationships between variables u and v, where a and n are constants
(a) $u^2 = av^2 + n$ (b) $v = nu(a + u)$
(c) $u = av^n$ (d) $v = na^{u.}$

9. The following values of x and y are believed to obey a law of the form $y = kb^x$ where k and b are constants:

x	1	2	3	4	5
y	0·8	2·3	6·7	20·2	60·9

Show graphically that this is so and determine approximate values of k and b.

                                                         (AEB 1976)

10. The table shows approximate values of a variable y corresponding to certain values of another variable x. By drawing a suitable linear graph, verify that these values of x and y satisfy approximately a relationship of the form $y = ax^k$. Use your graph to find approximate values of the constants a and k.

x	5	10	15	20	25	30	
y	45	63	77	89	100	110	(L)

11. Carry out the procedure given in the flow diagram below, tabulating the successive values of S, T and R as you proceed. State the printed value of S to the number of decimal places that you consider appropriate.　　　　　　(JMB)

Question 11　　　　　　　　　　　　　　　　Question 12

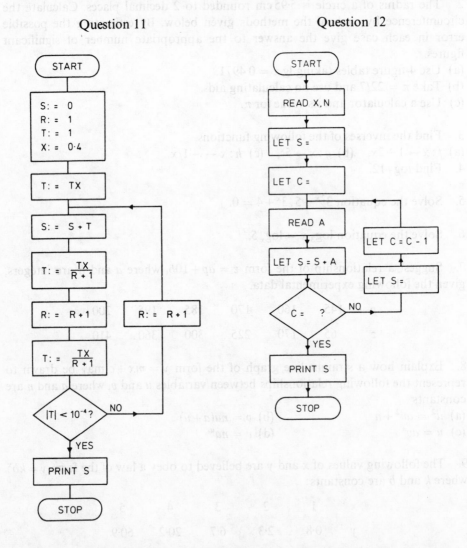

12. Copy and complete the given flow diagram designed to evaluate the polynomial $a_0x^n + a_1x^{n-1} + \ldots + a_{n-1}x + a_n$. Explain the function of the instruction 'READ A'. Demonstrate the use of the procedure to evaluate $2x^3 - 3x^2 + x - 7$ when $x = 2$, tabulating the values assigned to S, C and A throughout.

13. A *part* of a flow diagram is shown below. The purpose of the flow diagram is to find sets of positive integers x, y, z such that $x^2 + y^2 = z^2$, where $x < y$.

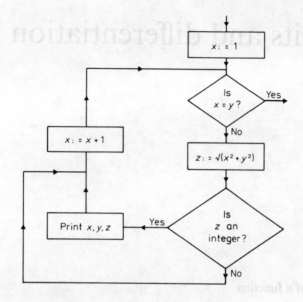

When the current value of y is 12, work through this section of the diagram, showing any values printed.

Complete the flow diagram so that y takes all integer values $1, 2, 3, \ldots, N$ in turn, where N is a positive integer to be read as data at the start.   (C)

14. Draw a flow diagram for a procedure to determine whether a given integer N is prime. [You may assume that N is greater than 1.]

15. Draw a flow diagram for the process of reading 100 positive numbers into a computer, calculating the largest difference between any pair of these numbers and printing out this difference.   (AEB 1975)

16. Construct a flow diagram to calculate the values of $3x^2 - 4x + 2$ using nested multiplication for $x = -1(0 \cdot 2)2$ (i.e. for $x = -1, -0 \cdot 8, -0 \cdot 6, \ldots, 1 \cdot 6, 1 \cdot 8, 2$) and to print out the least of these values.

5 Limits and differentiation

5.1 The limit of a function

This chapter deals with the foundations of the study of calculus. The basis of this branch of mathematics is the idea of a limit.

Consider the function $f(x) = x^2 - x - 2$.

x	-1	-0.5	-0.2	-0.1	-0.01	0.01	0.1	0.2	0.5	1
$f(x)$	0	-1.25	-1.76	-1.89	-1.9899	-2.0099	-2.09	-2.16	-2.25	-2

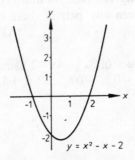

$y = x^2 - x - 2$

The table shows that as the value of x approaches zero, from either above or below, then the value of $f(x)$ approaches -2. Thus -2 is called the limit of $f(x)$ as x approaches zero. Using the symbol $\rightarrow$, which is read 'tends to', we write:

as $x \rightarrow 0$, $f(x) \rightarrow -2$.

In general, if, as we consider values of x closer and closer to $x = a$, the value of a function $f(x)$ approaches a finite value l, then l is called the *limit* of $f(x)$ as x tends to a. This may be written:

$$\lim_{x \to a} f(x) = l \quad \text{or} \quad \text{as } x \rightarrow a, f(x) \rightarrow l.$$

Example 1 Find the limit as $h \rightarrow 0$ of $2 - 3h + h^2$.

As $h \rightarrow 0$, $2 - 3h + h^2 \rightarrow 2$.

80

Example 2   Find $\lim\limits_{x \to 4} \left(\dfrac{x+3}{x-3} \right)$.

$$\lim_{x \to 4} \left(\frac{x+3}{x-3} \right) = \frac{4+3}{4-3} = 7.$$

As shown in these examples, we find that for many functions arising in elementary mathematics, $f(x) \to f(a)$ as $x \to a$. However, the notion of the limit of a function $f(x)$ as $x \to a$ is most useful when $f(x)$ is undefined at $x = a$.

Example 3   Find $\lim\limits_{x \to 1} \left(\dfrac{x^2+x-2}{x-1} \right)$.

Since there is no definition of division by zero, the function $f(x) = \dfrac{x^2+x-2}{x-1}$ is not defined for $x = 1$.

However, when $x \neq 1$, $f(x) = \dfrac{(x+2)(x-1)}{x-1} = x+2.$

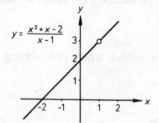

Hence we can obtain values of $f(x)$ as close as we like to 3, by taking values of x closer and closer to 1

$$\therefore \quad \lim_{x \to 1} \left(\frac{x^2+x-2}{x-1} \right) = \lim_{x \to 1} \left(x+2 \right) = 3.$$

If x is any real number, $[x]$ is defined as the greatest integer less than or equal to x, e.g. $[3\frac{3}{4}] = 3$, $[5] = 5$ and $[-1 \cdot 7] = -2$.

Example 4   Discuss the function $f(x) = [x]$ as $x \to 1$.

For values of x close to 1, but less than 1, $[x] = 0$.
For values of x close to 1, but greater then 1, $[x] = 1$
$\therefore \quad f(x) = [x]$ approaches no single value as $x \to 1$.
Hence, although $[x]$ is defined at $x = 1$, where it takes the value 1, the limit of $[x]$ as $x \to 1$ does not exist.

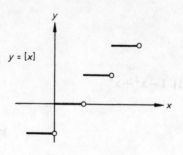

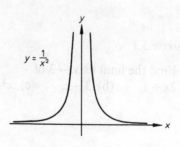

Example 5 Discuss the function $f(x) = 1/x^2$ as $x \to 0$.

As we examine values of x closer and closer to 0, $f(x)$ takes increasingly large values. Thus $f(x)$ has no limit as x tends to 0.

We may describe the behaviour of $f(x) = 1/x^2$ by writing:

as $x \to 0$, $f(x) \to \infty$, where $\to \infty$ is read 'tends to infinity'.

However, since a limit is a finite number, we may *not* state that the limit of $f(x)$ is infinity. It is sometimes convenient to say that $f(x)$ is infinite at $x = 0$, but it is *not* usually considered correct to write $f(0) = \infty$.

The concept of a limit may be extended to the value a function $f(x)$ approaches as x takes increasingly large values.

Example 6 Find the limits of $f(x) = 1/x$ as $x \to \infty$ and as $x \to -\infty$.

As x takes increasingly large positive values, $f(x)$ takes smaller and smaller positive values

$\therefore$ as $x \to \infty$, $f(x) \to 0$ from above.

Similarly, as x takes increasingly large negative values, $f(x)$ takes smaller and smaller negative values

$\therefore$ as $x \to -\infty$, $f(x) \to 0$ from below.

The following properties of limits are often useful when considering more complicated functions.

If, as $x \to a$, $f(x) \to l$ and $g(x) \to k$, then

(a) $f(x) + g(x) \to l + k$ (b) $f(x) - g(x) \to l - k$
(c) $f(x) . g(x) \to lk$ (d) $f(x)/g(x) \to l/k$ $(k \neq 0)$.

Example 7 Find the limit of $f(x) = \dfrac{3x}{x+3}$ as $x \to \infty$.

Dividing numerator and denominator by x,

$$f(x) = \frac{3x}{x+3} = \frac{3}{1 + 3/x}.$$

As $x \to \infty$, $3/x \to 0$ $\therefore$ as $x \to \infty$, $f(x) \to 3$.

Exercise 5.1

1. Find the limit as $x \to 3$ of
(a) $2x + 3$,   (b) $3 - x$,   (c) $x^2 + 1$,   (d) $1 - x^2 + x^4$.

2. Find the limit as $x \rightarrow 2$ of

(a) $\dfrac{1}{x+1}$,   (b) $1+\dfrac{1}{x}$,   (c) $\dfrac{x-4}{x+2}$,   (d) $\dfrac{x^2-4}{x-2}$.

3. Find the limit as $h \rightarrow 0$ of

(a) $3-h+h^2$,   (b) $\dfrac{h-2h^2}{h}$,   (c) $\dfrac{3h^3+2h^2}{h^2}$,   (d) $\dfrac{h^3+1}{h+1}$.

4. Find the limit as $x \rightarrow 0$ of

(a) $\dfrac{(x+1)^2-(x-1)^2}{2x}$,   (b) $\sqrt{\left(\dfrac{8x-5x^2+3x^3}{1-\{1-2x\}}\right)}$.

5. Discuss the function $f(x) = 1-[x]$ as $x \rightarrow 1$.

6. Discuss the function $f(x) = 1/x$ as $x \rightarrow 0$.

7. Discuss the values of the following functions as $x \rightarrow k$.

(a) $f(x) = (x-k)^2$,   (b) $g(x) = \dfrac{1}{(x-k)^2}$,   (c) $h(x) = \dfrac{1}{x-k}$.

8. Find the limit as $x \rightarrow \infty$ of

(a) $\dfrac{1}{x+1}$,   (b) $\dfrac{1}{x^2}$,   (c) $\dfrac{2x}{x-1}$,   (d) $\dfrac{2x^2}{x^2-1}$.

9. Find   (a) $\lim\limits_{x \rightarrow -1} \dfrac{3x^2+x-2}{2x^2+5x+3}$,   (b) $\lim\limits_{x \rightarrow \infty} \dfrac{3x^2+x-2}{2x^2+5x+3}$,

      (c) $\lim\limits_{x \rightarrow 1} \dfrac{x^3-1}{2x^3-3x+1}$,   (d) $\lim\limits_{x \rightarrow -\infty} \dfrac{x^3-1}{2x^3-3x+1}$.

5.2 The gradient of a curve

In §2.4 gradient was defined as a quantity which indicates the direction of a straight line. It was found that the gradient of the straight line passing through the points (x_1, y_1) and (x_2, y_2) is $(y_2-y_1)/(x_2-x_1)$. However, since the direction of a curve is not constant, there is no similar formula for the gradient of a curve. Instead, the gradient of the curve $y = f(x)$ at the point $x = a$ is defined to be the gradient of the tangent to the curve at that point.

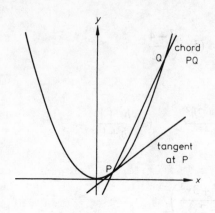

Consider the gradient of the curve $y = x^2$ at the point $P(1,1)$. We cannot find the gradient of the tangent at $(1,1)$ by the methods of Chapter 2, since we have the coordinates of only one point on it. However, we can obtain an approximate value for its gradient, by finding the gradient of a chord PQ, where Q is a point on the curve $y = x^2$ close to P. The table below gives successive approximations to the gradient of the tangent at P, obtained by taking Q closer and closer to P.

Value of x at Q	Value of y at Q	Gradient of PQ
2	4	3
1·5	2·25	2·5
1·1	1·21	2·1
1·01	1·0201	2·01
1·001	1·002001	2·001

This suggests that as Q approaches P, the values of the gradient of PQ approach 2.

To avoid the numerical work above, consider the point Q, where $x = 1+h$, $y = (1+h)^2$, then

$$\text{gradient of } PQ = \frac{(1+h)^2 - 1}{(1+h)-1} = \frac{2h+h^2}{h} = 2+h.$$

As $h \to 0$, $Q \to P$ and the gradient of PQ approaches that of the tangent at P.

$\therefore$ gradient of tangent at $P = \lim_{h \to 0} (\text{gradient of } PQ) = \lim_{h \to 0} (2+h) = 2.$

This limiting process also provides a method for finding the gradient of the curve $y = x^2$ at a general point $P(x, x^2)$.
Let Q be the point $(x+h, \{x+h\}^2)$.

The gradient of PQ is then $\dfrac{(x+h)^2 - x^2}{(x+h)-x} = 2x+h$

$\therefore$ gradient of tangent at $P = \lim_{h \to 0} (2x+h) = 2x.$

Hence the gradient of the curve $y = x^2$ at any point is given by the function $2x$. This function is sometimes referred to as the *gradient function* for the curve.
In general, for the curve $y = f(x)$, if P is the point $(x, f(x))$ and Q is the point $(x+h, f(x+h))$, then the gradient of $PQ = \dfrac{f(x+h)-f(x)}{(x+h)-x} = \dfrac{f(x+h)-f(x)}{h}.$

$\therefore$ the gradient of the curve at any point is given by

$$\lim_{h \to 0} \frac{f(x+h)-f(x)}{h}, \quad \text{if this limit exists.}$$

One important application of this principle is to the motion of a particle in a straight line. The velocity of such a particle is the rate at which its displacement from a fixed point is changing.

Example 1   An object moves in a straight line so that its displacement from its starting point after t seconds is s metres, where $s = 20t - 3t^2$. If the object passes through the points P and Q when $t = a$ and $t = a+h$, respectively, find the average velocity of the object as it moves from P to Q. Deduce its velocity at the instant it passes through P.

The displacement PQ (in metres)

$$= \{20(a+h)-3(a+h)^2\} - \{20a-3a^2\}$$
$$= 20a + 20h - 3a^2 - 6ah - 3h^2 - 20a + 3a^2$$
$$= 20h - 6ah - 3h^2.$$

The time taken to travel from P to $Q = h$ seconds

$\therefore$ the average velocity $= (20 - 6a - 3h)\,\mathrm{m\,s^{-1}}$.

The velocity at P is the limiting value of this average velocity as $h \to 0$.

$\therefore$ the velocity of the object as it passes through P is $(20 - 6a)\,\mathrm{m\,s^{-1}}$.

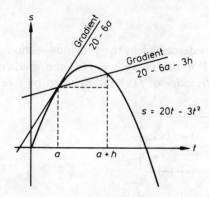

By comparing this example with the earlier work in this section, we see that the velocity of the particle at P is the same as the gradient of the graph $s = 20t - 3t^2$ at the point $t = a$.

Exercise 5.2

1.   Write down a series of approximations to the gradient of the tangent at the point $P(0, 1)$ to the curve $y = 1 - x^2$ by finding the gradient of PQ, where Q is the point on the curve given by $x = 1, 0{\cdot}5, 0{\cdot}1, 0{\cdot}01, 0{\cdot}001$.

2.   Repeat question 1 for the curve $y = 2x^2 - x + 1$.

3.   If P and Q are the points on the curve $y = x^2 + 3$ with x-coordinates 1 and $1 + h$ respectively, find the gradient of PQ. Deduce the gradient of the tangent to the curve at P.

4. Use the method of question 3 to find the gradients of the following curves at the given points
(a) $y = 3x^2$ at $(1, 3)$,   (b) $y = x - x^2$ at $(2, -2)$,
(c) $y = 2x^2 + x + 1$ at $(0, 1)$,   (d) $y = x^3$ at $(1, 1)$.

5. Find the gradient of the line joining the points $P(x, 3x^2 - 1)$ and $Q(x+h, 3\{x+h\}^2 - 1)$ on the curve $y = 3x^2 - 1$. By letting h tend to zero, find the gradient function for this curve.

6. Using the method of question 5 find the gradient functions for the following curves:
(a) $y = x^2 - x$,   (b) $y = 1/x$,   (c) $y = x^3$.

7. An object moves in a straight line so that its distance from its starting point after t seconds is s metres, where $s = 4t^2$. If the object passes through the points P and Q when $t = a$ and $t = a + h$ respectively, find the average velocity of the object as it moves from P to Q. Deduce its velocity at the instant it passes through P.

8. Repeat question 7 for (a) $s = 3t$, (b) $s = 12t - 5t^2$.

5.3 Differentiation from first principles

The process of finding the gradient function described in the previous section is called *differentiation* from first principles. For the curve $y = f(x)$ the gradient function is called the derived function or *derivative* of $f(x)$ and denoted by $f'(x)$, so that

$$f'(x) = \lim_{h \to 0} \frac{f(x+h) - f(x)}{h}.$$

For example, it has already been shown that if $f(x) = x^2$, then $f'(x) = 2x$.

An alternative expression for the derivative of the function $y = f(x)$ is obtained by using the Greek letter δ, 'delta', to mean 'a small increase in'.

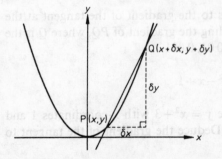

Consider the points $P(x, y)$ and $Q(x+\delta x, y+\delta y)$ on the curve $y = x^2$, where δx is a small increase in x and δy is the corresponding small increase in y.

At P $y = x^2$

At Q $y + \delta y = (x + \delta x)^2 = x^2 + 2x\delta x + (\delta x)^2$

∴ $\delta y = 2x\delta x + (\delta x)^2.$

The gradient of $PQ = \dfrac{\delta y}{\delta x} = 2x + \delta x.$

As $\delta x \to 0, \dfrac{\delta y}{\delta x} \to 2x$

∴   the gradient of the tangent at P is $2x$.

In this notation the derivative of y with respect to x is denoted by $\dfrac{dy}{dx}$, so that

$$\frac{dy}{dx} = \lim_{\delta x \to 0} \frac{\delta y}{\delta x}.$$

[Note that in this context d, dy, dx have no separate meaning.]

Both $f'(x)$ and dy/dx are widely used, so differentiation results may be written down using either notation.

Thus,   if $f(x) = x^2$,   then $f'(x) = 2x$

and,   if $y = x^2$,   then $\dfrac{dy}{dx} = 2x.$

We can also think of d/dx as a symbol indicating the operation of differentiation, writing $\dfrac{d}{dx}(x^2) = 2x.$

There is no need to refer to the graph of a function to carry out the process of differentiation.

Example 1   Differentiate from first principles the function $y = x^3$.

Let δx be a small increase in x and let δy be the corresponding small increase in y.

$y = x^3$

$\Rightarrow y + \delta y = (x + \delta x)^3 = x^3 + 3x^2\delta x + 3x(\delta x)^2 + (\delta x)^3$

$\Rightarrow \qquad \delta y = 3x^2\delta x + 3x(\delta x)^2 + (\delta x)^3$

$\Rightarrow \qquad \dfrac{\delta y}{\delta x} = 3x^2 + 3x\delta x + (\delta x)^2$

∴ $\dfrac{dy}{dx} = \lim_{\delta x \to 0} \dfrac{\delta y}{\delta x} = 3x^2.$

Alternative method

Let
$$f(x) = x^3$$
then
$$f(x+h) = (x+h)^3 = x^3 + 3x^2h + 3xh^2 + h^3$$
$$f(x+h) - f(x) = 3x^2h + 3xh^2 + h^3$$

$$\frac{f(x+h) - f(x)}{h} = 3x^2 + 3xh + h^2$$

$$\therefore \quad f'(x) = \lim_{h \to 0} \frac{f(x+h) - f(x)}{h} = 3x^2.$$

Example 2 Differentiate from first principles $y = 1/x$.

$$y = \frac{1}{x}$$

$$\Rightarrow y + \delta y = \frac{1}{x + \delta x}$$

$$\Rightarrow \quad \delta y = \frac{1}{x + \delta x} - \frac{1}{x} = \frac{x - (x + \delta x)}{x(x + \delta x)} = -\frac{\delta x}{x(x + \delta x)}$$

$$\Rightarrow \quad \frac{\delta y}{\delta x} = -\frac{1}{x(x + \delta x)}$$

$$\therefore \quad \frac{dy}{dx} = \lim_{\delta x \to 0} \frac{\delta y}{\delta x} = -\frac{1}{x^2}.$$

Exercise 5.3

1. If P is the point (x, y) and Q the point $(x + \delta x, y + \delta y)$ on the curve $y = x^2 + 2$, find the gradient of PQ and hence the gradient of the curve at P.

2. Repeat question 1 for the curves
(a) $y = 4 - x^2$,   (b) $y = x^2 + 2x$,   (c) $y = \dfrac{2}{x} + 3$.

In the remaining questions differentiate the given functions from first principles.

3. (a) $2x^2$ (b) $5x^2$ (c) $2x^2 - 1$.

4. (a) x (b) $4 - x$ (c) $x + x^2$.

5. (a) $3x - 1$ (b) $\frac{1}{2}x + 5$ (c) 7.

6. (a) $-x^3$ (b) $2x^3$ (c) x^4.

7. (a) $x - \dfrac{1}{x}$ (b) $\dfrac{1}{x^2}$ (c) $\dfrac{1}{x^3}$.

5.4 Differentiation rules

From the results obtained in Exercise 5.3 a table of derivatives of powers of x can be made.

y	$\dfrac{1}{x^3}$	$\dfrac{1}{x^2}$	$\dfrac{1}{x}$	1	x	x^2	x^3	x^4	$\dots$
$\dfrac{dy}{dx}$	$-\dfrac{3}{x^4}$	$-\dfrac{2}{x^3}$	$-\dfrac{1}{x^2}$	0	1	$2x$	$3x^2$	$4x^3$	$\dots$

A pattern emerges when we rewrite the table:

y	x^{-3}	x^{-2}	x^{-1}	x^0	x^1	x^2	x^3	x^4
$\dfrac{dy}{dx}$	$-3x^{-4}$	$-2x^{-3}$	$-1x^{-2}$	$0x^{-1}$	$1x^0$	$2x^1$	$3x^2$	$4x^3$

It now seems reasonable to assume that for any integer n,

$$\text{if } y = x^n, \quad \text{then } \frac{dy}{dx} = nx^{n-1}.$$

[A formal proof of this statement when n is a positive integer is given in §13.6. Negative values of n are considered in §10.1.]

Some readers may prefer to think of this rule for differentiating powers of x in words:

'multiply by the index and subtract 1 from it'.

Example 1   Find $\dfrac{dy}{dx}$ if (a) $y = x^7$ (b) $y = \dfrac{1}{x^7}$.

(a) If $y = x^7$, then $\dfrac{dy}{dx} = 7x^6$.

[Multiply by the index 7, then subtract 1 to obtain the new index 6.]

(b) If $y = \dfrac{1}{x^7} = x^{-7}$, then $\dfrac{dy}{dx} = -7x^{-8} = -\dfrac{7}{x^8}$.

[In this case the index is -7 and subtracting 1 gives the new index -8.]

It was also found in Exercise 5.3 that, for instance, the derivative of $5x^2$ is $10x$, which is 5 times the derivative of x^2,

$$\text{i.e.} \quad \text{if } y = 5u \text{ where } u = x^2, \text{ then } \frac{dy}{dx} = 10x = 5\frac{du}{dx}.$$

Other examples show that the derivative of a sum is the same as the sum of the separate derivatives, e.g.   if $y = x^2 + x = u + v$ where $u = x^2$ and $v = x$,

$$\text{then } \frac{dy}{dx} = 2x + 1 = \frac{du}{dx} + \frac{dv}{dx}.$$

These are examples of two general rules which we now prove using the properties of limits.

(1) If $y = ku$, where k is a constant and u is a function of x, then $\dfrac{dy}{dx} = k\dfrac{du}{dx}$.

Proof Let δx be a small increase in x and let δu and δy be the corresponding increases in u and y.

$$y = ku$$
$$\Rightarrow y + \delta y = k(u + \delta u) = ku + k\delta u$$
$$\Rightarrow \quad \delta y = k\delta u$$

$$\Rightarrow \quad \frac{\delta y}{\delta x} = k\frac{\delta u}{\delta x}$$

$$\therefore \quad \frac{dy}{dx} = \lim_{\delta x \to 0} \frac{\delta y}{\delta x} = \lim_{\delta x \to 0} k\frac{\delta u}{\delta x} = k \lim_{\delta x \to 0} \frac{\delta u}{\delta x} = k\frac{du}{dx}.$$

(2) If $y = u + v$, where u and v are functions of x, then

$$\frac{dy}{dx} = \frac{du}{dx} + \frac{dv}{dx}.$$

Proof Let δx be a small increase in x and let δu, δv and δy be the corresponding increases in u, v and y.

$$y = u + v$$
$$\Rightarrow y + \delta y = (u + \delta u) + (v + \delta v)$$
$$\Rightarrow \quad \delta y = \delta u + \delta v$$

$$\Rightarrow \quad \frac{\delta y}{\delta x} = \frac{\delta u}{\delta x} + \frac{\delta v}{\delta x}$$

$$\therefore \quad \frac{dy}{dx} = \lim_{\delta x \to 0} \frac{\delta y}{\delta x} = \lim_{\delta x \to 0} \left(\frac{\delta u}{\delta x} + \frac{\delta v}{\delta x} \right) = \lim_{\delta x \to 0} \frac{\delta u}{\delta x} + \lim_{\delta x \to 0} \frac{\delta v}{\delta x} = \frac{du}{dx} + \frac{dv}{dx}.$$

These results are used in the following examples.

Example 2 Find $\dfrac{dy}{dx}$ if (a) $y = x^3 - 4x^2$, (b) $y = 6 - \dfrac{7}{x^2}$.

(a) If $y = x^3 - 4x^2$, then $\dfrac{dy}{dx} = 3x^2 - 4.2x = 3x^2 - 8x.$

(b) If $y = 6 - \dfrac{7}{x^2} = 6 - 7x^{-2}$, then $\dfrac{dy}{dx} = 0 - 7(-2x^{-3}) = \dfrac{14}{x^3}.$

It is necessary to rearrange some functions in order to differentiate them.

Example 3 Find $f'(x)$ when (a) $f(x) = x(x-3)$ (b) $f(x) = \dfrac{x^2-4}{x}$.

(a) $f(x) = x(x-3) = x^2 - 3x$ $\qquad \therefore \quad f'(x) = 2x - 3$

(b) $f(x) = \dfrac{x^2+4}{x} = x + \dfrac{4}{x}$ $\qquad \therefore \quad f'(x) = 1 - \dfrac{4}{x^2}$.

[Note that differentiating (x^2+4) and x separately then dividing would not give the derivative of the quotient.]

Example 4 Find the gradient of the curve $y = 2x^2 + 3x - 1$ at the point $(1,4)$. Hence find the equation of the tangent to the curve at that point.

If $y = 2x^2 + 3x - 1$, $\dfrac{dy}{dx} = 4x + 3$ $\quad \therefore \quad$ when $x = 1$, $\dfrac{dy}{dx} = 7$.

Hence the gradient of the curve at the point $(1,4)$ is 7. Thus the tangent at this point is the straight line passing through $(1,4)$ with gradient 7

$\therefore \quad$ its equation is $y - 4 = 7(x-1)$, i.e. $y = 7x - 3$.

In §5.2 we saw that the process of differentiation could be used to find the instantaneous velocity of a moving object.

Example 5 A particle moves along a straight line such that after t seconds its displacement from a fixed point is s metres, where $s = 10t^2 - t^3$. Find (a) an expression for the velocity, $v\,\mathrm{m\,s^{-1}}$, after t seconds, (b) the velocity after 2 seconds and after 8 seconds.

(a) Since $s = 10t^2 - t^3$, $v = \dfrac{ds}{dt} = 20t - 3t^2$

$\therefore \quad$ the velocity after t seconds is given by $v = 20t - 3t^2$.

(b) When $t = 2$, $v = 20.2 - 3.4 = 28$

$\therefore \quad$ the velocity after 2 seconds is $28\,\mathrm{m\,s^{-1}}$.

When $t = 8$, $v = 20.8 - 3.64 = 160 - 192 = -32$

$\therefore \quad$ the velocity after 8 seconds is $-32\,\mathrm{m\,s^{-1}}$.

[The difference in sign shows that the direction of motion after 8 seconds is opposite to the direction after 2 seconds.]

It will be proved in §10.2 that the rule $\dfrac{d}{dx}(x^n) = nx^{n-1}$ can be applied to fractional powers of x.

Example 6 Differentiate (a) $x^{1/4}$, (b) $x^{-5/2}$, (c) $\sqrt{x}$, (d) $\dfrac{1}{\sqrt[3]{x}}$.

(a) If $y = x^{1/4}$, then $\dfrac{dy}{dx} = \tfrac{1}{4}x^{-3/4}$

(b) If $y = x^{-5/2}$, then $\dfrac{dy}{dx} = -\dfrac{5}{2}x^{-7/2}$

(c) If $y = \sqrt{x} = x^{1/2}$, then $\dfrac{dy}{dx} = \frac{1}{2}x^{-1/2} = \dfrac{1}{2\sqrt{x}}$

(d) If $y = \dfrac{1}{\sqrt[3]{x}} = x^{-1/3}$, then $\dfrac{dy}{dx} = -\frac{1}{3}x^{-4/3} = -\dfrac{1}{3\sqrt[3]{(x^4)}}$

[For revision of surds and indices see §1.5.]

Exercise 5.4

Differentiate the following functions with respect to x:

1. (a) x^5,   (b) x^{12},   (c) $3x^4$,   (d) -5

2. (a) $2x+7$,   (b) $3x^2-4x$,   (c) $2x^3-7x^6$.

3. (a) $3+4x-x^2$,   (b) $\frac{1}{2}x^3+\frac{1}{3}x^2$,   (c) $5x-4x^4$.

4. (a) $x(2x+3)$,   (b) $(3x-1)^2$,   (c) $x(x+2)^2$.

5. (a) x^{-2},   (b) $1/x^4$,   (c) $1/x^9$,   (d) $2/x^3$.

6. (a) $x^2 - \dfrac{1}{x}$,   (b) $x^4 + \dfrac{4}{x^2}$,   (c) $\dfrac{1}{2x^2} - \dfrac{1}{3x^3}$.

7. (a) $\dfrac{1+x^2}{x}$,   (b) $\dfrac{2x-5}{x^3}$,   (c) $\dfrac{(x-1)(x+2)}{x}$.

8. Find $f'(x)$, $f'(0)$ and $f'(-2)$ given that
(a) $f(x) = \frac{1}{2}(x^3+1)^2$,   (b) $f(x) = 3(x+1)^3$.

9. Find $f'(x)$, $f'(2)$ and $f'(-1)$ given that

(a) $f(x) = \dfrac{1}{x^2}(2x^3+1)$,   (b) $f(x) = \left(\dfrac{x^2+1}{x}\right)^2$.

10. Find the gradients of the following curves for the given values of x

(a) $y = 3x^2-x+2$; $x = 1$,   (b) $y = x^3-2x^2+5x$; $x = -2$,

(c) $y = \dfrac{x^4-1}{2x^3}$; $x = -1$,   (d) $y = \dfrac{(x+2)(1-2x)}{x^2}$; $x = 2$.

11. Find the equations of the tangents to the following curves at the points with given x-coordinates

(a) $y = x^2-3x$; $x = 2$,   (b) $y = 2+x-5x^2$; $x = -1$,

(c) $y = x^3 - 3x + 2; x = 0,$ (d) $y = (x^2 - 3)(2x^2 + 5); x = -\frac{1}{2},$

(e) $y = 1 - \dfrac{1}{x}; x = \frac{1}{2},$ (f) $y = \dfrac{1 - x^3}{x^4}; x = 2.$

12. A particle moves along a straight line such that after t seconds its displacement from a fixed point is s metres, where $s = 5t^2 + 8$. Find (a) an expression for the velocity after t seconds, (b) the velocity after 3 seconds and after 5 seconds.

13. Repeat question 12 for $s = 27t - 3t^2$.

14. Given that $A = \pi r^2$, find $\dfrac{dA}{dr}$ when $r = 2$.

15. Given that $pv^3 = 54$, find $\dfrac{dp}{dv}$ when $v = 3$.

16. The gradient of the curve $y = x^2 + ax + b$ at the point $(2, 6)$ is 7. Find the values of a and b.

17. The gradient of the curve $y = ax^2 + b/x^2$ at the point $(\frac{1}{2}, 2\frac{1}{2})$ is -6. Find the values of a and b.

18. Find $\dfrac{dy}{dx}$ if

(a) $y = x^{1/3},$ (b) $y = x^{3/2},$ (c) $y = x^{-1/4},$

(d) $y = \sqrt[5]{x},$ (e) $y = 1/\sqrt{x},$ (f) $y = \sqrt[3]{(8x)}.$

19. Differentiate with respect to x

(a) $x^{1/2} + x^{-3/2},$ (b) $(2x - 1)\sqrt{x},$ (c) $(1 + \sqrt{x})^2,$

(d) $\dfrac{x - 1}{\sqrt{x}},$ (e) $\dfrac{x^3 + x^2}{\sqrt{x}},$ (f) $\left(\sqrt{x} + \dfrac{1}{\sqrt{x}}\right)^3.$

20. Find the equation of the tangent to the curve $y = (\sqrt{x} + 1)\sqrt{x}$ at the point where $x = 4$.

5.5 Elementary curve sketching

In §3.1 it was shown that graphs of the form $y = ax^2 + bx + c$ all have the same general shape. Thus a quick sketch of a curve such as $y = x^2 - 5x + 4$ can be made by finding the points of intersection with the axes and checking the behaviour of the graph for large positive and large negative values of x.

$x = 0 \Rightarrow y = 4$ $\therefore$ the curve cuts the y-axis at $(0, 4)$

$y = 0 \Leftrightarrow x^2 - 5x + 4 = 0 \Leftrightarrow (x - 1)(x - 4) = 0$

              $\Leftrightarrow x = 1$ or $x = 4$

$\therefore$ the curve cuts the x-axis at the points $(1, 0)$ and $(4, 0)$.

As $x \to \infty$, $y \to \infty$ and as $x \to -\infty$, $y \to \infty$.

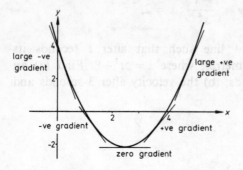

It is clear from the sketch that as x increases, the gradient of the curve moves through negative values to zero and then through positive values.

Differentiating $y = x^2 - 5x + 4$, $\dfrac{dy}{dx} = 2x - 5$.

Hence $2x - 5$ is the gradient function for the curve. As x increases, this does indeed behave as described above.

$$\frac{dy}{dx} = 0 \Leftrightarrow 2x - 5 = 0 \Leftrightarrow x = 2\tfrac{1}{2}$$

$\therefore$ the lowest point in the sketch occurs at $x = 2\tfrac{1}{2}$.

The graph of a more complicated function $y = f(x)$ is shown below.

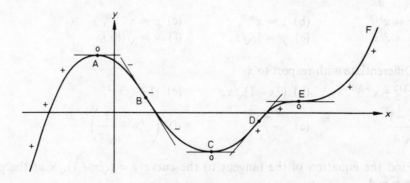

The sign of the gradient as x increases is shown in the diagram. At A, C and E the tangents to the curve are parallel to the x-axis and the gradient is zero. At these points, which are called *stationary points*, y is said to have a *stationary value*. The point A is a *maximum point* and y takes a *maximum value* at A. Similarly, C is called a *minimum point* and y has a *minimum value* there. It is clear from the sketch that these are local maximum and minimum values, since, for instance, the value of y at F is greater than its value at A.

A and C are both called *turning points*, but although y has a stationary value at E, E is not a turning point. The gradient of the curve is zero at E, but does not change sign as the curve passes through E. Such points are called *points of inflexion*. In general, a point of inflexion is a point at which a curve stops bending in one direction and starts bending the other way. In the diagram B, D and E are all points of inflexion and, as shown, the tangents at these points cross the curve.

> Summarising, a point at which $dy/dx = 0$ is
> (i)   a maximum point, if the sign of dy/dx changes from $+$ to $-$
> (ii) a minimum point, if the sign of dy/dx changes from $-$ to $+$
> (iii) a point of inflexion, if the sign of dy/dx does not change.

This provides a new approach to the sketching of graphs.

Example 1   Sketch the graph of $y = 2 + x - x^2$.

$x = 0 \Rightarrow y = 2$
$\therefore$ the curve cuts the y-axis at the point $(0, 2)$.
$y = 0 \Leftrightarrow 2 + x - x^2 = 0 \Leftrightarrow (2 - x)(1 + x) = 0$
$\qquad \Leftrightarrow x = -1 \quad \text{or} \quad x = 2$
$\therefore$ the curve cuts the x-axis at the points $(-1, 0)$ and $(2, 0)$.

Differentiating $\dfrac{dy}{dx} = 1 - 2x$

$\therefore \quad \dfrac{dy}{dx} = 0 \Leftrightarrow 1 - 2x = 0 \Leftrightarrow x = \frac{1}{2}$

When $x < \frac{1}{2}$, $\dfrac{dy}{dx} > 0$ and when $x > \frac{1}{2}$, $\dfrac{dy}{dx} < 0$

$\therefore$ when $x = \frac{1}{2}$, y takes the maximum value of $2\frac{1}{4}$.

As $x \to \infty$, $y \to -\infty$ and as $x \to -\infty$, $y \to -\infty$.

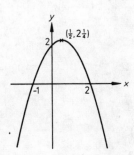

We are now able to sketch the curve and label the maximum point $(\frac{1}{2}, 2\frac{1}{4})$.

Example 2   Sketch the curve $y = x^3 - 6x^2 + 9x$.

$x = 0 \Rightarrow y = 0$
$\therefore$ the curve cuts the y-axis at the origin $(0, 0)$.
$y = 0 \Leftrightarrow x^3 - 6x^2 + 9x = 0 \Leftrightarrow x(x - 3)^2 = 0$
$\qquad \Leftrightarrow x = 0 \quad \text{or} \quad x = 3$
$\therefore$ the curve cuts the x-axis at the points $(0, 0)$ and $(3, 0)$.

Differentiating $\dfrac{dy}{dx} = 3x^2 - 12x + 9 = 3(x-1)(x-3)$

$\dfrac{dy}{dx} = 0 \Leftrightarrow (x-1)(x-3) = 0 \Leftrightarrow x = 1$ or $x = 3$

[We now determine the nature of the stationary points at $x = 1$ and $x = 3$, by drawing up a table showing the sign of dy/dx when x is less than 1, when x lies between 1 and 3 and when x is greater than 3.]

	$x < 1$	$1 < x < 3$	$x > 3$
$x - 1$	$-$	$+$	$+$
$x - 3$	$-$	$-$	$+$
dy/dx	$+$	$-$	$+$

∴   when $x = 1$, there is a maximum point $(1,4)$
   when $x = 3$, there is a minimum point $(3,0)$

As $x \to \infty, y \to \infty$ and as $x \to -\infty, y \to -\infty$.

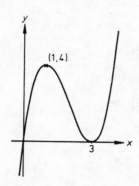

We can now sketch the curve $y = x^3 - 6x^2 + 9x = x(x-3)^2$ and we see that the repeated factor $(x-3)$ leads to a turning point at $x = 3$.

Example 3   Sketch the curve $y = (x+1)(x-3)^3$.

$x = 0 \Rightarrow y = -27$
∴   the curve cuts the y-axis at the point $(0, -27)$.

$y = 0 \Leftrightarrow (x+1)(x-3)^3 = 0 \Leftrightarrow x = -1$ or $x = 3$
∴   the curve cuts the x-axis at the points $(-1, 0)$ and $(3,0)$.

By multiplication $y = x^4 - 8x^3 + 18x^2 - 27$

Differentiating $\dfrac{dy}{dx} = 4x^3 - 24x^2 + 36x$

$= 4x(x^2 - 6x + 9) = 4x(x-3)^2.$

$\dfrac{dy}{dx} = 0 \Leftrightarrow 4x(x-3)^2 = 0 \Leftrightarrow x = 0$ or $x = 3$

	$x < 0$	$0 < x < 3$	$x > 3$
x	$-$	$+$	$+$
$(x-3)^2$	$+$	$+$	$+$
dy/dx	$-$	$+$	$+$

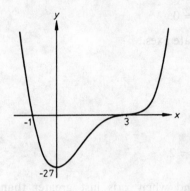

$\therefore$ when $x = 0$, there is a minimum point $(0, -27)$ and when $x = 3$, there is a point of inflexion $(3,0)$. As $x \to \infty$, $y \to \infty$ and as $x \to -\infty$, $y \to \infty$.

Example 4 Sketch the graph $y = \dfrac{2x-5}{x}$.

When $x = 0$ the value of y is undefined
$\therefore$ the curve does not cut the y-axis.

$y = 0 \Leftrightarrow 2x - 5 = 0 \Leftrightarrow x = 2\frac{1}{2}$
$\therefore$ the curve cuts the x-axis at the point $(2\frac{1}{2}, 0)$.

By division $y = 2 - \dfrac{5}{x}$.

Differentiating $\dfrac{dy}{dx} = \dfrac{5}{x^2}$.

Hence the gradient of the curve is always positive and there are no turning points.
As $x \to 0$ from above, $y \to -\infty$ and as $x \to 0$ from below, $y \to \infty$.
As $x \to \infty$, $y \to 2$ from below and as $x \to -\infty$, $y \to 2$ from above.

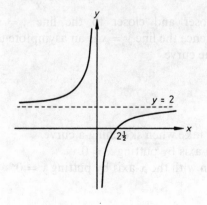

A straight line which a curve approaches more and more closely but never touches is called an *asymptote* to the curve. The curve $y = (2x - 5)/x$ has two asymptotes, the y-axis and the line $y = 2$.

Example 5   Sketch the graph $y = x + \dfrac{1}{x}$.

When $x = 0$, the value of y is undefined.

$$y = 0 \Leftrightarrow x + \frac{1}{x} = 0 \Leftrightarrow x^2 + 1 = 0$$

$\therefore$ there is no real value of x for which $y = 0$.

Hence the curve cuts neither of the coordinate axes.

Differentiating $\dfrac{dy}{dx} = 1 - \dfrac{1}{x^2} = \dfrac{x^2 - 1}{x^2}$

$\dfrac{dy}{dx} = 0 \Leftrightarrow x^2 - 1 = 0 \Leftrightarrow x = -1$ or $x = 1$.

When $x = -1$, $y = -2$ and when $x = 1$, $y = 2$.

When x is just less than -1, $\dfrac{dy}{dx} > 0$ and when x is just greater than -1,

$\dfrac{dy}{dx} < 0$ $\therefore$ the point $(-1, -2)$ is a maximum point.

When x is just less than 1, $\dfrac{dy}{dx} < 0$ and when x is just greater than 1, $\dfrac{dy}{dx} > 0$ $\therefore$ the

point $(1, 2)$ is a minimum point.
As $x \to 0$ from above, $y \to \infty$ and as $x \to 0$ from below, $y \to -\infty$.
$\therefore$ the y-axis is an asymptote to the curve.

As $x \to \infty$, $y \to \infty$ and as $x \to -\infty$, $y \to -\infty$.

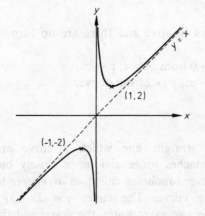

Although we are now ready to sketch the curve, a more accurate sketch will be obtained by noting the fact that as $x \to \pm\infty$, the curve $y = x + \dfrac{1}{x}$ draws closer and closer to the line $y = x$. Hence the line $y = x$ is an asymptote to the curve.

To summarise, here is a list of the steps to take when sketching a curve.
(1) Find the points of intersection with the y-axis by putting $x = 0$.
(2) Find, if possible, the points of intersection with the x-axis by putting $y = 0$.
(3) Find the points at which $dy/dx = 0$.

(4) Determine the nature of these points by considering the sign of dy/dx.

(5) Note any values of x for which y is not defined and examine the behaviour of y as x approaches such values.

(6) Consider the values of y as $x \to \infty$ and as $x \to -\infty$.

(7) If further checks are needed, determine the sign of y for all values of x.

It is important to remember that if differentiating and solving $dy/dx = 0$ is difficult, it is often still possible to sketch a curve fairly quickly using the remaining techniques.

Exercise 5.5

Sketch the following curves showing clearly on each sketch the nature of any stationary points.

1. $y = x^2 - 2x - 3$.

2. $y = 2 - 3x - 2x^2$.

3. $y = (x-1)(x+2)$.

4. $y = 4x^2 - 4x + 3$.

5. $y = x^2(x-3)$.

6. $y = x^3 + 1$.

7. $y = 6x^2 - 12x - x^3$.

8. $y = (x+2)^2(2x-5)$.

9. $y = 2x + x^2 - 4x^3$.

10. $y = 8x^3 + 9x^2 - 15x - 2$.

11. $y = x^4(x+5)$.

12. $y = 4x^3 - 3x^4$.

13. $y = \dfrac{x+1}{x}$.

14. $y = \dfrac{2-3x}{x}$.

15. $y = 9x^3 - 45x^2 + 48x - 11$.

16. $y = x^4 - 2x^3 - 5x^2 + 6$.

17. $y = 4x + \dfrac{9}{x}$.

18. $y = \dfrac{x^3 + 4}{x^2}$.

19. $y = 2x^5 - 15x^4 + 30x^3 - 64$.

20. $y = x - \sqrt{x}\ (x \geqslant 0)$.

21. The curve $y = x^3 + ax^2 + b$ has a minimum point at $(4, -11)$. Find the coordinates of the maximum point on the curve.

22. Given that the curve $y = x^3 + px^2 + qx + r$ passes through the point $(1, 1)$ and has turning points where $x = -1$ and $x = 3$, find the values of p, q and r.

23. Find the conditions that the curve $y = x^3 + ax^2 + bx + c$ should have (i) two distinct stationary points, (ii) one stationary point, (iii) no stationary points.

24. Write down the equations of the two asymptotes to the curve $y = (x^2 + k)/x$, where $k \neq 0$. Sketch the curve for (i) $k > 0$, (ii) $k < 0$.

5.6 The second derivative

For the function $y = f(x)$ the *first derivative* is $f'(x)$ or dy/dx. The *second derivative* is obtained by differentiating again and is written $f''(x)$ or $\dfrac{d^2y}{dx^2}$, which is shorthand for $\dfrac{d}{dx}\left(\dfrac{dy}{dx}\right)$.

Example 1   If $y = 3x + 2 + \dfrac{1}{x}$, find $\dfrac{d^2y}{dx^2}$.

Rearranging $y = 3x + 2 + x^{-1}$

Differentiating $\dfrac{dy}{dx} = 3 - x^{-2} = 3 - \dfrac{1}{x^2}$

and $\dfrac{d^2y}{dx^2} = -(-2)x^{-3} = \dfrac{2}{x^3}.$

Example 2   If $f(x) = x^4 - 6x^2 + 7$, find $f(1)$, $f'(1)$ and $f''(1)$.

$f(x) = x^4 - 6x^2 + 7$ $\therefore$ $f(1) = 1 - 6 + 7 = 2$
$f'(x) = 4x^3 - 12x$ $\therefore$ $f'(1) = 4 - 12 = -8$
$f''(x) = 12x^2 - 12$ $\therefore$ $f''(1) = 12 - 12 = 0.$

If a particle moves in a straight line so that at time t its displacement from a fixed point is s, then the first derivative ds/dt gives the velocity v after t seconds. The second derivative d^2s/dt^2 is also the first derivative of v, dv/dt. Hence it is a measure of the rate at which the velocity is changing, i.e. it represents the acceleration of the particle and we write

$$a = \frac{dv}{dt} = \frac{d^2s}{dt^2}.$$

Example 3   If a particle moves in a straight line, so that after t seconds its displacement from a fixed point is s metres, where $s = 8t^2 - t^4$, find its velocity and acceleration after 1 second.

Differentiating with respect to t: $v = \dfrac{ds}{dt} = 16t - 4t^3$

$$a = \frac{dv}{dt} = 16 - 12t^2$$

When $t = 1$, $v = 12$ and $a = 4$.
$\therefore$ after 1 second the velocity of the particle is $12\,\mathrm{m\,s^{-1}}$ and its acceleration is $4\,\mathrm{m\,s^{-2}}$.

In general, the second derivative, d^2y/dx^2, can be used to examine how the gradient function, dy/dx, changes as x increases.

For the curve $y = 2 + x - x^2$ sketched in Example 1, §5.5,

$$\frac{dy}{dx} = 1 - 2x \quad \text{and} \quad \frac{d^2y}{dx^2} = -2.$$

This means that the graph of this gradient function is a straight line, gradient -2.

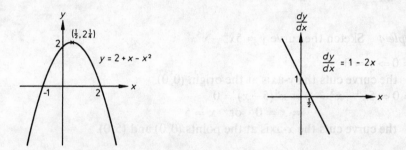

The turning point on the curve corresponds to the point at which the graph of dy/dx cuts the x-axis.

The diagrams below show the graph of a function $y = f(x)$ and the corresponding graph of the gradient function dy/dx or $f'(x)$. The gradient function for this second graph is the second derivative d^2y/dx^2 or $f''(x)$.

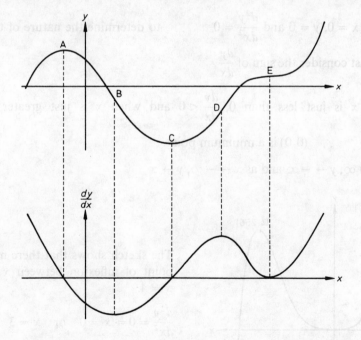

At the maximum point A, the gradient of the curve is decreasing through zero and d^2y/dx^2 is negative. At the minimum point C, the gradient of the curve is increasing through zero and d^2y/dx^2 is positive. Points of inflexion, such as B, D and E, are points where dy/dx reaches either a maximum or a minimum value.

Thus at these points $d^2y/dx^2 = 0$. However, $d^2y/dx^2 = 0$ does not necessarily imply the presence of a point of inflexion.

Summarising, a point where $\dfrac{dy}{dx} = 0$ is a maximum point if $\dfrac{d^2y}{dx^2} < 0$, a minimum point if $\dfrac{d^2y}{dx^2} > 0$. When $\dfrac{d^2y}{dx^2} = 0$, further investigation is needed.

Example 4   Sketch the curve $y = 5x^4 - x^5$.

$x = 0 \Rightarrow y = 0$

$\therefore$ the curve cuts the y-axis at the origin $(0,0)$.

$y = 0 \Leftrightarrow 5x^4 - x^5 = 0 \Leftrightarrow x^4(5-x) = 0$

$\Leftrightarrow x = 0$ or $x = 5$

$\therefore$ the curve cuts the x-axis at the points $(0,0)$ and $(5,0)$.

$\dfrac{dy}{dx} = 20x^3 - 5x^4 = 5x^3(4-x),\ \dfrac{d^2y}{dx^2} = 60x^2 - 20x^3 = 20x^2(3-x)$

$\therefore$ $\dfrac{dy}{dx} = 0 \Leftrightarrow 5x^3(4-x) = 0 \Leftrightarrow x = 0$ or $x = 4$.

When $x = 4$, $y = 256$ and $\dfrac{d^2y}{dx^2} < 0$ $\therefore$ $(4, 256)$ is a maximum point.

When $x = 0$, $y = 0$ and $\dfrac{d^2y}{dx^2} = 0$ $\therefore$ to determine the nature of this point we must consider the sign of $\dfrac{dy}{dx}$.

When x is just less than 0, $\dfrac{dy}{dx} < 0$ and when x is just greater than 0, $\dfrac{dy}{dx} > 0$ $\therefore$ $(0,0)$ is a minimum point.

As $x \to \infty$, $y \to -\infty$ and as $x \to -\infty$, $y \to \infty$.

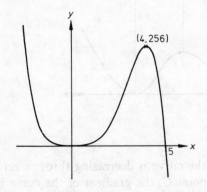

The sketch shows that there must be a point of inflexion between $x = 0$ and $x = 4$.

$\dfrac{d^2y}{dx^2} = 0 \Rightarrow x = 0$ or $x = 3$

and when $x = 3$, $y = 162$

$\therefore$ the coordinates of the point of inflexion are $(3, 162)$.

Exercise 5.6

In questions 1 to 6 find $\dfrac{d^2y}{dx^2}$.

1. $y = 3x^2 + 4x - 1$.

2. $y = 5x^3 - x^2 - x$.

3. $y = x^4 - 2x^3 + \dfrac{1}{x}$.

4. $y = \dfrac{(x^2 - 4)(x + 1)}{x^2}$.

5. $y = \sqrt{x} + \dfrac{1}{\sqrt{x}}$.

6. $y = \dfrac{(x - 2)(2x + 3)}{\sqrt{x}}$.

Sketch the following curves using the second derivative, where possible, to determine the nature of any stationary points.

7. $y = x^3 - 3x$.

8. $y = x^4 - 2x^2 + 1$.

9. $y = x^4 - 2x^3$.

10. $y = 4x - 3 + \dfrac{1}{x}$.

11. $y = 2x^3 - 9x^2 + 12x - 3$.

12. $y = 3x^4 - 4x^3 - 12x^2 + 5$.

13. In each of the following cases find $f(-1), f'(-1)$ and $f''(-1)$
(a) $f(x) = x^5 + 6x^4 - x^2$,   (b) $f(x) = (x^3 - 2)/x$.

14. If $f(x) = x^4 - 4x^3 + 16x - 16$, show that $f(2) = f'(2) = f''(2) = 0$. Sketch the graph of the function showing any turning points and points of inflexion.

15. Show that the curve $y = x^3 - 3x^2 + 6x - 4$ has one point of inflexion and find the gradient of the curve at this point. Sketch the curve.

16. A particle moves along a straight line so that after t seconds its displacement from a fixed point A on the line is s metres. If $s = 3t^2(3 - t)$, find (a) expressions for the velocity, v ms^{-1}, and the acceleration, a ms^{-2}, after t seconds, (b) the initial velocity and acceleration of the particle, (c) the velocity and acceleration after 3 seconds.

17. Repeat question 16 for $s = 8t^3 - 33t^2 + 27t$.

18. The curve $y = x^4 + ax^2 + bx + c$ passes through the point $(-1, 16)$ and at that point $\dfrac{d^2y}{dx^2} = -\dfrac{dy}{dx} = 16$. Find the values of a, b, c and sketch the curve.

19. Sketch the following curves, labelling any turning points and points of inflexion.

(a) $y = x^2 + \dfrac{1}{x}$,   (b) $y = \dfrac{1}{x} - \dfrac{1}{x^2}$,   (c) $y = \dfrac{1}{x} - \dfrac{1}{x^3}$.

20. Sketch the curve $y = x^4 + 4x$ and show that d^2y/dx^2 is zero at a point which is neither a turning point nor a point of inflexion.

Exercise 5.7   (miscellaneous)

1.   Find the limit as $h \to 0$ of

(a) $2 - 3h + 5h^2$,   (b) $\dfrac{h^2 - 4h}{h}$,   (c) $\dfrac{1 - h^2}{1 - 2h}$.

2.   Find the limit as $x \to \infty$ of

(a) $\dfrac{4}{2x - 3}$,   (b) $\dfrac{2x^2 + 1}{x^2 - 7}$,   (c) $\dfrac{x - 1}{x^2 - 3x + 5}$.

3.   (a) Prove that, as x tends to zero, the limit of the expression

$$\frac{(2 + 3x)^2 - 4(1 + x)^2}{6x} \text{ is } \frac{2}{3}.$$

(b) Find the limit, as n tends to infinity, of

$$\frac{[\sqrt{(4n + 3)} + 2\sqrt{(1 + n)}]}{\sqrt{n}}.$$ (AEB 1978)

4.   Differentiate from first principles the functions
(a) $(x + 1)^3$,   (b) $(x + 1)^{-1}$.

5.   Prove that $\sqrt{(a + b)} - \sqrt{a} = \dfrac{b}{\sqrt{(a + b)} + \sqrt{a}}$. Use this result to differentiate the function $y = \sqrt{x}$ from first principles.

6.   Differentiate with respect to x

(a) $(3x + 1)^2$,   (b) $\dfrac{1}{x}(x + 2)(x + 3)$,   (c) $(x + 2)\sqrt{x}$.

7.   Find the equations of the tangents to the curve $y = x^3 - 2x^2 - 3x$ at the points where the curve crosses the x-axis.

8.   Show that the tangent to the curve $y = (1 + x)^2(5 - x)$ at the point where $x = 1$ does not meet the curve again. Show also that the tangent at the point (0.5) cuts the curve at a turning point. Draw a rough sketch of the curve, showing these tangents.

9.   Sketch the following curves indicating the approximate positions of any turning points

(a) $y = x^2 - 4$,   (b) $x^3 - 4x$,   (c) $y = x^4 - 4x^2$,

(d) $y = x - \dfrac{4}{x}$,   (e) $y = 1 - \dfrac{4}{x^2}$,   (f) $y = \dfrac{1}{x} - \dfrac{4}{x^3}$.

10. Find any maxima, minima or horizontal points of inflexion of the curve $y = \dfrac{x^3 + 3x - 1}{x^2}$, stating, with reasons, the nature of each point. Sketch the curve, indicating clearly what happens as $x \to \pm\infty$.   (SU)

11. A particle moves along a straight line such that after t seconds its displacement from a fixed point on the line is s metres, where $s = 7t + 5t^2 - 2t^3$. Find (a) expressions for the velocity and acceleration of the particle after t seconds, (b) the velocity and acceleration of the particle initially and after 2 seconds.

12. A function $f(x)$ is defined as follows:
$$f(x) = 2x^3 - 9x^2 + 12x \qquad \text{when } 0 \leqslant x \leqslant 2$$
and $f(x) = 4(x-1)(3-x) \qquad \text{when } 2 < x \leqslant 3$.
Sketch the graph of the function.

13. If $f(x) = (x^2 - 1)(x - 3)$ show that the minimum value of $f'(x)$ is -4. Sketch the graphs of the functions $f(x)$ and $f'(x)$.

14. Show that the curve $y = ax^3 + bx^2 + cx + d$ $(a \neq 0)$ always has exactly one point of inflexion and write down its x-coordinate.

15. Show that there are no points of inflexion on the curve $y = x^4 - 4x^3 + 6x^2 - 4x$, then sketch the curve.

6 Introduction to integration

6.1 The reverse of differentiation

Any graph with gradient function given by $dy/dx = 2$ has gradient 2 at every point on it. Hence the graph must be a straight line with equation $y = 2x + c$, where c is some constant. Conversely, differentiating $y = 2x + c$, we obtain $dy/dx = 2$ for all values of c. Thus the differential equation, $dy/dx = 2$, is said to represent the family of all straight lines with gradient 2.

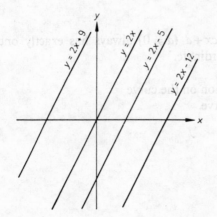

Consider now graphs with gradient function, $dy/dx = 3x^2$. Since $\dfrac{d}{dx}(x^3)$

$= 3x^2$, the result $\dfrac{dy}{dx} = 3x^2$ may be derived from any equation of the form, $y = x^3 + c$, where c is a constant. Thus the equation $dy/dx = 3x^2$ represents the family of curves $y = x^3 + c$, some of which are shown in the diagram.

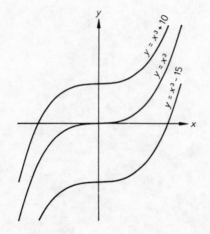

The operation of obtaining an expression for y in terms of x from the gradient function, dy/dx, is called *integration*. The function $x^3 + c$ is the *integral* of $3x^2$ with respect to x. Since the constant c may take any value, it is called an *arbitrary constant*.

The rule for integrating powers of x is found by reversing the rule for differentiation. We find that to integrate a power of x, we must add 1 to the index, then divide by the new index, i.e.

$$\text{if } \frac{dy}{dx} = x^n, \quad \text{then} \quad y = \frac{x^{n+1}}{n+1} + c \quad \text{provided that} \quad n+1 \neq 0.$$

This rule cannot be applied to the integration of x^{-1}, because there is no power of x whose derivative is x^{-1}.

Example 1   Find y if $\frac{dy}{dx}$ is (a) x^4, (b) $\frac{1}{x^3}$, (c) $6x$, (d) $x^{1/2}$.

(a) If $\frac{dy}{dx} = x^4$, then $y = \frac{1}{5}x^5 + c$.

(b) If $\frac{dy}{dx} = \frac{1}{x^3} = x^{-3}$, then $y = \frac{x^{-2}}{-2} + c = -\frac{1}{2x^2} + c$.

(c) If $\frac{dy}{dx} = 6x = 6.x^1$, then $y = 6.\frac{x^2}{2} + c = 3x^2 + c$.

(d) If $\frac{dy}{dx} = x^{1/2}$, then $y = \frac{x^{3/2}}{\frac{3}{2}} + c = \frac{2}{3}x^{3/2} + c$.

Example 2   Find $f(u)$, given that $f'(u) = (u-2)(2u+1)$.

If $\quad f'(u) = (u-2)(2u+1) = 2u^2 - 3u - 2$

then $\quad f(u) = \frac{2}{3}u^3 - \frac{3}{2}u^2 - 2u + c$.

It is sometimes possible to determine the value of the arbitrary constant in an integration problem, if additional information is given.

Example 3   Find V in terms of h, if $\frac{dV}{dh} = 4h^2 + h$ and $V = 2$ when $h = 1$.

$$\frac{dV}{dh} = 4h^2 + h \quad \Rightarrow \quad V = \frac{4}{3}h^3 + \frac{1}{2}h^2 + c$$

Since $V = 2$ when $h = 1$, $\quad 2 = \frac{4}{3} + \frac{1}{2} + c$

$$\therefore \quad c = 2 - \frac{4}{3} - \frac{1}{2} = \frac{1}{6}$$

Hence $V = \dfrac{4}{3}h^3 + \dfrac{1}{2}h^2 + \dfrac{1}{6} = \dfrac{1}{6}(8h^3 + 3h^2 + 1).$

Example 4   The gradient of a curve is given by $\dfrac{dy}{dx} = 1 - \dfrac{1}{x^2}$. If the curve passes through the point $(1, 1)$, find its equation.

Integrating $y = x + \dfrac{1}{x} + c$

Since $y = 1$, when $x = 1$, $1 = 1 + 1 + c$ $\therefore c = -1.$

Hence the equation of the curve is $y = x + \dfrac{1}{x} - 1.$

Exercise 6.1

1. Sketch the families of curves with the following gradient functions:
(a) 1, (b) $2x$, (c) $4x^3$.

2. Sketch the family of curves represented by each of the following differential equations

(a) $\dfrac{dy}{dx} = -\dfrac{1}{2}$,   (b) $\dfrac{dy}{dx} = 1 - 2x$,   (c) $\dfrac{dy}{dx} = 3x^2 - 6x.$

3. Find y if $\dfrac{dy}{dx}$ is   (a) x^2,   (b) $\dfrac{1}{x^2}$,   (c) $8x^3$,   (d) $\dfrac{6}{x^3}$.

In questions 4 to 12 integrate the given functions of x.

4. $3x^2 + 4x.$ 5. $x^5 - 1.$ 6. $(2x + 1)^2.$

7. $6x - \dfrac{1}{6x^3}.$ 8. $\left(x + \dfrac{1}{x}\right)^2.$ 9. $\dfrac{x^2 - 1}{x^4}.$

10. $x^{1/3} + x^{-1/3}.$ 11. $\dfrac{x - 1}{\sqrt{x}}.$ 12. $\sqrt{x^3} - \dfrac{1}{\sqrt{x^3}}.$

13. Find $f(t)$ given that $f'(t)$ is equal to

(a) $(t + 6)(3t - 4)$,   (b) $\dfrac{(2t + 1)^2}{t^4}$,   (c) $\dfrac{(t - 2)(2t - 1)}{\sqrt{t}}.$

14. Find an expression for y in terms of x, if

$\dfrac{dy}{dx} = (x - 1)(3x - 5)$ and $y = 0$ when $x = 1.$

15. Given that $\dfrac{dy}{dx} = 2\left(x + \dfrac{1}{x^3}\right)$ and that $y = 3$ when $x = 1$, find the value of y when $x = \frac{1}{2}$.

16. The gradient of a curve is given by $\dfrac{dy}{dx} = 3x^2 - 4$. If the curve passes through the point $(2, -1)$, find its equation.

17. The gradient of a certain curve at a typical point (x, y) is $4(1 - x)$. Given that the maximum value of y on the curve is 8, find its equation.

18. Find an expression for A in terms of h, given that

$\dfrac{dA}{dh} = 3\sqrt{h} - \dfrac{1}{2\sqrt{h}}$ and that $A = 10$ when $h = 4$.

19. Find an expression for y in terms of x, given that

$\dfrac{d^2y}{dx^2} = 6x - 10$ and that when $x = 1$, $y = 1$ and $\dfrac{dy}{dx} = 1$.

20. If y is a function of x and $\dfrac{d^2y}{dx^2} = 3 - \dfrac{5}{\sqrt[3]{x}}$, find the value of y when $x = 8$, given that $dy/dx = \frac{1}{2}$ and $y = 5$ when $x = 1$.

6.2 The area under a curve

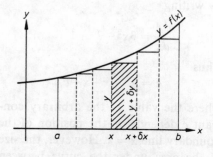

The diagram shows part of a curve $y = f(x)$. The area bounded by the curve, the x-axis and the lines $x = a$ and $x = b$ can be determined by dividing it into strips. These strips are assumed to be approximately rectangular, so that a typical strip of width δx and height y has area $y\,\delta x$. The total area is then estimated by finding the sum of all such areas between $x = a$ and $x = b$. The smaller the width of each strip, the more accurate this estimate will be. Thus, as δx approaches zero, the sum of the areas of the strips approaches the required area under the curve. Since the area is derived from the limit of a sum of terms of the form $y\,\delta x$, as $\delta x \rightarrow 0$, the standard notation for this area is

$$\int_a^b y\,dx \quad \text{or} \quad \int_a^b f(x)\,dx, \quad \text{where} \quad \int \text{ is an elongated S for sum.}$$

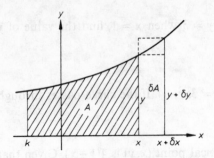

To find a way of evaluating this limit, consider the shaded area, A, between the curve $y = f(x)$ and the x-axis shown in the sketch. Since the value of A depends on the value of x, it may be possible to express A in terms of x.

Let δx be a small increase in x and let δy and δA be the corresponding increases in y and A. The area δA must lie between the areas of the two rectangles shown in the diagram, which have width δx and heights y and $y + \delta y$

i.e. $y\,\delta x < \delta A < (y + \delta y)\,\delta x$

$$\therefore \quad y < \frac{\delta A}{\delta x} < y + \delta y$$

As $\delta x \to 0$, $\delta y \to 0$ and $\dfrac{\delta A}{\delta x} \to \dfrac{dA}{dx}$

$$\therefore \quad \frac{dA}{dx} = y.$$

Hence an expression for A may be obtained by integrating $f(x)$.

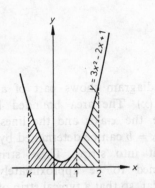

For example, the area function A for the curve $y = 3x^2 - 2x + 1$ is obtained by writing

$$\frac{dA}{dx} = 3x^2 - 2x + 1$$

Thus

$$A = x^3 - x + x + c,$$

where the value of the arbitrary constant c depends on the position of the boundary line $x = k$. However, the size of the area under the curve between $x = 1$ and $x = 2$ does not depend on the values of c and k.

At $x = 2$, $A = 8 - 4 + 2 + c = 6 + c$

At $x = 1$, $A = 1 - 1 + 1 + c = 1 + c$

$\therefore$ the area bounded by the curve $y = 3x^2 - 2x + 1$, the x-axis and the lines $x = 1$ and $x = 2$ is $(6 + c) - (1 + c)$, i.e. 5 square units.

More generally, if the area function for a curve $y = f(x)$ is $A = F(x) + c$, then the area under the curve between $x = a$ and $x = b$ is $F(b) - F(a)$.

Hence
$$\int_a^b y\,dx = \int_a^b f(x)\,dx = F(b) - F(a).$$

The expression $F(b) - F(a)$ is often written $\left[F(x)\right]_a^b$.

Example 1   Find the area bounded by the curve $y = x^2 - x + 3$, the x-axis and the lines $x = 2$, $x = 4$.

Required area $= \displaystyle\int_2^4 y\,dx$

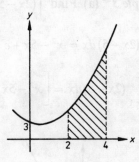

$$= \int_2^4 (x^2 - x + 3)\,dx$$

$$= \left[\tfrac{1}{3}x^3 - \tfrac{1}{2}x^2 + 3x\right]_2^4$$

$$= (\tfrac{1}{3}.4^3 - \tfrac{1}{2}.4^2 + 3.4) - (\tfrac{1}{3}.2^3 - \tfrac{1}{2}.2^2 + 3.2)$$

$$= (64/3 - 8 + 12) - (8/3 - 2 + 6) = 18\tfrac{2}{3}.$$

[We will assume that all areas obtained by integration are measured in square units.]

Example 2   Find the area of the region bounded by the curve $y = 2 + x - x^2$ and the straight line $y = x + 1$.

At the points of intersection of the line and the curve

$$y = 2 + x - x^2 \quad \text{and} \quad y = x + 1$$
$$2 + x - x^2 = x + 1$$
$$\Leftrightarrow \qquad\qquad x^2 = 1$$
$$\Leftrightarrow \quad x = -1 \quad \text{or} \quad x = 1$$

$\therefore$ the points of intersection are $(-1, 0)$ and $(1, 2)$.

The area under the curve from $x = -1$ to $x = 1$

$$= \int_{-1}^1 (2 + x - x^2)\,dx$$

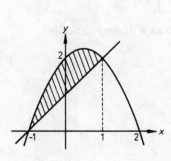

$$= \left[2x + \tfrac{1}{2}x^2 - \tfrac{1}{3}x^3\right]_{-1}^1$$

$$= (2 + \tfrac{1}{2} - \tfrac{1}{3}) - (-2 + \tfrac{1}{2} + \tfrac{1}{3}) = 3\tfrac{1}{3}$$

The area of the triangle under the line $= \tfrac{1}{2}.2.2 = 2$.

Hence the area bounded by the given curve and straight line is $3\tfrac{1}{3} - 2$, i.e. $1\tfrac{1}{3}$.

In §6.1 integration was described as the reverse of differentiation. However, we now see that it is also the process used to find areas under curves. Because of this relationship between integration and summation the integral of a function $f(x)$ is denoted by $\int f(x)\,dx$ and referred to as an *indefinite integral*. The expression $\int_a^b f(x)\,dx$ is called a *definite integral*. The constants a and b are the *limits of integration*, a being the lower limit and b the upper.

Example 3   (a) Find $\int (2x-5)\,dx$,   (b) Evaluate $\int_{-1}^2 (2x-5)\,dx$.

(a) $\int (2x-5)\,dx = x^2 - 5x + c$

(b) $\int_{-1}^2 (2x-5)\,dx = \left[x^2 - 5x \right]_{-1}^2 = (2^2 - 5.2) - (\{-1\}^2 - 5.\{-1\}) = -6-6$

$$= -12.$$

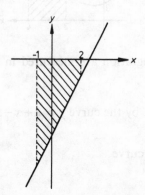

The diagram shows the significance of the negative value of the above definite integral. The line $y = 2x - 5$ is below the x-axis, i.e. y is negative, throughout the interval $x = -1$ to $x = 2$. This means that although the definite integral is negative, it is still numerically equal to the area bounded by the line $y = 2x - 5$, the x-axis and the lines $x = -1, x = 2$.

As shown in the examples, for any given function $f(x)$, the definite integral $\int_a^b f(x)\,dx$ is not itself a function of x, but has a numerical value which depends solely on the limits a and b. If a different variable is used the value is unchanged.

$$\int_a^b f(x)\,dx = \int_a^b f(t)\,dt = \int_a^b f(\theta)\,d\theta.$$

Thus x (or t, or θ) may sometimes be referred to as a *dummy variable*.

Example 4   Evaluate $\int_1^4 \left(\sqrt{u} + \dfrac{1}{\sqrt{u}} \right) du$.

$$\int_1^4 \left(\sqrt{u} + \frac{1}{\sqrt{u}} \right) du = \int_1^4 (u^{1/2} + u^{-1/2})\,du$$

$$= \left[\tfrac{2}{3} u^{3/2} + 2u^{1/2} \right]_1^4$$

$$= (\tfrac{2}{3}.4^{3/2} + 2.4^{1/2}) - (\tfrac{2}{3}.1^{3/2} + 2.1^{1/2})$$

$$= \frac{16}{3} + 4 - \frac{2}{3} - 2 = 6\tfrac{2}{3}.$$

Exercise 6.2

Find the following indefinite integrals

1. (a) $\int (6x+1)\,dx.$ (b) $\int (3x-1)^2\,dx.$ (c) $\int x(4x+1)\,dx.$

2. (a) $\int \left(3 - \dfrac{1}{x^2}\right)dx.$ (b) $\int \left(x - \dfrac{1}{x}\right)^2 dx.$ (c) $\int \dfrac{3x+1}{x^3}\,dx.$

3. (a) $\int 4\sqrt{x}\,dx.$ (b) $\int \dfrac{x-1}{\sqrt{x}}\,dx.$ (c) $\int 4(x^{1/3}+x^{-1/3})\,dx.$

4. (a) $\int \left(3t^2 - \dfrac{1}{t^2}\right)dt.$ (b) $\int u(1-\sqrt{u})\,du.$ (c) $\int \dfrac{s^3+1}{s^3}\,ds.$

Evaluate the following definite integrals

5. (a) $\int_{-1}^{1} (4x+3)\,dx$ (b) $\int_{1}^{3} (3x^2-x)\,dx.$ (c) $\int_{1}^{25} x^{1/2}\,dx.$

6. (a) $\int_{1}^{2} \left(x + \dfrac{1}{x}\right)^2 dx.$ (b) $\int_{-2}^{-1} \dfrac{2x^4+1}{x^4}\,dx.$ (c) $\int_{1}^{4} \dfrac{5x^2-4}{\sqrt{x}}\,dx.$

7. (a) $\int_{-3}^{3} u(u-1)^2\,du.$ (b) $\int_{1}^{27} y^{1/3}\,dy.$ (c) $\int_{1}^{2} \dfrac{3t^4-1}{t^2}\,dt.$

8. Find the areas bounded by the x-axis and the following curves and straight lines.
(a) $y = 4x^2,\ x = 0,\ x = 1,$ (b) $y = x^3 - x,\ x = 1,\ x = 2,$
(c) $y = 18/x^3,\ x = 1,\ x = 3,$ (d) $y = 3\sqrt{x},\ x = 4,\ x = 9.$

9. Find the areas enclosed by the x-axis and the following curves
(a) $y = (1-x)(x+2),$ (b) $y = 3x^2 - x^3,$
(c) $y = 4x^2 - 4x - 3$ (d) $y = x^4 - 8x.$

10. Find the areas of the regions bounded by the following curves and straight lines.
(a) $y = (5-x)(2+x),\ y = 10,$ (b) $y = (x-1)^2,\ y = 9,$
(c) $y = x(3-x),\ y = x,$ (d) $y = (x^2-1)(x-2),\ y = 2-2x,$
(e) $y = 2\sqrt{x},\ 2x-3y+4 = 0,$ (f) $y = 9\left(x + \dfrac{1}{x^2}\right),\ y = 7(x+1).$

11. Find the area of the smaller closed region bounded by the curve $y = x^2$, the straight line $2x + y = 8$ and the x-axis.

12. Sketch the curves $y = x^2$ and $y^2 = x$. Find the coordinates of the points of intersection of the curves. Calculate the area enclosed between the two curves.

6.3 Properties of definite integrals

As shown in the previous section, the definite integral produces positive values for areas above the x-axis but negative values for areas below the x-axis. Thus difficulties may arise when a curve crosses the x-axis inside the range of integration.

Example 1   (a) Evaluate $\displaystyle\int_0^2 x(x-1)\,dx.$ (b) Find the total area enclosed by the curve $y = x(x-1)$, the x-axis and the line $x = 2$.

(a) $\displaystyle\int_0^2 x(x-1)\,dx = \int_0^2 (x^2 - x)\,dx = \left[\tfrac{1}{3}x^3 - \tfrac{1}{2}x^2\right]_0^2 = (\tfrac{1}{3}.2^3 - \tfrac{1}{2}.2^2) - 0 = \tfrac{2}{3}.$

(b) $y = 0 \Leftrightarrow x(x-1) = 0$
$\qquad\quad \Leftrightarrow x = 0 \quad \text{or} \quad x = 1$

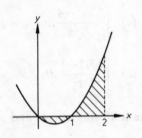

$\therefore$ the curve cuts the x-axis at the points $(0,0)$ and $(1,0)$.

$$\int_0^1 (x^2 - x)\,dx = \left[\tfrac{1}{3}x^3 - \tfrac{1}{2}x^2\right]_0^1$$

$$= \tfrac{1}{3} - \tfrac{1}{2} = -\frac{1}{6}$$

$\therefore$ the shaded area below the x-axis is 1/6.

$$\int_1^2 (x^2 - x)\,dx = \left[\tfrac{1}{3}x^3 - \tfrac{1}{2}x^2\right]_1^2$$

$$= \frac{2}{3} - \left(-\frac{1}{6}\right) = \frac{5}{6}$$

$\therefore$ the shaded area above the x-axis is 5/6.

Hence the total area enclosed by the curve $y = x(x-1)$, the x-axis and the line $x = 2$ is 1.

[Note that the definite integral gave the difference between the area above the x-axis and the area below it, i.e. $\dfrac{5}{6} - \dfrac{1}{6} = \dfrac{2}{3}$, instead of the sum $\dfrac{5}{6} + \dfrac{1}{6} = 1$, which we required.]

Another type of difficulty arises when we consider a curve such as $y = 1/x^2$.

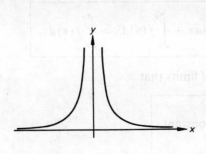

The integral $\displaystyle\int_a^b \frac{1}{x^2} dx$ can be used to find areas under the curve as long as a and b are either both positive or both negative. However, there is a break or *discontinuity* in the curve at $x = 0$, as shown in the sketch. It is, therefore, quite meaningless to talk about the area under the curve between such values as $x = -1$ and $x = 2$. Although the integral $\displaystyle\int_{-1}^2 \frac{1}{x^2} dx$ can be evaluated in the usual way, the result is not valid and does not represent an area under the curve $y = 1/x^2$.

The area bounded by a curve, the y-axis and lines $y = \alpha$ and $y = \beta$ is given by a definite integral of the form $\displaystyle\int_\alpha^\beta x \, dy$, in which the roles of x and y are interchanged.

Example 2   Find the area bounded by the curve $y = x^2$ and the line $y = 4$.

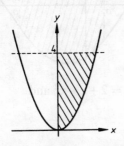

The required area is twice the shaded area shown in the sketch.

Shaded area

$$= \int_0^4 x \, dy = \int_0^4 y^{1/2} \, dy = \left[\tfrac{2}{3} y^{3/2} \right]_0^4$$

$$= 16/3 = 5\tfrac{1}{3}.$$

Hence the area bounded by the curve $y = x^2$ and the line $y = 4$ is $10\tfrac{2}{3}$.

Two general properties of the definite integral may be proved as follows:

Let $\displaystyle\int f(x) \, dx = F(x) + c$,   then

$$\int_b^a f(x) \, dx = \left[F(x) \right]_b^a = F(a) - F(b) = -\{F(b) - F(a)\} = -\left[F(x) \right]_a^b$$

$$= -\int_a^b f(x) \, dx.$$

$$\int_a^b f(x) \, dx + \int_b^c f(x) \, dx = \{F(b) - F(a)\} + \{F(c) - F(b)\} = F(c) - F(a)$$

$$= \int_a^c f(x) \, dx.$$

Summarising:

$$\int_b^a f(x)\,dx = -\int_a^b f(x)\,dx, \quad \int_a^b f(x)\,dx + \int_b^c f(x)\,dx = \int_a^c f(x)\,dx.$$

It may also be shown using the properties of limits that

$$\int_a^b kf(x)\,dx = k\int_a^b f(x)\,dx \quad \text{where } k \text{ is a constant}$$

$$\int_a^b f(x)\,dx + \int_a^b g(x)\,dx = \int_a^b \{f(x)+g(x)\}\,dx.$$

These properties can be used when finding the area between two curves. For instance, in the cases illustrated below, the shaded area is given by

$$\int_a^b \{f(x)-g(x)\}\,dx.$$

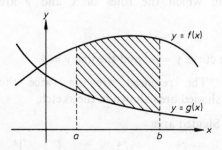
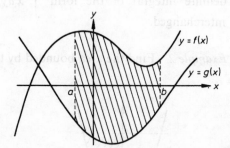

Example 3   Find the area enclosed by the curves $y = 2+x-x^2$ and $y = 2-3x+x^2$.

At the points of intersection of the two curves

$$2+x-x^2 = 2-3x+x^2$$
$$\therefore \quad 4x - 2x^2 = 0$$
$$\therefore \quad x(2-x) = 0$$

$\therefore$ either $x = 0, y = 2$ or $x = 2, y = 0$.

Hence the required area

$$= \int_0^2 (2+x-x^2)\,dx - \int_0^2 (2-3x+x^2)\,dx$$

$$= \int_0^2 (4x-2x^2)\,dx$$

$$= \left[2x^2 - \tfrac{2}{3}x^3 \right]_0^2$$

$$= 8 - 16/3 = 2\tfrac{2}{3}.$$

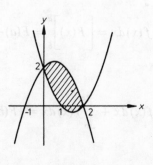

Exercise 6.3

1. Find the total areas of the regions enclosed by the following curves and straight lines

(a) $y = (x+1)(x-3)$, $y = 0$ and $x = -3$,
(b) $y = x^3 - 3x^2$, $y = 0$ and $x = 4$,
(c) $y = x^3 + x^2 - 2x$ and the x-axis,
(d) $y = x^2 - 5 + \dfrac{4}{x^2}$ and the x-axis.

2. Find the area bounded by the curve $y = x^2$ and the line $y = 9$.

3. Find the area bounded by the curve $y^2 = 4 - x$ and the y-axis.

4. Find the area bounded by the curve $y = (x-1)^3$, the y-axis and the line $y = 8$.

5. Find the area bounded by the curve $y = 1/(x+1)^2$, the y-axis and the line $y = 4$.

6. Find the areas of the finite regions bounded by the following curves and straight lines

(a) $y = x(4 - 3x)$ and $y = x$,
(b) $y = x^2 + 2x + 3$ and $y = 2(x+2)$,
(c) $y = 3 + 2x - x^2$ and $y = 3 - 2x$.

7. Sketch the following pairs of curves and find the area of the regions enclosed by them.

(a) $y = 2x^2$, $y = 3 - x^2$,   (b) $y = x^2 - 3x$, $y = 2 - x^2$,
(c) $y = 3x^2 + 9x + 5$, $y = x^2 + x - 1$.

6.4 Volumes of revolution

Consider the volume, V, generated when the shaded area between the curve $y = f(x)$ and the x-axis is rotated completely about the x-axis.

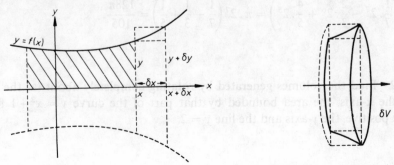

Let δx be a small increase in x and let δy and δV be the corresponding increases in y and V. The volume δV must lie between the volumes of two cylinders or discs of thickness δx and radii y and $y + \delta y$,

i.e. $\qquad \pi y^2 \, \delta x < \delta V < \pi (y + \delta y)^2 \, \delta x$

$$\therefore \quad \pi y^2 < \frac{\delta V}{\delta x} < \pi (y + \delta y)^2$$

As $\quad \delta x \to 0, \quad \delta y \to 0 \quad$ and $\quad \dfrac{\delta V}{\delta x} \to \dfrac{dV}{dx}$

$$\therefore \quad \frac{dV}{dx} = \pi y^2.$$

Hence the volume generated between $x = a$ and $x = b$ is given by

$$\int_a^b \pi y^2 \, dx.$$

Example 1 Find the volume generated by rotating completely about the x-axis the area bounded by the curve $y = x^3 - 2x^2$ and the x-axis.

$$y = 0 \Leftrightarrow x^3 - 2x^2 = 0 \Leftrightarrow x = 0 \quad \text{or} \quad x = 2$$

$\therefore$ the curve cuts the x-axis at $(0, 0)$ and $(2, 0)$.

Hence the required volume $= \displaystyle\int_0^2 \pi y^2 \, dx$

$$= \pi \int_0^2 (x^3 - 2x^2)^2 \, dx$$

$$= \pi \int_0^2 (x^6 - 4x^5 + 4x^4) \, dx$$

$$= \pi \left[\frac{1}{7} x^7 - \frac{4}{6} x^6 + \frac{4}{5} x^5 \right]_0^2$$

$$= \pi \left(\frac{1}{7} . 2^7 - \frac{2}{3} . 2^6 + \frac{4}{5} . 2^5 \right) = \pi . 2^7 \left(\frac{1}{7} - \frac{1}{3} + \frac{1}{5} \right) = \frac{128\pi}{105}.$$

Example 2 Find the volumes generated by rotating completely about (a) the y-axis, (b) the x-axis, the area bounded by that part of the curve $y = x^2 + 1$ for which x is positive, the y-axis and the line $y = 2$.

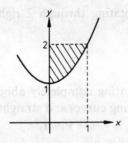

(a) The volume generated by rotation about the y-axis $= \displaystyle\int_1^2 \pi x^2 \, dy$

$$= \int_1^2 \pi(y-1)\,dy$$

$$= \pi\left[\tfrac{1}{2}y^2 - y\right]_1^2$$

$$= \pi\{(\tfrac{1}{2}.2^2 - 2) - (\tfrac{1}{2} - 1)\} = \tfrac{1}{2}\pi.$$

(b) [Note that in this case the volume generated by rotation about the x-axis cannot be calculated directly.]

Let V_1 be the volume of the cylinder generated by rotating about the x-axis the rectangle bounded by the axes and the lines $x = 1$, $y = 2$.

Thus $V_1 = \pi.2^2.1 = 4\pi$.

Let V_2 be the volume generated by rotating about the x-axis the area bounded by the curve, the axes and the line $x = 1$.

Thus $V_2 = \displaystyle\int_0^1 \pi y^2 \, dx = \pi \int_0^1 (x^2+1)^2 \, dx$

$$= \pi \int_0^1 (x^4 + 2x^2 + 1)\,dx$$

$$= \pi\left[\frac{1}{5}x^5 + \frac{2}{3}x^3 + x\right]_0^1$$

$$= \pi\left(\frac{1}{5} + \frac{2}{3} + 1\right) = \frac{28\pi}{15}$$

Hence the required volume $= V_1 - V_2 = \left(4 - \dfrac{28}{15}\right)\pi = \dfrac{32\pi}{15}.$

Exercise 6.4

[Answers may be left in terms of π.]

1. Find the volumes of the solids formed by rotating completely about the x-axis the areas bounded by the x-axis and the given curves and lines.
(a) $y = 5x^2$, $x = -1$, $x = 3$,   (b) $y = 3x - x^2$, $x = 1$, $x = 2$,
(c) $y = 2x - 5$, $x = 1$, $x = 4$,   (d) $y = x^3 + 1$, $x = 2$,
(e) $y = 1 + \sqrt{x}$, $x = 4$, $x = 9$,   (f) $y = x + \dfrac{1}{x}$, $x = \tfrac{1}{2}$, $x = 2$.

2. Find the volumes of the solids formed by rotating completely about the x-axis the areas enclosed by each of the following curves and the x-axis (a) $y = x^2 - 4$, (b) $3y = x^2(3 - x)$.

3. Find the volumes of the solids formed by rotating through 2 right angles about the x-axis the regions bounded by
(a) the curve $y^2 = x^3$ and the lines $x = 1$, $x = 2$,
(b) the curve $y^2 = 2(5-x)$ and the line $x = -1$.

4. Find the volumes of the solids formed by rotating completely about the y-axis the areas enclosed by the y-axis and the following curves and straight lines
(a) $y = \sqrt{x}$, $y = 2$,   (b) $y = x-1$, $y = 0$, $y = 1$,
(c) $y = 1/x$, $y = 1$, $y = 2$,   (d) $y = x^3$, $y = 8$.

5. Find the volumes of the solids formed when the region bounded by the curve $y = x^2+3$ and the straight lines $y = 0$, $x = 0$ and $x = 2$ is rotated completely about (a) the x-axis, (b) the y-axis.

6. Find the volumes of the solids formed when the smaller region enclosed by the curve $y^2 = 4-x$, the y-axis and the line $y = 1$ is rotated completely about (a) the x-axis, (b) the y-axis.

7. By considering a solid of revolution generated by the triangle with vertices $(0,0)$, (r,h) and $(0,h)$, find the volume of a cone height h, base radius r.

8. Given that the equation of the circle with radius a and centre the origin is $x^2+y^2 = a^2$, find by integration the volume of a sphere of radius a.

9. Find the volume generated by rotating completely about the x-axis the finite region bounded by the curve $y^2 = 4x$ and the straight line $y = x$.

10. Find the volume generated by rotating completely about the x-axis the finite region bounded by the curve $y = x^3$, the x-axis and the line $x+3y = 4$.

6.5 Integration as the limit of a sum

In §6.2 the definite integral $\displaystyle\int_a^b f(x)\,dx$ was introduced as the area bounded by the curve $y = f(x)$, the x-axis and the lines $x = a$ and $x = b$. We arrive at a formal definition of the definite integral by considering the area to be the sum of strips called *elements* of area.

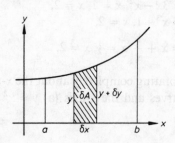

The diagram shows a typical element of area δA. The value of $\displaystyle\int_a^b f(x)\,dx$ is the sum of the areas of all such elements. Using the Greek capital letter 'sigma' Σ to mean 'the sum of', this may be written

$$\int_a^b f(x)\,dx = \sum_{x=a}^{x=b} \delta A.$$

For small values of δx the area δA is approximately equal to the area of a rectangle with height y and width δx. Similarly the total area $\Sigma \delta A$ is approximately equal to the sum of the areas of such rectangles $\Sigma y \delta x$. If the number of strips is increased so that $\delta x \rightarrow 0$, then the difference between the sums $\Sigma \delta A$ and $\Sigma y \delta x$ also approaches zero. Hence the area under the curve $y = f(x)$ is given by the limit as δx tends to zero of $\Sigma y \delta x$. Thus the intuitive approach to the definite integral through areas is consistent with the following formal definition:

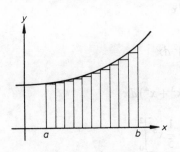

$$\int_a^b f(x)\,dx = \lim_{\delta x \to 0} \sum_{x=a}^{x=b} f(x)\,\delta x.$$

The fact that the definite integral, considered as the limit of a sum, can be found using a process which is the reverse of differentiation is called the *fundamental theorem of calculus*.

These results indicate that it is often possible to use integration to find a quantity expressed as a sum of elements of the form $f(x)\,\delta x$. For example, the formula for a volume of revolution derived in §6.5 may also be obtained by considering a typical element of volume $\delta V \approx \pi y^2\,\delta x$. The volume generated by rotating about the x-axis the area bounded by the curve $y = f(x)$, the x-axis and the lines $x = a$ and $x = b$, is then given by

$$\lim_{\delta x \to 0} \sum_{x=a}^{x=b} \pi y^2\,\delta x = \int_a^b \pi y^2\,dx.$$

Example 1   Find the volume generated by rotating completely about the line $y = 1$, the area bounded by the curve $y = 1 + 2x - x^2$ and the line $y = 1$.

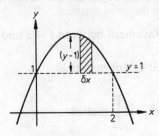

At the points of intersection of the curve $y = 1 + 2x - x^2$ and the line $y = 1$,

$$1 + 2x - x^2 = 1$$
$$2x - x^2 = 0$$
$$x(2 - x) = 0$$

$\therefore$ either $x = 0$ or $x = 2$.

A typical element of the required volume is a disc, radius $(y-1)$ and thickness δx

$\therefore$ element of volume $\approx \pi(y-1)^2\,\delta x$

Hence the required volume $= \lim_{\delta x \to 0} \Sigma \pi (y-1)^2 \, \delta x$

$$= \int_0^2 \pi (y-1)^2 \, dx$$

$$= \pi \int_0^2 (2x - x^2)^2 \, dx$$

$$= \pi \int_0^2 (4x^2 - 4x^3 + x^4) \, dx$$

$$= \pi \left[\frac{4}{3} x^3 - x^4 + \frac{1}{5} x^5 \right]_0^2$$

$$= \pi \left(\frac{4}{3} \cdot 2^3 - 2^4 + \frac{1}{5} \cdot 2^5 \right)$$

$$= \pi \left(\frac{32}{3} - 16 + \frac{32}{5} \right) = \frac{16\pi}{15}.$$

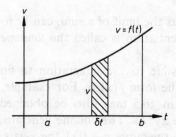

Consider now a particle moving along a straight line, so that its velocity at time t is given by $v = f(t)$. In a short interval of time δt, the displacement of the particle is approximately $v \, \delta t$. Hence the total displacement between $t = a$ and $t = b$ is given by $\lim_{\delta t \to 0} \sum_{t=a}^{t=b} v \, \delta t$.

Thus the total displacement of the particle in any given interval of time is represented by an area under the velocity-time graph and is found by evaluating a definite integral of the form $\int_a^b v \, dt$.

Example 2   A particle moves in a straight line so that after t seconds its velocity in $m \, s^{-1}$ is given by $v = 2t^3 + 3t + 5$. Find the distance moved in the third second of the motion.

Since the velocity of the particle is positive throughout the motion, the distance moved in the third second

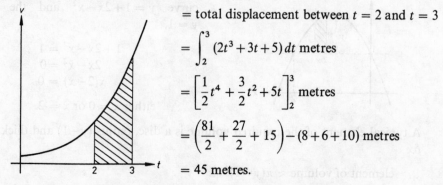

$= $ total displacement between $t = 2$ and $t = 3$

$$= \int_2^3 (2t^3 + 3t + 5) \, dt \text{ metres}$$

$$= \left[\frac{1}{2} t^4 + \frac{3}{2} t^2 + 5t \right]_2^3 \text{ metres}$$

$$= \left(\frac{81}{2} + \frac{27}{2} + 15 \right) - (8 + 6 + 10) \text{ metres}$$

$= 45$ metres.

[Note that if a particle moving along a straight line changes direction in the interval from $t = a$ to $t = b$ then the total distance travelled in that interval is *not* equal to the total displacement of the particle between $t = a$ and $t = b$.]

Exercise 6.5

1. Find the volume of the solid formed by rotating completely about the line $y = 1$ the area bounded by the curve $y = x^2 + 2$, the y-axis and the lines $x = 1$ and $y = 1$.

2. Find the volume generated by rotating completely about the line $y = 3$, the area enclosed by the curve $y = 4x - x^2$ and the line $y = 3$.

3. A particle moves in a straight line so that after t seconds its velocity is v ms^{-1}. In each of the following cases sketch the velocity-time graph for the motion and find the total distance moved in the given interval of time.
(a) $v = 10 + 2t$, $t = 0$ to $t = 2$,   (b) $v = 16t - 3t^2$, the 3rd second,
(c) $v = \frac{1}{2}t^2 + 5$, $t = 1$ to $t = 3$,   (d) $v = 18t^2 - 4t^3$, the 4th second,
(e) $v = 5 + 4t - t^2$, $t = 1$ to $t = 6$,   (f) $v = 4t^3 - 16t$, $t = 0$ to $t = 3$.

4. Find the volume of the solid formed by rotating completely about the line $y = 2$ the region enclosed by the curve $y = x(2 - x)$ and the x-axis.

5. Find the volume of the solid formed by rotating through 2 right angles about the line $x = 2$ the area bounded by the curve $y = x^2 - 4x + 5$ and the line $y = 5$.

6. Use integration to find a formula for the volume of a pyramid of height h cm with a square base of side a cm.

7. The horizontal cross-section of a bowl at a height h cm above its base is a regular hexagon of side x cm. Given that $x^2 = 16(h + 1)$, find the volume of liquid in the bowl when it is filled to a depth of 8 cm.

8. By considering the area under the curve $y = \sqrt{x}$ between $x = 0$ and $x = 81$ as a sum of strips of width 1 unit, show that

(a) $\displaystyle\int_0^{81} \sqrt{x}\,dx < \sqrt{1} + \sqrt{2} + \sqrt{3} + \ldots + \sqrt{81}$,

(b) $\sqrt{1} + \sqrt{2} + \sqrt{3} + \ldots + \sqrt{80} < \displaystyle\int_0^{81} \sqrt{x}\,dx$.

Deduce that $477 < \sqrt{1} + \sqrt{2} + \sqrt{3} + \ldots + \sqrt{80} < 486$.

9. By considering the area under the curve $y = 1/x^2$ between $x = 1$ and $x = 100$, show that

$$\frac{1}{1^2} + \frac{1}{2^2} + \frac{1}{3^2} + \ldots + \frac{1}{100^2} < 2.$$

6.6 Mean value

The mean value of a function $f(x)$ between $x = a$ and $x = b$ is a type of average of the values of the function in that interval. For example, the mean value of a function $f(t)$ which represents the velocity of a moving object after time t is the same as the average velocity.

Example 1   An object is fired vertically upwards so that after time t its velocity is given by $v = 40 - 10t$. Find the average velocity between $t = 1$ and $t = 3$.

The total displacement between $t = 1$ and $t = 3$

$$= \int_1^3 (40 - 10t)\,dt = \left[40t - 5t^2 \right]_1^3 = 75 - 35 = 40$$

∴   the average velocity between $t = 1$ and $t = 3$

$$= \frac{40}{3-1} = \frac{40}{2} = 20.$$

Similarly, the average or mean velocity of an object moving in a straight line, between $t = a$ and $t = b$, is found by evaluating $\dfrac{1}{(b-a)} \displaystyle\int_a^b v\,dt$. The general definition of mean value is framed along these lines.

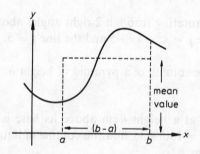

The *mean value* of a function $f(x)$ between $x = a$ and $x = b$ is

$$\frac{1}{(b-a)} \int_a^b f(x)\,dx.$$

Geometrically, this is the height of the rectangle, with base $(b-a)$, whose area is equal to the area under the curve from $x = a$ to $x = b$.

Example 2   The volume, $V\,\text{cm}^3$, of water in a hemispherical bowl is given by $V = \frac{1}{3}\pi(30h^2 - h^3)$ where $h\,\text{cm}$ is the depth of the water. Find the mean volume of water in the bowl as the depth increases from 0 to 4 cm.

$$\text{Mean volume (in cm}^3) = \frac{1}{4-0} \int_0^4 V\,dh = \frac{1}{4} \int_0^4 \frac{1}{3}\pi(30h^2 - h^3)\,dh$$

$$= \frac{1}{12}\pi \left[10h^3 - \frac{1}{4}h^4 \right]_0^4$$

$$= \frac{1}{12}\pi \left(10.4^3 - \frac{1}{4}.4^4 \right)$$

$$= \frac{1}{12}\pi.9.4^3 = 48\pi.$$

Exercise 6.6

1. A particle is moving in a straight line such that after t seconds its velocity is $v\,\mathrm{m\,s}^{-1}$, where $v = 6t + 12t^2$. Find
(a) the mean velocity during the first 2 seconds of the motion,
(b) the mean acceleration between $t = 1$ and $t = 5$.

2. Repeat question 1 for $v = 2t + \dfrac{5}{t^2}$.

3. Find the mean values of the following functions in the given intervals.
(a) $2x^3 - x + 1$, $-1 \leqslant x \leqslant 1$,
(b) $(x+3)(2x-5)$, $1 \leqslant x \leqslant 5$,
(c) $1 - \dfrac{1}{x^2}$, $0.1 \leqslant x \leqslant 1$,
(d) $(5x-3)\sqrt{x}$, $1 \leqslant x \leqslant 4$.

4. The volume, $V\,\mathrm{cm}^3$, of water in a conical vessel is given by $V = \pi h^3/12$, where $h\,\mathrm{cm}$ is the depth of the water. Find the mean volume of water in the bowl as the depth increases from $2\,\mathrm{cm}$ to $8\,\mathrm{cm}$.

5. A mass of gas of volume v at pressure p expands according to the law $pv^{3/4} = 30$. Find the mean pressure as the gas expands from $v = 1$ to $v = 16$.

6. Given that $x = 4t - 1$, find the mean values in the interval from $t = 1$ to $t = 4$ of (a) x^2, (b) $1/(x+1)^2$, (c) $(x+1)^{3/2}$.

Exercise 6.7   (miscellaneous)
[Answers may be left in terms of π, where appropriate.]

1. Sketch the families of curves with the following gradient functions
(a) $\dfrac{dy}{dx} = 2(1 - x)$,
(b) $\dfrac{dy}{dx} = \dfrac{1}{2\sqrt{x}}$,
(c) $\dfrac{dy}{dx} = 1 + \dfrac{1}{x^3}$.

2. Integrate with respect to x
(a) $4x^5 - x^3$,
(b) $4 - \dfrac{3}{x^2}$,
(c) $\dfrac{x^4 + 1}{x^3}$.

3. Find the following indefinite integrals
(a) $\displaystyle\int (2 - 3t)^2\, dt$,
(b) $\displaystyle\int \left(5x^4 - \dfrac{1}{5x^4}\right) dx$,
(c) $\displaystyle\int \dfrac{1}{\sqrt[3]{u}}\, du$.

4. Given that $\dfrac{dv}{dt} = (t+1)(3t-7)$ and that $v = 36$ when $t = 5$, show that $v = (t+1)^2(t-4)$.

5. The gradient of a curve is given by $\dfrac{dy}{dx} = ax + \dfrac{b}{x^2}$. If the curve passes through

the point $(-1, -4)$ and has a turning point at the point $(1, 0)$, find its equation and sketch the curve.

6. Evaluate   (a) $\int_1^2 \dfrac{(x+1)(x-2)}{x^4} dx$,   (b) $\int_1^4 \left(\sqrt{x} - \dfrac{1}{x} \right)^2 dx$.

7. Find the area enclosed by the curve $y = x - \dfrac{1}{x^2}$, the x-axis and the line $x = 2$.

8. Find the area enclosed by the curve $y = 2x^2 + 1$ and the line $y = 3$.

9. Find the total area of the regions enclosed by the curve $y = x^4 - x^3$, the x-axis and the line $x = 2$.

10. Find the area enclosed by the curve $y^2 - 2y = x$ and the y-axis.

11. Find the equation of the tangent at the point $(1, 0)$ to the curve $y = (x-1)(x^2+1)$. Find the area of the finite region enclosed by the curve and this tangent.

12. Sketch the region in the x-y plane within which the inequalities $y > (x-2)^2$ and $y < x$ are satisfied. Determine the area of this region.

13. Sketch the curves $y = x^2(4x - 5)$ and $y = x(3x - 4)$ on the same diagram, then find the area of the finite region enclosed between them.

14. When the area bounded by the curve $y = 15x(k - x)$ and the x-axis is rotated completely about the x-axis the volume of the solid generated is 240π. Find the value of k.

15. The region R is bounded by the curve $y = 4/x$, the x- and y-axes and the lines $x = 2$, $y = 4$. Find the volume of the solid formed when R is rotated completely about (a) the x-axis, (b) the y-axis.

16. The region R is bounded by the curve $4y = x^2$ and the lines $x = 4$, $y = 1$. Find the volume of the solid formed when R is rotated completely about (a) the x-axis, (b) the y-axis, (c) the line $y = 1$, (d) the line $x = 4$.

17. The region R is bounded by the curve $y^2 = 2x$ and the line $y = x$. Find the volume of the solid formed when R is rotated completely about (a) the x-axis, (b) the y-axis.

18. The curves $cy^2 = x^3$ and $y^2 = ax$ (where $a > 0$ and $c > 0$) intersect at the origin O and at a point P in the first quadrant. The areas of the regions enclosed by the arcs OP, the x-axis and the ordinate through P are A_1 and A_2 for the two curves; the volumes of the two solids formed by rotating these regions through four right angles about the x-axis are V_1 and V_2 respectively. Prove that $A_1/A_2 = 3/5$ and $V_1/V_2 = 1/2$.

19. Find dy/dx given that $y^2 = x(3-x)^2$. State the values of x for which dy/dx is (a) zero, (b) infinite. Sketch the curve $y^2 = x(3-x)^2$ and find the volume of the solid formed when the area enclosed by the loop of the curve is rotated through 180° about the x-axis.

20. Evaluate $\displaystyle\int_{-2}^{4} [x]\,dx$, where $[x]$ is defined as the greatest integer less than or equal to x. (See §5.1.)

21. Evaluate $\displaystyle\int_{-4}^{2} |x|\,dx$, where $|x|$ is defined as the magnitude of x. (See §1.4.)

22. A particle moves in a straight line such that after t seconds its velocity is $v\,\mathrm{m\,s^{-1}}$, where $v = 4 - 4t - 15t^2$. Find the *total* distance moved by the particle in (a) the first two seconds, (b) the third second of its motion.

23. Show that over the range $0 \leqslant x \leqslant 6$, the mean value of the function $9x(6-x)$ is two-thirds of the maximum value of the function.   (AEB 1975)

24. Find the mean area of vertical cross-sections of a sphere of radius a.

7 Elementary trigonometry

7.1 Trigonometric ratios for any angle

Elementary trigonometry is based on the fact that in any set of similar right-angled triangles the ratios of corresponding pairs of sides remain constant. Using the right-angled triangle in the diagram, the sine and cosine of angle θ are defined as follows:

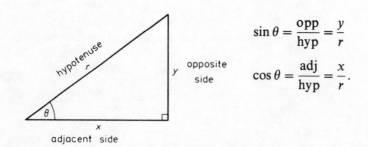

$$\sin \theta = \frac{\text{opp}}{\text{hyp}} = \frac{y}{r}$$

$$\cos \theta = \frac{\text{adj}}{\text{hyp}} = \frac{x}{r}.$$

In more advanced work it is useful to extend these definitions so that they can be applied to angles of any magnitude.

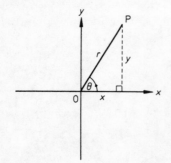

Consider a point P with coordinates (x, y). Let $OP = r$ and let θ be the angle OP makes with the positive direction of the x-axis. Positive angles are measured anti-clockwise from the x-axis and negative angles clockwise.

Sine and cosine may now be defined for any real value of θ by writing:

$$\sin \theta = \frac{y}{r} \qquad \cos \theta = \frac{x}{r}$$

The graphs of $\sin \theta$ and $\cos \theta$ may be plotted directly as shown below. Various points P on a circle of radius 1 unit are used, so that $\sin \theta = y$ and $\cos \theta = x$.

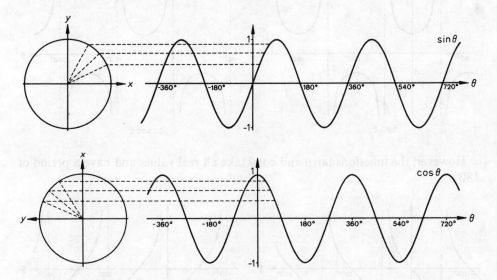

After OP has been rotated through $360°$, $\sin \theta$ and $\cos \theta$ pass through the sets of values they have already taken. For this reason $\sin \theta$ and $\cos \theta$ are described as *periodic functions* with *period* $360°$.

Example 1 Using a sketch graph if necessary, write down all the angles between $-360°$ and $720°$ with the same cosine as $70°$.

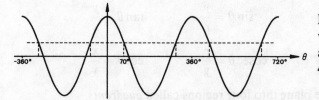

From the sketch the angles with the same cosine as $70°$ are: $-290°$, $-70°$, $70°$, $290°$, $430°$ and $650°$.

The sine and cosine of an angle can be used to define the remaining trigonometric ratios, tangent, cotangent, secant, cosecant.

$$\tan \theta = \frac{\sin \theta}{\cos \theta} \qquad \cot \theta = \frac{\cos \theta}{\sin \theta}$$

$$\sec \theta = \frac{1}{\cos \theta} \qquad \operatorname{cosec} \theta = \frac{1}{\sin \theta}.$$

Because of their relationship with $\cos \theta$ and $\sin \theta$, $\sec \theta$ and $\csc \theta$ must also be periodic functions with period 360°. Since the range of both $\cos \theta$ and $\sin \theta$ is the set of real numbers from -1 to $+1$, neither $\sec \theta$ nor $\csc \theta$ can take values between -1 and $+1$.

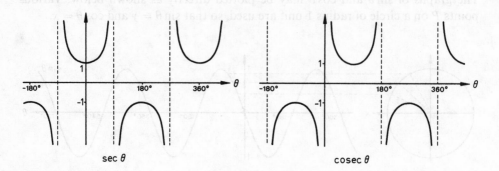

sec θ cosec θ

However, the functions $\tan \theta$ and $\cot \theta$ take all real values and have a period of 180°.

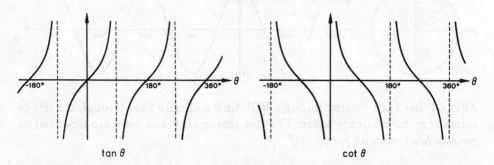

tan θ cot θ

In terms of the coordinates (x, y) of the point P considered earlier, the six trigonometric ratios may now be defined as follows:

$$\cos \theta = \frac{x}{r} \qquad \sin \theta = \frac{y}{r} \qquad \tan \theta = \frac{y}{x}$$

$$\sec \theta = \frac{r}{x} \qquad \csc \theta = \frac{r}{y} \qquad \cot \theta = \frac{x}{y}$$

The x- and y-axes divide the plane into four regions called *quadrants*.

Second quadrant	First quadrant	x −ve y +ve	x +ve y +ve
Third quadrant	Fourth quadrant	x −ve y −ve	x +ve y −ve

When P lies in the first quadrant, θ is acute and all the trigonometric ratios are positive. By examining the signs of x and y in the other quadrants, the signs of $\sin \theta$, $\cos \theta$ and $\tan \theta$ for any value of θ can be determined.

sin θ +ve	sin θ +ve	SIN	ALL
cos θ −ve	cos θ +ve	+ve	+ve
tan θ −ve	tan θ +ve		
sin θ −ve	sin θ −ve	TAN	COS
cos θ −ve	cos θ +ve	+ve	+ve
tan θ +ve	tan θ −ve		

The above diagrams show which ratios are positive in each quadrant. There are many mnemonics for the initial letters of All, Sin, Tan, Cos, e.g. All Stations To Crewe, All Steam Tugs Chug.

The trigonometric ratios for any angle θ are numerically equal to the corresponding ratios for the acute angle between OP and the x-axis. The quadrant in which OP lies determines the sign of the ratio, positive or negative.

Example 2   Express the following in terms of ratios of acute angles:
(a) sin 215°,   (b) cos (−70°),   (c) tan 95°.

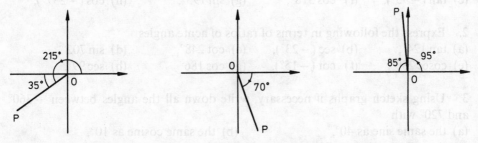

(a) [We note mentally that the acute angle between OP and the x-axis is 35° and that OP lies in the 3rd quadrant.] From the sketch, sin 215° = −sin 35°.
(b) cos (−70°) = cos 70°,   (c) tan 95° = −tan 85°.
[These results can also be obtained using sketch graphs of sin θ, cos θ and tan θ.]

In general calculators, slide rules or mathematical tables are used to write down values of trigonometric ratios. However, in some cases such aids are not needed.

$$\sin 0° = 0 \qquad \cos 0° = 1 \qquad \tan 0° = 0$$
$$\sin 90° = 1 \qquad \cos 90° = 0 \qquad \tan 90° \text{ is undefined.}$$

[Considering values of θ close to 90° we find that as θ → 90° from below, tan θ → ∞ and as θ → 90° from above, tan θ → −∞.]

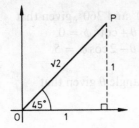

Let P be the point (1, 1), so that $OP = \sqrt{2}$ and θ = 45°.

Hence $\sin 45° = \cos 45° = \dfrac{1}{\sqrt{2}}$

and $\tan 45° = 1$.

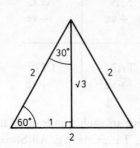

Using an equilateral triangle with sides each 2 units in length and height $\sqrt{3}$ units, we have

$$\sin 30° = \frac{1}{2} \qquad \sin 60° = \frac{\sqrt{3}}{2}$$

$$\cos 30° = \frac{\sqrt{3}}{2} \qquad \cos 60° = \frac{1}{2}$$

$$\tan 30° = \frac{1}{\sqrt{3}} \qquad \tan 60° = \sqrt{3}.$$

Exercise 7.1

1. Express the following in terms of ratios of acute angles
(a) $\cos 165°$,   (b) $\sin(-35°)$,   (c) $\tan 310°$,   (d) $\sin 112°$,
(e) $\tan(-95°)$,   (f) $\cos 318°$,   (g) $\sin 195°$,   (h) $\cos(-237°)$.

2. Express the following in terms of ratios of acute angles
(a) $\tan 124°$,   (b) $\sec(-23°)$,   (c) $\cot 248°$,   (d) $\sin 702°$,
(e) $\operatorname{cosec} 280°$,   (f) $\cot(-15°)$,   (g) $\cos 186°$ (h) $\sec 99°$.

3. Using sketch graphs if necessary, write down all the angles between $-360°$ and $720°$ with
(a) the same sine as $40°$,   (b) the same cosine as $10°$,
(c) the same tangent as $75°$,   (d) the same secant as $180°$.

4. Find all the values of θ between $0°$ and $360°$ such that
(a) $\cos\theta = \cos 25°$,   (b) $\sin\theta = \sin 50°$,
(c) $\tan\theta = \tan 42{\cdot}3°$,   (d) $\sin\theta = -\sin 63{\cdot}4°$.

5. Find, without using tables or a calculator, the values of the following
(a) $\sin 120°$,   (b) $\cot 30°$,   (c) $\cos(-210°)$,   (d) $\tan(-45°)$,
(e) $\cos 135°$,   (f) $\sin(-300°)$,   (g) $\operatorname{cosec} 210°$,   (h) $\sec 750°$.

6. Find, without using tables or a calculator, the values of the following
(a) $\cos 270°$,   (b) $\tan 120°$,   (c) $\sin(-180°)$,   (d) $\sec 240°$,
(e) $\cot 450°$,   (f) $\cos 540°$,   (g) $\operatorname{cosec} 225°$,   (h) $\sin(-90°)$.

7. Find the possible values of θ and ϕ between $0°$ and $360°$, given that
(a) $\cos^2\theta + \sin^2\phi = 0$,   (b) $\tan^2\theta + \cot^2\phi = 0$,
(c) $2\sin\theta + \cos\phi = 3$,   (d) $3\sin\theta - 2\cos\phi = 5$.

8. Find the range of possible values of an acute angle θ given that
(a) $\tan 2\theta > 0$,   (b) $\cos 3\theta < 0$,
(c) $\sin 5\theta < 0$,   (d) $\cot 6\theta > 0$.

9. In each of the following cases sketch the given pair of curves on the same diagram

(a) $y = 2\sin\theta$, $y = \sin 2\theta$, (b) $y = \frac{1}{2}\cos\theta$, $y = \cos\frac{1}{2}\theta$,

(c) $y = -\sin\theta$, $y = \sin(-\theta)$, (d) $y = -\cos\theta$, $y = \cos(-\theta)$.

7.2 The inverse functions and simple equations

In the previous section the trigonometric ratios were defined for any given angle. We now consider the reverse process of determining an angle given the value of one of the trigonometric ratios. One approach to this problem is through sketch graphs.

Example 1 Find all the values of θ between $-180°$ and $+180°$ such that $\tan\theta = 1$.

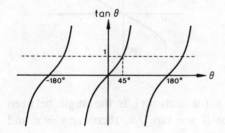

$\tan\theta = 1 = \tan 45°$

∴ from the sketch

$\theta = -135°$ or $45°$.

[Note that if there is no restriction on the value of θ, the equation $\tan\theta = 1$ has an infinite solution set

$$\{\ldots, -315°, -135°, 45°, 225°, 405°, \ldots\}.]$$

An alternative approach is to use the notion of the rotating line segment OP discussed in §7.1.

Example 2 Find all the values of θ between $0°$ and $360°$ such that $\sin\theta = -\frac{1}{2}$.

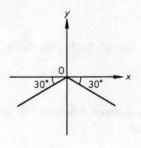

We note mentally that if $\sin\theta$ is $-$ve then OP is in the 3rd or 4th quadrant. If $\sin 30° = \frac{1}{2}$ then the acute angle between OP and the x-axis is $30°$. The sketch shows the two possible positions of OP.

$\sin\theta = -\frac{1}{2} = -\sin 30°$

∴ $\theta = 210°$ or $330°$.

[More generally, by considering further rotations of OP, the solution set of the equation $\sin\theta = -\frac{1}{2}$ is found to be

$$\{\ldots, -150°, -30°, 210°, 330°, 570°, \ldots\}.]$$

As illustrated in the above example, if $\sin a = b$ then for any given value of b there are many possible values of a. Thus, in the language of §4.2, the function $f : \theta \rightarrow \sin \theta$ has no true inverse. However, if the domain of the sine function is restricted so that $-90° \leqslant \theta \leqslant 90°$, then an inverse function can be defined. The *inverse sine* of x, written $\sin^{-1} x$ (or arcsin x), is the angle between $-90°$ and $90°$ whose sine is x. Hence if $y = \sin^{-1} x$, then $\sin y = x$ and $-90° \leqslant y \leqslant 90°$. These values, $-90°$ to $+90°$, are sometimes called the *principal values* of the inverse sine. [To avoid confusion between $\sin^{-1} x$ and $(\sin x)^{-1}$, i.e. $1/\sin x$, the symbol $\sin^{-1}$ may be read as 'inverse sine', 'sine inverse' or 'sine minus one', but *not* 'sine to the minus one'.] Similarly, the *inverse cosine* of x, written $\cos^{-1} x$ (or arccos x), is the angle between $0°$ and $180°$ whose cosine is x. Hence if $y = \cos^{-1} x$, then $\cos y = x$ and $0° \leqslant y \leqslant 180°$.

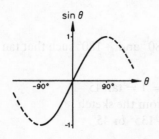
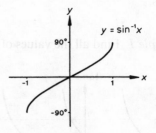

The *inverse tangent* of x, written $\tan^{-1} x$ (or arctan x), is the angle between $-90°$ and $90°$ whose tangent is x. Hence if $y = \tan^{-1} x$, then $\tan y = x$ and $-90° < y < 90°$.

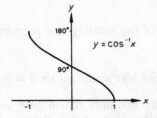
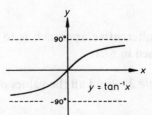

In the following example we demonstrate the use of both calculator inverse functions and mathematical tables.

Example 3 Solve the equation $\cos \theta = -0.4$ for values of θ between $0°$ and $360°$, giving your answers to the nearest tenth of a degree.

Method A (using calculator inverse cosine function)

We must first find the angle between $0°$ and $180°$ whose cosine is -0.4.
 As a first answer we write down the angle to three decimal places.

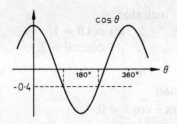

Thus $\cos\theta = -0\cdot4 = \cos 113\cdot578°$
$= 113\cdot6°$ (to nrst $0\cdot1°$)
$\therefore\quad \theta = 113\cdot6°$ or $360° - 113\cdot6°$
i.e. $\quad\theta = 113\cdot6°$ or $246\cdot4°$

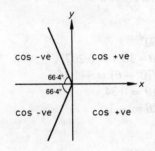

Method B (using table of cosines)
$\cos\theta = -0\cdot4 = -\cos 66\cdot422°$
$= -\cos 66\cdot4°$ (nrst $0\cdot1°$)
$\therefore\quad \theta = 180° - 66\cdot4°$ or
$180° + 66\cdot4°$
i.e. $\quad\theta = 113\cdot6°$ or $246\cdot4°$

Example 4 Find the values of θ between $0°$ and $360°$ such that $\tan 2\theta = -2$, giving your answer to the nearest tenth of a degree. [Note that since we require values of θ between $0°$ and $360°$, we must look for values of 2θ between $0°$ and $720°$.]

$\tan 2\theta = -2 = -\tan 63\cdot435°$
$\therefore\quad$ between $0°$ and $720°$, $2\theta = 116\cdot565°$, $296\cdot565°$, $476\cdot565°$ or $656\cdot565°$.
Hence, between $0°$ and $360°$, $\theta = 58\cdot3°$, $148\cdot3°$, $238\cdot3°$ or $328\cdot3°$.

The last example concerns a quadratic equation in $\cos\theta$. Since brackets would be rather cumbersome $(\cos\theta)^2$ is usually written $\cos^2\theta$.

Example 5 Solve the equation $2\cos^2\theta - 5\cos\theta + 2 = 0$ for values of θ from $0°$ to $360°$.

$2\cos^2\theta - 5\cos\theta + 2 = 0 \Leftrightarrow (2\cos\theta - 1)(\cos\theta - 2) = 0$
$\Leftrightarrow \cos\theta = \frac{1}{2}$ or $\cos\theta = 2$

Since there is no value of θ for which $\cos\theta = 2$, we must have $\cos\theta = \frac{1}{2} = \cos 60°$. Hence $\theta = 60°$ or $300°$.

Exercise 7.2

Give answers to the nearest tenth of a degree.

1. Find all the values of θ between $0°$ and $360°$ such that
(a) $\sin\theta = 0\cdot3$,
(b) $\tan\theta = 1\cdot5$,
(c) $\cos\theta = -0\cdot73$,
(d) $\sin\theta = -0\cdot62$.

2. Find all the values of θ between $-180°$ and $+180°$ such that
(a) $\cos\theta = 0\cdot6$,
(b) $\sin\theta = 0\cdot8$,
(c) $\tan\theta = -0\cdot62$,
(d) $\cos\theta = -0\cdot342$.

3. Find all the values of θ between $0°$ and $360°$ such that
    (a) $\sin \theta = 1/\sqrt{2}$,   (b) $\tan \theta = -1/\sqrt{3}$,   (c) $\cot \theta = 1$,
    (d) $\cos \theta = -\frac{1}{2}$,   (e) $\sec \theta = -1$,   (f) $\operatorname{cosec} \theta = 2$.

4. Solve the following equations for $0° \leqslant x \leqslant 360°$
    (a) $4 \sin x = 3 \cos x$,   (b) $\sin x + \cos x = 0$,
    (c) $4 \tan x = 3 \sec x$,   (d) $2 \tan x \operatorname{cosec} x = 3$.

5. Solve the following equations for $0° \leqslant \theta \leqslant 360°$
    (a) $\cos (\theta + 10°) = -0{\cdot}44$,   (b) $\sin (\theta - 30°) = 0{\cdot}207$,
    (c) $\sin (\theta + 50°) = 0{\cdot}541$,   (d) $\tan (70° - \theta) = -1{\cdot}16$,
    (e) $\tan 2\theta = 0{\cdot}7$,   (f) $\cos \frac{1}{3}\theta = 0{\cdot}34$,
    (g) $\sin \frac{1}{2}\theta = 0{\cdot}83$,   (h) $\sec 2\theta = -1$.

6. Solve the following equations for $-90° \leqslant x \leqslant 90°$
    (a) $\sin 3x = 1/\sqrt{2}$,   (b) $\tan 4x = 0$,
    (c) $\cot 5x + 1 = 0$,   (d) $2 \cos 3x + 1 = 0$.

7. Solve the following equations for $0° \leqslant x \leqslant 360°$
    (a) $4 \sin^2 x = 3$,   (b) $2 \cos^2 x = \cos x$,
    (c) $5 \sin x \cos x = \sin x$,   (d) $\sin^2 x - \sin x - 2 = 0$,
    (e) $2 \tan^2 x = \sec x \tan x$,   (f) $3 \cos^2 x = 2 \sin x \cos x$.

8. By rearranging as quadratic equations, solve the following for $-180° \leqslant \theta \leqslant 180°$
    (a) $2 \tan \theta - \cot \theta = 1$,   (b) $2 \operatorname{cosec} \theta + 7 = 4 \sin \theta$,
    (c) $2 \cos \theta + \sec \theta = 3$,   (d) $2 \sin \theta \tan \theta = 3 \sin \theta + 5 \cos \theta$.

9. Solve the given pairs of simultaneous equations, where x and y can take any values from $-180°$ to $+180°$ inclusive.
    (a) $x + y = 180°$ (b) $x - y = 120°$
         $\tan (x - y) = \sqrt{3}$ $\sin (x + y) = 0{\cdot}5$.

10. Draw flow charts for procedures to solve the equations (i) $a \sin x = b$, (ii) $a \cos x = b$, (iii) $a \sin x = b \cos x$, using a pocket calculator. Print out all possible values of x from $0°$ to $360°$ inclusive or an appropriate message if the equation has no solution. Check that your procedures deal with $a = 0$, $b = 0$ and $a = b$.

7.3 **Properties of trigonometric ratios**

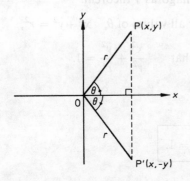

It follows from the definitions of $\sin\theta$, $\cos\theta$ and $\tan\theta$ that

$$\sin(-\theta) = -\sin\theta, \ \cos(-\theta) = \cos\theta,$$
$$\tan(-\theta) = -\tan\theta.$$

These results can also be obtained by considering the graphs of $\sin(-\theta)$, $\cos(-\theta)$ and $\tan(-\theta)$, which are the reflections in the y-axis of the graphs of $\sin\theta$, $\cos\theta$ and $\tan\theta$.

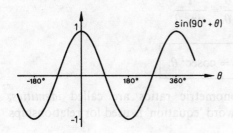

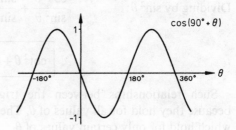

The diagrams above show that

$$\sin(90° + \theta) = \cos\theta \qquad\qquad \cos(90° + \theta) = -\sin\theta$$

By a similar process it is found that

$$\sin(180° + \theta) = -\sin\theta \qquad\qquad \cos(180° + \theta) = -\cos\theta$$

Substituting $-\theta$ for θ in these results

$$\sin(90° - \theta) = \cos(-\theta) \qquad\qquad \cos(90° - \theta) = -\sin(-\theta)$$
$$\therefore \quad \sin(90° - \theta) = \cos\theta \qquad\qquad \therefore \quad \cos(90° - \theta) = \sin\theta$$

Similarly $\sin(180° - \theta) = \sin\theta$, $\cos(180° - \theta) = -\cos\theta$.

[The graphs of $\sin(90° - \theta)$, $\cos(90° - \theta)$, $\sin(180° - \theta)$ and $\cos(180° - \theta)$ may be obtained by reflection then translation of the graphs of $\sin\theta$ and $\cos\theta$.]

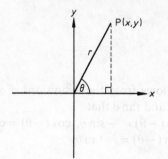

Three basic properties of the trigonometric ratios are derived from Pythagoras'† theorem.

For all values of θ, $x^2 + y^2 = r^2$,

so that $\dfrac{x^2}{r^2} + \dfrac{y^2}{r^2} = 1$.

Thus

$$\boxed{\cos^2\theta + \sin^2\theta = 1.}$$

Dividing by $\cos^2\theta$: $\dfrac{\cos^2\theta}{\cos^2\theta} + \dfrac{\sin^2\theta}{\cos^2\theta} = \dfrac{1}{\cos^2\theta}$

$$\therefore\quad \boxed{1 + \tan^2\theta = \sec^2\theta.}$$

Dividing by $\sin^2\theta$: $\dfrac{\cos^2\theta}{\sin^2\theta} + \dfrac{\sin^2\theta}{\sin^2\theta} = \dfrac{1}{\sin^2\theta}$

$$\therefore\quad \boxed{\cot^2\theta + 1 = \operatorname{cosec}^2\theta.}$$

Such relationships between the trigonometric ratios are called *identities*, because they hold for all values of θ. The word 'equation' is used for relationships which hold for only certain values of θ.

Example 1   If $\sin\theta = 5/13$, where θ is an obtuse angle, find $\cos\theta$ and $\tan\theta$.

$$\cos^2\theta = 1 - \sin^2\theta = 1 - \left(\frac{5}{13}\right)^2 = 1 - \frac{25}{169} = \frac{144}{169}$$

Since θ is obtuse, $\cos\theta = -12/13$

and $\tan\theta = \dfrac{\sin\theta}{\cos\theta} = \dfrac{5}{13}\Big/\left(-\dfrac{12}{13}\right) = -5/12.$

Alternative method

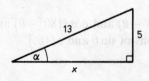

The diagram shows a right-angled triangle constructed so that $\sin\alpha = 5/13$.
By Pythagoras' theorem, $x = 12$.
Hence $\cos\alpha = 12/13$, $\tan\alpha = 5/12.$

† *Pythagoras* (6th cent. B.C.) Greek philosopher. He founded a religious brotherhood which devoted much of its attention to geometry and the theory of numbers. It is believed that Pythagoras or his early followers discovered the theorem that bears his name.

Since θ is an obtuse angle such that $\theta = 5/13$, $\cos\theta = -12/13$ and $\tan\theta = -5/12$.

Example 2 Simplify $\dfrac{\sin^2\theta}{1-\cos\theta}$.

$$\frac{\sin^2\theta}{1-\cos\theta} = \frac{1-\cos^2\theta}{1-\cos\theta} = \frac{(1-\cos\theta)(1+\cos\theta)}{1-\cos\theta} = 1+\cos\theta.$$

Example 3 Eliminate θ from the equations

$$x = 1+2\cos\theta, \; y = 3\sin\theta.$$

Rearranging $\qquad\dfrac{x-1}{2} = \cos\theta, \dfrac{y}{3} = \sin\theta$

Since $\cos^2\theta + \sin^2\theta = 1$, $\qquad\dfrac{(x-1)^2}{4} + \dfrac{y^2}{9} = 1.$

Example 4 Solve the equation $\sec^2\theta + \tan\theta - 1 = 0$ for $0° \leqslant \theta \leqslant 360°$.

Substituting $\sec^2\theta = 1+\tan^2\theta$,

$$\sec^2\theta + \tan\theta - 1 = 0 \Leftrightarrow (1+\tan^2\theta) + \tan\theta - 1 = 0$$
$$\Leftrightarrow \qquad \tan^2\theta + \tan\theta = 0$$
$$\Leftrightarrow \qquad \tan\theta(\tan\theta + 1) = 0$$

$\therefore$ either $\tan\theta = 0$ $\qquad\qquad$ or $\quad\tan\theta = -1$
$\qquad\quad \theta = 0°, 180°, 360°$ $\qquad\qquad \theta = 135°, 315°.$
Hence the required solutions are $0°, 135°, 180°, 315°$ and $360°$.

Exercise 7.3

1. Sketch the graphs of the following functions and use them to verify the results given in the text
(a) $\sin(-\theta)$, $\cos(-\theta)$,   (b) $\sin(180° + \theta)$, $\cos(180° + \theta)$,
(c) $\sin(90° - \theta)$, $\cos(90° - \theta)$,   (d) $\sin(180° - \theta)$, $\cos(180° - \theta)$.

2. By drawing sketch graphs, or otherwise, express the following in terms of $\sin\theta$ or $\cos\theta$
(a) $\sin(360° + \theta)$,   (b) $\cos(360° - \theta)$,   (c) $\cos(270° + \theta)$,
(d) $\sin(\theta - 90°)$,   (e) $\cos(\theta - 180°)$,   (f) $\sin(270° - \theta)$.

3. By drawing sketch graphs, or otherwise, express the following in terms of $\tan\theta$ or $\cot\theta$
(a) $\tan(90° + \theta)$,   (b) $\tan(180° + \theta)$,   (c) $\tan(90° - \theta)$,
(d) $\tan(180° - \theta)$,   (e) $\tan(\theta - 360°)$,   (f) $\tan(\theta - 90°)$.

In questions 4 to 7 do not use tables or calculators.

4.   If $\cos\theta = 4/5$ and θ is an acute angle, find $\sin\theta$, $\tan\theta$ and $\sec\theta$.

5.   If $\tan\theta = -8/15$ and θ is obtuse, find $\sin\theta$, $\sec\theta$ and $\cot\theta$.

6.   If $\cot x = 7/24$ and $90° < x < 360°$, find $\sin x$, $\cos x$ and $\operatorname{cosec} x$.

7.   If $\sin x = 12/13$ and $0° < x < 90°$, find $\cos x$, $\cos(x+90°)$ and $\tan(x+180°)$.

8.   Simplify the following expressions, where $0° < \theta < 90°$:

(a) $\dfrac{\sqrt{(1-\cos^2\theta)}}{\tan\theta}$,   (b) $\dfrac{\sin\theta}{\sqrt{(1-\sin^2\theta)}}$,   (c) $\dfrac{\tan\theta}{\sqrt{(1+\tan^2\theta)}}$.

9.   Simplify the following expressions
(a) $\sec^2\theta - \tan^2\theta$,   (b) $(\sin^2\theta - 2)^2 - 4\cos^2\theta$,

(c) $\dfrac{\cos^4\theta - \sin^4\theta}{\cos\theta - \sin\theta}$,   (d) $\dfrac{\sin\theta}{\operatorname{cosec}\theta - \cot\theta}$.

10. Prove the following identities
(a) $\sec\theta - \cos\theta = \sin\theta\tan\theta$,   (b) $\sec^2\theta + \operatorname{cosec}^2\theta = \sec^2\theta\operatorname{cosec}^2\theta$,

(c) $\dfrac{1-\sin\theta}{1+\sin\theta} = (\sec\theta - \tan\theta)^2$,   (d) $\dfrac{\cot^2\theta - 1}{\cot^2\theta + 1} = 1 - 2\sin^2\theta$.

11. Eliminate θ from the following pairs of equations
(a) $x = \cos\theta$, $y = \sin\theta$,   (b) $x = 1 - 2\sin\theta$, $y = 1 + 3\cos\theta$,
(c) $x = \sec\theta$, $y = \tan\theta$,   (d) $x = \sin\theta + \cos\theta$, $y = \sin\theta - \cos\theta$.

12. Solve for t and θ, where $0° \leqslant \theta \leqslant 360°$, the simultaneous equations $\sin\theta = 2t$, $2\cos\theta + 3t = 0$.

In questions 13 to 22 solve the given equations for $0° \leqslant \theta \leqslant 360°$.

13. $3\cos^2\theta + 5\sin\theta - 1 = 0$.   14. $8\sin^2\theta + 2\cos\theta - 5 = 0$.
15. $2\sin\theta = 3\cot\theta$.   16. $\sec\theta\tan\theta = 2$.

17. $\tan^2\theta = \sec\theta + 5$.   18. $7\sin^2\theta + \cos^2\theta = 5\sin\theta$.

19. $2\sec^2\theta + 3\tan\theta = 4$.   20. $4\cot^2\theta - 3\operatorname{cosec}^2\theta = 2\cot\theta$.

21. $\sec\theta = 3\cos\theta + \sin\theta$.   22. $4\sec^2\theta = 5\tan\theta + 3\tan^2\theta$.

23. Express $2\sin x - \cos^2 x$ in the form $(\sin x + a)^2 + b$ and hence find the maximum and minimum values of the expression.

24. Find the range of the function $f : x \to \sec^2 x - 2\tan x + 1$.

7.4 Addition formulae

This section deals with expressions for $\sin(A \pm B)$, $\cos(A \pm B)$ in terms of sines and cosines of A and B.

In the diagrams below, OP and OQ make angles A and B respectively with the positive direction of the x-axis, so that $\angle POQ = A - B$. Letting $OP = OQ = 1$, the coordinates of P and Q are $P(\cos A, \sin A)$ and $Q(\cos B, \sin B)$.

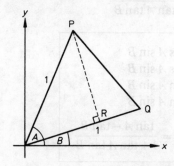
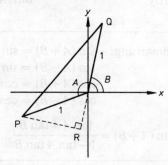

The distance between the points P and Q is given by

$$PQ^2 = (\cos A - \cos B)^2 + (\sin A - \sin B)^2$$
$$= \cos^2 A - 2\cos A \cos B + \cos^2 B + \sin^2 A - 2\sin A \sin B + \sin^2 B$$
$$= (\cos^2 A + \sin^2 A) + (\cos^2 B + \sin^2 B) - 2(\cos A \cos B + \sin A \sin B)$$
$$= 2 - 2(\cos A \cos B + \sin A \sin B).$$

Applying Pythagoras' theorem to $\triangle PQR$, $PQ^2 = PR^2 + RQ^2$

For all values of A and B this leads to

$$PQ^2 = \{\sin (A - B)\}^2 + \{1 - \cos (A - B)\}^2$$
$$= \sin^2 (A - B) + \cos^2 (A - B) + 1 - 2\cos (A - B)$$
$$= 2 - 2\cos (A - B).$$

Comparing these two expressions for PQ^2, we have

$$\cos(A - B) = \cos A \cos B + \sin A \sin B. \tag{1}$$

Substituting $-B$ for B in this expression

$$\cos (A + B) = \cos A \cos (-B) + \sin A \sin (-B)$$
$$\therefore \quad \cos (A + B) = \cos A \cos B - \sin A \sin B. \tag{2}$$

Substituting $90° - A$ for A in (1)

$$\cos (90° - A - B) = \cos (90° - A) \cos B + \sin (90° - A) \sin B$$
$$\therefore \quad \sin (A + B) = \sin A \cos B + \cos A \sin B. \tag{3}$$

Substituting $-B$ for B in (3)

$$\sin (A - B) = \sin A \cos (-B) + \cos A \sin (-B)$$
$$\therefore \quad \sin (A - B) = \sin A \cos B - \cos A \sin B. \tag{4}$$

Expressions for $\tan (A + B)$ and $\tan (A - B)$ can be deduced from identities (1) to (4).

$$\tan (A + B) = \frac{\sin (A + B)}{\cos (A + B)} = \frac{\sin A \cos B + \cos A \sin B}{\cos A \cos B - \sin A \sin B}.$$

Dividing numerator and denominator by $\cos A \cos B$

$$\tan (A+B) = \left(\frac{\sin A}{\cos A} + \frac{\sin B}{\cos B}\right) \bigg/ \left(1 - \frac{\sin A}{\cos A} \cdot \frac{\sin B}{\cos B}\right)$$

$$\therefore \quad \tan (A+B) = \frac{\tan A + \tan B}{1 - \tan A \tan B}.$$

Similarly,

$$\tan (A-B) = \frac{\tan A - \tan B}{1 + \tan A \tan B}.$$

Summarising:
$$\sin (A+B) = \sin A \cos B + \cos A \sin B$$
$$\sin (A-B) = \sin A \cos B - \cos A \sin B$$
$$\cos (A+B) = \cos A \cos B - \sin A \sin B$$
$$\cos (A-B) = \cos A \cos B + \sin A \sin B$$

$$\tan (A+B) = \frac{\tan A + \tan B}{1 - \tan A \tan B}, \quad \tan (A-B) = \frac{\tan A - \tan B}{1 + \tan A \tan B}.$$

Example 1 Find, without using tables, expressions in surd form for (a) $\sin 15°$, (b) $\tan 105°$.

(a) $\sin 15° = \sin (60° - 45°) = \sin 60° \cos 45° - \cos 60° \sin 45°$

$$= \frac{\sqrt{3}}{2} \cdot \frac{1}{\sqrt{2}} - \frac{1}{2} \cdot \frac{1}{\sqrt{2}} = \frac{\sqrt{3}-1}{2\sqrt{2}} \quad \text{or} \quad \frac{1}{4}(\sqrt{6}-\sqrt{2})$$

(b) $\tan 105° = \tan (60° + 45°) = \dfrac{\tan 60° + \tan 45°}{1 - \tan 60° \tan 45°}$

$$= \frac{\sqrt{3}+1}{1-\sqrt{3}} = \frac{(\sqrt{3}+1)^2}{(1-\sqrt{3})(1+\sqrt{3})} = \frac{3+2\sqrt{3}+1}{1-3} = -2-\sqrt{3}.$$

Example 2 Solve the equation $\cos (\theta - 30°) = 2 \sin \theta$ for values of θ between $0°$ and $360°$.

$$\cos (\theta - 30°) = 2 \sin \theta$$

$$\Rightarrow \qquad \cos \theta \cos 30° + \sin \theta \sin 30° = 2 \sin \theta$$

$$\Rightarrow \qquad \frac{\sqrt{3}}{2} \cos \theta + \frac{1}{2} \sin \theta = 2 \sin \theta$$

$$\Rightarrow \qquad \sqrt{3} \cos \theta = 3 \sin \theta$$

Hence $\tan \theta = \dfrac{1}{\sqrt{3}} = \tan 30°$, so that $\theta = 30°$ or $210°$.

Example 3 Find, without using tables, the values of

(a) $\dfrac{1}{\sqrt{2}} (\cos 75° - \sin 75°)$ (b) $\dfrac{1+\tan 15°}{1-\tan 15°}$

(a) $\dfrac{1}{\sqrt{2}}(\cos 75° - \sin 75°) = \cos 45° \cos 75° - \sin 45° \sin 75° = \cos (45° + 75°)$
$= \cos 120° = -\frac{1}{2}.$

(b) $\dfrac{1 + \tan 15°}{1 - \tan 15°} = \dfrac{\tan 45° + \tan 15°}{1 - \tan 45° \tan 15°} = \tan (45° + 15°) = \tan 60° = \sqrt{3}.$

Exercise 7.4

Answer questions 1 to 10 without using tables or calculators.

1. Find expressions in surd form for
   (a) $\sin 75°$,   (b) $\cos 105°$,   (c) $\tan (-15°)$,   (d) $\cot 75°$.

2. Find the values of
   (a) $\sin 80° \cos 70° + \cos 80° \sin 70°$,   (b) $\dfrac{1}{\sqrt{2}} \cos 15° - \dfrac{1}{\sqrt{2}} \sin 15°$,

   (c) $\cos 105° \cos 15° + \sin 105° \sin 15°$,   (d) $\dfrac{\sqrt{3}}{2} \sin 60° + \dfrac{1}{2} \cos 60°$.

3. Find the values of
   (a) $\dfrac{\tan 40° + \tan 20°}{1 - \tan 40° \tan 20°}$,   (b) $\dfrac{\tan 75° - 1}{\tan 75° + 1}$,

   (c) $\cos 75° + \sin 75°$,   (d) $\sqrt{3} \cos 15° - \sin 15°$.

4. If $\sin A = 12/13$ and $\sin B = 4/5$, where A and B are acute angles, find $\sin (A + B)$ and $\cos (A + B)$.

5. If $\cos A = 5/7$ and $\sin B = 1/5$, where A is acute and B is obtuse, find $\sin (A - B)$ and $\cos (A - B)$.

6. If $\tan A = 1/2$ and $\tan B = -1/3$, where $180° < A < 360°$ and $-90° < B < 90°$, find $A - B$.

7. If $\tan (A - B) = 2$ and $\tan B = \frac{1}{4}$, find $\tan A$.

8. Simplify the following expressions
   (a) $\sin (A + B) + \sin (A - B)$,   (b) $\cos (A + B) + \cos (A - B)$,
   (c) $\cos A \cos (A - B) + \sin A \sin (A - B)$.

9. Solve the equation $\cos 3x \cos 2x - \sin 3x \sin 2x = 0·5$ for $0° \leqslant x \leqslant 180°$.

10. Solve the equation $\sin 5x \cos 3x - \cos 5x \sin 3x = 1$ for $-180° \leqslant x \leqslant 180°$.

11. Solve the following equations for $0° \leqslant \theta \leqslant 360°$
    (a) $2 \tan \theta = 3 \tan (45° - \theta)$,   (b) $\sin \theta = 2 \sin (60° - \theta)$,
    (c) $\cos (\theta - 30°) = \cos (\theta + 30°)$,   (d) $\sin (\theta + 45°) = 5 \cos (\theta - 45°)$.

12. Express $\cot(A+B)$ in terms of $\cot A$ and $\cot B$.

13. By writing $A = \tan^{-1} x$ and $B = \tan^{-1} y$, show that under certain conditions
$\tan^{-1} x + \tan^{-1} y = \tan^{-1}\left(\dfrac{x+y}{1-xy}\right)$.

14. Use the result of question 13 to show that

(a) $\tan^{-1}\dfrac{1}{3} + \tan^{-1}\dfrac{1}{2} = \tan^{-1} 1$,   (b) $\tan^{-1}\dfrac{1}{5} + \tan^{-1}\dfrac{1}{8} = \tan^{-1}\dfrac{1}{3}$.

7.5   Double and half angle formulae

Substituting $B = A$ in the expressions obtained in the previous section for $\sin(A+B)$, $\cos(A+B)$ and $\tan(A+B)$:

$$\sin 2A = \sin(A+A) = \sin A \cos A + \cos A \sin A = 2\sin A \cos A$$
$$\cos 2A = \cos(A+A) = \cos A \cos A - \sin A \sin A = \cos^2 A - \sin^2 A$$
$$\tan 2A = \tan(A+A) = \frac{\tan A + \tan A}{1 - \tan A \tan A} = \frac{2\tan A}{1 - \tan^2 A}.$$

Using the identity $\cos^2 A + \sin^2 A = 1$,

$$\cos 2A = \cos^2 A - (1 - \cos^2 A) = 2\cos^2 A - 1$$
$$\cos 2A = (1 - \sin^2 A) - \sin^2 A = 1 - 2\sin^2 A.$$

Thus we have several useful results:

$$
\begin{array}{ll}
\cos 2A = \cos^2 A - \sin^2 A & \sin 2A = 2\sin A \cos A \\
\quad\quad\ = 2\cos^2 A - 1 & \\
\quad\quad\ = 1 - 2\sin^2 A & \tan 2A = \dfrac{2\tan A}{1 - \tan^2 A}.
\end{array}
$$

Example 1   Solve the equation $1 - 2\sin\theta - 4\cos 2\theta = 0$ for values of θ between $-180°$ and $+180°$.

Substituting $\cos 2\theta = 1 - 2\sin^2\theta$,
$$1 - 2\sin\theta - 4\cos 2\theta = 0 \Leftrightarrow 1 - 2\sin\theta - 4(1 - 2\sin^2\theta) = 0$$
$$\Leftrightarrow \quad 8\sin^2\theta - 2\sin\theta - 3 = 0$$
$$\Leftrightarrow \quad (4\sin\theta - 3)(2\sin\theta + 1) = 0$$
$$\therefore \quad \sin\theta = \tfrac{3}{4} = \sin 48\cdot6° \quad \text{or} \quad \sin\theta = -\tfrac{1}{2} = -\sin 30°$$
$$\theta = 48\cdot6°, \ 131\cdot4° \quad\quad\quad \theta = -150°, \ -30°.$$
Hence the required solutions are $-150°$, $-30°$, $48\cdot6°$, $131\cdot4°$.

Example 2   Express $\sin 3A$ in terms of $\sin A$.

$$\sin 3A = \sin(2A + A) = \sin 2A \cos A + \cos 2A \sin A$$
$$= 2\sin A \cos A \cos A + (\cos^2 A - \sin^2 A)\sin A$$

$$= 3 \sin A \cos^2 A - \sin^3 A$$
$$= 3 \sin A (1 - \sin^2 A) - \sin^3 A$$
$$\therefore \quad \sin 3A = 3 \sin A - 4 \sin^3 A.$$

Example 3   Simplify $\dfrac{\sin x}{1 + \cos x}$.

$$\sin x = 2 \sin \tfrac{1}{2} x \cos \tfrac{1}{2} x, \quad \cos x = 2 \cos^2 \tfrac{1}{2} x - 1$$

$$\therefore \quad \frac{\sin x}{1 + \cos x} = \frac{2 \sin \tfrac{1}{2} x \cos \tfrac{1}{2} x}{2 \cos^2 \tfrac{1}{2} x} = \frac{\sin \tfrac{1}{2} x}{\cos \tfrac{1}{2} x} = \tan \tfrac{1}{2} x.$$

Two further important identities are obtained by rearranging expressions for $\cos 2A$:

$$\boxed{\cos^2 A = \tfrac{1}{2}(1 + \cos 2A), \quad \sin^2 A = \tfrac{1}{2}(1 - \cos 2A).}$$

Example 4   Express $\cos^4 A$ in terms of cosines of multiples of A.

$$\cos^4 A = (\cos^2 A)^2 = \tfrac{1}{4}(1 + \cos 2A)^2 = \tfrac{1}{4}(1 + 2 \cos 2A + \cos^2 2A)$$
$$= \tfrac{1}{4}(1 + 2 \cos 2A + \tfrac{1}{2}\{1 + \cos 4A\}) = \tfrac{1}{8}(2 + 4 \cos 2A + 1 + \cos 4A)$$
$$\therefore \quad \cos^4 A = \tfrac{1}{8}(3 + 4 \cos 2A + \cos 4A).$$

If other methods fail, equations can often be solved and identities proved by expressing $\sin \theta$, $\cos \theta$ and $\tan \theta$ in terms of t, where $t = \tan \tfrac{1}{2}\theta$.

Using the formula for $\tan 2A$, $\tan \theta = \dfrac{2t}{1 - t^2}$.

$$\cos \theta = \cos^2 \tfrac{1}{2}\theta - \sin^2 \tfrac{1}{2}\theta = \cos^2 \tfrac{1}{2}\theta (1 - \tan^2 \tfrac{1}{2}\theta) = \frac{1 - \tan^2 \tfrac{1}{2}\theta}{\sec^2 \tfrac{1}{2}\theta} = \frac{1 - t^2}{1 + t^2}.$$

We may now write $\sin \theta = \cos \theta \tan \theta$ or obtain the result independently,

$$\sin \theta = 2 \sin \tfrac{1}{2}\theta \cos \tfrac{1}{2}\theta = 2 \tan \tfrac{1}{2}\theta \cos^2 \tfrac{1}{2}\theta = \frac{2 \tan \tfrac{1}{2}\theta}{\sec^2 \tfrac{1}{2}\theta} = \frac{2t}{1 + t^2}.$$

Thus
$$\boxed{\sin \theta = \frac{2t}{1 + t^2}, \quad \cos \theta = \frac{1 - t^2}{1 + t^2}, \quad \tan \theta = \frac{2t}{1 - t^2}.}$$

The main disadvantage of using these 't formulae' to solve trigonometric equations is that polynomial equations involving large powers of t may be produced. It is not always possible to solve these by elementary methods.

Example 5   Solve the equation $5 \tan \theta + \sec \theta + 5 = 0$ for values of θ between $0°$ and $360°$.

If $\tan\frac{1}{2}\theta = t$, then provided that $t^2 \neq 1$, the equation becomes

$$5\left(\frac{2t}{1-t^2}\right) + \left(\frac{1+t^2}{1-t^2}\right) + 5 = 0$$

$$10t + (1+t^2) + 5(1-t^2) = 0$$

$$-4t^2 + 10t + 6 = 0$$

$$2t^2 - 5t - 3 = 0$$

$$(t-3)(2t+1) = 0$$

$\therefore$ either $t = 3$ or $t = -\frac{1}{2}$

$\tan\frac{1}{2}\theta = \tan 71\cdot565°$ $\tan\frac{1}{2}\theta = -\tan 26\cdot565°$

Hence, between $0°$ and $180°$, $\frac{1}{2}\theta = 71\cdot565°$ or $153\cdot435°$.
Thus the required values of θ are $143\cdot1°$ or $306\cdot9°$ (nrst $0\cdot1°$).

Exercise 7.5

Answer questions 1 to 7 without using tables or calculators.

1.   Given that x is an acute angle such that $\cos x = 3/5$, find $\sin 2x$, $\cos 2x$ and $\sin 3x$.

2.   Given that θ is an obtuse angle such that $\sin\theta = 2/3$, find $\cos 2\theta$, $\tan 2\theta$ and $\cos 4\theta$.

3.   Given that A is an acute angle such that $\tan A = \frac{1}{2}$, find $\sin 2A$, $\tan 2A$ and $\tan 3A$.

4.   Given that x is an obtuse angle such that $\cos 2x = 1/8$, find $\cos x$, $\tan x$ and $\sec\frac{1}{2}x$.

5.   Given that $\sin A = -0\cdot8$ where $0° < A < 270°$, find $\cos\frac{1}{2}A$, $\sin\frac{1}{2}A$ and $\sin\frac{3}{2}A$.

6.   Find the values of the following expressions
(a) $(\sin 67\frac{1}{2}° + \cos 67\frac{1}{2}°)^2$,   (b) $\cos^2 15° - \sin^2 15°$,
(c) $\tan 75° \cos^2 75°$,   (d) $1 - 2\sin^2 22\frac{1}{2}°$.

7.   Solve the following equations for $0° \leqslant x \leqslant 180°$
(a) $\sin 2x = \sin x$,   (b) $\cos 2x = \cos x$,
(c) $\tan 2x + \tan x = 0$,   (d) $\sin 2x - \tan x = 0$.

In questions 8 to 15 prove the given identities.

8. $\cos^4 A - \sin^4 A = \cos 2A$.

9. $\cot\theta - \tan\theta = 2\cot 2\theta$.

10. $\dfrac{\sin 3A}{\sin A} + \dfrac{\cos 3A}{\cos A} = 4\cos 2A$.

11. $\dfrac{\cos\theta - \sin\theta}{\cos\theta + \sin\theta} = \dfrac{\cos 2\theta}{1+\sin 2\theta}$.

12. $\dfrac{\sec 2x - 1}{\sec 2x + 1} = \sec^2 x - 1$.

13. $\dfrac{\sin 2\theta - \cos 2\theta + 1}{\sin 2\theta + \cos 2\theta + 1} = \tan\theta$.

14. $\operatorname{cosec} x - \cot x = \tan \frac{1}{2} x$.

15. $\tan(\frac{1}{2}x + 45°) + \cot(\frac{1}{2}x + 45°) = 2 \sec x$.

16. Solve the following equations for $0° \leqslant x \leqslant 360°$
(a) $\cos 2x = 5 \cos x + 2$,
(b) $3 \cos 2x + 1 = 2 \sin x$,
(c) $4 \sin^2 x - \tan^2 x = 1$,
(d) $4 \sin x = 7 \tan 2x$.

17. By expressing $\cos 2\theta$ and $\sin 2\theta$ in terms of $\tan \theta$, solve the following equations for $0° \leqslant \theta \leqslant 360°$
(a) $\cos 2\theta - 2 \sin 2\theta = 2$,
(b) $5 \cos 2\theta - 2 \sin 2\theta = 2$.

18. Using the substitution $\tan \frac{1}{2} x = t$, solve the following equations for $-180° \leqslant x \leqslant 180°$
(a) $9 \cos x - 8 \sin x = 1$,
(b) $\sin x + 1 = 3 \cos x$,
(c) $2 \cos x - \sin x + 1 = 0$,
(d) $7 \sin x + 9 \cos x = 3$.

19. By squaring $\sin^2 \theta + \cos^2 \theta$, prove that $\sin^4 \theta + \cos^4 \theta = \frac{1}{4}(\cos 4\theta + 3)$. Hence solve the equation $\sin^4 \theta + \cos^4 \theta = \frac{1}{2}$ for $0° < \theta < 360°$.

20. Express $\cos 3\theta$ in terms of $\cos \theta$ and hence solve the equation $\cos 3\theta + 2 \cos 2\theta + 4 \cos \theta + 2 = 0$ for $0° < \theta < 360°$.

7.6 Sum and product formulae

In §7.4 it was shown that

$$\sin(A+B) = \sin A \cos B + \cos A \sin B$$
$$\sin(A-B) = \sin A \cos B - \cos A \sin B$$

Adding $\quad\quad \sin(A+B) + \sin(A-B) = 2 \sin A \cos B \quad\quad\quad (1)$
Subtracting $\quad \sin(A+B) - \sin(A-B) = 2 \cos A \sin B \quad\quad\quad (2)$

Similarly $\quad\quad \cos(A+B) = \cos A \cos B - \sin A \sin B$
$$\cos(A-B) = \cos A \cos B + \sin A \sin B$$

Adding $\quad\quad \cos(A+B) + \cos(A-B) = 2 \cos A \cos B \quad\quad\quad (3)$
Subtracting $\quad \cos(A+B) - \cos(A-B) = -2 \sin A \sin B. \quad\quad (4)$

These results provide a way of expressing a product of sines and cosines as a sum or a difference. Results (1), (3) and (4) cover all possible products.

$$2 \sin A \cos B = \sin(A+B) + \sin(A-B)$$
$$2 \cos A \cos B = \cos(A+B) + \cos(A-B)$$
$$2 \sin A \sin B = -\{\cos(A+B) - \cos(A-B)\}.$$

Example 1   Express as a sum or a difference (a) $2\cos 4\theta \cos \theta$, (b) $\sin 2x \cos 3x$.

(a) $2\cos 4\theta \cos \theta = \cos (4\theta + \theta) + \cos (4\theta - \theta) = \cos 5\theta + \cos 3\theta$.

(b) $\sin 2x \cos 3x = \frac{1}{2}\{\sin (2x + 3x) + \sin (2x - 3x)\}$
$= \frac{1}{2}\{\sin 5x + \sin (-x)\} = \frac{1}{2}\{\sin 5x - \sin x\}$.

Example 2   Find, without using tables, the value of $2\sin 15° \sin 45°$.

$2\sin 15° \sin 45° = -\{\cos (15° + 45°) - \cos (15° - 45°)\}$
$= -\cos 60° + \cos (-30°)$
$= -\frac{1}{2} + \frac{\sqrt{3}}{2} = \frac{1}{2}(\sqrt{3} - 1)$.

Results (1), (2), (3) and (4) can also be used to express sums and differences of sines and cosines as products.

Letting $A + B = X$, $A - B = Y$ so that $A = \frac{1}{2}(X + Y)$, $B = \frac{1}{2}(X - Y)$,

$$\sin X + \sin Y = 2\sin \tfrac{1}{2}(X + Y)\cos \tfrac{1}{2}(X - Y)$$
$$\sin X - \sin Y = 2\cos \tfrac{1}{2}(X + Y)\sin \tfrac{1}{2}(X - Y)$$
$$\cos X + \cos Y = 2\cos \tfrac{1}{2}(X + Y)\cos \tfrac{1}{2}(X - Y)$$
$$\cos X - \cos Y = -2\sin \tfrac{1}{2}(X + Y)\sin \tfrac{1}{2}(X - Y).$$

As these identities can be used to 'factorise' sums and differences, they are sometimes called the *factor formulae*.

Example 3   Simplify $\dfrac{\sin (A + B) - \sin A}{\cos (A + B) + \cos A}$.

$\sin (A + B) - \sin A = 2\cos \frac{1}{2}\{(A + B) + A\} \sin \frac{1}{2}\{(A + B) - A\}$
$= 2\cos (A + \frac{1}{2}B)\sin \frac{1}{2}B$.

Similarly $\cos (A + B) + \cos A = 2\cos (A + \frac{1}{2}B)\cos \frac{1}{2}B$

$\therefore \quad \dfrac{\sin (A + B) - \sin A}{\cos (A + B) + \cos A} = \dfrac{2\cos (A + \frac{1}{2}B)\sin \frac{1}{2}B}{2\cos (A + \frac{1}{2}B)\cos \frac{1}{2}B} = \tan \tfrac{1}{2}B.$

Example 4   Solve the equation $\sin 5\theta + \sin 3\theta = 0$ for values of θ between $0°$ and $180°$.

$\sin 5\theta + \sin 3\theta = 0 \Rightarrow 2\sin \frac{1}{2}(5\theta + 3\theta)\cos \frac{1}{2}(5\theta - 3\theta) = 0$
$\Rightarrow \qquad\qquad \sin 4\theta \cos \theta = 0$
$\therefore \qquad \sin 4\theta = 0 \qquad\qquad\qquad\qquad \text{or} \quad \cos \theta = 0$
$\qquad\qquad 4\theta = 0°, 180°, 360°, 540°, 720° \qquad\qquad \theta = 90°$
$\qquad\qquad \theta = 0°, 45°, 90°, 135°, 180°$

Hence the solutions are $\theta = 0°, 45°, 90°, 135°, 180°$.

Example 5 Solve the equation $\cos 5\theta + \cos 3\theta + \cos \theta = 0$ for values of θ between $0°$ and $180°$.

$$\cos 5\theta + \cos 3\theta + \cos \theta = 0$$
$$\Rightarrow \quad (\cos 5\theta + \cos \theta) + \cos 3\theta = 0$$
$$\Rightarrow \quad 2\cos 3\theta \cos 2\theta + \cos 3\theta = 0$$
$$\Rightarrow \quad \cos 3\theta (2\cos 2\theta + 1) = 0$$

$$\therefore \quad \cos 3\theta = 0 \qquad \text{or} \quad \cos 2\theta = -\tfrac{1}{2}$$
$$3\theta = 90°, 270°, 450° \qquad \qquad 2\theta = 120°, 240°$$
$$\theta = 30°, 90°, 150° \qquad \qquad \theta = 60°, 120°.$$

Hence the required values of θ are $30°$, $60°$, $90°$, $120°$, $150°$.

Exercise 7.6

1. Express as a sum or a difference
(a) $2\sin 2x \cos x$,
(b) $2\cos 3\theta \cos 5\theta$,
(c) $6\sin 3A \sin 2A$,
(d) $\sin 2t \cos 4t$,
(e) $2\cos (A+B)\cos (A-B)$,
(f) $\sin (x+75°)\sin (x+15°)$.

2. Find, without using tables, the values of
(a) $4\sin 75° \cos 45°$,
(b) $20\sin 22\tfrac{1}{2}° \sin 67\tfrac{1}{2}°$,
(c) $8\cos 52\tfrac{1}{2}° \cos 37\tfrac{1}{2}° \cos 15°$,
(d) $\tan 82\tfrac{1}{2}° \cot 52\tfrac{1}{2}°$.

3. Solve the following equations for $0° \leqslant \theta \leqslant 360°$
(a) $2\sin 2\theta \cos \theta = \sin 3\theta$,
(b) $2\cos (\theta + 120°)\cos (\theta + 60°) = 1$,
(c) $2\sin (\theta + 30°) = \sec \theta$,
(d) $\sin (\theta + 30°)\cos (\theta - 40°) = 0·2$.

4. Express as a product
(a) $\sin x + \sin 7x$,
(b) $\cos 3A + \cos 5A$,
(c) $\sin (\theta + \alpha) - \sin (\theta - \alpha)$,
(d) $\cos 3x + \sin (x - 90°)$.

5. Simplify the following expressions
(a) $\dfrac{\cos 3\theta + \cos 7\theta}{\sin 3\theta + \sin 7\theta}$,
(b) $\dfrac{\cos 5x - \cos x}{\sin 5x - \sin x}$,
(c) $\dfrac{\cos A - \cos 2A + \cos 3A}{\sin A - \sin 2A + \sin 3A}$,
(d) $\dfrac{\cos \theta - 2\cos 3\theta + \cos 5\theta}{\cos \theta + 2\cos 3\theta + \cos 5\theta}$.

6. Find the values of
(a) $\dfrac{\cos 50° - \cos 70°}{\sin 70° - \sin 50°}$,
(b) $\dfrac{\sin \theta + \sin (\theta + 120°)}{\cos (60° - \theta) + \cos \theta}$.

7. Solve the following equations for $0° \leqslant x \leqslant 180°$
(a) $\cos 3x = \cos x$,
(b) $\sin 5x = \sin x$,
(c) $\sin (3x + 60°) = \sin x$,
(d) $\sin 3x = \cos x$.

8. Solve the following equations for $0° \leqslant \theta \leqslant 180°$
(a) $\sin \theta + \sin 2\theta + \sin 3\theta = 0$,
(b) $\sin 5\theta - \sin \theta = \cos 3\theta$,
(c) $\cos 3\theta - \sin 3\theta = \cos 2\theta - \sin 2\theta$.

7.7 The expression $a \cos \theta + b \sin \theta$

A sketch of the graph of a function of the form $a \cos \theta + b \sin \theta$ can be made by combining the graphs of $a \cos \theta$ and $b \cos \theta$. The result for the function $\cos \theta + \sin \theta$ is shown below.

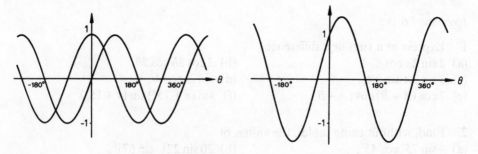

However, the exact form of the graph becomes clear when we apply one of the factor formulae derived in the previous section.

$$\cos \theta + \sin \theta = \cos \theta + \cos (90° - \theta) = 2 \cos 45° \cos (\theta - 45°)$$

$$= 2 \cdot \frac{1}{\sqrt{2}} \cos (\theta - 45°) = \sqrt{2} \cos (\theta - 45°).$$

It seems reasonable to investigate whether the function $a \cos \theta + b \sin \theta$ can be expressed in the form $r \cos (\theta - \alpha)$, where r is positive.

Since $r \cos (\theta - \alpha) = r(\cos \theta \cos \alpha + \sin \theta \sin \alpha)$
$$= (r \cos \alpha) \cos \theta + (r \sin \alpha) \sin \theta$$

the expressions $a \cos \theta + b \sin \theta$ and $r \cos (\theta - \alpha)$ will be equal for all values of θ if
$$r \cos \alpha = a, \qquad r \sin \alpha = b$$

$\therefore \quad a^2 + b^2 = r^2 (\cos^2 \alpha + \sin^2 \alpha) = r^2 \quad$ i.e. $r = \sqrt{(a^2 + b^2)}$

and $\quad \dfrac{b}{a} = \dfrac{r \sin \alpha}{r \cos \alpha} = \tan \alpha \qquad$ i.e. $\tan \alpha = b/a$.

Hence the function $a \cos \theta + b \sin \theta$ can be expressed in the form $r \cos (\theta - \alpha)$, where $r = \sqrt{(a^2 + b^2)}$, $\tan \alpha = b/a$.

[Note that since r is assumed positive, the value of α must be chosen so that $\cos \alpha$ has the same sign as a and $\sin \alpha$ the same sign as b.]

Example 1   Express $3 \cos \theta + 4 \sin \theta$ in the form $r \cos (\theta - \alpha)$. Hence find the maximum and minimum values of $3 \cos \theta + 4 \sin \theta$.

If $3\cos\theta + 4\sin\theta = r\cos(\theta-\alpha) = r\cos\alpha\cos\theta + r\sin\alpha\sin\theta$
then $r\cos\alpha = 3$ and $r\sin\alpha = 4$.

Since both $r\cos\alpha$ and $r\sin\alpha$ are positive, we may take $r > 0$ and $0° < \alpha < 90°$.

$\therefore \quad r = \sqrt{(3^2 + 4^2)} = 5$ and $\tan\alpha = 4/3, \alpha = 53\cdot13°$

Hence $3\cos\theta + 4\sin\theta = 5\cos(\theta - 53\cdot1°)$.

Since the maximum and minimum values of $\cos(\theta - 53\cdot1°)$ are $+1$ and -1 respectively, the maximum and minimum values of $3\cos\theta + 4\sin\theta$ must be $+5$ and -5.

Example 2   Solve the equation $3\cos\theta - \sin\theta = 1$ for values of θ between $0°$ and $360°$.

Let $3\cos\theta - \sin\theta = r\cos(\theta+\alpha) = r\cos\alpha\cos\theta - r\sin\alpha\sin\theta$
then $r\cos\alpha = 3$ and $r\sin\alpha = 1$

$\therefore \quad r = \sqrt{(3^2 + 1^2)} = \sqrt{10}$ and $\tan\alpha = 1/3, \alpha = 18\cdot435°$.

Hence the equation $3\cos\theta - \sin\theta = 1$
may be written $\sqrt{10}\cos(\theta + 18\cdot435°) = 1$
$\therefore \quad \cos(\theta + 18\cdot435°) = 1/\sqrt{10} = \cos 71\cdot565°$
$\therefore \quad \theta + 18\cdot435° = 71\cdot565°$ or $288\cdot435°$.

Hence the required solutions are $53\cdot1°$ and $270°$.

In the above example it was more convenient to use $r\cos(\theta+\alpha)$ instead of $r\cos(\theta-\alpha)$, because this led to a value of α between $0°$ and $90°$. The expressions $r\sin(\theta+\alpha)$ and $r\sin(\theta-\alpha)$ may also be used when appropriate.

Exercise 7.7

1.   Express each of the following functions in the form $r\cos(\theta\pm\alpha)$, where $r > 0$ and $0° < \alpha < 90°$. Hence find the maximum and minimum values of the function, giving the values of θ between $-360°$ and $+360°$ for which these occur. Sketch the graph of the function in this interval.
(a) $\cos\theta - \sin\theta$,   (b) $\sqrt{3}\cos\theta - \sin\theta$,
(c) $5\cos\theta + 12\sin\theta$,   (d) $2\cos\theta + \sin\theta$.

2.   Using an appropriate expression of the form $r\cos(\theta\pm\alpha)$, solve the following equations for $0° \leqslant \theta \leqslant 360°$.
(a) $4\cos\theta - 3\sin\theta = 1$,   (b) $2\cos\theta + 5\sin\theta = 4$,
(c) $3\cos\theta + 7\sin\theta + 3 = 0$,   (d) $15\cos\theta - 8\sin\theta + 10 = 0$.

3.   Express $5\sin\theta - 8\cos\theta$ in the form $r\sin(\theta-\alpha)$, where $r > 0$ and $0° < \alpha < 90°$. Hence solve the following equations for $0° \leqslant \theta \leqslant 360°$.
(a) $5\sin\theta - 8\cos\theta = 6$,   (b) $5\sin\theta - 8\cos\theta = 5$.

4.   Solve the following equations for $0° \leqslant x \leqslant 360°$,

(i) by expressing $\cos x$ and $\sin x$ in terms of $t = \tan \frac{1}{2}x$, (ii) using an expression of the form $r\cos(x-\alpha)$.

(a) $3\cos x - 5\sin x = 2$,　　　　　　(b) $4\cos x - 6\sin x = 5$.

5.　Construct a flow chart for a procedure to solve the equation $a\cos\theta + b\sin\theta = c$, where $a > 0$, using a pocket calculator. The output of your procedure should be the values of θ, for $0° \leqslant \theta \leqslant 360°$, or a suitable message if there are no solutions. Consider whether accuracy or efficiency would be improved by incorporating in your chart branches or jumps for special cases such as $a = b$ or $b = c$.

Exercise 7.8 (*miscellaneous*)

1.　Find all values of θ from $0°$ to $360°$ inclusive, such that
(a) $\sin\theta = \cos 20°$,　　　　　　　　(b) $\sin 2\theta = -\sin 50°$,
(c) $\cos\theta = -\cos(-35°)$,　　　　　　(d) $\tan 3\theta = \cot 15°$.

2.　Given that $\cos x = -0{\cdot}8$, where $0° < x < 180°$, find the values of
(a) $\cos(x - 180°)$,　　(b) $\cos(x + 90°)$,　　(c) $\sin(90° - x)$,
(d) $\sin(x + 180°)$,　　(e) $\tan(x + 360°)$,　　(f) $\cot(x - 90°)$.

3.　Solve the following equations for $0° \leqslant x \leqslant 360°$.
(a) $2\sin x = 3\cos x$,　　　　　　　　(b) $3\cos x - \sec x = \frac{1}{2}$,
(c) $3\tan x = 5\sin x$,　　　　　　　　(d) $5\cos 2x + 1 = 11\sin x$.

4.　Given that θ is an obtuse angle and that $\cos\theta = k$, find the following in terms of k.
(a) $\cos 2\theta$,　　(b) $\sin 3\theta$,　　(c) $\cos\frac{1}{2}\theta$,　　(d) $\tan\frac{1}{2}\theta$.

5.　Eliminate θ from the following pairs of equations.
(a) $x = 1 + \sin\theta$　　　　　　　　(b) $x = \tan\theta + \sec\theta$
　　$y = \frac{1}{2}\cos\theta$,　　　　　　　　　$y = \sec\theta - \tan\theta$,
(c) $x = \cos\theta$　　　　　　　　　(d) $x = 1 + \cos\theta$
　　$y = \cos 2\theta + 1$,　　　　　　　　$y = \sin 2\theta$.

6.　Solve the following equations for $0° \leqslant x \leqslant 180°$.
(a) $\dfrac{\tan x}{1 - \tan^2 x} = \dfrac{1}{5}$,　　　　　　(b) $\dfrac{\tan x}{1 + \tan^2 x} = \dfrac{1}{5}$,
(c) $\sin 3x = \sin x$,　　　　　　　　(d) $\sin 4x + \sin 2x = 0$.

7.　Sketch the curves $y = 2\sin x$ and $y = 3\cos x$ for $0° \leqslant x \leqslant 360°$. Find the range of values of x in this interval for which $2\sin x \geqslant 3\cos x$.

8.　Given that $\tan A = \frac{2}{3}$ and $\tan B = \frac{1}{2}$, find the value of

$$\frac{\cos 2A + \cos 2B}{\sin 2A - \sin 2B}.$$

9. Sketch the graphs of the following functions for $-360° \leqslant \theta \leqslant 360°$, showing clearly the maximum and minimum values of each function.
(a) $2\cos\theta\sin\theta$,
(b) $2\sin^2\theta$,
(c) $\cos\theta + \sqrt{3}\sin\theta$,
(d) $(\cos\theta + \sqrt{3}\sin\theta)^2$.

10. Prove the following identities

(a) $\dfrac{1-\cos 2A}{1+\cos 2A} = \tan^2 A = \dfrac{\tan^2 A+1}{\cot^2 A+1}$,

(b) $\dfrac{\sin\theta}{1+\cos\theta} + \dfrac{1-\cos\theta}{\sin\theta} = 2\tan\tfrac{1}{2}\theta$,

(c) $\dfrac{\cos^4 A+\sin^4 A}{\cos^4 A-\sin^4 A} = \tfrac{1}{2}(\cos 2A + \sec 2A)$,

(d) $\dfrac{\sin(\theta+15°)+\sin(\theta-15°)}{\cos(\theta-15°)+\cos(\theta+15°)} = \tan\theta$.

11. (a) Prove that $15\cos 2\theta + 20\sin 2\theta + 7 \equiv 2(11\cos\theta - 2\sin\theta)(\cos\theta + 2\sin\theta)$. Hence, or otherwise, find all angles θ between $0°$ and $180°$ for which $15\cos 2\theta + 20\sin 2\theta + 7 = 0$, giving your answers to the nearest tenth of a degree.
(b) If $\sin(\theta+\alpha) = \lambda\sin(\theta-\alpha)$, where λ is a numerical constant $(\lambda \neq 1)$, find an expression for $\tan\theta$ in terms of $\tan\alpha$ and λ. In the case when $\lambda = \tfrac{1}{2}$ and $\alpha = 30°$, find the values of θ which lie between $0°$ and $360°$. (C)

12. (a) Solve the equation $\cos x + \cos 2x + \cos 3x = 0$, giving all values between $0°$ and $360°$ (inclusive).
(b) Express $3\sin x + 4\cos x$ in the form $R\cos(x-\alpha)$, where R is a positive number. Hence, or otherwise, solve the equation $3\sin x + 4\cos x = 2$, giving all values between $0°$ and $360°$.
(c) If x and y are angles between $0°$ and $360°$ (inclusive), and $\sin^2 x + \cos^2 y = 2$, state what the possible values are of x and y. (SU)

13. Express $\tan 3\theta$ in terms of $\tan\theta$. Hence solve the equation $2\tan 3\theta = 9\tan\theta$ for $0° \leqslant \theta \leqslant 180°$.

14. Write down expressions for $\tan\theta$ and $\sec\theta$ in terms of t, where $t = \tan\dfrac{\theta}{2}$, and show that $\sec\theta + \tan\theta = \tan\left(45° + \dfrac{\theta}{2}\right)$. Find a solution in the interval $0° < \theta < 90°$ of the equation $\sec\theta + \tan\theta = \cot 2\theta$. (JMB)

15. (a) Express $7\sin x - 24\cos x$ in the form $R\sin(x-\alpha)$, where R is positive and α is an acute angle. Hence or otherwise solve the equation $7\sin x - 24\cos x = 15$, for $0° < x < 360°$.
(b) Solve the simultaneous equations $\cos x + \cos y = 1$, $\sec x + \sec y = 4$, for $0° < x < 180°, 0° < y < 180°$. (AEB)

16. By expressing $\sin\theta$ and $\cos\theta$ in terms of $\tan\frac{1}{2}\theta$, solve the equation $\sin\theta+2\cos\theta = 1$, for $0° \leqslant \theta \leqslant 360°$. Explain why the method breaks down for the equation $2\sin\theta-\cos\theta = 1$ and find the values of θ, between $0°$ and $360°$, which satisfy this equation.

17. Prove that (a) $\cos A\cos 2A - \cos 2A\cos 5A = \sin 3A\sin 4A$
    (b) $\sin A\cos 2A + \sin 2A\cos 5A = \sin 3A\cos 4A$.

18. (a) Prove the identities $\cos\theta+\cos 3\theta+\cos 5\theta+\cos 7\theta \equiv 4\cos\theta\cos 2\theta\cos 4\theta$
$\equiv \sin 8\theta/2\sin\theta$.
(b) Solve for $0° < \theta < 360°$ the equation $\sec\theta-3\tan\theta = 2$.   (W)

19. Find, to the nearest $0.1°$, the acute angle α for which $4\cos\theta - 3\sin\theta$ $\equiv 5\cos(\theta+\alpha)$. Calculate the values of θ in the interval $-180° \leqslant \theta \leqslant 180°$ for which the function $f(\theta) = 4\cos\theta-3\sin\theta-4$ attains its greatest value, its least value and the value zero.   (JMB)

20. Solve the following equations for $0° \leqslant x \leqslant 180°$.
(a) $2\tan 3x\cot x+1 = 0$,   (b) $3(\sec 2x-\tan 2x) = 2\tan x$,
(c) $\cot 5x+\tan 2x = 0$,   (d) $4\sin x\cos 2x\sin 3x = 1$.

21. Prove that, if the equation $a\sin x+b\cos x = c$ is to have a solution, then $a^2+b^2 \geqslant c^2$. Find all the solutions of the equation $7\sin x+6\cos x = 9$ between $0°$ and $360°$, giving your answers to the nearest tenth of a degree.   (O)

22. Write down the values of the following in degrees.
(a) $\sin^{-1}\frac{1}{2}$,   (b) $\cos^{-1}(-1)$,   (c) $\tan^{-1}(-1)$,   (d) $\cot^{-1}\sqrt{3}$,

(e) $\sin^{-1}x+\cos^{-1}x$,   (f) $\tan^{-1}x+\tan^{-1}\frac{1}{x}$,

(g) $\tan^{-1}\frac{2}{3}+\tan^{-1}\frac{1}{5}$,   (h) $\tan^{-1}\frac{5}{2}-\tan^{-1}\frac{3}{7}$.

23. Prove that $\cos 3\theta = 4\cos^3\theta-3\cos\theta$. Hence solve the equation
$$x^3-3x-\sqrt{2} = 0$$
by using a suitable substitution of the form $x = k\cos\theta$, then finding possible values of θ between $0°$ and $180°$. Give your answers in surd form.

24. (a) Find all solutions of the equation $\sin 3\theta = \sin^2\theta$ for which $0° \leqslant \theta < 360°$.
(b) Express $\lambda\sin\theta+(1-\lambda)\cos\theta$ in the form $R\sin(\theta+\phi)$, where $R(R > 0)$ and $\tan\phi$ are to be given in terms of λ. Write down an expression, in terms of λ, for the minimum value of $\lambda\sin\theta+(1-\lambda)\cos\theta$ as θ varies, and show that, for all λ, this minimum is less than or equal to $-\frac{1}{2}\sqrt{2}$.   (C)

8 Trigonometry of triangles

8.1 Review of elementary geometry

[This introductory section contains a review of some of the language and results of elementary geometry which may be required when solving trigonometrical problems.]

In elementary geometrical work the notions of points and distances, straight lines and angles are introduced. Development of these basic ideas leads to the study of plane figures such as triangles and parallelograms. One set of important results involving circles is illustrated here. In diagram (1) angles subtended by the

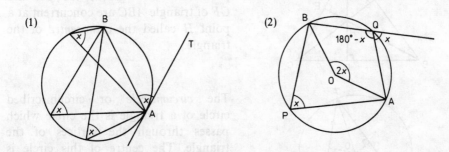

chord AB, lying in the same segment of the circle, are equal. The angle between the tangent AT and the chord AB is equal to any angle in the alternate segment. In diagram (2) the angle subtended by AB at the centre O is twice the angle subtended by AB at P on the circumference of the circle. Opposite angles of the cyclic quadrilateral $APBQ$ are supplementary and any exterior angle is equal to the opposite interior angle.

The ratio properties of similar figures have many applications. One result which may be proved using similar triangles is the angle bisector theorem. In the triangles ABC shown overleaf, BP bisects $\angle A$ internally in diagram (3) and externally in diagram (4).

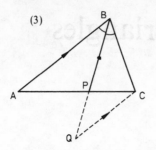

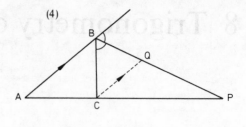

In both cases we have
$$\frac{AP}{PC} = \frac{AB}{BC}.$$

[The proof uses similar triangles ABP and CQP.]

We now list some further properties of the triangle.

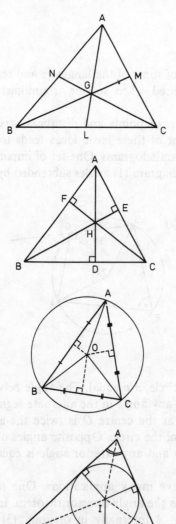

A *median* of a triangle is a line joining a vertex to the mid-point of the opposite side. The medians AL, BM and CN of triangle ABC are concurrent at a point G, called the *centroid* of the triangle. G divides each median in the ratio $2:1$.

An *altitude* of a triangle is a perpendicular from a vertex to the opposite side. The altitudes AD, BE and CF of triangle ABC are concurrent at a point H called the *orthocentre* of the triangle.

The *circumcircle* or circumscribed circle of a triangle is the circle which passes through the vertices of the triangle. The centre of this circle is called the *circumcentre*. It is the point of intersection of the perpendicular bisectors of the sides of the triangle.

The *inscribed circle* or incircle of a triangle is the circle which touches the three sides of the triangle internally. The centre of this circle is called the *incentre*. It is the point of intersection of the bisectors of the angles of the triangle.

Exercise 8.1

1.   The points A, B and C lie on a circle centre O. How are $\angle A$, $\angle B$ and $\angle C$ of the quadrilateral $OABC$ related?

2.   The points P, Q and R lie on a circle and $\angle PRQ$ is obtuse. The tangents to the circle at P and Q intersect at T. If $\angle TPQ = x$, $\angle PRQ = y$ and $\angle PTQ = z$, state the relationships between (a) x and y, (b) y and z.

3.   In triangle PQR the internal bisector of $\angle Q$ meets PR at X and the external bisector of $\angle Q$ meets PR produced at Y. Given that $PQ:QR = 3:2$, find the ratio $PR:XY$. Prove that $\angle XQY$ is a right-angle. Hence show that Q lies on the circle with diameter XY.

4.   A point P moves in a plane containing two fixed points A and B, such that the ratio AP/PB is a constant not equal to 1. Show that the locus of P is a circle. [This locus is called *Apollonius'†* circle.]

5.   By showing that the medians of a triangle divide the triangle into six smaller triangles of equal area, prove that the centroid of the triangle divides each median in the ratio $2:1$.

6.   Given that AD, BE and CF are the altitudes of an acute angled triangle ABC, prove that the orthocentre of $\triangle ABC$ is the incentre of $\triangle DEF$. Find the position of the incentre of $\triangle DEF$ when $\angle A$ is obtuse. [$\triangle DEF$ is called the *pedal triangle* of $\triangle ABC$ because its vertices are the 'feet' of the altitudes.]

8.2 Sine and cosine rules

To establish the sine rule, consider a triangle ABC as shown below. Let h be the height of the perpendicular (or altitude) from C to AB. In both diagrams,
$$\sin A = \frac{h}{b}, \sin B = \frac{h}{a}$$

$$\therefore \quad \frac{a}{\sin A} = \frac{b}{\sin B} \left(= \frac{ab}{h} \right).$$

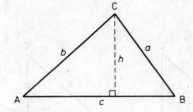
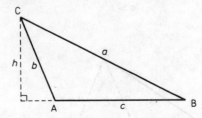

† *Apollonius of Perga* (3rd cent. B.C.) Greek mathematician known as 'the great geometer'. His treatise on conic sections forms the basis of much of the later work on the subject.

Similarly, it may be shown that $\dfrac{b}{\sin B} = \dfrac{c}{\sin C}$, leading to the *sine rule*:

$$\frac{a}{\sin A} = \frac{b}{\sin B} = \frac{c}{\sin C}.$$

Example 1 Solve the triangle ABC in which $A = 40°$, $B = 65°$ and $c = 10$.

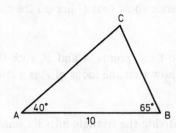

$$A + B + C = 180°$$

$$\therefore \quad C = 180° - 40° - 65° = 75°.$$

By the sine rule,

$$\frac{a}{\sin A} = \frac{b}{\sin B} = \frac{c}{\sin C}$$

$$\therefore \quad \frac{a}{\sin 40°} = \frac{b}{\sin 65°} = \frac{10}{\sin 75°}$$

Hence $\quad a = \dfrac{10 \sin 40°}{\sin 75°} \approx 6{\cdot}65, \quad b = \dfrac{10 \sin 65°}{\sin 75°} \approx 9{\cdot}38$

$\therefore$ the remaining sides and angles of the triangle are $C = 75°$, $a = 6{\cdot}65$ and $b = 9{\cdot}38$.

The sine rule can also be applied when two sides and one angle of a triangle are given. However, in this case it may sometimes be possible to construct two triangles satisfying the given conditions. For instance, let us assume that in $\triangle ABC$, the angle A and the sides a and b are given. These diagrams show that the ambiguous case arises when a is less than b, but greater than $b \sin A$.

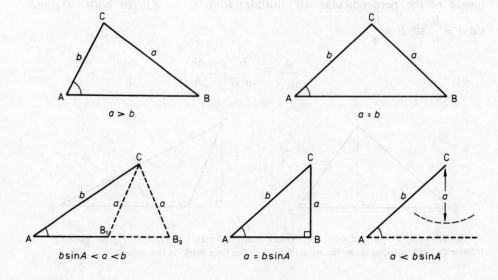

Example 2 If in triangle ABC, $a = 10$, $b = 16$ and $A = 30°$, find the two possible values of c.

$$\text{Using the sine rule}\quad \frac{a}{\sin A} = \frac{b}{\sin B} = \frac{c}{\sin C}$$

$$\therefore\quad \sin B = \frac{b \sin A}{a} = \frac{16 \sin 30°}{10} = \frac{16 . \frac{1}{2}}{10} = 0{\cdot}8.$$

Since $b > a$, $B > A$ and B may be either acute or obtuse

$\therefore$ either $B = 53{\cdot}13°$ or $B = 180° - 53{\cdot}13° = 126{\cdot}87°$
$\phantom{\therefore \text{ either } }C = 96{\cdot}87°$ $\phantom{\text{ or } }C = 23{\cdot}13°.$

If B is acute, $c = \dfrac{a \sin C}{\sin A} = \dfrac{10 \sin 96{\cdot}87°}{\frac{1}{2}} = 20 \sin 96{\cdot}87° \approx 19{\cdot}9$

If B is obtuse, $c = \dfrac{a \sin C}{\sin A} = \dfrac{10 \sin 23{\cdot}13°}{\frac{1}{2}} = 20 \sin 23{\cdot}13° \approx 7{\cdot}86.$

Hence the two possible values of c are $7{\cdot}86$ and $19{\cdot}9$.

Another proof of the sine rule involves the construction of the circumcircle of $\triangle ABC$. In both diagrams, CD is a diameter of the circle, so that $\angle CBD = 90°$. Using the geometrical properties of a circle, in (1) $\angle D = \angle A$ and in (2) $\angle D = 180° - \angle A$.

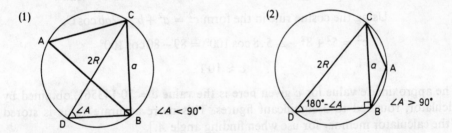

(1) $2R$ a $\angle A$ $\angle A < 90°$ (2) $2R$ a $180° - \angle A$ $\angle A > 90°$

Let R be the radius of the circumcircle of $\triangle ABC$, then using $\triangle BCD$, in (1) $\sin A = a/2R$ and in (2) $\sin A = \sin (180° - A) = a/2R$

$\therefore$ in both cases, $\qquad\qquad \dfrac{a}{\sin A} = 2R.$

By similar arguments it may be shown that

$$\boxed{\frac{a}{\sin A} = \frac{b}{\sin B} = \frac{c}{\sin C} = 2R,}$$

which is an extension of the basic sine rule.

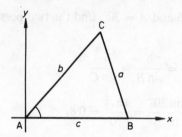
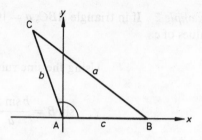

To prove the cosine rule we use Cartesian coordinates and the distance between two points. In both diagrams, the coordinates of B and C are $(c, 0)$ and $(b \cos A, b \sin A)$ respectively,

$$\therefore \quad a^2 = BC^2 = (b \cos A - c)^2 + (b \sin A - 0)^2$$
$$= b^2 \cos^2 A - 2bc \cos A + c^2 + b^2 \sin^2 A$$
$$= b^2 (\cos^2 A + \sin^2 A) + c^2 - 2bc \cos A.$$

Since $\cos^2 A + \sin^2 A = 1$, we have established the *cosine rule*

$$\boxed{a^2 = b^2 + c^2 - 2bc \cos A.}$$

[Note that this proof is valid for an angle A of any magnitude.]

Example 3   Solve the triangle ABC in which $a = 5$, $b = 8$ and $C = 100°$.

Using the cosine rule in the form $c^2 = a^2 + b^2 - 2ab \cos C$,

$$c^2 = 5^2 + 8^2 - 2.5.8 \cos 100° = 89 - 80 \cos 100°$$

$$\therefore \quad c \approx 10 \cdot 1.$$

[The approximate value for c given here is the value $c = 10 \cdot 143561$, obtained by calculator, rounded to 3 significant figures. This more accurate value is stored in the calculator memory for use when finding angle A.]

Using the sine rule, $\dfrac{\sin A}{a} = \dfrac{\sin C}{a}$

$$\therefore \quad \sin A = \frac{a \sin C}{c} = \frac{5 \sin 100°}{c} \quad \text{and} \quad A \approx 29 \cdot 04°.$$

Since $A + B + C = 180°$, $B = 50 \cdot 96°$.

Hence the remaining side and angles of the triangle are $c = 10 \cdot 1$, $A = 29 \cdot 0°$ and $B = 51 \cdot 0°$.

The cosine rule can be rearranged when finding unknown angles:

$$\boxed{\cos A = \frac{b^2 + c^2 - a^2}{2bc}.}$$

Example 4   Solve the triangle ABC in which $a = 8$, $b = 9$ and $c = 10$.

[Since any obtuse angle in the triangle will be opposite the longest side c it may be easier to find angles A and B first.]

Using the cosine rule, $\cos A = \dfrac{b^2 + c^2 - a^2}{2bc}$

$$\therefore \quad \cos A = \frac{9^2 + 10^2 - 8^2}{2.9.10} = \frac{117}{180} = \frac{13}{20} = 0.65.$$

$$\therefore \quad A \approx 49.458°$$

Using the cosine rule, $\cos B = \dfrac{a^2 + c^2 - b^2}{2ac}$

$$\therefore \quad \cos B = \frac{8^2 + 10^2 - 9^2}{2.8.10} = \frac{83}{160} = 0.51875$$

$$\therefore \quad B \approx 58.752°.$$

Since $A + B + C = 180°$, $C \approx 71.790°$.

$\therefore$ the angles of the triangle are $A = 49.5°$, $B = 58.8°$ and $C = 71.8°$.

[Some readers may prefer to find B using the sine rule. However, this does require the use of the approximate or even wrongly calculated value of A. As a check on accuracy, C can also be calculated independently.]

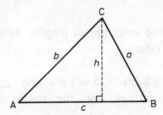

Let $\triangle$ represent the area of $\triangle ABC$ then

$$\triangle = \tfrac{1}{2}ch = \tfrac{1}{2}c.b\sin A$$

$\therefore$ the area of $\triangle ABC$ is $\tfrac{1}{2}bc\sin A$.

To obtain an expression for $\triangle$ in terms of a, b and c we write

$$\sin^2 A = 1 - \cos^2 A = (1 + \cos A)(1 - \cos A).$$

Using the cosine rule it can then be shown that

$$4b^2c^2\sin^2 A = (\{b+c\}^2 - a^2)(a^2 - \{b-c\}^2).$$

Hence $16\triangle^2 = (a+b+c)(b+c-a)(a+c-b)(a+b-c).$

This result is expressed in a more convenient form using the *semi-perimeter* of the triangle, $s = \tfrac{1}{2}(a+b+c)$.

$$\triangle = \sqrt{\{s(s-a)(s-b)(s-c)\}}$$

This is *Hero's†* formula for the area of a triangle.

† *Hero (Heron) of Alexandria* (1st cent. A.D.) Greek mathematician. He invented many machines and demonstrated the law of reflection. The derivation of his formula for the area of a triangle appears in *Metrica*, his most important geometrical work.

Exercise 8.2

In questions 1 to 12 solve the triangle ABC.

1. $A = 60°, B = 50°, c = 5.$ 2. $A = 47°, b = 8, C = 72°.$

3. $a = 5, b = 9, C = 51\cdot2°.$ 4. $a = 2\cdot4, B = 45°, c = 5\cdot1.$

5. $a = 6, b = 8, c = 9.$ 6. $a = 3\cdot6, b = 6, c = 4\cdot8.$

7. $A = 67\cdot3°, a = 10, b = 10.$ 8. $A = 121°, b = 6\cdot9, c = 4\cdot7.$

9. $a = 6\cdot4, B = 23°, C = 54°.$ 10. $B = 55°, b = 12, c = 9.$

11. $a = 15, b = 8, c = 10.$ 12. $b = 6, c = 3, C = 30°.$

13. In triangle ABC, $a = 4$, $b = 5$ and $A = 48°$. Find the two possible values of c.

14. In triangle ABC, $b = 12$, $c = 9$ and $C = 34\cdot3°$. Find the two possible values of a.

15. In triangle XYZ, $\angle X = 108°$, $\angle Y = 25°$ and $XY = 10\,\text{cm}$. Calculate the area of the triangle.

16. A triangle has sides $13\,\text{cm}$, $7\,\text{cm}$ and $5\sqrt{3}\,\text{cm}$. Without using tables or calculators, find the smallest angle of the triangle and the diameter of the circumcircle.

17. The area of a triangle is $10\,\text{cm}^2$. Two of the sides are of lengths $5\,\text{cm}$ and $7\,\text{cm}$. Calculate the possible lengths of the third side.

18. In quadrilateral $ABCD$, $AB = 7\,\text{cm}$, $BC = 8\,\text{cm}$, $CD = 5\,\text{cm}$ and $\angle ABC = 52°$. Given that $ABCD$ is a cyclic quadrilateral, find the radius of its circumscribing circle and the length of AD.

19. In triangle XYZ, $XY = p$, $XZ = q$ and M is the mid-point of YZ. If $\angle MXY = \theta$ and $\angle MXZ = \phi$, prove that $p \sin \theta = q \sin \phi$.

20. With the usual notation for a triangle ABC, prove that $a \cos B + b \cos A = c$.

21. Use the sine rule to prove, with the usual notation, that in triangle ABC,

$$\frac{b-c}{b+c} = \frac{\sin B - \sin C}{\sin B + \sin C}.$$

Deduce that $\tan\frac{1}{2}(B-C) = \dfrac{b-c}{b+c}\tan\frac{1}{2}(B+C) = \dfrac{b-c}{b+c}\cot\frac{1}{2}A$. Use this formula (called the *tangent rule*) to find B and C given (a) $A = 52°$, $b = 7$, $c = 5$, (b) $A = 40°$, $b = 4\cdot4$, $c = 2$.

22. The triangle ABC has incircle of radius r with centre at I. By considering triangles IBC, ICA and IAB, find an expression for the area of triangle ABC in terms of r and the semi-perimeter s. Calculate r given that $a = 5$, $b = 7$ and $c = 8$.

8.3 Problems in two dimensions

The next exercise provides further practice in the use of the sine and cosine rules. Some of the terms used in trigonometry problems are defined below.

(1)   *Bearings*

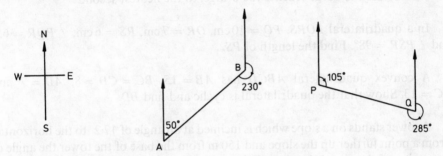

The bearing of B from A is $050°$ or N 50° E and that of A from B is $230°$ or S 50° W.

The bearing of Q from P is $105°$ or S 75° E and that of P from Q is $285°$ or N 75° W.

(2)   *Angle of depression*

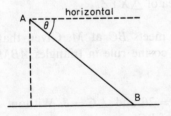

To an observer at A the angle of depression of an object at B is θ.

(3)   *Angle of elevation*

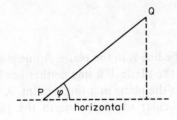

To an observer at P the angle of elevation of an object at Q is ϕ.
   The angle of elevation of the sun is sometimes called the *sun's altitude*.

Exercise 8.3

1.   A ship A is 6·7 km from a lightship on a bearing of 308°. A second ship B is 8·3 km from the lightship on a bearing of 074°. Calculate the distance AB and the bearing of B from A to the nearest degree.

2. A, B and C are three towns. B is 10 km from A in the direction N 51° E. C is 15 km from B in the direction N 64° W. Calculate the distance and the bearing of A from C.

3.   From a barge moving with constant speed along a straight canal the angle of elevation of a bridge is 10°. After 10 minutes the angle is 15°. How much longer will it be before the barge reaches the bridge, to the nearest second?

4.   In a quadrilateral $PQRS$, $PQ = 10$ cm, $QR = 7$ cm, $RS = 6$ cm, $\angle PQR = 65°$ and $\angle PSR = 98°$. Find the length of PS.

5.   A convex quadrilateral $ABCD$ has $AB = 15$, $BC = CD = 8$, $AD = 7$ and $AC = 13$. Show that the quadrilateral is cyclic and find BD.

6.   A tower stands on a slope which is inclined at an angle of 17·2° to the horizontal. From a point further up the slope and 150 m from the base of the tower the angle of depression of the top of the tower is found to be 9·6°. Find the height of the tower.

7. AB is a level straight road 1500 m long. C and D are the bases of two church spires on opposite sides of the road. The angles BAC, ABC, BAD, ABD are 43°, 57°, 29° and 37° respectively. Find the distance between the spires.

8.   The line ABC is the tangent to a circle at the point B. X, Y and Z are points on the circle, such that $\angle ABX = 24°$, $\angle ABY = 63°$ and $\angle CBZ = 51°$. Given that the radius of the circle is 8 cm, find the area of $\triangle XYZ$.

9.   In triangle ABC the median through A meets BC at M. Given that $AB = 8$ cm, $AM = 5$ cm and $AC = 6$ cm, use the cosine rule in triangles ABM and AMC to find BC. Find also $\angle ABC$.

10. In $\triangle ABC$, $AB = 9$ cm, $AC = 12$ cm, $\angle B = 2\theta$ and $\angle C = \theta$. Without using tables or calculators, find $\cos\theta$ and the length of BC.

8.4 Angles, lines and planes

A line is said to lie in a plane if every point of the line is in the plane. A line is said to be parallel to a plane if the line never meets the plane. If a line neither lies in a plane nor is parallel to it, then the line intersects the plane in a single point. A line which is perpendicular to a plane is perpendicular to every line in the plane

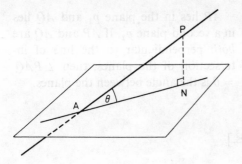

through this point of intersection. In general, a line and a plane intersect as shown in the diagram. If N is the foot of the perpendicular to the plane from a point P on the line, then AN is called the *projection* of AP on the plane. The angle between the line and the plane is defined as the angle θ between the line and its projection on the plane.

Example 1 The prism shown below has three identical rectangular faces. $AD = BE = CF = 12$ cm and the sides of triangles ABC, DEF are each 10 cm long. Find the angle x between the line CD and the plane $ABED$.

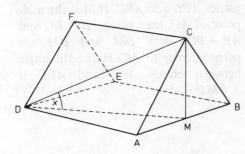

The perpendicular from C to the plane $ABED$ meets the plane at M, the midpoint of AB

$\therefore$ the angle between CD and the plane $ABED$ is $\angle CDM = x$.

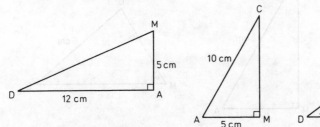

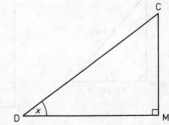

Using Pythagoras' theorem in $\triangle ADM$,

$$DM = \sqrt{(AM^2 + AD^2)} = \sqrt{(5^2 + 12^2)}\,\text{cm} = \sqrt{169}\,\text{cm} = 13\,\text{cm}$$

Using Pythagoras' theorem in $\triangle ACM$,

$$CM = \sqrt{(AC^2 - AM^2)} = \sqrt{(10^2 - 5^2)}\,\text{cm} = \sqrt{75}\,\text{cm} = 5\sqrt{3}\,\text{cm}$$

Hence, in $\triangle CMD$, $\tan x = CM/DM = 5\sqrt{3}/13$ $\therefore$ $x \approx 33.7°$.
The angle between CD and the plane $ABCD$ is $33.7°$.

Two planes are said to be parallel if they do not intersect. Two planes which are not parallel have a line of intersection (or common line) as shown below.

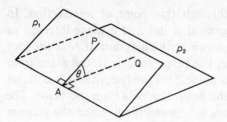

AP lies in the plane p_1 and AQ lies in a second plane p_2. If AP and AQ are *both* perpendicular to the line of intersection of the planes, then $\angle PAQ = \theta$ is the angle between the planes.

[θ is called the *dihedral angle* of the planes.]

Example 2   In a tetrahedron $ABCD$, $AD = BD = CD = 6$ cm and $AB = BC = CA = 8$ cm. Find the angle between the plane ACD and the plane ABC.

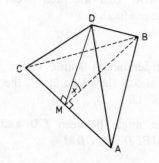

AC is the line of intersection of the planes ACD and ABC. If M is the mid-point of AC, then since $AD = DC$ and $AB = BC$, both DM and BM are perpendicular to AC. Hence the angle between planes ACD and ABC is $\angle BMD = x$.

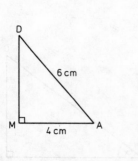
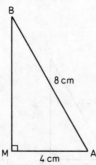
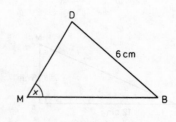

Using Pythagoras' theorem in $\triangle ADM$,

$$DM = \sqrt{(AD^2 - AM^2)} = \sqrt{(36-16)}\,\text{cm} = \sqrt{20}\,\text{cm} = 2\sqrt{5}\,\text{cm}.$$

Using Pythagoras' theorem in $\triangle ABM$,

$$BM = \sqrt{(AB^2 - AM^2)} = \sqrt{(64-16)}\,\text{cm} = \sqrt{48}\,\text{cm} = 4\sqrt{3}\,\text{cm}.$$

Using the cosine rule in $\triangle BDM$,

$$\cos x = \frac{BM^2 + DM^2 - BD^2}{2BM \cdot DM} = \frac{48 + 20 - 36}{2 \cdot 4\sqrt{3} \cdot 2\sqrt{5}} = \frac{32}{16\sqrt{15}} = \frac{2}{\sqrt{15}}$$

$$\therefore \quad x \approx 58 \cdot 9°.$$

Hence the angle between the planes ACD and ABC is $58 \cdot 9°$.

Two straight lines are said to be parallel if they are coplanar (i.e. lie in the same plane) but do not meet. Two lines which are not parallel and which do not meet are called *skew lines*. Skew lines l_1 and l_2 are shown below. The line l_3 is constructed so that l_3 intersects l_2 and is parallel to l_1. The angle between l_1 and l_2 is defined to be the angle θ between l_2 and l_3. BN is drawn perpendicular to the

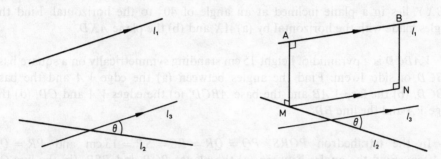

plane containing l_2 and l_3. If M is the point on l_2 such that MN is parallel to l_1, then $ABNM$ is a rectangle. This shows that it is always possible to construct a common perpendicular AM to the two skew lines l_1 and l_2. It can also be shown that AM is the shortest distance between l_1 and l_2.

Example 3 In the prism given in Example 1, find the angle between CD and BE.

Since AD is parallel to BE, the angle between CD and BE is equal to the angle between CD and AD, y.

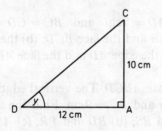

In triangle ACD, $\tan y = \dfrac{10}{12} = \dfrac{5}{6}$,

$$\therefore \quad y \approx 39 \cdot 8°$$

Hence the angle between the skew lines CD and BE is $39 \cdot 8°$.

Exercise 8.4

1. Triangles ABC and XYZ are two faces of a right triangular prism. $AB = AC = XY = XZ = 7$ cm and $BC = YZ = 10$ cm. The plane of each triangle is perpendicular to the edges AX, BY and CZ, which are of length 15 cm. Find the angles between the plane $BCZY$ and (a) the line AY, (b) the plane ABY and (c) the plane AYZ.

2. A triangle PQR lies in a horizontal plane and S is a point vertically above P. Given that $PQ = 5$ cm, $PR = 10$ cm, $RS = 14$ cm and $\angle RPQ = 60°$, find the angles between (a) RS and the plane PQR, (b) the planes QRS and PQR, (c) the lines PS and QR.

3.   A triangle ABC lies in a horizontal plane. The points X, Y and Z are 8 cm vertically above A, B and C respectively. M is the mid-point of YZ. $AB = 5$ cm, $BC = 6$ cm and $\angle ABC = 90°$. Find the angles between (a) the planes AYZ and ABC, (b) the line AM and the plane ABC, (c) the lines AB and XC.

4.   A square $ABCD$ of side 10 cm lies in a horizontal plane. A second square $ABXY$ lies in a plane inclined at an angle of 40° to the horizontal. Find the angles made with the horizontal by (a) AX and (b) the plane AXD.

5. $VABCD$ is a pyramid of height 15 cm standing symmetrically on a square base $ABCD$ of side 16 cm. Find the angles between (a) the edge VA and the base $ABCD$, (b) the face VAB and the base $ABCD$, (c) the edges VA and CD, (d) the edge VA and the line BD.

6.   In the tetrahedron $PQRS$, $PQ = QR = RS = SP = 13$ cm and $PR = QS = 10$ cm. Find the angles between (a) the planes PQR and PSR, (b) the line QS and the plane PSR.

7.   A pyramid $VABCD$ stands on a horizontal square base $ABCD$. The faces VAB, VBC, VCD,VDA are equilateral triangles of side $2a$. Find (a) the height of the vertex V above the base, (b) the angle between the faces VAB and VCD, (c) the angle between the faces VAB and VBC.

8.   Each face of a tetrahedron $ABCD$ is an equilateral triangle of side 6 units. Without using tables or calculators, find (a) the cosine of the angle between any two faces, (b) the perpendicular distance of any vertex from the opposite face.

9.   In a tetrahedron $ABCD$, $AB = AC = AD = 5$ cm and $BC = CD = DB = 8$ cm. Find the angles between (a) the edge AB and the face BCD, (b) the faces ABC and BCD, (c) the faces ABC and ACD, (d) the edge AD and the face ABC.

10. $ABCDPQRS$ is a cuboid on a horizontal base $ABCD$. The vertical edges PA, QB, RC and SD are of length 6 cm. $AB = 8$ cm and $BC = 9$ cm. Find the angles between the following pairs of lines (a) AR and BS, (b) BD and PR, (c) AS and DR, (d) AC and BS.

8.5 Problems in three dimensions

In some problems it is necessary to obtain a general expression connecting the lengths and angles involved.

Example 1   A man at A observes a tower CD due north of him, with height h and angle of elevation α. At a point B, due east of the tower and a distance d from A, the angle of elevation is β. If A, B and C lie in the same horizontal plane, find an expression connecting h, d, α and β.

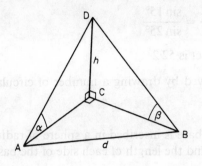

In $\triangle ACD$, $\cot \alpha = \dfrac{AC}{CD} = \dfrac{AC}{h}$

$$\therefore \quad AC = h \cot \alpha.$$

In $\triangle BCD$, $\cot \beta = \dfrac{BC}{CD} = \dfrac{BC}{h}$

$$\therefore \quad BC = h \cot \beta.$$

Using Pythagoras' theorem in $\triangle ABC$,

$$AB^2 = AC^2 + BC^2$$

$$\therefore \quad d^2 = h^2 \cot^2 \alpha + h^2 \cot^2 \beta.$$

Hence the required expression is $d^2 = h^2(\cot^2 \alpha + \cot^2 \beta)$.

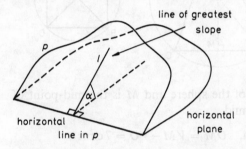

Consider a plane p inclined at an angle α to the horizontal. The diagram shows the plane p and its intersection with a horizontal plane. The inclination to the horizontal of any line l in p which is perpendicular to the line of intersection is α. Since no line in p can be inclined to the horizontal at an angle greater than α, l is called a *line of greatest slope*.

Example 2 On a plane hillside which slopes at an angle $25°$ to the horizontal, there are two straight roads. One lies along a line of greatest slope and the other makes an angle of $15°$ with the horizontal. Find the angle θ at which the roads intersect.

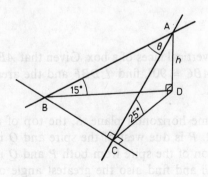

In the diagram AB and AC are segments of the two roads. Their point of intersection A is at a height h above the point D, which lies in the horizontal plane through BC.

In $\triangle ACD$, $\sin 25° = \dfrac{AD}{AC} = \dfrac{h}{AC} \quad \therefore \quad AC = \dfrac{h}{\sin 25°}$

In $\triangle ABD$, $\sin 15° = \dfrac{AD}{AB} = \dfrac{h}{AB} \quad \therefore \quad AB = \dfrac{h}{\sin 15°}$

In $\triangle ABC$, $\cos \theta = \dfrac{AC}{AB} = \dfrac{h}{\sin 25°} \cdot \dfrac{\sin 15°}{h} = \dfrac{\sin 15°}{\sin 25°}$

$\therefore$ the angle θ at which the roads intersect is 52·2°.

Problems involving spheres are often solved by drawing a number of circular sections through the sphere.

Example 3   A right pyramid with a square base is inscribed in a sphere of radius 9 cm. If the height of the pyramid is 16 cm, find the length of each side of the base.

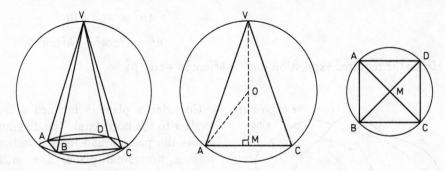

In the diagrams above, O is the centre of the sphere and M is the mid-point of AC, so that VM is the height of the pyramid.

$\therefore$ $AO = VO = 9$ cm, $VM = 16$ cm, $OM = VM - VO = 7$ cm.

Using Pythagoras' theorem in $\triangle AOM$,

$$AM^2 = AO^2 - OM^2 = 9^2 - 7^2 = 81 - 49 = 32.$$

Using Pythagoras' theorem in $\triangle ABM$,

$$AB^2 = AM^2 + MB^2 = 2AM^2 = 64.$$

Hence each side of the base of the pyramid is 8 cm long.

Exercise 8.5

1.   Rectangles $ABED$ and $BCFE$ form two vertical faces of a box. Given that $AB = 20$ cm, $BC = 36$ cm, $AD = 15$ cm and $\angle ABC = 90°$, find $\angle DBF$ and the area of $\triangle DBF$.

2.   Three points P, Q and R lie in the same horizontal plane. S, the top of a church spire, is h metres vertically above R. P is due west of the spire and Q is south-east of the spire. The angle of elevation of the spire from both P and Q is 30°. If the distance $PQ = 300$ m, calculate h and find also the greatest angle of elevation of S from any point on PQ.

3.   A clock rests on a stand so that its face makes an angle of 68° with the horizontal. Find the angle made with the horizontal by the minute hand at (a) 08.10, (b) 07.25.

4.   A straight path up a hillside, which may be considered as a plane at 25° to the horizontal, makes an angle of 53° with a line of greatest slope. Find the angle the path makes with the horizontal. A second path making an angle of 19° with the horizontal cuts the first path. Find the angle between the two paths.

5.   An observer on the ground notes that an aircraft on a bearing of 340° is at a height of 200 m and at an angle of elevation of 45°. The aircraft then travels 400 m due east rising to a height of 300 m. Find the new bearing and angle of elevation of the aircraft.

6.   A small boat is due south of a lighthouse and to an observer at the top of the lighthouse, 40 m above sea level, its angle of depression is 30°. After travelling 200 m on a steady course and passing to the east of the lighthouse, the new angle of depression of the boat is 15°. Find the new bearing of the boat from the lighthouse. Find also the bearing of the boat from the lighthouse at its closest point of approach.

7.   Two pylons 50 m high stand at points X and Y in the same horizontal plane as an observer at Z. The point Y is 100 m due east of X. The bearings of X and Y from Z are S 70° W and S 30° W respectively. Find the angles of elevation of the tops of the pylons from Z.

8.   The triangle ABC lies in a horizontal plane and M is the mid-point of BC. $AM = 5$ m, $AC = 4$ m and $\angle ACB = 90°$. A vertical pole CD of height h metres stands at C. The angle of elevation of D from A is α and the angle of elevation of D from B is β. Given that $\alpha + \beta = 45°$, find h, α and β.

9. A, B and C are three points in a horizontal plane. There are vertical posts AP and BQ at A and B, both of height h. The angles of elevation of P and Q from C are α and β respectively. Angles PCQ and ACB are θ and ϕ respectively. Show that
(a) if $\phi = 90°$, then $\cos \theta = \sin \alpha \sin \beta$,
(b) if $\theta = 90°$, then $\cos \phi = -\tan \alpha \tan \beta$.

10. A, B and C are three points on a plane which slopes at an angle of 30° to the horizontal, B and C being above the horizontal plane containing A. The line of greatest slope through A passes through the mid-point M of BC. $AM = 10$ m, $BC = 16$ m and $\angle AMB = 60°$. Find the lengths of AB and AC. By adding to your diagram a horizontal line through A and lines of greatest slope through B and C, or otherwise, find the angles made by AB and AC with the horizontal plane through A.

11. A right pyramid with a square base is inscribed in a sphere. If the height of the pyramid is 10 cm and the length of each side of the base is 8 cm, find (without using tables or calculators) the radius of the sphere.

Exercise 8.6   (*miscellaneous*)

1.   The points A, B, C and D lie on the circumference of a circle. $AB = 7\,\text{cm}$, $BC = 9\,\text{cm}$, $CA = 5\,\text{cm}$ and AD is a diameter of the circle. Find $\angle ABC$ and the length of CD.

2.   Use the sine rule to prove that if P is a point on the side XZ of $\triangle XYZ$ such that $\angle XYP = \angle PYZ$, then $XP:PZ = XY:YZ$. By letting $\angle XYZ = 30°$, $\angle YZX = 60°$ and $YZ = 2$ units, show that $\cot 15° = 2 + \sqrt{3}$.

3.   The points X, Y and Z lie on a circle with centre O. If $XY = 8\,\text{cm}$, $YZ = 11\,\text{cm}$ and $ZX = 15\,\text{cm}$, find angles XOY, YOZ and ZOX. Find also the radius of the circle.

4.   In the triangle ABC, X, Y and Z are the mid-points of BC, CA and AB, respectively. Using the cosine rule or otherwise, prove that $b^2 + c^2 = 2AX^2 + 2BX^2$. Write down two other similar results, and hence show that $AX^2 + BY^2 + CZ^2 = \frac{3}{4}(a^2 + b^2 + c^2)$.   (JMB)

5.   In each of the following cases find (giving reasons for your answers) the number of triangles ABC satisfying the given conditions and, where possible, find by calculation the value(s) of c, leaving your answers in surd form, if you wish.
(i) $a = 5, b = 3, B = 30°$;   (ii) $a = 5, b = 2, B = 30°$;
(iii) $a = 2, b = 3, B = 30°$;   (iv) $a = 2, b = 3, B = 150°$.   (C)

6.   Construct a flow diagram for finding $\angle ABC$ in triangle ABC given a, b and $\angle BAC = x°$. Your diagram should produce an appropriate output for all cases.

7.   The point P divides the side BC of $\triangle ABC$ internally in the ratio $m:n$. If $\angle B = \theta$, $\angle C = \phi$ and $\angle APC = \alpha$, show that $(m+n)\cot \alpha = n\cot \theta - m\cot \phi$.

8.   Using the usual notation in $\triangle ABC$, prove that
$$\frac{a\cos A + b\cos B}{a\cos B + b\cos A} = \cos(A-B).$$

9.   With the usual notation in $\triangle ABC$, write down an expression for $\cos A$ in terms of a, b and c. Using this result show that $\sin^2 \frac{1}{2}A = \dfrac{(s-b)(s-c)}{bc}$ and $\cos^2 \frac{1}{2}A = \dfrac{s(s-a)}{bc}$ where $s = \frac{1}{2}(a+b+c)$. Hence find expressions for $\tan^2 \frac{1}{2}A$ and the area of the triangle in terms of a, b, c and s.

10.   An isosceles triangle ABC, in which $AB = AC$ and $\angle A = 2\theta$, is inscribed in a circle of radius $5\,\text{cm}$. Prove that the two equal altitudes of the triangle have length $10\cos \theta \sin 2\theta\,\text{cm}$. If the sum of the lengths of the three altitudes is $10\,\text{cm}$, find the three angles of the triangle to the nearest degree.   (O & C)

11. From a point A on level ground due S of a church the angle of elevation of the top T of its steeple is $\beta°$. From a point B on the ground whose distance from A is $2a$ on a bearing of $N\theta°E$ $(0 < \theta < 90)$ the angle of elevation of T is also $\beta°$. Show that the height of T above the ground is $a\sec\theta° \tan\beta°$ and find the bearing of the church from B. If D is the point on AB produced distant a from B show that the distance of D from the steeple is $a\sqrt{(3+\sec^2\theta°)}$ and that the bearing of the church from D is $S(\theta+\phi)°W$, where $\sin\phi = \tan\theta/\sqrt{(3+\sec^2\theta)}$.   (SU)

12. A, B, C are three landmarks. B is $15\,\text{km}$ from A on a bearing of $140°$ and C is $15\,\text{km}$ from B on a bearing of $216°$. An observer on a ship finds that B is directly behind C and that A bears $015°$. After sailing for 30 minutes directly towards A, the observer finds that C bears due east. Find the speed of the ship.

13. A and B are two points on level ground, and B is a metres due east of A; a tower, h metres high, is also on the same level ground. From A, the tower is in a direction $N\theta E$ and from B it is $N\phi W$. From the top of the tower, the angle of depression of A is α and of B is β. Prove the following (in any order):
(i) $h\sin(\theta+\phi) = a\cos\phi\tan\alpha$,
(ii) $\cos\phi\tan\alpha = \cos\theta\tan\beta$,
(iii) $h^2(\cot^2\alpha - \cot^2\beta) - 2ha\cot\alpha\sin\theta + a^2 = 0$.   (SU)

14.

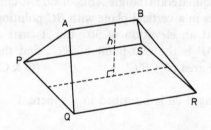

The sketch represents a roof with a horizontal ridge AB at a height h above the (horizontal) ceiling level $PQRS$. $PQRS$ is a rectangle, and AB is parallel to PS and QR. The side of the roof $ABRQ$ makes an angle α with the horizontal, the end APQ makes an angle β with the horizontal, and θ is the angle between AQ and the horizontal. Prove that $\cot^2\alpha + \cot^2\beta = \cot^2\theta$. Prove also that $\cos^2\gamma + \cos^2\delta + \sin^2\theta = 1$, where γ and δ are the angles that AQ makes with PQ and QR respectively.   (SU)

15. A rectangular lamina $ABCD$ has sides $AB = CD = 2a$ and $BC = AD = a$. The mid-point of CD is M and the mid-point of BM is N. The lamina is folded along BM so that the planes BMC and $BMDA$ are at right angles. For this folded figure, find, leaving your answers in surd form if desired, (i) the distance AN, (ii) the distance AC, (iii) the angle ACB, (iv) the tangent of the angle between the planes ADC and ADB.   (O)

16. $ABCD$ is a regular tetrahedron (that is, a triangular pyramid with all its edges equal), and E, F are the midpoints of AB, CD respectively. Find the angles between (i) the planes $ABEF$ and $CDEF$, (ii) the plane $ABEF$ and the line AC, (iii) the lines AC and EF.   (C)

17. A triangle ABC is in a horizontal plane and has $AB = 5$ cm, $BC = 7$ cm and $AC = 8$ cm. The points X, Y and Z are vertically above A, B and C respectively, such that $AX = 10$ cm, $BY = 5$ cm and $CZ = 2$ cm. Find $\angle BAC$ and $\angle YXZ$. If the lines AB and XY, AC and XZ intersect at the points P and Q respectively, show that triangles PAQ and PXQ are isosceles. Find the angle between the planes ABC and XYZ.

18. PTQ is the tangent to a circle at the point T. The points A and B on the circumference of the circle are such that TA and TB make acute angles α and β with TP and TQ respectively. If AB meets the diameter through T at N, prove that $TN = a \sin \alpha \sin \beta / \cos (\alpha - \beta)$, where a is the length of the diameter. If the points C and D on the circumference of the circle are such that TC and TD make acute angles γ and δ with TP and TQ respectively and CD meets the diameter through T at the same point N, prove that $\tan \alpha \tan \beta = \tan \gamma \tan \delta$.   (O)

19. Prove that, for any triangle ABC, with the usual notation and for all values of the angle θ

$$c \sin \theta = a \sin (\theta - B) + b \sin (\theta + A).$$

A quadrilateral $ABCD$ is inscribed in a circle. By applying the above result to the triangle ABC and taking for θ the angle CAD, prove that
$AB \cdot CD + AD \cdot BC = AC \cdot BD.$ (JMB)

20. A road sign is surmounted by a plane equilateral triangle ABC of side 40 cm; its base BC is horizontal and the triangle lies in a vertical plane with BC pointing in the direction N 80° E. The sun is SW at an elevation of 30° and it casts a shadow $A'B'C'$ on a horizontal plane. If M' is the mid-point of $B'C'$, find the length of $A'M'$; hence, or otherwise, find the area of $A'B'C'$.   (O & C)

21. A regular tetrahedron with edges of length $2a$ is inscribed in a sphere. Find the diameter of the sphere.

22. A pyramid has a horizontal square base $ABCD$ of side $2a$. Its vertex V is vertically above the centre O of the base, and the length of VO is $2a$. The line through V perpendicular to the face VAD meets the plane of the base at X. Find (i) the length of VX; (ii) the cosine of the angle between the faces VAB and VAD; (iii) the sine of the angle between the edge VC and the face VAB.   (O)

23. In the region of three fixed buoys A, B and C at sea there is a plane stratum of oil-bearing rock. The depths of the rock below A, B and C are 900 m, 800 m and 1000 m respectively. B is 600 m due east of A and the bearings of C from A and B are 190° and 235° respectively. Calculate (i) the distance BC, (ii) the direction of the horizontal projection of the line of greatest slope of the plane, (iii) the angle this plane makes with the horizontal.   (AEB 1978)

[It may be helpful to consider a horizontal plane at a depth of 900 m.]

9 Vectors

9.1 Introduction to vectors

Some physical quantities, such as temperature, may be completely specified by a number referred to some unit of measurement, e.g. 25°C, 350°F. Such quantities, which have magnitude but which are not related to any definite direction in space, are called *scalar quantities*. Similarly, a number representing the magnitude of some physical quantity is called a *scalar*.

When measuring other quantities, such as wind velocity, it is necessary to give a direction as well as a number and a unit of measurement, e.g. 40 km/h from the north-east. These quantities, which have both magnitude and a definite direction in space, are called *vector quantities*. In general, a *vector* may be described as a number associated with a particular direction in space.

Any vector may be represented by a *directed line segment*, whose direction is that of the vector and whose length represents the magnitude of the vector.

The vector represented here is denoted by **PQ** in bold type (or $\underset{\sim}{PQ}$ in manuscript). The *magnitude* or modulus of the vector is written |**PQ**| or PQ. The directed line segment joining P to Q is denoted by $\vec{PQ}$. However, since it is not usually necessary to distinguish between the line segment and the vector it represents, the notation $\vec{PQ}$ is in common use for both vector and line segment.

The magnitude of a vector is usually positive but may be zero, in which case the vector is called the *zero* or *null vector* and written **0** in bold type. The zero vector is the only vector with indeterminate direction.

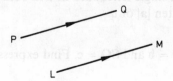

Two vectors are *equal* if they have the same magnitude and direction. Since PQ and LM are parallel and equal in length, **PQ** = **LM**.

175

A *displacement* is one of the simplest examples of a vector quantity. For instance, a car journey from a town A to a town B may be represented by a displacement vector **AB**. Its magnitude is the distance between A and B. Its direction is that of the straight line joining A to B.

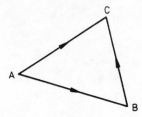

Let us suppose that a man drives from A to B and then from B to C. On another occasion he drives directly from A to C. Since the result of these two journeys is the same, we may write **AB + BC = AC**.

The displacement **AC** is the *sum* or *resultant* of the displacements **AB** and **BC**.

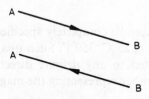

Consider now a journey from A to B, followed by the return journey from B to A. Since the result of these two journeys is a zero displacement, it is reasonable to write, **AB + BA = 0** and **BA = −AB**.

All vectors represented by directed line segments may be manipulated in the same way as displacement vectors. For instance, given any three vectors **AB**, **BC** and **AC** represented by the sides of triangle ABC, we may write **AB + BC = AC**. A vector which has the same magnitude as **AB**, but the opposite direction, is denoted by **BA** or −**AB**.

Example 1   Simplify **EF + FG − HG**.

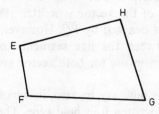

$$EF + FG - HG = EG - HG$$
$$= EG + GH$$
$$= EH.$$

It is often convenient to denote a vector by a single letter such as **a** in bold type (or $\underline{a}$ in manuscript). Its magnitude is then written |**a**| or a.

Example 2   In the given diagram **PQ = a**, **RS = b** and **SQ = c**. Find expressions for **RQ**, **PS** and **PR** in terms of **a**, **b** and **c**.

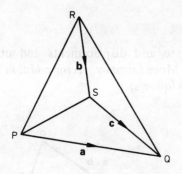

In $\triangle QRS$, $\mathbf{RQ} = \mathbf{RS} + \mathbf{SQ} = \mathbf{b} + \mathbf{c}$

In $\triangle PQS$, $\mathbf{PS} = \mathbf{PQ} + \mathbf{QS} = \mathbf{PQ} - \mathbf{SQ}$
$$= \mathbf{a} - \mathbf{c}$$

In $\triangle PQR$, $\mathbf{PR} = \mathbf{PQ} + \mathbf{QR} = \mathbf{PQ} - \mathbf{RQ}$
$$= \mathbf{a} - (\mathbf{b} + \mathbf{c})$$
$$= \mathbf{a} - \mathbf{b} - \mathbf{c}.$$

In general vectors do not have any definite position in space. However, certain vector quantities may be associated with a particular location. For instance, in mechanics, when considering the motion of an object, it may be necessary to take into account the line of action of a force as well as its magnitude and direction. Equal forces with different points of application may produce different effects. A vector which may be represented by any line segment of the appropriate magnitude and direction is sometimes called a *free vector*.

Exercise 9.1

1. Simplify   (a) $\mathbf{PQ} + \mathbf{QR} + \mathbf{RS}$,   (b) $\mathbf{AB} + \mathbf{DE} + \mathbf{CD} + \mathbf{BC}$,
             (c) $\mathbf{AC} - \mathbf{BC}$,   (d) $\mathbf{XY} + \mathbf{YX}$,
             (e) $\mathbf{MN} - \mathbf{RP} - \mathbf{PN}$,   (f) $\mathbf{QT} - \mathbf{QR} + \mathbf{PR} - \mathbf{ST}$.

2. Given that $ABCDEF$ is a regular hexagon, decide whether the following statements are true or false.
(a) $\mathbf{BC} = \mathbf{EF}$,   (b) $\mathbf{BF} = \mathbf{CE}$,   (c) $|\mathbf{BE}| = |\mathbf{CF}|$,   (d) $|\mathbf{AB}| = |\mathbf{DE}|$,
(e) $\mathbf{AC}$ and $\mathbf{DF}$ are in the same direction,   (f) $\mathbf{AD}$ is parallel to $\mathbf{EF}$.

3. Given that $ABCDPQRS$ is a cuboid lettered so that AP, BQ, CR and DS are edges, decide whether the following statements are true or false.
(a) $\mathbf{PQ} = \mathbf{DC}$,   (b) $\mathbf{BR} = \mathbf{PD}$,   (c) $|\mathbf{RA}| = |\mathbf{BS}|$,   (d) $|\mathbf{PA}| = |\mathbf{CR}|$,
(e) $\mathbf{DQ}$ and $\mathbf{AR}$ are in the same direction,   (f) $\mathbf{AQ}$ is parallel to $\mathbf{CS}$.

4. In the given diagram $\mathbf{AB} = \mathbf{x}$, $\mathbf{BC}$ $= \mathbf{y}$ and $\mathbf{CD} = \mathbf{z}$. Find expressions for $\mathbf{AC}$, $\mathbf{BD}$ and $\mathbf{AD}$ in terms of $\mathbf{x}$, $\mathbf{y}$ and $\mathbf{z}$.

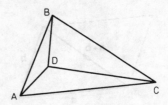

5. In the pentagon $PQRST$ $\mathbf{PQ} = \mathbf{a}$, $\mathbf{QR} = \mathbf{b}$, $\mathbf{ST} = \mathbf{c}$ and $\mathbf{QT} = \mathbf{d}$. Find expressions for $\mathbf{PT}$, $\mathbf{RT}$, $\mathbf{RS}$ and $\mathbf{PS}$ in terms of $\mathbf{a}$, $\mathbf{b}$, $\mathbf{c}$ and $\mathbf{d}$.

9.2 Elementary operations on vectors

In the previous section triangles were used to add displacements and other vectors represented by directed line segments. More formally, *vector addition* is a binary operation defined by the *triangle law*, as follows:

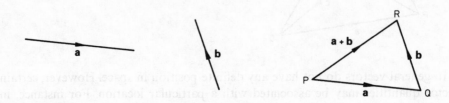

If two vectors **a** and **b** are represented by the sides $\vec{PQ}$ and $\vec{QR}$ of a triangle, then **a** + **b** is represented by the third side $\vec{PR}$.

In physics and mechanics it is sometimes more convenient to use the *parallelogram law* for vector addition, which states:

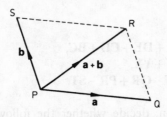

If two vectors **a** and **b** are represented by the sides $\vec{PQ}$ and $\vec{PS}$ of a parallelogram, then **a** + **b** is represented by the diagonal $\vec{PR}$. [Since the line segments $\vec{PS}$ and $\vec{QR}$ are equal in magnitude and direction, the two addition laws are equivalent.]

In $\triangle PQR$ shown above, |**a**|, |**b**| and |**a** + **b**| are represented by the lengths of the sides PQ, QR and PR respectively. For any points P, Q and R we have

$$PR \leqslant PQ + QR.$$

Hence
$$|\mathbf{a} + \mathbf{b}| \leqslant |\mathbf{a}| + |\mathbf{b}|.$$

$[|\mathbf{a} + \mathbf{b}| = |\mathbf{a}| + |\mathbf{b}|$ when P, Q and R are collinear.]

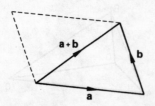 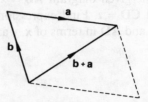

The two diagrams above show that **a** + **b** = **b** + **a**. Thus the *commutative law* holds for vector addition.

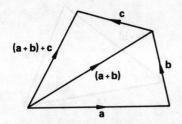

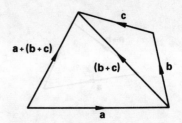

These diagrams show that $(\mathbf{a}+\mathbf{b})+\mathbf{c} = \mathbf{a}+(\mathbf{b}+\mathbf{c})$. Thus the *associative law* holds for vector addition. Hence the sum of a set of vectors is not affected by changes in the order or the grouping of the terms.

The *subtraction* of **b** from **a** may be defined as the address of $-\mathbf{b}$ to **a**, i.e. $\mathbf{a}-\mathbf{b} = \mathbf{a}+(-\mathbf{b})$.

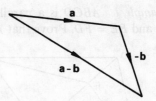

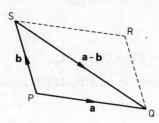

If the vectors **a** and **b** are represented by the sides $\overrightarrow{PQ}$ and $\overrightarrow{PS}$ of a parallelogram, then $\mathbf{a}-\mathbf{b}$ is represented by the diagonal $\overrightarrow{SQ}$.

Scalar multiples of a vector **a**, such as $3\mathbf{a}$ and $-2\mathbf{a}$, can be defined using vector addition. For instance, $3\mathbf{a} = \mathbf{a}+\mathbf{a}+\mathbf{a}$ and $-2\mathbf{a} = -(\mathbf{a}+\mathbf{a})$. This leads to the following more general definition of *multiplication* of a vector by a scalar.

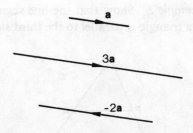

If λ is a scalar and **a** is a vector, then the magnitude of $\lambda\mathbf{a}$ is $|\lambda|$ times the magnitude of **a**, i.e. $|\lambda\mathbf{a}| = |\lambda|a$. The direction of $\lambda\mathbf{a}$ is the same as that of **a** if λ is positive, but opposite to that of **a** if λ is negative.

[*Division* of a vector by a scalar λ (not equal to zero) is defined as multiplication by $1/\lambda$.]

It follows from the associative and distributive properties of real numbers that

$$\lambda(\mu\mathbf{a}) = (\lambda\mu)\mathbf{a} \quad \text{and} \quad (\lambda+\mu)\mathbf{a} = \lambda\mathbf{a}+\mu\mathbf{a}.$$

We obtain a further distributive law by constructing a pair of similar triangles.

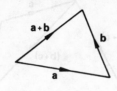
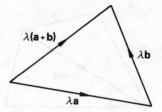

By applying the triangle law of addition to the second triangle, we find that

$$\lambda(\mathbf{a}+\mathbf{b}) = \lambda\mathbf{a}+\lambda\mathbf{b}.$$

We conclude this section with two examples showing vector methods applied to geometrical problems.

Example 1   *ABCD* is a parallelogram. The points *E* and *F* lie on the diagonal *BD* and *BE* = *FD*. Prove that *AECF* is a parallelogram.

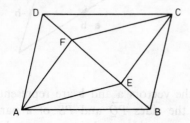

Since *ABCD* is a parallelogram,

$$\mathbf{AB} = \mathbf{DC}.$$

Since *B*, *E*, *F* and *D* are collinear and *BE* = *FD*, $\mathbf{BE} = \mathbf{FD}$.

$$\therefore \quad \mathbf{AE} = \mathbf{AB}+\mathbf{BE} = \mathbf{DC}+\mathbf{FD} = \mathbf{FD}+\mathbf{DC} = \mathbf{FC}.$$

Hence, since *AE* and *FC* are parallel and equal in length, *AECF* must be a parallelogram.

Example 2   Show that the line segment joining the mid-points of any two sides of a triangle is parallel to the third side and equal to half its length.

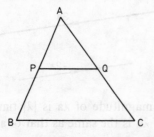

Consider the triangle *ABC*, where *P* and *Q* are the mid-points of the sides *AB* and *AC* respectively.

$$\mathbf{PQ} = \mathbf{PA}+\mathbf{AQ} = \tfrac{1}{2}\mathbf{BA}+\tfrac{1}{2}\mathbf{AC}$$
$$= \tfrac{1}{2}(\mathbf{BA}+\mathbf{AC})$$
$$= \tfrac{1}{2}\mathbf{BC}.$$

Hence *PQ* is parallel to *BC* and half its length.

Exercise 9.2

If **a**, **b** and **c** are displacements of 1 km due east, 2 km due north and 1 km in the direction S 30° W respectively, find the magnitudes and directions of the displacements given in questions 1 to 3. (You may leave your answers in surd form.)

1.   (a) $3\mathbf{a}$,   (b) $5\mathbf{b}$,   (c) $-\mathbf{c}$,   (d) $-\frac{1}{2}\mathbf{b}$.

2.   (a) $2\mathbf{a}+\mathbf{b}$,   (b) $\mathbf{b}+2\mathbf{a}$,   (c) $2\mathbf{a}-\mathbf{b}$,   (d) $\mathbf{b}-2\mathbf{a}$.

3.   (a) $\mathbf{a}+\mathbf{c}$,   (b) $\mathbf{a}+2\mathbf{c}$,   (c) $2\mathbf{a}+\mathbf{c}$,   (d) $\mathbf{a}-\mathbf{c}$.

4.   The diagonals of a parallelogram $ABCD$ intersect at M. If $\mathbf{AB}=\mathbf{p}$ and $\mathbf{AD}=\mathbf{q}$, express in terms of $\mathbf{p}$ and $\mathbf{q}$ the vectors $\mathbf{AC}$, $\mathbf{BD}$, $\mathbf{AM}$ and $\mathbf{MD}$.

5.   In a regular hexagon $ABCDEF$ $\mathbf{AB}=\mathbf{a}$ and $\mathbf{BC}=\mathbf{b}$. Find expressions in terms of $\mathbf{a}$ and $\mathbf{b}$ for $\mathbf{DE}$, $\mathbf{DC}$, $\mathbf{AD}$ and $\mathbf{BD}$.

6.   In the pentagon $PQRST$ $\mathbf{PQ}=\mathbf{a}$ and $\mathbf{RS}=\mathbf{b}$. If $\mathbf{PT}=2\mathbf{RS}$ and $\mathbf{TS}=2\mathbf{PQ}$, find expressions for $\mathbf{PR}$ and $\mathbf{QR}$ in terms of $\mathbf{a}$ and $\mathbf{b}$.

7. $PQRS$ is a parallelogram with $\mathbf{PQ}=2\mathbf{a}$ and $\mathbf{PS}=\mathbf{b}$. The point T is such that $\mathbf{PT}=2\mathbf{b}$. If the lines PR and QS intersect at X and the lines RS and QT intersect at Y, find expressions for the vectors $\mathbf{TR}$, $\mathbf{PY}$, $\mathbf{QY}$ and $\mathbf{XY}$ in terms of $\mathbf{a}$ and $\mathbf{b}$.

8.   Simplify the following expressions, stating which vector property is being used at each stage.
(a) $\mathbf{x}+(\mathbf{y}+\mathbf{x})$,   (b) $(\mathbf{u}-2\mathbf{v})+2(\mathbf{v}-\mathbf{w})$,   (c) $3(\mathbf{p}+\mathbf{q})+4\mathbf{q}$.

9.   Given that $\mathbf{HL}+\mathbf{KN}=\mathbf{KL}+\mathbf{HM}$, show that the points M and N are coincident.

10.   Given that $\mathbf{OA}+\mathbf{OC}=\mathbf{OB}+\mathbf{OD}$, show that the quadrilateral $ABCD$ is a parallelogram.

11.   If $ABCDEF$ is a hexagon in which $\mathbf{AB}=\mathbf{ED}$ and $\mathbf{BC}=\mathbf{FE}$, prove that $CDFA$ is a parallelogram.

12.   If $PQRST$ is a pentagon in which $\mathbf{QR}+\mathbf{RS}=\mathbf{PT}$, prove that $\mathbf{PQ}=\mathbf{TS}$.

13.   In a parallelogram $ABCD$, if M and N are the mid-points of AB and CD respectively, show that $AMCN$ is a parallelogram.

14.   Prove that in any quadrilateral $PQRS$,
(a) $\mathbf{PQ}+\mathbf{RS}=\mathbf{PS}+\mathbf{RQ}$,   (b) $\mathbf{PR}+\mathbf{QS}=\mathbf{PS}+\mathbf{QR}$.

15.   In quadrilateral $ABCD$ the points H, K, L and M are the mid-points of the sides AB, BC, CD and DA respectively. Prove that $HKLM$ is a parallelogram.

16.   Prove that for any vectors $\mathbf{a}$ and $\mathbf{b}$ (i) $|\mathbf{a}-\mathbf{b}| \geqslant |\mathbf{a}|-|\mathbf{b}|$, (ii) $|\mathbf{a}-\mathbf{b}| \geqslant |\mathbf{b}|-|\mathbf{a}|$. Deduce that $|\mathbf{a}-\mathbf{b}| \geqslant ||\mathbf{a}|-|\mathbf{b}||$. Under what conditions does $|\mathbf{a}-\mathbf{b}| = ||\mathbf{a}|-|\mathbf{b}||$?

9.3 Unit vectors and Cartesian components

Resolving a vector into *component vectors* means expressing it as a sum of two or more non-parallel vectors.

Given two non-parallel vectors **a** and **b**, then for any vector **r** in the same plane it is possible to construct a parallelogram in which one diagonal represents **r** and the sides represent scalar multiples of **a** and **b**. For any particular vectors **a**, **b** and **r** there is only one way of constructing this parallelogram. This suggests that there is a unique expression for **r** of the form $\lambda\mathbf{a} + \mu\mathbf{b}$. Thus a vector **r** may be resolved into component vectors, $\lambda\mathbf{a}$ and $\mu\mathbf{b}$, in the directions of any two non-parallel vectors **a** and **b** in a plane containing **r**.

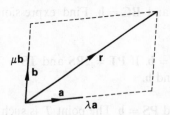
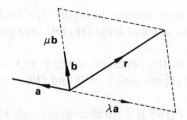

In three-dimensional problems it may be necessary to resolve a vector **r** into component vectors in three given directions. It may be demonstrated that this is possible, provided that the directions are not coplanar, by constructing a parallelepiped with **r** represented by a diagonal.

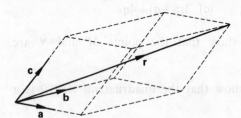

For any vectors **a**, **b** and **c** which are not coplanar, there is a unique expression for **r** of the form $\lambda\mathbf{a} + \mu\mathbf{b} + \nu\mathbf{c}$.

It is often convenient to resolve vectors into component vectors in the directions of the Cartesian coordinate axes. In three-dimensional work the third axis is the *z*-axis, which is constructed perpendicular to the *x*- and *y*-axes to form a *right-handed system*. This means that if we point the thumb of the right hand in the direction of the *z*-axis, then bend the fingers slightly, they will indicate the direction of a rotation from the *x*-axis to the *y*-axis. Two standard ways of drawing these axes are shown below.

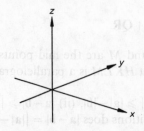
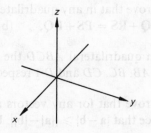

Any vector with magnitude 1 is called a *unit vector*. The unit vectors in the directions of the *x*-, *y*- and *z*-axes are denoted by **i**, **j** and **k** respectively.

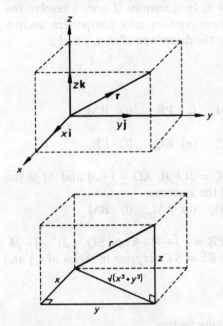

By constructing a cuboid with one diagonal representing **r** and sides parallel to the coordinate axes, we can demonstrate that there is a unique expression for any vector **r** of the form $x\mathbf{i} + y\mathbf{j} + z\mathbf{k}$. The scalars *x*, *y* and *z* are called the *components* of **r** in the directions of **i**, **j** and **k**, or simply the *Cartesian components* of **r**.

Since **i**, **j** and **k** are unit vectors, *x*, *y* and *z* are the lengths of the sides of the cuboid constructed here. Applying Pythagoras' theorem in the two right-angled triangles illustrated, we find that the magnitude of **r** is given by

$$r = \sqrt{(x^2 + y^2 + z^2)}.$$

Example 1 If $\mathbf{a} = 3\mathbf{i} + 2\mathbf{j} + 7\mathbf{k}$ and $\mathbf{b} = 2\mathbf{i} + 4\mathbf{j} - 5\mathbf{k}$, find $|\mathbf{a}|$ and $|\mathbf{a} - \mathbf{b}|$.

$|\mathbf{a}| = \sqrt{(3^2 + 2^2 + 7^2)} = \sqrt{(9 + 4 + 49)} = \sqrt{62}$

$\mathbf{a} - \mathbf{b} = (3\mathbf{i} + 2\mathbf{j} + 7\mathbf{k}) - (2\mathbf{i} + 4\mathbf{j} - 5\mathbf{k}) = \mathbf{i} - 2\mathbf{j} + 12\mathbf{k}$

$\therefore\quad |\mathbf{a} - \mathbf{b}| = \sqrt{(1^2 + \{-2\}^2 + 12^2)} = \sqrt{(1 + 4 + 144)} = \sqrt{149}$.

Since *a* represents the magnitude of a vector **a**, the vector $\mathbf{a}/a$ has magnitude 1 and the same direction as **a**. Thus the unit vector in the direction of a given vector **a** (sometimes denoted by **â**) may be expressed in the form $\mathbf{a}/a$.

Example 2 Find the unit vector in the direction of $\mathbf{a} = 2\mathbf{i} + 2\mathbf{j} - \mathbf{k}$.

$a = \sqrt{(2^2 + 2^2 + \{-1\}^2)} = \sqrt{(4 + 4 + 1)} = \sqrt{9} = 3$

$\therefore\quad$ the unit vector in the direction of **a**

$$= \tfrac{1}{3}(2\mathbf{i} + 2\mathbf{j} - \mathbf{k}) = \tfrac{2}{3}\mathbf{i} + \tfrac{2}{3}\mathbf{j} - \tfrac{1}{3}\mathbf{k}.$$

Exercise 9.3

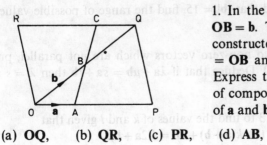

1. In the given diagram $\mathbf{OA} = \mathbf{a}$ and $\mathbf{OB} = \mathbf{b}$. The points *P*, *Q* and *R* are constructed so that $\mathbf{AP} = 2\mathbf{OA}$, $\mathbf{BQ} = \mathbf{OB}$ and *OPQR* is a parallelogram. Express the following vectors as sums of component vectors in the directions of **a** and **b**

(a) **OQ**,   (b) **QR**,   (c) **PR**,   (d) **AB**,   (e) **CQ**,   (f) **OC**.

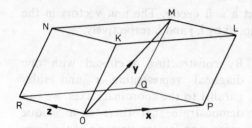

In the parallelepiped shown in the diagram $OP = x$, $OM = y$ and $OR = z$. In questions 2 and 3 resolve the given vectors into component vectors in the directions of of x, y and z.

2. (a) **PQ**.   (b) **RQ**,   (c) **MN**,   (d) **LM**,   (e) **PR**,   (f) **RM**.

3. (a) **ON**,   (b) **KM**,   (c) **OK**,   (d) **NP**,   (e) **KQ**,   (f) **LR**.

4. In quadrilateral $ABCD$, $AB = 2i - j$, $BC = 3i + 4j$, $AD = i + 5j$ and M is the mid-point of CD. Express in terms of **i** and **j** the vectors
(a) **AC**,   (b) **BD**,   (c) **CD**,   (d) **DM**,   (e) **AM**,   (f) **BM**.

5. In tetrahedron $PQRS$, $PQ = 3i - j - k$, $PR = -i + 4j + k$ and $SQ = 3i - 4j - 3k$. The point T lies on RS produced such that $RS = ST$. Express in terms of **i**, **j** and **k** the vectors
(a) **QR**,   (b) **PS**,   (c) **RS**,   (d) **PT**.

6. Find the magnitude of each of the following vectors
(a) $5i - 12j$,   (b) $-i + 2k$,   (c) $8j + 6k$,
(d) $2i + j - 2k$,   (e) $2i - 6j + 3k$,   (f) $-i + 7j - 5k$.

7. Find unit vectors in the direction of
(a) $8i - 4j - k$,   (b) $16i - 8j - 2k$,   (c) $-8i + 4j + k$.

In questions 8 to 10 take $a = i - 2j + k$, $b = 3i - j - k$, $c = i + 3j - 2k$.

8. Find (a) $|a + b|$,   (b) $|a - b|$,   (c) $|2b - 2a|$.

9. Find (a) $|b + c|$,   (b) $|a + b + c|$,   (c) $|5a - b + 3c|$.

10. Find unit vectors in the directions of
(a) $2b - c$,   (b) $5a - 5b + 3c$,   (c) $5a - b + 3c$.

11. If $a = \lambda i - 3j + 3\lambda k$ and $|a| = 7$, find the possible values of λ.

12. Given that $a = 24i - 7j$ and that $|b| = 15$, find the range of possible values of $|a + b|$.

13. Given that **a** and **b** are two non-zero vectors which are not parallel, prove that if $pa = qb$, then $p = q = 0$. Deduce that if $\lambda a + \mu b = sa + tb$ then $\lambda = s$ and $\mu = t$.

14. Use the result of question 13 to find the values of k and l given that
(a) $ka + (1 - k)b = l(a + b)$,   (b) $k(a + b) + 2b = l(2a + b)$.

9.4 Position vectors

Taking a fixed point O as origin, the position of any point P can be specified by giving the vector $\mathbf{OP}$, which is then called the *position vector* of P.

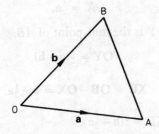

If A and B are two points with position vectors $\mathbf{a}$ and $\mathbf{b}$ respectively, then

$$\mathbf{AB} = \mathbf{AO} + \mathbf{OB} = -\mathbf{OA} + \mathbf{OB} = \mathbf{OB} - \mathbf{OA}$$
$$\therefore \quad \mathbf{AB} = \mathbf{b} - \mathbf{a}.$$

Hence the distance between the points A and B is given by $|\mathbf{b} - \mathbf{a}|$.

Consider now the mid-point M of AB.

$$\mathbf{AM} = \mathbf{MB}$$
$$\Rightarrow \mathbf{OM} - \mathbf{OA} = \mathbf{OB} - \mathbf{OM}$$
$$\Rightarrow \quad 2\mathbf{OM} = \mathbf{OA} + \mathbf{OB}$$
$$\Rightarrow \quad \mathbf{OM} = \tfrac{1}{2}(\mathbf{OA} + \mathbf{OB})$$

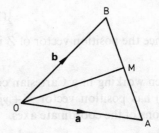

$\therefore$ the position vector of the mid-point of AB is $\tfrac{1}{2}(\mathbf{a} + \mathbf{b})$.

Example 1 Prove that the diagonals of a parallelogram bisect each other.

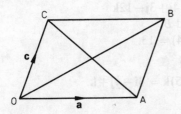

In parallelogram $OABC$, let $\mathbf{a}$ and $\mathbf{c}$ be the position vectors of A and C, then the position vector of the mid-point of AC is $\tfrac{1}{2}(\mathbf{a} + \mathbf{c})$.

By the parallelogram law, $\mathbf{OB} = \mathbf{a} + \mathbf{c}$.
$\therefore$ the position vector of the mid-point of OB is $\tfrac{1}{2}(\mathbf{a} + \mathbf{c})$.
Since the diagonals have the same mid-point, they must bisect each other.

If P is a point on the straight line through given points A and B, then there must exist some scalar t, such that $\mathbf{AP} = t\mathbf{AB}$. It is often helpful to assume a relationship of this form when dealing with collinear points.

Example 2   In the given diagram X and Y are the mid-points of OA and AB respectively. If **a** and **b** are the position vectors of the points A and B, find the position vector of the point Z.

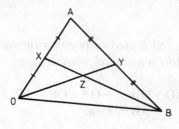

Since X is the mid-point of OA,

$$OX = \tfrac{1}{2}\mathbf{a}.$$

Since Y is the mid-point of AB,

$$OY = \tfrac{1}{2}(\mathbf{a} + \mathbf{b}).$$

$$\mathbf{XB} = \mathbf{OB} - \mathbf{OX} = \mathbf{b} - \tfrac{1}{2}\mathbf{a}.$$

Since Z lies on XB, for some scalar t, $\mathbf{XZ} = t\mathbf{XB} = t(\mathbf{b} - \tfrac{1}{2}\mathbf{a})$.

$\therefore$ $\mathbf{OZ} = \mathbf{OX} + \mathbf{XZ} = \tfrac{1}{2}\mathbf{a} + t(\mathbf{b} - \tfrac{1}{2}\mathbf{a}) = \tfrac{1}{2}(1-t)\mathbf{a} + t\mathbf{b}$.

However, since Z also lies on OY, its position vector $\mathbf{OZ}$ must also be a scalar multiple of $(\mathbf{a} + \mathbf{b})$

$\therefore$ $\tfrac{1}{2}(1-t) = t$ and $t = \tfrac{1}{3}$.

Hence the position vector of Z is $\tfrac{1}{3}(\mathbf{a} + \mathbf{b})$.

When working in a Cartesian coordinate system, the point P with coordinates (x, y, z) has position vector $x\mathbf{i} + y\mathbf{j} + z\mathbf{k}$, where $\mathbf{i}$, $\mathbf{j}$ and $\mathbf{k}$ are unit vectors in the directions of the coordinate axes.

Example 3   The position vectors of points A and B with respect to an origin O are $\mathbf{a} = \mathbf{i} - 2\mathbf{j} + 7\mathbf{k}$ and $\mathbf{b} = 5\mathbf{i} + \mathbf{j} - 5\mathbf{k}$. Find (i) the distance between the origin and the point A, (ii) the distance between the points A and B, (iii) the position vector of the mid-point of AB.

(i)   the distance between the origin and the point A
$= |\mathbf{a}| = \sqrt{(1^2 + \{-2\}^2 + 7^2)} = \sqrt{(1 + 4 + 49)} = \sqrt{54}$.

(ii) $\mathbf{AB} = \mathbf{b} - \mathbf{a} = (5\mathbf{i} + \mathbf{j} - 5\mathbf{k}) - (\mathbf{i} - 2\mathbf{j} + 7\mathbf{k}) = 4\mathbf{i} + 3\mathbf{j} - 12\mathbf{k}$
$\therefore$ the distance between the points A and B
$= |\mathbf{b} - \mathbf{a}| = |4\mathbf{i} + 3\mathbf{j} - 12\mathbf{k}| = \sqrt{(16 + 9 + 144)} = 13$.

(iii)   the position vector of the mid-point of AB
$= \tfrac{1}{2}(\mathbf{a} + \mathbf{b}) = \tfrac{1}{2}(1 + 5)\mathbf{i} + \tfrac{1}{2}(-2 + 1)\mathbf{j} + \tfrac{1}{2}(7 - 5)\mathbf{k} = 3\mathbf{i} - \tfrac{1}{2}\mathbf{j} + \mathbf{k}$.

Exercise 9.4

1.   In a regular hexagon $OABCDE$ the position vectors of A and B relative to O are **a** and **b** respectively. Find expressions in terms of **a** and **b** for the vectors **AB** and **BC**. Find also the position vectors of the points C, D and E.

2.   In a quadrilateral $ABCD$ the point M is the mid-point of the diagonal BD. Given that the position vectors of A, B and C are **a**, **b** and **c** respectively and that

ABCM is a parallelogram, find in terms of **a**, **b** and **c** the vectors **BA**, **BC** and **BM**. Hence find the position vector of the point *D*.

3.   The points *A*, *B*, *C*, *D* have position vectors **a**, **b**, **c** and **d** respectively. Prove that the lines joining the mid-points of opposite edges of the tetrahedron *ABCD* bisect each other and give the position vector of the point of intersection.

4.   Write down, in terms of unit vectors **i** and **j** in the directions of the *x*- and *y*-axes, the position vectors of the points *A*(2, 3), *B*(5, −1) and *C*(4, 4). If *D* is the fourth vertex of the parallelogram *ABCD*, find the vector **AD**. Hence find the position vector and the coordinates of the point *D*.

5.   The points *A* and *B* have position vectors **a** and **b** respectively. In each of the following cases, find the distance between *A* and *B*, the unit vector in the direction of **AB** and the position vector of the mid-point *M* of *AB*.
(a) $\mathbf{a} = 3\mathbf{i} - 5\mathbf{j} - \mathbf{k}$, $\mathbf{b} = \mathbf{i} - \mathbf{j} + 3\mathbf{k}$,
(b) $\mathbf{a} = -7\mathbf{i} + 13\mathbf{j}$, $\mathbf{b} = 5\mathbf{i} - 5\mathbf{j} - 4\mathbf{k}$,
(c) $\mathbf{a} = \mathbf{i} - \mathbf{j} + 3\mathbf{k}$, $\mathbf{b} = \mathbf{i} + 2\mathbf{j} + 2\mathbf{k}$,
(d) $\mathbf{a} = 5\mathbf{i} + 4\mathbf{j} + \mathbf{k}$, $\mathbf{b} = -\mathbf{i} + \mathbf{j} - 2\mathbf{k}$.

6.   Write down in terms of **i**, **j** and **k** the position vectors of the points *A*(2, −1, 5), *B*(0, 2, −1) and *C*(−2, 4, 3). Hence find the length of *AB* and the coordinates of the mid-point of *BC*. Find also the coordinates of the point *D*, given that it is the fourth vertex of the parallelogram *ABCD*.

7.   The points *X*, *Y* and *Z* have position vectors $-2\mathbf{i} + 2\mathbf{j} - 3\mathbf{k}$, $2\mathbf{i} + 4\mathbf{j} - 5\mathbf{k}$ and $-4\mathbf{i} + \mathbf{j} - 2\mathbf{k}$ respectively. By finding **XY** and **XZ**, show that *X*, *Y* and *Z* are collinear.

8.   Use vector methods to show that the points *X*(3, −4, 0), *Y*(−1, 8, −8) and *Z*(6, −13, 6) are collinear.

9.   The points *A*, *B* and *C* have position vectors $\mathbf{a} = -\mathbf{i} + 2\mathbf{j} + 3\mathbf{k}$, $\mathbf{b} = 8\mathbf{i} + 7\mathbf{j} - 9\mathbf{k}$ and $\mathbf{c} = 2\mathbf{i} - 3\mathbf{j} - \mathbf{k}$. Prove that the triangle *ABC* is right-angled and find its area.

10.   The points *A*, *B*, *C* and *D* have position vectors **a**, **b**, 4**b** and $k(\mathbf{a} - \mathbf{b})$ respectively. Find the value of *k* given that
(a) **AD** is parallel to **b**,   (b) **BD** is parallel to **a**,
(c) **CD** is parallel to $\mathbf{a} + \mathbf{b}$,   (d) *A*, *C* and *D* are collinear.

11.   The points *P* and *Q* have position vectors **p** and **q** with respect to an origin *O*. *X* is the mid-point of *PQ* and *Y* is the point on *OX* such that $OY = 2YX$. If *PY* meets *OQ* at *Z*, find expressions in terms of **p** and **q** for **OX**, **OY** and **PY**. If $\mathbf{PZ} = k\mathbf{PY}$ find **OZ** in terms of **p**, **q** and *k*. Deduce that the position vector of *Z* is $\frac{1}{2}\mathbf{q}$.

12.   The points *A* and *B* have position vectors **a** and **b** with respect to an origin *O*.

The points P, Q and R are defined such that $3\mathbf{OP} = \mathbf{OA}$, $3\mathbf{OQ} = 2\mathbf{OB}$, $2\mathbf{PR} = \mathbf{RQ}$ and S is the point of intersection of AB and OR produced. Find the position vector of R. If $\mathbf{AS} = k\mathbf{AB}$ and $\mathbf{OS} = l\mathbf{OR}$, find the values of k and l. Hence write down the position vector of S.

13. The points A, B, P and Q are defined as in question 12. X is the point of intersection of AQ and BP. Y is the point of intersection of AB and OX produced. Find the position vectors of X and Y.

Exercise 9.5   *(miscellaneous)*

1.   Given that $\mathbf{SR} + \mathbf{QT} = \mathbf{SQ} + \mathbf{PT}$, show that the points P, Q and R are collinear.

2.   If P is any point and D, E, F are the mid-points of the sides BC, CA and AB respectively of the triangle ABC, show that $\mathbf{PA} + \mathbf{PB} + \mathbf{PC} = \mathbf{PD} + \mathbf{PE} + \mathbf{PF}$.

3.   In a tetrahedron $PQRS$, if H and K are the mid-points of the edges PQ and RS respectively, show that

$$\mathbf{PR} + \mathbf{QR} + \mathbf{PS} + \mathbf{QS} = 4\mathbf{HK}.$$

4.   (i) In the quadrilateral $ABCD$, X and Y are the mid-points of the diagonals AC and BD respectively. Show that (a) $\vec{BA} + \vec{BC} = 2\vec{BX}$,
$$\text{(b) } \vec{BA} + \vec{BC} + \vec{DA} + \vec{DC} = 4\vec{YX}.$$
(ii) The point P lies on the circle through the vertices of a rectangle $QRST$. The point X on the diagonal QS is such that $\vec{QX} = 2\vec{XS}$. Express $\vec{PX}$, $\vec{QX}$ and $(\vec{RX} + \vec{TX})$ in terms of $\vec{PQ}$ and $\vec{PS}$.   (L)

5.   If $\mathbf{a}$, $\mathbf{b}$ and $\mathbf{c}$ are vectors representing the edges of a parallelepiped, find vectors representing the four diagonals.

6.   In a tetrahedron $OABC$ $\mathbf{OA} = \mathbf{a}$, $\mathbf{OB} = \mathbf{b}$ and $\mathbf{OC} = \mathbf{c}$. The points P and Q are constructed such that $\mathbf{OA} = \mathbf{AP}$ and $2\mathbf{OB} = \mathbf{BQ}$. The point M is the mid-point of PQ. Find, in terms of $\mathbf{a}$, $\mathbf{b}$ and $\mathbf{c}$, expressions for (a) $\mathbf{AB}$, (b) $\mathbf{PQ}$, (c) $\mathbf{CQ}$, (d) $\mathbf{QM}$, (e) $\mathbf{MB}$, (f) $\mathbf{OM}$.

7.   If $\mathbf{a} = 2\mathbf{i} - 4\mathbf{j} + 2\mathbf{k}$ and $\mathbf{b} = 3\mathbf{i} + 4\mathbf{j} - 5\mathbf{k}$, find (a) the magnitudes of $\mathbf{a}$, $\mathbf{b}$ and $5\mathbf{a} + 2\mathbf{b}$, (b) the unit vector in the direction of $\mathbf{a} + 2\mathbf{b}$.

8.   If P and Q are the points with position vectors

$$\mathbf{p} = -\mathbf{i} + 3\mathbf{j} + 2\mathbf{k} \text{ and } \mathbf{q} = \mathbf{i} - 7\mathbf{j} + 4\mathbf{k}$$

respectively, find (a) the distance PQ, (b) the unit vector in the direction of PQ, (c) the position vector of the mid-point of PQ.

9.   Given that $\mathbf{a} = 6\mathbf{i} + (p - 10)\mathbf{j} + (3p - 5)\mathbf{k}$ and that $|\mathbf{a}| = 11$, find the possible values of p.

10. Given that the points A, B and C have position vectors $\mathbf{a} = \mathbf{i} - 2\mathbf{j} + 2\mathbf{k}$, $\mathbf{b} = 3\mathbf{i} - \mathbf{k}$ and $\mathbf{c} = -\mathbf{i} + \mathbf{j} + 4\mathbf{k}$, prove that the triangle ABC is isosceles.

11. In the parallelogram $OPQR$, the position vectors of P and R with respect to O are $6\mathbf{i}+\mathbf{j}$ and $3\mathbf{i}+4\mathbf{j}$ respectively. M and N are the mid-points of the sides PQ and QR respectively. Find (a) the unit vector in the direction of $\overrightarrow{MN}$, (b) the magnitude of the vector $\overrightarrow{OM}$. (L)

12. In triangle OAB, $\mathbf{OA} = \mathbf{a}$ and $\mathbf{OB} = \mathbf{b}$. Points X, Y and Z are constructed so that $2\mathbf{AX} = 3\mathbf{AB}$, $\mathbf{OB} = \mathbf{BY}$ and Z is the point of intersection of OX and AY. If $\mathbf{AZ} = k\mathbf{AY}$, express $\mathbf{OZ}$ in terms of $\mathbf{a}$, $\mathbf{b}$ and k. Show that $\mathbf{OZ}$ is a scalar multiple of $3\mathbf{b}-\mathbf{a}$. Hence find the value of k and the position vector of Z.

13. In a parallelogram $OABC$, M is the mid-point of AB and P is the point of intersection of OM and AC. If the position vectors of A and B with respect to O as origin are $\mathbf{a}$ and $\mathbf{b}$, find the position vector of P.

14. The points $A(3, -2,0)$, $B(-2,5, -4)$ and $C(-1,0,4)$ are three vertices of a rhombus. Use vector methods to find the fourth vertex and the area of the rhombus.

15. Prove that three distinct points A, B, C with position vectors $\mathbf{a}$, $\mathbf{b}$, $\mathbf{c}$ are collinear if and only if there exist non-zero scalars l, m, n such that $l\mathbf{a}+m\mathbf{b}+n\mathbf{c} = 0$ where $l+m+n = 0$. Find the condition that the point with position vector $s\mathbf{a}+t\mathbf{b}$ should lie on the straight line which passes through A and B.

16. In triangle ABC $\mathbf{AB} = \mathbf{p}$ and $\mathbf{AC} = \mathbf{q}$. If G is the point of intersection of the medians of the triangle, find an expression for $\mathbf{AG}$ in terms of $\mathbf{p}$ and $\mathbf{q}$. Use your result to find the position vector of G, given that $\mathbf{a}$, $\mathbf{b}$ and $\mathbf{c}$ are the position vectors of A, B and C respectively.

10 Further differentiation

10.1 Composite functions

If f and g are functions defined on the set of real numbers, such that $f : x \rightarrow u$ and $g : u \rightarrow y$, then the *composite function* gf is defined by writing $gf : x \rightarrow y$. Thus $gf(x)$, the image of x under gf, is obtained by applying f followed by g.

For example, if $f : x \rightarrow x - 2$ and $g : u \rightarrow 3u$, then $f(5) = 3$ and $g(3) = 9$
$\therefore$ $gf(5) = 9$.

In this case a general expression for $gf(x)$ can be obtained by writing $gf(x) = g(u)$, where $u = f(x) = x - 2$. Hence $gf(x) = 3u = 3(x - 2)$, i.e. $gf : x \rightarrow 3(x - 2)$.
[Note that since $gf(x) = g(f(x))$, the function gf may also be described as a *function of a function*.]

Example 1 If $f(x) = x^2$ and $g(x) = x + 1$, find $fg(x)$, $gf(x)$, $f^2(x)$ and $g^2(x)$.

$$fg(x) = f(u) \qquad \text{where} \qquad u = g(x)$$
i.e. $\qquad fg(x) = u^2 \qquad \text{where} \qquad u = x + 1$
$\therefore \qquad fg(x) = (x + 1)^2 = x^2 + 2x + 1.$

Similarly $\qquad gf(x) = g(x^2) = x^2 + 1$
$\qquad\qquad\qquad f^2(x) = ff(x) = f(x^2) = (x^2)^2 = x^4$
$\qquad\qquad\qquad g^2(x) = g(x + 1) = (x + 1) + 1 = x + 2.$

It is sometimes convenient to reverse the process and consider a function as a composite function. If y is a given function of x, then this may be done by expressing y in terms of u, where u is a function of x. For instance, given $y = (2x + 1)^5$, then $y = u^5$ where $u = 2x + 1$.

In general, for a composite function of the form $y = fg(x)$, we may write $y = f(u)$ where $u = g(x)$.

To obtain a rule for differentiating functions of this type, let δx be a small increase in x and let δu and δy be the corresponding increases in u and y.

As δx, δu and δy tend to zero,

$$\frac{\delta y}{\delta x} \to \frac{dy}{dx}, \quad \frac{\delta y}{\delta u} \to \frac{dy}{du} \quad \text{and} \quad \frac{\delta u}{\delta x} \to \frac{du}{dx}$$

$\therefore$ since $\dfrac{\delta y}{\delta x} = \dfrac{\delta y}{\delta u} \cdot \dfrac{\delta u}{\delta x}$ we find that $\boxed{\dfrac{dy}{dx} = \dfrac{dy}{du} \cdot \dfrac{du}{dx}}$.

This formula is known as the *chain rule*.

Example 2 Find $\dfrac{dy}{dx}$ if $y = (2x+1)^5$.

Let $\qquad\qquad y = u^5 \qquad$ where $\qquad u = 2x+1$

then $\qquad\qquad \dfrac{dy}{du} = 5u^4 \qquad\qquad\qquad \dfrac{du}{dx} = 2$

$\therefore \qquad\qquad \dfrac{dy}{dx} = \dfrac{dy}{du} \cdot \dfrac{du}{dx} = 5u^4 \cdot 2 = 10(2x+1)^4.$

Example 3 Find $\dfrac{dy}{dx}$ if $y = \sqrt{\left(1 - \dfrac{1}{x^2}\right)^3}$

Let $\qquad y = \sqrt{(u^3)} = u^{3/2} \qquad$ where $\qquad u = 1 - \dfrac{1}{x^2} = 1 - x^{-2}$

then $\qquad \dfrac{dy}{du} = \dfrac{3}{2} u^{1/2} = \dfrac{3}{2}\sqrt{u} \qquad\qquad \dfrac{du}{dx} = 2x^{-3} = \dfrac{2}{x^3}$

$\therefore \qquad \dfrac{dy}{dx} = \dfrac{dy}{du} \cdot \dfrac{du}{dx} = \dfrac{3}{2}\sqrt{u} \cdot \dfrac{2}{x^3} = \dfrac{3}{x^3}\sqrt{\left(1 - \dfrac{1}{x^2}\right)}.$

A student who is confident that he understands this technique may write down solutions in one of the following ways.

Example 4 Differentiate $\dfrac{1}{1+x^3}$.

Either If $\qquad y = \dfrac{1}{1+x^3} = (1+x^3)^{-1}$

then $\qquad \dfrac{dy}{dx} = -1 \cdot (1+x^3)^{-2} \cdot 3x^2 = -\dfrac{3x^2}{(1+x^3)^2}$

or $\qquad \dfrac{d}{dx}\left(\dfrac{1}{1+x^3}\right) = \dfrac{d}{dx}\{(1+x^3)\}^{-1} = -1 \cdot (1+x^3)^{-2} \cdot \dfrac{d}{dx}(1+x^3)$

$$= -(1+x^3)^{-2} \cdot 3x^2 = -\dfrac{3x^2}{(1+x^3)^2}.$$

This rule can be extended to 'chains' of three or more functions.

Example 5   Find $\dfrac{dy}{dx}$ if $y = \{1+(x^2-1)^3\}^{1/3}$.

Let $\qquad\qquad y = u^{1/3}, \qquad\qquad u = 1+v^3, \qquad\qquad v = x^2-1$

$$\frac{dy}{du} = \tfrac{1}{3}u^{-2/3} \qquad\qquad \frac{du}{dv} = 3v^2 \qquad\qquad \frac{dv}{dx} = 2x$$

$$\therefore \qquad \frac{dy}{dx} = \frac{dy}{du}\cdot\frac{du}{dv}\cdot\frac{dv}{dx} = \tfrac{1}{3}u^{-2/3}\cdot 3v^2 \cdot 2x = 2xv^2/u^{2/3}.$$

Hence $\qquad\qquad \dfrac{dy}{dx} = 2x(x^2-1)^2/\{1+(x^2-1)^3\}^{2/3}.$

The differentiation rule $\dfrac{d}{dx}(x^n) = nx^{n-1}$ can now be proved for negative values

of n, assuming that the rule holds for positive values of n and that

$$\frac{d}{dx}\left(\frac{1}{x}\right) = -\frac{1}{x^2}.$$

Let $\qquad\qquad y = x^n = x^{-m} \qquad$ where m is positive,

then $\qquad\qquad y = u^m \qquad$ where $\quad u = x^{-1}$

$$\frac{dy}{du} = mu^{m-1} \qquad\qquad \frac{du}{dx} = -x^{-2}$$

$$\therefore \qquad \frac{dy}{dx} = \frac{dy}{du}\cdot\frac{du}{dx} = mu^{m-1}\cdot(-x^{-2}) = -mx^{-m+1}\cdot x^{-2}$$

Hence $\qquad\qquad \dfrac{dy}{dx} = -mx^{-m-1} = nx^{n-1}.$

Exercise 10.1

1. If $f(x) = x^2-1$ and $g(x) = 2x+1$, find
(a) $gf(x)$,   (b) $fg(x)$,   (c) $f^2(x)$,   (d) $g^2(x)$.

2. If $f(x) = 2x$, $g(x) = x-1$ and $h(x) = x^2$, find
(a) $fgh(x)$,   (b) $f^2g(x)$,   (c) $hgf(x)$,   (d) $gh^2(x)$.

3. If $f(x) = 2x-3$ and $fg(x) = 2x+1$, find $g(x)$.

4. If $f(x) = x-1$ and $gf(x) = 3+2x-x^2$, find $g(x)$.

5. Express y in terms of u, given that $u = 2x-1$ and
(a) $y = \sqrt{(2x-1)}$ (b) $y = (x-\tfrac{1}{2})^5$
(c) $y = 1/(1-2x)$ (d) $y = x(2x-1)^8$.

Differentiate with respect to x:

6. $(x+3)^6$.   7. $(2x-1)^4$.   8. $(5-3x)^7$.

9. $(3x-2)^{-2}$.   10. $(x^3-1)^5$.   11. $(4-x^2)^{-4}$.

12. $(1+3x)^{1/2}$.   13. $(6x+1)^{-1/3}$.   14. $(3x^2-1)^{5/2}$.

15. $\left(x-\dfrac{1}{x}\right)^{-3}$.   16. $\dfrac{1}{\sqrt{(1-x^2)}}$.   17. $\dfrac{1}{(1+\sqrt{x})^2}$.

18. Find the gradient of the curve $y=(2x^2-1)^3$ at the point where $x=-1$. Hence find the equation of the tangent to the curve at this point.

19. Find the equation of the tangent to the curve $y=\sqrt{\left(1+\dfrac{6}{x}\right)}$ at the point where $x=2$.

20. A particle moves along a straight line so that after t seconds its displacement, s metres, from a fixed point on the line is given by $s^3=3t-2$. Find the velocity and acceleration of the particle when $t=1$.

21. An object moves along a straight line such that after t seconds its velocity is $v\,\mathrm{ms}^{-1}$, where $v=t+4/(t+1)$. Find an expression for its acceleration after t seconds. Find also the minimum speed of the object during its motion.

22. Differentiate the following functions with respect to x by substituting $u=x+1$.

(a) $x(x+1)^5$,   (b) $\dfrac{x-1}{x+1}$,   (c) $\dfrac{x}{\sqrt{(x+1)}}$.

23. Differentiate with respect to x:

(a) $\sqrt{\{(2x-3)^4-1\}}$,   (b) $\dfrac{1}{4+\sqrt{(4x^2+1)}}$.

24. Find the turning points on the curve $y=x(5-x)^4$ and determine their nature. Sketch the curve.

25. Find any turning points on the curve $y=4/(x^2-2x+5)$ and show that the x-axis is an asymptote to the curve. Hence sketch the curve.

10.2 Functions defined implicitly

In previous sections we have considered functions defined explicitly by equations of the form $y=f(x)$. Sometimes a function $f:x\rightarrow y$ is defined *implicitly* using an equation such as $x^2+2y-y^2=5$.

   [Note that since a function is a rule assigning one and only one value of y to every value of x, restrictions on the values of x and y are often required to complete such a definition.

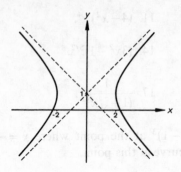

The sketch of the curve $x^2 + 2y - y^2 = 5$ shows that in this case possible restrictions would be $|x| > 2$, $y > 1$. However, in general an expression for dy/dx can be obtained without considering such restrictions.]

Given $x^2 + 2y - y^2 = 5$, dy/dx is found by differentiating both sides of the equation with respect to x.

$$\frac{d}{dx}(x^2) = 2x, \quad \frac{d}{dx}(2y) = 2\frac{dy}{dx}, \quad \frac{d}{dx}(5) = 0.$$

The derivative of y^2 is obtained using the chain rule:

$$\frac{d}{dx}(y^2) = \frac{d}{dy}(y^2) \cdot \frac{dy}{dx} = 2y\frac{dy}{dx}.$$

Thus $x^2 + 2y - y^2 = 5 \Rightarrow 2x + 2\frac{dy}{dx} - 2y\frac{dy}{dx} = 0$

$$\Rightarrow \quad \frac{dy}{dx} - y\frac{dy}{dx} = -x$$

$\therefore$ provided that $y \neq 1$, $\dfrac{dy}{dx} = \dfrac{x}{y-1}$.

Example 1   Given that $(x+1)^2 + (y-2)^2 = 1$, find $\dfrac{dy}{dx}$.

Differentiating with respect to x:

$$2(x+1) + 2(y-2)\frac{dy}{dx} = 0$$

$\therefore$ $(y-2)\dfrac{dy}{dx} = -(x+1)$.

Hence provided that $y \neq 2$ $\dfrac{dy}{dx} = -\dfrac{x+1}{y-2}$.

Example 2   Find the gradient of the curve $x^3 + y^3 = 4y^2$ at the point $(2, 2)$.

Differentiating with respect to x: $3x^2 + 3y^2\dfrac{dy}{dx} = 8y\dfrac{dy}{dx}$

Substituting $x = 2$, $y = 2$: $12 + 12\dfrac{dy}{dx} = 16\dfrac{dy}{dx}$

$$\therefore \quad \frac{dy}{dx} = 3$$

Hence at the point $(2, 2)$ the gradient of the curve is 3.

Using this approach it may be proved that if $\dfrac{d}{dx}(x^n) = nx^{n-1}$ for integral values of n, then the result also holds for fractional values of the form $n = p/q$, where p and q are integers.

Let $y = x^n = x^{p/q}$ then $y^q = x^p$.

Differentiating with respect to x, $qy^{q-1}\dfrac{dy}{dx} = px^{p-1}$

$$\therefore \quad \frac{dy}{dx} = \frac{px^{p-1}}{qy^{q-1}} = \frac{px^p y}{qxy^q} = \frac{px^p x^n}{qx \cdot x^p} = nx^{n-1}.$$

Given an equation connecting x and y, dy/dx is a measure of the rate of change of y as x increases. Similarly dx/dy is the rate of change of x as y increases. To establish the relationship between these derivatives, let δx and δy be corresponding small increases in x and y, then $\dfrac{\delta y}{\delta x} \cdot \dfrac{\delta x}{\delta y} = 1$.

As $\delta x \to 0$, $\delta y \to 0$, $\dfrac{\delta y}{\delta x} \to \dfrac{dy}{dx}$ and $\dfrac{\delta x}{\delta y} \to \dfrac{dx}{dy}$

$$\therefore \quad \frac{dy}{dx} \cdot \frac{dx}{dy} = 1 \quad \text{so that} \quad \frac{dx}{dy} = 1 \bigg/ \frac{dy}{dx}.$$

Consider, for example, the relation $x^2 - y = 0$ for positive values of x and y.

$$y = x^2 \qquad \text{and} \qquad x = y^{1/2}$$

$$\frac{dy}{dx} = 2x \qquad\qquad \frac{dx}{dy} = \tfrac{1}{2}y^{-1/2} = \frac{1}{2x}$$

$$\frac{d^2 y}{dx^2} = 2 \qquad\qquad \frac{d^2 x}{dy^2} = -\frac{1}{4}y^{-3/2} = -\frac{1}{4x^3}$$

Hence $\dfrac{dx}{dy} = 1 \bigg/ \dfrac{dy}{dx}$ but $\dfrac{d^2 x}{dy^2} \neq 1 \bigg/ \dfrac{d^2 y}{dx^2}$.

Thus although it is tempting to think of derivatives such as dy/dx as fractions, higher derivatives clearly do *not* behave like fractions.

Exercise 10.2

Find $\dfrac{dy}{dx}$ in terms of x and y when

1. $y^2 = 6x$.   2. $x^2 + y^2 = 5$.   3. $4x^2 + y^2 = 4$.

4. $y^3 = x^2 + 1$. 　　5. $(y-1)^2 = 2x$. 　　6. $3y^2 = x(x^2 - 3)$.

7. $x^2 + y^2 - 2x + y + 1 = 0$ 　　8. $(x+y)^3 = 3x + 5$.

9. Find the gradient of the curve $(x-3)^2 + (y+4)^2 = 5$ at the point $(1, -3)$.

10. Find the gradient of the curve $y(y+2) = 4x - 1$ at each of the points on it where $x = 4$.

11. Find the equation of the tangent to the curve $y^2 = 3x + 1$ at the point $(1, -2)$.

12. Find the equation of the tangent to the curve $x^2 - y^2 = 9$ at the point $(5, 4)$.

13. Find the x-coordinates of the stationary points on the curve $x^3 + 4x^2 + 3y^2 + 5x - 2 = 0$.

14. Find the coordinates of the stationary points on the curve $x^2 + y^2 - 6x - 8y = 0$.

10.3 Products and quotients

Consider a function of x, y, which can be expressed as a product of two other functions of x, u and v. Let δx be a small increase in x and let δu, δv and δy be the corresponding small increases in u, v and y, then

$$y = uv$$
$$\Rightarrow \quad y + \delta y = (u + \delta u)(v + \delta v) = uv + u\delta v + v\delta u + \delta u \delta v$$
$$\Rightarrow \quad \delta y = u\delta v + v\delta u + \delta u \delta v$$
$$\Rightarrow \quad \frac{\delta y}{\delta x} = u\frac{\delta v}{\delta x} + v\frac{\delta u}{\delta x} + \delta u\frac{\delta v}{\delta x}.$$

As $\delta x \to 0$, $\delta u \to 0$, $\dfrac{\delta y}{\delta x} \to \dfrac{dy}{dx}, \dfrac{\delta u}{\delta x} \to \dfrac{du}{dx}, \dfrac{\delta v}{\delta x} \to \dfrac{dv}{dx}$

$$\therefore \quad \boxed{\frac{dy}{dx} = u\frac{dv}{dx} + v\frac{du}{dx}.}$$

Example 1　Find $\dfrac{dy}{dx}$ if $y = (x^2 + 4)(x^5 + 7)$.

Let $y = uv$ where $u = x^2 + 4$ 　$v = x^5 + 7$

$$\frac{du}{dx} = 2x \qquad \frac{dv}{dx} = 5x^4$$

$$\therefore \quad \frac{dy}{dx} = u\frac{dv}{dx} + v\frac{du}{dx} = (x^2+4).5x^4 + (x^5+7).2x = 5x^6 + 20x^4 + 2x^6 + 14x$$

$$\therefore \quad \frac{dy}{dx} = 7x^6 + 20x^4 + 14x.$$

Clearly, this result could have been obtained by writing $y = x^7 + 4x^5 + 7x^2 + 28$, then differentiating. The next two examples show how the product rule and the chain rule can be used together to differentiate more complicated functions.

Example 2   Find $\dfrac{dy}{dx}$ if $y = (x^2 - 1)^3 (3x+1)^4$.

Let $u = (x^2 - 1)^3$ $v = (3x+1)^4$

then $\dfrac{du}{dx} = 3(x^2-1)^2 . 2x$ $\dfrac{dv}{dx} = 4(3x+1)^3 . 3$

$\qquad\quad = 6x(x^2-1)^2$ $\qquad = 12(3x+1)^3.$

$$\therefore \quad \frac{dy}{dx} = u\frac{dv}{dx} + v\frac{du}{dx} = (x^2-1)^3 . 12(3x+1)^3 + (3x+1)^4 . 6x(x^2-1)^2$$

$$= 6(x^2-1)^2 (3x+1)^3 \{2(x^2-1) + x(3x+1)\}$$

$$= 6(x^2-1)^2 (3x+1)^3 (5x^2 + x - 2).$$

Example 3   Find $\dfrac{dy}{dx}$ if $y = (x+4)\sqrt{(x^2-1)}$.

Let $u = x+4$ $v = \sqrt{(x^2-1)} = (x^2-1)^{1/2}$

$\dfrac{du}{dx} = 1$ $\dfrac{dv}{dx} = \frac{1}{2}(x^2-1)^{-1/2} . 2x = \dfrac{x}{\sqrt{(x^2-1)}}$

$$\therefore \quad \frac{dy}{dx} = u\frac{dv}{dx} + v\frac{du}{dx} = (x+4).\frac{x}{\sqrt{(x^2-1)}} + \sqrt{(x^2-1)}.1$$

$$= \frac{x(x+4)}{\sqrt{(x^2-1)}} + \frac{x^2-1}{\sqrt{(x^2-1)}}$$

$$= (2x^2 + 4x - 1)/\sqrt{(x^2-1)}.$$

Consider now a quotient, $y = u/v$, where u and v are functions of x. Let δx be a small increase in x and let δu, δv and δy be the corresponding small increases in u, v and y, then

$$y = \frac{u}{v}$$

$$\Rightarrow \quad y + \delta y = \frac{u + \delta u}{v + \delta v}$$

$$\Rightarrow \quad \delta y = \frac{u + \delta u}{v + \delta v} - \frac{u}{v} = \frac{v(u + \delta u) - u(v + \delta v)}{v(v + \delta v)} = \frac{v\delta u - u\delta v}{v(v + \delta v)}$$

$$\Rightarrow \quad \frac{\delta y}{\delta x} = \frac{v\dfrac{\delta u}{\delta x} - u\dfrac{\delta v}{\delta x}}{v(v + \delta v)}.$$

As $\delta x \to 0$, $\delta v \to 0$, $\dfrac{\delta y}{\delta x} \to \dfrac{dy}{dx}$, $\dfrac{\delta u}{\delta x} \to \dfrac{du}{dx}$ and $\dfrac{\delta v}{\delta x} \to \dfrac{dv}{dx}$

$$\therefore \frac{dy}{dx} = \frac{v\dfrac{du}{dx} - u\dfrac{dv}{dx}}{v^2}.$$

Example 4   Find $\dfrac{dy}{dx}$ if $y = \dfrac{x}{x+1}$.

Method 1 using the quotient rule:

Let $y = \dfrac{u}{v}$ where $u = x$ $\qquad\qquad$ $v = x+1$

$$\frac{du}{dx} = 1 \qquad\qquad \frac{dv}{dx} = 1$$

$$\therefore \quad \frac{dy}{dx} = \frac{v\dfrac{du}{dx} - u\dfrac{dv}{dx}}{v^2} = \frac{(x+1).1 - x.1}{(x+1)^2} = \frac{x+1-x}{(x+1)^2} = \frac{1}{(x+1)^2}.$$

Method 2 using the product rule:

Let $y = uv$ where $u = x$ $\qquad\qquad$ $v = (x+1)^{-1}$

$$\frac{du}{dx} = 1 \qquad\qquad \frac{dv}{dx} = -1.(x+1)^{-2}.1$$

$$= -1/(x+1)^2$$

$$\therefore \quad \frac{dy}{dx} = u\frac{dv}{dx} + v\frac{du}{dx} = x.\frac{-1}{(x+1)^2} + \frac{1}{(x+1)}.1$$

$$= \frac{-x+(x+1)}{(x+1)^2} = \frac{1}{(x+1)^2}$$

Example 5   Find $\dfrac{dy}{dx}$ if $y = \sqrt{\left(\dfrac{x+1}{x^2+1}\right)}$.

$$y = \sqrt{\left(\frac{x+1}{x^2+1}\right)} \qquad y^2 = \frac{x+1}{x^2+1}.$$

Differentiating: $$2y\frac{dy}{dx} = \frac{(x^2+1).1 - (x+1).2x}{(x^2+1)^2}$$

$$\therefore \quad \frac{dy}{dx} = \frac{1}{2y}.\frac{(x^2+1-2x^2-2x)}{(x^2+1)^2} = \left(\frac{x^2+1}{x+1}\right)^{1/2}.\frac{(1-2x-x^2)}{2(x^2+1)^2}.$$

Hence $$\frac{dy}{dx} = \frac{1-2x-x^2}{2(x+1)^{1/2}(x^2+1)^{3/2}}.$$

[This function can also be differentiated by writing $y = \sqrt{u}$ where $u = (x+1)/(x^2+1)$ and using the chain rule.]

The next two examples show the use of the product formula when y is an implicit function of x.

Example 6   Find $\dfrac{dy}{dx}$ if $y^3 - xy^2 - x^3 = 1$.

Differentiating with respect to x:

$$\frac{d}{dx}(y^3) - \frac{d}{dx}(xy^2) - \frac{d}{dx}(x^3) = 0$$

$$3y^2\frac{dy}{dx} - \left(x \cdot 2y\frac{dy}{dx} + y^2 \cdot 1\right) - 3x^2 = 0$$

$$(3y^2 - 2xy)\frac{dy}{dx} - y^2 - 3x^2 = 0$$

$$\therefore \quad \frac{dy}{dx} = \frac{3x^2 + y^2}{3y^2 - 2xy}.$$

Example 7   If $y^3 + x^3 = 3x + 7$ show that

$$y^2\frac{d^2y}{dx^2} + 2y\left(\frac{dy}{dx}\right)^2 + 2x = 0.$$

Differentiating with respect to x: $3y^2\dfrac{dy}{dx} + 3x^2 = 3$

$$\therefore \quad y^2\frac{dy}{dx} + x^2 = 1.$$

Differentiating again with respect to x:

$$y^2\frac{d}{dx}\left(\frac{dy}{dx}\right) + \frac{dy}{dx} \cdot \frac{d}{dx}(y^2) + 2x = 0$$

$$y^2\frac{d^2y}{dx^2} + \frac{dy}{dx} \cdot 2y\frac{dy}{dx} + 2x = 0$$

$$\therefore \quad y^2\frac{d^2y}{dx^2} + 2y\left(\frac{dy}{dx}\right)^2 + 2x = 0.$$

Exercise 10.3

Differentiate the following with respect to x, simplifying your answers when possible.

1. $(x+3)(x^4-1)$.

2. $(x-1)(x^2+x-6)$.

3. $(3x^2-1)(2-5x^3)$.

4. $(x^2-2)(x^2+2+1/x^2)$.

5. $x^2(x+3)^3$.

6. $x(3x-1)^5$.

7. $(x+1)^2(x+2)^5$.

8. $(2x+3)^3(1-x)^4$.

9. $x^2\sqrt{(1+x^2)}$.

10. $(x+3)\sqrt{(1-x^3)}$.

11. $\dfrac{x-2}{x+2}$.

12. $\dfrac{x^2}{2x+1}$.

13. $\dfrac{x+3}{2-3x}$.

14. $\dfrac{x^2+1}{x^3+1}$.

15. $\dfrac{x^2-2}{x^2+1}$.

16. $\dfrac{x^2+x-1}{1-x^2}$.

17. $\dfrac{x^2-2}{(x+2)^2}$.

18. $\dfrac{x^2}{(x-1)^3}$.

19. $\dfrac{(2x+1)^2}{(4x+3)^3}$.

20. $\dfrac{x}{\sqrt{(1-x^2)}}$.

21. $\dfrac{x^3}{\sqrt{(1-2x^2)}}$.

22. $\dfrac{\sqrt{(x^2+4)}}{x+1}$.

23. $\left(\dfrac{x-1}{2-x}\right)^2$.

24. $\sqrt{\left(\dfrac{2x}{x-1}\right)}$.

25. $\sqrt{\left(\dfrac{1+x^2}{x}\right)}$.

26. Find $\dfrac{dy}{dx}$ in terms of x and y, given that (a) $x^2-xy+y^2 = 1$, (b) $x^2y+y^3 = 4$, (c) $x^2+y^2-6xy+3x-2y+5 = 0$.

27. Find the gradient of the curve $x^2+2xy-2y^2+x = 2$ at the point $(-4, 1)$.

28. Find the equation of the tangent to the curve $(x+1)y^2 = x-2$ at the point $(-2, 2)$.

29. Find $\dfrac{d^2y}{dx^2}$ given that

(a) $y = \dfrac{1}{x^2+1}$,

(b) $y = \dfrac{x}{x-1}$,

(c) $y = \sqrt{(x^2+1)}$.

30. Differentiate the following with respect to x

(a) $\dfrac{(x^2+1)(x-1)^2}{2x-1}$,

(b) $\dfrac{x\sqrt{(x-1)}}{x+1}$,

(c) $\sqrt{\left\{\dfrac{x^3+1}{(x+1)^3}\right\}}$.

31. If $x^2-y^2 = 1$, prove that $y\dfrac{d^2y}{dx^2}+\left(\dfrac{dy}{dx}\right)^2 = 1$.

32. Find the values of $\dfrac{dy}{dx}$ and $\dfrac{d^2y}{dx^2}$ at the point $(1, 3)$ on the curve $3x^2+y^2 = 4y$.

33. If $y = \sqrt{\left(\dfrac{6x}{x+2}\right)}$, find the values of $\dfrac{dy}{dx}$ and $\dfrac{d^2y}{dx^2}$ when $x = 4$.

34. If $y^2 - 2xy = 2x$, prove that $(x-y)\dfrac{d^2y}{dx^2} + 2\dfrac{dy}{dx} = \left(\dfrac{dy}{dx}\right)^2$.

10.4 Maxima and minima

In Chapter 5 it was shown that maximum and minimum points on a curve $y = f(x)$ can be found by examining points at which $dy/dx = 0$. Thus any maximum or minimum values of the function $f(x)$ occur when $f'(x) = 0$. The nature of such stationary values is determined either by studying the behaviour of $f'(x)$ or by finding the sign of the second derivative $f''(x)$.

Example 1   Find the maximum and minimum values of the function $f(x) = \dfrac{4x}{x^2 + 4}$ and sketch its graph.

Differentiating, $f'(x) = \dfrac{4\{(x^2+4).1 - x.2x\}}{(x^2+4)^2} = \dfrac{4(4-x^2)}{(x^2+4)^2}$

$$f'(x) = 0 \Leftrightarrow 4 - x^2 = 0 \Leftrightarrow x = -2 \quad \text{or} \quad x = 2.$$

When x is just less than -2, $f'(x) < 0$ and when x is just greater than -2, $f'(x) > 0$
$\therefore$ when $x = -2$, $f(x)$ takes the minimum value $f(-2) = -1$.
When x is just less than 2, $f'(x) > 0$ and when x is just greater than 2, $f'(x) < 0$
$\therefore$ when $x = 2$, $f(x)$ takes the maximum value $f(2) = 1$.

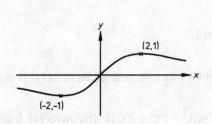

Hence the curve $y = \dfrac{4x}{x^2+4}$ has a minimum point $(-2, -1)$ and a maximum point $(2, 1)$. The curve cuts the axes only at the origin. As $x \to \infty$, $y \to 0$ from above and as $x \to -\infty$, $y \to 0$ from below,
$\therefore$ the x-axis is an asymptote to the curve.

These methods can also be applied to finding maximum and minimum values in practical problems.

Example 2   A carton of volume $V\,\text{m}^3$ is made from a piece of cardboard as shown below. If the area of cardboard used is $6\,\text{m}^3$, find expressions for h and V in terms of x and the value of x which produces a box of maximum volume.

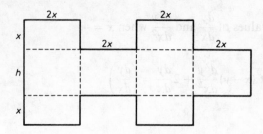 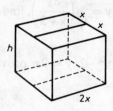

The area of cardboard used $= (4.2x.h + 4.2x.x)\,\text{m}^2$
$$= 8x(h+x)\,\text{m}^2$$

$\therefore$ $8x(h+x) = 6$ and $h+x = 6/8x = 3/4x$

$\therefore$ in terms of x, $h = \dfrac{3}{4x} - x$.

The volume of the box $= V\,\text{m}^3 = 4hx^2\,\text{m}^3$

$\therefore$ in terms of x, $V = 4x^2 \left(\dfrac{3}{4x} - x \right) = 3x - 4x^3$.

Differentiating with respect to x,

$$\frac{dV}{dx} = 3 - 12x^2, \quad \frac{d^2V}{dx^2} = -24x$$

$\dfrac{dV}{dx} = 0 \Leftrightarrow 3 - 12x^2 = 0 \Leftrightarrow x^2 = \tfrac{1}{4}$

$\therefore$ the only positive value of x for which $\dfrac{dV}{dx} = 0$ is $x = \tfrac{1}{2}$.

When $x = \tfrac{1}{2}$, $\dfrac{d^2V}{dx^2} < 0$ and $V = 1$

$\therefore$ $x = \tfrac{1}{2}$ gives a maximum value for V of 1.

It is important to note the greatest value of a function in a given interval is not always a 'maximum value'.

Example 3   Find the greatest value of $y = x^3 - 5x^2 + 7x$ in the interval from $x = 0$ to $x = 4$.

Differentiating, $\dfrac{dy}{dx} = 3x^2 - 10x + 7 = (3x-7)(x-1)$

$$\frac{d^2y}{dx^2} = 6x - 10$$

$\dfrac{dy}{dx} = 0 \Leftrightarrow (3x-7)(x-1) = 0 \Leftrightarrow x = 1 \text{ or } x = 2\tfrac{1}{3}$

When $x = 1$, $\dfrac{d^2y}{dx^2} < 0$ $\therefore$ y takes a maximum value.

When $x = 2\tfrac{1}{3}$, $\dfrac{d^2y}{dx^2} > 0$ $\therefore$ y takes a minimum value.

However, in the interval from $x = 2\tfrac{1}{3}$ to $x = 4$, dy/dx is positive, so that the value of y must be increasing.

When $x = 1$, $y = 1 - 5 + 7 = 3$.

When $x = 4$, $y = 64 - 80 + 28 = 12$.

Hence although the function has a 'local' maximum value of 3 when $x = 1$, its greatest value in the interval $x = 0$ to $x = 4$ is 12.

Exercise 10.4

In questions 1 to 6 find any maximum or minimum values of the given function and sketch its graph.

1. $(2x - 5)^4$.

2. $x(x + 4)^3$.

3. $x^2(x - 3)^4$.

4. $\dfrac{2x - 1}{x^2 + 2}$.

5. $\dfrac{3x}{x^2 + x + 1}$.

6. $\dfrac{x^2 - 1}{x^2 + 1}$.

7. Find the greatest and least values of $y = x^3 + x^2 - 5x - 4$ in the interval from $x = -3$ to $x = 3$.

8. Find the greatest and least values of $y = x^2 + 16/x$ in the interval from $x = \tfrac{2}{3}$ to $x = 3$.

9. Find the range of values taken by y on the curve $y = 12/(x^2 + 3)$. Find also the coordinates of the points of inflexion on the curve.

10. Repeat question 9 for the curve $y = 12x/(x^2 + 3)$.

11. The line $x = t$ meets the curves $y = x(x - 3)$ and $y = 5x - x^2$ at the points A and B. Find the maximum length of AB as t varies between 0 and 4.

12. A square of side x cm is cut from each of the corners of a rectangular piece of cardboard 15 cm by 24 cm. The cardboard is then folded to form an open box of depth x cm. Show that the volume of the box is $(4x^3 - 78x^2 + 360x)$ cm^3. Find the value of x for which the volume is a maximum.

13. A man wishes to fence in a rectangular enclosure of area 200 m^2. One side of the enclosure is formed by part of a wall already in position. What is the least possible length of fencing required for the other three sides?

14. A lump of modelling clay of volume 72 cm^3 is moulded into the shape of a cuboid with edges of lengths x cm, $2x$ cm and y cm. Find the minimum surface area of this cuboid.

15. A right circular cylinder of height $2h$ is contained in a sphere of radius R, the circular edges of the cylinder touching the sphere. The volumes of the cylinder and the sphere are denoted by V and W respectively. Express V in terms of R and h. By finding the maximum value of V, as h varies, show that $V/W \leqslant 1/\sqrt{3}$.   (W)

16. A closed hollow right-circular cone has internal height a and the internal radius of its base is also a. A solid circular cyclinder of height h just fits inside the cone with the axis of the cylinder lying along the axis of the cone. Show that the volume of the cylinder is $V = \pi h(a-h)^2$. If a is fixed, but h may vary, find h in terms of a when V is maximum.   (JMB)

17. $ABCDE$ is a pentagon of fixed perimeter P cm. Its shape is such that ABE is an equilateral triangle and $BCDE$ is a rectangle. If the length of AB is x cm, find the value of P/x for which the area of the pentagon is a maximum.

18. A right circular cylinder is of radius r cm and height pr cm. The total surface area of the cylinder is S cm^2 and its volume is V cm^3. Find an expression for V in terms of p and S. If the value of S is fixed, find the value of p for which V is a maximum.

10.5 Related rates of change

The chain rule can be used to solve many practical problems involving the rates of change of more than two variables.

Example 1   A piece of paper is burning round the circumference of a circular hole. After t seconds, the radius, r cm, of the hole is increasing at the rate of 0.5 cm s^{-1}. Find the rate at which the area, A cm^2, of the hole is increasing when $r = 5$.

The rate of increase of the radius of the hole in cm s^{-1} is given by

$$\frac{dr}{dt} = 0.5$$

The area of the hole in cm^2 is $A = \pi r^2$

$$\therefore \quad \frac{dA}{dr} = 2\pi r = 10\pi \quad \text{when} \quad r = 5.$$

The rate of increase of the area of the hole in cm^2 s^{-1} is

$$\frac{dA}{dt} = \frac{dA}{dr} \cdot \frac{dr}{dt} = 10\pi \times 0.5 = 5\pi.$$

Hence the area of the hole is increasing at a rate of 5π cm^2 s^{-1} when the radius is 5 cm.

Example 2 Water is being poured into a conical vessel at a rate of $10\,\text{cm}^3\,\text{s}^{-1}$. After t seconds, the volume, $V\,\text{cm}^3$, of water in the vessel is given by $V = \frac{1}{6}\pi x^3$, where $x\,\text{cm}$ is the depth of the water. Find, in terms of x, the rate at which the water is rising.

Since $V = \frac{1}{6}\pi x^3$ where x is a function of t, $\dfrac{dV}{dt} = \dfrac{dV}{dx} \cdot \dfrac{dx}{dt}$.

The rate at which the volume is increasing is the rate at which the water is being poured into the vessel

$$\therefore \quad \frac{dV}{dt} = 10.$$

By differentiation $\dfrac{dV}{dx} = \frac{1}{2}\pi x^2$.

Hence $10 = \frac{1}{2}\pi x^2 \cdot \dfrac{dx}{dt}$, i.e. $\dfrac{dx}{dt} = \dfrac{20}{\pi x^2}$

$\therefore$ the rate at which the water is rising is $20/\pi x^2\,\text{cm}\,\text{s}^{-1}$.

Example 3 A particle moves along a straight line so that its velocity, $v\,\text{m}\,\text{s}^{-1}$, when it is $s\,\text{m}$ from a fixed point, is given by $v = s^2 + 3$. Find an expression for its acceleration, $a\,\text{m}\,\text{s}^{-2}$, in terms of s.

$$a = \frac{dv}{dt} = \frac{dv}{ds} \cdot \frac{ds}{dt} = v\frac{dv}{ds}.$$

By differentiation, $\dfrac{dv}{ds} = 2s$

$$\therefore \quad a = v\frac{dv}{ds} = 2s(s^2 + 3).$$

Exercise 10.5

[Answers may be left in terms of π where appropriate.]

1. The side of a square is increasing at the rate of $3\,\text{cm/s}$. Find the rate of increase of the area when the length of the side is $10\,\text{cm}$.

2. The volume of a cube is increasing at the rate of $12\,\text{cm}^3/\text{s}$. Find the rate of increase of the length of an edge when the volume of the cube is $125\,\text{cm}^3$.

3. The area of a circle is increasing at the rate of $12\,\text{cm}^2/\text{s}$. Find the rate of increase of the circumference when the radius is $3\,\text{cm}$.

4. The area of a rectangle $x\,\text{cm}$ by $y\,\text{cm}$ is constant. If $dx/dt = 2$ when $3x = y$, find the corresponding value of dy/dt.

5. If $M = (2p+3)^4$, find $\dfrac{dM}{dt}$ when $p = 1$, given that $\dfrac{dp}{dt} = 2$.

6. If $r = \dfrac{1+\theta}{1+\theta^2}$, find $\dfrac{d\theta}{dt}$ when $\theta = 2$, given that $\dfrac{dr}{dt} = 14$.

7. A particle moves along a straight line so that its velocity, $v\,\text{m s}^{-1}$, when it is $s\,\text{m}$ from a fixed point, is given by $v = (1+s^2)/s$. Find an expression for the acceleration of the particle in terms of s.

8. A particle moves along a straight line so that after t seconds its displacement $s\,\text{m}$ from a fixed point satisfies the equation $s^2 + s = t$. Find an expression for its acceleration after t seconds in terms of s.

9. The volume of a spherical bubble is increasing at the rate of $6\,\text{cm}^3/\text{s}$. Find the rate at which the surface area of the bubble is increasing when the radius is $3\,\text{cm}$.

10. The radius of the base of a right circular cylinder is $r\,\text{cm}$ and its height is $2r\,\text{cm}$. Find (a) the rate at which its volume is increasing, when the radius is $2\,\text{cm}$ and is increasing at $0{\cdot}25\,\text{cm/s}$, (b) the rate at which the total surface area is increasing when the radius is $5\,\text{cm}$ and the volume is increasing at $5\pi\,\text{cm}^3/\text{s}$.

11. A horizontal trough is $4\,\text{m}$ long and $1\,\text{m}$ deep. Its cross-section is an isosceles triangle of base $1{\cdot}5\,\text{m}$ with its vertex downwards. Water runs into the trough at the rate of $0{\cdot}03\,\text{m}^3\,\text{s}^{-1}$. Find the rate at which the water level is rising after the water has been running for 25 seconds.

12. Water runs into a conical vessel fixed with its vertex downwards at the rate of $3\pi\,\text{cm}^3/\text{s}$, filling the vessel to a depth of $15\,\text{cm}$ in a time of one minute. Find the rate at which the depth of water in the vessel is increasing when the water has been running for $7{\cdot}5$ seconds.

10.6 Small changes and errors

If δx is a small change in x and δy is the corresponding small change in y,

$$\text{then} \quad \frac{\delta y}{\delta x} \approx \frac{dy}{dx}, \quad \text{i.e.} \quad \boxed{\delta y \approx \frac{dy}{dx}\,\delta x.}$$

Example 1   In an experiment, the diameter, x cm, of a sphere is measured and the volume, $V\,\text{cm}^3$, calculated using the formula $V = \dfrac{1}{6}\pi x^3$. If the diameter is found to be 10 cm with a possible error of 0·1 cm, estimate the possible error in the volume calculated from this reading.

$$\frac{dV}{dx} = \tfrac{1}{2}\pi x^2 = 50\pi \quad \text{when} \quad x = 10$$

$$\therefore \quad \text{if} \quad \delta x = 0\cdot 1 \quad \text{then} \quad \delta V \approx \frac{dV}{dx}\delta x \approx 50\pi \times 0\cdot 1 \approx 5\pi.$$

Hence the possible error in the volume is $5\pi\,\text{cm}^3$.

Example 2 The time, T seconds, taken for one complete swing of a pendulum, length l m, is given by $T = 2\pi\sqrt{\dfrac{l}{g}}$, where g is constant. If a 1% error is made in measuring the length of a pendulum, estimate the percentage error in the value of T.

$$T = 2\pi\sqrt{\frac{l}{g}} = \frac{2\pi}{\sqrt{g}}\cdot l^{1/2} \qquad \therefore \quad \frac{dT}{dl} = \frac{2\pi}{\sqrt{g}}\cdot \tfrac{1}{2}l^{-1/2} = \frac{\pi}{\sqrt{(gl)}}$$

$$\therefore \quad \delta T \approx \frac{dT}{dl}\delta l = \frac{\pi}{\sqrt{(gl)}}\cdot \delta l \quad \text{and} \quad \frac{\delta T}{T} \approx \frac{\pi}{\sqrt{(gl)}}\cdot\frac{1}{2\pi}\sqrt{\frac{g}{l}}\cdot \delta l = \frac{1}{2}\cdot\frac{\delta l}{l}.$$

Since $\dfrac{\delta l}{l} = \dfrac{1}{100}$, $\dfrac{\delta T}{T} \approx \dfrac{1}{200}$

$\therefore$ the error in the value of T is approximately 0·5%.

In the next example we find an approximate value for $y + \delta y$ rather than just δy.

Example 3 Find an approximate value for $\sqrt[3]{(1003)}$.

Let $y = \sqrt[3]{x} = x^{1/3}$, then $\dfrac{dy}{dx} = \tfrac{1}{3}x^{-2/3}$

$$\therefore \quad \delta y \approx \frac{dy}{dx}\delta x = \tfrac{1}{3}x^{-2/3}\delta x.$$

Substituting $x = 1000$ and $\delta x = 3$, $\delta y \approx \dfrac{1}{3}\times\dfrac{1}{100}\times 3 = 0\cdot 01.$

Hence $\sqrt[3]{(1003)} \approx 10 + 0\cdot 01 = 10\cdot 01.$

Exercise 10.6

[Answers may be left in terms of π where appropriate.]

1. If $y = x^2(x-2)$, find the approximate increase in y when x increases from 3 to 3·02.

2.   If $y = 2x^3 + 1$, find the approximate increase in x which causes y to increase from 3 to 3·06.

3.   If $T = 2\pi \sqrt{\dfrac{l}{10}}$, find the approximate decrease in T if l is reduced from 2·5 to 2·4.

4.   The radius of a circle is 6 cm. Find the approximate reduction in the area of the circle, if the radius is reduced by 0·1 cm.

5.   A cylindrical hole is said to be 25 cm deep and 6 cm in diameter. Find the error in the calculated volume if there is an error of (a) 0·1 cm in the diameter, (b) 0·3 cm in the depth.

6.   If $y = 3x^4$, find the approximate percentage increase in y when x in increased by 0·5%.

7.   If a 2% error is made in measuring the diameter of a sphere, find approximately the resulting percentage errors in the volume and surface area of the sphere.

8.   The length of a rectangle is twice its breadth. If the area of the rectangle increases by 5%, find the percentage increase in its perimeter.

9.   The pressure P and volume V of a certain mass of gas are connected by the formula $PV = k$ where k is constant. If the pressure increases by 1%, what is the approximate change in the volume?

10.   If $y = x^{3/2}$, find $\dfrac{dy}{dx}$ when $x = 4$. Hence find approximate values for (a) $(4 \cdot 01)^{3/2}$, (b) $(3 \cdot 98)^{3/2}$.

11.   Find approximately the values of $7x^2 - 3x + \dfrac{4}{x}$ when (a) $x = 2 \cdot 01$, (b) $x = 1 \cdot 98$.

12.   Find approximately the values of

(a) $\sqrt{(4 \cdot 004)}$, (b) $\dfrac{1}{5 \cdot 05}$, (c) $\sqrt[3]{(124 \cdot 7)}$, (d) $\dfrac{1}{\sqrt{(0 \cdot 96)}}$.

Exercise 10.7 (miscellaneous)

1.   Differentiate with respect to x

(a) $\dfrac{1}{(5 + 2x - x^2)^3}$,

(b) $\sqrt{(2x^3 + 5)}$.

2. If $y = \left(1 - \dfrac{1}{x}\right)^4$, prove that $(x^2 - x)\dfrac{dy}{dx} = 4y$.

3. Find the equation of the tangent to the curve $y = 1/(x-1)^2$ at the point where $x = 2$.

4. Find the gradient of the curve $x^2 + y^2 = 10y$ at each of the points where $x = 3$.

5. Find the equation of the tangent to the curve $(x+3)^2 - 4(y-2)^2 = 9$ at the point $(2, 4)$.

6. Differentiate with respect to x:

(a) $(2x+3)(x^2+1)^4$,

(b) $(x^2-2)\sqrt{(2x-1)}$,

(c) $\dfrac{4x^2+3x+5}{(x+1)^2}$,

(d) $\sqrt{\left(\dfrac{x+5}{x+3}\right)}$.

7. Find $\dfrac{dy}{dx}$ and $\dfrac{d^2y}{dx^2}$ when $y = \sqrt{(1+4x^2)}$.

8. If $x^4 - x^2y^2 + y^4 = 5$, find $\dfrac{dy}{dx}$ in terms of x and y.

9. Find the values of $\dfrac{dy}{dx}$ and $\dfrac{d^2y}{dx^2}$ at the point $(1, -2)$ on the curve $3x^2 + 2xy + y^2 = 3$.

10. Prove that if $y = \sqrt{(3x^2+2)}$, then $y\dfrac{d^2y}{dx^2} + \left(\dfrac{dy}{dx}\right)^2 = 3$.

11. Find any stationary values of the function $x^2(x-5)^3$ and sketch its graph.

12. Find any turning points and points of inflexion on the graph $y = x/(x^2+1)$. Hence sketch the curve.

13. In each of the following cases, express f', the derivative of f (with respect to x) in terms of g'. The number a is constant. (i) $f(x) = g(x+g(a))$. (ii) $f(x) = g(a+g(x))$. (iii) $f(x) = g(x^2)$.   (AEB 1975)

14. Given that $(x+y) = (x-y)^2$, prove by differentiating implicitly, or otherwise, that $1 - \dfrac{dy}{dx} = \dfrac{2}{2x-2y+1}$. Hence, or otherwise, prove that $\dfrac{d^2y}{dx^2} = \left(1 - \dfrac{dy}{dx}\right)^3$.   (JMB)

15. A piece of wire 80 cm in length is cut into three parts, two of which are bent into equal circles and the third into a square. Find the radius of the circles if the sum of the enclosed areas is a minimum.   (AEB 1975)

16. The diagonals of a rhombus are of lengths $2x$ cm and $(10-x)$ cm. As x varies, find (a) the maximum area of the rhombus, (b) the minimum length of its perimeter.

17. The height h and the base radius r of a right circular cone vary in such a way that the volume remains constant. Find the rate of change of h with respect to r at the instant when h and r are equal.

18. A right circular cone is of height 4 cm. The radius of the base is increasing at the rate of 0.5 cm/s. When the radius is 3 cm, find the rate of increase of (a) the volume of the cone, (b) the curved surface area.

19. Find approximate values for

(a) $(8.003)^{2/3}$, (b) $\dfrac{1}{4.98}$, (c) $\sqrt[4]{(16.032)}$.

20. Find approximately the values of $x^3 + 2x - \dfrac{16}{x^2}$ when

(a) $x = 4.02$, (b) $x = 3.96$.

21. Find the percentage increase in the circumference of a circle, which will result in an increase in the area of the circle of approximately 3%.

22. In an experiment the value of a quantity f is calculated using the formula $\dfrac{1}{f}$ $= \dfrac{1}{u} + \dfrac{1}{v}$. When $u = 20$, the value of v is found to be 30 with a possible error of 0.5. Find the corresponding error in the value of f.

23. A right pyramid having a square base is inscribed in a sphere of radius R, all five vertices of the pyramid lying on the sphere. The height of the pyramid is x; show that the four vertices forming the base of the pyramid lie on a circle of radius r, where $r^2 = 2Rx - x^2$. Hence, or otherwise, show that the volume V, of the pyramid is given by the formula $V = \frac{2}{3}x^2(2R - x)$. If R is fixed but x may vary, find the greatest possible value of V.   (C)

24. Water starts running into an empty basin at the rate of 6π cm^3/s. The basin is in the shape of the surface formed when the curve $4y = x^2$ is rotated completely about the y-axis. Show that when the depth of the water is y cm, the volume of water in the basin is $2\pi y^2$ cm^3. Find the rate at which the water level is rising when the water has been running for 3 seconds.

25. A hemispherical bowl of radius a cm is initially full of water. The water runs out of a small hole at the bottom of the bowl at a constant rate which is such that it would empty the bowl in 24 s. Given that, when the depth of the water is x cm, the volume of water is $\frac{1}{3}\pi x^2(3a - x)$ cm^3, prove that the depth is decreasing at a rate of $a^3/\{36x(2a - x)\}$ cm/s. Find after what time the depth of water is $\frac{1}{2}a$ cm, and the rate at which the water level is then decreasing.   (O&C)

11 Trigonometric functions

11.1 Circular measure

In elementary work, angles are usually measured in degrees, but it is often more convenient to use another unit called a radian.

An angle of 1 *radian* at the centre of a circle is subtended by an arc equal in length to the radius of the circle. Since the circumference of the circle is an arc of length $2\pi r$, it subtends an angle of 2π radians at the centre

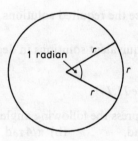

∴ | one complete revolution $= 360° = 2\pi$ radians.

Hence $\quad 1 \text{ rad} = \dfrac{360°}{2\pi} \approx 57 \cdot 3° \quad$ and $\quad 1° = \dfrac{2\pi}{360} \text{ rad} \approx 0 \cdot 0175 \text{ rad}.$

Because of their relation to circular arcs, radians are referred to as *circular measure* and sometimes denoted by ^{c}, e.g. $2\pi^c = 360°$. This symbol and the abbreviation rad are used only when it is necessary to distinguish between radians and degrees. Usually it is assumed that an angle is measured in radians unless otherwise stated.

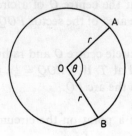

Consider now two points A and B on a circle, centre O and radius r. Let $\angle AOB = \theta$ (in radians). Since an arc of length r subtends an angle of 1 radian at O, the length of arc AB must be $r\theta$.

Since the area of the circle is πr^2, the area of sector AOB must be $\dfrac{\theta}{2\pi} \times \pi r^2$, i.e. $\frac{1}{2}r^2\theta$.

$$\therefore \quad \boxed{\text{length of arc } AB = r\theta, \quad \text{area of sector } AOB = \tfrac{1}{2}r^2\theta.}$$

Solutions of trigonometric equations are sometimes given in radians.

Example 1   Solve the equation $\cos 2\theta + \cos \theta + 1 = 0$ where $0 \leqslant \theta \leqslant 2\pi$.

$$\cos 2\theta + \cos \theta + 1 = 0 \Leftrightarrow (2\cos^2 \theta - 1) + \cos \theta + 1 = 0$$
$$\Leftrightarrow \qquad 2\cos^2 \theta + \cos \theta = 0$$
$$\Leftrightarrow \qquad \cos \theta (2\cos \theta + 1) = 0$$

$\therefore \quad \cos \theta = 0 \qquad \text{or} \qquad \cos \theta = -\tfrac{1}{2} = -\cos\tfrac{1}{3}\pi$

$\qquad \theta = \dfrac{1}{2}\pi, \dfrac{3}{2}\pi \qquad\qquad\qquad \theta = \dfrac{2}{3}\pi, \dfrac{4}{3}\pi$

Hence the required solutions are $\dfrac{1}{2}\pi, \dfrac{2}{3}\pi, \dfrac{4}{3}\pi$ and $\dfrac{3}{2}\pi$.

[The equivalent solutions in degrees are 90°, 120°, 240° and 270°.]

Exercise 11.1

1. Express the following angles in degrees:
(a) π rad,   (b) $\pi/4$ rad,   (c) $\pi/6$ rad,   (d) $4\pi/3$ rad.

2. Express the following angles in radians (as multiples of π):
(a) 90°,   (b) 60°,   (c) 150°,   (d) 315°.

3. Find, without using tables
(a) $\sin \dfrac{3\pi}{2}$,   (b) $\cos \dfrac{2\pi}{3}$,   (c) $\tan \dfrac{5\pi}{4}$,   (d) $\sec\left(-\dfrac{\pi}{6}\right)$.

4. Give the values in radians of
(a) $\cos^{-1} \dfrac{1}{\sqrt{2}}$,   (b) $\tan^{-1}(-\sqrt{3})$,   (c) $\sin^{-1} \dfrac{1}{2}$,   (d) $\cos^{-1}(-1)$.

5. An arc PQ subtends an angle of 1·5 radians at the centre O of a circle with radius 10 cm. Find the length of the arc PQ and the area of the sector POQ.

6. P and Q are points on the circumference of a circle centre O and radius 4 cm. The tangent to the circle at P meets OQ produced at T. If $\angle POQ = \frac{1}{4}\pi$ radians, find the area of the region bounded by PT, TQ and the arc PQ.

7. AB is a diameter of a circle radius r and C is a point on the circumference

such that $\angle ABC = \theta$ radians. Find expressions for the area and the perimeter of the region bounded by AB, BC and the arc AC.

8. A and B are points on the circumference of a circle centre O, radius 5 cm. If $\angle AOB = \theta$ radians, find the values of θ for which (a) the area of sector OAB is 15 cm², (b) the length of the perimeter of sector OAB is 12 cm, (c) the chord AB is of length $5\sqrt{3}$ cm, (d) the area of triangle OAB is 6·25 cm².

9. AB is an arc of a circle with centre O and radius 12 cm. A second circle with centre O and radius $(12+x)$ cm cuts OA and OB produced at the points C and D. If $\angle AOB = 0.8$ radians and the difference between the areas of the sectors AOB and COD is 72 cm², find the value of x.

10. Solve the following equations in radians for $0 \leqslant \theta \leqslant 2\pi$
(a) $2\sin\theta = 1$,   (b) $4\cos^2\theta = 1$,   (c) $\sec^2\theta = 2\tan\theta$.

11. Solve the following equations in radians for $0 \leqslant \theta \leqslant \pi$
(a) $\sin 2\theta = \cos 4\theta$,   (b) $\sin 6\theta = \cos 3\theta$.

12. Sketch on the same diagram the graphs $y = \sqrt{2}\cos x$ and $y = \sin 2x$, for $-\pi \leqslant x \leqslant 2\pi$. Find the ranges of values of x in that interval for which $\sin 2x > \sqrt{2}\cos x$.

In questions 13 to 15 you may use a calculator, giving your answers to 3 significant figures. Check that the calculator is adjusted for work in radians.

13. A chord AB subtends an angle of 0·75 rad at the centre of a circle of radius 20 cm. Find the area and the length of the perimeter of the minor segment of the circle cut off by AB.

14. AB is the diameter of a circle radius 12 cm and P is a point on the circumference such that $\angle PAB = 0.6$ rad. The tangent to the circle at P cuts AB produced at T. Find the area of the region bounded by BT, TP and arc PB.

15. A chord AB of a circle of radius 5 cm subtends an angle θ at the centre O. A second chord CD is parallel to AB and on the same side of O as AB. If $AB = 2$ cm and $\angle COD = \theta + \frac{1}{2}\pi$, find θ and the area of the part of the circle lying between AB and CD.

11.2 General solutions of trigonometric equations

The trigonometric equation $\sin\theta = 0$ has an infinite solution set $\{\ldots, -2\pi, -\pi, 0, \pi, \ldots\}$. Since all the solutions are of the form $n\pi$ where n is an integer, $\theta = n\pi$ is said to be the *general solution* of the equation. We now consider three more general cases.

(1) $\cos \theta = \cos \alpha$

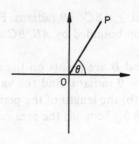

Geometrically, the roots of this equation are represented by the possible positions of a line OP, which rotates about the origin as shown in the diagram. In every complete revolution of OP, θ passes through two values which satisfy $\cos \theta = \cos \alpha$. These values correspond with the positions of OP given by $\theta = \alpha$ and $\theta = -\alpha$. Hence every root takes the form $\alpha + 2n\pi$ or $-\alpha + 2n\pi$ where n is an integer, $\therefore$ the general solution of the equation $\cos \theta = \cos \alpha$ is

$$\theta = 2n\pi \pm \alpha, \quad \text{where } n \text{ is an integer.}$$

(2) $\sin \theta = \sin \alpha$

In this case, since $\sin (\pi - \alpha) = \sin \alpha$, the two possible positions of OP in every complete revolution are given by $\theta = \alpha$ and $\theta = \pi - \alpha$, $\therefore$ every root of the equation takes either the form $\alpha + 2n\pi$ or $(\pi - \alpha) + 2n\pi$, where n is an integer. Hence the general solution of the equation $\sin \theta = \sin \alpha$ is

$$\theta = 2n\pi + \alpha \quad \text{or} \quad 2n\pi + (\pi - \alpha) \quad \text{where } n \text{ is an integer.}$$

This means that θ is either an even multiple of π plus α or an odd multiple of π minus α. Hence the general solution of the equation $\sin \theta = \sin \alpha$ can also be written in the form

$$\theta = n\pi + (-1)^n \alpha, \quad \text{where } n \text{ is an integer.}$$

(3) $\tan \theta = \tan \alpha$

The function $\tan \theta$ takes every real value exactly once in every rotation of OP through π radians. Since one solution of the equation is $\theta = \alpha$, the general solution of $\tan \theta = \tan \alpha$ is

$$\theta = n\pi + \alpha \quad \text{where } n \text{ is an integer.}$$

Summarising:

$$\boxed{\begin{aligned} \cos \theta = \cos \alpha &\Rightarrow \theta = 2n\pi \pm \alpha \\ \sin \theta = \sin \alpha &\Rightarrow \theta = n\pi + (-1)^n \alpha \\ \tan \theta = \tan \alpha &\Rightarrow \theta = n\pi + \alpha \end{aligned}}$$

where in every case n is an integer.

There are a few special cases in which these general forms can be simplified.

$$\cos \theta = 0 \quad \Rightarrow \theta = (2n+1)\frac{\pi}{2} \qquad\qquad \sin \theta = 0 \quad \Rightarrow \theta = n\pi$$

$$\cos \theta = 1 \quad \Rightarrow \theta = 2n\pi \qquad\qquad \sin \theta = 1 \quad \Rightarrow \theta = (4n+1)\frac{\pi}{2}$$

$$\cos \theta = -1 \Rightarrow \theta = (2n+1)\pi \qquad\qquad \sin \theta = -1 \Rightarrow \theta = (4n-1)\frac{\pi}{2}$$

Example 1   Find the general solution of the equation $\sin 2\theta - \sqrt{3}\cos\theta = 0$.

$$\sin 2\theta - \sqrt{3}\cos\theta = 0 \Leftrightarrow 2\sin\theta\cos\theta - \sqrt{3}\cos\theta = 0$$
$$\Leftrightarrow \quad \cos\theta(2\sin\theta - \sqrt{3}) = 0$$

$\therefore$ either $\cos\theta = 0$ or $\sin\theta = \dfrac{\sqrt{3}}{2} = \sin\dfrac{\pi}{3}$

$$\theta = n\pi + \dfrac{\pi}{2} \qquad\qquad \theta = n\pi + (-1)^n\dfrac{\pi}{3}$$

Hence the general solution of the equation is

$$\theta = (2n+1)\dfrac{\pi}{2} \quad \text{or} \quad n\pi + (-1)^n\dfrac{\pi}{3}, \quad \text{where } n \text{ is an integer.}$$

Example 2   Find the general solution of the equation $\sin 3\theta = \sin\theta$.

$$\sin 3\theta = \sin\theta$$

$\therefore$ either $3\theta = 2n\pi + \theta$ or $3\theta = 2n\pi + \pi - \theta$
$\qquad\qquad 2\theta = 2n\pi \qquad\qquad\quad\; 4\theta = (2n+1)\pi$
$$\theta = n\pi \qquad\qquad\qquad \theta = (2n+1)\dfrac{\pi}{4}$$

Hence the general solution is $\theta = n\pi$ or $\theta = (2n+1)\dfrac{\pi}{4}$ where n is an integer.

Example 3   Find the general solution of the equation $\cos 4\theta = \sin 5\theta$ giving your answer in degrees.

$$\cos 4\theta = \sin 5\theta \Leftrightarrow \cos 4\theta = \cos(90° - 5\theta)$$

$\therefore$ either $4\theta = 360n° + 90° - 5\theta$ or $4\theta = 360n° - (90° - 5\theta)$
$\qquad\qquad\; 9\theta = 360n° + 90° \qquad\qquad\qquad -\theta = 360n° - 90°$
$\qquad\qquad\; \theta = 40n° + 10° \qquad\qquad\qquad\;\; \theta = 90° - 360n°.$

Since every solution of the form $90° - 360n°$ can also be expressed in the form $40n° + 10°$, the required general solution is simply $\theta = 40n° + 10°$, where n is an integer.

Example 4   Find the general solution of the equation $3\cos\theta + 4\sin\theta = 2$, giving your answer in degrees and minutes.

Let $3\cos\theta + 4\sin\theta \equiv r\cos(\theta - \alpha) \equiv r\cos\alpha\cos\theta + r\sin\alpha\sin\theta$

then $r\cos\alpha = 3$ and $r\sin\alpha = 4$

$\therefore$ $r = \sqrt{(3^2 + 4^2)} = 5$ and $\tan\alpha = 4/3, \quad \alpha = 53\cdot13°.$

Hence $3\cos\theta + 4\sin\theta = 2 \Leftrightarrow 5\cos(\theta - 53\cdot13°) = 2$

$\therefore$ $\cos(\theta - 53\cdot13°) = 0\cdot4 = \cos 66\cdot42°$

$\therefore$ either $\theta - 53 \cdot 13° = 360n° + 66 \cdot 42°$
$$\theta = 360n° + 119 \cdot 6°$$
   or $\theta - 53 \cdot 13° = 360n° - 66 \cdot 42°$
$$\theta = 360n° - 13 \cdot 3°.$$

Thus the general solution is $\theta = 360n° + 119 \cdot 6°$ or $\theta = 360n° - 13 \cdot 3°$ where n is an integer.

Exercise 11.2

Find, in radians, the general solutions of the following equations.

1. $\cos \theta = \cos \dfrac{2}{5}\pi.$

2. $\tan \theta = \tan \dfrac{1}{3}\pi.$

3. $\sin \theta = \sin \dfrac{\pi}{8}.$

4. $\cos \theta = \cos \pi.$

5. $\tan \theta = -1.$

6. $2 \sin \theta = 1.$

7. $\sin^2 \theta = 1.$

8. $2 \cos^2 \theta = 1.$

9. $\sin 2x = \sin x.$

10. $\cos 2x = \cos x.$

11. $2 \cos 2x = 1 - 4 \cos x.$

12. $\sec^2 x = 2 \tan x.$

13. $\tan \theta = \tan 4\theta.$

14. $\tan 2\theta = \tan (\frac{1}{2}\pi - 3\theta).$

15. $\tan 3\theta = \cot \theta.$

16. $\cos 3\theta = \sin 5\theta.$

Find, to the nearest $0 \cdot 1°$, the general solutions of the following equations.

17. $\cos \theta + 3 \sin \theta = 2.$

18. $16 \cos \theta + 30 \sin \theta = 17.$

11.3 Useful limits and approximations

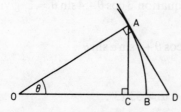

If $OA = OB = 1$ and θ is measured in radians, then

$$OC = \cos \theta. \quad \text{arc } AB = \theta$$
$$AC = \sin \theta, \quad AD = \tan \theta$$

When θ is small, $OC \approx OB$ and $AC \approx AB \approx AD$.
Hence $\cos \theta \approx 1$ and $\sin \theta \approx \theta \approx \tan \theta$.

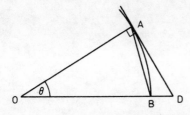

In a more formal approach to small values of θ, areas are considered.

$$\triangle AOB \; < \; \text{sector } AOB \; < \; \triangle AOD$$
$$\Rightarrow \tfrac{1}{2}r^2 \sin \theta \; < \; \tfrac{1}{2}r^2\theta \; < \; \tfrac{1}{2}r^2 \tan \theta$$
$$\Rightarrow \quad \sin \theta \; < \; \theta \; < \; \tan \theta$$
$$\Rightarrow \quad \frac{\sin \theta}{\sin \theta} \; < \; \frac{\theta}{\sin \theta} \; < \; \frac{\tan \theta}{\sin \theta}$$
$$\Rightarrow \quad 1 \; < \; \frac{\theta}{\sin \theta} \; < \; \frac{1}{\cos \theta}$$

As $\quad \theta \to 0, \quad \cos \theta \to 1 \qquad \therefore \quad \dfrac{1}{\cos \theta} \to 1$

Hence, as $\quad \theta \to 0, \qquad \dfrac{\theta}{\sin \theta} \to 1.$

Thus

$$\lim_{\theta \to 0} \frac{\theta}{\sin \theta} = 1 \quad \text{and} \quad \lim_{\theta \to 0} \frac{\sin \theta}{\theta} = 1.$$

As before, we see that for small values of θ, $\sin \theta \approx \theta$.
Similarly $\sin \tfrac{1}{2}\theta \approx \tfrac{1}{2}\theta \quad \therefore \cos \theta = 1 - 2\sin^2 \tfrac{1}{2}\theta \approx 1 - 2(\tfrac{1}{2}\theta)^2 \approx 1 - \tfrac{1}{2}\theta^2.$

$\therefore \quad$ for small values of θ in radians, we write

$$\sin \theta \approx \theta, \quad \tan \theta \approx \theta \quad \text{and} \quad \cos \theta \approx 1 - \tfrac{1}{2}\theta^2$$

[or $\cos \theta \approx 1$ when less accuracy is required].

These limits and approximations have many applications especially in calculus. Some of their uses are simply illustrated in the following examples.

Example 1　Find an approximate value for $\sin 2°$ given $\pi = 3.1416$.

$$2° = \frac{2}{360} \times 2\pi = \frac{\pi}{90} \approx \frac{3.1416}{90} \approx 0.0349$$

$\therefore \quad$ an approximate value for $\sin 2°$ is 0.0349.

[The true value of $\sin 2°$ correct to 6 significant figures is 0.0348995.]

Example 2　Find an approximation for the expression $\dfrac{\sin 2\theta \tan 2\theta}{1 - \cos \theta}$ when θ is small.

$$\sin 2\theta \approx 2\theta, \quad \tan 2\theta \approx 2\theta, \quad \cos \theta \approx 1 - \tfrac{1}{2}\theta^2$$

$$\therefore \quad \frac{\sin 2\theta \tan 2\theta}{1 - \cos \theta} \approx \frac{2\theta \cdot 2\theta}{1 - (1 - \tfrac{1}{2}\theta^2)} = \frac{4\theta^2}{\tfrac{1}{2}\theta^2} = 8.$$

Hence when θ is small $\dfrac{\sin 2\theta \tan 2\theta}{1 - \cos \theta} \approx 8.$

Example 3   Evaluate $\lim\limits_{\theta \to 0} \dfrac{\sin 2\theta + \sin 4\theta}{\theta}$

$$\frac{\sin 2\theta + \sin 4\theta}{\theta} = \frac{\sin 2\theta}{\theta} + \frac{\sin 4\theta}{\theta} = 2 \cdot \frac{\sin 2\theta}{2\theta} + 4 \cdot \frac{\sin 4\theta}{4\theta}$$

$$\therefore \quad \lim_{\theta \to 0} \frac{\sin 2\theta + \sin 4\theta}{\theta} = 2\left(\lim_{\theta \to 0} \frac{\sin 2\theta}{2\theta} \right) + 4\left(\lim_{\theta \to 0} \frac{\sin 4\theta}{4\theta} \right)$$

$$= 2 \cdot 1 + 4 \cdot 1 = 6.$$

Exercise 11.3

1.   Find approximate values for the following expressions without using tables or calculators, given that $\pi = 3 \cdot 1416$.
(a) $\sin 1 \cdot 2°$
(b) $\tan 0 \cdot 7°$
(c) $\sin 0 \cdot 015°$.

2.   Find approximate values of the following expressions when θ is small,
(a) $\dfrac{\theta \sin \theta}{1 - \cos \theta}$,
(b) $\dfrac{\tan 3\theta}{2\theta}$,
(c) $\dfrac{\sin 2\theta \tan \theta}{1 - \cos 3\theta}$.

3.   Find an expression of the form $a + b\theta + c\theta^2$ which is approximately equal to the following when θ is small,
(a) $\sin (\theta + \tfrac{1}{3}\pi)$,
(b) $\cos (\theta - \tfrac{1}{4}\pi)$,
(c) $\cos \theta \cos 2\theta$.

4.   Find the limit as $\theta \to 0$ of
(a) $\dfrac{\sin \theta}{2\theta}$,
(b) $\dfrac{\sin 3\theta}{\theta}$,
(c) $\dfrac{\sin 5\theta}{\sin 4\theta}$.

5.   Find the limit as $x \to 0$ of
(a) $\dfrac{1 - \cos 2x}{x^2}$,
(b) $\dfrac{\cos 3x - \cos x}{\cos 4x - \cos 2x}$.

6.   Use areas to prove that as $\theta \to 0$, $\dfrac{\tan \theta}{\theta} \to 1$.

11.4 Derivatives of trigonometric functions

The function $\sin x$ is differentiated from first principles as follows:

$$y = \sin x \quad \text{(where } x \text{ is in radians)}$$
$$\Rightarrow y + \delta y = \sin(x + \delta x)$$
$$\Rightarrow \quad \delta y = \sin(x + \delta x) - \sin x = 2\cos(x + \tfrac{1}{2}\delta x)\sin\tfrac{1}{2}\delta x$$
$$\Rightarrow \quad \frac{\delta y}{\delta x} = \frac{2\cos(x + \tfrac{1}{2}\delta x)\sin\tfrac{1}{2}\delta x}{\delta x} = \cos(x + \tfrac{1}{2}\delta x) \cdot \frac{\sin\tfrac{1}{2}\delta x}{\tfrac{1}{2}\delta x}.$$

As $\delta x \to 0$, $\cos(x + \tfrac{1}{2}\delta x) \to \cos x$ and $\dfrac{\sin\tfrac{1}{2}\delta x}{\tfrac{1}{2}\delta x} \to 1$

$$\therefore \quad \frac{dy}{dx} = \lim_{\delta x \to 0} \frac{\delta y}{\delta x} = \cos x \cdot 1.$$

Hence $\qquad \dfrac{d}{dx}(\sin x) = \cos x.$

Similarly it can be shown that $\dfrac{d}{dx}(\cos x) = -\sin x.$

Example 1   Differentiate (a) $\sin^3 x$, (b) $\cos(4 - 3x)$, (c) $\sin x°$.

(a) Let $y = \sin^3 x = u^3$ where $u = \sin x$

$$\frac{dy}{du} = 3u^2 \qquad\qquad \frac{du}{dx} = \cos x$$

$$\therefore \quad \frac{dy}{dx} = \frac{dy}{du} \cdot \frac{du}{dx} = 3u^2 \cdot \cos x = 3\sin^2 x \cos x.$$

Hence $\quad \dfrac{d}{dx}(\sin^3 x) = 3\sin^2 x \cos x.$

(b) Let $y = \cos(4 - 3x) = \cos u$ where $u = 4 - 3x$

$$\frac{dy}{du} = -\sin u \qquad\qquad \frac{du}{dx} = -3$$

$$\therefore \quad \frac{dy}{dx} = \frac{dy}{du} \cdot \frac{du}{dx} = -\sin u \cdot (-3) = 3\sin u.$$

Hence $\quad \dfrac{d}{dx}(\cos(4 - 3x)) = 3\sin(4 - 3x).$

(c) Let $y = \sin x°$, then expressing $x°$ in radians $y = \sin \dfrac{\pi}{180} x$

$$\therefore \quad \frac{dy}{dx} = \cos \frac{\pi}{180} x \cdot \frac{\pi}{180} = \frac{\pi}{180}\cos x°.$$

Hence $\quad \dfrac{d}{dx}(\sin x°) = \dfrac{\pi}{180}\cos x°.$

Example 2   Find the maximum and minimum values of the function $f(x) = 2 \sin x + \cos 2x$ for $0 < x < \pi$.

Differentiating, $f'(x) = 2 \cos x - 2 \sin 2x = 2 \cos x - 4 \sin x \cos x$
$$= 2 \cos x (1 - 2 \sin x)$$

$f'(x) = 0 \Leftrightarrow \cos x (1 - 2 \sin x) = 0$
$$\Leftrightarrow \cos x = 0 \quad \text{or} \quad \sin x = \tfrac{1}{2}$$

$\therefore$ for $0 < x < \pi, f'(x) = 0$ when $x = \dfrac{1}{6}\pi, \dfrac{1}{2}\pi$ or $\dfrac{5}{6}\pi$.

	$0 < x < \dfrac{1}{6}\pi$	$\dfrac{1}{6}\pi < x < \dfrac{1}{2}\pi$	$\dfrac{1}{2}\pi < x < \dfrac{5}{6}\pi$	$\dfrac{5}{6}\pi < x < \pi$
$\cos x$	$+$	$+$	$-$	$-$
$1 - 2 \sin x$	$+$	$-$	$-$	$+$
$f'(x)$	$+$	$-$	$+$	$-$

$\therefore$ at $x = \dfrac{1}{6}\pi, f(x)$ takes the maximum value $f\left(\dfrac{1}{6}\pi\right) = 1\tfrac{1}{2}$,

at $x = \dfrac{1}{2}\pi, f(x)$ takes the minimum value $f\left(\dfrac{1}{2}\pi\right) = 1$.

at $x = \dfrac{5}{6}\pi, f(x)$ takes the maximum value $f\left(\dfrac{5}{6}\pi\right) = 1\tfrac{1}{2}$.

The function $\tan x$ is differentiated by expressing it as the quotient $\dfrac{\sin x}{\cos x}$ and using the formula $\dfrac{d}{dx}\left(\dfrac{u}{v}\right) = \left(v\dfrac{du}{dx} - u\dfrac{dv}{dx}\right)\Big/ v^2$ derived in §10.3.

If $y = \tan x = \dfrac{\sin x}{\cos x} = \dfrac{u}{v}$ where $u = \sin x, \quad v = \cos x$

then $\dfrac{du}{dx} = \cos x, \quad \dfrac{dv}{dx} = -\sin x$

$\therefore \quad \dfrac{dy}{dx} = \dfrac{\cos x . \cos x - \sin x . (-\sin x)}{\cos^2 x} = \dfrac{\cos^2 x + \sin^2 x}{\cos^2 x} = \dfrac{1}{\cos^2 x} = \sec^2 x$

$\therefore \quad \dfrac{d}{dx}(\tan x) = \sec^2 x.$

Similarly it can be shown that $\dfrac{d}{dx}(\cot x) = -\operatorname{cosec}^2 x.$

To differentiate $\sec x$ we write:

$$y = \sec x = (\cos x)^{-1} = u^{-1} \quad \text{where} \quad u = \cos x$$

$\therefore \quad \dfrac{dy}{du} = -\dfrac{1}{u^2} \quad \text{and} \quad \dfrac{du}{dx} = -\sin x.$

Hence $\dfrac{dy}{dx} = \dfrac{dy}{du} \cdot \dfrac{du}{dx} = -\dfrac{1}{u^2}(-\sin x) = \dfrac{\sin x}{\cos^2 x} = \dfrac{1}{\cos x} \times \dfrac{\sin x}{\cos x}$

$$\therefore \quad \dfrac{d}{dx}(\sec x) = \sec x \tan x.$$

Similarly it can be shown that $\dfrac{d}{dx}(\cosec x) = -\cosec x \cot x.$

Example 3 If $y^2 = \tan 2x + \sec 2x$, show that when $y \neq 0$, $\dfrac{dy}{dx} = y \sec 2x$.

Differentiating with respect to x,

$$y^2 = \tan 2x + \sec 2x \Leftrightarrow 2y\frac{dy}{dx} = 2\sec^2 2x + 2\sec 2x \tan 2x$$

$$\therefore \quad y\frac{dy}{dx} = \sec 2x(\sec 2x + \tan 2x) = y^2 \sec 2x.$$

Hence, when $y \neq 0$, $\dfrac{dy}{dx} = y \sec 2x$.

The table below shows the results obtained in this section.

y	$\sin x$	$\cos x$	$\tan x$	$\cot x$	$\sec x$	$\cosec x$
$\dfrac{dy}{dx}$	$\cos x$	$-\sin x$	$\sec^2 x$	$-\cosec^2 x$	$\sec x \tan x$	$-\cosec x \cot x$

Exercise 11.4

Differentiate the following with respect to x, simplifying your answers where possible.

1. (a) $\sin 2x$, (b) $3\cos 4x$, (c) $4\tan \frac{1}{2}x$.

2. (a) $\cos^4 x$, (b) $\sqrt{(\sin x)}$, (c) $\sin^2 5x$.

3. (a) $(x + \sin x)^3$, (b) $\sin (x^2)$, (c) $\tan (6x°)$.

4. (a) $x^4 \cos x$, (b) $(4x^2 + 1)\tan x$, (c) $x^2 \sin 3x$.

5. (a) $\cosec (x + 1)$, (b) $2\cot (1 - 2x)$, (c) $\sec (3x - 4)$.

6. (a) $\tan (\cos x)$, (b) $\sec (1 + \sqrt{x})$, (c) $\cot (1/x)$.

7. (a) $\sin x \cos 2x$, (b) $\cos^3 x \sin 3x$, (c) $\cos x \tan x$.

8. (a) $\dfrac{\sin x}{x^2}$,   (b) $\dfrac{1}{\cos x - \sin x}$,   (c) $\dfrac{\cos 3x}{1 + \sin 3x}$.

In questions 9 to 12 find the coordinates of any stationary points on the given curve for $0 \leqslant x \leqslant 2\pi$. Hence sketch the curve in that interval.

9. $y = 4 \sin x - \cos 2x$.

10. $y = x - 2 \sin x$.

11. $y = \tan x (\tan x + 2)$.

12. $y = \sin^3 x \cos x$.

13. A particle P moves in a straight line such that after t seconds its displacement from a fixed point O is s metres, where $s = 10 \sin 3t$. Find (a) the time at which P first returns to O, (b) the maximum distance from O reached by P, (c) the maximum speed attained by the particle and its position each time this speed is reached.

14. A right circular cone has semi-vertical angle θ and height $15 \,\text{cm}$. If θ is increasing at the rate of $k \,\text{rad/s}$, where k is constant, find the rate of change of the volume of the cone when $\theta = \frac{1}{4}\pi$.

15. Points A and B lie on the circumference of a circle with centre O and radius $10 \,\text{cm}$. If $\angle AOB = \theta$ and θ is increasing at the rate of $0{\cdot}1 \,\text{rad/s}$, find the rate of increase when $\theta = \frac{1}{3}\pi$ of (a) the area of $\triangle AOB$, (b) the perimeter of the region enclosed by the chord AB and the arc AB.

16. Given that $\sqrt{3} \approx 1{\cdot}7321$ and $0{\cdot}1° \approx 0{\cdot}00175 \,\text{rad}$, find approximate values for (a) $\cos 30{\cdot}7°$,   (b) $\tan 45{\cdot}3°$,   (c) $\sin 60{\cdot}5°$.

17. In a trapezium $ABCD$ the sides AB, DC are parallel and $\angle ABC$ is a right angle. If $AD = DB = 10 \,\text{cm}$ and $\angle DAB = \theta$, find the value of $\tan \theta$ for which the perimeter, $p \,\text{cm}$, is a maximum. Hence find the range of values taken by p for $0 < \theta < \frac{1}{2}\pi$.

18. A particle moves in a straight line such that after t seconds its displacement from a fixed point is s metres, where $s = 4 \cos t - \cos 2t$. If the particle first comes to rest after T seconds, where $T > 0$, find (a) its acceleration at time T, (b) the maximum speed it attains for $0 < t < T$.

11.5 Integration of trigonometric functions

From the differentiation results obtained so far:

$$\int \sin x \, dx = -\cos x + c \qquad \int \cos x \, dx = \sin x + c$$

$$\int \sec^2 x \, dx = \tan x + c \qquad \int \cosec^2 x \, dx = -\cot x + c$$

$$\int \sec x \tan x \, dx = \sec x + c \qquad\qquad \int \csc x \cot x \, dx = -\csc x + c.$$

These results can be extended as shown in the following examples.

Example 1 Integrate (a) $\cos 2x$, (b) $\sin^4 x \cos x$.

(a) Since $\dfrac{d}{dx}(\sin 2x) = 2\cos 2x$, $\displaystyle\int \cos 2x \, dx = \tfrac{1}{2}\sin 2x + c.$

(b) Since $\dfrac{d}{dx}(\sin^5 x) = 5\sin^4 x \cos x$, $\displaystyle\int \sin^4 x \cos x \, dx = \frac{1}{5}\sin^5 x + c.$

In some cases trigonometric identities are used to change the form of the integrand (i.e. the function to be integrated).

Example 2 Integrate (a) $\tan^2 x$, (b) $\sin^2 x$.

(a) $\displaystyle\int \tan^2 x \, dx = \int (\sec^2 x - 1)\, dx = \tan x - x + c.$

(b) $\displaystyle\int \sin^2 x \, dx = \int \tfrac{1}{2}(1 - \cos 2x)\, dx = \tfrac{1}{2}(x - \tfrac{1}{2}\sin 2x) + c = \tfrac{1}{2}x - \tfrac{1}{4}\sin 2x + c.$

Example 3 Find $\displaystyle\int \sin 5x \cos x \, dx.$

$$2\sin 5x \cos x = \sin 6x + \sin 4x$$

$$\therefore \quad \int \sin 5x \cos x \, dx = \int (\tfrac{1}{2}\sin 6x + \tfrac{1}{2}\sin 4x)\, dx$$

$$= \frac{1}{2}\cdot\frac{1}{6}(-\cos 6x) + \frac{1}{2}\cdot\frac{1}{4}(-\cos 4x) + c$$

$$= -\frac{1}{12}\cos 6x - \frac{1}{8}\cos 4x + c.$$

Example 4 Evaluate $\displaystyle\int_0^{\pi/6} \cos^5 x \, dx.$

$$\cos^5 x = (\cos^2 x)^2 \cos x = (1 - \sin^2 x)^2 \cos x = (1 - 2\sin^2 x + \sin^4 x)\cos x,$$

$$\therefore \quad \int_0^{\pi/6} \cos^5 x \, dx = \int_0^{\pi/6} (\cos x - 2\sin^2 x \cos x + \sin^4 x \cos x)\, dx$$

$$= \left[\sin x - \frac{2}{3}\sin^3 x + \frac{1}{5}\sin^5 x \right]_0^{\pi/6}$$

$$= \left(\frac{1}{2} - \frac{2}{3}\left(\frac{1}{2}\right)^3 + \frac{1}{5}\left(\frac{1}{2}\right)^5 \right) - 0 = \frac{1}{2} - \frac{1}{12} + \frac{1}{160} = \frac{203}{480}.$$

Exercise 11.5

Find the following indefinite integrals

1. (a) $\int \sin 3x \, dx$,   (b) $\int \cos \frac{1}{2}x \, dx$,   (c) $\int 4 \sec^2 2x \, dx$.

2. (a) $\int \cos^2 x \, dx$,   (b) $\int \cot^2 x \, dx$,   (c) $\int \sin^2 x \cos x \, dx$.

3. (a) $\int \sin x \cos^3 x \, dx$,   (b) $\int \sin x \cos 3x \, dx$,   (c) $\int \cos 2x \cos x \, dx$.

Evaluate the following definite integrals

4. (a) $\int_0^{\pi/4} \cos 2x \, dx$,   (b) $\int_0^{\pi/12} \sin^2 3x \, dx$,   (c) $\int_0^{\pi/2} \sin x \cos^2 x \, dx$.

5. (a) $\int_0^{\pi/3} \tan^2 x \, dx$,   (b) $\int_0^{\pi/3} \sin 3x \cos 2x \, dx$,   (c) $\int_0^{\pi/4} \sin 3x \sin x \, dx$.

6. (a) $\int_0^{\pi/3} \frac{\sin x}{\cos^2 x} \, dx$,   (b) $\int_{\pi/4}^{\pi/2} \frac{\cos 2x}{\sin^2 x} \, dx$,   (c) $\int_0^{\pi/2} \cos^3 x \, dx$.

7. Differentiate $\tan^3 x$ with respect to x and use your result to find $\int \tan^4 x \, dx$.

8. Show that   (a) $\int 4 \sin x \cos x \, dx = 2 \sin^2 x + \text{constant}$,

    (b) $\int 4 \sin x \cos x \, dx = -\cos 2x + \text{constant}$.

Write down a third expression for the same integral and explain how all three expressions can be correct.

9. Express $\cos^4 x$ in terms of $\cos 2x$ and $\cos 4x$. Hence evaluate $\int_0^{\pi/4} \cos^4 x \, dx$.

10. Find the area of the region bounded by the curve $y = 2/(1 + \cos 2x)$, the x-axis, the y-axis and the line $x = \frac{1}{4}\pi$.

11. Find the volume of the solid formed when the region bounded by the curve $y = 3 - 2\cos x$, the x-axis, the y-axis and the line $x = \pi$ is rotated completely about the x-axis.

12. Find the mean value of $\sin^3 x$ over the interval $0 \leqslant x \leqslant \pi$.

11.6 Inverse trigonometric functions

The inverse trigonometric functions $\sin^{-1}x$, $\cos^{-1}x$ and $\tan^{-1}x$ were introduced in §7.2. At that stage it was convenient to use angles measured in degrees. However, in more advanced work, these functions are usually evaluated in radians.

To differentiate the function $\sin^{-1}x$,

let $\quad y = \sin^{-1}x$, then $\quad \sin y = x$

Differentiating $\qquad \cos y \dfrac{dy}{dx} = 1$

$$\therefore \quad \frac{dy}{dx} = \frac{1}{\cos y}$$

But $\quad \cos^2 y + \sin^2 y = 1 \qquad \therefore \quad \cos^2 y = 1 - \sin^2 y$

Since $\cos y$ is positive for $-\frac{1}{2}\pi < y < \frac{1}{2}\pi$,

$$\cos y = \sqrt{(1 - \sin^2 y)} = \sqrt{(1 - x^2)}.$$

Hence $\quad \dfrac{dy}{dx} = \dfrac{1}{\sqrt{(1-x^2)}}$, i.e. $\dfrac{d}{dx}(\sin^{-1}x) = \dfrac{1}{\sqrt{(1-x^2)}}.$

By a similar method, it can be shown that

$$\frac{d}{dx}(\cos^{-1}x) = -\frac{1}{\sqrt{(1-x^2)}}$$

[This result can also be obtained by using the fact that $\sin^{-1}x + \cos^{-1}x = \frac{1}{2}\pi$.]

To differentiate the function $\tan^{-1}x$,

let $\quad y = \tan^{-1}x$, then $\quad \tan y = x$

Differentiating $\qquad \sec^2 y \dfrac{dy}{dx} = 1$

$$\therefore \quad \frac{dy}{dx} = \frac{1}{\sec^2 y}.$$

But $\qquad\qquad\qquad \sec^2 y = 1 + \tan^2 y = 1 + x^2$

$$\therefore \quad \frac{dy}{dx} = \frac{1}{1+x^2}, \quad \text{i.e.} \quad \frac{d}{dx}(\tan^{-1}x) = \frac{1}{1+x^2}.$$

Summarising:

$$\frac{d}{dx}(\sin^{-1}x) = \frac{1}{\sqrt{(1-x^2)}} \quad \text{and} \quad \int \frac{dx}{\sqrt{(1-x^2)}} = \sin^{-1}x + c$$

$$\frac{d}{dx}(\tan^{-1}x) = \frac{1}{1+x^2} \quad \text{and} \quad \int \frac{dx}{1+x^2} = \tan^{-1}x + c.$$

Example 1   Find $\dfrac{dy}{dx}$ if $y = \sin^{-1}(3x-1)$.

Let $\quad y = \sin^{-1} u$ $\qquad\qquad$ where $\quad u = 3x-1$

then $\quad \dfrac{dy}{du} = \dfrac{1}{\sqrt{(1-u^2)}}$ $\qquad\qquad \dfrac{du}{dx} = 3$

$\therefore \quad \dfrac{dy}{dx} = \dfrac{dy}{du}\cdot\dfrac{du}{dx} = \dfrac{3}{\sqrt{(1-u^2)}} = \dfrac{3}{\sqrt{(1-\{3x-1\}^2)}} = \dfrac{3}{\sqrt{(6x-9x^2)}}.$

To obtain more general integration results, we consider the functions $\sin^{-1}\dfrac{x}{a}$ and $\tan^{-1}\dfrac{x}{a}$.

Let $\quad y = \sin^{-1} u$ $\qquad\qquad$ where $\quad u = \dfrac{x}{a}$

$\quad \dfrac{dy}{du} = \dfrac{1}{\sqrt{(1-u^2)}}$ $\qquad\qquad \dfrac{du}{dx} = \dfrac{1}{a}$

$\therefore \quad \dfrac{dy}{dx} = \dfrac{dy}{du}\cdot\dfrac{du}{dx} = \dfrac{1}{\sqrt{(1-u^2)}}\cdot\dfrac{1}{a} = \dfrac{1}{a\sqrt{\left(1-\dfrac{x^2}{a^2}\right)}} = \dfrac{1}{\sqrt{(a^2-x^2)}}.$

Hence $\qquad\qquad\qquad \dfrac{d}{dx}\left(\sin^{-1}\dfrac{x}{a}\right) = \dfrac{1}{\sqrt{(a^2-x^2)}}.$

Similarly, $\quad \dfrac{d}{dx}\left(\tan^{-1}\dfrac{x}{a}\right) = \dfrac{1}{\left(1+\dfrac{x^2}{a^2}\right)}\cdot\dfrac{1}{a} = \dfrac{a}{a^2\left(1+\dfrac{x^2}{a^2}\right)} = \dfrac{a}{a^2+x^2}.$

Thus $\qquad \boxed{\displaystyle\int\dfrac{dx}{\sqrt{(a^2-x^2)}} = \sin^{-1}\dfrac{x}{a}+c, \quad \int\dfrac{dx}{a^2+x^2} = \dfrac{1}{a}\tan^{-1}\dfrac{x}{a}+c.}$

Example 2   Evaluate $\displaystyle\int_0^3 \dfrac{dx}{\sqrt{(9-x^2)}}$.

$$\int_0^3 \dfrac{dx}{\sqrt{(9-x^2)}} = \left[\sin^{-1}\dfrac{x}{3}\right]_0^3 = \sin^{-1}1 - \sin^{-1}0 = \tfrac{1}{2}\pi.$$

Example 3   Find   (a) $\displaystyle\int\dfrac{dx}{1+4x^2}$,   (b) $\displaystyle\int\dfrac{dx}{\sqrt{(4-9x^2)}}$.

(a) [The fact that $4x^2 = (2x)^2$ suggests that the answer may involve $\tan^{-1} 2x$.]

$$\frac{d}{dx}(\tan^{-1} 2x) = \frac{1}{1+(2x)^2}\cdot 2 = \frac{2}{1+4x^2}$$

$$\therefore \quad \int \frac{dx}{1+4x^2} = \tfrac{1}{2}\tan^{-1} 2x + c.$$

(b) [The fact that $4-9x^2 = 2^2-(3x)^2$ suggests that the answer may involve $\sin^{-1}\dfrac{3x}{2}$.]

$$\frac{d}{dx}\left(\sin^{-1}\frac{3x}{2}\right) = \frac{1}{\sqrt{\left(1-\dfrac{9x^2}{4}\right)}}\cdot\frac{3}{2} = \frac{3}{\sqrt{\left\{4\left(1-\dfrac{9x^2}{4}\right)\right\}}} = \frac{3}{\sqrt{(4-9x^2)}}$$

$$\therefore \quad \int \frac{dx}{\sqrt{(4-9x^2)}} = \frac{1}{3}\sin^{-1}\frac{3x}{2} + c.$$

Exercise 11.6

Differentiate with respect to x:

1. $\sin^{-1}\tfrac{1}{2}x$.

2. $\tan^{-1} 3x$.

3. $\cos^{-1}(2x+1)$

4. $x\tan^{-1} x$.

5. $\sin^{-1}(\cos x)$.

6. $(1-x^2)^{1/2}\sin^{-1} x$.

7. $\sin^{-1}\left(\dfrac{1}{x}\right)$.

8. $\dfrac{\tan^{-1} 2x}{1+4x^2}$.

9. $\tan^{-1}\left(\dfrac{1+x}{1-x}\right)$.

Integrate the following functions:

10. $\dfrac{1}{\sqrt{(25-x^2)}}$.

11. $\dfrac{1}{9+x^2}$.

12. $\dfrac{1}{\sqrt{(1-4x^2)}}$.

13. $\dfrac{1}{1+9x^2}$.

14. $\dfrac{1}{\sqrt{(16-9x^2)}}$.

15. $\dfrac{1}{9+4x^2}$.

Evaluate the following definite integrals:

16. $\displaystyle\int_0^1 \frac{dx}{\sqrt{(4-x^2)}}$.

17. $\displaystyle\int_0^2 \frac{dx}{4+x^2}$.

18. $\displaystyle\int_{1/6}^{1/3} \frac{dx}{\sqrt{(1-9x^2)}}$.

19. $\displaystyle\int_0^{\sqrt{3}/5} \frac{dx}{1+25x^2}$.

20. $\displaystyle\int_0^{\sqrt{3}/4} \frac{dx}{16x^2+9}$.

21. $\displaystyle\int_{-3/4}^0 \frac{dx}{\sqrt{(9-16x^2)}}$.

Exercise 11.7 (miscellaneous)

1. Two circles with centres A and B intersect at points P and Q, such that $\angle APB$ is a right angle. If $AB = x\,$cm and $\angle PAQ = \frac{1}{3}\pi$ radians, find in terms of x the length of the perimeter and the area of the region common to the two circles.

2. The points A, B and C lie on a circle and $\angle ACB = \frac{1}{3}\pi$ radians. Show that AB divides the circle into major and minor segments whose areas are in the ratio $(8\pi + 3\sqrt{3}) : (4\pi - 3\sqrt{3})$.

3. Two parallel chords of lengths $x\,$cm and $y\,$cm lie on the same side of the centre of a circle with radius $r\,$cm. Construct a flow chart for a procedure to determine the perimeter and the area of the part of the circle between the two chords.

4. Solve, for $0 \leqslant \theta \leqslant 2\pi$, the equations
(a) $\cos 3\theta = \cos \theta$,
(b) $\sin \theta + \sin 2\theta = \sin 3\theta$.

5. Find, in radians, the general solutions of the equations
(a) $\cos 2x = \sin x$,
(b) $\cos x + \cos 3x + \cos 5x = 0$.

6. Find, in degrees, the general solution of the equation $6 \cos \theta - 4 \sin \theta = 5$.

7. Find the limit as $x \to 0$ of $\dfrac{\sin(x + \alpha) - \sin \alpha}{\sin 2x}$.

8. Differentiate the function $\cos x$ from first principles.

9. Write down the derivatives of $\sin x$ and $\cos x$. Hence find the derivatives of $\cot x$ and $\operatorname{cosec} x$.

10. Differentiate with respect to x
(a) $\sin^2 (2x - 5)$,
(b) $x^4 \tan 4x$,
(c) $\dfrac{\sec x + \tan x}{\sec x - \tan x}$,
(d) $\dfrac{\sin x}{\sqrt{(\cos 2x)}}$.

11. Sketch the following curves for $0 \leqslant x \leqslant 2\pi$, showing clearly the positions of any stationary points
(a) $y = 2 \cos x + \sin 2x$,
(b) $y = 3 \sin x - \sin 3x$.

12. Find the following indefinite integrals
(a) $\displaystyle\int \cos (2x - 1)\,dx$,
(b) $\displaystyle\int \sin^2 \tfrac{1}{2}x\,dx$,
(c) $\displaystyle\int \tan x \sec^2 x\,dx$,
(d) $\displaystyle\int \sin 4x \cos x\,dx$.

13. Evaluate (a) $\displaystyle\int_{\pi/6}^{\pi/2} \sin^5 x \cos x \, dx$, (b) $\displaystyle\int_0^{\pi/4} \cos x \cos 2x \cos 3x \, dx$.

14. Differentiate $x \sin x$ with respect to x and use your result to find $\displaystyle\int x \cos x \, dx$.

By a similar method find $\displaystyle\int x^2 \sin x \, dx$.

15. A particle moves in a straight line such that after t seconds its acceleration is $a\,\mathrm{m\,s^{-2}}$, where $a = 8 \sin 2t$. If the velocity of the particle after $\pi/3$ seconds is $5\,\mathrm{m\,s^{-1}}$, find its displacement from its initial position at that instant.

16. Given that R is the region in the first quadrant enclosed by the curves $y = 2 \cos x$, $y = \sin 2x$ and the y-axis, find the volume of the solid formed by rotating R completely about the x-axis.

17. Use the identity $1 - \sin^2 x = \cos^2 x$ to find the integral $\displaystyle\int \frac{dx}{1 - \sin x}$. Hence find the mean value of the function $1/(1 - \sin x)$ over the interval $-\pi/3 \leqslant x \leqslant \pi/6$.

18. Differentiate with respect to x
(a) $x/\sin^{-1} x$, (b) $\tan^{-1}(\sec x)$, (c) $\cos(\sin^{-1} x)$.

19. Find (a) $\displaystyle\int \frac{dx}{\sqrt{(9 - x^2)}}$, (b) $\displaystyle\int \frac{dx}{9x^2 + 25}$.

20. Evaluate (a) $\displaystyle\int_0^1 \frac{dx}{1 + 3x^2}$, (b) $\displaystyle\int_{\sqrt{2}}^2 \frac{dx}{\sqrt{(8 - x^2)}}$.

21. Given that p and q are solutions of the equation $x \tan x = 1$,
(i) show that $\displaystyle\int_0^1 \cos px \cos qx \, dx = 0$ when $p \neq q$,

(ii) find an expression for $\displaystyle\int_0^1 \cos^2 px \, dx$ entirely in terms of p, not involving any trigonometric functions. (AEB 1976)

22. The equal sides AB and AC of an isosceles triangle have length a, and the angle at A is denoted by 2θ. Show that the radius of the inscribed circle of the triangle is given by $r = \dfrac{a \sin \theta \cos \theta}{1 + \sin \theta}$. Show that, if a is constant and θ varies between $0°$ and $90°$, the maximum value of r occurs when $\sin \theta = (\sqrt{5} - 1)/2$. [You need not verify that this value of θ gives a maximum rather than a minimum.] (W)

23. The points A and B are on the same horizontal level, and at a distance b apart. A particle P falls vertically from rest at B, so that, at time t, its depth below

B is kt^2, where k is constant. At this time, the angle of depression of P from A is θ.

Prove that $\dfrac{d\theta}{dt} = \dfrac{2bkt}{b^2 + k^2 t^4}$. Show that $\dfrac{d\theta}{dt}$ is greatest (and not least) when $\theta = \dfrac{1}{6}\pi$.

(C)

24. Differentiate $\tan^{-1}(x+a)$ with respect to x and use your result to find

(a) $\displaystyle\int \frac{dx}{x^2 + 4x + 5}$,

(b) $\displaystyle\int \frac{dx}{x^2 + 2x + 5}$.

25. A rectangular sheet of paper $ABCD$ is folded about the line joining points P on AB and Q on AD so that the new position of A is on CD. If $AB = a$ and $AD = b$, where $a \geqslant 2b/\sqrt{3}$, show that the least possible area of the triangle APQ is obtained when the angle AQP is equal to $\pi/3$. What is the significance of the condition $a \geqslant 2b/\sqrt{3}$?

(O)

12 Permutations and combinations

12.1 Permutations

A *permutation* is an arrangement of objects chosen from a given set. In this section we discuss ways of finding the total number of permutations of a set of objects under various conditions. For example, consider the number of ways in which we could arrange four guests in a row of four numbered chairs at a concert.

Any one of the 4 people may sit in the first chair. When the first person is seated, there are 3 people to be considered for the second place. This means that for each of the 4 ways of choosing the first person, there are 3 ways of choosing the second person to be seated. Similarly, in each of these $4 \times 3 = 12$ cases, we are left with 2 ways of choosing the occupant of the third chair. When 3 people are seated, the fourth chair must be filled by the 1 remaining person. Hence the total number of ways of seating the 4 people is $4 \cdot 3 \cdot 2 \cdot 1$, i.e. 24.

Using the letters A, B, C, D to represent the 4 people, these 24 arrangements are as follows:

A B C D	B A C D	C A B D	D A B C
A B D C	B A D C	C A D B	D A C B
A C B D	B C A D	C B A D	D B A C
A C D B	B C D A	C B D A	D B C A
A D B C	B D A C	C D A B	D C A B
A D C B	B D C A	C D B A	D C B A

Since products of the type $4 \cdot 3 \cdot 2 \cdot 1$ frequently arise in this type of work, the *factorial* notation is used. We write $4 \cdot 3 \cdot 2 \cdot 1 = 4!$ which is read 'four factorial' or 'factorial four'. Thus for any positive integer n, $n! = n(n-1)(n-2)\ldots 3 \cdot 2 \cdot 1$.

The result of the above seating problem can now be generalised.

The number of permutations or arrangements of n different objects is $n!$.

231

Example 1   In how many different ways can 4 people chosen from a set of 6 be seated in a row of four chairs?

There are 6 possible choices for the first chair, then 5 choices for the second, 4 for the third and 3 for the fourth. Hence the total number of ways of seating 4 people out of a set of six is $6.5.4.3$, i.e. 360.
[In factorial notation this number is $6!/2!$]

In general, the number of permutations or arrangements of r different objects chosen from a set of n objects, written $_nP_r$, is given by $_nP_r = \dfrac{n!}{(n-r)!}$.

When $r = n$ this expression becomes $_nP_n = n!/0!$, but as shown above $_nP_n = n!$. Hence, it is convenient to define $0!$ to be 1. This is equivalent to assuming that there is exactly one way of arranging a set containing no objects.

These methods can be extended to other types of problem.

Example 2   How many different three-digit numbers can be formed using the digits 0, 1, 2, 3, 4 (excluding numbers which begin with 0) if (a) no digit may be repeated, (b) repetitions are allowed?

(a) Since the first digit must not be 0, the number of ways of choosing the first digit is 4. As no digit may be repeated, there are 4 digits to choose from for the second position, then 3 for the third. Hence the total number of ways of forming the three-digit number is $4.4.3$, i.e. 48.
(b) If repetitions are allowed, any of the 5 digits may be used in the second and third positions. Hence the total number of three-digit numbers is $4.5.5$, i.e. 100.

Difficulties arise when some of the objects to be arranged are identical. For instance, let us consider the number of ways of arranging the letters of the word TOTTER.

If we label the Ts with suffixes, then for the word $T_1OT_2T_3ER$ there are $6!$, i.e. 120 different arrangements. However, many of these would be indistinguishable with the suffixes removed, e.g. the set

$$RT_1ET_2T_3O, \quad RT_2ET_1T_3O, \quad RT_3ET_1T_2O,$$
$$RT_1ET_3T_2O, \quad RT_2ET_3T_1O, \quad RT_3ET_2T_1O.$$

Since T_1, T_2, T_3 can be arranged in $3!$, i.e. 6 different ways, all 120 arrangements can be grouped into sets of 6, like the one already listed. Hence, with no suffixes, the number of different arrangements will be $6!/3! = 120/6 = 20$.

In general, the number of permutations of n objects, r of which are identical, is $n!/r!$.

Example 3   In how many ways can the letters of the word NECESSITIES be arranged?

The total number of letters in the word is 11.
The letters E and S each occur 3 times. The letter I occurs twice.

Hence the total number of arrangements $= \dfrac{11!}{3!3!2!} = 554\,400.$

Exercise 12.1

1.   Without using a calculator, find the values of

(a) $7!$,   (b) $6! - 5!$,   (c) $\dfrac{8!}{4!}$,   (d) $\dfrac{10!}{3!7!}$,   (e) $_4P_1$,   (f) $_8P_5$.

2.   Express in factorial notation
(a) $5.4.3.2$,   (b) $10.9.8.7$,   (c) $n(n-1)(n-2)$.

3.   Find the number of ways of arranging 6 different books on a shelf.

4.   Find the number of arrangements of 8 items on a shopping list.

5.   A lady has 8 house plants. In how many ways can she arrange 6 of them in a line on a window sill?

6.   In a competition 6 household products chosen from 10 are to be listed in order of preference. In how many ways can this be done?

7.   There are 25 entrants in a gymnastics competition. In how many different ways can the gold, silver and bronze medals be awarded?

8.   Find the number of arrangements of 4 different letters chosen from the word PROBLEM which (a) begin with a vowel, (b) end with a consonant.

9.   How many different four-digit numbers greater than 6000 can be formed using the digits 1, 2, 4, 5, 6, 8, if (a) no digit can be repeated, (b) repetitions are allowed?

10. In how many ways can 3 books be distributed among 10 people if (a) each person can receive any number of books, (b) nobody can be given more than 1 book, (c) nobody can be given more than 2 books?

11. Find the number of different ways in which the letters of the following words can be arranged
(a) NUMBER,   (b) POSSIBLE,   (c) PEPPER,   (d) STATISTICS.

12. How many different six-digit numbers can be formed using the digits 2, 3, 3, 3, 4, 4? How many of these are even?

13. In how many different ways can 8 books be arranged on a shelf if 2 particular books must be placed next to each other?

14. Three girls and 4 boys are to sit in a row of 7 chairs. If the girls wish to sit in adjacent chairs, how many different arrangements are possible?

15. In how many ways can 6 children form a circle to play a game? If Joan refuses to stand next to Tom, how many possible arrangements are there?

16. Find the number of permutations of the word PARABOLA. In how many of these permutations are (a) all three As together, (b) no two As together?

17. How many numbers less than 3500 can be formed using one or more of the digits 1, 3, 5, 7, if (a) no digit can be repeated, (b) repetitions are allowed?

18. Find the total number of possible arrangements of 3 letters chosen from the word CALCULUS.

19. A set of 10 flags, 5 red, 3 blue and 2 yellow, are to be arranged in a line along a balcony. If flags of the same colour are indistinguishable, find the number of arrangements in which (a) the three blue flags are together, (b) the yellow flags are not together, (c) the red flags occupy alternate positions in the line. If there is room for only 9 of the flags, find the total number of possible arrangements.

20. On a shelf there are 4 saucers of different colours and 4 matching cups. In how many ways can the cups be arranged on the saucers, so that no cup is on a matching saucer?

12.2 Combinations

In some problems the order in which objects are arranged is not important. The number of *combinations* of r different objects out of a set of n is the number of different selections, irrespective of order, and is denoted by $_nC_r$, or sometimes $\binom{n}{r}$.

Let us suppose that a set of 3 cards is to be dealt from a pack of 52 playing cards. The number of permutations of 3 cards chosen from $52 = 52!/49!$ $= 52.51.50$. However, since any set of 3 cards can be arranged in 3! different ways, each set of 3 cards will appear 6 times in the list of all possible arrangements. For instance, the set containing cards X, Y and Z will appear as XYZ, XZY, YXZ, YZX, ZXY and ZYX. Hence the total number of ways of selecting 3 cards $= \dfrac{52!}{3!49!} = \dfrac{52.51.50}{3.2.1} = 22\,100.$

In general, the number of ways of selecting r objects from n unlike objects $= {}_nC_r = \dfrac{n!}{r!(n-r)!}.$

Example 1   A committee of 5 is to be formed from 12 men and 8 women. In how many ways can the committee be chosen so that there are 3 men and 2 women on it?

Number of ways of choosing 3 men from 12

$$= {}_{12}C_3 = \frac{12!}{3!9!} = \frac{12.11.10}{3.2.1} = 220.$$

Number of ways of choosing 2 women from 8

$$= {}_8C_2 = \frac{8!}{2!6!} = \frac{8.7}{2.1} = 28.$$

∴   the total number of ways of forming the committee

$$= {}_{12}C_3 \times {}_8C_2 = 220 \times 28 = 6160.$$

There is no general formula for dealing with selections made from sets containing objects which are not all different, as there was for permutations of such sets.

Example 2   How many ways are there of selecting 4 letters from the letters in the word TOTTER?

Number of selections containing one T and three other letters = 1.
Number of selections containing two Ts and two letters from the remaining three = ${}_3C_2 = 3$.
Number of selections containing three Ts and one letter from the remaining three = ${}_3C_1 = 3$.
Hence the total number of ways of selecting 4 letters from TOTTER is 7.

When we select r objects from n, we are dividing the set containing n objects into 2 sets containing r and $n-r$ objects respectively. It is not, therefore, surprising to find that the number of ways of selecting $n-r$ objects from n unlike objects is the same as the number of ways of selecting r objects.

$$_nC_{n-r} = \frac{n!}{(n-r)!(n-\{n-r\})!} = \frac{n!}{(n-r)!r!} = {}_nC_r.$$

Another identity involving the quantity $_nC_r$ is proved in the next example.

Example 3   Prove that $_nC_r + {}_nC_{r-1} = {}_{n+1}C_r$.

$$_nC_r + {}_nC_{r-1} = \frac{n!}{r!(n-r)!} + \frac{n!}{(r-1)!(n-\{r-1\})!}$$

$$= \frac{n!}{r!(n-r+1)!}\{(n-r+1)+r\}$$

$$= \frac{(n+1)!}{r!(n+1-r)!} = {}_{n+1}C_r.$$

Exercise 12.2

1. Evaluate (a) $_7C_4$,   (b) $_5C_4$,   (c) $_6C_1$,   (d) $_8C_0$.

2. Verify that $_nC_{n-r} = {_nC_r}$ for the cases
(a) $n = 8, r = 5$;   (b) $n = 10, r = 2$.

3. In how many ways can
(a) 4 photographs be chosen from 10 proofs,
(b) 3 representatives be chosen from 20 students,
(c) a hand of 5 cards be dealt from a set of 13,
(d) 11 players be selected from 12 cricketers?

4. Nine people are to go on a journey in cars which can take 2, 3 and 4 passengers respectively. In how many different ways can the party travel, assuming that the seating arrangements inside the cars are not important?

5. In how many ways can a set of 12 unlike objects be divided into (a) 2 sets of 6, (b) 3 sets of 4, (c) 6 sets of 2?

6. A team of 5 students, including a captain and a reserve, is to be selected for a general knowledge contest. In how many ways can the team be chosen from a short list of 12?

7. Find the number of different selections of two letters which can be made from the letters of the word PROBABILITY. How many of these selections do not contain a vowel?

8. A chess team of 5 players is to be selected from 15 boys. In how many ways can the team be chosen if (a) no more than one of the three best players is to be included, (b) at least one of the four youngest players is to be included?

9. Find the number of ways in which 8 books can be distributed to 2 boys, if each boy is to receive at least 2 books.

10. Find the number of different selections of three letters which can be made from the letters of the word PARALLELOGRAM. How many of these selections contain the letter P?

11. A tennis team of 6 players consists of a 1st pair, a 2nd pair and a 3rd pair. In how many ways can the team be selected, if there are (a) only 6 players available, (b) 9 players available?

12. A committee of 6 is to be formed from 13 men and 7 women. In how many ways can the committee be selected given that (a) it must consist of 4 men and 2 women, (b) it must have at least one member of each sex?

12.3 Elementary theory of probability

In mathematics probability is the numerical value assigned to the likelihood that a particular event will take place. For instance, if we throw an unbiased die, we have equal chances of scoring any of the numbers 1, 2, 3, 4, 5 and 6. Since there is one chance in six of throwing a 3 the probability of the event occurring is said to be 1/6. Similarly when tossing a coin the probability that it lands heads is considered to be 1/2. This does not, of course, mean that in any two tosses we expect the coin to fall heads once, only that in a long series of tosses the number of heads will be approximately half the total number of throws.

To arrive at a formal definition, consider the set S of all possible *outcomes* of an experiment or *trial*. A set of this kind is sometimes called a *possibility space* or *sample space*. Any *event A* can be represented by the subset A of S, which contains all the outcomes in which the event occurs. If S contains a finite number of *equally likely* outcomes, then the probability $P(A)$ that the event A will occur is given by

$$P(A) = \frac{n(A)}{n(S)}, \quad \text{i.e.} \quad \frac{\text{no. of favourable outcomes}}{\text{no. of possible outcomes}}.$$

If the event A is impossible, then $A = \varnothing$ and $P(A) = 0$. However, if the event A is certain to occur, then $A = S$ and $P(A) = 1$. Otherwise $P(A)$ will take some value between 0 and 1.

[When probabilities are calculated from experimental data, a definition such as the following may be used.

$$\text{Estimated probability} = \frac{\text{no. of successes}}{\text{no. of trials}}.$$

However, this value for the probability could be unreliable unless large numbers of observations are used.]

Example 1 What is the probability of drawing an ace at random from a pack of cards?

Since there are 4 aces in a pack of 52 cards, the probability of drawing an ace is 4/52, i.e. 1/13.

Example 2 If a letter is chosen at random from the word FACETIOUS, what is the probability that it is a vowel?

Since there are 5 vowels out of a total of 9 letters, the probability of choosing a vowel is 5/9.

Returning to the problem of throwing an unbiased die, the probability of throwing a 3 is 1/6, but the probability of not throwing a 3 is 5/6. We notice that the sum of these probabilities is 1. More generally, in a set S of equally likely possible outcomes, if A' denotes the subset of outcomes in which the event A does not occur, then A and A' are called *complementary* events and

$$P(A') = \frac{n(A')}{n(S)} = \frac{n(S) - n(A)}{n(S)} = 1 - \frac{n(A)}{n(S)}$$

$$\therefore \quad \boxed{P(A') = 1 - P(A).}$$

Hence, it seems reasonable to assume that in any sample space, if p is the probability that an event occurs and q is the probability that the event does not occur, then $p + q = 1$.

For experiments in which a trial is a throw of two or more dice, we can construct the sample space from the set of outcomes for a single die, $S = \{1, 2, 3, 4, 5, 6\}$. For instance, in the two-dice case, the possible outcomes can be expressed as ordered pairs such as $(1, 3)$, $(4, 6)$ and $(6, 4)$ formed from the elements of S.

A *sample space diagram* can be used to find probabilities as shown in the next example.

Example 3 If two dice are thrown together, what is the probability of the following events?

A: scoring a total of 2 B: scoring a total of 3
C: the same score on both dice D: 3 or more on each die.

Score on 1st die

The diagram shows that when two dice are thrown, there are 36 possible outcomes. A score of 2 is obtained only when the score on each die is 1

$$\therefore \quad P(A) = \frac{1}{36}.$$

There are two outcomes $(1, 2)$ and $(2, 1)$ which produce a score of 3

$$\therefore \quad P(B) = \frac{2}{36} = \frac{1}{18}.$$

The set of outcomes in which both dice show the same score has 6 elements, as indicated in the diagram

$$\therefore \quad P(C) = \frac{6}{36} = \frac{1}{6}.$$

The diagram also shows that there are 16 outcomes in which both dice show 3 or more

$$\therefore \quad P(D) = \frac{16}{36} = \frac{4}{9}.$$

Example 4 If 4 cards are selected at random from a pack of 52, what is the probability that exactly 3 of them are diamonds?

The number of ways of selecting 3 diamonds from $13 = {}_{13}C_3$.
The number of ways of selecting 1 card from the 39 which are not diamonds $= 39$.
∴ the number of ways of selecting 4 cards, 3 of which are diamonds $= 39 \times {}_{13}C_3$.
The number of ways of selecting any 4 cards from $52 = {}_{52}C_4$.
Hence the probability that exactly 3 cards out of 4 are diamonds

$$= 39 \times {}_{13}C_3 \div {}_{52}C_4 = 39 \times \frac{13!}{3!10!} \times \frac{4!48!}{52!} \approx 0{\cdot}0412.$$

For a trial in which the possible outcomes are not equally likely, it is more difficult to arrive at a precise definition of the probability of an event. However, the subsets of a sample space S are regarded as events whatever the exact nature of the set S. In all cases $P(A)$, the probability of an event A, is a number or a weighting associated with the subset A. We can consider P to be a *probability mapping* which maps any subset A onto a real number p, where $0 \leqslant p \leqslant 1$. In any experiment the set of events (i.e. the set of subsets of the sample space) to be considered together with the appropriate probability mapping may be referred to as the *probability space*.

Exercise 12.3

In questions 1 to 4 find the probability of events A, B and C.

1. A die is thrown. A: scoring a four, B: scoring an odd number, C: scoring four or less.

2. A card is drawn from a pack. A: drawing a red card, B: drawing a seven, C: drawing a king, a queen or a jack.

3. Three coins are tossed. A: three heads, B: at least two tails, C: at least one of each.

4. It rained on exactly two days last week. A: it rained on Monday and Tuesday, B: it rained on two consecutive days, C: it rained on neither Monday nor Tuesday.

5. Two unbiased dice are thrown. Find the probability that the product of the scores is (a) odd, (b) a multiple of 3, (c) a multiple of 12.

6. A domino is drawn from a standard set of 28. Find the probability that the sum of its spots is (a) 2, (b) 8, (c) odd, (d) even.

7. An integer is chosen at random from the first 200 positive integers. Find the probability that it is (a) not divisible by 5, (b) a perfect square, (c) divisible by both 5 and 2, (d) divisible by neither 2 nor 7.

8. In a cafeteria 80% of the customers order chips and 60% order peas. If 20% of those ordering peas do not want chips, find the probability that a customer chosen at random orders chips but not peas.

9. The points A, B, C, D and E are the vertices of a regular pentagon. All possible lines joining pairs of these points are drawn. If two of these lines are chosen at random, that is the probability that their point of intersection is (a) inside the pentagon, (b) one of the points A, B, C, D, E.

10. A box contains 4 discs numbered 1, 2, 2, 3. A disc is drawn from the box then replaced and a second disc is drawn. With the aid of a sample space diagram or otherwise, find the probability that (a) the total score is 6, (b) the total score is 4, (c) the numbers drawn are different, (d) the difference between the two numbers drawn is less than two.

11. Two cards are selected at random without replacement from a set of five numbered 2, 3, 4, 4, 5. With the aid of a diagram or otherwise, find the probability that the numbers on the cards (a) are both even, (b) have a difference of 2, (c) have a sum of 7, (d) have a sum of 8.

12. Write down in factorial form the number of different arrangements of the letters of the word EQUILIBRIUM. One of these arrangements is chosen at random. Find the probability that (a) the first two letters of the arrangement are consonants, (b) all the vowels are together.

13. A hand of three cards is dealt from a well shuffled pack of 52. Find the probability that the hand contains (a) exactly one ace, (b) three cards of the same suit, (c) no two cards of the same suit.

14. On a plate of 12 assorted cakes, 3 are doughnuts. If 3 cakes are selected at random, find the probabilities that 0, 1, 2, 3 doughnuts are chosen.

15. A bag contains 25 clothes pegs, 15 plastic pegs and 10 wooden pegs. If 4 pegs are taken from the bag at random, find the probability that (a) all 4 are plastic, (b) 2 are plastic and 2 are wooden.

16. Four books are selected at random from a shelf containing 3 cookery books, 5 novels and 2 biographies. Find the probability that the four books (a) are all novels, (b) are 2 novels and 2 cookery books, (c) include at least one biography, (d) include at least one of each type.

Exercise 12.4 (miscellaneous)

1. How many even five-digit numbers can be formed using the digits 0, 1, 2, 3, 4, 5, 6 (excluding numbers which start with 0) if (a) no digit may be repeated, (b) repetition is allowed?

2. Find the number of different ways in which the letters of the word ISOSCELES can be arranged. How many of these arrangements (a) begin and end with E, (b) begin with S, (c) end with a vowel?

3. A man has found 6 records that he likes in a shop, but cannot decide which of them to buy. Assuming that he buys at least one, find the number of different selections he could make.

4. Six lines are drawn, no two of which are parallel. If no more than two of the lines pass through any one point, find the number of triangles formed.

5. In how many ways can a group of 9 people attending a conference be split into three sets of 3 people for discussion? Later the same people form new sets of 3. In how many ways can this be done if no two people remain together?

6. Find the number of ways in which 5 books can be distributed between three people A, B and C if the books are (a) all different, (b) indistinguishable.

7. A drawer contains 4 different pairs of socks. Find the probability that (a) if 2 socks are selected at random they will form a pair, (b) if 4 socks are selected at random they will form two pairs.

8. (a) Two dice are thrown together, and the scores added. What is the probability that (i) the total score exceeds 8, (ii) the total score is 9, or the individual scores differ by 1, or both?
(b) A bag contains 3 red balls and 4 black ones. 3 balls are picked out, one at a time and not replaced. What is the probability that there will be 2 red and 1 black in the sample?
(c) A committee of 4 is to be chosen from 6 men and 5 women. One particular man and one particular woman refuse to serve if the other person is on the committee. How many different committees may be formed?   (SU)

9. Two cards are drawn simultaneously from a pack of 52. What is the probability that both are spades if one card is known to be (a) black, (b) red, (c) a spade, (d) a king?

10. A pack of 52 cards contains 4 suits each of 13 cards. If 13 cards are taken at random from the pack what is the probability that exactly 10 of them are spades? [You may take $\binom{52}{13} = 6\cdot35 \times 10^{11}$.]   (O&C)

13 Series and the binomial theorem

13.1 Sequences and series

Below are some sets of numbers given in a definite order. In each case the numbers are produced according to some simple rule.

(a) $2, 4, 6, 8, 10, \ldots$ (b) $1, 4, 9, 16, 25, \ldots$

(c) $1, -1, 1, -1, 1, \ldots$ (d) $8, -4, 2, -1, \frac{1}{2}, \ldots$

(e) $10, 11, 9, 12, 8, 13, \ldots$ (f) $1, 1, 2, 3, 5, 8, \ldots$

These sets of numbers are called *sequences*. Each member of a sequence is a *term*. For instance, in (a) 6 is the third term of the sequence.

One way of stating the rule by which a sequence is obtained is to write down a formula for the *nth term*, often denoted by u_n. For sequences (a), (b) and (c) given above we may write,

(a) $u_n = 2n$ and $u_6 = 12, u_7 = 14$,

(b) $u_n = n^2$ and $u_6 = 36, u_7 = 49$,

(c) $u_n = (-1)^{n+1}$ and $u_6 = -1, u_7 = 1$.

In some cases the formula for u_n is not obvious. In (d) to obtain each successive term we divide by 2, then change the sign. Thus, at each stage we are multiplying by $-\frac{1}{2}$, which means that

$$u_n = 8 \cdot (-\tfrac{1}{2})^{n-1}, \text{ so that } u_6 = 8 \cdot (-\tfrac{1}{2})^5 = -\frac{8}{2^5} = -\frac{1}{4}.$$

In (e) a general formula for u_n would be difficult to find, but we can give separate formulae for odd and even terms of the sequence.

$u_{2n+1} = 10 - n$ and for $n = 3, u_7 = 7$,

$u_{2n} = 10 + n$ and for $n = 4, u_8 = 14$.

In (f) each term is the sum of the two previous terms. This can be expressed formally as a relation between u_n and u_{n-1}, u_{n-2}:

$$u_n = u_{n-1} + u_{n-2} \qquad (n \geqslant 3).$$

242

In this case more advanced techniques are needed to find a formula for u_n in terms of n.

If a sequence ends after a certain number of terms it is said to be *finite*. A sequence which continues indefinitely is said to be *infinite*. The sequence $1, 3, 5, \ldots, 2n-1$ is finite with n terms, whereas $1, 3, 5, \ldots, 2n-1, \ldots$ denotes an infinite sequence.

A sum of a sequence of numbers is called a *series*. $1 + 3 + 5 + \ldots + 97 + 99$ is a finite series and $1 + 3 + 5 + \ldots$ indicates an infinite series. The nth term of both these series is $u_n = 2n-1$, where $1 \leqslant n \leqslant 50$ in the finite case.

S_n is used to denote the sum of the first n terms of a series, so that $S_n = u_1 + u_2 + \ldots + u_n$.

Example 1 Find S_1, S_5 and S_6 for the series $1 + \dfrac{1}{2} + \dfrac{1}{4} + \dfrac{1}{8} + \ldots$.

S_1 is simply the first term $\therefore$ $S_1 = 1$

$$S_5 = 1 + \frac{1}{2} + \frac{1}{4} + \frac{1}{8} + \frac{1}{16} \quad \therefore \quad S_5 = 1\frac{15}{16}$$

$$S_6 = S_5 + \frac{1}{32} = 1\frac{15}{16} + \frac{1}{32} \quad \therefore \quad S_6 = 1\frac{31}{32}.$$

Example 2   The sum of the first n terms of a series is given by $S_n = n^2 + n$. Write down the first three terms of the series and find an expression for the nth term, u_n.

$$S_1 = 1^2 + 1 = 2, \quad S_2 = 2^2 + 2 = 6, \quad S_3 = 3^2 + 3 = 12,$$

$\therefore$ the first three terms of the series must be $2 + 4 + 6 + \ldots$.

$$S_n = n^2 + n, \quad S_{n-1} = (n-1)^2 + (n-1) = n^2 - n$$

$$\therefore \quad u_n = S_n - S_{n-1} = n^2 + n - (n^2 - n) = 2n.$$

Hence the nth term of the series is $2n$.

Exercise 13.1

In questions 1 to 10 write down the next two terms of the given sequence and an expression for the nth term.

1. $5, 10, 15, 20, \ldots$

2. $4, 7, 10, 13, \ldots$

3. $1, \dfrac{1}{2}, \dfrac{1}{3}, \dfrac{1}{4}, \ldots$

4. $\dfrac{1}{2}, \dfrac{2}{3}, \dfrac{3}{4}, \dfrac{4}{5}, \ldots$

5. $1, 2, 4, 8, \ldots$

6. $0, 3, 8, 15, 24, \ldots$

7. $\dfrac{1}{12}, \dfrac{1}{6}, \dfrac{1}{3}, \dfrac{2}{3}, \ldots$

8. $\dfrac{1}{2}, \dfrac{1}{6}, \dfrac{1}{12}, \dfrac{1}{20}, \ldots$

9. $1, -2, 3, -4, \ldots$ 　　　　　　　　　10. $11, 8, 13, 6, 15, \ldots$

In questions 11 to 16 find the first three terms and the nth term of the series with the given sum to n terms.

11. $S_n = 4 + 7n^2$. 　　　　　　　　　　12. $S_n = 3n - 7n^3$.

13. $S_n = 2^n$. 　　　　　　　　　　　　14. $S_n = \dfrac{1}{n}$.

15. $S_n = \dfrac{1}{4}n^2(n+1)^2$. 　　　　　　16. $S_n = \dfrac{1}{6}n(n+1)(2n+1)$.

17. Given that $1^3 + 2^3 + 3^3 + \ldots + n^3 = \dfrac{1}{4}n^2(n+1)^2$, find the sum of the first 20 terms of the series $2 + 16 + 54 + 128 + 250 + \ldots$.

18. Given that $1^2 + 2^2 + 3^2 + \ldots + n^2 = \dfrac{1}{6}n(n+1)(2n+1)$, find the sum of the series $2^2 + 4^2 + 6^2 + \ldots + 50^2$. Use your result to find the sum of the series $1^2 + 3^2 + 5^2 + \ldots + 49^2$.

13.2 Arithmetic progressions

An *arithmetic progression* is a series in which one term is obtained from the previous term by adding a fixed number.

For example:　(a)　$1 + 2 + 3 + 4 + \ldots + 98 + 99$,
　　　　　　　(b)　$6 + 10 + 14 + 18 + \ldots + 46 + 50$,
　　　　　　　(c)　$10 + 7 + 4 + 1 + \ldots - 47 - 50$.

This fixed number is called the *common difference*. In the above examples the common differences are $1, 4$ and -3 respectively.

An arithmetic progression is completely defined when the first term a and the common difference d are given:

$$a + (a+d) + (a+2d) + \ldots.$$

Example 1　Write down the first three terms, the 10th term and the nth term of the A.P. (arithmetic progression) with first term -20 and common difference 3.

The first three terms are $-20, -17$ and -14.
The 10th term, $u_{10} = -20 + (3 \times 9) = 7$.
The nth term, $u_n = -20 + 3(n-1) = 3n - 23$.

More generally, the nth term of the A.P. with first term a and common difference d is $\boxed{u_n = a + (n-1)d.}$

To illustrate the general approach to the summation of arithmetic progressions, we consider the following:

$$1 + \quad 2 + \quad 3 + \ldots + \quad 98 + \quad 99$$
$$99 + \quad 98 + \quad 97 + \ldots + \quad 2 + \quad 1$$

$$\overline{100 + 100 + 100 + \ldots + 100 + 100}$$

Since there are 99 columns,

$$2(1 + 2 + 3 + \ldots + 99) = 99 \times 100.$$

Hence $1 + 2 + 3 + \ldots + 99 = 4950.$

Applying this method to an A.P. with n terms, first term a, last term l and common difference d:

$$S_n = a + (a+d) + \ldots + (l-d) + l$$
$$S_n = l + (l-d) + \ldots + (a+d) + a$$
$$\therefore \quad 2S_n = (a+l) + (a+l) + \ldots + (a+l) + (a+l) = n(a+l)$$

$$\therefore \quad \text{the sum of the first } n \text{ terms,} \boxed{S_n = \tfrac{1}{2}n(a+l).}$$

As l is the nth term of the series, $l = a + (n-1)d$

$$\therefore \quad S_n = \tfrac{1}{2}n\{a + a + (n-1)d\} = \tfrac{1}{2}n\{2a + (n-1)d\}.$$

Hence the sum of the first n terms of an arithmetic progression with first term a and common difference d is $\tfrac{1}{2}n\{2a + (n-1)d\}$.

Example 2   Find the sums of the series
(a) $6 + 10 + 14 + \ldots + 50$,   (b) $10 + 7 + 4 + \ldots - 50$.

(a) The series has first term 6, common difference 4

$$\therefore \quad \text{the number of terms} = \frac{50-6}{4} + 1 = 12.$$

Hence the sum of the series $= \tfrac{1}{2} . 12(6+50) = 336.$
(b) The series has first term 10, common difference -3

$$\therefore \quad \text{the number of terms} = \frac{-50-10}{-3} + 1 = 21.$$

Hence the sum of the series $= \tfrac{1}{2} . 21(10-50) = -420.$

Example 3   Find the sum of the first 20 terms of the A.P. with first term 3 and common difference $\tfrac{1}{2}$.

$$S_{20} = \tfrac{1}{2} . 20(2 . 3 + 19 . \tfrac{1}{2}) = 10\left(6 + \frac{19}{2}\right) = 60 + 95 = 155$$

$\therefore$ the sum of the first twenty terms is 155.

Example 4   In an A.P. the sum of the first 10 terms is 520 and the 7th term is double the 3rd term. Find the first term a and the common difference d.

$$S_{10} = \tfrac{1}{2}.10(2a+9d) = 520 \qquad \therefore \quad 2a+9d = 104. \tag{1}$$

The 7th term, $u_7 = a+6d$, and the 3rd term, $u_3 = a+2d$

$$\therefore \quad a+6d = 2(a+2d), \quad \text{i.e.} \quad 2d = a \tag{2}$$

Substituting in (1) $13d = 104 \qquad \therefore \quad d = 8$
Substituting in (2) $a = 16.$

Hence the first term of the A.P. is 16 and the common difference is 8.

If three numbers a, b and c are in arithmetic progression, then b is called the *arithmetic mean* of a and c.

The common difference $= b-a = c-b$, $\therefore \quad b = \tfrac{1}{2}(a+c)$. Thus the arithmetic mean of any two numbers, p and q, is the 'average', $\tfrac{1}{2}(p+q)$.

Exercise 13.2
1.   Write down the stated term and the nth term of the following A.P.s
(a) $7+11+15+ \dots$ (7th),   (b) $18+11+4+ \dots$ (6th),
(c) $-7-5-3- \dots$ (23rd),   (d) $3+3\tfrac{1}{2}+4+ \dots$ (16th).

2.   Find the sums of the following series
(a) $5+9+13+ \dots +101.$ (b) $83+80+77+ \dots +5,$
(c) $-17-12-7- \dots +33,$ (d) $1+1\tfrac{1}{4}+1\tfrac{1}{2}+ \dots +9\tfrac{3}{4}.$

3.   Find the sums of the following A.P.s
(a) $4+11+ \dots$ to 16 terms,   (b) $3+8\tfrac{1}{2}+ \dots$ to 20 terms,
(c) $19+13+ \dots$ to 10 terms,   (d) $-9-1+ \dots$ to 8 terms.

4.   Find the sum of the A.P. $-7-3+1+ \dots$ from the seventh to the thirtieth term inclusive.

5.   Find the sum of all odd numbers between 0 and 500 which are divisible by 7.

6.   Show that the sum $1+3+5+ \dots +(2n-1)$ is always a perfect square.

7.   The first and last terms of an A.P. with 25 terms are 29 and 179. Find the sum of the series and its common difference.

8.   The rth term of a series is $10-3r$. Find the first three terms of the series and the sum of the first 18 terms.

9.   Given that the first and third terms of an A.P. are 13 and 25 respectively, find the 100th term and the sum of the first 15 terms.

10. A piece of string of length 5 m is cut into n pieces in such a way that the lengths of the pieces are in arithmetic progression. If the lengths of the longest and the shortest pieces are 1 m and 25 cm respectively, calculate n.

11. The second and seventh terms of an A.P. are -5 and 10 respectively. Find the fifth term and the least number of terms that must be taken for their sum to exceed 200.

12. The tenth term of an A.P. is 10 and the sum of the first 10 terms is -35. Find the first term and the common difference of the progression.

13. The sum of the first four terms of an A.P. is twice the fifth term. Show that the common difference is equal to the first term.

14. In an A.P. the sum of the first 15 terms is 615 and the 13th term is six times the 2nd term. Find the first three terms.

15. Find the arithmetic mean of

(a) 3 and 27,   (b) 3 and -27,   (c) $\dfrac{1}{3}$ and $\dfrac{1}{27}$,   (d) lg 3 and lg 27.

16. Three numbers in A.P. have sum 33 and product 1232. Find the numbers.

17. The sum of three numbers in A.P. is 30 and the sum of their squares is 398. Find the numbers.

18. The sum of the first n terms of a certain series is $3n^2 + n$. Show that the series is an A.P. and find the first term and the common difference.

19. Show that the sum to 20 terms of the series

$$\log a + \log(ab) + \log(ab^2) + \log(ab^3) + \dots$$

can be written in the form $\log(a^x b^y)$ and find the values of x and y.

20. In an A.P. the sum of the first $2n$ terms is equal to the sum of the next n terms. If the first term is 12 and the common difference is 3, find the non-zero value of n.

13.3 Geometric progressions

A *geometric progression* (G.P.) is a series in which any term is obtained from the previous term by multiplying by a fixed number.

For example: (a) $1 + 2 + 4 + 8 + \dots + 128 + 256$,

(b) $27 - 9 + 3 - 1 + \dots + \dfrac{1}{27} - \dfrac{1}{81}$.

This fixed number is called the *common ratio*. In the above examples the common ratios are 2 and $-\frac{1}{3}$ respectively.

A geometric progression is completely defined when the first term a and the common ratio r are given:

$$a + ar + ar^2 + ar^3 + \ldots .$$

The nth term of this G.P. is $\boxed{u_n = ar^{n-1}.}$

Example 1 Write down the formula for the nth term and find the number of terms in series (a) and (b) above.

(a) The nth term $= 1 \times 2^{n-1} = 2^{n-1}$.

If $2^{n-1} = 256 = 2^8$, then $n = 9$

$\therefore$ the series has 9 terms.

(b) The nth term $= 27 \times (-\frac{1}{3})^{n-1}$

If $27 \times (-\frac{1}{3})^{n-1} = -\dfrac{1}{81}$, then $(-\frac{1}{3})^{n-1} = -\dfrac{1}{3^7} = (-\frac{1}{3})^7$

$\therefore$ $n = 8$ and the series must have 8 terms.

We illustrate the method by which G.P.s are summed by considering the sum S of series (a).

$$S = 1 + 2 + 4 + \ldots + 256$$
$$2S =\quad 2 + 4 + 8 + \ldots \quad + 512.$$

Subtracting: $2S - S = 512 - 1$
$$\therefore\quad S = 511.$$

Applying this method to a G.P. with n terms, first term a and common ratio r, we have

$$S_n = a + ar + ar^2 + \ldots + ar^{n-1}$$
$$rS_n =\quad ar + ar^2 + \ldots + ar^{n-1} + ar^n.$$

Subtracting: $S_n - rS_n = a - ar^n$
$$S_n(1 - r) = a(1 - r^n)$$
$$\therefore\ S_n = \frac{a(1 - r^n)}{1 - r} \qquad (r \neq 1)$$

$\therefore$ the sum of the first n terms of a geometric progression with first term a and common ratio r is given by

$$\boxed{S_n = \frac{a(1 - r^n)}{1 - r} \quad \text{or} \quad S_n = \frac{a(r^n - 1)}{r - 1}.}$$

[The second expression is more convenient if $r > 1$.]

Example 2 Find the sum of the first 6 terms of the series
(a) $2-6+18-\ldots$ (b) $14+7+3\frac{1}{2}+\ldots$

(a) The series is a G.P. with first term 2 and common ratio -3

$$\therefore \quad \text{the sum} = \frac{2\{1-(-3)^6\}}{1-(-3)} = \frac{2(1-729)}{4} = -364.$$

(b) The series is a G.P. with first term 14 and common ratio $\frac{1}{2}$

$$\therefore \quad \text{the sum} = \frac{14\{1-(\frac{1}{2})^6\}}{1-\frac{1}{2}} = \frac{14(1-1/64)}{\frac{1}{2}} = 14\cdot2\cdot\frac{63}{64} = \frac{441}{16}.$$

Example 3 A G.P. has first term 10 and common ratio 1·5. How many terms of the series are needed to reach a sum greater than 200?

$$\text{The sum of } n \text{ terms} = \frac{10\{(1\cdot5)^n-1\}}{1\cdot5-1} = 20\{(1\cdot5)^n-1\}$$

$$20\{(1\cdot5)^n-1\} > 200 \Rightarrow (1\cdot5)^n - 1 > 10$$
$$\Rightarrow \quad (1\cdot5)^n > 11$$
$$\Rightarrow \quad \lg(1\cdot5)^n > \lg 11$$
$$\Rightarrow \quad n\lg 1\cdot5 > \lg 11$$
$$\Rightarrow \quad n > \frac{\lg 11}{\lg 1\cdot5} \approx 5\cdot9.$$

Hence 6 terms are needed to reach a sum greater than 200.

If three positive numbers a, b and c are in geometric progression, then b is called the *geometric mean* of a and c.

$$\text{The common ratio} = \frac{b}{a} = \frac{c}{b} \qquad \therefore \quad b^2 = ac.$$

Hence the geometric mean of two numbers, p and q, is $\sqrt{(pq)}$.

Exercise 13.3

1. Write down the stated term and the nth term of the following G.P.s
(a) $\frac{1}{2}+1+2+\ldots$ (8th),   (b) $162+54+18+\ldots$ (6th),
(c) $200-50+12\frac{1}{2}-\ldots$ (5th),   (d) $-\frac{4}{9}-\frac{2}{3}-1-\ldots$ (7th).

2. Find the number of terms in each of the following G.P.s and the sum of the series.
(a) $\frac{1}{4}+\frac{1}{2}+\ldots+64$,   (b) $\frac{1}{4}-\frac{1}{2}+\ldots+64$,
(c) $1000+200+\ldots+0\cdot32$,   (d) $2-3+\ldots+22\frac{25}{32}$.

3. Find the sums of the following G.P.s
(a) $100+10+\ldots$ to 7 terms,   (b) $1-\frac{1}{3}+\ldots$ to 6 terms,
(c) $3-6+\ldots$ to n terms,   (d) $a^p+a^{p+3}+a^{p+6}+\ldots$ to k terms.

4.   The first term of a G.P. with positive terms is 80. If the sum of the first three terms is 185, find the common ratio.

5.   Find two distinct numbers p and q such that p, q, 10 are in arithmetic progression and q, p, 10 are in geometric progression.

6.   Find the geometric mean of

(a) 3 and 27,   (b) $\dfrac{1}{3}$ and $\dfrac{1}{27}$,   (c) 10^3 and 10^{27}.

7.   Given that the geometric mean of the numbers $4x-3$ and $9x+4$ is $6x-1$, find the value of x.

8.   The second and fifth terms in a G.P. are 405 and -120 respectively. Find the seventh term and the sum of the first seven terms.

9.   In a G.P. the second term exceeds the first by 20 and the fourth term exceeds the second by 15. Find the two possible values of the first term.

10. If the sum of the first two terms of a G.P. is 162 and the sum of its first four terms is 180, find the sum of the first six terms. Find also the two possible values of the sixth term.

11. The sum of the first six terms of a G.P. is nine times the sum of the first three terms. Find the common ratio.

12. The sum of $(n+12)$ terms of the G.P. $2+4+8+ \ldots$ is twice the sum of n terms of the G.P. $3+12+48+ \ldots$. Calculate the value of n.

13. The sum of the first seven terms of a G.P. is 7 and the sum of the next seven terms is 896. Find the common ratio of the progression. If the kth term is the first term of the G.P. which is greater than 1, find k.

14. Find the sum of the first n terms of the G.P. $\dfrac{1}{12}+\dfrac{1}{4}+\dfrac{3}{4}+ \ldots$. How many terms of the series are needed to reach a sum greater than 100?

15. A G.P. has first term 16 and common ratio $\frac{3}{4}$. If the sum of the first n terms is greater than 60, find the least possible value of n.

13.4 Infinite geometric series

Consider the infinite geometric progression (or geometric series)

$$1+\frac{1}{2}+\frac{1}{4}+\frac{1}{8}+ \ldots +\left(\frac{1}{2}\right)^{n-1}+ \ldots.$$

The sum of the first n terms is

$$S_n = \frac{1\{1-(\frac{1}{2})^n\}}{1-\frac{1}{2}} = 2\{1-(\frac{1}{2})^n\} = 2 - \frac{1}{2^{n-1}}.$$

As n increases, $\frac{1}{2^{n-1}}$ approaches 0 and S_n takes values closer and closer to 2.

Thus as $n \to \infty$, $1/2^{n-1} \to 0$ and $S_n \to 2$.

Since S_n approaches a finite limit, as n increases, the infinite series is said to be *convergent* with sum 2.

More generally, for a geometric series with first term a and common ratio r,

$$S_n = \frac{a(1-r^n)}{1-r} = \frac{a}{1-r} - r^n\left(\frac{a}{1-r}\right).$$

The value of S_n, as n increases, depends on the value of r^n. If

$|r| < 1$,   i.e. if $-1 < r < 1$,   then as $n \to \infty$, $r^n \to 0$ and $S_n \to a/(1-r)$.

In this case, we say that the series $a + ar + ar^2 + \ldots$ *converges* and its *sum to infinity*, denoted by S or S_∞, is $\frac{a}{1-r}$.

[If $r > 1$, then as $n \to \infty$, $r^n \to \infty$. If $r < -1$, then as $n \to \infty$, r^n oscillates between large positive and large negative values. If $r = 1$, then $S_n = na$. If $r = -1$, then either $S_n = a$ or $S_n = 0$. In none of these cases does S_n approach a finite limit and the series is said to be *divergent*.]

Hence, provided that $|r| < 1$, the sum to infinity of the geometric series $a + ar + ar^2 + \ldots$ is $\frac{a}{1-r}$.

Example 1   Find the sum to infinity of the series $18 - 6 + 2 - \ldots$.

This is a geometric series with first term 18 and common ratio $-\frac{1}{3}$

$\therefore$ the sum to infinity $= \dfrac{18}{1-(-\frac{1}{3})} = 18 \Big/ \dfrac{4}{3} = 18 \cdot \dfrac{3}{4} = 13\frac{1}{2}$.

Example 2   Express as a fraction in its lowest terms the recurring decimal $0\cdot37\dot{0}$.

$0\cdot37\dot{0} = 0\cdot370370370\ldots = 0\cdot37 + 0\cdot00037 + 0\cdot00000037 + \ldots$.

This is a geometric series with first term $0\cdot37$ and common ratio $1/1000$, i.e. $0\cdot001$

$\therefore$ $0\cdot37\dot{0} = \dfrac{0\cdot37}{1-0\cdot001} = \dfrac{0\cdot37}{0\cdot999} = \dfrac{370}{999} = \dfrac{10}{27}$.

Example 3 Find the sum of the infinite series $1 + 2x + 4x^2 + 8x^3 + \ldots$, stating for which values of x your result is valid.

This is a geometric series with first term 1 and common ratio $2x$

$\therefore$ its sum is $1/(1 - 2x)$.

The result is valid for $|2x| < 1$, i.e. for $|x| < \frac{1}{2}$.

Exercise 13.4

1.   Find the sums to infinity of the following geometric series
(a) $6 + 2 + \frac{2}{3} + \ldots$,   (b) $1 - \frac{1}{2} + \frac{1}{4} - \ldots$,
(c) $10 + 1 + 0 \cdot 1 + \ldots$,   (d) $45 - 30 + 20 - \ldots$.

2.   Express as fractions in their lowest terms
(a) $0 \cdot \dot{5}\dot{4}$,   (b) $0 \cdot 0\dot{7}\dot{2}$,   (c) $0 \cdot 5\dot{7}4\dot{0}$.

3.   A geometric series with common ratio $0 \cdot 8$ converges to the sum 250. Find the fourth term of the series.

4.   The first and fourth terms of a geometric series are 135 and -40 respectively. Find the common ratio of the series and its sum to infinity.

5.   The sum of the first n terms of a geometric series is $8 - 2^{3-2n}$. Find the first term of the series, its common ratio and its sum to infinity.

6.   Find the sums of the following infinite series, stating the values of x for which your results are valid.
(a) $1 + 3x + 9x^2 + \ldots$,   (b) $1 - \frac{1}{2}x + \frac{1}{4}x^2 - \ldots$,

(c) $2 - 4x + 8x^2 - \ldots$,   (d) $x + \frac{1}{3}x^2 + \frac{1}{9}x^3 + \ldots$.

7. A geometric series has first term 35 and common ratio 2^x. State the set of values of x for which the series is convergent. Find the value of x for which the sum to infinity of the series is 40.

8.   Find the sum to n terms of the geometric series $108 + 60 + 33\frac{1}{3} + \ldots$. If k is the least number which exceeds this sum for all values of n, find k. Find also the least value of n for which the sum exceeds 99% of k.

13.5 The Σ notation

As writing out a series can often be cumbersome, the Greek capital letter Σ (pronounced 'sigma') is used to mean 'the sum of'.

$$\sum_{r=1}^{n} u_r \left(\text{or} \sum_{1}^{n} u_r \right) \text{ means 'the sum of all the terms } u_r \text{ from } r = 1 \text{ to } r = n', \text{ i.e.}$$

$$S_n = \sum_{r=1}^{n} u_r = u_1 + u_2 + u_3 + \dots + u_n.$$

Example 1 Find $\displaystyle\sum_{r=3}^{6} r(r-1)$.

$$\sum_{r=3}^{6} r(r-1) = 3(3-1) + 4(4-1) + 5(5-1) + 6(6-1)$$
$$= 6 + 12 + 20 + 30 = 68.$$

Example 2 Write in Σ notation the series
(a) $2 + 5 + 10 + 17 + 26 + \dots + 401$
(b) $3 + 2 + \dfrac{11}{7} + \dfrac{12}{9} + \dfrac{13}{11} + \dots + \dfrac{20}{25}$.

(a) The rth term of the series, $u_r = r^2 + 1$.
Since 401 is given by $r = 20$, the series has 20 terms.
Hence in Σ notation the series is $\displaystyle\sum_{r=1}^{20} (r^2 + 1)$.

(b) The rth term, $u_r = \dfrac{r+8}{2r+1}$.

The final term, $\dfrac{20}{25}$, is given by $r = 12$.

Hence in Σ notation the series is $\displaystyle\sum_{r=1}^{12} \dfrac{r+8}{2r+1}$.

Some basic rules for manipulating expressions involving Σ can be established as follows:

$$\sum_{1}^{n} (ku_r) = ku_1 + ku_2 + \dots + ku_n$$
$$= k(u_1 + u_2 + \dots + u_n) = k \sum_{1}^{n} u_r.$$

In particular $\displaystyle\sum_{1}^{n} k = k + k + \dots + k = kn.$

$$\sum_{1}^{n} (u_r + v_r) = (u_1 + v_1) + (u_2 + v_2) + \dots + (u_n + v_n)$$
$$= (u_1 + u_2 + \dots + u_n) + (v_1 + v_2 + \dots + v_n)$$
$$= \sum_{1}^{n} u_r + \sum_{1}^{n} v_r.$$

Similarly
$$\sum_1^n (u_r - v_r) = \sum_1^n u_r - \sum_1^n v_r.$$

$\Bigg[$ Note that, in general, $\sum_1^n u_r v_r = u_1 v_1 + u_2 v_2 + \dots + u_n v_n$ is *not* equal to

$\left(\sum_1^n u_r\right)\left(\sum_1^n v_r\right).\Bigg]$

Exercise 13.5

1. Write in full and hence evaluate:

(a) $\displaystyle\sum_{r=1}^4 (r^3 + 3r)$,

(b) $\displaystyle\sum_{r=10}^{12} (150 - r^2)$,

(c) $\displaystyle\sum_{r=2}^7 (4r + 3)$,

(d) $\displaystyle\sum_{r=1}^6 \frac{120}{r}$,

(e) $\displaystyle\sum_{r=1}^6 \sin\frac{r\pi}{3}$,

(f) $\displaystyle\sum_{r=0}^5 (-1)^r (1 + 2^{r+1})$.

2. Find expressions for the following series in the form $\displaystyle\sum_1^n f(r)$.

(a) $5 + 7 + 9 + \dots + 27$,

(b) $1 + 8 + 27 + \dots + 4096$

(c) $-2 + 3 - 4 + 5 - \dots + 41$,

(d) $360 - 180 + 90 - \dots + 5\frac{5}{8}$,

(e) $\dfrac{1}{2} + \dfrac{3}{4} + \dfrac{5}{6} + \dots + \dfrac{19}{20}$,

(f) $\dfrac{1}{4} + \dfrac{4}{7} + \dfrac{9}{10} + \dots + \dfrac{144}{37}$.

3. Evaluate the following without writing down the series in full.

(a) $\displaystyle\sum_1^{20} (4r + 5)$,

(b) $\displaystyle\sum_1^{16} (-1)^r (2r - 1)$,

(c) $\displaystyle\sum_0^{50} (25 - 2r)$

(d) $\displaystyle\sum_1^9 5(-2)^{r-1}$,

(e) $\displaystyle\sum_0^{\infty} (\tfrac{1}{2})^r$,

(f) $\displaystyle\sum_2^{\infty} (0.1)^r$.

4. By expressing r in terms of s, or otherwise, show that

(a) $\displaystyle\sum_{r=0}^{n-1} r(r+1) = \sum_{s=1}^n s(s-1)$,

(b) $\displaystyle\sum_{r=1}^n (3r+2) = \sum_{s=3}^{n+2} (3s-4)$.

5. Show that   (a) $\displaystyle\sum_1^{100} (2-r)(2+r) = 400 - \sum_1^{100} r^2$

(b) $\displaystyle\sum_{21}^{40} (r-5) = 300 + \sum_1^{20} r$.

6. Show that $1^3 + 3^3 + 5^3 + \dots + 25^3 = \displaystyle\sum_1^{25} r^3 - 8\sum_1^{12} r^3.$

7. Prove that $\sum_{1}^{n}(au_r + bv_r) = a\sum_{1}^{n}u_r + b\sum_{1}^{n}v_r.$

13.6 The binomial theorem

This section concerns powers of binomial (or 'two term') expressions such as $(a+b)$. By multiplication it is found that

$$
\begin{aligned}
(a+b)^0 &= 1 \\
(a+b)^1 &= a+b \\
(a+b)^2 &= a^2 + 2ab + b^2 \\
(a+b)^3 &= a^3 + 3a^2b + 3ab^2 + b^3 \\
(a+b)^4 &= a^4 + 4a^3b + 6a^2b^2 + 4ab^3 + b^4 \\
(a+b)^5 &= a^5 + 5a^4b + 10a^3b^2 + 10a^2b^3 + 5ab^4 + b^5
\end{aligned}
$$

These coefficients form an array known as Pascal's† triangle:

$$
\begin{array}{ccccccccccc}
& & & & & 1 & & & & & \\
& & & & 1 & & 1 & & & & \\
& & & 1 & & 2 & & 1 & & & \\
& & 1 & & 3 & & 3 & & 1 & & \\
& 1 & & 4 & & 6 & & 4 & & 1 & \\
1 & & 5 & & 10 & & 10 & & 5 & & 1
\end{array}
$$

....

Each entry in the array is the sum of the two entries on either side of it in the previous line. This means that the triangle can easily be extended to provide the coefficients in the expansions of higher powers of $(a+b)$. To see why coefficients in successive lines are related in this way, we consider

$$(a+b)^6 = (a+b)(a^5 + 5a^4b + 10a^3b^2 + 10a^2b^3 + 5ab^4 + b^5)$$

In the product there are two terms in a^4b^2, $b.5a^4b = 5a^4b^2$ and $a.10a^3b^2 = 10a^4b^2$. Hence the coefficient of $a^4b^2 = 5 + 10 = 15$.

Although Pascal's triangle can always be used to obtain expansions of $(a+b)^n$, for large values of n the method becomes rather long. To find another approach, we consider the product

$$
\begin{aligned}
(a_1 + b_1)&(a_2 + b_2)(a_3 + b_3) \\
&= (a_1 + b_1)(a_2a_3 + a_2b_3 + b_2a_3 + b_2b_3) \\
&= a_1a_2a_3 + a_1a_2b_3 + a_1b_2a_3 + a_1b_2b_3 + b_1a_2a_3 + b_1a_2b_3 + b_1b_2a_3 + b_1b_2b_3.
\end{aligned}
$$

Writing $a_1 = a_2 = a_3 = a$ and $b_1 = b_2 = b_3 = b$, we see that the terms a^2b and ab^2 each appear three times, giving

$$(a+b)^3 = a^3 + 3a^2b + 3ab^2 + b^3.$$

† *Pascal, Blaise* (1623–1662) French theologian, mathematician and inventor. His *Traité du Triangle Arithmétique* is one of several essays on mathematical subjects. He also anticipated the invention of differential calculus and contributed to the foundation of the theory of probability.

Extending this method to the product

$$(a+b)^6 = (a+b)(a+b)(a+b)(a+b)(a+b)(a+b)$$

we find that each individual term in the expansion is the product of an '*a*' or a '*b*' from each of the six brackets. A term in a^4b^2 arises when 4 *a*'s and 2 *b*'s are selected. Since there are $_6C_2$ ways of selecting *b*'s from 2 of the 6 brackets and *a*'s from the rest, the term a^4b^2 must be produced $_6C_2$ times. (See §12.2.) Hence the coefficient of a^4b^2 is $_6C_2 = \dfrac{6!}{2!4!} = 15$, as shown above. This approach leads to the general result:

$$\boxed{(a+b)^n = a^n + {_nC_1}a^{n-1}b + {_nC_2}a^{n-2}b^2 + \ldots + {_nC_{n-1}}ab^{n-1} + b^n}$$

i.e. $(a+b)^n = a^n + na^{n-1}b + \dfrac{n(n-1)}{2!}a^{n-2}b^2 + \ldots + nab^{n-1} + b^n$. This is called the *binomial theorem*.

A general term in the expansion, such as the term in $a^{n-r}b^r$, takes the form:

$$_nC_r a^{n-r}b^r = \frac{n!}{r!(n-r)!}a^{n-r}b^r = \frac{n(n-1)\ldots(n-r+1)}{r!}a^{n-r}b^r.$$

Example 1   Use the binomial theorem to expand $(1+x)^7$.

$$(1+x)^7 = 1 + {_7C_1}x + {_7C_2}x^2 + {_7C_3}x^3 + {_7C_4}x^4 + {_7C_5}x^5 + {_7C_6}x^6 + x^7$$

$$= 1 + \frac{7!}{1!6!}x + \frac{7!}{2!5!}x^2 + \frac{7!}{3!4!}x^3 + \frac{7!}{4!3!}x^4 + \frac{7!}{5!2!}x^5 + \frac{7!}{6!1!}x^6 + x^7$$

$$= 1 + 7x + \frac{7.6}{1.2}x^2 + \frac{7.6.5}{1.2.3}x^3 + \frac{7.6.5}{1.2.3}x^4 + \frac{7.6}{1.2}x^5 + 7x^6 + x^7$$

$$= 1 + 7x + 21x^2 + 35x^3 + 35x^4 + 21x^5 + 7x^6 + x^7.$$

Example 2   Use the binomial theorem to expand $(3p+2q)^4$.

$$(3p+2q)^4 = (3p)^4 + {_4C_1}(3p)^3 2q + {_4C_2}(3p)^2(2q)^2 + {_4C_3}3p(2q)^3 + (2q)^4$$

$$= 3^4p^4 + 4.3^3.2p^3q + 6.3^2.2^2p^2q^2 + 4.3.2^3pq^3 + 2^4q^4$$

$$\therefore \quad (3p+2q)^4 = 81p^4 + 216p^3q + 216p^2q^2 + 96pq^3 + 16q^4.$$

Example 3   Find the coefficient of x^4 in the expansion of $(2x-1)^{15}$.

By the binomial theorem the term in $x^4 = {_{15}C_{11}}(2x)^4(-1)^{11}$.

Hence the coefficient of $x^4 = -{_{15}C_{11}}.2^4 = -\frac{15.14.13.12}{4.3.2.1}.2^4$

$$= -21\,840.$$

Example 4   Write down the first three terms in the expansion of $(1-x)^{10}$. Hence find an approximate value for $(0\cdot99)^{10}$.

Using the binomial theorem

$$(1-x)^{10} = 1^{10} + {}_{10}C_1 1^9(-x) + {}_{10}C_2 1^8(-x)^2 + \ldots$$

$$= 1 - 10x + \frac{10.9}{2.1}x^2 - \ldots$$

$$\therefore \quad (1-x)^{10} = 1 - 10x + 45x^2 - \ldots$$

Substituting $x = 0\cdot01$, we find that

$$(0\cdot99)^{10} \approx 1 - 10(0\cdot01) + 45(0\cdot01)^2 = 1 - 0\cdot1 + 0\cdot0045$$

$$\therefore \quad (0\cdot99)^{10} \approx 0\cdot9045.$$

Example 5   Expand $(1+x+2x^2)^6$ as far as the term in x^3.

$$(1+x+2x^2)^6 = 1 + 6(x+2x^2) + \frac{6.5}{2.1}(x+2x^2)^2$$

$$+ \frac{6.5.4}{3.2.1}(x+2x^2)^3 + \ldots.$$

Neglecting terms in x^4 and higher powers:

$$(1+x+2x^2)^6 = 1 + 6(x+2x^2) + 15(x^2+4x^3) + 20x^3 + \ldots$$

$$= 1 + 6x + 27x^2 + 80x^3 + \ldots.$$

One important application of the binomial theorem is to the proof of the rule for differentiating powers of x introduced in §5.4, namely

$$\frac{d}{dx}(x^n) = nx^{n-1}, \quad \text{where } n \text{ is a positive integer.}$$

Let δx be a small increase in x and let δy be the corresponding small increase in y, then

$$y = x^n$$

$$\Rightarrow y + \delta y = (x + \delta x)^n$$

$$= x^n + {}_nC_1 x^{n-1}\delta x + {}_nC_2 x^{n-2}(\delta x)^2 + \ldots + (\delta x)^n$$

$$\Rightarrow \quad \delta y = nx^{n-1}\delta x + \frac{n(n-1)}{2}x^{n-2}(\delta x)^2 + \ldots + (\delta x)^n$$

$$\Rightarrow \quad \frac{\delta y}{\delta x} = nx^{n-1} + \frac{n(n-1)}{2}x^{n-2}\delta x + \ldots + (\delta x)^{n-1}$$

$$\therefore \quad \frac{dy}{dx} = \lim_{\delta x \to 0} \frac{\delta y}{\delta x} = nx^{n-1}.$$

Exercise 13.6

1. Use the binomial theorem to expand:
    (a) $(x+y)^4$,　　　　(b) $(a-b)^7$,　　　　(c) $(2+p^2)^6$,
    (d) $(2h-k)^5$,　　　　(e) $\left(x+\dfrac{1}{x}\right)^3$,　　　　(f) $\left(z-\dfrac{1}{2z}\right)^8$.

2. Find the given terms in the following expansions:
    (a) $(1+x)^{10}$, 5th term,　　　　　　(b) $(2-3x)^8$, term in x^2,
    (c) $(2a+b)^{12}$, 10th term,　　　　　(d) $(p-3q^2)^7$, term in p^4q^6,
    (e) $\left(x-\dfrac{1}{x}\right)^6$, constant term,　　(f) $\left(x^2+\dfrac{1}{x}\right)^9$, term in $\dfrac{1}{x^3}$.

3. Expand and simplify $\left(2x+\dfrac{1}{x^2}\right)^5+\left(2x-\dfrac{1}{x^2}\right)^5$.

4. The coefficient of x^3 in the expansion of $(1+x)^n$ is four times the coefficient of x^2. Find the value of n.

5. In the binomial expansion of $(1+\tfrac{1}{3})^n$ the fourth and fifth terms are equal. Find the value of n.

6. The coefficient of x^5 in the expansion of $(1+5x)^8$ is equal to the coefficient of x^4 in the expansion of $(a+5x)^7$. Find the value of a.

7. If the first three terms of the expansion of $(1+ax)^n$ in ascending powers of x are $1-4x+7x^2$, find n and a.

8. Use the expansion of $(a+b)^4$ to evaluate $(1\cdot03)^4$ correct to 2 decimal places.

9. Use the expansion of $(2-x)^5$ to evaluate $(1\cdot98)^5$ correct to 5 decimal places.

10. Obtain the expansion in ascending powers of x of $(1+2x)^{15}$ as far as the term in x^3. Hence evaluate $(1\cdot002)^{15}$ correct to 5 decimal places.

11. Find the first four terms in the expansions, in ascending powers of x, of
    (a) $(1+x)^7$, (b) $(1+x-x^2)^7$.

12. Expand $(1+2x+3x^2)^8$ in ascending powers of x as far as the term in x^3.

13. Find the first three terms in the expansion in ascending powers of x of $(1-3x)(1+2x)^6$.

14. Find the coefficient of the given power of x in the expansion of
    (a) $(1+x^2)(2-3x)^7$, x^3,　　　　(b) $(1-3x-2x^2)(1+x^2)^{10}$, x^{20},
    (c) $x\left(x-\dfrac{2}{x^2}\right)^{12}$, x^4,　　　　(d) $\left(x+\dfrac{1}{x}\right)^2(1-x)^5$, x^2.

13.7 Use of the binomial series

By the binomial theorem, if n is a positive integer

$$(1+x)^n = 1 + nx + \frac{n(n-1)}{2!}x^2 + \frac{n(n-1)(n-2)}{3!}x^3 + \ldots + x^n.$$

This result can be extended to other values of n by writing

$$(1+x)^n = 1 + nx + \frac{n(n-1)}{2!}x^2 + \frac{n(n-1)(n-2)}{3!}x^3 + \ldots$$

$$\ldots + \frac{n(n-1)\ldots(n-r+1)}{r!}x^r + \ldots.$$

When n is a positive integer this expansion is the same as that obtained using the binomial theorem. Otherwise the expansion produces an infinite series called the *binomial series*. It can be shown that this series is a valid expansion of $(1+x)^n$ when $|x| < 1$, i.e. when $-1 < x < 1$.

Example 1   Expand $1/(1-x)^2$ in ascending powers of x, giving the first four terms and the term in x^r.

$$\frac{1}{(1-x)^2} = (1-x)^{-2} = 1 + (-2)(-x) + \frac{(-2)(-3)}{2!}(-x)^2$$

$$+ \frac{(-2)(-3)(-4)}{3!}(-x)^3 + \ldots$$

$$+ \frac{(-2)(-3)\ldots(-2-r+1)}{r!}(-x)^r + \ldots$$

$$\therefore \quad \frac{1}{(1-x)^2} = 1 + 2x + 3x^2 + 4x^3 + \ldots + (r+1)x^r + \ldots$$

[Note: The coefficients of the terms in the expansions of $(1-x)^{-1}$, $(1-x)^{-2}$, $(1-x)^{-3}$, ... form the diagonal lines in Pascal's triangle given in §13.6.]

Example 2   Find the expansion of $(1+2x)^{3/2}$ in ascending powers of x as far as the term in x^3. State the range of values of x for which the expansion is valid.

$$(1+2x)^{3/2} = 1 + \frac{3}{2} \cdot 2x + \frac{\frac{3}{2} \cdot \frac{1}{2}}{2!}(2x)^2 + \frac{\frac{3}{2} \cdot \frac{1}{2} \cdot (-\frac{1}{2})}{3!}(2x)^3 + \ldots$$

$$= 1 + 3x + \frac{3}{2}x^2 - \frac{1}{2}x^3 + \ldots$$

The expansion is valid for $|2x| < 1$, i.e. for $|x| < \frac{1}{2}$.

Example 3   Find the first three terms in the expansion of $(4+x)^{-1/2}$ in ascending powers of x. Deduce an approximate value of $1/\sqrt{(4 \cdot 16)}$.

[Note that the binomial series cannot be used to expand $(4+x)^{-1/2}$ directly. We must rearrange to create an expression of the form $(1+\ldots)^{-1/2}$.]

$$(4+x)^{-1/2} = \{4(1+\tfrac{1}{4}x)\}^{-1/2} = 4^{-1/2}(1+\tfrac{1}{4}x)^{-1/2} = \tfrac{1}{2}(1+\tfrac{1}{4}x)^{-1/2}$$

$$\therefore \quad (4+x)^{-1/2} = \tfrac{1}{2}\left\{1 + (-\tfrac{1}{2})(\tfrac{1}{4}x) + \frac{(-\tfrac{1}{2})(-\tfrac{3}{2})}{2!}(\tfrac{1}{4}x)^2 + \ldots\right\}$$

$$= \frac{1}{2} - \frac{1}{16}x + \frac{3}{256}x^2 - \ldots$$

Substituting $x = 0.16$, we have

$$(4.16)^{-1/2} = \frac{1}{2} - \frac{1}{16}(0.16) + \frac{3}{256}(0.16)^2 - \ldots = 0.5 - 0.01 + 0.0003 - \ldots .$$

Hence $1/\sqrt{(4.16)} \approx 0.4903.$

Exercise 13.7

In questions 1 to 3 expand the given function in a series of ascending powers of x giving the first three terms and the term in x^r.

1. $(1+x)^{-2}$,   2. $(1-x)^{-1}$,   3. $1/(1+2x)^3$.

In questions 4 to 9 expand the given function in a series of ascending powers of x giving the first three terms. State the values of x for which each expansion is valid.

4. $(1+x)^{1/2}$.   5. $\sqrt[3]{(1-3x)}$.   6. $1/\sqrt{(1+\tfrac{1}{2}x)}$.

7. $1/(3+x)$.   8. $\sqrt{(4-x)}$.   9. $(9-4x)^{3/2}$.

10. Find the first four non-zero terms in the expansion of $(1+2x^2)^{-1/2}$ in ascending powers of x.

11. Find the first four terms in the expansion of $(1-x)^{1/2}$ in ascending powers of x. Deduce the value of $\sqrt{(0.9)}$ correct to 4 decimal places.

12. Expand $(1+3x)^{-1/3} + (1-4x)^{-1/4}$ as a series in ascending powers of x, giving the first three non-zero terms.

13. Expand $(2-x)^{-2}$ as a series of ascending powers of x as far as the term in x^4. Deduce the value of $1/(1.8)^2$ correct to 3 significant figures.

14. Expand $(1+2x)^{1/2}$ in ascending powers of x as far as the term in x^3. By substituting $x = 1/25$, find an approximate value for $\sqrt{3}$ giving your answer to 3 decimal places.

15. Expand $(1-3x)/(1+4x)$ in ascending powers of x as far as the term in x^3, stating the values of x for which the expansion is valid.

16. Expand the following in ascending powers of x as far as the term in x^3
(a) $1/(1+x-x^2)$,   (b) $\sqrt{(1+x+2x^2)}$.

Exercise 13.8 (miscellaneous)

1. Write down an expression for the nth term of the sequence 0, 2, 6, 12, 20, ...
Find which term of the sequence is equal to 210.

2. Find the first three terms and the nth term of the series whose sums are given
by

(a) $S_n = 4n - \dfrac{1}{n}$,   (b) $S_n = (n+1)!$

3. Evaluate the following:

(a) $\displaystyle\sum_{r=1}^{20} (r+2)$,   (b) $\displaystyle\sum_{r=1}^{8} 2^r$,   (c) $\displaystyle\sum_{r=1}^{n} 2r$.

4. Given that the arithmetic mean of $1/(a+b)$ and $1/(b+c)$ is $1/(a+c)$, find in terms of b the arithmetic mean of a^2 and c^2.

5. Find the least value of n for which the nth term of the series $12+10\cdot7+9\cdot4$ $+8\cdot1+...$ is negative. Find also the least value of n for which the sum to n terms is negative.

6. The sum of the first twenty terms of an arithmetic progression is 45, and the sum of the first forty terms is 290. Find the first term and the common difference. Find the number of terms in the progression which are less than 100.   (JMB)

7. The second, fourth and ninth terms of an arithmetic progression are in geometric progression. Find the common ratio of the geometric progression.

8. A rod one metre in length is divided into ten pieces whose lengths are in geometrical progression. The length of the longest piece is eight times the length of the shortest piece. Find, to the nearest millimetre, the length of the shortest piece.
(JMB)

9. (i) The sum to infinity of a geometric progression is 3. When the terms of this geometric progression are squared a new geometric progression is obtained whose sum to infinity is 1·8. Find the first term and the common ratio of each series.
(ii) Express the recurring decimal $0\cdot32\dot{1}$ in the form p/q, where p and q are integers with no common factor.   (AEB 1978)

10. (i) Write down the first four terms of a geometric series with sum to infinity 4/3 and first term 1.

(ii) Find the values of r for which the series

$$r^2 + \frac{r^2}{1+r^2} + \frac{r^2}{(1+r^2)^2} + \dots \text{ is convergent, and find its sum.} \qquad \text{(AEB 1975)}$$

11. (i) Given that the sum of the first and second terms of an arithmetical progression is x and that the sum of the $(n-1)$th and nth terms is y, prove that the sum of the first n terms is $\frac{1}{4}n(x+y)$.

(ii) The sum of the first four terms of a geometric series of positive terms is 15 and the sum to infinity of the series is 16. Show that the sum of the first eight terms of the series differs from the sum to infinity by 1/16. (L)

12. (a) Prove that the sum of all the integers between m and n inclusive $(m, n \in \mathbb{Z}_+, n > m)$ is $\frac{1}{2}(m+n)(n-m+1)$. Find the sum of all the integers between 1000 and 2000 which are not divisible by 5.

(b) A geometric series has first term 2 and common ratio 0·95. The sum of the first n terms of the series is denoted by S_n and the sum to infinity is denoted by S. Calculate the least value of n for which $S - S_n < 1$. (C)

13. The first term of a geometric series is 2 and the second term is x. State the set of values of x for which the series is convergent. Show that when convergent the series converges to a sum greater than 1. If $x = \frac{1}{2}$, find the smallest positive integer n such that the sum of the first n terms differs from the sum to infinity by less than 2^{-10}. (L)

14. An arithmetic series and a geometric series have r as the common difference and the common ratio respectively. The first term of the arithmetic series is 1 and the first term of the geometric series is 2. If the fourth term of the arithmetic series is equal to the sum of the third and fourth terms of the geometric series, find the three possible values of r. When $|r| < 1$ find, in the form $p + q\sqrt{2}$, (i) the sum to infinity of the geometric series, (ii) the sum of the first ten terms of the arithmetic series. (AEB 1978)

15. If S is the sum of the series $1 + 3x + 5x^2 + \dots + (2n+1)x^n$, prove, by considering $(1-x)S$, or otherwise, that if $x \neq 1$,

$$S = \frac{1 + x - (2n+3)x^{n+1} + (2n+1)x^{n+2}}{(1-x)^2}. \qquad \text{(O)}$$

16. (i) Find the set of values of x for which the series $\displaystyle\sum_{n=0}^{\infty} \left(\frac{2x}{x+1}\right)^n$ is convergent. If the sum to infinity is 3, find x.

(ii) Without using tables, find the value of

$$\left(2+\frac{1}{\sqrt{2}}\right)^5 + \left(2-\frac{1}{\sqrt{2}}\right)^5.$$ (L)

17. Obtain the first three terms in the expansion in ascending powers of x of
(a) $(1+2x-x^2)^6$,   (b) $(1-2x)^5(1+x)^7$.

18. Find the term independent of x in the expansion of

(a) $\left(x^2-\frac{1}{3x}\right)^9$,   (b) $\left(x-\frac{1}{x}\right)^8\left(x+\frac{1}{x^2}\right)^4$.

19. The coefficients of x^4 in the expansions of $(1+x)^{2n}$ and $(1+15x^2)^n$ are equal. Given that n is a positive integer, find its value.

20. By substituting $a = b = 1$ in the binomial expansion of $(a+b)^8$, find the sum of $_8C_1 + {_8C_2} + {_8C_3} + \ldots + {_8C_8}$. Using a similar method, evaluate $_8C_1 - {_8C_2} + {_8C_3} - \ldots - {_8C_8}$.

21. The first three terms in the expansion of $(1+ax)^n$ are $1+12x+81x^2$. Find the values of a and n. Find also the coefficient of x^3 in the expansion.

22. Show that $\dfrac{1}{1-2x} - \dfrac{2}{2+x} = \dfrac{5x}{(1-2x)(2+x)}$. Hence expand $\dfrac{5x}{(1-2x)(2+x)}$ in ascending powers of x as far as the term in x^3.

23. Write down the first five terms of the expansion of $(1+3x)^{1/3}$ in ascending powers of x and state the range of values of x for which the infinite expansion of this form is valid. Hence find an approximation to the cube root of 0·97, correct to five places of decimals.   (AEB 1976)

24. Write down the first four terms in the binomial expansion of $(1+2x)^{-3}$ in ascending powers of x. State the range of values of x for which it is valid. By putting $x = -0·01$, find a value for 7^{-6} correct to four significant figures.   (AEB 1978)

25. Write down the expansion in ascending powers of x up to the term in x^2 of (i) $(1+x)^{1/2}$, (ii) $(1-x)^{-1/2}$ and simplify the coefficients. Hence, or otherwise, expand $\sqrt{\left(\dfrac{1+x}{1-x}\right)}$ in ascending powers of x up to the term in x^2. By using $x = 1/10$ obtain an estimate, to three decimal places, for $\sqrt{11}$.   (JMB)

26. (a) If $x - \dfrac{1}{x} = u$, express $x^3 - \dfrac{1}{x^3}$ and $x^5 - \dfrac{1}{x^5}$ in terms of u.
(b) Assuming that $(1-2kx+x^2)^{-1/2}$ may be expanded in a series of ascending powers of x, obtain the expansion as far as the term in x^3, simplifying the coefficients.   (C)

27. For each of the following series construct a flow diagram for a procedure to list the first 10 terms of the series and determine their sum.

(a) An arithmetic progression with the first term a and common difference d given as data.

(b) A geometric progression with the first term a and common ratio r given as data.

(c) The series $1 + 2x + 3x^2 + \ldots$ with the value of x given as data.

28. Construct a flow diagram to output the terms of the binomial expansion of $(\frac{1}{4} + \frac{3}{4})^n$, where n is a given positive integer. Test your procedure using a calculator and the value $n = 3$.

14 Graphs and parameters

14.1 Odd and even functions

The diagrams below show the graphs of $y = x^n$ for various integral values of n: in (1) odd values of n and in (2) even values.

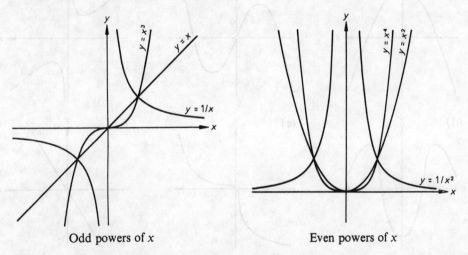

Odd powers of x Even powers of x

In diagram (1) each of the curves is symmetrical about the origin, i.e. each curve remains unchanged when rotated through 180° about the origin. In (2) the graphs of even powers of x are symmetrical about the y-axis, i.e. the curves remain unchanged when reflected in the y-axis. These symmetries arise because for odd powers $(-x)^n = -x^n$ and for even powers $(-x)^n = x^n$.

The words 'odd' and 'even' are used to describe functions with the same symmetries as the odd and even powers of x. Thus $f(x)$ is called an *odd function* if $f(-x) = -f(x)$. The graph is symmetrical about the origin, so that if (a, b) lies on the graph so does $(-a, -b)$. Similarly $f(x)$ is called an *even function* if $f(-x) = f(x)$. In this case the graph is symmetrical about the y-axis, so that if (a, b) lies on the graph so does $(-a, b)$.

Example 1   Decide whether the following functions are odd, even or neither.
(a) $f(x) = x^3 + x$,   (b) $g(x) = x^3 + 1$,   (c) $h(x) = \cos 3x$.

(a) $f(-x) = (-x)^3 + (-x) = -x^3 - x = -(x^3 + x) = -f(x)$
    $\therefore$ $f(x)$ is an odd function.
(b) $g(-x) = (-x)^3 + 1 = -x^3 + 1$
    $\therefore$ $g(-x) \neq g(x)$ and $g(-x) \neq -g(x)$.
    Hence $g(x)$ is neither odd nor even.
(c) $h(-x) = \cos 3(-x) = \cos(-3x) = \cos 3x = h(x)$
    $\therefore$ $h(x)$ is an even function.

When sketching the graphs of odd and even functions, it is only necessary to consider positive values of x. The sketch is then completed using the symmetry of the function.

Exercise 14.1

1.   State which of the following graphs represent odd or even functions.

(a)   (b)   (c)

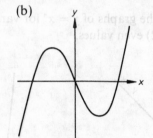

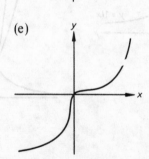

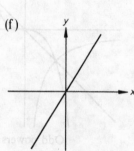

(d)   (e)   (f)

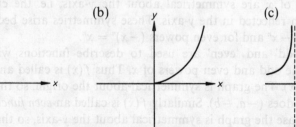

2.   Copy and complete each of the following sketches so that it represents (i) an odd function, (ii) an even function.

(a)   (b)   (c)

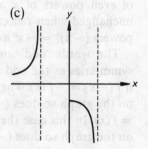

3. Decide whether the following functions are odd, even or neither.
(a) $3x^2+5$,   (b) $2x-x^3$,   (c) $(x-2)(x+4)$,
(d) $\dfrac{x^3+1}{x}$,   (e) $\dfrac{x^3+x}{x^2}$,   (f) $\dfrac{x}{x^3-x}$.

4. Decide whether the following functions are odd, even or neither.
(a) $\sin 2x$,   (b) $\cos 5x$,   (c) $\tan \pi x$,
(d) $\sin^2 x$,   (e) $\cos (x+\tfrac{1}{4}\pi)$,   (f) $1+\cos x$.

14.2 Composite functions

When investigating the properties of a function it is sometimes helpful to think of it as a composite function. This approach was used in §10.1 when differentiating various types of function. It can also be used when sketching graphs.

To illustrate the method let us suppose that $y=f(x)$ is the equation of a graph already familiar to us or relatively easy to sketch. We will now consider how our knowledge can be used to sketch composite functions of the form $f(x)+k$, $f(x-k)$, $1/f(x)$ and $|f(x)|$.

The graph of $f(x)+k$ is produced from the graph of $f(x)$ by performing a translation of k units in the direction of the y-axis. Similarly a translation of k units in the direction of the x-axis gives the graph of $f(x-k)$. This is readily verified by considering some examples.

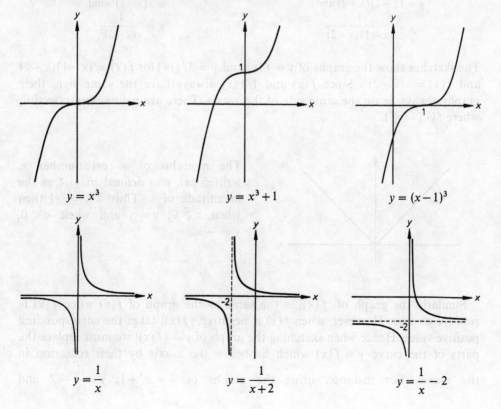

$$y = x^3 \qquad\qquad y = x^3+1 \qquad\qquad y = (x-1)^3$$

$$y = \dfrac{1}{x} \qquad\qquad y = \dfrac{1}{x+2} \qquad\qquad y = \dfrac{1}{x} - 2$$

When comparing the graphs of $f(x)$ and $1/f(x)$ it is useful to note the values of x for which $f(x) = 0$. If $f(a) = 0$ then the curve $y = f(x)$ cuts the x-axis at $(a, 0)$. However as $x \to a$, $1/f(x) \to \pm\infty$, which means that the line $x = a$ is an asymptote to the curve $y = 1/f(x)$.

Since as $f(x)$ increases, $1/f(x)$ must decrease, a non-zero maximum value of $f(x)$ corresponds to a minimum value of $1/f(x)$. Similarly when there is a minimum point on the curve $y = f(x)$, the corresponding point on the curve $y = 1/f(x)$, if defined, will be a maximum point.

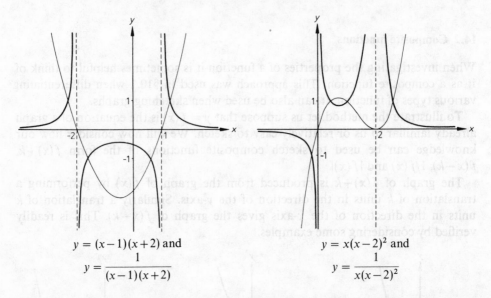

$y = (x-1)(x+2)$ and
$$y = \frac{1}{(x-1)(x+2)}$$

$y = x(x-2)^2$ and
$$y = \frac{1}{x(x-2)^2}$$

The sketches show the graphs of $y = f(x)$ and $y = 1/f(x)$ for $f(x) = (x-1)(x+2)$ and $f(x) = x(x-2)^2$. Since $f(x)$ and $1/f(x)$ always have the same sign, their graphs always lie on the same side of the x-axis. There are points of intersection where $f(x) = \pm 1$.

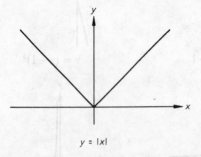

$y = |x|$

The modulus of a real number x, written $|x|$, was defined in §1.4 as the magnitude of x. Thus if $y = |x|$ then when $x \geqslant 0$, $y = x$ and when $x < 0$, $y = -x$.

Similarly the graph of $|f(x)|$ is the same as the graph of $f(x)$ when $f(x)$ is positive or zero. However, when $f(x)$ is negative, $|f(x)|$ takes the corresponding positive value. Hence when sketching the graph of $y = |f(x)|$ we must replace the parts of the curve $y = f(x)$ which lie below the x-axis by their reflection in the x-axis. For instance, using the graphs of $y = x^3 + 1$, $y = \dfrac{1}{x} - 2$ and

$y = (x-1)(x+2)$ which appear earlier in this section, the graphs of $y = |x^3+1|$, $y = \left|\dfrac{1}{x} - 2\right|$ and $y = |(x-1)(x+2)|$ can be produced.

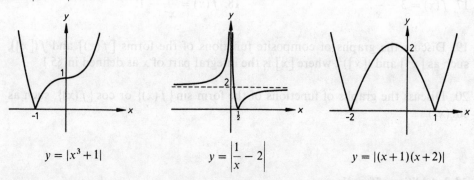

$$y = |x^3+1| \qquad\qquad y = \left|\frac{1}{x} - 2\right| \qquad\qquad y = |(x+1)(x+2)|$$

Finally we note that when the turning points on the graph of $y = f(x)$ have been found, the coordinates of turning points on the graph of a composite function, such as $y = 1/f(x)$ or $y = |f(x)|$, can usually be deduced. Further differentiation should not be necessary.

Exercise 14.2

In questions 1 to 4 sketch the graphs with given equations

1. (a) $y = x^2$, (b) $y = x^2+3$, (c) $y = (x-3)^2$.

2. (a) $y = \dfrac{1}{x^2}$, (b) $y = \dfrac{1}{x^2} + 4$, (c) $y = \dfrac{1}{(x+4)^2}$.

3. (a) $y = \sin x$, (b) $y = 1+\sin x$, (c) $y = \sin\left(x - \tfrac{1}{3}\pi\right)$.

4. (a) $y = |x|$, (b) $y = |x|-1$, (c) $y = |x-1|$.

In questions 5 to 12 sketch the graphs of $f(x)$ and $1/f(x)$, giving the coordinates of any stationary points.

5. $f(x) = x^2-1$.   6. $f(x) = x^2+1$.

7. $f(x) = x(x-2)$.   8. $f(x) = (x+2)^2$.

9. $f(x) = x^2-4x+5$.   10. $f(x) = 2+x-x^2$.

11. $f(x) = x^2(x+3)$.   12. $f(x) = x^3-12x$.

In questions 13 to 18 sketch the graphs of $f(x)$ and $|f(x)|$, giving the coordinates of any stationary points.

13. $f(x) = x+2$.   14. $f(x) = 5-2x$.

15. $f(x) = x^2 - 2x - 3$.

16. $f(x) = 6x - x^2 - 9$.

17. $f(x) = 3 - \dfrac{1}{x}$.

18. $f(x) = \dfrac{1}{x^2} - 1$.

19. Discuss the graphs of composite functions of the forms $[f(x)]$ and $f([x])$, such as $[x^2]$ and $([x])^2$, where $[x]$ is the integral part of x as defined in §5.1.

20. Discuss the graphs of functions of the form $\sin\{f(x)\}$ or $\cos\{f(x)\}$, such as $\sin(x^2)$.

14.3 Addition of functions

When a function $f(x)$ can be expressed as the sum of two simpler functions $g(x)$ and $h(x)$, it is sometimes possible to sketch the graph of $f(x)$ by combining the graphs of $g(x)$ and $h(x)$. This approach can be particularly useful when dealing with a function such as $y = (x^2 + 3x + 2)/2x$. Rearranging we find that (i) $y = \dfrac{(x+1)(x+2)}{2x}$ and (ii) $y = \dfrac{1}{2}x + \dfrac{3}{2} + \dfrac{1}{x}$. The equation in form (i) tells us that the curve cuts the x-axis at the points $(-1, 0)$ and $(-2, 0)$ and that the y-axis is an asymptote to the curve. Form (ii) shows that the graph can be sketched by combining the graphs $y = \dfrac{1}{2}x + \dfrac{3}{2}$ and $y = \dfrac{1}{x}$.

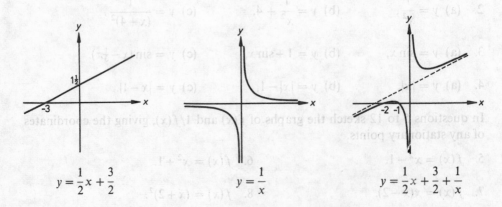

$$y = \frac{1}{2}x + \frac{3}{2}$$

$$y = \frac{1}{x}$$

$$y = \frac{1}{2}x + \frac{3}{2} + \frac{1}{x}$$

The sketches show that the line $y = \dfrac{1}{2}x + \dfrac{3}{2}$ is an asymptote to the curve. The coordinates of the two turning points can be obtained using dy/dx in the usual way.

The next set of sketches show the same method applied to the curve $y = (x^3 - 1)/x$, i.e. $y = x^2 - \dfrac{1}{x}$.

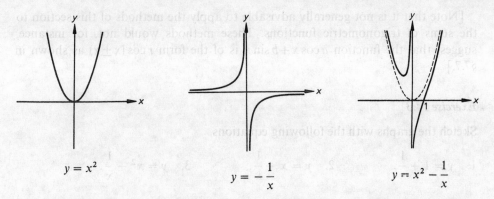

$$y = x^2 \qquad y = -\frac{1}{x} \qquad y = x^2 - \frac{1}{x}$$

The sums of modulus functions need a different approach. For instance, consider the function $f(x) = |x+1| + |x-2|$.

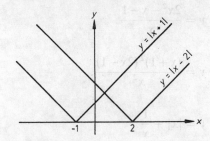

The sketch of the graphs of $|x+1|$ and $|x-2|$ shows that the behaviour of $f(x)$ is likely to change when $x = -1$ and again when $x = 2$.

When $x < -1$, $x+1 < 0$ and $x-2 < 0$
$\qquad \therefore \quad |x+1| = -(x+1)$ and $|x-2| = -(x-2)$
$\therefore \quad f(x) = -(x+1)-(x-2) = -2x+1.$

When $-1 < x < 2$, $x+1 > 0$ and $x-2 < 0$
$\qquad \therefore \quad |x+1| = x+1$ and $|x-2| = -(x-2)$
$\therefore \quad f(x) = (x+1)-(x-2) = 3.$

When $x > 2$, $x+1 > 0$ and $x-2 > 0$
$\qquad \therefore \quad |x+1| = x+1$ and $|x-2| = x-2$
$\therefore \quad f(x) = (x+1)+(x-2) = 2x-1.$

Thus the graph of $f(x) = |x+1| + |x-2|$ can now be sketched.

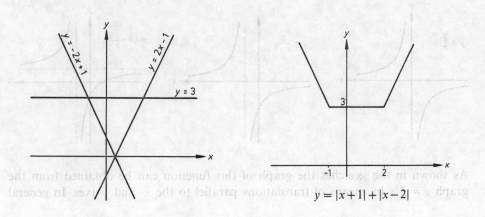

$$y = |x+1| + |x-2|$$

[Note that it is not generally advisable to apply the methods of this section to the sums of trigonometric functions. These methods would not, for instance, suggest that the function $a\cos x + b\sin x$ is of the form $r\cos(x\pm\alpha)$ as shown in §7.7.]

Exercise 14.3

Sketch the graphs with the following equations.

1. $y = 1 + \dfrac{1}{x}$.

2. $y = x - \dfrac{1}{x}$.

3. $y = x^2 + \dfrac{1}{x}$.

4. $y = 1 - \dfrac{1}{x^2}$.

5. $y = x + \dfrac{1}{x^2}$.

6. $y = x^2 + \dfrac{1}{x^2}$.

7. $y = \dfrac{x^2 + x + 1}{x}$.

8. $y = \dfrac{2x^2 - x - 1}{x}$.

9. $y = \dfrac{(x^2 - 1)^2}{x^2}$.

10. $y = \dfrac{(x+1)^2(2x-1)}{x^2}$.

11. $y = x + \dfrac{1}{x-1}$.

12. $y = |x| + \dfrac{1}{x}$.

13. $y = |x| + |x - 4|$.

14. $y = |x - 1| + |2x - 1|$.

14.4 The function $(ax+b)/(cx+d)$

We consider first a typical function of this type, namely $y = \dfrac{x+1}{x-1}$, i.e.

$$y = 1 + \frac{2}{x-1}.$$

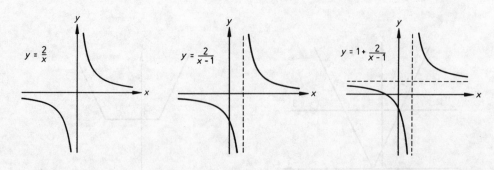

$y = \dfrac{2}{x}$ $y = \dfrac{2}{x-1}$ $y = 1 + \dfrac{2}{x-1}$

As shown in the sketches the graph of this function can be obtained from the graph $y = 2/x$ by means of translations parallel to the x- and y-axes. In general the function $y = (ax+b)/(cx+d)$ has a graph related to the graph $y = 1/x$ in a similar way. Thus to sketch such a graph it is usually sufficient to determine the points of intersection with the coordinate axes and the equations of the asymptotes.

Example 1   Sketch the curve $y = \dfrac{2x-9}{x+3}$.

$$x = 0 \Rightarrow y = -\frac{9}{3} = -3$$

∴   the curve cuts the y-axis at the point $(0, -3)$

$$y = 0 \Rightarrow 2x-9 = 0 \Rightarrow x = 4\tfrac{1}{2}$$

∴   the curve cuts the x-axis at the point $(4\tfrac{1}{2}, 0)$.

As $x \to -3$, $y \to \pm\infty$ ∴   the line $x = -3$ is an asymptote.

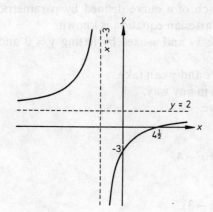

$$y = \frac{2x-9}{x+3} = \frac{2-9/x}{1+3/x}$$

∴   as $x \to \pm\infty$, $y \to 2$.
Hence the line $y = 2$ is an asymptote.

Exercise 14.4

In questions 1 to 9 sketch the given curve, stating the equations of the asymptotes.

1. $y = \dfrac{1}{x+2}$.

2. $y = \dfrac{3}{x-4}$.

3. $y = \dfrac{2}{2x-3}$.

4. $y = \dfrac{x}{x+2}$.

5. $y = \dfrac{x-2}{x+2}$.

6. $y = \dfrac{2x+3}{2x-3}$.

7. $y = \dfrac{2x-5}{x+2}$.

8. $y = \dfrac{1-3x}{3-x}$.

9. $y = \dfrac{5+2x}{2-5x}$.

10. Sketch the curve $y = x/(x-1)$ and write down the equation of its reflection in the y-axis.

11. Sketch the curve $y = (x-1)/(x+1)$ and write down the equation of its reflection in the x-axis.

12. If a, b, c and d are all positive, sketch the curve $y = \dfrac{ax+b}{cx+d}$ when (i) $ad - bc < 0$, (ii) $ad - bc = 0$, (iii) $ad - bc > 0$.

14.5 Parametric equations

In this and earlier chapters we have considered lines and curves defined by equations connecting the coordinates (x, y) of a typical point. It is sometimes more convenient to express x and y in terms of a third variable called a *parameter*. For instance, the equations $x = 1 - t$, $y = t^2 - 4$ are the *parametric equations* of a curve. The same curve may also be referred to as the *locus* or path of the point $(1 - t, t^2 - 4)$ as the parameter t varies.

The procedure used when making a sketch of a curve defined by parametric equations is similar to that used when the Cartesian equation is known.
(1) Find the points of intersection with the x- and y-axes by letting $y = 0$ and then $x = 0$.
(2) Note any restrictions on the values that x and y can take.
(3) Decide whether the curve is symmetrical in any way.
(4) If necessary plot a few points on the curve.

Example 1   Sketch the curve $x = 1 - t$, $y = t^2 - 4$.

$x = 0 \Rightarrow 1 - t = 0 \Rightarrow t = 1 \Rightarrow y = -3$

∴   the curve cuts the y-axis at the point $(0, -3)$.
$y = 0 \Rightarrow t^2 - 4 = 0 \Rightarrow$ either $t = -2$, $x = 3$ or $t = 2$, $x = -1$
∴   the curve cuts the x-axis at $(-1, 0)$ and $(3, 0)$.

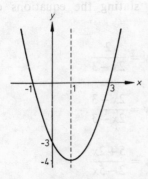

As t varies x may take any value, but since t^2 is never negative the minimum value of y is -4. For any given value of y greater than -4, there are two possible values of x of the form $1 \pm k$. Hence the curve is symmetrical about the line $x = 1$.

It is sometimes easier to work with the Cartesian equation of a curve. This is obtained from the parametric equations by eliminating the parameter.

Example 2   Find the Cartesian equation of the curve $x = 1 - t$, $y = t^2 - 4$.

$x = 1 - t \Leftrightarrow t = 1 - x$
$\therefore \quad y = t^2 - 4 = (1 - x)^2 - 4 = 1 - 2x + x^2 - 4$.
Hence the Cartesian equation is $y = x^2 - 2x - 3$.

Example 3   Find the Cartesian equation of the locus of the point $(2t^2, 1 - t^2)$ as t varies. Sketch the locus.

The parametric equations of the locus are
$$x = 2t^2 \qquad\qquad (1)$$
$$y = 1 - t^2 \qquad\qquad (2)$$
Adding (1) to $2 \times$ (2) $x + 2y = 2$.
However, since t^2 can never be negative, $x \geqslant 0$.
Hence the Cartesian equation of the locus is $x + 2y = 2$, where $x \geqslant 0$.

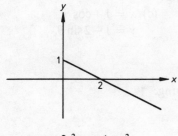

$x = 2t^2, y = 1 - t^2$

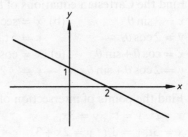

$x + 2y = 2$

Example 4   Find the Cartesian equation of the curve $x = 2\cos\theta + \sin\theta$, $y = \cos\theta - 2\sin\theta$.

Eliminating $\sin\theta$, $2x + y = 5\cos\theta$
Eliminating $\cos\theta$, $x - 2y = 5\sin\theta$.
Squaring and adding these equations

$$(2x + y)^2 + (x - 2y)^2 = 25\cos^2\theta + 25\sin^2\theta$$
$$4x^2 + 4xy + y^2 + x^2 - 4xy + 4y^2 = 25(\cos^2\theta + \sin^2\theta)$$
$$\therefore \quad 5x^2 + 5y^2 = 25.$$

Hence the required Cartesian equation is $x^2 + y^2 = 5$.

The parametric equations of a curve may be used to find points of intersection with other lines or curves.

Example 5   Find the points of intersection of the line $3x - 2y = 2$ with the curve $x = t - 1$, $y = 1/t$.

Substituting for x and y in the equation of the line,

$$3x - 2y = 2 \Rightarrow 3(t-1) - 2.\frac{1}{t} = 2$$

$$\Rightarrow 3t(t-1) - 2 = 2t$$
$$\Rightarrow 3t^2 - 5t - 2 = 0$$
$$\Rightarrow (3t+1)(t-2) = 0$$
$$\Rightarrow t = -\tfrac{1}{3} \text{ or } t = 2$$

Hence the points of intersection are $(-1\tfrac{1}{3}, -3)$ and $(1, \tfrac{1}{2})$.

Exercise 14.5

1. Sketch the following graphs
(a) $x = 4t, y = 3 - t$,   (b) $x = t - 1, y = t^2 + 1$,
(c) $x = 2t^2, y = 4(t-1)$,   (d) $x = t^2 - 1, y = t^2 + 1$,
(e) $x = t + 2, y = 1/t$,   (f) $x = t^2 - 1, y = t^4 + 1$.

2. Find the Cartesian equations of the graphs in question 1.

3. Find the Cartesian equations of the following:
(a) $x = 3 \sin \theta$ (b) $x = \sec \theta$ (c) $x = 1 + \cos \theta$
    $y = 2 \cos \theta$, $y = 5 \tan \theta$, $y = 1 - 2 \sin \theta$,
(d) $x = \cos \theta + \sin \theta$ (e) $x = \cos(\theta + \tfrac{1}{4}\pi)$
    $y = 2 \cos \theta + \sin \theta$, $y = \sqrt{2} \sin \theta$.

4. Find the points of intersection of the following:
(a) $x = t^2, y = t^3; y = 3x$,
(b) $x = 3t, y = 3/t; y = 2x + 3$,
(c) $x = 4t^2, y = 8t; 3y + 16 = 4x$,
(d) $x = 2t + 1, y = t^2; 2x - 3y + 13 = 0$,
(e) $x = \dfrac{1}{1+t^2}, y = \dfrac{t}{1+t^2}; x + y = 1$,
(f) $x = \dfrac{t}{t+1}, y = \dfrac{1}{t+1}; x^2 + y^2 = 25$.

5. Draw sketches of the following curves on graph paper. Plot sufficient points to give a good indication of the general shape of the curve.
(a) The semi-cubical parabola $x = t^2, y = t^3$.
(b) The ellipse $x = 3 \cos \theta, y = 2 \sin \theta$.
(c) The hyperbola $x = t - \dfrac{1}{t}, y = 2\left(t + \dfrac{1}{t}\right)$.
(d) The astroid $x = \cos^3 t, y = \sin^3 t$.
(e) The cycloid $x = \theta - \sin \theta, y = 1 - \cos \theta$.

14.6 Differentiation and parameters

When a curve is defined by parametric equations of the form $x = f(t), y = g(t)$, $\dfrac{dy}{dx}$ can be obtained as a function of t by writing

$$\frac{dy}{dx} = \frac{dy}{dt} \cdot \frac{dt}{dx} = \frac{dy}{dt} \cdot \left(1 \bigg/ \frac{dx}{dt}\right) = \frac{dy}{dt} \bigg/ \frac{dx}{dt}$$

Example 1 Find $\dfrac{dy}{dx}$ in terms of t if $x = 3t - 2$, $y = t^3 + 1$.

$$\frac{dx}{dt} = 3 \qquad \frac{dy}{dt} = 3t^2$$

$$\therefore \quad \frac{dy}{dx} = \frac{dy}{dt} \bigg/ \frac{dx}{dt} = \frac{3t^2}{3} = t^2.$$

When expressed as a function of t, dy/dx represents the gradient of a curve at the point with parameter t.

Example 2 Find the equation of the tangent to the curve $y^2 = x - 5$ at the point $(4t^2 + 5, 2t)$.

This curve can be represented by the parametric equations

$$x = 4t^2 + 5 \qquad\qquad y = 2t$$

$$\frac{dx}{dt} = 8t \qquad\qquad \frac{dy}{dt} = 2$$

$$\therefore \quad \frac{dy}{dx} = \frac{dy}{dt} \bigg/ \frac{dx}{dt} = \frac{2}{8t} = \frac{1}{4t}.$$

Hence the gradient of the tangent to the curve at the point $(4t^2 + 5, 2t)$ is $1/4t$.

The equation of the tangent is $y - 2t = \dfrac{1}{4t}\left(x - \left\{4t^2 + 5\right\}\right)$,

i.e. $4ty - 8t^2 = x - 4t^2 - 5.$

Thus the required equation is $x - 4ty + 4t^2 - 5 = 0$.

Remembering that second derivatives do *not* behave like fractions, we now obtain d^2y/dx^2 for the equations of Example 1, $x = 3t - 2$, $y = t^3 + 1$. We look again at the method used to find dy/dx, then use a similar method to find d^2y/dx^2.

$$\frac{dy}{dx} = \frac{d}{dx}\left(t^3 + 1\right) = \frac{d}{dt}\left(t^3 + 1\right) \cdot \frac{dt}{dx} = \frac{d}{dt}\left(t^3 + 1\right) \bigg/ \frac{dx}{dt} = \frac{3t^2}{3} = t^2.$$

Similarly $\dfrac{d^2y}{dx^2} = \dfrac{d}{dx}\left(\dfrac{dy}{dx}\right) = \dfrac{d}{dx}\left(t^2\right) = \dfrac{d}{dt}\left(t^2\right) \cdot \dfrac{dt}{dx} = \dfrac{d}{dt}\left(t^2\right) \bigg/ \dfrac{dx}{dt} = \dfrac{2t}{3}.$

Example 3 If $x = 1 + \dfrac{1}{t}$ and $y = t + \dfrac{1}{t}$, find $\dfrac{dy}{dx}$ and $\dfrac{d^2y}{dx^2}$ in terms of t.

$$\frac{dx}{dt} = -\frac{1}{t^2} \qquad\qquad \frac{dy}{dt} = 1 - \frac{1}{t^2}$$

$$\therefore \quad \frac{dy}{dx} = \frac{dy}{dt} \Big/ \frac{dx}{dt} = \left(1 - \frac{1}{t^2}\right) \Big/ \left(-\frac{1}{t^2}\right) = 1 - t^2.$$

$$\frac{d^2y}{dx^2} = \frac{d}{dx}\left(1 - t^2\right) = \frac{d}{dt}\left(1 - t^2\right) \Big/ \frac{dx}{dt} = -2t \Big/ \left(-\frac{1}{t^2}\right) = 2t^3.$$

Exercise 14.6

Find $\dfrac{dy}{dx}$ in terms of t if:

1. $x = 2t + 1,\ y = t^2 - 1.$ 2. $x = t^3,\ y = 3t^2 + 2.$

3. $x = 4t,\ y = 1 - \dfrac{1}{t}.$ 4. $x = (1 - 2t)^3,\ y = t^2 - t.$

5. $x = 4\cos t,\ y = 3\sin t.$ 6. $x = 2\cos^3 t,\ y = 2\sin^3 t.$

Find $\dfrac{dy}{dx}$ and $\dfrac{d^2y}{dx^2}$ in terms of t if:

7. $x = \dfrac{1}{t^2},\ y = 1 + t.$ 8. $x = 6t^2,\ y = 12t - 3t^4.$

9. $x = t^3,\ y = t^2 + t.$ 10. $x = (t + 1)^2,\ y = t^2 - 1.$

11. $x = 2\sin t,\ y = \cos 2t.$ 12. $x = \cos^2 t,\ y = \sin 2t.$

13.   Given that $x = t^3 - 2t,\ y = 5t^2 + \dfrac{1}{t}$, find the value of $\dfrac{dy}{dx}$ when $t = 1$.

14.   The parametric equations of a curve are $x = t(t^2 + 1),\ y = t^2 + 1$. Find, in its simplest form, the equation of the tangent to the curve at the point with parameter t.

15.   Find the equation of the tangent to the curve $x^2 - y^2 = 1$ at the point $(\sec\theta, \tan\theta)$.

16.   The parametric equations of a curve are $x = (5 - 3t)^2,\ y = 6t - t^2$. Find dy/dx in terms of t and the coordinates of the stationary point on the curve.

17.   Find the coordinates of the stationary points and the point of inflexion on the curve with parametric equations $x = t^2 + 1,\ y = t(t - 3)^2$.

18.   Given that $x = \theta - \sin\theta,\ y = 1 - \cos\theta$, show that $y^2 \dfrac{d^2y}{dx^2} + 1 = 0$.

Exercise 14.7 (miscellaneous)

1.   Decide whether the following functions are odd, even or neither
(a) $2x^5 - 3x^3 + 1$,   (b) $\sin 2x - \sin x$,   (c) $|x|$,

(d) $\dfrac{x}{2x^5 - 3x^3}$,   (e) $x^3 \tan x$,   (f) $[x + \frac{1}{2}]$.

2.   Given that $f(x) = ax^3 + bx^2 + cx + d$, state what can be deduced about the values of a, b, c, d in each of the following cases
(a) $f(x)$ is an even function,
(b) $f(x)$ is an odd function,
(c) $f(x) = |f(x)|$ for all values of x,
(d) $f(x) = -|f(x)|$ for all values of x.

3.   Let $f(x) = \dfrac{ax+b}{x+c}$ where x, a, b, c are real and $x \neq \pm c$. Show that if f is an even function then $ac = b$. Deduce that if f is an even function then $f(x)$ must reduce to the form $f(x) = k$, where k is constant. Find all odd functions of the form $\dfrac{ax+b}{x+c}$.   (JMB)

4.   Sketch on the same diagram the graphs of $f(x)$ and $1/f(x)$ where (a) $f(x) = 4x - x^2$, (b) $f(x) = (x-1)^2$, (c) $f(x) = x^2 + 2x + 3$.

5.   Sketch the graphs with the following equations
(a) $y = |2x - 3|$,   (b) $y = |x^2 + 3x|$,

(c) $y = \left| x + 3 + \dfrac{2}{x} \right|$,   (d) $y = \left| \dfrac{x-2}{x+2} \right|$.

6.   Find the coordinates of the point of intersection of the curve $y = \dfrac{x^3 + 1}{x}$ and the x-axis. Find also the gradients when $x = 1$ and $x = -1$, the value of x at the stationary point, and the nature of this stationary point. Sketch this curve and also the curve $y = \dfrac{x}{x^3 + 1}$.   (L)

7.   Find the local maxima and minima, and the points of inflexion, if any, of the functions f and g defined by $f(x) = \dfrac{x^4}{4(x^2 - 1)}$, $g(x) = \dfrac{4(x^2 - 1)}{x^4}$, and sketch the graphs of these two functions on one diagram.   (W)

8.   Sketch the following curves

(a) $y = \dfrac{2x+1}{x-1}$,   (b) $y = \dfrac{x-1}{2x+1}$,

(c) $y = \left| \dfrac{2x+1}{x-1} \right|$,   (d) $y = \dfrac{2|x|+1}{|x|-1}$.

9. Below are listed five functions, numbered (1)–(5), and five graphs, lettered (A)–(E). *Four* of the graphs correspond to *four* of the functions.

$$(1)\ y = \frac{(x+1)^2}{x} \qquad (2)\ y = \frac{x}{(x+1)^2} \qquad (3)\ y = \frac{x}{x+1}$$

$$(4)\ y = \left|\frac{x}{x+1}\right| \qquad (5)\ y = \frac{x^2}{x+1}.$$

(A)   (B)   (C)

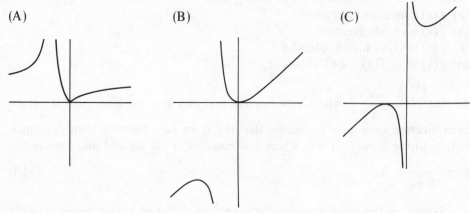

(D)   (E)

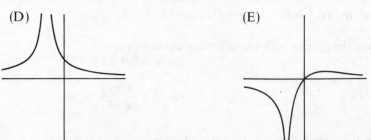

(a) Pair off the four corresponding functions and graphs. (Give your answers as four ordered pairs (n, X), n being a number and X a letter.)

(b) Sketch the graph of the fifth remaining function.

(c) Suggest a suitable function which could fit the fifth remaining graph.   (O&C)

10. Sketch the following graphs
(a) $y = |x| + |2x - 3|$,   (b) $y = |x + 3| - |x - 2|$.

11. Show that the equation $|x + 2| + |x| + |x - 1| + |x - 3| = 6$ has an infinite number of real solutions.   (C)

12. The function f is defined by $f : x \to |x - 2| + a/x$ where $x \in \mathbb{R}$, $x \neq 0$, and $a \in \mathbb{R}$, $a \neq \pm 4$ or 0. Determine the number of turning points of f for different sets of values of a. (A turning point exists for $x = c$ if $f'(c) = 0$ and $f'(x)$ changes sign as x passes through the value c.)

Sketch a graph of f (i) for $a = 3$ and (ii) for $a = -1$, showing carefully the nature of the curve near the point at which $x = 2$, and also for large values of $|x|$.

(JMB)

13. Find the Cartesian equations of the following curves

(a) $x = 2\left(t + \dfrac{1}{t}\right), y = 3\left(t - \dfrac{1}{t}\right),$

(b) $x = \dfrac{1+t^2}{1-t^2}, y = \dfrac{2t}{1-t^2},$

(c) $x = \cos\theta - 2\sin\theta$
$y = 3\cos\theta + \sin\theta,$

(d) $x = 3\sin(\theta + \frac{1}{3}\pi)$
$y = 2\sin(\theta + \frac{1}{6}\pi).$

14. The parametric equations of a curve are $x = 4 - t^2$, $y = 4t - t^3$. Find dy/dx in terms of t and hence find the coordinates of any turning points on the curve. Sketch the curve.

15. A curve is given parametrically by the equations $x = (1+t)^2$, $y = (1-t)^2$. Find dy/dx in terms of t, and hence find the point on the curve at which the gradient is zero. Find also the equation of the tangent to the curve at the point where $x = y$.

(C)

16. A locus is defined parametrically by the equations $x = \dfrac{3}{t+1}, y = \dfrac{1-5t}{t+1}$. Find

the points of intersection between this locus and the curve $xy = 3$. Find dy/dx for the locus and hence its Cartesian equation.

17. Given that $x + y = \sin(\theta + 75°)$, $x - y = \sin(\theta + 15°)$, express x and y each in terms of the sine or cosine of $\theta + 45°$. If x and y are the coordinates of a point P and θ varies, obtain in a simplified form the Cartesian equation of the locus of P. Sketch this locus.

(JMB)

18. Find $\dfrac{dy}{dx}$ and $\dfrac{d^2y}{dx^2}$ in terms of t, given that

(a) $x = 3t(3 - 4t^2)$, $y = (3 - 2t)(1 - 2t)^2$,
(b) $x = 2\cos t + \cos 2t$, $y = 2\sin t + \sin 2t$.

19. A curve joining the points $(0, 1)$ and $(0, -1)$ is represented parametrically by the equations

$$x = \sin\theta, y = (1 + \sin\theta)\cos\theta, \text{ where } 0 \leqslant \theta \leqslant \pi.$$

Find dy/dx in terms of θ, and determine the x, y coordinates of the points on the curve at which the tangents are parallel to the x-axis and of the point at which the tangent is perpendicular to the x-axis. Sketch the curve.

The region in the quadrant $x \geqslant 0$, $y \geqslant 0$ bounded by the curve and the coordinate axes is rotated about the x-axis through an angle of 2π. Show that the

volume swept out is given by $V = \pi \displaystyle\int_0^1 (1+x)^2(1-x^2)dx$. Evaluate V, leaving your result in terms of π.

(JMB)

15 Coordinate geometry

15.1 The locus of a point

A *locus* is the set of all points satisfying some condition. The Cartesian equation of a locus is obtained by expressing this condition as a relationship between the x- and y-coordinates of a typical point.

Example 1 Find the equation of the locus of points at a distance of 2 units from the point $C(-1, 2)$.

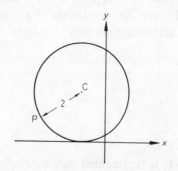

Let $P(x, y)$ be a point on the locus then
$$PC^2 = 2^2$$
$$\therefore \quad (x+1)^2 + (y-2)^2 = 2^2$$
$$x^2 + 2x + 1 + y^2 - 4y + 4 = 4$$
$$\therefore \quad \text{the equation of the locus is}$$
$$x^2 + y^2 + 2x - 4y + 1 = 0.$$

Clearly this equation must represent a circle with centre $(-1, 2)$ and radius 2.

Example 2 Find the equation of the locus of points 5 units above the x-axis.

For any point $P(x, y)$ on the locus, $y = 5$ and there is no restriction on the value of x. Hence the equation of the locus is simply $y = 5$.

Example 3 Find the equation of the locus of points equidistant from the x- and y-axes.

The distance of a point $P(x, y)$ from the x-axis is $|y|$. Similarly the distance of P from the y-axis is $|x|$. Since these distances are equal,

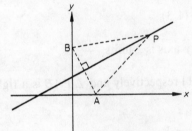

$$|x| = |y|.$$

Squaring to avoid the use of moduli, the equation of the locus may be written

$$x^2 = y^2 \quad \text{or} \quad x^2 - y^2 = 0.$$

This equation represents the pair of lines which bisect the angles between the x- and y-axes.

Example 4   Find the equation of the locus of a point which moves so that it is equidistant from the points $A(1, 0)$ and $B(0, 2)$.

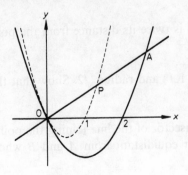

If $P(x, y)$ is any point on the locus then

$$PA^2 = PB^2$$
$$\therefore \quad (x-1)^2 + y^2 = x^2 + (y-2)^2$$
$$x^2 - 2x + 1 + y^2 = x^2 + y^2 - 4y + 4$$
$$\therefore \quad \text{the equation of the locus is}$$

$$2x - 4y + 3 = 0.$$

This equation must represent the perpendicular bisector of AB.

In some problems it is necessary to express the coordinates of a general point on a locus in terms of a parameter. The Cartesian equation is then obtained by eliminating the parameter.

Example 5   The line $y = mx$ and the curve $y = x^2 - 2x$ intersect at the origin O and meet again at a point A. If P is the mid-point of OA, find the equation of the locus of P as m varies.

At the points of intersection

$$x^2 - 2x = mx$$
$$x(x - m - 2) = 0$$
$$\therefore \quad x = 0 \quad \text{or} \quad x = m + 2$$
$$\therefore \quad \text{the coordinates of } A \text{ are}$$
$(m + 2, m\{m + 2\})$ and the coordinates of P are $(\frac{1}{2}\{m + 2\}, \frac{1}{2}m\{m + 2\})$.

Hence in parametric form the equations of the locus of P are

$$x = \tfrac{1}{2}(m+2) \qquad (1)$$

$$y = \tfrac{1}{2}m(m+2) \qquad (2)$$

Rearranging (1) $m = 2x - 2$

Substituting in (2) $y = (x-1)2x.$

Hence the equation of the locus of P is $y = 2x(x-1)$.

Exercise 15.1

In questions 1 to 10 find the equation of the locus of a point P as it moves subject to the stated condition. In each case draw a sketch to illustrate your answer.

1.   The distance of P from the point $(-3, 4)$ is 5 units.

2. P is equidistant from the points $(1,0)$ and $(4,3)$.

3.   The perpendicular distance of P from the y-axis is 2 units.

4. A and B are the points $(-3,1)$ and $(5, -1)$ respectively and $\angle PAB$ is a right angle.

5. P is equidistant from the lines $x = 1$ and $y = 1$.

6.   The distance of P from the point $(0,2)$ is equal to its distance from the x-axis.

7.   The area of the rectangle with sides parallel to the axes and with diagonal OP is 9 square units.

8. A and B are the points $(-1,2)$ and $(3,2)$ respectively and $\angle APB$ is a right angle.

9.   The distance of P from point $(3,0)$ is equal to its perpendicular distance from the line $x + 3 = 0$.

10. The distance of P from the point $(-2,1)$ is twice its distance from the point $(4,1)$.

11. Find the equation of the circle centre $(-1,1)$ and radius $\sqrt{2}$. Show that this circle passes through the origin.

12. Find the equation of the perpendicular bisector of the line joining the points $A(2,1)$ and $B(-4, -1)$. Hence find the point equidistant from A and B whose x-coordinate is -3.

13. The line $y = mx$ meets the curve $y^2 = 4x$ at the origin O and at a point A. Find the equation of the locus of the mid-point of OA as m varies.

14. If P is the point $(t, t^2 - 4)$ and Q is the point $(2, 0)$, find the coordinates of the mid-point R of PQ. Deduce the equation of the locus of R as t varies.

15. A and B are the points $(a, 0)$ and $(0, b)$ respectively and P is the mid-point of AB. Find the equation of the locus of P as a and b vary given that (a) $a + b = c$, where c is constant, (b) triangle OAB is of constant area k, (c) AB is of constant length l.

16. The line $y = mx$ intersects the curve $y = x^2 - 1$ at the points A and B. Find the equation of the locus of the mid-point of AB as m varies.

15.2 The circle

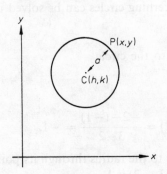

Let $P(x, y)$ be a point on the circle, centre (h, k) and radius a, then $PC^2 = a^2$

$$\therefore \quad (x - h)^2 + (y - k)^2 = a^2.$$

Thus the equation of the circle, centre (h, k), radius a, is

$$\boxed{(x - h)^2 + (y - k)^2 = a^2.}$$

In particular, the equation of the circle with centre the origin and radius a is

$$\boxed{x^2 + y^2 = a^2.}$$

Example 1   Find the equation of the circle with centre $(1, -2)$ and radius 3.

The equation is
$$(x - 1)^2 + (y + 2)^2 = 3^2$$
$$x^2 - 2x + 1 + y^2 + 4y + 4 = 9$$
i.e. $\qquad x^2 + y^2 - 2x + 4y - 4 = 0.$

Given the equation of a circle, it can be expressed in the form $(x - h)^2 + (y - k)^2 = a^2$ in order to write down its centre and radius.

Example 2   Find the centre and radius of the circle $x^2 + y^2 + 6x - 2y - 6 = 0$.

[The aim is to rearrange the equation by completing squares of the form $(x - h)^2$ and $(y - k)^2$.]

The equation of the circle may be rearranged as

$$x^2 + 6x + y^2 - 2y = 6$$
$$x^2 + 6x + 9 + y^2 - 2y + 1 = 6 + 9 + 1$$

i.e. $$(x+3)^2 + (y-1)^2 = 4^2.$$

Hence the circle has centre $(-3, 1)$ and radius 4.

We see that the equation $x^2 + y^2 + 2gx + 2fy + c = 0$ represents a circle for suitable values of g, f and c. Rearranging

$$x^2 + 2gx + y^2 + 2fy = -c$$
$$x^2 + 2gx + g^2 + y^2 + 2fy + f^2 = f^2 + g^2 - c$$

i.e. $$(x+g)^2 + (y+f)^2 = f^2 + g^2 - c.$$

Thus the equation $x^2 + y^2 + 2gx + 2fy + c = 0$ represents a circle with centre $(-g, -f)$ and radius $\sqrt{(f^2 + g^2 - c)}$ provided that this is real.

Many problems in coordinate geometry concerning circles can be solved using their elementary properties.

Example 3   Find the equation of the tangent to the circle $x^2 + y^2 - 4x + 2y + 3 = 0$ at the point $(3, -2)$.

The centre of the circle is the point $(2, -1)$

$\therefore$ the gradient of the radius through $(3, -2) = \dfrac{-2 - (-1)}{3 - 2} = -1$.

Since any tangent to a circle is perpendicular to the radius through its point of contact, the gradient of the tangent through $(3, -2)$ is 1.

Hence its equation is $y + 2 = 1(x - 3)$, i.e. $y = x - 5$.

Example 4   Find the length of a tangent drawn from the point $A(3, -4)$ to the circle $x^2 + y^2 + 6x - 8y = 0$.

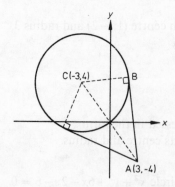

Rearranging the equation of the circle

$$x^2 + 6x + 9 + y^2 - 8y + 16 = 9 + 16$$

i.e. $$(x+3)^2 + (y-4)^2 = 5^2$$

$\therefore$ the circle has centre $(-3, 4)$ and radius 5.

If C is the centre of the circle and B is the point of contact of a tangent through A, then

$$AC^2 = (3 - \{-3\})^2 + (-4 - 4)^2 = 6^2 + 8^2 = 100 \quad \text{and}$$
BC, a radius of the circle, is of length 5.

Hence, using Pythagoras' theorem,

$$AB^2 = AC^2 - BC^2 = 100 - 25 = 75 \qquad \therefore \quad AB = 5\sqrt{3}.$$

Thus the length of the tangents from A to the given circle is $5\sqrt{3}$.

Example 5 Find the equation of the circle whose diameter is the line joining the points $A(1,3)$ and $B(-2,5)$.

[One way of doing this is to write down the centre and the radius of the circle, then use these to obtain the equation. We give here an alternative method.]

If $P(x, y)$ is any point on the circle, then since AB is a diameter, the angle APB is a right angle.

Gradient of $AP = \dfrac{y-3}{x-1}$, gradient of $BP = \dfrac{y-5}{x+2}$.

Since AP is perpendicular to BP, $\dfrac{y-3}{x-1} \times \dfrac{y-5}{x+2} = -1$

$$\therefore \quad (x-1)(x+2) + (y-3)(y-5) = 0$$
$$x^2 + x - 2 + y^2 - 8y + 15 = 0.$$

Hence the equation of the circle is $x^2 + y^2 + x - 8y + 13 = 0.$

Example 6 Find the equation of the circle which passes through the points $(-1,0)$, $(1,2)$ and $(-5,4)$.

Let the equation of the circle be $x^2 + y^2 + 2gx + 2fy + c = 0$, then since the coordinates $(-1,0)$, $(1,2)$ and $(-5,4)$ must satisfy this equation

$1 + 0 - 2g + c = 0$	$\therefore \qquad -2g + c = -1$	(1)
$1 + 4 + 2g + 4f + c = 0$	$\therefore \qquad 2g + 4f + c = -5$	(2)
$25 + 16 - 10g + 8f + c = 0$	$\therefore \quad -10g + 8f + c = -41$	(3)

$2 \times (2) - (3)$ $\qquad\qquad 14g + c = 31$

Subtracting (1) $\qquad\qquad\quad 16g = 32 \qquad \therefore \quad g = 2$

Using (1) and (2) $c = 3$ and $f = -3$.

Hence the required equation is $x^2 + y^2 + 4x - 6y + 3 = 0.$

Another way of finding the equation of a circle through three given points is to use the fact that if points A and B lie on a circle then the centre of the circle lies on the perpendicular bisector of AB.

Example 7 Find the equation of the circle that touches the line $y = x$ at the point $A(3,3)$ and passes through the point $B(5,9)$.

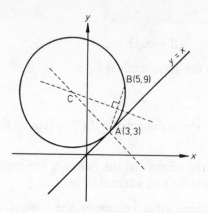

If C is the centre of the circle then C must lie on the perpendicular bisector of AB. Since the line $y = x$ is a tangent to the circle, C must also lie on the line through A perpendicular to $y = x$.

The gradient of $AB = \dfrac{9-3}{5-3} = 3.$

The coordinates of the mid-point of AB are $(4, 6)$

$\therefore$ the perpendicular bisector passes through $(4, 6)$ and has gradient $-\frac{1}{3}$.

Hence its equation is $y - 6 = -\frac{1}{3}(x-4)$ i.e. $x + 3y = 22$ $\qquad$ (1)

The line through A perpendicular to $y = x$ has gradient -1

$\therefore$ its equation is $y - 3 = -1(x-3)$,   i.e. $x + y = 6$ $\qquad$ (2)

Subtracting (2) from (1) $2y = 16$ $\therefore$ $y = 8, x = -2.$

Hence the centre of the circle is the point $(-2, 8)$.

The radius of the circle $= AC = \sqrt{\{(-2-3)^2 + (8-3)^2\}} = \sqrt{50}$

Thus the equation of the circle is $(x+2)^2 + (y-8)^2 = 50$

i.e. $x^2 + y^2 + 4x - 16y + 18 = 0.$

Exercise 15.2

1. Find the equations of the circles with the following centres and radii
(a) $(3, 2)$, 4, $\qquad$ (b) $(-1, -2)$, 1, $\qquad$ (c) $(0, 0)$, 5,
(d) $(\frac{1}{2}, 0)$, 3/2, $\qquad$ (e) $(4, -1)$, $\sqrt{3}$, $\qquad$ (f) $(-3, 5)$, $2\sqrt{5}$.

2. Find the centres and radii of the following circles
(a) $x^2 + y^2 - 2x - 6y + 1 = 0$, $\qquad$ (b) $x^2 + y^2 = 4$,
(c) $x^2 + y^2 + 6x + 8y = 0$, $\qquad$ (d) $x^2 + y^2 - 4x + 2y + 4 = 0$,
(e) $4x^2 + 4y^2 - 5 = 0$, $\qquad$ (f) $2x^2 + 2y^2 - 6x + 10y + 7 = 0$.

3. Find the range of values of k for which each of the following equations represents a circle with non-zero radius.
(a) $x^2 + y^2 = k$ $\qquad$ (b) $x^2 + ky^2 - 2x - 8 = 0$,
(c) $kx^2 + y^2 + 4y + 9 = 0$, $\qquad$ (d) $2x^2 + 2y^2 + kxy - 9 = 0$,
(e) $x^2 + y^2 + 2x - 6y + k = 0$, $\qquad$ (f) $x^2 + y^2 + kx - 2y + 5 = 0$.

4. Find the equations of the tangents to the following circles at the given points
(a) $x^2 + y^2 = 5$, $(-2, 1)$,　　　(b) $x^2 + y^2 - 4x + 2y = 3$, $(0, -3)$,
(c) $x^2 + y^2 + 6y - 1 = 0$, $(3, -4)$,　(d) $2x^2 + 2y^2 + 9x - 4y + 4 = 0$, $(-2, 3)$.

5. Find the lengths of the tangents drawn from the following points to the given circles
(a) $(6, -1)$, $x^2 + y^2 = 12$,
(b) $(-1, 3)$, $x^2 + y^2 - 8x + 4y + 19 = 0$,
(c) $(4, -2)$, $x^2 + y^2 - 10y - 4 = 0$,
(d) $(3, -4)$, $x^2 + y^2 + x - 3y = 0$.

6. Find the equations of the circles which pass through the following sets of points
(a) $(0, 0)$, $(2, 0)$, $(0, 6)$,　　　(b) $(5, 6)$, $(5, -2)$, $(1, 6)$,
(c) $(5, 0)$, $(3, 2)$, $(-3, -4)$,　　(d) $(2, 3)$, $(-2, 1)$, $(4, 7)$.

7. Find the greatest and the least distance of a point P from the origin as it moves round the circle
(a) $x^2 + y^2 - 24x - 10y + 48 = 0$,
(b) $x^2 + y^2 + 6x - 8y - 24 = 0$.

8. Find the equation of the circle which has the points $(-7, 3)$ and $(1, 9)$ at the ends of a diameter. Find also the equations of the tangents to this circle which are parallel (a) to the x-axis, (b) to the y-axis.

9. Find the equation of the locus of a point P which moves so that its distance from the point $A(1, 3)$ is twice its distance from the point $B(4, 6)$. Show that the locus is a circle giving its centre and radius.

10. Find the equation of the circle which passes through the point $A(6, 1)$ and touches the x-axis at the point $B(3, 0)$. If this circle cuts the y-axis at the points P and Q, find the area of the quadrilateral $ABPQ$.

11. Find the equation of the circle which touches the line $3x - 4y = 3$ at the point $(5, 3)$ and passes through the point $(-2, 4)$.

12. Show that the circle $x^2 + y^2 - 6x - 4y + 9 = 0$ touches the x-axis and that the circle $x^2 + y^2 - 2x - 6y + 9 = 0$ touches the y-axis. Find the coordinates of their points of intersection, showing that these lie on a straight line through the origin.

13. Find the equation of the circle C_1 which has as the ends of a diameter the points $P(1, 1)$ and $Q(6, 2)$. Show that the point $R(7, -3)$ lies outside this circle and find the equation of the circle C_2 which passes through P, Q and R. Hence show that the centre of C_2 lies on C_1.

15.3 Tangents and normals

As we have seen in previous chapters, the gradient of the tangent at any point on a curve in the x, y plane is given by dy/dx. The *normal* to a curve at any point is the line perpendicular to the tangent. Thus if the gradients of the tangent and the normal at a particular point are m_1 and m_2, then $m_1 m_2 = -1$.

Example 1 Find the equations of the tangent and the normal to the curve $x^2 - 3xy + y^2 = 5$ at the point $(1, 4)$.

Differentiating the equation with respect to x

$$2x - 3x\frac{dy}{dx} - 3y + 2y\frac{dy}{dx} = 0$$

$\therefore$ at the point $(1, 4)$ $2 - 3\frac{dy}{dx} - 12 + 8\frac{dy}{dx} = 0$

i.e. $5\frac{dy}{dx} - 10 = 0$ so that $\frac{dy}{dx} = 2.$

Hence the gradients of the tangent and normal at $(1, 4)$ are 2 and $-\frac{1}{2}$ respectively.

The equation of the tangent is $y - 4 = 2(x - 1)$

i.e. $y = 2x + 2.$

The equation of the normal is $y - 4 = -\frac{1}{2}(x - 1)$

i.e. $x + 2y = 9.$

Example 2 Find the equation of the normal to the curve with parametric equations $x = 3t + 5$, $y = 1 - t^2$, which is parallel to the line $3x + 4y = 7$.

Differentiating $\frac{dx}{dt} = 3$ $\frac{dy}{dt} = -2t$

$$\therefore \quad \frac{dy}{dx} = \frac{dy}{dt} \Big/ \frac{dx}{dt} = -\frac{2t}{3}.$$

Hence the gradient of the normal at the point with parameter t is $3/2t$.

The gradient of the line $3x + 4y = 7$ is $-\frac{3}{4}$

$\therefore$ the normal to the curve is parallel to this line

when $\dfrac{3}{2t} = -\dfrac{3}{4}$,   i.e.   when $t = -2$.

Thus the required normal passes through the point $(-1, -3)$ on the curve.

$\therefore$ its equation is $3x + 4y = 3(-1) + 4(-3)$
      i.e. $3x + 4y + 15 = 0$.

The next example shows a different way of obtaining the equation of a tangent to a curve.

Example 3 $P(2p, 2/p)$ and $Q(2q, 2/q)$ are two points on the curve $xy = 4$. Find the equation of the chord PQ. Deduce the equation of the tangent to the curve at P.

The gradient of $PQ = \dfrac{2/q - 2/p}{2q - 2p} = \dfrac{p - q}{pq(q - p)} = -\dfrac{1}{pq}$, assuming $p \neq q$.

$\therefore$ the equation of the chord PQ is

$$y - \frac{2}{p} = -\frac{1}{pq}(x - 2p)$$
$$pqy - 2q = -x + 2p$$
i.e. $$x + pqy = 2(p + q).$$

As we consider points Q closer and closer to P, the chord PQ approaches the tangent at P

$\therefore$ letting $q \to p$, we obtain the equation of the tangent at P,

$$x + p^2 y = 4p.$$

We now consider the equations of tangents to a curve through a given point not on the curve.

Example 4   Using the result of Example 3, find the equations of the tangents to the curve $xy = 4$ which pass through the point $(3, 1)$ and give the coordinates of their points of contact.

The tangent at the point $(2p, 2/p)$ has equation $x + p^2 y = 4p$. If this tangent passes through $(3, 1)$ then $3 + p^2 = 4p$

i.e. $$p^2 - 4p + 3 = 0$$
         $$(p - 1)(p - 3) = 0$$

$\therefore$ either $p = 1$ or $p = 3$.

Hence the required tangents have equations $x + y = 4$ and $x + 9y = 12$, their points of contact being $(2, 2)$ and $(6, \frac{2}{3})$ respectively.

Example 5   Find the equations of the tangents to the circle $x^2 + y^2 = 5$ which pass through the point $(5, 0)$. Find also the equation of the chord of contact

The equation of the line through $(5, 0)$ with gradient m is $y = m(x - 5)$.

Substituting in the equation $x^2 + y^2 = 5$ to find the points of intersection

$$x^2 + m^2(x-5)^2 = 5$$
$$x^2 + m^2x^2 - 10m^2x + 25m^2 = 5$$
$$(1+m^2)x^2 - 10m^2x + 25m^2 - 5 = 0 \qquad (1)$$

The line will be a tangent to the circle if this quadratic equation in x has equal roots

i.e. if $\quad (-10m^2)^2 - 4(1+m^2)(25m^2 - 5) = 0 \qquad [\,b^2 - 4ac = 0\,]$

$\therefore \qquad 100m^4 - 100m^4 - 80m^2 + 20 = 0$

$\therefore \qquad 1 - 4m^2 = 0$

$\therefore$ either $\quad m = \frac{1}{2}$ or $\quad m = -\frac{1}{2}$.

Hence the equations of the tangents through $(5,0)$ are

$$y = \tfrac{1}{2}(x-5) \quad \text{and} \quad y = -\tfrac{1}{2}(x-5)$$
i.e. $\quad x - 2y = 5 \quad$ and $\quad x + 2y = 5.$

When equation (1) has equal roots

$$x = \frac{10m^2}{2(1+m^2)} = \frac{10 \cdot \frac{1}{4}}{2(1+\frac{1}{4})} = 1 \qquad \left[x = \frac{-b}{2a} \right]$$

$\therefore$ the x-coordinate of both points of contact is 1.

Hence the equation of the chord of contact is $x = 1$.

Example 6   Show that the line $y = 3x - 4$ is a tangent to the curve $y = x^2 - x$. Find also the condition that the line $y = mx + c$ should be a tangent to the curve.

At the points of intersection between the curve $y = x^2 - x$ and the line $y = 3x - 4$,

$$x^2 - x = 3x - 4$$
$$x^2 - 4x + 4 = 0$$
$$(x-2)^2 = 0.$$

Since this equation has equal roots the line is a tangent to the curve.

At any points of intersection between the curve $y = x^2 - x$ and the line $y = mx + c$,

$$x^2 - x = mx + c$$
$$\therefore \quad x^2 - (m+1)x - c = 0$$

The condition that this equation has equal roots is

$$(m+1)^2 - 4.1.(-c) = 0, \quad \text{i.e.} \quad (m+1)^2 + 4c = 0.$$

Hence the line $y = mx + c$ will be a tangent to the curve $y = x^2 - x$ if $(m+1)^2 + 4c = 0$.

Exercise 15.3

In questions 1 to 10 find the equations of the tangent and normal to the given curve at the stated point.

1. $y = 3 + 5x - x^2$; $(4, 7)$.

2. $y = x\sqrt{(x-1)}$; $(2, 2)$.

3. $y = x^2 - \dfrac{1}{x}$; $(-1, 2)$.

4. $y = \dfrac{2x-1}{x+2}$; $(-3, 7)$.

5. $3x^2 + y^2 = 39$; $(1, -6)$.

6. $x^2 + 5xy + 2y^2 = 8$; $(1, 1)$.

7. $y^2 = x^3 - 2$; $(3, 5)$.

8. $\dfrac{1}{x} - \dfrac{1}{y} = \dfrac{1}{6}$; $(2, 3)$.

9. $x = (2t+1)^2$, $y = t^2 - t$; $t = -1$.

10. $x = t(t^2 + 4)$, $y = t^2 + 4$; $t = 2$.

11. Show that the following lines are tangents to the given curves and find their points of contact
(a) $x + y = 4$; $y = 3x - x^2$,
(b) $2x + y = 5$; $x^2 + y^2 - 2x + 4y = 0$,
(c) $5x - 3y = 8$; $x = t + \dfrac{1}{t}$, $y = t - \dfrac{1}{t}$.

12. Find the equation of the normal to the curve $x = 3t - 2t^2$, $y = 2 + t^2$ which is parallel to the line $5x - 4y = 0$.

13. Find the equations of the tangents to the curve $y = x^3 - 10x + 5$ which are parallel to the line $2x - y = 5$.

14. Find the values of m for which the line $y = m(2x - 1)$ touches the curve $y = x^2 + 4x$.

15. Find the equations of the tangents to the curve $y = x^2 + 2x + 4$ which pass through the point $(2, 3)$ and the coordinates of the points of contact.

16. Find the equations of the tangents from the origin to the circle $x^2 + y^2 - 4x - 2y + 4 = 0$. Find also the length of the chord of contact.

17. Find the values of c for which the line $y = x + c$ is a tangent to the circle $x^2 + y^2 - 4x + 2y - 3 = 0$.

18. Find the values of c for which the line $2x - 3y = c$ is a tangent to the curve $x^2 + 2y^2 = 2$ and find the equation of the line joining the points of contact.

19. Find the equations of the tangents to the circle $x^2 + y^2 = 10$ which are parallel to the line $y = 3x$.

20. Find the equations of the tangents to the circle $x^2 + y^2 = 9$ which pass

through the point $(0, 5)$. Find also the acute angle between these tangents, giving your answer in degrees.

21. Show that the equation of the tangent to the curve $x = 4\cos\theta$, $y = 2\sin\theta$ at the point with parameter θ is $x\cos\theta + 2y\sin\theta = 4$. Hence find the equations of the tangents which pass through the point $(5, 0)$ and the coordinates of their points of contact.

22. Find the equation of the normal to the curve $x = 2t$, $y = t^2$ at the point with parameter t. If this normal meets the x- and y-axes at the points A and B respectively, find the equation of the locus of the mid-point of AB.

23. $P(p-1, p^2)$ and $Q(q-1, q^2)$ are two points on the curve $y = (x+1)^2$. Find the equation of the chord PQ and hence the equation of the tangent at P. If the tangent at P meets the line $x = -1$ at the point R, find the equation of the locus of the mid-point of PR.

24. $P(p^2, p^3)$ and $Q(q^2, q^3)$ are two points on the curve $y^2 = x^3$. Find the equation of the chord PQ and deduce the equation of the tangent at P. Given that the tangent at P passes through Q and is normal to the curve at Q, find the values of p and q.

15.4 The parabola

The locus of a point equidistant from a fixed point and a fixed line is called a *parabola*. The fixed point is the *focus* of the parabola and the fixed line is called the *directrix*.

The standard form of the equation of a parabola is obtained by letting the focus be the point $S(a, 0)$ and the directrix the line $x = -a$.

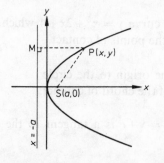

If $P(x, y)$ is any point on the parabola and M is the foot of the perpendicular from P to the directrix, then

$$SP^2 = PM^2$$

$$\therefore \quad (x-a)^2 + y^2 = (x+a)^2$$

$$\therefore \quad y^2 = 4ax$$

Thus the equation $y^2 = 4ax$ represents a parabola with focus $(a, 0)$, directrix $x = -a$.

The line of symmetry of the curve, in this case the x-axis, is called the *axis* of the parabola. The point where the curve cuts the axis, the origin $(0, 0)$, is referred to as the *vertex*.

Example 1   Find the equation of the tangent to the parabola $y^2 = 8x$ at the point $(2, 4)$.

$$y^2 = 8x$$

Differentiating with respect to x: $2y\dfrac{dy}{dx} = 8$

$$\therefore \quad \dfrac{dy}{dx} = \dfrac{8}{2y} = \dfrac{4}{y}.$$

$\therefore$ the gradient of the tangent at the point $(2, 4)$ is 1.

Hence its equation is $y - 4 = 1(x - 2)$, i.e. $y = x + 2$.

By the same method it can be shown that the tangent at (x_1, y_1) to the curve $y^2 = 4ax$ has equation $yy_1 = 2a(x + x_1)$.

It is usually more convenient to express the equation $y^2 = 4ax$ in the parametric form $x = at^2$, $y = 2at$. Substituting in the original equation, we find that the point $(at^2, 2at)$ lies on the parabola for all values of the parameter t.

Example 2   Find the equations of the tangent and the normal to the curve $y^2 = 4ax$ at the point $(at^2, 2at)$.

Differentiating the parametric equations

$$x = at^2 \qquad y = 2at$$

$$\dfrac{dx}{dt} = 2at \qquad \dfrac{dy}{dt} = 2a$$

$$\therefore \quad \dfrac{dy}{dx} = \dfrac{dy}{dt}\bigg/\dfrac{dx}{dt} = \dfrac{2a}{2at} = \dfrac{1}{t}$$

$\therefore$ the gradient of the tangent at the point $(at^2, 2at)$ is $1/t$.

Hence its equation is $y - 2at = \dfrac{1}{t}(x - at^2)$, i.e.

$$ty - x = at^2.$$

The gradient of the normal at $(at^2, 2at)$ is $-t$.

Hence the equation of the normal is $y - 2at = -t(x - at^2)$,
i.e. $y + tx = 2at + at^3$.

A *chord* of a parabola is a straight line which joins any two points on the curve. A chord which passes through the focus is a *focal chord*. The focal chord parallel to the directrix is called the *latus rectum*.

Example 3   Find the equation of the chord PQ of the parabola $x = at^2$, $y = 2at$, where P and Q are the points with parameters p and q respectively. Given that the chord PQ passes through the focus of the parabola, find the equation of the locus of the mid-point M of PQ as p and q vary.

The coordinates of P and Q are $(ap^2, 2ap)$ and $(aq^2, 2aq)$

$$\therefore \quad \text{the gradient of } PQ = \frac{2ap - 2aq}{ap^2 - aq^2} = \frac{2}{p+q}.$$

Hence the equation of PQ is $y - 2ap = \dfrac{2}{p+q}(x - ap^2)$

$$(p+q)(y - 2ap) = 2(x - ap^2)$$
$$(p+q)y - 2ap^2 - 2apq = 2x - 2ap^2$$

i.e.
$$(p+q)y - 2x = 2apq.$$

Given that the focus $(a, 0)$ lies on this line

$$-2a = 2apq \qquad \therefore \quad pq = -1$$

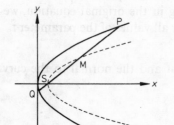

The coordinates of M are

$$(\tfrac{1}{2}\{ap^2 + aq^2\}, \tfrac{1}{2}\{2ap + 2aq\})$$

$\therefore$ the equations of the locus of M are

$$x = \tfrac{1}{2}a(p^2 + q^2), \quad y = a(p+q)$$

where $pq = -1$.

[To obtain the Cartesian equation of the locus, p and q must be eliminated from these three equations.]

Expressing x in terms of $p+q$ and pq,

$$x = \tfrac{1}{2}a\{(p+q)^2 - 2pq\}$$

$$\therefore \quad x = \tfrac{1}{2}a\left\{\frac{y^2}{a^2} - 2(-1)\right\} = \frac{y^2}{2a} + a.$$

Hence the equation of the locus of M is $y^2 = 2a(x - a)$.

Exercise 15.4

1. Sketch the following parabolas showing their foci and directrices
(a) $y^2 = 4x$,
(b) $y^2 = 12x$,
(c) $y^2 = -8x$,
(d) $y^2 = 4x + 1$,
(e) $y^2 = x$,
(f) $y = x^2$,
(g) $x = 2t^2, y = 4t$,
(h) $x = 3t^2, y = -6t$.

2. Write down the equations of the parabolas with the following foci and directrices
(a) $(2, 0); x = -2$,
(b) $(5, 0); x = -5$,
(c) $(0, 1); y = -1$,
(d) $(-3, 0); x = 3$,
(e) $(1, 1); x = -1$,
(f) $(0, 2); y = 0$.

3. Derive the equations of the parabolas with the following foci and directrices

(a) $(3, 0)$; $x = 1$,
(c) $(-1, 1)$; $x = -3$,

(b) $(3, 1)$; $x = -3$,
(d) $(4, 2)$; $y = 3$.

4. Write down the parametric coordinates of a point on each of the following curves

(a) $y^2 = 8x$,
(b) $y^2 = 24x$,
(c) $y^2 = -16x$.

5. Find the equations of the tangents and normals to the following curves at the given points

(a) $y^2 = 16x$; $(1, 4)$,
(c) $x = t^2$, $y = 2t$; $t = 2$,

(b) $y^2 = 6x$; $(6, -6)$,
(d) $x = 3t^2$, $y = 6t$; $t = -1$.

6. The normal to the parabola $y^2 = 4ax$ at the point $P(at^2, 2at)$ meets the x-axis at A. Find the equation of the locus of the mid-point of AP as t varies.

7. The tangent to the parabola $y^2 = 4ax$ at the point $P(at^2, 2at)$ meets the x-axis at A and the y-axis at B. Find the equation of the locus of the mid-point of AB as t varies.

8. Show that, if the chord joining the points $P(ap^2, 2ap)$, $Q(aq^2, 2aq)$ on the parabola $y^2 = 4ax$ passes through $(a, 0)$, then $pq = -1$. Further, the tangent at P meets the line through Q parallel to the axis of the parabola at R. Prove that the line $x + a = 0$ bisects PR. (O & C)

9. Find the condition that the line $y = mx + c$ should be a tangent to the parabola $y^2 = 4ax$. Use this result to find the equations of the tangents to the curve $y^2 = 4x$ which pass through the point $(-2, 1)$.

10. The tangents at $P(ap^2, 2ap)$ and $Q(aq^2, 2aq)$ to the parabola $y^2 = 4ax$ meet at a point R. Find the coordinates of R. If R lies on the line $2x + a = 0$, find the equation of the locus of the mid-point of PQ.

11. The points $P(ap^2, 2ap)$ and $Q(aq^2, 2aq)$ lie on the parabola $y^2 = 4ax$. Prove that if PQ is a focal chord then the tangents to the curve at P and Q intersect at right angles at a point on the directrix.

12. Find the gradient of the normal to the parabola $y^2 = 4ax$ at the point $P(ap^2, 2ap)$. Find the slope of the chord joining the point $P(ap^2, 2ap)$ to another point $Q(aq^2, 2aq)$. The normal at a point $P(ap^2, 2ap)$ meets the parabola again at a point $Q(aq^2, 2aq)$. By treating this line both as a normal and a chord, or otherwise, prove that $p^2 + pq + 2 = 0$.
   The normal at a point $R(4a, 4a)$ meets the parabola again at a point S. The normal at S meets the parabola again at T. What are the coordinates of T? Find the length of RS, giving your answer in simplified surd form. (SU)

13. The tangents at the points $P(ap^2, 2ap)$ and $Q(aq^2, 2aq)$ on the parabola $y^2 = 4ax$ intersect at the point R. Given that the tangent at P is perpendicular to the chord OQ, where O is the origin, find the equation of the locus of R as p varies.

14. Find the equation of the tangent to the parabola $y^2 = 4ax$ at the point $P(at^2, 2at)$. The line through O, parallel to this tangent, meets the parabola again at Q. Show that the line through P, parallel to the axis of the parabola, passes through the midpoint of OQ. Show also that, if the tangent and normal at P meet the x-axis at T and N respectively, the area of the triangle TPN is $2a^2t(1+t^2)$. (L)

15. The tangent to the parabola $y^2 = 4ax$ at the point $P(at^2, 2at)$ meets the x-axis at T. The straight line through P parallel to the axis of the parabola meets the directrix at Q. If S is the focus of the parabola, show that $PQTS$ is a rhombus. If M is the mid-point of PT and N is the mid-point of PM, find the equation of the locus of (i) M, (ii) N. (AEB 1978)

15.5 Translations and change of origin

In the previous section the parabola $y^2 = 4ax$ was considered in some detail. We now look at ways of using our knowledge of this 'standard' parabola to determine the properties of a parabola whose vertex is not at the origin.

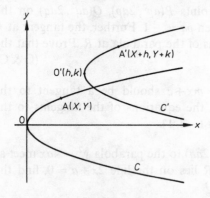

The sketch shows the curve C with equation $y^2 = 4ax$ and its image C' under a translation with column vector $\begin{pmatrix} h \\ k \end{pmatrix}$. The image of the origin O under this translation is the point $O'(h, k)$. The image of a typical point $A(X, Y)$ on the curve C is the point $A'(X+h, Y+k)$. Thus at a typical point A' on C'

$$x = X+h, \quad y = Y+k \quad \text{where} \quad Y^2 = 4aX.$$

Eliminating X and Y we find that the Cartesian equation of C' is

$$(y-k)^2 = 4a(x-h).$$

Hence the equation $(y-k)^2 = 4a(x-h)$ represents the image of the parabola $y^2 = 4ax$ under a translation in which the point $(0,0)$ is mapped to the point (h, k).

Example 1 Show that the equation $y^2 = 4x-8$ represents a parabola. Find its focus and directrix.

The equation may be written in the form $y^2 = 4(x-2)$.

Hence the equation represents the image of the curve $y^2 = 4x$ under a translation which maps the point $(0,0)$ to the point $(2,0)$. The curve $y^2 = 4x$ is a parabola with focus $(1,0)$ and directrix $x = -1$.

$\therefore$ the curve $y^2 = 4x-8$ is a parabola with focus $(3,0)$ and directrix $x = 1$.

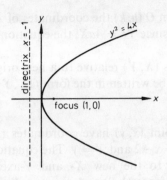

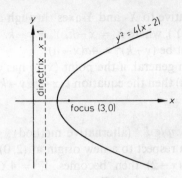

The result obtained for the parabola can be generalised. If the equation $f(x, y) = 0$ represents a curve in the x, y plane, then the equation $f(x-h, y-k) = 0$ represents the image of that curve under a translation with column vector $\begin{pmatrix} h \\ k \end{pmatrix}$.

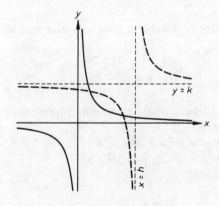

For instance, the curve $x^2 + y^2 = a^2$ is a circle, centre $(0, 0)$, radius a. The curve $(x-h)^2 + (y-k)^2 = a^2$ is a circle, centre (h, k), radius a.

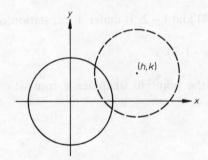

Similarly, the equation $xy = c^2$ represents a curve called a rectangular hyperbola with the lines $x = 0$, $y = 0$ as asymptotes. The curve $(x-h)(y-k) = c^2$ is a rectangular hyperbola with asymptotes $x = h$, $y = k$.

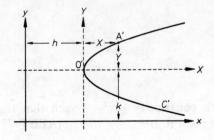

We now look briefly at a different approach to curves with equations of the form $f(x-h, y-k) = 0$. Consider again a typical point $A'(x, y)$ on the curve C' as defined earlier.

Relative to X- and Y-axes through a new origin $O'(h, k)$ the coordinates of A' are (X, Y), where $X = x - h$, $Y = y - k$. As before, since $Y^2 = 4aX$, the equation of C' must be $(y - k)^2 = 4a(x - h)$.

In general, if the point (x, y) has coordinates (X, Y) relative to a new origin at (h, k) then the equation $f(x - h, y - k) = 0$ may be written in the form $f(X, Y) = 0$.

Example 1 (alternative method)   Let the point (x, y) have coordinates (X, Y) with respect to a new origin at $(2, 0)$, then $X = x - 2$ and $Y = y$. The equation $y^2 = 4(x - 2)$ then becomes $Y^2 = 4X$. Relative to the new X- and Y-axes the equation $Y^2 = 4X$ represents a parabola with focus $(1, 0)$ and directrix $X = -1$. Hence, relative to the original x- and y-axes, the equation $y^2 = 4x - 8$ represents a parabola with focus $(3, 0)$ and directrix $x = 1$.

Exercise 15.5

1.   Find the images of the points $(1, 3)$, $(0, 4)$ and $(-2, 5)$ under a translation in which the point $(0, 0)$ is mapped to the point
(a) $(1, 0)$,   (b) $(0, -2)$,   (c) $(-1, 2)$.

2.   Find the coordinates of the image of the point $(0, 0)$ under a translation which maps the given curves as follows:
(a) $x^2 + y^2 = 4 \rightarrow (x - 1)^2 + (y - 2)^2 = 4$,
(b) $y^2 = 4x \rightarrow (y + 1)^2 = 4(x - 3)$,
(c) $x^2 + y^2 = 1 \rightarrow x^2 + y^2 - 2y = 0$,
(d) $xy = 4 \rightarrow xy + 3x + 2y + 6 = 4$.

3.   Show that each of the following equations represents a parabola and find its vertex, focus and directrix
(a) $y^2 = 4(x - 3)$,   (b) $(y - 1)^2 = 8x$,   (c) $y^2 = 4x + 20$,
(d) $y^2 + 4y = x$,   (e) $4y = x^2 + 4$,   (f) $y = x^2 - 2x$.

4.   Show that each of the following pairs of parametric equations represents a parabola and find its vertex, focus and directrix.
(a) $x = t^2 + 1$, $y = 2t + 3$,   (b) $x = 3t^2 - 2$, $y = 6t + 5$,
(c) $x = 1 - t^2$, $y = 2t$,   (d) $x = 4t - 3$, $y = 2t^2 - 1$.

5.   Sketch the following pairs of related curves
(a) $y = x^3$, $y = x^3 - 3x^2 + 3x + 1$,
(b) $xy = 1$, $xy = 2x + y - 1$,
(c) $y^2 = -12x$, $y^2 = 12(y - x)$.

Exercise 15.6 (*miscellaneous*)

1.   Find those points P on the curve with equation $y = x^2 - 2$ such that the normal to the curve at P passes through the point $(0, 0)$.   (AEB 1977)

2.   Find the condition that the line $y = mx + c$ should be a tangent to the circle $x^2 + y^2 = a^2$.

3.   A curve is defined by the parametric equations

$$x = \theta - \sin \theta, \quad y = 1 - \cos \theta, \quad 0 < \theta < 2\pi.$$

Show that $dy/dx = \cot \theta/2$, and find the equation of the tangent and of the normal to the curve at the point where $\theta = \pi/2$.   (JMB)

4.   Find the equations of the tangent and the normal to the curve $y^2(y-1) = x^2(x+3)$ at the point $(1, 2)$.

5.   Find the centres and radii of the circles C_1 and C_2 whose equations are $x^2 + y^2 - 2x = 0$ and $x^2 + y^2 - 2y = 0$ respectively. Draw a figure to illustrate the circles. The line $y = mx$ through the origin O meets C_1 and C_2 again at P and Q. Find the coordinates of P and Q. Let A denote the second point of intersection of the two circles. Show that AP and AQ are perpendicular.   (W)

6.   Find the equation of the circle which passes through the points $A(2, 0)$, $B(10, 4)$ and $C(5, 9)$ and show that it touches the y-axis. If the tangents at A and B intersect at D find the coordinates of D, the length BD and the angle ADB correct to the nearest degree.   (SU)

7.   The circle S has the equation $x^2 + y^2 - 6x - 8y = 0$. (i) Find the coordinates of the centre, and the radius, of S. (ii) Prove, by calculation, that the point A, with coordinates $(7, 2)$, lies inside the circle S. (iii) Show that the chord of S which is bisected at A has equation $y - 2x + 12 = 0$. (iv) Find the equations of the two tangents to S which are parallel to the line $y = 2x$.   (C)

8.   Prove that the point $B(1, 0)$ is the mirror-image of the point $A(5, 6)$ in the line $2x + 3y = 15$. Find the equation of (a) the circle on AB as diameter, (b) the circle which passes through A and B and touches the x-axis.   (L)

9.   Find the equation of the tangent to the circle $x^2 + y^2 = a^2$ at the point $T(a \cos \theta, a \sin \theta)$. This tangent meets the line $x + a = 0$ at R. If RT is produced to P so that $RT = TP$, find the coordinates of P in terms of θ and find the coordinates of the points in which the locus of P meets the y-axis.   (L)

10.   A circle passes through the points A, B and C which have coordinates $(0, 3)$, $(\sqrt{3}, 0)$ and $(-\sqrt{3}, 0)$ respectively. Find: (i) the equation of the circle, (ii) the length of the minor arc BC, (iii) the equation of the circle on AB as diameter. A line $y = mx - 3$ of variable gradient m cuts the circle ABC in two points L and M. Find in cartesian form the equation of the locus of the mid-point of LM.   (AEB 1976)

11.   Find the equations of the two circles each of which touches both coordinate axes and passes through the point $(9, 2)$. Find (i) the coordinates of the second

point of intersection of these circles, (ii) the equation of the common chord of the two circles. (C)

12. The point $A(4, 1)$ lies on the line whose equation is $3x - 4y - 8 = 0$. A circle touches this line at A and passes through the point $B(5, 3)$. Find the equation of the circle, and show that it touches the y-axis. Find also the equation of the line parallel to AB on which the circle cuts off a chord equal in length to AB. (C)

13. Sketch for $0 \leqslant t \leqslant 2\pi$ the curve given parametrically by $x = a\cos^3 t$, $y = a\sin^3 t$. Show that $dy/dx = -\tan t$. Find and simplify the equation of the tangent at the point where $t = \alpha$. If this tangent meets the axes at A and B, show that the length of AB is independent of x. (L)

14. A curve is given parametrically by the equations $x = a(2 + t^2)$, $y = 2at$. Find the values of the parameter t at the points P and Q in which this curve is cut by the circle with centre $(3a, 0)$ and radius $5a$. Show that the tangents to the curve at P and Q meet on the circle, and that the normals to the curve at P and Q also meet on the circle. (L)

15. The parametric equations of a curve are $x = \cos 2t$, $y = 4 \sin t$. Sketch the curve for $0 \leqslant t \leqslant \frac{1}{2}\pi$. Show that $dy/dx = -\operatorname{cosec} t$ and find the equation of the tangent to the curve at the point $A(\cos 2T, 4 \sin T)$. The tangent at A crosses the x-axis at the point M and the normal at A crosses the x-axis at the point N. If the area of the triangle AMN is $12 \sin T$, find the value of T between 0 and $\frac{1}{2}\pi$.
(AEB 1976)

16. A curve is defined by the parametric form $x = a(\cos 3\theta - 3 \cos \theta)$, $y = a(\sin 3\theta + 3 \sin \theta)$. Prove that $dy/dx = -\cot \theta$, and hence show that the normal to the curve at the point with parameter θ is given by $x \sin \theta - y \cos \theta + 4a \sin 2\theta = 0$. Prove that the distance between the points where the normal meets the coordinate axes is independent of θ. (O)

17. Find the equation of the tangent to the curve $y = \dfrac{5}{12}x^3 - \dfrac{13}{9}x$ at the point P at which $x = x_0$. Show that the x-coordinate of the point Q where this tangent meets the curve again is $-2x_0$, and find the values of x_0 for which the tangent at P is the normal at Q. (O)

18. Find the equations of the tangent and the normal to the parabola $y^2 = 4ax$ at the point P with parameter p. (i) Show that, if the tangent at P meets the directrix at L, then $PL = a(p^2 + 1)^{3/2}/p$. (ii) Show that, if the tangent at P is parallel to the normal at a point Q, then PQ passes through the focus of the parabola. (SU)

19. Find the equation of the normal to the parabola $y^2 = 4ax$ at the point $(at^2, 2at)$ and the coordinates of the point at which this normal cuts the x-axis. Show that the equation of the circle which touches this parabola at the points $(at^2, 2at)$ and $(at^2, -2at)$ is $(x - 2a - at^2)^2 + y^2 = 4a^2(1 + t^2)$. Find the values of t for which this circle passes through the point $(9a, 0)$. (L)

20. Prove that the chord joining the points $P(ap^2, 2ap)$ and $Q(aq^2, 2aq)$ on the parabola $y^2 = 4ax$ has the equation $(p+q)y = 2x + 2apq$. A variable chord PQ of the parabola is such that the lines OP and OQ are perpendicular, where O is the origin. (i) Prove that the chord PQ cuts the axis of x at a fixed point, and give the x-coordinate of this point. (ii) Find the equation of the locus of the mid-point of PQ. (C)

21. Prove that the tangent at the point $(at^2, 2at)$ on the parabola $y^2 = 4ax$ has the equation $ty = x + at^2$. Find, in their simplest form, the coordinates of T, the point of intersection of the tangents at the points $P(ap^2, 2ap)$ and $Q(aq^2, 2aq)$ on the parabola $y^2 = 4ax$. If PQ is of constant length d, show that T lies on the curve whose equation is

$$(y^2 - 4ax)(y^2 + 4a^2) = a^2 d^2.$$ (C)

22. Show that the equation of the normal to the parabola $y^2 = 4ax$ at the point $P(ap^2, 2ap)$ is $y + px = 2ap + ap^3$. Find the coordinates of R, the point of intersection of the normal at P and the normal at $Q(aq^2, 2aq)$. Given that the chord PQ passes through $S(a, 0)$, show that $pq = -1$ and find the equation of the locus of R. (AEB 1978)

23. Show that the equation of the normal to the parabola $y^2 = 4ax$ at the point $P(ap^2, 2ap)$ is $px + y = 2ap + ap^3$. The tangent at P meets the x-axis at A and the y-axis at B. The normal at P meets the x-axis at C and S is the point $(a, 0)$. Show that the areas of the triangles APS and SPC are equal. Show also that the locus of the mid-point of PS is a parabola through the mid-point of OS. If BS and OP meet at Q, show that the equation of the locus of Q is $2x^2 + y^2 = 2ax$. (AEB 1977)

24. Prove that the mid-points of chords of the parabola $y^2 = 4ax$ that are parallel to the line $y = mx$ lie on the line $y = 2a/m$. Hence, or otherwise, find the equation of the tangent to the parabola that is parallel to the line $y = mx$. (O)

25. Find the equation of the tangent to the parabola $y^2 = 4ax$ at the point $P(ap^2, 2ap)$. Show that the equation of the normal at P is $y = p(2a - x) + ap^3$. If the tangents at P and $Q(aq^2, 2aq)$ meet at T show that T is the point $(apq, ap + aq)$. The point N is the intersection of the normals at P and Q. Given that T lies on the line $x + 2a = 0$ show that N lies on the parabola with equation $y^2 = 4a(x - 4a)$. (L)

26. Prove that the line $y = mx + 15/4m$ is a tangent to the parabola $y^2 = 15x$ for all non-zero values of m. Using this result or otherwise find the equations of the common tangents to this parabola and the circle $x^2 + y^2 = 16$. (L)

27. Find the equation of the normal at the point $P(at^2, 2at)$ to the parabola $y^2 = 4ax$. The focus of the given parabola is the point S, $(a, 0)$. If PN is the normal at the point P and SN is parallel to the tangent at P, find the coordinates of the point N. Deduce that the locus of N for variable P is a parabola and find the coordinates of its vertex. (O & C)

28. Prove that the normal to the parabola $y^2 = 4ax$ at the point $(at^2, 2at)$ has equation $y + tx = 2at + at^3$. The normals at the points $P(ap^2, 2ap)$ and $Q(aq^2, 2aq)$ intersect at the point R. Find the coordinates of R in terms of $(p+q)$ and pq. If O is the vertex of the parabola and P and Q are variable points such that $P\hat{O}Q$ is a right angle, find the locus of R; verify that it is a parabola, and find the coordinates of its vertex.   (O & C)

29. A fixed point $P(ap^2, 2ap)$ is taken on the parabola $y^2 = 4ax$. Two points Q and R are chosen on the parabola so that the lines PQ and PR are perpendicular. Prove that the line QR passes through a fixed point F, independent of Q and R, and that PF is normal to the parabola at P.   (O)

30. A circle with centre at the point $P(h, k)$ touches the y-axis, and passes through the point $S(2, 0)$. Show that P lies on the curve $y^2 = 4x - 4$, and sketch this curve. Show that the straight line joining $P(h, k)$ to the point $Q(2 + h, 0)$ cuts the curve $y^2 = 4x - 4$ at right angles at P.   (L)

31. Find the equation of the normal to the parabola $y^2 = 4x$ at the point $P(p^2, 2p)$. If the normals at P and $Q(q^2, 2q)$ meet at $R(\alpha, \beta)$ show that $\alpha = 2 + p^2 + pq + q^2$, $\beta = -pq(p+q)$. The point of intersection of PQ with the x-axis divides PQ internally in the ratio $1 : \lambda$. Prove that $q = -\lambda p$. Given that $\lambda = 2$, find the Cartesian equation of the locus of R as p varies. Determine the coordinates of the point on this locus which is nearest the origin.   (JMB)

32. Find the equations of the tangents to the curve $27y^2 = 4x^3$ at the points $P(3p^2, 2p^3)$ and $Q(3q^2, 2q^3)$. Show that these tangents intersect at the point $R(\alpha, \beta)$ where $\alpha = p^2 + pq + q^2$, $\beta = pq(p+q)$. The points P and Q move along the curve in such a way that the tangents at P and Q are always perpendicular. Prove that R moves on the parabola $y^2 = x - 1$. Verify that this parabola touches the curve $27y^2 = 4x^3$ at the points $(3/2, \pm 1/\sqrt{2})$.   (JMB)

33. The straight line through the point $A(-a, 0)$ at an angle θ to the positive direction of the x-axis meets the circle $x^2 + y^2 = a^2$ at P, distinct from A. The circle on AP as diameter is denoted by C. (i) By finding the equation of C, or otherwise, show that if C touches the y-axis, then $\cos 2\theta = 2 - \sqrt{5}$. (ii) C meets the x-axis at M, distinct from A, and the tangents to C at A and M meet at Q. Find the coordinates of Q in terms of θ and show that, as θ varies, Q always lies on the curve $y^2 x + (x + a)^3 = 0$.   (JMB)

16 Inequalities

16.1 Basic inequalities

The most important rules for manipulating inequalities are as follows:
(1) Any number may be added to or subtracted from both sides of an inequality,
e.g.

$$x < y \Rightarrow x + 3 < y + 3.$$

(2) Both sides of an inequality may be multiplied or divided by the same *positive* number, e.g.

$$x < y \Rightarrow 3x < 3y.$$

(3) If both sides of an inequality are multiplied or divided by the same *negative* number, the inequality is reversed, e.g.

$$-2x < 6y \Rightarrow x > -3y.$$

[For further examples of the use of these rules see §1.4.]

In this chapter we will be considering two main types of inequality. This section deals briefly with basic inequalities which hold for all values of the variables involved. Later sections are concerned with finding the solution sets of inequalities which hold for only certain values of the variables. The distinction between these two types of inequality broadly corresponds to that made in earlier work between identities and equations.

Most basic inequalities are established using the fact that the square of a real number is never negative.

Example 1 Prove that $a^2 + b^2 \geqslant 2ab$ for all real values of a and b.

As any square is positive or zero, $\qquad (a - b)^2 \geqslant 0$
$$\therefore \qquad a^2 - 2ab + b^2 \geqslant 0$$
Hence $\qquad\qquad\qquad a^2 + b^2 \geqslant 2ab.$

The result of Example 1 can be used to derive further inequalities.

305

Example 2 Prove that $a^2+b^2+c^2 \geqslant ab+bc+ca$ for all real values of a, b and c.

$$a^2+b^2 \geqslant 2ab, \quad b^2+c^2 \geqslant 2bc, \quad c^2+a^2 \geqslant 2ca.$$

Adding $2(a^2+b^2+c^2) \geqslant 2(ab+bc+ca).$

Hence $a^2+b^2+c^2 \geqslant ab+bc+ca.$

Example 3 Prove that $\dfrac{1}{a}+\dfrac{1}{b} \geqslant \dfrac{4}{a+b}$ for all positive values of a and b.

$$\frac{1}{a}+\frac{1}{b}-\frac{4}{a+b} = \frac{b(a+b)+a(a+b)-4ab}{ab(a+b)}$$

$$= \frac{a^2-2ab+b^2}{ab(a+b)} = \frac{(a-b)^2}{ab(a+b)}$$

$\therefore$ provided that a and b are positive $\dfrac{1}{a}+\dfrac{1}{b}-\dfrac{4}{a+b} \geqslant 0$

i.e. $\dfrac{1}{a}+\dfrac{1}{b} \geqslant \dfrac{4}{a+b}.$

Alternative method

$$a^2+b^2 \geqslant 2ab \Rightarrow (a+b)^2 \geqslant 4ab.$$

Dividing both sides by $ab(a+b)$, assumed positive

$$\frac{a+b}{ab} \geqslant \frac{4}{a+b}$$

$\therefore$ $\dfrac{1}{a}+\dfrac{1}{b} \geqslant \dfrac{4}{a+b}.$

Exercise 16.1

1.   State whether each of the following statements is true or false. If you decide that a statement is false, show, by a numerical example, that this is so.

(a) $x^2 < 4 \Rightarrow x < 2,$ (b) $x^2 > 4 \Rightarrow x > 2,$

(c) $x < 4 \Rightarrow \dfrac{1}{x} > \dfrac{1}{4},$ (d) $x > 4 \Rightarrow \dfrac{1}{x} < \dfrac{1}{4}.$

2.   Given that a and b are positive, state the range of values of x for which the following statements are true.

(a) $ax \leqslant bx \Rightarrow a \leqslant b,$ (b) $x-a < x-b \Rightarrow a > b,$

(c) $\dfrac{x}{a} \geqslant \dfrac{x}{b} \Rightarrow a \geqslant b,$ (d) $a > b \Rightarrow \dfrac{1}{x+a} < \dfrac{1}{x+b}.$

3.   Prove that for any real numbers p and q

(a) $p^2+q^2 \geqslant 2pq,$ (b) $p^2+4q^2 \geqslant 4pq,$

(c) $(p+q)^2 \geqslant 4pq,$ (d) $(p+q)^2 \leqslant 2(p^2+q^2).$

4. Prove that if a and b are positive, then

(a) $\dfrac{a}{b} + \dfrac{b}{a} \geqslant 2,$ (b) $a^3 + b^3 \geqslant ab(a+b).$

5. Prove that for any real numbers p, q, r, s
(a) $p^4 + q^4 \geqslant 2p^2 q^2,$ (b) $p^4 + q^4 + r^4 + s^4 \geqslant 4pqrs.$

6. Prove that for any real numbers x, y, z
$3(xy + yz + zx) \leqslant (x+y+z)^2 \leqslant 3(x^2 + y^2 + z^2).$

16.2 Graphical approach

We now consider the graphical approach to finding the set of values of x which satisfy an inequality of the form $f(x) < g(x)$. This method is particularly useful when the graphs of the functions $f(x)$ and $g(x)$ are fairly easy to sketch.

Example 1   Find the values of x for which $x^2 - 4x < 1$.

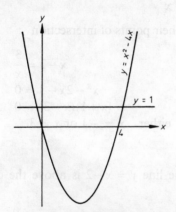

Consider the graphs of $y = x^2 - 4x$ and $y = 1$.
At their points of intersection

$$x^2 - 4x = 1$$
$$x^2 - 4x - 1 = 0$$
$$\therefore \quad x = \frac{4 \pm \sqrt{(4^2 - 4.1\{-1\})}}{2}$$
$$= \frac{4 \pm \sqrt{20}}{2} = 2 \pm \sqrt{5}.$$

The inequality $x^2 - 4x < 1$ is satisfied when the curve $y = x^2 - 4x$ is below the line $y = 1$

i.e.   when $2 - \sqrt{5} < x < 2 + \sqrt{5}.$

Example 2   Find the values of x for which $0 \leqslant \dfrac{x-1}{x+2} \leqslant 2.$

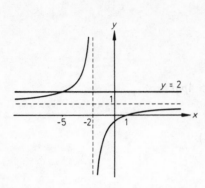

Consider the curve $y = \dfrac{x-1}{x+2}$.

It cuts the axes at the points $(1,0)$ and $(0, -\frac{1}{2})$. The lines $x = -2$ and $y = 1$ are asymptotes to the curve. [See §20.4.]

$$\frac{x-1}{x+2} = 2 \Rightarrow x - 1 = 2x + 4$$
$$\Rightarrow x = -5$$

$\therefore$ the curve cuts the line $y = 2$ when $x = -5$.

Hence, from the sketch, $0 \leqslant \dfrac{x-1}{x+2} \leqslant 2$ when $x \leqslant -5$ and when $x \geqslant 1$.

Example 3   Find the values of x for which $x - 2 > \dfrac{3}{x}$.

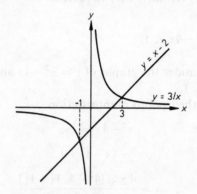

Consider the graphs $y = x - 2$ and $y = \dfrac{3}{x}$.

At their points of intersection

$$x - 2 = \frac{3}{x}$$

i.e.
$$x^2 - 2x - 3 = 0$$
$$(x+1)(x-3) = 0$$

$\therefore$ either $x = -1$ or $x = 3$.

The inequality $x - 2 > \dfrac{3}{x}$ is satisfied when the line $y = x - 2$ is above the curve $y = \dfrac{3}{x}$, i.e. when

$-1 < x < 0$ and when $x > 3$.

Exercise 16.2

With the aid of sketch graphs find the values of x which satisfy the following inequalities.

1. $x^2 - x - 6 < 0$.

2. $2x^2 + 7x + 3 \geqslant 0$.

3. $6x - x^2 \geqslant 5$.

4. $x^2 - 2x > 5$.

5. $4x < 3 - x^2$.

6. $x^3 - 3x^2 \leqslant 10x$.

7. $\dfrac{1}{x-3} > 1$.

8. $\dfrac{x}{x+1} < 2$.

9. $0 < \dfrac{2x-4}{x-1} < 1$.

10. $2 < \dfrac{x-7}{x-2} < 3$.

11. $3 - x > \dfrac{2}{x}$.

12. $2x + 5 < \dfrac{3}{x}$.

13. $\dfrac{3}{x+2} < x$.

14. $x - 2 > \dfrac{2}{x-1}$.

15. $\dfrac{12}{x-3} < x + 1$.

16. $\dfrac{1}{x-1} < \dfrac{1}{x+1}$.

17. $\dfrac{x+1}{2x-3} < \dfrac{1}{x-3}$.

18. $\dfrac{1}{x^2} < \dfrac{1}{x+2}$.

19. $\pi \sin x > 2x$.

20. $2\pi \cos x < 3x$.

16.3 Analytical methods

If $(x - a)$ is a factor of $f(x)$ then $f(x)$ may change sign as x passes through the value a. This statement forms the basis of the analytical approach to inequalities.

Example 1   Find the values of x for which $x(2x - 5) > 3$.

$$x(2x - 5) > 3 \Leftrightarrow \quad 2x^2 - 5x - 3 > 0$$
$$\Leftrightarrow (2x + 1)(x - 3) > 0.$$

[We now construct a table of signs for the function $(2x + 1)(x - 3)$, noting that sign changes may occur at $x = -\frac{1}{2}$ and $x = 3$.]

	$x < -\frac{1}{2}$	$-\frac{1}{2} < x < 3$	$x > 3$
$2x + 1$	$-$	$+$	$+$
$x - 3$	$-$	$-$	$+$
$(2x + 1)(x + 3)$	$+$	$-$	$+$

Hence $x(2x - 5) > 3$ when $x < -\frac{1}{2}$ or $x > 3$.

Example 2   Find the values of x for which $x(x^2-2) < x^2$.

$$x(x^2-2) < x^2 \Leftrightarrow \quad x^3-x^2-2x < 0$$
$$\Leftrightarrow x(x+1)(x-2) < 0.$$

The function $f(x) = x(x+1)(x-2)$ changes sign at $x = -1$, $x = 0$ and $x = 2$.

	$x < -1$	$-1 < x < 0$	$0 < x < 2$	$x > 2$
$x+1$	$-$	$+$	$+$	$+$
x	$-$	$-$	$+$	$+$
$x-2$	$-$	$-$	$-$	$+$
$f(x)$	$-$	$+$	$-$	$+$

Hence the inequality holds for $x < -1$ and $0 < x < 2$.

Great care must be taken when dealing with inequalities involving fractions. In general, it is inadvisable to 'multiply through' by a variable denominator which may be positive or negative. The most reliable method is to collect all the terms on one side of the inequality.

Example 3   Find the values of x for which $\dfrac{x^2-12}{x} > -1$.

$$\frac{x^2-12}{x} > -1 \Leftrightarrow \frac{x^2-12}{x} + 1 > 0$$

$$\Leftrightarrow \frac{x^2+x-12}{x} > 0$$

$$\Leftrightarrow \frac{(x+4)(x-3)}{x} > 0.$$

The function $f(x) = (x+4)(x-3)/x$ changes sign as x passes through the values -4, 0 and 3.

	$x < -4$	$-4 < x < 0$	$0 < x < 3$	$x > 3$
$x+4$	$-$	$+$	$+$	$+$
x	$-$	$-$	$+$	$+$
$x-3$	$-$	$-$	$-$	$+$
$f(x)$	$-$	$+$	$-$	$+$

Hence the inequality holds for $-4 < x < 0$ and $x > 3$.

Example 4   For what values of x is $\dfrac{x}{x+8} \leqslant \dfrac{1}{x-1}$?

$$\frac{x}{x+8} \leqslant \frac{1}{x-1} \Leftrightarrow \frac{x}{x+8} - \frac{1}{x-1} \leqslant 0$$

$$\Leftrightarrow \frac{x(x-1)-(x+8)}{(x+8)(x-1)} \leqslant 0$$

$$\Leftrightarrow \frac{x^2-2x-8}{(x+8)(x-1)} \leqslant 0$$

$$\Leftrightarrow \frac{(x+2)(x-4)}{(x+8)(x-1)} \leqslant 0.$$

The function $f(x) = \dfrac{(x+2)(x-4)}{(x+8)(x-1)}$ passes through the value zero when $x = -2$ and when $x = 4$. The function is undefined at $x = -8$ and $x = 1$ and has different signs on either side of these values.

	$x < -8$	$-8 < x < -2$	$-2 < x < 1$	$1 < x < 4$	$x > 4$
$x+8$	$-$	$+$	$+$	$+$	$+$
$x+2$	$-$	$-$	$+$	$+$	$+$
$x-1$	$-$	$-$	$-$	$+$	$+$
$x-4$	$-$	$-$	$-$	$-$	$+$
$f(x)$	$+$	$-$	$+$	$-$	$+$

Hence $\dfrac{x}{x+8} \leqslant \dfrac{1}{x-1}$ when $-8 < x \leqslant -2$ and $1 < x \leqslant 4$.

Exercise 16.3

Find the values of x which satisfy the following inequalities.

1. $x^2 + 2x < 15$.

2. $3x^2 + 2 > 7x$.

3. $x^2(x-5) > 6x$.

4. $x(x^2+4) < 5x^2$.

5. $\dfrac{x^2+12}{x} > 7$.

6. $\dfrac{x^2+6}{x} > 5$.

7. $\dfrac{(x-1)(x+3)}{(x-2)} < 0$.

8. $\dfrac{(2x-3)}{(x+2)(x-5)} > 0$.

9. $\dfrac{6}{x-1} > 1$.

10. $\dfrac{2x-4}{x-1} < 1$.

11. $\dfrac{8}{x+2} > x.$

12. $\dfrac{6}{x-4} < x+1.$

13. $\dfrac{5-x}{x^2-3x+2} < 1.$

14. $\dfrac{x+6}{x(x+1)} < 6.$

15. $\dfrac{1}{x+1} < \dfrac{1}{x+4}.$

16. $\dfrac{1}{x+2} > \dfrac{1}{2x-3}.$

17. $\dfrac{x}{x-2} > \dfrac{1}{x}.$

18. $\dfrac{x+1}{2x-3} < \dfrac{1}{x-3}.$

16.4 Modulus inequalities

The modulus notation was introduced in §1.4. From the definition it follows that if $|f(x)| < a$, where a is a positive constant, then $-a < f(x) < a$.

Example 1   Find the values of x for which $|2x+1| < 3$.

$$|2x+1| < 3 \Leftrightarrow -3 < 2x+1 < 3$$
$$\Leftrightarrow -4 < 2x < 2$$
$$\Leftrightarrow -2 < x < 1.$$

Hence the inequality is satisfied when $-2 < x < 1$.

Some inequalities can be simplified by squaring both sides. However, it is important to remember that this method is valid only when both sides of the inequality are positive or zero for all values of x.

Example 2   Find the values of x for which $2|x-1| < |x+3|$.

Since both sides of the inequality are positive or zero for all values of x

$$2|x-1| < |x+3| \Leftrightarrow 4(x-1)^2 < (x+3)^2$$
$$\Leftrightarrow 4x^2 - 8x + 4 < x^2 + 6x + 9$$
$$\Leftrightarrow 3x^2 - 14x - 5 < 0$$
$$\Leftrightarrow (3x+1)(x-5) < 0.$$

Hence the inequality holds if $-\frac{1}{3} < x < 5$.

In harder examples it may be possible to adapt the methods of Examples 1 and 2 or to use sketch graphs. [For work on graphs with equations of the form $y = |f(x)|$ see §§14.2, 14.3.]

Example 3   Find the values of x for which $|2x-3| > x$.

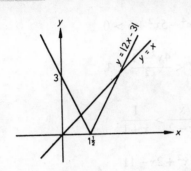

The graphs of $y = |2x-3|$ and $y = x$ have two points of intersection, where $2x-3 = x$, i.e. $x = 3$ and where $-(2x-3) = x$, i.e. $x = 1$. Hence, from the sketch, $|2x-3| > x$ when $x < 1$ and when $x > 3$.

Alternative method

Since $|2x-3|$ is never negative the inequality must hold when $x < 0$.

When $x \geqslant 0$, $|2x-3| > x \Leftrightarrow$ $\quad (2x-3)^2 > x^2$

$\Leftrightarrow 4x^2 - 12x + 9 > x^2$

$\Leftrightarrow 3x^2 - 12x + 9 > 0$

$\Leftrightarrow \quad x^2 - 4x + 3 > 0$

$\Leftrightarrow (x-1)(x-3) > 0$

$\Leftrightarrow \quad x < 1 \text{ or } x > 3.$

Thus, considering all values of x, the inequality holds for $x < 1$ and $x > 3$.

Exercise 16.4

Find the values of x which satisfy the following inequalities.

1. $|x-2| > 1$.

2. $|x+3| \leqslant 5$.

3. $|3x+5| < 4$.

4. $|2x-1| \geqslant 11$.

5. $|x| \leqslant |x-1|$.

6. $2|x+2| > |x+3|$.

7. $3|x-2| \geqslant |x+6|$.

8. $5|2x-3| < 4|x-5|$.

9. $2|x-2| > x$.

10. $|3x+4| \leqslant x+2$.

11. $|2x+1| < 3x+2$.

12. $|x+1| > x-3$.

13. $|x^2-3x-2| < 2$.

14. $|x(x-5)| > 6$.

15. $\left|\dfrac{x}{x+4}\right| < 2$.

16. $\left|\dfrac{x^2-4}{x}\right| \leqslant 3$.

Exercise 16.5 *(miscellaneous)*

In questions 1 to 18 find the set of values of x which satisfy the given inequalities.

1. $x(x+6) \geqslant 7$.

2. $x(x-2) < 1$.

3. $(x^2-1)(2x+1) < 0.$

4. $x(x^2+10) < 7x^2.$

5. $x^4-3x^2-4 > 0.$

6. $x^4-5x^2+6 > 0.$

7. $0 < \dfrac{x}{2x-3} < 1.$

8. $2 < \dfrac{4x^2-1}{x^2} < 3.$

9. $\dfrac{5}{x+1} < x-3.$

10. $\dfrac{x}{x-2} > \dfrac{1}{x+1}.$

11. $\dfrac{4x-1}{x^2-2x-3} < 3.$

12. $\dfrac{5x^2+2x-11}{x^2+1} > 4.$

13. $|3-2x| \leqslant |x+4|.$

14. $|x^2+1| < |x^2-9|.$

15. $|3x-2| < x.$

16. $|5x-6| > x^2.$

17. $\left|\dfrac{x+1}{x-1}\right| < 1.$

18. $\left|\dfrac{x}{x-2}\right| < 2.$

19. Find the values of x between $-\pi/2$ and $+5\pi/2$ for which
(a) $\cos x > \tfrac{1}{2},$ (b) $|\tan x| \leqslant 1,$ (c) $4\sin^2 x < 1.$

20. By considering $(a^2+b^2)^2$ or otherwise, prove that $a^4+b^4 \geqslant a^3b+ab^3$ for all real values of a and b.

21. Prove that the geometric mean of two positive real numbers p and q is less than or equal to their arithmetic mean.

22. Find the ranges of values of x between 0 and 2π for which $\sin 2x > \cos x$.   (O)

23. For each of the following expressions, state, with reasons, for what set of values of x it is greater than -1:

(i) $\dfrac{1}{x},$ (ii) $-(x-1)^2,$ (iii) $\dfrac{2x-1}{x-2}.$ (O&C)

24. Determine the range of values of x for which

(i) $\dfrac{6}{x+1} < x,$ (ii) $\dfrac{6}{|x|+1} < |x|.$ (O&C)

17 Mathematical reasoning

17.1 Deductive and inductive processes

Pure mathematics is the study of pattern and structure in systems involving sets of objects such as numbers or points in space. The theory of the subject is developed by logical argument based on precise definitions of the terms used. In general, the type of reasoning used in scientific work is different from that used in mathematics. A scientist observes some natural phenomenon, then uses the data he has collected to formulate laws governing the behaviour of the objects concerned. If results obtained from later experiments also satisfy these laws, they may be accepted by other scientists and used as the basis of further work. This process, by which particular items of data lead to a general theory, is called *inductive* reasoning. Scientific laws obtained in this way cannot be regarded as absolute truths. New evidence may be found which shows that the theory is untenable or that it needs modification.

A mathematician may use inductive processes to produce *conjectures* which he then attempts to prove. One such conjecture is that there are no positive integers a, b and c such that $a^n + b^n = c^n$, where n is any positive integer greater than 2. It is believed that the mathematician Fermat[†] may have proved this, but he left no record of his method of proof. The conjecture has since been proved for certain values of n, but the general statement has yet to be proved or disproved. Another famous mathematical conjecture, known as the "four colour problem", has only recently been proved. This is the statement that any geographical map (or division of a plane into regions) can be coloured using only four different colours, so that no two countries (or regions) with a common boundary have the same colour.

To *prove* a mathematical statement, we must establish its truth by logical reasoning. A mathematical *proof* is a chain of reasoning in which a statement or theorem is shown to follow from previously proved statements or from initial assumptions called premises, axioms or postulates. This process, in which one

---

[†]*Fermat, Pierre de* (1601–1665) French mathematician. He made important contributions to probability theory and the theory of numbers. He wrote his famous conjecture in the margin of his copy of the *Arithmetica* written by the Greek mathematician Diophantus in about A.D. 275.

statement follows logically from another, is called *deductive* reasoning or *deduction*. We now give a simple example to illustrate the use of the process.

Example 1 What can be deduced from the following three statements?

(a) John always enjoys a boiled egg for breakfast.
(b) There was no bacon left for breakfast today.
(c) If there is no bacon, John boils an egg for breakfast.

If we form these statements into a chain, taking (b) then (c) then (a), we may deduce that John enjoyed his breakfast today.

The next example shows that an apparently logical argument may be invalid.

Example 2 Decide whether the conclusion drawn from the three given statements is valid.

(a) There is a robin in Mrs. Brown's garden.
(b) No other bird in Mrs. Brown's garden has a red breast.
(c) Mrs. Brown can see a bird with a red breast.
    Conclusion: Mrs. Brown can see a robin.

The argument is invalid for various reasons. Robins are not the only birds with red breasts. Mrs. Brown may not be watching the birds in her own garden. She may, for instance, be looking at a bullfinch in a neighbour's garden.

We now demonstrate an invalid mathematical argument.

Consider the equation:

$$x + \frac{1}{x} = 1 \tag{1}$$

Multiply (1) by x, $\qquad\qquad\qquad x^2 + 1 = x \tag{2}$

Multiply (2) by x, $\qquad\qquad\qquad x^3 + x = x^2 \tag{3}$

Rearranging (3), $\qquad\qquad\qquad x^3 = x^2 - x$

Rearranging (2), $\qquad\qquad\qquad x^2 - x = -1$

$\therefore \qquad\qquad\qquad\qquad\qquad x^3 = -1 \tag{4}$

Hence $\qquad\qquad\qquad\qquad\qquad x = -1$

Clearly $x = -1$ does not satisfy the original equation. The flaw in the argument becomes apparent when we consider the steps in more detail.

Rearranging (2), $\qquad\qquad\qquad x^2 - x + 1 = 0$

Rearranging (3), $\qquad\qquad\qquad x(x^2 - x + 1) = 0$

Adding, $\qquad\qquad\qquad\qquad (x + 1)(x^2 - x + 1) = 0$

i.e. $\qquad\qquad\qquad\qquad\qquad x^3 + 1 = 0$

We can now see that combining equations (2) and (3) to produce equation (4) results in the introduction of the factor $(x + 1)$. It is this extra factor which leads to the invalid solution $x = -1$.

[It can be shown that the equation $x + \dfrac{1}{x} = 1$ has no real roots.]

The way in which deductive reasoning is used in various types of mathematical proof is discussed later in the chapter. However, although deduction forms the basis of mathematical reasoning, in such fields as problem solving and original research less reliable processes such as intuition or "trial and error" may be involved.

In applied mathematics both inductive and deductive processes are used. An applied mathematician states in mathematical form laws obtained from experimental data. He may be interested in such things as the performance of an aircraft, the growth of a population of bacteria or the current in an electrical circuit. Using the laws governing the system under consideration, he sets up a mathematical model, often in the form of a set of equations. Predictions about the behaviour of the system can now be made using this model. In general, setting up a mathematical model is an inductive process, but using the model to make predictions involves mainly deductive reasoning.

Exercise 17.1

1. Decide what conclusion can be deduced from the following sets of statements.
(a) Most people disapprove of immorality.
   Stealing is immoral.
   The Knave of Hearts stole some tarts.
(b) N is an even number greater than 2.
   A prime number has only itself and 1 as factors.
   Any even number is divisible by 2.
(c) Boycott was the vice-captain of the England cricket team.
   It is impossible to play cricket with a broken arm.
   If the captain cannot play, the vice-captain takes over.
   The England cricket captain broke his arm.

2. Decide whether the conclusions drawn from the following sets of statements are valid. Give reasons for your answer in each case.
(a) Swallow-tail butterflies feed on Milk Parsley.
   Milk Parsley grows in the Norfolk fens.
Conclusion: There are swallow-tail butterflies in Norfolk.
(b) Mathematicians are highly intelligent.
   People who are not absent-minded never wear odd socks.
   Highly intelligent people are thought to be absent-minded.
Conclusion: Mathematicians are thought to wear odd socks.
(c) Opposite angles of a parallelogram are equal.
   A rhombus is a parallelogram whose diagonals cut at right angles.
   $ABCD$ has two pairs of equal angles.
   The diagonals of $ABCD$ cut at right angles.
Conclusion: $ABCD$ is a rhombus.

3.   Find the flaw in the following argument:

Let $x = y$
then $x^2 = xy$
and $x^2 - y^2 = xy - y^2$
Factorising, $(x + y)(x - y) = y(x - y)$
$\therefore$ $x + y = y$
Since $x = y$, $2x = x$
Hence $2 = 1$

4.   Read the short story given below, then consider the statements which follow it. In each case decide whether the statement is (a) true, (b) false or (c) could be either true or false.

A pedestrian had just stepped off the pavement when a vehicle, travelling at high speed, came round the corner. The car driver quickly applied his brakes and the man on the zebra crossing narrowly escaped serious injury. The police were called to the scene of the incident and later the guilty party was prosecuted for dangerous driving.

(1)   At the beginning of the story a man stepped off the pavement.
(2)   The car was travelling at high speed.
(3)   The man on the zebra crossing was not injured.
(4)   After the incident the police were called to the scene.
(5)   A driver was found guilty of dangerous driving.
(6)   A man escaped serious injury because the car driver braked quickly.
(7)   A vehicle came round the corner just after a pedestrian had stepped off the pavement.
(8)   A man was crossing the road at the time of the incident.
(9)   The car stopped on or near the zebra crossing.
(10) The car stopped.
(11) The car driver was prosecuted for dangerous driving.
(12) The incident involved at least one driver.
(13) The zebra crossing was near a bend in the road.
(14) The events described in the story could not have taken place on a dual carriageway.
(15) None of the people referred to in the story could have been riding a bicycle.
(16) It is possible that the incident involved two vehicles.
(17) The story states that a vehicle being driven at high speed knocked down a man on a zebra crossing, injuring him only slightly.
(18) Three people are mentioned in the story, apart from the police.

17.2   Implication and equivalence

It is sometimes convenient to use letters and symbols to represent statements and relations between them.

For two statements denoted by p and q,

$p \Rightarrow q$ means   "p implies q"   or   "if p, then q",
$p \Leftarrow q$ means   "p is implied by q"   or   "if q, then p",
$p \Leftrightarrow q$ means   "p implies q and q implies p"   i.e.   "the statements p and q are equivalent".

Example 1 Use the symbols ⇒ and ⇔ to connect the following statements:

a: $\triangle ABC$ is isosceles   b: In $\triangle ABC$, $\angle B = \angle C$
c: $\triangle ABC$ is equilateral   d: In $\triangle ABC$, $AB = AC$

We see that $b \Rightarrow a, b \Rightarrow d; c \Rightarrow a, c \Rightarrow b, c \Rightarrow d; d \Rightarrow a, d \Rightarrow b$.
Since $b \Rightarrow d$ and $d \Rightarrow b$, we have $b \Leftrightarrow d$
i.e. the statements b and d are equivalent.

The symbols $\not\Rightarrow$ "does not imply" and $\not\Leftrightarrow$ "is not equivalent to" may also be used.

Example 2 Use the symbols $\not\Rightarrow$ and $\not\Leftrightarrow$ to connect statements a, b, c and d.

By considering an isosceles triangle ABC in which $AB = BC$, we see that $a \not\Rightarrow b$ and $a \not\Rightarrow d$. We also find that $a \not\Rightarrow c, b \not\Rightarrow c$ and $d \not\Rightarrow c$. Hence $a \not\Leftrightarrow b$, $a \not\Leftrightarrow c, a \not\Leftrightarrow d, b \not\Leftrightarrow c, c \not\Leftrightarrow d$.

The *negation* of a statement p is denoted by $\sim p$ (or sometimes p') and read "not p". The negations of a, b, c and d in *Example 1* are as follows:

$\sim a$: $\triangle ABC$ is not isosceles $\sim b$: In $\triangle ABC$, $\angle B, \neq \angle C$
$\sim c$: $\triangle ABC$ is not equilateral $\sim d$: In $\triangle ABC$, $AB \neq AC$

Here are some of the connections between these new statements:
$$\sim a \Rightarrow \sim c, \quad \sim b \Leftrightarrow \sim d, \quad \sim d \Rightarrow \sim c, \quad \sim d \not\Rightarrow \sim a.$$

These examples illustrate some basic properties of negation and implication.
(1) If $p \Rightarrow q$, then $\sim q \Rightarrow \sim p$.
(2) If $p \Leftrightarrow q$, then $\sim p \Leftrightarrow \sim q$.
It is also important to notice that writing $p \not\Rightarrow q$ is *not* equivalent to writing $p \Rightarrow \sim q$. For instance in *Example 2*, the statement $a \not\Rightarrow d$ means: "if $\triangle ABC$ is isosceles, then it does not necessarily follow that $AB = AC$". However, writing $a \Rightarrow \sim d$ would mean: "if $\triangle ABC$ is isosceles, then $AB \neq AC$", which is clearly false.

Other phrases which are used in mathematical statements, such as "if and only if" or "necessary and sufficient condition", can be replaced by implication symbols. The table below shows some sets of equivalent statements.

$p \Rightarrow q$	p only if q	q is a necessary condition that p
$p \Leftarrow q$	p if q	q is a sufficient condition that p
$p \Leftrightarrow q$	p if and only if q	q is a necessary and sufficient condition that p

Consider now the following statements concerning a positive integer n.

a: n is the square of an even number
b: n is a multiple of 4
c: n is an even number

We see that $a \Rightarrow b \Rightarrow c$ and that, using the phrases in the given table:

the statement b is true if a is true, but b is true only if c is true;
the truth of c is a necessary condition for b to be true, but a is a sufficient condition for b to be true.

Clearly implication signs provide the most economical way of expressing connections between statements. The process of deduction is based on a *law of implication* which we can now state in the form:

$$\boxed{\text{if } a \Rightarrow b \text{ and } b \Rightarrow c, \text{ then } a \Rightarrow c.}$$

A deductive proof can always be reduced to a series of these steps or closely related ones such as, "if $a \Rightarrow b$ and $a \Rightarrow c$, where b and c together imply d, then $a \Rightarrow d$."

Exercise 17.2

1. Use the symbols $\Rightarrow$ and $\Leftrightarrow$ to connect the statements p, q and r.
(a) p: *ABCD* is a square
    q: *ABCD* has four equal sides
    r: *ABCD* is a parallelogram
(b) p: Ivor is Welsh
    q: Ivor lives in Cardiff
    r: Ivor is British
(c) p: *KLMN* is a rectangle 3 cm by 4 cm
    q: The area of rectangle *KLMN* is 12 cm^2
    r: *KLMN* is a rectangle with diagonals 5 cm long
(d) p: The integer n is an even multiple of 5
    q: The integer n has final digit 0
    r: The integer n has a pair of prime factors which differ by 3.

2. Use the symbol $\nRightarrow$ to connect the statements given in question 1.

3. Use the symbols $\Rightarrow$ and $\Leftrightarrow$ to connect the negations $\sim p$, $\sim q$ and $\sim r$ of the statements given in question 1.

4. Write down all possible connections between the statements p, q, $\sim p$ and $\sim q$ using the symbols $\Rightarrow$ and $\Leftrightarrow$.
(a) p: In quadrilateral *ABCD*, $AC = BD$
    q: *ABCD* is a rectangle
(b) p: In $\triangle ABC$, $\angle A$ is obtuse
    q: In $\triangle ABC$, $\angle B = 90°$
(c) p: For integers x and y, $x - y$ is odd
    q: For integers x and y, $x^2 - y^2$ is divisible by 4

(d) *p*: *C* lies on the circle with *AB* as diameter

  q: In △*ABC*, ∠*C* is not a right angle.

5.   Using only the terms and symbols *p*, *q*, ~*p*, ~*q*, ⇒, ⇔, ⇏ and ⇎, write down a statement equivalent to each of the following:

(a) ~*p* ⇒ ~*q*,   (b) *p* ⇔ ~*q*,   (c) ~*p* ⇏ *q*,

(d) *p* ⇎ *q*,   (e) *p* ⇒ ~*q*,   (f) ~*p* ⇔ *q*,

6.   Use the symbol ⇒ to state the connection between the statements *p* and *q* in each of the following cases.

(a) *q* is true only if *p* is true,

(b) *p* is a necessary condition that *q*,

(c) *q* is a sufficient condition that *p*,

(d) *p* is true if *q* is true,

(e) *p* is a sufficient condition that *q*,

(f) *p* is true only if *q* is true.

7.   Use the terms "if", "only if", "necessary condition" and "sufficient condition" to express the connection between the statements, "△*ABC* is equilateral" and "*AB* = *AC*" in four different ways.

17.3 Types of proof

We first give an example of an elementary deductive proof.

Example 1   Prove that $a \times 0 = 0$ for all real values of *a*.

   [You may assume the following properties of real numbers:

(i) $a + (b + c) = (a + b) + c$ associative law for addition

(ii) $a(b + c) = ab + ac$ distributive law

(iii) $a + 0 = a = 0 + a$ for all real *a*

(iv)   any real number *a* has an additive inverse $(-a)$, such that $a + (-a) = 0 = (-a) + a$.]

$$b + 0 = b$$ property (iii)

⇒ $a(b + 0) = ab$ both sides multiplied by *a*

⇒ $ab + a \times 0 = ab$ distributive law

⇒ $-ab + (ab + a \times 0) = -ab + ab$ $-ab$ added to both sides

⇒ $(-ab + ab) + a \times 0 = -ab + ab$ associative law for +

⇒ $0 + a \times 0 = 0$ property (iv)

⇒ $a \times 0 = 0$ property (iii)

Another important type of proof is called *proof by contradiction* (or "reductio ad absurdum".) To prove a theorem by this method we assume that the theorem does not hold, then show that this assumption leads to a contradiction. In its simplest form this process is equivalent to proving a statement *p* true by showing ~*p* to be false. For instance, the standard proof of the statement "$\sqrt{2}$ is irrational" begins with the assumption that $\sqrt{2}$ is rational. In the example given here a statement of the form $p \Rightarrow q$ is proved by showing that $\sim q \Rightarrow \sim p$.

Example 2   Prove that in $\triangle ABC$, if $AB^2 + BC^2 = AC^2$, then $\angle ABC = 90°$.

[You may assume Pythagoras' theorem.]

Let us assume that in $\triangle ABC$, $\angle ABC \neq 90°$.

(1) $\angle ABC < 90°$ (2) $\angle ABC > 90°$

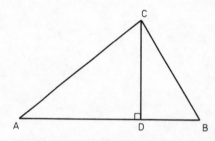   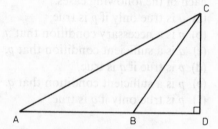

Case (1):   By Pythagoras' theorem in $\triangle ADC$, $AC^2 = AD^2 + DC^2$

But $AD < AB$ and $DC < BC$, $\therefore$ $AC^2 < AB^2 + BC^2$.

Case (2):   By Pythagoras' theorem in $\triangle ADC$, $AC^2 = AD^2 + DC^2$

$\therefore$ $AC^2 = (AB + BD)^2 + DC^2 = AB^2 + 2AB.BD + BD^2 + DC^2$

By Pythagoras' theorem in $\triangle BDC$, $BD^2 + DC^2 = BC^2$

$\therefore$ $AC^2 = AB^2 + 2AB.BD + BC^2 > AB^2 + BC^2$.

Thus, in both cases, if $AB^2 + BC^2 = AC^2$, the assumption that $\angle ABC \neq 90°$ leads to a contradiction.

Hence, if $AB^2 + BC^2 = AC^2$, then $\angle ABC = 90°$.

This result is, of course, the converse of Pythagoras' theorem. In general, the *converse* of the statement $p \Rightarrow q$ is the statement $q \Rightarrow p$.

As in the case of Fermat's famous conjecture, mentioned in §17.1, it is sometimes difficult to establish the truth of a general statement about such objects as real numbers or sets. However, a statement can be proved false by producing just one *counter-example*.

Example 3   Discuss the statement that if n is a positive integer, then $n^2 - n + 17$ is prime.

[To prove that this statement is true it would be necessary to show that it holds for all positive integral values of n. However, the statement can be proved false by finding one value of n, such that $n^2 - n + 17$ is not prime.]

If we test the statement by writing $n = 1, 2, 3, 4, 5 \ldots$, we obtain the prime numbers $17, 19, 23, 29, 37, \ldots$. This suggests that the statement could be true. However, if $n = 17$, $n^2 - n + 17 = 17^2$, which is not prime. Hence the statement is false.

Exercise 17.3

1. Using the given diagrams, show that if $\angle ABC = \angle CAT$, the assumption that AT cuts the circle again at a point D leads to a contradiction. What conclusion can be drawn from this?

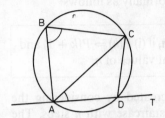 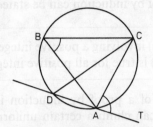 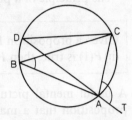

2. Show that if $p_1, p_2, p_3, \ldots, p_n$ are prime numbers, then the number $p_1 p_2 p_3 \ldots p_n + 1$ is either a prime not already listed or a multiple of such a prime. Hence prove by contradiction that there are infinitely many prime numbers.

3. Write down the converses of the following statements. In each case decide whether (i) the statement, (ii) its converse are true or false.
(a) If a diameter of a circle bisects a chord, it is perpendicular to that chord.
(b) If $2x - 3 = 0$, then $2x^2 - x - 3 = 0$.
(c) If a pentagon is regular, it must be equilateral.
(d) If x is greater than y, then x^2 is greater than y^2.
(e) If a positive integer N is divisible by 9, then the sum of its digits is divisible by 9.
(f) If any set of six socks taken from a drawer contains a pair, then there must be five pairs of socks in the drawer.

In questions 4, 5 and 6 decide whether the given statements are true or false. If a statement is true, prove it; if it is false, give a counter-example.

4. (a) The square of any odd number is of the form $4k + 1$, where k is a non-negative integer.
   (b) Any number of the form $4k + 1$ is the square of an odd number.

5. (a) If $0 < p < q$, then $\log p < \log q$.

   (b) If $0 < p < q$, then $\displaystyle\int_0^p f(x)dx < \int_0^q f(x)dx.$

6. (a) If $n^3 - n$ is divisible by 4, then n must be divisible by 4.
   (b) If n is a positive integer, then $n^3 - n$ is divisible by 3.

17.4 Proof by induction

The elementary deductive methods discussed so far are sometimes found to be inadequate when attempting to prove that a proposition, such as "the number $4^n + 5$ is divisible by 3", holds for all positive integral values of n. The difficulty is that this general statements is equivalent to the infinite sequence of propositions "3 is a factor of $4^1 + 5, 4^2 + 5, 4^3 + 5, 4^4 + 5, \ldots$" However, propositions of this kind can often be proved using *mathematical induction*. Although the method is related to the type of inductive reasoning used in science, it is nevertheless a rigorous procedure in which conclusions are reached by sound deductive reasoning.

The principle of a proof by induction can be stated formally as follows:

Given a proposition $P(n)$ involving a positive integer n, if (i) $P(k) \Rightarrow P(k + 1)$ and (ii) $P(1)$ is true, then $P(n)$ is true for all positive integral values of n.

A useful mental picture of a proof by induction is created by considering the proposition that a man can climb a certain uniform staircase with n steps. The statement will be proved if we can show

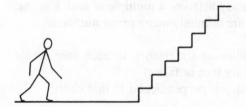

(i) that the man is capable of climbing from any step to the one above and
(ii) that the man can reach the foot of the staircase.

Thus it may be helpful to think of a general proposition $P(n)$ as a staircase to be climbed. The steps of the staircase are the propositions $P(1), P(2), P(3), \ldots$. It is possible to proceed from one "step" to the next if we can prove that for any k, $P(k + 1)$ may be deduced from $P(k)$. If, in addition, it is shown that $P(1)$ is true (i.e. that it is possible to set foot on the first step of the staircase), then it follows that $P(2)$ is true, then $P(3)$ is true and so on for all positive integral values of n.

Example 1   Prove that the number, $a_n = 4^n + 5$, is divisible by 3 for all positive integral values of n.

Consider the numbers $a_k = 4^k + 5$ and $a_{k+1} = 4^{k+1} + 5$.

$$a_{k+1} - a_k = (4^{k+1} + 5) - (4^k + 5)$$
$$= 4^{k+1} - 4^k = 4^k(4 - 1) = 4^k \times 3$$
$$\therefore \quad a_{k+1} = a_k + 4^k \times 3$$

Hence, if a_k is divisible by 3, so is a_{k+1}.
$\therefore$ if the proposition is true for $n = k$, it is also true for $n = k + 1$.
$a_1 = 4^1 + 5 = 9$, which is divisible by 3,
$\therefore$ the proposition is true for $n = 1$.
Hence, by induction, the number $4^n + 5$ must be divisible by 3 for all positive integral values of n.

When dealing with a finite series, it is sometimes possible to suggest a formula for the sum to n terms by examining the first few sums, $S_1, S_2, S_3, \ldots$. Such a result can often be proved by the method of induction.

Example 2   If S_n is the sum of the first n terms of the series

$$\frac{1}{1 \times 2} + \frac{1}{2 \times 3} + \frac{1}{3 \times 4} + \ldots + \frac{1}{n(n+1)} + \ldots,$$

find S_1, S_2 and S_3, then suggest a formula for S_n. Prove that the result is correct by the method of induction.

$$S_1 = \frac{1}{1 \times 2} = \frac{1}{2}, \qquad S_2 = S_1 + \frac{1}{2 \times 3} = \frac{1}{2} + \frac{1}{6} = \frac{2}{3},$$

$$S_3 = S_2 + \frac{1}{3 \times 4} = \frac{2}{3} + \frac{1}{12} = \frac{3}{4}.$$

These results suggests that $S_n = \dfrac{n}{n+1}$.

Assuming that this result is true for $n = k$, $S_k = \dfrac{k}{k+1}$.

$$\therefore \quad S_{k+1} = S_k + \frac{1}{(k+1)(k+2)}$$

$$= \frac{k}{k+1} + \frac{1}{(k+1)(k+2)}$$

$$= \frac{k(k+2) + 1}{(k+1)(k+2)}$$

$$= \frac{k^2 + 2k + 1}{(k+1)(k+2)} = \frac{(k+1)^2}{(k+1)(k+2)} = \frac{k+1}{k+2}$$

$\therefore$ if the result holds for $n = k$, it also holds for $n = k + 1$.

When $n = 1$, $S_n = S_1 = \dfrac{1}{2}$ and $\dfrac{n}{n+1} = \dfrac{1}{1+1} = \dfrac{1}{2}$.

$\therefore$ the result holds for $n = 1$.

Hence, by induction, it is true that $S_n = n/(n + 1)$ for all positive integral values of n.

The method of induction can also be used to prove the binomial theorem:

$$(a + b)^n = a^n + {}_nC_1 a^{n-1}b + {}_nC_2 a^{n-2}b^2 + \ldots$$
$$+ {}_nC_r a^{n-r}b^r + \ldots + {}_nC_{n-1}ab^{n-1} + b^n.$$

Assuming that the theorem is true for $n = k$,

$$(a + b)^k = a^k + {}_kC_1 a^{k-1}b + {}_kC_2 a^{k-2}b^2 + \ldots$$
$$+ {}_kC_{r-1}a^{k-r+1}b^{r-1} + {}_kC_r a^{k-r}b^r + \ldots + b^k,$$

then, multiplying by $(a + b)$,

$$(a + b)^{k+1} = a^{k+1} + {}_kC_1 a^k b + {}_kC_2 a^{k-1}b^2 + \ldots + {}_kC_r a^{k-r+1}b^r \quad + \ldots$$
$$+ a^k b + {}_kC_1 a^{k-1}b^2 + \ldots + {}_kC_{r-1}a^{k-r+1}b^r + \ldots + b^{k+1}.$$

But $_kC_1 + 1 = k + 1 = {_{k+1}}C_1$, and

$$_kC_r + {_k}C_{r-1} = \frac{k!}{r!(k-r)!} + \frac{k!}{(r-1)!(k-\{r-1\})!}$$

$$= \frac{k!}{r!(k-r+1)!}\{(k-r+1) + r\}$$

$$= \frac{(k+1)!}{r!(k+1-r)!} = {_{k+1}}C_r$$

$\therefore \quad (a+b)^{k+1} = a^{k+1} + {_{k+1}}C_1 a^k b + {_{k+1}}C_2 a^{k-1}b^2 + \ldots$

$$\ldots + {_{k+1}}C_r a^{k+1-r}b^r + \ldots + b^{k+1}.$$

$\therefore \quad$ if the theorem is true for $n = k$ it is also true for $n = k + 1$.

Since $(a+b)^1 = a^1 + b^1$, the theorem is true for $n = 1$. Hence, by induction, the binomial theorem is true for all positive integral values of n.

[Note that the basic principle of induction can be extended in various ways. Suppose, for instance, that for some proposition $P(n)$, where n is a positive integer, it can be shown that $P(k) \Rightarrow P(k + 1)$, but that the proposition $P(1)$ is false or meaningless. Clearly $P(n)$ cannot be proved true for all positive integral values of n. However, provided that there is some positive integer m such that $P(m)$ is true, then by induction, $P(n)$ holds for all integral values of n greater than or equal to m.]

Exercise 17.4

In questions 1 to 8 prove, by induction, that the given statements are true for all positive integral values of n.

1. The sum of the first n terms of the series
$(1 \times 3) + (2 \times 4) + (3 \times 5) + \ldots + r(r + 2) + \ldots$ is $\frac{1}{6}n(n + 1)(2n + 7)$.

2. The sum of the first n terms of the series
$$\frac{1}{1 \times 3} + \frac{1}{3 \times 5} + \frac{1}{5 \times 7} + \ldots + \frac{1}{(2r-1)(2r+1)} + \ldots \text{is } \frac{n}{2n+1}.$$

3. $\displaystyle\sum_{r=1}^{n} r(r+1) = \frac{1}{3}n(n+1)(n+2)$.

4. $\displaystyle\sum_{r=1}^{n} \frac{r}{2^r} = 2 - \frac{n+2}{2^n}$.

5. $n^3 + 3n^2 - 10n$ is divisible by 3.

6. $3^{2n} - 1$ is a multiple of 8.

7. $7^n + 4^n + 1^n$ is divisible by 6.

8. If $\mathbf{M} = \begin{pmatrix} 1 & 0 \\ 3 & 1 \end{pmatrix}$, then $\mathbf{M}^n = \begin{pmatrix} 1 & 0 \\ 3n & 1 \end{pmatrix}$.

9. Prove that $\sum_{r=1}^{n} r^2 = \frac{1}{6}n(n + 1)(2n + 1)$ for all positive integers n. Hence find the following sums:
(a) $1^2 + 2^2 + 3^2 + \ldots + 20^2$,
(b) $21^2 + 22^2 + 23^2 + \ldots + 40^2$,
(c) $2^2 + 4^2 + 6^2 + \ldots + 40^2$,
(d) $1^2 + 3^2 + 5^2 + \ldots + 39^2$.

10. Prove that the sum to n terms of the series

$$\frac{1}{1 \times 2 \times 3} + \frac{1}{2 \times 3 \times 4} + \frac{1}{3 \times 4 \times 5} + \ldots \text{ is } \frac{1}{4} - \frac{1}{2(n + 1)(n + 2)}.$$

Hence find the sum to infinity of the series.

11. If $\mathbf{A} = \begin{pmatrix} 3 & -1 \\ 4 & -1 \end{pmatrix}$, prove that $\mathbf{A}^n = \begin{pmatrix} 2n + 1 & -n \\ 4n & 1 - 2n \end{pmatrix}$, where n is a positive integer. Given that the transformation represented by $\mathbf{A}$ is applied to the points of the x, y plane n times in succession, find the image of
(a) the point $(0, -1)$,
(b) the line $y = x$.

12. Given that $f(x) = x/(x + 1)$, find $f^2(x)$ i.e. $f(f(x))$. Find also $f^3(x)$ and suggest a possible form for $f^n(x)$. Prove that your result is correct by mathematical induction.

Exercise 17.5 (miscellaneous)

In questions 1 to 6 explain why the given chain of reasoning is unsound.

1.
$$-6x + 9 = 2x + 1$$
$$\Rightarrow \quad x^2 - 6x + 9 = x^2 + 2x + 1$$
$$\Rightarrow \quad (x - 3)^2 = (x + 1)^2$$
$$\Rightarrow \quad x - 3 = x + 1$$
$$\Rightarrow \quad -3 = 1$$

2.
$$2 > 1$$
$$\Rightarrow \quad 2\lg(0 \cdot 2) > \lg(0 \cdot 2)$$
$$\Rightarrow \quad \lg(0 \cdot 2)^2 > \lg(0 \cdot 2)$$
$$\Rightarrow \quad \lg(0 \cdot 04) > \lg(0 \cdot 2)$$
$$\Rightarrow \quad 0 \cdot 04 > 0 \cdot 2$$

3.
$$(2x + 3)(3x + 1) = (6x + 5)(x + 1)$$
$$\Rightarrow \quad 6x^2 + 11x + 3 = 6x^2 + 11x + 5$$
$$\Rightarrow \quad 3 = 5$$

4.
$$a + b > 0$$
$$\Rightarrow \qquad a^2 + ab > 0$$
$$\Rightarrow \qquad a^2 + 2ab + b^2 > ab + b^2$$
$$\Rightarrow \qquad (a + b)^2 > (a + b)b$$
$$\Rightarrow \qquad a + b > b$$

Hence if $a + b > 0$, then $a + b > b$.

5.

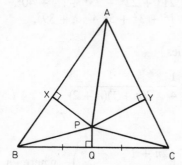

In $\triangle ABC$ the point P is constructed such that AP bisects $\angle A$ and PQ is the perpendicular bisector of BC. PX and PY are drawn perpendicular to AB and AC respectively.

In $\triangle$s APX and APY, $\angle AXP = \angle AYP$, $\angle PAX = \angle PAY$ and AP is common,
$\therefore \quad \triangle$s APX and APY are congruent.
Hence $PX = PY$ and $AX = AY$.
In $\triangle$s PXB and PYC, $\angle BXP = \angle CYP = 90°$, $PX = PY$ and $PB = PC$.
$\therefore \quad \triangle$s PXB and PYC are congruent and hence $XB = YC$.
Thus $AX + XB = AY + YC$ i.e. $AB = AC$.
Hence any triangle is isosceles.

6. To prove that $a_n = 7^n - 11$ is divisible by 6, where n is an integer greater than 1.

Proof: $a_{k+1} - a_k = (7^{k+1} - 11) - (7^k - 11)$
$$= 7^{k+1} - 7^k = 7^k(7 - 1) = 7^k \times 6,$$

$\therefore \quad$ if a_k is divisible by 6, so is a_{k+1}.
Hence, by induction, a_n is divisible by 6 for all integral values of n greater than 1.

7. In proving a statement of the form $p \Rightarrow q$, it has been shown that p implies either r or s. What further steps are required to complete the proof?

8. In proving that the proposition $P(n)$ is true for all positive integral values of n, it has been shown that $P(k) \Rightarrow P(k + 2)$. What further steps are required to complete the proof?

9. Prove that if n is any positive integer,
$1 \times 2 \times 3 + 2 \times 3 \times 4 + \dots + n(n + 1)(n + 2) = \frac{1}{4}n(n + 1)(n + 2)(n + 3)$.

10. Prove that $\dfrac{d}{dx}(x^n) = nx^{n-1}$ for all positive integral values of n.

11. Prove that $\displaystyle\sum_{r=2}^{n} \frac{1}{r^2 - 1} = \frac{3}{4} - \frac{2n + 1}{2n(n + 1)}$.

12. Given that $A = \begin{pmatrix} 1 + \cos\theta & \sin\theta \\ \sin\theta & 1 - \cos\theta \end{pmatrix}$, prove that $A^{n+1} = 2^n \times A$, where n is a positive integer.

13. If $u_{n+1} = 2u_n + 1$ where n is a positive integer and $u_1 = 5$, prove by induction that $u_n = 3 \times 2^n - 1$.

14. If $A = \begin{pmatrix} 1 & 1 \\ 0 & 2 \end{pmatrix}$, find A^2, A^3 and conjecture a form for A^n where n is any positive integer. Prove the truth of your conjecture by mathematical induction.   (O & C)

15. Prove by induction that the sum of the first n terms of the series
$$\frac{1}{1 \times 2 \times 3} + \frac{4}{2 \times 3 \times 4} + \frac{7}{3 \times 4 \times 5} + \dots \text{ is } \frac{n^2}{(n+1)(n+2)}.$$
Find the limit of this sum as n tends to infinity.

16. If $S_n = 1.n + 2(n-1) + 3(n-2) + \dots + (n-1).2 + n.1$, where n is a positive integer, prove that $S_{n+1} - S_n = \frac{1}{2}(n+1)(n+2)$. By induction, or otherwise, prove that $S_n = \frac{1}{6}n(n+1)(n+2)$.   (O)

17. Prove that, if n is a positive integer greater than one, $n^5 - n$ is a multiple of 5. Hence, or otherwise, prove that all square numbers are of the form $5r$ or $5r \pm 1$ where r is an integer.   (JMB)

18. Let A, B and C be subsets of some universal set $\mathscr{E}$. For the three statements below, prove those that are true and, by taking $\mathscr{E}$ to be the set of all positive integers, provide counter-examples to demonstrate the falsity of the others:
(i) $(A \cap B = A \cap C) \Rightarrow (B = C)$,   (ii) $(A \cap B = A \cup B) \Rightarrow (A = B)$,
(iii) $(A \cap B) \cup C = (A \cup C) \cap B$.

[In this question Venn diagrams may be used to examine the plausibility of a statement but will not be accepted as proofs of truth or falsity.]   (C)

19. The real function f, defined for all $x \in \mathbb{R}$, is said to be multiplicative if, for all $x \in \mathbb{R}$, $y \in \mathbb{R}$, $f(xy) = f(x)f(y)$. [$\mathbb{R}$ denotes the set of real numbers.] Prove that if f is a multiplicative function then
(i) either $f(0) = 0$ or $f(x) \equiv 1$,
(ii) either $f(1) = 1$ or $f(x) \equiv 0$,
(iii) $f(x^n) = \{f(x)\}^n$ for all positive integers n.
Give an example of a non-constant multiplicative function.   (C)

20. The matrix $X = \begin{pmatrix} p & q \\ r & s \end{pmatrix}$ has real non-zero elements; the matrix P is of the form $\begin{pmatrix} a & 0 \\ 0 & b \end{pmatrix}$ where $a \neq b$, and $M = \begin{pmatrix} 4 & 2 \\ -3 & -1 \end{pmatrix}$. Given that $XM = PX$, show

that $\dfrac{q}{p} = \dfrac{4-a}{3} = \dfrac{2}{1+a}$ and find a possible matrix **P** and a possible corres-

ponding matrix **X**. Show that, if n is a positive integer, $\mathbf{M}^n = \mathbf{X}^{-1}\mathbf{P}^n\mathbf{X}$. Deduce the elements of $\mathbf{M}^n$ in terms of n.   (JMB)

21. Prove that if n is a positive integer, $10^n - 1$ is divisible by 9. Hence prove that a necessary and sufficient condition for a positive integer to be divisible by 9 is that the sum of its digits is divisible by 9.

18 Some functions and their properties

18.1 Symmetry, continuity and differentiability

A *function* f with *domain* X and *codomain* Y is a rule which assigns to each element $x \in X$ exactly one *image* $y \in Y$. The set containing the images under f of all the elements of the domain is called the *range* (or image set). In this chapter we will be considering functions with domain the set of real numbers $\mathbb{R}$ (or some subset of $\mathbb{R}$), and codomain $\mathbb{R}$. The notation used to define such functions will take one of the following forms: $f(x) = x^2 + 1$, $y = x^2 + 1$ or $f : x \to x^2 + 1$. Unless otherwise stated, the domain of a function f is assumed to be the set of all real numbers for which an image is defined. For instance, the domain of the function $f(x) = x/(x^2 - 1)$ is taken to be the set $\mathbb{R} - \{-1, 1\}$ i.e. all real numbers except -1 and $+1$. We now examine some of the properties possessed by various functions defined in $\mathbb{R}$.

A function $f(x)$ is said to be *odd* if $f(-x) = -f(x)$. The graph of an odd function is symmetrical about the origin, i.e. if (a, b) lies on the graph so does $(-a, -b)$. The function $f(x)$ is said to be *even* if $f(-x) = f(x)$. The graph of an even function is symmetrical about the y-axis i.e. if (a, b) lies on the graph so does $(-a, b)$.

Example 1 Decide whether each of the functions f, g and h is odd, even or neither, given that

$$f(x) = x + 1/x, \ x \in \mathbb{R}, \ x \neq 0,$$
$$g(x) = 2 \cos x - x, \ x \in \mathbb{R},$$
$$h(x) = \sqrt{(4 - x^2)}, \ x \in \mathbb{R}, \ |x| \leqslant 2.$$

$$f(-x) = (-x) + 1/(-x) = -x - 1/x = -f(x)$$

$\therefore$ f is an odd function.

$$g(-x) = 2 \cos(-x) - (-x) = 2 \cos x + x$$

$\therefore$ g is neither odd nor even.

$$h(-x) = \sqrt{(4 - \{-x\}^2)} = \sqrt{(4 - x^2)} = h(x)$$

$\therefore$ h is an even function.

The sketches below show the graphs of f, g and h.

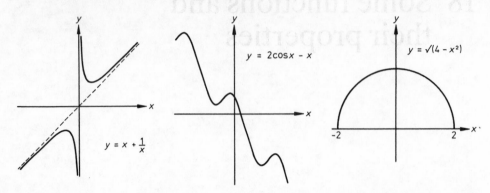

A function $f(x)$ is said to be *periodic* if there is a constant k such that $f(x + k) = f(x)$ for all values of x. The graph of the function forms a repeating pattern such that any translation parallel to the x-axis through k units leaves the pattern unchanged. The *period* of the function is the least positive constant a such that $f(x + a) = f(x)$ for all values of x. The trigonometric functions $\sin x$ and $\cos x$ are periodic and have period 2π. The function $\tan x$ is also periodic, but has period π.

Example 2   Sketch the graph of the function $f(x) = x - [x]$ and decide whether it is periodic. [Note that $[x]$ denotes the greatest integer less than or equal to x.]

When x is an integer, $[x] = x$, $\therefore$ $f(x) = x - x = 0$
When $0 \leqslant x < 1$, $[x] = 0$, $\therefore$ $f(x) = x$
For all values of x, $f(x + 1) = (x + 1) - [x + 1]$
$$= x + 1 - ([x] + 1)$$
$$= x - [x] = f(x)$$

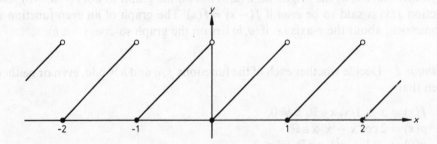

The sketch shows that $f(x)$ is periodic with period 1.
[Open and closed circles are used to show that, for instance, the value of $f(1)$ is 0 rather than 1.]

Example 3   Given that f is a periodic function such that for $0 \leqslant x \leqslant 4$, $f(x) = x(4 - x)$, sketch the graph $y = f(x)$ in each of the following cases,

(a) the period of f is 4,
(b) f is an odd function and has period 8.

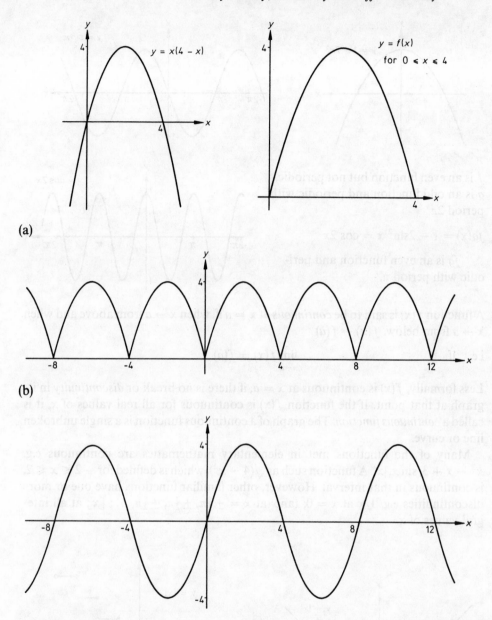

(a)

(b)

If f and g are functions defined on $\mathbb{R}$, then the *composite function fg* (also written $f \circ g$) is defined by $fg(x) = f(g(x))$.

Example 4 The functions f and g are defined by $f: x \to 1 - 2x^2$ and $g: x \to \sin x$. Sketch the graphs of the functions f, g and fg. State whether each of these functions is

(a) odd, even or neither,

(b) periodic, and if so give the period.

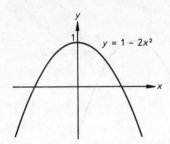

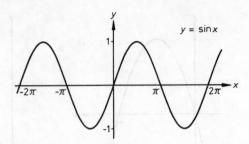

f is an even function but not periodic.
g is an odd function and periodic with
period 2π.

$$fg(x) = 1 - 2\sin^2 x = \cos 2x$$

$\therefore$ *fg* is an even function and periodic with period π.

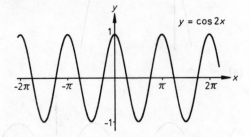

A function $f(x)$ is said to be *continuous* at $x = a$ if, when $x \to a$ from above and when
$x \to a$ from below, $f(x) \to f(a)$

i.e.   if $$\lim_{x \to a} f(x) = f(a).$$

Less formally, $f(x)$ is continuous at $x = a$, if there is no break or *discontinuity* in its
graph at that point. If the function $f(x)$ is continuous for all real values of x, it is
called a *continuous function*. The graph of a continuous function is a single unbroken
line or curve.

Many of the functions met in elementary mathematics are continuous e.g.
$x^3 - x + 3, \sin x, |x|$. A function such as $\sqrt{(4 - x^2)}$, which is defined for $-2 \leqslant x \leqslant 2$,
is continuous in that interval. However, other familiar functions have one or more
discontinuities e.g. $1/x$ at $x = 0$; $\tan x$ at $x = \pm\frac{1}{2}\pi, \pm\frac{3}{2}\pi, \pm\frac{5}{2}\pi, \ldots$; $[x]$ at all integral values of x.

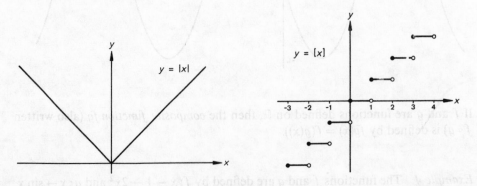

The *derivative* of a function $f(x)$ at $x = a$ is defined as

$$f'(a) = \lim_{h \to 0} \frac{f(a + h) - f(a)}{h}.$$

If this limit exists $f(x)$ is said to be *differentiable* at $x = a$. Given a function $f(x)$ the *derived function* $f'(x)$ can often be found using the standard rules for differentiation. However, any general formula for $f'(x)$ will be invalid where $f(x)$ has a discontinuity and possibly at certain other points. For instance, if $f(x) = 1/x$, the result $f'(x) = -1/x^2$ is meaningless when $x = 0$. The function $f(x) = [x]$ is not differentiable when x is an integer, but for non-integral values of x, $f'(x) = 0$. If we consider the function $f(x) = |x|$ near $x = 0$, we find that

for $h > 0$,
$$\frac{f(0 + h) - f(0)}{h} = \frac{h - 0}{h} = 1,$$

but for $h < 0$,
$$\frac{f(0 + h) - f(0)}{h} = \frac{-h - 0}{h} = -1.$$

Hence the expression $\dfrac{f(0 + h) - f(0)}{h}$ approaches no single value as $h \to 0$. Thus although $|x|$ is a continuous function it is not differentiable at $x = 0$.

Exercise 18.1

In questions 1 to 4 decide whether the given functions are odd, even or neither.

1. (a) $x^4 - 6$,   (b) $x^3 + 5$,   (c) $x^3 + 5x$.

2. (a) $1 + \dfrac{1}{x^2}$,   (b) $\dfrac{1}{1 + x^2}$,   (c) $\dfrac{x}{1 + x^2}$.

3. (a) $1 - \cos x$,   (b) $x^2 \sin x$,   (c) $\sec x + \tan x$.

4. (a) $[x]$,   (b) $[x] + \tfrac{1}{2}$,   (c) $[x^2]$.

In questions 5 to 8 decide whether the given functions are periodic and if so state the period.

5. (a) $\sin 3x$,   (b) $1 + \tan 2x$,   (c) $\cos \tfrac{1}{4}(x + \pi)$.

6. (a) $x + \cos x$,   (b) $\sin x + \cos x$,   (c) $\sin x \cos x$.

7. (a) $\sin 2x - \sin 3x$,   (b) $x \sin 3x$,   (c) $\sin 3x \cos 2x$.

8. (a) $|\cos x|$,   (b) $\sin |x|$,   (c) $[\tan x]$.

In questions 9 to 12 sketch the graphs of the functions f, g, fg and gf. In each case state whether the function is odd, even or neither, give its range and, if periodic, its period.

9. $f(x) = x^2 - 1, g(x) = 2x + 1$.

10. $f(x) = \tfrac{1}{2}(\pi - x), g(x) = \sin x$.

11. $f(x) = \cos x$, $g(x) = x^2$.

12. $f(x) = |x|$, $g(x) = x(x^2 - 3)$.

In questions 13 to 16 sketch the graphs of the given periodic functions.

13. $f(x) = x^2$ for $-2 < x \leqslant 2$, f has period 4.

14. $f(x) = |x|$ for $-1 < x \leqslant 1$, f has period 2.

15. $f(x) = x^3$ for $0 \leqslant x \leqslant 1$,
$f(x) = -x$ for $-1 < x < 0$, f has period 2.

16. $f(x) = x$ for $0 \leqslant x \leqslant k$,
$f(x) = k$ for $k < x < 2k$, f has period $2k$.

In questions 17 to 20 sketch the graphs of the given functions. State any values of x at which
(a) there is a discontinuity,
(b) the function is not differentiable.

17. $1/(x^2 - 1)$.   18. $|x^2 - 1|$.   19. $x + [x]$.

20. $f(x) = x$ for $|x| \leqslant 1$, $f(x) = x^2 - 2$ for $|x| > 1$.

21. Given that f is a periodic function such that for $0 \leqslant x \leqslant 1$, $f(x) = x^2 - 2x$, sketch the graph of the function in each of the following cases
(a) f has period 1,
(b) f is an even function and has period 2,
(c) f is an odd function and has period 2.

22. A function f is defined by $f(x) = x^2 + 3x$ for $x < 0$, $f(x) = kx$ for $x \geqslant 0$. Show that $f(x)$ is differentiable at $x = 0$ for only one value of k and state this value.

18.2 Some graphs with related equations

In this section we consider some graphs with equations of the form $y = f(x)$ together with graphs which have related equations such as $y = |f(x)|$, $y = 1/f(x)$, $y = \{f(x)\}^2$, $y^2 = f(x)$.

However, we first digress a little to note that not all graphs represent functions. There are many ways in which two real numbers x and y may be related, e.g. "$x < y$", "$y^2 = x$" or perhaps "$x - y$ is an integer". Each of these statements is said to define a *relation* on the set of real numbers. The graph of the relation is the set of points (x, y) such that x and y are related in the stated manner.

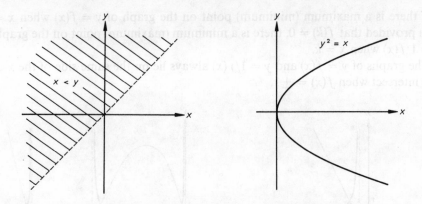

Thus, in general, an equation (or inequality) connecting x and y defines a relation on $\mathbb{R}$. Such an equation defines a function of x with domain $\mathbb{R}$ (or a subset of $\mathbb{R}$) only if there is at most one value of y corresponding to any given value of x. For instance the equation $y^2 = x$ specifies a relation, but not a function of the form $f:x \to y$, whereas the equation $y = \sqrt{x}$ defines a function with domain $\{x \in \mathbb{R}: x \geqslant 0\}$.

The equation $\quad y = |f(x)|$

When $f(x) \geqslant 0$, the graph of $y = |f(x)|$ coincides with the graph of $y = f(x)$. When $f(x) < 0$, the graph of $y = |f(x)|$ is the reflection in the x-axis of the graph of $y = f(x)$.

[In the following sketches broken lines are used for the graph of $y = f(x)$ and unbroken lines for the graph of $y = |f(x)|.$]

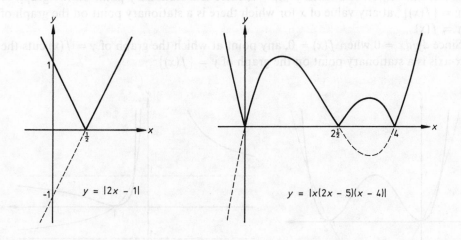

The equation $\quad y = 1/f(x)$

If the graph of $y = f(x)$ meets the x-axis at $x = a$, then the line $x = a$ is an asymptote to the graph of $y = 1/f(x)$ and vice versa.

If there is a maximum (minimum) point on the graph of $y = f(x)$ when $x = k$, then provided that $f(k) \neq 0$, there is a minimum (maximum) point on the graph of $y = 1/f(x)$ when $x = k$.

The graphs of $y = f(x)$ and $y = 1/f(x)$ always lie on the same side of the x-axis and intersect when $f(x) = \pm 1$.

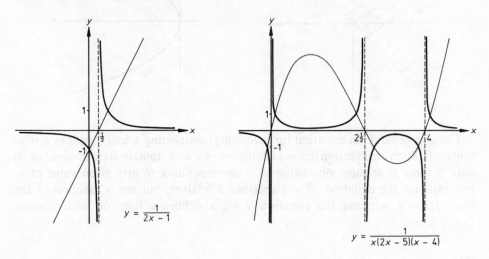

The equation $y = \{f(x)\}^2$

The graph of $y = \{f(x)\}^2$ lies entirely on or above the x-axis and cuts the graph of $y = f(x)$ when $f(x) = 0$ or 1.

$$y = \{f(x)\}^2 \quad \Rightarrow \quad \frac{dy}{dx} = 2f(x)f'(x)$$

Thus, since $dy/dx = 0$ when $f'(x) = 0$, there is a stationary point on the graph of $y = \{f(x)\}^2$ at any value of x for which there is a stationary point on the graph of $y = f(x)$.

Since $dy/dx = 0$ when $f(x) = 0$, any point at which the graph of $y = f(x)$ cuts the x-axis is a stationary point on the graph of $y = \{f(x)\}^2$.

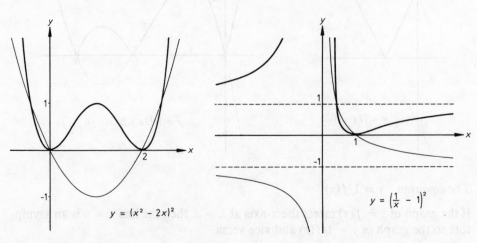

The equation $y^2 = f(x)$

At values of x such that $f(x) < 0$, there are no points on the graph of $y^2 = f(x)$.

At values of x such that $f(x) > 0$, there are two possible values of y, namely $\pm\sqrt{\{f(x)\}}$. Hence the graph of $y^2 = f(x)$ is symmetrical about the x-axis.

It is also useful to note that if $0 < f(x) < 1$, then $\sqrt{\{f(x)\}} > f(x)$ and if $f(x) > 1$, then $\sqrt{\{f(x)\}} < f(x)$.

$$y^2 = f(x) \;\Rightarrow\; 2y\frac{dy}{dx} = f'(x)$$

$\therefore$ if $f'(x) = 0$, and $f(x) > 0$, then $\dfrac{dy}{dx} = 0.$

Thus, any stationary point above the x-axis on the curve $y = f(x)$ gives rise to a pair of stationary points on the curve $y^2 = f(x)$.

To determine how the graph of $y^2 = f(x)$ behaves near the x-axis, the expression for dy/dx must be considered further. For instance, suppose that $f(x) = x(x-3)^2$.

If $$y^2 = x(x-3)^2 = x^3 - 6x^2 + 9x$$

then differentiating with respect to x,

$$2y\frac{dy}{dx} = 3x^2 - 12x + 9 = 3(x-1)(x-3)$$

But $y = \pm(x-3)\sqrt{x}$
$\therefore$ provided that $x \neq 3$,

$$\frac{dy}{dx} = \pm\frac{3(x-1)}{2\sqrt{x}}$$

As $x \to 0$, $\dfrac{dy}{dx} \to \pm\infty.$

As $x \to 3$, $\dfrac{dy}{dx} \to \pm\sqrt{3}.$

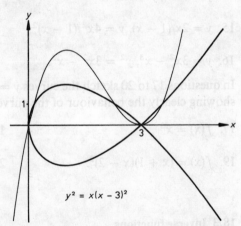

$y^2 = x(x-3)^2$

Exercise 18.2

In questions 1 to 6 sketch the graphs with given equations

1. (a) $y = x^2$,   (b) $y = \frac{1}{2}x^2$,   (c) $y = x^2 - 4$,   (d) $y = (x+2)^2$.

2. (a) $y = \sin x$,   (b) $y = 2\sin x$,   (c) $y = \sin 2x$,   (d) $y = \sin(x + \frac{1}{2}\pi)$.

3. (a) $y = \dfrac{1}{x}$,   (b) $y = \dfrac{4}{x}$,   (c) $y = \dfrac{1}{x+1}$,   (d) $y = \dfrac{x+2}{x+1}$.

4. (a) $y = |3 - 2x|$,   (b) $y = |x^2 - 4|$,   (c) $y = |x^3 - 3x^2|$.

5. (a) $y = |\cos x|$,   (b) $y = |\cos x| - 1$,   (c) $y = |2\cos x + 1|$.

6. (a) $y = \dfrac{1}{x - 2}$,   (b) $y = \dfrac{1}{2 - x}$,   (c) $y = \dfrac{1}{|x - 2|}$.

In questions 7 to 16 sketch the given pair of curves in the same diagram. Label clearly any stationary points and asymptotes.

7. $y = x^2 + 2x$, $y = 1/(x^2 + 2x)$.

8. $y = x^2 + 2x + 1$, $y = 1/(x^2 + 2x + 1)$.

9. $y = x^2 + 2x + 2$, $y = 1/(x^2 + 2x + 2)$.

10. $y = x^3 + 2x^2 - 15x$, $y = 1/(x^3 - 2x^2 - 15x)$.

11. $y = (2x - 1)/(x + 2)$, $y = (x + 2)/(2x - 1)$.

12. $y = 2x - 3$, $y = (2x - 3)^2$.

13. $y = 4 - x^2$, $y = (4 - x^2)^2$.

14. $y = \sin x$, $y = \sin^2 x$.

15. $y = 2x/(1 - x)$, $y = 4x^2/(1 - x)^2$.

16. $y = 3x^2 - x^3$, $y^2 = 3x^2 - x^3$.

In questions 17 to 20 sketch the curves $y = f(x)$ and $y^2 = f(x)$ in the same diagram, showing clearly the behaviour of the curves near the x-axis.

17. $f(x) = x^3$.   18. $f(x) = x(x + 3)^2$.

19. $f(x) = (x + 1)(x - 2)^2$.   20. $f(x) = x^2(4 - x^2)$.

18.3 Inverse functions

Consider a function f with domain X and range Y. If every element of Y is the image of one and only one element of X, then f is said to be *one-one*. For any one-one function $f : X \to Y$ we define an *inverse function* $f^{-1} : Y \to X$ such that if $y = f(x)$ then $f^{-1}(y) = x$.

It follows from the definition that

$$f^{-1}f(x) = f^{-1}(y) = x \quad \text{and} \quad ff^{-1}(y) = f(x) = y$$

i.e. the composite functions $f^{-1}f$ and ff^{-1} are the identity mappings on the sets X and Y respectively.

Example 1 One-one functions f and g are defined on $\mathbb{R}$ by $f : x \to 3x - 1$ and $g : x \to \lg(1 - x)$, $x < 1$. Find expressions for f^{-1} and g^{-1}.

Let $y = f^{-1}(x)$ then $f(y) = x$

$\therefore$ $3y - 1 = x$

$\qquad y = \tfrac{1}{3}(x + 1)$

Hence $f^{-1} : x \to \tfrac{1}{3}(x + 1)$.

Let $y = g^{-1}(x)$ then $g(y) = x$

$\therefore$ $\lg(1 - y) = x$

$\qquad 1 - y = 10^x$

$\qquad\quad y = 1 - 10^x$

Hence $g^{-1} : x \to 1 - 10^x$.

Example 2 A one-one function f is defined by $f : x \to 1/\sqrt{(x - 1)}$ where $x \in \mathbb{R}$, $x > 1$.

Find an expression for f^{-1}, stating its domain. Verify that $f^{-1}f(x) = x$ where $x \in \mathbb{R}$, $x > 1$.

$\begin{aligned}
y = f^{-1}(x) &\Rightarrow & f(y) &= x \\
&\Rightarrow & 1/\sqrt{(y - 1)} &= x \\
&\Rightarrow & 1/(y - 1) &= x^2 \\
&\Rightarrow & 1 &= x^2(y - 1) \\
&\Rightarrow & y - 1 &= 1/x^2 \\
&\Rightarrow & y &= 1 + 1/x^2
\end{aligned}$

$\therefore$ $f^{-1} : x \to 1 + 1/x^2$.

The domain of f^{-1} is the same as the range of f
i.e. $\mathbb{R}^+$, the set of positive real numbers.

$f^{-1}f(x) = f^{-1}(u)$, where $u = f(x) = 1/\sqrt{(x - 1)}$

$\therefore$ $f^{-1}f(x) = 1 + 1/u^2 = 1 + (x - 1) = x$.

Example 3 A function f is defined on $\mathbb{R}$ by $f : x \to x^2 - 2x$. Explain why f^{-1} does not exist. Suggest a restricted domain for which f^{-1} does exist.

$f(0) = f(2) = 0$ i.e. 0 is the image under f of both 0 and 2,

$\therefore$ the function f defined over $\mathbb{R}$ is not one-one and has no inverse.

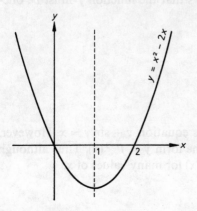

The sketch of the graph $y = x^2 - 2x$ shows that for $x \geqslant 1$ there is only one value of x corresponding to each value of y; $\therefore$ over the domain $\{x \in \mathbb{R} : x \geqslant 1\}$ the function f is one-one and f^{-1} does exist. [Note that f^{-1} also exists for the restricted domain $\{x \in \mathbb{R} : x \leqslant 1\}$.]

In general, a function f has an inverse if and only if any line drawn parallel to the x-axis cuts the graph $y = f(x)$ exactly once. Clearly a function whose graph has one or more turning points does not have an inverse.

If a point (a, b) lies on the graph $y = f(x)$ then the point (b, a) lies on the graph $y = f^{-1}(x)$. Hence each graph is the reflection of the other in the line $y = x$.

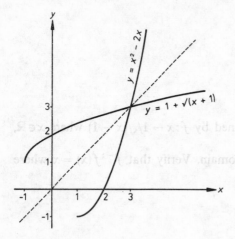

The diagram illustrates this relationship for the function

$$f : x \rightarrow x^2 - 2x, \quad x \geqslant 1.$$

The equation of the graph of f^{-1} is $y^2 - 2y = x, y \geqslant 1$, which may be rearranged as

$$(y - 1)^2 = x + 1, \, y \geqslant 1$$

i.e. $y - 1 = \sqrt{(x + 1)}$

i.e. $y = 1 + \sqrt{(x + 1)}.$

In some cases it is possible to show that a function f has an inverse, but difficult to find an expression for $f^{-1}(x)$. Consider, for example, the function $f : x \rightarrow x + \sin x$.

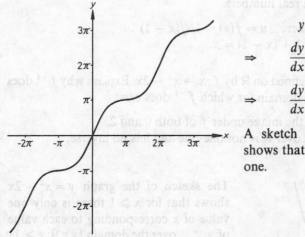

$$y = x + \sin x$$

$$\Rightarrow \quad \frac{dy}{dx} = 1 + \cos x$$

$$\Rightarrow \quad \frac{dy}{dx} \geqslant 0 \quad \text{for all} \quad x \in \mathbb{R}.$$

A sketch of the graph $y = x + \sin x$ shows that the function f must be one-one.

Hence the inverse f^{-1} exists and its graph has equation $y + \sin y = x$. However, it is impossible to rearrange this equation in the form $y = f^{-1}(x)$. Thus although f^{-1} exists, in practice it is difficult to find $f^{-1}(x)$ for many values of x.

Exercise 18.3

In questions 1 to 14 state whether or not the function f is one-one. If the function f is one-one, find an expression for f^{-1}, stating its domain. For any function that is not one-one, give two distinct values of x which have the same image.

1. $f: x \to 2x + 1$.

2. $f: x \to 5 - x$.

3. $f: x \to x(x + 2)$.

4. $f: x \to x^2 - 2, \; x \geqslant 0$.

5. $f: x \to 1 + \dfrac{1}{x}, \; x \neq 0$.

6. $f: x \to \dfrac{1}{9 - x}, \; x \neq 9$.

7. $f: x \to \sqrt{(3 - x)}, \; x \leqslant 3$.

8. $f: x \to \sqrt{(1 - x^2)}, \; -1 \leqslant x \leqslant 1$.

9. $f: x \to 3^x$.

10. $f: x \to \lg(x + 2), \; x > -2$.

11. $f: x \to \dfrac{1}{x^2 + 4}$.

12. $f: x \to \dfrac{2x}{x - 1}, \; x \neq 1$.

13. $f: x \to \cos 3x$.

14. $f: x \to \sin^{-1} x, \; -1 \leqslant x \leqslant 1$.

15. One-one functions f and g are defined on $\mathbb{R}$ by $f: x \to 5 - 4x$ and $g: x \to 1 - x^2, \; x \geqslant 0$. Given that h is the composite function fg, find expressions for $h(x)$ and $h^{-1}(x)$. Verify that $h^{-1} = g^{-1} f^{-1}$.

16. Functions f, g and h are defined on $\mathbb{R}$ by $f: x \to 3 - x$, $g: x \to 3x/(x - 3)$, $x \neq 3$ and $h: x \to \sqrt{(4 - x^2)}, \; 0 \leqslant x \leqslant 2$. Show that each of the functions is its own inverse. Find the composite function gf and verify that its inverse is fg.

17. Find the inverse of each of the following functions defined on $\mathbb{R}$. Verify that, over the appropriate domains, $f^{-1}f(x) = x$ and $ff^{-1}(x) = x$.
(a) $f: x \to (x - 2)^2, \; x \geqslant 2$,
(b) $f: x \to 1 + \lg(x - 1), \; x > 1$,
(c) $f: x \to \dfrac{1 - x}{1 + x}, \; x \neq -1$,
(d) $f: x \to \dfrac{1}{\sqrt{(x^2 - 1)}}, \; x > 1$.

In questions 18 to 23 the function f has domain $\mathbb{R}^+$, the set of positive real numbers. In each case sketch the graph of f and explain why no inverse function exists. Find the maximum domain of the form $\{x \in \mathbb{R} : x \geqslant k\}$ for which f would have an inverse f^{-1} and state the domain of the inverse.

18. $f: x \to x^2 - 4x + 8$.

19. $f: x \to 6x - x^2$.

20. $f: x \to |x - 4|$.

21. $f: x \to 2x^3 - 3x^2$.

22. $f: x \to x + \dfrac{1}{x}$.

23. $f: x \to x - \sqrt{x}$.

24. Decide whether the following functions have inverses, giving brief reasons for your answers.

(a) $f: x \rightarrow x^3 + 3x^2, x \in \mathbb{R}$,　　　　(b) $f: x \rightarrow x^3 + 3x, x \in \mathbb{R}$,

(c) $f: x \rightarrow 2x + \cos x, x \in \mathbb{R}$,　　　(d) $f: x \rightarrow x + 2\sin x, x \in \mathbb{R}$,

(e) $f: x \rightarrow |\lg x|, x \in \mathbb{R}^+$,　　　　(f) $f: x \rightarrow |x| + 2x, x \in \mathbb{R}$.

25. Differentiable functions f and g are defined on $\mathbb{R}$ such that f is the inverse of g. Prove that, if $f(a) = b$, then $f'(a)g'(b) = 1$.

18.4 Polynomials; remainders and factors

If, when a polynomial $P(x)$ is divided by $(x - a)$, the quotient is $Q(x)$ and the remainder is R, then

$$P(x) \equiv (x - a)Q(x) + R.$$

This identity leads to two familiar results.

The remainder theorem:　When $P(x)$ is divided by $(x - a)$ the remainder is $P(a)$.

The factor theorem:　If $P(a) = 0$, then $(x - a)$ is a factor of $P(x)$.

This approach can be extended to the division of a polynomial $f(x)$ by a polynomial $g(x)$ of degree less than or equal to the degree of $f(x)$. If the division gives quotient $Q(x)$ and remainder $R(x)$ then

$$f(x) \equiv g(x)Q(x) + R(x)$$

where $R(x)$ is of lower degree than $g(x)$.

[In particular, if $g(x)$ is a quadratic function then $R(x)$ is of the form $Ax + B$.]

Example 1　A polynomial $P(x)$ is a multiple of $x - 3$ and the remainder when $P(x)$ is divided by $x + 3$ is 12. Find the remainder when $P(x)$ is divided by $x^2 - 9$.

When $P(x)$ is divided by $x^2 - 9$, let the quotient be $Q(x)$ and the remainder $Ax + B$, then

$$P(x) \equiv (x^2 - 9)Q(x) + Ax + B.$$

Since $x - 3$ is a factor of $P(x)$, by the factor theorem,

$$P(3) = 0 \quad \therefore \quad 3A + B = 0 \tag{1}$$

Since when $P(x)$ is divided by $x + 3$ the remainder is 12, by the remainder theorem,

$$P(-3) = 12 \quad \therefore \quad -3A + B = 12 \tag{2}$$

Using (1) and (2),　$A = -2$,　$B = 6$.

Hence the remainder when $P(x)$ is divided by $x^2 - 9$ is $-2x + 6$.

Suppose now that a polynomial $f(x)$ has a repeated factor $(x - a)$,

so that $\qquad f(x) \equiv (x - a)^2 g(x)$

Differentiating, $\qquad f'(x) = (x - a)^2 g'(x) + 2(x - a)g(x)$

$$= (x - a)\{(x - a)g'(x) + 2g(x)\}$$

Hence, if $f(x)$ has a repeated factor $(x - a)$, then $(x - a)$ is also a factor of $f'(x)$.

It can further be shown, by the method of question 21, Exercise 18.4, that $(x - a)^2$ is a factor of a polynomial $f(x)$ if and only if $f(a) = f'(a) = 0$.

Example 2   Given that the polynomial $f(x) = x^3 + 3x^2 - 9x + k$ has a repeated linear factor, find the possible values of k.

Differentiating, $\quad f'(x) = 3x^2 + 6x - 9$

$$= 3(x^2 + 2x - 3) = 3(x - 1)(x + 3)$$

$\therefore$ the repeated factor of $f(x)$ is $(x - 1)$ or $(x + 3)$.

If $(x - 1)$ is a factor of $f(x)$, then $f(1) = 0$

i.e. $1 + 3 - 9 + k = 0$ giving $k = 5$.

If $(x + 3)$ is a factor of $f(x)$, then $f(-3) = 0$

i.e. $-27 + 27 + 27 + k = 0$ giving $k = -27$.

Thus the possible values of k are 5 and -27.

When dealing with polynomial equations it may be helpful to use the relationships between roots and coefficients. In the case of the cubic equation $ax^3 + bx^2 + cx + d = 0$ with roots α, β and γ,

$$\alpha + \beta + \gamma = -\frac{b}{a}, \quad \alpha\beta + \beta\gamma + \gamma\alpha = \frac{c}{a}, \quad \alpha\beta\gamma = -\frac{d}{a}.$$

Similar results can be obtained for equations of higher degree.

Example 3   Find the roots of the equation $4x^3 + 12x^2 - 15x + 4 = 0$ given that it has a repeated root.

Let $\quad f(x) = 4x^3 + 12x^2 - 15x + 4$

then $\quad f'(x) = 12x^2 + 24x - 15$

$$= 3(4x^2 + 8x - 5) = 3(2x - 1)(2x + 5)$$

Any repeated root of the equation $f(x) = 0$ is also a root of the equation $f'(x) = 0$

$\therefore$ the repeated root must be either $-5/2$ or $1/2$.

[It is possible to decide which of these values is the required root by evaluating $f(-5/2)$ and $f(1/2)$. However, the method given below may be quicker.]

The product of the roots of $f(x) = 0$ is $-4/4$ i.e. -1.

Thus, if the repeated root is $-5/2$, the remaining root is $-1 \div (-5/2)^2$ i.e. $-4/25$.

If the repeated root is $1/2$, the remaining root is $-1 \div (1/2)^2$ i.e. -4.

Since the sum of the roots of $f(x) = 0$ is $-12/4$ i.e. -3, the roots must be $1/2$, $1/2$, -4.

Let us consider two polynomials $P(x) = a_0x^n + a_1x^{n-1} + \ldots + a_n$ and

$$Q(x) = b_0x^n + b_1x^{n-1} + \ldots + b_n.$$

It can be shown that if $P(x) \equiv Q(x)$ i.e. if $P(x)$ and $Q(x)$ are equal for all values of x, then $a_0 = b_0, a_1 = b_1, \ldots, a_n = b_n$.

One way of proving this result uses the fact that if $P(x) \equiv Q(x)$, then $P'(x) \equiv Q'(x)$, $P''(x) \equiv Q''(x), \ldots, P^{(n)}(x) \equiv Q^{(n)}(x)$.

Substituting $x = 0$, we find that $P(0) = Q(0) \Rightarrow a_n = b_n$,
$P'(0) = Q'(0) \Rightarrow a_{n-1} = b_{n-1}, \ldots, P^{(n)}(0) = Q^{(n)}(0) \Rightarrow a_0 = b_0$.

We deduce that if two polynomials are identically equal, then corresponding coefficients are equal. Problems involving such identities are solved by *comparing coefficients*, by substituting suitable values of x, or by a combination of these methods.

Example 4   Given that $x^2 - 3x + 7 \equiv a(x - 1)^2 + b(x - 1) + c$, find the values of a, b and c.

Comparing coefficients of x^2: $1 = a$ $\therefore \quad a = 1$
Putting $x = 1$: $1 - 3 + 7 = 0 + 0 + c$ $\therefore \quad c = 5$
Putting $x = 0$: $7 = a - b + c$ $\therefore \quad b = -1$
Hence $x^2 - 3x + 7 \equiv (x - 1)^2 - (x - 1) + 5$.

[Note that putting $x = 0$ is equivalent to comparing constant terms.]

Example 5   If $x^2 + 1$ is a factor of $3x^4 + x^3 - 4x^2 + px + q$, find the values of p and q.

Let $3x^4 + x^3 - 4x^2 + px + q \equiv (x^2 + 1)(ax^2 + bx + c)$.

Comparing coefficients of x^4: $3 = a$
$\qquad\qquad\qquad\qquad\quad x^3$: $1 = b$
$\qquad\qquad\qquad\qquad\quad x^2$: $-4 = a + c$
$\qquad\qquad\qquad\qquad\quad x$: $p = b$
Comparing constant terms: $q = c$
Hence $p = 1$ and $q = -7$.

Exercise 18.4

1.   Find the remainder when
(a) $x^3 - 4x^2 + 3x - 7$ is divided by $x - 4$,
(b) $x^4 + 2x^3 + 5x - 8$ is divided by $x + 3$,
(c) $2x^3 - 5x^2 + 3x + 1$ is divided by $2x + 1$,
(d) $x^3 - 2x^2 - 5$ is divided by $(x + 1)(x - 2)$,
(e) $x^4 + 3x^3 - 12x - 16$ is divided by $x^2 - 4$,
(f) $2x^4 - 3x^3 - 9x^2 - 7$ is divided by $x^2 - x - 6$.

2. When a polynomial $f(x)$ is divided by $(x - 2)$ the remainder is -2, and when it is divided by $(x - 3)$ the remainder is 3. Given that the remainder when $f(x)$ is divided by $(x - 2)(x - 3)$ is $px + q$, find the values of p and q.

3. When a polynomial is divided by $(x + 1)$ the remainder is 7, and when it is divided by $(x - 4)$ the remainder is -8. Find the remainder when the polynomial is divided by $(x + 1)(x - 4)$.

4. When the polynomial $x^3 + px^2 + qx + 7$ is divided by $x^2 - 3x + 2$, the remainder is $5x - 3$. Find the values of p and q.

5. When $P(x) = x^3 + ax^2 + bx + c$ is divided by $x^2 - 4$ the remainder is $2x + 11$. Given that $x + 1$ is a factor of $P(x)$, find the values of a, b and c.

6. Show, by putting $a = -b$, that $a + b$ is a factor of $(a + b + c)^3 - (a^3 + b^3 + c^3)$. Factorise the expression completely.

7. Show, by putting $x = y$, that $x - y$ is a factor of $(x - y)^3 + (y - z)^3 + (z - x)^3$. Factorise the expression completely.

8. Given that the polynomial $f(x) = 2x^3 - 3x^2 - 12x + k$ has a repeated linear factor, find the possible values of k and factorise $f(x)$ in each case.

9. Factorise the polynomial $3x^4 + 8x^3 + 16$ given that it has a repeated linear factor.

10. Find the values of a and b and factorise the polynomial

$$f(x) = x^3 + 4ax^2 + bx + 3a$$

given that it is divisible by $(x - 1)^2$.

11. Find the roots of the equation $x^3 - 6x^2 - 63x - 108 = 0$ given that it has a repeated root.

12. Given that $P(x) = 8x^3 - 12x^2 - 18x + k$, find the values of k such that the equation $P(x) = 0$ has a repeated root. Give the roots of the equation in each case.

13. The roots of the equation $2x^3 + 3x^2 + kx - 6 = 0$ are in arithmetic progression. By letting the roots be $\alpha - \lambda, \alpha, \alpha + \lambda$, or otherwise, find the value of k and solve the equation.

14. Given that the roots of the equation $3x^3 - 7x^2 + px + 24 = 0$ are in geometric progression, find the value of p and solve the equation.

15. If $ax^3 + 2x^2 + bx + 2b - c \equiv x^3 + 2x^2 + (c + 2)x + b + c$, find the values of a, b and c.

16. If $x^3 - 2x + 7 \equiv a(x - 1)^3 + b(x - 1)^2 + c(x - 1) + d$, find the values of a, b, c and d.

17. Find constants a, b, c and d such that

$$n^3 \equiv an(n + 1)(n + 2) + bn(n + 1) + cn + d.$$

18. Show that no constants a and b can be found such that

$$n^2 \equiv a(n + 1)^2 + b(n + 1).$$

19. Given that $x^4 - 6x^3 + 10x^2 + ax + b$ is a perfect square, find the values of a and b.

20. Given that $x^2 - x + 1$ is a factor of $2x^4 - 3x^3 + px^2 + qx - 3$, find the values of p and q.

21. If $f(x)$ and $g(x)$ are polynomials and $f(x) \equiv (x - a)^2 g(x) + Ax + B$, find $f'(x)$ and hence find A and B in terms of $f(a)$ and $f'(a)$. Deduce that $(x - a)$ is a repeated factor of $f(x)$ if and only if $f(a) = f'(a) = 0$.

   Find all real values of k for which the equation $x^3 - 3kx^2 + 2k + 2 = 0$ has repeated roots and, for each such k, solve the equation completely.   (O & C)

18.5 Graphs of rational functions

A rational function is a function of the form $P(x)/Q(x)$, where $P(x)$ and $Q(x)$ are polynomials. The graph of this function cuts the x-axis where $P(x) = 0$ and has asymptotes parallel to the y-axis where $Q(x) = 0$.

One of the simplest types of rational function takes the form $(ax + b)/(cx + d)$. In general, the graph of this function is a curve called a *rectangular hyperbola* with asymptotes parallel to the x- and y-axes.

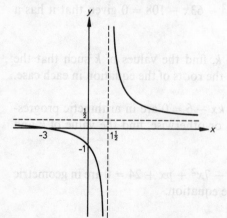

The diagram shows the graph of $y = (x + 3)/(2x - 3)$.

The curve cuts the axes at $(-3, 0)$ and $(0, -1)$.

As $x \to 1\frac{1}{2}$, $y \to \pm\infty$.

$$y = \frac{x + 3}{2x - 3} = \frac{1 + 3/x}{2 - 3/x}$$

$\therefore$ as $x \to \pm\infty$, $y \to \frac{1}{2}$.

Hence the lines $x = 1\frac{1}{2}$ and $y = \frac{1}{2}$ are asymptotes to the curve.

[If necessary, we can verify that such curves have no turning points by finding dy/dx.

In this case

$$\frac{dy}{dx} = \frac{(2x - 3)1 - (x + 3)2}{(2x - 3)^2} = -\frac{9}{(2x - 3)^2}.$$

Thus the gradient of the curve is always negative.]

Another important set of rational functions are defined by expressions of the form $y = (ax + b)/(px^2 + qx + r)$. When sketching the graphs of these functions it is helpful to find the range of values taken by y and also to note where changes in the sign of y occur.

We illustrate this approach by considering the graph of $y = 4x/(x^2 + 1)$.
The graph cuts the axes only at the origin $(0, 0)$.
Since $(x^2 + 1)$ is always positive, there can be no asymptotes parallel to the y-axis and the sign of y will always be the same as the sign of x.
As $x \to \infty$, $y \to 0$ from above and as $x \to -\infty$, $y \to 0$ from below,
$\therefore$ the x-axis is an asymptote to the curve.
To find the range of the function $y = 4x/(x^2 + 1)$, we rearrange the equation as a quadratic equation in x:

$$y(x^2 + 1) = 4x \quad \text{i.e.} \quad yx^2 - 4x + y = 0.$$

Since we are concerned only with values of y given by real values of x, the range of values taken by y is the set of values for which this quadratic equation has real roots. The equation $ax^2 + bx + c = 0$ has real roots if $b^2 - 4ac \geqslant 0$,
$\therefore$ for real values of x, $\quad (-4)^2 - 4y \cdot y \geqslant 0$
$$16 - 4y^2 \geqslant 0$$
$$y^2 \leqslant 4$$

i.e. for real values of x, $\quad -2 \leqslant y \leqslant 2$.

Thus all points of the graph lie on or between the lines $y = \pm 2$.

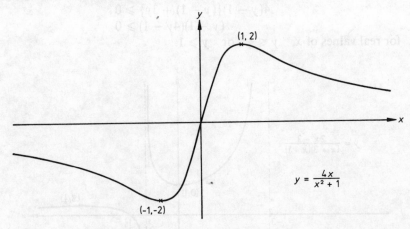

When $y = -2$ and when $y = 2$ the quadratic equation in x has equal roots, $x = -1$ and $x = 1$ respectively. Hence the line $y = -2$ is a tangent to the curve at the point $(-1, -2)$ and the line $y = 2$ is a tangent to the curve at the point $(1, 2)$. It follows that $(-1, -2)$ must be a minimum point on the curve and $(1, 2)$ a maximum point.

For every non-zero value of y in the interval $-2 < y < 2$ the quadratic equation in x has two distinct real roots. Hence there are no other turning points on the curve. [Note that a graph of similar form will be obtained for any function $(ax + b)/(px^2 + qx + r)$ if the denominator $(px^2 + qx + r)$ is never zero.]

Example 1   Sketch the curve $y = \dfrac{2x - 3}{x^2 + 2x - 3}$.

$x = 0 \Rightarrow y = 1$ $\therefore$ the curve cuts the y-axis at the point $(0; 1)$.

$y = 0 \Leftrightarrow 2x - 3 = 0 \Leftrightarrow x = 1\frac{1}{2}$

$\therefore$ the curve cuts the x-axis at the point $(1\frac{1}{2}, 0)$.

$x^2 + 2x - 3 = 0 \Leftrightarrow (x + 3)(x - 1) = 0 \Leftrightarrow x = -3$ or $x = 1$

$\therefore$ the lines $x = -3$ and $x = 1$ are asymptotes to the curve.

As $x \to \pm\infty, y \to 0$ $\therefore$ the x-axis is an asymptote to the curve.

The following table shows the changes in the sign of y.

	$x < -3$	$-3 < x < 1$	$1 < x < 1\frac{1}{2}$	$x > 1\frac{1}{2}$
$x + 3$	$-$	$+$	$+$	$+$
$x - 1$	$-$	$-$	$+$	$+$
$2x - 3$	$-$	$-$	$-$	$+$
y	$-$	$+$	$-$	$+$

Rearranging the equation as a quadratic in x:

$$y(x^2 + 2x - 3) = 2x - 3 \quad \text{i.e.} \quad yx^2 + (2y - 2)x - 3y + 3 = 0$$

$\therefore$ for real values of x, $(2y - 2)^2 - 4y(-3y + 3) \geqslant 0$

$$4(y - 1)^2 + 12y(y - 1) \geqslant 0$$

$$4(y - 1)\{(y - 1) + 3y\} \geqslant 0$$

$$(y - 1)(4y - 1) \geqslant 0$$

$\therefore$ for real values of x, $y \leqslant \frac{1}{4}$ or $y \geqslant 1$.

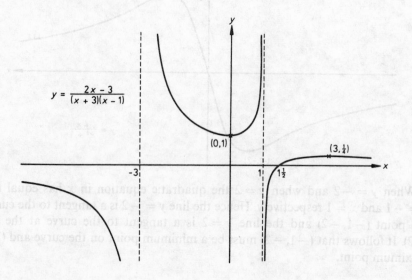

$$y = \frac{2x - 3}{(x + 3)(x - 1)}$$

$(0, 1)$

$(3, \frac{1}{4})$

Hence there are no points on the curve between the lines $y = \frac{1}{4}$ and $y = 1$.
There is a stationary point on the curve whenever the quadratic equation in x has
repeated roots, i.e. when $y = \frac{1}{4}$, $x = 3$ and when $y = 1$, $x = 0$. Since y cannot take
values between $\frac{1}{4}$ and 1, $(3, \frac{1}{4})$ is a maximum point and $(0, 1)$ a minimum point.

There is one other form that the graph of $y = (ax + b)/(px^2 + qx + r)$ can take.
Consider, for example, the curve $y = x/(x + 2)(x - 1)$.
This curve cuts the axes only at the origin $(0, 0)$.
The asymptotes to the curve are the lines $x = -2$, $x = 1$ and the x-axis.
Rearranging the equation as a quadratic in x:

$$y(x^2 + x - 2) = x \quad \text{i.e.} \quad yx^2 + (y - 1)x - 2y = 0.$$

The nature of the roots of this quadratic equation depends on the sign of
the expression

$$(y - 1)^2 - 4y(-2y) \quad \text{i.e.} \quad (y - 1)^2 + 8y^2.$$

Since this expression is always positive, the equation must have two real distinct roots for all non-zero values of y. Hence there are no stationary points on the
curve and no restrictions on the values of y.
  Again it is useful to determine the sign of y throughout the domain of the function.

	$x < -2$	$-2 < x < 0$	$0 < x < 1$	$x > 1$
$x + 2$	$-$	$+$	$+$	$+$
x	$-$	$-$	$+$	$+$
$x - 1$	$-$	$-$	$-$	$+$
y	$-$	$+$	$-$	$+$

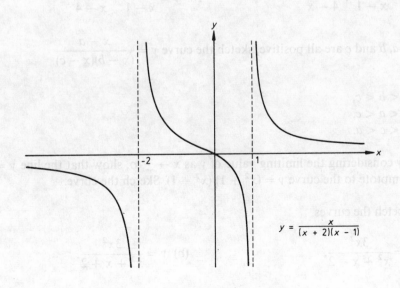

$$y = \frac{x}{(x + 2)(x - 1)}$$

[These methods can be extended to functions of the form $P(x)/Q(x)$ where both $P(x)$ and $Q(x)$ are quadratic functions.]

Exercise 18.5

In questions 1 to 6 sketch the given curve.

1. $y = \dfrac{1}{x - 1}$

2. $y = \dfrac{x}{x - 1}$

3. $y = \dfrac{x - 1}{x}$

4. $y = \dfrac{3 - x}{2 + x}$

5. $y = \dfrac{2x + 1}{x - 2}$

6. $y = \dfrac{x}{3x + 4}$

In questions 7 to 16 find the range of possible values of y. Sketch each curve showing clearly any asymptotes and turning points.

7. $y = \dfrac{5x - 25}{x^2 + 3x - 4}$

8. $y = \dfrac{2x + 1}{x^2 + 2}$

9. $y = \dfrac{x + 1}{x(x + 3)}$

10. $y = \dfrac{x - 1}{x(x + 3)}$

11. $y = \dfrac{2 - 3x}{x^2 - 3x + 2}$

12. $y = \dfrac{15 - 10x}{4 + x^2}$

13. $y = \dfrac{1 - x}{1 - x + x^2}$

14. $y = \dfrac{x + 6}{x^2 + 7x + 10}$

15. $y = \dfrac{1}{x - 1} + \dfrac{1}{4 - x}$

16. $y = \dfrac{1}{x - 1} + \dfrac{1}{x - 4}$

17. If a, b and c are all positive, sketch the curve $y = \dfrac{x - a}{(x - b)(x - c)}$

when

(i) $a < b < c$,
(ii) $b < a < c$,
(iii) $b < c < a$.

18. By considering the limiting value of y as $x \to \pm \infty$, show that the line $y = 1$ is an asymptote to the curve $y = (x^2 + 1)/(x^2 - 1)$. Sketch the curve.

19. Sketch the curves

(a) $y = \dfrac{3x^2}{x^2 + x - 2}$,

(b) $y = \dfrac{3x^2}{x^2 + x + 2}$.

20. Sketch the curve $y = \dfrac{x^2 - 3x + 4}{x - 3}$ showing clearly any asymptotes and turning points.

18.6 Partial fractions

A sum of two fractions can be expressed as a single fraction by a method such as the following:

$$\frac{3}{3x - 2} - \frac{x}{x^2 + 1} \equiv \frac{3(x^2 + 1) - x(3x - 2)}{(3x - 2)(x^2 + 1)} \equiv \frac{2x + 3}{(3x - 2)(x^2 + 1)}.$$

In this section we consider the reverse process by which a rational function is expressed as a sum of two or more simpler fractions called *partial fractions*.

We will deal first with *proper fractions* i.e. fractions in which the degree of the numerator is less than the degree of the denominator. The methods used in the examples which follow are based on the assumption that a proper fraction can be expressed as a sum of partial fractions which are also proper, such as

$$\frac{A}{x - a}, \quad \frac{Ax + B}{ax^2 + bx + c}.$$

[A rigorous proof of this statement is beyond the scope of this course.]

Example 1 Express $\dfrac{2x - 5}{(x + 2)(x - 1)}$ in partial fractions.

Let $$\frac{2x - 5}{(x + 2)(x - 1)} \equiv \frac{A}{x + 2} + \frac{B}{x - 1}$$

then, multiplying both sides of the identity by $(x + 2)(x - 1)$,

$$2x - 5 \equiv A(x - 1) + B(x + 2)$$

Putting $x = 1$: $\qquad\qquad 2 - 5 = 3B \qquad\qquad \therefore \quad B = -1$
Putting $x = -2$: $\qquad -4 - 5 = -3A \qquad\qquad \therefore \quad A = 3$

$$\therefore \quad \frac{2x - 5}{(x + 2)(x - 1)} \equiv \frac{3}{x + 2} - \frac{1}{x - 1}.$$

Example 2 Express $\dfrac{x + 1}{2x^3 - 5x^2 + 2x}$ in partial fractions.

$$2x^3 - 5x^2 + 2x \equiv x(2x^2 - 5x + 2) \equiv x(x - 2)(2x - 1)$$

$\therefore$ let $$\frac{x + 1}{2x^3 - 5x^2 + 2x} \equiv \frac{A}{x} + \frac{B}{x - 2} + \frac{C}{2x - 1}$$

then $$x + 1 \equiv A(x - 2)(2x - 1) + Bx(2x - 1) + Cx(x - 2)$$

Putting $x = 0$: $1 = 2A$ $\qquad$ $\therefore$ $A = \frac{1}{2}$

Putting $x = 2$: $3 = 6B$ $\qquad$ $\therefore$ $B = \frac{1}{2}$

Putting $x = \frac{1}{2}$: $\frac{3}{2} = C \times \frac{1}{2} \times (-\frac{3}{2})$ $\qquad$ $\therefore$ $C = -2$

$\therefore$ $\dfrac{x + 1}{2x^3 - 5x^2 + 2x} \equiv \dfrac{1}{2x} + \dfrac{1}{2(x - 2)} - \dfrac{2}{2x - 1}$.

So far we have determined unknown constants by substituting suitable values of x. In examples involving quadratic factors some constants can be obtained more quickly by comparing coefficients of powers of x.

Example 3 Express $\dfrac{4x^2}{(x - 3)(x^2 + 3)}$ in partial fractions.

Let $\qquad \dfrac{4x^2}{(x - 3)(x^2 + 3)} \equiv \dfrac{A}{x - 3} + \dfrac{Bx + C}{x^2 + 3}$

then $\qquad 4x^2 \equiv A(x^2 + 3) + (Bx + C)(x - 3)$

Putting $x = 3$: $\qquad 36 = 12A$ $\qquad$ $\therefore$ $A = 3$

Putting $x = 0$: $\qquad 0 = 3A - 3C$ $\qquad$ $\therefore$ $C = 3$

Comparing coefficients of x^2:

$$4 = A + B \qquad\qquad \therefore \quad B = 1$$

$\therefore$ $\dfrac{4x^2}{(x - 3)(x^2 + 3)} \equiv \dfrac{3}{x - 3} + \dfrac{x + 3}{x^2 + 3}$

In the next example we consider a fraction with the repeated factor $(x + 1)^2$ in the denominator. Using the "proper fraction" rule, there will be a corresponding partial fraction of the form $(Ax + K)/(x + 1)^2$. However, we obtained simpler partial fractions by writing $K = A + B$:

$$\frac{Ax + K}{(x + 1)^2} \equiv \frac{Ax + A + B}{(x + 1)^2} \equiv \frac{A(x + 1) + B}{(x + 1)^2} \equiv \frac{A}{x + 1} + \frac{B}{(x + 1)^2}.$$

Example 4 Express $\dfrac{x - 5}{(x + 1)^2(x - 1)}$ in partial fractions.

Let $\qquad \dfrac{x - 5}{(x + 1)^2(x - 1)} \equiv \dfrac{A}{x + 1} + \dfrac{B}{(x + 1)^2} + \dfrac{C}{x - 1}$

then $\qquad x - 5 \equiv A(x + 1)(x - 1) + B(x - 1) + C(x + 1)^2$

Putting $x = 1$: $\qquad -4 = 4C$ $\qquad$ $\therefore$ $C = -1$

Putting $x = -1$: $\qquad -6 = -2B$ $\qquad$ $\therefore$ $B = 3$

Comparing coefficients of x^2:

$$0 = A + C \qquad\qquad \therefore \quad A = 1$$

$\therefore$ $\dfrac{x - 5}{(x + 1)^2(x - 1)} \equiv \dfrac{1}{x + 1} + \dfrac{3}{(x + 1)^2} - \dfrac{1}{x - 1}$

A fraction in which the degrees of the numerator and denominator are equal can be expressed as the sum of a constant and a proper fraction,

e.g.
$$\frac{x^2 + 1}{x^2 - 1} \equiv 1 + \frac{2}{x^2 - 1}.$$

We use this fact in the next example.

Example 5   Express $\dfrac{x^2 + 2}{(x - 1)(2x + 1)}$ in partial fractions.

Let
$$\frac{x^2 + 2}{(x - 1)(2x + 1)} \equiv A + \frac{B}{x - 1} + \frac{C}{2x + 1}$$

then $x^2 + 2 \equiv A(x - 1)(2x + 1) + B(2x + 1) + C(x - 1)$

Putting $x = 1$: $3 = 3B$ $\therefore \quad B = 1$

Putting $x = -\frac{1}{2}$: $\frac{9}{4} = -\frac{3}{2}C$ $\therefore \quad C = -\frac{3}{2}$

Comparing coefficients of x^2:

$$1 = 2A \qquad\qquad\qquad \therefore \quad A = \tfrac{1}{2}$$

$$\therefore \quad \frac{x^2 + 2}{(x - 1)(2x + 1)} \equiv \frac{1}{2} + \frac{1}{x - 1} - \frac{3}{2(2x + 1)}.$$

When dealing with fractions in which the degree of the numerator is greater than the degree of the denominator, we may either use long division to express the fraction as the sum of a polynomial and a proper fraction or extend the method of Example 5. If the degree of the numerator exceeds that of the denominator by n, then the expression in partial fractions must include a polynomial of degree n.

Example 6   Express $\dfrac{x^3 - 3x^2 + 1}{x^2 - x - 2}$ in partial fractions.

Method 1

$$
\begin{array}{r}
x - 2 \\
x^2 - x - 2 \overline{\smash{)}\, x^3 - 3x^2 + 1} \\
\underline{x^3 - x^2 - 2x} \\
-2x^2 + 2x + 1 \\
\underline{-2x^2 + 2x + 4} \\
- 3
\end{array}
$$

$$\therefore \quad \frac{x^3 - 3x^2 + 1}{x^2 - x - 2} \equiv x - 2 - \frac{3}{x^2 - x - 2}$$

Let
$$\frac{-3}{x^2 - x - 2} \equiv \frac{A}{x + 1} + \frac{B}{x - 2}$$

then $-3 \equiv A(x - 2) + B(x + 1)$

Putting $x = -1$: $-3 = -3A$ $\therefore \quad A = 1$

Putting $x = 2$: $-3 = 3B$ $\therefore \quad B = -1$

$$\therefore \qquad \frac{x^3 - 3x^2 + 1}{x^2 - x - 2} \equiv x - 2 + \frac{1}{x + 1} - \frac{1}{x - 2}$$

Method 2

Let $\dfrac{x^3 - 3x^2 + 1}{x^2 - x - 2} \equiv Ax + B + \dfrac{C}{x + 1} + \dfrac{D}{x - 2}$

then $x^3 - 3x^2 + 1 \equiv (Ax + B)(x + 1)(x - 2)$
$$+ C(x - 2) + D(x + 1)$$

Putting $x = -1$: $-3 = -3C$ $\therefore \quad C = 1$

Putting $x = 2$: $-3 = 3D$ $\therefore \quad D = -1$

Putting $x = 0$: $1 = -2B - 2C + D$ $\therefore \quad B = -2$

Comparing coefficients of x^3:

$$1 = A$$

$$\therefore \qquad \frac{x^3 - 3x^2 + 1}{x^2 - x - 2} \equiv x - 2 + \frac{1}{x + 1} - \frac{1}{x - 2}.$$

We now summarise the rules for expressing a rational function in partial fractions.

(1) To a linear factor $(x - a)$ in the denominator, there corresponds a fraction of the form $A/(x - a)$.

(2) To a quadratic factor $(ax^2 + bx + c)$, there corresponds a fraction of the form $(Ax + B)/(ax^2 + bx + c)$.

(3) To a repeated factor $(x - a)^n$, there correspond n fractions of the form $A_1/(x - a), A_2/(x - a)^2, \ldots, A_n/(x - a)^n$.

(4) To a repeated factor $(ax^2 + bx + c)^n$, there correspond n fractions

$$\frac{A_1 x + B_1}{(ax^2 + bx + c)}, \frac{A_2 x + B_2}{(ax^2 + bx + c)^2}, \ldots, \frac{A_n x + B_n}{(ax^2 + bx + c)^n}.$$

[Note that there are many ways of expressing a rational function as a sum of two or more fractions e.g. $\dfrac{1}{(x + 1)(x + 2)} \equiv \dfrac{x + 1}{x + 2} - \dfrac{x}{x + 1} \equiv \dfrac{x^2}{x + 1} - \dfrac{x^2 + x - 1}{x + 2}.$

However, the simplest and most useful form is the expression in partial fractions according to rules (1) to (4) above.]

Exercise 18.6

Express in partial fractions

1. $\dfrac{1}{(x + 1)(x + 2)}$

2. $\dfrac{4 - x}{(x - 1)(x + 2)}$

3. $\dfrac{3x - 10}{(x - 2)(x - 4)}$

4. $\dfrac{4x - 9}{x(x - 3)}$

5. $\dfrac{x + 7}{(x - 2)(x + 1)}$

6. $\dfrac{5x + 3}{(x + 1)(2x + 1)}$

7. $\dfrac{x}{x^2 - 1}$

8. $\dfrac{5}{6 - x - x^2}$

9. $\dfrac{10x - 1}{(2x + 1)(4x - 1)}$

10. $\dfrac{4 - 2x}{(2x - 1)(2x + 5)}$

11. $\dfrac{17x + 11}{(x - 2)(x + 3)(x + 1)}$

12. $\dfrac{5x^2 - 12x - 5}{(x^2 - 1)(x - 2)}$

13. $\dfrac{3x + 1}{(x + 1)(x^2 + 1)}$

14. $\dfrac{x + 2}{(2x - 1)(x^2 + 1)}$

15. $\dfrac{3x + 1}{x(2x^2 + 1)}$

16. $\dfrac{x^2 - 10}{(x^2 + 3)(2x - 1)}$

17. $\dfrac{x^2 - 13}{(x - 1)^2(x + 2)}$

18. $\dfrac{3x^2 + 7x + 1}{x^3 + 2x^2 + x}$

19. $\dfrac{2x^2 - 3x - 2}{x^3 - x^2}$

20. $\dfrac{x^2 + 23}{(x + 1)^3(x - 2)}$

21. $\dfrac{2x^2 - 5x - 5}{(2x^2 + 5)(4x - 5)}$

22. $\dfrac{x + 2}{(x - 2)(x^2 - x + 2)}$

23. $\dfrac{x^2 + 1}{x^2 - 1}$

24. $\dfrac{x^2}{x^2 - x - 2}$

25. $\dfrac{x(x - 2)}{(3x - 1)(x - 1)}$

26. $\dfrac{x^3}{x^2 - 4}$

27. $\dfrac{x^2 - x}{(x^2 + 3)(x^2 + 2)}$

28. $\dfrac{3x^3 + 2x^2 + 2x - 3}{(x^2 + 2)(x + 1)^2}$

29. $\dfrac{2x^4 - 2x^3 + x}{(2x - 1)^2(x - 2)}$

30. $\dfrac{x^6 - x^5 - 4x^2 + x}{x^4 + 3x^2 + 2}$

31. Express $f(x) = \dfrac{4x + 5}{(x + 1)(2x + 3)}$ in partial fractions. Hence find $f'(x)$ and $f''(x)$.

32. Find the coordinates of the points of inflexion on the curves

(a) $y = \dfrac{2x}{1 - x^2}$,

(b) $y = \dfrac{7(x + 1)}{x(x - 7)}$.

Exercise 18.7 (miscellaneous)

1.   The functions f, g, h and k are defined by

$$f : x \rightarrow \sin^2 3x, \quad x \in \mathbb{R},$$
$$g : x \rightarrow 1/(1 - x), \quad x \in \mathbb{R}, \, x \neq 1,$$
$$h : x \rightarrow \sqrt{(1 - x^2)}, \, x \in \mathbb{R}, \, |x| \leqslant 1,$$
$$k : x \rightarrow \operatorname{cosec} \tfrac{1}{2} x, \quad x \in \mathbb{R}, \, x \neq 2n\pi (n \in \mathbb{Z}).$$

For each function, state whether it is even, odd or neither. State also whether or not it is periodic, giving the period where appropriate.

2.   Sketch the graphs of the following functions. State any values of x at which
(a) there is a discontinuity,
(b) the function is not differentiable.

$$f(x) = |x - 2|, \qquad g(x) = [\tfrac{1}{2} x],$$
$$h(x) = 1/(x^2 - x - 2), \quad k(x) = |x^4 - x^3|.$$

3.   The functions f and g are defined by $f : x \rightarrow \sin 2x, x \in \mathbb{R}$, $g : x \rightarrow \cot x$, $x \in \mathbb{R}$, $x \neq k\pi (k \in \mathbb{Z})$. State the periods of f and g. Find the period of the function $f.g$. On separate axes, sketch the graph of f, g and $f.g$ for the interval $\{x : -\pi < x < \pi, x \neq 0\}$. Find the range of the function $f.g$.   (JMB)

4.   Determine whether each of the three functions, f, g, h defined in $\mathbb{R}$ is an even function, an odd function or neither, given that $f(x) = \pi/2 - \sin(x/2)$, $g(x) = \pi/2 - \cos(x/3)$, $h(x) = \cos(\sin x)$. Determine the period, if it exists, of each of the two functions $G(x) = g(x) - f(x)$, $H(x) = g(x) - h(x) + \sin[f(2x)]$.   (L)

5.   Find the ranges of the given functions f, g, h and k. State whether f^{-1}, g^{-1}, h^{-1}, k^{-1} exist, giving brief reasons for each answer.

$$f : x \rightarrow x^2 + 4, \qquad x \in \mathbb{R}, \, 0 \leqslant x \leqslant 4;$$
$$g : x \rightarrow x^2 - 4x, \qquad x \in \mathbb{R}, \, 0 \leqslant x \leqslant 4;$$
$$h : x \rightarrow 3 \cos x + 4 \sin x, \quad x \in \mathbb{R};$$
$$k : x \rightarrow 1 - \lg(x + 1), \qquad x \in \mathbb{R}, \, x \geqslant 0.$$

6.   Sketch the graph of the function f defined by $f(x) = 4x/(1 + x^2)$, x real. Let g denote the function f restricted to the domain $[-a, a]$, so that $g(x) = 4x/(1 + x^2)$, $-a \leqslant x \leqslant a$, where a is the largest positive number such that the function g is one-one. What is the value of a? Obtain an expression for the inverse function g^{-1}, and state the domain and range of g^{-1}.   (W)

7.   The function ϕ is defined by $\phi(x) = x^3 + 2x - 1$, and the inverse function ϕ^{-1} is denoted by ψ. Find the values of $\psi(2)$ and $\psi'(2)$.   (W)

8. The domain of the function f is the set $D = \{x : x \in \mathbb{R}, -2 < x < 3\}$. The function $f : D \rightarrow \mathbb{R}$ is defined by

$$f(x) = \begin{cases} 2x - 1 & \text{for} & -2 < x \leqslant 1, \\ x^2 & \text{for} & 1 < x \leqslant 2, \\ 10 - 3x & \text{for} & 2 < x < 3. \end{cases}$$

Find the range of this function and sketch its graph. Explain why there is no inverse function to f. Suggest an interval such that f, restricted to this interval, will have an inverse function. Give an expression for the inverse function in this case.   (L)

9.   Explain what is meant by the statement "f is a function from a set A to a set B." A function $f : \mathbb{R} \rightarrow \mathbb{R}$ is defined by

$$\begin{cases} f(x) = \sin 2x, & 0 \leqslant x \leqslant \pi/4, \\ f(x) = 2 - 4x/\pi, & \pi/4 < x \leqslant \pi/2, \\ f \text{ is an odd function, } f \text{ is periodic with period } \pi. \end{cases}$$

Sketch the graph of $y = f(x)$ for $-\pi \leqslant x \leqslant \pi$. Find two different intervals, each of length $\pi/2$, such that f, restricted to either interval, will have an inverse. In each case, give an expression for the inverse function.   (L)

10. (i) f_1 is a periodic odd function with a period 2π and f_2 is a periodic even function with a period 3π. Functions F and G are defined by $F(x) = f_2(x) \cdot f_1(x), G(x) = f_2[f_1(x)]$. State whether the functions F and G are
   (a) odd, even or neither,
   (b) periodic, and if periodic state a period.
   Functions f_3 and f_4 are defined by $f_3(x) = x \cos x, f_4(x) = \cos(\sin 3x)$. State whether f_3 and f_4 are odd, even or neither and if periodic state a period.
   (ii) A mapping $f : A \rightarrow \mathbb{R}$, where $A = \{x : x \in \mathbb{R} \text{ and } -\pi/4 \leqslant x \leqslant \pi/4\}$, is defined by $f(x) = \cos x + \sin x$. Find $f^{-1}(1)$.   (L)

11. A function f is defined on $\mathbb{R}$ by $f : x \rightarrow |x + [x]|$ where $[x]$ indicates the greatest integer less than or equal to x, e.g. $[3] = 3, [2\cdot4] = 2, [-3\cdot6] = -4$. Sketch the graph of the function for $-3 \leqslant x \leqslant 3$. What is the range of f? Is the mapping one-one?
The function g is defined by $g : x \rightarrow |x + [x]|, x \in \mathbb{R}^+, x \notin \mathbb{Z}^+$. Find the rule and domain of the inverse function g^{-1}.   (C)

12. Sketch the curve $y = |x^2 - 5x|$. Find the ranges of values of x for which $|x^2 - 5x| < 6$.

13. Sketch the curves $y = x^2(3 - x)$ and $y^2 = x^2(3 - x)$, showing clearly the behaviour of the curves near the x-axis.

14. Using a sketch graph, or otherwise, solve the inequality $\left|\dfrac{1}{1 + 2x}\right| < 1$.

15. Prove that the curves $y = \dfrac{x}{x + 1}$ and $y = \left(\dfrac{x}{x + 1}\right)^2$ intersect at only one point.

Sketch these curves in the same diagram. Label your sketch so that it is immediately clear which curve is which.   (O&C)

16. Given that $f(x) \equiv 6x^2 + x - 12$, find the minimum value of $f(x)$ and the values of x for which $f(x) = 0$. Using the same axes, sketch the curves $y = f(x)$ and $y = 1/f(x)$, labelling each clearly. Deduce that there are four values of x for which $[f(x)]^2 = 1$. Find these values, each to two decimal places.   (L)

17. The polynomial $P(x)$ leaves a remainder of 2 when divided by $(x - 1)$ and a remainder of 3 when divided by $(x - 2)$. The remainder when $P(x)$ is divided by $(x - 1)(x - 2)$ is $ax + b$. By writing $P(x) \equiv (x - 1)(x - 2)Q(x) + ax + b$, find the values of a and b. Given also that $P(x)$ is a cubic polynomial with coefficient of x^3 equal to unity, and that -1 is a root of the equation $P(x) = 0$, obtain $P(x)$. Show that the equation $P(x) = 0$ has no other real roots.   (JMB)

18. Find the remainder when the polynomial $P(x) = x^3 - 5x + 2$ is divided by
(a) $x^2 + 1$,
(b) $(x - 1)^2$.

19. Using the remainder theorem, or otherwise, show that $x + a + b + c$ is a factor of

$$(x + a)(x + b)(x + c) + (b + c)(c + a)(a + b).$$

Hence, or otherwise, solve the equation

$$(x + 2)(x - 3)(x - 1) + 4 = 0. \qquad \text{(C)}$$

20. Factorise completely the expressions
(a) $x(y^3 - z^3) + y(z^3 - x^3) + z(x^3 - y^3)$,
(b) $12abc + 4(a^3 + b^3 + c^3) - (a + b + c)^3$.

21. If $f(x)$ is a polynomial in x, show that when $f(x)$ is divided by $x - a$ the remainder is $f(a)$.
When $x^3 + ax^2 + bx + c$ is divided by $x + 3$ the remainder is -26 and when divided by $x^2 - x - 2$ the remainder is 14. Find the values of a, b and c.
                                                                    (AEB 1978)

22. Show that if a polynomial $f(x)$ is divided by $(x - a)(x - b)$, where $a \neq b$, then the remainder is $\left\{\dfrac{f(a) - f(b)}{a - b}\right\}x + \left\{\dfrac{af(b) - bf(a)}{a - b}\right\}$.

23. Solve the equation $x^4 - 4x^3 - 20x^2 + 32 = 0$ given that it has a repeated root.

24. Given that the polynomial $f(x) = x^4 - 8x^3 + 10x^2 + p$ has a repeated linear factor, find the possible values of p.

25. The equation $x^3 - px^2 + qx - r = 0$ is such that its roots are in geometric progression. Show that
(a) one root is $\sqrt[3]{r}$,
(b) $p^3 r = q^3$.

26. If the expression $2x^2 - xy - y^2 + 2x + ky - 4$ is the product of two linear factors, find the possible values of k.

27. (i) Given that $x + 1$ is a factor of $x^3 + 2x^2 + 3x + c$, find c.

(ii) In the algebraic operation of polynomial division, one polynomial $f(x)$ is divided by another polynomial $g(x)$ of order equal to or lower than that of $f(x)$. Polynomials $Q(x)$ and $R(x)$ are found such that $f(x) = g(x)Q(x) + R(x)$ and $R(x)$ is of lower order than $g(x)$. Carry out the process described in the flow chart when $A(x) = x^3 + 2x^2 + 3x + 2$ and $B(x) = x^2 - x - 2$.

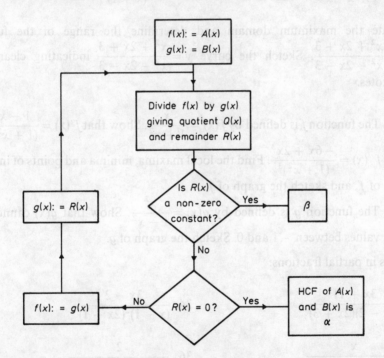

State what should be written in the spaces α and β for the flow chart to be applicable to any two polynomials of suitable degree.   (AEB 1980)

28. By considering the equation $yx^2 + (y - 1)x + (y - 1) = 0$, where $y \neq 0$, as a quadratic equation in x, find the range of values of y for which this equation has real roots. State the value of x which satisfies this equation when $y = 0$. Using these results, or otherwise, determine the range of the function $f : x \to \dfrac{x + 1}{x^2 + x + 1}$, where x is real. Sketch the graph of $f(x)$ giving the coordinates of any turning points. Explain why f has no inverse function.   (JMB)

29. In each of the following cases find the range of the function f. Sketch the graph of f, showing clearly any asymptotes and turning points.

(a) $f(x) = \dfrac{x-1}{2x+1}$,

(b) $f(x) = \dfrac{4}{(1-x)(3+x)}$,

(c) $f(x) = \dfrac{3(x+1)}{x(x-3)}$,

(d) $f(x) = \dfrac{2x-1}{x^2-4}$.

30. Sketch each of the following curves, showing any stationary points and indicating clearly the form of the curve when $|x|$ becomes large.

(a) $y = x - \dfrac{1}{x+1}$,

(b) $y = \dfrac{x^2}{x-1}$,

(c) $y = \dfrac{x^2}{1+x^2}$,

(d) $y = \dfrac{x-1}{(x+1)^2}$.

31. State the maximum domain and determine the range of the function $f(x) = \dfrac{x^2+2x+3}{x^2-2x-3}$. Sketch the curve $y = \dfrac{x^2+2x+3}{x^2-2x-3}$ indicating clearly any asymptotes. (O)

32. (a) The function f is defined by $f(x) = \dfrac{x}{1+x^2}$. Show that $f'(x) = \dfrac{1-x^2}{(1+x^2)^2}$ and $f''(x) = \dfrac{-6x+2x^3}{(1+x^2)^3}$. Find the local maxima, minima and points of inflexion of f, and sketch the graph of f.

(b) The function g is defined by $g(x) = \dfrac{x^2}{1-x^2}$. Show that $g(x)$ cannot take values between -1 and 0. Sketch the graph of g. (W)

Express in partial fractions:

33. $\dfrac{3x+11}{(3x-2)(2x+3)}$

34. $\dfrac{3x-2}{(x-1)^2(2x-1)}$

35. $\dfrac{x}{x^3-x^2+x-1}$

36. $\dfrac{2}{x^3-2x^2-x+2}$

37. $\dfrac{5+x^2}{3+5x-2x^2}$

38. $\dfrac{3x}{1-x^3}$

39. $\dfrac{x(x+1)(x-2)}{(x-1)(x+2)}$

40. $\dfrac{7x^2-2x+3}{(x^2-1)^2}$

19 Exponential and logarithmic functions

19.1 Exponential functions

Exponent is another word for index. A function such as 2^x, in which the index is variable, is called *an exponential function.*

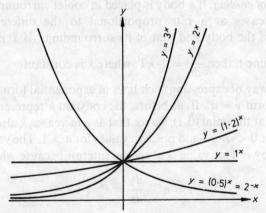

The diagram shows the graphs of $y = a^x$ for various positive values of a. We see that each graph lies entirely above the x-axis and cuts the y-axis at the point $(0, 1)$. We now consider how to differentiate the function a^x.

Let
$$f(x) = a^x, \quad \text{then} \quad f(x + h) = a^{x+h}$$

$$\therefore \quad f(x + h) - f(x) = a^{x+h} - a^x = a^x(a^h - 1)$$

$$\therefore \quad f'(x) = \lim_{h \to 0} \frac{f(x + h) - f(x)}{h}$$

$$= \lim_{h \to 0} \frac{a^x(a^h - 1)}{h} = a^x \lim_{h \to 0} \left(\frac{a^h - 1}{h} \right).$$

In particular, $f'(0) = a^0 \lim_{h \to 0} \left(\frac{a^h - 1}{h} \right) = \lim_{h \to 0} \left(\frac{a^h - 1}{h} \right)$. Since $f'(0)$ is the gradient of the curve $y = a^x$ at the point $(0, 1)$, it seems reasonable to assume that this limit exists and is equal to some constant k.

Thus, if $f(x) = a^x$, then $f'(x) = ka^x$, where the value of k depends on the value of a.

It follows that if $y = a^x$, then $\dfrac{dy}{dx} = ky$, i.e. the rate of change of y is proportional to y.

Because of this property the theory of exponential functions has many important applications. There are various scientific laws which state that the rate of change of a certain quantity is proportional to the quantity itself. We give here three simple examples of such laws.

(1) *Law of growth.* If a population of simple organisms such as bacteria is allowed to increase without restriction, then the rate of growth is proportional to the size of the population. If n is the number of organisms present at time t, then $\dfrac{dn}{dt} = kn$, where k is constant.

(2) *Law of radio-active decay.* The rate at which a radio-active substance decays is proportional to the quantity of the substance present. If a mass m is present at time t, then $\dfrac{dm}{dt} = -km$, where k is constant.

(3) *Newton's law of cooling.* If a body is placed in cooler surroundings then its temperature decreases at a rate proportional to the difference between the temperature of the body and that of its surroundings. If T is the temperature difference at time t, then $\dfrac{dT}{dt} = -kT$, where k is constant.

We arrive at a way of expressing such laws in exponential form by looking again at graphs of the form $y = a^x$. If, as before, the constant k represents the gradient of a particular curve at the point $(0, 1)$, we see that as a increases, k also increases, taking negative values for $0 < a < 1$ and positive values for $a > 1$. The value of a for which $k = 1$ is denoted by e. This value is of special interest because when

$$y = e^x, \quad \frac{dy}{dx} = e^x = y.$$

It can be shown that e is an irrational number approximately equal to $2 \cdot 718$.

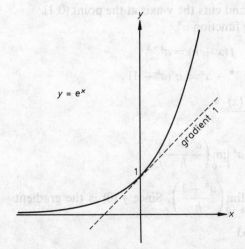

$y = e^x$

gradient 1

The function e^x is called *the exponential function* and is sometimes written exp x. [In numerical work values of e^x are found using a scientific calculator or mathematical tables.]

The result $\dfrac{d}{dx}(e^x) = e^x$ can be extended as follows.

Let $$y = e^u, \quad \text{where} \quad u = kx \ .$$

then $$\frac{dy}{du} = e^u \quad \text{and} \quad \frac{du}{dx} = k$$

$$\frac{dy}{dx} = \frac{dy}{du} \times \frac{du}{dx} = ke^u.$$

Hence, if $y = e^{kx}$, then $\dfrac{dy}{dx} = ke^{kx} = ky.$

It is now possible to express the scientific laws mentioned earlier in exponential form:

(1) $n = n_0 e^{kt}$,   (2) $m = m_0 e^{-kt}$,   (3) $T = T_0 e^{-kt}$,

where n_0, m_0 and T_0 are the values of the variables when $t = 0$.

Some useful results to remember:

$$\frac{d}{dx}(e^x) = e^x, \qquad \int e^x \, dx = e^x + c$$

$$\frac{d}{dx}(e^{kx}) = ke^{kx}, \qquad \int e^{kx} \, dx = \frac{1}{k}e^{kx} + c.$$

Example 1   Differentiate e^{x^2+1} with respect to x.

Let $y = e^u$,   where $u = x^2 + 1$

$$\frac{dy}{du} = e^u, \qquad \frac{du}{dx} = 2x$$

$$\frac{dy}{dx} = \frac{dy}{du} \times \frac{du}{dx} = e^u \times 2x = 2xe^{x^2+1}.$$

[Students thoroughly familiar with the differentiation of composite functions may write:

$$\frac{d}{dx}(e^{x^2+1}) = e^{x^2+1}\frac{d}{dx}(x^2 + 1) = 2xe^{x^2+1}.]$$

Example 2   Find $\displaystyle\int \sin x \, e^{\cos x} \, dx.$

$$\frac{d}{dx}(e^{\cos x}) = e^{\cos x}\frac{d}{dx}(\cos x) = -\sin x \, e^{\cos x}$$

$$\therefore \int \sin x \, e^{\cos x} \, dx = -e^{\cos x} + c.$$

Example 3   Sketch the curve $y = x^2 e^{-x}$.

$$x = 0 \iff x^2 e^{-x} = 0 \iff y = 0$$

∴   the curve cuts the x- and y-axes at the origin.
Differentiating (using the product rule),

$$\frac{dy}{dx} = x^2(-e^{-x}) + 2xe^{-x} = (-x^2 + 2x)e^{-x} = x(2 - x)e^{-x}$$

∴ $\frac{dy}{dx} = 0 \iff x(2 - x)e^{-x} = 0 \iff x = 0$ or $x = 2$.

	$x < 0$	$0 < x < 2$	$x > 2$
x	$-$	$+$	$+$
$2 - x$	$+$	$+$	$-$
e^{-x}	$+$	$+$	$+$
$\frac{dy}{dx}$	$-$	$+$	$-$

∴   when $x = 0$, there is a minimum point $(0, 0)$,
when $x = 2$, there is a maximum point $(2, 4e^{-2})$.

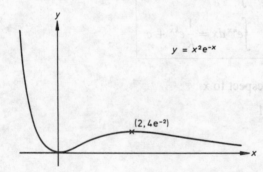

$y = x^2 e^{-x}$

$(2, 4e^{-2})$

As $x \to -\infty$, $y \to \infty$.
As x increases through positive values, e^x increases at a much greater rate than x^2,
∴   as $x \to \infty$, $y \to 0$.

[The behaviour of the function $x^n e^{-x}$ as $x \to \infty$ is also considered in *Exercise 22.4*, question 12.]

Exercise 19.1

In questions 1 to 7 differentiate the given functions with respect to x.

1. (a) e^{2x} (b) $5e^{-x}$ (c) e^{3x+5}

2. (a) e^{2x^3} (b) $e^{\sqrt{x}}$ (c) $e^{-1/x}$

3. (a) $e^{\sin x}$ (b) $e^{\cos 2x}$ (c) $e^{4 \tan x}$

4. (a) xe^{x^2} (b) $x^2 e^{5x}$ (c) $e^{x \cos x}$

5. (a) $e^{2x}\cos 3x$ (b) $e^{-x^2}\sin x$ (c) $(x+1)^3 e^{x/2}$

6. (a) $\sqrt{(1-e^{4x})}$ (b) $e^{(e^x)}$ (c) $\sin(e^x)$

7. (a) $\frac{1}{2}(e^x - e^{-x})^2$ (b) $\dfrac{e^x}{1+e^{-x}}$ (c) $\dfrac{e^{\sin^2 x}}{e^{-\cos^2 x}}$

8. Find (a) $\displaystyle\int e^{3x}\,dx$, (b) $\displaystyle\int e^{-x}\,dx$, (c) $\displaystyle\int e^{x+4}\,dx$.

9. Evaluate, leaving your answers in terms of e,

(a) $\displaystyle\int_0^1 6e^{2x}\,dx$ (b) $\displaystyle\int_{-2}^0 e^{(-x/2)}\,dx$,   (c) $\displaystyle\int_{-1}^1 \{3/e^{3(x-1)}\}\,dx$.

10. Find dy/dx in terms of x when y is defined implicitly by:
(a) $e^y = x$,   (b) $xe^y = 1$,   (c) $e^{x+y} = x^2$.

11. If $y = e^x \sin x$, show that $\dfrac{d^2y}{dx^2} - 2\dfrac{dy}{dx} + 2y = 0$.

12. Find the equation of the tangent to the curve $y = e^{3x-5}$ at the point where $x = 2$.

13. Find in terms of e the area enclosed by the curve $y = e^{1-x}$, the axes and the line $x = 1$.

14. By considering the graphs of $y = e^x$ and $y = e^{-x}$, or otherwise, make rough sketches of:
(a) $y = e^x + e^{-x}$,   (b) $y = e^x - e^{-x}$,   (c) $y = e^x - x$.

In questions 15 to 20 sketch the given curves. Give the coordinates of any turning points and show clearly the behaviour of the curve when $|x|$ is large.

15. $y = xe^{-x}$.   16. $y = (x+1)e^x$.   17. $y = xe^{-x^2/2}$.

18. $y = (x-1)^2 e^{2x}$.   19. $y = e^x/x$.   20. $y = e^{1-\cos x}$.

21. A particle moves in a straight line so that after t seconds its distance from a fixed point O is s metres, where $s = t^2 e^{2-t}$. Find the distance of the particle from O when it first comes to rest and its acceleration at that point.

22. Find the values of x for which the function $(x^2 - 2x - 1)e^{2x}$ has maximum or minimum values, distinguishing between them.

23. Find the values of x between 0 and 2π for which the function $e^x \cos x$ has maximum or minimum values, distinguishing between them.

24. Find the area of the finite region bounded by the curves $y = e^{2x}$, $y = e^{-x}$ and the line $x = 1$. If this region is rotated completely about the x-axis, find the volume of the solid formed.   (AEB 1976)

19.2 Logarithmic functions

If a and x are positive real numbers such that $x = a^p$, then p is the logarithm of x to the base a,

i.e. $x = a^p \iff \log_a x = p.$

The laws of logarithms can be summarised as follows:

$$\log_a xy = \log_a x + \log_a y$$
$$\log_a x/y = \log_a x - \log_a y$$
$$\log_a x^n = n \log_a x$$
$$(\log_a b)(\log_b c) = \log_a c$$

The relationship between logarithms to different bases leads to two useful formulae:

$$\log_a x = \frac{1}{\log_x a}, \quad \log_a x = \frac{\log_b x}{\log_b a}.$$

Now that the exponential function e^x has been defined, we can introduce logarithms to the base e. These are called *natural logarithms* or *Napierian logarithms*[†]. The natural logarithm of x may be written $\log_e x$, but is more often denoted by $\ln x$.

Thus $x = e^p \iff \ln x = p.$

In numerical work values of $\ln x$ are found using a calculator or mathematical tables.

Example 1   Solve the equation $e^x - 2 - 3e^{-x} = 0$.

Letting $y = e^x$, $e^x - 2 - 3e^{-x} = 0$.
$$\Rightarrow \quad y - 2 - 3/y = 0$$
$$\Rightarrow \quad y^2 - 2y - 3 = 0$$
$$\Rightarrow \quad (y - 3)(y + 1) = 0$$
$$\Rightarrow \quad y = 3 \quad \text{or} \quad y = -1$$
$$\Rightarrow \quad e^x = 3, \quad \text{since} \quad e^x > 0$$
$$\Rightarrow \quad x = \ln 3 \approx 1 \cdot 1$$

To investigate the properties of logarithmic functions we use our knowledge of exponential functions.

If $f(x) = a^x$, then $y = f^{-1}(x) \Rightarrow f(y) = x \Rightarrow a^y = x \Rightarrow y = \log_a x.$

[†] *Napier, John* (1550–1617) Scottish mathematician. He was the inventor of logarithms and spent 25 years producing tables. He also invented the calculating apparatus known as "Napier's Bones".

Hence the function $\log_a x$ is the inverse of the function a^x.

Thus $\qquad\qquad a^{\log_a x} = x \quad$ and $\quad \log_a(a^x) = x.$

It also follows that the graph of $y = \log_a x$ is the reflection in the line $y = x$ of the graph of $y = a^x$.

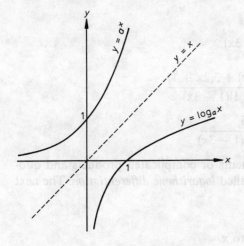

Since $\log_a x$ is defined only when $x > 0$, there are no points on the graph of $y = \log_a x$ for $x \leqslant 0$.

When $x = 1$, $y = \log_a 1 = 0$

$\therefore$ the graph of $y = \log_a x$ passes through the point $(1, 0)$ for all values of a.

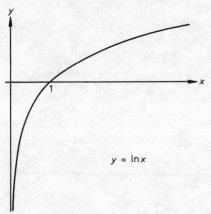

$y = \ln x$

If $y = \ln x$, then $e^y = x$.

Differentiating with respect to x,

$$\frac{d}{dx}(e^y) = 1$$

But $\quad \dfrac{d}{dx}(e^y) = \dfrac{d}{dy}(e^y)\dfrac{dy}{dx}$

$$= e^y \frac{dy}{dx} = x \frac{dy}{dx}$$

$\therefore \qquad x\dfrac{dy}{dx} = 1 \quad$ i.e. $\quad \dfrac{dy}{dx} = \dfrac{1}{x}.$

Hence, $\qquad$ for $\ x > 0, \ \dfrac{d}{dx}(\ln x) = \dfrac{1}{x} \ $ and $\ \displaystyle\int \frac{1}{x}\,dx = \ln x + c.$

Example 2 Differentiate $\ln(x^2 + 1)$ with respect to x.

Let $\quad y = \ln u,$ where $\quad u = x^2 + 1$

$\dfrac{dy}{du} = \dfrac{1}{u} \qquad\qquad\qquad \dfrac{du}{dx} = 2x$

$$\therefore \quad \frac{dy}{dx} = \frac{dy}{du} \times \frac{du}{dx} = \frac{1}{u} \times 2x = \frac{2x}{x^2 + 1}.$$

Some problems may be simplified by using the laws of logarithms.

Example 3   If $y = \ln\left(\dfrac{2x + 1}{1 - 3x}\right)$, find $\dfrac{dy}{dx}$.

$$y = \ln\left(\frac{2x + 1}{1 - 3x}\right) = \ln(2x + 1) - \ln(1 - 3x)$$

$$\therefore \quad \frac{dy}{dx} = \frac{2}{2x + 1} - \frac{(-3)}{1 - 3x} = \frac{2(1 - 3x) + 3(2x + 1)}{(2x + 1)(1 - 3x)}$$

$$= \frac{5}{(2x + 1)(1 - 3x)}$$

Some functions involving variable exponents or complicated products and quotients are differentiated using a process called *logarithmic differentiation*. The next two examples illustrate the method.

Example 4   Differentiate 2^x with respect to x.

Let $y = 2^x$,   then $\ln y = \ln(2^x) = x \ln 2$.

Differentiating, $\dfrac{1}{y}\dfrac{dy}{dx} = \ln 2$

$$\therefore \quad \frac{dy}{dx} = y \ln 2 = 2^x \ln 2.$$

Example 5   If $y = \dfrac{x}{\sqrt{(x^2 - 2)}}$, find $\dfrac{dy}{dx}$.

$$\ln y = \ln x - \ln\sqrt{(x^2 - 2)} = \ln x - \tfrac{1}{2}\ln(x^2 - 2)$$

$$\therefore \quad \frac{1}{y}\frac{dy}{dx} = \frac{1}{x} - \frac{1}{2}\left(\frac{2x}{x^2 - 2}\right) = \frac{x^2 - 2 - x^2}{x(x^2 - 2)} = \frac{-2}{x(x^2 - 2)}$$

$$\therefore \quad \frac{dy}{dx} = y\left\{\frac{-2}{x(x^2 - 2)}\right\} = \frac{x}{\sqrt{(x^2 - 2)}}\left\{\frac{-2}{x(x^2 - 2)}\right\} = -\frac{2}{(x^2 - 2)^{3/2}}$$

Example 6   Sketch the curve $y = \dfrac{1}{x}\ln x$.

$\ln x$ is not defined for $x \leqslant 0$,

$\therefore$ the curve lies entirely to the right of the y-axis.

$$y = 0 \quad \Rightarrow \quad \frac{1}{x}\ln x = 0 \quad \Rightarrow \quad x = 1$$

∴   the curve cuts the x-axis at the point $(1, 0)$.

Differentiating (using the product rule),

$$\frac{dy}{dx} = \frac{1}{x} \times \frac{1}{x} + \left(-\frac{1}{x^2}\right) \ln x = \frac{1}{x^2}(1 - \ln x)$$

$$\therefore \quad \frac{dy}{dx} = 0 \quad \Leftrightarrow \quad 1 - \ln x = 0 \quad \Leftrightarrow \quad x = e$$

When $x < e$, $\dfrac{dy}{dx} > 0$ and when $x > e$, $\dfrac{dy}{dx} < 0$,

∴   the point $(e, 1/e)$ is a maximum point.

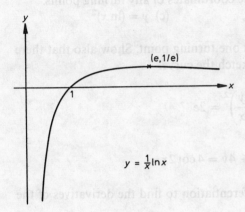

As $x \to 0$, $1/x \to \infty$ and $\ln x \to -\infty$

∴ $y \to -\infty$.

When x is large, the rate of increase of $\ln x$ is very small

∴   as $x \to \infty$, $y \to 0$.

[The behaviour of the function $\dfrac{1}{x} \ln x$ as $x \to \infty$ is also considered in *Exercise 22.4*, question 12.]

Exercise 19.2

In questions 1 to 7 differentiate the given functions with respect to x.

1. (a) $\ln 3x$,   (b) $\ln(x + 3)$,   (c) $\ln(2x - 1)$.

2. (a) $\ln(x^3 + 4)$,   (b) $\ln(\sin 2x)$,   (c) $\ln(\sec x)$.

3. (a) $x^2 \ln x$,   (b) $(\ln x)/x^2$,   (c) $\ln(\ln x)$.

4. (a) $\ln(x^3)$,   (b) $\ln\sqrt{(4x + 5)}$,   (c) $x \ln(1/x)$.

5. (a) $\ln(\sec x + \tan x)$, (b) $\ln(x^2 + 4)^2$,   (c) $\log_{10} x$.

6. (a) $\ln\left(\dfrac{x^2}{3x - 2}\right)$,   (b) $\ln\sqrt{\left(\dfrac{x}{1 + x}\right)}$,   (c) $\ln\dfrac{\cos x}{\sqrt{(1 - x^2)}}$.

7. (a) $e^{2 \ln x}$,   (b) $\ln(e^{\tan x})$,   (c) $\ln(3x^2 e^{-x})$.

8. Find the equation of the tangent to the curve $y = \ln(3x - 5)$ at the point where $x = 2$.

9. If $x = 1 + \ln t$ and $y = \ln(1 + t)$, find dy/dx in terms of t.

10. By considering the graph of $y = \ln x$, or otherwise, sketch the following:
(a) $y = \ln(-x)$,   (b) $y = \ln(1/x)$,   (c) $y = \ln(1 + x)$.

11. Given that $\ln 2 = p$ and $\ln 3 = q$, express the following in terms of p and q.
(a) $\ln 12e$,   (b) $\log_3 2$,   (c) $\log_6 e$,   (d) 6.

12. Solve the following equations
(a) $e^{3t} + 2e^t = 3e^{2t}$,   (b) $2e^x + 5 = 3e^{-x}$.

13. Sketch the following curves, giving the coordinates of any turning points.
(a) $y = |\ln x|$,   (b) $y = 1/\ln x$,   (c) $y = (\ln x)^2$.

14. Show that the curve $y = x - \ln x$ has one turning point. Show also that there are no points of inflexion on the curve. Sketch the curve.

15. If $y = \ln(x^2 - 5)$, show that $\dfrac{d^2y}{dx^2} + \left(\dfrac{dy}{dx}\right)^2 = 2e^{-y}$.

16. If $y = \sin 2x \ln(\tan x)$, show that $\dfrac{d^2y}{dx^2} + 4y = 4\cot 2x$.

In questions 17 to 20 use logarithmic differentiation to find the derivatives of the given functions.

17. (a) 3^x,   (b) 5^{2x},   (c) $10^{\sin x}$.

18. (a) x^x,   (b) $x^{\ln x}$,   (c) $(\ln x)^x$.

19. (a) $\dfrac{x^2 + 1}{(2x + 1)^2}$,   (b) $\dfrac{x^3}{\sqrt{(1 - x)}}$,   (c) $\dfrac{(x - 1)^2 e^{4x}}{(x + 1)^2}$

20. (a) $\sqrt{\left\{\dfrac{(x + 2)^3}{1 - 5x}\right\}}$,   (b) $\sqrt[3]{\left\{\dfrac{x^2 - 2}{x^2 + 4}\right\}}$,   (c) $\dfrac{\sqrt{(\sin 2x)}}{\cos^3 x}$.

19.3 ln x defined in integral form

In this section we consider a more rigorous approach to the theory of exponential and logarithmic functions. In §19.1 we assumed with little justification that a^x is a continuous differentiable function defined for all real values of x. However, any elementary definition of a^x is valid only for rational values of x. Similarly, the laws of indices and the rule for differentiating x^n can be proved by elementary methods only for rational values of the exponents. We avoid these difficulties by using definitions of $\ln x$ and $\exp x$ which are valid for both rational and irrational values of x.

We define $\ln x$ as a definite integral by writing:

$$\ln x = \int_1^x \frac{1}{t} dt, \quad \text{where } x \text{ is real and positive.}$$

It follows that when $x = 1$, $\ln x = 0$. Other values of $\ln x$ are related to areas under the curve $y = 1/t$ as shown in the diagrams below.

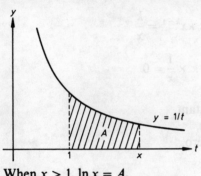

When $x > 1$, $\ln x = A$.

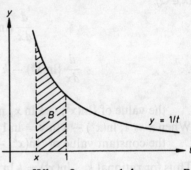

When $0 < x < 1$, $\ln x = -B$.

Thus the domain of the function $\ln x$ is the set of positive real numbers and its range is the set of all real numbers.

We can now define $\exp x$ for all real values of x by letting the function $\exp x$ be the inverse of the function $\ln x$, so that

$$y = \exp x \iff \ln y = x$$

To differentiate the function $\ln x$, let $f(x) = \ln x$, then

$$f(x + h) - f(x) = \ln(x + h) - \ln x$$

$$= \int_1^{x+h} \frac{1}{t} dt - \int_1^x \frac{1}{t} dt = \int_x^{x+h} \frac{1}{t} dt.$$

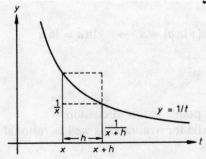

From the sketch we see that

$$h \times \frac{1}{x+h} < \int_x^{x+h} \frac{1}{t} dt < h \times \frac{1}{x}$$

$$\therefore \quad \frac{1}{x+h} < \frac{f(x+h) - f(x)}{h} < \frac{1}{x}$$

As $h \to 0$, $\dfrac{1}{x+h} \to \dfrac{1}{x}$,

$$\therefore \quad f'(x) = \lim_{h \to 0} \frac{f(x+h) - f(x)}{h} = \frac{1}{x}$$

i.e.

$$\frac{d}{dx}(\ln x) = \frac{1}{x}$$

To differentiate the function $\exp x$, let $y = \exp x$, then

$$\ln y = x \;\Rightarrow\; \frac{1}{y}\frac{dy}{dx} = 1 \;\Rightarrow\; \frac{dy}{dx} = y$$

i.e.
$$\frac{d}{dx}(\exp x) = \exp x$$

We develop the theory further by considering $\ln(x^k)$, where k is any rational number $(k \in \mathbb{Q})$.

$$\frac{d}{dx}\{\ln(x^k)\} = \frac{1}{x^k} \times kx^{k-1} = \frac{k}{x}$$

$\therefore$
$$\frac{d}{dx}\{\ln(x^k) - k\ln x\} = \frac{k}{x} - k \times \frac{1}{x} = 0$$

$\therefore$ the value of $\{\ln(x^k) - k\ln x\}$ must be constant.
When $x = 1$, $\ln(x^k) - k\ln x = \ln 1 - k\ln 1 = 0$,
$\therefore$ the constant value of $\{\ln(x^k) - k\ln x\}$ is zero.

Thus for rational k, $\quad \ln(x^k) = k\ln x$
and hence $\qquad\qquad x^k = \exp(k\ln x) \qquad\qquad\qquad\qquad (1)$

The constant e is now defined as the real number such that $\ln e = 1$. Substituting $x = e$ in equation (1) we have

$$e^k = \exp(k\ln e) = \exp k, \quad \text{for rational } k.$$

Thus it seems reasonable to give a meaning to the expression e^x when x is irrational by letting $e^x = \exp x$ for all real x.
It follows from this definition that $\log_e x = \ln x$.
More generally, it is consistent with equation (1) to define a^x by writing

$$\boxed{a^x = \exp(x\ln a) \quad \text{for all real } x}$$

It is a consequence of this definition that

$$y = \log_a x \;\Rightarrow\; a^y = x \;\Rightarrow\; \exp(y\ln a) = x \;\Rightarrow\; y\ln a = \ln x$$

$$\therefore \quad \boxed{\log_a x = (\ln x)/(\ln a).}$$

We conclude by summarising the important points in this discussion.
We needed definitions of e^x and $a^x (a > 0)$ valid for irrational as well as rational values of x. We found that using the definitions

$$\ln x = \int_1^x \frac{1}{t}\,dt, \quad y = \exp x \;\Leftrightarrow\; \ln y = x,$$

it followed that, for rational values of k,

$$e^k = \exp k, \quad a^k = \exp(k\ln a).$$

Thus suitable definitions of e^x and a^x are

$$e^x = \exp x, \quad a^x = \exp(x \ln a).$$

We deduce from these definitions that

$$\log_e x = \ln x, \quad \log_a x = (\ln x)/(\ln a).$$

These results provide a firmer basis for the work of §19.1 and §19.2.

[Note that the theory of exponential and logarithmic functions defined in terms of $\exp x$ and $\ln x$ is extended in *Exercise 19.3* and in *Exercise 20.6*, question 11.]

Exercise 19.3

1. (a) Use the result $\dfrac{d}{dx}(\ln x) = \dfrac{1}{x}$ to prove that

$$\frac{d}{dx}(\ln xy - \ln x - \ln y) = 0.$$

(b) Deduce that $\ln xy = \ln x + \ln y$.
(c) By substituting $u = \ln x, v = \ln y$, show that

$$(\exp u)(\exp v) = \exp(u + v).$$

2. Use the methods of question 1 to show that
    (a) $\ln(x/y) = \ln x - \ln y$.
    (b) $(\exp u)/(\exp v) = \exp(u - v)$.

3. Use the definition $x^p = \exp(p \ln x)$ or the equivalent statement $\ln(x^p) = p \ln x$ to prove that, for all real values of p,

$$y = x^p \quad \Rightarrow \quad \frac{dy}{dx} = px^{p-1}.$$

19.4 Integration using logarithms

By differentiating logarithmic functions we can obtain various useful integration results.

For $x > 0, \dfrac{d}{dx}(\ln x) = \dfrac{1}{x}$,

$\therefore$ for $x > 0$, $\displaystyle\int \frac{1}{x} dx = \ln x + c.$ (1)

For $x < 0, \dfrac{d}{dx}\{\ln(-x)\} = \dfrac{1}{(-x)} \times (-1) = \dfrac{1}{x}$

$\therefore$ for $x < 0$, $\displaystyle\int \frac{1}{x} dx = \ln(-x) + c.$ (2)

For $ax + b > 0$, $\dfrac{d}{dx}\{\ln(ax + b)\} = \dfrac{1}{ax + b} \times a = \dfrac{a}{ax + b}$

$\therefore$ for $ax + b > 0$, $\displaystyle\int \dfrac{1}{ax + b}\, dx = \dfrac{1}{a}\ln(ax + b) + c.$

Example 1 Find $\displaystyle\int \dfrac{1}{3x - 2}\, dx$ when (a) $3x - 2 > 0$, (b) $3x - 2 < 0$.

(a) $\displaystyle\int \dfrac{1}{3x - 2}\, dx = \dfrac{1}{3}\ln(3x - 2) + c$, for $3x - 2 > 0$.

(b) $\displaystyle\int \dfrac{1}{3x - 2}\, dx = -\int \dfrac{1}{2 - 3x}\, dx = -\dfrac{1}{(-3)}\ln(2 - 3x) + c$

$$= \dfrac{1}{3}\ln(2 - 3x) + c, \quad \text{for}\quad 3x - 2 < 0.$$

Example 2 Evaluate (a) $\displaystyle\int_5^9 \dfrac{1}{x - 3}\, dx$, (b) $\displaystyle\int_1^2 \dfrac{1}{x - 3}\, dx$.

(a) Within the limits of integration $x - 3 > 0$,

$\therefore$ $\displaystyle\int_5^9 \dfrac{1}{x - 3}\, dx = \Big[\ln(x - 3)\Big]_5^9 = \ln 6 - \ln 2 = \ln(6/2) = \ln 3.$

(b) Within the limits of integration $x - 3 < 0$,

$\therefore$ $\displaystyle\int_1^2 \dfrac{1}{x - 3}\, dx = -\int_1^2 \dfrac{1}{3 - x}\, dx = \Big[\ln(3 - x)\Big]_1^2 = \ln 1 - \ln 2 = -\ln 2.$

When there are no stated restrictions on the values of x, results (1) and (2) can be combined in the statement:

$$\int \dfrac{1}{x}\, dx = \ln|x| + c$$

Similarly
$$\boxed{\int \dfrac{1}{ax + b}\, dx = \dfrac{1}{a}\ln|ax + b| + c.}$$

We stress, however, that it should not be necessary to use modulus signs when evaluating definite integrals.

Example 3 Find $\displaystyle\int \dfrac{x - 1}{x + 1}\, dx$.

$$\int \dfrac{x - 1}{x + 1}\, dx = \int \left\{1 - \dfrac{2}{x + 1}\right\} dx = x - 2\ln|x + 1| + c.$$

Example 4 Find $\displaystyle\int_1^3 \frac{2x^2 + 3x}{2x - 1}\, dx.$

$$
\begin{array}{r}
x + 2 \\
2x - 1 \overline{\smash{\big)}\ 2x^2 + 3x} \\
\underline{2x^2 - x} \\
4x \\
\underline{4x - 2} \\
2
\end{array}
$$

By division

$$\frac{2x^2 + 3x}{2x - 1} = x + 2 + \frac{2}{2x - 1}$$

Noting that within the limits of integration $2x - 1 > 0$,

$$\int_1^3 \frac{2x^2 + 3x}{2x - 1}\, dx = \int_1^3 \left\{ x + 2 + \frac{2}{2x - 1} \right\} dx$$

$$= \left[\tfrac{1}{2}x^2 + 2x + \ln(2x - 1) \right]_1^3$$

$$= (\tfrac{9}{2} + 6 + \ln 5) - (\tfrac{1}{2} + 2 + \ln 1) = 8 + \ln 5.$$

To obtain a general integration formula, let $y = \ln\{f(x)\}$, then

$$\frac{dy}{dx} = \frac{1}{f(x)} \times \frac{d}{dx}\{f(x)\} = \frac{f'(x)}{f(x)}$$

$\therefore$ for $f(x) > 0$, $\displaystyle\int \frac{f'(x)}{f(x)}\, dx = \ln\{f(x)\} + c.$

When the sign of $f(x)$ is unknown we may write

$$\boxed{\int \frac{f'(x)}{f(x)}\, dx = \ln|f(x)| + c.}$$

Example 5 Find $\displaystyle\int \frac{x}{3x^2 + 5}\, dx.$

If $f(x) = 3x^2 + 5$, then $f'(x) = 6x$,
$\therefore$ noting that $3x^2 + 5 > 0$ for all values of x,

$$\int \frac{x}{3x^2 + 5}\, dx = \frac{1}{6}\int \frac{6x}{3x^2 + 5}\, dx = \frac{1}{6}\ln(3x^2 + 5) + c.$$

Example 6 Find $\displaystyle\int \tan x\, dx.$

If $f(x) = \cos x$, then $f'(x) = -\sin x$,

$$\therefore \quad \int \tan x\, dx = -\int \frac{(-\sin x)}{\cos x}\, dx = -\ln|\cos x| + c$$

$$= \ln \frac{1}{|\cos x|} + c = \ln|\sec x| + c.$$

Exercise 19.4

Find the following indefinite integrals.

1. (a) $\int \dfrac{1}{2x+7} dx$ for $2x+7>0$,   (b) $\int \dfrac{1}{5x-2} dx$ for $5x-2>0$.

2. (a) $\int \dfrac{1}{1-x} dx$ for $1-x>0$,   (b) $\int \dfrac{1}{2x-1} dx$ for $2x-1<0$.

3. (a) $\int \dfrac{3}{3x-2} dx$ for $3x<2$,   (b) $\int \dfrac{8}{3-4x} dx$ for $4x<3$.

4. (a) $\int \dfrac{1}{x+3} dx$,   (b) $\int \dfrac{3}{3-x} dx$,   (c) $\int \dfrac{2}{4x+5} dx$.

5. (a) $\int \dfrac{x}{x-1} dx$,   (b) $\int \dfrac{x-2}{x-4} dx$,   (c) $\int \dfrac{x+1}{2x+1} dx$.

6. (a) $\int \dfrac{x^2-1}{x} dx$,   (b) $\int \dfrac{(1-x)^2}{1+x^2} dx$,   (c) $\int \dfrac{1-x+x^2}{1-x} dx$.

7. (a) $\int \dfrac{x}{1-x^2} dx$,   (b) $\int \dfrac{x^2}{x^3+8} dx$,   (c) $\int \dfrac{x+1}{2x^2+4x-1} dx$.

8. (a) $\int \dfrac{\cos x}{1+\sin x} dx$,   (b) $\int \cot x\, dx$,   (c) $\int (1+\tan 2x)\, dx$.

9. (a) $\int \dfrac{e^x}{1+e^x} dx$,   (b) $\int \dfrac{1}{x\ln x} dx$,   (c) $\int \dfrac{1}{(1+\sqrt{x})\sqrt{x}} dx$.

Evaluate the following definite integrals.

10. (a) $\displaystyle\int_2^4 \dfrac{5}{x} dx$,   (b) $\displaystyle\int_3^9 \dfrac{1}{x-1} dx$,   (c) $\displaystyle\int_{-4}^0 \dfrac{1}{1-2x} dx$.

11. (a) $\displaystyle\int_0^1 \dfrac{1}{3x+2} dx$,   (b) $\displaystyle\int_0^3 \dfrac{1}{x-4} dx$,   (c) $\displaystyle\int_3^5 \dfrac{x}{x+1} dx$.

12. (a) $\displaystyle\int_0^{\pi/2} \tan{\tfrac{1}{2}}x\, dx$,   (b) $\displaystyle\int_3^4 \dfrac{2x-3}{x^2-3x+1} dx$,   (c) $\displaystyle\int_0^{\ln 2} \dfrac{e^{-x}}{1+e^{-x}} dx$.

13. Evaluate, giving answers correct to 3 significant figures.

(a) $\displaystyle\int_2^4 \dfrac{x+2}{x^2+4x-7} dx$,   (b) $\displaystyle\int_{\pi/6}^{\pi/3} \dfrac{\sec^2 x}{\tan x} dx$.

14. Express $\dfrac{1}{2x - 1} - \dfrac{2}{3 - x}$ as a single fraction and hence evaluate, correct to

3 decimal places, $\displaystyle\int_{1}^{2} \dfrac{1 - x}{(2x - 1)(3 - x)}\,dx.$

15. Find the area enclosed by the curve $y = 1/(x - 2)$ and the line $y = 7 - 2x$.

16. Find the volume of the solid formed by rotating about the x-axis the area bounded by the curve $y = \sqrt{x} + 1/\sqrt{x}$, the x-axis and the lines $x = 1$, $x = 3$.

19.5 Introduction to hyperbolic functions

Hyperbolic sine and cosine are defined as follows:

$$\sinh x = \tfrac{1}{2}(e^x - e^{-x}), \quad \cosh x = \tfrac{1}{2}(e^x + e^{-x})$$

The remaining hyperbolic functions can be expressed in terms of $\sinh x$ and $\cosh x$.

$$\tanh x = \dfrac{\sinh x}{\cosh x}, \quad \coth x = \dfrac{\cosh x}{\sinh x}, \quad \operatorname{sech} x = \dfrac{1}{\cosh x}, \quad \operatorname{cosech} x = \dfrac{1}{\sinh x}$$

[Note that cosh, sech, cosech, coth are pronounced as they are written, tanh is pronounced 'tanch' and sinh as 'shine' or sometimes 'sinch'.]

The graphs of $y = \sinh x$ and $y = \cosh x$ may be sketched from the graphs of $y = e^x$ and $y = e^{-x}$.

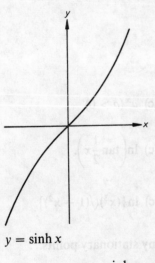

$y = \sinh x$

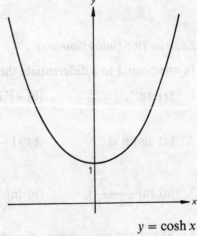

$y = \cosh x$

$$y = \sinh x = \tfrac{1}{2}(e^x - e^{-x}) \Rightarrow \dfrac{dy}{dx} = \tfrac{1}{2}(e^x + e^{-x}) = \cosh x$$

$$y = \cosh x = \tfrac{1}{2}(e^x + e^{-x}) \Rightarrow \dfrac{dy}{dx} = \tfrac{1}{2}(e^x - e^{-x}) = \sinh x$$

$$\therefore \quad \dfrac{d}{dx}(\sinh x) = \cosh x, \quad \dfrac{d}{dx}(\cosh x) = \sinh x.$$

We now establish one of the most useful identities connecting hyperbolic functions.

$$\cosh^2 x - \sinh^2 x = \{\tfrac{1}{2}(e^x + e^{-x})\}^2 - \{\tfrac{1}{2}(e^x - e^{-x})\}^2$$
$$= \tfrac{1}{4}\{(e^{2x} + 2 + e^{-2x}) - (e^{2x} - 2 + e^{-2x})\}$$
$$= \tfrac{1}{4} \times 4 = 1$$

i.e. $$\cosh^2 x - \sinh^2 x = 1.$$

Exercise 19.5

1. Differentiate with respect to x
   (a) $\sinh 2x$,   (b) $\cosh 3x$,   (c) $\sinh^2 x$,   (d) $\sqrt{(\cosh x)}$.

2. Find (a) $\int \sinh x \, dx$,   (b) $\int \cosh 2x \, dx$,   (c) $\int \tanh x \, dx$.

3. Differentiate with respect to x
   (a) $\tanh x$,   (b) $\coth x$,   (c) $\operatorname{sech} x$,   (d) $\operatorname{cosech} x$.

4. Use the definitions of $\sinh x$ and $\cosh x$ to prove
   (a) $\sinh 2x = 2 \sinh x \cosh x$,   (b) $\cosh 2x = \cosh^2 x + \sinh^2 x$.

5. By substituting $y = e^x$, solve the equations
   (a) $3 \cosh x - 2 \sinh x = 3$,   (b) $5 \cosh x + 7 \sinh x = 1$.

Exercise 19.6 (*miscellaneous*)

In questions 1 to 3 differentiate the given functions.

1. (a) xe^{3x},   (b) $e^{2x} \ln 4x$,   (c) $a^x (a > 0)$.

2. (a) $\sin(\ln x)$,   (b) $(1 - x^2)\ln x$,   (c) $\ln\left(\tan\tfrac{1}{2}x\right)$.

3. (a) $\ln\left(\dfrac{x-3}{3x-1}\right)$,   (b) $\ln\left(\dfrac{1 + \sin x}{1 - \sin x}\right)$,   (c) $\ln\{(x^3)\sqrt{(1 - x^2)}\}$.

4. Sketch the given curves, giving the coordinates of any stationary points.
   (a) $y = e^x + 4e^{-x}$,   (b) $y = x^3 e^{-x}$.

5. Find the value of x for which the curve $y = x^{1/x} (x > 0)$ has a stationary point. State the nature of this point.

6. Show that if $y = e^{4x} \cos 3x$, then $d^2 y/dx^2$ can be expressed in the form $25e^{4x} \cos(3x + \alpha)$. Give the value of $\tan \alpha$.

7. Sketch the curves

(a) $y = \dfrac{x+1}{x-1}$,   (b) $y = \left|\dfrac{x+1}{x-1}\right|$,   (c) $y = \ln\left|\dfrac{x+1}{x-1}\right|$.

8. Given that $x \ln x \to 0$ as $x \to 0$, sketch the curves

(a) $y = x \ln x$,   (b) $y = \dfrac{1}{x} + \ln x$.

9. Find the coordinates of any turning points on the curve $y = e^{-x/2}(x^2 + x - 2)$. Sketch this curve and the curve $y = x^2 + x - 2$ on the same axes.

10. Evaluate (a) $\displaystyle\int_2^6 \dfrac{1}{2x-3}\,dx$,   (b) $\displaystyle\int_0^5 \dfrac{x}{x^2+5}\,dx$,   (c) $\displaystyle\int_{\pi/2}^{\pi} \cot\dfrac{1}{3}x\,dx$.

11. Find (a) $\displaystyle\int \dfrac{x}{3x+1}\,dx$,   (b) $\displaystyle\int \dfrac{(x-2)(x+2)}{x^3}\,dx$,   (c) $\displaystyle\int \dfrac{2x^2+1}{x^2+x+1}\,dx$

12. Simplify $\log_e\left[\dfrac{(1+x)e^{-2x}}{1-x}\right]^{1/2}$ and show that its derivative is $x^2/(1-x^2)$.

Hence, or otherwise, evaluate dy/dx at $x = 0$ for the function $y = \left[\dfrac{(1+x)e^{-2x}}{1-x}\right]^{1/2}$.

(JMB)

13. If $\tan y = \log_e x^2$, show that $x\dfrac{dy}{dx} = 2\cos^2 y$. Hence show that

$$x^2\dfrac{d^2y}{dx^2} + 2(1 + 2\sin 2y)\cos^2 y = 0.$$

(AEB 1980)

14. If $y = (x - 0.5)e^{2x}$, find dy/dx and hence or otherwise calculate, correct to one decimal place, the mean value of xe^{2x} in the interval $0 \leqslant x \leqslant 2.5$.   (AEB 1980)

15. The coordinates of a point on a curve are given in terms of a parameter θ by $x = a\{\ln(\cot\frac{1}{2}\theta) - \cos\theta\}$, $y = a\sin\theta$, where a is a positive constant and $0 < \theta \leqslant \frac{1}{2}\pi$.

Show that, if $\theta \neq \frac{1}{2}\pi$, $\dfrac{dy}{dx} = -\tan\theta$.

The tangent at any point P of the curve meets the x-axis at T. Prove that the length of PT is equal to a.   (C)

16. Sketch the region in the x-y plane within which all three of the following inequalities are satisfied:
(i) $y < x + 1$,   (ii) $y > (x - 1)^2$,   (iii) $xy < 2$.
Determine the area of this region.   (JMB)

17. Sketch the curve $y = 1 + 2e^{-x}$, showing clearly the behaviour of the curve as $x \to +\infty$. Find the area of the finite region enclosed by the curve and the lines $x = 0$, $x = 1$, $y = 1$. Find also the volume formed when this region is rotated completely about the line $y = 1$.   (L)

18. Sketch the curve whose equation is $y + 3 = \dfrac{6}{x - 1}$. Find the coordinates of the points where the line $y + 3x = 9$ intersects the curve and show that the area of the region enclosed between the curve and the line is $\dfrac{3}{2}(3 - 4\log_e 2)$. Determine the equations of the two tangents to the curve which are parallel to the line.   (JMB)

19. Sketch the curve $y = x/(1 + x^2)$, finding its turning points, showing that the origin is a point of inflexion, and indicating the behaviour of y when $|x|$ is large. Calculate the area of the region defined by the inequalities

$$0 \leqslant x \leqslant a, 0 \leqslant y \leqslant x/(1 + x^2),$$

and show that this area has the value 1 when $a = \sqrt{(e^2 - 1)}$.   (L)

20. A curve has the equation $y = a/(b + e^{-cx})$, $(a \neq 0, b > 0, c > 0)$. Show that it has one point of inflexion, and that the value of y at the point of inflexion is half the limiting value y as $x \to \infty$.   (O)

21. Sketch the curve $y = (x^2 - 7x + 10)/(x - 6)$, indicating clearly any vertical asymptotes and turning values. Determine the finite area bounded by the x-axis and that part of the curve between the points where it crosses the x-axis.   (O)

22. Sketch the curve $y = \log_e(x - 2)$. The inner surface of a bowl is of the shape formed by rotating completely about the y-axis that part of the x-axis between $x = 0$ and $x = 3$ and that part of the curve $y = \log_e(x - 2)$ between $y = 0$ and $y = 2$. The bowl is placed with its axis vertical and water is poured in. Calculate the volume of water in the bowl when the bowl is filled to a depth $h(<2)$. If water is poured into the bowl at a rate of 50 cubic units per second, find the rate at which the water level is rising when the depth of the water is 1·5 units.   (AEB 1979)

23. By means of a diagram, or otherwise, show that

$$\frac{1}{r + 1} < \int_r^{r+1} \frac{1}{x}\,dx < \frac{1}{r}.$$

Deduce that the sum to N terms of the series $1 + \dfrac{1}{2} + \dfrac{1}{3} + \ldots + \dfrac{1}{r} + \ldots$ lies between $\log_e(1 + N)$ and $1 + \log_e N$, where $N > 1$. Show that the sum of one hundred million terms of this series lies between 18·4 and 19·5.   (JMB)

20 Methods of integration

20.1 Standard forms

We first list some important integration results.

$$\int x^n \, dx = \frac{1}{n+1} x^{n+1} + c, \quad (n \neq -1)$$

$$\int \sin x \, dx = -\cos x + c, \qquad \int \cos x \, dx = \sin x + c$$

$$\int \sec^2 x \, dx = \tan x + c, \qquad \int \cosec^2 x \, dx = -\cot x + c$$

$$\int e^x \, dx = e^x + c, \qquad \int \frac{1}{x} \, dx = \ln x + c, \quad (x > 0)$$

When using these standard forms it is worth noting that if we can integrate a function $f(x)$, we should also be able to integrate $f(ax + b)$. For instance, remembering that $\int \cos x \, dx = \sin x + c$, to find $\int \cos (2x - 3) \, dx$ we try differentiating $\sin (2x - 3)$:

$$y = \sin u, \quad \text{where} \quad u = 2x - 3$$

$$\Rightarrow \quad \frac{dy}{du} = \cos u \qquad \frac{du}{dx} = 2$$

$$\Rightarrow \quad \frac{dy}{dx} = \frac{dy}{du} \times \frac{du}{dx} = 2\cos u = 2 \cos (2x - 3)$$

Hence
$$\int \cos (2x - 3) \, dx = \tfrac{1}{2} \sin (2x - 3) + c.$$

Example 1   Find (a) $\int e^{x/2}\,dx$, (b) $\int (1-2x)^3\,dx$, (c) $\int \dfrac{1}{(3x+4)^4}\,dx$.

(a) $\dfrac{d}{dx}\{e^{x/2}\} = e^{x/2} \times \tfrac{1}{2} = \tfrac{1}{2}e^{x/2}$

$$\therefore \qquad \int e^{x/2}\,dx = 2e^{x/2} + c.$$

(b) $\dfrac{d}{dx}\{(1-2x)^4\} = 4(1-2x)^3 \times (-2) = -8(1-2x)^3$

$$\therefore \qquad \int (1-2x)^3\,dx = -\tfrac{1}{8}(1-2x)^4 + c.$$

(c) $\dfrac{d}{dx}\{(3x+4)^{-3}\} = -3(3x+4)^{-4} \times 3 = -\dfrac{9}{(3x+4)^4}$

$$\therefore \qquad \int \dfrac{1}{(3x+4)^4}\,dx = -\dfrac{1}{9(3x+4)^3} + c.$$

Integrals involving trigonometric functions can often be found using basic trigonometric identities.

$$\int \tan^2 x\,dx = \int (\sec^2 x - 1)\,dx = \tan x - x + c.$$

$$\int \cos^2 x\,dx = \int \tfrac{1}{2}(1 + \cos 2x)\,dx = \tfrac{1}{2}x + \tfrac{1}{4}\sin 2x + c.$$

$$\int \sin 3x \cos 2x\,dx = \int \tfrac{1}{2}(\sin 5x + \sin x)\,dx = -\tfrac{1}{10}\cos 5x - \tfrac{1}{2}\cos x + c.$$

In the next two examples we consider integrals of the form

$$\int \{f(x)\}^n f'(x)\,dx.$$

Example 2   Find $\int \sin^2 x \cos x\,dx$ and hence $\int \cos^3 x\,dx$.

[We note that $f(x) = \sin x \Rightarrow f'(x) = \cos x$ and therefore try differentiating $\sin^3 x$.]

$$\dfrac{d}{dx}(\sin^3 x) = 3\sin^2 x \cos x$$

$$\therefore \qquad \int \sin^2 x \cos x\,dx = \tfrac{1}{3}\sin^3 x + c.$$

Hence
$$\int \cos^3 x \, dx = \int (\cos^2 x) \cos x \, dx$$

$$= \int (1 - \sin^2 x) \cos x \, dx$$

$$= \int (\cos x - \sin^2 x \cos x) \, dx$$

$$= \sin x - \tfrac{1}{3} \sin^3 x + c.$$

Example 3 Find $\int 2x(1 + x^2)^4 \, dx$.

[We note that $f(x) = 1 + x^2 \Rightarrow f'(x) = 2x$ and therefore try differentiating $(1 + x^2)^5$.]

$$\frac{d}{dx}\{(1 + x^2)^5\} = 5(1 + x^2)^4 \times 2x$$

$$\therefore \quad \int 2x(1 + x^2)^4 \, dx = \tfrac{1}{5}(1 + x^2)^5 + c.$$

Two general results involving logarithms were derived in §19.4:

$$\int \frac{1}{ax + b} \, dx = \frac{1}{a} \ln(ax + b) + c, \quad \text{for} \quad ax + b > 0$$

$$\int \frac{f'(x)}{f(x)} \, dx = \ln\{f(x)\} + c, \quad \text{for} \quad f(x) > 0$$

or
$$\int \frac{f'(x)}{f(x)} \, dx = \ln|f(x)| + c.$$

These were used to integrate functions such as:

$$\frac{1}{3x - 2}, \quad \frac{x - 1}{x + 1}, \quad \frac{2x^2 + 3x}{2x - 1}, \quad \frac{x}{3x^2 + 5} \quad \text{and} \quad \tan x.$$

Finally we note that when obtaining an indefinite integral it may be possible to produce several different answers.

(i) $\int (2x + 2) \, dx = x^2 + 2x + c$

or $\int (2x + 2) \, dx = \int 2(x + 1) \, dx = (x + 1)^2 + c.$

(ii) $\int 2 \sin x \cos x \, dx = \sin^2 x + c$ or $\int 2 \sin x \cos x \, dx = -\cos^2 x + c$

or $\int 2 \sin x \cos x \, dx = \int \sin 2x \, dx = -\tfrac{1}{2} \cos 2x + c.$

However, apparently dissimilar results turn out to differ only by a constant. For example, in (ii)

$$\sin^2 x = -\cos^2 x + 1 = -\tfrac{1}{2}\cos 2x + \tfrac{1}{2}.$$

Exercise 20.1

Find the given indefinite integrals.

1. $\displaystyle\int \frac{x-3}{x^3}\,dx$

2. $\displaystyle\int (x^3 - 1)^2\,dx$

3. $\displaystyle\int (x+1)\sqrt{x}\,dx$

4. $\displaystyle\int \cos 3x\,dx$

5. $\displaystyle\int e^{4x-3}\,dx$

6. $\displaystyle\int \sin(1-2x)\,dx$

7. $\displaystyle\int (1-x)^4\,dx$

8. $\displaystyle\int \frac{1}{(x+4)^2}\,dx$

9. $\displaystyle\int \frac{1}{(2x-5)^3}\,dx$

10. $\displaystyle\int \frac{1}{2x-5}\,dx$

11. $\displaystyle\int \sec^2 5x\,dx$

12. $\displaystyle\int \cot \tfrac{1}{2}x\,dx$

13. $\displaystyle\int \sin^2 x\,dx$

14. $\displaystyle\int \sin x \cos 3x\,dx$

15. $\displaystyle\int \cot^2 x\,dx$

16. $\displaystyle\int \sin x \cos^2 x\,dx$

17. $\displaystyle\int \frac{\sin x}{\cos^2 x}\,dx$

18. $\displaystyle\int \sin^3 x\,dx$

19. $\displaystyle\int \frac{x+1}{x+2}\,dx$

20. $\displaystyle\int \frac{x^2}{x-1}\,dx$

21. $\displaystyle\int \frac{x^3 - x}{x^2 + 5}\,dx$

22. $\displaystyle\int \frac{1}{\sqrt{(5x+3)}}\,dx$

23. $\displaystyle\int \frac{x^3}{1+x^4}\,dx$

24. $\displaystyle\int x^3(1+x^4)^3\,dx$

Evaluate the given definite integrals.

25. $\displaystyle\int_0^1 e^{1-x}\,dx$

26. $\displaystyle\int_{-2/3}^{1/3} (2+3x)^5\,dx$

27. $\displaystyle\int_0^{\pi/4} \cos^3 x \sin x\,dx$

28. $\displaystyle\int_0^{\pi/2} \sin 2x \sin 5x\,dx$

29. $\displaystyle\int_0^{\pi/12} \cos^2 3x\,dx$

30. $\displaystyle\int_0^{\pi/2} \sin^3 x \cos^2 x\,dx$

31. $\displaystyle\int_0^{\pi/3} \tan x \sec^2 x\,dx$

32. $\displaystyle\int_0^{\pi/4} \cos 3x \cos x\,dx$

33. $\displaystyle\int_0^{\pi/2} \tan^2\!\left(x - \frac{\pi}{4}\right)dx$

34. $\displaystyle\int_0^{\pi/2} \frac{\cos x}{1+\sin x}\,dx$

35. $\displaystyle\int_1^2 \frac{6}{(1-2x)^2}\,dx$

36. $\displaystyle\int_0^{1/2} \frac{x}{1-x^2}\,dx$

37. Show that $\displaystyle\int_0^{\pi/4} (1 + \tan x)^2 \, dx = 1 + \ln 2$.

38. Find $\dfrac{d}{dx}\{\ln(\sec x + \tan x)\}$ and hence evaluate $\displaystyle\int_0^{\pi/6} \sec x \, dx$.

39. By expressing $\cos x$ in terms of $\cos\frac{1}{2}x$, or otherwise, find

$$\int \frac{1}{1 + \cos x} \, dx.$$

40. Prove that $\sin^4 x = \frac{1}{8}(\cos 4x - 4\cos 2x + 3)$. Hence evaluate

$$\int_0^{\pi} \sin^4 x \, dx.$$

20.2 Use of partial fractions

Most rational functions of the form $P(x)/Q(x)$, where $P(x)$ and $Q(x)$ are polynomials, are more easily integrated when expressed in partial fractions.

As shown in §18.6, a linear factor of the form $(ax + b)$ in the denominator of a rational function leads to a partial fraction $A/(ax + b)$. Such fractions are integrated using the rule:

$$\int \frac{1}{ax + b} \, dx = \frac{1}{a}\ln(ax + b) + c, \quad \text{for} \quad ax + b > 0.$$

Example 1   Find $\displaystyle\int \frac{1}{(x - 2)(x + 1)} \, dx$ for $x > 2$.

Let
$$\frac{1}{(x - 2)(x + 1)} \equiv \frac{A}{x - 2} + \frac{B}{x + 1}$$

then
$$1 \equiv A(x + 1) + B(x - 2)$$

Putting $x = 2$: $1 = 3A \qquad \therefore \quad A = \frac{1}{3}$

Putting $x = -1$: $1 = -3B \qquad \therefore \quad B = -\frac{1}{3}$

$$\therefore \quad \int \frac{1}{(x - 2)(x + 1)} \, dx = \int \left\{ \frac{1}{3(x - 2)} - \frac{1}{3(x + 1)} \right\} dx$$

$$= \tfrac{1}{3}\ln(x - 2) - \tfrac{1}{3}\ln(x + 1) + c$$

$$= \tfrac{1}{3}\ln\left(\frac{x - 2}{x + 1} \right) + c, \quad \text{for} \quad x > 2.$$

Partial fractions are not needed when integrating rational functions of the form $f'(x)/f(x)$.

Example 2   Find $\displaystyle\int \frac{2x-1}{(x-2)(x+1)}\,dx.$

If $f(x) = (x-2)(x+1) = x^2 - x - 2$, then $f'(x) = 2x - 1$

$$\therefore \quad \int \frac{2x-1}{(x-2)(x+1)}\,dx = \ln|(x-2)(x+1)| + c.$$

A quadratic factor in the denominator of a rational function may give rise to a partial fraction of the form $f'(x)/f(x)$.

Example 3   Find $\displaystyle\int \frac{1-x^2}{x(x^2+1)}\,dx$, for $x > 0$.

Let
$$\frac{1-x^2}{x(x^2+1)} \equiv \frac{A}{x} + \frac{Bx+C}{x^2+1}$$

then $1 - x^2 \equiv A(x^2+1) + (Bx+C)x$
Putting $x = 0$ $1 = A$ $\therefore \quad A = 1$
Comparing coefficients, x^2: $-1 = A + B$ $\therefore \quad B = -2$
                    x: $0 = C$ $\therefore \quad C = 0$

$$\therefore \quad \int \frac{1-x^2}{x(x^2+1)}\,dx = \int \left\{ \frac{1}{x} - \frac{2x}{x^2+1} \right\} dx$$

$$= \ln x - \ln(x^2+1) + c$$

$$= \ln\left(\frac{x}{x^2+1} \right) + c, \quad \text{for} \quad x > 0.$$

Example 4   Evaluate $\displaystyle\int_0^1 \frac{1}{(x+1)(x^2+2x+2)}\,dx.$

Let
$$\frac{1}{(x+1)(x^2+2x+2)} \equiv \frac{A}{x+1} + \frac{Bx+C}{x^2+2x+2}$$

then $1 \equiv A(x^2+2x+2) + (Bx+C)(x+1)$
Putting $x = -1$: $1 = A$ $\therefore \quad A = 1$
Putting $x = 0$: $1 = 2A + C$ $\therefore \quad C = -1$
Comparing coefficients of x^2: $0 = A + B$ $\therefore \quad B = -1$

$$\therefore \quad \int_0^1 \frac{1}{(x+1)(x^2+2x+2)}\,dx = \int_0^1 \left\{ \frac{1}{x+1} - \frac{x+1}{x^2+2x+2} \right\} dx$$

$$= \int_0^1 \left\{ \frac{1}{x+1} - \frac{1}{2}\left(\frac{2x+2}{x^2+2x+2} \right) \right\} dx$$

$$= \left[\ln(x+1) - \tfrac{1}{2}\ln(x^2+2x+2) \right]_0^1$$

$$= (\ln 2 - \tfrac{1}{2}\ln 5) - (\ln 1 - \tfrac{1}{2}\ln 2)$$

$$= \tfrac{3}{2}\ln 2 - \tfrac{1}{2}\ln 5$$

$$= \tfrac{1}{2}(3\ln 2 - \ln 5) = \tfrac{1}{2}\ln(8/5).$$

Example 5   Find $\int \dfrac{x-4}{(x-1)^2(2x+1)}\,dx$.

Let
$$\frac{x-4}{(x-1)^2(2x+1)} \equiv \frac{A}{x-1} + \frac{B}{(x-1)^2} + \frac{C}{(2x+1)}$$

then $x - 4 \equiv A(x-1)(2x+1) + B(2x+1) + C(x-1)^2$

Putting $x = 1$: $-3 = 3B$ $\therefore\quad B = -1$

Putting $x = -\frac{1}{2}$: $-\frac{9}{2} = \frac{9}{4}C$ $\therefore\quad C = -2$

Comparing coefficients of x^2: $0 = 2A + C$ $\therefore\quad A = 1$

$$\therefore \int \frac{x-4}{(x-1)^2(2x+1)}\,dx = \int \left\{ \frac{1}{x-1} - \frac{1}{(x-1)^2} - \frac{2}{2x+1} \right\} dx$$

$$= \ln|x-1| + \frac{1}{x-1} - \ln|2x+1| + c$$

$$= \frac{1}{x-1} + \ln\left| \frac{x-1}{2x+1} \right| + c.$$

Exercise 20.2

Find the following indefinite integrals.

1. $\displaystyle\int \frac{3}{(x-1)(x+2)}\,dx$

2. $\displaystyle\int \frac{1}{1-x^2}\,dx$

3. $\displaystyle\int \frac{1}{x(x-3)}\,dx$

4. $\displaystyle\int \frac{x}{x^2-4}\,dx$

5. $\displaystyle\int \frac{4x}{x^2-2x-3}\,dx$

6. $\displaystyle\int \frac{2x-5}{(x-2)(x-3)}\,dx$

7. $\displaystyle\int \frac{3x+5}{(x+1)(x+3)}\,dx$

8. $\displaystyle\int \frac{x-1}{x(2x-1)}\,dx$

9. $\displaystyle\int \frac{2x-11}{x^2-5x+4}\,dx$

10. $\displaystyle\int \frac{x^2}{1-x^2}\,dx$

11. $\displaystyle\int \frac{x-2}{x^2-4x-8}\,dx$

12. $\displaystyle\int \frac{x^3}{x^2-4}\,dx$

13. $\int \dfrac{2x^2 + 1}{(x + 1)^2(x - 2)} \, dx$

14. $\int \dfrac{x + 2}{x^2(x - 1)} \, dx$

15. $\int \dfrac{x}{(x + 3)^2} \, dx$

16. $\int \dfrac{x^2 + 2x - 1}{(x + 1)(x^2 + 1)} \, dx$

17. $\int \dfrac{x + 1}{(x^2 + 1)(x - 1)} \, dx$

18. $\int \dfrac{x}{(x^2 + 3)(x^2 + 5)} \, dx$

19. $\int \dfrac{4x^2 + x + 4}{(2x + 1)(x^2 + 2)} \, dx$

20. $\int \dfrac{x^3 - 3x - 4}{x^3 - 1} \, dx$

Evaluate the following definite integrals.

21. $\displaystyle\int_1^2 \dfrac{x}{(x + 1)(x + 2)} \, dx$

22. $\displaystyle\int_3^4 \dfrac{5}{x^2 + x - 6} \, dx$

23. $\displaystyle\int_4^5 \dfrac{2x}{x^2 - 4x + 3} \, dx$

24. $\displaystyle\int_0^{1/3} \dfrac{3x}{1 - x^2} \, dx$

25. $\displaystyle\int_0^{1/3} \dfrac{3 + x}{(1 - x)(1 + 3x)} \, dx$

26. $\displaystyle\int_2^3 \dfrac{1}{x(x - 1)} \, dx$

27. $\displaystyle\int_1^2 \dfrac{x - 3}{x(x + 1)(x + 3)} \, dx$

28. $\displaystyle\int_0^2 \dfrac{x^3 + 4x^2 + 3x - 2}{x^2 + 4x + 3} \, dx$

29. $\displaystyle\int_1^2 \dfrac{1}{x^2(x + 1)} \, dx$

30. $\displaystyle\int_3^4 \dfrac{x^2 + x - 3}{(x - 2)^2(x - 1)} \, dx$

31. $\displaystyle\int_3^4 \dfrac{x^3}{(x - 1)(x - 2)} \, dx$

32. $\displaystyle\int_4^5 \dfrac{2x^2 + 10x + 40}{(x - 3)^2(x + 1)} \, dx$

33. $\displaystyle\int_3^4 \dfrac{2x + 1}{(x - 2)(x^2 + 1)} \, dx$

34. $\displaystyle\int_1^2 \dfrac{2(x + 2)^2}{x^2(x^2 + 4)} \, dx$

35. $\displaystyle\int_0^1 \dfrac{(x - 2)^2}{x^3 + 1} \, dx$

36. $\displaystyle\int_2^3 \dfrac{x + 3}{(x - 1)(x^2 - x + 2)} \, dx$

37. Find $\displaystyle\int \frac{4}{(x-1)(x+3)}\,dx$ for (a) $x>1$, (b) $-3<x<1$, (c) $x<-3$.

38. Find $\displaystyle\int \frac{x-4}{2x^2-x-3}\,dx$ for (a) $x>1\frac{1}{2}$, (b) $x<1\frac{1}{2}$.

20.3 Integration by substitution

The integration methods considered so far rely on the use of differentiation results in reverse. Integrating by substitution is a more systematic procedure, roughly equivalent to reversing the "chain rule" method for differentiating composite functions.

Suppose that as a result of applying the chain rule we have:

$$\frac{dy}{dx} = 10(2x+3)^4$$

We can work "backwards" to an expression for y as follows:

$$\frac{dy}{dx} = \frac{dy}{du} \times \frac{du}{dx}$$

$\therefore$ substituting $u = 2x+3$ gives $\dfrac{dy}{dx} = 10u^4$, $\dfrac{du}{dx} = 2$ and thus

$$10u^4 = \frac{dy}{du} \times 2 \quad \text{i.e.} \quad \frac{dy}{du} = 5u^4.$$

Hence $y = u^5 + c = (2x+3)^5 + c.$

The above method can be modified to produce a useful general result.

Let $\dfrac{dy}{dx} = F(x)$,   so that $y = \displaystyle\int F(x)\,dx.$

If, in terms of another variable u, $F(x) = G(u)$,

then $\dfrac{dy}{du} = \dfrac{dy}{dx} \times \dfrac{dx}{du} = F(x)\dfrac{dx}{du} = G(u)\dfrac{dx}{du}$

$\therefore$ $y = \displaystyle\int G(u)\frac{dx}{du}\,du$

i.e. $\boxed{\text{if} \quad F(x) = G(u), \quad \text{then} \quad \displaystyle\int F(x)\,dx = \int G(u)\frac{dx}{du}\,du.}$

Hence, when simplifying an integral $\displaystyle\int F(x)\,dx$ by a change to a new variable u, we must express $F(x)$ in terms of u and replace dx by $\dfrac{dx}{du}\,du$.

[Note that in this context a statement such as $dx = \dfrac{dx}{du}\,du$ is often used as shorthand for "dx may be replaced by $\dfrac{dx}{du}\,du$".]

There are three different ways of expressing suitable substitutions.

(i)   If $f(x) = u$, then $f'(x) = \dfrac{du}{dx}$,

and
$$dx = \frac{dx}{du}\,du = \frac{1}{f'(x)}\,du$$

$\therefore$ we write
$$f'(x)\,dx = du.$$

(ii) If $x = g(u)$, then $\dfrac{dx}{du} = g'(u)$,

$\therefore$ we write
$$dx = g'(u)du.$$

(iii) If $f(x) = g(u)$, then $f'(x)\dfrac{dx}{du} = g'(u)$,

$\therefore$ we write
$$f'(x)\,dx = g'(u)\,du.$$

Example 1   Find $\displaystyle\int 10(2x + 3)^4\,dx$.

Let $2x + 3 = u$,   then $2dx = du$.

$\therefore$ $\displaystyle\int 10(2x + 3)^4\,dx = \int 5(2x + 3)^4 \times 2\,dx$

$$= \int 5u^4\,du$$

$$= u^5 + c = (2x + 3)^5 + c.$$

Example 2   Find $\displaystyle\int \sin^3 2x \cos 2x\,dx$.

Let $\sin 2x = u$,   then $2\cos 2x\,dx = du$.

$\therefore$ $\displaystyle\int \sin^3 2x \cos 2x\,dx = \int \tfrac{1}{2}\sin^3 2x \times 2\cos 2x\,dx$

$$= \int \tfrac{1}{2}u^3\,du$$

$$= \tfrac{1}{8}u^4 + c = \tfrac{1}{8}\sin^4 2x + c.$$

Example 3 Find $\int x\sqrt{(2x-1)}\,dx$.

Let $\qquad 2x-1=u^2,$ $\qquad\qquad\qquad\qquad 2x=u^2+1$

then $\qquad 2dx=2u\,du,$ $\qquad\qquad\qquad\qquad x=\frac{1}{2}(u^2+1)$

$\therefore \qquad\quad dx=u\,du$

$$\int x\sqrt{(2x-1)}\,dx = \int \frac{1}{2}(u^2+1)\times u\times u\,du$$

$$= \frac{1}{2}\int(u^4+u^2)\,du$$

$$= \frac{1}{2}(\frac{1}{5}u^5+\frac{1}{3}u^3)+c$$

$$= \frac{1}{30}u^3(3u^2+5)+c$$

$\therefore \quad \int x\sqrt{(2x-1)}\,dx = \frac{1}{30}(2x-1)^{3/2}(3\{2x-1\}+5)+c$

$$= \frac{1}{15}(2x-1)^{3/2}(3x+1)+c.$$

When the method of substitution is applied to a definite integral, the limits of integration must be changed as well as the variable.

Example 4 Evaluate $\int_0^1 4x(3x^2-1)^3\,dx$.

Let $\qquad 3x^2-1=u,$ $\qquad\qquad\qquad\qquad x=1\Rightarrow u=2$

then $\qquad 6x\,dx=du$ $\qquad\qquad\qquad\qquad x=0\Rightarrow u=-1$

$$\int_0^1 4x(3x^2-1)^3\,dx = \int_0^1 \frac{2}{3}(3x^2-1)^3\times 6x\,dx$$

$$= \int_{-1}^2 \frac{2}{3}u^3\,du$$

$$= \left[\frac{1}{6}u^4\right]_{-1}^2$$

$$= \frac{1}{6}\{2^4-(-1)^4\} = \frac{15}{6} = 2\frac{1}{2}.$$

Example 5 Evaluate $\int_0^2 \sqrt{(4-x^2)}\,dx$.

$$\int_0^2 \sqrt{(4 - x^2)}\, dx$$

$$= \int_0^{\pi/2} 2\cos\theta \times 2\cos\theta\, d\theta$$

$$= \int_0^{\pi/2} 4\cos^2\theta\, d\theta$$

$$= \int_0^{\pi/2} (2 + 2\cos 2\theta)\, d\theta$$

$$= \left[2\theta + \sin 2\theta \right]_0^{\pi/2}$$

$$= \pi$$

Let $x = 2\sin\theta$
then $dx = 2\cos\theta\, d\theta$

$4 - x^2 = 4 - 4\sin^2\theta$
$\qquad = 4(1 - \sin^2\theta)$
$\qquad = 4\cos^2\theta$

$\therefore \quad \sqrt{(4 - x^2)} = 2\cos\theta$

$x = 2 \;\Rightarrow\; \theta = \tfrac{1}{2}\pi$
$x = 0 \;\Rightarrow\; \theta = 0$

When integrating trigonometric functions one useful substitution is $\tan\tfrac{1}{2}\theta = t$, where

$$\sin\theta = \frac{2t}{1 + t^2}, \quad \cos\theta = \frac{1 - t^2}{1 + t^2}, \quad \tan\theta = \frac{2t}{1 - t^2}$$

Example 6   Evaluate $\displaystyle\int_0^{\pi/2} \frac{4}{3 + 5\cos\theta}\, d\theta$.

$$\int_0^{\pi/2} \frac{4}{3 + 5\cos\theta}\, d\theta$$

$$= \int_0^1 \frac{4(1 + t^2)}{8 - 2t^2} \times \frac{2}{1 + t^2}\, dt$$

$$= \int_0^1 \frac{4}{4 - t^2}\, dt$$

$$= \int_0^1 \left\{ \frac{1}{2 + t} + \frac{1}{2 - t} \right\} dt$$

$$= \left[\ln(2 + t) - \ln(2 - t) \right]_0^1$$

$$= (\ln 3 - \ln 1) - (\ln 2 - \ln 2)$$

$$= \ln 3$$

Let $\tan\tfrac{1}{2}\theta = t$
then $\tfrac{1}{2}\sec^2\tfrac{1}{2}\theta\, d\theta = dt$
$\therefore \quad (1 + \tan^2\tfrac{1}{2}\theta)\, d\theta = 2dt$

$\therefore \qquad d\theta = \dfrac{2}{1 + t^2}\, dt$

$$3 + 5\cos\theta = 3 + 5\left(\frac{1 - t^2}{1 + t^2} \right)$$

$$= \frac{3(1 + t^2) + 5(1 - t^2)}{1 + t^2}$$

$$= \frac{8 - 2t^2}{1 + t^2}$$

$\theta = \tfrac{1}{2}\pi \;\Rightarrow\; t = 1$
$\theta = 0 \;\Rightarrow\; t = 0$

A change of variable may be helpful when finding areas and volumes by integration. For instance, to evaluate $\displaystyle\int_a^b y\, dx$ it may be simpler to work in terms of y rather than x. If x and y are given in parametric form it will usually be best to use the parameter as variable in any integrations.

Example 7   Find the area bounded by the curve $x = t^3 - 1$, $y = 5t^2 - 4$, the x- and y-axes and the line $x = 7$.

As shown in the sketch below, values of x from 0 to 7 are given by values of t from 1 to 2.

Since $x = t^3 - 1$, we have $dx = 3t^2 \, dt$.

Required area $= \displaystyle\int_0^7 y \, dx$

$= \displaystyle\int_1^2 (5t^2 - 4) \times 3t^2 \, dt$

$= \displaystyle\int_1^2 (15t^4 - 12t^2) \, dt$

$= \left[3t^5 - 4t^3 \right]_1^2$

$= (96 - 32) - (3 - 4) = 65.$

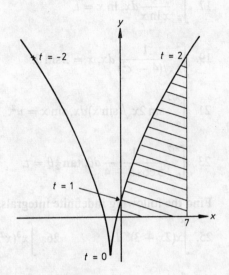

Exercise 20.3

Use the given substitutions to find the following indefinite integrals.

1. $\displaystyle\int (3x - 2)^3 \, dx, \, 3x - 2 = u.$

2. $\displaystyle\int (1 - 2x)^4 \, dx, \, 1 - 2x = u.$

3. $\displaystyle\int x(1 - x)^5 \, dx, \, 1 - x = u.$

4. $\displaystyle\int 2x^2(x^3 - 1)^3 \, dx, \, x^3 - 1 = u.$

5. $\displaystyle\int \tan^2 x \sec^2 x \, dx, \, \tan x = u.$

6. $\displaystyle\int \sin x \cos^5 x \, dx, \, \cos x = u.$

7. $\displaystyle\int x\sqrt{(x^2 + 4)} \, dx, \, x^2 + 4 = t^2.$

8. $\displaystyle\int x\sqrt{(1 - x)} \, dx, \, 1 - x = t^2.$

9. $\displaystyle\int \frac{x}{\sqrt{(2x + 1)}} \, dx, \, 2x + 1 = t^2.$

10. $\displaystyle\int \frac{e^x}{1 + e^x} \, dx, \, e^x = t.$

11. $\displaystyle\int \cos^3 \theta \, d\theta, \, \sin \theta = x.$

12. $\displaystyle\int \sin^3 \theta \cos^2 \theta \, d\theta, \, \cos \theta = x.$

13. $\displaystyle\int \frac{\sin \theta}{1 + \cos 2\theta} \, d\theta, \, \cos \theta = x.$

14. $\displaystyle\int \frac{\sec^2(\sqrt{x})}{\sqrt{x}} \, dx, \, \sqrt{x} = \theta.$

Use the given substitutions to find the following definite integrals.

15. $\int_4^5 (x - 1)\sqrt{(x - 4)}\, dx$, $x - 4 = u^2$.

16. $\int_0^1 x^2(1 - x)^{1/2}\, dx$, $1 - x = u^2$.

17. $\int_e^{e^2} \frac{1}{x \ln x}\, dx$, $\ln x = t$.

18. $\int_0^1 \frac{e^x}{(1 + e^x)^2}\, dx$, $e^x = t$.

19. $\int_0^2 \frac{1}{\sqrt{(4 - x^2)}}\, dx$, $x = 2 \sin \theta$.

20. $\int_0^{\sqrt{3}} \frac{1}{9 + x^2}\, dx$, $x = 3 \tan \theta$.

21. $\int_0^{\pi/2} \sin 2x \sqrt{(\sin x)}\, dx$, $\sin x = u^2$.

22. $\int_0^{1/2} (1 - x^2)^{1/2}\, dx$, $x = \sin u$.

23. $\int_0^{\pi/2} \frac{1}{5 \cos \theta + 4}\, d\theta$, $\tan \tfrac{1}{2}\theta = t$.

24. $\int_0^{\pi/4} \frac{1}{5 \cos^2 \theta - 1}\, d\theta$, $\tan \theta = t$.

Find the following indefinite integrals.

25. $\int x(2x + 3)^4\, dx$

26. $\int x^3(x^2 - 1)^3\, dx$

27. $\int \sqrt{(1 + 3x)}\, dx$

28. $\int \frac{x}{\sqrt{(3 + x)}}\, dx$

29. $\int \frac{x^2}{(x^3 - 1)^2}\, dx$

30. $\int \frac{x + 1}{(x - 1)^3}\, dx$

31. $\int xe^{x^2}\, dx$

32. $\int \frac{1}{x\sqrt{(\ln x)}}\, dx$

33. $\int \frac{e^x}{4 - e^{2x}}\, dx$

Find the following definite integrals

34. $\int_{-1}^2 x^2\sqrt{(x^3 + 1)}\, dx$

35. $\int_0^3 x\sqrt{(9 - x^2)}\, dx$

36. $\int_0^3 \sqrt{(9 - x^2)}\, dx$

37. $\int_1^2 \frac{x}{\sqrt{(4 - x^2)}}\, dx$

38. $\int_1^2 \frac{x^2}{\sqrt{(4 - x^2)}}\, dx$

39. $\int_0^{\ln 2} \frac{1}{1 + e^x}\, dx$

40. Find the area between the x-axis and the curve $x = 2t^3 - 1$, $y = t^2 - 1$ for $1 \leqslant t \leqslant 2$.

41. Find the area of the finite region bounded by the curve $x = 5t^2$, $y = 2t^3$ and the line $x = 5$. Find also the volume of the solid formed when this region is rotated through π radians about the x-axis.

42. Find the area bounded by the x-axis and the curve $x = \theta - \sin \theta$, $y = 1 - \cos \theta$ for $0 \leqslant \theta \leqslant 2\pi$.

43. Using the substitution $\tan\frac{1}{2}x = t$, or otherwise, show that

$$\int_{\pi/3}^{\pi/2} \frac{1}{1 + \sin x + \cos x}\, dx = 0.237$$

correct to 3 significant figures.

44. Using the substitution $x = 2\cos^2\theta + 5\sin^2\theta$, or otherwise, evaluate

$$\int_2^{7/2} \frac{1}{\sqrt{\{(x-2)(5-x)\}}}\, dx.$$

45. Using the substitution $\tan x = t$, or otherwise, show that

$$\int \frac{1}{1 - 2\sin^2 x}\, dx = \tfrac{1}{2}\ln\{\tan(x + \tfrac{1}{4}\pi)\} + c.$$

20.4 Integration by parts

A further general method of integration is obtained by considering the formula for differentiating a product. If u and v are functions of x, then

$$\frac{d}{dx}(uv) = u\frac{dv}{dx} + v\frac{du}{dx}$$

Integrating,

$$uv = \int u\frac{dv}{dx}\, dx + \int v\frac{du}{dx}\, dx$$

Rearranging,

$$\boxed{\int u\frac{dv}{dx}\, dx = uv - \int v\frac{du}{dx}\, dx} \tag{1}$$

This rule provides a way of expressing the integral of a product in terms of a second integral, which may be easier to find. The method is called *integration by parts*.

Example 1 Find $\int x\cos x\, dx$.

In rule (1), let $\quad u = x, \quad \dfrac{dv}{dx} = \cos x,$

$$\frac{du}{dx} = 1, \quad v = \sin x,$$

$$\therefore \int x\cos x\, dx = x\sin x - \int (\sin x \times 1)\, dx$$

$$= x\sin x - \int \sin x\, dx = x\sin x + \cos x + c.$$

[Note that it is not necessary to introduce an arbitrary constant when integrating $\dfrac{dv}{dx}$ to give v, since rule (1) is valid for any function v such that $\dfrac{dv}{dx} = \cos x$.]

Example 2   Find $\displaystyle\int x \ln x \, dx$.

In rule (1), let $u = \ln x, \quad \dfrac{dv}{dx} = x$,

$$\dfrac{du}{dx} = \dfrac{1}{x}, \quad v = \tfrac{1}{2}x^2,$$

$\therefore \quad \displaystyle\int x \ln x \, dx = \tfrac{1}{2}x^2 \ln x - \int \left(\tfrac{1}{2}x^2 \times \dfrac{1}{x} \right) dx$

$$= \tfrac{1}{2}x^2 \ln x - \int \tfrac{1}{2}x \, dx = \tfrac{1}{2}x^2 \ln x - \tfrac{1}{4}x^2 + c.$$

For definite integrals the rule for integration by parts becomes

$$\int_a^b u \dfrac{dv}{dx} \, dx = \left[uv \right]_a^b - \int_a^b v \dfrac{du}{dx} \, dx \qquad (2)$$

Example 3   Evaluate $\displaystyle\int_0^1 x^2 e^x \, dx$.

In rule (2), let $u = x^2, \quad \dfrac{dv}{dx} = e^x$,

$$\dfrac{du}{dx} = 2x, \quad v = e^x,$$

$\therefore \quad \displaystyle\int_0^1 x^2 e^x \, dx = \left[x^2 e^x \right]_0^1 - \int_0^1 (e^x \times 2x) \, dx$

$$= e - 2 \int_0^1 x e^x \, dx.$$

In rule (2), let $u = x, \quad \dfrac{dv}{dx} = e^x$,

$$\dfrac{du}{dx} = 1, \quad v = e^x,$$

$\therefore \quad \displaystyle\int_0^1 x e^x \, dx = \left[x e^x \right]_0^1 - \int_0^1 e^x \, dx$

$$= e - \left[e^x \right]_0^1 = e - (e - 1) = 1.$$

Hence $\displaystyle\int_0^1 x^2 e^x \, dx = e - 2\int_0^1 xe^x \, dx = e - 2.$

Integration by parts is also used to integrate functions which are not products.

Example 4   Find $\displaystyle\int \ln x \, dx.$

In rule (1), let $u = \ln x, \quad \dfrac{dv}{dx} = 1,$

$$\dfrac{du}{dx} = \dfrac{1}{x}, \qquad v = x,$$

$\displaystyle\therefore \quad \int \ln x \, dx = x \ln x - \int \left(x \times \dfrac{1}{x} \right) dx$

$$= x \ln x - \int dx = x \ln x - x + c.$$

The next example illustrates a further way in which integration by parts may be used.

Example 5   Find $\displaystyle\int e^x \cos x \, dx.$

Integrating by parts,

$$\int e^x \cos x \, dx = e^x \sin x - \int e^x \sin x \, dx \qquad\qquad \text{(i)}$$

Integrating by parts,

$$\int e^x \sin x \, dx = e^x(-\cos x) - \int (-\cos x) e^x \, dx$$

$$= -e^x \cos x + \int e^x \cos x \, dx$$

Substituting this expression for $\displaystyle\int e^x \sin x \, dx$ in (i),

$$\int e^x \cos x \, dx = e^x \sin x - \left(-e^x \cos x + \int e^x \cos x \, dx \right)$$

$$= e^x \sin x + e^x \cos x - \int e^x \cos x \, dx$$

$\displaystyle\therefore \quad 2\int e^x \cos x \, dx = e^x \sin x + e^x \cos x + k$

Hence $\displaystyle\int e^x \cos x \, dx = \tfrac{1}{2} e^x (\sin x + \cos x) + c.$

Exercise 20.4

Find the following indefinite integrals.

1. $\int x \sin x \, dx$

2. $\int x \cos \frac{1}{2} x \, dx$

3. $\int x e^{-x} \, dx$

4. $\int x \ln 2x \, dx$

5. $\int x e^{2x} \, dx$

6. $\int x \sec^2 x \, dx$

7. $\int x \sin x \cos x \, dx$

8. $\int x \tan^2 x \, dx$

9. $\int x \cos^2 x \, dx$

10. $\int x^2 \cos x \, dx$

11. $\int x^3 e^x \, dx$

12. $\int x^3 \ln x \, dx$

13. $\int x(\ln x)^2 \, dx$

14. $\int \ln(x-1) \, dx$

15. $\int e^{-x} \sin x \, dx$

Find the following definite integrals.

16. $\int_0^\pi x \cos x \, dx$

17. $\int_{-1}^1 x e^x \, dx$

18. $\int_0^{\pi/3} x \sin 3x \, dx$

19. $\int_1^e \ln x \, dx$

20. $\int_0^\pi x \sin^2 x \, dx$

21. $\int_1^2 x^2 \ln x \, dx$

22. $\int_2^3 x^2 e^{-x} \, dx$

23. $\int_1^e \frac{1}{x^3} \ln x \, dx$

24. $\int_0^{\pi/2} x^2 \sin x \, dx$

25. $\int_0^\pi e^x \sin x \, dx$

26. $\int_1^2 x^2 e^{2x} \, dx$

27. $\int_e^{e^2} \ln(\sqrt{x}) \, dx$

28. Find $\int x(x+1)^4 \, dx$ using (a) integration by parts, (b) the substitution $x + 1 = t$.

29. Find, using integration by parts or otherwise,

(a) $\int x \sqrt{(x-1)} \, dx$,

(b) $\int \frac{x}{(x+2)^3} \, dx$.

30. Use integration by parts to show that

(a) $2 \int \cos^2 x \, dx = \cos x \sin x + x + c$,

(b) $3 \int \cos^3 x \, dx = \cos^2 x \sin x + 2 \sin x + c$.

20.5 Use of inverse trigonometric functions

The inverse trigonometric functions $\sin^{-1}x$ and $\tan^{-1}x$ are defined as follows:

$$y = \sin^{-1}x \Rightarrow \sin y = x \quad \text{and} \quad -\tfrac{1}{2}\pi \leqslant y \leqslant \tfrac{1}{2}\pi$$
$$y = \tan^{-1}x \Rightarrow \tan y = x \quad \text{and} \quad -\tfrac{1}{2}\pi < y < \tfrac{1}{2}\pi$$

In §11.6 two important integration results were obtained by differentiating $\sin^{-1}\dfrac{x}{a}$ and $\tan^{-1}\dfrac{x}{a}$.

$$\int \frac{1}{\sqrt{(a^2 - x^2)}}\,dx = \sin^{-1}\frac{x}{a} + c, \quad \int \frac{1}{a^2 + x^2}\,dx = \frac{1}{a}\tan^{-1}\frac{x}{a} + c.$$

[These integrals can also be found by substituting $x = a\sin\theta$ and $x = a\tan\theta$ respectively.]

Example 1 Evaluate (a) $\displaystyle\int_0^1 \frac{1}{\sqrt{(4 - x^2)}}\,dx$, (b) $\displaystyle\int_0^2 \frac{1}{4 + x^2}\,dx$.

(a) $\displaystyle\int_0^1 \frac{1}{\sqrt{(4 - x^2)}}\,dx = \left[\sin^{-1}\frac{x}{2}\right]_0^1 = \sin^{-1}\frac{1}{2} - \sin^{-1}0 = \frac{\pi}{6}$.

(b) $\displaystyle\int_0^2 \frac{1}{4 + x^2}\,dx = \left[\frac{1}{2}\tan^{-1}\frac{x}{2}\right]_0^2 = \frac{1}{2}\tan^{-1}1 - \frac{1}{2}\tan^{-1}0 = \frac{\pi}{8}$.

Example 2 Find (a) $\displaystyle\int \frac{1}{\sqrt{(9 - 4x^2)}}\,dx$, (b) $\displaystyle\int \frac{1}{25 + 16x^2}\,dx$.

(a) Let $2x = u$, then $4x^2 = u^2$ and $2dx = du$,

$$\therefore \int \frac{1}{\sqrt{(9 - 4x^2)}}\,dx = \frac{1}{2}\int \frac{1}{\sqrt{(9 - u^2)}}\,du$$

$$= \frac{1}{2}\sin^{-1}\frac{u}{3} + c.$$

$$= \frac{1}{2}\sin^{-1}\frac{2x}{3} + c.$$

(b) Let $4x = u$, then $16x^2 = u^2$ and $4dx = du$,

$$\therefore \int \frac{1}{25 + 16x^2}\,dx = \frac{1}{4}\int \frac{1}{25 + u^2}\,du$$

$$= \frac{1}{4} \times \frac{1}{5}\tan^{-1}\frac{u}{5} + c$$

$$= \frac{1}{20}\tan^{-1}\frac{4x}{5} + c.$$

The method of Example 2 can be extended to integrals of the form

$$\int \frac{1}{\sqrt{(ax^2 + bx + c)}} dx, \qquad \int \frac{1}{ax^2 + bx + c} dx.$$

Example 3   Find $\int \dfrac{1}{x^2 - 2x + 2} dx.$

$$x^2 - 2x + 2 = (x^2 - 2x + 1) + 1 = (x - 1)^2 + 1$$

$$\therefore \quad \int \frac{1}{x^2 - 2x + 2} dx = \int \frac{1}{(x - 1)^2 + 1} dx$$

$$= \int \frac{1}{u^2 + 1} du \qquad\qquad \text{letting } x - 1 = u$$
$$\qquad\qquad\qquad\qquad\qquad\qquad dx = du$$

$$= \tan^{-1} u + c$$
$$= \tan^{-1}(x - 1) + c.$$

The remaining examples illustrate further uses of inverse trigonometric functions.

Example 4   Find $\int \dfrac{x + 3}{x^2 + 9} dx.$

$$\int \frac{x + 3}{x^2 + 9} dx = \int \left\{ \frac{x}{x^2 + 9} + \frac{3}{x^2 + 9} \right\} dx = \frac{1}{2} \int \frac{2x}{x^2 + 9} dx + 3 \int \frac{1}{x^2 + 9} dx$$

$$= \frac{1}{2} \ln(x^2 + 9) + \tan^{-1} \frac{x}{3} + c.$$

Example 5   Evaluate $\displaystyle\int_0^1 \frac{3 - x}{(x + 1)(x^2 + 1)} dx.$

Let $\quad \dfrac{3 - x}{(x + 1)(x^2 + 1)} \equiv \dfrac{A}{x + 1} + \dfrac{Bx + C}{x^2 + 1}$

then $\qquad\qquad 3 - x \equiv A(x^2 + 1) + (Bx + C)(x + 1)$

Putting $x = -1$: $4 = 2A \qquad\qquad \therefore \quad A = 2$

Putting $x = 0$: $3 = A + C \qquad\qquad \therefore \quad C = 1$

Comparing coefficients of x^2:

$$0 = A + B \qquad\qquad \therefore \quad B = -2$$

$$\therefore \quad \int_0^1 \frac{3 - x}{(x + 1)(x^2 + 1)} dx = \int_0^1 \left\{ \frac{2}{x + 1} + \frac{(-2x + 1)}{x^2 + 1} \right\} dx$$

$$= \int_0^1 \left\{ \frac{2}{x + 1} - \frac{2x}{x^2 + 1} + \frac{1}{x^2 + 1} \right\} dx$$

$$= \left[2\ln(x + 1) - \ln(x^2 + 1) + \tan^{-1} x \right]_0^1$$

$$= (2\ln 2 - \ln 2 + \tan^{-1} 1) - (2\ln 1 - \ln 1 + \tan^{-1} 0)$$
$$= \ln 2 + \tfrac{1}{4}\pi.$$

Example 6   Find $\displaystyle\int \frac{2x^2}{\sqrt{(1-x^2)}}\,dx$.

$$\int \frac{2x^2}{\sqrt{(1-x^2)}}\,dx$$

$$= \int \frac{2\sin^2\theta}{\cos\theta} \times \cos\theta\,d\theta$$

$$= \int (1 - \cos 2\theta)\,d\theta$$

$$= \theta - \tfrac{1}{2}\sin 2\theta + c$$

$$= \theta - \sin\theta\cos\theta + c$$

$$= \sin^{-1}x - x\sqrt{(1-x^2)} + c.$$

Let $\qquad x = \sin\theta$

then $\qquad dx = \cos\theta\,d\theta$

$$1 - x^2 = 1 - \sin^2\theta$$
$$= \cos^2\theta$$
$$\therefore \ \sqrt{(1-x^2)} = \cos\theta$$

Exercise 20.5

Find the following indefinite integrals.

1. $\displaystyle\int \frac{1}{\sqrt{(16 - x^2)}}\,dx$

2. $\displaystyle\int \frac{1}{x^2 + 25}\,dx$

3. $\displaystyle\int \frac{1}{\sqrt{(1 - 4x^2)}}\,dx$

4. $\displaystyle\int \frac{x + 1}{x^2 + 1}\,dx$

5. $\displaystyle\int \frac{1}{\sqrt{(4 - 25x^2)}}\,dx$

6. $\displaystyle\int \frac{1}{4 + 9x^2}\,dx$

7. $\displaystyle\int \frac{x^2 - x}{(x + 1)(x^2 + 1)}\,dx$

8. $\displaystyle\int \frac{4}{(1 - x)(1 + x^2)}\,dx$

9. $\displaystyle\int \frac{6(x - 3)}{x(x^2 + 9)}\,dx$

10. $\displaystyle\int \frac{5x^2 + 4x - 20}{(x + 2)(x^2 + 4)}\,dx$

11. $\displaystyle\int \frac{1}{x^2 + 2x + 5}\,dx$

12. $\displaystyle\int \frac{1}{\sqrt{(5 + 4x - x^2)}}\,dx$

Evaluate the following definite integrals.

13. $\displaystyle\int_0^{\sqrt{3}} \frac{1}{x^2 + 9}\,dx$

14. $\displaystyle\int_0^5 \frac{1}{\sqrt{(25 - x^2)}}\,dx$

15. $\displaystyle\int_0^{1/2} \frac{1}{4x^2 + 1}\,dx$

16. $\displaystyle\int_{-2}^2 \frac{x + 2}{x^2 + 4}\,dx$

17. $\displaystyle\int_0^1 \frac{4}{(x + 1)(x^2 + 1)}\,dx$

18. $\displaystyle\int_3^4 \frac{1}{x^2 - 6x + 10}\,dx$

19. $\displaystyle\int_{-1/2}^{1/2} \frac{1}{\sqrt{(3 - 4x - 4x^2)}}\,dx$

Use appropriate substitutions to find the following indefinite integrals.

29. $\int \dfrac{e^x + e^{2x}}{1 + e^{2x}} dx$

21. $\int \dfrac{1}{e^x + e^{-x}} dx$

22. $\int \sqrt{(1 - x^2)} \, dx$

23. $\int \dfrac{1 - x}{\sqrt{(1 - x^2)}} dx$

Use the given substitutions to find the following indefinite integrals.

24. $\int \dfrac{2x}{x^2 - 2x + 10} dx, \; x = u + 1.$

25. $\int \dfrac{x}{x^4 + 2x^2 + 2} dx, \; x^2 = u - 1.$

26. $\int \dfrac{1}{x\sqrt{(x^2 - 1)}} dx, \; x = \dfrac{1}{u}.$

27. Evaluate correct to 3 significant figures

(a) $\displaystyle\int_1^3 \dfrac{4 - 3x}{(2x - 1)(x^2 + 1)} dx,$

(b) $\displaystyle\int_0^1 \dfrac{7x + 2}{(x + 1)^2(x^2 + 4)} dx$

28. Use integration by parts to show that

$$\int \sin^{-1} x \, dx = x \sin^{-1} x + \sqrt{(1 - x^2)} + c.$$

20.6 Properties of the definite integral

The definite integral is defined formally as the limit of a sum by considering a function $f(x)$ in the interval $a \leqslant x \leqslant b$.

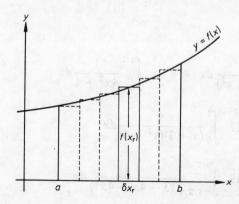

Suppose that this interval is divided into n subintervals of lengths $\delta x_1, \delta x_2, \ldots, \delta x_n$. If n is increased in such a way that the values of $\delta x_1, \delta x_2, \ldots, \delta x_n$ tend to zero, then

$$\int_a^b f(x) \, dx = \lim_{n \to \infty} \left\{ \sum_{r=1}^n f(x_r) \, \delta x_r \right\},$$

where x_r lies in the interval of length δx_r.

This definition may be expressed more simply as

$$\int_a^b y\,dx = \lim_{\delta x \to 0} \sum y\,\delta x.$$

In general the value of this integral represents the area bounded by the curve $y = f(x)$, the x-axis, the lines $x = a$ and $x = b$. We must remember, however, that areas above the x-axis are positive and areas below the x-axis are negative.

The most important properties of the definite integral are as follows:

$$\int_a^b f(x)\,dx + \int_a^b g(x)\,dx = \int_a^b \{f(x) + g(x)\}\,dx.$$

$$\int_a^b kf(x)\,dx = k\int_a^b f(x)\,dx, \quad \text{where } k \text{ is a constant.}$$

$$\int_b^a f(x)\,dx = -\int_a^b f(x)\,dx,$$

$$\int_a^b f(x)\,dx + \int_b^c f(x)\,dx = \int_a^c f(x)\,dx.$$

If $f(x)$ is an *even function* then the curve $y = f(x)$ will be symmetrical about the y-axis. Hence the area under the curve between $x = -a$ and $x = 0$ is equal to the area between $x = 0$ and $x = a$.

∴

$$\text{if} f(x) \text{ is an even function } \int_{-a}^a f(x)\,dx = 2\int_0^a f(x)\,dx.$$

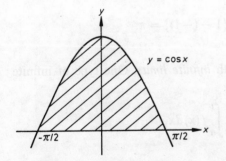

$y = \cos x$

For instance, if $f(x) = \cos x$,
$$f(-x) = \cos(-x) = \cos x = f(x)$$

∴
$$\int_{-\pi/2}^{\pi/2} \cos x\,dx = 2\int_0^{\pi/2} \cos x\,dx$$

$$= 2\left[\sin x\right]_0^{\pi/2} = 2.$$

If $f(x)$ is an *odd function*, the areas bounded by the curve $y = f(x)$ and the x-axis between $x = -a$ and $x = 0$ and between $x = 0$ and $x = a$ are numerically equal but opposite in sign,

∴

$$\text{if } f(x) \text{ is an odd function } \int_{-a}^a f(x)\,dx = 0.$$

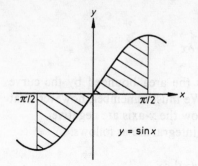

For instance, if $f(x) = \sin x$,
$$f(-x) = \sin(-x) = -\sin x = -f(x)$$

$$\therefore \quad \int_{-\pi/2}^{\pi/2} \sin x \, dx = 0.$$

The symmetries of the sine function can also be used when integrating functions of the form $xf(\sin x)$. We illustrate the method by a simple example.

Example 1   Evaluate $I = \displaystyle\int_0^\pi x \sin x \, dx$.

$$I = -\int_\pi^0 (\pi - u)\sin(\pi - u)\,du \qquad\qquad \text{Let} \quad x = \pi - u$$
$$\text{then} \quad dx = -du$$

$$= \int_0^\pi (\pi - u)\sin u \, du \qquad\qquad\qquad x = \pi \;\Rightarrow\; u = 0$$
$$x = 0 \;\Rightarrow\; u = \pi$$

$$= \int_0^\pi \pi \sin u \, du - \int_0^\pi u \sin u \, du$$

$$= \pi \int_0^\pi \sin u \, du - I$$

$$\therefore \quad I = \tfrac{1}{2}\pi \int_0^\pi \sin u \, du = \tfrac{1}{2}\pi \Big[-\cos u \Big]_0^\pi = \tfrac{1}{2}\pi\{1 - (-1)\} = \pi.$$

Finally we consider definite integrals with *infinite limits*. One type of infinite integral is defined as follows:

$$\int_0^\infty f(x)\,dx = \lim_{t \to \infty} \int_0^t f(x)\,dx,$$

provided that this limit exists.

Example 2   Evaluate $\displaystyle\int_0^\infty e^{-x}\,dx$.

$$\int_0^t e^{-x}\,dx = \Big[-e^{-x} \Big]_0^t = -e^{-t} + 1$$

$$\therefore \quad \int_0^\infty e^{-x}\,dx = \lim_{t \to \infty}(-e^{-t} + 1) = 1.$$

Exercise 20.6

1. Evaluate the following integrals using the properties of odd and even functions.

(a) $\displaystyle\int_{-1}^{1} x^4\, dx,$ (b) $\displaystyle\int_{-3}^{3} x(x^2 - 1)\, dx,$ (c) $\displaystyle\int_{-\pi}^{\pi} \sin^2 x\, dx,$

(d) $\displaystyle\int_{-\pi/3}^{\pi/3} \frac{1}{1 + \cos 2x}\, dx,$ (e) $\displaystyle\int_{-4}^{4} \frac{x}{x^2 - 25}\, dx,$ (f) $\displaystyle\int_{-1}^{1} \frac{x \cos x}{1 + \tan^2 x}\, dx.$

2. Sketch the curve $y = (x^2 - 1)(x - 3)$. Hence evaluate $\displaystyle\int_{-7}^{9} (x^2 - 1)(x - 3)\, dx.$

3. Using sketch graphs, or otherwise, evaluate

(a) $\displaystyle\int_{-2}^{2} [x]\, dx,$ (b) $\displaystyle\int_{-2}^{2} |x|\, dx,$ (c) $\displaystyle\int_{-2}^{2} (x + |x|)\, dx.$

4. Evaluate (a) $\displaystyle\int_{0}^{3} (x - 2)\, dx,$ (b) $\displaystyle\left| \int_{0}^{3} (x - 2)\, dx \right|,$ (c) $\displaystyle\int_{0}^{3} |x - 2|\, dx.$

5. Evaluate (a) $\displaystyle\int_{0}^{3} x(x - 2)\, dx,$ (b) $\displaystyle\int_{0}^{3} |x(x - 2)|\, dx.$

6. Prove that $\displaystyle\int_{0}^{a} f(x)\, dx = \int_{0}^{a} f(a - x)\, dx.$ Hence, or otherwise, show that

(a) $\displaystyle\int_{0}^{\pi} \frac{x \sin x}{4 - \cos^2 x}\, dx = \tfrac{1}{4}\pi \ln 3,$ (b) $\displaystyle\int_{0}^{\pi} \frac{x \sin x}{1 + \cos^2 x}\, dx = \tfrac{1}{4}\pi^2.$

7. Evaluate $\displaystyle\int_{0}^{1} e^x\, dx.$ Hence show that

$$\lim_{n \to \infty} \frac{1}{n}\left\{ e^{1/n} + e^{2/n} + e^{3/n} + \ldots + e \right\} = e - 1.$$

8. Evaluate $\displaystyle\int_{0}^{1} \frac{x\, dx}{\sqrt{(1 + x)}}.$ By considering integration as the limit of a sum, or otherwise, show that

$$\lim_{n \to \infty} \frac{1}{n\sqrt{n}} \left\{ \frac{1}{\sqrt{(n + 1)}} + \frac{2}{\sqrt{(n + 2)}} + \ldots + \frac{n}{\sqrt{(2n)}} \right\} = \tfrac{2}{3}(2 - \sqrt{2}). \qquad \text{(JMB)}$$

9. Explain what is wrong with the following mathematical arguments and evaluate the integrals I and J correctly:

(i) Let $I = \displaystyle\int_{0}^{2} \frac{1}{x^2 - 2x + 2}\, dx.$ Then putting $x - 1 = \cot \theta$ we have

$$I = \int_{\cot^{-1}(-1)}^{\cot^{-1}(1)} \frac{-\csc^2 \theta}{\cot^2 \theta + 1}\, d\theta = -\int_{-\pi/4}^{\pi/4} d\theta = -\tfrac{1}{2}\pi.$$

(ii) Let $J = \displaystyle\int_0^\pi e^{|\sin x|}|\cos x|\, dx$. Then putting $u = |\sin x|$ we have $du = |\cos x|\, dx$ and

so $J = \displaystyle\int_0^0 e^u\, du = 0$.   (C)

10. Evaluate (a) $\displaystyle\int_0^\infty e^{-x/2}\, dx$, (b) $\displaystyle\int_1^\infty \frac{1}{x^2}\, dx$, (c) $\displaystyle\int_{-\infty}^\infty \frac{1}{1+x^2}\, dx$.

11. Use appropriate substitutions to show that

(i) $\displaystyle\int_1^{ak} \frac{1}{t}\, dt = k\int_1^a \frac{1}{u}\, du$,

(ii) $\displaystyle\int_a^{ab} \frac{1}{t}\, dt = \int_1^b \frac{1}{u}\, du$.

Defining $\ln x$ as $\displaystyle\int_1^x \frac{1}{t}\, dt$, deduce that

(iii) $\ln(a^k) = k\ln a$,

(iv) $\ln(ab) = \ln a + \ln b$.

Exercise 20.7 (miscellaneous)

In questions 1 to 15 evaluate the given definite integrals.

1. $\displaystyle\int_0^4 \frac{x}{2x+1}\, dx$

2. $\displaystyle\int_{-1/2}^0 \frac{x}{(x+1)^2}\, dx$

3. $\displaystyle\int_1^2 \frac{1}{4x^2-1}\, dx$

4. $\displaystyle\int_{-1}^4 \frac{1}{\sqrt{(3x+4)}}\, dx$

5. $\displaystyle\int_2^3 \frac{x^2+1}{x(x-1)}\, dx$

6. $\displaystyle\int_0^2 (4-x^2)\sqrt{x}\, dx$

7. $\displaystyle\int_0^2 x\sqrt{(4-x^2)}\, dx$

8. $\displaystyle\int_0^\pi (\sin x + \cos x)^2\, dx$

9. $\displaystyle\int_0^{\pi/3} 2\sin 2x \cos x\, dx$

10. $\displaystyle\int_0^{\pi/4} \tan^3 x\, dx$

11. $\displaystyle\int_0^{\pi/4} \sin^3 x \cos^3 x\, dx$

12. $\displaystyle\int_{\ln 2}^{\ln 5} \frac{2}{e^x - e^{-x}}\, dx$

13. $\displaystyle\int_0^{\pi/4} \frac{\sin 2x}{1+\cos^2 x}\, dx$

14. $\displaystyle\int_0^1 x^2\sqrt{(1-x^2)}\, dx$

15. $\displaystyle\int_0^1 2^x\, dx$

16. Find $\displaystyle\int \frac{2x-1}{(x+2)(x-3)^2}\,dx$, given that $x > 3$.

17. Show that $\displaystyle\int_0^3 \frac{x+3}{x^2+3}\,dx = \ln 2 + \frac{\pi\sqrt{3}}{3}$.

In questions 18 to 21 use the given substitutions to evaluate the definite integrals.

18. $\displaystyle\int_{\sqrt{2}}^2 \frac{1}{x\sqrt{(x^2-1)}}\,dx$, $x = \sec\theta$.

19. $\displaystyle\int_0^{1/2} \sqrt{\left(\frac{x}{1-x}\right)}\,dx$, $x = \sin^2\theta$.

20. $\displaystyle\int_0^1 \frac{1}{(1+x^2)}\,dx$, $x = \tan\theta$.

21. $\displaystyle\int_0^{\pi/6} \sec x \, dx$, $\sin x = u$.

22. Use integration by parts and the result of question 21 to show that

$$\int_0^{\pi/6} \sec^3 x \, dx = \tfrac{1}{3} + \tfrac{1}{4}\ln 3.$$

23. Show that the curve $y = \dfrac{3}{(2x+1)(1-x)}$ has only one turning point. Find the coordinates of this point and determine its nature. Sketch the curve. Find the area of the region enclosed by the curve and the line $y = 3$.   (JMB)

24. Find the coordinates of the turning point of the curve $y = (x^2-4)/(x+1)^2$ and ascertain the nature of this turning point. Calculate the area of the region enclosed by the curve, the y-axis and the x-axis between $x = 0$ and $x = 2$.   (AEB 1978)

25. If $f(x) = \dfrac{x^2+x+2}{(x^2+1)(x-1)}$ express $f(x)$ in partial fractions and hence evaluate $\displaystyle\int_2^3 f(x)\,dx$ and $\displaystyle\int_{-3}^{-2} f(x)\,dx$ each correct to 2 places of decimals.   (SU)

26. The region enclosed by the loop of the curve $y^2(3-x) = x^2(3+x)$ is rotated about the x-axis through four right angles. Show that the volume of the solid of revolution is $18\pi(3\ln 2 - 2)$.   (C)

27. (i) Given that $0 < a < b$, sketch the graph of $y = |x-a|$ for $-b \leqslant x \leqslant b$. Hence, or otherwise, find $\displaystyle\int_{-b}^b |x-a|\,dx$.

  (ii) Find the value of $\displaystyle\int_1^2 \log_{10} x \, dx$ leaving your answer in terms of logarithms.

  (iii) Using the substitution $x = \tfrac{1}{2}\sin\theta$, or otherwise, evaluate $\displaystyle\int_0^{1/4} \sqrt{(1-4x^2)}\,dx$.
     (L)

28. Sketch the curve given in terms of a parameter t by $x = 2a + at^2$, $y = 2at$ where a is a positive constant. Find the equation of the tangent and of the normal to the curve at the point where $t = 1$. Determine the area of the finite region bounded by the curve and the straight line joining the points at which $t = \pm 1$.   (L)

29. A curve is defined parametrically by the equations $x = \cos t$, $y = \sin^3 t$, $-\pi \leqslant t < \pi$. Show that the curve is symmetrical about each of the coordinate axes. Find dy/dx in terms of t and deduce the equation of the tangent to the curve at the point with parameter t_1. Sketch the curve. Show that the area, A, of the region enclosed by the curve is given by $A = 4 \int_0^{\pi/2} \sin^4 t \, dt$ and use the relation $2 \sin^2 \theta = 1 - \cos 2\theta$ to deduce that $A = 3\pi/4$.   (L)

30. The curve whose equation is $y = (1 - x)e^x$ meets the x-axis at A and the y-axis at B. The region bounded by the arc AB of the curve and the line segments OA and OB, where O is the origin, is rotated through a complete revolution about the x-axis. Show that the volume swept out is $\frac{1}{4}\pi(e^2 - 5)$.   (JMB)

31. Obtain $\int x^2 \cos 2x \, dx$ and hence prove that $\int_0^\pi x^2 \cos 2x \, dx = \frac{1}{2}\pi$. Find the area of the region enclosed by the curve $y = x \sin x$, for $0 \leqslant x \leqslant \pi$, and the x-axis. The region is rotated through 2π radians about the x-axis. Find the volume of the solid of revolution thus generated. From your results, or otherwise, find the volume of the solid of revolution generated by rotation of the same region through 2π radians about the line $y = -\frac{1}{8}$.   (O&C)

32. Express $y = \dfrac{2x^2 + 3x + 5}{(x + 1)(x^2 + 3)}$ in partial fractions and hence show that $\dfrac{dy}{dx} = -\dfrac{2}{3}$ when $x = 0$. Evaluate $\int_0^{\sqrt{3}} y \, dx$ and state the mean value of y in the interval $0 \leqslant x \leqslant \sqrt{3}$.   (AEB 1979)

33. Determine the values of p and q for which $x^2 - 4x + 5 \equiv (x - p)^2 + q$ and hence evaluate $\int_2^3 \dfrac{1}{x^2 - 4x + 5} \, dx$. Calculate also $\int_2^3 \dfrac{2x - 4}{x^2 - 4x + 5} \, dx$ and deduce, or find otherwise, the value of $\int_2^3 \dfrac{2x}{x^2 - 4x + 5} \, dx$.   (JMB)

34. (a) Using the formula for $\cos(A + B)$, express $\cos \theta$ in terms of $t = \tan \frac{1}{2}\theta$.
    (b) Express $\dfrac{10(1 + t^2)}{(1 - t^2)(1 + 9t^2)}$ in partial fractions.
    (c) With the help of (a) and (b), and using the substitution $t = \tan \frac{1}{2}\theta$, show that $\int_0^{\pi/3} \dfrac{5 \, d\theta}{5 \cos \theta - 4 \cos^2 \theta} = \log_e(2 + \sqrt{3}) + \frac{8}{9}\pi$.   (W)

35. (a) Using integration by parts, or otherwise, evaluate

$$\int \log_e x \, dx \quad \text{and} \quad \int (\log_e x)^2 \, dx.$$

(b) Sketch the graph of the function $\log_e x$. Let A and C denote the points $(1, 0)$ and $(e, 1)$ on the graph, and let B denote the point $(e, 0)$. The region bounded by the graph and the lines, AB, BC is rotated about the x-axis; find the volume of the solid so formed. Show that the volume of the solid formed by rotating the same region about the y-axis is $\frac{1}{2}\pi(e^2 + 1)$.

(W)

36. Evaluate (i) $\displaystyle\int_0^{\pi/2} \frac{\sin^3 \theta}{2 - \sin^2 \theta} \, d\theta$, (ii) $\displaystyle\int_0^{\sqrt{2}} xe^{-x^2} \, dx$.

37. Let $I = \displaystyle\int_0^\pi \frac{x \, dx}{1 + \sin x}$. Show, by means of the substitution $y = \pi - x$ that $I = \pi \displaystyle\int_0^{\pi/2} \frac{dx}{1 + \sin x}$. Hence, by means of the substitution $t = \tan \frac{1}{2}x$, or otherwise, evaluate I.

(JMB)

38. Draw the circle $x^2 + y^2 = a^2$ and, on the same diagram, the line $x = a/2$. Find by integration the smaller area between the line and the circumference of the circle and the volume generated when this area is rotated through 4 right-angles about the x-axis.

(SU)

39. The area A in the first quadrant bounded by the curve $(2 - x)y^2 = x$, the x-axis and the line $x = 1$ is rotated completely about the x-axis to form a solid of volume V. Find: (i) the volume V, (ii) the area A.

(AEB 1976)

40. Find the area of the region enclosed between the curves $y = x^2/2a$ and $y = a - x^4/2a^3$ $(a > 0)$. Find also the volume of the solid obtained by rotating this region through two right angles about the y-axis.

(O)

41. Sketch the curve $y^2 = x^2(4 - x^2)$. Find the area enclosed by one loop of the curve. Find also the volume of the solid generated when this loop is rotated through two right angles about the x-axis.

42. The domain of the function defined by $f(x) = e^{-x} \sin x$ is the set of real numbers in the interval $0 \le x \le 4\pi$. Show that stationary values of this function occur for values of x for which $\tan x = 1$. Determine the nature of these stationary values. Sketch the graph of the function. By integrating by parts twice, or otherwise, evaluate $\displaystyle\int_0^\pi f(x) \, dx$. Show that the ratio of $f(a + 2\pi)$ to $f(a)$ is independent of the value of a, and hence write down the value of $\displaystyle\int_{2\pi}^{3\pi} f(x) \, dx$.

(JMB)

43. By interpreting $\int_a^b f(x)\,dx$ as an area, show that

(i) $\displaystyle\int_0^\pi \sin^5 x \cos^5 x \, dx = 0$,   (ii) $\displaystyle\int_0^\pi e^{2x} \cos x \, dx < 0$,

(iii) for $n > 1$, $\dfrac{1}{n+1}\left(\dfrac{\pi}{4}\right)^{n+1} < \displaystyle\int_0^{\pi/4} \tan^n x \, dx < \dfrac{\pi}{8}$.   (JMB)

44. (a) By considering $\int x^{1/2}\,dx$ between suitable limits, or otherwise, prove that

$$\tfrac{2}{3}n^{3/2} < \sqrt{1} + \sqrt{2} + \cdots + \sqrt{n} < \tfrac{2}{3}\{(n+1)^{3/2} - 1\}.$$

(b) By considering an appropriate integral, prove that

$$\frac{1}{k}\left\{1 - \frac{1}{(n+1)^k}\right\} < \sum_{r=1}^n \frac{1}{r^{k+1}} < \frac{1}{k}\left\{k + 1 - \frac{1}{n^k}\right\}, \text{ where } k > 0.$$ (O&C)

21 Vectors and scalar product

21.1 Properties of vectors

We begin by reviewing some of the basic properties of vectors.

(1) The sum or resultant of two vectors
may be found using the triangle law
for vector addition

e.g. $\qquad$ $\mathbf{a} + \mathbf{b} = \mathbf{c}$.

Vector addition is both commutative and associative

i.e. $\qquad$ $\mathbf{a} + \mathbf{b} = \mathbf{b} + \mathbf{a}, \quad (\mathbf{a} + \mathbf{b}) + \mathbf{c} = \mathbf{a} + (\mathbf{b} + \mathbf{c})$.

(2) For any scalar λ, the vector $\lambda\mathbf{a}$ is parallel to $\mathbf{a}$ and has magnitude $|\lambda|$ times the magnitude of $\mathbf{a}$.

It can be shown that $\qquad$ $\lambda(\mu\mathbf{a}) = (\lambda\mu)\mathbf{a}$,
$$(\lambda + \mu)\mathbf{a} = \lambda\mathbf{a} + \mu\mathbf{a}, \quad \lambda(\mathbf{a} + \mathbf{b}) = \lambda\mathbf{a} + \lambda\mathbf{b}.$$

(3) Given two non-zero vectors $\mathbf{a}$ and $\mathbf{b}$, which are not parallel, any vector $\mathbf{r}$ in the plane of $\mathbf{a}$ and $\mathbf{b}$ can be expressed in the form $\lambda\mathbf{a} + \mu\mathbf{b}$. The vectors $\lambda\mathbf{a}$ and $\mu\mathbf{b}$ are the *component vectors* of $\mathbf{r}$ in the directions of *base vectors* $\mathbf{a}$ and $\mathbf{b}$.
   (i) If vectors $\lambda\mathbf{a} + \mu\mathbf{b}$ and $l\mathbf{a} + m\mathbf{b}$ are equal, then $\lambda = l$ and $\mu = m$.
   (ii) If vectors $\lambda\mathbf{a} + \mu\mathbf{b}$ and $l\mathbf{a} + m\mathbf{b}$ are parallel, then for some scalar t,
$$\lambda\mathbf{a} + \mu\mathbf{b} = t(l\mathbf{a} + m\mathbf{b}) \text{ and thus } \frac{\lambda}{l} = \frac{\mu}{m} = t.$$

(4) Given three non-zero vectors $\mathbf{a}$, $\mathbf{b}$ and $\mathbf{c}$, which are not coplanar, any vector $\mathbf{r}$ can be expressed in the form $\lambda\mathbf{a} + \mu\mathbf{b} + v\mathbf{c}$.
   (i) If vectors $\lambda\mathbf{a} + \mu\mathbf{b} + v\mathbf{c}$ and $l\mathbf{a} + m\mathbf{b} + n\mathbf{c}$ are equal, then $\lambda = l$, $\mu = m$ and $v = n$.
   (ii) If vectors $\lambda\mathbf{a} + \mu\mathbf{b} + v\mathbf{c}$ and $l\mathbf{a} + m\mathbf{b} + n\mathbf{c}$ are parallel, then for some scalar t,
$$\lambda\mathbf{a} + \mu\mathbf{b} + v\mathbf{c} = t(l\mathbf{a} + m\mathbf{b} + n\mathbf{c}) \text{ and thus } \frac{\lambda}{l} = \frac{\mu}{m} = \frac{v}{n} = t.$$

(5) If $\mathbf{r} = x\mathbf{i} + y\mathbf{j} + z\mathbf{k}$, where $\mathbf{i}, \mathbf{j}$ and $\mathbf{k}$ are unit vectors in the directions of the x-, y- and z-axes respectively then,

(i) the magnitude of $\mathbf{r}$ is given by $r = \sqrt{(x^2 + y^2 + z^2)}$,

(ii) the unit vector in the direction of $\mathbf{r}$ is $\hat{\mathbf{r}} = \dfrac{x}{r}\mathbf{i} + \dfrac{y}{r}\mathbf{j} + \dfrac{z}{r}\mathbf{k}$.

(6)

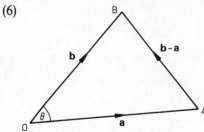

If the position vectors of points A and B with respect to O are $\mathbf{a}$ and $\mathbf{b}$ respectively, then $\mathbf{OA} = \mathbf{a}$, $\mathbf{OB} = \mathbf{b}$ and $\mathbf{AB} = \mathbf{b} - \mathbf{a}$.

(i) The distance between A and B is given by $|\mathbf{b} - \mathbf{a}|$ (or $|\mathbf{a} - \mathbf{b}|$).

(ii) If θ is the angle between $\mathbf{a}$ and $\mathbf{b}$, then the cosine rule can be used to express $\cos\theta$ in terms of $|\mathbf{a}|, |\mathbf{b}|$ and $|\mathbf{a} - \mathbf{b}|$.

(iii) A point C, with position vector $\mathbf{c}$, lies on the straight line passing through A and B if and only if there is a scalar λ such that $\mathbf{AC} = \lambda\mathbf{AB}$ i.e. $\mathbf{c} - \mathbf{a} = \lambda(\mathbf{b} - \mathbf{a})$.

The fundamental ideas summarised in paragraphs (1) to (6) form the foundation for the work of this chapter.

(i)

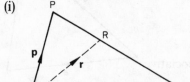

(ii)

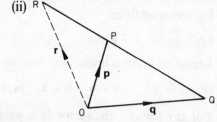

Let us consider three points P, Q and R such that R divides PQ in the ratio $\mu:\lambda$. We will observe the convention that (i) if λ and μ have the same sign then R lies between P and Q, and (ii) if λ and μ have opposite signs then R does not lie between P and Q.

In both cases
$$\lambda\mathbf{PR} = \mu\mathbf{RQ}$$
$$\therefore \quad \lambda(\mathbf{OR} - \mathbf{OP}) = \mu(\mathbf{OQ} - \mathbf{OR})$$
$$\therefore \quad \lambda\mathbf{OR} - \lambda\mathbf{OP} = \mu\mathbf{OQ} - \mu\mathbf{OR}$$
Hence
$$(\lambda + \mu)\mathbf{OR} = \lambda\mathbf{OP} + \mu\mathbf{OQ}$$

This result is called the *ratio theorem* and may also be stated as follows:

The resultant of the vectors $\lambda\mathbf{OP}$ and $\mu\mathbf{OQ}$ is $(\lambda + \mu)\mathbf{OR}$, where R is the point which divides PQ in the ratio $\mu:\lambda$

If the position vectors of P, Q and R with respect to O are $\mathbf{p}, \mathbf{q}$ and $\mathbf{r}$ respectively then
$$(\lambda + \mu)\mathbf{r} = \lambda\mathbf{p} + \mu\mathbf{q}.$$

Thus the point R which divides PQ in the ratio $\mu:\lambda$ has position vector

$$\mathbf{r} = \frac{\lambda\mathbf{p} + \mu\mathbf{q}}{\lambda + \mu}$$

In particular, if R is the *mid-point* of PQ, then $\mathbf{r} = \frac{1}{2}(\mathbf{p} + \mathbf{q})$.

Example 1 The points A and B have position vectors $\mathbf{a} = \mathbf{i} + 3\mathbf{j} - 2\mathbf{k}$ and $\mathbf{b} = 6\mathbf{i} - 2\mathbf{j} + 3\mathbf{k}$ respectively. Find the position vectors of the point P which divides AB internally in the ratio $1:4$ and the point Q which divides AB externally in the ratio $3:2$.

Observing the usual sign convention, P divides AB in the ratio $1:4$ and Q divides AB in the ratio $3:-2$.
Thus the position vector of P

$$= \frac{4\mathbf{a} + \mathbf{b}}{4 + 1} = \frac{4(\mathbf{i} + 3\mathbf{j} - 2\mathbf{k}) + (6\mathbf{i} - 2\mathbf{j} + 3\mathbf{k})}{5} = 2\mathbf{i} + 2\mathbf{j} - \mathbf{k}.$$

Similarly, the position vector of Q

$$= \frac{-2\mathbf{a} + 3\mathbf{b}}{-2 + 3} = -2(\mathbf{i} + 3\mathbf{j} - 2\mathbf{k}) + 3(6\mathbf{i} - 2\mathbf{j} + 3\mathbf{k}) = 16\mathbf{i} - 12\mathbf{j} + 13\mathbf{k}.$$

[Note that the same result will be obtained for the position vector of Q if the ratio $-3:2$ is used instead of the ratio $3:-2$.]

Example 2 Prove that the medians of a triangle meet at a point which divides each median in the ratio $2:1$.

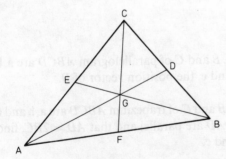

In $\triangle ABC$ let D, E and F be the mid-points of BC, CA and AB respectively. If the position vectors of A, B and C are $\mathbf{a}, \mathbf{b}$ and $\mathbf{c}$, then the position vectors of D, E and F are $\frac{1}{2}(\mathbf{b} + \mathbf{c}), \frac{1}{2}(\mathbf{c} + \mathbf{a})$ and $\frac{1}{2}(\mathbf{a} + \mathbf{b})$ respectively.

Let G be the point which divides AD in the ratio $2:1$, then its position vector is $\dfrac{1 \times \mathbf{a} + 2 \times \frac{1}{2}(\mathbf{b} + \mathbf{c})}{1 + 2}$ i.e. $\frac{1}{3}(\mathbf{a} + \mathbf{b} + \mathbf{c})$.

Since this expression is symmetrical in $\mathbf{a}, \mathbf{b}$ and $\mathbf{c}$, G must also be the point which divides BE and CF in the ratio $2:1$. Hence the medians meet at a point which divides each median in the ratio $2:1$.

[As stated in §8.1 the point G with position vector $\frac{1}{3}(\mathbf{a} + \mathbf{b} + \mathbf{c})$ is the centroid of $\triangle ABC$.]

Let us consider again the points P, Q and R with position vectors $\mathbf{p}, \mathbf{q}$ and $\mathbf{r}$ respectively. It follows from the ratio theorem that if $(\lambda + \mu)\mathbf{r} = \lambda\mathbf{p} + \mu\mathbf{q}$, then R is the point which divides PQ in the ratio $\mu:\lambda$. If $\lambda + \mu = 1$, we obtain the following useful result.

If $\mathbf{r} = \lambda\mathbf{p} + \mu\mathbf{q}$ for scalars λ and μ such that $\lambda + \mu = 1$, then R is the point which divides PQ in the ratio $\mu:\lambda$.

Example 3 In a parallelogram $OABC$, P is the mid-point of AB and Q divides OP in the ratio $2:1$. Show that Q lies on AC and find the ratio $AQ:QC$.

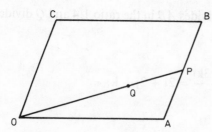

Let the position vectors of A, B, C, P and Q with respect to O be $\mathbf{a}, \mathbf{b}, \mathbf{c}, \mathbf{p}$ and $\mathbf{q}$ respectively.

P is the mid-point of AB

$$\therefore \quad \mathbf{p} = \tfrac{1}{2}(\mathbf{a} + \mathbf{b})$$

Q divides OP in the ratio $2:1$

$$\therefore \quad \mathbf{q} = \tfrac{2}{3}\mathbf{p} = \tfrac{2}{3} \times \tfrac{1}{2}(\mathbf{a} + \mathbf{b}) = \tfrac{1}{3}\mathbf{a} + \tfrac{1}{3}\mathbf{b}$$

However, since $OABC$ is a parallelogram, $\mathbf{b} = \mathbf{a} + \mathbf{c}$,

$$\therefore \quad \mathbf{q} = \tfrac{1}{3}\mathbf{a} + \tfrac{1}{3}(\mathbf{a} + \mathbf{c}) = \tfrac{2}{3}\mathbf{a} + \tfrac{1}{3}\mathbf{c}$$

Hence, by the ratio theorem, Q is the point on AC such that $AQ:QC = 1:2$.

Exercise 21.1

1.   The position vectors of the vertices A, B and C of parallelogram $ABCD$ are $\mathbf{a}, \mathbf{b}$ and $\mathbf{c}$ respectively. Find, in terms of $\mathbf{a}, \mathbf{b}$ and $\mathbf{c}$, the position vector of D.

2.   The position vectors of the vertices A, B and C of trapezium $ABCD$ are $\mathbf{a}, \mathbf{b}$ and $\mathbf{c}$ respectively. Given that the sides BC and AD are parallel and that $AD = 2BC$, find the position vector of D in terms of $\mathbf{a}, \mathbf{b}$ and $\mathbf{c}$.

3.   Find the angle between the vectors $\mathbf{a}$ and $\mathbf{b}$ given that $|\mathbf{a}| = 3$, $|\mathbf{b}| = 8$ and $|\mathbf{a} - \mathbf{b}| = 7$.

4.   The angle between the vectors $\mathbf{a}$ and $\mathbf{b}$ is $120°$. If $|\mathbf{a}| = 5$ and $|\mathbf{b}| = 3$, find $|\mathbf{a} - \mathbf{b}|$ and $|\mathbf{a} + \mathbf{b}|$.

5.   The points A and B have position vectors $\mathbf{a}$ and $\mathbf{b}$ respectively relative to an origin O, where $\mathbf{a} = 2\mathbf{i} + \mathbf{j} - 3\mathbf{k}$ and $\mathbf{b} = -4\mathbf{i} + s\mathbf{j} + t\mathbf{k}$. Find the possible values of s and t if (a) the points O, A and B are collinear, (b) $|AB| = 7$ and $s = 2t$.

6. Given that $\mathbf{a} = 2\mathbf{i} + 6\mathbf{j}$ and $\mathbf{b} = 3\mathbf{i} + t\mathbf{j}$, find the value of t such that (a) $\mathbf{a}$ and $\mathbf{b}$ are parallel, (b) $\mathbf{a}$ and $\mathbf{b}$ are at right angles.

7. If the points A and B have position vectors $\mathbf{a}$ and $\mathbf{b}$ respectively, find in terms of $\mathbf{a}$ and $\mathbf{b}$ the position vectors of (a) the point P which divides AB internally in the ratio $5:3$, (b) the point Q which divides AB externally in the ratio $3:1$, (c) the point R such that A is the mid-point of BR.

8. The points A and B have position vectors $\mathbf{a} = 5\mathbf{i} + 4\mathbf{j} + \mathbf{k}$ and $\mathbf{b} = -\mathbf{i} + \mathbf{j} - 2\mathbf{k}$ respectively. Find the position vectors of (a) the point C on AB such that $AC = 2CB$, (b) the point D on AB produced such that $AD = 2BD$.

9. Write down, in terms of $\mathbf{i}, \mathbf{j}$ and $\mathbf{k}$, the position vectors of the points $A(2, -5, 3)$ and $B(7, 0, -2)$. Hence find the coordinates of the point C which divides AB internally in the ratio $2:3$ and the point D which divides AB externally in the ratio $3:8$.

10. The vertices A, B and C of a triangle have position vectors $\mathbf{a}, \mathbf{b}$ and $\mathbf{c}$ respectively. Points P, Q and R have position vectors given respectively by $\mathbf{p} = \mathbf{a} - \mathbf{b} + \mathbf{c}$, $\mathbf{q} = \frac{3}{7}\mathbf{a} + \frac{4}{7}\mathbf{c}, \mathbf{r} = 3\mathbf{b} - 2\mathbf{c}$. Describe geometrically the positions of P, Q and R relative to A, B and C.

11. The diagonals AC and BD of a quadrilateral $ABCD$ intersect at a point P such that $AP:PC = 2:7$ and $BP:PD = 5:4$. Show that

$$\frac{7\mathbf{a} - 4\mathbf{b}}{7 - 4} = \frac{5\mathbf{d} - 2\mathbf{c}}{5 - 2}$$

where $\mathbf{a}, \mathbf{b}, \mathbf{c}$ and $\mathbf{d}$ are the position vectors of A, B, C and D respectively. Explain the geometrical significance of this result.

12. The vertices A, B and C of a triangle have position vectors $\mathbf{a}, \mathbf{b}$ and $\mathbf{c}$ respectively. The point P divides BC internally in the ratio $3:1$, the point Q is the mid-point of CA and the point R divides AB externally in the ratio $1:3$. If the position vectors of P, Q and R are $\mathbf{p}, \mathbf{q}$ and $\mathbf{r}$ respectively, express $\mathbf{r}$ in terms of $\mathbf{p}$ and $\mathbf{q}$. Hence show that R lies on PQ produced and find the ratio $PR:QR$.

21.2 Equations of lines and planes

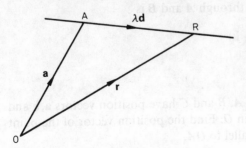

The diagram shows a straight line which passes through a fixed point A with position vector $\mathbf{a}$ and which is parallel to a given vector $\mathbf{d}$. Let $\mathbf{r}$ be the position vector of a point R on the line.

Since **AR** is parallel to **d**, then, for some scalar λ,

$$\mathbf{AR} = \lambda\mathbf{d}$$

i.e.
$$\mathbf{r} - \mathbf{a} = \lambda\mathbf{d}$$
$$\mathbf{r} = \mathbf{a} + \lambda\mathbf{d}$$

Thus every point on the line has a position vector of the form $\mathbf{a} + \lambda\mathbf{d}$. Moreover, each real value of the parameter λ corresponds to some point on the line.

The equation $\mathbf{r} = \mathbf{a} + \lambda\mathbf{d}$ is called the *vector equation* of the line through A parallel to **d**. The vector **d** is a *direction vector* of the line.

Example 1   Find the vector equation of the line which passes through the point with position vector $2\mathbf{i} - \mathbf{j} + 3\mathbf{k}$ and which is parallel to the vector $2\mathbf{j} - \mathbf{k}$.

The vector equation of the given line is

$$\mathbf{r} = 2\mathbf{i} - \mathbf{j} + 3\mathbf{k} + \lambda(2\mathbf{j} - \mathbf{k})$$

i.e.
$$\mathbf{r} = 2\mathbf{i} + (2\lambda - 1)\mathbf{j} + (3 - \lambda)\mathbf{k}.$$

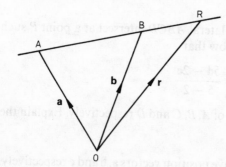

Consider now the line through two points A and B with position vectors **a** and **b** respectively. If a point R, with position vector **r**, lies on this line, then for some scalar λ,

$$\mathbf{AR} = \lambda\mathbf{AB}$$
$$\therefore \quad \mathbf{r} - \mathbf{a} = \lambda(\mathbf{b} - \mathbf{a})$$
$$\therefore \quad \mathbf{r} = \mathbf{a} + \lambda(\mathbf{b} - \mathbf{a}).$$

Hence the vector equation of the line through A and B is $\mathbf{r} = (1 - \lambda)\mathbf{a} + \lambda\mathbf{b}$.

Example 2   Find the vector equation of the straight line which passes through the points $A(1, 0, -2)$ and $B(2, 3, -1)$.

The position vectors of A and B are $\mathbf{i} - 2\mathbf{k}$ and $2\mathbf{i} + 3\mathbf{j} - \mathbf{k}$ respectively.
Hence the vector equation of the line through A and B is

$$\mathbf{r} = (1 - \lambda)(\mathbf{i} - 2\mathbf{k}) + \lambda(2\mathbf{i} + 3\mathbf{j} - \mathbf{k})$$

i.e.
$$\mathbf{r} = (\lambda + 1)\mathbf{i} + 3\lambda\mathbf{j} + (\lambda - 2)\mathbf{k}.$$

Example 3   Three non-collinear points A, B and C have position vectors $\mathbf{a}, \mathbf{b}$ and $\frac{4}{3}\mathbf{a} - \frac{2}{3}\mathbf{b}$ respectively, relative to an origin O. Find the position vector of the point D on CA produced, such that BD is parallel to OA.

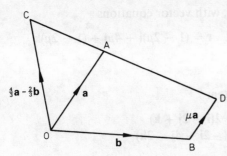

The vector equation of the line through A and C is

$$\mathbf{r} = (1 - \lambda)\mathbf{a} + \lambda(\tfrac{4}{3}\mathbf{a} - \tfrac{2}{3}\mathbf{b})$$
i.e. $\mathbf{r} = (1 + \tfrac{1}{3}\lambda)\mathbf{a} - \tfrac{2}{3}\lambda\mathbf{b}.$

The vector equation of the line through B parallel to OA is

$$\mathbf{r} = \mathbf{b} + \mu\mathbf{a}$$

At the point D where these lines intersect

$$(1 + \tfrac{1}{3}\lambda)\mathbf{a} - \tfrac{2}{3}\lambda\mathbf{b} = \mu\mathbf{a} + \mathbf{b}$$

Since the vectors $\mathbf{a}$ and $\mathbf{b}$ are not parallel, it follows that

$1 + \tfrac{1}{3}\lambda = \mu$ and $-\tfrac{2}{3}\lambda = 1$

$\therefore \qquad \lambda = -\tfrac{3}{2}, \quad \mu = \tfrac{1}{2}$

Hence the position vector of D is $\tfrac{1}{2}\mathbf{a} + \mathbf{b}$.

In three dimensional space a pair of vector equations such as $\mathbf{r} = \mathbf{a} + \lambda\mathbf{p}$ and $\mathbf{r} = \mathbf{b} + \mu\mathbf{q}$ may represent
(i)   the same line,   (ii)   parallel lines,
(iii) intersecting lines,   (iv)   skew lines.

Example 4   Show that the lines l_1 and l_2, with vector equations $\mathbf{r} = \mathbf{k} + \lambda(\mathbf{i} - \mathbf{j} - 3\mathbf{k})$ and $\mathbf{r} = 2\mathbf{i} + \mathbf{j} + \mu(3\mathbf{j} + 5\mathbf{k})$ respectively, intersect, and find the position vector of their point of intersection.

The equations of l_1 and l_2 may be written:

$$\mathbf{r} = \lambda\mathbf{i} - \lambda\mathbf{j} + (1 - 3\lambda)\mathbf{k}$$
$$\mathbf{r} = 2\mathbf{i} + (1 + 3\mu)\mathbf{j} + 5\mu\mathbf{k}$$

At any point of intersection

$$\lambda\mathbf{i} - \lambda\mathbf{j} + (1 - 3\lambda)\mathbf{k} = 2\mathbf{i} + (1 + 3\mu)\mathbf{j} + 5\mu\mathbf{k}$$
Thus
$$\lambda = 2 \qquad\qquad\qquad\qquad\qquad (1)$$
$$-\lambda = 1 + 3\mu \qquad\qquad\qquad\quad (2)$$
$$1 - 3\lambda = 5\mu \qquad\qquad\qquad\qquad (3)$$

From (1) and (2), $\lambda = 2, \mu = -1.$

Since these values also satisfy equation (3), the lines do have a point of intersection. Its position vector, given by substituting $\lambda = 2$ in the equation of l_1, is $2\mathbf{i} - 2\mathbf{j} - 5\mathbf{k}$.

[Note that we can check this result by substituting $\mu = -1$ in the equation of l_2.]

Example 5   Show that the lines l_1 and l_2, with vector equations

$$\mathbf{r} = \lambda\mathbf{i} + (3 - 2\lambda)\mathbf{j} + (2 + \lambda)\mathbf{k} \quad \text{and} \quad \mathbf{r} = (1 - 2\mu)\mathbf{i} + 4\mu\mathbf{j} + (1 - 2\mu)\mathbf{k}$$

respectively, are distinct parallel lines.

The equations of l_1 and l_2 may be written:

$$\mathbf{r} = 3\mathbf{j} + 2\mathbf{k} + \lambda(\mathbf{i} - 2\mathbf{j} + \mathbf{k})$$
$$\mathbf{r} = \mathbf{i} + \mathbf{k} + \mu(-2\mathbf{i} + 4\mathbf{j} - 2\mathbf{k})$$

Thus l_1 passes through a point A with position vector $\mathbf{a} = 3\mathbf{j} + 2\mathbf{k}$ and is parallel to the vector $\mathbf{p} = \mathbf{i} - 2\mathbf{j} + \mathbf{k}$.
Similarly l_2 passes through a point B with position vector $\mathbf{b} = \mathbf{i} + \mathbf{k}$ and is parallel to the vector $\mathbf{q} = -2\mathbf{i} + 4\mathbf{j} - 2\mathbf{k}$.
Since $\mathbf{q} = -2\mathbf{p}$, the vectors $\mathbf{p}$ and $\mathbf{q}$ are parallel.
Hence the lines l_1 and l_2 are parallel or coincident.
Since $\mathbf{AB} = \mathbf{b} - \mathbf{a} = \mathbf{i} - 3\mathbf{j} - \mathbf{k}$, which is not a scalar multiple of $\mathbf{p}$, the line through A and B is not parallel to $\mathbf{p}$.
Hence the lines l_1 and l_2 must be distinct parallel lines.

Example 6   Show that the lines with vector equations $\mathbf{r} = 2\lambda\mathbf{i} - 3\mathbf{j} + (\lambda - 2)\mathbf{k}$ and $\mathbf{r} = (\mu + 1)\mathbf{i} + (2 - \mu)\mathbf{j} + (2\mu - 5)\mathbf{k}$ do not intersect.

At any point of intersection

$$2\lambda\mathbf{i} - 3\mathbf{j} + (\lambda - 2)\mathbf{k} = (\mu + 1)\mathbf{i} + (2 - \mu)\mathbf{j} + (2\mu - 5)\mathbf{k}$$

Thus
$$2\lambda = \mu + 1 \tag{1}$$
$$-3 = 2 - \mu \tag{2}$$
$$\lambda - 2 = 2\mu - 5 \tag{3}$$

From (2), $\mu = 5$
Using (1), $2\lambda = 5 + 1$ $\therefore$ $\lambda = 3$

Testing these values in (3):

$$\lambda - 2 = 1, \quad 2\mu - 5 = 5$$

$\therefore$ no values of λ and μ can be found which satisfy all three equations.
Hence the given lines do not intersect.

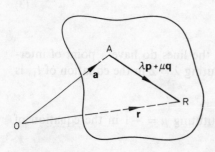

Consider now a plane which passes through a point A with position vector $\mathbf{a}$ and which contains non-parallel vectors $\mathbf{p}$ and $\mathbf{q}$. Let $\mathbf{r}$ be the position vector of a point R in the plane.

Since **AR** lies in the plane, there are scalars λ and μ such that

$$\mathbf{AR} = \lambda\mathbf{p} + \mu\mathbf{q}$$
$$\mathbf{r} - \mathbf{a} = \lambda\mathbf{p} + \mu\mathbf{q}$$

i.e.
$$\mathbf{r} = \mathbf{a} + \lambda\mathbf{p} + \mu\mathbf{q}.$$

This equation is called the *vector equation* of the plane in *parametric form*.

Example 7   Write down the vector equation of the plane through the point with position vector $\mathbf{i} - 2\mathbf{k}$ which is parallel to the vectors $\mathbf{i} + \mathbf{j}$ and $\mathbf{k}$.

The vector equation of the given plane is

$$\mathbf{r} = \mathbf{i} - 2\mathbf{k} + \lambda(\mathbf{i} + \mathbf{j}) + \mu\mathbf{k}$$

i.e. $\mathbf{r} = (\lambda + 1)\mathbf{i} + \lambda\mathbf{j} + (\mu - 2)\mathbf{k}.$

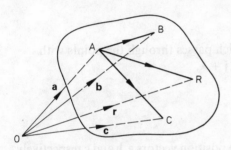

Suppose that $\mathbf{r}$ is the position vector of a point R which lies in the plane containing three non-collinear points A, B and C with position vectors $\mathbf{a}, \mathbf{b}$ and $\mathbf{c}$ respectively.

Since **AR** lies in the plane containing **AB** and **AC**, there are scalars λ and μ such that

$$\mathbf{AR} = \lambda\mathbf{AB} + \mu\mathbf{AC}$$
$$\mathbf{r} - \mathbf{a} = \lambda(\mathbf{b} - \mathbf{a}) + \mu(\mathbf{c} - \mathbf{a})$$

i.e.
$$\mathbf{r} = (1 - \lambda - \mu)\mathbf{a} + \lambda\mathbf{b} + \mu\mathbf{c}$$

This is the vector equation of the plane through given points A, B and C.

Example 8   Find a vector equation of the plane through the points $A(1, 0, 0)$, $B(2, -6, 1)$ and $C(-3, 0, 4)$. Hence find the coordinates of the point of intersection of the plane ABC and the line with vector equation $\mathbf{r} = 2t\mathbf{i} + (1 - 5t)\mathbf{j} + (t - 2)\mathbf{k}$.

The points A, B and C have position vectors $\mathbf{i}, 2\mathbf{i} - 6\mathbf{j} + \mathbf{k}$ and $-3\mathbf{i} + 4\mathbf{k}$ respectively.

∴   the vector equation of the plane ABC is

$$\mathbf{r} = (1 - \lambda - \mu)\mathbf{i} + \lambda(2\mathbf{i} - 6\mathbf{j} + \mathbf{k}) + \mu(-3\mathbf{i} + 4\mathbf{k})$$

i.e. $\mathbf{r} = (1 + \lambda - 4\mu)\mathbf{i} - 6\lambda\mathbf{j} + (\lambda + 4\mu)\mathbf{k}.$

The point of intersection of this plane with the line $\mathbf{r} = 2t\mathbf{i} + (1 - 5t)\mathbf{j} + (t - 2)\mathbf{k}$ is given by

$$1 + \lambda - 4\mu = 2t \qquad (1)$$
$$-6\lambda \qquad = -5t + 1 \qquad (2)$$
$$\lambda + 4\mu = t - 2 \qquad (3)$$

Adding (1) to (3), $1 + 2\lambda = 3t - 2$

$\therefore$ $2\lambda = 3t - 3$ (4)

Substituting in (2), $-3(3t - 3) = -5t + 1$

i.e. $-9t + 9 = -5t + 1$ $\therefore$ $t = 2$

Substituting in the equation of the line, $\mathbf{r} = 4\mathbf{i} - 9\mathbf{j}$.

Hence the coordinates of the point of intersection are $(4, -9, 0)$.

Exercise 21.2

1.   Find the vector equation of the line with direction vector $\mathbf{d}$ which passes through the point with position vector $\mathbf{a}$ given that

(a) $\mathbf{a} = \mathbf{i} + 2\mathbf{j} - \mathbf{k}, \mathbf{d} = 3\mathbf{i} - \mathbf{k}$,

(b) $\mathbf{a} = 4\mathbf{i} - 3\mathbf{k}, \mathbf{d} = \mathbf{i} - 3\mathbf{j} + 3\mathbf{k}$.

2.   Find the vector equation of the line which passes through the points with

(a) position vectors $2\mathbf{i} - 3\mathbf{j} + \mathbf{k}$ and $-2\mathbf{i} + \mathbf{j} + \mathbf{k}$,

(b) position vectors $\mathbf{i} + 5\mathbf{j}$ and $3\mathbf{i} - \mathbf{j} + 2\mathbf{k}$,

(c) coordinates $(0, 6, -8)$ and $(5, -7, 2)$,

(d) coordinates $(0, 0, 0)$ and $(5, -2, 3)$.

3.   The vertices A, B and C of a triangle have position vectors $\mathbf{a}, \mathbf{b}$ and $\mathbf{c}$ respectively. The point P divides BC internally in the ratio $2:1$ and the point Q divides AC externally in the ratio $2:1$. Find vector equations for the lines AP and BQ. Hence find the position vector of the point of intersection of the lines AP and BQ.

4.   The position vectors of points A and B with respect to an origin O are $\mathbf{a}$ and $\mathbf{b}$ respectively. P is the mid-point of OA and $APBQ$ is a parallelogram. The lines AB and OQ intersect at T. Find the position vectors of P, Q and T.

5.   The position vectors relative to an origin O of the points A and B are $\mathbf{a}$ and $\mathbf{b}$ respectively. The point P on AB is such that $3AP = PB$. The point Q on OP produced is such that AQ is parallel to OB. Find the position vector of the point of intersection of the lines OA and BQ.

6.   The position vectors of four points A, B, C, D are $\mathbf{a} = 5\mathbf{j}, \mathbf{b} = -6\mathbf{i} + \mathbf{j}, \mathbf{c} = 6\mathbf{i} - \mathbf{j}$, $\mathbf{d} = -3\mathbf{i} + 5\mathbf{j}$ respectively. The lines AB and CD intersect at a point X. Find the ratio $AX:XB$.

7.   Decide whether the following pairs of straight lines are intersecting, parallel or skew. If the lines intersect give the position vector of their point of intersection.

(a) $\mathbf{r} = (1 - \lambda)\mathbf{i} + 3\lambda\mathbf{j} + (2\lambda + 5)\mathbf{k}$,

   $\mathbf{r} = 2\mu\mathbf{i} + (\mu - 4)\mathbf{j} + 3\mathbf{k}$.

(b) $\mathbf{r} = -7\mathbf{i} + 4\mathbf{j} + 3\mathbf{k} + \lambda(2\mathbf{i} + \mathbf{k})$,

   $\mathbf{r} = 5\mathbf{i} + 8\mathbf{j} + \mathbf{k} + \mu(-4\mathbf{i} + 3\mathbf{k})$.

(c) $\mathbf{r} = 2\lambda\mathbf{i} + 3\mathbf{j} - (2\lambda + 5)\mathbf{k}$,

   $\mathbf{r} = (2 - 3\mu)\mathbf{i} - 4\mathbf{j} + 3\mu\mathbf{k}$.

(d) $\mathbf{r} = 2\lambda\mathbf{i} + (4\lambda + 1)\mathbf{j} + (5 - 3\lambda)\mathbf{k}$,

   $\mathbf{r} = (\mu + 4)\mathbf{i} + (5\mu + 3)\mathbf{j} + (\mu - 6)\mathbf{k}$.

8. Decide which of the points A, B and C, with position vectors $\mathbf{a} = \mathbf{i} - 2\mathbf{j}$, $\mathbf{b} = 3\mathbf{i} - \mathbf{j} - \mathbf{k}$ and $\mathbf{c} = \mathbf{i} + \mathbf{j} + 2\mathbf{k}$ respectively, lie on the following lines and planes.
(a) $\mathbf{r} = (2\lambda + 5)\mathbf{i} + \lambda\mathbf{j} - (\lambda + 2)\mathbf{k}$,
(b) $\mathbf{r} = 2\mathbf{i} - 3\mathbf{j} + 2\mathbf{k} + \lambda(\mathbf{i} + 2\mathbf{j} - 3\mathbf{k})$,
(c) $\mathbf{r} = (2\lambda - \mu - 2)\mathbf{i} + (1 - \lambda + 2\mu)\mathbf{j} + \lambda\mathbf{k}$,
(d) $\mathbf{r} = -3\mathbf{i} - \mathbf{j} + 4\mathbf{k} + \lambda(2\mathbf{i} + \mathbf{j} - \mathbf{k}) + \mu(3\mathbf{j} + 2\mathbf{k})$.

9. Write down in parametric form the vector equations of the planes through the given points parallel to the given pairs of vectors.
(a) $(1, -2, 0)$; $\mathbf{i} + 3\mathbf{j}$ and $-\mathbf{j} + 2\mathbf{k}$,
(b) the origin; $2\mathbf{i} - \mathbf{j}$ and $-\mathbf{i} + 2\mathbf{j} - 7\mathbf{k}$,
(c) $(3, 1, -1)$; $\mathbf{j}$ and $\mathbf{i} + \mathbf{j} + \mathbf{k}$.

10. Find a vector equation for the plane passing through the points with position vectors $2\mathbf{k}, \mathbf{i} - 3\mathbf{j} + \mathbf{k}$ and $5\mathbf{i} + 2\mathbf{j}$.

11. Write down direction vectors for the lines l_1 and l_2 with equations $\mathbf{r} = (2 - \lambda)\mathbf{i} + 5\mathbf{j} + 3\lambda\mathbf{k}$ and $\mathbf{r} = 4\mathbf{i} + 5\mu\mathbf{j} - 2\mathbf{k}$ respectively. By writing down the position vector of a particular point on l_1, find a vector equation for the plane which contains l_1 and is parallel to l_2.

12. Find a vector equation for the plane through the points $A(1, 0, -2)$ and $B(3, -1, 1)$ which is parallel to the line with vector equation

$$\mathbf{r} = 3\mathbf{i} + (2\lambda - 1)\mathbf{j} + (5 - \lambda)\mathbf{k}.$$

Hence find the coordinates of the point of intersection of this plane and the line $\mathbf{r} = \mu\mathbf{i} + (5 - \mu)\mathbf{j} + (2\mu - 7)\mathbf{k}$.

13. The position vectors of three non-collinear points A, B and C, with respect to an origin O, are $\mathbf{a}, \mathbf{b}$ and $\mathbf{c}$ respectively. Given that O does not lie in the plane ABC, show that
(a) if the point P with position vector $\mathbf{p} = \lambda\mathbf{a} + \mu\mathbf{b}$ lies on the line AB, then $\lambda + \mu = 1$;
(b) if the point Q with position vector $\mathbf{q} = \alpha\mathbf{a} + \beta\mathbf{b} + \gamma\mathbf{c}$ lies in the plane ABC, then $\alpha + \beta + \gamma = 1$.

14. OAD, OBE, OCF are three distinct straight lines. The position vectors with respect to O of the points A, B, C, D, E, F are $\mathbf{a}, \mathbf{b}, \mathbf{c}, p\mathbf{a}, q\mathbf{b}, r\mathbf{c}$ respectively, where p, q, r are scalars, no two of which are equal. Show that any point on BC has position vector given parametrically by $(1 - t)\mathbf{b} + t\mathbf{c}$. The intersections of the pairs of lines BC, EF; CA, FD; AB, DE (produced if necessary) are the points L, M, N respectively. Show that the position vector of L is $[q(1 - r)\mathbf{b} + r(q - 1)\mathbf{c}]/(q - r)$ and find the position vectors of M and N. Taking the values $p = 4, q = 3, r = 2$, show that L, M, N are collinear points.   (C)

21.3 Scalar product

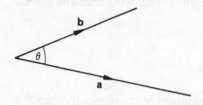

The *scalar product* (or dot product) of two vectors **a** and **b** is defined as the scalar $ab \cos \theta$, where θ is the angle between **a** and **b**.

The scalar product is denoted by **a** . **b**, which is read "a dot b".

Thus $$\mathbf{a} . \mathbf{b} = ab \cos \theta$$

The scalar product **a** . **a** is sometimes written as $\mathbf{a}^2$.

[Note that although a product of three real numbers a, b, c can be evaluated by writing $abc = (ab)c$, it is not possible to define a scalar product of three vectors in a similar way. Since **a** . **b** is a scalar, the expressions (**a** . **b**) . **c** and **a** . **b** . **c** are meaningless. Similarly, since **a** . **a** is a scalar, the expression $\mathbf{a}^3$ cannot be defined as (**a** . **a**) . **a**.]

The commutative, associative and distributive properties of multiplication of real numbers can be used to establish various properties of the scalar product.

(1) $\mathbf{a} . \mathbf{b} = ab \cos \theta = ba \cos \theta = \mathbf{b} . \mathbf{a}$

Hence the scalar product is *commutative*.

(2) Since we cannot form products such as (**a** . **b**) . **c** there is no true associative law for the scalar product. However, for any scalar λ,

$$\lambda(\mathbf{a} . \mathbf{b}) = (\lambda \mathbf{a}) . \mathbf{b} = \mathbf{a} . (\lambda \mathbf{b}) = \lambda ab \cos \theta.$$

(3)

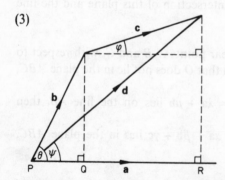

For vectors **a**, **b**, **c** and **d** shown in the diagram,

$$\mathbf{a} . (\mathbf{b} + \mathbf{c}) = \mathbf{a} . \mathbf{d}$$

Since $PR = PQ + QR$

$d \cos \psi = b \cos \theta + c \cos \phi$

$\therefore \quad ad \cos \psi = ab \cos \theta + ac \cos \phi$

$\therefore \qquad \mathbf{a} . \mathbf{d} = \mathbf{a} . \mathbf{b} + \mathbf{a} . \mathbf{c}$

$\therefore \quad \mathbf{a} . (\mathbf{b} + \mathbf{c}) = \mathbf{a} . \mathbf{b} + \mathbf{a} . \mathbf{c}$

Hence the scalar product is *distributive* over vector addition.

The definition of the scalar product gives rise to further useful properties.

(4) For any vector **a**, $\mathbf{a} . \mathbf{a} = a^2 \cos 0° = a^2.$

(5) If non-zero vectors **a** and **b** are perpendicular, then

$$\mathbf{a} . \mathbf{b} = ab \cos 90° = 0.$$

Conversely, if non-zero vectors **a** and **b** are such that **a** . **b** = 0, then **a** is perpendicular to **b**.

These results can be summarised as follows:

(1) $\mathbf{a} \cdot \mathbf{b} = \mathbf{b} \cdot \mathbf{a}$,
(2) $\lambda(\mathbf{a} \cdot \mathbf{b}) = (\lambda\mathbf{a}) \cdot \mathbf{b} = \mathbf{a} \cdot (\lambda\mathbf{b})$,

(3) $\mathbf{a} \cdot (\mathbf{b} + \mathbf{c}) = \mathbf{a} \cdot \mathbf{b} + \mathbf{a} \cdot \mathbf{c}$,
(4) $\mathbf{a} \cdot \mathbf{a} = a^2$.

(5) $\mathbf{a} \cdot \mathbf{b} = 0 \quad \Leftrightarrow \quad \mathbf{a} = \mathbf{0}$ or $\mathbf{b} = \mathbf{0}$ or $\mathbf{a}$ is perpendicular to $\mathbf{b}$.

The scalar product has important applications in geometrical proofs.

Example 1 Prove the cosine rule in the form
$$a^2 = b^2 + c^2 - 2bc \cos A.$$

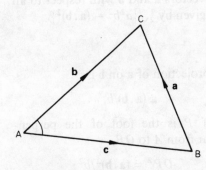

In $\triangle ABC$, let $\mathbf{a} = \vec{BC}$, $\mathbf{b} = \vec{AC}$ and $\mathbf{c} = \vec{AB}$, then

$$\begin{aligned}
a^2 = \mathbf{a} \cdot \mathbf{a} &= (\mathbf{b} - \mathbf{c}) \cdot (\mathbf{b} - \mathbf{c}) \\
&= \mathbf{b} \cdot (\mathbf{b} - \mathbf{c}) - \mathbf{c} \cdot (\mathbf{b} - \mathbf{c}) \\
&= \mathbf{b} \cdot \mathbf{b} - \mathbf{b} \cdot \mathbf{c} - \mathbf{c} \cdot \mathbf{b} + \mathbf{c} \cdot \mathbf{c} \\
&= b^2 + c^2 - 2\mathbf{b} \cdot \mathbf{c} \\
\therefore \quad a^2 &= b^2 + c^2 - 2bc \cos A.
\end{aligned}$$

Example 2 Show that any angle inscribed in a semi-circle is a right angle.

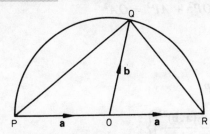

In the diagram, PR is a diameter of a circle with centre O. Let $\vec{PO} = \vec{OR} = \mathbf{a}$ and let Q be a point on the circle such that $\vec{OQ} = \mathbf{b}$, then $\vec{PQ} = \mathbf{a} + \mathbf{b}$, $\vec{QR} = \mathbf{a} - \mathbf{b}$.

$$\therefore \quad \vec{PQ} \cdot \vec{QR} = (\mathbf{a} + \mathbf{b}) \cdot (\mathbf{a} - \mathbf{b})$$
$$= \mathbf{a} \cdot \mathbf{a} - \mathbf{a} \cdot \mathbf{b} + \mathbf{b} \cdot \mathbf{a} - \mathbf{b} \cdot \mathbf{b} = a^2 - b^2$$

Since PO and OQ are radii of the circle, $a = b$,

$$\therefore \quad \vec{PQ} \cdot \vec{QR} = 0$$

Hence $\vec{PQ}$ is perpendicular to $\vec{QR}$ i.e. $\angle PQR = 90°$.

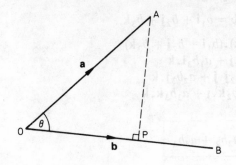

The diagram shows two vectors $\mathbf{a}$ and $\mathbf{b}$ represented by line segments $\vec{OA}$ and $\vec{OB}$ respectively. If the vector $\mathbf{a}$ is resolved along and perpendicular to $\mathbf{b}$, then its component in the direction of $\mathbf{b}$ is $a \cos \theta$.

Thus the component of $\mathbf{a}$ in the direction of $\mathbf{b}$ is $\dfrac{\mathbf{a} \cdot \mathbf{b}}{b}$ or $\mathbf{a} \cdot \hat{\mathbf{b}}$, where $\hat{\mathbf{b}}$ is the unit vector in the direction of $\mathbf{b}$.

In geometrical work the quantity $\mathbf{a} \cdot \hat{\mathbf{b}}$ is called the *projection* of $\mathbf{a}$ on $\mathbf{b}$. In the diagram the length of this projection is represented by the distance OP.

Example 3   The points A and B have position vectors $\mathbf{a}$ and $\mathbf{b}$ with respect to an origin O. Show that the area of triangle OAB is given by $\frac{1}{2}\sqrt{\{a^2 b^2 - (\mathbf{a} \cdot \mathbf{b})^2\}}$.

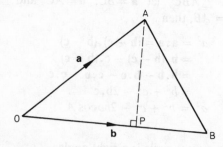

The projection of $\mathbf{a}$ on $\mathbf{b}$ is

$$(\mathbf{a} \cdot \mathbf{b})/b,$$

$\therefore$ if P is the foot of the perpendicular from A to OB,

$$OP^2 = (\mathbf{a} \cdot \mathbf{b})^2/b^2$$

Using Pythagoras' theorem in $\triangle OAP$, $OP^2 + AP^2 = OA^2$

$$\therefore \quad AP^2 = OA^2 - OP^2 = a^2 - \frac{(\mathbf{a} \cdot \mathbf{b})^2}{b^2}$$

Hence the area of $\triangle OAB = \frac{1}{2} \times OB \times AP$

$$= \frac{1}{2}\sqrt{\left\{ b^2 \times \left(a^2 - \frac{(\mathbf{a} \cdot \mathbf{b})^2}{b^2} \right) \right\}}$$

$$= \frac{1}{2}\sqrt{\{a^2 b^2 - (\mathbf{a} \cdot \mathbf{b})^2\}}.$$

When considering the unit vectors $\mathbf{i}, \mathbf{j}$ and $\mathbf{k}$ the definition of scalar product leads to the results

$$\mathbf{i} \cdot \mathbf{i} = \mathbf{j} \cdot \mathbf{j} = \mathbf{k} \cdot \mathbf{k} = 1, \quad \mathbf{i} \cdot \mathbf{j} = \mathbf{j} \cdot \mathbf{k} = \mathbf{k} \cdot \mathbf{i} = 0$$

Thus for vectors $\mathbf{a} = a_1\mathbf{i} + a_2\mathbf{j} + a_3\mathbf{k}$ and $\mathbf{b} = b_1\mathbf{i} + b_2\mathbf{j} + b_3\mathbf{k}$,

$$\mathbf{a} \cdot \mathbf{b} = (a_1\mathbf{i} + a_2\mathbf{j} + a_3\mathbf{k}) \cdot (b_1\mathbf{i} + b_2\mathbf{j} + b_3\mathbf{k})$$
$$= a_1 b_1 \mathbf{i} \cdot \mathbf{i} + a_1 b_2 \mathbf{i} \cdot \mathbf{j} + a_1 b_3 \mathbf{i} \cdot \mathbf{k}$$
$$+ a_2 b_1 \mathbf{j} \cdot \mathbf{i} + a_2 b_2 \mathbf{j} \cdot \mathbf{j} + a_2 b_3 \mathbf{j} \cdot \mathbf{k}$$
$$+ a_3 b_1 \mathbf{k} \cdot \mathbf{i} + a_3 b_2 \mathbf{k} \cdot \mathbf{j} + a_3 b_3 \mathbf{k} \cdot \mathbf{k}$$

$\therefore$

$$\mathbf{a} \cdot \mathbf{b} = a_1 b_1 + a_2 b_2 + a_3 b_3$$

If the angle between **a** and **b** is θ, then $\mathbf{a}.\mathbf{b} = ab\cos\theta$.

Thus
$$\cos\theta = \frac{\mathbf{a}.\mathbf{b}}{ab} = \frac{a_1b_1 + a_2b_2 + a_3b_3}{ab}$$

It follows that non-zero vectors **a** and **b** are perpendicular if and only if

$$a_1b_1 + a_2b_2 + a_3b_3 = 0.$$

Example 4   Find the angle θ between the vectors $\mathbf{a} = 4\mathbf{i} + 5\mathbf{j} + 3\mathbf{k}$ and $\mathbf{b} = 3\mathbf{i} - 5\mathbf{j} - 4\mathbf{k}$.

$\mathbf{a}.\mathbf{b} = 4 \times 3 + 5 \times (-5) + 3 \times (-4) = 12 - 25 - 12 = -25$
$a = \sqrt{\{4^2 + 5^2 + 3^2\}} = \sqrt{\{16 + 25 + 9\}} = \sqrt{50}$
$b = \sqrt{\{3^2 + (-5)^2 + (-4)^2\}} = \sqrt{\{9 + 25 + 16\}} = \sqrt{50}$

$$\therefore \quad \cos\theta = \frac{\mathbf{a}.\mathbf{b}}{ab} = \frac{-25}{\sqrt{50} \times \sqrt{50}} = -\frac{25}{50} = -\frac{1}{2}$$

Hence the angle between the vectors is $120°$.

Example 5   The points A, B and C have position vectors $\mathbf{a} = 5\mathbf{i} + 3\mathbf{j} + 2\mathbf{k}$, $\mathbf{b} = 2\mathbf{i} - \mathbf{j} + 3\mathbf{k}$ and $\mathbf{c} = 7\mathbf{i} - 3\mathbf{j} + 10\mathbf{k}$ respectively. Show that $\angle ABC$ is a right angle.

$$\mathbf{BA} = \mathbf{a} - \mathbf{b} = 3\mathbf{i} + 4\mathbf{j} - \mathbf{k}, \quad \mathbf{BC} = \mathbf{c} - \mathbf{b} = 5\mathbf{i} - 2\mathbf{j} + 7\mathbf{k},$$
$$\therefore \quad \mathbf{BA}.\mathbf{BC} = 3 \times 5 + 4 \times (-2) + (-1) \times 7 = 15 - 8 - 7 = 0$$

Hence BA is perpendicular to BC i.e. $\angle ABC$ is a right angle.

Exercise 21.3

1.   Use the properties of the scalar product to simplify
(a) $(\mathbf{p} + \mathbf{q}).(\mathbf{p} + \mathbf{q})$,
(b) $(\mathbf{p} + \mathbf{q}).(\mathbf{p} - \mathbf{q})$,
(c) $\mathbf{p}.(\mathbf{q} + \mathbf{r}) - \mathbf{p}.(\mathbf{q} - \mathbf{r})$,
(d) $|\mathbf{p} - \mathbf{q}|^2$.

2.   Given that **x** is perpendicular to **y**, simplify
(a) $\mathbf{x}.(\mathbf{x} + \mathbf{y})$,
(b) $(2\mathbf{x} + \mathbf{y}).(\mathbf{x} - 3\mathbf{y})$.

3.   Given that $|\mathbf{a}| = 7, |\mathbf{b}| = 4$ and $\mathbf{a}.\mathbf{b} = 8$, calculate $(\mathbf{a} + \mathbf{b}).(\mathbf{a} + \mathbf{b})$ and $(\mathbf{a} - \mathbf{b}).(\mathbf{a} - \mathbf{b})$. Hence find $|\mathbf{a} + \mathbf{b}|$ and $|\mathbf{a} - \mathbf{b}|$.

4.   Given that $|\mathbf{x}| = 5, |\mathbf{y}| = 10$ and $\mathbf{x}.\mathbf{y} = 22$, calculate $|\mathbf{x} + \mathbf{y}|$ and $|\mathbf{x} - \mathbf{y}|$.

5.   Show that if **a** and **b** are non-zero parallel vectors, then either $\mathbf{a}.\mathbf{b} = ab$ or $\mathbf{a}.\mathbf{b} = -ab$.

6. Show that if non-zero vectors **a** and **b** are of the same magnitude, then (**a** + **b**) is perpendicular to (**a** − **b**).

7. Show that if **a**, **b** and **c** are non-zero vectors such that **a.b** = **a.c**, then either **b** = **c** or **a** is perpendicular to (**b** − **c**).

8. Vectors **a**, **b** and **c** are such that **a.c** = 3 and **b.c** = 4. Given that the vector **d** = **a** + λ**b** is perpendicular to **c**, find the value of λ.

9. Coplanar vectors **a**, **b** and **c** are such $|$**a**$|$ = $|$**b**$|$ = 1, **a.b** = $\frac{1}{2}$, **b.c** = $-\frac{1}{2}$ and **a.c** = 2. Find an expression for **c** in terms of **a** and **b**.

10. Use vector methods to prove Pythagoras' theorem.

11. Use vector methods to prove that the diagonals of a rhombus bisect each other at right angles.

12. In triangle ABC the point D is the mid-point of BC. By letting $\overrightarrow{AB}$ = **x** and $\overrightarrow{BD}$ = **y**, prove Apollonius' theorem, which states that

$$AB^2 + AC^2 = 2(AD^2 + BD^2).$$

13. In triangle ABC the altitudes through A and B intersect at a point H. Show that if $\overrightarrow{HA}$ = **a**, $\overrightarrow{HB}$ = **b** and $\overrightarrow{HC}$ = **c** then **a.b** = **a.c** and **b.a** = **b.c**. Deduce that the altitudes of a triangle are concurrent.

14. Find the angles between the following pairs of vectors
(a) $8\mathbf{i} - \mathbf{j} + 4\mathbf{k}$, $2\mathbf{i} + 2\mathbf{j} - \mathbf{k}$,   (b) $\mathbf{j} + 7\mathbf{k}$, $-5\mathbf{i} + 4\mathbf{j} + 3\mathbf{k}$,
(c) $2\mathbf{i} - 3\mathbf{j} + 8\mathbf{k}$, $6\mathbf{i} - 4\mathbf{j} - 3\mathbf{k}$,   (d) $\mathbf{i} - \mathbf{j} + \mathbf{k}$, $\mathbf{i} + \mathbf{k}$.

15. Find the cosine of the angle BAC, given that .
(a) the points A, B and C have position vectors $\mathbf{i} - \mathbf{j}$, $5\mathbf{i} - 2\mathbf{j} - \mathbf{k}$ and $\mathbf{i} - 2\mathbf{j} - \mathbf{k}$ respectively;
(b) the points A, B and C have coordinates $(0, -2, 1), (1, -1, -2)$ and $(-1, 1, 0)$ respectively.

16. Find the component of the vector $\mathbf{i} + 3\mathbf{j} - 2\mathbf{k}$ in the direction of
(a) $\mathbf{j}$,   (b) $-\mathbf{k}$,   (c) $-4\mathbf{i} + 3\mathbf{j}$ (d) $6\mathbf{i} - 3\mathbf{j} + 2\mathbf{k}$.

17. Given the points $A(1, -5, 3)$, $B(0, 2, -4)$, $C(-1, 1, 0)$ and $D(7, -2, -8)$, find the lengths of the projections of AB on AC and BD.

18. If $\mathbf{a} = \lambda\mathbf{i} + \mu\mathbf{j}$ and $\mathbf{b} = \mu\mathbf{i} - \lambda\mathbf{j}$, show that **a** is perpendicular to **b**. Hence write down vectors perpendicular to
(a) $3\mathbf{i} + 4\mathbf{j}$,   (b) $5\mathbf{i} - 2\mathbf{j}$,   (c) $-2\mathbf{i} - 3\mathbf{j}$.

19. Points A and B have position vectors $4\mathbf{i} - 5\mathbf{j} - 2\mathbf{k}$ and $8\mathbf{i} - 5\mathbf{j} + 6\mathbf{k}$ respectively relative to an origin O. Find the angles of triangle AOB and also its area.

20. Given the points $A(7, 3, -1)$, $B(1, 5, 2)$ and $C(3, -1, 1)$, find the cosine of $\angle BAC$ and the area of triangle ABC.

21. Show that the lines with vector equations $\mathbf{r} = (1 + 4\lambda)\mathbf{i} + (1 - \lambda)\mathbf{j} + 2\lambda\mathbf{k}$ and $\mathbf{r} = (5 + 3\mu)\mathbf{i} + 2\mu\mathbf{j} + (2 - 5\mu)\mathbf{k}$ cut at right angles and give the position vector of their point of intersection.

22. The points A, B, C and D have coordinates $(3, -2, 0), (-1, 2, 4), (0, 1, -1)$ and $(5, -4, 4)$ respectively. Find (a) the point of intersection of the lines AB and CD, (b) the acute angle between these lines.

23. $ABCDA'B'C'D'$ is a cube with horizontal faces $ABCD$ and $A'B'C'D'$ and vertical edges AA', BB', CC', DD'. Taking $\mathbf{AB} = \mathbf{i}, \mathbf{AD} = \mathbf{j}, \mathbf{AA}' = \mathbf{k}$, obtain vectors (in terms of $\mathbf{i}, \mathbf{j}, \mathbf{k}$) perpendicular to the planes $ACC'A'$ and $CDA'B'$, and hence find the angle between these two planes.   (O&C)

24. A plane p contains the vectors $\mathbf{a} = \mathbf{i} + 2\mathbf{j} - 3\mathbf{k}$ and $\mathbf{b} = 3\mathbf{i} - \mathbf{j} + 2\mathbf{k}$. If $\mathbf{c} = \mathbf{i} + \lambda\mathbf{j} + \mu\mathbf{k}$, find the values of λ and μ such that $\mathbf{c}$ is perpendicular to the plane p. If $\mathbf{d} = -3\mathbf{i} + \mathbf{j} - 3\mathbf{k}$, find $\mathbf{c} \cdot \mathbf{d}$. Hence find the sine of the angle between the plane p and the vector $\mathbf{d}$.

25. Prove that if the vectors $\mathbf{a}$ and $\mathbf{b}$ are differentiable functions of a scalar variable t, then $\dfrac{d}{dt}(\mathbf{a} \cdot \mathbf{b}) = \mathbf{a} \cdot \dfrac{d\mathbf{b}}{dt} + \dfrac{d\mathbf{a}}{dt} \cdot \mathbf{b}$.

21.4 Further lines and planes

As shown in §21.2 the vector equation of the straight line which passes through the point with position vector $\mathbf{a}$ and has direction vector $\mathbf{d}$ is

$$\mathbf{r} = \mathbf{a} + \lambda\mathbf{d}.$$

Similarly the vector equation of the straight line passing through the points with position vectors $\mathbf{a}$ and $\mathbf{b}$ is
$$\mathbf{r} = (1 - \lambda)\mathbf{a} + \lambda\mathbf{b}.$$

The scalar product can be used to find vectors perpendicular to such lines.

Example 1   The points A, B and C have position vectors $\mathbf{a} = 3\mathbf{i} - \mathbf{j} + 4\mathbf{k}$, $\mathbf{b} = \mathbf{j} - 4\mathbf{k}$ and $\mathbf{c} = 6\mathbf{i} + 4\mathbf{j} + 5\mathbf{k}$ respectively. Find the position vector of the point R on BC such that AR is perpendicular to BC. Hence find the perpendicular distance of A from the line BC.

Since R lies on BC its position vector is of the form

$$\mathbf{r} = (1 - \lambda)(\mathbf{j} - 4\mathbf{k}) + \lambda(6\mathbf{i} + 4\mathbf{j} + 5\mathbf{k})$$
i.e. $\mathbf{r} = 6\lambda\mathbf{i} + (3\lambda + 1)\mathbf{j} + (9\lambda - 4)\mathbf{k}$ (1)

Since AR is perpendicular to BC, $AR.BC = 0$.

But $BC = c - b = 6i + 3j + 9k$

and $AR = r - a = (6\lambda - 3)i + (3\lambda + 2)j + (9\lambda - 8)k$ (2)

$\therefore$ $6(6\lambda - 3) + 3(3\lambda + 2) + 9(9\lambda - 8) = 0$

$\therefore$ $36\lambda - 18 + 9\lambda + 6 + 81\lambda - 72 = 0$

$\therefore$ $126\lambda - 84 = 0$ $\therefore$ $\lambda = \frac{2}{3}$

From (1), the position vector of R is $4i + 3j + 2k$

From (2), $AR = i + 4j - 2k$

Hence the perpendicular distance of A from BC

$= |AR| = \sqrt{\{1^2 + 4^2 + (-2)^2\}} = \sqrt{\{1 + 16 + 4\}} = \sqrt{21}.$

The parametric form of the vector equation of the plane which passes through a point A with position vector $\mathbf{a}$ and which contains non-parallel vectors $\mathbf{p}$ and $\mathbf{q}$ is

$$\mathbf{r} = \mathbf{a} + \lambda\mathbf{p} + \mu\mathbf{q}.$$

Another form of the equation of a plane is obtained by using the scalar product.

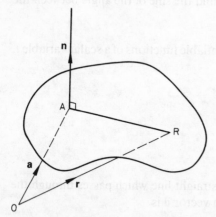

Consider a plane which passes through a point A with position vector $\mathbf{a}$ and which is perpendicular to a vector $\mathbf{n}$. If $\mathbf{r}$ is the position vector of a point R in the plane, then since AR is perpendicular to $\mathbf{n}$,

$$AR.\mathbf{n} = 0$$

$\therefore$ $(\mathbf{r} - \mathbf{a}).\mathbf{n} = 0$

This is the vector equation of the plane through A perpendicular to $\mathbf{n}$, in scalar product form.

$(\mathbf{r} - \mathbf{a}).\mathbf{n} = 0$ $\Leftrightarrow$ $\mathbf{r}.\mathbf{n} - \mathbf{a}.\mathbf{n} = 0$

$\Leftrightarrow$ $\mathbf{r}.\mathbf{n} = \mathbf{a}.\mathbf{n}$

$\Leftrightarrow$ $\mathbf{r}.\mathbf{n} = p$,   where $p = \mathbf{a}.\mathbf{n}.$

Hence the equation of any plane perpendicular to a vector $\mathbf{n}$ may be written in the form $\mathbf{r}.\mathbf{n} = p$.

If the point D with position vector $\mathbf{d}$ is the foot of the perpendicular from the origin to the plane $\mathbf{r}.\mathbf{n} = p$, then the perpendicular distance of the origin from the plane is d.

Since D lies in the plane, $\mathbf{d}.\mathbf{n} = p.$

However, $\mathbf{d}$ is parallel to $\mathbf{n}$,

$\therefore$ either $\mathbf{d}.\mathbf{n} = dn$ or $\mathbf{d}.\mathbf{n} = -dn.$

Hence $dn = |p|$ giving $d = |p|/n.$

Thus the plane $\mathbf{r} \cdot \mathbf{n} = p$ is perpendicular to the vector $\mathbf{n}$ and lies at a distance $\dfrac{|p|}{n}$ from the origin.

Example 2   Find the vector equation of the plane which passes through the point with position vector $2\mathbf{i} - \mathbf{j} + \mathbf{k}$ and is perpendicular to the vector $3\mathbf{i} + \mathbf{j} - 4\mathbf{k}$.

The vector equation of the given plane is

$$(\mathbf{r} - \{2\mathbf{i} - \mathbf{j} + \mathbf{k}\}) \cdot (3\mathbf{i} + \mathbf{j} - 4\mathbf{k}) = 0$$
$$\mathbf{r} \cdot (3\mathbf{i} + \mathbf{j} - 4\mathbf{k}) - (2\mathbf{i} - \mathbf{j} + \mathbf{k}) \cdot (3\mathbf{i} + \mathbf{j} - 4\mathbf{k}) = 0$$
$$\mathbf{r} \cdot (3\mathbf{i} + \mathbf{j} - 4\mathbf{k}) - (6 - 1 - 4) = 0$$
i.e $$\mathbf{r} \cdot (3\mathbf{i} + \mathbf{j} - 4\mathbf{k}) = 1.$$

Example 3   Find in scalar product form the equation of the plane

$$\mathbf{r} = (1 + 3\lambda + 2\mu)\mathbf{i} + (1 + \lambda + 4\mu)\mathbf{j} + (\mu - \lambda)\mathbf{k}.$$

Rearranging the given equation, we have

$$\mathbf{r} = \mathbf{i} + \mathbf{j} + \lambda(3\mathbf{i} + \mathbf{j} - \mathbf{k}) + \mu(2\mathbf{i} + 4\mathbf{j} + \mathbf{k})$$

∴   the given plane passes through the point with position vectors $\mathbf{i} + \mathbf{j}$ and is parallel to the vectors $3\mathbf{i} + \mathbf{j} - \mathbf{k}$ and $2\mathbf{i} + 4\mathbf{j} + \mathbf{k}$.
Let $\mathbf{n} = n_1\mathbf{i} + n_2\mathbf{j} + n_3\mathbf{k}$ be a vector perpendicular to $3\mathbf{i} + \mathbf{j} - \mathbf{k}$ and $2\mathbf{i} + 4\mathbf{j} + \mathbf{k}$, then

$$\mathbf{n} \cdot (3\mathbf{i} + \mathbf{j} - \mathbf{k}) = 0 \quad \text{i.e.} \quad 3n_1 + n_2 - n_3 = 0 \tag{1}$$
$$\mathbf{n} \cdot (2\mathbf{i} + 4\mathbf{j} + \mathbf{k}) = 0 \quad \text{i.e.} \quad 2n_1 + 4n_2 + n_3 = 0 \tag{2}$$

Adding (1) to (2): $5n_1 + 5n_2 = 0$ ∴ $n_2 = -n_1$
Substituting in (1): $3n_1 - n_1 - n_3 = 0$ ∴ $n_3 = 2n_1$

∴ $n_1 : n_2 : n_3 = n_1 : -n_1 : 2n_1 = 1 : -1 : 2$

Thus one vector perpendicular to the given plane is $\mathbf{i} - \mathbf{j} + 2\mathbf{k}$. Hence the equation of the plane in scalar product form is

$$(\mathbf{r} - \{\mathbf{i} + \mathbf{j}\}) \cdot (\mathbf{i} - \mathbf{j} + 2\mathbf{k}) = 0$$
$$\mathbf{r} \cdot (\mathbf{i} - \mathbf{j} + 2\mathbf{k}) - (\mathbf{i} + \mathbf{j}) \cdot (\mathbf{i} - \mathbf{j} + 2\mathbf{k}) = 0$$
i.e. $$\mathbf{r} \cdot (\mathbf{i} - \mathbf{j} + 2\mathbf{k}) = 0$$

Example 4   Find the angle between the planes $\mathbf{r} \cdot (2\mathbf{i} - \mathbf{j} - 3\mathbf{k}) = 10$ and $\mathbf{r} \cdot (\mathbf{i} + 3\mathbf{j} - 2\mathbf{k}) = 16$.

The given planes are perpendicular to the vectors $\mathbf{n}_1 = 2\mathbf{i} - \mathbf{j} - 3\mathbf{k}$ and $\mathbf{n}_2 = \mathbf{i} + 3\mathbf{j} - 2\mathbf{k}$ respectively.
∴   the angle θ between the planes is equal to the angle between $\mathbf{n}_1$ and $\mathbf{n}_2$.

$$\mathbf{n}_1 . \mathbf{n}_2 = 2 \times 1 + (-1) \times 3 + (-3) \times (-2) = 2 - 3 + 6 = 5$$
$$n_1 = \sqrt{\{2^2 + (-1)^2 + (-3)^2\}} = \sqrt{\{4 + 1 + 9\}} = \sqrt{14}$$
$$n_2 = \sqrt{\{1^2 + 3^2 + (-2)^2\}} = \sqrt{\{1 + 9 + 4\}} = \sqrt{14}$$

$$\therefore \quad \cos \theta = \frac{\mathbf{n}_1 . \mathbf{n}_2}{n_1 n_2} = \frac{5}{\sqrt{14} \times \sqrt{14}} = \frac{5}{14}$$

Hence the angle between the planes is 69·1°.

Example 5   Find the angle between the line $\mathbf{r} = 3\mathbf{k} + \lambda(7\mathbf{i} - \mathbf{j} + 4\mathbf{k})$ and the plane $\mathbf{r} . (2\mathbf{i} - 5\mathbf{j} - 2\mathbf{k}) = 8$.

The given line is parallel to the vector $\mathbf{d} = 7\mathbf{i} - \mathbf{j} + 4\mathbf{k}$ and the given plane is perpendicular to the vector $\mathbf{n} = 2\mathbf{i} - 5\mathbf{j} - 2\mathbf{k}$.

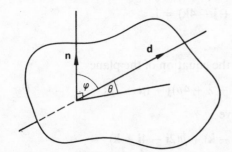

If the angle between the line and the plane is θ and the angle between $\mathbf{d}$ and $\mathbf{n}$ is ϕ then

$$\theta + \phi = 90°,$$

$$\therefore \quad \sin \theta = \cos \phi = \frac{\mathbf{d} . \mathbf{n}}{dn}$$

$$\mathbf{d} . \mathbf{n} = 7 \times 2 + (-1) \times (-5) + 4 \times (-2) = 14 + 5 - 8 = 11$$
$$d = \sqrt{\{7^2 + (-1)^2 + 4^2\}} = \sqrt{\{49 + 1 + 16\}} = \sqrt{66}$$
$$n = \sqrt{\{2^2 + (-5)^2 + (-2)^2\}} = \sqrt{\{4 + 25 + 4\}} = \sqrt{33}$$

$$\therefore \quad \sin \theta = \frac{11}{\sqrt{66} \times \sqrt{33}} = \frac{11}{33\sqrt{2}} = \frac{1}{3\sqrt{2}}$$

Hence the angle between the line and the plane is 13·6°.

Example 6   Find the position vector of the point of intersection of the line $\mathbf{r} = (2\mathbf{i} - \mathbf{k}) + \lambda(\mathbf{i} + 3\mathbf{j})$ and the plane $\mathbf{r} . (5\mathbf{i} - \mathbf{j} + 7\mathbf{k}) = 9$.

At the point of intersection

$$\{(2\mathbf{i} - \mathbf{k}) + \lambda(\mathbf{i} + 3\mathbf{j})\} . (5\mathbf{i} - \mathbf{j} + 7\mathbf{k}) = 9$$
$$\therefore \quad (2\mathbf{i} - \mathbf{k}) . (5\mathbf{i} - \mathbf{j} + 7\mathbf{k}) + \lambda(\mathbf{i} + 3\mathbf{j}) . (5\mathbf{i} - \mathbf{j} + 7\mathbf{k}) = 9$$
$$\therefore \quad (10 + 0 - 7) + \lambda(5 - 3 + 0) = 9$$
$$\therefore \quad 3 + 2\lambda = 9$$
$$\therefore \quad \lambda = 3$$

Hence the position vector of the point of intersection is

$$2\mathbf{i} - \mathbf{k} + 3(\mathbf{i} + 3\mathbf{j}) \quad \text{i.e.} \quad 5\mathbf{i} + 9\mathbf{j} - \mathbf{k}.$$

By writing $\mathbf{r} = x\mathbf{i} + y\mathbf{j} + z\mathbf{k}$ we can express the equations of lines and planes in Cartesian form.

Consider first the straight line $\mathbf{r} = \mathbf{a} + \lambda\mathbf{d}$, which passes through the point with position vector $\mathbf{a} = a_1\mathbf{i} + a_2\mathbf{j} + a_3\mathbf{k}$ and is parallel to the vector $\mathbf{d} = d_1\mathbf{i} + d_2\mathbf{j} + d_3\mathbf{k}$.

$$\mathbf{r} = \mathbf{a} + \lambda\mathbf{d} \quad \Leftrightarrow \quad \left. \begin{array}{l} x = a_1 + \lambda d_1 \\ y = a_2 + \lambda d_2 \\ z = a_3 + \lambda d_3 \end{array} \right\} \begin{array}{l} \text{These are the } \textit{parametric} \\ \textit{equations} \text{ of the line.} \end{array}$$

Assuming that d_1, d_2 and d_3 are non-zero, we have

$$\frac{x - a_1}{d_1} = \lambda, \quad \frac{y - a_2}{d_2} = \lambda, \quad \frac{z - a_3}{d_3} = \lambda$$

$$\therefore \qquad \frac{x - a_1}{d_1} = \frac{y - a_2}{d_2} = \frac{z - a_3}{d_3}$$

These are the *Cartesian equations* of the line.

Any line parallel to the vector $d_1\mathbf{i} + d_2\mathbf{j} + d_3\mathbf{k}$ is said to have *direction ratios* $d_1 : d_2 : d_3$.

Thus the equations $\dfrac{x - a_1}{d_1} = \dfrac{y - a_2}{d_2} = \dfrac{z - a_3}{d_3}$ represent the straight line through the point (a_1, a_2, a_3) with direction ratios $d_1 : d_2 : d_3$.

By convention the Cartesian equations of a straight line may be given in the above form for all values of d_1, d_2, d_3 including zero. For instance, the equations $\dfrac{x - 2}{3} = \dfrac{y + 1}{0} = \dfrac{z}{-2}$ represent the straight line through the point $(2, -1, 0)$, with direction ratios $3 : 0 : -2$ i.e. in a direction parallel to the vector $3\mathbf{i} - 2\mathbf{k}$.

Consider now the plane which passes through the point with position vector $\mathbf{a} = a_1\mathbf{i} + a_2\mathbf{j} + a_3\mathbf{k}$ and is perpendicular to the vector $\mathbf{n} = n_1\mathbf{i} + n_2\mathbf{j} + n_3\mathbf{k}$. Writing $\mathbf{r} = x\mathbf{i} + y\mathbf{j} + z\mathbf{k}$, its vector equation $(\mathbf{r} - \mathbf{a}) \cdot \mathbf{n} = 0$ becomes

$$\{(x - a_1)\mathbf{i} + (y - a_2)\mathbf{j} + (z - a_3)\mathbf{k}\} \cdot (n_1\mathbf{i} + n_2\mathbf{j} + n_3\mathbf{k}) = 0.$$

Hence the Cartesian equation of this plane is

$$n_1 (x - a_1) + n_2 (y - a_2) + n_3 (z - a_3) = 0.$$

Similarly the vector equation $\mathbf{r} \cdot \mathbf{n} = p$ gives rise to the Cartesian form

$$n_1 x + n_2 y + n_3 z - p = 0.$$

For instance, the Cartesian equation of the plane $\mathbf{r} \cdot (3\mathbf{i} - \mathbf{j} + 4\mathbf{k}) = 5$ is $3x - y + 4z - 5 = 0$.

It follows that the equation $Ax + By + Cz + D = 0$ is the Cartesian equation of a plane perpendicular to the vector $A\mathbf{i} + B\mathbf{j} + C\mathbf{k}$.

Thus the equation $Ax + By + Cz + D = 0$ represents a plane, the direction ratios of the normal to the plane being $A : B : C$.

Exercise 21.4

1. The equation of a line l is $\mathbf{r} = \lambda\mathbf{i} - (\lambda + 4)\mathbf{j} + \mathbf{k}$. Find the position vector with respect to the origin O of the point A on l, given that OA is perpendicular to l. Hence find the perpendicular distance of O from the line l.

2. The position vectors of points A and B are $3\mathbf{i} - 8\mathbf{j} + \mathbf{k}$ and $4\mathbf{j} - 2\mathbf{k}$ respectively. Find the position vector of the foot of the perpendicular from the origin O to AB. Hence find the area of the triangle OAB.

3. The points A and B have position vectors $2\mathbf{j} + 7\mathbf{k}$ and $5\mathbf{i} - 3\mathbf{j} + 2\mathbf{k}$ respectively relative to an origin O. Find the position vector of the point R on AB such that OR is perpendicular to AB. Hence find the position vector of the reflection of O in AB.

4. A point A has position vector $2\mathbf{i} + 3\mathbf{j} - 6\mathbf{k}$ and a line l has equation $\mathbf{r} = \mathbf{i} - \mathbf{j} + 7\mathbf{k} + \lambda(4\mathbf{i} - \mathbf{k})$. Find the position vector of a point R on l such that AR is perpendicular to l. Hence find the perpendicular distance of A from the line l.

5. Find, in scalar product form, the equation of the plane through the point with position vector $\mathbf{a}$ and perpendicular to the vector $\mathbf{n}$, given that
(a) $\mathbf{a} = \mathbf{i} - 2\mathbf{j} + \mathbf{k}, \mathbf{n} = 4\mathbf{i} - \mathbf{k}$,   (b) $\mathbf{a} = 3\mathbf{j} - 2\mathbf{k}, \mathbf{n} = \mathbf{i} - \mathbf{j} - 2\mathbf{k}$.

6. Find, in the form $\mathbf{r} \cdot \mathbf{n} = p$, the equations of the planes through the given points and perpendicular to the given vectors
(a) $(0, 0, 1), \mathbf{k}$,   (b) $(2, -1, 1), 3\mathbf{i} + 4\mathbf{j} - 2\mathbf{k}$.

7. Find the perpendicular distances from the origin of the following planes
(a) $\mathbf{r} \cdot (\mathbf{i} - 2\mathbf{j} + 2\mathbf{k}) = 15$,   (b) $\mathbf{r} \cdot \mathbf{i} = 3$,
(c) $\mathbf{r} \cdot (3\mathbf{i} - 4\mathbf{k}) = 20$,   (d) $\mathbf{r} \cdot (\mathbf{i} + \mathbf{j} + \mathbf{k}) = 0$.

8. Find a vector which is perpendicular to both $\mathbf{i} + 2\mathbf{k}$ and $3\mathbf{i} + \mathbf{j} + \mathbf{k}$. Hence find the vector equation in scalar product form of the plane parallel to these vectors which passes through the point with position vector $\mathbf{i} - \mathbf{j}$.

9. Find in scalar product form the equation of the plane
$$\mathbf{r} = (3 + 3\lambda + 4\mu)\mathbf{i} + (\lambda + 2\mu)\mathbf{j} + (1 + 3\lambda + 5\mu)\mathbf{k}.$$

10. Find in scalar product form the equation of the plane containing the lines
$$\mathbf{r} = (\lambda + 1)\mathbf{i} - 2\mathbf{j} + 3\mathbf{k} \text{ and } \mathbf{r} = 3\mu\mathbf{i} + (2\mu - 4)\mathbf{j} + (\mu + 2)\mathbf{k}.$$

11. Find the acute angles between the following pairs of planes.
(a) $\mathbf{r} \cdot (\mathbf{i} - \mathbf{j}) = 4, \mathbf{r} \cdot (\mathbf{j} + \mathbf{k}) = 1$,
(b) $\mathbf{r} \cdot (\mathbf{i} - 2\mathbf{j} - 2\mathbf{k}) = 5, \mathbf{r} \cdot \mathbf{j} = 0$,
(c) $\mathbf{r} \cdot (\mathbf{i} + \mathbf{j} + \mathbf{k}) = 1, \mathbf{r} \cdot (\mathbf{i} - \mathbf{j} \div \mathbf{k}) = 0$.

12. In each of the following cases find the sine of the angle between the given line and plane.
(a) $\mathbf{r} = \mathbf{i} - 3\mathbf{j} + \lambda(2\mathbf{i} - \mathbf{j} - \mathbf{k})$, $\mathbf{r} \cdot (\mathbf{i} - 2\mathbf{j} - 7\mathbf{k}) = 10$,
(b) $\mathbf{r} = (2 + \lambda)\mathbf{i} - 3\mathbf{j} + (1 - \lambda)\mathbf{k}$, $\mathbf{r} \cdot (4\mathbf{i} + \mathbf{j} - \mathbf{k}) = 6$,
(c) $\mathbf{r} = 3\lambda\mathbf{i} + 2\lambda\mathbf{j} - 6\lambda\mathbf{k}$, $\mathbf{r} \cdot (4\mathbf{i} - 3\mathbf{k}) = 20$.

13. Find the position vectors of points of intersection of the line $\mathbf{r} = \lambda\mathbf{i} - 2\mathbf{j} + (2\lambda - 1)\mathbf{k}$ with the planes $\mathbf{r} \cdot (2\mathbf{i} + \mathbf{j} - 3\mathbf{k}) = 5$ and $\mathbf{r} \cdot (\mathbf{i} + 5\mathbf{j} + 2\mathbf{k}) = -2$.

14. Find the vector equation of the line through the point A with position vector $5\mathbf{i} - 3\mathbf{j} + 4\mathbf{k}$ which is perpendicular to the plane $\mathbf{r} \cdot (3\mathbf{i} - 4\mathbf{j} + \mathbf{k}) = 5$. Hence find the position vector of the foot of the perpendicular from A to this plane.

15. Find the Cartesian equations of the straight line which
(a) has vector equation $\mathbf{r} = \mathbf{i} - 2\mathbf{j} + \mathbf{k} + \lambda(2\mathbf{i} + 3\mathbf{j} + 4\mathbf{k})$,
(b) has vector equation $\mathbf{r} = \lambda\mathbf{i} + (2 - \lambda)\mathbf{j} + (3 + 2\lambda)\mathbf{k}$,
(c) passes through the point $(2, -3, 1)$ and has direction ratios $5 : -6 : 3$,
(d) passes through the point $(5, 0, -4)$ and has direction ratios $1 : 3 : 0$.

16. Write down the Cartesian equations of the planes
(a) $\mathbf{r} \cdot (2\mathbf{i} - 3\mathbf{j} + \mathbf{k}) = 5$,   (b) $\mathbf{r} \cdot (3\mathbf{i} + \mathbf{j} - 5\mathbf{k}) = 9$.

17. Find the Cartesian equation of the plane which passes through the point with position vector $\mathbf{i} - 2\mathbf{j} + 3\mathbf{k}$ and is perpendicular to the vector $5\mathbf{i} + \mathbf{j} + \mathbf{k}$.

18. Find the Cartesian equation of a plane which passes through the point $(4, 0, -1)$, given that the normal to the plane has direction ratios $2 : -1 : 5$.

19. The points A, B and C have position vectors $3\mathbf{i} + 2\mathbf{j} - \mathbf{k}$, $\mathbf{i} + 2\mathbf{j}$ and $4\mathbf{i} + \mathbf{j} - 3\mathbf{k}$ respectively. Find a vector perpendicular to both $\mathbf{AB}$ and $\mathbf{AC}$. Hence find the equation of the plane containing A, B and C in (a) scalar product form, (b) Cartesian form.

20. Find the Cartesian equation of the plane containing the points $A(2, -1, 1)$, $B(1, -2, 0)$ and $C(-3, 6, -1)$.

21. Find the acute angle between
(a) the lines $\dfrac{x - 1}{1} = \dfrac{y + 2}{-2} = \dfrac{z}{2}$, $\dfrac{x + 3}{3} = \dfrac{y + 1}{0} = \dfrac{z - 2}{-4}$;

(b) the planes $x - 2y - 3z = 1$, $2x - 4y + z = 3$;

(c) the line $\dfrac{x}{4} = \dfrac{y - 1}{-1} = \dfrac{z + 3}{-5}$, the plane $x - 2y + 4z + 3 = 0$.

22. The points A and B are fixed points with position vectors $\mathbf{a}$ and $\mathbf{b}$ respectively relative to an origin O. If R is a variable point with position vector $\mathbf{r}$, describe

the locus of R in each of the following cases

(a) $\mathbf{r} \cdot \mathbf{a} = 0$,

(b) $(\mathbf{r} - \mathbf{a}) \cdot \mathbf{a} = 0$,

(c) $(\mathbf{r} - \mathbf{a}) \cdot (\mathbf{r} - \mathbf{a}) = 1$,

(d) $\mathbf{r} \cdot \mathbf{a} = \mathbf{r} \cdot \mathbf{b}$,

(e) $(\mathbf{r} - \mathbf{a}) \cdot \mathbf{r} = 0$,

(f) $(\mathbf{r} - \mathbf{a}) \cdot (\mathbf{r} - \mathbf{b}) = 0$.

Exercise 21.5 (miscellaneous)

1. A cube $OPQRABCD$ has OA, PB, QC and RD perpendicular to the base $OPQR$; M is the centre of the face $ABCD$. The position vectors of A, B, C relative to O are $\mathbf{a}, \mathbf{b}, \mathbf{c}$ respectively. Find in terms of $\mathbf{a}, \mathbf{b}$, and $\mathbf{c}$ the vectors $\mathbf{AB}, \mathbf{OM}, \mathbf{OD}$. If $|\mathbf{OP}| = 2$, express $\mathbf{a}, \mathbf{b}, \mathbf{c}, \mathbf{OM}, \mathbf{OD}$ in terms of unit vectors $\mathbf{i}, \mathbf{j}, \mathbf{k}$ along $\mathbf{OP}, \mathbf{OR}, \mathbf{OA}$ respectively. Find the cosine of the angle MOC.   (L)

2. Points A and B have position vectors $\mathbf{a}$ and $\mathbf{b}$ respectively with respect to a given origin O. Prove that the position vector of the point P dividing the line segment AB in the ratio λ to μ is $(\mu\mathbf{a} + \lambda\mathbf{b})/(\lambda + \mu)$. The position vectors of A, B, C and D, the vertices of a plane quadrilateral, are $\mathbf{a}, \mathbf{b}, \mathbf{c}$ and $\mathbf{d}$ respectively. Find the position vectors of P, Q, R, S, T and U, the mid-points of AB, BC, CD, DA, AC and BD respectively. Hence show that the point with position vector $\frac{1}{4}(\mathbf{a} + \mathbf{b} + \mathbf{c} + \mathbf{d})$ lies on each of the lines PR, QS and TU and that these lines bisect each other. If $\mathbf{a} = 2\mathbf{i} + 3\mathbf{j}, \mathbf{b} = 6\mathbf{i} + 5\mathbf{j}, \mathbf{c} = 8\mathbf{i} - \mathbf{j}$ and $\mathbf{d} = \mathbf{j}$, where $\mathbf{i}$ and $\mathbf{j}$ are orthogonal unit vectors, show that the acute angle between AC and BD is $\cos^{-1}(5/13)$. Find a unit vector orthogonal to the line TU.   (W)

3. The points A, B and C have position vectors $\mathbf{a}, \mathbf{b}$ and $\mathbf{c}$ with respect to an origin O. The point R in the plane ABC has position vector $\mathbf{r}$ where $\mathbf{r} = \frac{1}{2}(\frac{2}{3}\mathbf{a} + \frac{1}{3}\mathbf{b}) + \frac{1}{2}\mathbf{c}$. Use the ratio theorem to obtain a geometrical description of the position of R with reference to the points A, B and C. Illustrate your answer with a diagram. By writing $\mathbf{r}$ in the form $\lambda\mathbf{a} + \mu(m\mathbf{b} + n\mathbf{c})$ where $\lambda + \mu = 1$, obtain an alternative description of the position of R. Given that the point S has position vector $\frac{2}{3}\mathbf{a} + \frac{1}{12}\mathbf{b} + \frac{1}{4}\mathbf{c}$, show that S bisects the line segment AR.   (JMB)

4.

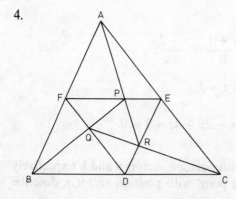

The diagram shows a triangle ABC, with D, E, F as the mid-points of the sides. The points P, Q, R are chosen on EF, FD, DE so that RP, PQ, QR pass through A, B, C. If the position vectors of A, B, C are $\mathbf{a}, \mathbf{b}, \mathbf{c}$ and if

$$\frac{PF}{EP} = \frac{QD}{FQ} = \frac{RE}{DR} = \lambda,$$

find the position vectors of P, Q, R and hence the value of λ.   (O)

5.　The position vectors of two points A and B relative to an origin O are $\mathbf{a}$ and $\mathbf{b}$ respectively. Show that the vector equation of the line bisecting angle AOB is $\mathbf{r} = \lambda(\hat{\mathbf{a}} + \hat{\mathbf{b}})$, where $\hat{\mathbf{a}}$ and $\hat{\mathbf{b}}$ are unit vectors in the directions of $\mathbf{a}$ and $\mathbf{b}$. Hence prove that the bisector of an interior angle of a triangle divides the opposite side into segments proportional to the adjacent sides.

6.　Three lines l_1, l_2 and l_3 have vector equations $\mathbf{r} = 2\mathbf{i} - \mathbf{j} + \mathbf{k} + \lambda(\mathbf{i} + 3\mathbf{j} + 3\mathbf{k})$, $\mathbf{r} = \mathbf{i} - 3\mathbf{j} + \mu(2\mathbf{i} + 5\mathbf{j} + 4\mathbf{k})$ and $\mathbf{r} = 3\mathbf{i} + v(\mathbf{j} + 2\mathbf{k})$ respectively. Find the position vector of the point of intersection of l_1 and l_2. Hence show that the three lines are concurrent. Write down, in parametric form, a vector equation of the plane containing l_2 and l_3. Hence show that the three lines are coplanar.

7.　Two planes p_1 and p_2 have vector equations $\mathbf{r} = (1 - \lambda)\mathbf{i} + (2\lambda + \mu)\mathbf{j} + (\mu - 1)\mathbf{k}$ and $\mathbf{r} = (s - t)\mathbf{i} + (2s - 3)\mathbf{j} + t\mathbf{k}$ respectively. Show that if a point in p_1 also lies in p_2, then $\mu = 4\lambda + 3$. Hence find a vector equation of the line of intersection of the two planes.

8.　Given non-zero vectors $\mathbf{a}$ and $\mathbf{b}$, show that $|\mathbf{a} + \mathbf{b}| = |\mathbf{a} - \mathbf{b}|$ if and only if $\mathbf{a}$ is perpendicular to $\mathbf{b}$. Deduce that a parallelogram is a rectangle if and only if its diagonals are equal in length.

9.　Use vector methods to find the acute angle between two diagonals of a cube.

10.　A tetrahedron $OABC$ with vertex O at the origin is such that $\vec{OA} = \mathbf{a}$, $\vec{OB} = \mathbf{b}$ and $\vec{OC} = \mathbf{c}$. Show that the line segments joining the mid-points of opposite edges bisect one another. Given that two pairs of opposite edges are perpendicular prove that $\mathbf{a} \cdot \mathbf{b} = \mathbf{b} \cdot \mathbf{c} = \mathbf{c} \cdot \mathbf{a}$ and show that the third pair of opposite edges is also perpendicular. Prove also that, in this case, $OA^2 + BC^2 = OB^2 + AC^2$.
(L)

11.　ABC is a given triangle, and the centre of the circle through A, B, C is O. Relative to O, the position vectors of A, B, C are $\mathbf{a}, \mathbf{b}, \mathbf{c}$. If H is the point with position vector $\mathbf{a} + \mathbf{b} + \mathbf{c}$, prove that AH, BH, CH are perpendicular to BC, CA, AB respectively. If A', B', C' are the mid-points of BC, CA, AB respectively, prove that AA', BB' and CC' are concurrent in G, and find the position vector of G. Prove that O, G, H lie on a straight line.
(O)

12.　Let $\mathbf{a} = \mathbf{i} - 2\mathbf{j} + \mathbf{k}, \mathbf{b} = 2\mathbf{i} + \mathbf{j} - \mathbf{k}$. Given that $\mathbf{c} = \lambda\mathbf{a} + \mu\mathbf{b}$ and that $\mathbf{c}$ is perpendicular to $\mathbf{a}$, find the ratio of λ to μ. Let A, B be the points with position vectors $\mathbf{a}, \mathbf{b}$ respectively with respect to an origin O. Write down, in terms of $\mathbf{a}$ and $\mathbf{b}$, a vector equation of the line l through A, in the plane of O, A and B, which is perpendicular to OA. Find the position vector of P, the point of intersection of l and OB.
(JMB)

13. The position vectors of A, B, C are $\mathbf{i}, 2\mathbf{j}, 3\mathbf{k}$ respectively. The perpendicular from the origin O to the plane ABC meets the plane at the point D. Find (i) the vector equation of the plane ABC, (ii) the vector equation of the line OD, (iii) the position vector of the point D.   (AEB 1980)

14. A straight line passes through the point $(2, 0, -1)$ and is parallel to the vector $\mathbf{i} + 2\mathbf{j} - \mathbf{k}$. The feet of the perpendiculars from the points $A(2, -2, 1)$ and $B(1, 7, 0)$ to this line are P and Q. Find (i) the coordinates of P and Q, (ii) the angles APB and AQB, (iii) the Cartesian equations of the planes PAQ and PBQ, (iv) the angle between the planes PAQ and PBQ.

15. Interpret geometrically the equations $\mathbf{r} \cdot \mathbf{n} = p$ and $\mathbf{r} = \mathbf{a} + t\mathbf{b}$ where $\mathbf{n}, \mathbf{a}$ and $\mathbf{b}$ are constant vectors, p is a constant scalar and t is a parameter which can take all real values. Find the value of t in terms of $\mathbf{a}, \mathbf{b}, \mathbf{n}$ and p if the value of $\mathbf{r}$ given by the second equation also satisfies the first. Explain the geometrical significance of the point given by this value of t, giving special attention to the cases when (i) $\mathbf{b} \cdot \mathbf{n} = 0$ and (ii) $\mathbf{b} = \mathbf{n}$.

The point A has coordinates $(1, 1, 2)$. Determine the coordinates of the point A' which is the reflection of A in the plane $2x + 2y + z = 9$.   (AEB 1979)

16. The lines l_1 and l_2 have equations $\mathbf{r}_1 = (2\lambda + 3)\mathbf{i} + (2 - 3\lambda)\mathbf{j} + \lambda\mathbf{k}$ and $\mathbf{r}_2 = (\mu - 4)\mathbf{i} + (2\mu + 1)\mathbf{j} + (4\mu - 3)\mathbf{k}$ respectively. Show that l_1 is perpendicular to l_2. Find the values of λ and μ such that the vector $\mathbf{r}_1 - \mathbf{r}_2$ is perpendicular to both l_1 and l_2. Hence find the position vectors of the ends of the common perpendicular to l_1 and l_2. Find also the length of this common perpendicular.

17. A pyramid has a square base $OABC$ and vertex V. The position vectors of A, B, C, V referred to O as origin are given by $\mathbf{OA} = 2\mathbf{i}, \mathbf{OB} = 2\mathbf{i} + 2\mathbf{j}, \mathbf{OC} = 2\mathbf{j}, \mathbf{OV} = \mathbf{i} + \mathbf{j} + 3\mathbf{k}$. (i) Express $\mathbf{AV}$ in terms of $\mathbf{i}, \mathbf{j}$ and $\mathbf{k}$. (ii) Using scalar products, or otherwise, find a vector $\mathbf{x}$ which is perpendicular to both $\mathbf{OV}$ and $\mathbf{AV}$. (iii) Calculate the angle between the vector $\mathbf{x}$, found in (ii), and $\mathbf{VB}$, giving your answer to the nearest degree. (iv) Write down the acute angle between VB and the plane OVA.   (C)

22 Series and expansions

22.1 Summation of finite series

There are various standard results that can be used to find the sums of finite series. Two of these are the formula for the sums of arithmetic and geometric progressions obtained in Chapter 13.

The sum to n terms of the A.P. with first term a and common difference d is $\frac{1}{2}n\{2a + (n-1)d\}$.

The sum to n terms of the G.P. with first term a and common ratio r is $a(1 - r^n)/(1 - r)$.

The series $\sum_{r=1}^{n} r = 1 + 2 + 3 + \ldots + n$ is an arithmetic progression with first term 1 and common difference 1.

$$\therefore \qquad \sum_{r=1}^{n} r = \tfrac{1}{2}n\{2 + (n-1)\} = \tfrac{1}{2}n(n+1).$$

The series $\sum_{r=1}^{n} r^2 = 1^2 + 2^2 + 3^2 + \ldots + n^2$ can be summed using the identity

$$(r+1)^3 - r^3 \equiv 3r^2 + 3r + 1.$$

Substituting $r = 1, 2, 3, \ldots, n$, we have

$$2^3 - 1^3 = 3 \cdot 1^2 + 3 \cdot 1 + 1$$
$$3^3 - 2^3 = 3 \cdot 2^2 + 3 \cdot 2 + 1$$
$$4^3 - 3^3 = 3 \cdot 3^2 + 3 \cdot 3 + 1$$
$$\cdots\cdots\cdots\cdots\cdots\cdots\cdots\cdots$$
$$(n+1)^3 - n^3 = 3n^2 + 3n + 1$$

Adding together all n equations, we find that most of the terms on the left may be

439

cancelled out to give:

$$(n + 1)^3 - 1^3 = 3 \sum_{r=1}^{n} r^2 + 3 \sum_{r=1}^{n} r + n$$

$$\therefore \quad 3 \sum_{r=1}^{n} r^2 = (n + 1)^3 - 1^3 - 3 \sum_{r=1}^{n} r - n$$

$$= (n + 1)^3 - 1 - \tfrac{3}{2}n(n + 1) - n$$
$$= n^3 + \tfrac{3}{2}n^2 + \tfrac{1}{2}n = \tfrac{1}{2}n(2n^2 + 3n + 1)$$

Hence $\qquad \displaystyle\sum_{r=1}^{n} r^2 = \tfrac{1}{6}n(n + 1)(2n + 1).$

By a similar method it can be shown that

$$\sum_{r=1}^{n} r^3 = \tfrac{1}{4}n^2(n + 1)^2 = \left(\sum_{r=1}^{n} r \right)^2$$

To summarise, we now have three further important results:

$$\sum_{r=1}^{n} r = \tfrac{1}{2}n(n + 1), \quad \sum_{r=1}^{n} r^2 = \tfrac{1}{6}n(n + 1)(2n + 1), \quad \sum_{r=1}^{n} r^3 = \tfrac{1}{4}n^2(n + 1)^2$$

Example 1   Find the sum of the first n terms of the series

$$1.3.5 + 2.4.6 + 3.5.7 + \dots.$$

The rth term of the series $= r(r + 2)(r + 4) = r^3 + 6r^2 + 8r$
$\therefore \quad$ the sum of the first n terms

$$= \sum_{r=1}^{n} (r^3 + 6r^2 + 8r)$$

$$= \sum_{r=1}^{n} r^3 + 6 \sum_{r=1}^{n} r^2 + 8 \sum_{r=1}^{n} r$$

$$= \tfrac{1}{4}n^2(n + 1)^2 + 6.\tfrac{1}{6}n(n + 1)(2n + 1) + 8.\tfrac{1}{2}n(n + 1)$$
$$= \tfrac{1}{4}n(n + 1)\{n(n + 1) + 4(2n + 1) + 16\}$$
$$= \tfrac{1}{4}n(n + 1)(n^2 + n + 8n + 4 + 16)$$
$$= \tfrac{1}{4}n(n + 1)(n^2 + 9n + 20)$$
$$= \tfrac{1}{4}n(n + 1)(n + 4)(n + 5)$$

Example 2   Find the sum of the series $(n + 1)^2 + (n + 2)^2 + (n + 3)^2 + \dots + (2n)^2$.

The sum of the series $= \displaystyle\sum_{r=1}^{2n} r^2 - \sum_{r=1}^{n} r^2$

$$= \tfrac{1}{6}.2n(2n + 1)(4n + 1) - \tfrac{1}{6}n(n + 1)(2n + 1)$$
$$= \tfrac{1}{6}n(2n + 1)\{2(4n + 1) - (n + 1)\}$$
$$= \tfrac{1}{6}n(2n + 1)(7n + 1).$$

Example 3 Find the sum of the series $1^3 + 3^3 + 5^3 + \ldots + (2n - 1)^3$.

$$1^3 + 2^3 + 3^3 + \ldots + (2n)^3 = \sum_{r=1}^{2n} r^3$$

$$= \tfrac{1}{4}(2n)^2(2n + 1)^2$$
$$= n^2(2n + 1)^2$$
$$2^3 + 4^3 + 6^3 + \ldots + (2n)^3 = 2^3(1^3 + 2^3 + 3^3 + \ldots + n^3)$$

$$= 8 \sum_{r=1}^{n} r^3$$

$$= 2n^2(n + 1)^2$$

$$\therefore \quad 1^3 + 3^3 + 5^3 + \ldots + (2n - 1)^3$$
$$= n^2(2n + 1)^2 - 2n^2(n + 1)^2$$
$$= n^2\{(2n + 1)^2 - 2(n + 1)^2\} = n^2(2n^2 - 1)$$

In the next example we use the *method of differences* to find the sum of the given series. We express each term of the series as a difference, in such a way that most terms of the series cancel each other out. A similar process was used earlier in the section to show that $\sum_{r=1}^{n} \{(r + 1)^3 - r^3\} = (n + 1)^3 - 1^3$.

Example 4 Show that $\dfrac{1}{r} - \dfrac{1}{r + 1} \equiv \dfrac{1}{r(r + 1)}$. Hence evaluate $\sum_{r=1}^{n} \dfrac{1}{r(r + 1)}$.

$$\frac{1}{r} - \frac{1}{r + 1} \equiv \frac{(r + 1) - 1}{r(r + 1)} \equiv \frac{1}{r(r + 1)}$$

$$\therefore \quad \sum_{r=1}^{n} \frac{1}{r(r + 1)} = \sum_{r=1}^{n} \left(\frac{1}{r} - \frac{1}{r + 1} \right)$$

$$= \left(1 - \frac{1}{2} \right) + \left(\frac{1}{2} - \frac{1}{3} \right) + \left(\frac{1}{3} - \frac{1}{4} \right) + \ldots$$

$$\ldots + \left(\frac{1}{n - 1} - \frac{1}{n} \right) + \left(\frac{1}{n} - \frac{1}{n + 1} \right)$$

$$= 1 - \frac{1}{n + 1} = \frac{n}{n + 1}$$

[Note that as $n \to \infty$, $\dfrac{1}{n + 1} \to 0$, $\quad \therefore \quad 1 - \dfrac{1}{n + 1} \to 1$. Thus the sum to infinity of this series is 1.]

We can extend the method of Example 4 to other series by using partial fractions.

Example 5 Find

$$\sum_{r=1}^{n} \frac{1}{r(r + 1)(r + 2)} = \frac{1}{1.2.3} + \frac{1}{2.3.4} + \ldots + \frac{1}{n(n + 1)(n + 2)}.$$

Let $\dfrac{1}{r(r+1)(r+2)} \equiv \dfrac{A}{r} + \dfrac{B}{r+1} + \dfrac{C}{r+2}$

then $\qquad\qquad 1 \equiv A(r+1)(r+2) + Br(r+2) + Cr(r+1)$

Putting $r = 0$: $\qquad 1 = 2A \qquad \therefore \quad A = \tfrac{1}{2}$

Putting $r = -1$: $\qquad 1 = -B \qquad \therefore \quad B = -1$

Putting $r = -2$: $\qquad 1 = 2C \qquad \therefore \quad C = \tfrac{1}{2}$

Hence $\dfrac{1}{r(r+1)(r+2)} \equiv \dfrac{1}{2r} - \dfrac{1}{r+1} + \dfrac{1}{2(r+2)}$

$$\therefore \quad \sum_{r=1}^{n} \frac{1}{r(r+1)(r+2)} = \frac{1}{2.1} - \frac{1}{2} + \frac{1}{2.3}$$

$$+ \frac{1}{2.2} - \frac{1}{3} + \frac{1}{2.4}$$

$$+ \frac{1}{2.3} - \frac{1}{4} + \frac{1}{2.5}$$

$$\cdots\cdots\cdots\cdots\cdots$$

$$+ \frac{1}{2(n-1)} - \frac{1}{n} + \frac{1}{2(n+1)}$$

$$+ \frac{1}{2n} - \frac{1}{n+1} + \frac{1}{2(n+2)}$$

$$\therefore \quad \sum_{r=1}^{n} \frac{1}{r(r+1)(r+2)} = \frac{1}{2.1} - \frac{1}{2} + \frac{1}{2.2} + \frac{1}{2(n+1)} - \frac{1}{n+1} + \frac{1}{2(n+2)}$$

$$= \frac{1}{4} - \frac{1}{2(n+1)} + \frac{1}{2(n+2)}$$

[Note that the results obtained in this section can also be proved by the method of mathematical induction, as shown in §17.4.]

Exercise 22.1

1. Use standard results to find the sums of the following series.

(a) $\displaystyle\sum_{r=1}^{n} (2r+1)$ 　　　　(b) $\displaystyle\sum_{r=1}^{n} (r-1)(r+1)$ 　　　　(c) $\displaystyle\sum_{r=1}^{n} 2^r$

(d) $\displaystyle\sum_{r=1}^{n} r^2(r+1)$ 　　　　(e) $\displaystyle\sum_{r=1}^{n} 3^{1-r}$ 　　　　(f) $\displaystyle\sum_{r=1}^{n} (r+4)^3$

2. Use partial fractions to find the sums of the following series.

(a) $\displaystyle\sum_{r=1}^{n} \frac{1}{(r+1)(r+2)}$ 　　(b) $\displaystyle\sum_{r=1}^{n} \frac{1}{r(r+2)}$ 　　(c) $\displaystyle\sum_{r=1}^{n} \frac{1}{(r+1)(r+2)(r+3)}$

3. Find the sums of the following series (i) to $2n$ terms, (ii) to $(2n + 1)$ terms.
(a) $1 - 1 + 1 - 1 + \ldots$ (b) $1 - 2 + 3 - 4 + \ldots$

4. Show that $r(r + 1)(r + 2) - (r - 1)r(r + 1) \equiv 3r(r + 1)$.

Hence find the sum of the series $\sum_{r=1}^{n} r(r + 1)$.

5. Use the method of question 4 to show that

$$\sum_{r=1}^{n} r(r + 1)(r + 2) = \tfrac{1}{4}n(n + 1)(n + 2)(n + 3).$$

6. Show that $(r + 1)^4 - r^4 \equiv 4r^3 + 6r^2 + 4r + 1$. Use this identity and the standard formulae for $\sum_{r=1}^{n} r$ and $\sum_{r=1}^{n} r^2$ to prove that $\sum_{r=1}^{n} r^3 = \tfrac{1}{4}n^2(n + 1)^2$.

7. Use the method of question 6 to find $\sum_{r=1}^{n} r^4$.

8. Use the method of differences to find the sum to n terms of the series
$1(1!) + 2(2!) + 3(3!) + \ldots$.

[Hint: express each term in the form $p! - q!$.]

9. Find the sum of (a) the integers from $2n$ to $3n$ inclusive, (b) the squares of the integers from $2n$ to $3n$ inclusive.

10. Find the sum of (a) the first n odd positive integers, (b) the squares of the first n odd positive integers.

11. Find the sums of the following series
(a) $21^3 + 22^3 + 23^3 + \ldots + 35^3$,
(b) $1^3 + 3^3 + 5^3 + \ldots + 25^3$,
(c) $(n + 1)^3 + (n + 2)^3 + (n + 3)^3 + \ldots + (2n)^3$,
(d) $1^3 - 2^3 + 3^3 - 4^3 + \ldots + (2n - 1)^3 - (2n)^3$.

In questions 12 to 19 write down an expression for the rth term of the given series and hence find the sum of the first n terms of the series.

12. $1.4 + 2.5 + 3.6 + \ldots$ 13. $2^2 + 5^2 + 8^2 + 11^2 + \ldots$

14. $1.2 + 3.4 + 5.6 + \ldots$ 15. $1.2.5 + 2.3.6 + 3.4.7 + \ldots$

16. $\dfrac{1}{1.4} + \dfrac{1}{2.5} + \dfrac{1}{3.6} + \ldots$ 17. $\dfrac{1}{1.3} + \dfrac{1}{3.5} + \dfrac{1}{5.7} + \ldots$

18. $\dfrac{1}{1.3.5} + \dfrac{1}{3.5.7} + \dfrac{1}{5.7.9} + \ldots$ 19. $\dfrac{1}{2.3.4} + \dfrac{2}{3.4.5} + \dfrac{3}{4.5.6} + \ldots$

20. Find the sum of the series $1 + x + x^2 + \ldots + x^n$, where $x \neq 1$. By differentiating your result, find the sum of the series $1 + 2x + 3x^2 + \ldots + nx^{n-1}$ for $x \neq 1$.

21. Find the sum $S = x + 2x^2 + 3x^3 + \ldots + nx^n$, where $x \neq 1$, by considering the expression $S - xS$.

22. Find the sum $S = 1 - 3a + 5a^2 - \ldots + (2n + 1)(-a)^n$, where $a \neq -1$, by considering the expression $(1 + a)S$.

22.2 Maclaurin's theorem

Under certain conditions a function $f(x)$ can be expressed as an infinite series of ascending powers of x. Assuming that such a series exists, we may write

$$f(x) = a_0 + a_1 x + a_2 x^2 + a_3 x^3 + a_4 x^4 + \ldots + a_r x^r + \ldots$$

Differentiating with respect to x, we have

$$f'(x) = a_1 + 2a_2 x + 3a_3 x^2 + 4a_4 x^3 + \ldots + ra_r x^{r-1} + \ldots$$
$$f''(x) = 2a_2 + 3.2a_3 x + 4.3a_4 x^2 + \ldots + r(r-1)a_r x^{r-2} + \ldots$$
$$f'''(x) = 3.2a_3 + 4.3.2a_4 x + \ldots + r(r-1)(r-2)a_r x^{r-3} + \ldots$$

....

$$f^{(r)}(x) = r(r-1)(r-2)\ldots3.2a_r + \ldots$$

Substituting $x = 0$, we find that

$$f(0) = a_0 \qquad\qquad \therefore\; a_0 = f(0)$$
$$f'(0) = a_1 \qquad\qquad \therefore\; a_1 = f'(0)$$

$$f''(0) = 2a_2 \qquad\qquad \therefore\; a_2 = \frac{f''(0)}{2!}$$

$$f'''(0) = 3.2a_3 \qquad\qquad \therefore\; a_3 = \frac{f'''(0)}{3!}$$

and $\quad f^{(r)}(0) = r(r-1)(r-2)\ldots3.2a_r \qquad \therefore\; a_r = \frac{f^{(r)}(0)}{r!}$

Thus $\quad \boxed{f(x) = f(0) + f'(0)x + \dfrac{f''(0)}{2!}x^2 + \dfrac{f'''(0)}{3!}x^3 + \ldots + \dfrac{f^{(r)}(0)}{r!}x^r + \ldots}$

This result is called *Maclaurin's theorem*[†] and the series obtained is known as the *Maclaurin series* for $f(x)$.

It is possible to find a Maclaurin series for any function $f(x)$ whose derivatives $f'(0), f''(0), f'''(0), \ldots$ can be determined. The series obtained may converge to the

[†]*Maclaurin, Colin* (1698–1746) Scottish mathematician. He became professor of Mathematics at Aberdeen at the age of 19. His most important work was his *Treatise on fluxions* (1742).

sum $f(x)$ for all values of x. However, for many functions, Maclaurin's theorem holds only within a restricted range of values of x.

We now use Maclaurin's theorem to obtain various important expansions.

Let $\quad f(x) = (1 + x)^n$, where n is a real number,

then $\quad f'(x) = n(1 + x)^{n-1}$,

$\qquad f''(x) = n(n - 1)(1 + x)^{n-2}$,

$\qquad f'''(x) = n(n - 1)(n - 2)(1 + x)^{n-3}$,

$$\cdots\cdots\cdots\cdots\cdots\cdots\cdots\cdots\cdots\cdots\cdots\cdots\cdots\cdots\cdots$$

$\qquad f^{(r)}(x) = n(n - 1)(n - 2)\ldots(n - r + 1)(1 + x)^{n-r}$,

$\therefore \quad f(0) = 1, \quad f'(0) = n, \quad f''(0) = n(n - 1), \quad f'''(0) = n(n - 1)(n - 2)$

and $\qquad\qquad f^{(r)}(0) = n(n - 1)(n - 2)\ldots(n - r + 1)$.

Thus

$$(1 + x)^n = 1 + nx + \frac{n(n - 1)}{2!}x^2 + \frac{n(n - 1)(n - 2)}{3!}x^3 + \cdots$$
$$\cdots + \frac{n(n - 1)(n - 2)\ldots(n - r + 1)}{r!}x^r + \cdots$$

This result was introduced in §13.7 as an extension of the binomial theorem. When n is a positive integer the expansion is valid for all values of x. It can be shown that, for other values of n, the result holds only when $|x| < 1$, i.e. when $-1 < x < 1$.

If $\qquad\qquad\qquad\qquad f(x) = e^x, \quad$ then $\quad f(0) = 1$

$\qquad\qquad\qquad\qquad\qquad f'(x) = e^x, \qquad\qquad\quad f'(0) = 1$

$\qquad\qquad\qquad\qquad\qquad f''(x) = e^x, \qquad\qquad\quad f''(0) = 1$

$$\cdots\cdots\cdots\cdots\cdots\cdots\qquad\cdots\cdots\cdots\cdots\cdots\cdots$$

$\qquad\qquad\qquad\qquad\qquad f^{(r)}(x) = e^x, \qquad\qquad\quad f^{(r)}(0) = 1$

Thus

$$e^x = 1 + x + \frac{x^2}{2!} + \cdots + \frac{x^r}{r!} + \cdots$$

This expansion is valid for all values of x.

The function $\ln x$ is not defined for $x = 0$ and therefore has no Maclaurin series. However, an expansion of $\ln(1 + x)$ can be obtained.

If $\qquad\qquad f(x) = \ln(1 + x), \qquad\qquad$ then $\qquad f(0) = \ln 1 = 0$

$\qquad\qquad\quad f'(x) = (1 + x)^{-1}, \qquad\qquad\qquad\qquad f'(0) = 1$

$\qquad\qquad\quad f''(x) = -(1 + x)^{-2}, \qquad\qquad\qquad\quad f''(0) = -1$

$\qquad\qquad\quad f'''(x) = 2(1 + x)^{-3}, \qquad\qquad\qquad\quad f'''(0) = 2$

$\qquad\qquad\quad f^{(4)}(x) = -3.2(1 + x)^{-4}, \qquad\qquad\quad f^{(4)}(0) = -3!$

$$\cdots\cdots\cdots\cdots\cdots\cdots\cdots\cdots\qquad\qquad\cdots\cdots\cdots\cdots\cdots\cdots\cdots$$

$\qquad f^{(r)}(x) = (-1)^{r+1}(r - 1)!(1 + x)^{-r}, \qquad f^{(r)}(0) = (-1)^{r+1}(r - 1)!$

Thus $\quad \ln(1 + x) = 0 + x - \frac{x^2}{2!} + \frac{2x^3}{3!} - \frac{3!x^4}{4!} + \cdots + \frac{(-1)^{r+1}(r - 1)!x^r}{r!} + \cdots$

i.e.

$$\ln(1 + x) = x - \frac{x^2}{2} + \frac{x^3}{3} - \frac{x^4}{4} + \ldots + (-1)^{r+1}\frac{x^r}{r} + \ldots$$

This result is valid for $-1 < x \leqslant 1$.

If

$$\begin{aligned}
f(x) &= \sin x, & \text{then} && f(0) &= 0 \\
f'(x) &= \cos x, &&& f'(0) &= 1 \\
f''(x) &= -\sin x, &&& f''(0) &= 0 \\
f'''(x) &= -\cos x, &&& f'''(0) &= -1 \\
f^{(4)}(x) &= \sin x, &&& f^{(4)}(0) &= 0 \\
f^{(5)}(x) &= \cos x, &&& f^{(5)}(0) &= 1
\end{aligned}$$

Since we can now see a pattern emerging, we may write

$$\sin x = x - \frac{x^3}{3!} + \frac{x^5}{5!} - \frac{x^7}{7!} + \ldots$$

A similar result can be obtained for $\cos x$:

$$\cos x = 1 - \frac{x^2}{2!} + \frac{x^4}{4!} - \frac{x^6}{6!} + \ldots$$

The expansions of $\sin x$ and $\cos x$ are valid for all values of x (in radians).

Exercise 22.2

In questions 1 to 9 use Maclaurin's theorem to expand the given function in ascending powers of x as far as the term in x^4.

1. $\cos x$ 2. $\tan x$ 3. $\sec x$

4. $\ln(\cos x)$ 5. $\sin^2 x$ 6. $\ln(1 + \sin x)$

7. $\tan^{-1} x$ 8. $e^{\sin x}$ 9. $\sin^{-1} x$

10. If $y = e^x \sin x$, show that $\dfrac{d^2y}{dx^2} = 2\left(\dfrac{dy}{dx} - y\right)$. By further differentiation of this result, find the Maclaurin expansion of the function $e^x \sin x$ as far as the term in x^6.

22.3 The binomial series

The *binomial series* is the expansion of $(1 + x)^n$ in ascending powers of x, as follows:

$$(1 + x)^n = 1 + nx + \frac{n(n-1)}{2!}x^2 + \frac{n(n-1)(n-2)}{3!}x^3 + \dots$$

$$\dots + \frac{n(n-1)(n-2)\dots(n-r+1)}{r!}x^r + \dots$$

where n is a real number and $|x| < 1$.

Simple applications of this expansion were discussed in §13.7. We now consider further uses of the series.

First we recall that the expression $(a + x)^n$ cannot be expanded directly using the binomial series. Provided that $|x| < |a|$, we write

$$(a + x)^n = a^n\left(1 + \frac{x}{a}\right)^n = a^n\left\{1 + n\left(\frac{x}{a}\right) + \frac{n(n-1)}{2!}\left(\frac{x}{a}\right)^2 + \dots\right\}$$

Example 1 Expand $(8 + 3x)^{1/3}$ in ascending powers of x as far as the term in x^3, stating the values of x for which the expansion is valid. Hence obtain an approximate value for $\sqrt[3]{8\cdot72}$.

$$(8 + 3x)^{1/3} = 8^{1/3}\left(1 + \frac{3}{8}x\right)^{1/3}$$

$$= 2\left\{1 + \frac{1}{3}\left(\frac{3}{8}x\right) + \frac{1}{2!} \times \frac{1}{3}\left(\frac{1}{3} - 1\right)\left(\frac{3}{8}x\right)^2\right.$$

$$\left. + \frac{1}{3!} \times \frac{1}{3}\left(\frac{1}{3} - 1\right)\left(\frac{1}{3} - 2\right)\left(\frac{3}{8}x\right)^3 - \dots\right\}$$

$$= 2\left\{1 + \frac{1}{8}x - \frac{1}{2}\cdot\frac{1}{3}\cdot\frac{2}{3}\cdot\frac{3^2}{8^2}x^2 + \frac{1}{6}\cdot\frac{1}{3}\cdot\frac{2}{3}\cdot\frac{5}{3}\cdot\frac{3^3}{8^3}x^3 - \dots\right\}$$

$$= 2\left\{1 + \frac{1}{8}x - \frac{1}{8^2}x^2 + \frac{5}{3\cdot8^3}x^3 - \dots\right\}$$

$$= 2 + \frac{1}{4}x - \frac{1}{32}x^2 + \frac{5}{768}x^3 - \dots$$

The expansion is valid for $|\frac{3}{8}x| < 1$ i.e. for $|x| < \frac{8}{3}$.
Substituting $x = 0\cdot24$, we have

$$(8\cdot72)^{1/3} = 2 + \tfrac{1}{4}(0\cdot24) - \tfrac{1}{32}(0\cdot24)^2 + \tfrac{5}{768}(0\cdot24)^3 - \dots$$
$$= 2 + 0\cdot06 - 0\cdot0018 + 0\cdot00009 - \dots$$
$$\approx 2\cdot05829.$$

Hence the approximate value of $\sqrt[3]{8\cdot72}$ is $2\cdot05829$.

[To decide whether it is reasonable to give this result to 5 decimal places, we may consider the sum, S_n, of the first n terms in the expansion, for $n = 1, 2, 3, \dots$.

$$S_1 = 2$$
$$S_2 = 2{\cdot}06$$
$$S_3 = 2{\cdot}0582$$
$$S_4 = 2{\cdot}05829$$
$$S_5 = 2{\cdot}0582846$$

Each term in the expansion of $(8{\cdot}72)^{1/3}$ is smaller than the previous term but opposite in sign. It follows that $\sqrt[3]{8{\cdot}72}$ lies between S_4 and S_5. Thus the difference between $2{\cdot}05829$ and the true value of $\sqrt[3]{8{\cdot}72}$ must be less than 1×10^{-5}.]

Example 2   Given that the first three terms in the expansion in ascending powers of x of $(1 - 8x)^{1/4}$ are the same as the first three terms in the expansion of $(1 + ax)/(1 + bx)$, find the values of a and b. Hence find an approximation to $(0{\cdot}6)^{1/4}$ in the form p/q, where p and q are integers.

$$(1 - 8x)^{1/4} = 1 + \frac{1}{4}(-8x) + \frac{1}{2!} \times \frac{1}{4}\left(\frac{1}{4} - 1\right)(-8x)^2 + \dots$$

$$= 1 - 2x - \frac{1}{2} \cdot \frac{1}{4} \cdot \frac{3}{4} \cdot 8^2 x^2 - \dots$$

$$= 1 - 2x - 6x^2 - \dots$$

$$\frac{1 + ax}{1 + bx} = (1 + ax)(1 + bx)^{-1}$$

$$= (1 + ax)\left\{1 + (-1)bx + \frac{1}{2!}(-1)(-2)b^2x^2 + \dots\right\}$$

$$= (1 + ax)(1 - bx + b^2x^2 + \dots)$$
$$= 1 + ax - bx - abx^2 + b^2x^2 + \dots$$
$$= 1 + (a - b)x + (b^2 - ab)x^2 + \dots$$

Since the first three terms of the expansions are the same.

$$a - b = -2, \quad b^2 - ab = -6$$

i.e. $b - a = 2, \qquad b(b - a) = -6$

Hence $b = -3$ and $a = -5$.

Thus
$$(1 - 8x)^{1/4} \approx \frac{1 - 5x}{1 - 3x}.$$

Substituting $x = 0{\cdot}05$, we have

$$(1 - 0{\cdot}4)^{1/4} \approx \frac{1 - 0{\cdot}25}{1 - 0{\cdot}15} = \frac{0{\cdot}75}{0{\cdot}85}.$$

Hence $(0{\cdot}6)^{1/4}$ is approximately equal to $15/17$.

Example 3   Assuming that x is so small that terms in x^3 and higher powers may be neglected, find a quadratic approximation to $\sqrt{\left(\dfrac{1 - x}{1 + 2x}\right)}$.

$$\sqrt{\left(\frac{1-x}{1+2x}\right)} = (1-x)^{1/2}(1+2x)^{-1/2}$$

$$(1-x)^{1/2} = 1 + \frac{1}{2}(-x) + \frac{1}{2!} \times \frac{1}{2}\left(-\frac{1}{2}\right)(-x)^2 + \cdots$$

$$= 1 - \frac{1}{2}x - \frac{1}{8}x^2 - \cdots$$

$$(1+2x)^{-1/2} = 1 + \left(-\frac{1}{2}\right)(2x) + \frac{1}{2!} \times \left(-\frac{1}{2}\right)\left(-\frac{3}{2}\right)(2x)^2 + \cdots$$

$$= 1 - x + \frac{3}{2}x^2 - \cdots$$

∴   neglecting terms in x^3 and higher powers,

$$\sqrt{\left(\frac{1-x}{1+2x}\right)} \approx \left(1 - \frac{1}{2}x - \frac{1}{8}x^2\right)\left(1 - x + \frac{3}{2}x^2\right)$$

$$\approx 1 - x + \frac{3}{2}x^2 - \frac{1}{2}x + \frac{1}{2}x^2 - \frac{1}{8}x^2$$

Hence $\sqrt{\left(\frac{1-x}{1+2x}\right)} \approx 1 - \frac{3}{2}x + \frac{15}{8}x^2.$

Example 4   Expand $\dfrac{1}{1+x+2x^2}$ in ascending powers of x up to and including the term in x^3.

$$\frac{1}{1+y} = (1+y)^{-1}$$

$$= 1 + (-1)y + \frac{(-1)(-2)}{2!}y^2 + \frac{(-1)(-2)(-3)}{3!}y^3 + \cdots$$

$$= 1 - y + y^2 - y^3 + \cdots$$

Substituting $y = x + 2x^2$, we obtain

$$\frac{1}{1+x+2x^2} = 1 - (x + 2x^2) + (x + 2x^2)^2 - (x + 2x^2)^3 + \cdots$$

$$= 1 - x - 2x^2 + x^2 + 4x^3 - x^3 + \cdots$$
$$= 1 - x - x^2 + 3x^3 + \cdots$$

Suppose that we now wish to expand $\dfrac{1}{(1-x)(1+2x)}$ in ascending powers of x. We could use the method of Example 4:

$$\frac{1}{(1-x)(1+2x)} = (1 + x - 2x^2)^{-1} = 1 - (x - 2x^2) + (x - 2x^2)^2 - \cdots$$

or we could write:

$$\frac{1}{(1-x)(1+2x)} = (1-x)^{-1}(1+2x)^{-1}$$

$$= (1 + x + x^2 + \ldots)(1 - 2x + 4x^2 - \ldots)$$

We may quickly obtain the first few terms of the expansion using either of these methods. However, if a general formula for the term in x^r is required, we must adopt a different approach. This further method involves the use of partial fractions. (See §18.6)

Example 5   Expand $\dfrac{1}{(1-x)(1+2x)}$ in ascending powers of x, giving the first three terms and the term in x^r. State the values of x for which the expansion is valid.

$$(1-x)^{-1} = 1 + (-1)(-x) + \frac{(-1)(-2)}{2!}(-x)^2 + \ldots$$

$$+ \frac{(-1)(-2)\ldots(-r)}{r!}(-x)^r + \ldots$$

Thus $\qquad (1-x)^{-1} = 1 + x + x^2 + \ldots + x^r + \ldots$

Similarly $\quad (1+2x)^{-1} = 1 - 2x + 4x^2 + \ldots + (-2)^r x^r + \ldots$

Let $\qquad \dfrac{1}{(1-x)(1+2x)} \equiv \dfrac{A}{1-x} + \dfrac{B}{1+2x}$

then $\qquad\qquad 1 \equiv A(1+2x) + B(1-x)$

Putting $x = 1$: $\qquad 1 = 3A \quad \therefore \quad A = \frac{1}{3}$

Putting $x = -\frac{1}{2}$: $\quad 1 = \frac{3}{2}B \quad \therefore \quad B = \frac{2}{3}$

$$\therefore \quad \frac{1}{(1-x)(1+2x)} = \tfrac{1}{3}(1-x)^{-1} + \tfrac{2}{3}(1+2x)^{-1}$$

$$= \tfrac{1}{3}(1 + x + x^2 + \ldots + x^r + \ldots)$$
$$+ \tfrac{2}{3}(1 - 2x + 4x^2 + \ldots + (-2)^r x^r + \ldots)$$
$$= 1 - x + 3x^2 + \ldots + \{\tfrac{1}{3} + \tfrac{2}{3}(-2)^r\}x^r + \ldots$$
$$= 1 - x + 3x^2 + \ldots + \tfrac{1}{3}\{1 - (-2)^{r+1}\}x^r + \ldots$$

The expansion of $(1-x)^{-1}$ is valid for $|x| < 1$ and the expansion of $(1+2x)^{-1}$ is valid for $|2x| < 1$, i.e. $|x| < \frac{1}{2}$.

Thus the expansion of $\dfrac{1}{(1-x)(1+2x)}$ is valid when $|x| < \frac{1}{2}$.

Exercise 22.3

In questions 1 to 9 expand the given function in ascending powers of x up to and including the term in x^3.

1. $(1+x)^{-3}$ $\qquad\qquad$ 2. $(1+2x)^{1/2}$ $\qquad\qquad$ 3. $(4+x)^{-3/2}$

4. $\dfrac{1 + 2x}{1 - 2x}$ 5. $\dfrac{1 - x}{(2 + x)^2}$ 6. $\dfrac{1 - 2x}{\sqrt{(1 - 4x)}}$

7. $\dfrac{1}{1 + x + x^2}$ 8. $\dfrac{1}{\sqrt{(1 + x - 2x^2)}}$ 9. $\sqrt[3]{(1 + x + 3x^2)}$

In questions 10 to 15 assume that x is so small that terms in x^3 and higher powers of x may be neglected. Hence find a quadratic approximation to the given function, stating the values of x for which your answer is valid.

10. $\sqrt{\left(\dfrac{1 - x}{1 + x}\right)}$ 11. $\sqrt[3]{\left(\dfrac{8 + x}{1 - 3x}\right)}$ 12. $\dfrac{(1 + 4x)^{1/4}}{(1 + 5x)^{1/5}}$

13. $\dfrac{1}{(1 + x)(3 - x)}$ 14. $\dfrac{1}{(1 - x)(1 + 2x)^2}$ 15. $\dfrac{1}{(1 - 2x)\sqrt{(1 - x)}}$

In questions 16 to 21 use partial fractions to find the first five non-zero terms in the expansion of the given function in ascending powers of x. State the values of x for which the expansion is valid.

16. $\dfrac{3 - 5x}{(1 - 3x)(1 + x)}$ 17. $\dfrac{4x}{(1 - x)(3 + x)}$ 18. $\dfrac{1 + x}{(1 + x^2)(1 - x)}$

19. $\dfrac{4 - x}{(1 - x)^2(1 + 2x)}$ 20. $\dfrac{2}{(1 + x)(1 + x^2)}$ 21. $\dfrac{8(2x - 1)}{(x - 2)^2(x^2 + 2)}$

In questions 22 to 24 expand the given function in ascending powers of x, giving the first three non-zero terms and the term in x^r.

22. $\dfrac{3}{(1 + x)(1 - 2x)}$ 23. $\dfrac{4x}{(1 - x)(1 + 3x)}$ 24. $\dfrac{4 + 3x}{(2 - x)(1 + 2x)}$

25. Expand $(1 + 2x)^{1/4}$ in ascending powers of x as far as the term in x^3, stating the values of x for which the expansion is valid. Hence obtain approximate values for (a) $\sqrt[4]{1\cdot4}$, (b) $\sqrt[4]{1\cdot08}$. Obtain the values of $\sqrt[4]{1\cdot4}$ and $\sqrt[4]{1\cdot08}$ by calculator, (using the function $x^{1/y}$ if available). Explain why the error in answer (a) is greater than the error in answer (b).

26. Expand $(a + 2x)\sqrt{(1 - 4x)} + \dfrac{b}{(1 - x)^2}$ in ascending powers of x as far as the term in x^3. Given that the coefficients of x and x^2 are zero, find the first term in the expansion and the coefficient of x^3.

27. Given that the first three terms in the expansion in ascending powers of x of $(1 + x + x^2)^n$ are the same as the first three terms in the expansion of $\left(\dfrac{1 + ax}{1 - 3ax}\right)^3$,

find the non-zero values of n and a. Show that the coefficients of x^3 in the two expansions differ by 7·5.

28. If x is so small that x^3 and higher powers of x may be neglected, find the values of a and b such that

$$\sqrt{(1 + 4x)} \approx \frac{1 + ax}{1 + bx}.$$

By letting $x = 0.04$ find an approximation to $\sqrt{29}$ in the form p/q, where p and q are integers.

22.4 Exponential and logarithmic series

As shown in §22.2 the expansion in ascending powers of x of the exponential function e^x is as follows:

$$e^x = 1 + x + \frac{x^2}{2!} + \frac{x^3}{3!} + \dots + \frac{x^r}{r!} + \dots \text{ for all real values of } x.$$

Example 1 Expand e^{2x} in ascending powers of x giving the first three terms and the term in x^r.

$$e^{2x} = 1 + (2x) + \frac{(2x)^2}{2!} + \dots + \frac{(2x)^r}{r!} + \dots$$

$$= 1 + 2x + 2x^2 + \dots + \frac{2^r}{r!} x^r + \dots$$

Example 2 Find the first three terms in the expansion of e^{x+x^2} in ascending powers of x.

$$e^{x+x^2} = 1 + (x + x^2) + \frac{(x + x^2)^2}{2!} + \dots$$

$$= 1 + x + x^2 + \frac{1}{2}x^2 + \text{higher powers of } x$$

$$= 1 + x + \frac{3}{2}x^2 + \dots$$

Example 3 Expand e^{2-x} in ascending powers of x as far as the term in x^3.

$$e^{2-x} = e^2 \times e^{-x} = e^2 \left\{ 1 + (-x) + \frac{(-x)^2}{2!} + \frac{(-x)^3}{3!} + \dots \right\}$$

$$= e^2 \left\{ 1 - x + \frac{1}{2}x^2 - \frac{1}{6}x^3 + \dots \right\}$$

Example 4   Find the coefficient of x^r in the expansion of $(x^2 + 2x + 3)e^x$ in ascending powers of x.

Considering the terms $\ldots + \dfrac{x^{r-2}}{(r-2)!} + \dfrac{x^{r-1}}{(r-1)!} + \dfrac{x^r}{r!} + \ldots$ in the expansion of e^x, we find that the terms in x^r in the expansion of $(x^2 + 2x + 3)e^x$ must be

$$\ldots + x^2 \times \frac{x^{r-2}}{(r-2)!} + 2x \times \frac{x^{r-1}}{(r-1)!} + 3 \times \frac{x^r}{r!} + \ldots$$

Hence the coefficient of x^r in the expansion

$$= \frac{1}{(r-2)!} + \frac{2}{(r-1)!} + \frac{3}{r!}$$

$$= \frac{r(r-1)}{r!} + \frac{2r}{r!} + \frac{3}{r!}$$

$$= \frac{r^2 - r + 2r + 3}{r!}$$

$$= \frac{r^2 + r + 3}{r!}$$

In §22.2 we also obtained the logarithmic series:

$$\ln(1+x) = x - \frac{x^2}{2} \pm \frac{x^3}{3} - \ldots + (-1)^{r+1}\frac{x^r}{r} + \ldots \text{ where } -1 < x \leqslant 1.$$

Replacing x by $-x$ in this expansion gives:

$$\ln(1-x) = -x - \frac{x^2}{2} - \frac{x^3}{3} - \ldots - \frac{x^r}{r} - \ldots \text{ where } -1 \leqslant x < 1.$$

When these series are used to find numerical values of logarithms, large numbers of terms are needed to produce accurate results. A much better expansion for this purpose is given by:

$$\ln\left(\frac{1+x}{1-x}\right) = \ln(1+x) - \ln(1-x)$$

$$= \left(x - \frac{x^2}{2} + \frac{x^2}{3} - \ldots\right) - \left(-x - \frac{x^2}{2} - \frac{x^3}{3} - \ldots\right)$$

i.e.

$$\ln\left(\frac{1+x}{1-x}\right) = 2\left(x + \frac{x^3}{3} + \frac{x^5}{5} + \ldots\right)$$

We demonstrate the advantages of using this series rather than the expansion of $\ln(1 + x)$ by calculating a sequence of approximate values for $\ln 1\cdot 5$.

	$\ln(1 + x), x = \frac{1}{2}$	$\ln\left(\dfrac{1 + x}{1 - x}\right), x = \frac{1}{5}$
1 term	0·5	0·4
2 terms	0·375	0·40533333
3 terms	0·41666667	0·40546133
4 terms	0·40104167	0·40546499
5 terms	0·40729167	0·40546510
6 terms	0·40468750	0·40546511

Using the figures on the left we can give $\ln 1\cdot 5$ to 1 decimal place, but not to 2. However, the figures on the right give a result correct to 8 decimal places.

We now use the laws of logarithms to obtain some further expansions.

Example 5 Expand $\ln(2 + 3x)$ in ascending powers of x as far as the term in x^3. State the values of x for which the expansion is valid.

$$\ln(2 + 3x) = \ln 2\left(1 + \frac{3}{2}x\right)$$

$$= \ln 2 + \ln\left(1 + \frac{3}{2}x\right)$$

$$= \ln 2 + \left(\frac{3}{2}x\right) - \frac{1}{2}\left(\frac{3}{2}x\right)^2 + \frac{1}{3}\left(\frac{3}{2}x\right)^3 - \ldots$$

$$= \ln 2 + \frac{3}{2}x - \frac{9}{8}x^2 + \frac{9}{8}x^3 - \ldots$$

The expansion is valid for $-1 < \frac{3}{2}x \leqslant 1$ i.e. $-\frac{2}{3} < x \leqslant \frac{2}{3}$.

Example 6 Expand $\ln\dfrac{1 + x}{\sqrt{(1 - 2x)}}$ in ascending powers of x as far as the term in x^3, stating the values of x for which the expansion is valid.

$$\ln\frac{1 + x}{\sqrt{(1 - 2x)}} = \ln(1 + x) - \frac{1}{2}\ln(1 - 2x)$$

$$= \left\{x - \frac{1}{2}x^2 + \frac{1}{3}x^3 - \ldots\right\}$$

$$\quad - \frac{1}{2}\left\{(-2x) - \frac{1}{2}(-2x)^2 + \frac{1}{3}(-2x)^3 - \ldots\right\}$$

$$= \left\{x - \frac{1}{2}x^2 + \frac{1}{3}x^3 - \ldots\right\} + \left\{x + x^2 + \frac{4}{3}x^3 + \ldots\right\}$$

$$= 2x + \frac{1}{2}x^2 + \frac{5}{3}x^3 + \ldots$$

The expansion of $\ln(1 + x)$ is valid for $-1 < x \leqslant 1$ and the expansion of $\ln(1 - 2x)$ is valid for $-1 < -2x \leqslant 1$, i.e. $-\frac{1}{2} \leqslant x < \frac{1}{2}$.

Hence the expansion of $\ln \dfrac{1+x}{\sqrt{(1-2x)}}$ is valid for $-\frac{1}{2} \leqslant x < \frac{1}{2}$.

Example 7 Assuming that x is so small that x^3 and higher powers may be neglected, obtain a quadratic approximation to the function

$$\frac{1 + e^x}{1 + \ln(1 + x)}.$$

$$1 + e^x = 1 + \left(1 + x + \frac{x^2}{2!} + \ldots\right) \approx 2 + x + \frac{1}{2}x^2$$

$$1 + \ln(1 + x) = 1 + \left(x - \frac{x^2}{2} + \ldots\right) \approx 1 + x - \frac{1}{2}x^2$$

Using the binomial expansion,

$$(1 + y)^{-1} = 1 + (-1)y + \frac{(-1)(-2)}{2!}y^2 + \ldots = 1 - y + y^2 - \ldots$$

Substituting $y = x - \frac{1}{2}x^2$,

$$\frac{1}{1 + \ln(1 + x)} \approx \left\{1 + \left(x - \frac{1}{2}x^2\right)\right\}^{-1}$$

$$= 1 - \left(x - \frac{1}{2}x^2\right) + \left(x - \frac{1}{2}x^2\right)^2 - \ldots$$

$$= 1 - x + \frac{1}{2}x^2 + x^2 + \ldots$$

$$\approx 1 - x + \frac{3}{2}x^2$$

$$\therefore \quad \frac{1 + e^x}{1 + \ln(1 + x)} \approx \left(2 + x + \frac{1}{2}x^2\right)\left(1 - x + \frac{3}{2}x^2\right)$$

$$\approx 2 - 2x + 3x^2 + x - x^2 + \frac{1}{2}x^2$$

i.e. $\dfrac{1 + e^x}{1 + \ln(1 + x)} \approx 2 - x + \dfrac{5}{2}x^2$.

Exercise 22.4

1. Find the first three non-zero terms and the general terms in the expansions in ascending powers of x of:
(a) e^{-x} (b) e^{3x} (c) e^{x^2} (d) e^{1+x}

2. Find the first four terms in the expansions of:
(a) $(1 + 2x)e^{2x}$
(b) $(1 - x)^2 e^{-x}$
(c) $e^{(x^2 - x)}$

3. Use the exponential series to calculate the values of e and $1/e$ correct to 4 decimal places.

4. Find the first three non-zero terms and the general terms in the expansions of the following functions, stating the values of x for which the expansions are valid:
(a) $\ln(1 + 3x)$
(b) $\ln(1 - \frac{1}{2}x)$
(c) $\ln(3 + x)$
(d) $\ln(e - x)$

5. Find the first four terms in the expansions of:
(a) $\ln\left(\dfrac{1 + x}{1 + x^2}\right)$
(b) $\ln(1 + x - 2x^2)$
(c) $\ln\dfrac{(1 - x)^2}{\sqrt{(1 + 4x)}}$

6. Use the expansion of $\ln\left(\dfrac{1 + x}{1 - x}\right)$ to calculate the value of $\ln 3$ correct to 4 decimal places.

7. Find the coefficient of x^r in the expansions of each of the following functions in ascending powers of x:
(a) $(1 - x)e^x$
(b) $(1 + x - 3x^2)e^{2x}$
(c) $(1 + x)^2 e^{x/2}$

8. Given that x is so small that terms in x^3 and higher powers of x may be neglected, find quadratic approximations to the following functions:
(a) $e^x \ln(1 + x)$
(b) $(1 + e^{-x})^2$
(c) $(1 + x)^8 e^{-x/2}$
(d) $\dfrac{e^{3x} - e^x}{e^{2x}}$
(e) $\dfrac{1 - \ln(1 - x)}{1 - x}$
(f) $\dfrac{\ln(1 - 2x)}{1 - e^x}$

9. Show that, if $n > 1$, $\ln\left(\dfrac{n + 1}{n - 1}\right) = 2\left(\dfrac{1}{n} + \dfrac{1}{3n^3} + \dfrac{1}{5n^5} + \dots\right)$. Hence calculate the value of $\ln 2$ correct to 4 decimal places.

10. The expansion of $(1 - x)^n$ in ascending powers of x is the same as the expansion of $e^{ax + x^2}$ as far as the term in x^2. Find the values of a and n.

11. The expansion of $(3x + ax^2)/(3 + bx)$ in ascending powers of x is the same as the expansion of $\ln(1 + x)$ as far as the term in x^3. Find the values of a and b. Hence find a rational approximation to $\ln 1 \cdot 2$.

12. (a) Use the expansion of e^x to show that if n is a positive integer, then $x^n e^{-x} \to 0$ as $x \to \infty$.
(b) By letting $x = e^y$, show that $\dfrac{1}{x}\ln x \to 0$ as $x \to \infty$.

13.   Show that, if $n > 1$, $\ln\left(1 + \dfrac{1}{n}\right)^n = 1 - \dfrac{1}{2n} + \dfrac{1}{3n^2} - \cdots$

Use the expansion of e^x to deduce that

$$\left(1 + \frac{1}{n}\right)^n = e\left(1 - \frac{1}{2n} + \frac{11}{24n^2} - \cdots\right).$$

Deduce that, as $n \to \infty$, $\left(1 + \dfrac{1}{n}\right)^n \to e$.

22.5 The expansions of sin x and cos x

$$\sin x = x - \frac{x^3}{3!} + \frac{x^5}{5!} - \cdots, \quad \cos x = 1 - \frac{x^2}{2!} + \frac{x^4}{4!} - \cdots$$

for all real values of x.

The expansions of $\sin x$ and $\cos x$ are used in the same ways as the various series discussed in previous sections.

Example 1   Expand $e^{\sin x}$ in ascending powers of x, neglecting terms in x^4 and higher powers of x.

$$\sin x = x - \frac{x^3}{3!} + \cdots = x - \frac{1}{6}x^3 + \cdots$$

$$e^y = 1 + y + \frac{y^2}{2!} + \frac{y^3}{3!} + \cdots = 1 + y + \frac{1}{2}y^2 + \frac{1}{6}x^3 + \cdots$$

Substituting $y = x - \frac{1}{6}x^3$,

$$e^{\sin x} = 1 + \left(x - \frac{1}{6}x^3\right) + \frac{1}{2}\left(x - \frac{1}{6}x^3\right)^2 + \frac{1}{6}\left(x - \frac{1}{6}x^3\right)^3 + \cdots$$

$$= 1 + x - \frac{1}{6}x^3 + \frac{1}{2}x^2 + \frac{1}{6}x^3 + \cdots$$

$$= 1 + x + \frac{1}{2}x^2 + \cdots$$

Example 2   Expand $\sec x$ in ascending powers of x, as far as the term in x^4.

$$\sec x = (\cos x)^{-1} = \left(1 - \frac{x^2}{2!} + \frac{x^4}{4!} - \cdots\right)^{-1} = \left(1 - \frac{x^2}{2} + \frac{x^4}{24} - \cdots\right)^{-1}$$

Using the binomial expansion, $(1 + y)^{-1} = 1 - y + y^2 - \cdots$

Thus, substituting $y = -\dfrac{x^2}{2} + \dfrac{x^4}{24}$,

$$\sec x = 1 - \left(-\frac{x^2}{2} + \frac{x^4}{24}\right) + \left(-\frac{x^2}{2} + \frac{x^4}{24}\right)^2 - \cdots$$

$$= 1 + \frac{x^2}{2} - \frac{x^4}{24} + \frac{x^4}{4} + \cdots$$

$$= 1 + \frac{x^2}{2} + \frac{5x^4}{24} + \cdots$$

Exercise 22.5

1. Evaluate, correct to 4 decimal places,
   (a) $\sin 0{\cdot}3$ (b) $\cos 0{\cdot}4$ (c) $\cos 2$ (d) $\sin 1$

2. Find the first three non-zero terms in the expansions of the following functions in ascending powers of x:
   (a) $\sin 3x$ (b) $\cos 2x$ (c) $\ln(1 + \sin x)$
   (d) $e^{\cos x}$ (e) $x \operatorname{cosec} x$ (f) $\tan x$

3. Find approximations to the following functions, given that powers of x higher than the fourth are negligible:
   (a) $\sin x(x + \cos x)$ (b) $\sin \{\ln(1 + 2x)\}$
   (c) $\cos (\sin 2x) - e^{-2x^2}$ (d) $e^{2x} \cos^2 x$

Exercise 22.6 (*miscellaneous*)

1. Find the sums of the following series
   (a) $\displaystyle\sum_{r=2}^{n} r(r-1)$ (b) $\displaystyle\sum_{r=0}^{n} (2r+1)(2r+3)$

   (c) $\displaystyle\sum_{r=n}^{2n} \frac{1}{r(r+1)}$ (d) $\displaystyle\sum_{r=2}^{n} \frac{1}{r^2 - 1}$

2. Find the sum to n terms of each of the following series
   (a) $1 \cdot 2^2 + 2 \cdot 3^2 + 3 \cdot 4^2 + \cdots$ (b) $1 \cdot 2 \cdot 3 + 3 \cdot 4 \cdot 5 + 5 \cdot 6 \cdot 7 + \cdots$

3. Find the sum of all possible products of the form rs^2, where r and s are distinct positive integers such that $1 \leqslant r, s \leqslant n$.

4. The sum of the first n terms of the series $1 + 2x^2 + 3x^4 + \cdots$, where $x^2 \neq 1$, is S. Find an expression for S by considering $S - x^2 S$.

5. Using the remainder theorem, or otherwise, factorise $x^3 + 6x^2 + 11x + 6$. Express $\dfrac{4x + 6}{x^3 + 6x^2 + 11x + 6}$ in partial fractions. Hence show that

$$\sum_{n=0}^{18} \frac{4n + 6}{n^3 + 6n^2 + 11n + 6} = 2\frac{43}{140}. \tag{L}$$

6. (a) Find the sum of the first n terms of the series whose rth term is $2^r + 2r - 1$.
    (b) If x is so small that terms in x^n, $n \geqslant 3$, can be neglected and
    $\dfrac{3 + ax}{3 + bx} = (1 - x)^{1/3}$, find the values of a and b. Hence, without the use of
    tables, find an approximation in the form p/q, where p and q are integers,
    for $\sqrt[3]{0.96}$.   (AEB 1979)

7. Find the expansions of $\left(1 + \dfrac{1}{x^2}\right)^{1/2}$ and $\left(1 - \dfrac{1}{x^2}\right)^{1/2}$ in ascending powers of
    $1/x^2$ up to and including the term in $1/x^4$. Hence, or otherwise, show that, if the
    positive number x is very large compared with 1, then $(x^2 + 1)^{1/2} - (x^2 + 1)^{1/2} \approx \dfrac{1}{x}$.
                                                                            (C)

8. Expand $\sqrt{(4 - x)}$ as a series in ascending powers of x up to and including the
    terms in x^2. If terms in x^n, $n \geqslant 3$, can be neglected, find the quadratic approximation
    to $\sqrt{\left(\dfrac{4 - x}{1 - 2x}\right)}$. State the range of values of x for which this approximation is valid.
                                                                            (AEB 1980)

9. Expand the function $(2 - x)\sqrt{(1 + 2x + 2x^2)}$ in ascending powers of x as far as
    the term in x^3.

10. Use partial fractions to expand the following functions in ascending powers of
    x, giving the first three non-zero terms and the term in x^r. State the values of x for
    which the expansions are valid.

    (a) $\dfrac{3x}{(1 + 2x)(1 - x)}$ (b) $\dfrac{x}{(x - 3)(x - 2)}$ (c) $\dfrac{1 - x - x^2}{(1 - 3x)(1 - 2x)(1 - x)}$

11. Expand the following functions in ascending powers of x, as far as the term in x^4.
    State the values of x for which the expansions are valid.

    (a) $\dfrac{1 - 2x}{\sqrt{(1 + 2x^2)}}$ (b) $\dfrac{1 + 2x^2}{(1 - 2x)^2}$ (c) $\dfrac{3}{(1 + 2x^2)(1 - 2x)}$

12. (a) Expand $e^{x/2} \log_e(1 + x)$ in ascending powers of x as far as the term
    in x^4 and hence show that, for certain values of x to be stated,
    $e^{x/2} \log_e(1 + x) + e^{-x/2} \log_e(1 - x) = ax^4 + \ldots$ and give the value of a.
    (b) Expand $(1 + x)^{-1/2}$ in ascending powers of x, giving the first four terms and
    the general term. Hence, without using tables or calculator, obtain the value
    of $1/\sqrt{101}$, correct to 6 decimal places, showing all working.   (SU)

13. (a) Draw rough sketches of the following graphs, showing quite clearly their
    general shape, and where they cross any axis:
    (i) $y = e^x$ (ii) $y = e^{-x}$ (iii) $y = \log_e x$ (iv) $y = \log_e(1 + x)$

(b) Expand $\log_e \dfrac{(1 + 2x)^2}{1 - 3x}$ in ascending powers of x, as far as the term in x^4, giving the range of values of x for which the expansion is valid. What is the nth term?

(c) Prove that the coefficient of x^n in the expansion of $e^{2x}(x^2 + 3x - 7)$ is
$$\frac{2^{n-2}(n^2 + 5n - 28)}{n!}$$
(SU)

14. Obtain the series expansion of $\dfrac{e^{2x}}{1 + x}$ in ascending powers of x up to and including the term in x^3. Using these terms find an approximation to the value of $\displaystyle\int_0^{1/4} \frac{e^{2x}dx}{1 + x}$, giving your answer correct to three places of decimals. (O)

15. State the series expansion in ascending powers of x, including the general term, of $\log_e(1 + x)$ for $|x| < 1$. Show that

(i) $\log_e\left(\dfrac{1 + x}{1 - x}\right) = 2\left[x + \dfrac{1}{3}x^3 + \dfrac{1}{5}x^5 + \ldots\right]$,

(ii) $\log_e m = 2\left[\left(\dfrac{m - 1}{m + 1}\right) + \dfrac{1}{3}\left(\dfrac{m - 1}{m + 1}\right)^3 + \dfrac{1}{5}\left(\dfrac{m - 1}{m + 1}\right)^5 + \ldots\right]$.

Hence evaluate $\log_e 2$ to four decimal places, showing all your working.

If $\log_e\left(\dfrac{1 + x}{1 - x}\right) - \left(\dfrac{e^{2x} - 1}{e^x}\right) = ax^3 + bx^5$, when terms in x^n, $n \geqslant 6$, are neglected, find the values of a and b. (AEB 1978)

16. Given that $1 - px + x^2 \equiv (1 - \alpha x)(1 - \beta x)$, obtain expressions for $\alpha^2 + \beta^2$ and $\alpha^3 + \beta^3$ in terms of p. Hence, or otherwise, find the first three terms in the expansion of $\log_e(1 - px + x^2)$ in ascending powers of x. (JMB)

17. Find the values of positive constants a, b and c given that the expansions of $e^{-ax}\sin 2x$ and $\cos bx \ln(1 + cx)$ in ascending powers of x are the same as far as the term in x^3.

23 Some numerical methods

23.1 Numerical integration

When a function $f(x)$ is difficult to integrate, it may be possible to estimate the value of the definite integral $\int_a^b f(x)\,dx$ by numerical methods. Such methods are also useful when, instead of a formula for $f(x)$, we have a set of values obtained experimentally.

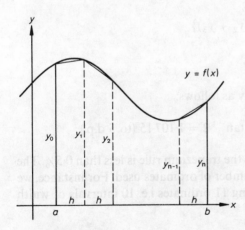

The integral $\int_a^b f(x)\,dx$ is represented by the area under the curve $y = f(x)$ between $x = a$ and $x = b$. Suppose that the area is divided into n strips of width h, as shown in the diagram. The ordinates $y_0, y_1, y_2, \ldots, y_n$ represent the values of $f(x)$ at $x_0 = a, x_1 = a + h,$ $x_2 = a + 2h, \ldots, x_n = b.$

An approximate value for the area is obtained by regarding each strip as a trapezium, so that

$$\int_a^b f(x)\,dx \approx \tfrac{1}{2}h(y_0 + y_1) + \tfrac{1}{2}h(y_1 + y_2) + \ldots + \tfrac{1}{2}h(y_{n-1} + y_n)$$

i.e.
$$\int_a^b f(x)\,dx \approx \tfrac{1}{2}h(y_0 + 2y_1 + 2y_2 + \ldots + 2y_{n-1} + y_n)$$

461

Thus we have the *trapezium rule* for n strips ($n + 1$ ordinates)

$$\int_a^b f(x)\,dx \approx \tfrac{1}{2}h\{(y_0 + y_n) + 2(y_1 + y_2 + \ldots + y_{n-1})\},$$

where $h = (b - a)/n$.

Example 1 Use the trapezium rule with 5 ordinates to find an approximate value for $\int_0^2 \dfrac{1}{1 + x^2}\,dx$.

Using 5 ordinates in the interval from $x = 0$ to $x = 2$ gives 4 strips of width $h = 0.5$.

n	x_n	y_n (rounded to 5 d.p.)
0	0	1
1	0.5	0.8
2	1	0.5
3	1.5	0.307 69
4	2	0.2

$$\begin{array}{cc} & \underline{1.2} \\ & \underline{1.607\,69} \\ 3.215\,38 & \times\ 2 \\ \hline 4.415\,38 & 3.215\,38 \end{array}$$

By the trapezium rule,

$$\int_0^2 \frac{1}{1 + x^2}\,dx \approx \tfrac{1}{2}h\{(y_0 + y_4) + 2(y_1 + y_2 + y_3)\}$$
$$\approx \tfrac{1}{2} \times 0.5 \times 4.415\,38$$
$$\approx 1.104$$

This integral can also be evaluated directly as follows:

$$\int_0^2 \frac{1}{1 + x^2}\,dx = \left[\, \tan^{-1} x \,\right]_0^2 = \tan^{-1} 2 = 1.107\,15 \text{ (to 5 d.p.)}$$

Thus the error in the value obtained using the trapezium rule is less than 0.5%. The error may be reduced by increasing the number of ordinates used. For instance, we can obtain a better approximation by using 11 ordinates i.e. 10 intervals of width $h = 0.2$.

n	x_n	y_n (rounded to 5 d.p.)
0	0	1
1	0.2	0.961 54
2	0.4	0.862 07
3	0.6	0.735 29
4	0.8	0.609 76
5	1	0.5
6	1.2	0.409 84
7	1.4	0.337 84

8	1·6		0·280 90
9	1·8		0·235 85
10	2	0·2	
		1·2	4·933 09
		9·866 18	× 2
		11·066 18	9·866 18

By the trapezium rule, $\displaystyle\int_0^2 \frac{1}{1+x^2}\,dx \approx \tfrac{1}{2}h\{(y_0 + y_{10}) + 2(y_1 + y_2 + \ldots + y_9)\}$

$$\approx \tfrac{1}{2} \times 0{\cdot}2 \times 11{\cdot}066\,18$$
$$\approx 1{\cdot}1066$$

Using 21 ordinates the value 1·1070 is obtained. However, rounding errors in the values of y_n will limit further improvements in accuracy.

Evaluating the integral $\displaystyle\int_a^b f(x)\,dx$ by the trapezium rule is equivalent to replacing the curve $y = f(x)$ by a series of straight lines joining the tops of the ordinates $y_0, y_1, y_2, \ldots$ A better estimate of the area under the curve is usually obtained using *Simpson's rule*.[†] In this case the curve $y = f(x)$ is regarded as a series of parabolic arcs joining the tops of the ordinates y_0, y_1 and $y_2; y_2, y_3$ and $y_4; \ldots$

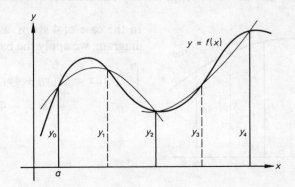

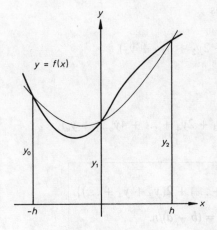

We consider first the integral $\displaystyle\int_{-h}^{h} f(x)\,dx$, letting y_0, y_1, y_2 be the ordinates at $x_0 = -h, x_1 = 0$ and $x_2 = h$. If $y = px^2 + qx + r$ is the parabola which joins the tops of the ordinates y_0, y_1, y_2, then

$$y_0 = ph^2 - qh + r,$$
$$y_1 = r,$$
$$y_2 = ph^2 + qh + r.$$

[†]*Simpson, Thomas* (1710–1761) English mathematician known as 'the oracle of Nuneaton'. The rule which bears his name was used by earlier mathematicians, but Simpson was credited with its discovery when he published it in 1743.

The area under this parabola between $x = -h$ and $x = h$

$$= \int_{-h}^{h} (px^2 + qx + r)\, dx = \left[\tfrac{1}{3}px^3 + \tfrac{1}{2}qx^2 + rx \right]_{-h}^{h}$$

$$= (\tfrac{1}{3}ph^3 + \tfrac{1}{2}qh^2 + rh) - (-\tfrac{1}{3}ph^3 + \tfrac{1}{2}qh^2 - rh)$$

$$= \tfrac{2}{3}ph^3 + 2rh$$

$$= \tfrac{1}{3}h(2ph^2 + 6r)$$

$$= \tfrac{1}{3}h(y_0 + 4y_1 + y_2)$$

Thus
$$\int_{-h}^{h} f(x)\, dx \approx \tfrac{1}{3}h(y_0 + 4y_1 + y_2).$$

Since this result depends only on the values of the ordinates y_0, y_1, y_2 and the interval h between them, we may also write:

$$\int_{a}^{b} f(x)\, dx \approx \tfrac{1}{3}h(y_0 + 4y_1 + y_2)$$

where $h = \tfrac{1}{2}(b - a)$ and $y_0 = f(a)$, $y_1 = f(a + h)$, $y_2 = f(b)$.

This is Simpson's rule in its simplest form. The rule for 2 strips (3 ordinates) can be extended to any even number of strips (or any odd number of ordinates.)

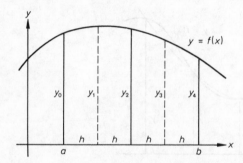

In the case of 4 strips, as shown in the diagram, we apply the basic rule twice:

$$\int_{a}^{b} f(x)\, dx \approx \tfrac{1}{3}h(y_0 + 4y_1 + y_2)$$
$$+ \tfrac{1}{3}h(y_2 + 4y_3 + y_4)$$

Thus Simpson's rule for 4 strips (5 ordinates) is

$$\int_{a}^{b} f(x)\, dx \approx \tfrac{1}{3}h(y_0 + 4y_1 + 2y_2 + 4y_3 + y_4)$$

More generally, Simpson's rule states that:

$$\int_{a}^{b} f(x)\, dx \approx \tfrac{1}{3}h(y_0 + 4y_1 + 2y_2 + 4y_3 + 2y_4 + \ldots + 4y_{n-1} + y_n)$$

i.e.
$$\int_{a}^{b} f(x)\, dx \approx \tfrac{1}{3}h\{(y_0 + y_n) + 4(y_1 + y_3 + \ldots) + 2(y_2 + y_4 + \ldots)\}$$

where n is even and $h = (b - a)/n$.

Example 2 Use Simpson's rule with 5 ordinates to find an approximate value for $\int_0^2 \dfrac{1}{1+x^2}\,dx.$

Using 5 ordinates in the interval from $x = 0$ to $x = 2$ gives 4 strips of width $h = 0 \cdot 5$.

n	x_n	y_n (rounded to 5 d.p.)		
0	0	1		
1	0·5		0·8	
2	1			0·5
3	1·5		0·307 69	
4	2	0·2		
		$\overline{1\cdot2}$	$\overline{1\cdot107\,69}$	$\overline{0\cdot5}$
		4·430 76	× 4 ×	2
		1·0	4·430 76	1·0
		$\overline{6\cdot630\,76}$		

By Simpson's rule,

$$\int_0^2 \frac{1}{1+x^2}\,dx \approx \tfrac{1}{3}h\{(y_0 + y_4) + 4(y_1 + y_3) + 2y_2\}$$

$$\approx \tfrac{1}{3} \times 0\cdot5 \times 6\cdot630\,76$$
$$\approx 1\cdot105$$

This is closer to the true value of the integral than the result obtained in Example 1 using the trapezium rule. Accuracy can again be improved by increasing the number of ordinates to 11.

n	x_n	y_n (rounded to 5 d.p.)		
0	0	1		
1	0·2		0·961 54	
2	0·4			0·862 07
3	0·6		0.735 29	
4	0·8			0·609 76
5	1		0·5	
6	1·2			0·409 84
7	1·4		0·337 84	
8	1·6			0·280 90
9	1·8		0·235 85	
10	2	0·2		
		$\overline{1\cdot2}$	$\overline{2\cdot770\,52}$	$\overline{2\cdot162\,57}$
		11·082 08	× 4	× 2
		4·325 14	11·082 08	4·325 14
		$\overline{16\cdot607\,22}$		

By Simpson's rule,

$$\int_0^2 \frac{1}{1+x^2}\,dx \approx \tfrac{1}{3}h\{(y_0 + y_{10}) + 4(y_1 + y_3 + \ldots) + 2(y_2 + y_4 + \ldots)\}$$

$$\approx \tfrac{1}{3} \times 0{\cdot}2 \times 16{\cdot}607\,22$$

$$\approx 1{\cdot}1071$$

[Unless more accurate values of y_n can be obtained, there is little point in making further increases in the number of ordinates.]

Under certain conditions an approximate value for $\int_a^b f(x)\,dx$ can be obtained by expanding $f(x)$ in ascending powers of x, then integrating term by term. Clearly the method cannot be used unless the expansion of $f(x)$ is valid throughout the interval $a \leqslant x \leqslant b$.

Since the binomial series for $(1 + x^2)^{-1}$ is valid only when $|x| < 1$, this expansion will not produce a good approximation to the value of $\int_0^2 \frac{1}{1+x^2}\,dx$. We consider instead $\int_0^{0{\cdot}4} \frac{1}{1+x^2}\,dx$. Using the binomial expansion,

$$(1 + x^2)^{-1} = 1 - x^2 + x^4 - x^6 + \cdots$$

$$\therefore \quad \int_0^{0{\cdot}4} \frac{1}{1+x^2}\,dx \approx \int_0^{0{\cdot}4} (1 - x^2 + x^4 - x^6 + \ldots)\,dx$$

$$\approx \left[x - \frac{x^3}{3} + \frac{x^5}{5} - \frac{x^7}{7} + \cdots \right]_0^{0{\cdot}4}$$

$$\approx 0{\cdot}4 - \frac{(0{\cdot}4)^3}{3} + \frac{(0{\cdot}4)^5}{5} - \frac{(0{\cdot}4)^7}{7}$$

$$\approx 0{\cdot}3805.$$

Exercise 23.1

Use the trapezium rule to obtain approximate values of the following integrals, giving your answers to 3 decimal places.

1. $\int_1^3 \frac{1}{1+x}\,dx$, 5 ordinates.

2. $\int_0^3 \sqrt{(1 + x^2)}\,dx$, 4 ordinates.

3. $\int_0^2 10^x\,dx$, 5 strips.

4. $\int_1^8 \lg x\,dx$, 7 strips.

5. $\int_0^{\pi/6} \tan x\,dx$, 7 ordinates.

6. $\int_0^4 xe^{-x}\,dx$, 5 ordinates.

Questions 7 to 12. Use sketches to decide whether the results obtained in questions 1 to 6 are greater than or less than the true values of the given integrals.

Use Simpson's rule to obtain approximate values of the following integrals, giving your answers to 4 decimal places.

13. $\int_0^1 \dfrac{1}{1 + x^3}$, 5 ordinates.

14. $\int_0^{\frac{1}{2}} \sqrt{(1 - x^2)}\,dx$, 4 strips.

15. $\int_0^{\pi/3} \sqrt{(\sin x)}\,dx$, 6 strips.

16. $\int_0^4 xe^{-x}\,dx$, 5 ordinates.

17. $\int_1^2 x\lg x\,dx$, 11 ordinates.

18. $\int_0^2 \sqrt{(1 + x^3)}\,dx$, 11 ordinates.

19. Expand $(1 + x^2)^{12}$ in ascending powers of x as far as the term in x^8. Hence find an approximate value for the integral $\int_0^{0.5} (1 + x^2)^{12}\,dx$. Using the trapezium rule with 6 ordinates, obtain a second estimate for the value of this integral. Give your answers to 4 decimal places.

20. Use Simpson's rule with 5 ordinates to estimate the value of $\int_0^{0.4} \ln(1 + x)\,dx$. By expanding $\ln(1 + x)$ in ascending powers of x as far as the term in x^3 and integrating term by term, obtain a second estimate for the value of this integral. Give your answers to 4 decimal places.

21. Values of a continuous function $f(x)$ were obtained experimentally as follows:

x	1	1·5	2	2·5	3
$f(x)$	8·01	6·02	4·69	3·80	3·27

Estimate the value of $\int_1^3 f(x)\,dx$ using (a) the trapezium rule, (b) Simpson's rule.

22. A car of mass 1000 kg starts from rest and accelerates continuously along a straight road for 20 seconds. After t seconds the resultant force acting on the car is P newtons. The table below gives values of P at intervals of 5 seconds.

t	0	5	10	15	20
P	800	740	590	460	360

Use the trapezium rule to estimate (a) the speed of the car after 10 seconds, (b) the speed of the car after 20 seconds. Use the trapezium rule and your answers to (a) and (b) to estimate the distance travelled in the first 20 seconds.

23. A particle moves in a straight line under the action of a variable force of magnitude F newtons. The value of F after the particle has travelled a distance of s metres is given in the table below.

s	0	1	2	3	4	5	6
F	54	61	67	72	76	79	81

Estimate the work done when the particle has travelled a distance of 6 metres using (a) the trapezium rule, (b) Simpson's rule.

24. Construct a flow diagram to evaluate $\int_0^1 e^{-x^2}\,dx$ using the trapezium rule with 6 ordinates. Test your procedure using a pocket calculator.

25. Construct a flow diagram to evaluate $\int_2^3 \sqrt{(x^2 - 4)}\,dx$ using Simpson's rule with 11 ordinates. Test your procedure using a pocket calculator.

26.

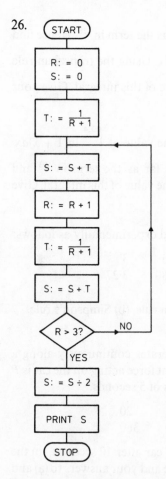

The following flow diagram is designed for the calculation of an approximate value of $\int_0^4 \dfrac{1}{1 + x}\,dx$ using the trapezium rule. Carry out the procedure indicated, tabulating the successive value of R, S and T in simplified fractional form as you proceed. State the printed value of S giving two decimal places in your answers.

By referring to a sketch graph of

$$y = \frac{1}{x + 1} \text{ for } 0 \leqslant x \leqslant 4,$$ give a reason why the printed value of S will be an over-estimate of the value of the integral.

(JMB)

27. Show that the formula $\int_0^{2h} f(x)\,dx \approx \tfrac{1}{3}h\{f(0) + 4f(h) + f(2h)\}$ is exact when $f(x)$ is a cubic polynomial in x. Use the formula given above to obtain an approximate value of I where $I = \int_0^{\frac{1}{2}} \dfrac{1}{\sqrt{(1 - x^2)}}\,dx$, giving your result to three decimal places. Show, by direct integration, that $I = \pi/6$.   (L)

23.2 Approximate solutions to equations

The roots of the equation $f(x) = 0$ are the values of x at which the curve $y = f(x)$ cuts the x-axis. Thus approximate values for the roots can be obtained by drawing the graph of $y = f(x)$. However, it is sometimes better to estimate the roots by rearranging the equation and finding the points of intersection of two graphs.

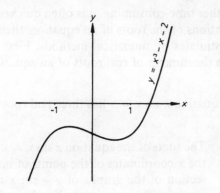
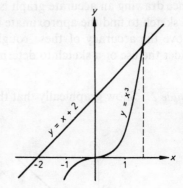

Consider, for instance, the equation $x^3 - x - 2 = 0$. An accurate graph of $y = x^3 - x - 2$ shows that the equation has one real root approximately equal to $1 \cdot 5$. Rearranging the equation as $x^3 = x + 2$, we see that we can also find this root by drawing the graphs of $y = x^3$ and $y = x + 2$.

Example 1 By drawing the graphs of $y = \ln x$ and $y = 2 - x$ in the interval $1 \leqslant x \leqslant 2$, find the solution of the equation $\ln x + x - 2 = 0$, correct to 1 decimal place.

x	1·0	1·2	1·4	1·6	1·8	2·0
$\ln x$	0	0·182	0·336	0·470	0·588	0·693

x	1	1·5	2
$2 - x$	1	0·5	0

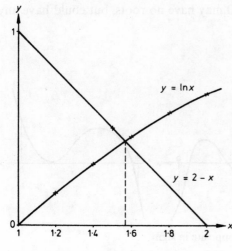

At the point of intersection of the graphs of $y = \ln x$ and $y = 2 - x$ the approximate value of x is $1 \cdot 6$.

Hence if $\ln x + x - 2 = 0$, then $x \approx 1 \cdot 6$.

We can check that this result is accurate to one decimal place as follows:

If $x = 1{\cdot}55$, $\ln x \approx 0{\cdot}438$ and $2 - x = 0{\cdot}45$ $\qquad \therefore \quad \ln x < 2 - x.$
If $x = 1{\cdot}65$, $\ln x \approx 0{\cdot}501$ and $2 - x = 0{\cdot}35$ $\qquad \therefore \quad \ln x > 2 - x.$

Hence $\ln x = 2 - x$ for some value of x between $1{\cdot}55$ and $1{\cdot}65$ i.e. when $x = 1{\cdot}6$ correct to 1 decimal place.

Since drawing an accurate graph is rather time-consuming, it is often quicker to use a sketch to find the approximate locations of the roots of an equation, then to improve the accuracy of these rough estimates by numerical methods. First we consider the use of a sketch to determine the number of real roots of an equation.

Example 2   Show graphically that the equation $\pi \sin x = x$ has three real roots.

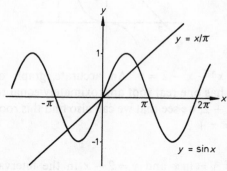

The roots of the equation $\pi \sin x = x$ are the x-coordinates of the points of inter-section of the graphs of $y = \sin x$ and $y = x/\pi$. The curve $y = \sin x$ always lies between the lines $y = -1$ and $y = 1$. The straight line $y = x/\pi$ passes through the origin and the points $(-\pi, -1)$, $(\pi, 1)$. Thus, as shown in the sketch, the graphs intersect at three points. Hence the equation $\pi \sin x = x$ has three real roots.

Roots of the equation $f(x) = 0$ can be located by considering the sign changes of the function $f(x)$. Each of the following diagrams shows a function $f(x)$ which is continuous between $x = a$ and $x = b$. We see that if $f(a)$ and $f(b)$ are *opposite* in sign then, in the interval $a < x < b$, the equation $f(x) = 0$ must have at least one root, but may have any *odd* number of roots. If $f(a)$ and $f(b)$ have the *same* sign then, in the interval $a < x < b$, the equation $f(x) = 0$ may have no roots, but could have any *even* number of roots.

[Some of the roots may be coincident.]

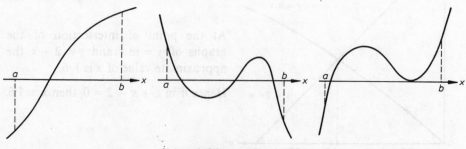

$f(a)$ and $f(b)$ opposite in sign

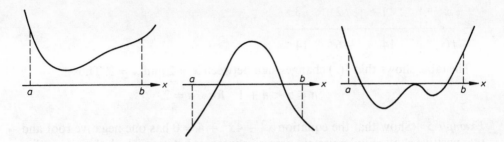

$f(a)$ and $f(b)$ have the same sign

Example 3   Show that the equation $x^3 - 3x^2 + 5 = 0$ has only one real root and that this root lies between -2 and -1.

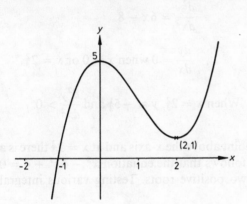

Let $y = x^3 - 3x^2 + 5,$

then $\dfrac{dy}{dx} = 3x^2 - 6x = 3x(x - 2)$

and $\dfrac{d^2y}{dx^2} = 6x - 6 = 6(x - 1)$

$\therefore \ \dfrac{dy}{dx} = 0$ when $x = 0$ or $x = 2.$

When $x = 0$, $y = 5$ and $\dfrac{d^2y}{dx^2} < 0.$

When $x = 2$, $y = 1$ and $\dfrac{d^2y}{dx^2} > 0.$

Hence on the curve $y = x^3 - 3x^2 + 5$ there is a maximum point at $(0, 5)$ and a minimum point at $(2, 1)$.
Since both turning points are above the x-axis, if follows that the equation $x^3 - 3x^2 + 5 = 0$ has only one real root.
When $x = -2$, $y = -15$ and when $x = -1$, $y = 1$
$\therefore$ y changes sign in the interval $-2 < x < -1$.
Hence the root of the given equation lies between -2 and -1.

Example 4   Show that the equation $x^3 + x - 16 = 0$ has only one real root α and find the integer n such that $n \leqslant \alpha < n + 1$.

Let $f(x) = x^3 + x - 16$, then $f'(x) = 3x^2 + 1.$
Since $f'(x)$ is always positive, the curve $y = f(x)$ has no turning points and cannot cut the x-axis more than once. For large negative values of x, $f(x)$ is negative and for large positive values of x, $f(x)$ is positive,
$\therefore$ the curve $y = f(x)$ cuts the x-axis exactly once.
Hence the equation $x^3 + x - 16 = 0$ has only one real root α.
When $x \leqslant 0$, $f(x) < 0$ $\therefore$ $\alpha > 0$.

x	1	2	3
$f(x)$	-14	-6	14

The table shows that $f(x)$ changes sign between $x = 2$ and $x = 3$. Thus

$$n \leqslant \alpha < n + 1 \quad \text{for} \quad n = 2.$$

Example 5   Show that the equation $x^3 - 4x^2 + 4 = 0$ has one negative root and two positive roots. Find pairs of successive integers between which these roots lie.

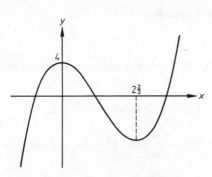

Let $f(x) = x^3 - 4x^2 + 4$ and consider the curve $y = f(x)$.

$$\frac{dy}{dx} = 3x^2 - 8x = x(3x - 8)$$

$$\frac{d^2y}{dx^2} = 6x - 8$$

$$\therefore \quad \frac{dy}{dx} = 0 \text{ when } x = 0 \text{ or } x = 2\tfrac{2}{3}$$

When $x = 0$, $y = 4$ and $\dfrac{d^2y}{dx^2} < 0$.   When $x = 2\tfrac{2}{3}$, $y \approx -5\tfrac{1}{2}$ and $\dfrac{d^2y}{dx^2} > 0$.

Hence at $x = 0$ there is a maximum point above the x-axis and at $x = 2\tfrac{2}{3}$ there is a minimum point below the x-axis. It follows that the equation $x^3 - 4x^2 + 4 = 0$ must have one negative root and two positive roots. Testing various integral values of x, we have:

x	-1	0	1	2	3	4
$f(x)$	-1	4	1	-4	-5	4

Using the sign changes shown in the table, we deduce that the roots of the given equation lie between -1 and 0, 1 and 2, 3 and 4.

When it has been shown that an equation $f(x) = 0$ has a root α in the interval $a < x < b$, then *linear interpolation* can be used to estimate the value of α.

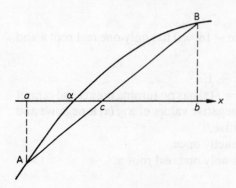

Let us suppose that A and B are the points on the curve $y = f(x)$ at which $x = a$ and $x = b$ respectively. If the straight line joining A to B cuts the x-axis at $(c, 0)$, then c is taken as an approximate value of the root α.

We illustrate the method by letting $f(x) = x^3 + x - 16$. As shown in Example 4, the equation $x^3 + x - 16 = 0$ has a root α in the interval $2 < x < 3$ and the

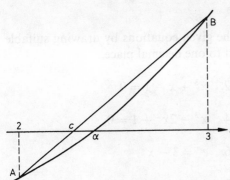

curve $y = x^3 + x - 16$ passes through the points $A(2, -6)$ and $B(3, 14)$. If the straight line joining A to B cuts the x-axis at $(c, 0)$, then using similar triangles, we find that c divides the interval from $x = 2$ to $x = 3$ in the ratio $6:14$

Hence, by linear interpolation,

$$\alpha \approx 2 + \frac{6}{6 + 14} = 2 \cdot 3.$$

[Note that since $f(2 \cdot 3) \approx -1 \cdot 5$, the true value of α lies between $2 \cdot 3$ and 3.]

If the equation $f(x) = 0$ is known to have a root so small that, for values of x close to the root, x^3 and higher powers of x are negligible, then the root can be estimated using a *quadratic approximation* to $f(x)$.

Example 6 Given that the equation $(1 - x)e^x = 0 \cdot 7(2x + 1)$ has a small root, use a quadratic approximation to estimate its value.

$$(1 - x)e^x = (1 - x)\left(1 + x + \frac{x^2}{2!} + \ldots\right)$$

$$= 1 + x + \tfrac{1}{2}x^2 - x - x^2 + \ldots$$

$$\therefore \quad (1 - x)e^x \approx 1 - \tfrac{1}{2}x^2.$$

Hence the small root of the equation $(1 - x)e^x = 0 \cdot 7(2x + 1)$ is approximately equal to the small root of the equation $1 - \tfrac{1}{2}x^2 = 0 \cdot 7(2x + 1)$.
Multiplying both sides of this equation by 10, we have

$$10 - 5x^2 = 7(2x + 1)$$

i.e. $\quad 5x^2 + 14x - 3 = 0$

$$(5x - 1)(x + 3) = 0$$

$$\therefore \quad x = 0 \cdot 2 \quad \text{or} \quad x = -3.$$

Hence the approximate value of the small root of the given equation is $0 \cdot 2$.

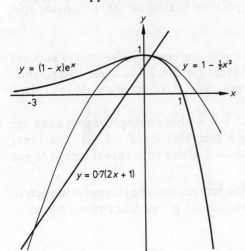

$y = (1 - x)e^x$

$y = 1 - \tfrac{1}{2}x^2$

$y = 0 \cdot 7(2x + 1)$

[We see from the sketch that the approximation $(1 - x)e^x \approx 1 - \tfrac{1}{2}x^2$ is valid for only a small range of values of x. Thus the second root, $x = -3$, obtained using this approximation has no real significance.]

Exercise 23.2

In questions 1 to 10 obtain the roots of the given equations by drawing suitable accurate graphs. Give your answers correct to one decimal place.

1. $x^2 - 2x - 2 = 0$ 2. $x^3 + x - 1 = 0$

3. $x^3 - 3x + 3 = 0$ 4. $x^3 - 2x^2 + 1 = 0$

5. $x^3 + x^2 - 2x - 1 = 0$ 6. $e^x = 3 - x$

7. $2 \sin x = x$ 8. $4 \cos x = x$

9. $\dfrac{4}{x^2} = 2x + 1$ 10. $(x - 2)\ln x = x - 1$

In questions 11 to 14 use a sketch to find the number of real roots of the given equation.

11. $e^{-x} = x - 1$ 12. $2e^x = 5x + 1$

13. $\cos 2x = 1 - x$ 14. $\sin \pi x = \frac{1}{2}(x - 1)$

In questions 15 to 22 determine the number of real roots of the given equation and find pairs of successive integers between which the roots lie.

15. $x^3 - 6x^2 + 36 = 0$ 16. $x^3 + 5x - 10 = 0$

17. $x^3 - 12x + 12 = 0$ 18. $x^3 + 2x^2 - 4x - 4 = 0$

19. $2x^3 + 4x - 15 = 0$ 20. $x^3 - x - 3 = 0$

21. $e^x = x + 3$ 22. $\sin x = \ln x$

23. Show that the equation $x^3 - 7x - 12 = 0$ has one real root and show that this root lies between 3 and 4. Use linear interpolation to estimate the root, giving your answer to one decimal place.

24. Show that the equation $x^4 - 4x - 4 = 0$ has one negative root α and one positive root β. Show that $-1 < \alpha < 0$ and that $1 < \beta < 2$. Use linear interpolation to estimate the values of α and β, giving your answers correct to one decimal place.

25. Show that the equation $x^4 + 3x^3 + x^2 - 9 = 0$ has one negative root α and one positive root β. Find α and the integer k such that $k < \beta < k + 1$. Use linear interpolation to find an approximate value for β, giving your answer correct to one decimal place.

In questions 26 to 31 use linear interpolation between suitable successive integers to obtain estimates for the roots of the given equations, giving your answers correct to one decimal place.

26. $2x^3 - 25 = 0$ 27. $x^3 + 3x^2 - 14x - 10 = 0$

28. $4x^3 - 9x^2 + 3 = 0$ 29. $x^3 + 3x^2 - 4x + 3 = 0$

30. $\ln x = x^2 - 6x + 8$ 31. $6\cos x + x = 0$

32. Draw an accurate graph of $y = 2x^3 - 5x + 2$ for values of x between -2 and $+2$. Estimate the roots of the equation $2x^3 - 5x + 2 = 0$ (a) from your graph, (b) by linear interpolation between suitable successive integers. Why does linear interpolation give poor approximations to the roots in this case?

33. Each of the following equations has a root so small that, for values of x close to the root, x^3 and higher powers of x are negligible. Use quadratic approximations to estimate these roots.
(a) $2(1 - x)^5 = 18x + 5$ (b) $8\ln(1 + x) = 3x + 1$
(c) $10(1 - \cos x) = 2 - 3x$ (d) $5\sqrt[3]{(1 + 3x)} = 14x + 3$

23.3 The Newton–Raphson method

If $x = a$ is an approximate value of a root of an equation $f(x) = 0$, then the tangent to the curve $y = f(x)$ at $x = a$ can be used to find a second approximation to the root. As shown in the diagrams, the x-coordinate of the point of intersection of this tangent with the x-axis is usually closer to the true root than the first approximation $x = a$.

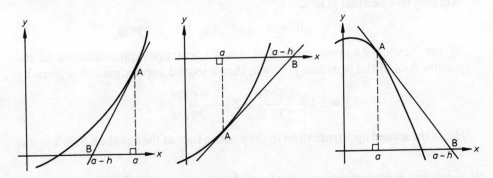

Let A be the point $(a, f(a))$ on the curve $y = f(x)$ and let the point of intersection of the tangent at A with the x-axis be the point B with coordinates $(a - h, 0)$, then:

$$\text{gradient of } AB = \frac{f(a) - 0}{a - (a - h)} = \frac{f(a)}{h}.$$

However, since AB is the tangent to the curve $y = f(x)$ at $x = a$, its gradient is also equal to $f'(a)$,

$$\therefore \qquad f'(a) = \frac{f(a)}{h} \quad \text{which gives} \quad h = \frac{f(a)}{f'(a)}.$$

Thus the tangent at A cuts the x-axis where $x = a - \dfrac{f(a)}{f'(a)}$. This result forms the basis of the procedure known as the *Newton-Raphson*[†] *method* (or simply Newton's method).

> If $x = a$ is a first approximation to a root of the equation $f(x) = 0$, then a second approximation to the root is given by $x = a - \dfrac{f(a)}{f'(a)}$.

The following diagrams show that the method may fail to produce a better approximation to the root when the value of $f'(a)$ is small or when the first approximation to the root is poor.

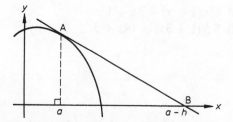 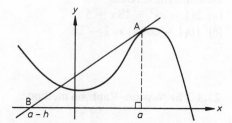

Example 1   Taking $x = 2 \cdot 3$ as a first approximation to the positive root of the equation $3 \sin x = x$, use the Newton-Raphson method to find a second approximation to this root, giving your answer to 2 decimal places.

Let $f(x) = 3 \sin x - x$, then $f'(x) = 3 \cos x - 1$.
Working to 4 decimal places,

$$f(2 \cdot 3) \approx -0 \cdot 0629 \quad \text{and} \quad f'(2 \cdot 3) \approx -2 \cdot 9988.$$

By the Newton-Raphson method, if $x = 2 \cdot 3$ is a first approximation to the positive root of the equation $f(x) = 0$, then a second approximation is given by

$$x = 2 \cdot 3 - \frac{f(2 \cdot 3)}{f'(2 \cdot 3)} \approx 2 \cdot 3 - \frac{0 \cdot 0629}{2 \cdot 9988} \approx 2 \cdot 28.$$

Hence the second approximation to the positive root of the equation $3 \sin x = x$ is $x = 2 \cdot 28$.

If x_0 is a first approximation to a root α of the equation $f(x) = 0$, then the Newton-Raphson method can be used to produce a sequence of approximations $x_1, x_2, x_3, \ldots$ by writing:

$$x_{n+1} = x_n - \frac{f(x_n)}{f'(x_n)}$$

The following diagrams show that, in general, the sequence $x_0, x_1, x_2, x_3, \ldots$ converges quickly to the required root.

[†]*Raphson, Joseph* (1648–1715) English mathematician. His account of the Newton-Raphson method was published in 1690 and was based on earlier work by Newton. Raphson produced many other mathematical works including a *History of Fluxions* (1715).

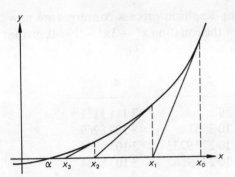
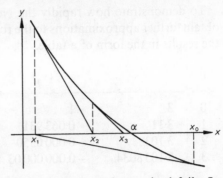

The next two diagrams show that in certain circumstances the method fails. In (1) the sequence x_0, x_1, x_2, x_3, ... converges to a different root β and in (2) the sequence diverges.

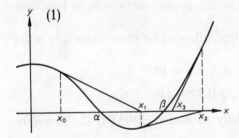
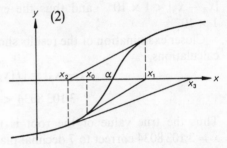

Example 2   The equation $x^3 - 3x^2 - 1 = 0$ has one real root. Starting with $x = 3$, use two iterations of Newton's method to find an approximate value for this root, correct to 3 decimal places.

Let $f(x) = x^3 - 3x^2 - 1$, then $f'(x) = 3x^2 - 6x$.
Using Newton's method and working to 5 decimal places,

let $x_0 = 3$,   then $f(x_0) = -1$, $f'(x_0) = 9$

$\therefore$ $x_1 = x_0 - \dfrac{f(x_0)}{f'(x_0)} = 3 - \dfrac{(-1)}{9} \approx 3{\cdot}11111$

Let $x_1 = 3{\cdot}11$,   then $f(x_1) \approx 0{\cdot}063\,93$, $f'(x_1) = 10{\cdot}3563$

$\therefore$ $x_2 = x_1 - \dfrac{f(x_1)}{f'(x_1)} = 3{\cdot}11 - \dfrac{0{\cdot}063\,93}{10{\cdot}3563} \approx 3{\cdot}103\,83$

Hence an approximate value for the root is $3{\cdot}104$.

Checking the accuracy of this result we find that

$$f(3{\cdot}1035) \approx -0{\cdot}003 \quad \text{and} \quad f(3{\cdot}1045) \approx 0{\cdot}007,$$

$\therefore$ the root is $3{\cdot}104$ correct to 3 decimal places.

[Note that when evaluating a function $f(x)$ by calculator it is usually best to store the value of x in the memory. If $f(x)$ is a polynomial more accurate results will be obtained by using nested multiplication as described in §4.4.]

To demonstrate how rapidly the Newton-Raphson process converges we now obtain further approximations to the root of the equation $x^3 - 3x^2 - 1 = 0$, giving the results in the form of a table.

n	x_n	$f(x_n)$	$f'(x_n)$	x_{n+1}
0	3	-1	9	3·111 1111
1	3·11	0·063 931	10·3563	3·103 8269
2	3·1038	$-0·000 0350$	10·277 9233	3·103 8034
3	3·103 8034	$-0·000 000 03$	10·277 9662	3·103 8034

When using the Newton-Raphson process it is usually reasonable to assume that if $|x_{n+1} - x_n| < \varepsilon$, then the error in the approximation x_{n+1} is less than ε.

In the given table the values of x_3 and x_4 agree to 7 decimal places. It follows that $|x_4 - x_3| < 1 \times 10^{-7}$ and thus the error in the approximation x_4 is less than 1×10^{-7}.

Closer examination of the results shows that, allowing for rounding errors in the calculations,

$$|x_4 - x_3| = |f(x_3)/f'(x_3)| < 1 \times 10^{-8}$$

$\therefore$
$$3·103 8034 < x_4 < 3·103 803 41$$

Thus the true value of the root is unlikely to exceed 3·103 803 42. Therefore $x = 3·103 8034$ correct to 7 decimal places.

Exercise 23.3

In questions 1 to 8 use the Newton-Raphson method to find a second approximation to a root of the given equation taking the stated value of a as a first approximation. Give your answers to 2 decimal places.

1. $x^3 - 4x^2 + 4 = 0, a = 1.$

2. $x^3 - 3x^2 + 5 = 0, a = -1.$

3. $x^3 - x + 2 = 0, a = -1·5.$

4. $x^3 + x - 16 = 0, a = 2·3.$

5. $\ln x + x - 2 = 0, a = 1·6.$

6. $e^x + x - 3 = 0, a = 0·8.$

7. $2 \sin x = x, a = -2.$

8. $3 \cos x = x, a = 1·2.$

In questions 9 to 14 use two iterations of the Newton-Raphson method to find an approximate value for a root of the given equation, taking the stated value of x_0 as a first approximation. Give your answers to 3 decimal places.

9. $x^3 - 5x - 8 = 0, x_0 = 3.$

10. $x^3 - 9x^2 + 20 = 0, x_0 = 2.$

11. $4x^3 + 6x^2 - 5x - 6 = 0, x_0 = -1.$

12. $x^3 + x + 8 = 0, x_0 = -2.$

13. $e^{-x} = x - 1, x_0 = 1·2.$

14. $\sin x = \ln x, x_0 = 2·3.$

15. Show that the equation $x^3 + 2x - 1 = 0$ has only one real root and that this root lies between 0 and 1. Find the approximate value of this root correct to 3 decimal places.

16. Show that the equation $x^3 - 12x - 6 = 0$ has one positive and two negative roots. Use linear interpolation between suitable successive integers to find a first approximation to the positive root. Hence find the approximate value of this root correct to 4 decimal places.

17. Give, on the same diagram, a sketch of the graph of $y = 3e^{x/2}$ and of the graph of $y = 4x + 6$. State the number of roots of the equation $3e^{x/2} = 4x + 6$. Taking 4 as a first approximation to one root α of this equation, find a second approximation to α, giving three significant figures in your answer and showing clearly how this answer has been obtained. Using a suitable integer as first approximation to another root β of the equation, find a second approximation to β, again giving three significant figures in your answer and showing clearly how this answer has been determined.   (C)

18. Show that the equation $e^x = 2(1 + x)$ has only one positive root. Find the nearest integer to this root. Rewrite the flow chart shown below and complete it to specify a process which will find the root of the above equation, with an error of less than 0·01, starting from the integer nearest to the root. Evaluate the root to this degree of accuracy.

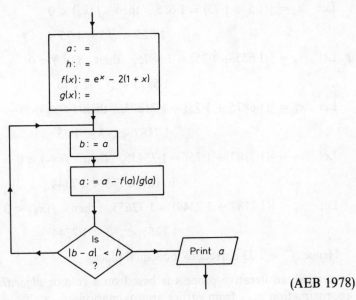

(AEB 1978)

23.4 Other iterative processes

An *iterative process* is a repetitive procedure designed to produce a sequence of approximations to some numerical quantity. The Newton-Raphson method described in the previous section is one example of such a process.

Interval bisection is another iterative process used to obtain approximations to a root α of an equation $f(x) = 0$. To use this method it is necessary to locate an interval containing the root, i.e. to find values x_0 and x_1 such that $x_0 < \alpha < x_1$. The length of this interval is halved by taking $x_2 = \frac{1}{2}(x_0 + x_1)$ and then determining whether α lies between x_0 and x_2 or between x_2 and x_1. The new interval is then bisected to produce a further approximation x_3. The bisection process is repeated until the interval containing α is small enough to ensure a result to the required degree of accuracy. We will see in the following example that this method converges much more slowly than the Newton-Raphson method.

Example 1 Use interval bisection to obtain a sequence of approximations to the positive root of the equation $x^2 - 3 = 0$. Hence evaluate $\sqrt{3}$ correct to 2 decimal places.

Let $f(x) = x^2 - 3$, then the positive root of the equation $f(x) = 0$ is $\sqrt{3}$.
Since $f(1) < 0$ and $f(2) > 0$, we have $1 < \sqrt{3} < 2$.
Taking $x_0 = 1$ and $x_1 = 2$ as first approximations to $\sqrt{3}$,

let $x_2 = \frac{1}{2}(x_0 + x_1) = \frac{1}{2}(1 + 2) = 1 \cdot 5$, then $f(x_2) < 0$

$\therefore$ $$1 \cdot 5 < \sqrt{3} < 2$$

Let $x_3 = \frac{1}{2}(1 \cdot 5 + 2) = 1 \cdot 75$, then $f(x_3) > 0$

$\therefore$ $$1 \cdot 5 < \sqrt{3} < 1 \cdot 75$$

Let $x_4 = \frac{1}{2}(1 \cdot 5 + 1 \cdot 75) = 1 \cdot 625$, then $f(x_4) < 0$

$\therefore$ $$1 \cdot 625 < \sqrt{3} < 1 \cdot 75$$

Let $x_5 = \frac{1}{2}(1 \cdot 625 + 1 \cdot 75) = 1 \cdot 6875$, then $f(x_5) < 0$

$\therefore$ $$1 \cdot 6875 < \sqrt{3} < 1 \cdot 75$$

Let $x_6 = \frac{1}{2}(1 \cdot 6875 + 1 \cdot 75) = 1 \cdot 71875$, then $f(x_6) < 0$

$\therefore$ $$1 \cdot 7187 < \sqrt{3} < 1 \cdot 75$$

Let $x_7 = \frac{1}{2}(1 \cdot 7187 + 1 \cdot 75) = 1 \cdot 73435$, then $f(x_7) < 0$

$\therefore$ $$1 \cdot 7187 < \sqrt{3} < 1 \cdot 7344$$

Let $x_8 = \frac{1}{2}(1 \cdot 7187 + 1 \cdot 7344) = 1 \cdot 72655$, then $f(x_8) < 0$

$\therefore$ $$1 \cdot 7265 < \sqrt{3} < 1 \cdot 7344$$

Hence $\sqrt{3} = 1 \cdot 73$ correct to 2 decimal places.

In general, an iterative process is based on a rule or *algorithm* for obtaining an approximation x_{n+1} from earlier approximations $x_0, x_1, x_2, \ldots, x_n$. In many cases this rule can be expressed as an iterative formula giving x_{n+1} in terms of x_n. In section §23.3 we showed that the Newton-Raphson method can be used to produce such a formula. We now discuss an alternative method.

Let us consider the general iterative formula

$$x_{n+1} = f(x_n)$$

If the sequence $x_0, x_1, x_2, x_3, \ldots$ converges to a finite limit α, then as $n \to \infty$, $x_{n+1} \to \alpha$ and $f(x_n) \to f(\alpha)$

giving
$$\alpha = f(\alpha).$$

Thus, if the iteration $x_{n+1} = f(x_n)$ is convergent, it will produce a sequence of approximations to a root of the equation $x = f(x)$.

When solving an equation we may be able to obtain a suitable iterative formula by writing the equation in the form $x = f(x)$. For any particular equation several different rearrangements will be possible, but not all the corresponding iterative processes will converge to the required root. It is difficult to predict which rearrangements will be most successful. However, it can be shown that, in general, the iteration $x_{n+1} = f(x_n)$ converges to a root α, provided that (i) x_0 is a fairly good approximation to α, and that (ii) $-1 < f'(\alpha) < 1$.

To illustrate the various possibilities we consider the equation $x^2 - 4x - 8 = 0$. This has one root α between -2 and -1 and another root β between 5 and 6. We will attempt to calculate these roots using iterative formulae based on the rearrangements:

(a) $x = \frac{1}{4}x^2 - 2$, (b) $x = \dfrac{8}{x - 4}$, (c) $x = 2\sqrt{(x + 2)}$.

(a) The following table shows the sequences obtained using the formula $x_{n+1} = \frac{1}{4}x_n^2 - 2$, taking x_0 as -2, -1, 5 and 6, then working to 3 decimal places.

x_0	-2	-1	5	6
x_1	-1	-1.75	4.25	7
x_2	-1.75	-1.234	2.516	10.25
x_3	-1.234	-1.619	-0.417	24.266
x_4	-1.619	-1.345	-1.957	145.210
x_5	-1.345	-1.548	-1.043	$\vdots$
x_6	-1.548	-1.401	-1.728	$\vdots$

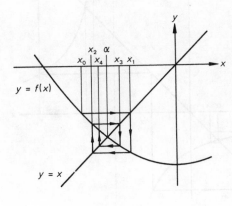

$x_0 = -2, \; f(x) = \frac{1}{4}x^2 - 2$

The sketch graphs show that three of the sequences converge slowly to the root α and that the other sequence diverges. Writing $f(x) = \frac{1}{4}x^2 - 2$, we find that

$$f'(\alpha) \approx f'(-1.5) = -0.75$$
$$\text{and} \qquad f'(\beta) \approx f'(5.5) = 2.75.$$

These results tend to confirm that the rate of convergence depends on the value of $f'(x)$.

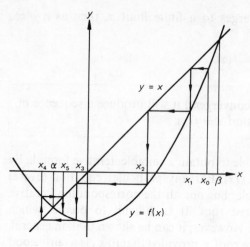

$$x_0 = 5, f(x) = \tfrac{1}{4}x^2 - 2$$

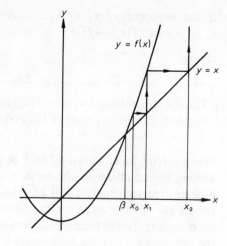

$$x_0 = 6, f(x) = \tfrac{1}{4}x^2 - 2$$

(b) Next we work with the formula $x_{n+1} = \dfrac{8}{x_n - 4}$

x_0	-2	-1	5	6
x_1	$-1{\cdot}333$	$-1{\cdot}6$	8	4
x_2	$-1{\cdot}500$	$-1{\cdot}429$	2	—
x_3	$-1{\cdot}455$	$-1{\cdot}474$	-4	
x_4	$-1{\cdot}467$	$-1{\cdot}461$	-1	
x_5	$-1{\cdot}463$	$-1{\cdot}465$	$-1{\cdot}6$	
x_6	$-1{\cdot}464$	$-1{\cdot}464$	$-1{\cdot}429$	

In this case three of the sequences converge fairly quickly to the root α. In the remaining sequence the value of x_2 is undefined. Writing $g(x) = 8/(x - 4)$, we have $g'(\alpha) \approx -0{\cdot}25$ and $g'(\beta) \approx -4$.

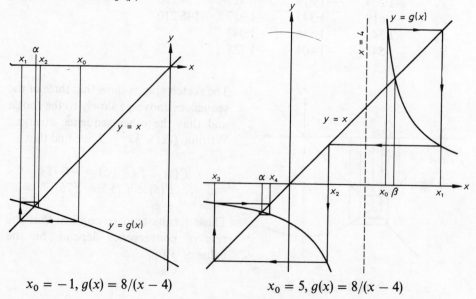

$$x_0 = -1, g(x) = 8/(x - 4) \qquad\qquad x_0 = 5, g(x) = 8/(x - 4)$$

(c) Since the rearrangement $x = 2\sqrt{(x + 2)}$ is not valid for the negative root α of the original equation, we hope to use the formula $x_{n+1} = 2\sqrt{(x_n + 2)}$ to obtain the positive root β.

x_0	5	6
x_1	5·292	5·657
x_2	5·401	5·534
x_3	5·441	5·490
x_4	5·456	5·474
x_5	5·461	5·468
x_6	5·463	5·466

Both sequences converge to the root β, one from below, the other from above. Letting $h(x) = 2\sqrt{(x + 2)}$, we find that $h'(\beta) \approx 0·37$.

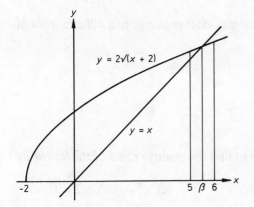

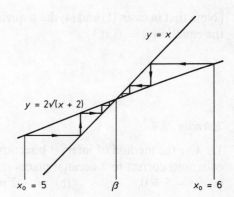

Returning to the general formula $x_{n+1} = f(x_n)$, we conclude that there are four ways in which the sequence of approximations $x_0, x_1, x_2, \ldots$ may behave close to a root α of the equation $x = f(x)$.

(1)

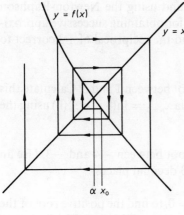

$$f'(\alpha) < -1$$

(2)

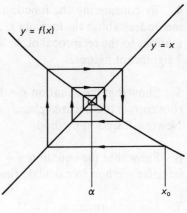

$$-1 < f'(\alpha) < 0$$

(3)

(4)

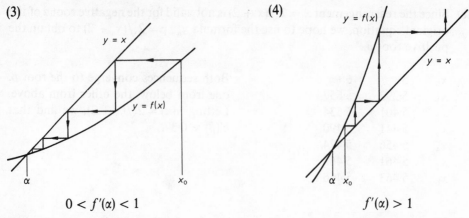

$$0 < f'(\alpha) < 1 \qquad\qquad f'(\alpha) > 1$$

[Note that in cases (1) and (4) the sequence may later converge to a different root of the equation $x = f(x)$.]

Exercise 23.4

1. Use the method of interval bisection to find the positive roots of the following equations correct to 2 decimal places.
(a) $x^2 - 5 = 0$,   (b) $x^3 - 2 = 0$,   (c) $x^3 - 4x^2 + 2 = 0$.

2. The iterative formula $x_{n+1} = \frac{1}{2}(x_n + a/x_n)$ gives successive approximations to the square root of a. Use this formula and the given values of x_0 to calculate correct to 3 decimal places.
(a) $\sqrt{2}, x_0 = 1$,   (b) $\sqrt{10}, x_0 = 3$,   (c) $\sqrt{13}, x_0 = 4$.

3. The iterative formula $x_{r+1} = \frac{1}{2}(x_r + N/x_r^2)$ can be used to find an approximate cube root of a number N. Letting $x_0 = 2$, find $\sqrt[3]{5}$ correct to 3 significant figures.

4. By considering the function $f(x) = N - 1/x$ and using the Newton-Raphson method, establish the formula $x_{r+1} = x_r(2 - Nx_r)$ for obtaining successive approximations to the reciprocal of N. Taking $x_0 = 1$, find the reciprocal of 1.3 correct to 3 significant figures.

5. Show that the equation $x = \ln(8 - x)$ has a root between 1 and 2. Calculate this root correct to 3 decimal places (a) using the formula $x_{n+1} = \ln(8 - x_n)$, (b) using the Newton-Raphson method.

6. Show that the equation $x = \cos x - 3$ has a root between -4 and -3. Use an iterative method to calculate this root correct to 3 decimal places.

7. Use the formula $x_{r+1} = (1 - x_r^2)/5$, where $x_0 = 0$, to find the positive root of the equation $x^2 + 5x - 1 = 0$, correct to 4 decimal places. Discuss with the aid of

sketch graphs the behaviour of the sequence $x_0, x_1, x_2, \dots$ when $x_0 = -6$ and when $x_0 = -5$.

8. Show graphically, or otherwise, that the equation $x^3 - x - 1 = 0$ has only one real root and find the integer n such that the root α satisfies $n < \alpha < n + 1$. An iterative process for finding this root is defined by

$$x_1 = 1, \quad x_{m+1} = (x_m + 1)^{1/3} \quad \text{for all} \quad m \in \mathbb{N}.$$

Obtain, to 3 places of decimals, the values of x_2 and x_3. Show, on a sketch graph, the line $y = x$ and the curve $y = (x + 1)^{1/3}$, indicating on this graph the relation between x_1, x_2, x_3 and the root α. (L)

9. Verify by sketching graphs of $y = x$ and $y = 2(1 + 1/x)$ that, in general, the sequence defined by $x_{n+1} = 2(1 + 1/x_n)$ converges to the root $1 + \sqrt{3}$ of the equation $x^2 - 2x - 2 = 0$. Hence find $\sqrt{3}$ to 4 significant figures, taking a suitable integer as first approximation.

10. Demonstrate graphically that neither

$$x_{n+1} = \tfrac{2}{5}(4 - x_n^3) \quad \text{nor} \quad x_{n+1} = (8 - 5x_n)/2x_n^2$$

can be used to find the real root of the equation $2x^3 + 5x - 8 = 0$. Derive a suitable iteration formula and hence obtain the root to 3 decimal places.

11.

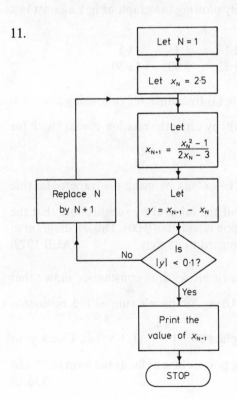

The flow diagram shown represents the steps involved in finding an estimate of a solution of the equation $x^2 - 3x + 1 = 0$, using an iterative method. Follow the steps to their conclusion and obtain the estimate of the root. Indicate clearly everything that is to be printed and work to three decimal places. Indicate the purpose of the decision box.

(L)

12. The equation $f(x) = 0$ is known to have precisely one root in the interval $a \leqslant x \leqslant b$. Construct a flow diagram giving an algorithm to estimate this root, using the method of interval bisection. The following are given: the numbers a and b (with $a < b$), the function f, and the positive number δ which is the maximum permissible magnitude of the error in the root. Demonstrate the working of your flow diagram by applying it to the equation $\cos x - x = 0$ with $a = 0$, $b = 1$ and $\delta = 0.1$, giving your answer correct to one decimal place.   (C)

Exercise 23.5 (miscellaneous)

1.   Values of a continuous function f were found experimentally as given below.

t	0	0·3	0·6	0·9	1·2	1·5	1·8
$f(t)$	2·72	3·00	3·32		4·06	4·48	4·95

Use linear interpolation to estimate $f(0.9)$. Then use Simpson's rule with seven ordinates to estimate $\int_0^{1.8} f(t)\,dt$, tabulating your working and giving your answer to two places of decimals.   (JMB)

2.   The following pairs of values of x and y satisfy approximately a relation of the form $y = ax^n$, where a and n are integers. By plotting the graph of $\lg y$ against $\lg x$ find the values of the integers a and n.

x	0·7	0·9	1·1	1·3	1·5
y	1·37	2·92	5·32	8·80	13·50

Estimate the value of the integral $\int_{0.7}^{1.5} y\,dx$ (a) by Simpson's rule, using five ordinates and clearly indicating your method, (b) by using the relation $y = ax^n$ with the values found for a and n.   (L)

3.   Find an approximate value of $\int_0^{1/2} \sqrt{(1 - x^2)}\,dx$ by using the trapezoidal rule with intervals of 0·1. Show, by working out the integral by substitution, that the magnitude of the error in your approximation is less than 0·001. Draw a diagram to illustrate the reason for this error, having regard to its sign.   (AEB 1979)

4.   If $f(x) = a + bx + cx^2 + kx^3$, where a, b, c, k are constants, show that $\int_{-h}^{h} f(x)\,dx = \frac{1}{3}h\{f(-h) + 4f(0) + f(h)\}$. Using Simpson's rule with 5 ordinates, obtain an approximate value, to 3 decimal places, for $\int_0^{0.4} \sqrt{(1 + x^2)}\,dx$. Check your result by expanding $\sqrt{(1 + x^2)}$ in ascending powers of x as far as the term in x^6 and integrating term by term.   (O&C)

5.   Plot the graph of $y = x^3$ for x from -3 to $+3$. Use the graph to obtain solutions to the following equations (i) $x^3 - 2x - 5 = 0$, (ii) $2x^3 - 4x + 1 = 0$. By writing the equation $5x^3 + 2x^2 - 1 = 0$ in terms of $1/x$, obtain its solution, correct to one decimal place.   (AEB 1979)

6.   Sketch the graph of $y = \tan x$ for values of x between 0 and 2π. Use your sketch graph, together with additional straight line graphs, to solve the following problems:
(i) If $a > 0$ and $b > 0$, find the number of roots, between 0 and 2π, of the equation $\tan x = ax + b$.
(ii) If m can take all real values, find the set of values of m such that the equation $\tan x = mx + \pi$ has exactly three roots lying in the interval $0 < x < 2\pi$.   (C)

7.   Sketch the graph of $y = x^2 e^{-x}$ giving the coordinates of the turning points. Explain, from your graph, why, if $0 < k < 4/e^2$, the equation $ke^x = x^2$ has three real roots.   (O&C)

8.   By considering the graph of $y = x^3 - 3px - q$, where p and q are real constants, show that the condition for the equation $x^3 - 3px - q = 0$ to have three distinct real roots is $4p^3 > q^2$. Find the additional condition necessary for two of the roots to be positive.   (JMB)

9.   The least positive root of the equation $x^3 - 10x^2 + 12x + 16 = 0$ is denoted by α. Use linear interpolation between two suitable successive integers to obtain an estimate for α, giving your answer to one decimal place. Will your answer be an underestimate or overestimate of the exact root? Explain your reasoning.   (O&C)

10. Sketch the graph of $y = \cos x$ for $0 \leqslant x \leqslant 4\pi$. Use your sketch to find the number of positive roots of the equation $\cos x = x/10$. Prove that the equation of the tangent to the curve $y = \cos x$ at $(\frac{1}{2}\pi, 0)$ is $y = \frac{1}{2}\pi - x$. By using $\frac{1}{2}\pi - x$ as an approximation for $\cos x$ (valid for x near $\frac{1}{2}\pi$), calculate an estimate of the smallest positive root of the equation $\cos x = x/10$, giving your answer to 2 decimal places. Show on a new sketch the part of the curve $y = \cos x$ near $x = \frac{1}{2}\pi$ and the tangent at $x = \frac{1}{2}\pi$. Hence determine whether the estimate of the root calculated above is larger or smaller than the correct value.   (C)

11. The given flow diagram is designed to search for a root of the equation $f(x) = 0$ in the range $0 < x < 10$. (i) If x reaches 10 explain why the message printed has to be "No root found" and not "There is no root between 0 and 10". (ii) Work through the flow diagram in the case where $f(x) = e^x - 3x - 4$. (iii) Extend the flow diagram so that, when a root is located between two consecutive integers, a further search is carried out which will narrow the range in which the root lies to 0·1.

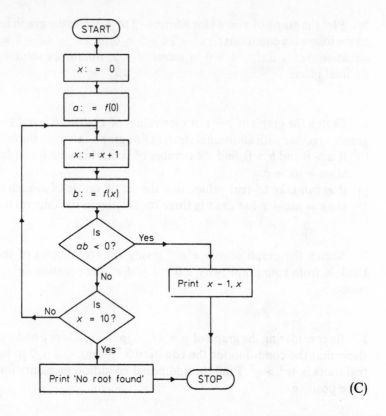

START

$x: = 0$

$a: = f(0)$

$x: = x + 1$

$b: = f(x)$

Is $ab < 0$? —Yes→

No ↓

Print $x - 1, x$

Is $x = 10$? ←No

Yes ↓

Print 'No root found' → STOP

(C)

12. Using the same axes draw accurate graphs of $y = \ln x$ and $y = 3 - x$ in the interval $1 \leqslant x \leqslant 4$. Deduce that the equation $x + \ln x - 3 = 0$ has a root near $x = 2\cdot2$. Clearly showing your method, obtain alternative approximations to the root of the equation (a) by linear interpolation between $x = 2\cdot2$ and $x = 2\cdot3$, (b) by one application of the Newton-Raphson procedure using $x = 2\cdot2$ as the initial value.   (L)

13. Given that $P(x) = x^3 - 6x^2 + 9x + a$ for all real x, find the values of x for which $P'(x) = 0$. Determine the values of the constant a such that the equation $P(x) = 0$ has a repeated root. By sketching graphs of $y = P(x)$ for these values of a, or otherwise, find the set of values of a for which $P(x) = 0$ has only one real root. Given now that $a = -5$, and that 4 is an approximation to the root of the equation $P(x) = 0$, use Newton's method once to obtain another approximation to the root, giving your answer correct to one decimal place.   (JMB)

14. Use linear interpolation to find an approximation x_1 to the root of the equation $f(x) = 0$ lying between 3 and 4, where $f(x) \equiv x^4 - 4x^3 + x + 12$. Use one application of the Newton-Raphson process applied to $f(x)$ starting with $x = 4$ to find another approximation x_2 to the same root. Use one application of the same process starting with $x = 3$ to find another approximation x_3 to the same root. Correct to 2 decimal places the root is $x = 3\cdot69$. Indicate on a diagram how each of the approximations is related to the graph of $f(x)$ for $3 \leqslant x \leqslant 4$.   (C)

15. Explain, with the use of diagrams, the use of Newton's method for obtaining the numerical solutions of an equation. Draw a diagram to show how the method can break down.

Obtain the real factors, with integer coefficients, of $x^4 - 4x^3 + 3x^2 - 4x + 12$. Hence or otherwise obtain the greater real root of the equation

$$x^4 - 4x^3 + 3x^2 - 4x + 11 = 0,$$

correct to 3 decimal places. (AEB 1979)

16. Show that the equation $x^3 + 3x - 3 = 0$ has only one real root and that it lies between $x = 0.8$ and $x = 1$. Obtain approximations to the root (a) by performing one application of the Newton-Raphson procedure using $x = 0.8$ as the first approximation, (b) by performing two iterations, using the procedure defined by $x_{n+1} = (3 - x_n^3)/3$, and starting with $x = 0.8$. (L)

17. Using the same axes and scales, draw graphs of $y = \cos x$ and $y = x$ for the interval $0 \leqslant x \leqslant 1.4$. (A scale of 10 cm to a unit on each axis is recommended.) On your graph mark as A, B, C and D the first four points whose coordinates are printed when the following section of a flow diagram is executed.

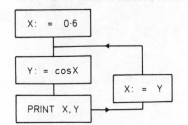

The procedure indicated in the flow diagram is an iterative method of solving a particular equation. Write down this equation and obtain from your graph an approximation solution to it. (JMB)

18. Given that $f(x) = x^3 + x^2 + 2x - 2$, show that the equation $f(x) = 0$ has only one root and that this root lies between 0 and 1. Use the iterative procedure

$$x_{n+1} = \frac{2}{x_n^2 + x_n + 2}, \quad x_1 = 1,$$

to obtain x_2 and x_3. By means of a sketch, illustrate how the successive values of x_n converge to the desired root. (L)

19. A solution of the equation $x = \phi(x)$ is to be attempted by using the iteration $x_{n+1} = \phi(x_n)$, starting with an initial estimate x_1. Draw sketch graphs showing $y = x$ and $y = \phi(x)$ to illustrate the following possibilities regarding convergence towards, or divergence from, the root $x = \alpha$. (i) $x_1 > \alpha$ and successive iterates steadily decrease, with the value α as a limit. (ii) $x_1 > \alpha$ and successive iterates are alternately less than α and greater than α, but approach α as a limit. (iii) $x_1 > \alpha$ and successive iterates get steadily larger. Use an iterative method to find a non-zero root of the equation $x = \tan^{-1}(2x)$ correct to 2 significant figures. (C)

20. 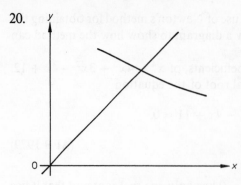 The equation $\sin x = \cos^{-1} x$ has a root in the neighbourhood of $x = \frac{1}{4}\pi$, and the iteration $x_{n+1} = \cos(\sin x_n)$ is to be employed to calculate this root. The diagram shows the appropriate parts of the graphs of $y = x$ and $y = \cos(\sin x)$. Explain with reference to this diagram why successive iterates are alternately greater than and less than the root. Use the given iteration to determine the root correct to 2 decimal places, showing clearly that you have achieved this degree of accuracy. Construct a flow diagram to show how the iteration may be continued until successive iterates differ by less than a given quantity δ. (C)

21. Show that the equation $x^3 - 3x + 1 = 0$ has one negative root and two positive roots. Rearrange the equation in the form $x = F(x)$ in such a way that the iteration $x_{n+1} = F(x_n)$ will converge to the larger positive root, showing clearly that the condition for convergence is satisfied by your function F. Show by means of a sketch how the iterates converge to the root if the initial estimate x_1 is taken to be 1. Use your iteration to calculate the root correct to two decimal places, taking 1·5 as your initial approximation. (C)

24 Differential equations

24.1 Differential equations and their solution curves

An equation connecting a function and one or more of its derivatives is called a *differential equation*. We shall see in §24.4 that many physical laws, such as the laws of natural growth or decay, can be expressed as differential equations.

The *order* of a differential equation is the order of the highest derivative which appears in it. For instance, the equations $\dfrac{dx}{dt} = -4x$ and $\left(\dfrac{dy}{dx}\right)^2 = x + y$ are first order equations and the equation $\dfrac{d^2y}{dx^2} - 3\dfrac{dy}{dx} = e^{2x}$ is a second order equation.

Let us consider a simple differential equation of the first order:

$$\frac{dy}{dx} = x - 1.$$

Any equation connecting x and y which satisfies this differential equation is a solution. Thus $y = \frac{1}{2}x^2 - x$, $y = \frac{1}{2}x^2 - x + 5$ and $y = \frac{1}{2}x^2 - x - 28$ are all solutions. The *general solution* of the differential equation is $y = \frac{1}{2}x^2 - x + c$, where c is an arbitrary constant. Since c can take any real value, this general solution can be represented graphically by an infinite set of curves called the *solution curves* or *integral curves* of the equation. Each member of this "family" of curves represents a particular solution, or *particular integral*, of the differential equation.

Given the equation of a family of curves, we can obtain the corresponding differential equation by differentiating and then eliminating any arbitrary constants.

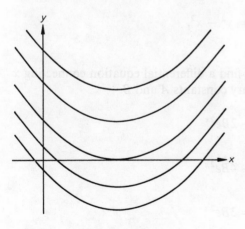

The solution curves of $\dfrac{dy}{dx} = x - 1$.

491

Example 1   Find the differential equation representing the family of curves, $y = Ax^3$, where A is an arbitrary constant.

If $y = Ax^3$, then $\dfrac{dy}{dx} = 3Ax^2$

$\therefore \quad x\dfrac{dy}{dx} = 3Ax^3 = 3y$

Hence the required differential equation is $x\dfrac{dy}{dx} = 3y$.

Example 2   Sketch some of the curves given by the equation $x^2 + y^2 - 2kx = 0$. Obtain the differential equation which represents this family of curves.

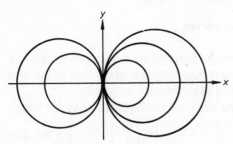

The equation $x^2 + y^2 - 2kx = 0$ may be written in the form

$$(x - k)^2 + y^2 = k^2.$$

Hence each curve in the family is a circle, centre $(k, 0)$ and radius $|k|$.

Differentiating the equation $\qquad x^2 + y^2 - 2kx = 0$

we obtain $\qquad\qquad\qquad 2x + 2y\dfrac{dy}{dx} - 2k = 0$

$\therefore \quad 2x^2 + 2xy\dfrac{dy}{dx} = x^2 + y^2 \quad (= 2kx)$

Hence this family of circles is represented by the differential equation

$$2xy\dfrac{dy}{dx} = y^2 - x^2.$$

Example 3   Given that $y = Ae^x + Be^{2x}$, find a differential equation connecting x and y which is independent of the arbitrary constants A and B.

If $y = Ae^x + Be^{2x}$, then $\quad \dfrac{dy}{dx} = Ae^x + 2Be^{2x}$

and $\quad \dfrac{d^2y}{dx^2} = Ae^x + 4Be^{2x}$

$\therefore \quad \dfrac{dy}{dx} - y = Be^{2x} \quad$ and $\quad \dfrac{d^2y}{dx^2} - y = 3Be^{2x}$

$\therefore \quad \dfrac{d^2y}{dx^2} - y = 3\left(\dfrac{dy}{dx} - y\right)$

Hence the required differential equation is

$$\frac{d^2y}{dx^2} - 3\frac{dy}{dx} + 2y = 0.$$

In Examples 1 and 2 equations involving one arbitrary constant gave rise to differential equations of the first order. However, in Example 3 it was necessary to introduce two derivatives to eliminate the two arbitrary constants. This suggests that in general an equation containing n arbitrary constants should lead to an nth order differential equation. Conversely, it seems reasonable to assume that the general solution of a differential equation of order n should contain n arbitrary constants.

We now consider ways of sketching the solution curves of a differential equation when the general solution of the equation is not available. We take as an example the differential equation

$$\frac{dy}{dx} = x - y.$$

A general impression of the solution curves can be gained by calculating values of dy/dx at various points of the x, y plane, then plotting the directions on a sketch graph.

	3	-6	-5	-4	-3	-2	-1	0
	2	-5	-4	-3	-2	-1	0	1
	1	-4	-3	-2	-1	0	1	2
y	0	-3	-2	-1	0	1	2	3
	-1	-2	-1	0	1	2	3	4
	-2	-1	0	1	2	3	4	5
	-3	0	1	2	3	4	5	6
		-3	-2	-1	0	1	2	3
					x			

Table showing values of $\dfrac{dy}{dx}$

Sketch graph showing directions of the solution curves

We see that $\dfrac{dy}{dx} = 0$ on the line $y = x$. Above this line $\dfrac{dy}{dx} < 0$ and below the line

$\dfrac{dy}{dx} > 0$. Hence the points on the line $y = x$ are minimum points on the solution curves.

The diagram also suggests that the line $y = x - 1$ could be one of the solution curves. Substituting $y = x - 1$ in the differential equation confirms that this is so.

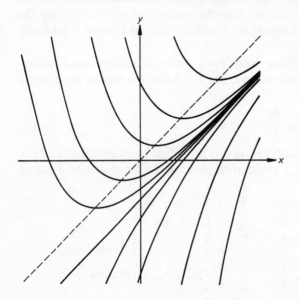

It is now possible to make a rough sketch of the solution curves.

Exercise 24.1

1.   Verify that the following are solutions of the differential equation

$$x\frac{dy}{dx} = x^2 + y,$$

(a) $y = x^2$,   (b) $y = x^2 - x$,   (c) $y = x^2 + 5x$.

2.   Verify that the following are solutions of the differential equation $\dfrac{d^2y}{dx^2} = 1 - y$,

(a) $y = 1 + 2\cos x$,   (b) $y = 1$,   (c) $y = 1 - 3\sin x$.

3.   Decide which of the following are solutions of the differential equation

$$\frac{d^2y}{dx^2} + \frac{dy}{dx} = 6y.$$

(a) $y = 3e^{2x}$,   (b) $y = 6e^x$,   (c) $y = 2e^{3x}$,   (d) $y = e^{2x} - e^{-3x}$.

4.   Given that $y = ax + b$ is a solution of the differential equation $\dfrac{dy}{dx} = 4x - 2y$, find a and b.

5. Given that $y = ax^2 + bx + c$ is a solution of the differential equation

$$\frac{d^2y}{dx^2} = y - x^2,$$

find a, b and c.

In questions 6 to 11 sketch some of the curves represented by the given equation and obtain a differential equation for y which does not contain the arbitrary constant A.

6. $y = x^3 + A$ 7. $y = x^2 - Ax$ 8. $y = A/x$

9. $y = Ae^{-x}$ 10. $x^2 + y^2 = A^2$ 11. $y^2 = 4Ax$

In questions 12 to 19 form differential equations by eliminating the arbitrary constant A, B and C.

12. $y = x + \dfrac{A}{x}$ 13. $y = x^2 \ln x + Ax^2$

14. $y^2 = A \cos x$ 15. $y = x^A$

16. $y = A \cos x + B \sin x$ 17. $y = Ae^{-x} + Be^{3x}$

18. $y^2 = Ax^2 + Bx + C$ 19. $y = (Ax + B)e^x + C$

In questions 20 to 25 sketch the solution curves of the given differential equation.

20. $\dfrac{dy}{dx} = \dfrac{x}{y}$ 21. $\dfrac{dy}{dx} = \dfrac{y}{x}$ 22. $\dfrac{dy}{dx} = -\dfrac{x}{2y}$

23. $\dfrac{dy}{dx} = x + y$ 24. $x\dfrac{dy}{dx} = x - y$ 25. $2y\dfrac{dy}{dx} = x + y$

24.2 Elementary methods of solution

Differential equations of the form $\dfrac{dy}{dx} = f(x)$ may be solved by direct integration.

Example 1 Solve the differential equation $\dfrac{dy}{dx} = 6x^2 - 5$.

By integration the general solution is $y = 2x^3 - 5x + c$, where c is an arbitrary constant.

Example 2   Solve the differential equation $\cos^2 x \dfrac{dy}{dx} = \sin x$.

Rearranging, we have: $\dfrac{dy}{dx} = \dfrac{\sin x}{\cos^2 x} = \sec x \tan x$

Integrating, we obtain the general solution $y = \sec x + c$, where c is an arbitrary constant.

Sometimes we require a solution which satisfies certain given conditions. We then use these conditions to determine the values of any arbitrary constants in the general solution.

Example 3   Solve the differential equation $e^x \dfrac{dy}{dx} + x = 0$, given that $y = 2$ when $x = 0$.

Rearranging we obtain: $\dfrac{dy}{dx} = -xe^{-x}$

Integrating by parts using the formula

$$\int u \frac{dv}{dx} dx = uv - \int v \frac{du}{dx} dx,$$

where $u = x$ and $\dfrac{dv}{dx} = -e^{-x}$

$\dfrac{du}{dx} = 1$ $v = e^{-x}$

$$\int (-xe^{-x}) dx = xe^{-x} - \int e^{-x} dx$$

$$= xe^{-x} + e^{-x} + c$$

∴   the general solution of the differential equation is

$$y = xe^{-x} + e^{-x} + c.$$

Since $y = 2$ when $x = 0$, $2 = 0 \times 1 + 1 + c$ ∴ $c = 1$
Hence the required solution is $y = xe^{-x} + e^{-x} + 1$.

When the integration of a differential equation leads to a general solution involving logarithmic functions, any restrictions on the values of x and y should be clearly stated.

Example 4   Solve the differential equation $\dfrac{dy}{dx} = \dfrac{x}{x-1}$, given that $y = 2$ when $x = 2$.

Rearranging: $\dfrac{dy}{dx} = \dfrac{x}{x-1} = 1 + \dfrac{1}{x-1}$

[Since we require a solution valid for $x = 2$, we will assume that x is greater than 1 when integrating.]

For $x > 1$, the general solution of this differential equation is

$$y = x + \ln(x - 1) + c$$

Since $y = 2$ when $x = 2$, $2 = 2 + \ln 1 + c$ $\therefore$ $c = 0$

Hence the required solution is $y = x + \ln(x - 1)$.

Second order differential equations of the form $\dfrac{d^2y}{dx^2} = f(x)$ can also be solved by direct integration.

Example 5   Solve the differential equation $\dfrac{d^2y}{dx^2} = 6x^3 + \dfrac{1}{x^3}$

Integrating we have: $\dfrac{dy}{dx} = \dfrac{3}{2}x^4 - \dfrac{1}{2x^2} + A$

Integrating again we obtain the general solution

$$y = \frac{3}{10}x^5 + \frac{1}{2x} + Ax + B,$$

where A and B are arbitrary constants.

Example 6   Solve the differential equation $\dfrac{d^2x}{dt^2} = -\sin t + \cos t$, subject to the conditions that $x = 0$, $\dfrac{dx}{dt} = 4$ when $t = 0$.

Integrating: $\dfrac{dx}{dt} = \cos t + \sin t + A$

$$x = \sin t - \cos t + At + B$$

Since $\dfrac{dx}{dt} = 4$ when $t = 0$, $4 = 1 + 0 + A$ $\therefore$ $A = 3$

Since $x = 0$ when $t = 0$, $0 = 0 - 1 + 0 + B$ $\therefore$ $B = 1$

Hence the required solution is $x = \sin t - \cos t + 3t + 1$.

To solve differential equations of the form $\dfrac{dy}{dx} = f(y)$, we use the fact that

$$\frac{dy}{dx} = 1 \bigg/ \frac{dx}{dy}.$$

Example 7   Solve the differential equation $\dfrac{dy}{dx} = y^2$.

The equation may be written as: $\dfrac{dx}{dy} = \dfrac{1}{y^2}$

Integrating with respect to y: $x = -\dfrac{1}{y} + c$

$\therefore \qquad \dfrac{1}{y} = c - x$

Hence the general solution is $y = \dfrac{1}{c - x}$.

A substitution is sometimes used to reduce a differential equation to a simpler form.

Example 8   Use the substitution $y = vx$, where v is a function of x, to solve the differential equation $x\dfrac{dy}{dx} = x + y$, given that $y = -1$ when $x = 1$.

If $y = vx$, then using the product rule, $\dfrac{dy}{dx} = v + x\dfrac{dv}{dx}$

Substituting in the given differential equation we have,

$$x\left(v + x\dfrac{dv}{dx}\right) = x + vx$$

i.e. $vx + x^2\dfrac{dv}{dx} = x + vx$

$\therefore \qquad \dfrac{dv}{dx} = \dfrac{1}{x}$

For $x > 0$, the general solution of this differential equation is

$v = \ln x + c$
$\therefore \quad y = vx = x(\ln x + c)$

Since $y = -1$ when $x = 1$, $-1 = 1(0 + c)$ $\therefore \quad c = -1$
Hence the required solution is $y = x(\ln x - 1)$.

In Example 8 we again dealt with an integration involving logarithms by considering a restricted set of values of x. However, in some problems it is better to avoid placing restrictions on the values of x and y by using modulus signs, as described in §19.4.
    For instance, in the case of the differential equation

$$\dfrac{dy}{dx} = \dfrac{1}{x - 5}$$

the general solution may be given as

$$y = \ln|x - 5| + c \tag{1}$$

Suppose now that we require the particular solution which satisfies the condition $y = -2$ when $x = 6$.

Substituting these values in the general solution (1),

$$-2 = \ln 1 + c \qquad \therefore \quad c = -2$$

Hence
$$y = \ln|x - 5| - 2.$$

But, using the method of Examples 4 and 8,

for $x > 5$, $$y = \ln(x - 5) + c \qquad (2)$$

As before, since $y = -2$ when $x = 6$, we have $c = -2$

Hence
$$y = \ln(x - 5) - 2.$$

Thus, although equation (1) provides a neat general solution, equation (2) leads to a simpler particular integral.

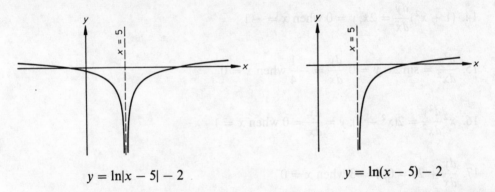

$$y = \ln|x - 5| - 2 \qquad\qquad\qquad y = \ln(x - 5) - 2$$

The sketch graphs show that solution (1) represents a family of curves with two branches, whereas solution (2) produces single curves lying to the right of the line $x = 5$. A question requiring a particular integral is probably best answered by a solution of type (2).

Exercise 24.2

Solve the following differential equations giving y in terms of x.

1. $\dfrac{dy}{dx} = 3x^2 + 1$

2. $\dfrac{dy}{dx} = \cos\frac{1}{2}x$

3. $x\dfrac{dy}{dx} = x^2 + 1$

4. $(x - 1)\dfrac{dy}{dx} = x + 1$

5. $\dfrac{d^2y}{dx^2} + \cos x = 2x$

6. $e^x\dfrac{d^2y}{dx^2} = 1 - e^{2x}$

7. $\dfrac{dy}{dx} + 2y^2 = 0$

8. $\dfrac{dy}{dx} = \cos^2 y$

9. $\dfrac{dy}{dx} = e^{-y}$

10. $3\dfrac{dy}{dx} = y^4$

Solve the following differential equations, subject to the given conditions.

11. $\dfrac{dy}{dx} = (x + 1)^2$; $y = 0$ when $x = 2$

12. $\dfrac{dy}{dx} = \dfrac{1}{\sqrt{(2x + 3)}}$; $y = 4$ when $x = 3$

13. $\sec x \dfrac{dy}{dx} = x$; $y = 0$ when $x = \pi$

14. $(1 + x^2)\dfrac{dy}{dx} = 2x$; $y = 0$ when $x = -1$

15. $\dfrac{d^2y}{dx^2} = \sin 2x$; $y = 0$, $\dfrac{dy}{dx} = -\dfrac{1}{4}$ when $x = 0$

16. $x^2\dfrac{d^2y}{dx^2} = 2(x^2 - 1)$; $y = \dfrac{dy}{dx} = 0$ when $x = 1$

17. $\dfrac{dy}{dx} + 2y = 0$; $y = 3$ when $x = 0$

18. $\dfrac{dy}{dx} = y - 1$; $y = 0$ when $x = 0$

19. $\dfrac{dy}{dx} = 1 + y^2$; $y = 1$ when $x = 0$

20. $2\dfrac{dy}{dx} = y^2 - 1$; $y = 2$ when $x = 0$

21. Use the substitution $y = 1/z$ to solve the differential equation $x^2\dfrac{dy}{dx} = y^2$.

22. Use the substitution $y = vx$, where v is a function of x, to solve the differential equation $x\dfrac{dy}{dx} - y = x^2 \cos x$.

23. Use the substitution $y = vx^2$, where v is a function of x, to solve the differential equation $x\dfrac{dy}{dx} - 2y = x$.

24. Use the substitution $dy/dx = p$, where p is a function of x, to solve the differential equation $\dfrac{d^2y}{dx^2} + \dfrac{dy}{dx} = 1$, given that $y = \dfrac{dy}{dx} = 2$ when $x = 1$.

25. If $z = xe^y$, where y is a function of x, find an expression for dz/dx. Hence find y in terms of x given that $xe^y\dfrac{dy}{dx} + e^y = 2x$ and that $y = 0$ when $x = 2$.

24.3 Equations with separable variables

If a first order differential equation can be expressed in the form

$$f(y)\frac{dy}{dx} = g(x)$$

then the variables x and y are said to be *separable*.
Integrating both sides of the equation with respect to x:

$$\int f(y)\frac{dy}{dx}\,dx = \int g(x)\,dx$$

As shown in §20.3, $\dfrac{dy}{dx}\,dx$ may be replaced by dy.

Thus

$$\int f(y)\,dy = \int g(x)\,dx$$

Example 1   Find the general solution of the equation $2y\dfrac{dy}{dx} = \cos x$.

Integrating both sides of the equation: $\displaystyle\int 2y\,dy = \int \cos x\,dx$

Hence the general solution of the equation is

$$y^2 = \sin x + c.$$

Example 2   Find the general solution of the equation

$$\frac{dy}{dx} = 2xy^2 - y^2.$$

Rearranging: $\dfrac{dy}{dx} = (2x - 1)y^2$

$$\frac{1}{y^2}\frac{dy}{dx} = 2x - 1$$

$\therefore$ $\displaystyle\int \frac{1}{y^2}\,dy = \int (2x - 1)\,dx$ $\therefore$ $-\dfrac{1}{y} = x^2 - x + c$

Hence the general solution of the equation is

$$y = -1/(x^2 - x + c).$$

Example 3   Find y in terms of x given that $2\dfrac{dy}{dx} = e^{x-2y}$ and that $y = 1$ when $x = 2$.

Rearranging:
$$2\frac{dy}{dx} = e^x \times e^{-2y}$$

$$2e^{2y}\frac{dy}{dx} = e^x$$

$\therefore$
$$\int 2e^{2y}\,dy = \int e^x\,dx$$

$\therefore$
$$e^{2y} = e^x + c$$

Since $y = 1$ when $x = 2$, $e^2 = e^2 + c$ $\therefore$ $c = 0$

Thus $e^{2y} = e^x$

$\therefore$ $2y = x$

Hence $y = \tfrac{1}{2}x$.

Example 4   Express y in terms of x given that $\dfrac{dy}{dx} = xy - x$ and that $y = 4$ when $x = 0$.

Rearranging:
$$\frac{dy}{dx} = x(y - 1)$$

$$\frac{1}{(y-1)}\frac{dy}{dx} = x$$

$\therefore$
$$\int \frac{1}{y-1}\,dy = \int x\,dx$$

$\therefore$ $\ln|y - 1| = \tfrac{1}{2}x^2 + c$
$\therefore$ $|y - 1| = e^{x^2/2 + c}$

Thus $y - 1 = Ae^{x^2/2}$,   where $|A| = e^c$

Since $y = 4$ when $x = 0$, $3 = Ae^0 = A$

Hence $y - 1 = 3e^{x^2/2}$

i.e. $y = 1 + 3e^{x^2/2}$.

Example 5   Find the general solution of the equation

$$(x^2 - 1)\frac{dy}{dx} = xy.$$

Rearranging: $\dfrac{1}{y}\dfrac{dy}{dx} = \dfrac{x}{x^2 - 1}$

$\therefore$
$$\int \frac{1}{y}\,dy = \int \frac{x}{x^2 - 1}\,dx$$

$$\therefore \qquad \ln|y| = \tfrac{1}{2}\ln|x^2 - 1| + c$$
$$\therefore \quad 2\ln|y| - \ln|x^2 - 1| = 2c$$

Using the laws of logarithms:

$$\ln\left|\frac{y^2}{x^2 - 1}\right| = 2c$$

$$\therefore \qquad \frac{y^2}{x^2 - 1} = A, \quad \text{where} \quad \ln|A| = 2c$$

Hence the general solution of the equation is $y^2 = A(x^2 - 1)$.

Example 6 Find the general solution of the equation

$$2x\frac{dy}{dx} - (2y + 1)(x + 1) = 0$$

Rearranging: $\qquad 2x\dfrac{dy}{dx} = (2y + 1)(x + 1)$

$$\frac{2}{(2y + 1)}\frac{dy}{dx} = 1 + \frac{1}{x}$$

$$\therefore \qquad \int \frac{2}{2y + 1}\,dy = \int\left(1 + \frac{1}{x}\right)dx$$

$$\therefore \qquad \ln|2y + 1| = x + \ln|x| + c$$
$$\therefore \quad \ln|2y + 1| - \ln|x| = x + c$$

i.e. $\qquad \ln\left|\dfrac{2y + 1}{x}\right| = x + c$

$$\therefore \qquad \left|\frac{2y + 1}{x}\right| = e^{x+c}$$

Thus $\qquad \dfrac{2y + 1}{x} = Ae^x, \quad \text{where} \quad |A| = e^c$

$$\therefore \qquad 2y + 1 = Axe^x$$

Hence the required general solution is $y = \tfrac{1}{2}(Axe^x - 1)$.

Example 7 Find y in terms of x given that $x(x - 1)\dfrac{dy}{dx} = y$ and that $y = 1$ when $x = 2$.

Rearranging: $\qquad \dfrac{1}{y}\dfrac{dy}{dx} = \dfrac{1}{x(x - 1)}$

$$\therefore \qquad \int \frac{1}{y} dy = \int \frac{1}{x(x-1)} dx$$

$$\therefore \qquad \int \frac{1}{y} dy = \int \left\{ \frac{1}{x-1} - \frac{1}{x} \right\} dx$$

$$\therefore \qquad \ln|y| = \ln|x-1| - \ln|x| + c$$

i.e. $\ln|y| - \ln|x-1| + \ln|x| = c$

Thus $\qquad \ln \left| \frac{xy}{x-1} \right| = c$

$$\therefore \qquad \frac{xy}{x-1} = A, \quad \text{where} \quad \ln|A| = c$$

Since $y = 1$ when $x = 2$, $2 = A$

Hence $\quad \dfrac{xy}{x-1} = 2$

i.e. $\qquad y = 2\left(1 - \dfrac{1}{x}\right).$

Exercise 24.3

In questions 1 to 10 find the general solutions of the given differential equations, expressing y in terms of x in each case.

1. $3y^2 \dfrac{dy}{dx} = 2x - 1$

2. $\dfrac{dy}{dx} = 6xy^2$

3. $\dfrac{dy}{dx} = e^y \sin x$

4. $\dfrac{dy}{dx} = e^{x-y}$

5. $\dfrac{dy}{dx} = x \sec y$

6. $\dfrac{dy}{dx} = 3 \cos^2 y$

7. $x \dfrac{dy}{dx} = y$

8. $(1 - x)\dfrac{dy}{dx} = y$

9. $\dfrac{dy}{dx} = \dfrac{4xy}{x^2 + 1}$

10. $\dfrac{dy}{dx} = \dfrac{2y}{x^2 - 1}$

In questions 11 to 20 find expressions for y in terms of x.

11. $x^2 \dfrac{dy}{dx} - y^2 = 0$; $y = -1$ when $x = 1$.

12. $\dfrac{dy}{dx} + 2xy = 0$; $y = 5$ when $x = 0$.

13. $\cot x \dfrac{dy}{dx} = y$; $y = 2$ when $x = 0$.

14. $\dfrac{dy}{dx} = xe^{-2y}$; $y = 0$ when $x = 0$.

15. $\dfrac{dy}{dx} - 2xy = 2x$; $y = 1$ when $x = 0$.

16. $x\dfrac{dy}{dx} = xy + y$; $y = 1$ when $x = 1$.

17. $(1 + x^3)\dfrac{dy}{dx} = 3x^2 \tan y$; $y = \frac{1}{2}\pi$ when $x = 0$.

18. $x \cos y \dfrac{dy}{dx} = 1 + \sin y$; $y = 0$ when $x = 1$.

19. $x\dfrac{dy}{dx} = 2y(y - 1)$; $y = 2$ when $x = \frac{1}{2}$.

20. $2x\dfrac{dy}{dx} = 1 - y^2$; $y = 0$ when $x = 1$.

In questions 21 to 24 find the general solutions of the given differential equations, expressing y in terms of x.

21. $(1 - x)\dfrac{dy}{dx} = xy$

22. $(x^2 - 1)\dfrac{dy}{dx} = (x^2 + 1)y$

23. $\dfrac{dy}{dx} = e^x(1 + y^2)$

24. $e^y\dfrac{dy}{dx} + 2x = 2xe^y$

25. Find y in terms of x given that $e^{2x}y\dfrac{dy}{dx} + 2x = 0$ and that $y = 1$ when $x = 0$.

26. Find y in terms of x given that $xy\dfrac{dy}{dx} = \sqrt{(y^2 - 9)}$ and that $y = 5$ when $x = e^4$.

27. Use the substitution $x + y = z$ to obtain the general solution of the differential equation $(x + y - 1)\dfrac{dy}{dx} = x - y + 1$.

28. Use the substitution $y = vx$, where v is a function of x, to obtain the general solution of the differential equation $xy\dfrac{dy}{dx} = 2x^2 - y^2$.

24.4 Formulation of differential equations

In our first example information about the tangent to a curve is expressed in the form of a differential equation. This equation is then solved to find the equation of the curve.

Example 1   The tangent at any point P on a curve in the first quadrant cuts the x-axis at Q. Given that $OP = PQ$, where O is the origin, and that the point $(1, 4)$ lies on the curve, find the equation of the curve.

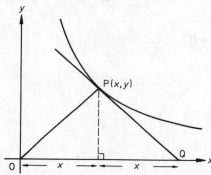

Since $OP = PQ$ the triangle OPQ is isosceles. Thus if P is the point (x, y), the coordinate of Q must be $(2x, 0)$.

∴   the gradient of PQ

$$= \frac{y - 0}{x - 2x} = -\frac{y}{x}$$

However, since PQ is the tangent at P its gradient is also given by dy/dx.

∴ $\dfrac{dy}{dx} = -\dfrac{y}{x}$

i.e. $\dfrac{1}{y}\dfrac{dy}{dx} = -\dfrac{1}{x}$

∴ $\displaystyle\int \frac{1}{y}\,dy = -\int \frac{1}{x}\,dx$

Since the curve lies in the first quadrant, $x > 0$ and $y > 0$

∴ $\ln y = -\ln x + c$

i.e. $\ln y + \ln x = c$

∴ $\ln xy = c$

∴ $xy = k,$ where $\ln k = c$

Since the curve passes through the point $(1, 4)$, $1 \times 4 = k$
Hence the equation of the curve is $xy = 4$.

Many scientific laws can be expressed as differential equations. For instance, as we saw in §19.1, Newton's law of cooling and certain laws of growth and decay lead to differential equations of the form $dx/dt = \pm kx$, where k is a positive constant. The solutions of such equations are used to make predictions about the behaviour of the variables involved.

Example 2 A liquid is being heated in an oven maintained at a constant temperature of 180°C. It is assumed that the rate of increase in the temperature of the liquid is proportional to $(180 - \theta)$, where θ°C is the temperature of the liquid at time t minutes. If the temperature of the liquid rises from 0°C to 120°C in 5 minutes, find the temperature of the liquid after a further 5 minutes.

The rate of increase in the temperature of the liquid is $d\theta/dt$,

$$\therefore \quad \frac{d\theta}{dt} = k(180 - \theta), \text{ where } k \text{ is constant.}$$

Rearranging, $\quad \dfrac{1}{(180 - \theta)} \dfrac{d\theta}{dt} = k$

$$\therefore \quad \int \frac{1}{180 - \theta} d\theta = \int k \, dt$$

$$\therefore \quad \int \frac{-1}{180 - \theta} d\theta = -\int k \, dt$$

Thus for $\theta < 180$, $\quad \ln(180 - \theta) = -kt + c$

$$180 - \theta = e^{-kt+c}$$

Writing $A = e^c$, $\qquad 180 - \theta = Ae^{-kt}$

Hence $\qquad\qquad\qquad \theta = 180 - Ae^{-kt}$

Letting $t = 0$ when $\theta = 0$, $0 = 180 - A$

$$\therefore \qquad\qquad \theta = 180(1 - e^{-kt})$$

Since $\theta = 120$ when $t = 5$, $120 = 180(1 - e^{-5k})$

$$\therefore \qquad\qquad \tfrac{2}{3} = 1 - e^{-5k}$$

i.e. $\qquad\qquad\qquad e^{-5k} = \tfrac{1}{3}$

Hence when $t = 10$, $\theta = 180(1 - e^{-10k})$

$$= 180(1 - \{e^{-5k}\}^2)$$

$$= 180(1 - \{\tfrac{1}{3}\}^2) = 160$$

Thus the temperature of the liquid after a further 5 minutes is 160°C.

Exercise 24.4

1. The tangent at any point P on a curve cuts the x-axis at the point Q. Given that $\angle OPQ = 90°$, where O is the origin, and that the point $(1, 2)$ lies on the curve, find the equation of the curve.

2. The tangent at any point P on a curve cuts the x-axis at A and the y-axis at B. Given that $2\overrightarrow{AP} = \overrightarrow{PB}$ and that the curve passes through the point $(1, 1)$, find the equation of the curve.

3.   At time t, the rate of increase in the concentration C of micro-organisms in a controlled environment is equal to k times the concentration, where k is a positive constant. When $t = 0$, $C = C_0$. Write down a differential equation involving C, t and k. Hence find C in terms of C_0, t and k. Find also, in terms of k, the time at which the concentration has increased by 50% from its value at $t = 0$.   (L)

4.   A body is placed in a room which is kept at a constant temperature. The temperature of the body falls at a rate $k\theta$ C per minute, where k is a constant and θ is the difference between the temperature of the body and that of the room at time t. Express this information in the form of a differential equation and hence show that $\theta = \theta_0 e^{-kt}$, where θ_0 is the temperature difference at time $t = 0$. The temperature of the body falls $5°C$ in the first minute and $4°C$ in the second minute. Show that the fall of temperature in the third minute is $3 \cdot 2°C$.   (L)

5.   A rectangular tank with its base horizontal is filled with water to a depth h at time $t = 0$. Water leaks out of the tank from a small hole in the base at a rate proportional to the square root of the depth of the water. If the depth of water is $\frac{1}{2}h$ at time t, find the further time it will take before the tank is empty.   (O)

6.   A radioactive substance decays so that the rate of decrease of mass at any time is proportional to the mass present at that time. Denoting by x the mass remaining at time t, write down a differential equation satisfied by x, and show that $x = x_0 e^{-kt}$, where x_0 is the initial mass and k is a constant. The mass is reduced to 4/5 of its initial value in 30 days. Calculate, correct to the nearest day, the time required for the mass to be reduced to half its initial value. A mass of 625 milligrammes of the substance is prepared. Determine the mass which is present 90 days after the preparation.
                     (JMB)

7.   According to Newton's law, the rate of cooling of a body in air is proportional to the difference between the temperature T of the body and the temperature T_0 of the air. If the air temperature is kept constant at $20°C$ and the body cools from $100°C$ to $60°C$ in 20 minutes, in what further time will the body cool to $30°C$?   (O)

8.   Two liquids, X and Y, are flowing into a trough at the constant rate of 10 and 20 litres per minute respectively. The liquid in the trough is stirred continuously and pumped out at the rate of 30 litres per minute. Initially the trough contains 200 litres of X and 100 litres of Y. After t minutes the tank contains x litres of X. By considering the change in x in a small interval of time δt, show that

$$\frac{dx}{dt} = 10 - \frac{x}{10}.$$

Hence find an expression for x in terms of t. Find, correct to the nearest litre, the quantity of liquid X in the trough after 10 minutes. After how long, to the nearest second, will there be less of liquid X in the mixture than of liquid Y?

9.   A tank being cleaned initially contains 3900 litres of water and 100 kg of dissolved dye. The mixture is kept uniform by stirring. Pure water is run in at the rate

of 130 litres per minute and the mixture is removed at the same rate. If the mass of dissolved dye remaining after t minutes is x kg, show that

$$\frac{dx}{dt} = -\frac{x}{30}.$$

How long will it be before half the dye has been removed? Determine how much dye remains after 30 minutes.
                                                                                    (L)

10. In a certain chemical reaction, in which a compound X is formed from a compound Y, the masses of X, Y present at time t are x, y respectively. The sum of the masses of X and Y is a, where a is constant, and at any time the rate at which x is increasing is proportional to the product of the two masses at that time. Show that

$\dfrac{dx}{dt} = kx(a - x)$, where k is constant. If $x = a/5$ at $t = 0$ and $x = a/2$ at $t = \ln 2$, show

that $k = 2/a$. Hence find t, correct to three significant figures, when $x = 99a/100$.
                                                                            (O & C)

11. A plant grows in a pot which contains a volume V of soil. At time t the mass of the plant is m and the volume of soil utilised by the roots is αm, where α is constant. The rate of increase of the mass of the plant is proportional to the mass of the plant times the volume of soil not yet utilised by the roots. Obtain a differential equation for m,

and verify that it can be written in the form $V\beta \dfrac{dt}{dm} = \dfrac{1}{m} + \dfrac{\alpha}{V - \alpha m}$, where β is a

constant. The mass of the plant is initially $V/4\alpha$. Find, in terms of V and β, the time taken for the plant to double its mass. Find also the mass of the plant at time t.
                                                                                (JMB)

12. At any instant, a spherical meteorite is gaining mass because of two effects: (i) mass is condensing onto it at a rate which is proportional to the surface area of the meteorite at that instant, (ii) the gravitational field of the meteorite attracts mass onto itself, the rate being proportional to the meteorite mass at that instant. Assuming that the two effects can be added together and that the meteorite remains spherical and of constant density, show that its radius r at time t satisfies the

differential equation $\dfrac{dr}{dt} = A + Br$, where A and B are constants. If $r = r_0$ at $t = 0$,

show that $r = r_0 e^{Bt} + \dfrac{A}{B}(e^{Bt} - 1)$.   (L)

24.5 The equations $d^2y/dx^2 \pm n^2y = constant$

We now consider some second order differential equations which have important applications especially in mechanics.

Type 1: $\dfrac{d^2y}{dx^2} + n^2y = 0$, where n is constant.

Multiplying both sides by $2\dfrac{dy}{dx}$ we obtain:

$$2\frac{dy}{dx}\frac{d^2y}{dx^2} + n^2\left(2y\frac{dy}{dx}\right) = 0.$$

But $\qquad 2\dfrac{dy}{dx}\dfrac{d^2y}{dx^2} = \dfrac{d}{dx}\left\{\left(\dfrac{dy}{dx}\right)^2\right\}$ and $2y\dfrac{dy}{dx} = \dfrac{d}{dx}(y^2)$,

so integrating both sides with respect to x:

$$\left(\frac{dy}{dx}\right)^2 + n^2y^2 = \text{constant}$$

Letting $y = a$ when $\dfrac{dy}{dx} = 0$, this becomes

$$\left(\frac{dy}{dx}\right)^2 + n^2y^2 = n^2a^2$$

$$\therefore \qquad \frac{dy}{dx} = \pm n\sqrt{(a^2 - y^2)}$$

Hence $\qquad \displaystyle\int \frac{1}{\sqrt{(a^2 - y^2)}}\,dy = \pm\int n\,dx$

$$\therefore \qquad \sin^{-1}\frac{y}{a} = \pm(nx + b)$$

$$\therefore \qquad \frac{y}{a} = \sin\{\pm(nx + b)\}$$

$$\therefore \qquad y = \pm a\sin(nx + b)$$

Since a is an arbitrary constant which may take any real value, positive or negative, there is no loss of generality in writing:

$$y = a\sin(nx + b)$$

Letting $b = c + \tfrac{1}{2}\pi$, we obtain:

$$y = a\sin(nx + c + \tfrac{1}{2}\pi)$$

i.e. $$y = a\cos(nx + c)$$

But $\qquad a\cos(nx + c) = a\cos nx \cos c - a\sin nx \sin c,$

thus the solution can also be expressed in the form

$$y = A\cos nx + B\sin nx$$

Thus the general solution of the differential equation

$$\frac{d^2y}{dx^2} + n^2y = 0$$

may be expressed in three possible forms:

$$y = a \sin(nx + b), \quad y = a \cos(nx + c)$$

or
$$y = A \cos nx + B \sin nx,$$

where a, b, c, A and B are arbitrary constants.

Example 1   Solve the differential equation $\dfrac{d^2y}{dx^2} + 9y = 0$ given that $y = 1$ when

$x = 0$ and that $y = 2$ when $x = \frac{1}{2}\pi$.

The general solution of the given equation is

$$y = A \cos 3x + B \sin 3x$$
Since $y = 1$ when $x = 0$, $1 = A + 0$ i.e. $A = 1$
Since $y = 2$ when $x = \frac{1}{2}\pi$, $2 = 0 - B$ i.e. $B = -2$

Hence the required solution is $y = \cos 3x - 2 \sin 3x$.

Example 2   Solve the differential equation $9\dfrac{d^2y}{dx^2} + 4y = 0$ given that $y = \dfrac{dy}{dx} = 2$

when $x = 0$.

Rearranging the equation, $\dfrac{d^2y}{dx^2} + \dfrac{4}{9}y = 0$

Hence the general solution is

$$y = A \cos\tfrac{2}{3}x + B \sin\tfrac{2}{3}x$$
$$\therefore \quad \frac{dy}{dx} = -\tfrac{2}{3}A \sin\tfrac{2}{3}x + \tfrac{2}{3}B \cos\tfrac{2}{3}x$$

Since $y = 2$ when $x = 0$, $2 = A$

Since $\dfrac{dy}{dx} = 2$ when $x = 0$, $2 = \tfrac{2}{3}B$

$\therefore \quad A = 2$ and $B = 3$

Hence the required solution is $y = 2 \cos\tfrac{2}{3}x + 3 \sin\tfrac{2}{3}x$.

Type 2: $\dfrac{d^2y}{dx^2} + n^2y = k$, where n and k are constant.

Rearranging: $\dfrac{d^2y}{dx^2} + n^2\left(y - \dfrac{k}{n^2}\right) = 0$

Letting $z = y - \dfrac{k}{n^2}$, we find that $\dfrac{d^2z}{dx^2} = \dfrac{d^2y}{dx^2}$

so the equation becomes: $\dfrac{d^2z}{dx^2} + n^2z = 0$

∴   the general solution is $z = A \cos nx + B \sin nx$

i.e. $y - \dfrac{k}{n^2} = A \cos nx + B \sin nx$

Thus the general solution of the differential equation

$$\dfrac{d^2y}{dx^2} + n^2y = k$$

is $y = A \cos nx + B \sin nx + k/n^2,$

where A and B are arbitrary constants.

Type 3: $\dfrac{d^2y}{dx^2} - n^2y = 0$, where n is constant.

Since $y = e^{nx}$ is a solution of this equation, we try the substitution $y = e^{nx}v$, where v is a function of x.

Differentiating: $\dfrac{dy}{dx} = e^{nx}\dfrac{dv}{dx} + ne^{nx}v$

∴ $\dfrac{d^2y}{dx^2} = e^{nx}\dfrac{d^2v}{dx^2} + 2ne^{nx}\dfrac{dv}{dx} + n^2e^{nx}v$

Hence the differential equation becomes

$$e^{nx}\dfrac{d^2v}{dx^2} + 2ne^{nx}\dfrac{dv}{dx} + n^2e^{nx}v - n^2e^{nx}v = 0$$

i.e. $\dfrac{d^2v}{dx^2} + 2n\dfrac{dv}{dx} = 0$

Integrating with respect to x,

$$\dfrac{dv}{dx} + 2nv = a$$

Rearranging: $\dfrac{dv}{dx} = a - 2nv$

∴ $\dfrac{1}{(a - 2nv)}\dfrac{dv}{dx} = 1$

∴ $\displaystyle\int\dfrac{-2n}{(a - 2nv)}\,dv = \int(-2n)\,dx$

i.e. $\ln|a - 2nv| = -2nx + c$
    $|a - 2nv| = e^{-2nx+c}$

Thus
$$a - 2nv = ke^{-2nx}, \quad \text{where } |k| = e^c.$$

$$\therefore \quad v = \frac{a}{2n} - \frac{k}{2n}e^{-2nx}$$

$$\therefore \quad y = e^{nx}v = \frac{a}{2n}e^{nx} - \frac{k}{2n}e^{-nx}$$

Thus the general solution of the differential equation

$$\frac{d^2y}{dx^2} - n^2y = 0$$

is of the form $\qquad y = Ae^{nx} + Be^{-nx},$

where A and B are arbitrary constants.

Example 3   Solve the differential equation $\dfrac{d^2y}{dx^2} - 100y = 0$, given that $y = 6$,

$\dfrac{dy}{dx} = 40$ when $x = 0$.

The general solution of the given equation is

$$y = Ae^{10x} + Be^{-10x}$$

$$\therefore \quad \frac{dy}{dx} = 10Ae^{10x} - 10Be^{-10x}$$

Since $y = 6$ when $x = 0$, $\qquad 6 = A + B$

Since $\dfrac{dy}{dx} = 40$ when $x = 0$, $\quad 40 = 10A - 10B$

$\therefore \quad A = 5 \quad$ and $\quad B = 1$

Hence the required solution is $y = 5e^{10x} + e^{-10x}$.

Type 4: $\dfrac{d^2y}{dx^2} - n^2y = k$, where n and k are constant.

By the method applied to equations of type 2 it can be shown that

$$y + \frac{k}{n^2} = Ae^{nx} + Be^{-nx}$$

Thus the general solution of the differential equation

$$\frac{d^2y}{dx^2} - n^2y = k$$

is $\qquad y = Ae^{nx} + Be^{-nx} - \dfrac{k}{n^2},$

where A and B are arbitrary constants.

Exercise 24.5

[In this exercise the general solutions of the given differential equations may be quoted without proof.]

Write down the general solutions of the following differential equations:

1. $\dfrac{d^2y}{dx^2} = -16y$

2. $4\dfrac{d^2y}{dx^2} + 7y = 0$

3. $\dfrac{d^2y}{dx^2} + 9y = 18$

4. $\dfrac{d^2y}{dx^2} = 10 - 10y$

5. $\dfrac{d^2y}{dx^2} = 36y$

6. $\dfrac{d^2y}{dx^2} - 8y = 0$

7. $9\dfrac{d^2y}{dx^2} = 1 + 27y$

8. $\dfrac{d^2y}{dx^2} - 4y + 1 = 0$

Solve the following differential equations subject to the given conditions.

9. $\dfrac{d^2y}{dx^2} + 4y = 0$; $y = 4$ when $x = 0$ and $y = 3$ when $x = 3\pi/4$.

10. $\dfrac{d^2y}{dx^2} - 16y = 0$; $y = 10$ and $\dfrac{dy}{dx} = -16$ when $x = 0$.

11. $36\dfrac{d^2y}{dx^2} + y = 0$; $y = 6$ and $\dfrac{dy}{dx} = 0$ when $x = 0$.

12. $9\dfrac{d^2y}{dx^2} + 16y = 0$; $y = -5$ when $x = 0$ and $y = 4$ when $x = 3\pi/8$.

13. $4\dfrac{d^2y}{dx^2} - 25y = 0$; $y = -9$ and $\dfrac{dy}{dx} = 12\frac{1}{2}$ when $x = 0$.

14. $\dfrac{d^2y}{dx^2} - 12y = 0$; $y = 4/e^2$ when $x = 1/\sqrt{3}$ and $y = 4$ when $x = 0$.

15. $9\dfrac{d^2y}{dx^2} - 49y = 28$; $y = 8\frac{3}{7}$ and $\dfrac{dy}{dx} = -7$ when $x = 0$.

16. $4\dfrac{d^2y}{dx^2} + 25y = 40$; $y = 5{\cdot}6$ and $\dfrac{dy}{dx} = 22{\cdot}5$ when $x = 0$.

17. $\dfrac{d^2y}{dx^2} + 3y = 6$; $y = 2$ when $x = 0$ and $y = 3$ when $x = \pi/2\sqrt{3}$.

18. $16\dfrac{d^2y}{dx^2} - 81y = 243$; $y = -1$ and $\dfrac{dy}{dx} = 0$ when $x = 0$.

19. $\dfrac{d^2y}{dx^2} - 18y = 54$; $y = -3 + \sqrt{2}$ and $\dfrac{dy}{dx} = 6$ when $x = 0$.

20. $\dfrac{d^2y}{dx^2} + 12y = 6$; $\dfrac{dy}{dx} = 24$ when $x = \pi/4\sqrt{3}$ and $\dfrac{dy}{dx} = -18$ when $x = 0$.

Exercise 24.6 (miscellaneous)

1. Sketch some of the straight lines represented by the equation $y = k(2x - k)$, where k is any constant. Obtain the differential equation for this family of lines.

2. Find a second order differential equation of which the general solution is $y = Axe^x + Be^{-x}$, where A and B are arbitrary constants.

3. The differential equation of a family of curves is $\dfrac{dy}{dx} = y - x^2$. Find the equations of the loci of points where $\dfrac{dy}{dx} = 0$ and where $\dfrac{d^2y}{dx^2} = 0$. Hence sketch the integral curves of the differential equation.

4. (a) Find, in any form, the solution of the differential equation $\dfrac{du}{dt} - 7u + 3 = 0$, given that $u = 0$ when $t = 5$.

   (b) Solve the differential equation $\dfrac{dy}{dx} = x\sqrt{(x^2 + 9)}$ given that $y = -9$ when $x = 0$.   (C)

5. (a) Solve the differential equation $\dfrac{dx}{dt} = \dfrac{1}{x + 2} - \dfrac{3}{3x + 5}$, given that $x = 1$ when $t = 2$.

   (b) Solve the differential equation $\dfrac{dy}{dx} = \dfrac{2y^2 + 3}{4y}$, given that $y = 1$ when $x = -1$. Give your answer in a form expressing y in terms of x.   (C)

6. The temperature y degrees of a body, t minutes after being placed in a certain room, satisfies the differential equation $6\dfrac{d^2y}{dt^2} + \dfrac{dy}{dt} = 0$. By using the substitution $z = dy/dt$, or otherwise, find y in terms of t, given that $y = 63$ when $t = 0$ and $y = 36$ when $t = 6\ln 4$. Find after how many minutes the rate of cooling of the body will have fallen below one degree per minute, giving your answer correct to the nearest minute. How cool does the body get?   (O&C)

7. By substituting $z = (1 + x)y$, solve the differential equation

$$\frac{dy}{dx} + \frac{y}{1 + x} = \cos x,$$

given that $y = 0$ when $x = 0$. In your answer give y in terms of x.

8. (a) Solve the differential equation $xy\frac{dy}{dx} = 1 + y^2$, given that, when $x = 2$, $y = 0$. Find the equation of the tangent to the curve at the point in the first quadrant where $x = 4$.

   (b) If $Ax^2 - By^2 = C$, where A, B and C are constants, prove that

$$xy\frac{d^2y}{dx^2} + x\left(\frac{dy}{dx}\right)^2 - y\frac{dy}{dx} = 0. \tag{SU}$$

9. (a) Solve the differential equation $dy/dx = \sin x \cos^2 y$, given that, when $x = \pi/2$, $y = \pi/4$.

   (b) A curve passes through the origin and is such that $dy/dx = e^{2x-y}$. Obtain the equation of the curve in the form $y = f(x)$ and give a rough sketch of its graph. \hfill (SU)

10. (i) Find y in terms of x given that $(1 + x)\frac{dy}{dx} = (1 - x)y$ and that $y = 1$ when $x = 0$.

   (ii) A curve passes through $(2, 2)$ and has gradient at (x, y) given by the differential equation $ye^{y^2}\frac{dy}{dx} = e^{2x}$. Find the equation of the curve. Show that the curve also passes through the point $(1, \sqrt{2})$ and sketch the curve. \hfill (L)

11. If y is a solution of the differential equation $\frac{dy}{dx} = \frac{1 + y^2}{1 + x^2}$ deduce that

$$y = x + k(1 + xy)$$

where k is a constant.

(You may assume that $\tan^{-1} a - \tan^{-1} b = \tan^{-1}\left(\frac{a - b}{1 + ab}\right) + n\pi$, n an integer.) \hfill (W)

12. Obtain the general solution of the differential equation $2x^2\frac{dy}{dx} + x^2y^2 = y^2$.

Find the three particular solutions such that (a) when $x = 1$, $y = 1$, (b) when $x = 1$, $y = \frac{2}{3}$, (c) when $x = 1$, $y = \frac{1}{2}$. Show that each of the integral curves given by these particular solutions has a maximum point on the line $x = 1$. Sketch the three curves on the same axes. \hfill (L)

13. In a chemical reaction there are present, at time, t, x kg of substance X and y kg of substance Y, and initially there is 1 kg of X and 2 kg of Y. The variables x and y satisfy the equations $\dfrac{dx}{dt} = -x^2 y, \dfrac{dy}{dt} = -xy^2$. Find $\dfrac{dy}{dx}$ in terms of x and y, and express y in terms of x. Hence obtain a differential equation in x and t only, and so find an expression for x in terms of t. (JMB)

14. (a) The equation of the family of all parabolas whose axes lie along the x-axis has the form $y^2 = 4a(x - h)$ where each parabola is specified by values of a and h. Form a differential equation (*not* involving a or h) satisfied by any point (x, y) lying on any one of these parabolas.

(b) The tangent to a curve at the point (x, y) cuts the x-axis at Q. If $OQ = kx$ (where O is the origin of the coordinate system) show that points on the curve satisfy the differential equation

$$\frac{dy}{dx} = \frac{y}{x - kx}.$$

By solving this differential equation show that the equation of the curve has the form $y = Ax^{1/(1-k)}$ where A is an arbitrary constant. (AEB 1975)

15. (i) Obtain the general solution of the differential equation $x \ln x \dfrac{dy}{dx} = 1$

(a) where $0 < x < 1$ and (b) where $x > 1$.

(ii) Sketch the family of integral curves for the differential equation

$$\frac{dy}{dx} = x(y + 1).$$

(iii) Find the equations of the two curves which pass through the point $(1, 1)$ and which satisfy the differential equation

$$\tan(y - 1)\frac{dy}{dx} = \tan(x - 1). \tag{L}$$

16. According to Newton's law of cooling, the rate at which a hot object cools is proportional to the difference between the temperature of the object and the temperature of the surrounding air (assumed to be constant). If an object cools from $100°$ to $80°$ in 10 minutes, and from $80°$ to $65°$ in another 10 minutes, find the temperature of the surrounding air and the temperature of the object after a further 10 minutes. (O)

17. (a) Given that $\dfrac{dy}{dx} = 9y^2 - 4$ and that $y = 1$ when $x = 2$, find an equation expressing x in terms of y.

(b) In a certain country, the price p of a particular commodity increases with the time t at a rate equal to kp where k is a positive constant. Write down a differential equation expressing this information. Show that if $p = 1$ when $t = 0$ and $p = \alpha$ when $t = 1$, then, at time t, $p = \alpha^t$.   (C)

18. (a) Solve the differential equation $\dfrac{dy}{dx} = 3y + 2$ given that $y = 1$ when $x = 2$, expressing your answer in a form giving y as a function of x.

(b) The rate of decomposition of a radioactive substance is proportional to the mass of the substance remaining. Write down a differential equation which expresses this law, stating the meaning of each symbol used. If one third of the mass is left after 12 years, how much was left after 3 years?   (C)

19. Social scientists studying the growth of population in an urban region use a model in which the rate of growth of population is proportional to $P(N - P)$, where P is the current size of the population (regarded as a continuous variable) and N is a constant. Set up a differential equation for this model and find its general solution expressing P as a function of time t. In a particular region, the population at a certain time was 100 000. Fifty years later the population was 200 000 and fifty years after that it was 300 000. Using the above model determine the value of N in this case. What is the significance of N?   (C)

20. A water reservoir is in the shape of the surface obtained by rotating a parabola $y = kx^2$ about its vertical axis, $x = 0$. Show that when the central depth of the water in the reservoir is h, the surface area A of the water is proportional to h and the volume V is proportional to h^2. In a dry period the rate of loss of water, due entirely to evaporation, is λA per day. Obtain a differential equation for h after t days and deduce that the depth decreases at a constant rate. If, in addition to the evaporation a constant volume C of water is now used per day, obtain the new differential equation and show that the time to empty the reservoir from a depth H will be $\displaystyle\int_0^H \dfrac{\pi h\,dh}{Ck + \pi\lambda h}$ days. Verify that when $H = 20$, $\lambda = \frac{1}{2}$, $C = 500$ and $k = 0\cdot0025$ this amounts to just under 35 days.   (AEB 1979)

21. (i) An electrically charged body loses its charge, Q coulombs, at a rate kQ coulombs per second, where k is a constant. Write down a differential equation involving Q and t, where t seconds is the time since the discharge started. Solve this equation for Q, given that the initial charge was Q_0 coulombs. If $Q_0 = 0\cdot001$, and $Q = 0\cdot0005$ when $t = 10$, find the value of Q when $t = 20$.

(ii) Solve the differential equation $\dfrac{d^2y}{dx^2} - 25y = 0$, given that $y = 4$, $\dfrac{dy}{dx} = 10$ when $x = 0$.   (L)

22. Find the solution of the differential equation $\dfrac{d^2y}{dx^2} + 9y = 18$, for which y has

a maximum at $(\frac{1}{2}\pi, 6)$. Find the minimum value of y, and the values of x for which $y = 0$. (O)

23. (i) Solve the differential equation $\dfrac{dy}{dx} = \left(\dfrac{x}{y}\right)e^{x+y}$ in the form $f(y) = g(x)$, given that $y = 0$ when $x = 0$.

(ii) Solve the differential equation $\dfrac{d^2y}{dx^2} + 4y = 16$, given that $y = 4$ and

$\dfrac{dy}{dx} = -4$ when $x = 0$. For which values of x does the graph of y have points of inflexion? (O)

24. (i) Find the general solution of the differential equation

$$(1 + x)\frac{dy}{dx} = xy.$$

(ii) By using the substitution $z = dy/dx$, or otherwise, solve the differential equation $\dfrac{d^3y}{dx^3} + 4\dfrac{dy}{dx} = 0$, given that y takes the values $0, 0, 1$ for $x = 0, \frac{1}{4}\pi$, $\frac{1}{2}\pi$ respectively. (O&C)

25. Prove that, if $y = \cos^2(x^2)$, then

$$x\frac{d^2y}{dx^2} - \frac{dy}{dx} + 16x^3y = 8x^3.$$

Prove that changing the independent variable in this differential equation from x to t, where $t = x^2$, gives the equation

$$\frac{d^2y}{dt^2} + ky = C,$$

where k, C are constants and hence, or otherwise, find the general solution of the first equation in terms of x. What is the general solution of the differential equation

$$x\frac{d^2y}{dx^2} - \frac{dy}{dx} - 16x^3y = 8x^3?$$ (O&C)

25 Further coordinate geometry

25.1 Angles, distances and areas

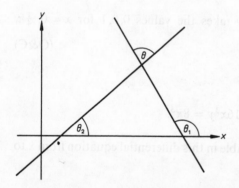

The diagram shows two lines which make angles θ_1 and θ_2 with the positive direction of the x-axis. If the gradients of these lines are m_1 and m_2 respectively, then

$$m_1 = \tan \theta_1, \qquad m_2 = \tan \theta_2.$$

One angle between the lines is θ, where $\theta = \theta_1 - \theta_2$,

$$\therefore \qquad \tan \theta = \tan(\theta_1 - \theta_2) = \frac{\tan \theta_1 - \tan \theta_2}{1 + \tan \theta_1 \tan \theta_2}.$$

Hence the angle θ between two lines with gradients m_1 and m_2 is given by

$$\boxed{\tan \theta = \frac{m_1 - m_2}{1 + m_1 m_2}}$$

Example 1 Find the acute angle between the straight lines $3x - y + 2 = 0$ and $x - 2y - 1 = 0$.

The equations of the lines may be re-written as:

$$y = 3x + 2 \quad \text{and} \quad y = \tfrac{1}{2}x - \tfrac{1}{2}.$$

Hence the gradients of the lines are 3 and $\tfrac{1}{2}$.

If θ is one angle between the lines, then

$$\tan \theta = \frac{3 - \frac{1}{2}}{1 + 3 \times \frac{1}{2}} = \frac{2\frac{1}{2}}{2\frac{1}{2}} = 1$$

∴ the acute angle between the lines is $45°$.

[Note that the angle between two curves at any point of intersection is defined as the angle between the tangents to the curves at the point.]

Consider now the line joining the points $A(x_1, y_1)$ and $B(x_2, y_2)$. Let P be the point which divides AB in the ratio $\mu : \lambda$. Then if C, D and Q are the feet of the perpendiculars from A, B and P to the x-axis, Q must divide CD in the ratio $\mu : \lambda$. It follows that the x-coordinate of P

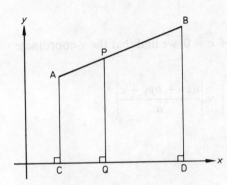

$$= x_1 + \frac{\mu}{\lambda + \mu}(x_2 - x_1) = \frac{\lambda x_1 + \mu x_2}{\lambda + \mu}$$

A similar expression is obtained for the y-coordinate of P.

i.e.

> The point dividing the line AB in the ratio $\mu : \lambda$ has coordinates
> $$\left(\frac{\lambda x_1 + \mu x_2}{\lambda + \mu}, \frac{\lambda y_1 + \mu y_2}{\lambda + \mu} \right).$$

This formula can be used when P divides AB externally in a given ratio if μ and λ are taken to have opposite signs.

[We recall that the corresponding formula for the position vector of a point which divides a lines in the ratio $\mu : \lambda$ was obtained in §21.1.]

Example 2 If A and B are the points $(2, 1)$ and $(-4, 4)$ respectively, find the coordinates of the point C which divides AB internally in the ratio $2:1$ and of the point D which divides AB externally in the ratio $3:2$.

The coordinates of C are

$$\left(\frac{1 \times 2 + 2(-4)}{1 + 2}, \frac{1 \times 1 + 2 \times 4}{1 + 2} \right) \quad \text{i.e.} \quad (-2, 3)$$

Regarding D as the point which divides AB in the ratio $3 : -2$, the coordinates of D are

$$\left(\frac{(-2)2 + 3(-4)}{-2 + 3}, \frac{(-2)1 + 3 \times 4}{-2 + 3} \right) \quad \text{i.e.} \quad (-16, 10).$$

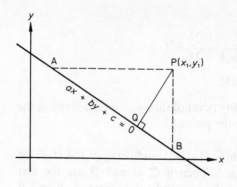

Next we derive a formula for the perpendicular distance from a point $P(x_1, y_1)$ to a straight line $ax + by + c = 0$. In the diagram A and B are points on the line $ax + by + c = 0$, such that AP is parallel to the x-axis and BP is parallel to the y-axis. The point Q is the foot of the perpendicular from P to the line and so PQ is the required perpendicular distance.

Substituting $y = y_1$ in the equation $ax + by + c = 0$, we find that the x-coordinate of A is $-(by_1 + c)/a$.

$$\therefore \qquad AP = \left| x_1 - \left\{ -\frac{(by_1 + c)}{a} \right\} \right| = \left| \frac{ax_1 + by_1 + c}{a} \right|$$

Similarly $BP = \left| \dfrac{ax_1 + by_1 + c}{b} \right|$

$$\therefore \qquad AB = \sqrt{\{AP^2 + BP^2\}}$$

$$= \sqrt{\left\{ \frac{(ax_1 + by_1 + c)^2}{a^2} + \frac{(ax_1 + by_1 + c)^2}{b^2} \right\}}$$

$$= \sqrt{\left\{ \frac{(ax_1 + by_1 + c)^2(a^2 + b^2)}{a^2 b^2} \right\}}$$

$$= \left| \frac{(ax_1 + by_1 + c)\sqrt{(a^2 + b^2)}}{ab} \right|$$

However, the area of $\triangle APB = \tfrac{1}{2} \times PQ \times AB = \tfrac{1}{2} \times AP \times BP$

$$\therefore \qquad PQ = \frac{AP \times BP}{AB}$$

$$= \left| \frac{(ax_1 + by_1 + c)^2}{ab} \times \frac{ab}{(ax_1 + by_1 + c)\sqrt{(a^2 + b^2)}} \right|$$

$$= \left| \frac{ax_1 + by_1 + c}{\sqrt{(a^2 + b^2)}} \right|$$

i.e.

> The perpendicular distance from the point (x_1, y_1) to the line
>
> $$ax + by + c = 0 \quad \text{is} \quad \left| \frac{ax_1 + by_1 + c}{\sqrt{(a^2 + b^2)}} \right|$$

Example 3   Find the distance of the point $(3, -5)$ from the line $2x - y = 1$.

The distance of the point $(3, -5)$ from the line $2x - y - 1 = 0$ is

$$\left|\frac{2 \times 3 - (-5) - 1}{\sqrt{\{2^2 + (-1)^2\}}}\right| = \frac{10}{\sqrt{5}} = 2\sqrt{5}.$$

Example 4   Find the locus of points equidistant from the lines $y = 2x$ and $2x + 4y - 3 = 0$.

Let $P(x_1, y_1)$ be a point equidistant from the lines $2x - y = 0$ and $2x + 4y - 3 = 0$, then

$$\left|\frac{2x_1 - y_1}{\sqrt{\{2^2 + (-1)^2\}}}\right| = \left|\frac{2x_1 + 4y_1 - 3}{\sqrt{\{2^2 + 4^2\}}}\right|$$

$$\therefore \quad \frac{1}{\sqrt{5}}|2x_1 - y_1| = \frac{1}{\sqrt{20}}|2x_1 + 4y_1 - 3|$$

$$\therefore \quad 2|2x_1 - y_1| = |2x_1 + 4y_1 - 3|$$

Thus either

$$2(2x_1 - y_1) = 2x_1 + 4y_1 - 3$$
$$4x_1 - 2y_1 = 2x_1 + 4y_1 - 3$$
$$2x_1 - 6y_1 + 3 = 0$$

or

$$2(2x_1 - y_1) = -(2x_1 + 4y_1 - 3)$$
$$4x_1 - 2y_1 = -2x_1 - 4y_1 + 3$$
$$6x_1 + 2y_1 - 3 = 0$$

Hence the locus of all points P equidistant from the given lines is the pair of straight lines

$$2x - 6y + 3 = 0, \qquad 6x + 2y - 3 = 0.$$

It follows that these lines are the bisectors of the angles between the given lines.

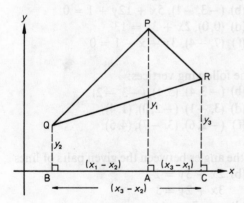

Finally we consider the area of the triangle whose vertices are $P(x_1, y_1)$, $Q(x_2, y_2)$ and $R(x_3, y_3)$.

As shown in the diagram, the area of $\triangle PQR$ = area $PQBA$ + area $PACR$ − area $QBCR$.

Since each of these areas is a trapezium,

area of $\triangle PQR = \frac{1}{2}(x_1 - x_2)(y_1 + y_2) + \frac{1}{2}(x_3 - x_1)(y_1 + y_3) - \frac{1}{2}(x_3 - x_2)(y_2 + y_3)$

$= \frac{1}{2}\{x_1(y_2 - y_3) + x_2(y_3 - y_1) + x_3(y_1 - y_2)\}$

It is found that, although this result holds for any points P, Q and R, it sometimes gives a negative value for the area. We must therefore include modulus signs in the general formula.

$$\text{Area of triangle} = \tfrac{1}{2}|x_1(y_2 - y_3) + x_2(y_3 - y_1) + x_3(y_1 - y_2)|$$

[Note that this formula is rarely needed in elementary work. Problems on area usually involve right-angled triangles, isosceles triangles or other triangles whose heights and bases are easily calculated.]

Exercise 25.1

1.   Find the tangent of the acute angle between the following pairs of lines
(a) $y = 2x - 3$, $y = 3x + 1$
(b) $3x - 2y + 1 = 0$, $2x - y - 7 = 0$
(c) $x + 3y - 2 = 0$, $5x - 6y + 2 = 0$
(d) $7x + 4y + 5 = 0$, $y = 0$
(e) $y = 4x$, $2x - 8y - 5 = 0$
(f) $4x + 3y + 2 = 0$, $x = 0$.

2.   Find the coordinates of the points which divide the lines joining the given pairs of points internally in the stated ratio.
(a) $(7, 3)$, $(1, -6)$; $1:2$
(b) $(2, -4)$, $(-8, 1)$; $2:3$
(c) $(0, 6)$, $(2\tfrac{1}{2}, -4)$; $4:1$
(d) $(-3, 5)$, $(1, -1)$; $5:3$

3.   Find the coordinates of the points which divide the lines joining the given pairs of points externally in the stated ratio.
(a) $(5, -1)$, $(-2, 3)$; $1:2$
(b) $(2, -3)$, $(0, 5)$; $2:3$
(c) $(4, 3)$, $(-2, 0)$; $4:1$
(d) $(-3, 4)$, $(1, -1)$; $5:3$

4.   Find the distances between the given points and the given lines.
(a) $(1, 2)$, $4x - 3y - 3 = 0$
(b) $(-3, -1)$, $5x + 12y + 1 = 0$
(c) $(2, 5)$, $x - y + 5 = 0$
(d) $(0, 0)$, $2x + 3y = 13$
(e) $(-6, 10)$, $x = 3$
(f) $(7, -4)$, $3y - x - 1 = 0$

5.   Find the areas of the triangles with the following vertices:
(a) $(2, 3)$, $(5, -1)$, $(2, -1)$
(b) $(-3, 4)$, $(5, 1)$, $(-3, -2)$
(c) $(-1, 3)$, $(2, -3)$, $(4, 5)$
(d) $(3, -1)$, $(-2, 0)$, $(1, 4)$
(e) $(5, 7)$, $(-4, -11)$, $(0, -3)$
(f) $(-2, 6)$, $(3, -7)$, $(4, 5)$

6.   Find the equations of the bisectors of the angles between the given pairs of lines
(a) $3x - y - 3 = 0$
      $x + 3y + 1 = 0$
(b) $2x + 3y = 2$
      $3x + 2y = 3$
(c) $3x + 6y - 1 = 0$
      $x - 2y + 1 = 0$
(d) $y = 7x - 1$
      $y = x + 5$

7.   Find the angles of the triangle PQR with vertices $P(1, 4)$, $Q(3, -2)$ and $R(5, 2)$.

8. Find the angles of the triangle ABC with vertices $A(1, -3)$, $B(4, 6)$ and $C(-1, 1)$.

9. A triangle has vertices $A(-4, 1)$, $B(3, 0)$ and $C(1, 2)$. If the internal bisector of $\angle B$ meets AC at P, use the fact that $AP : PC = AB : BC$ to find the coordinates of P.

10. A triangle has vertices $P(1, -2)$, $Q(5, 1)$ and $R(6, 10)$. Find the coordinates of the point on QR which is equidistant from the sides PQ and PR.

11. Find the tangent of the acute angle between the parabola $y^2 = 4x$ and the circle $x^2 + y^2 = 5$ at their points of intersection.

12. The curves $y = x^2$ and $y^2 = 8x$ intersect at the origin and at a point A. Find the angle between the curves at A.

13. Find the incentre of the triangle with vertices $(-1, 4)$, $(2, -2)$ and $(7, 8)$.

14. Find the incentre of the triangle whose sides have equations $x - y + 1 = 0$, $x + 7y + 9 = 0$ and $7x - y - 2 = 0$.

15. The points $A(-8, 9)$ and $C(1, 2)$ are opposite vertices of a parallelogram $ABCD$. The sides BC, CD of the parallelogram lie along the lines $x + 7y - 15 = 0$, $x - y + 1 = 0$, respectively. Calculate (i) the coordinates of D, (ii) the tangent of the acute angle between the diagonals of the parallelogram, (iii) the length of the perpendicular from A to the side CD, (iv) the area of the parallelogram.
(JMB)

25.2 Further work on circles

When a problem involves two circles, of radii a and b, the relative positions of the circles can be determined by finding the distance c between their centres. Assuming that $a > b$, there are various different possibilities.

(1)   (2)

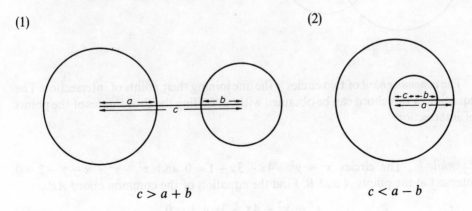

$c > a + b$ $c < a - b$

In diagrams (1) and (2) the circles do not intersect.

(3)   (4)

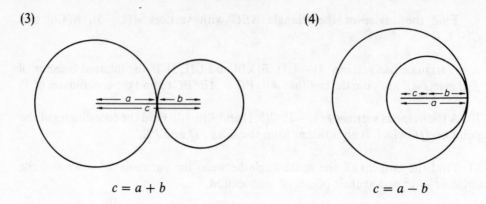

$$c = a + b \qquad\qquad\qquad\qquad c = a - b$$

In diagrams (3) and (4) the circles touch either externally or internally.

(5)

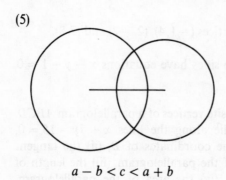

In diagram (5) the circles have two distinct points of intersection.

$$a - b < c < a + b$$

(6)

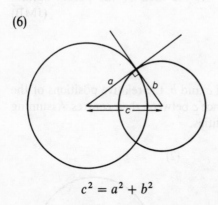

Two circles which cut at right-angles are called *orthogonal* circles. Diagram (6) shows two such circles.

$$c^2 = a^2 + b^2$$

The *common chord* of two circles is the line joining their points of intersection. The equation of this chord can be obtained without finding the coordinates of the points of intersection.

Example 1   The circles $x^2 + y^2 + 4x - 3y + 1 = 0$ and $x^2 + y^2 + x - y - 2 = 0$ intersect at the points A and B. Find the equation of the common chord AB.

$$x^2 + y^2 + 4x - 3y + 1 = 0 \qquad\qquad (1)$$
$$x^2 + y^2 + x - y - 2 = 0 \qquad\qquad (2)$$

Subtracting (2) from (1) we obtain:

$$3x - 2y + 3 = 0$$

Since the coordinates of A and B satisfy equations (1) and (2), they must also satisfy this new equation, which represents a straight line.

Hence $3x - 2y + 3 = 0$ is the equation of AB.

We now extend the method of Example 1 by considering two intersecting circles with equations:

$$x^2 + y^2 + 2gx + 2fy + c = 0 \qquad \text{(i)}$$
$$x^2 + y^2 + 2Gx + 2Fy + C = 0 \qquad \text{(ii)}$$

From these equations we can form a new equation:

$$x^2 + y^2 + 2gx + 2fy + c + k(x^2 + y^2 + 2Gx + 2Fy + C) = 0 \qquad \text{(iii)}$$

i.e. $\quad (1 + k)x^2 + (1 + k)y^2 + 2(g + kG)x + 2(f + kF)y + c + kC = 0$

This is the equation of a circle for all values of k, except $k = -1$. Moreover, any pair of values of x and y which satisfy equations (i) and (ii) must also satisfy equation (iii). Hence, in general, equation (iii) represents a circle passing through the points of intersection of circles (i) and (ii). When $k = -1$ equation (iii) represents a straight line through the points of intersection i.e. the common chord of the circles.

Example 2   The circles $x^2 + y^2 + 3x - y - 5 = 0$ and $x^2 + y^2 - 2x + y - 1 = 0$ intersect at points A and B. Find the equation of the circle which passes through the origin and the points A and B.

Any circle which passes through A and B has an equation of the form:

$$x^2 + y^2 + 3x - y - 5 + k(x^2 + y^2 - 2x + y - 1) = 0$$

If this circle also passes through the origin,

$$-5 + k(-1) = 0 \quad \text{i.e.} \quad k = -5$$

Hence the equation of the circle which passes through the origin and the points A and B is

$$x^2 + y^2 + 3x - y - 5 - 5(x^2 + y^2 - 2x + y - 1) = 0$$

i.e. $\qquad\qquad\qquad 4x^2 + 4y^2 - 13x + 6y = 0.$

Exercise 25.2

1.   Two circles have equations $\quad x^2 + y^2 - 2x - 6y - 54 = 0$ and
$$x^2 + y^2 - 8x + 2y + 13 = 0.$$
Show that one circle lies entirely inside the other.

2.   Prove that the circles whose equations are $x^2 + y^2 - 2x - 2y - 2 = 0$, $x^2 + y^2 - 6x - 10y + 33 = 0$ lie entirely outside one another.

3.   A circle C_1 has equation $x^2 + y^2 - 32x - 24y + 300 = 0$ and a second circle C_2 has as diameter the line joining the points $(8, 0)$ and $(0, 6)$. Show that the circles C_1 and C_2 touch externally.

4. A circle C has equation $x^2 + y^2 - 4x + 2y = 40$. Find the equations of the circles with centre $(3, 1)$ which touch circle C. Find also the coordinates of the points of contact.

5. Show that the circles $x^2 + y^2 - 2x - 2y - 2 = 0$ and
$$x^2 - y^2 - 8x - 10y + 32 = 0$$
touch externally and find the coordinates of the point of contact.

6. Find the equations of the two circles with centres $A(1, 1)$ and $B(9, 7)$ which have equal radii and touch each other externally. Find also the equations of the common tangents to these circles.

7. Two circles with centres $(3, -5)$ and $(-6, 7)$ pass through the point $(4, 2)$. Find the equations of these circles. Find also the equation and the length of their common chord.

8. Prove that the circles whose equations are $x^2 + y^2 - 4y - 5 = 0$, $x^2 + y^2 - 8x + 2y + 1 = 0$ cut orthogonally and find the equation of the common chord.

9. Find the equation of the circle with centre $(3, -2)$ and radius 5 units. Find also the equation of the circle with centre $(-7, 3)$ which intersects the original circle at right angles.

10. Show that any circle which passes through the points $(1, 0)$ and $(-1, 0)$ has an equation of the form $x^2 + y^2 - 2\lambda y - 1 = 0$. Prove also that if the circles given by $\lambda = \lambda_1$ and $\lambda = \lambda_2$ cut orthogonally then $\lambda_1 \lambda_2 = -1$.

11. Show that if the circles $x^2 + y^2 + 2gx + 2fy + c = 0$ and
$$x^2 + y^2 + 2Gx + 2Fy + C = 0$$
cut orthogonally, then $2gG + 2fF = c + C$.

12. The circles $x^2 + y^2 - 2x = 0$ and $x^2 + y^2 + 4x - 6y - 3 = 0$ intersect at the points A and B. Find (a) the equation of AB, (b) the equation of the circle which passes through A, B and the point $(1, 2)$.

13. Given that the circles $x^2 + y^2 - 3y = 0$ and $x^2 + y^2 + 5x - 8y + 5 = 0$ intersect at P and Q, find the equation of the circle which passes through P, Q and (a) the point $(1, 1)$, (b) the origin, (c) touches the x-axis.

14. The circle $x^2 + y^2 + 3x - 5y - 4 = 0$ and the straight line $y = 2x + 5$ intersect at the points A and B. Find the equation of the circle which passes through A, B and (a) the point $(3, 1)$, (b) the origin, (c) has its centre on the y-axis.

15. Show that the circles $x^2 + y^2 + 8x + 2y + 8 = 0$, $x^2 + y^2 - 2x + 2y - 2 = 0$ have three common tangents, and find their equations.   (C)

25.3 Loci using parametric forms

Many problems in coordinate geometry are best solved using the parametric equations of curves. The basic techniques involved were introduced earlier and used to investigate the properties of various curves including the parabola $y^2 = 4ax$. We now consider further applications of these methods. As clear diagrams are often useful in this type of work, we begin by giving sketches of several important curves together with the most commonly used parametric forms of their equations.

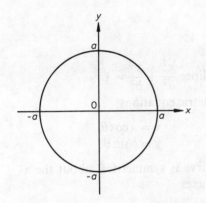

The circle $x^2 + y^2 = a^2$.
Parametric equations:

$$x = a \cos \theta,$$
$$y = a \sin \theta.$$

This is the circle with centre O and radius a.

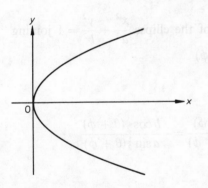

The parabola $y^2 = 4ax$.
Parametric equations:

$$x = at^2,$$
$$y = 2at.$$

This parabola has vertex O and is symmetrical about the x-axis.

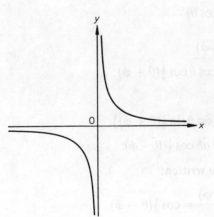

The rectangular hyperbola $xy = c^2$.
Parametric equations:

$$x = ct,$$
$$y = c/t.$$

The x- and y-axes are asymptotes to the curve and the curve is symmetrical about the lines $y = \pm x$.

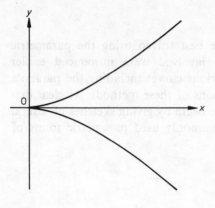

The semi-cubical parabola $ay^2 = x^3$.

Parametric equations:

$$x = at^2,$$
$$y = at^3.$$

The curve has a *cusp* at O and is symmetrical about the x-axis.

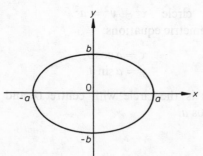

The ellipse $\dfrac{x^2}{a^2} + \dfrac{y^2}{b^2} = 1$.

Parametric equations:

$$x = a\cos\theta,$$
$$y = b\sin\theta.$$

The curve is symmetrical about the x- and y-axes.

Example 1   Find the equation of the chord of the ellipse $\dfrac{x^2}{a^2} + \dfrac{y^2}{b^2} = 1$ joining the points $P(a\cos\theta, b\sin\theta)$ and $Q(a\cos\phi, b\sin\phi)$.

Gradient of $PQ = \dfrac{b\sin\theta - b\sin\phi}{a\cos\theta - a\cos\phi}$

$$= \frac{2b\cos\frac{1}{2}(\theta + \phi)\sin\frac{1}{2}(\theta - \phi)}{-2a\sin\frac{1}{2}(\theta + \phi)\sin\frac{1}{2}(\theta - \phi)} = -\frac{b\cos\frac{1}{2}(\theta + \phi)}{a\sin\frac{1}{2}(\theta + \phi)}$$

Thus the equation of the chord PQ is

$$y - b\sin\theta = -\frac{b\cos\frac{1}{2}(\theta + \phi)}{a\sin\frac{1}{2}(\theta + \phi)}(x - a\cos\theta)$$

i.e. $ay\sin\frac{1}{2}(\theta + \phi) - ab\sin\theta\sin\frac{1}{2}(\theta + \phi)$

$$= -bx\cos\frac{1}{2}(\theta + \phi) + ab\cos\theta\cos\frac{1}{2}(\theta + \phi)$$

$\therefore \quad bx\cos\frac{1}{2}(\theta + \phi) + ay\sin\frac{1}{2}(\theta + \phi)$

$$= ab\{\cos\theta\cos\frac{1}{2}(\theta + \phi) + \sin\theta\sin\frac{1}{2}(\theta + \phi)\}$$

$$= ab\cos\{\theta - \frac{1}{2}(\theta + \phi)\} = ab\cos\frac{1}{2}(\theta - \phi).$$

Hence the equation of the chord PQ may be written:

$$\frac{x\cos\frac{1}{2}(\theta + \phi)}{a} + \frac{y\sin\frac{1}{2}(\theta + \phi)}{b} = \cos\frac{1}{2}(\theta - \phi).$$

Example 2   Find the equations of the tangent and the normal to the curve $xy = c^2$ at the point $P(ct, c/t)$. Given that the normal at P meets the curve again at Q, find the coordinates of Q. If the tangent at P meets the y-axis at R, find the equation of the locus of the mid-point M of PR.

The parametric equations of the curve are

$$x = ct, \qquad y = \frac{c}{t}$$

Differentiating with respect to t we have

$$\frac{dx}{dt} = c, \qquad \frac{dy}{dt} = -\frac{c}{t^2}$$

$$\therefore \quad \frac{dy}{dx} = \frac{dy}{dt} \bigg/ \frac{dx}{dt} = \left(-\frac{c}{t^2}\right) \bigg/ c = -\frac{1}{t^2}$$

Hence the gradients of the tangent and the normal to the curve at P are $-1/t^2$ and t^2 respectively.

$\therefore$ the equation of the tangent at P is

$$y - \frac{c}{t} = -\frac{1}{t^2}(x - ct)$$

i.e. $t^2 y - ct = -x + ct$

i.e. $x + t^2 y = 2ct$ (1)

The equation of the normal at P is

$$y - \frac{c}{t} = t^2(x - ct)$$

i.e. $ty - c = t^3 x - ct^4$

i.e. $t^3 x - ty = c(t^4 - 1)$ (2)

Let $(cu, c/u)$ be a point which lies on the curve $xy = c^2$ and on the normal at P, then from equation (2)

$$t^3 \times cu - t \times \frac{c}{u} = c(t^4 - 1)$$

$$\therefore \quad t^3 u^2 + (1 - t^4)u - t = 0$$

$$\therefore \quad (u - t)(t^3 u + 1) = 0$$

$$\therefore \quad \text{either } u = t \quad \text{or} \quad u = -1/t^3$$

Since the solution $u = t$ gives the point P, the remaining solution $u = -1/t^3$ must give the point Q.

Hence the coordinates of Q are $(-c/t^3, -ct^3)$.

Substituting $x = 0$ in equation (1) we have,

$$t^2 y = 2ct \quad \text{i.e.} \quad y = 2c/t$$

$\therefore$ the coordinates of the point R are $(0, 2c/t)$.

Thus the coordinates of the mid-point M of PR are

$$\left(\frac{1}{2}\{ct + 0\}, \frac{1}{2}\left\{\frac{c}{t} + \frac{2c}{t}\right\}\right) \quad \text{i.e.} \quad \left(\frac{1}{2}ct, \frac{3c}{2t}\right)$$

Hence as t varies the parametric equations of the locus of M are

$$x = \frac{1}{2}ct, \qquad y = \frac{3c}{2t}$$

Eliminating t from these equations we obtain the Cartesian equation of the locus, namely $xy = \frac{3}{4}c^2$.

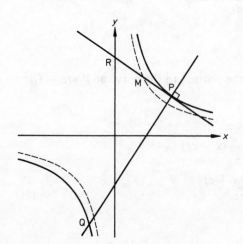

As shown in the diagram the locus of M is another rectangular hyperbola.

Exercise 25.3

1.   Write down parametric coordinates for a point on each of the following curves and sketch the curves.
(a) $y^2 = 12x$,   (b) $xy = 9$,   (c) $y^2 = x^3$,
(d) $4xy = 25$,   (e) $4y^2 = x^3$,   (f) $y^2 = 10x$.

2.   Write down parametric coordinates for a point on each of the following curves and sketch the curves.

(a) $\dfrac{x^2}{9} + \dfrac{y^2}{4} = 1$,   (b) $x^2 + y^2 = 9$,   (c) $\dfrac{x^2}{5} + y^2 = 1$,
(d) $4x^2 + 9y^2 = 4$,   (e) $9x^2 + y^2 = 9$,   (f) $x^2 + (y - 1)^2 = 25$.

3.   Find the equations of the tangent and normal to the curve $xy = 16$ at the point $(4t, 4/t)$.

4.   Find the equations of the tangent and normal to the curve $x = t$, $y = 1/t$ at the point where $t = 2$.

5. Find the equations of the tangent and normal to the curve $x = 2\cos\theta$, $y = \sin\theta$ at the point where $\theta = \frac{1}{3}\pi$.

6. P is the point $(5\cos\theta, 4\sin\theta)$ on the curve $x^2/25 + y^2/16 = 1$. Given that S and S' are the points with coordinates $(-3, 0)$ and $(3, 0)$, show that the value of $PS + PS'$ is independent of θ.

7. Find the equations of the tangents to the curve $xy = c^2$ which have gradient -4 and write down the coordinates of their points of contact.

8. The points $P(cp, c/p)$, $Q(cq, c/q)$ and $R(cr, c/r)$ lie on the curve $xy = c^2$. Show that if $\angle RPQ$ is a right angle, then $p^2qr = -1$. Prove further that QR is perpendicular to the tangent at P to the curve.

9. The parametric equations of a curve are $x = 2t$, $y = 2/t$. The tangent to the curve at $P(2t, 2/t)$ meets the x-axis at A; the normal to the curve at P meets the y-axis at B. The point Q divides AB in the ratio $3:1$. Find the parametric equations of the locus of Q as P moves on the given curve.   (JMB)

10. Let P and Q be points on the rectangular hyperbola $xy = a^2$, with coordinates $(ap, a/p)$ and $(aq, a/q)$. Obtain the equation of the line PQ, and deduce, or obtain otherwise, the equation of the tangent at P to the hyperbola. Show that, if the line PQ meets the coordinate axes at A and B, then the mid-point M of AB is the mid-point of PQ also. Obtain the coordinates of the point T where the tangents at P and Q meet, and show that the line MT passes through the origin.   (W)

11. Prove that the normal to the hyperbola $xy = c^2$ at the point $P(ct, c/t)$ has equation $y = t^2x + \dfrac{c}{t} - ct^3$. If the normal at P meets the line $y = x$ at N, and O is the origin, show that $OP = PN$ provided that $t^2 \neq 1$. The tangent to the hyperbola at P meets the line $y = x$ at T. Prove that $OT.ON = 4c^2$.   (O&C)

12. The normal at the point $P(ct, c/t)$ on the rectangular hyperbola $xy = c^2$ meets the curve again at Q. If the normal meets the x-axis at A and the y-axis at B, show that the mid-point of AB is also the mid-point of PQ.

13. Show that the tangent at $P(cp, c/p)$ to the rectangular hyperbola $xy = c^2$ has the equation $p^2y + x = 2cp$. The perpendicular from the origin to this tangent meets it at N, and meets the hyperbola again at Q and R. Prove that (i) the angle QPR is a right angle, (ii) as p varies, the point N lies on the curve whose equation is $(x^2 + y^2)^2 = 4c^2xy$.   (C)

14. The tangents at the points $P(cp, c/p)$ and $Q(cq, c/q)$ on the rectangular hyperbolar $xy = c^2$ intersect at the point R. Given that R lies on the rectangular hyperbola $xy = \frac{1}{2}c^2$, find the equation of the locus of the mid-point M of PQ as p and q vary.

15. Find the equation of the tangent to the curve $ay^2 = x^3$ at the point (at^2, at^3) and prove that, apart from one exceptional case, the tangent meets the curve again. Find the coordinates of the point of intersection. What is the exceptional case?   (O&C)

16. The tangents to the curve $9y^2 = x^3$ at the points $P(9p^2, 9p^3)$ and $Q(9q^2, 9q^3)$ intersect at the point R. Find the coordinates of R. If p and q vary in such a way that $\angle PRQ$ is always a right angle, find the equation of the locus of R.

17. Show that the equation of the tangent to the curve $x = a\cos t$, $y = b\sin t$ at the point $P(a\cos p, b\sin p)$ is $\dfrac{x}{a}\cos p + \dfrac{y}{b}\sin p = 1$. This tangent meets the curve $x = 2a\cos\theta$, $y = 2b\sin\theta$ at the points Q and R, which are given by $\theta = q$ and $\theta = r$ respectively. Show that p differs from each of q and r by $\pi/3$.   (JMB)

18. Show that if the tangents to the ellipse $x^2/a + y^2/b = 1$ at the points $P(a\cos\theta, b\sin\theta)$ and $Q(a\cos\phi, b\sin\phi)$ intersect at the point R, then the coordinates of R are $\left(\dfrac{a\cos\frac{1}{2}(\theta + \phi)}{\cos\frac{1}{2}(\theta - \phi)}, \dfrac{b\sin\frac{1}{2}(\theta + \phi)}{\cos\frac{1}{2}(\theta - \phi)}\right)$. If P and Q move on the ellipse in such a way that $\phi = \theta + \frac{1}{2}\pi$, find the equation of the locus of R.

19. Find the equation of the normal to the curve $x^2 - y^2 = 1$ at the point $P(\sec\theta, \tan\theta)$, where $-\frac{1}{2}\pi < \theta < \frac{1}{2}\pi$. If this normal cuts the x-axis at A and the y-axis at B, show that P is the centre of the circle which passes through A, B and the origin O. If the line OP cuts this circle again at the point Q, find the equation of the locus of Q as θ varies.

20. (a) The points $A(d, 0)$, $B(-d, 0)$ and $P(d\cos\theta,\ d\sin\theta)$ lie on the circle $x^2 + y^2 = d^2$. Show that the equation of the tangent to the circle at P is $x\cos\theta + y\sin\theta = d$. Show that the sum of the perpendicular distances from A and B to this tangent is independent of θ, and calculate the product of these distances.
(b) The point $P(p, p^3)$ lies on the curve $y = x^3$. Show that the equation of the tangent to the curve at P is $y - 3p^2x + 2p^3 = 0$. Show that when $p = 3$ this tangent passes through the point $A(7/3, 9)$, and find the other two values of p for which the tangent passes through A.   (W)

21. A curve has the parametric equations $x = a(\theta - \sin\theta)$, $y = a(1 - \cos\theta)$, where $0 \le \theta \le \pi$. A point P of the curve has parameter ϕ, where $\phi \ne 0$.

(i)   Show that, at P, $\dfrac{dy}{dx} = \dfrac{\sin\phi}{1 - \cos\phi}$.

(ii) The normal to the curve at P meets the x-axis at G, and O is the origin. Show that $OG = a\phi$.

(iii) The tangent to the curve at P meets at K the line through G parallel to the y-axis. Show that $GK = 2a$.   (C)

25.4 Conic sections

Some of the curves we have been studying arise naturally as cross-sections of a circular cone. The following diagrams show the sections produced when a double cone of semi-vertical angle θ is cut by a plane which does not pass through the vertex. The nature of the curve obtained in each case is determined by the value of the angle α between the plane and the axis of the cone, where $0 \leqslant \alpha \leqslant \frac{1}{2}\pi$.

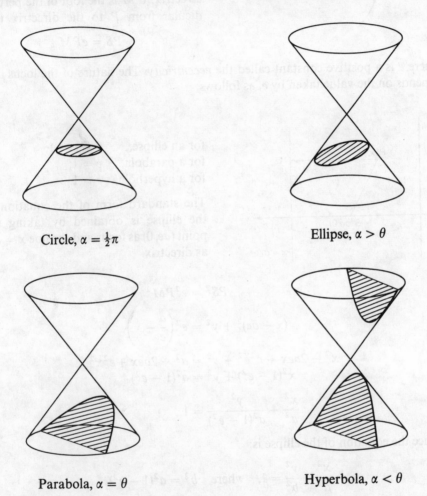

Circle, $\alpha = \frac{1}{2}\pi$ Ellipse, $\alpha > \theta$

Parabola, $\alpha = \theta$ Hyperbola, $\alpha < \theta$

The complete set of conics includes the sections produced by planes through the vertex of the double cone, namely:

for $\alpha < \theta$, a pair of straight lines;
for $\alpha = \theta$, a single straight line;
for $\alpha > \theta$, a single point.

It can be shown that the definition of a parabola as a conic section is consistent with the locus definition used in §15.4. We now consider the corresponding locus definitions of the ellipse and hyperbola.

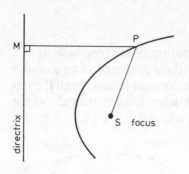

Suppose that P is a point which moves so that its distance from a fixed point S, the *focus*, is a constant multiple of its distance from a fixed line called the *directrix*. If M is the foot of the perpendicular from P to the directrix then

$$PS = ePM$$

where e is a positive constant called the *eccentricity*. The nature of the locus of P depends on the value taken by e, as follows:

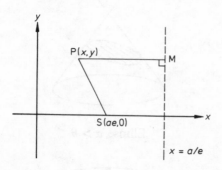

for an ellipse, $0 < e < 1$;
for a parabola, $e = 1$;
for a hyperbola, $e > 1$.

The standard form of the equation of the ellipse is obtained by taking the point $(ae, 0)$ as focus and the line $x = a/e$ as directrix.

$$PS^2 = e^2 PM^2$$

$$\therefore \qquad (x - ae)^2 + y^2 = e^2 \left(\frac{a}{e} - x \right)^2$$

$$x^2 - 2aex + a^2 e^2 + y^2 = a^2 - 2aex + e^2 x^2$$
$$x^2(1 - e^2) + y^2 = a^2(1 - e^2)$$

i.e.
$$\frac{x^2}{a^2} + \frac{y^2}{a^2(1 - e^2)} = 1$$

Hence the equation of the ellipse is:

$$\frac{x^2}{a^2} + \frac{y^2}{b^2} = 1, \quad \text{where} \quad b^2 = a^2(1 - e^2).$$

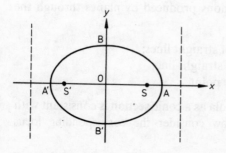

From this equation we see that the ellipse is symmetrical about both x- and y-axes. It cuts the x-axis at the points $A(a, 0)$ and $A'(-a, 0)$. It cuts the y-axis at the points $B(b, 0)$ and $B'(-b, 0)$. AA' is called the *major axis* and BB' the *minor axis*. The origin O is the *centre*

of the ellipse and any chord through O is a *diameter*. From symmetry of the curve it is clear that the same locus would have been produced using the point $S'(-ae, 0)$ as focus and the line $x = -a/e$ as directrix. Thus the ellipse is said to have foci $(\pm ae, 0)$ and directrices $x = \pm ae$.

[Note that in terms of a and b the coordinates of the foci are $(\pm\sqrt{\{a^2 - b^2\}}, 0)$ and the equations of the directrices are $x = \pm a^2/\sqrt{(a^2 - b^2)}$.]

Example 1 Find the eccentricity, the foci and the directrices of the ellipse $\dfrac{x^2}{9} + y^2 = 1$.

For the ellipse $\dfrac{x^2}{a^2} + \dfrac{y^2}{b^2} = 1$, we have $b^2 = a^2(1 - e^2)$.

Substituting $a = 3$, $b = 1$ we find that for the given ellipse,

$$1 = 9(1 - e^2)$$
$$\therefore \quad 1 = 9 - 9e^2$$
$$\therefore \quad e^2 = 8/9$$

Hence the eccentricity of the ellipse is $\tfrac{2}{3}\sqrt{2}$. Thus the foci are the points $(\pm 2\sqrt{2}, 0)$ and the directrices are the lines $x = \pm\tfrac{9}{4}\sqrt{2}$.

The standard form of the equation of the hyperbola is

$$\frac{x^2}{a^2} - \frac{y^2}{b^2} = 1, \quad \text{where} \quad b^2 = a^2(e^2 - 1).$$

Using the methods applied to the ellipse it can be shown that this hyperbola has foci $(\pm ae, 0)$ and directrices $x = \pm a/e$.

From the equation we see that the hyperbola is also symmetrical about both x- and y-axes. It cuts the x-axis at the points $A(a, 0)$ and $A'(-a, 0)$, but does not cut the y-axis.

Rearranging the equation we have:

$$\frac{y^2}{b^2} = \frac{x^2}{a^2} - 1$$

$$\therefore \quad \frac{y^2}{x^2} = \frac{b^2}{a^2} - \frac{b^2}{x^2}$$

$$\therefore \quad \text{as } |x| \to \infty, \quad \frac{y^2}{x^2} \to \frac{b^2}{a^2} \quad \text{and} \quad \frac{y}{x} \to \pm\frac{b}{a}$$

i.e. as $|x|$ increases the curve approaches the lines $y = \pm\dfrac{b}{a}x$.

Hence the lines $y = \pm\dfrac{b}{a}x$ are asymptotes to the hyperbola.

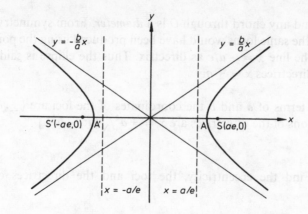

A hyperbola with perpendicular asymptotes is called a *rectangular hyperbola*. Since the lines $y = \pm \dfrac{b}{a}x$ are perpendicular when $a = b$, the equation of a rectangular hyperbola is of the form

$$x^2 - y^2 = a^2.$$

When the asymptotes are used as x- and y-axes the equation of the rectangular hyperbola takes the more familiar form $xy = c^2$.

Exercise 25.4

1. Find the eccentricities, the foci and the directrices of the following ellipses.

(a) $\dfrac{x^2}{25} + \dfrac{y^2}{9} = 1$,

(b) $16x^2 + 25y^2 = 100$,

(c) $\dfrac{x^2}{4} + y^2 = 1$,

(d) $\dfrac{x^2}{9} + \dfrac{y^2}{5} = 1$,

(e) $\dfrac{x^2}{4} + \dfrac{y^2}{9} = 1$,

(f) $4x^2 + y^2 = 1$.

2. Find the eccentricities, the foci, the directrices and the asymptotes of the following hyperbolas.

(a) $\dfrac{x^2}{16} - \dfrac{y^2}{9} = 1$,

(b) $x^2 - y^2 = 4$,

(c) $x^2 - 4y^2 = 4$

3. Find the eccentricities of the following ellipses

(a) $x = 2\cos\theta,\ y = \sin\theta$,

(b) $x = 5\cos\theta,\ y = 3\sin\theta$,

(c) $x = 2\cos\theta,\ y = 3\sin\theta$,

(d) $x = 5\sin\theta,\ y = 3\cos\theta$.

4. Find in the form $x^2/a^2 + y^2/b^2 = 1$ the equations of the ellipses with
(a) eccentricity 1/2, foci $(\pm 2, 0)$, (b) eccentricity 3/5, foci $(\pm 9, 0)$.

5. Use the locus definition of the ellipse to find the equation of the ellipse with eccentricity $\frac{2}{3}$, focus $(2, 1)$ and directrix $x = -\frac{1}{2}$.

6. Find the equations of the tangent and the normal to each of the following ellipses at the given point:

(a) $\dfrac{x^2}{9} + \dfrac{y^2}{4} = 1$; $(3, 0)$,

(b) $\dfrac{x^2}{8} + \dfrac{y^2}{2} = 1$; $(-2, 1)$,

(c) $9x^2 + 16y^2 = 40$; $(2, \frac{1}{2})$,

(d) $4x^2 + 5y^2 = 120$; $(-5, -2)$.

7. Find the equations of the tangents at the point (x_1, y_1) to the following curves:

(a) $4x^2 + 9y^2 = 36$,

(b) $\dfrac{x^2}{a^2} + \dfrac{y^2}{b^2} = 1$,

(c) $\dfrac{x^2}{3} - \dfrac{y^2}{2} = 1$.

8. Use the locus definition of the hyperbola to find the equation of the hyperbola with eccentricity $\sqrt{2}$, focus $(2k, 2k)$ and directrix $x + y = k$.

9. The line $y = mx + c$ is a tangent to the ellipse $\dfrac{x^2}{a^2} + \dfrac{y^2}{b^2} - 1 = 0$, $(a > b > 0)$.

Show that $c^2 = a^2 m^2 + b^2$. The perpendicular distances from the points $(\sqrt{(a^2 - b^2)}, 0)$ and $(-\sqrt{(a^2 - b^2)}, 0)$ to any tangent to the ellipse are p_1, p_2. Show that $p_1 p_2 = b^2$.   (C)

10. A line with gradient m is drawn through the fixed point $C(h, 0)$, where $0 < h < a$, to meet the ellipse $x^2/a^2 + y^2/b^2 = 1$ at the points P and Q. Prove that the mid-point R of PQ has the coordinates $\left(\dfrac{a^2 h m^2}{a^2 m^2 + b^2}, \dfrac{-b^2 hm}{a^2 m^2 + b^2}\right)$. Show that, as m varies, R always lies on the curve whose equation is $\dfrac{x^2}{a^2} + \dfrac{y^2}{b^2} = \dfrac{hx}{a^2}$.   (C)

11. The ellipse $x^2/a^2 + y^2/b^2 = 1$ intersects the positive x-axis at A and the positive y-axis at B. Determine the equation of the perpendicular bisector of AB.
(i) Given that this line intersects the x-axis at P and that M is the mid-point of AB, prove that the area of triangle PMA is $b(a^2 + b^2)/8a$. (ii) If $a^2 = 3b^2$, find, in terms of b, the coordinates of the points where the perpendicular bisector of AB intersects the ellipse.   (JMB)

12. Prove that the hyperbola H_1, with equation $x^2 - y^2 = a^2$, cuts the hyperbola H_2, with equation $xy = c^2$, at right angles at two points P and Q. If the distance between the tangents to H_1 at P and Q is equal to the distance between the tangents to H_2 at P and Q, find the relation between a and c.   (O)

Exercise 25.5 (miscellaneous)

1.   A straight line parallel to the line $2x + y = 0$ intersects the x-axis at A and the y-axis at B. The perpendicular bisector of AB cuts the y-axis at C. Prove that the gradient of the line AC is $-\frac{3}{4}$. Find also the tangent of the acute angle between the line AC and the bisector of the angle AOB, where O is the origin.
(JMB)

2.   The triangle ABC has vertices $A(0, 12)$, $B(-9, 0)$, $C(16, 0)$. Find the equations of the internal bisectors of the angles ABC and ACB. Hence, or otherwise, find the equation of the inscribed circle of the triangle ABC. Find also the equation of the circle passing through A, B and C.
(C)

3.   Write down the perpendicular distance from the point (a, a) to the line $4x - 3y + 4 = 0$. The circle, with centre (a, a) and radius a, touches the line $4x - 3y + 4 = 0$ at the point P. Find a, and the equation of the normal to the circle at P. Show that P is the point $(1/5, 8/5)$. Show that the equation of the circle which has centre P and which passes through the origin is $5(x^2 + y^2) - 2x - 16y = 0$.
(L)

4.   Find the centre and the radius of the circle C which passes through the points $(4, 2)$, $(2, 4)$ and $(2, 6)$. If the line $y = mx$ is a tangent to C, obtain the quadratic equation satisfied by m. Hence or otherwise find the equations of the tangents to C which pass through the origin O. Find also (i) the angle between the two tangents, (ii) the equation of the circle which is the reflection of C in the line $y = 3x$.
(AEB 1977)

5.   Show that the equation of the tangent to the curve $y^2 = 4ax$ at the point $(at^2, 2at)$ is $ty = x + at^2$ and the equation of the tangent to the curve $x^2 = 4by$ at the point $(2bp, bp^2)$ is $y = px - bp^2$. The curves $y^2 = 32x$ and $x^2 = 4y$ intersect at the origin and at A. Find the equation of the common tangent to these curves and the coordinates of the points of contact B and C between the tangent and the curves. Calculate the area of the triangle ABC.
(AEB 1976)

6.   On the same diagram sketch the circles $x^2 + y^2 = 4$ and $x^2 + y^2 - 10x = 0$. The line $ax + by + 1 = 0$ is a tangent to both these circles. State the distances of the centres of the circles from this tangent. Hence, or otherwise, find the possible values of a and b and show that, if 2ϕ is the angle between the common tangents, then $\tan \phi = \frac{3}{4}$.
(L)

7.   Find the centre and radius of each of the circles C_1 and C_2 whose equations are $x^2 + y^2 - 16y + 32 = 0$ and $x^2 + y^2 - 18x + 2y + 32 = 0$ respectively and show that the circles touch externally. Find the coordinates of their point of contact and show that the common tangent at that point passes through the origin. The other tangents from the origin, one to each circle, are drawn. Find, correct to the nearest degree, the angle between these tangents.
(SU)

8. Two circles, C_1 and C_2, have equations $x^2 + y^2 - 4x - 8y - 5 = 0$ and $x^2 + y^2 - 6x - 10y + 9 = 0$, respectively. Find the x-coordinates of the points P and Q at which the line $y = 0$ cuts C_1, and show that this line touches C_2. Find the tangent of the acute angle made by the line $y = 0$ with the tangents to C_1 at P and Q. Show that, for all values of the constant λ, the circle C_3 whose equation is $\lambda(x^2 + y^2 - 4x - 8y - 5) + x^2 + y^2 - 6x - 10y + 9 = 0$ passes through the points of intersection of C_1 and C_2. Find the two possible values of λ for which the line $y = 0$ is a tangent to C_3. (JMB)

9. The circles whose equations are $\quad x^2 + y^2 - x + 6y + 7 = 0$

$$\text{and} \quad x^2 + y^2 + 2x + 2y - 2 = 0$$

intersect at the points A and B. Find (i) the equation of the line AB, (ii) the coordinates of A and B. Show that the two given circles intersect at right angles and obtain the equation of the circle which passes through A and B and which also passes through the centres of the two circles. (AEB 1978)

10. A curve C_1 has equation $2y^2 = x$; a curve C_2 is given by the parametric equations $x = 4t$, $y = 4/t$. Sketch C_1 and C_2 on the same diagram and calculate the coordinates of their point of intersection, P. The tangent to C_1 at P crosses the x-axis at T and meets C_2 again at Q. (a) Show that T is a point of trisection of PQ. (b) Find the area of the finite region bounded by the x-axis, the line PT and the curve C_1. (L)

11. Show that the tangent at the point P, with parameter t, on the curve $x = ct$, $y = c/t$ has equation $x + t^2y = 2ct$. This tangent meets the x-axis in a point Q and the line through P parallel to the x-axis cuts the y-axis in a point R. Show that, for any position of P on the curve, QR is a tangent to the curve with parametric equations $x = ct$, $y = c/(2t)$. (L)

12. Prove that the equation of the normal to the rectangular hyperbola $xy = c^2$ at the point $P(ct, c/t)$ is $ty - t^3x = c(1 - t^4)$. The normal at P and the normal at the point $Q(c/t, ct)$, where $t > 1$, intersect at the point N. Show that $OPNQ$ is a rhombus, where O is the origin. Hence, or otherwise, find the coordinates of N. If the tangents to the hyperbola at P and Q intersect at T, prove that the product of the lengths of OT and ON is independent of t. (JMB)

13. The line of gradient $m(\neq 0)$ through the point $A(a, O)$ is a tangent to the rectangular hyperbola $xy = c^2$ at the point P. Find m in terms of a and c, and show that the coordinates of P are $(\frac{1}{2}a, 2c^2/a)$. The line through A parallel to the y-axis meets the hyperbola at Q, and the line joining Q to the origin O intersects AP at R. Given that OQ and AP are perpendicular to each other, find the numerical value of c^2/a^2 and the numerical value of the ratio $AR:RP$. (JMB)

14. The point P in the first quadrant lies on the curve with parametric equations $x = t^2$, $y = t^3$. The tangent to the curve at P meets the curve again at Q and is normal to the curve at Q. Find the coordinates of P and of Q. (L)

15. Sketch the parabola whose parametric equations are $x = t^2$, $y = 2t$ and on the same diagram sketch the curve with parametric equations $x = 10(1 + \cos \theta)$, $y = 10 \sin \theta$. These curves touch at the origin and meet again at two other points A and B. The normals at A and B to the parabola meet at P and the tangents to the other curve at A and B meet at Q. Calculate the length of PQ. (L)

16. Obtain an equation of the tangent, at the point with parameter t, to the curve $\mathscr{C}$ whose parametric equations are given by

$$x = 2 \sin^3 t, \quad y = 2 \cos^3 t, \quad 0 \leqslant t \leqslant \pi/2.$$

Show that, if the tangent meets the coordinate axes in points R and S, then RS is of constant length. Sketch the curve $\mathscr{C}$. Find the area of the finite region enclosed by the curve $\mathscr{C}$ and the coordinate axes.

(L)

17. Sketch the curve whose parametric equations are $x = a \cos \phi$, $y = b \sin \phi$, $0 \leqslant \phi \leqslant 2\pi$, where a and b are positive constants. The point P is given by $\phi = \pi/4$. Find (a) the equation of the tangent to the curve at P, (b) the equation of the normal to the curve at P. By evaluating a suitable integral, calculate the area of the region in the first quadrant between the curve and the coordinate axes. Hence deduce the area of the region enclosed by the curve.

(L)

18. Prove that the equation of the tangent at the point (x_1, y_1) on the ellipse $\dfrac{x^2}{a^2} + \dfrac{y^2}{b^2} = 1$ is $\dfrac{xx_1}{a^2} + \dfrac{yy_1}{b^2} = 1$. The tangent at the point $(2 \cos \theta, \sqrt{3} \sin \theta)$ on the ellipse $\dfrac{x^2}{4} + \dfrac{y^2}{3} = 1$ passes through the point $P(2, 1)$. Show that $\sqrt{3} \cos \theta + \sin \theta = \sqrt{3}$. Without using tables, calculator or slide rule, find all the solutions of this equation which are in the range $0° \leqslant \theta < 360°$. Hence obtain the coordinates of the points of contact, Q and R, of the tangents to the ellipse from P. Verify that the line through the origin and the point P passes through the mid-point of the line QR.

(JMB)

19. Prove that the equation of the normal at $(\alpha \cos \phi, \beta \sin \phi)$ to the ellipse $\dfrac{x^2}{\alpha^2} + \dfrac{y^2}{\beta^2} = 1$ is $\alpha x \sec \phi - \beta y \operatorname{cosec} \phi = \alpha^2 - \beta^2$. P is the point $(a \cos \theta, b \sin \theta)$ on the ellipse $\dfrac{x^2}{a^2} + \dfrac{y^2}{b^2} = 1$. M and N are the feet of the perpendiculars from P to the axes. Find the equation of MN. Prove that, for variable θ, MN is always normal to a fixed concentric ellipse and find the equation of this ellipse. (O&C)

20. Prove that the equation of the tangent to the curve $xy^2 = c^3$ $(c > 0)$ at the point $P(ct^2, c/t)$ is $2t^3 y + x = 3ct^2$. Prove that the parameters of the points of contact of the tangents which pass through the point $Q(h, k)$ $(k \neq 0)$ satisfy a cubic equation and, by considering the turning values of this cubic, or otherwise, prove that there are three distinct tangents to the curve which pass through Q if $hk^2 < c^3$

and $h > 0$. State a necessary and sufficient condition on the parameters t_1, t_2, t_3 for the tangents at the corresponding points to be concurrent.

When Q lies on the curve, the tangent at Q cuts the curve again at R; if the parameter of Q is t, determine the parameter of R. Prove that, if the tangents Q_1, Q_2, Q_3 are concurrent and cut the curve again at R_1, R_2, R_3 then the tangents at R_1, R_2, R_3 are concurrent. (O&C)

26 Complex numbers

26.1 Algebraic form

We are already familiar with various types of real number, such as integers, rationals and irrationals. However, since the square of any non-zero real number is positive, there are no solutions within the real number system of the equations such as $x^2 + 2 = 0$ and $x^2 + 2x + 2 = 0$. To deal with these equations we must extend the number system to include the square roots of negative numbers, e.g. $\sqrt{(-1)}$, $-\sqrt{(-5)}$, $\sqrt{(-7/3)}$. Numbers of the form $\pm\sqrt{(-k^2)}$, where k is real, are called *imaginary numbers*. If the number $\sqrt{(-1)}$ is denoted by i, so that $i^2 = -1$, then any imaginary number can be expressed as a multiple of i. For instance:

$$\sqrt{(-4)} = \sqrt{\{4 \times (-1)\}} = \sqrt{4} \times \sqrt{(-1)} = 2i,$$
$$\sqrt{(-7)} = \sqrt{\{7 \times (-1)\}} = \sqrt{7} \times \sqrt{(-1)} = i\sqrt{7}.$$

The set of all numbers of the form $a + ib$, where a and b are real, is called the set of *complex numbers* and denoted by $\mathbb{C}$. The number a is called the *real part* of $a + ib$ and b is the *imaginary part* of $a + ib$. Since $a + ib$ is real when $b = 0$, the set of real numbers $\mathbb{R}$ is a subset of $\mathbb{C}$.

Let us now consider the roots of the quadratic equation $ax^2 + bx + c = 0$, given by $x = \dfrac{-b \pm \sqrt{(b^2 - 4ac)}}{2a}$. As we know, when $b^2 - 4ac \geqslant 0$, this equation has real roots, but when $b^2 - 4ac < 0$ the formula for x involves the square root of a negative number. We can write this square root as a multiple of i, thus obtaining the roots of the quadratic equations in the form of complex numbers.

Example 1 Find the roots of the equations (a) $x^2 + 9 = 0$, (b) $x^2 + 2x + 2 = 0$, (c) $2x^2 - 2x + 5 = 0$.

(a) $x^2 + 9 = 0 \implies x^2 = -9 \implies x = \pm\sqrt{(-9)} = \pm 3i$.

(b) $x^2 + 2x + 2 = 0 \Rightarrow x = \dfrac{-2 \pm \sqrt{(4-8)}}{2}$

$$= \dfrac{-2 \pm \sqrt{(-4)}}{2}$$

$$= \dfrac{-2 \pm 2i}{2} = -1 \pm i.$$

(c) $2x^2 - 2x + 5 = 0 \Rightarrow x = \dfrac{2 \pm \sqrt{(4-40)}}{4}$

$$= \dfrac{2 \pm \sqrt{(-36)}}{4}$$

$$= \dfrac{2 \pm 6i}{4} = \dfrac{1}{2} \pm \dfrac{3}{2}i.$$

Each of the equations in Example 1 has a pair of roots of the form $p \pm iq$. The numbers $p + iq$, $p - iq$ are called *conjugate complex numbers* and $p - iq$ is described as the *conjugate* of $p + iq$. Further consideration of the general formula for the roots of a quadratic equation with real coefficients shows that complex roots must always occur in conjugate pairs. Thus if $p + iq$ is one root of a given quadratic equation, then the other root is $p - iq$.

It is assumed that complex numbers can be combined according to the usual laws of algebra, together with the property $i^2 = -1$.

Example 2 Express, in the form $a + ib$, (a) $(2 - 3i) + (-1 + 4i)$, (b) $(2 - 3i) - (-1 + 4i)$, (c) $(2 - 3i)(-1 + 4i)$, (d) $(2 - 3i)(2 + 3i)$.

(a) $(2 - 3i) + (-1 + 4i) = (2 - 1) + (-3 + 4)i = 1 + i$,

(b) $(2 - 3i) - (-1 + 4i) = (2 + 1) + (-3 - 4)i = 3 - 7i$,

(c) $(2 - 3i)(-1 + 4i) \quad = -2 + 8i + 3i - 12i^2$
$$= -2 + 8i + 3i + 12 = 10 + 11i,$$

(d) $(2 - 3i)(2 + 3i) \quad = 4 + 6i - 6i - 9i^2 = 4 + 9 = 13.$

This last result illustrates the fact that the product of a pair of conjugate complex numbers is real. In general,

$$(a + ib)(a - ib) = a^2 + b^2.$$

This property is used to simplify a quotient of complex numbers.

Example 3 Express $\dfrac{-1 + 2i}{1 + 3i}$ in the form $a + ib$.

Multiplying numerator and denominator by the conjugate of $1 + 3i$:

$$\frac{(-1 + 2i)(1 - 3i)}{(1 + 3i)(1 - 3i)} = \frac{-1 + 3i + 2i - 6i^2}{1 - 3i + 3i - 9i^2} = \frac{-1 + 5i + 6}{1 + 9} = \frac{5 + 5i}{10}$$

$$\therefore \quad \frac{-1 + 2i}{1 + 3i} = \frac{1}{2} + \frac{1}{2}i$$

We next consider two *equal* complex numbers $a + ib$ and $c + id$, where a, b, c, d are real.

$$a + ib = c + id \ \Rightarrow \quad a - c = i(d - b)$$
$$\Rightarrow \ (a - c)^2 = i^2(d - b)^2$$
$$\Rightarrow \ (a - c)^2 = -(d - b)^2$$
$$\Rightarrow \quad a - c = d - b = 0$$
$$\Rightarrow \qquad a = c \quad \text{and} \quad b = d$$

Hence $a + ib$ and $c + id$ are equal if and only if $a = c$ and $b = d$. This means that if two complex numbers are known to be equal, we may equate real and imaginary parts.

Example 4 Find the square roots of the complex number $5 - 12i$, giving your answers in the form $a + ib$.

Let $\qquad (a + ib)^2 = 5 - 12i$

then $\quad a^2 - b^2 + 2abi = 5 - 12i$

Equating real and imaginary parts:

$$a^2 - b^2 = 5, \quad 2ab = -12$$
i.e. $\quad a^2 - b^2 = 5, \qquad ab = -6$

By inspection, either $a = 3, b = -2$ or $a = -3, b = 2$.

$\therefore \quad$ the square roots of $5 - 12i$ are $3 - 2i$ and $-3 + 2i$.

[Note that the equations $a^2 - b^2 = 5$, $ab = -6$ could also be solved by eliminating b to obtain a quadratic equation in a^2.]

It is often convenient to use a single letter, such as z, to represent a complex number. The complex conjugate of z is then denoted by z^* (or sometimes $\bar{z}$). The real and imaginary parts of z are denoted by $\text{Re}(z)$ and $\text{Im}(z)$ respectively.

Thus, if $z = x + iy$, $z^* = x - iy$, $\text{Re}(z) = x$ and $\text{Im}(z) = y$.

Exercise 26.1

1. Express the following in terms of i:
(a) $\sqrt{(-25)}$, \qquad (b) $\sqrt{(-5)}$, \qquad (c) $\sqrt{9} - \sqrt{(-16)}$, \quad (d) $2 - \sqrt{(-18)}$

2. Write down the roots of the following equations:
(a) $x^2 - 4 = 0$, \qquad\qquad (b) $x^2 + 4 = 0$, \qquad\qquad (c) $x^2 + 2 = 0$,
(d) $4x^2 + 9 = 0$, \qquad\qquad (e) $x^3 + 3x = 0$, \qquad\qquad (f) $x^4 - 1 = 0$.

3. Find the roots of the following equations:
(a) $x^2 - 2x + 2 = 0$, \qquad (b) $x^2 - 6x + 10 = 0$, \qquad (c) $x^2 - 4x + 13 = 0$,
(d) $4x^2 - 4x + 5 = 0$, \qquad (e) $2x^2 + 3x + 2 = 0$, \qquad (f) $x^2 - x + 1 = 0$.

4. Write down the conjugates of the following complex numbers:
(a) $3 + 5i$, \qquad (b) $4 - 7i$, \qquad (c) $3i$, \qquad\qquad (d) -4, \qquad\qquad (e) $-1 + i$.

5. Find $z_1 + z_2$ and $z_1 - z_2$ in each of the following cases:
(a) $z_1 = 5 + 8i$, $z_2 = 2 + i$,   (b) $z_1 = 2 + 3i$, $z_2 = 1 - 4i$,
(c) $z_1 = 3 - i$, $z_2 = 5 - 3i$,   (d) $z_1 = -1 + 2i$, $z_2 = 3 + 5i$.

6. Express in the form $a + ib$:
(a) $(3 + i)(2 + 3i)$,   (b) $(1 - 2i)(5 + i)$,   (c) $(2 - i)(3 - 2i)$,
(d) $(3 - 4i)(3 + 4i)$,   (e) $(2 - 5i)^2$,   (f) $(1 - i)^3$.

7. Simplify (a) i^3, (b) i^5, (c) i^8, (d) $\dfrac{1}{i^2}$, (e) $\dfrac{1}{i}$, (f) $\dfrac{1}{i^3}$.

8. Express in the form $a + ib$:

(a) $\dfrac{3 + 4i}{1 - 2i}$,   (b) $\dfrac{2i}{3 + i}$,   (c) $\dfrac{3 - 2i}{1 - i}$,

(d) $\dfrac{\sqrt{3} - i}{\sqrt{3} + i}$,   (e) $\dfrac{1}{(1 + i)^2}$,   (f) $\dfrac{1}{(2 - i)(1 + 2i)}$.

9. Express in the form $a + ib$:

(a) $\dfrac{1}{2 + 3i} + \dfrac{1}{2 - 3i}$,   (b) $\dfrac{1}{3 + i} - \dfrac{1}{1 + 7i}$,   (c) $3 + 4i + \dfrac{25}{3 + 4i}$.

10. Find the values of a and b given that
(a) $(a + ib)(2 - i) = a + 3i$,   (b) $(a + i)(1 + ib) = 3b + ia$.

11. Find the square roots of the following complex numbers
(a) $3 - 4i$,   (b) $2i$,   (c) $8 + 6i$,   (d) $21 - 20i$.

12. Find the values of real numbers p and q given that one root of the equation $x^2 + px + q = 0$ is
(a) $2 + i$,   (b) $-1 + 3i$,   (c) $4i$,   (d) $3 - 5i$.

13. Find the complex factors of the following quadratic expressions.
(a) $x^2 + 1$,   (b) $x^2 + 25$,   (c) $9x^2 + 4$,
(d) $x^2 + 2x + 5$,   (e) $x^2 + 6x + 13$,   (f) $4x^2 - 12x + 25$.

14. Given that the complex number $a + ib$ is conjugate to its own square, find all possible pairs of values of a and b.

15. Given that $\dfrac{5}{x + iy} + \dfrac{2}{1 + 3i} = 1$, where x and y are real, find x and y.

16. If $(1 + i)z - iw + i = iz + (1 - i)w - 3i = 6$, find the complex numbers z, w, expressing each in the form $a + bi$ where a, b are real.   (O&C)

17. Express $(6 + 5i)(7 + 2i)$ in the form $a + ib$. Write down $(6 - 5i)(7 - 2i)$ in a similar form. Hence find the prime factors of $32^2 + 47^2$.   (JMB)

18. The roots of the quadratic equation $z^2 + pz + q = 0$ are $1 + i$ and $4 + 3i$. Find the complex numbers p and q. It is given that $1 + i$ is also a root of the equation $z^2 + (a + 2i)z + 5 + ib = 0$, where a and b are real. Determine the values of a and b.   (JMB)

19. Given that $z = (p + i)^4$, where p is real, find the values of p for which (a) z is real, (b) z is a real multiple of i.

20. Find the two square roots of $5 + 12i$. Hence find the roots of the equation $z^2 - (1 + 6i)z - 10 = 0$.

21. Prove that for any complex number z,

$$\text{Re}(z) = \tfrac{1}{2}(z + z^*) \quad \text{and} \quad \text{Im}(z) = \frac{1}{2i}(z - z^*).$$

26.2 Roots of polynomial equations

In the previous section we saw that a quadratic equation with real coefficients has either real roots or a pair of conjugate complex roots. This result can be extended to polynomial equations of higher degree by considering further the properties of conjugate complex numbers.

For two complex numbers $z_1 = x_1 + iy_1$, $z_2 = x_2 + iy_2$, we have

$$
\begin{aligned}
(z_1 + z_2)^* &= \{(x_1 + iy_1) + (x_2 + iy_2)\}^* \\
&= \{(x_1 + x_2) + i(y_1 + y_2)\}^* \\
&= (x_1 + x_2) - i(y_1 + y_2) \\
&= (x_1 - iy_1) + (x_2 - iy_2) = z_1^* + z_2^* \\
(z_1 z_2)^* &= \{(x_1 + iy_1)(x_2 + iy_2)\}^* \\
&= \{(x_1 x_2 - y_1 y_2) + i(x_1 y_2 + x_2 y_1)\}^* \\
&= (x_1 x_2 - y_1 y_2) - i(x_1 y_2 + x_2 y_1) \\
&= (x_1 - iy_1)(x_2 - iy_2) = z_1^* z_2^*
\end{aligned}
$$

i.e.

$$\boxed{(z_1 + z_2)^* = z_1^* + z_2^*, \qquad (z_1 z_2)^* = z_1^* z_2^*}$$

It follows that $(z^2)^* = (z^*)^2$ and $(z^3)^* = (z^*)^3$.
Thus, if $f(z) = az^3 + bz^2 + cz + d$, where a, b, c, d are real, then

$$
\begin{aligned}
\{f(z)\}^* &= \{az^3 + bz^2 + cz + d\}^* \\
&= (az^3)^* + (bz^2)^* + (cz)^* + d^* \\
&= a(z^3)^* + b(z^2)^* + cz^* + d \\
&= a(z^*)^3 + b(z^*)^2 + cz^* + d = f(z^*)
\end{aligned}
$$

More generally, it can be shown that $(z^n)^* = (z^*)^n$, where n is a positive integer.

Hence if $P(z)$ is a polynomial of degree n with real coefficients, then

$$\{P(z)\}^* = P(z^*)$$

Suppose now that α is a complex root of the polynomial equation $P(z) = 0$.

$$P(\alpha) = 0 \quad \Leftrightarrow \quad \{P(\alpha)\}^* = \{0\}^* \quad \Leftrightarrow \quad P(\alpha^*) = 0$$

$\therefore$ if α is a root of the equation $P(z) = 0$, its conjugate α^* is also a root.

Thus complex roots of polynomial equations with real coefficients occur in conjugate pairs.

Much of the general theory of polynomial equations is too difficult to discuss here. However, because of its importance, we will state one basic theorem.

Every polynomial equation of degree n has exactly n roots of the form $a + ib$, where a and b are real. Some of these roots may be repeated.

If the polynomial equation $P(z) = 0$ has a real root a, then $P(z)$ has a linear factor $z - a$. Thus, if the equation $P(z) = 0$ has r real roots, then $P(z)$ has r real linear factors.

Similarly, if the equation has a complex root $a + ib$, then since $a - ib$ is also a root, the polynomial $P(z)$ has factors $z - a - ib$ and $z - a + ib$. The product of these factors is $z^2 - 2az + a^2 + b^2$, which is a quadratic factor with real coefficients. Thus, if the equation $P(z) = 0$ has k pairs of conjugate complex roots, then $P(z)$ has k real quadratic factors which cannot be split into real linear factors.

Hence any polynomial with real coefficients is a product of real linear and quadratic factors.

When solving problems it is useful to remember that the formulae for sums and products of roots of polynomial equations remain valid for equations with complex roots.

Example 1   Find the real root of the equation $3z^3 - 10z^2 + 7z + 10 = 0$ given that one root is $2 - i$.

Since $2 - i$ is a root, its complex conjugate $2 + i$ is also a root.

The equation has three roots with sum $-\dfrac{(-10)}{3}$ i.e. $\dfrac{10}{3}$

$\therefore$ the real root of the equation $= \frac{10}{3} - (2 - i + 2 + i) = -\frac{2}{3}$

One cubic equation of special interest is the equation $z^3 = 1$, whose roots are the *cube roots of unity*.

$$z^3 - 1 = 0$$

$\Rightarrow$ $\qquad\qquad (z - 1)(z^2 + z + 1) = 0$

$\Rightarrow$ $\qquad\qquad$ either $z - 1 = 0$ or $z^2 + z + 1 = 0$

Hence the complex cube roots of unity are the roots of the equation $z^2 + z + 1 = 0$. Let ω be one of these complex roots, then

$$\omega^3 = 1 \quad \text{and} \quad \omega^2 + \omega + 1 = 0.$$

But $(\omega^2)^3 = \omega^6 = (\omega^3)^2 = 1^2 = 1$,

$\therefore$ $\quad \omega^2$ must also be a complex cube root of unity.

Thus the cube roots of 1 are 1, ω, ω^2, where $\omega^3 = 1$ and $\omega^2 + \omega + 1 = 0$.

By solving the equation $z^2 + z + 1 = 0$ we find that the complex cube roots of 1 are $\frac{1}{2}(-1 \pm i\sqrt{3})$. However, when solving problems involving these roots it is often easier to use ω and its properties, rather than the numerical values of the roots.

Example 2   If ω is a complex cube root of unity, find the value of $\omega^3 + \omega^4 + \omega^5$.

Since $\omega^3 = 1$ and $\omega^2 + \omega + 1 = 0$,
$\omega^3 + \omega^4 + \omega^5 = \omega^3(1 + \omega + \omega^2) = 0.$

Example 3   Given that ω is a complex cube root of unity find the equation whose roots are i, $i\omega$, $i\omega^2$.

The roots of the required equation are given by $z = i\alpha$, where α is a cube root of unity.

$\therefore$ $\quad z^3 = (i\alpha)^3 = i^3\alpha^3 = -i$

Hence the equation with roots i, $i\omega$, $i\omega^2$ is $z^3 + i = 0$.

Exercise 26.2

1.   Prove that a number z is real if and only if $z = z^*$.

2.   Prove that if z is a complex number and k is real, $(kz)^* = kz^*$.

3.   If z_1 and z_2 are two complex numbers, prove that

(a) $(z_1 - z_2)^* = z_1^* - z_2^*$, $\qquad\qquad$ (b) if $z_2 \neq 0$, then $\left(\dfrac{z_1}{z_2}\right)^* = \dfrac{z_1^*}{z_2^*}.$

4.   Prove by induction that if z is a complex number then $(z^n)^* = (z^*)^n$, where n is a positive integer.

5. Find the real root of the equation $z^3 + z + 10 = 0$ given that one root is $1 - 2i$.

6. Given that $3 + i$ is a root of the equation $z^3 - 3z^2 - 8z + 30 = 0$, find the remaining roots.

7. Given that $1 + i$ is a root of the equation $z^3 - 2z + k = 0$, find the other two roots and the value of the real constant k.

8. Given that $2 - 3i$ is a root of the equation $z^3 + pz^2 + qz + 13 = 0$, find the other two roots and the value of the real constants p and q.

9. Show that $z = i$ is a root of the equation $z^4 + z^3 + z - 1 = 0$. Find the three other roots.

10. Show that $z = -1 + i$ is a root of the equation $z^4 - 2z^3 - z^2 + 2z + 10 = 0$. Find the remaining roots.

11. Given that $1, \omega_1, \omega_2$ are the roots of the equation $z^3 = 1$, express ω_1 and ω_2 in the form $a + ib$. Hence show that
(a) $(\omega_1)^2 = \omega_2$,   (b) $(\omega_2)^2 = \omega_1$,   (c) $1/\omega_1 = \omega_2$.

12. Express the roots of the equation $z^3 - \alpha^3 = 0$ in terms of α and ω, where ω is a complex cube root of unity. Use your answer to find the roots of the following equations in the form $a + ib$:
(a) $z^3 - 27 = 0$,   (b) $z^3 + 8 = 0$,   (c) $z^3 - i = 0$.

13. Find the roots of the following equations in the form $a + ib$:
(a) $z^3 - 8 = 0$,   (b) $z^3 + 1 = 0$,   (c) $(z + 1)^3 = 1$.

14. Evaluate the following expressions given that ω is a complex cube root of unity.

(a) $\omega + \omega^3 + \omega^5$,   (b) $\dfrac{1}{\omega^2 + \omega^4}$,   (c) $\dfrac{\omega^2}{\omega + \omega^3}$.

15. Given that ω is a complex cube root of unity, show that $\omega^* = \omega^2$. Hence write down in terms of ω the conjugates of
(a) $1 + \omega$,   (b) $1 - \omega^2$,   (c) $3 + 4\omega + 5\omega^2$.

16. Given that ω is a complex cube root of unity, simplify the expression
$$(a + b + c)(a + \omega b + \omega^2 c)(a + \omega^2 b + \omega c).$$

17. Given that $1, \omega, \omega^2$ are the cube roots of unity, find the equation whose roots are
$\dfrac{1}{3}, \dfrac{1}{2 + \omega}, \dfrac{1}{2 + \omega^2}$.

18. Given that ω denotes either one of the non-real roots of the equation $z^3 = 1$, show that (i) $1 + \omega + \omega^2 = 0$, and (ii) the other non-real root is ω^2.

Show that the non-real roots of the equation $\left(\dfrac{1-u}{u}\right)^3 = 1$ can be expressed in '

the form $A\omega$ and $B\omega^2$, where A and B are real numbers, and find A and B.

(JMB)

26.3 Geometrical representation

The complex number $z = x + iy$ is completely specified by the ordered pair of real numbers (x, y). Thus to any complex number z there corresponds a unique point $P(x, y)$ in the x, y plane. This suggests that z may be represented by

(1) the point P with coordinates (x, y),
or (2) the vector $\overrightarrow{OP}$, where O is the origin,
or (3) any vector equal to $\overrightarrow{OP}$ in magnitude and direction.

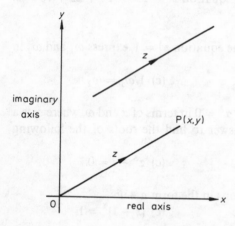

A diagram showing complex numbers represented by points or vectors is called an *Argand*[†] *diagram*.

Since real numbers are represented along the x-axis and imaginary numbers along the y-axis, in an Argand diagram these axes are often referred to as the *real axis* and the *imaginary axis* respectively.

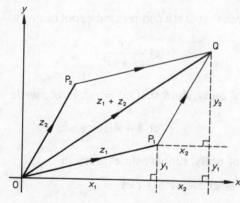

If $z_1 = x_1 + iy_1$ and $z_2 = x_2 + iy_2$, then $z_1 + z_2 = (x_1 + x_2) + i(y_1 + y_2)$. Let z_1, z_2 and $z_1 + z_2$ be represented by the vectors $\overrightarrow{OP_1}$, $\overrightarrow{OP_2}$ and $\overrightarrow{OQ}$ respectively. The diagram shows that $\overrightarrow{P_1Q}$ is equal to $\overrightarrow{OP_2}$ in magnitude and direction

$$\therefore \quad \overrightarrow{OQ} = \overrightarrow{OP_1} + \overrightarrow{P_1Q} = \overrightarrow{OP_1} + \overrightarrow{OP_2}.$$

Thus the sum of two complex numbers z_1 and z_2 is represented in an Argand diagram by the sum of the corresponding vectors $\overrightarrow{OP_1}$ and $\overrightarrow{OP_2}$.

[†] *Argand, Jean Robert* (1768–1822) Swiss mathematician. He published the geometrical representation of complex numbers in an "Essai" in 1806.

There are two ways of obtaining a geometrical representation of $z_1 - z_2$. If the complex number $(-z_2)$ is represented by the vector $\overrightarrow{OP_3}$, then $z_1 - z_2$ is represented by the sum of the vectors $\overrightarrow{OP_1}$ and $\overrightarrow{OP_3}$, as shown in diagram (i). However, since $\overrightarrow{OP_1} - \overrightarrow{OP_2} = \overrightarrow{P_2P_1}$, $z_1 - z_2$ can also be represented by $\overrightarrow{P_2P_1}$, as shown in diagram (ii).

(i)

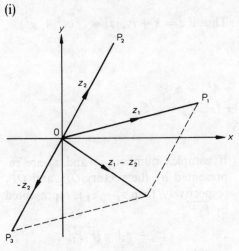

(ii)

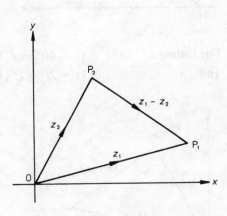

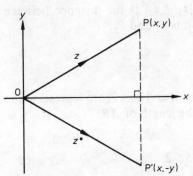

Let the complex number $z = x + iy$ and its conjugate $z^* = x - iy$ be represented by $\overrightarrow{OP}$ and $\overrightarrow{OP'}$ respectively. Since the coordinates of P and P' are (x, y) and $(x, -y)$ respectively, P' must be the reflection of P in the real axis.

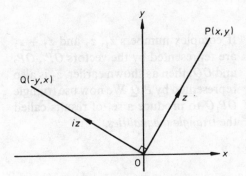

If $z = x + iy$, then

$$iz = i(x + iy) = -y + ix.$$

Thus if z and iz are represented by the vectors $\overrightarrow{OP}$ and $\overrightarrow{OQ}$, then the coordinates of P and Q are (x, y) and $(-y, x)$ respectively.

Since the gradient of OP is y/x and the gradient of OQ is $-x/y$, OP must be perpendicular to OQ. Hence multiplication of a complex number z by i results in an anti-clockwise rotation of the vector $\overrightarrow{OP}$ through $\frac{1}{2}\pi$ radians.

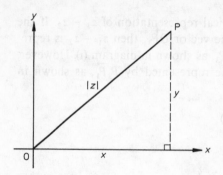

The *modulus* of a complex number z is defined as the length of the corresponding vector $\overrightarrow{OP}$ and is denoted by $|z|$.

Thus if $z = x + iy$, $|z| = \sqrt{(x^2 + y^2)}$.

For instance,
and
$$|3 + 4i| = \sqrt{\{3^2 + 4^2\}} = 5$$
$$|1 - 2i| = \sqrt{\{1^2 + (-2)^2\}} = \sqrt{5}.$$

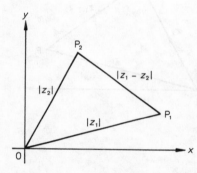

If complex numbers z_1 and z_2 are represented by the vectors $\overrightarrow{OP_1}$ and $\overrightarrow{OP_2}$ respectively, then $z_1 - z_2$ is represented by $\overrightarrow{P_2P_1}$.

$$\therefore \qquad |z_1 - z_2| = |\overrightarrow{P_2P_1}|$$

Thus $|z_1 - z_2|$ is the distance between the points P_1 and P_2.

Example 1   Given that the complex numbers $2 + 5i$ and $3 - 2i$ are represented in an Argand diagram by the points A and B, find the length of AB.

$$AB = |(2 + 5i) - (3 - 2i)|$$
$$= |-1 + 7i| = \sqrt{\{(-1)^2 + 7^2\}} = \sqrt{50} = 5\sqrt{2}.$$

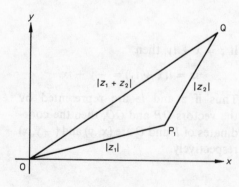

If complex numbers z_1, z_2 and $z_1 + z_2$ are represented by the vectors $\overrightarrow{OP_1}$, $\overrightarrow{OP_2}$ and $\overrightarrow{OQ}$, then as shown earlier, z_2 is also represented by $\overrightarrow{P_1Q}$. We now use triangle OP_1Q to produce a set of results called the *triangle inequalities*.

Since $OQ \leqslant OP_1 + P_1Q,$ $|z_1 + z_2| \leqslant |z_1| + |z_2|$
Since $OP_1 \leqslant P_1Q + OQ,$ $|z_1| \leqslant |z_2| + |z_1 + z_2|$
$\therefore$ $|z_1| - |z_2| \leqslant |z_1 + z_2|$

Since $P_1Q \leqslant OP_1 + OQ$, $|z_2| \leqslant |z_1| + |z_1 + z_2|$

$\therefore$ $|z_2| - |z_1| \leqslant |z_1 + z_2|$

Combining these three results, we have

$$||z_1| - |z_2|| \leqslant |z_1 + z_2| \leqslant |z_1| + |z_2|$$

[For an alternative method of proof see Exercise 26.4 question 14.]

Exercise 26.3

1.   Write down the complex numbers corresponding to the following points in an Argand diagram.
(a) $(3, 2)$,   (b) $(-2, 4)$,   (c) $(0, 5)$,   (d) $(1, -2)$,   (e) $(-2, 0)$.

2.   Represent the following complex numbers by vectors in an Argand diagram and find the modulus of the complex number in each case.
(a) $4 + 3i$,   (b) $2 - 5i$,   (c) $3i$,   (d) $-1 - i$,   (e) -4.

3.   Represent the complex number $z = 2 + i$ by a vector in an Argand diagram. Find and represent in the same diagram $-z, z^*, -z^*, iz$ and $-iz$.

4.   Represent the complex number $z = 1 + i$ by a vector in an Argand diagram. Find and represent in the same diagram z^2, z^3 and $1/z$.

5.   If $z_1 = 1 + 3i$ and $z_2 = 3 - i$, find $z_1 z_2$ and z_1/z_2 in the form $a + ib$. Show on an Argand diagram the vectors representing $z_1, z_2, z_1 z_2$ and z_1/z_2.

6.   Find and represent in an Argand diagram the square roots of
(a) -1,   (b) $-2i$,   (c) $3 + 4i$,   (d) $15 + 8i$.

7.   In each of the following cases represent z_1, z_2 and $z_1 + z_2$ in an Argand diagram and verify that

$$||z_1| - |z_2|| \leqslant |z_1 + z_2| \leqslant |z_1| + |z_2|.$$

(a) $z_1 = 12 + 5i, z_2 = -3 + 4i$,   (b) $z_1 = -1 - i, z_2 = 7 - i$.

8.   If $z_1 = 1 + 2i$, find the set of values of z_2 for which
(a) $|z_1 + z_2| = |z_1| + |z_2|$,   (b) $|z_1 + z_2| = |z_1| - |z_2|$,
(c) $|z_1 + z_2| = |z_2| - |z_1|$.

9.   If z_1 and z_2 are complex numbers, show geometrically that

$$||z_1| - |z_2|| \leqslant |z_1 - z_2| \leqslant |z_1| + |z_2|.$$

10. In each of the following cases find the distance between points in the Argand diagram representing the given pair of complex numbers.

(a) $2 + i, 5 - 3i$,   (b) $1 - 2i, 3 + 7i$,   (c) $2 - 5i, -1 - 3i$.

11. The points A, B, C and D in the Argand diagram correspond to the complex numbers $8 - i, 3 + 11i, -9 + 6i, -4 - 6i$. Prove that $ABCD$ is a square.

12. Given that $z = 1 + i\sqrt{2}$, express in the form $a + ib$ each of the complex numbers $p = z + \dfrac{1}{z}, q = z - \dfrac{1}{z}$. In an Argand diagram, P and Q are the points which represent p and q respectively, O is the origin, M is the midpoint of PQ and G is the point on OM such that $OG = \frac{2}{3}OM$. Prove that the angle PGQ is a right angle.   (JMB)

26.4 Modulus–argument form

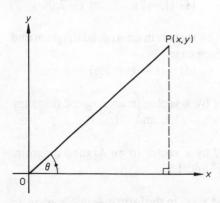

Let us suppose that a complex number $z = x + iy$ is represented in an Argand diagram by the vector $\overrightarrow{OP}$, where r is the length of $\overrightarrow{OP}$ and θ is the angle $\overrightarrow{OP}$ makes with the positive direction of the real axis.

From the diagram we see that

$$x = r\cos\theta, \qquad y = r\sin\theta,$$
$$r^2 = x^2 + y^2, \quad \tan\theta = y/x.$$

As we already know, the length r is called the modulus of z and written $|z|$,

$$\therefore \qquad \boxed{|z| = r = \sqrt{(x^2 + y^2)}}$$

The angle θ is called the *argument* of z (or less commonly, the *amplitude*), positive values of θ being measured anti-clockwise from the real axis and negative values clockwise. The problem with this definition is that for any given z there is an infinite set of possible values for θ. To avoid confusion we usually work with the value of θ for which $-\pi < \theta \leqslant \pi$. This is called the *principal argument* of z and denoted by arg z.

$$\therefore \qquad \boxed{\arg z = \theta, \quad \text{where} \quad \sin\theta = \frac{x}{r}, \qquad \cos\theta = \frac{y}{r} \quad \text{and} \quad -\pi < \theta \leqslant \pi.}$$

In practice the formula $\tan \theta = y/x$ is often used to find the principal argument of a complex number z, despite the fact that it leads to two possible values for θ in the permitted range. The correct value of arg z is then chosen with the aid of a sketch showing the approximate position of the corresponding vector $\overrightarrow{OP}$.

Example 1 Find the moduli and principal arguments of the complex numbers
(a) $1 + i$, (b) $-1 - i\sqrt{3}$, (c) -5.

(a)

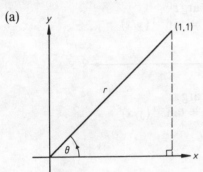

$|1 + i| = \sqrt{(1^2 + 1^2)} = \sqrt{2}$
If arg $(1 + i) = \theta$,
then $\tan \theta = \frac{1}{1} = 1 = \tan\frac{1}{4}\pi$
Since the point representing $1 + i$ lies in the first quadrant, $0 < \theta < \frac{1}{2}\pi$.

$\therefore \quad \theta = \frac{1}{4}\pi$

Hence $|1 + i| = \sqrt{2}$ and arg $(1 + i) = \frac{1}{4}\pi$.

(b)

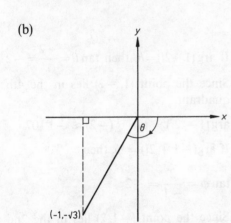

$|-1 - i\sqrt{3}| = \sqrt{\{(-1)^2 + (-\sqrt{3})^2\}}$
$= \sqrt{\{1 + 3\}} = 2$

If arg $(-1 - i\sqrt{3}) = \theta$, then

$\tan \theta = \dfrac{-\sqrt{3}}{-1} = \sqrt{3} = \tan\frac{1}{3}\pi$

Since the point representing $-1 - i\sqrt{3}$ lies in the third quadrant,

$$-\pi < \theta < -\tfrac{1}{2}\pi.$$

$\therefore \quad \theta = \tfrac{1}{3}\pi - \pi = -\tfrac{2}{3}\pi.$

Hence $|-1 - i\sqrt{3}| = 2$ and arg $(-1 - i\sqrt{3}) = -\tfrac{2}{3}\pi$.

(c)

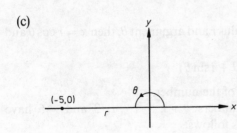

Since the point representing -5 lies on the negative part of the real axis, at a distance of 5 units from the origin, $|-5| = 5$ and arg $(-5) = \pi$.

When obtaining the argument of a complex number by calculator, care must be taken to use the inverse tangent function properly. Since this function always takes values between $-\frac{1}{2}\pi$ and $+\frac{1}{2}\pi$, it gives the correct value of arg z only when z is represented by a point in the first or fourth quadrants. When the point representing z lies in the second or third quadrants, it will be necessary to add $\pm\pi$ to the value obtained for $\tan^{-1}(y/x)$.

$$\arg z = \tan^{-1}(y/x) + \pi \qquad \arg z = \tan^{-1}(y/x)$$

$$\arg z = \tan^{-1}(y/x) - \pi \qquad \arg z = \tan^{-1}(y/x)$$

Example 2   Find in radians the principal arguments of the complex numbers $1 - 2i$ and $-1 + 2i$.

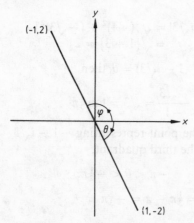

If $\arg(1-2i)=\theta$, then $\tan\theta=\dfrac{-2}{1}=-2$

Since the point $(1, -2)$ lies in the 4th quadrant,

$$\arg(1 - 2i) = \tan^{-1}(-2) \approx -1{\cdot}107$$

If $\arg(-1 + 2i) = \phi$, then

$$\tan\phi = \dfrac{2}{-1} = -2$$

Since the point $(-1, 2)$ lies in the 2nd quadrant,

$$\arg(-1 + 2i) = \tan^{-1}(-2) + \pi \approx 2{\cdot}034.$$

If a complex number $z = x + iy$ has modulus r and argument θ, then $x = r\cos\theta$ and $y = r\sin\theta$

$$\therefore \qquad z = r(\cos\theta + i\sin\theta)$$

This is called the *modulus-argument* form of the number.
Using the results of Example 1 the numbers $1 + i$, $-1 - i\sqrt{3}$ and -5 have expressions in modulus-argument form as follows:

$$1 + i = \sqrt{2}(\cos\tfrac{1}{4}\pi + i\sin\tfrac{1}{4}\pi),$$
$$-1 - i\sqrt{3} = 2\{\cos(-\tfrac{2}{3}\pi) + i\sin(-\tfrac{2}{3}\pi)\},$$
$$-5 = 5(\cos\pi + i\sin\pi).$$

Example 3   Write down the moduli and arguments of (a) $3(\cos 2\alpha + i \sin 2\alpha)$, (b) $\cos \frac{2}{3}\pi + i \sin \frac{2}{3}\pi$, (c) $a(\cos \phi - i \sin \phi)$.

(a) Since $r(\cos \theta + i \sin \theta)$ has modulus r and argument θ, $3(\cos 2\alpha + i \sin 2\alpha)$ has modulus 3 and argument 2α.

(b) Since $\cos \frac{2}{3}\pi + i \sin \frac{2}{3}\pi = 1(\cos \frac{2}{3}\pi + i \sin \frac{2}{3}\pi)$, this number has modulus 1 and argument $\frac{2}{3}\pi$.

(c) Since $a(\cos \phi - i \sin \phi) = a\{\cos(-\phi) + i \sin(-\phi)\}$, its modulus is a and its argument is $(-\phi)$.

We now investigate the general properties of complex numbers in modulus-argument form.

If $z = r(\cos \theta + i \sin \theta)$, then $z^* = r(\cos \theta - i \sin \theta)$.

$\therefore \quad zz^* = r^2(\cos \theta + i \sin \theta)(\cos \theta - i \sin \theta) = r^2(\cos^2 \theta + \sin^2 \theta) = r^2.$

Since z^* may also be written as $r\{\cos(-\theta) + i \sin(-\theta)\}$, the modulus of z^* is r and its argument is $(-\theta)$. It follows that:

$$zz^* = |z|^2, |z^*| = |z| \text{ and, for } -\pi < \arg z < \pi, \arg z^* = -\arg z.$$

If $z = r(\cos \theta + i \sin \theta)$, then $\dfrac{1}{z} = \dfrac{1}{r(\cos \theta + i \sin \theta)}$

$\therefore \quad \dfrac{1}{z} = \dfrac{\cos \theta - i \sin \theta}{r(\cos \theta + i \sin \theta)(\cos \theta - i \sin \theta)}$

$= \dfrac{\cos \theta - i \sin \theta}{r(\cos^2 \theta + \sin^2 \theta)} = \dfrac{1}{r}\{\cos(-\theta) + i \sin(-\theta)\}$

$$\left|\frac{1}{z}\right| = \frac{1}{|z|} \text{ and, for } -\pi < \arg z < \pi, \arg\left(\frac{1}{z}\right) = -\arg z.$$

If $z_1 = r_1(\cos \theta_1 + i \sin \theta_1)$ and $z_2 = r_2(\cos \theta_2 + i \sin \theta_2)$, then

$z_1 z_2 = r_1 r_2(\cos \theta_1 + i \sin \theta_1)(\cos \theta_2 + i \sin \theta_2)$
$= r_1 r_2\{(\cos \theta_1 \cos \theta_2 - \sin \theta_1 \sin \theta_2) + i(\sin \theta_1 \cos \theta_2 + \cos \theta_1 \sin \theta_2)\}$
$= r_1 r_2\{\cos(\theta_1 + \theta_2) + i \sin(\theta_1 + \theta_2)\}$

Hence $z_1 z_2$ has modulus $r_1 r_2$ and argument $\theta_1 + \theta_2$.

$\dfrac{z_1}{z_2} = \dfrac{r_1(\cos \theta_1 + i \sin \theta_1)(\cos \theta_2 - i \sin \theta_2)}{r_2(\cos \theta_2 + i \sin \theta_2)(\cos \theta_2 - i \sin \theta_2)}$

$= \dfrac{r_1\{(\cos \theta_1 \cos \theta_2 + \sin \theta_1 \sin \theta_2) + i(\sin \theta_1 \cos \theta_2 - \cos \theta_1 \sin \theta_2)\}}{r_2(\cos^2 \theta_2 + \sin^2 \theta_2)}$

$= \dfrac{r_1}{r_2}\{\cos(\theta_1 - \theta_2) + i \sin(\theta_1 - \theta_2)\}$

Hence z_1/z_2 has modulus r_1/r_2 and argument $\theta_1 - \theta_2$.

∴

$$|z_1 z_2| = |z_1||z_2| \quad \text{and} \quad \left|\frac{z_1}{z_2}\right| = \frac{|z_1|}{|z_2|}$$

If $\theta_1 = \arg z_1$ and $\theta_2 = \arg z_2$, it follows that $z_1 z_2$ has argument

$$\theta_1 + \theta_2 = \arg z_1 + \arg z_2.$$

However, since $-\pi < \theta_1 \leqslant \pi$ and $-\pi < \theta_2 \leqslant \pi$, $\theta_1 + \theta_2$ may itself lie outside the interval from $-\pi$ to π. In such cases $\arg z_1 + \arg z_2$ does not give the principal argument of $z_1 z_2$ and it is necessary to add or subtract 2π to obtain $\arg(z_1 z_2)$. Similar adjustments may be needed when finding $\arg(z_1/z_2)$.

∴

$$\arg(z_2 z_2) = \arg z_1 + \arg z_2 \ (\pm 2\pi \text{ if necessary}),$$
$$\arg(z_1/z_2) = \arg z_1 - \arg z_2 \ (\pm 2\pi \text{ if necessary}).$$

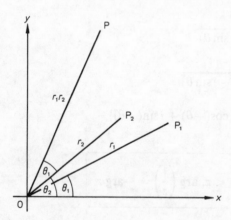

Let z_1 and z_2 be represented in an Argand diagram by the vectors $\overrightarrow{OP}_1$ and $\overrightarrow{OP}_2$ respectively. When z_2 is multiplied by z_1 the vector $\overrightarrow{OP}_2$ is rotated through an angle θ_1 and its length is multiplied by r_1 to produce the vector $\overrightarrow{OP}$ representing $z_1 z_2$.

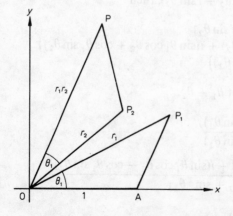

In this diagram we see that if A is the point $(1, 0)$, then triangles OAP_1 and OP_2P are similar.

[There are similar geometrical representations of the quotient z_1/z_2.]

Example 4 If $z_1 = 6(\cos\frac{5}{12}\pi + i\sin\frac{5}{12}\pi)$ and $z_2 = 3(\cos\frac{1}{4}\pi + i\sin\frac{1}{4}\pi)$, find z_1z_2 and z_1/z_2 in the form $a + ib$.

$$z_1z_2 = 6 \times 3\{\cos(\tfrac{5}{12}\pi + \tfrac{1}{4}\pi) + i\sin(\tfrac{5}{12}\pi + \tfrac{1}{4}\pi)\}$$

$$= 18\{\cos\tfrac{2}{3}\pi + i\sin\tfrac{2}{3}\pi\} = 18\left\{-\frac{1}{2} + \frac{\sqrt{3}}{2}i\right\} = -9 + 9\sqrt{3}i$$

$$\frac{z_1}{z_2} = \frac{6}{3}\{\cos(\tfrac{5}{12}\pi - \tfrac{1}{4}\pi) + i\sin(\tfrac{5}{12}\pi - \tfrac{1}{4}\pi)\}$$

$$= 2\{\cos\tfrac{1}{6}\pi + i\sin\tfrac{1}{6}\pi\} = 2\left\{\frac{\sqrt{3}}{2} + \frac{1}{2}i\right\} = \sqrt{3} + i.$$

Exercise 26.4

In questions 1 to 4 find the modulus and principal argument of each of the given complex numbers. Give the argument in radians, either as a multiple of π or correct to 3 decimal places.

1. (a) $\sqrt{3} + i$ (b) $1 - i$ (c) $4i$ (d) -3

2. (a) $3 - 4i$ (b) $-2 + i$ (c) $-1 - 3i$ (d) $5 - 3i$

3. (a) $\dfrac{10}{\sqrt{3} - i}$ (b) $\dfrac{1}{1 + i\sqrt{3}}$ (c) $\dfrac{2 + 3i}{5 + i}$ (d) $\dfrac{7 - i}{-4 - 3i}$

4. (a) $5(\cos\frac{1}{3}\pi + i\sin\frac{1}{3}\pi)$ (b) $\cos\frac{3}{2}\pi + i\sin\frac{3}{2}\pi$
    (c) $\cos\frac{2}{3}\pi - i\sin\frac{2}{3}\pi$ (d) $-2(\cos\frac{1}{4}\pi + i\sin\frac{1}{4}\pi)$

5. Express the following in the form $r(\cos\theta + i\sin\theta)$, where $r > 0$ and $-\pi < \theta \leqslant \pi$,
    (a) $\sqrt{3} - 3i$ (b) 8 (c) $-2 - 2i$ (d) $-i$

6. If $z = r(\cos\theta + i\sin\theta)$, where $r > 0$ and $0 < \theta < \frac{1}{2}\pi$, find in terms of r and θ the modulus and principal argument of
    (a) $-z$ (b) iz (c) z^2 (d) z/z^*

7. Simplify the following expressions:
    (a) $(\cos\frac{1}{4}\pi + i\sin\frac{1}{4}\pi)(\cos\frac{3}{4}\pi + i\sin\frac{3}{4}\pi)$ (b) $(\cos\frac{5}{12}\pi + i\sin\frac{5}{12}\pi)^2$
    (c) $(\cos\frac{2}{3}\pi + i\sin\frac{2}{3}\pi)(\cos\frac{7}{12}\pi + i\sin\frac{7}{12}\pi)$ (d) $(\cos\frac{2}{9}\pi + i\sin\frac{2}{9}\pi)^3$

    (e) $\dfrac{(\cos\frac{1}{3}\pi + i\sin\frac{1}{3}\pi)}{(\cos\frac{5}{6}\pi + i\sin\frac{5}{6}\pi)}$ (f) $\dfrac{(\cos\frac{1}{4}\pi + i\sin\frac{1}{4}\pi)^2}{(\cos\frac{1}{6}\pi + i\sin\frac{1}{6}\pi)}$

8. Find the moduli and principal arguments of w, z, wz and w/z, given that:
    (a) $w = 10i$, $z = 1 + i\sqrt{3}$, (b) $w = -2\sqrt{3} + 2i$, $z = 1 - i$.

9.   Given that $z = 2/(1 + \cos 2\theta - i \sin 2\theta)$, where $-\frac{1}{2}\pi < \theta < \frac{1}{2}\pi$, find expressions for $|z|$ and $\arg z$ in terms of θ.

10. Given that $z = \cos\theta + i\sin\theta$, where $0 < \theta < \pi$, find the moduli and principal arguments of $1 - z$, $z - 1$, $1/(1 - z)$, $z/(z - 1)$.

11. If $z_1 = 1 + i\sqrt{3}$ and $z_2 = 2i$, find $|z_1|$ and $\arg z_1$, $|z_2|$ and $\arg z_2$. Using an Argand diagram, deduce that $\arg(z_1 + z_2) = 5\pi/12$. Hence show that $\tan(5\pi/12) = 2 + \sqrt{3}$.

12. Two non-zero complex numbers z_1 and z_2 are such that $|z_1 + z_2| = |z_1 - z_2|$. Represent $z_1, z_2, z_1 + z_2$ and $z_1 - z_2$ by vectors on an Argand diagram. Hence, or otherwise, find the possible values of $\arg(z_1/z_2)$.   (JMB)

13. (a) Express the complex number $z = \dfrac{1 + i}{3 - 2i}$ in the form $a + bi$ $(a, b \in \mathbb{R})$, and find the argument of z, giving your answer in radians correct to 3 significiant figures. Write down the argument of z^2, and find the exact value of $|z^2|$.
(b) The conjugate of the non-zero complex number z is denoted by z^*. In an Argand diagram with origin O, the point P represents z and Q represents $1/z^*$. Prove that O, P and Q are collinear, and find the ratio $OP:OQ$ in terms of $|z|$.
(C)

14. Show that, for any complex number z, (a) $zz^* = |z|^2$, (b) $z + z^* = 2\operatorname{Re}(z)$, (c) $\operatorname{Re}(z) \leqslant |z|$. Hence show that
(i) $|z_1 + z_2|^2 = |z_1|^2 + |z_2|^2 + 2\operatorname{Re}(z_1 z_2^*)$,
(ii) $|z_1 + z_2| \leqslant |z_1| + |z_2|$.

26.5 Loci in the Argand diagram

Let us consider again a complex number $z = x + iy$ represented by the vector $\overrightarrow{OP}$, where P is the point (x, y). If z varies subject to some given condition, then the corresponding set of points in the Argand diagram is called the *locus* of P. Since many loci can be defined using either distances or angles, equations of loci in the Argand diagram often involve moduli or arguments of complex variables.

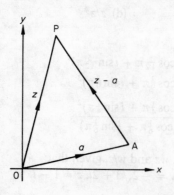
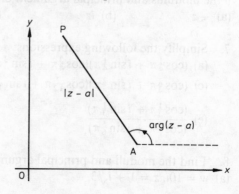

If a is constant complex number represented by a fixed vector $\overrightarrow{OA}$, then $z - a$ is represented by $\overrightarrow{AP}$. Hence $|z - a|$ is represented by the distance AP and $\arg(z - a)$ is the angle $\overrightarrow{AP}$ makes the positive direction of the real axis.

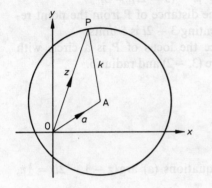

It follows that if $|z - a| = k$, where k is a positive constant, then the distance of P from A is constant. Thus

---

$|z - a| = k$ is the equation of the circle with centre at the point A and radius k.

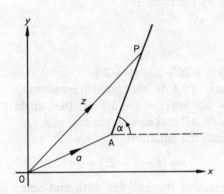

However, if $\arg(z - a) = \alpha$, where α is constant and $-\pi < \alpha \leqslant \pi$, then the direction of $\overrightarrow{AP}$ is constant. Thus

---

$\arg(z - a) = \alpha$ is the equation of a *half-line* with end-point A, inclined at an angle α to the real axis.

Example 1 Sketch the loci defined by the equations (a) $|z| = 2$, (b) $|z - 3 + 2i| = 5$.

Let z be represented in the Argand diagram by the point P.

(a)

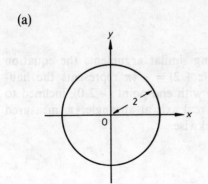

If $|z| = 2$, then the distance of P from the origin is 2 units.
Hence the locus of P is a circle with centre the origin and radius 2.

(b)

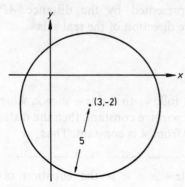

If $|z - 3 + 2i| = 5$,

then $|z - (3 - 2i)| = 5$,

i.e. the distance of P from the point representing $3 - 2i$ is 5 units.

Hence the locus of P is a circle with centre $(3, -2)$ and radius 5.

Example 2   Sketch the loci defined by the equations (a) $\arg(z - 1 - 2i) = \frac{1}{4}\pi$, (b) $\arg(z + 2) = -\frac{2}{3}\pi$.

Let z be represented in the Argand diagram by the point P.

(a)

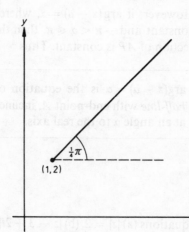

$z - 1 - 2i = z - (1 + 2i)$

Thus, if A is the point representing $1 + 2i$, $\arg(z - 1 - 2i)$ is the angle which $\overrightarrow{AP}$ makes with the real axis. Hence the equation

$$\arg(z - 1 - 2i) = \frac{1}{4}\pi$$

represents the half-line with end-point $(1, 2)$, inclined at an angle $\frac{1}{4}\pi$ to the real axis.

(b)

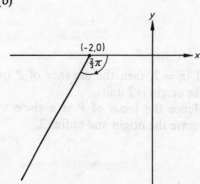

Using similar arguments the equation $\arg(z + 2) = -\frac{2}{3}\pi$ represents the half-line with end-point $(-2, 0)$, inclined to the real axis at an angle $\frac{2}{3}\pi$, measured clockwise.

Example 3   Sketch the locus of the point $P(x, y)$ representing the complex number $z = x + iy$, given that $|z - 1| = |z + i|$. Write down the Cartesian equation of the locus.

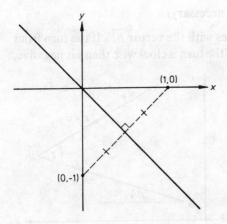

$|z - 1|$ and $|z + i|$ are the distances between the point P and the points representing 1 and $-i$ respectively. Hence the equation

$$|z - 1| = |z + i|$$

represents the locus of points equidistant from $(1, 0)$ and $(0, -1)$ i.e. the perpendicular bisector of the line joining the points $(1, 0)$ and $(0, -1)$. From the sketch it is clear that the Cartesian equation of the locus is $y = -x$.

Example 4   Find the Cartesian equation of the locus of the point $P(x, y)$ representing the complex number z, given that $2|z - 3i| = |z|$. Show that the locus is a circle, giving its centre and radius.

$$2|z - 3i| = |z| \Rightarrow \qquad 2|x + iy - 3i| = |x + iy|$$
$$\Rightarrow \qquad 2|x + i(y - 3)| = |x + iy|$$
$$\Rightarrow \qquad 4\{x^2 + (y - 3)^2\} = x^2 + y^2$$
$$\Rightarrow 4x^2 + 4y^2 - 24y + 36 = x^2 + y^2$$
$$\Rightarrow 3x^2 + 3y^2 - 24y + 36 = 0$$

Hence the Cartesian equation of the locus is

$$x^2 + y^2 - 8y + 12 = 0$$

Rearranging: $x^2 + (y - 4)^2 = 4$

This equation represents a circle with centre $(0, 4)$ and radius 2.

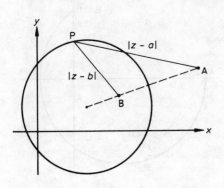

In general, if a point P moves so that the ratio of its distances from two fixed points A and B is constant, then the locus of P is a circle. This locus is referred to as Apollonius' circle and is represented in the Argand diagram by an equation of the form

$$|z - a| = k|z - b| \quad \text{or} \quad \left|\frac{z - a}{z - b}\right| = k,$$

$$(k \neq 1).$$

As shown in Example 3, when $k = 1$, the equation represents the perpendicular bisector of the line joining A to B.

Equations involving $\arg\left(\dfrac{z-a}{z-b}\right)$ are more difficult to interpret.

If $\arg(z-a) = \alpha$, $\arg(z-b) = \beta$ and $\arg\left(\dfrac{z-a}{z-b}\right) = \gamma$,

then
$$\gamma = \alpha - \beta(\pm 2\pi \text{ if necessary}).$$

Thus γ is the angle which the vector $\overrightarrow{AP}$ makes with the vector $\overrightarrow{BP}$. If the turn from $\overrightarrow{BP}$ to $\overrightarrow{AP}$ is anti-clockwise then γ is positive; if the turn is clockwise then γ is negative.

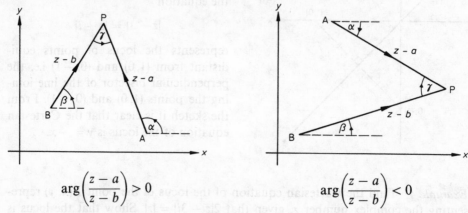

$$\arg\left(\dfrac{z-a}{z-b}\right) > 0 \qquad\qquad \arg\left(\dfrac{z-a}{z-b}\right) < 0$$

It follows that the equation $\arg\left(\dfrac{z-a}{z-b}\right) = \lambda$, where λ is constant, represents a circular arc with end-points A and B.

For instance, if $\arg\left(\dfrac{z-3}{z-1}\right) = \frac{1}{4}\pi$, then the locus of P is a circular arc with end-points $A(3,0)$ and $B(1,0)$, such that $\angle APB = \frac{1}{4}\pi$.

Similarly, if $\arg\left(\dfrac{z+2}{z-i}\right) = \frac{1}{3}\pi$, then the locus of P is a circular arc with end-points $A(-2,0)$ and $B(0,1)$, such that $\angle APB = \frac{1}{3}\pi$. Since in both cases the given arguments are positive, the arcs must be drawn so that the turn from $\overrightarrow{BP}$ to $\overrightarrow{AP}$ is anti-clockwise.

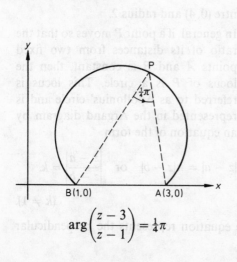

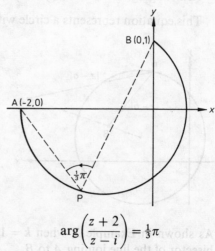

$$\arg\left(\dfrac{z-3}{z-1}\right) = \frac{1}{4}\pi \qquad\qquad \arg\left(\dfrac{z+2}{z-i}\right) = \frac{1}{3}\pi$$

We use a worked example to illustrate the use of equations involving parameters to represent loci in the Argand diagram.

Example 5   If z is represented in an Argand diagram by the point P and $z - 6i = \lambda iz$, where λ is real, find the Cartesian equation of the locus of P as λ varies.

Let $z = x + iy$, then the equation of the locus becomes

$$x + iy - 6i = \lambda i(x + iy)$$
i.e. $x + i(y - 6) = -\lambda y + i\lambda x$

Equating real and imaginary parts,

$$x = -\lambda y, \qquad y - 6 = \lambda x$$

$\therefore$ provided that $x \neq 0$ and $y \neq 0, \dfrac{x}{-y} = \dfrac{y - 6}{x} = \lambda$

i.e. $$x^2 = -y^2 + 6y$$
Hence the Cartesian equation of the locus of P is $x^2 + y^2 - 6y = 0$, which represents a circle with centre $(0, 3)$ and radius 3.

[Investigating the excluded values $x = 0, y = 0$, we find that there is no finite value of λ such that $z = 0$ satisfies the equation $z - 6i = \lambda iz$. This means that strictly speaking the origin $(0, 0)$ is not part of the locus.]

Inequalities involving the modulus or argument of a complex variable can be used to represent regions of an Argand diagram.

Example 6   Shade in separate Argand diagrams the regions in which
(a) $|z - 1 - i| < 3,$ (b) $\tfrac{1}{3}\pi \leqslant \arg(z - 2) \leqslant \pi.$

(a)

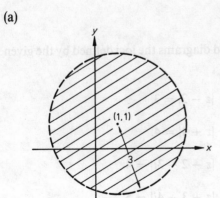

Since $z - 1 - i = z - (1 + i)$, the equation $|z - 1 - i| = 3$ represents a circle with centre $(1, 1)$ and radius 3. Hence the inequality $|z - 1 - i| < 3$ represents the interior of this circle, but not the circle itself.

(b)

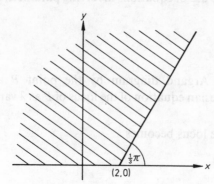

The equations $\arg(z - 2) = \frac{1}{3}\pi$ and $\arg(z - 2) = \pi$ represent half-lines with end-point $(2, 0)$. Hence the inequality

$$\tfrac{1}{3}\pi \leqslant \arg(z - 2) \leqslant \pi$$

represents these two lines and the region between them.

A geometrical approach is sometimes helpful when solving problems.

Example 7   Given that z is a complex number which varies such that $|z - i| = 1$, find the greatest and least values of $|z + 1|$.

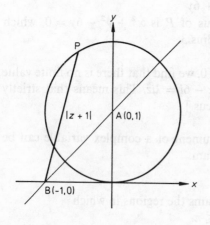

Let z be represented in an Argand diagram by the point P. Given that $|z - i| = 1$, the locus of P is a circle with centre $A(0, 1)$ and radius 1. Since $|z + 1|$ is the distance of P from the point $B(-1, 0)$, its greatest and least values occur when P lies on the straight line through A and B. As $AB = \sqrt{2}$ and the radius of the circle is 1, these greatest and least values must be $\sqrt{2} + 1$ and $\sqrt{2} - 1$.

Exercise 26.5

In questions 1 to 11 sketch in separate Argand diagrams the loci defined by the given equations.

1. (a) $|z| = 5$,   (b) $|z - 2| = 3$.

2. (a) $|z - 3i| = 2$,   (b) $|z + 4| = 4$.

3. (a) $|z - 1 + i| = 1$,   (b) $|z - 2 - 3i| = 4$.

4. (a) $|z + 1 + 2i| = 3$,   (b) $|z + 3 - 4i| = 5$.

5. (a) $\arg z = \frac{1}{4}\pi$,   (b) $\arg(z - i) = \frac{1}{3}\pi$.

6. (a) $\arg(z + 1 - 3i) = -\frac{1}{6}\pi$,   (b) $\arg(z - 3 + 2i) = \pi$.

7. (a) $\arg(z + 2 + i) = \frac{1}{2}\pi$,   (b) $\arg(z - 1 - i) = -\frac{3}{4}\pi$.

8. (a) $|z + 1| = |z - 3|$,   (b) $|z| = |z - 6i|$.

9. (a) $\left|\dfrac{z - i}{z - 1}\right| = 1$,   (b) $\left|\dfrac{z - 2 - 3i}{z + 2 + i}\right| = 1$.

10. (a) $\arg\left(\dfrac{z - 1}{z + 1}\right) = \frac{1}{3}\pi$,   (b) $\arg\left(\dfrac{z + 1}{z - 1}\right) = \frac{1}{3}\pi$.

11. (a) $\arg\left(\dfrac{z - 3}{z - 2i}\right) = \frac{1}{4}\pi$,   (b) $\arg\left(\dfrac{z}{z - 4 + 2i}\right) = \frac{1}{2}\pi$.

In questions 12 to 24 find the Cartesian equation of the locus of the point P representing the complex number z. Sketch the locus of P in each case.

12. $2|z + 1| = |z - 2|$ 13. $|z + 4i| = 3|z - 4|$

14. $\left|\dfrac{z}{z - 4}\right| = 5$ 15. $\left|\dfrac{z + i}{z - 5 - 2i}\right| = 1$

16. $\left|\dfrac{z}{z + 6}\right| = 5$ 17. $\left|\dfrac{z - 1}{z + 1 - i}\right| = \frac{2}{3}$

18. $z - 5 = \lambda i(z + 5)$, where λ is a real parameter.

19. $\dfrac{z + 2i}{z - 2} = \lambda i$, where λ is a real parameter.

20. $z = 3i + \lambda(2 + 5i)$, where λ is a real parameter.

21. $\text{Im}(z^2) = 2$ 22. $\text{Re}(z^2) = 1$

23. $\text{Re}\left(z - \dfrac{1}{z}\right) = 0$ 24. $\text{Im}\left(z + \dfrac{9}{z}\right) = 0$.

In questions 25 to 34 shade in separate Argand diagrams the regions represented by the given inequalities. Indicate in each case whether the boundaries are to be included in the region.

25. $|z| > 5$ 26. $1 \leqslant |z| \leqslant 2$

27. $|z - i| \leqslant 3$ 28. $|z - 4 + 3i| < 4$

29. $0 \leqslant \arg z \leqslant \frac{1}{3}\pi$ 30. $\frac{1}{4}\pi < \arg z < \frac{3}{4}\pi$

31. $-\frac{1}{6}\pi < \arg(z - 1) < \frac{1}{6}\pi$ 32. $-\frac{1}{2}\pi \leqslant \arg(z + i) \leqslant \frac{2}{3}\pi$

33. $|z| > |z + 2|$ 34. $|z + i| \leqslant |z - 3i|$

35. Represent each of the following loci in an Argand diagram.
(a) $\arg(z - 1) = \arg(z + 1)$,   (b) $\arg z = \arg(z - 1 - i)$,
(c) $\arg(z - 2) = \pi + \arg z$,   (d) $\arg(z - 1) = \pi + \arg(z - i)$.

36. Find the least value of $|z + 4|$ for which
(a) $\text{Re}(z) = 5$,   (b) $\text{Im}(z) = 3$,   (c) $|z| = 1$,   (d) $\arg z = \frac{1}{4}\pi$.

37. Given that the complex number z varies such that $|z - 7| = 3$, find the greatest and least values of $|z - i|$.

38. Given that the complex numbers w and z vary subject to the conditions $|w - 12| = 7$ and $|z - 5i| = 4$, find the greatest and least values of $|w - z|$.

39. In an Argand diagram, the point P represents the complex number z, where $z = x + iy$. Given that $z + 2 = \lambda i(z + 8)$, where λ is a real parameter, find the Cartesian equation of the locus of P as λ varies. If also $z = \mu(4 + 3i)$, where μ is real, prove that there is only one possible position for P.   (JMB)

40. (i) Represent on the same Argand diagram the loci given by the equations $|z - 3| = 3$ and $|z| = |z - 2|$. Obtain the complex numbers corresponding to the points of intersection of these loci. (ii) Find a complex number z whose argument is $\pi/4$ and which satisfies the equation $|z + 2 + i| = |z - 4 + i|$.   (L)

26.6 De Moivre's theorem for an integral index

In §26.4 it was shown that

$$(\cos \theta_1 + i \sin \theta_1)(\cos \theta_2 + i \sin \theta_2) = \cos(\theta_1 + \theta_2) + i \sin(\theta_1 + \theta_2).$$

Writing $\theta_1 = \theta_2 = \theta$, we find that

$$(\cos \theta + i \sin \theta)^2 = \cos 2\theta + i \sin 2\theta$$
$$(\cos \theta + i \sin \theta)^3 = (\cos 2\theta + i \sin 2\theta)(\cos \theta + i \sin \theta)$$
$$\text{Thus} \quad (\cos \theta + i \sin \theta)^3 = \cos 3\theta + i \sin 3\theta$$

These results suggest a general formula,

$$\boxed{(\cos \theta + i \sin \theta)^n = \cos n\theta + i \sin n\theta}$$

This statement, known as *De Moivre's*[†] theorem, may be proved for positive integral values of n by the method of induction.

Assuming that the theorem holds for $n = k$,

$$(\cos\theta + i\sin\theta)^k = \cos k\theta + i\sin k\theta$$

$$\therefore \quad (\cos\theta + i\sin\theta)^{k+1} = (\cos\theta + i\sin\theta)^k(\cos\theta + i\sin\theta)$$

$$= (\cos k\theta + i\sin k\theta)(\cos\theta + i\sin\theta)$$

$$= \cos(k\theta + \theta) + i\sin(k\theta + \theta)$$

$$= \cos(k+1)\theta + i\sin(k+1)\theta$$

$\therefore$ if the theorem holds for $n = k$, it also holds for $n = k + 1$.

When $n = 1$, $(\cos\theta + i\sin\theta)^n = \cos\theta + i\sin\theta$

and $\cos n\theta + i\sin n\theta = \cos\theta + i\sin\theta$

$\therefore$ the theorem holds for $n = 1$.

Hence, by induction, De Moivre's theorem holds when n is a positive integer.

Example 1   Find the value of $(\cos\frac{1}{4}\pi + i\sin\frac{1}{4}\pi)^{12}$.

By De Moivre's theorem,

$$(\cos\tfrac{1}{4}\pi + i\sin\tfrac{1}{4}\pi)^{12} = \cos(12 \times \tfrac{1}{4}\pi) + i\sin(12 \times \tfrac{1}{4}\pi)$$

$$= \cos 3\pi + i\sin 3\pi = -1.$$

Example 2   Express $(1 - i\sqrt{3})^4$ in the form $a + ib$.

$$|1 - i\sqrt{3}| = \sqrt{\{1^2 + (-\sqrt{3})^2\}} = \sqrt{\{1 + 3\}} = 2$$

If $\arg(1 - i\sqrt{3}) = \theta$, then $\tan\theta = \dfrac{-\sqrt{3}}{1} = -\sqrt{3}$

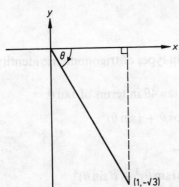

Since the point representing $1 - i\sqrt{3}$ lies in the fourth quadrant, $\arg(1 - i\sqrt{3}) = -\frac{1}{3}\pi$.

$\therefore$ $1 - i\sqrt{3} = 2\{\cos(-\frac{1}{3}\pi) + i\sin(-\frac{1}{3}\pi)\}$

By De Moivre's theorem,

$$(1 - i\sqrt{3})^4 = 2^4\{\cos(-\tfrac{1}{3}\pi) + i\sin(-\tfrac{1}{3}\pi)\}^4$$

$$= 16\{\cos(-\tfrac{4}{3}\pi) + i\sin(-\tfrac{4}{3}\pi)\} = 16\left\{-\frac{1}{2} + \frac{\sqrt{3}}{2}i\right\}$$

[†] *De Moivre, Abraham* (1667–1754) French mathematician of Huguenot extraction who settled in England, and was a friend of Newton. He published his theorem in *Miscellanea Analytica* in 1730.

Hence $(1 - i\sqrt{3})^4 = -8 + 8\sqrt{3}i$.

To prove De Moivre's theorem when n is a negative integer, let $n = -m$ where m is a positive integer, then

$$(\cos\theta + i\sin\theta)^n = (\cos\theta + i\sin\theta)^{-m}$$
$$= \frac{1}{(\cos\theta + i\sin\theta)^m}$$

Applying De Moivre's theorem for positive integral index,

$$(\cos\theta + i\sin\theta)^n = \frac{1}{\cos m\theta + i\sin m\theta}$$
$$= \cos m\theta - i\sin m\theta$$
$$= \cos(-m\theta) + i\sin(-m\theta)$$
$$= \cos n\theta + i\sin n\theta$$

Hence De Moivre's theorem holds for all integral values of n.

Example 3   Evaluate $\dfrac{1}{(1 - i\sqrt{3})^3}$.

As shown in Example 2, $1 - i\sqrt{3} = 2\{\cos(-\tfrac{1}{3}\pi) + i\sin(-\tfrac{1}{3}\pi)\}$
By De Moivre's theorem,

$$(1 - i\sqrt{3})^{-3} = 2^{-3}\{\cos(-\tfrac{1}{3}\pi) + i\sin(-\tfrac{1}{3}\pi)\}^{-3}$$
$$= \tfrac{1}{8}\{\cos[(-3)(-\tfrac{1}{3}\pi)] + i\sin[(-3)(-\tfrac{1}{3}\pi)]\}$$
$$= \tfrac{1}{8}\{\cos\pi + i\sin\pi\}$$

Hence $\dfrac{1}{(1 - i\sqrt{3})^3} = -\tfrac{1}{8}$

De Moivre's theorem may be used to obtain certain types of trigonometric identity.

Example 4   Express $\cos 4\theta$ in terms of $\cos\theta$ and $\tan 4\theta$ in terms of $\tan\theta$.

By De Moivre's theorem, $\cos 4\theta + i\sin 4\theta = (\cos\theta + i\sin\theta)^4$
Using the binomial expansion,

$$\cos 4\theta + i\sin 4\theta = \cos^4\theta + 4\cos^3\theta(i\sin\theta)$$
$$+ 6\cos^2\theta(i\sin\theta)^2 + 4\cos\theta(i\sin\theta)^3 + (i\sin\theta)^4$$
$$= (\cos^4\theta - 6\cos^2\theta\sin^2\theta + \sin^4\theta)$$
$$+ i(4\cos^3\theta\sin\theta - 4\cos\theta\sin^3\theta)$$

Equating real and imaginary parts,

$$\cos 4\theta = \cos^4\theta - 6\cos^2\theta\sin^2\theta + \sin^4\theta \tag{1}$$
$$\sin 4\theta = 4\cos^3\theta\sin\theta - 4\cos\theta\sin^3\theta \tag{2}$$

From (1): $\cos 4\theta = \cos^4\theta - 6\cos^2\theta(1 - \cos^2\theta) + (1 - \cos^2\theta)^2$
$$= \cos^4\theta - 6\cos^2\theta + 6\cos^4\theta + 1 - 2\cos^2\theta + \cos^4\theta$$
$\therefore\qquad \cos 4\theta = 8\cos^4\theta - 8\cos^2\theta + 1$

Using (1) and (2): $\tan 4\theta = \dfrac{4\cos^3\theta\sin\theta - 4\cos\theta\sin^3\theta}{\cos^4\theta - 6\cos^2\theta\sin^2\theta + \sin^4\theta}$

Dividing numerator and denominator by $\cos^4\theta$,

$$\tan 4\theta = \frac{4\tan\theta - 4\tan^3\theta}{1 - 6\tan^2\theta + \tan^4\theta}$$

Expressions for powers of $\sin\theta$ and $\cos\theta$ in terms of sines and cosines of multiples of θ can be derived using the following results.

If $\quad z = \cos\theta + i\sin\theta, \quad$ then $\quad \dfrac{1}{z} = \cos\theta - i\sin\theta$

$\therefore \quad z + \dfrac{1}{z} = 2\cos\theta \quad$ and $\quad z - \dfrac{1}{z} = 2i\sin\theta$

By De Moivre's theorem,

$$z^n = \cos n\theta + i\sin n\theta, \quad \text{so that} \quad \frac{1}{z^n} = \cos n\theta - i\sin n\theta$$

$$\boxed{z^n + \frac{1}{z^n} = 2\cos n\theta \quad \text{and} \quad z^n - \frac{1}{z^n} = 2i\sin n\theta}$$

Example 5 Express $\cos^4\theta$ in terms of cosines of multiples of θ.

$$\left(z + \frac{1}{z}\right)^4 = z^4 + 4z^3\cdot\frac{1}{z} + 6z^2\cdot\frac{1}{z^2} + 4z\cdot\frac{1}{z^3} + \frac{1}{z^4}$$

$$= z^4 + 4z^2 + 6 + \frac{4}{z^2} + \frac{1}{z^4}$$

$$= \left(z^4 + \frac{1}{z^4}\right) + 4\left(z^2 + \frac{1}{z^2}\right) + 6$$

If $z = \cos\theta + i\sin\theta$, $z^n + \dfrac{1}{z^n} = 2\cos n\theta$

$\therefore \quad (2\cos\theta)^4 = 2\cos 4\theta + 4\times 2\cos 2\theta + 6$

i.e. $\quad 16\cos^4\theta = 2\cos 4\theta + 8\cos 2\theta + 6$

Hence $\quad \cos^4\theta = \frac{1}{8}(\cos 4\theta + 4\cos 2\theta + 3)$

Exercise 26.6

1. Use De Moivre's theorem to simplify the following:

(a) $\left(\cos\dfrac{\pi}{5} + i\sin\dfrac{\pi}{5}\right)^{10}$ (b) $\left(\cos\dfrac{\pi}{8} + i\sin\dfrac{\pi}{8}\right)^{12}$

(c) $\left(\cos\dfrac{\pi}{9} + i\sin\dfrac{\pi}{9}\right)^{-3}$ (d) $\left\{\cos\left(-\dfrac{\pi}{6}\right) + i\sin\left(-\dfrac{\pi}{6}\right)\right\}^{-4}$

2. Express $\sqrt{3} + i$ in modulus-argument form. Hence find $(\sqrt{3} + i)^{10}$ and $1/(\sqrt{3} + i)^7$ in the form $a + ib$.

3. Express $-1 + i$ in modulus-argument form. Hence show that $(-1 + i)^{16}$ is real and that $1/(-1 + i)^6$ is purely imaginary, giving the value of each.

4. Simplify the following expressions:

(a) $\dfrac{\left(\cos\dfrac{2\pi}{7} - i\sin\dfrac{2\pi}{7}\right)^3}{\left(\cos\dfrac{2\pi}{7} + i\sin\dfrac{2\pi}{7}\right)^4}$ (b) $\dfrac{\left(\cos\dfrac{2\pi}{5} + i\sin\dfrac{2\pi}{5}\right)^8}{\left(\cos\dfrac{3\pi}{5} - i\sin\dfrac{3\pi}{5}\right)^3}$

5. Find expressions for $\cos 3\theta$ in terms of $\cos\theta$, $\sin 3\theta$ in terms of $\sin\theta$ and $\tan 3\theta$ in terms of $\tan\theta$.

6. Express $\sin 5\theta$ and $\cos 5\theta/\cos\theta$ in terms of $\sin\theta$.

7. Prove that $\tan 5\theta = \dfrac{5\tan\theta - 10\tan^3\theta + \tan^5\theta}{1 - 10\tan^2\theta + 5\tan^4\theta}$. By considering the equation $\tan 5\theta = 0$, show that $\tan^2(\pi/5) = 5 - 2\sqrt{5}$.

8. Find expressions for $\cos 6\theta$ and $\sin 6\theta/\sin\theta$ in terms of $\cos\theta$ and for $\tan 6\theta$ in terms of $\tan\theta$.

9. Express in terms of cosines of multiples of θ:
(a) $\cos^5\theta$ (b) $\cos^7\theta$ (c) $\sin^2\theta\cos^3\theta$

10. Express in terms of sines of multiples of θ:
(a) $\sin^3\theta$ (b) $\sin^7\theta$ (c) $\cos^4\theta\sin^3\theta$

11. Prove that $\cos^6\theta + \sin^6\theta = \frac{1}{8}(3\cos 4\theta + 5)$.

12. Evaluate (a) $\displaystyle\int_0^\pi \sin^4\theta\,d\theta$, (b) $\displaystyle\int_0^{\pi/2} \cos^4\theta\sin^2\theta\,d\theta$.

Exercise 26.7 (miscellaneous)

1. Let $z = x + iy$ be any non-zero complex number. Express $\dfrac{1}{z}$ in the form $u + iv$.

Given that $z + \dfrac{1}{z} = k$ with k real, prove that either $y = 0$ or $x^2 + y^2 = 1$. Show
(i) that if $y = 0$ then $|k| \geqslant 2$, (ii) that if $x^2 + y^2 = 1$ then $|k| \leqslant 2$.   (JMB)

2. In the quadratic equation $x^2 + (p + iq)x + 3i = 0$, p and q are real. Given that the sum of the squares of the roots is 8, find all possible pairs of values of p and q.
(JMB)

3. Express the complex number $z_1 = \dfrac{11 + 2i}{3 - 4i}$ in the form $x + iy$ where x and y are real. Given that $z_2 = 2 - 5i$, find the distance between the points in the Argand diagram which represent z_1 and z_2. Determine the real numbers α, β such that $\alpha z_1 + \beta z_2 = -4 + i$.
(JMB)

4. (i) Find two complex numbers z satisfying the equation $z^2 = -8 - 6i$.
   (ii) Solve the equation $z^2 - (3 - i)z + 4 = 0$ and represent the solutions on an Argand diagram by vectors $\overrightarrow{OA}$ and $\overrightarrow{OB}$, where O is the origin. Show that triangle OAB is right-angled.

5. If z and w are complex numbers, show that
$$|z - w|^2 + |z + w|^2 = 2\{|z|^2 + |w|^2\}.$$
Interpret your results geometrically.
(AEB 1977)

6. A regular octagon is inscribed in the circle $|z| = 1$ in the complex plane and one of its vertices represents the number $\dfrac{1}{\sqrt{2}}(1 + i)$. Find the numbers represented by the other vertices.
(AEB 1977)

7. (i) Two complex numbers z_1 and z_2 each have arguments between 0 and π. If $z_1 z_2 = i - \sqrt{3}$ and $z_1/z_2 = 2i$ find the values of z_1 and z_2 giving the modulus and argument of each.
   (ii) Obtain in the form $a + ib$ the solutions of the equation $z^2 - 2z + 5 = 0$, and represent the solutions on an Argand diagram by the points A and B.
   The equation $z^2 - 2pz + q = 0$ is such that p and q are real, and its solutions in the Argand diagram are represented by the points C and D. Find in the simplest form the algebraic relation satisfied by p and q in each of the following cases:
   (a) $p^2 < q$, $p \neq 1$ and A, B, C, D are the vertices of a rectangle;
   (b) $p^2 > q$ and $\angle CAD = \tfrac{1}{2}\pi$.
(O&C)

8. (a) If $-\pi < \arg z_1 + \arg z_2 \leqslant \pi$ show that $\arg(z_1 z_2) = \arg z_1 + \arg z_2$. The complex numbers $a = 4\sqrt{3} + 2i$ and $b = \sqrt{3} + 7i$ are represented in the Argand diagram by points A and B respectively. O is the origin. Show that triangle OAB is equilateral and find the complex number c which the point C represents where $OABC$ is a rhombus. Calculate $|c|$ and $\arg c$. (You may leave answers in surd form.)
   (b) z is a complex number such that $z = \dfrac{p}{2 - i} + \dfrac{q}{1 + 3i}$ where p and q are real. If $\arg z = \pi/2$ and $|z| = 7$ find the values of p and q.
(SU)

9. (i) Given that $z_1 = 3 + 4i$ and $z_2 = -1 + 2i$, represent z_1, z_2, $(z_1 + z_2)$ and $(z_2 - z_1)$ by vectors in the Argand diagram. Express $(z_1 + z_2)/(z_2 - z_1)$ in the form $a + ib$, where a and b are real. Find the magnitude of the angle between the vectors representing $(z_1 + z_2)$ and $(z_2 - z_1)$.

   (ii) One root of the equation $z^3 - 6z^2 + 13z + k = 0$, where k is real, is $z = 2 + i$. Find the other roots and the value of k. (L)

10. (a) Show that $(1 + 3i)^3 = -(26 + 18i)$.
   (b) Find the three roots z_1, z_2, z_3 of the equation $z^3 = -1$.
   (c) Find, in the form $a + ib$, the three roots z_1', z_2', z_3' of the equation $z^3 = 26 + 18i$.
   (d) Indicate in the same Argand diagram the points represented by z_r and z_r' for $r = 1, 2, 3$, and prove that the roots of the equations may be paired so that $|z_1 - z_1'| = |z_2 - z_2'| = |z_3 - z_3'| = 3$. (O&C)

11. Write down, or obtain, the non-real cube roots of unity, ω_1 and ω_2, in the form $a + ib$, where a and b are real. A regular hexagon is drawn in an Argand diagram such that two adjacent vertices represent ω_1 and ω_2, respectively, and the centre of the circumscribing circle of the hexagon is the point $(1, 0)$. Determine, in the form $a + ib$, the complex numbers represented by the other four vertices of the hexagon and find the product of these four complex numbers. (JMB)

12. A complex number ω is such that $\omega^3 = 1$ and $\omega \neq 1$. Show that

(i) $\omega^2 + \omega + 1 = 0$,   (ii) $(x + a + b)(x + \omega a + \omega^2 b)(x + \omega^2 a + \omega b)$

is real for real x, a and b, and simplify this product. Hence, or otherwise, find the three roots of the equation $x^3 - 6x + 6 = 0$, giving your answers in terms of ω, ω^2 and cube roots of integers. (JMB)

13. (i) Find, without the use of tables, the two square roots of $5 - 12i$ in the form $x + iy$, where x and y are real.
   (ii) Represent on an Argand diagram the loci $|z - 2| = 2$ and $|z - 4| = 2$. Calculate the complex numbers corresponding to the points of intersection of these loci. (L)

14. (i) Given that $(1 + 5i)p - 2q = 3 + 7i$, find p and q when (a) p and q are real, (b) p and q are conjugate complex numbers.
   (ii) Shade on the Argand diagram the region for which $3\pi/4 < \arg z < \pi$ and $0 < |z| < 1$. Choose a point in the region and label it A. If A represents the complex number z, label clearly the points B, C, D and E which represent $-z$, iz, $z + 1$ and z^2 respectively. (L)

15. (i) Show that $z = 1 + i$ is a root of the equation $z^4 + 3z^2 - 6z + 10 = 0$. Find the other roots of this equation.
   (ii) Sketch the curve in the Argand diagram defined by $|z - 1| = 1$, $\operatorname{Im} z \geqslant 0$. Find the value of z at the point P in which this curve is cut by the line $|z - 1| = |z - 2|$. Find also the value of $\arg z$ and $\arg(z - 2)$ at P. (L)

16. (i) If $z = 1 + i\sqrt{3}$, find $|z|$ and $|z^5|$, and also the values of $\arg z$ and $\arg(z^5)$ lying between $-\pi$ and π. Show that $\text{Re}(z^5) = 16$ and find the value of $\text{Im}(z^5)$.

(ii) Draw the line $|z| = |z - 4|$ and the half-line $\arg(z - i) = \pi/4$ in the Argand diagram. Hence find the complex number that satisfies both equations.

(L)

17. (i) Without using tables, simplify $\dfrac{\left(\cos\dfrac{\pi}{9} + i\sin\dfrac{\pi}{9}\right)^4}{\left(\cos\dfrac{\pi}{9} - i\sin\dfrac{\pi}{9}\right)^5}$.

(ii) Express $z_1 = \dfrac{7 + 4i}{3 - 2i}$ in the form $p + qi$, where p and q are real.

Sketch in an Argand diagram the locus of points representing complex numbers z such that $|z - z_1| = \sqrt{5}$. Find the greatest value of $|z|$ subject to this condition.

(L)

18. (i) Given that $z = 1 - i$, find the values of $r(>0)$ and θ, $-\pi < \theta \leqslant \pi$, such that $z = r(\cos\theta + i\sin\theta)$. Hence, or otherwise, find $1/z$ and z^6, expressing your answers in the form $p + iq$, where $p, q \in \mathbb{R}$.

(ii) Sketch on an Argand diagram the set of points corresponding to the set A, where $A = \{z : z \in \mathbb{C}, \ \arg(z - i) = \pi/4\}$. Show that the set of points corresponding to the set B, where $B = \{z : z \in \mathbb{C}, \ |z + 7i| = 2|z - 1|\}$, forms a circle in the Argand diagram. If the centre of this circle represents the numbers z_1, show that $z_1 \in A$.

(L)

19. Use De Moivre's theorem to show that

$$\cos 7\theta = 64\cos^7\theta - 112\cos^5\theta + 56\cos^3\theta - 7\cos\theta.$$

20. (i) If $(1 + 3i)z_1 = 5(1 + i)$, express z_1 and z_1^2 in the form $x + iy$, where x and y are real. Sketch in an Argand diagram the circle $|z - z_1| = |z_1|$ giving the coordinates of its centre.

(ii) If $z = \cos\theta + i\sin\theta$. show that

$$z - \frac{1}{z} = 2i\sin\theta. \qquad z^n - \frac{1}{z^n} = 2i\sin n\theta.$$

Hence, or otherwise, show that

$$16\sin^5\theta = \sin 5\theta - 5\sin 3\theta + 10\sin\theta. \qquad (L)$$

21. (i) Given that $(1 + i)^n = x + iy$. where x and y are real and n is an integer, prove that $x^2 + y^2 = 2^n$.

(ii) Given that $\left|\dfrac{z - 1}{z + 1}\right| = 2$, find the cartesian equation of the locus of z and represent the locus by a sketch in the Argand diagram. Shade the region for which the inequalities $\left|\dfrac{z-1}{z+1}\right| > 2$ and $0 < \arg z < 3\pi/4$ are both satisfied.

(L)

22. (i) Given that x and y are real, find the values of x and y which satisfy the
    equation $\dfrac{2y+4i}{2x+y} - \dfrac{y}{x-i} = 0.$

(ii) Given that $z = x + iy$, where x and y are real, (a) show that, when $\operatorname{Im}\left(\dfrac{z+i}{z+2}\right) = 0$, the point (x, y) lies on a straight line, (b) Show that, when $\operatorname{Re}\left(\dfrac{z+i}{z+2}\right) = 0$, the point (x, y) lies on a circle with centre $(-1, -\tfrac{1}{2})$ and radius $\tfrac{1}{2}\sqrt{5}$.

(L)

23. (i) Find $|z|$ and $\arg z$ for each of the complex numbers z given by (a) $12 - 5i$, (b) $(1 + 2i)/(2 - i)$, giving the argument in degrees (to the nearest degree) such that $-180° < \arg z \leqslant 180°$.

(ii) By expressing $\sqrt{3} - i$ in modulus-argument form, or otherwise, find the least positive integer n such that $(\sqrt{3} - i)^n$ is real and positive.

(iii) The point P in the Argand diagram lies outside or on the circle of radius 4 with centre at $(-1, -1)$. Write down in modulus form the condition satisfied by the complex number z represented by the point P.

(L)

24. Sketch the circle C with Cartesian equation $x^2 + (y - 1)^2 = 1$. The point P, representing the non-zero complex number z, lies on C. Express $|z|$ in terms of θ, the argument of z. Given that $z' = 1/z$, find the modulus and argument of z' in terms of θ. Show that, whatever the position of P on the circle C, the point P' representing z' lies on a certain line, the equation of which is to be determined.

(JMB)

25. (a) The sum of the infinite series $1 + z + z^2 + z^3 + \ldots$ for values of z such that $|z| < 1$ is $1/(1 - z)$. By substituting $z = \tfrac{1}{2}(\cos\theta + i\sin\theta)$ in this result and using De Moivre's theorem, or otherwise, prove that

$$\frac{1}{2}\sin\theta + \frac{1}{2^2}\sin 2\theta + \ldots + \frac{1}{2^n}\sin n\theta + \ldots = \frac{2\sin\theta}{5 - 4\cos\theta}.$$

(b) Two variable complex numbers z and w are such that $|z - i| = |z - 1|$ and $|w - 4| = 2$. Show on the same Argand diagram the loci of the points representing z and w. Mark on the diagram the points A and B representing z and w respectively for which $|z - w|$ has its least value and find this value.

(O&C)

26. The point representing the complex number z in an Argand diagram describes the circle $|z - 1| = 1$. Show that $z = 1 + \cos\theta + i\sin\theta$, where $-\pi < \theta \leqslant \pi$, and deduce that the point representing the complex number $1/z$ describes a straight line. Find the modulus and argument of z and hence, or otherwise, express

$(1 + \cos\theta + i\sin\theta)^n$ in the form $x + iy$, where n is a positive integer, and x and y are real. By writing $\cos\theta + i\sin\theta = \omega$, and using the binomial expansion of $(1 + \omega)^n$, prove that

$$1 + \binom{n}{1}\cos\theta + \binom{n}{2}\cos 2\theta + \ldots + \cos n\theta \equiv \left[2\cos\left(\frac{\theta}{2}\right)\right]^n \cos\left(\frac{n\theta}{2}\right). \quad \text{(L)}$$

Formulae for reference

Logarithms

$$x = a^p \iff \log_a x = p; \quad \log_a x = \log_b x / \log_b a.$$

Series

Sum of A.P. $= \frac{1}{2}n\{2a + (n-1)d\}$, sum of G.P. $= \dfrac{a(1-r^n)}{1-r}$

For $|r| < 1$, sum to infinity of G.P. $= a/(1-r)$

$$(a+b)^n = a^n + na^{n-1}b + \frac{n(n-1)}{2!}a^{n-2}b^2 + \cdots + \binom{n}{r}a^{n-r}b^r + \cdots + b^n,$$

where n is a positive integer.

$$\sum_1^n r = \tfrac{1}{2}n(n+1); \quad \sum_1^n r^2 = \tfrac{1}{6}n(n+1)(2n+1); \quad \sum_1^n r^3 = \tfrac{1}{4}n^2(n+1)^2$$

Trigonometry

$$\cos^2\theta + \sin^2\theta = 1; \quad 1 + \tan^2\theta = \sec^2\theta; \quad \cot^2\theta + 1 = \csc^2\theta.$$

$\sin(A+B) = \sin A \cos B + \cos A \sin B$
$\sin(A-B) = \sin A \cos B - \cos A \sin B$
$\cos(A+B) = \cos A \cos B - \sin A \sin B$
$\cos(A-B) = \cos A \cos B + \sin A \sin B$

$\tan(A+B) = \dfrac{\tan A + \tan B}{1 - \tan A \tan B}$

$\tan(A-B) = \dfrac{\tan A - \tan B}{1 + \tan A \tan B}$

$\sin 2A = 2 \sin A \cos A; \quad \tan 2A = 2 \tan A/(1 - \tan^2 A)$

$\cos 2A = \cos^2 A - \sin^2 A = 2 \cos^2 A - 1 = 1 - 2 \sin^2 A$

$\cos^2 A = \frac{1}{2}(1 + \cos 2A), \quad \sin^2 A = \frac{1}{2}(1 - \cos 2A)$

$$\sin \theta = \frac{2t}{1 + t^2}, \quad \cos \theta = \frac{1 - t^2}{1 + t^2}, \quad \tan \theta = \frac{2t}{1 - t^2}, \quad \text{where} \quad t = \tan \frac{1}{2}\theta.$$

$$2 \sin A \cos B = \sin (A + B) + \sin (A - B)$$
$$2 \cos A \cos B = \cos (A + B) + \cos (A - B)$$
$$2 \sin A \sin B = -\{\cos (A + B) - \cos (A - B)\}$$
$$\sin X + \sin Y = 2 \sin \tfrac{1}{2}(X + Y) \cos \tfrac{1}{2}(X - Y)$$
$$\sin X - \sin Y = 2 \cos \tfrac{1}{2}(X + Y) \sin \tfrac{1}{2}(X - Y)$$
$$\cos X + \cos Y = 2 \cos \tfrac{1}{2}(X + Y) \cos \tfrac{1}{2}(X - Y)$$
$$\cos X - \cos Y = -2 \sin \tfrac{1}{2}(X + Y) \sin \tfrac{1}{2}(X - Y)$$

$$\frac{a}{\sin A} = \frac{b}{\sin B} = \frac{c}{\sin C} = 2R, \quad a^2 = b^2 + c^2 - 2bc \cos A$$

Area of $\triangle ABC = \frac{1}{2}bc \sin A = \sqrt{\{s(s - a)(s - b)(s - c)\}}$,
where $s = \frac{1}{2}(a + b + c)$.

Length of circular arc $= r\theta$, area of sector $= \frac{1}{2}r^2\theta$ (θ in radians)

Calculus

$$\frac{d}{dx}(uv) = u\frac{dv}{dx} + v\frac{du}{dx}, \qquad \frac{d}{dx}\left(\frac{u}{v}\right) = \frac{v\dfrac{du}{dx} - u\dfrac{dv}{dx}}{v^2}$$

y	$\sin x$	$\cos x$	$\tan x$	$\cot x$	$\sec x$	$\operatorname{cosec} x$
dy/dx	$\cos x$	$-\sin x$	$\sec^2 x$	$-\operatorname{cosec}^2 x$	$\sec x \tan x$	$-\operatorname{cosec} x \cot x$

$$\int u\frac{dv}{dx}dx = uv - \int v\frac{du}{dx}dx$$

$$\int e^{kx}dx = \frac{1}{k}e^{kx} + c, \qquad \int \frac{dx}{ax + b} = \frac{1}{a}\ln|ax + b| + c,$$

$$\int \frac{dx}{\sqrt{(a^2 - x^2)}} = \sin^{-1}\frac{x}{a} + c, \qquad \int \frac{dx}{a^2 + x^2} = \frac{1}{a}\tan^{-1}\frac{x}{a} + c.$$

If $\dfrac{d^2y}{dx^2} + n^2 y = k$, then $y = A \cos nx + B \sin nx + \dfrac{k}{n^2}$.

If $\dfrac{d^2y}{dx^2} - n^2 y = k$, then $y = Ae^{nx} + Be^{-nx} - \dfrac{k}{n^2}$.

Expansions

$$(1 + x)^n = 1 + nx + \frac{1}{2!}n(n - 1)x^2 + \ldots + \binom{n}{r}x^r + \ldots \quad (|x| < 1)$$

$$e^x = 1 + x + \frac{x^2}{2!} + \ldots + \frac{x^r}{r!} + \ldots \qquad (\text{all } x)$$

$$\ln(1 + x) = x - \frac{x^2}{2} + \frac{x^3}{3} - \ldots + \frac{(-1)^{r+1}x^r}{r} + \ldots \qquad (-1 < x \leqslant 1)$$

$$\sin x = x - \frac{x^3}{3!} + \frac{x^5}{5!} - \ldots, \quad \cos x = 1 - \frac{x^2}{2!} + \frac{x^4}{4!} - \ldots$$

Maclaurin's series: $f(x) = f(0) + f'(0)x + \dfrac{f''(0)}{2!}x^2 + \dfrac{f'''(0)}{3!}x^3 + \ldots$

Hyperbolic functions

$$\cosh x = \tfrac{1}{2}(e^x + e^{-x}), \quad \sinh x = \tfrac{1}{2}(e^x - e^{-x})$$

$$\cosh^2 x - \sinh^2 x = 1.$$

Numerical methods

Newton-Raphson process: $x_{n+1} = x_n - \dfrac{f(x_n)}{f'(x_n)}$

Trapezium rule:

$$\int_a^b f(x)\,dx \approx \tfrac{1}{2}h\{(y_0 + y_n) + 2(y_1 + y_2 + \ldots + y_{n-1})\}$$

Simpson's rule:

$$\int_a^b f(x)\,dx \approx \tfrac{1}{3}h\{(y_0 + y_n) + 4(y_1 + y_3 + \ldots) + 2(y_2 + y_4 + \ldots)\}$$

Coordinate geometry

Point dividing line joining (x_1, y_2) to (x_2, y_2) in ratio $\mu : \lambda$ is

$$\left(\frac{\lambda x_1 + \mu x_2}{\lambda + \mu}, \ \frac{\lambda y_1 + \mu y_2}{\lambda + \mu}\right)$$

Distance of (x_1, y_1) from $ax + by + c = 0$ is $\dfrac{|ax_1 + by_1 + c|}{\sqrt{(a^2 + b^2)}}$

Area of triangle $= \frac{1}{2}|x_1(y_2 - y_3) + x_2(y_3 - y_1) + x_3(y_1 - y_2)|$

Circle: $(x - h)^2 + (y - k)^2 = a^2$, centre (h, k), radius a;
$x^2 + y^2 + 2gx + 2fy + c = 0$, centre $(-g, -f)$, radius $\sqrt{(f^2 + g^2 - c)}$.

Rectangular hyperbola: $\quad xy = c^2, \quad (ct, c/t)$

Semicubical parabola: $\quad ay^2 = x^3, \quad (at^2, at^3)$

Parabola: $\qquad\qquad\qquad y^2 = 4ax, \quad (at^2, 2at) \quad$ focus $(a, 0)$, directrix $x = -a$.

Ellipse: $\dfrac{x^2}{a^2} + \dfrac{y^2}{b^2} = 1$, $(a \cos \theta, b \sin \theta)$, where $b^2 = a^2(1 - e^2)$, $e < 1$, foci $(\pm ae, 0)$ or $(\pm\sqrt{\{a^2 - b^2\}}, 0)$, directrices $x = \pm a/e$ or $\pm a^2/\sqrt{(a^2 - b^2)}$

Hyperbola: $\dfrac{x^2}{a^2} - \dfrac{y^2}{b^2} = 1$, $(a \sec \theta, b \tan \theta)$, where $b^2 = a^2(e^2 - 1)$, $e > 1$, foci $(\pm ae, 0)$, directrices $x = \pm a/e$, asymptotes $y = \pm bx/a$

Answers

1. (a) True, (b) False, (c) True, (d) True,
   (e) False, (f) False, (g) True, (h) False.
2. $A = C$; $B \subset A$, $B \subset C$, $E \subset D$.
3. $\varnothing \subset X$, $\varnothing \subset Y$, $\varnothing \subset P$, $\varnothing \subset Q$, $X \subset Y$; $\varnothing \in Q$, $0 \in X$, $0 \in Y$, $X \in P$.
4. (a) $p \Rightarrow q$ (b) $p \Leftrightarrow q$ (c) $p \Rightarrow q$ (d) $p \neq q$.
5. (a) $X \subset Z$ (b) $X = Z$.
6. $A = \varnothing$, $B = \{2\}$, $C = \{2,3\}$, $D = \{1,2\}$.
7. (a) $(x,f), (x,g), (x,h)$, (b) $(x,p), (x,q)$, (c) $(p,x), (q,x)$, (d) (x,x).
8. $A = \{1,2,3\}$, $B = \{1,2\}$.
9. (a) $\{0,2\}$, (b) $\mathscr{E}$, (c) $\{2\}$, (d) $\varnothing$.
10. (a) True, (b) True only if $\mathscr{E} = \{\text{integers}\}$, (c) True, (d) False. A could be a subset of C.

Exercise 1.2 (pp. 4–5)

1. (a) $2, 0, -2$, (b) $2, 0, -2, 0\cdot 7, 7\cdot 3,$ (c) $\sqrt[3]{2}, \pi$ (d) $2, 0, -2, 0\cdot 7. \sqrt[3]{2}, 7\cdot 3$, (e) π.
2. (a) $7, -1$, (b) $7, -1, 4/3, 3\cdot 142$, (c) $\pi + 2, \sqrt{\pi}, \sqrt{3} + 2$,
   (d) $7, -1, 4/3, 3\cdot 142, \sqrt{3} + 2$, (e) $\pi + 2, \sqrt{\pi}$.
3. (i) (a) $\{4\}$ (b) $\{\ \}$ (c) $\{1\}$ (d) $\{\ \}$
   (ii) (a) $\{4, -1\}$ (b) $\{\ \}$ (c) $\{1\}$ (d) $\{\ \}$
   (iii) (a) $\{4, -1\}$ (b) $\{\ \}$ (c) $\{1, \frac{1}{2}\}$ (d) $\{\ \}$
   (iv) (a) $\{4, -1\}$ (b) $\{-\sqrt{5}, \sqrt{5}\}$ (c) $\{1, \frac{1}{2}\}$ (d) $\{\ \}$.
4. $\dfrac{1}{2}, \dfrac{7}{16}, \dfrac{1}{25}, \dfrac{1}{625}, \dfrac{5}{64}, \dfrac{51}{75}$.
5. (a) $\dfrac{5}{9}$, (b) $\dfrac{1}{2}$, (c) $\dfrac{3}{11}$, (d) $\dfrac{1}{27}$, (e) $\dfrac{1}{7}$.

Exercise 1.3 (pp. 6–7)

1. $-5, -\frac{1}{4}, 2, -k, n$.

2. $\frac{1}{2}, -3, -1, 5/4, x.$
3. (a) not commutative, (b) not associative.
4. (a) commutative, (b) associative.
5. (a) commutative, (b) not associative.
6. (a) 4, (b) 9, (c) 2, (d) −2, (e) −3, (f) 0 or 2.

Exercise 1.4 (p. 8)

2. (a) $x < 7$, (b) $x \geqslant 5$, (c) $x < -1$, (d) $x \leqslant 4$, (e) $x < -2$, (f) $x < -\frac{3}{4}$.
3. (a) $x < 1$, (b) $x \geqslant 8$, (c) $x < -3$, (d) $x \geqslant 7$, (e) $x \leqslant -5$ or $x \geqslant 5$,
   (f) $-6 < x < 6$.
4. (a) $-\frac{1}{2} < x < \frac{1}{2}$, (b) $-2 \leqslant x \leqslant 0$, (c) $1 < x < 2$, (d) $-\frac{1}{2} < x \leqslant 1$,
   (e) $-1 < x < 3$, (f) $-10 \leqslant x \leqslant 4$.
5. (a) False, (b) True, (c) False, (d) True, (e) False,
   (f) True, (g) False, (h) True, (i) False, (j) True.

Exercise 1.5 (pp. 11–12)

1. (a) 49, (b) 1, (c) 1/5, (d) 6, (e) 2, (f) 1/8, (g) $3\frac{1}{2}$, (h) $\frac{1}{3}$.
2. (a) 8, (b) $\frac{2}{3}$, (c) 16, (d) $\frac{1}{3}$, (e) $2\frac{7}{9}$, (f) $1\frac{1}{2}$, (g) 1, (h) 8.
3. (a) $3\sqrt{6}$, (b) $7\sqrt{2}$, (c) $6\sqrt{2}$, (d) $2\sqrt{17}$, (e) 18, (f) 2, (g) $\sqrt{3}$, (h) $\sqrt{2}$.
4. (a) $2\sqrt{5}$, (b) $5\sqrt{5}$, (c) $7\sqrt{2}$, (d) $-\sqrt{7}$.
5. (a) $\sqrt{18}$, (b) $\sqrt{125}$, (c) $\sqrt{x^2 y}$, (d) $\sqrt{4a^4 b}$.
6. (a) $2\sqrt{5}$, (b) $\dfrac{3\sqrt{7}+14}{7}$, (c) $\sqrt{15}-\sqrt{5}$, (d) $\dfrac{7+3\sqrt{5}}{4}$,
   (e) $\dfrac{17+13\sqrt{2}}{7}$, (f) $5+2\sqrt{6}$.
7. (a) $1\frac{1}{2}$, (b) $3\frac{1}{2}$, (c) −3.
8. (a) −5, (b) 1, (c) −1, (d) 2.
9. (a) 0, 3, (b) 0, 2, (c) 1, 2, (d) −1, 2, (e) 1, 2, (f) $\frac{1}{2}, -\frac{1}{2}$.
10. (a) $\sqrt{(x^4-x)}$, (b) $\sqrt{(1+x^2)}$, (c) $x(x-2)^{1/2}$, (d) $2x(2x-1)^{-1/2}$.

Exercise 1.6 (pp. 14–15)

1. (a) $\log_2 16 = 4$, (b) $\log_3 (1/9) = -2$, (c) $\log_{16} 4 = \frac{1}{2}$.
2. (a) $64 = 4^3$, (b) $0.2 = 5^{-1}$, (c) $27 = 9^{1.5}$.
3. (a) 3, (b) −2, (c) 0, (d) 1, (e) $\frac{1}{2}$.
4. (a) 2, (b) $\frac{1}{2}$, (c) −1, (d) $1\frac{1}{2}$, (e) 0.
5. (a) 4, (b) $\frac{1}{3}$, (c) $-\frac{1}{2}$, (d) $\frac{1}{2}$, (e) $-\frac{2}{3}$, (f) −3, (g) $1\frac{1}{2}$, (h) −2.
6. (a) $2\log x + \log y$, (b) $\frac{1}{2}\log x + \frac{1}{2}\log y$, (c) $4\log x - 3\log y$.
7. (a) $\log A + 2\log B - 3\log C$, (b) $\log A + \frac{1}{2}\log B + 2\log C$,
   (c) $\frac{3}{2}\log A + \log B + \frac{1}{2}\log C$.
8. (a) $\log 4$, (b) $\log 80$, (c) $\log \frac{3}{4}$, (d) $\log \frac{1}{2}$.
9. (a) 5, (b) $1\frac{1}{2}$, (c) 2.
10. (a) $1+2p+q$, (b) $5p-q$, (c) $p/(p+q)$.
11. (a) $1+2t$, (b) $1/t$, (c) $\frac{1}{2}t$, (d) $-1/t$.

12. (a) 4,   (b) 1/5.
13. (a) 3,   (b) 1.
14. (a) 9, 1/9,   (b) 2, 64,   (c) $\frac{1}{2}$, 64,   (d) 5, 25.
15. $x = 4, y = \frac{1}{2}$.

Exercise 1.7 (pp. 15–16)

1. (a) False,   (b) True,   (c) False,   (d) True.
2. (a) False,   (b) True,   (c) True,   (d) False.
3. (a) True,   (b) False,   (c) False,   (d) True.
4. (a) True,   (b) False,   (c) False,   (d) False.
5. (a) {irrational numbers},   (b) {non-negative numbers},
    (c) $\{x : x > 4\}$,   (d) $\{0\}$,   (e) $\mathbb{R}$,   (f) $\{x : x^2 \geqslant 1\}$.
6. (a) commutative,   (b) not associative.
8. (a) $x < -3$,   (b) $x \leqslant -8$,   (c) $\frac{1}{2} < x \leqslant 2$,   (d) $x > 3$ or $x < -3$,
    (e) $-7 < x < 3$,   (f) $x \leqslant 1$ or $x \geqslant 5$.
9. $2\sqrt{11}, 3\sqrt{5}, 4\sqrt{3}, 7, 5\sqrt{2}$.
10. (a) $1\frac{1}{2}$,   (b) 10,   (c) $\sqrt[3]{2}$.
11. (a) $3 + 2\sqrt{2}$,   (b) $17 - 12\sqrt{2}$,   (c) $1 - \sqrt{2}, -1 + \sqrt{2}$.
12. $x = 2, y = 0$.
13. (a) $-1\cdot89$,   (b) $0\cdot63$,   (c) $0\cdot26$ or $0\cdot37$.
14. (a) 16,   (b) 10,   (c) $\frac{1}{3}$,   (d) 2.
15. (a) -3,   (b) 2,   (c) 0.
16. (a) 4,   1/16,   (b) 1/9.

Exercise 2.1 (pp. 18–19)

1. (a) Yes,   (b) no,   (c) no.
2. (a) Yes,   (b) no,   (c) yes.
3. (a) 4, 10, 4,   (b) many-to-one,   (c) no,   (d) yes.
4. (a) 8, 38, 602,   (b) one-one,   (c) yes,   (d) no.
5. (a) 13, 343, 90301,   (b) one-one,   (c) yes,   (d) no.
6. (a) 7, 20, 352,   (b) many-to-one,   (c) yes,   (d) no.
7. $\mathbb{R}$ (a) yes,   (b) yes,   (c) yes.
8. $\{2\}$ (a) no,   (b) no,   (c) no.
9. $\mathbb{R}$ (a) yes,   (b) yes,   (c) yes.
10. $\{x \in \mathbb{R} : x \geqslant 0\}$ (a) no,   (b) no,   (c) no.
11. $\mathbb{Z}$ (a) yes,   (b) yes,   (c) yes.
12. $\mathbb{Z}$ (a) yes,   (b) yes,   (c) yes.
13. $\{x \in \mathbb{R} : x > 0\}$ (a) yes,   (b) no,   (c) no.
14. $\{x \in \mathbb{R} : x > 1\}$ (a) no,   (b) yes,   (c) no.
15. $\{1, 2, 4, 8, 16, \ldots\}$ (a) no,   (b) no,   (c) no.

Exercise 2.2 (p. 21)

1. $y = 2 - x$.
2. $y = 2x + 1$.
3. $y = 4 - x^2$.
4. $y = x^3 - 2x^2$.
5. $y = 1/x^2$.
6. $y = 1/(1 - x)$.

7. Yes; $\mathbb{R},\mathbb{R}$; one-one.
8. Yes; $\mathbb{R},\mathbb{R}$; one-one.
9. Yes; $\mathbb{R},\mathbb{R}$; one-one.
10. Yes; $\mathbb{R}$, $\{y \in \mathbb{R} : y \geqslant 4\}$; many-to-one.
11. No.
12. Yes; $\mathbb{R}$, $\{y \in \mathbb{R} : y \leqslant 1\}$; many-to-one.
13. Yes; $\mathbb{R} - \{0\}, \mathbb{R} - \{0\}$; many-to-one.
14. Yes; $\mathbb{R} - \{1\}, \mathbb{R} - \{0\}$; one-one.
15. Yes; $\mathbb{R} - \{4\}, \mathbb{R} - \{0\}$; one-one.
16. No.
17. Yes; $\{x \in \mathbb{R} : x \geqslant 0\}, \{y \in \mathbb{R} : y \geqslant 0\}$; one-one.
18. Yes; $\mathbb{R}$, $\{y \in \mathbb{R} : y \geqslant 0\}$; many-to-one.

Exercise 2.3 (pp. 24–25)

1. (a) $(0, -1)$, $(1, 0)$,   (b) $(0, 5)$, $(-2\frac{1}{2}, 0)$,   (c) $(0, 0)$, $(-3, 0)$,
    (d) $(0, -2)$, $(-2, 0)$, $(\frac{1}{2}, 0)$,   (e) $(0, -1)$,   (f) $(0, \frac{1}{2})$, $(3, 0)$.
2. (a) $(-3, 6)$,   (b) $(3, 1)$,   (c) $(2, 3)$, $(-5, 115)$,   (d) $(-2, -7)$, $(4, 35)$, $(-1, -5)$,
    (e) $(-2, 2)$, $(-1, -4)$,   (f) $(7, -6)$, $(0, 1)$.
3. (a) 15,   (b) 5,   (c) 13,   (d) 10,   (e) 17,   (f) 25,   (g) $\sqrt{13}$,   (h) $3\sqrt{5}$.
4. (a) $(6, 2\frac{1}{2})$,   (b) $(-5, -6\frac{1}{2})$,   (c) $(\frac{1}{2}, 8)$,   (d) $(8, 3)$,   (e) $(0, -2\frac{1}{2})$,
    (f) $(-\frac{1}{2}, 8)$,   (g) $(6, -2\frac{1}{2})$,   (h) $(-\frac{1}{2}, 0)$.
5. (a) $(5, 0)$,   (b) $(0, -6)$,   (c) $(1, -6)$,   (d) $(2, 1)$.
6. (a) $(9, -8)$,   (b) $(0, 1)$,   (c) $(5, 8)$,   (d) $(2, -4)$.
7. (a) isosceles,   (b) neither,   (c) right-angled,   (d) both.
9. 5.
10. 50.
11. $(9, 4)$; 126.
12. $(-4, 1)$; 80.
13. $S(7, 0)$, $T(3, -6)$.
14. 2; $(10, 5)$, 10.
15. 20.

Exercise 2.4 (pp. 27–28)

1. (a) $\frac{3}{4}$,   (b) -7,   (c) -2,   (d) $3/7$,   (e) 5,   (f) 1.
2. (a) $-4/3$,   (b) $1/7$,   (c) $\frac{1}{2}$,   (d) $-7/3$,   (e) $-1/5$,   (f) -1.
3. (a) No,   (b) yes,   (c) yes,   (d) no.
6. (a) -1,   (b) -5,   (c) 3 or -4.
7. (a) $(4, 0)$,   (b) $(9, 0)$,   (c) $(-1, 0)$.
8. $2\sqrt{10}$, $\sqrt{10}$, $\sqrt{10}$; 15 sq. units.
10. 0, -1; $7\frac{1}{2}$ sq. units, 10 sq. units.
11. 123 sq. units.

Exercise 2.5 (pp. 31–32)

1. (a) $y = 4x + 11$,   (b) $x + 2y + 4 = 0$,   (c) $3x + y = 11$,

(d) $2x-3y-11 = 0$,   (e) $5x+12y = 0$,   (f) $x-ty+t^2 = 0$.

2. (a) $y = x-7$,   (b) $2x+y = 2$,   (c) $y = 7$,   (d) $3x-4y = 0$,
    (e) $3x-7y = 15$,   (f) $x = 6$,   (g) $(p+q)y = 2x+2pq$,   (h) $x+pqy = p+q$.

3. (a) $5/2, 9/2$,   (b) $7/4, -13/4$,   (c) $-1/4, -19/8$,   (d) $1/2, -17/6$,
    (e) $0, -5/2$,   (f) $-5/9, 3$.

4. (a) $(1,1)$,   (b) $(3,2)$,   (c) $(0,-3)$,   (d) none,   (e) $(2,1)$,   (f) $(-\frac{2}{3},\frac{1}{3})$.

5. (a) perpendicular,   (b) perpendicular,   (c) neither,
    (d) parallel,   (e) perpendicular,   (f) neither.

6. (a) $y = 2x+5, x+2y = 5$,   (b) $3x+2y = 4, 3y-2x = 6$,
    (c) $x = 3, y+4 = 0$,   (d) $x-3y = 1, 3x+y+7 = 0$.

7. $(1,-2)$.   8. $(2,0)$.

9. $y = 3x+5$.   10. $y = x-5$.

12. (a) $2y+x = 13, y = 2x+9$,   (b) $(-1,7)$.

13. $(2,-4)$.   14. $B(3,-1), D(1,1)$.

15. $(-3,7)$.   16. $(-1,3), y = 7x+10$.

Exercise 2.6 (p. 34)

3. $y > -2$.

4. $x < 3$.

5. (a) $-1\frac{1}{2} < x < 6$,   (b) $0 < y < 3$,   (c) $0 < x+y < 9$.

6. (a) $-14/3 < x < 0$,   (b) $0 < y \leqslant 5$,   (c) $-14/3 < x+y < 17/4$.

Exercise 2.7 (pp. 34–35)

1. (a) $\{y \in \mathbb{R} : y \geqslant -4\}$; neither,
    (b) $\{y \in \mathbb{Q} : y = 1/n, n \in \mathbb{N}\}$; one-one,
    (c) $\mathbb{R}$; onto.

2. $-2\frac{1}{4} \leqslant y \leqslant 10$; $\{x \in \mathbb{R} : -3 \leqslant x \leqslant 0 \text{ or } 3 \leqslant x \leqslant 6\}$.

3. $A(-4,0), B(0,2); 2\sqrt{5}$.

6. $(10,-1), (2,15), (-6,-1)$.

7. (a) $y = 2x+1$,   (b) $9x+5y-2 = 0$,   (c) $4x-3y = 11$,
    (d) $5x+3y = 3$.

8. $A(2,-5), B(1,-2), C(4,13)$.

9. $(3,\frac{2}{3})$.

10. $(6,-4)$; 50 sq. units.

11. $(5,1), (-1,7), (-1,-3)$.

12. (a) $\frac{1}{2}, 8\frac{1}{2}, -3$,   (b) 25 sq. units.

13. (a) $(\frac{1}{2}\{h+3\}, \frac{1}{2}\{k+10\})$,   (b) $(k-10)/(h-3)$.

14. (a) $(6,2)$,   (b) $x+7y = 45$.

16. (a) 6,   (b) $16x-12y = 35$.

17. (a) $2x+3y = 1$,   (b) $3\sqrt{13}$.

18. (a) $(2,6)$,   (b) 20 sq. units.

19. $(0,2), 5$.

20. $(2,5), (5,3), (6,1); 19k/(2+3k)$.

Exercise 3.1 (p. 39)

1. (a) Min, -9, (b) Max, 1, (c) Min, 7/4, (d) Min, 4, (e) Min, -12,
   (f) Min, 0, (g) Max, 25/12, (h) Max, $-25/3$.
2. (a) $\{y \in \mathbb{R} : y \geqslant -5\}$, (b) $\{y \in \mathbb{R} : y \geqslant -9\}$, (c) $\{y \in \mathbb{R} : y \geqslant \frac{1}{2}\}$,
   (d) $\{y \in \mathbb{R} : y \leqslant 12\frac{1}{4}\}$.
3. $(x-2)^2 + 4$.
6. (a) $0 < x < 2$, (b) $1 \leqslant x \leqslant 5$, (c) $x \leqslant -2$ or $x \geqslant 2$,
   (d) $x < 1$ or $x > 3$, (e) $-1 < x < \frac{1}{3}$. (f) $x \leqslant -3$ or $x \geqslant -\frac{1}{2}$.
7. $-7; c > 12$.
8. $k \geqslant 9/4$.
9. (a) $-3, 8$, (b) $\frac{1}{2}, -5$, (c) 1, 3.
10. 8.

Exercise 3.2 (pp. 41–42)

1. (a) $\frac{1}{2}(3 \pm \sqrt{5})$, (b) $\frac{1}{4}(-3 \pm \sqrt{17})$, (c) $1 \pm \sqrt{2}$, (d) no real roots,
   (e) $-3/2, 9/2$, (f) $\frac{1}{2}(3 \pm \sqrt{3})$.
2. (a) $3, -2$, (b) -1.
3. (a) $p < -5$ or $p > 0$, (b) $-2 < p < 2$, (c) $p < 1$ or $p > 9$,
   (d) all real $p \neq 0$.
4. (a) $a < -1$ or $a > 0$, (b) all real $a \neq 0$, (c) $0 < a < 3$,
   (d) $a > 1$.
5. $3, -1$.
7. 3.
8. $0 < k < 1$.
9. $k \leqslant -6$ or $2 \leqslant k < 3$.

Exercise 3.3 (pp. 44–45)

1. (a) $5/2, -3/2$, (b) $1, -6$, (c) $0, -5/3$, (d) $-p, -p$, (e) 7, 5,
   (f) $\frac{3}{4}, -\frac{1}{4}$.
2. (a) $x^2 - 3x + 2 = 0$, (b) $4x^2 + 2x + 3 = 0$, (c) $x^2 - 4 = 0$,
   (d) $14x^2 - 6x - 1 = 0$, (e) $x^2 - (p-q)x + p + q = 0$,
   (f) $abx^2 - a^2x + 1 = 0$.
3. 9.   4. 4, 6.
6. (i) 3, (ii) -2, (iii) 13, (iv) 45.
7. (i) 4, (ii) 24, (iii) $2\sqrt{6}$, (iv) $-4\sqrt{6}$.
8. (a) 17/4, (b) 33/4, (c) 25/8, (d) $-1/4$, (e) 17/16, (f) 25/32.
9. $3; x^2 - 5x + 3 = 0$.   10. $x^2 \pm 11x + 28 = 0$.
11. (a) $x^2 - 12x + 18 = 0$, (b) $x^2 - 10x + 23 = 0$,
    (c) $x^2 - 16x + 56 = 0$.
12. (a) $x^2 + (2k-1)x + k^2 = 0$, (b) $x^2 - x + k = 0$,
    (c) $x^2 + 3x + (k+2) = 0$.
13. (a) $cx^2 + bx + a = 0$, (b) $a^2x^2 + 4ac - b^2 = 0$,
    (c) $b^2x^2 - b^2x + ac = 0$.
14. $2 + 2p - q, 2\frac{1}{2} + 2p - q$.   15. 0, 1.

Exercise 3.4 (p. 47)

1. (a) $(1,2)$, $(4,17)$,   (b) $(2,-1)$ repeated (i.e. tangent),
    (c) $(1,-2)$, $(2,-1)$,   (d) none,   (e) $(2,-3)$, $(-5/4,-19/2)$,
    (f) $(-5,8/3)$.
2. $4,-3$; $-3,4$.   3. $4,6$; $-4,-6$.
4. $3,-2$.   5. $3,-1$; $-2,-2$.
6. $1,2$ (repeated).   7. $3,\frac{1}{2}$; $5/3,5/2$.
8. $5,1$.   9. $1,-2$; $-2,1$.
10. $1,-1$; $\frac{1}{4},\frac{1}{2}$.   11. $6,-5$; $-5,6$.
12. $-1,5/3$; $5/2,-2/3$.
13. $2,1$; $-2,-1$; $\sqrt{3},2/\sqrt{3}$; $-\sqrt{3},-2/\sqrt{3}$.
14. $5/2,-3/2$; $-3/2,5/2$.   15. $-1,4$ (repeated).
16. $-2,0$; $-2,-2$; $2/3,2/3$; $2/3,-8/3$.
17. $\pm\sqrt{3},0$; $2,-1$; $-2,1$.
18. $0,3$ (repeated); $1+2\sqrt{2}$, $-1-\sqrt{2}$; $1-2\sqrt{2}$, $-1+\sqrt{2}$.

Exercise 3.5 (pp. 50–51)

1. (a) $2x^3+3x^2+5x+14$,   (b) $6x^4-13x^3+16x^2-17x+3$,
    (c) $4x^4+11x^3-10x^2+5x-2$,   (d) $5x^5-7x^3+3x^2+2x-3$,
    (e) $9x^5-4x^3+18x^2-8$,   (f) x^6-1.
2. (a) $-16,-7$,   (b) $7,5$,   (c) $-5,3$,   (d) $-4,5$.
3. (a) $\dfrac{3}{(1-x)(2x-5)}$,   (b) $\dfrac{x+2}{x^2-2x+4}$,   (c) x^2+x+1,   (d) $\dfrac{2x+1}{2x-3}$.
4. (a) 19,   (b) 112,   (c) 15,   (d) -16,   (e) a^2,   (f) 0.
5. (a) $3x-5$; 10,   (b) $2x^2+x+4$; 13,   (c) x^2-3x+9; -30,
    (d) x^4-2x^2+3x+1; 0,   (e) x^2-x; $5x-5$,   (f) $2x^2-x+7$; $-2x+7$.
6. (a) $(x-1)^2(2x+1)$,   (b) $(x+1)(x-2)(3x+1)$,
    (c) $(x+3)(x-3)(x^2+8)$,   (d) $x(x^4+x^2+1)$,
    (e) $(x+2)(2x-1)(2x-3)$,   (f) $(x+1)(x-2)(2x+1)(2x-1)$.
7. $2/3,7/3$.   8. $3,-6$.   9. $-5,7$.
10. $3,-5$.   11. $3,-2$.   12. $0,6,-6$.
13. $a=3$: $3(x-3)(x+1)^2$; $a=-3$: $-3(x+3)(x-1)^2$.
14. (a) 10,   (b) 3.
15. (a) $(2x-1)(2x-3)(2x-5)$,   (b) $(2x+1)^2(3x-2)$,
    (c) $(3x+2)(x^2-x+2)$.

Exercise 3.6 (pp. 53–54)

1. $-1,2,7$.   2. $1,-2,-3$.
3. $4,-1$ (repeated).   4. $-2,-2/3,-5/2$.
5. $\pm\frac{1}{2}$.   6. $\pm3,\pm\sqrt{2}$.
7. $-2,1\pm\sqrt{3}$.   8. 3.
9. $-\frac{1}{2},\pm\sqrt{3}$.   10. $2,-1,2\pm\sqrt{2}$.
11. 3.   12. 4.
13. $1,5$.   14. -4.

15. $-7, -6; 3, -2, -1.$ 16. $4; 2/3, -3/2.$

17. (a) $-3/2, 6,$ (b) $-5/2, 0,$ (c) $-4/3, 2/3,$ (d) $0, 6.$

18. $-8; a = -28, b = -32.$ 19. $\frac{1}{2}; p = -9, q = 12.$

20. (a) $6, -4,$ (b) $1/2, 3/2,$ (c) $0, 0,$ (d) $3/2, 1/2.$

21. 1 (repeated), $-3, -\frac{1}{3}.$ 22. $2, \frac{1}{2}.$

Exercise 3.7 (pp. 54–55)

1. (a) Min $(-1, -1),$ (b) Min $(-\frac{1}{4}, -3\frac{1}{8}),$ (c) Max $(\frac{1}{2}, 4),$ (d) Min $(3, 1).$

2. $x > -1.$ 3. $5, -2, \frac{1}{2}(3 \pm \sqrt{5}).$

4. (a) $0, 3,$ (b) $4, -1.$

5. $x^2 + (2q - p - p^2)x + q(p + q + 1) = 0.$

6. $3x^2 + 10x - 9 = 0.$ 7. $p = -3, q = 19.$

8. (a) $p = 7, q = -3\frac{1}{2}$ or $p = -8, q = 4.$

9. (b) $k \leqslant 0$ or $k \geqslant 3,$ (c) $k \geqslant 3.$

11. $(1\frac{1}{2}, 8).$ 12. $(k + 2, 2k\{k + 2\}).$

13. $2, -1; 3/5, 2/5.$

14. $1, 2; -1, -2; 1/2, 5/2; -1/2, -5/2.$

15. $-13, 4; (x + 1), (x + 2), (2x - 1).$

16. $-2, 2, -8.$

17. $2x^2 + 5x - 3; x = -3$ or $\frac{1}{2}.$

18. $n(n - 1)(n + 1)(n + 2).$

20. $-2 \leqslant c \leqslant 2.$

21. (a) $1, 4, -1 \pm \sqrt{5}, 1 \pm \sqrt{5},$ (b) $\frac{1}{4}b^2(b^4 + 6a^2b^2 - 3a^4).$

22. $b = 1 - a; ax^2 + (1 - a)x + 1.$

Exercise 4.1 (pp. 58–59)

1. $44 \cdot 72 < z < 47 \cdot 52; z = 46 \pm 2.$

2. $92 \cdot 885 < z < 95 \cdot 625; z = 94 \pm 2.$

3. $0 \cdot 3883 < z < 0 \cdot 3900; z = 0 \cdot 389 \pm 0 \cdot 001.$

4. $4 \cdot 000 < z < 4 \cdot 243; z = 4 \cdot 1 \pm 0 \cdot 2.$

5. (a) $10 \cdot 65, 10 \cdot 73; 10 \cdot 7,$ (b) $10 \cdot 69, 10 \cdot 77; 11.$

6. (a) $1 \cdot 691, 1 \cdot 703; 1 \cdot 7,$ (b) $1 \cdot 690, 1 \cdot 702; 1 \cdot 7.$

7. (a) $20,$ (b) $0 \cdot 0720,$ (c) $14 \cdot 3,$ (d) $12 \cdot 7.$

Exercise 4.2 (pp. 62–63)

1. (a) $f^{-1} : x \to x/3,$ (b) $f^{-1} : x \to 2x,$ (c) $f^{-1} : x \to x + 1.$
    (d) $f^{-1} : x \to 1 - x,$ (e) $f^{-1} : x \to \frac{1}{2}(x - 3),$ (f) $f^{-1} : x \to \frac{1}{4}(x + 4).$

2. (a) $y = \frac{1}{2}x,$ (b) $y = 2/x,$ (c) $y = 2 - x,$ (d) $y = x + 2,$
    (e) $y = \log_2 x,$ (f) $y = 10^x + 2.$

4. (a) $1 \cdot 172,$ (b) $64 \cdot 82,$ (c) $19\,840,$ (d) $6 \cdot 463.$

5. (a) $1 \cdot 404,$ (b) $2 \cdot 096,$ (c) $0 \cdot 4307.$

6. (a) $3 \cdot 170,$ (b) $0 \cdot 3920,$ (c) $0 \cdot 5377.$

8. (a) $1 \cdot 292,$ (b) $1 \cdot 295,$ (c) $1 \cdot 613,$ (d) $4 \cdot 962.$

9. (a) $8 \cdot 432,$ (b) $1 \cdot 453.$

10. $1 \cdot 921.$

Exercise 4.3 (pp. 67–68)

1. (a) 1·2,   (b) 3·36.
2. (a) REAL AND DISTINCT; 5, −3,   (b) REAL AND EQUAL; −0·5,
    (c) NO REAL ROOTS,   (d) REAL AND DISTINCT; 8, −0·6.

Exercise 4.4 (pp. 70–71)

1. (a) 12, −3,   (b) 3, 6,   (c) 16, 40.
2. (a) 10·52, 5·080,   (b) 4·696, 20·84,   (c) 18·10, 4·102,
    (d) 93·16, −5·533.
3. (a) 9·487,   (b) 1·225,   (c) 0·5435.
4. (a) 0·3832,   (b) 3·889.
5. (a) 5·477,   (b) 35·36.
6. (a) 1·556,   (b) 9·595.   (c) 9·595
7. (a) 255,   (b) −4058,   (c) 4·335.
8. (a) 3·922,   (b) 2·900,   (c) 6·423.

Exercise 4.5 (pp. 75–76)

1. $y = 0·30x + 0·60$.
2. $R = 88 + 2·3V$.
3. $E = 0·054L + 0·53$.
4. $\theta = 7·6 − 0·32T$.
5. 16.
6. −2·7, 11.
7. 1·5, 10.
8. 0·65, 1·4.
9. 2·5, 4·8.
10. 5·0, −2·0.

Exercise 4.6 (pp. 77–79)

1. $180·12 \text{ cm}^2$, $187·92 \text{ cm}^2$; $184 \pm 4 \text{ cm}^2$.
2. (a) 37 cm^2,   (b) $37·4 \text{ cm}^2$,   (c) $37·4 \text{ cm}^2$.
3. (a) $f^{-1} : x \to \frac{1}{2}(1 − x)$,   (b) $g^{-1} : x \to \log_5 x$,   (c) $h^{-1} : x \to −1/x$.
4. 1·277.   5.   0, 1·262.
6. 3·78.   7. $z = 6p − 800$.
8. (a) $x = v^2, y = u^2$,   (b) $x = u, y = v/u$,   (c) $x = \lg v, y = \lg u$,
    (d) $x = u, y = \lg v$.
9. 0·25, 3.   10. 20, 0·50.
11. 0·411.
12. LET $S = 0$, LET $C = N, C = 0$?, LET $S = SX$; −1.
13. 5, 12, 13; 9, 12, 15.

Exercise 5.1 (pp. 82–83)

1. (a) 9,   (b) 0,   (c) 10,   (d) 73.
2. (a) $\frac{1}{3}$,   (b) $1\frac{1}{2}$,   (c) $−\frac{1}{2}$,   (d) 4.
3. (a) 3,   (b) 1,   (c) 2,   (d) 1.
4. (a) 2,   (b) 2.
5. As $x \to 1$ from above, $f(x) \to 0$; as $x \to 1$ from below, $f(x) \to 1$.

6. As $x \to 0$ from above, $f(x) \to \infty$; as $x \to 0$ from below, $f(x) \to -\infty$.
7. (a) $f(x) \to 0$, (b) $g(x) \to \infty$, (c) as $x \to k$ from above, $h(x) \to \infty$;
    as $x \to k$ from below, $h(x) \to -\infty$.
8. (a) 0, (b) 0, (c) 2, (d) 2.
9. (a) -5, (b) 3/2, (c) 1, (d) $\frac{1}{2}$.

Exercise 5.2 (pp. 85–86)

1. $-1, -0\cdot5, -0\cdot1, -0\cdot01, -0\cdot001$.
2. $1, 0, -0\cdot8, -0\cdot98, -0\cdot998$.
3. $2+h$; 2.
4. (a) 6, (b) -3, (c) 1, (d) 3.
5. $6x+3h$; $6x$.
6. (a) $2x-1$, (b) $-1/x^2$, (c) $3x^2$.
7. $8a+4h$; $8a$.
8. (a) 3; 3, (b) $12-10a-5h$; $12-10a$.

Exercise 5.3 (p. 88)

1. $2x+\delta x$; $2x$.

2. (a) $-2x-\delta x$; $-2x$, (b) $2x+2+\delta x$; $2x+2$, (c) $\dfrac{-2}{x(x+\delta x)}$; $-\dfrac{2}{x^2}$.

3. (a) $4x$, (b) $10x$, (c) $4x$.
4. (a) 1, (b) -1, (c) $1+2x$.
5. (a) 3, (b) $\frac{1}{2}$, (c) 0.
6. (a) $-3x^2$, (b) $6x^2$, (c) $4x^3$.

7. (a) $1+\dfrac{1}{x^2}$, (b) $-\dfrac{2}{x^3}$, (c) $-\dfrac{3}{x^4}$.

Exercise 5.4 (pp. 92–93)

1. (a) $5x^4$, (b) $12x^{11}$, (c) $12x^3$, (d) 0.
2. (a) 2, (b) $6x-4$, (c) $6x^2-42x^5$.

3. (a) $4-2x$, (b) $\dfrac{3}{2}x^2 +\dfrac{2}{3}x$, (c) $5-16x^3$.

4. (a) $4x+3$, (b) $18x-6$, (c) $3x^2+8x+4$.
5. (a) $-2x^{-3}$, (b) $-4/x^5$, (c) $-9/x^{10}$, (d) $-6/x^4$.

6. (a) $2x + \dfrac{1}{x^2}$, (b) $4x^3 - \dfrac{8}{x^3}$, (c) $-\dfrac{1}{x^3}+\dfrac{1}{x^4}$.

7. (a) $1 - \dfrac{1}{x^2}$, (b) $\dfrac{15}{x^4} - \dfrac{4}{x^3}$, (c) $1 + \dfrac{2}{x^2}$.

8. (a) $3x^2(x^3+1), 0, -84$, (b) $9(x+1)^2, 9, 9$.

9. (a) $2 - \dfrac{2}{x^3}, 1\frac{3}{4}, 4$, (b) $2x - \dfrac{2}{x^3}, 3\frac{3}{4}, 0$.

10. (a) 5, (b) 25, (c) 2, (d) $\frac{1}{4}$.

11. (a) $y = x - 4$,   (b) $y = 11x + 7$,   (c) $3x + y = 2$,
    (d) $8y + 121 = 0$,   (e) $y = 4x - 3$,   (f) $16y = 2x - 11$.
12. (a) $10t\,\mathrm{m\,s^{-1}}$,   (b) $30\,\mathrm{m\,s^{-1}}$, $50\,\mathrm{m\,s^{-1}}$.
13. (a) $27 - 6t\,\mathrm{m\,s^{-1}}$,   (b) $9\,\mathrm{m\,s^{-1}}$, $-3\,\mathrm{m\,s^{-1}}$.
14. 4π.   15. -2.
16. $3, -4$.   17. $2, \frac{1}{2}$.

18. (a) $\frac{1}{3}x^{-2/3}$,   (b) $\frac{3}{2}x^{1/2}$,   (c) $-\frac{1}{4}x^{-5/4}$,   (d) $\frac{1}{5}x^{-4/5} = 1/(5\sqrt[5]{x^4})$,

    (e) $-\frac{1}{2}x^{-3/2} = -1/(2\sqrt{x^3})$,   (f) $\frac{2}{3}x^{-2/3} = 2/(3\sqrt[3]{x^2})$.

19. (a) $\frac{1}{2}x^{-1/2} - \frac{3}{2}x^{-5/2}$,   (b) $3x^{1/2} - \frac{1}{2}x^{-1/2}$,   (c) $1 + \frac{1}{\sqrt{x}}$,

    (d) $\frac{1}{2\sqrt{x}} + \frac{1}{2\sqrt{x^3}}$,   (e) $\frac{5}{2}x\sqrt{x} + \frac{3}{2}\sqrt{x}$,   (f) $\frac{3}{2}\sqrt{x} + \frac{3}{2\sqrt{x}} - \frac{3}{2x\sqrt{x}} - \frac{3}{2x^2\sqrt{x}}$.

20. $4y = 5x + 4$.

Exercise 5.5 (p. 99)

1. $(1, -4)\,$min.   2. $(-\frac{3}{4}, 3\frac{1}{8})\,$max.
3. $(-\frac{1}{2}, -2\frac{1}{4})\,$min.   4. $(\frac{1}{2}, 2)\,$min.
5. $(0,0)\,$max, $(2, -4)\,$min.   6. $(0, 1)\,$inflexion.
7. $(2, -8)\,$inflexion.   8. $(-2,0)\,$max, $(1, -27)\,$min.
9. $(-1/3, -11/27)\,$min, $(\frac{2}{3}, \frac{3}{4})\,$max.
10. $(-1\frac{1}{4}, 15\frac{3}{16})\,$max, $(\frac{1}{2}, -6\frac{1}{4})\,$min.
11. $(-4, 256)\,$max, $(0,0)\,$min.   12. $(0,0)\,$inflexion, $(1,1)\,$max.
13. None.   14. None.
15. $(\frac{2}{3}, 3\frac{2}{3})\,$max, $(2\frac{2}{3}, -32\frac{1}{3})\,$min.
16. $(-1, 4)\,$min, $(0, 6)\,$max, $(2\frac{1}{2}, -17\frac{7}{16})\,$min.
17. $(-1\frac{1}{2}, -12)\,$max, $(1\frac{1}{2}, 12)\,$min.   18. $(2, 3)\,$min.
19. $(0, -64)\,$inflexion, $(3, 17)\,$inflexion.
20. $(\frac{1}{4}, -\frac{1}{4})\,$min.
21. $(0, 21)$.   22. $-3, -9, 12$.
23. (i) $a^2 > 3b$,   (ii) $a^2 = 3b$,   (iii) $a^2 < 3b$.
24. $x = 0, y = x$.

Exercise 5.6 (pp. 103–104)

1. 6.   2. $30x - 2$.

3. $12x^2 - 12x + \dfrac{2}{x^3}$.   4. $-\dfrac{8}{x^3} - \dfrac{24}{x^4}$.

5. $-\dfrac{1}{4}x^{-3/2} + \dfrac{3}{4}x^{-5/2}$.   6. $\dfrac{3}{2}x^{-1/2} + \dfrac{1}{4}x^{-3/2} - \dfrac{9}{2}x^{-5/2}$.

7. $(-1, 2)\,$max; $(1, -2)\,$min.
8. $(-1, 0)\,$min; $(0, 1)\,$max; $(1, 0)\,$min.
9. $(0, 0)\,$inflexion; $(1\frac{1}{2}, -1\frac{11}{16})\,$min.
10. $(-\frac{1}{2}, -7)\,$max; $(\frac{1}{2}, 1)\,$min.
11. $(1, 2)\,$max; $(2, 1)\,$min.

12. $(-1,0)$ min; $(0,5)$ max; $(2,-27)$ min.
13. (a) $4, -17, 50,$ (b) $3, 0, 6.$
14. $(-1, -27)$ min; $(2,0)$ inflexion.
15. $(1,0), 3.$
16. (a) $v = 18t - 9t^2, a = 18 - 18t,$ (b) $0\,\mathrm{m\,s}^{-1}, 18\,\mathrm{m\,s}^{-2},$
    (c) $-27\,\mathrm{m\,s}^{-1}, -36\,\mathrm{m\,s}^{-2}.$
17. (a) $v = 24t^2 - 66t + 27, a = 48t - 66,$ (b) $27\,\mathrm{m\,s}^{-1}, -66\,\mathrm{m\,s}^{-2},$
    (c) $45\,\mathrm{m\,s}^{-1}, 78\,\mathrm{m\,s}^{-2}.$
18. $2, -8, 5.$
19. (a) $\left(\dfrac{1}{\sqrt[3]{2}}, \dfrac{3}{2}\sqrt[3]{2}\right)$ min, $(-1,0)$ inflexion.

    (b) $(2,\frac{1}{4})$ max, $(3,\frac{2}{9})$ inflexion.

    (c) $\left(-\sqrt{3}, -\dfrac{2}{9}\sqrt{3}\right)$ min, $\left(\sqrt{3}, \dfrac{2}{9}\sqrt{3}\right)$ max, $\left(-\sqrt{6}, -\dfrac{5}{36}\sqrt{6}\right)$ inflexion,

    $\left(\sqrt{6}, \dfrac{5}{36}\sqrt{6}\right)$ inflexion.
20. $(0,0).$

Exercise 5.7 (pp. 104–105)

1. (a) 2, (b) -4, (c) 1.
2. (a) 0, (b) 2, (c) 0.
3. (b) 4.
4. (a) $3(x+1)^2$, (b) $-(x+1)^{-2}.$
5. $\frac{1}{2}x^{-1/2}.$

6. (a) $6(3x+1)$, (b) $1 - \dfrac{6}{x^2}$, (c) $\dfrac{3}{2}\sqrt{x} - \dfrac{1}{\sqrt{x}}.$

7. $y = 4(x+1), y = -3x, y = 12(x-3).$

9. (a) $(0, -4)$ min, (b) $\left(-\dfrac{2}{3}\sqrt{3}, \dfrac{16}{9}\sqrt{3}\right)$ max; $\left(\dfrac{2}{3}\sqrt{3}, -\dfrac{16}{9}\sqrt{3}\right)$ min,

    (c) $(-\sqrt{2}, -4)$ min; $(0,0)$ max; $(\sqrt{2}, -4)$ min, (d) no turning points,

    (e) no turning points, (f) $\left(2\sqrt{3}, \dfrac{1}{9}\sqrt{3}\right)$ max; $\left(-2\sqrt{3}, \dfrac{-1}{9}\sqrt{3}\right)$ min.

10. $(-2, -3\frac{3}{4})$ max; $(1,3)$ inflexion.
11. (a) $v = 7 + 10t - 6t^2\,\mathrm{m\,s}^{-1}, a = 10 - 12t\,\mathrm{m\,s}^{-2},$
    (b) $7\,\mathrm{m\,s}^{-1}, 10\,\mathrm{m\,s}^{-2}; 3\,\mathrm{m\,s}^{-1}, -14\,\mathrm{m\,s}^{-2}.$
14. $-b/3a.$

Exercise 6.1 (pp. 108–109)

3. (a) $\frac{1}{3}x^3 + c$, (b) $-\dfrac{1}{x} + c$, (c) $2x^4 + c$, (d) $-\dfrac{3}{x^2} + c.$

4. $x^3 + 2x^2 + c.$ 5. $\dfrac{1}{6}x^6 - x + c.$

6. $\dfrac{4}{3}x^3 + 2x^2 + x + c.$ 7. $3x^2 + \dfrac{1}{12x^2} + c.$

8. $\frac{1}{3}x^3 + 2x - \frac{1}{x} + c.$ 9. $-\frac{1}{x} + \frac{1}{3x^3} + c.$

10. $\frac{3}{4}x^{4/3} + \frac{3}{2}x^{2/3} + c.$ 11. $\frac{2}{3}x^{3/2} - 2x^{1/2} + c.$

12. $\frac{2}{5}x^{5/2} + 2x^{-1/2} + c.$

13. (a) $t^3 + 7t^2 - 24t + c,$ (b) $-\frac{4}{t} - \frac{2}{t^2} - \frac{1}{3t^3} + c,$

   (c) $\frac{4}{5}t^{5/2} - \frac{10}{3}t^{3/2} + 4t^{1/2} + c.$

14. $x^3 - 4x^2 + 5x - 2.$ 15. $-\frac{3}{4}.$

16. $y = x^3 - 4x - 1.$ 17. $y = 6 + 4x - 2x^2.$

18. $2\sqrt{h^3} - \sqrt{h} - 4.$ 19. $x^3 - 5x^2 + 8x - 3.$

20. $-5.$

Exercise 6.2 (pp. 113–114)

1. (a) $3x^2 + x + c,$ (b) $3x^3 - 3x^2 + x + c,$ (c) $\frac{4}{3}x^3 + \frac{1}{2}x^2 + c.$

2. (a) $3x + \frac{1}{x} + c,$ (b) $\frac{1}{3}x^3 - 2x - \frac{1}{x} + c,$ (c) $-\frac{3}{x} - \frac{1}{2x^2} + c.$

3. (a) $\frac{8}{3}x^{3/2} + c,$ (b) $\frac{2}{3}x^{3/2} - 2x^{1/2} + c,$ (c) $3x^{4/3} + 6x^{2/3} + c.$

4. (a) $t^3 + \frac{1}{t} + c,$ (b) $\frac{1}{2}u^2 - \frac{2}{5}u^{5/2} + c,$ (c) $s - \frac{1}{2s^2} + c.$

5. (a) 6, (b) 22, (c) $82\frac{2}{3}.$

6. (a) $4\frac{5}{6},$ (b) $2\frac{7}{24},$ (c) 54.

7. (a) $-36,$ (b) 60, (c) $6\frac{1}{2}.$

8. (a) $1\frac{1}{3},$ (b) $2\frac{1}{4},$ (c) 8, (d) 38.

9. (a) $4\frac{1}{2},$ (b) $6\frac{3}{4},$ (c) $-5\frac{1}{3},$ (d) $-9\frac{3}{5}.$

10. (a) $4\frac{1}{2},$ (b) 36, (c) $1\frac{1}{3},$ (d) 1/12, (e) $\frac{1}{3},$ (f) $\frac{3}{4}.$

11. $6\frac{2}{3}.$

12. $(0,0), (1,1); \frac{1}{3}.$

Exercise 6.3 (p. 117)

1. (a) $21\frac{1}{3},$ (b) $13\frac{1}{2},$ (c) $3\frac{1}{12},$ (d) $1\frac{1}{3}.$

2. 36.   3. $10\frac{2}{3}.$

4. $20\frac{1}{4}.$ 5. 1.

6. (a) $\frac{1}{2},$ (b) $1\frac{1}{3},$ (c) $10\frac{2}{3}.$

7. (a) 4, (b) $5\frac{5}{24},$ (c) $2\frac{2}{3}.$

Exercise 6.4 (pp. 119–120)

1. (a) $1220\pi,$ (b) $47\pi/10,$ (c) $9\pi,$ (d) $405\pi/14,$ (e) $377\pi/6,$ (f) $57\pi/8.$

2. (a) $512\pi/15,$ (b) $81\pi/35.$

3. (a) $15\pi/4$, (b) 36π.
4. (a) $32\pi/5$, (b) $7\pi/3$, (c) $\pi/2$, (d) $96\pi/5$.
5. (a) $202\pi/5$, (b) 20π.
6. (a) $9\pi/2$, (b) $53\pi/15$.
7. $\frac{1}{3}\pi r^2 h$.
8. $\frac{4}{3}\pi a^3$.
9. $32\pi/3$.
10. $8\pi/7$.

Exercise 6.5 (p. 123)

1. $28\pi/15$.
2. $16\pi/15$.
3. (a) $24\,\text{m}$, (b) $21\,\text{m}$, (c) $14\frac{1}{3}\,\text{m}$, (d) $47\,\text{m}$, (e) $30\,\text{m}$, (f) $41\,\text{m}$.
4. $64\pi/15$.
5. 8π.
6. $\frac{1}{3}a^2 h\,\text{cm}^3$.
7. $960\sqrt{3}\,\text{cm}^3$.

Exercise 6.6 (p. 125)

1. (a) $22\,\text{m s}^{-1}$, (b) $78\,\text{m s}^{-2}$.
2. (a) $3/4\,\text{m s}^{-1}$, (b) $4/5\,\text{m s}^{-2}$.
3. (a) 1, (b) $8\frac{2}{3}$, (c) -9, (d) 16.
4. $85\pi/6$.
5. 8.
6. (a) 93, (b) $1/64$, (c) $496/15$.

Exercise 6.7 (pp. 125–127)

1. (a) $y = 2x - x^2 + c$, (b) $y = x^{1/2} + c$, (c) $y = x - \dfrac{1}{2x^2} + c$.

2. (a) $\dfrac{2}{3}x^6 - \dfrac{1}{4}x^4 + c$, (b) $4x + \dfrac{1}{x} + c$, (c) $\dfrac{1}{2}x^2 - \dfrac{1}{2x^2} + c$.

3. (a) $4t - 6t^2 + 3t^3 + c$, (b) $x^5 + \dfrac{1}{15x^3} + c$, (c) $\dfrac{3}{2}u^{2/3} + c$.

5. $y = x^2 + \dfrac{2}{x} - 3$.
6. (a) $-\frac{11}{24}$, (b) $4\frac{1}{4}$.

7. 1.
8. $2\frac{2}{3}$.
9. $2\frac{1}{2}$.
10. $1\frac{1}{3}$.
11. $y = 2x - 2$; $1\frac{1}{3}$.
12. $4\frac{1}{2}$.
13. $\frac{1}{3}$.
14. 2.
15. (a) 24π, (b) 12π.
16. (a) $52\pi/5$, (b) 18π, (c) $76\pi/15$, (d) $10\pi/3$.
17. (a) $4\pi/3$, (b) $16\pi/15$.

19. $\pm\left(\dfrac{3}{2\sqrt{x}} - \dfrac{3}{2}\sqrt{x}\right)$; (a) 1, (b) 0; $27\pi/4$.

20. 3.
21. 10.
22. (a) $41\frac{23}{25}\,\text{m}$, (b) $101\,\text{m}$.
24. $\frac{2}{3}\pi a^2$.

Exercise 7.1 (pp. 132–133)

1. (a) $-\cos 15°$, (b) $-\sin 35°$, (c) $-\tan 50°$, (d) $\sin 68°$,
   (e) $\tan 85°$, (f) $\cos 42°$, (g) $-\sin 15°$, (h) $-\cos 57°$.
2. (a) $-\tan 56°$, (b) $\sec 23°$, (c) $\cot 68°$, (d) $-\sin 18°$,
   (e) $-\operatorname{cosec} 80°$, (f) $-\cot 15°$, (g) $-\cos 6°$, (h) $-\sec 81°$.
3. (a) $-320°$, $-220°$, $40°$, $140°$, $400°$, $500°$,
   (b) $-350°$, $-10°$, $10°$, $350°$, $370°$, $710°$,
   (c) $-285°$, $-105°$, $75°$, $255°$, $435°$, $615°$,
   (d) $-180°$, $180°$, $540°$.
4. (a) $25°$, $335°$, (b) $50°$, $130°$, (c) $42·3°$, $222·3°$,
   (d) $243·5°$, $296·5°$.
5. (a) $\sqrt{3}/2$, (b) $\sqrt{3}$, (c) $-\sqrt{3}/2$, (d) -1, (e) $-1/\sqrt{2}$, (f) $\sqrt{3}/2$,
   (g) -2, (h) $2/\sqrt{3}$.
6. (a) 0, (b) $-\sqrt{3}$, (c) 0, (d) -2, (e) 0, (f) -1, (g) $-\sqrt{2}$, (h) -1.
7. (a) $\theta = 90°$, $270°$, $\phi = 0°$, $180°$, $360°$,
   (b) $\theta = 0°$, $180°$, $360°$, $\phi = 90°$, $270°$,
   (c) $\theta = 90°$, $\phi = 0°$, $360°$,
   (d) $\theta = 90°$, $\phi = 180°$.
8. (a) $0° < \theta < 45°$, (b) $30° < \theta < 90°$, (c) $36° < \theta < 72°$,
   (d) $0° < \theta < 15°$, $30° < \theta < 45°$, $60° < \theta < 75°$.

Exercise 7.2 (pp. 135–136)

1. (a) $17·5°$, $162·5°$, (b) $56·3°$, $236·3°$, (c) $136·9°$, $223·1°$,
   (d) $218·3°$, $321·7°$.
2. (a) $-53·1°$, $53·1°$, (b) $53·1°$, $126·9°$, (c) $-31·8°$, $148·2°$,
   (d) $-110°$, $110°$.
3. (a) $45°$, $135°$, (b) $150°$, $330°$, (c) $45°$, $225°$, (d) $120°$, $240°$,
   (e) $180°$, (f) $30°$, $150°$.
4. (a) $36·9°$, $216·9°$, (b) $135°$, $315°$, (c) $48·6°$, $131·4°$
   (d) $48·2°$, $311·8°$.
5. (a) $106·1°$, $233·9°$, (b) $41·9°$, $198·1°$, (c) $97·2°$, $342·8°$,
   (d) $119·2°$, $299·2°$, (e) $17·5°$, $107·5°$, $197·5°$, $287·5°$,
   (f) $210·4°$, (g) $112·2°$, $247·8°$, (h) $90°$, $270°$
6. (a) $-75°$, $15°$, $45°$, (b) $-90°$, $-45°$, $0°$, $45°$, $90°$,
   (c) $-81°$, $-45°$, $-9°$, $27°$, $63°$, (d) $-80°$, $-40°$, $40°$, $80°$.
7. (a) $60°$, $120°$, $240°$, $300°$, (b) $60°$, $90°$, $270°$, $300°$,
   (c) $0°$, $78·5°$, $180°$, $281·5°$, $360°$, (d) $270°$,
   (e) $0°$, $30°$, $150°$, $180°$, $360°$, (f) $56·3°$, $90°$, $236·3°$, $270°$.
8. (a) $-135°$, $-26·6°$, $45°$, $153·4°$, (b) $-165·5°$, $-14·5°$,
   (c) $-60°$, $0°$, $60°$, (d) $-111·8°$, $-45°$, $68·2°$, $135°$.
9. (a) $x = 30°$, $y = 150°$; $x = 120°$, $y = 60°$,
   (b) $x = -45°$, $y = -165°$; $x = 75°$, $y = -45°$; $x = 135°$, $y = 15°$.

Exercise 7.3 (pp. 139–140)

2. (a) $\sin \theta$, (b) $\cos \theta$, (c) $\sin \theta$, (d) $-\cos \theta$, (e) $-\cos \theta$, (f) $-\cos \theta$.

3. (a) $-\cot\theta$, (b) $\tan\theta$, (c) $\cot\theta$, (d) $-\tan\theta$, (e) $\tan\theta$, (f) $-\cot\theta$.

4. 3/5, 3/4, 5/4.   5.   8/17, $-17/15$, $-15/8$.

6. $-24/25$, $-7/25$, $-25/24$.   7.   5/13, $-12/13$, 12/5.

8. (a) $\cos\theta$, (b) $\tan\theta$, (c) $\sin\theta$.

9. (a) 1, (b) $\sin^4\theta$, (c) $\cos\theta+\sin\theta$, (d) $1+\cos\theta$.

11. (a) $x^2+y^2=1$, (b) $(x-1)^2/4+(y-1)^2/9=1$,

    (c) $x^2-y^2=1$, (d) $x^2+y^2=2$.

12. $t=2/5$, $\theta=126\cdot9°$ or $t=-2/5$, $\theta=306\cdot9°$.

13. $199\cdot5°$, $340\cdot5°$.   14. $41\cdot4°$, $120°$, $240°$, $318\cdot6°$.

15. $60°$, $300°$.   16. $51\cdot3°$, $128\cdot7°$.

17. $70\cdot5°$, $120°$, $240°$, $289\cdot5°$.   18. $19\cdot5°$, $30°$, $150°$, $160\cdot5°$.

19. $26\cdot6°$, $116\cdot6°$, $206\cdot6°$, $296\cdot6°$.

20. $18\cdot4°$, $135°$, $198\cdot4°$, $315°$.   21. $63\cdot4°$, $135°$, $243\cdot4°$, $315°$.

22. $45°$, $76°$, $225°$, $256°$.

23. $(\sin x + 1)^2 - 2; 2, -2$.   24. $\{y:y\geqslant 1\}$.

Exercise 7.4 (pp. 143–144)

1. (a) $\frac14(\sqrt6+\sqrt2)$, (b) $\frac14(\sqrt2-\sqrt6)$, (c) $\sqrt3-2$, (d) $2-\sqrt3$.

2. (a) $\frac12$, (b) $\frac12$, (c) 0, (d) 1.

3. (a) $\sqrt3$, (b) $1/\sqrt3$, (c) $\frac12\sqrt6$, (d) $\sqrt2$.

4. 56/65, $-33/65$.   5. $-29/35$, $-8\sqrt6/35$.

6. $225°$.   7. $4\frac12$.

8. (a) $2\sin A\cos B$, (b) $2\cos A\cos B$, (c) $\cos B$.

9. $12°$, $60°$, $84°$, $132°$, $156°$.

10. $-135°$, $45°$.

11. (a) $26\cdot6°$, $108\cdot4°$, $206\cdot6°$, $288\cdot4°$,

    (b) $40\cdot9°$, $220\cdot9°$, (c) $0°$, $180°$, $360°$, (d) $135°$, $315°$.

12. $\dfrac{\cot A\cot B - 1}{\cot A + \cot B}$.

Exercise 7.5 (pp. 146–147)

1. 24/25. $-7/25$, 44/125.   2.   1/9, $-4\sqrt5$, $-79/81$.

3. 4/5, 4/3, $5\frac12$.   4. $-3/4$, $-\sqrt{7/3}$, $2\sqrt2$.

5. $-1/\sqrt5$, $2/\sqrt5$, $-2/5\sqrt5$.

6. (a) $1+1/\sqrt2$, (b) $\sqrt3/2$, (c) 1/4, (d) $1/\sqrt2$.

7. (a) $0°$, $60°$, $180°$, (b) $0°$, $120°$, (c) $0°$, $60°$, $120°$, $180°$,

    (d) $0°$, $45°$, $135°$, $180°$.

16. (a) $120°$, $240°$, (b) $41\cdot8°$, $138\cdot2°$, $270°$,

    (c) $45°$, $135°$, $225°$, $315°$, (d) $0°$, $104\cdot5°$, $180°$, $255\cdot5°$, $360°$.

17. (a) $135°$, $161\cdot6°$, $315°$, $341\cdot6°$,

    (b) $23\cdot2°$, $135°$, $203\cdot2°$, $315°$.

18. (a) $-126\cdot9°$, $43\cdot6°$, (b) $-90°$, $53\cdot1°$, (c) $-143\cdot1°$, $90°$,

    (d) $-36\cdot9°$, $112\cdot6°$.

19. $45°$, $135°$, $225°$, $315°$.

20. $4\cos^3\theta - 3\cos\theta$; $90°$, $120°$, $240°$, $270°$.

Exercise 7.6 (pp. 149–150)

1. (a) $\sin 3x + \sin x$, (b) $\cos 8\theta + \cos 2\theta$, (c) $3(\cos A - \cos 5A)$,
   (d) $\frac{1}{2}(\sin 6t - \sin 2t)$, (e) $\cos 2A + \cos 2B$, (f) $\frac{1}{4}(1 + 2\sin 2x)$.
2. (a) $1 + \sqrt{3}$, (b) $5\sqrt{2}$, (c) $2 + \sqrt{3}$, (d) $3 + 2\sqrt{2}$.
3. (a) $0°$, $180°$, $360°$, (b) $60°$, $120°$, $240°$, $300°$,
   (c) $0°$, $60°$, $180°$, $240°$, $360°$,
   (d) $111·3°$, $168·7°$, $291·3°$, $348·7°$.
4. (a) $2\sin 4x \cos 3x$, (b) $2\cos 4A \cos A$, (c) $2\cos\theta\sin\alpha$,
   (d) $-2\sin 2x \sin x$.
5. (a) $\cot 5\theta$, (b) $-\tan 3x$, (c) $\cot 2A$, (d) $-\tan^2\theta$.
6. (a) $\sqrt{3}$, (b) $1/\sqrt{3}$.
7. (a) $0°$, $90°$, $180°$, (b) $0°$, $30°$, $90°$, $150°$, $180°$,
   (c) $30°$, $120°$, $150°$, (d) $22\frac{1}{2}°$, $45°$, $112\frac{1}{2}°$.
8. (a) $0°$, $90°$, $120°$, $180°$, (b) $15°$, $30°$, $75°$, $90°$, $150°$,
   (c) $0°$, $54°$ $126°$.

Exercise 7.7 (pp. 151–152)

1. (a) $\sqrt{2}\cos(\theta + 45°)$; $\sqrt{2}$, $\theta = -45°$, $315°$; $-\sqrt{2}$, $\theta = -225°$, $135°$,
   (b) $2\cos(\theta + 30°)$; 2, $\theta = -30°$, $330°$; -2, $\theta = -210°$, $150°$,
   (c) $13\cos(\theta - 67·4°)$; 13, $\theta = -292·6°$, $67·4°$; -13, $\theta = -112·6°$,
   $247·4°$,
   (d) $\sqrt{5}\cos(\theta - 26·6°)$; $\sqrt{5}$, $\theta = -333·4°$, $26·6°$; $-\sqrt{5}$, $\theta = -153·4°$,
   $206·6°$.
2. (a) $41·6°$, $244·7°$, (b) $26·2°$, $110·2°$, (c) $180°$, $313·6°$,
   (d) $98°$, $205·9°$.
3. $\sqrt{89}\sin(\theta - 58°)$; (a) $97·5°$, $198·5°$, (b) $90°$, $206°$.
4. (a) $10·9°$, $231°$, (b) $257·6°$, $349·8°$.

Exercise 7.8 (pp. 152–154)

1. (a) $70°$, $110°$, (b) $115°$, $155°$, $295°$, $335°$, (c) $145°$, $215°$,
   (d) $25°$, $85°$, $145°$, $205°$, $265°$, $325°$.
2. (a) $0·8$, (b) $-0·6$, (c) $-0·8$, (d) $-0·6$, (e) $-0·75$, (f) $0·75$.
3. (a) $56·3°$, $236·3°$, (b) $48·2°$, $120°$, $240°$, $311·8°$,
   (c) $0°$, $53·1°$, $180°$, $306·9°$, $360°$, (d) $23·6°$, $156·4°$.
4. (a) $2k^2 - 1$, (b) $(4k^2 - 1)\sqrt{(1 - k^2)}$, (c) $\sqrt{\left(\dfrac{1 + k}{2}\right)}$, (d) $\sqrt{\left(\dfrac{1 - k}{1 + k}\right)}$.
5. (a) $(x - 1)^2 + 4y^2 = 1$, (b) $xy = 1$, (c) $y = 2x^2$,
   (d) $y^2 = 4x(2 - x)(x - 1)^2$.
6. (a) $10·9°$, $100·9°$, (b) $11·8°$, $78·2°$,
   (c) $0°$, $45°$, $135°$, $180°$,
   (d) $0°$, $60°$, $90°$, $120°$, $180°$.
7. $56·3° \leqslant x \leqslant 236·3°$.   8. 8.
9. (a) max 1, min -1, (b) max 2, min 0, (c) max 2, min -2,
   (d) max 4, min 0.

11. (a) 79·7°, 153·4°,   (b) $\left(\dfrac{\lambda + 1}{\lambda - 1}\right)$ tan α; 120°, 300°.

12. (a) 45°, 120°, 135°, 225°, 240°, 315°,
    (b) $5\cos(x - 36·9°)$; 103·3°, 330·4°,
    (c) 90°, 270°; 0°, 180°, 360°.

13. $\dfrac{3\tan\theta - \tan^3\theta}{1 - 3\tan^2\theta}$; 0°, 19·1°, 160·9°, 180°.

14. $\dfrac{2t}{1 - t^2}, \dfrac{1 + t^2}{1 - t^2}$; 18°.

15. (a) $25\sin(x - 73·7°)$; 110·6°, 216·9°,   (b) 60°, 60°.

16. 90°, 323·1°; 53·1°, 180°.   18. (b) 130·2°, 342·4°.

19. 36·9°; −36·9°, 143·1°; 0°, −73·7°.

20. (a) 49·8°, 130·2°,   (b) 26·6°, 108·4°,   (c) 30°, 90°, 150°,
    (d) 22½°, 30°, 67½°, 112½°, 150°, 157½°.

21. 36·9°, 61·9°.

22. (a) 30°,   (b) 180°,   (c) −45°,   (d) 30°,   (e) 90°,   (f) 90° or −90°,
    (g) 45°,   (h) 45°.

23. $k = 2$; $-\sqrt{2}, \frac{1}{2}(\sqrt{2} \pm \sqrt{6})$.

24. (a) 0°, 48·6°, 131·4°, 180°, 270°,
    (b) $R = \sqrt{(2\lambda^2 - 2\lambda + 1)}$, $\tan\phi = (1 - \lambda)/\lambda$; min $-\sqrt{(2\lambda^2 - 2\lambda + 1)}$.

Exercise 8.1 (p. 157)

1. $\angle B = \angle A + \angle C$.
2. (a) $x + y = 180°$,   (b) $z = 2y - 180°$.
3. 5:12.
6. A is the incentre of $\triangle DEF$ when $\angle A$ is obtuse.

Exercise 8.2 (pp. 162–163)

1. $C = 70°, a = 4·61, b = 4·08$.
2. $B = 61°, a = 6·69, c = 8·70$.
3. $A = 33·6°, B = 95·2°, c = 7·04$.
4. $A = 26·5°, C = 108·5°, b = 3·80$.
5. $A = 40·8°, B = 60·6°, C = 78·6°$.
6. $A = 36·9°, B = 90°, C = 53·1°$.
7. $B = 67·3°, C = 45·4°, c = 7·72$.
8. $B = 35·6°, C = 23·4°, a = 10·2$.
9. $A = 103°, b = 2·57, c = 5·31$.
10. $A = 87·1°, C = 37·9°, a = 14·6$.
11. $A = 112·4°, B = 29·5°, C = 38°$.
12. $A = 60°, B = 90°, a = 5·20$.
13. 4·83, 1·86.   14. 15·9, 3·97.
15. 27·5 cm².   16. 30°; 14 cm.
17. 4·07 cm, 11·5 cm.   18. 4·21 cm, 2·26 cm.
21. (a) 82·9°, 45·1°,   (b) 115·9°, 24·1°.
22. $\triangle = rs$; $r = \sqrt{3} = 1·73$.

Exercise 8.3 (p. 164)

1. 13·4 km; 098°.
3. 19 min 15 sec.
5. 13·5.
7. 1350 m.
9. 10 cm; 36·9°.

2. 14·1 km; S 23·9° E.
4. 6·55 cm.
6. 20·2 m.
8. 71·1 cm².
10. 2/3, 7 cm.

Exercise 8.4 (pp. 167–168)

1. (a) 17·2°, (b) 44·4°, (c) 18·1°.
2. (a) 44·4°, (b) 63°, (c) 90°.
3. (a) 58°, (b) 53·9°, (c) 63·4°.
4. (a) 27°, (b) 32·7°.
5. (a) 53°, (b) 61·9°, (c) 64·8°, (d) 90°.
6. (a) 49·2°, (b) 65·4°.
7. (a) $a\sqrt{2}$, (b) 70·5°, (c) 109·5°.
8. (a) 1/3, (b) $2\sqrt{6}$.
9. (a) 22·5°, (b) 39·7°, (c) 112·9°, (d) 117·8°.
10. (a) 73°, (b) 83·3°, (c) 70·6°, (d) 96°.

Exercise 8.5 (pp. 170–171)

1. 76·7°, 474 cm².
3. (a) 27·6°, (b) 53·4°.
5. 060·5°, 38·2°.
7. 20·4°, 43·2°.
10. 9·17 m, 15·6 m; 19·1°, 26·6°.
11. 6·6.

2. 93·7 m, 56·5°.
4. 14·7°; 13·4° or 87·4°.
6. 051·4°, 125·7°.
8. 2, 26·6°, 18·4°.

Exercise 8.6 (pp. 172–174)

1. 33·6°, 7·54 cm.
3. 62·6°, 91·1°, 153·7°; 7·70 cm.
5. (i) 2; $c = \frac{1}{2}(5\sqrt{3} \pm \sqrt{11})$, (ii) none, (iii) 1; $c = \sqrt{3} + 2\sqrt{2}$,
    (iv) 1; $c = 2\sqrt{2} - \sqrt{3}$.
9. $\tan^2 \frac{1}{2}A = \dfrac{(s-b)(s-c)}{s(s-a)}$; area $= \sqrt{\{s(s-a)(s-b)(s-c)\}}$.
10. 124°, 28°, 28°.   11. S2θ° W.
12. 32·3 km h⁻¹.
15. (i) $\frac{1}{2}a\sqrt{10}$, (ii) $a\sqrt{3}$, (iii) 90°, (iv) $\frac{1}{3}\sqrt{2}$.
16. (i) 90°, (ii) 30°, (iii) 45°.
17. 60°, 41·4°; 49·1°.   20. 60 cm; 688 cm².
21. $a\sqrt{6}$.
22. (i) $2a\sqrt{5}$, (ii) $-1/5$, (iii) $4/\sqrt{30}$.
23. (i) 836 m, (ii) 042·9°, (iii) 13·8°.

Exercise 9.1 (p. 177)

1. (a) **PS**, (b) **AE**, (c) **AB**, (d) **0**, (e) **MR**, (f) **PS**.
2. (a) false, (b) true, (c) true, (d) true, (e) false, (f) true.
3. (a) true, (b) false, (c) true, (d) true, (e) false, (f) false.
4. $\mathbf{x}+\mathbf{y}, \mathbf{y}+\mathbf{z}, \mathbf{x}+\mathbf{y}+\mathbf{z}$.
5. $\mathbf{a}+\mathbf{d}, \mathbf{d}-\mathbf{b}, \mathbf{d}-\mathbf{b}-\mathbf{c}, \mathbf{a}+\mathbf{d}-\mathbf{c}$.

Exercise 9.2 (pp. 180–181)

1. (a) 3 km E, (b) 10 km N, (c) 1 km N 30° E, (d) 1 km S.
2. (a) $2\sqrt{2}$ km NE, (b) $2\sqrt{2}$ km NE, (c) $2\sqrt{2}$ km SE, (d) $2\sqrt{2}$ km NW.
3. (a) 1 km S 30° E, (b) $\sqrt{3}$ km S, (c) $\sqrt{3}$ km S 60° E, (d) $\sqrt{3}$ km N 60° E.
4. $\mathbf{p}+\mathbf{q}, \mathbf{q}-\mathbf{p}, \frac{1}{2}(\mathbf{p}+\mathbf{q}), \frac{1}{2}(\mathbf{q}-\mathbf{p})$.
5. $-\mathbf{a}, \mathbf{a}-\mathbf{b}, 2\mathbf{b}, 2\mathbf{b}-\mathbf{a}$.   6. $2\mathbf{a}+\mathbf{b}, \mathbf{a}+\mathbf{b}$.
7. $2\mathbf{a}-\mathbf{b}, \mathbf{a}+\mathbf{b}, \mathbf{b}-\mathbf{a}, \frac{1}{2}\mathbf{b}$.
8. (a) $2\mathbf{x}+\mathbf{y}$, (b) $\mathbf{u}-2\mathbf{w}$, (c) $3\mathbf{p}+7\mathbf{q}$.
16. **a** must be a positive multiple of **b**.

Exercise 9.3 (pp. 183–184)

1. (a) $2\mathbf{b}$, (b) $-3\mathbf{a}$, (c) $2\mathbf{b}-6\mathbf{a}$, (d) $\mathbf{b}-\mathbf{a}$, (e) $\mathbf{a}$, (f) $2\mathbf{b}-\mathbf{a}$.
2. (a) $\mathbf{z}$, (b) $\mathbf{x}$, (c) $-\mathbf{x}$, (d) $\mathbf{z}$, (e) $-\mathbf{x}+\mathbf{z}$, (f) $\mathbf{y}-\mathbf{z}$.
3. (a) $-\mathbf{x}+\mathbf{y}$, (b) $\mathbf{x}+\mathbf{z}$, (c) $-\mathbf{x}+\mathbf{y}-\mathbf{z}$, (d) $2\mathbf{x}-\mathbf{y}$,
   (e) $2\mathbf{x}-\mathbf{y}+2\mathbf{z}$, (f) $-\mathbf{y}+2\mathbf{z}$.
4. (a) $5\mathbf{i}+3\mathbf{j}$, (b) $-\mathbf{i}+6\mathbf{j}$, (c) $-4\mathbf{i}+2\mathbf{j}$, (d) $2\mathbf{i}-\mathbf{j}$,
   (e) $3\mathbf{i}+4\mathbf{j}$, (f) $\mathbf{i}+5\mathbf{j}$.
5. (a) $-4\mathbf{i}+5\mathbf{j}+2\mathbf{k}$, (b) $3\mathbf{j}+2\mathbf{k}$, (c) $\mathbf{i}-\mathbf{j}+\mathbf{k}$, (d) $\mathbf{i}+2\mathbf{j}+3\mathbf{k}$.
6. (a) 13, (b) $\sqrt{5}$, (c) 10, (d) 3, (e) 7, (f) $5\sqrt{3}$.
7. (a) $\frac{8}{9}\mathbf{i}-\frac{4}{9}\mathbf{j}-\frac{1}{9}\mathbf{k}$, (b) $\frac{8}{9}\mathbf{i}-\frac{4}{9}\mathbf{j}-\frac{1}{9}\mathbf{k}$, (c) $-\frac{8}{9}\mathbf{i}+\frac{4}{9}\mathbf{j}+\frac{1}{9}\mathbf{k}$.
8. (a) 5, (b) 3, (c) 6.   9. (a) $\sqrt{29}$, (b) $\sqrt{29}$, (c) 5.
10. (a) $\frac{1}{\sqrt{2}}\mathbf{i}-\frac{1}{\sqrt{2}}\mathbf{j}$, (b) $-\frac{7}{9}\mathbf{i}+\frac{4}{9}\mathbf{j}+\frac{4}{9}\mathbf{k}$, (c) $\mathbf{i}$.
11. ± 2.   12. $10 \leqslant |\mathbf{a}+\mathbf{b}| \leqslant 40$.
14. (a) $\frac{1}{2},\frac{1}{2}$, (b) $-4, -2$.

Exercise 9.4 (pp. 186–188)

1. $\mathbf{b}-\mathbf{a}, \mathbf{b}-2\mathbf{a}; 2\mathbf{b}-2\mathbf{a}, 2\mathbf{b}-3\mathbf{a}, \mathbf{b}-2\mathbf{a}$.
2. $\mathbf{a}-\mathbf{b}, \mathbf{c}-\mathbf{b}, \mathbf{a}-2\mathbf{b}+\mathbf{c}; 2\mathbf{a}-3\mathbf{b}+2\mathbf{c}$.
3. $\frac{1}{4}(\mathbf{a}+\mathbf{b}+\mathbf{c}+\mathbf{d})$.
4. $2\mathbf{i}+3\mathbf{j}, 5\mathbf{i}-\mathbf{j}, 4\mathbf{i}+4\mathbf{j}; -\mathbf{i}+5\mathbf{j}; \mathbf{i}+8\mathbf{j}, (1,8)$.
5. (a) 6, $-\frac{1}{3}\mathbf{i}+\frac{2}{3}\mathbf{j}+\frac{2}{3}\mathbf{k}, 2\mathbf{i}-3\mathbf{j}+\mathbf{k}$,
   (b) 22, $\frac{6}{11}\mathbf{i}-\frac{9}{11}\mathbf{j}-\frac{2}{11}\mathbf{k}, -\mathbf{i}+4\mathbf{j}-2\mathbf{k}$,

(c) $\sqrt{10}, \dfrac{3}{\sqrt{10}}\mathbf{j} - \dfrac{1}{\sqrt{10}}\mathbf{k}, \mathbf{i} + \dfrac{1}{2}\mathbf{j} + \dfrac{5}{2}\mathbf{k},$

(d) $3\sqrt{6}, -\dfrac{2}{\sqrt{6}}\mathbf{i} - \dfrac{1}{\sqrt{6}}\mathbf{j} - \dfrac{1}{\sqrt{6}}\mathbf{k}, 2\mathbf{i} + \dfrac{5}{2}\mathbf{j} - \dfrac{1}{2}\mathbf{k}.$

6. $2\mathbf{i} - \mathbf{j} + 5\mathbf{k}, 2\mathbf{j} - \mathbf{k}, -2\mathbf{i} + 4\mathbf{j} + 3\mathbf{k}$; 7, $(-1, 3, 1)$; $(0, 1, 9)$.

7. $\mathbf{XY} = 4\mathbf{i} + 2\mathbf{j} - 2\mathbf{k}, \mathbf{XZ} = -2\mathbf{i} - \mathbf{j} + \mathbf{k}.$

9. 50.

10. (a) 1, (b) -1, (c) -2, (d) 4/3.

11. $\frac{1}{2}(\mathbf{p} + \mathbf{q}), \frac{1}{3}(\mathbf{p} + \mathbf{q}), -\frac{2}{3}\mathbf{p} + \frac{1}{3}\mathbf{q}$; $(1 - \frac{2}{3}k)\mathbf{p} + \frac{1}{3}k\mathbf{q}.$

12. $\dfrac{2}{9}(\mathbf{a} + \mathbf{b}); \dfrac{1}{2}, \dfrac{9}{4}; \dfrac{1}{2}(\mathbf{a} + \mathbf{b}).$

13. $\dfrac{1}{7}\mathbf{a} + \dfrac{4}{7}\mathbf{b}; \dfrac{1}{5}\mathbf{a} + \dfrac{4}{5}\mathbf{b}.$

Exercise 9.5 (pp. 188–189)

4. (ii) $\frac{1}{3}\mathbf{PQ} + \frac{2}{3}\mathbf{PS}, -\frac{2}{3}\mathbf{PQ} + \frac{2}{3}\mathbf{PS}, -\frac{1}{3}\mathbf{PQ} + \frac{1}{3}\mathbf{PS}.$

5. $\mathbf{a} + \mathbf{b} + \mathbf{c}, \mathbf{b} + \mathbf{c} - \mathbf{a}, \mathbf{a} + \mathbf{c} - \mathbf{b}, \mathbf{a} + \mathbf{b} - \mathbf{c}.$

6. (a) $\mathbf{b} - \mathbf{a}$, (b) $3\mathbf{b} - 2\mathbf{a}$, (c) $3\mathbf{b} - \mathbf{c}$, (d) $\mathbf{a} - \dfrac{3}{2}\mathbf{b}$, (e) $-\mathbf{a} - \dfrac{1}{2}\mathbf{b}$,

(f) $\mathbf{a} + \dfrac{3}{2}\mathbf{b}.$

7. (a) $2\sqrt{6}, 5\sqrt{2}, 20$, (b) $\frac{2}{3}\mathbf{i} + \frac{1}{3}\mathbf{j} - \frac{2}{3}\mathbf{k}.$

8. (a) $6\sqrt{3}$, (b) $\dfrac{1}{9}\sqrt{3}\mathbf{i} - \dfrac{5}{9}\sqrt{3}\mathbf{j} + \dfrac{1}{9}\sqrt{3}\mathbf{k}$, (c) $-2\mathbf{j} + 3\mathbf{k}.$

9. 1, 4.

11. (a) $-\dfrac{1}{\sqrt{2}}\mathbf{i} + \dfrac{1}{\sqrt{2}}\mathbf{j}$, (b) $\dfrac{3}{2}\sqrt{29}.$

12. $\mathbf{a} + k(2\mathbf{b} - \mathbf{a})$; 3, $6\mathbf{b} - 2\mathbf{a}.$

13. $\frac{1}{3}\mathbf{a} + \frac{1}{3}\mathbf{b}.$

14. $(4, -7, 8)$: 54 sq. units.

15. $s + t = 1.$

16. $\frac{1}{3}\mathbf{p} + \frac{1}{3}\mathbf{q}; \frac{1}{3}\mathbf{a} + \frac{1}{3}\mathbf{b} + \frac{1}{3}\mathbf{c}.$

Exercise 10.1 (pp. 192–193)

1. (a) $2x^2 - 1$, (b) $4x^2 + 4x$, (c) $x^4 - 2x^2$, (d) $4x + 3.$

2. (a) $2x^2 - 2$, (b) $4x - 4$, (c) $4x^2 - 4x + 1$, (d) $x^4 - 1.$

3. $x + 2.$ 4. $4 - x^2.$

5. (a) $\sqrt{u}$, (b) $u^5/32$, (c) $-1/u$, (d) $\frac{1}{2}u^8(u + 1).$

6. $6(x + 3)^5.$ 7. $8(2x - 1)^3.$

8. $-21(5 - 3x)^6.$ 9. $-6(3x - 2)^{-3}.$

10. $15x^2(x^3 - 1)^4.$ 11. $8x(4 - x^2)^{-5}.$

12. $\frac{3}{2}(1+3x)^{-1/2}$.

13. $-2(6x+1)^{-4/3}$.

14. $15x(3x^2-1)^{3/2}$.

15. $-3\left(1+\frac{1}{x^2}\right)\left(x-\frac{1}{x}\right)^{-4}$.

16. $\frac{x}{\sqrt{(1-x^2)^3}}$.

17. $\frac{-1}{\sqrt{x}(1+\sqrt{x})^3}$.

18. -12; $12x+y+11=0$.

19. $3x+8y=22$.

20. $1\,\mathrm{m\,s}^{-1}$, $-2\,\mathrm{m\,s}^{-2}$.

21. $1-4/(t+1)^2$, $3\,\mathrm{m\,s}^{-1}$.

22. (a) $(6x+1)(x+1)^4$, (b) $2/(x+1)^2$, (c) $\frac{1}{2}(x+2)(x+1)^{-3/2}$.

23. (a) $\frac{4(2x-3)^3}{\sqrt{\{(2x-3)^4-1\}}}$, (b) $\frac{-4x}{\{4+\sqrt{(4x^2+1)}\}^2\sqrt{(4x^2+1)}}$.

24. $(1,256)\,\mathrm{max}$, $(5,0)\,\mathrm{min}$.

25. $(1,1)\,\mathrm{max}$.

Exercise 10.2 (pp. 195–196)

1. $3/y$.

2. $-x/y$.

3. $-4x/y$.

4. $2x/3y^2$.

5. $1/(y-1)$.

6. $(x^2-1)/2y$.

7. $\frac{2-2x}{1+2y}$.

8. $\frac{1}{(x+y)^2}-1$.

9. 2.

10. $\frac{1}{2}$, $-\frac{1}{2}$.

11. $3x+4y+5=0$.

12. $4y=5x-9$.

13. $-5/3$, -1.

14. $(3,9)$, $(3,-1)$.

Exercise 10.3 (pp. 199–201)

1. $5x^4+12x^3-1$.

2. $3x^2-7$.

3. $12x+15x^2-75x^4$.

4. $4x^3+4/x^3$.

5. $x(5x+6)(x+3)^2$.

6. $(18x-1)(3x-1)^4$.

7. $(x+1)(7x+9)(x+2)^4$.

8. $-2(3+7x)(2x+3)^2(1-x)^3$.

9. $\frac{x(2+3x^2)}{\sqrt{(1+x^2)}}$.

10. $\frac{2-9x^2-5x^3}{2\sqrt{(1-x^3)}}$.

11. $\frac{4}{(x+2)^2}$.

12. $\frac{2x(x+1)}{(2x+1)^2}$.

13. $\frac{11}{(2-3x)^2}$.

14. $\frac{x(2-3x-x^3)}{(x^3+1)^2}$.

15. $\frac{6x}{(x^2+1)^2}$.

16. $\frac{1+x^2}{(1-x^2)^2}$.

17. $\frac{4(x+1)}{(x+2)^3}$.

18. $\frac{-x(2+x)}{(x-1)^4}$.

19. $-\frac{8x(2x+1)}{(4x+3)^4}$.

20. $\frac{1}{(1-x^2)^{3/2}}$.

21. $\dfrac{x^2(3-4x^2)}{(1-2x^2)^{3/2}}$.

22. $\dfrac{x-4}{(x+1)^2\sqrt{(x^2+4)}}$.

23. $\dfrac{2(x-1)}{(2-x)^3}$.

24. $\dfrac{-1}{\sqrt{\{2x(x-1)^3\}}}$.

25. $\dfrac{x^2-1}{2x\sqrt{(x+x^3)}}$.

26. (a) $\dfrac{2x-y}{x-2y}$,   (b) $-\dfrac{2xy}{x^2+3y^2}$,   (c) $\dfrac{2x-6y+3}{6x-2y+2}$.

27. $-5/12$.

28. $4y=3x+14$.

29. (a) $\dfrac{2(3x^2-1)}{(x^2+1)^3}$,   (b) $\dfrac{2}{(x-1)^3}$,   (c) $\dfrac{1}{(x^2+1)^{3/2}}$.

30. (a) $\dfrac{2x(x-1)(3x^2-3x+2)}{(2x-1)^2}$,   (b) $\dfrac{x^2+3x-2}{2(x+1)^2\sqrt{(x-1)}}$,

   (c) $\dfrac{3(x-1)}{2\sqrt{\{(x+1)^3(x^3+1)\}}}$.

32. $-3, -12$.

33. $1/12, -1/32$.

Exercise 10.4 (pp. 203–204)

1. Min. 0 when $x=2\frac12$.   2.   Min. -27 when $x=-1$.
3. Min. 0 when $x=0$ and 3; max. 16 when $x=1$.
4. Min. -1 when $x=-1$; max. $\frac12$ when $x=2$.
5. Min. -3 when $x=-1$; max. 1 when $x=1$.
6. Min. -1 when $x=0$.   7. $17, -7$.
8. $24\frac49, 12$.
9. $0<y\leqslant 4$; $(-1,3), (1,3)$.
10. $-2\sqrt3\leqslant y\leqslant 2\sqrt3$; $(-3,-3), (0,0), (3,3)$.
11. 8.   12. 3.
13. 40 m.   14. 108 cm^2.
15. $V=2\pi h(R^2-h^2)$.   16. $\frac13 a$.
17. $6-\sqrt3$.   18. $\sqrt{\left(\dfrac{S^3p^2}{8\pi(1+p)^3}\right)}$; 2.

Exercise 10.5 (pp. 205–206)

1. 60 cm^2/s.   2. 4/25 cm/s.
3. 4 cm/s.   4. -6.
5. 2000.   6. -50.
7. $(s^4-1)/s^3$ m s^{-2}.   8. $-2/(2s+1)^3$ m s^{-2}.
9. 4 cm^2/s.
10. (a) 6π cm^3/s,   (b) 2π cm^2/s.
11. 0·01 m/s.   12. $\frac13$ cm/s.

Exercise 10.6 (pp. 207–208)

1. 0·3.
2. 0·01.
3. $\pi/50$.
4. $1\cdot2\pi\,\text{cm}^2$.
5. (a) $7\cdot5\pi\,\text{cm}^3$, (b) $2\cdot7\pi\,\text{cm}^3$.
6. 2%.
7. 6%, 4%.
8. $2\frac{1}{2}$%.
9. 1% decrease.
10. 3; (a) 8·03, (b) 7·94.
11. (a) 24·24, (b) 23·52.
12. (a) 2·001, (b) 0·198, (c) 4·996, (d) 1·02.

Exercise 10.7 (pp. 208–210)

1. (a) $\dfrac{6(x-1)}{(5+2x-x^2)^4}$, (b) $\dfrac{3x^2}{\sqrt{(2x^3+5)}}$.
3. $2x+y=5$.
4. $\pm\frac{3}{4}$.
5. $5x-8y+22=0$.

6. (a) $2(9x^2+12x+1)(x^2+1)^3$, (b) $\dfrac{5x^2-2x-2}{\sqrt{(2x-1}}$,

   (c) $\dfrac{5x-7}{(x+1)^3}$, (d) $-\dfrac{1}{\sqrt{\{(x+3)^3(x+5)\}}}$.

7. $\dfrac{4x}{\sqrt{(1+4x^2)}}$, $\dfrac{4}{\sqrt{(1+4x^2)^3}}$,

8. $\dfrac{x(2x^2-y^2)}{y(x^2-2y^2)}$.
9. 1, 6.

11. $(0,0)$ max, $(2,-108)$ min, $(5,0)$ inflexion.
12. $(1,\frac{1}{2})$ max, $(-1,-\frac{1}{2})$ min; $(0,0)$ inflexion, $(\sqrt{3},\frac{1}{4}\sqrt{3})$ inflexion, $(-\sqrt{3},-\frac{1}{4}\sqrt{3})$ inflexion.
13. (i) $g'(x+g(a))$. (ii) $g'(x)\cdot g'(a+g(x))$, (iii) $2xg'(x^2)$.
15. $20/(\pi+2)$.
16. (a) $25\,\text{cm}^2$, (b) $8\sqrt{5}\,\text{cm}$.
17. -2.
18. (a) $4\pi\,\text{cm}^3/\text{s}$, (b) $17\pi/5\,\text{cm}^2/\text{s}$.
19. (a) 4·001, (b) 0·2008, (c) 2·001.
20. (a) 72·01, (b) 68·98.
21. $1\frac{1}{2}$%.
22. 0·08.
23. $64R^3/81$.
24. 0·5 cm/s.
25. $16\frac{1}{2}$ s, $a/27$ cm/s.

Exercise 11.1 (pp. 212–213)

1. (a) 180°, (b) 45°, (c) 30°, (d) 240°.
2. (a) $\pi/2$, (b) $\pi/3$, (c) $5\pi/6$, (d) $7\pi/4$.
3. (a) -1, (b) $-\frac{1}{2}$, (c) 1, (d) $2/\sqrt{3}$.
4. (a) $\pi/4$, (b) $-\pi/3$, (c) $\pi/6$, (d) π.
5. 15 cm, 75 cm².
6. $8-2\pi\,\text{cm}^2$.
7. $\frac{1}{2}r^2(2\theta+\sin 2\theta)$, $2r(1+\theta+\cos\theta)$.
8. (a) 1·2, (b) 0·4, (c) $2\pi/3$, (d) $\pi/6$.
9. 6.

10. (a) $\pi/6$, $5\pi/6$, (b) $\pi/3$, $2\pi/3$, $4\pi/3$, $5\pi/3$, (c) $\pi/4$, $5\pi/4$.
11. (a) $\pi/12$, $5\pi/12$, $3\pi/4$, (b) $\pi/18$, $\pi/6$, $5\pi/18$, $\pi/2$, $13\pi/18$, $5\pi/6$, $17\pi/18$.
12. $-\pi < x < -\pi/2$, $\pi/4 < x < \pi/2$, $3\pi/4 < x < 3\pi/2$.
13. $13{\cdot}7\,\text{cm}^2$, $29{\cdot}7\,\text{cm}$.   14. $98{\cdot}8\,\text{cm}^2$.
15. $0{\cdot}403$, $13{\cdot}0\,\text{cm}^2$.

Exercise 11.2 (p. 216)

1. $2n\pi \pm 2\pi/5$.
2. $n\pi + \pi/3$.
3. $n\pi + (-1)^n\pi/8$.
4. $(2n+1)\pi$.
5. $n\pi - \pi/4$.
6. $n\pi + (-1)^n\pi/6$.
7. $(2n+1)\pi/2$.
8. $(2n+1)\pi/4$.
9. $n\pi$, $2n\pi \pm \pi/3$.
10. $2n\pi/3$.
11. $2n\pi \pm \pi/3$.
12. $n\pi + \pi/4$.
13. $n\pi/3$.
14. $(2n+1)\pi/10$.
15. $(2n+1)\pi/8$.
16. $(4n+1)\pi/16$, $(4n+1)\pi/4$.
17. $360n° + 122{\cdot}3°$, $360n° + 20{\cdot}8°$.
18. $360n° + 121{\cdot}9°$, $360n° + 1{\cdot}9°$.

Exercise 11.3 (p. 218)

1. (a) $0{\cdot}0209$, (b) $0{\cdot}0122$, (c) $0{\cdot}000262$.
2. (a) 2, (b) 3/2, (c) 4/9.
3. (a) $\dfrac{\sqrt{3}}{2} + \dfrac{1}{2}\theta - \dfrac{\sqrt{3}}{4}\theta^2$, (b) $\dfrac{\sqrt{2}}{2} + \dfrac{\sqrt{2}}{2}\theta - \dfrac{\sqrt{2}}{4}\theta^2$, (c) $1 - \dfrac{5}{2}\theta^2$.
4. (a) 1/2, (b) 3, (c) 5/4.
5. (a) 2, (b) 2/3.

Exercise 11.4 (pp. 221–222)

1. (a) $2\cos 2x$, (b) $-12\sin 4x$, (c) $2\sec^2 \tfrac{1}{2}x$.
2. (a) $-4\cos^3 x \sin x$, (b) $\cos x/2\sqrt{(\sin x)}$, (c) $5\sin 10x$.

3. (a) $3(x+\sin x)^2(1+\cos x)$, (b) $2x\cos(x^2)$, (c) $\dfrac{\pi}{30}\sec^2(6x°)$.

4. (a) $x^3(4\cos x - x\sin x)$, (b) $8x\tan x + (4x^2+1)\sec^2 x$,
   (c) $x(2\sin 3x + 3x\cos 3x)$.

5. (a) $-\csc(x+1)\cot(x+1)$, (b) $4\csc^2(1-2x)$,
   (c) $3\sec(3x-4)\tan(3x-4)$.

6. (a) $-\sin x \sec^2(\cos x)$, (b) $\dfrac{1}{2\sqrt{x}}\sec(1+\sqrt{x})\tan(1+\sqrt{x})$,

   (c) $\dfrac{1}{x^2}\csc^2\left(\dfrac{1}{x}\right)$.

7. (a) $\cos x \cos 2x - 2\sin x \sin 2x$, (b) $3\cos^2 x \cos 4x$, (c) $\cos x$.

8. (a) $\dfrac{x\cos x - 2\sin x}{x^3}$, (b) $\dfrac{\sin x + \cos x}{(\cos x - \sin x)^2}$, (c) $-\dfrac{3}{1+\sin 3x}$.

9. $(\pi/2, 5)$ max; $(3\pi/2, -3)$ min.

10. $(\pi/3, \pi/3 - \sqrt{3})$ min; $(5\pi/3, 5\pi/3 + \sqrt{3})$ max.
11. $(3\pi/4, -1)$ min; $(7\pi/4, -1)$ min.
12. $(0,0)$ inflexion; $(\pi/3, 3\sqrt{3}/16)$ max; $(2\pi/3, -3\sqrt{3}/16)$ min; $(\pi, 0)$ inflexion; $(4\pi/3, 3\sqrt{3}/16)$ max; $(5\pi/3, -3\sqrt{3}/16)$ min; $(2\pi, 0)$ inflexion.
13. (a) $\pi/3$, (b) $10\,\mathrm{m}$, (c) $30\,\mathrm{m\,s^{-1}}$, at O.
14. $4500\,k\pi\,\mathrm{cm^3/s}$.
15. (a) $2{\cdot}5\,\mathrm{cm^2/s}$, (b) $\frac{1}{2}\sqrt{3} + 1\,\mathrm{cm/s}$.
16. (a) $0{\cdot}860$, (b) $1{\cdot}0105$, (c) $0{\cdot}870$.
17. $\frac{1}{3}$; $20 < P \leqslant 10(1 + \sqrt{10})$.
18. (a) $8\,\mathrm{m\,s^{-2}}$, (b) $3\sqrt{3}\,\mathrm{m\,s^{-1}}$.

Exercise 11.5 (p. 224)

1. (a) $-\frac{1}{3}\cos 3x + c$, (b) $2\sin\frac{1}{2}x + c$, (c) $2\tan 2x + c$.
2. (a) $\frac{1}{2}x + \frac{1}{4}\sin 2x + c$, (b) $-\cot x - x + c$, (c) $\frac{1}{3}\sin^3 x + c$.
3. (a) $-\dfrac{1}{4}\cos^4 x + c$, (b) $\dfrac{1}{4}\cos 2x - \dfrac{1}{8}\cos 4x + c$,

   (c) $\dfrac{1}{6}\sin 3x + \dfrac{1}{2}\sin x + c$.

4. (a) $\frac{1}{2}$, (b) $(\pi - 2)/24$, (c) $\frac{1}{3}$.
5. (a) $\sqrt{3} - \pi/3$, (b) $3/10$, (c) $1/4$.
6. (a) 1, (b) $1 - \pi/2$, (c) $2/3$.
7. $\frac{1}{3}\tan^3 x - \tan x + x + c$.
8. $-2\cos^2 x + \text{constant}$.
9. $\dfrac{3}{8} + \dfrac{1}{2}\cos 2x + \dfrac{1}{8}\cos 4x$; $(3\pi + 8)/32$.
10. 1.
11. $11\pi^2$.
12. $4/3\pi$.

Exercise 11.6 (p. 227)

1. $\dfrac{1}{\sqrt{(4 - x^2)}}$.

2. $\dfrac{3}{1 + 9x^2}$.

3. $-\dfrac{1}{\sqrt{(-x - x^2)}}$.

4. $\dfrac{x}{1 + x^2} + \tan^{-1} x$.

5. -1.

6. $1 - \dfrac{x\sin^{-1} x}{\sqrt{(1 - x^2)}}$.

7. $-\dfrac{1}{x\sqrt{(x^2 - 1)}}$.

8. $\dfrac{2 - 8x\tan^{-1} 2x}{(1 + 4x^2)^2}$.

9. $\dfrac{1}{1 + x^2}$.

10. $\sin^{-1}\dfrac{x}{5} + c$.

11. $\dfrac{1}{3}\tan^{-1}\dfrac{x}{3} + c$.

12. $\dfrac{1}{2}\sin^{-1} 2x + c$.

13. $\dfrac{1}{3}\tan^{-1} 3x + c$.

14. $\dfrac{1}{3}\sin^{-1}\dfrac{3x}{4} + c$.

15. $\dfrac{1}{6}\tan^{-1}\dfrac{2x}{3} + c$.

16. $\pi/6$.

17. $\pi/8$.

18. $\pi/9$.

19. $\pi/15$.

20. $\pi/72$.

21. $\pi/8$.

Exercise 11.7 (pp. 228–230)

1. $(2+\sqrt{3})\pi x/6$, $(5\pi-6\sqrt{3})x^2/24$.
4. (a) 0, $\pi/2$, π, $3\pi/2$, 2π, (b) 0, $2\pi/3$, π, $4\pi/3$, 2π.
5. (a) $(4n+1)\pi/6$, (b) $(2n+1)\pi/6$, $n\pi\pm\pi/3$.
6. $360n° + 12\cdot4°$, $360n° - 79\cdot8°$.
7. $\frac{1}{2}\cos\alpha$.
9. $\cos x$, $-\sin x$; $-\operatorname{cosec}^2 x$, $-\operatorname{cosec} x \cot x$.
10. (a) $2\sin(4x-10)$, (b) $4x^3(\tan 4x + x\sec^2 4x)$,
    (c) $\dfrac{2\sec x}{(\sec x - \tan x)^2}$, (d) $\dfrac{\cos x}{(\cos 2x)^{3/2}}$.
11. (a) $(\pi/6, 2\sqrt{3})$ max; $(5\pi/6, -2\sqrt{3})$ min; $(3\pi/2, 0)$ inflexion,
    (b) $(0,0)$ inflexion; $(\pi/2, 4)$ max; $(\pi, 0)$ inflexion;
    $(3\pi/2, -4)$ min; $(2\pi, 0)$ inflexion.
12. (a) $\frac{1}{2}\sin(2x-1)+c$, (b) $\frac{1}{2}x - \frac{1}{2}\sin x + c$,
    (c) $\frac{1}{2}\tan^2 x + c$, (d) $-\dfrac{1}{10}\cos 5x - \dfrac{1}{6}\cos 3x + c$.
13. (a) $21/128$, (b) $(3\pi+4)/48$.
14. $x\sin x + \cos x + c$; $2\cos x + 2x\sin x - x^2\cos x + c$.
15. $\pi - \sqrt{3}$.   16. $\frac{3}{4}\pi^2$.
17. $\tan x + \sec x + c$; $4(\sqrt{3}-1)/\pi$.
18. (a) $\dfrac{(\sin^{-1} x)\sqrt{(1-x^2)}-x}{(\sin^{-1} x)^2\sqrt{(1-x^2)}}$, (b) $\dfrac{\sec x \tan x}{1+\sec^2 x}$, (c) $-\dfrac{x}{\sqrt{(1-x^2)}}$.
19. (a) $\sin^{-1}\dfrac{x}{3}+c$, (b) $\dfrac{1}{15}\tan^{-1}\dfrac{3x}{5}+c$.
20. (a) $\pi/3\sqrt{3}$, (b) $\pi/12$.
21. (ii) $\dfrac{2+p^2}{2(1+p^2)}$.
24. $\dfrac{1}{x^2+2ax+a^2+1}$; (a) $\tan^{-1}(x+2)+c$, (b) $\dfrac{1}{2}\tan^{-1}\left(\dfrac{x+1}{2}\right)+c$.

Exercise 12.1 (pp. 233–234)

1. (a) 5040, (b) 600, (c) 1680, (d) 120, (e) 4, (f) 6720.
2. (a) 5!, (b) 10!/6!, (c) $n!/(n-3)!$.
3. 720.   4. 40 320.
5. 20 160.   6. 151 200.
7. 13 800.   8. (a) 240, (b) 600.
9. (a) 120, (b) 432.   10. (a) 1000, (b) 720, (c) 990.
11. (a) 720, (b) 20 160, (c) 60, (d) 50 400.
12. 60, 30.   13. 10 080.
14. 720.   15. 120, 72.
16. 6720; (a) 720, (b) 2400.   17. (a) 48, (b) 180.
18. 96.
19. (a) 168, (b) 2016, (c) 20; 2520.
20. 9.

Exercise 12.2 (p. 236)

1. (a) 35, (b) 5, (c) 6, (d) 1.
3. (a) 210, (b) 1140, (c) 1287, (d) 12.
4. 1260.
5. (a) 462, (b) 5775, (c) 10 395.
6. 15 840.   7. 38, 16.
8. (a) 2277, (b) 2541.   9. 238.
10. 79, 24.   11. (a) 90, (b) 7560.
12. (a) 15 015, (b) 37 037.

Exercise 12.3 (pp. 239–240)

1. $\frac{1}{6}, \frac{1}{2}, \frac{2}{3}$.   2. $\frac{1}{2}, \frac{1}{13}, \frac{3}{13}$.

3. $\frac{1}{8}, \frac{1}{2}, \frac{3}{4}$.   4. $\frac{1}{21}, \frac{2}{7}, \frac{10}{21}$.

5. (a) $\frac{1}{4}$, (b) $\frac{5}{9}$, (c) $\frac{7}{36}$.   6. (a) $\frac{1}{14}$, (b) $\frac{3}{28}$, (c) $\frac{3}{7}$, (d) $\frac{4}{7}$.

7. (a) 0·8, (b) 0·07, (c) 0·1, (d) 0·43.

8. 0·32.   9. (a) $\frac{1}{9}$, (b) $\frac{2}{3}$.

10. (a) $\frac{1}{16}$, (b) $\frac{3}{8}$, (c) $\frac{5}{8}$, (d) $\frac{7}{8}$.

11. (a) $\frac{3}{10}$, (b) $\frac{3}{10}$, (c) $\frac{3}{10}$, (d) $\frac{1}{5}$.

12. $\frac{11!}{3!2!}$; (a) $\frac{2}{11}$, (b) $\frac{1}{77}$.

13. (a) 0·204, (b) 0·052, (c) 0·398.

14. $\frac{21}{55}, \frac{27}{55}, \frac{27}{220}, \frac{1}{220}$.   15. (a) 0·108, (b) 0·374.

16. (a) $\frac{1}{42}$, (b) $\frac{1}{7}$, (c) $\frac{2}{3}$, (d) $\frac{1}{2}$.

Exercise 12.4 (p. 241)

1. (a) 1260, (b) 8232.
2. 30 240; (a) 840, (b) 10 080, (c) 13 440.
3. 63.   4. 20.
5. 280, 36.   6. (a) 243, (b) 21.

7. (a) $\frac{1}{7}$, (b) $\frac{3}{35}$.

8. (a) (i) $\frac{5}{18}$, (ii) $\frac{1}{3}$, (b) $\frac{12}{35}$, (c) 294.

9. (a) $\dfrac{6}{77}$, (b) 0, (c) $\dfrac{2}{15}$, (d) $\dfrac{2}{33}$.

10. 4.12×10^{-6}.

Exercise 13.1 (pp. 243–244)

1. $25, 30; 5n.$

2. $16, 19; 3n+1.$

3. $\dfrac{1}{5}, \dfrac{1}{6}; \dfrac{1}{n}.$

4. $\dfrac{5}{6}, \dfrac{6}{7}; \dfrac{n}{n+1}.$

5. $16, 32; 2^{n-1}.$

6. $35, 48; n^2 - 1.$

7. $\dfrac{4}{3}, \dfrac{8}{3}; \dfrac{1}{3} \cdot 2^{n-3}.$

8. $\dfrac{1}{30}, \dfrac{1}{42}; \dfrac{1}{n(n+1)}.$

9. $5, -6; (-1)^{n-1}n.$

10. $4, 17; 10+(-1)^{n+1}n.$

11. $11, 21, 35; 14n-7 \ (n \geqslant 2).$

12. $-4, -46, -130; -21n^2+21n-4.$

13. $2, 2, 4; 2^{n-1} \ (n \geqslant 2).$

14. $1, -\dfrac{1}{2}, -\dfrac{1}{6}; -\dfrac{1}{n(n-1)} \ (n \geqslant 2).$

15. $1, 8, 27; n^3.$

16. $1, 4, 9; n^2.$

17. $88\,200.$

18. $22\,100, 20\,825.$

Exercise 13.2 (pp. 246–247)

1. (a) $31, 4n+3$, (b) $-17, 25-7n$, (c) $37, 2n-9$,
   (d) $10\frac{1}{2}, \frac{1}{2}(n+5)$.

2. (a) 1325, (b) 1188, (c) 88, (d) $193\frac{1}{2}$.

3. (a) 904, (b) 1105, (c) -80, (d) 152.

4. 1512.

5. 9072.

7. $2600, 6\frac{1}{4}.$

8. $7, 4, 1; -333.$

9. $607, 825.$

10. 8.

11. $4, 16.$

12. $-17, 3.$

14. $6, 11, 16.$

15. (a) 15, (b) -12, (c) $\dfrac{5}{27}$, (d) $\lg 9$.

16. $8, 11, 14.$

17. $3, 10, 17.$

18. $4, 6.$

19. $20, 190.$

20. 7.

Exercise 13.3 (pp. 249–250)

1. (a) $64, 2^{n-2}$, (b) $\frac{2}{3}, 2 \cdot 3^{5-n}$, (c) $\frac{25}{32}, 200(-4)^{1-n}$, (d) $-\frac{81}{16}, -\left(\frac{3}{2}\right)^{n-3}$.

2. (a) $9, 127\frac{3}{4}$, (b) $9, 42\frac{3}{4}$, (c) $6, 1249 \cdot 92$, (d) $7, 14\frac{15}{32}$.

3. (a) $111 \cdot 1111$, (b) $\frac{182}{243}$, (c) $1 - (-2)^n$, (d) $a^p(a^{3k}-1)/(a^3-1)$.

4. $\frac{3}{4}$.   5. $-5, 2\frac{1}{2}$.

6. (a) 9, (b) $\frac{1}{9}$, (c) 10^{15}.   7. 13.

8. $-53\frac{1}{3}, -385\frac{5}{6}$.   9. $-40, -8$.

10. $182; \frac{1}{2}, -1$.   11. 2.

12. 12.   13. 2, 6.

14. $(3^n - 1)/24; 8$.   15. 10.

Exercise 13.4 (p. 252)

1. (a) 9, (b) $\frac{2}{3}$, (c) $11\frac{1}{9}$, (d) 27.

2. (a) $6/11$, (b) $8/111$, (c) $31/54$.

3. $25 \cdot 6$.   4. $-\frac{2}{3}, 81$.

5. $6, \frac{1}{4}, 8$.

6. (a) $\dfrac{1}{1-3x}, |x| < \frac{1}{3}$, (b) $\dfrac{2}{2+x}, |x| < 2$,

   (c) $\dfrac{2}{1+2x}, |x| < \frac{1}{2}$, (d) $\dfrac{3x}{3-x}, |x| < 3$.

7. $x < 0, -3$.   8. $243\left\{1 - \left(\dfrac{5}{9}\right)^n\right\}; 243; 8$.

Exercise 13.5 (pp. 254–255)

1. (a) $4 + 14 + 36 + 76 = 130$, (b) $50 + 29 + 6 = 85$,
   (c) $11 + 15 + 19 + 23 + 27 + 31 = 126$,
   (d) $120 + 60 + 40 + 30 + 24 + 20 = 294$,
   (e) $\sin\dfrac{\pi}{3} + \sin\dfrac{2\pi}{3} + \sin\pi + \sin\dfrac{4\pi}{3} + \sin\dfrac{5\pi}{3} + \sin 2\pi = 0$,
   (f) $3 - 5 + 9 - 17 + 33 - 65 = -42$.

2. (a) $\sum_{1}^{12}(2r+3)$,   (b) $\sum_{1}^{16}r^3$,   (c) $\sum_{1}^{40}(-1)^r(r+1)$,

    (d) $\sum_{1}^{7}360(-\tfrac{1}{2})^{r-1}$,   (e) $\sum_{1}^{10}\dfrac{2r-1}{2r}$,   (f) $\sum_{1}^{12}\dfrac{r^2}{3r+1}$.

3. (a) 940,   (b) 16,   (c) -1275,   (d) 855,   (e) 2,   (f) 1/90.

Exercise 13.6 (p. 258)

1. (a) $x^4+4x^3y+6x^2y^2+4xy^3+y^4$,
    (b) $a^7-7a^6b+21a^5b^2-35a^4b^3+35a^3b^4-21a^2b^5+7ab^6-b^7$,
    (c) $64+192p^2+240p^4+160p^6+60p^8+12p^{10}+p^{12}$,
    (d) $32h^5-80h^4k+80h^3k^2-40h^2k^3+10hk^4-k^5$,

    (e) $x^3+3x+\dfrac{3}{x}+\dfrac{1}{x^3}$,

    (f) $z^8-4z^6+7z^4-7z^2+\dfrac{35}{8}-\dfrac{7}{4z^2}+\dfrac{7}{16z^4}-\dfrac{1}{16z^6}+\dfrac{1}{256z^8}$.

2. (a) $210x^4$,   (b) $16\,128x^2$,   (c) $1760a^3b^9$,   (d) $-945p^4q^6$,   (e) -20,
    (f) $36/x^3$.

3. $64x^5+\dfrac{160}{x}+\dfrac{20}{x^7}$. $\qquad\qquad$ 4.   14.

5. 15. $\qquad\qquad\qquad\qquad\qquad$ 6.   2.
7. $8,\ -\tfrac{1}{2}$. $\qquad\qquad\qquad\qquad\quad$ 8.   1·13.
9. 30·43168.
10. $1+30x+420x^2+3640x^3$; 1·03042.
11. (a) $1+7x+21x^2+35x^3$,   (b) $1+7x+14x^2-7x^3$.
12. $1+16x+136x^2+784x^3$. $\qquad$ 13. $1+9x+24x^2$.
14. (a) $-16\,464$,   (b) -19,   (c) -1760,   (d) 26.

Exercise 13.7 (pp. 260–261)

1. $1-2x+3x^2$; $(-1)^r(r+1)x^r$.
2. $1+x+x^2$; x^r.
3. $1-6x+24x^2$; $(-1)^r(r+1)(r+2)2^{r-1}x^r$.

4. $1+\dfrac{1}{2}x-\dfrac{1}{8}x^2$; $|x|<1$. $\qquad$ 5. $1-x-x^2$; $|x|<\tfrac{1}{3}$.

6. $1-\dfrac{1}{4}x+\dfrac{3}{32}x^2$; $|x|<2$. $\qquad$ 7. $\dfrac{1}{3}-\dfrac{1}{9}x+\dfrac{1}{27}x^2$; $|x|<3$.

8. $2-\dfrac{1}{4}x-\dfrac{1}{64}x^2$; $|x|<4$. $\qquad$ 9. $27-18x+2x^2$; $|x|<\dfrac{9}{4}$.

10. $1-x^2+\dfrac{3}{2}x^4-\dfrac{5}{2}x^6$. $\qquad$ 11. $1-\dfrac{1}{2}x-\dfrac{1}{8}x^2-\dfrac{1}{16}x^3$; 0·9487.

12. $2+\dfrac{9}{2}x^2+\dfrac{17}{6}x^3$.

13. $\dfrac{1}{4}+\dfrac{1}{4}x+\dfrac{3}{16}x^2+\dfrac{1}{8}x^3+\dfrac{5}{64}x^4$; 0·309.

14. $1+x-\frac{1}{2}x^2+\frac{1}{2}x^3$; 1·732.   15. $1-7x+28x^2-112x^3$; $|x|<\frac{1}{4}$.

16. (a) $1-x+2x^2-3x^3$,   (b) $1+\frac{1}{2}x+\frac{7}{8}x^2-\frac{7}{16}x^3$.

Exercise 13.8 (pp. 261–264)

1. $n(n-1)$; 15th.

2. (a) $3, 4\frac{1}{2}, 4\frac{1}{6}, 4+\dfrac{1}{n(n-1)}$,   (b) $2, 4, 18, n \cdot n!$.

3. (a) 250,   (b) 510,   (c) $n(n+1)$.

4. b^2.   5.   11, 20.

6. $-2\frac{1}{2}, \frac{1}{2}$; 205.   7. $2\frac{1}{2}$.

8. 29 mm.   9.   (i) $1, \dfrac{2}{3}$,   (ii) $\dfrac{53}{165}$.

10. (i) $1+\dfrac{1}{4}+\dfrac{1}{16}+\dfrac{1}{64}$, (ii) all values of r; $1+r^2$ for $r \neq 0$, 0 for $r = 0$.

12. (a) 1 200 000,   (b) 72.   13. $-2 < x < 2$; 6.

14. $1, -1+\frac{1}{2}\sqrt{2}, -1-\frac{1}{2}\sqrt{2}$; (i) $\dfrac{8}{7}+\dfrac{2}{7}\sqrt{2}$, (ii) $-35+\dfrac{45}{2}\sqrt{2}$.

16. (i) $-\frac{1}{3} < x < 1, \frac{1}{2}$, (ii) 149.

17. (a) $1+12x+54x^2$,   (b) $1-3x-9x^2$.

18. (a) 28/243,   (b) -307.   19.   14.

20. 255, 1.   21. $-\dfrac{3}{2}, -8$; 405.

22. $\dfrac{5}{2}x+\dfrac{15}{4}x^2+\dfrac{65}{8}x^3$.

23. $1+x-x^2+\dfrac{5}{3}x^3-\dfrac{10}{3}x^4$; $|x|<\frac{1}{3}$; 0·98990.

24. $1-6x+24x^2-80x^3$, $|x|<\frac{1}{2}$; 0·000008500.

25. (i) $1+\dfrac{1}{2}x-\dfrac{1}{8}x^2$, (ii) $1+\dfrac{1}{2}x+\dfrac{3}{8}x^2$; $1+x+\dfrac{1}{2}x^2$; 3·315.

26. (a) u^3+3u, u^5+5u^3+5u,

    (b) $1+kx+\dfrac{1}{2}(3k^2-1)x^2+\dfrac{k}{2}(5k^2-3)x^3$.

28. 0·015625, 0·140625, 0·421875, 0·421875.

Exercise 14.1 (pp. 266–267)

1. (a) even,   (b) odd,   (c) odd,   (d) even,   (e) neither,   (f) odd.

3. (a) even,   (b) odd,   (c) neither,   (d) neither,   (e) odd,   (f) even.

4. (a) odd,   (b) even,   (c) odd,   (d) even,   (e) neither,   (f) even.

Exercise 14.2 (pp. 269–270)

5. $(0, -1)$; $(0, -1)$.   6. $(0, 1)$; $(0, 1)$.
7. $(1, -1)$; $(1, -1)$.   8. $(-2, 0)$; none.
9. $(2, 1)$; $(2, 1)$.   10. $(\frac{1}{2}, 2\frac{1}{4})$; $(\frac{1}{2}, \frac{4}{9})$.
11. $(-2, 4)$, $(0, 0)$; $(-2, \frac{1}{4})$.
12. $(-2, 16)$, $(2, -16)$; $(-2, \frac{1}{16})$, $(2, -\frac{1}{16})$.
15. $(1, -4)$; $(1, 4)$.   16. $(3, 0)$; $(3, 0)$.

Exercise 14.4 (pp. 273–274)

1. $x = -2$, $y = 0$.   2. $x = 4$, $y = 0$.
3. $x = 1\frac{1}{2}$, $y = 0$.   4. $x = -2$, $y = 1$.
5. $x = -2$, $y = 1$.   6. $x = 1\frac{1}{2}$, $y = 1$.
7. $x = -2$, $y = 2$.   8. $x = 3$, $y = 3$.
9. $x = \dfrac{2}{5}$, $y = -\dfrac{2}{5}$. 10. $y = \dfrac{x}{x+1}$.

11. $y = \dfrac{1-x}{1+x}$.

Exercise 14.5 (p. 276)

2. (a) $x + 4y = 12$, (b) $y = x^2 + 2x + 2$, (c) $8x = (y+4)^2$,
    (d) $y = x + 2$ $(x \geqslant -1)$, (e) $y = 1/(x-2)$, (f) $y = x^2 + 2x + 2$ $(x \geqslant -1)$.
3. (a) $4x^2 + 9y^2 = 36$, (b) $25x^2 - y^2 = 25$,
    (c) $4x^2 + y^2 - 8x - 2y + 1 = 0$, (d) $5x^2 - 6xy + 2y^2 = 1$,
    (e) $2x^2 + 2xy + y^2 = 1$.
4. (a) $(0,0)$, $(9,27)$, (b) $(-3, -3)$, $(1\frac{1}{2}, 6)$, (c) $(1, -4)$, $(16, 16)$,
    (d) $(7, 9)$, $(-\frac{7}{3}, \frac{25}{9})$, (e) $(1, 0)$, $(\frac{1}{2}, \frac{1}{2})$, (f) $(-3, 4)$, $(4, -3)$.

Exercise 14.6 (p. 278)

1. t.   2. $2/t$.
3. $1/4t^2$.   4. $1/6(1 - 2t)$.
5. $-\frac{3}{4} \cot t$.   6. $-\tan t$.
7. $-\frac{1}{2}t^3$, $\frac{3}{4}t^5$.   8. $\dfrac{1}{t} - t^2$, $-\dfrac{1}{12t^3} - \dfrac{1}{6}$.
9. $\dfrac{2t+1}{3t^2}$, $-\dfrac{2(t+1)}{9t^5}$.   10. $\dfrac{t}{t+1}$, $\dfrac{1}{2(t+1)^3}$.
11. $-2\sin t$, -1.   12. $-2\cot 2t$, $-4\cosec^3 2t$.
13. 9.   14. $(3t^2 + 1)y = 2tx + (t^2 + 1)^2$.

15. $y = x\cosec\theta - \cot\theta$.   16. $\dfrac{t-3}{15 - 9t}$; $(16, 9)$.
17. $(2, 4)$, $(10, 0)$; $(4, 12\sqrt{3} - 18)$, $(4, -12\sqrt{3} - 18)$.

Exercise 14.7 (pp. 279–281)

1. (a) neither, (b) odd, (c) even, (d) even, (e) even, (f) neither.
2. (a) $a = c = 0$, (b) $b = d = 0$, (c) $a = 0, b > 0, c^2 < 4bd$,
   (or $a = b = c = 0, d \geqslant 0$), (d) $a = 0, b < 0, c^2 < 4bd$ (or $a = b = c = 0, d \leqslant 0$).
3. $f(x) = k/x$.   6. $(-1, 0); 1, -3; 1/\sqrt[3]{2}$, minimum.
7. $f(x)$: max $(0, 0)$, min $(\pm \sqrt{2}, 1)$,

   $g(x)$: max $(\pm \sqrt{2}, 1)$, inflexion $\left(\pm \sqrt{\dfrac{10}{3}, \dfrac{21}{25}} \right)$.

9. (a) $(1, C), (2, E), (4, A), (5, B)$, (c) $y = \left| \dfrac{1}{x+1} \right|$ is a possibility.

12. $a > 4$: one; $0 < a < 4$: none; $-4 < a < 0$: two; $a < -4$: one.
13. (a) $9x^2 - 4y^2 = 144$, (b) $x^2 - y^2 = 1$,
    (c) $10x^2 - 2xy + 5y^2 = 49$, (d) $4x^2 - 6\sqrt{3}xy + 9y^2 = 9$.

14. $\dfrac{3t^2 - 4}{2t}; \left(\dfrac{8}{3}, \pm \dfrac{16}{9}\sqrt{3} \right)$.   15. $\dfrac{t-1}{t+1}, (4, 0); x + y = 2$.

16. $(-\frac{1}{2}, -6), (3, 1); 2, y = 2x - 5 \ (x \neq 0)$.

17. $x = \dfrac{\sqrt{3}}{2} \sin(\theta + 45°), y = \dfrac{1}{2} \cos(\theta + 45°); 4x^2 + 12y^2 = 3$.

18. (a) $\dfrac{12t - 14}{9 + 18t}, \dfrac{40}{81(1 - 2t)(1 + 2t)^3}$.

    (b) $-\cot \left(\dfrac{3t}{2} \right), -\dfrac{3}{8} \operatorname{cosec}^3 \left(\dfrac{3t}{2} \right) \sec \left(\dfrac{t}{2} \right)$.

19. $(1 - \sin \theta - 2 \sin^2 \theta)/\cos \theta, (\frac{1}{2}, \pm\frac{3}{4}\sqrt{3}), (1, 0); 1 \cdot 3\pi$.

Exercise 15.1 (pp. 284–285)

1. $x^2 + y^2 + 6x - 8y = 0$.   2. $x + y = 4$.
3. $x^2 = 4$.   4. $y = 4x + 13$.
5. $(x - y)(x + y - 2) = 0$.   6. $x^2 = 4(y - 1)$.
7. $xy = 9$.   8. $x^2 + y^2 - 2x - 4y + 1 = 0$.
9. $y^2 = 12x$.   10. $x^2 + y^2 - 12x - 2y + 21 = 0$.
11. $x^2 + y^2 + 2x - 2y = 0$.   12. $3x + y + 3 = 0; (-3, 6)$.
13. $y^2 = 2x$.   14. $(\frac{1}{2}t + 1, \frac{1}{2}t^2 - 2); y = 2x^2 - 4x$.
15. (a) $x + y = \frac{1}{2}c$, (b) $xy = \frac{1}{4}k$, (c) $x^2 + y^2 = \frac{1}{4}l^2$.
16. $y = 2x^2$.

Exercise 15.2 (pp. 288–289)

1. (a) $x^2 + y^2 - 6x - 4y - 3 = 0$, (b) $x^2 + y^2 + 2x + 4y + 4 = 0$,
   (c) $x^2 + y^2 = 25$, (d) $x^2 + y^2 - x - 2 = 0$,
   (e) $x^2 + y^2 - 8x + 2y + 14 = 0$, (f) $x^2 + y^2 + 6x - 10y + 14 = 0$.
2. (a) $(1, 3), 3$, (b) $(0, 0), 2$, (c) $(-3, -4), 5$,
   (d) $(2, -1), 1$, (e) $(0, 0), \frac{1}{2}\sqrt{5}$, (f) $(1\frac{1}{2}, -2\frac{1}{2}), \sqrt{5}$.

3. (a) $k > 0$, (b) $k = 1$, (c) No values of k,
    (d) $k = 0$, (e) $k < 10$, (f) $k > 4$ or $k < -4$.
4. (a) $y = 2x + 5$, (b) $x + y + 3 = 0$, (c) $y = 3x - 13$,
    (d) $x + 8y = 22$.
5. (a) 5, (b) 7, (c) 6, (d) $2\sqrt{10}$.
6. (a) $x^2 + y^2 - 2x - 6y = 0$, (b) $x^2 + y^2 - 6x - 4y - 7 = 0$,
    (c) $x^2 + y^2 - 2x + 4y - 15 = 0$, (d) $x^2 + y^2 + 6x - 16y + 23 = 0$.
7. (a) 24, 2, (b) 12, 2.
8. $x^2 + y^2 + 6x - 12y + 20 = 0$; (a) $y = 1, y = 11$, (b) $x = 2, x = -8$.
9. $x^2 + y^2 - 10x - 14y + 66 = 0$; $(5,7), 2\sqrt{2}$.
10. $x^2 + y^2 - 6x - 10y + 9 = 0$; 27 sq. units.
11. $x^2 + y^2 - 4x - 14y + 28 = 0$.
12. $(1,2), (9/5, 18/5)$.
13. $x^2 + y^2 - 7x - 3y + 8 = 0$; $x^2 + y^2 - 8x + 2y + 4 = 0$.

Exercise 15.3 (pp. 293–294)

1. $y + 3x = 19$; $3y = x + 17$.
2. $y = 2x - 2$; $2y + x = 6$.
3. $x + y = 1$; $y = x + 3$.
4. $y = 5x + 22$; $5y + x = 32$.
5. $2y = x - 13$; $2x + y + 4 = 0$.
6. $9y + 7x = 16$; $7y = 9x - 2$.
7. $10y = 27x - 31$; $27y + 10x = 165$.
8. $4y = 9x - 6$; $9y + 4x = 35$.
9. $4y = 3x + 5$; $3y + 4x = 10$.
10. $4y = x + 16$; $y + 4x = 72$.
11. (a) $(2,2)$, (b) $(3, -1)$, (c) $(2\frac{1}{2}, 1\frac{1}{2})$.
12. $5x - 4y + 34 = 0$.
13. $2x - y = 11, 2x - y + 21 = 0$.
14. 1, 4.
15. $y = 3$ at $(-1,3)$, $y = 12x - 21$ at $(5,39)$.
16. $y = 0, 3y = 4x$; $4/\sqrt{5}$.
17. 1, -7.
18. $\pm\sqrt{17}, 3x + 4y = 0$.
19. $y = 3x \pm 10$.
20. $3y = 15 \pm 4x$; $73 \cdot 7°$.
21. $2x \pm 3y = 10$; $(16/5, 6/5), (16/5, -6/5)$.
22. $x + ty = 2t + t^3$; $x^2 = 2y^2(y - 1)$.
23. $y = (p + q)x + p + q - pq$, $y = 2px + 2p - p^2$; $y = 0$.
24. $(p + q)y = (p^2 + pq + q^2)x - p^2q^2$; $2y = 3px - p^3$;
    $p = \frac{2}{3}\sqrt{2}, q = -\frac{1}{3}\sqrt{2}$ or $p = -\frac{2}{3}\sqrt{2}, q = \frac{1}{3}\sqrt{2}$.

Exercise 15.4 (pp. 296–297)

1. (a) $(1,0)$; $x = -1$, (b) $(3,0)$; $x = -3$, (c) $(-2,0)$; $x = 2$,
    (d) $(\frac{3}{4},0)$; $x = -5/4$, (e) $(\frac{1}{4},0)$; $x = -\frac{1}{4}$, (f) $(0,\frac{1}{4})$; $y = -\frac{1}{4}$,
    (g) $(2,0)$; $x = -2$, (h) $(3,0)$; $x = -3$.
2. (a) $y^2 = 8x$, (b) $y^2 = 20x$, (c) $x^2 = 4y$,
    (d) $y^2 + 12x = 0$, (e) $(y - 1)^2 = 4x$, (f) $x^2 = 4(y - 1)$.
3. (a) $y^2 = 4(x - 2)$, (b) $(y - 1)^2 = 12x$, (c) $(y - 1)^2 = 4(x + 2)$,
    (d) $x^2 - 8x + 2y + 11 = 0$.
4. (a) $(2t^2, 4t)$, (b) $(6t^2, 12t)$, (c) $(-4t^2, -8t)$.

5. (a) $y = 2x+2$, $x+2y = 9$, (b) $x+2y+6 = 0$, $y = 2x-18$,
(c) $2y = x+4$, $2x+y = 12$, (d) $x+y+3 = 0$, $y = x-9$.
6. $y^2 = a(x-a)$.   7. $2y^2 + ax = 0$.
9. $mc = a$; $x+y+1 = 0$, $2y = x+4$.
10. $(apq, a(p+q))$; $y^2 = a(2x-a)$.
12. $-p$; $\dfrac{2}{p+q}$; $\left(\dfrac{121a}{9}, \dfrac{22a}{3}\right)$; $5\sqrt{5}a$.
13. $x+2a = 0$.   14. $ty = x+at^2$.
15. (i) $x = 0$,   (ii) $2y^2 = 9ax$.

Exercise 15.5 (p. 300)

1. (a) $(2,3)$, $(1,4)$, $(-1,5)$,   (b) $(1,1)$, $(0,2)$, $(-2,3)$,
(c) $(0,5)$, $(-1,6)$, $(-3,7)$.
2. (a) $(1,2)$,   (b) $(3,-1)$,   (c) $(0,1)$,   (d) $(-2,-3)$.
3. (a) $(3,0)$, $(4,0)$, $x = 2$,   (b) $(0,1)$, $(2,1)$, $x = -2$,
(c) $(-5,0)$, $(-4,0)$, $x = -6$,   (d) $(-4,-2)$, $(-3\frac{3}{4}, -2)$, $x = -4\frac{1}{4}$,
(e) $(0,1)$, $(0,2)$, $y = 0$,   (f) $(1,-1)$, $(1,-\frac{3}{4})$, $y = -1\frac{1}{4}$.
4. (a) $(1,3)$, $(2,3)$, $x = 0$,   (b) $(-2,5)$, $(1,5)$, $x = -5$,
(c) $(1,0)$, $(0,0)$, $x = 2$,   (d) $(-3,-1)$, $(-3,1)$, $y = -3$.

Exercise 15.6 (pp. 300–304)

1. $(0,-2)$, $\left(\sqrt{\dfrac{3}{2}}, -\dfrac{1}{2}\right)$, $\left(-\sqrt{\dfrac{3}{2}}, -\dfrac{1}{2}\right)$.   2. $c^2 = a^2(1+m^2)$.

3. $y = x+2-\frac{1}{2}\pi$, $x+y = \frac{1}{2}\pi$.   4. $8y = 9x+7$, $8x+9y = 26$.

5. $(1,0)$, 1; $(0,1)$, 1; $\left(\dfrac{2}{1+m^2}, \dfrac{2m}{1+m^2}\right)$, $\left(\dfrac{2m}{1+m^2}, \dfrac{2m^2}{1+m^2}\right)$.

6. $x^2+y^2-10x-8y+16 = 0$; $(10,-6)$, 10, $53°$.
7. (i) $(3,4)$, 5,   (iv) $y = 2x-2+5\sqrt{5}$, $y = 2x-2-5\sqrt{5}$.
8. (a) $x^2+y^2-6x-6y+5 = 0$,   (b) $3x^2+3y^2-6x-26y+3 = 0$.
9. $x\cos\theta+y\sin\theta = a$; $(a(2\cos\theta+1), a(1-\cos\theta-2\cos^2\theta)/\sin\theta)$;
$(0, 2a/\sqrt{3})$, $(0, -2a/\sqrt{3})$.
10. (i) $x^2+y^2-2y-3 = 0$,   (ii) $4\pi/3$,
(iii) $x^2+y^2-\sqrt{3}x-3y = 0$; $x^2+y^2+2y-3 = 0$.
11. $x^2+y^2-10x-10y+25 = 0$; $x^2+y^2-34x-34y+289 = 0$;
(i) $(2,9)$,   (ii) $x+y = 11$.

12. $x^2+y^2-5x-6y+9 = 0$; $y = 2x+3$.
13. $y\cos\alpha+x\sin\alpha = a\sin\alpha\cos\alpha$.   14. ± 2.
15. $y\sin T+x = 1+2\sin^2 T$; $\frac{1}{4}\pi$.

17. $y = \left(\dfrac{5}{4}x_0^2 - \dfrac{13}{9}\right)x - \dfrac{5}{6}x_0^3$; $\pm\frac{1}{3}\sqrt{5}$, $\pm\frac{2}{3}\sqrt{2}$.

18. $py = x+ap^2$, $y+px = 2ap+ap^3$.
19. $y+tx = 2at+at^3$, $(2a+at^2, 0)$; $\pm\sqrt{3}$, $\pm\sqrt{15}$.
20. (i) $4a$,   (ii) $y^2 = 2a(x-4a)$.   21. $(apq, a(p+q))$.
22. $(a(2+p^2+pq+q^2), -apq(p+q))$; $y^2 = a(x-3a)$.

24. $y = mx + a/m.$

25. $py = x + ap^2.$

26. $y = \frac{3}{4}x + 5, y = -\frac{3}{4}x - 5.$

27. $(a(1+t^2), at); (a, 0).$

28. $(a\{2 + (p+q)^2 - pq\}, -apq(p+q)); y^2 = 16a(x-6a); (6a, 0).$

31. $y + px = 2p + p^3; 27y^2 = 4(x-2)^3, (2, 0).$

32. $y = px - p^3, y = qx - q^3.$

33. (ii) $(-a\sin^2\theta, -a\cos^3\theta/\sin\theta).$

Exercise 16.1 (pp. 306–307)

1. (a) True,   (b) False,   (c) False,   (d) True.
2. (a) $x > 0$,   (b) all x,   (c) $x < 0$,   (d) $x < -a$ or $x > -b$.

Exercise 16.2 (pp. 308–309)

1. $-2 < x < 3.$

2. $x \leqslant -3$ or $x \geqslant -\frac{1}{2}.$

3. $1 \leqslant x \leqslant 5.$

4. $x < 1 - \sqrt{6}$ or $x > 1 + \sqrt{6}.$

5. $-2 - \sqrt{7} < x < -2 + \sqrt{7}.$

6. $x \leqslant -2$ or $0 \leqslant x \leqslant 5.$

7. $3 < x < 4.$

8. $x < -2$ or $x > -1.$

9. $2 < x < 3.$

10. $-3 < x < -\frac{1}{2}.$

11. $x < 0$ or $1 < x < 2.$

12. $x < -3$ or $0 < x < \frac{1}{2}.$

13. $-3 < x < -2$ or $x > 1.$

14. $0 < x < 1$ or $x > 3.$

15. $-3 < x < 3$ or $x > 5.$

16. $-1 < x < 1.$

17. $0 < x < 1\frac{1}{2}$ or $3 < x < 4.$

18. $-2 < x < -1$ or $x > 2.$

19. $x < -\frac{1}{3}\pi$ or $0 < x < \frac{1}{2}\pi.$

20. $x > \frac{1}{3}\pi.$

Exercise 16.3 (pp. 311–312)

1. $-5 < x < 3.$

2. $x < \frac{1}{3}$ or $x > 2.$

3. $-1 < x < 0$ or $x > 6.$

4. $x < 0$ or $1 < x < 4.$

5. $0 < x < 3$ or $x > 4.$

6. $0 < x < 2$ or $x > 3.$

7. $x < -3$ or $1 < x < 2.$

8. $-2 < x < 1\frac{1}{2}$ or $x > 5.$

9. $1 < x < 7.$

10. $1 < x < 3.$

11. $x < -4$ or $-2 < x < 2.$

12. $-2 < x < 4$ or $x > 5.$

13. $x < -1, 1 < x < 2, x > 3.$

14. $x < -1\frac{1}{2}, -1 < x < 0, x > \frac{2}{3}.$

15. $-4 < x < -1.$

16. $-2 < x < 1\frac{1}{2}$ or $x > 5.$

17. $x < 0$ or $x > 2.$

18. $0 < x < 1\frac{1}{2}$ or $3 < x < 4.$

Exercise 16.4 (p. 313)

1. $x < 1$ or $x > 3.$

2. $-8 \leqslant x \leqslant 2.$

3. $-3 < x < -\frac{1}{3}.$

4. $x \leqslant -5$ or $x \geqslant 6.$

5. $x \leqslant \frac{1}{2}.$

6. $x < -7/3$ or $x > -1.$

7. $x \leqslant 0$ or $x \geqslant 6.$

8. $-5/6 < x < 5/2.$

9. $x < 4/3$ or $x > 4.$

10. $-3/2 \leqslant x \leqslant -1.$

11. $x > -3/5$.
12. All real x.
13. $-1 < x < 0$ or $3 < x < 4$.
14. $x < -1, 2 < x < 3, x > 6$.
15. $x < -8$ or $x > -8/3$.
16. $-4 \leqslant x \leqslant -1$ or $1 \leqslant x \leqslant 4$.

Exercise 16.5 (pp. 313–314)

1. $x \leqslant -7$ or $x \geqslant 1$.
2. $1 - \sqrt{2} < x < 1 + \sqrt{2}$.
3. $x < -1$ or $-\frac{1}{2} < x < 1$.
4. $x < 0$ or $2 < x < 5$.
5. $x < -2$ or $x > 2$.
6. $x < -\sqrt{3}, -\sqrt{2} < x < \sqrt{2}, x > \sqrt{3}$.
7. $x < 0$ or $x > 3$.
8. $-1 < x < -1/\sqrt{2}$ or $1/\sqrt{2} < x < 1$.
9. $-2 < x < -1$ or $x > 4$.
10. $x < -1$ or $x > 2$.
11. $x < -1, -\frac{2}{3} < x < 3, x > 4$.
12. $x < -5$ or $x > 3$.
13. $-\frac{1}{3} \leqslant x \leqslant 7$.
14. $-2 < x < 2$.
15. $\frac{1}{2} < x < 1$.
16. $-6 < x < 1$ or $2 < x < 3$.
17. $x < 0$.
18. $x < 4/3$ or $x > 4$.

19. (a) $-\dfrac{\pi}{3} < x < \dfrac{\pi}{3}, \dfrac{5\pi}{3} < x < \dfrac{7\pi}{3}$,

(b) $-\dfrac{\pi}{4} \leqslant x \leqslant \dfrac{\pi}{4}, \dfrac{3\pi}{4} \leqslant x \leqslant \dfrac{5\pi}{4}, \dfrac{7\pi}{4} \leqslant x \leqslant \dfrac{9\pi}{4}$,

(c) $-\dfrac{\pi}{6} < x < \dfrac{\pi}{6}, \dfrac{5\pi}{6} < x < \dfrac{7\pi}{6}, \dfrac{11\pi}{6} < x < \dfrac{13\pi}{6}$.

22. $\dfrac{\pi}{6} < x < \dfrac{\pi}{2}$ or $\dfrac{5\pi}{6} < x < \dfrac{3\pi}{2}$.

23. (i) $x < -1$ or $x > 0$, (ii) $0 < x < 2$, (iii) $x < 1$ or $x > 2$.
24. $-3 < x < -1$ or $x > 2$, (ii) $x < -2$ or $x > 2$.

Exercise 17.1 (pp. 317–318)

1. (a) Most people disapprove of the Knave of Hearts.
   (b) N is not prime.
   (c) Boycott took over as England cricket captain.
2. (a) Not valid. There could be swallow-tail butterflies in Norfolk, but there may not be.
   (b) Not valid. We are not told that absent-minded people do wear odd socks.
   (c) Not valid. *ABCD* could be an isosceles trapezium.
3. Since $x - y = 0$, we cannot divide by $(x - y)$ to obtain $x + y = y$.
4. (1) Either, (2) Either, (3) Either, (4) True, (5) Either, (6) Either, (7) True, (8) Either, (9) Either, (10) Either, (11) Either, (12) True, (13) Either, (14) False, (15) False (16) True (17) False (18) Either.

Exercise 17.2 (pp. 320–321)

1. (a) $p \Rightarrow q, p \Rightarrow r, q \Rightarrow r$ (b) $p \Rightarrow r$ (c) $p \Rightarrow q, p \Rightarrow r$ (d) $p \Leftrightarrow q, p \Leftrightarrow r, q \Leftrightarrow r$
2. (a) $q \nRightarrow p, r \nRightarrow p, r \nRightarrow q$ (b) $p \nRightarrow q, q \nRightarrow p, q \nRightarrow r, r \nRightarrow p, r \nRightarrow q$ (c) $q \nRightarrow p, q \nRightarrow r, r \nRightarrow p, r \nRightarrow q$ (d) none

3. (a) $\sim q \Rightarrow \sim p$, $\sim r \Rightarrow \sim p$, $\sim r \Rightarrow \sim q$ (b) $\sim r \Rightarrow \sim p$ (c) $\sim q \Rightarrow \sim p$,
    $\sim r \Rightarrow \sim p$ (d) $\sim p \Leftrightarrow \sim q$, $\sim p \Leftrightarrow \sim r$, $\sim q \Leftrightarrow \sim r$
4. (a) $q \Rightarrow p$, $\sim p \Rightarrow \sim q$ (b) $p \Rightarrow \sim q$, $q \Rightarrow \sim p$ (c) $p \Leftrightarrow \sim q$, $\sim p \Leftrightarrow q$
    (d) $p \Leftrightarrow \sim q$, $\sim p \Leftrightarrow q$
5. (a) $q \Rightarrow p$ (b) $\sim p \Leftrightarrow q$ (c) $\sim q \not\Rightarrow p$ (d) $\sim p \not\Leftrightarrow \sim q$ (e) $q \Rightarrow \sim p$
    (f) $p \Leftrightarrow \sim q$
6. (a) $q \Rightarrow p$ (b) $q \Rightarrow p$ (c) $q \Rightarrow p$ (d) $q \Rightarrow p$ (e) $p \Rightarrow q$ (f) $p \Rightarrow q$
7. $AB = AC$ if $\triangle ABC$ is equilateral.
    $\triangle ABC$ is equilateral only if $AB = AC$.
    $\triangle ABC$ being equilateral is a sufficient condition for $AB = AC$.
    $AB = AC$ is a necessary condition for $\triangle ABC$ to be equilateral.

Exercise 17.3 (p. 323)

1. If $\angle ABC = \angle CAT$, then AT must be a tangent to the circle.
3. (a) If a diameter of a circle is perpendicular to a chord then it bisects that chord;
    (i) True, (ii) True.
    (b) If $2x^2 - x - 3 = 0$, then $2x - 3 = 0$; (i) True, (ii) False.
    (c) If a pentagon is equilateral, it must be regular; (i) True, (ii) False.
    (d) If x^2 is greater than y^2, then x is greater than y; (i) False, (ii) False.
    (e) If the sum of the digits of a positive integer N is divisible by 9, then N is
    divisible by 9; (i) True, (ii) True.
    (f) If there are five pairs of socks in a drawer, then any set of six socks taken
    from the drawer will contain a pair; (i) False, (ii) True.
4. (a) True, (b) False.   5.   (a) True, (b) False.
6. (a) False, (b) True.

Exercise 17.4 (pp. 326–327)

9. (a) 2870 (b) 19 270 (c) 11 480 (d) 10 660   10. $\frac{1}{4}$
11. (a) $(n, 2n - 1)$ (b) $(n + 1)y = (2n + 1)x$

12. $\dfrac{x}{2x + 1}$, $\dfrac{x}{3x + 1}$, $\dfrac{x}{nx + 1}$

Exercise 17.5 (pp. 327–330)

1. If $(x - 3)^2 = (x + 1)^2$, then $x - 3 = \pm(x + 1)$.
2. Since $\lg(0 \cdot 2) < 0$, $2\lg(0 \cdot 2) < \lg(0 \cdot 2)$.
3. No value of x satisfies the initial statement.
4. $a + b > 0$ implies $a^2 + ab > 0$ only if $a > 0$.
5. The diagram is incorrect. P lies outside $\triangle ABC$.
6. There is no value of n for which a_n is divisible by 6.
7. It is necessary to prove that $r \Rightarrow q$ and that $s \Rightarrow q$.

8. It is necessary to prove that $P(1)$ and $P(2)$ are true.

14. $\begin{pmatrix} 1 & 3 \\ 0 & 4 \end{pmatrix}, \begin{pmatrix} 1 & 7 \\ 0 & 8 \end{pmatrix}, \begin{pmatrix} 1 & 2^n - 1 \\ 0 & 2^n \end{pmatrix}$ 15. 1.

18. (i) False, (ii) True, (iii) False.   19. One example is $f(x) \equiv x$.

20. One possibility is $\mathbf{P} = \begin{pmatrix} 1 & 0 \\ 0 & 2 \end{pmatrix}$, $\mathbf{X} = \begin{pmatrix} 1 & 1 \\ 3 & 2 \end{pmatrix}$; $\begin{pmatrix} -2 + 2^n.3 & -2 + 2^{n+1} \\ 3 - 2^n.3 & 3 - 2^{n+1} \end{pmatrix}$.

Exercise 18.1 (pp. 335–336)

1. (a) Even, (b) neither, (c) odd.   2. (a) Even, (b) even, (c) odd.
3. (a) Even, (b) odd, (c) neither.   4. (a) Neither, (b) neither, (c) even.
5. (a) Yes, $2\pi/3$; (b) yes, $\pi/2$; (c) yes, 8π.
6. (a) No; (b) yes, 2π; (c) yes, π.
7. (a) Yes, 2π; (b) no; (c) yes, 2π.
8. (a) Yes, π; (b) no; (c) yes, π.
9. f: even, $f(x) \geqslant -1$; g: neither, $\mathbb{R}$; fg: neither, $fg(x) \geqslant -1$; gf: even, $gf(x) \geqslant -1$.
10. f: neither, $\mathbb{R}$; g: odd, $-1 \leqslant g(x) \leqslant 1$, 2π; fg: neither, $\frac{1}{2}(\pi - 1) \leqslant fg(x) \leqslant \frac{1}{2}(\pi + 1)$, 2π; gf: even, $-1 \leqslant gf(x) \leqslant 1$, 4π.
11. f: even, $-1 \leqslant f(x) \leqslant 1$, 2π; g: even, $g(x) \geqslant 0$; fg: even, $-1 \leqslant fg(x) \leqslant 1$; gf: even, $0 \leqslant gf(x) \leqslant 1$, π.
12. f: even, $f(x) \geqslant 0$; g: odd, $\mathbb{R}$; fg: even, $fg(x) \geqslant 0$; gf: even, $gf(x) \geqslant -2$.
17. (a) $-1, 1$, (b) $-1, 1$.   18. (a) none, (b) $-1, 1$.
19. (a) $x \in \mathbb{Z}$, (b) $x \in \mathbb{Z}$.   20. (a) 1, (b) $-1, 1$.   22. 3.

Exercise 18.2 (pp. 339–340)

7. $(-1, -1)$ min; $(-1, -1)$ max, $x = -2$, $x = 0$, $y = 0$.
8. $(-1, 0)$ min; $x = -1$, $y = 0$.   9. $(-1, 1)$ min; $(-1, 1)$ max, $y = 0$.
10. $(-3, 36)$ max, $(5/3, -400/27)$ min; $(-3, 1/36)$ min, $(5/3, -27/400)$ max, $x = -5$, $x = 0$, $x = 3$, $y = 0$.
11. $x = -2$, $y = 2$; $x = \frac{1}{2}$, $y = \frac{1}{2}$.   12. None, $(3/2, 0)$ min.
13. (0.4) max; $(-2, 0)$ min, $(0, 16)$ max, $(2, 0)$ min.
14. $(2n\pi + \frac{1}{2}\pi, 1)$ max, $(2n\pi - \frac{1}{2}\pi, -1)$ min; $(n\pi, 0)$ min, $(n\pi + \frac{1}{2}\pi, 1)$ max.
15. $x = 1$, $y = -2$; $(0, 0)$ min, $x = 1$, $y = 4$.
16. $(0, 0)$ min, $(2, 4)$ max; $(2, -2)$ min, $(2, 2)$ max.

Exercise 18.3 (pp. 343–344)

1. Yes; $\frac{1}{2}(x - 1)$; $\mathbb{R}$.   2. Yes; $5 - x$; $\mathbb{R}$.   3. No; e.g. $-2, 0$.
4. Yes; $\sqrt{(x + 2)}$; $\{x \in \mathbb{R} : x \geqslant -2\}$.
5. Yes; $1/(x - 1)$; $\mathbb{R} - \{1\}$.

6. Yes, $9 - 1/x$; $\mathbb{R} - \{0\}$.   7.   Yes; $3 - x^2$; $\{x \in \mathbb{R} : x \geqslant 0\}$.
8. No; e.g. $-1, 1$.   9.   Yes; $\log_3 x$; $\mathbb{R}^+$.   10. Yes, $10^x - 2$; $\mathbb{R}$.
11. No; e.g. $-1, 1$.   12. Yes; $x/(x - 2)$; $\mathbb{R} - \{2\}$.
13. No; e.g. $0, 2\pi$.   14. Yes; $\sin x$; $\{x \in \mathbb{R} : -\tfrac{1}{2}\pi \leqslant x \leqslant \tfrac{1}{2}\pi\}$
15. $1 + 4x^2$; $\tfrac{1}{2}\sqrt{(x - 1)}$.   16. $gf : x \to 3 - 9/x$.

17. (a) $f^{-1} : x \to 2 + \sqrt{x}, x \geqslant 0$,   (b) $f^{-1} : x \to 1 + 10^{x-1}$,

    (c) $f^{-1} : x \to \dfrac{1 - x}{1 + x}, x \neq -1$ (d) $f^{-1} : x \to \sqrt{\left(1 + \dfrac{1}{x^2}\right)}, x > 0$.

18. $k = 2$, $\{x \in \mathbb{R} : x \geqslant 4\}$.   19. $k = 3$, $\{x \in \mathbb{R} : x \leqslant 9\}$.
20. $k = 4$, $\{x \in \mathbb{R} : x \geqslant 0\}$.   21. $k = 1$, $\{x \in \mathbb{R} : x \geqslant -1\}$.
22. $k = 1$, $\{x \in \mathbb{R} : x \geqslant 2\}$.   23. $k = \tfrac{1}{4}$, $\{x \in \mathbb{R} : x \geqslant -\tfrac{1}{4}\}$.
24. (a) No,   (b) Yes,   (c) Yes,   (d) No,   (e) No,   (f) Yes.

Exercise 18.4 (pp. 346–348)

1. (a) 5, (b) 4, (c) -2, (d) $x - 7$, (e) 0, (f) $-4x + 5$.
2. $5, -12$.   3. $-3x + 4$.   4. $2, -8$.   5. $4, -2, -5$.
6. $3(a + b)(b + c)(c + a)$.   7. $3(x - y)(y - z)(z - x)$.
8. $k = -7$, $(x + 1)^2(2x - 7)$; $k = 20$, $(x - 2)^2(2x + 5)$.
9. $(x + 2)^2(3x^2 - 4x + 4)$.   10. $-2, 13$; $(x - 1)^2(x - 6)$.
11. $-3, -3, 12$.   12. $k = -5$: $-1/2, -1/2, 5/2$; $k = 27$: $3/2, 3/2, -3/2$.
13. -11; $-3, -\tfrac{1}{2}, 2$.   14. -14; $3, -2, 4/3$.   15. $1, 4, 2$.
16. $1, 3, 1, 6$.   17. $1, -3, 1, 0$.   19. $-3, \tfrac{1}{4}$.   20. $0, 2$.
21. $(x - a)^2 g'(x) + 2(x - a)g(x) + A$; $f'(a)$, $f(a) - af'(a)$; $k = -1$: $-3, 0, 0$;
    $k = 1$; $-1, 2, 2$.

Exercise 18.5 (pp. 352–353)

7. $y \leqslant 1/5$ or $y \geqslant 5$; $x = -4$, $x = 1$, $y = 0$; $(-1, 5)$ min, $(11, 1/5)$ max.
8. $-\tfrac{1}{2} \leqslant y \leqslant 1$; $y = 0$; $(-2, -\tfrac{1}{2})$ min, $(1, 1)$ max.
9. All real values; $x = -3$, $x = 0$, $y = 0$; no turning points.
10. $y \leqslant 1/9$ or $y \geqslant 1$; $x = -3$, $x = 0$, $y = 0$; $(-1, 1)$ min, $(3, 1/9)$ max.
11. $y \leqslant 1$ or $y \geqslant 9$; $x = 1$, $x = 2$, $y = 0$; $(0, 1)$ max, $(4/3, 9)$ min.
12. $-5/4 \leqslant y \leqslant 5$; $y = 0$; $(4, -5/4)$ min, $(-1, 5)$ max.
13. $-\tfrac{1}{3} \leqslant y \leqslant 1$; $y = 0$; $(0, 1)$ max, $(2, -\tfrac{1}{3})$ min.
14. $y \leqslant -1$ or $y \geqslant -1/9$; $x = -5$, $x = -2$, $y = 0$; $(-8, -1/9)$ min,
    $(-4, -1)$ max.
15. $y \leqslant 0$ or $y \geqslant 4/3$; $x = 1$, $x = 4$, $y = 0$; $(5/2, 4/3)$ min.
16. All real values; $x = 1$, $x = 4$, $y = 0$; no turning points.
20. $x = 3$, $y = x$; $(1, -1)$ max, $(5, 7)$ min.

Exercise 18.6 (pp. 356–358)

1. $\dfrac{1}{x+1} - \dfrac{1}{x+2}$.

2. $\dfrac{1}{x-1} - \dfrac{2}{x+2}$.

3. $\dfrac{2}{x-2} + \dfrac{1}{x-4}$.

4. $\dfrac{3}{x} + \dfrac{1}{x-3}$.

5. $\dfrac{3}{x-2} - \dfrac{2}{x+1}$.

6. $\dfrac{2}{x+1} + \dfrac{1}{2x+1}$.

7. $\dfrac{1}{2(x-1)} + \dfrac{1}{2(x+1)}$.

8. $\dfrac{1}{3+x} + \dfrac{1}{2-x}$.

9. $\dfrac{1}{4x-1} + \dfrac{2}{2x+1}$.

10. $\dfrac{1}{2(2x-1)} - \dfrac{3}{2(2x+5)}$.

11. $\dfrac{3}{x-2} - \dfrac{4}{x+3} + \dfrac{1}{x+1}$.

12. $\dfrac{6}{x-1} + \dfrac{2}{x+1} - \dfrac{3}{x-2}$.

13. $\dfrac{x+2}{x^2+1} - \dfrac{1}{x+1}$.

14. $\dfrac{2}{2x-1} - \dfrac{x}{x^2+1}$.

15. $\dfrac{1}{x} + \dfrac{3-2x}{2x^2+1}$.

16. $\dfrac{2x+1}{x^2+3} - \dfrac{3}{2x-1}$.

17. $\dfrac{2}{x-1} - \dfrac{4}{(x-1)^2} - \dfrac{1}{x+2}$.

18. $\dfrac{1}{x} + \dfrac{2}{x+1} + \dfrac{3}{(x+1)^2}$.

19. $\dfrac{5}{x} + \dfrac{2}{x^2} - \dfrac{3}{x-1}$.

20. $\dfrac{1}{x-2} - \dfrac{1}{x+1} - \dfrac{2}{(x+1)^2} - \dfrac{8}{(x+1)^3}$.

21. $\dfrac{x}{2x^2+5} - \dfrac{1}{4x-5}$.

22. $\dfrac{1}{x-2} - \dfrac{x}{x^2-x+2}$.

23. $1 + \dfrac{1}{x-1} - \dfrac{1}{x+1}$.

24. $1 + \dfrac{4}{3(x-2)} - \dfrac{1}{3(x+1)}$.

25. $\dfrac{1}{3} + \dfrac{5}{6(3x-1)} - \dfrac{1}{2(x-1)}$.

26. $x + \dfrac{2}{x-2} + \dfrac{2}{x+2}$.

27. $\dfrac{x+3}{x^2+3} - \dfrac{x+2}{x^2+2}$.

28. $\dfrac{2x-1}{x^2+2} + \dfrac{1}{x+1} - \dfrac{2}{(x+1)^2}$.

29. $\dfrac{x}{2} + 1 - \dfrac{1}{4(2x-1)} - \dfrac{1}{4(2x-1)^2} + \dfrac{2}{x-2}$.

30. $x^2 - x - 3 + \dfrac{3}{x^2+1} + \dfrac{3x}{x^2+2}$.

31. $\dfrac{2}{2x+3} + \dfrac{1}{x+1}; \ -\dfrac{4}{(2x+3)^2} - \dfrac{1}{(x+1)^2}; \dfrac{16}{(2x+3)^3} + \dfrac{2}{(x+1)^3}.$

32. (a) $(0,0)$,   (b) $(-7, -3/7)$.

Exercise 18.7 (pp. 358–362)

1. f: even, periodic, $\frac{1}{3}\pi$; g: neither, not periodic; h: even, not periodic; k: odd, periodic, 4π.

2. f: none; 2; g: x an even integer; x an even integer; h: $-1, 2$; $-1, 2$; k: none; 1.

3. $\pi, \pi; \pi; 0 \leqslant f(x).g(x) < 2.$ 4. f: neither; g: even; h: even; $12\pi, 6\pi$.

5. $4 \leqslant f(x) \leqslant 20, \ f^{-1}$ exists; $-4 \leqslant g(x) \leqslant 0$, no inverse; $-5 \leqslant h(x) \leqslant 5$, no inverse; $k(x) \leqslant 1, k^{-1}$ exists.

6. $a = 1; g^{-1}(x) = (2 - \sqrt{\{4 - x^2\}})/x, \ -2 \leqslant x \leqslant 2, \ -1 \leqslant g^{-1}(x) \leqslant 1.$

7. $1, 1/5.$

8. $-5 < f(x) \leqslant 4; \ -2 < x \leqslant 1: f^{-1}(y) = \frac{1}{2}(y + 1), \ 1 < x \leqslant 2: f^{-1}(y) = \sqrt{y}, \ 2 \leqslant x < 3: f^{-1}(y) = \frac{1}{3}(10 - y).$

9. $-\frac{1}{4}\pi \leqslant x \leqslant \frac{1}{4}\pi, f^{-1}(y) = \frac{1}{2}\sin^{-1} y; \frac{1}{4}\pi \leqslant x \leqslant \frac{3}{4}\pi, f^{-1}(y) = \frac{1}{4}\pi(2 - y).$

10. (i) F: odd, periodic, 6π; G: even, periodic, 2π; f_3: odd; f_4: even, period $\frac{1}{3}\pi$,   (ii) 0.

11. $\{y \in \mathbb{R}: y \geqslant 0, \ y \neq 2r + 1, r \in \mathbb{Z}\}$; not one-one; $g^{-1}: x \to x - \frac{1}{2}[x]$;
    $\{x \in \mathbb{R}^+: 2r < x < 2r + 1, r \in \mathbb{Z}\}.$

12. $-1 < x < 2, 3 < x < 6.$ 14. $x < -1$ or $x > 0.$

16. $-12\frac{1}{24}; \ -3/2, 4/3; \ -1.56, -1.44, 1.27, 1.39.$

17. $a = b = 1; x^3 - 2x^2 + 3.$ 18. (a) $-6x + 2$,   (b) $-2x.$

19. $2, \pm\sqrt{5}.$

20. (a) $(x + y + z)(x - y)(y - z)(z - x)$,   (b) $3(a - b - c)(b - c - a)(c - a - b).$

21. $a = -2, b = -1, c = 16.$ 23. $-2, -2, 4 \pm 2\sqrt{2}.$ 24. $0, -3, 125.$

26. $4, -5.$

27. (i) 2,   (ii) HCF of $A(x)$ and $B(x)$ is $8x + 8$; $\alpha: g(x)$, $\beta: A(x)$ and $B(x)$ have no common factor.

28. $-\frac{1}{3} \leqslant y \leqslant 1, x = -1; \ -\frac{1}{3} \leqslant f(x) \leqslant 1; (-2, -\frac{1}{3}), (0, 1).$

29. (a) $\mathbb{R} - \{\frac{1}{2}\}$; $x = -\frac{1}{2}, \ y = \frac{1}{2}$; none,   (b) $\{y \in \mathbb{R}: y < 0$ or $y \geqslant 1\}$; $x = -3$, $x = 1, \ y = 0$; $(-1, 1)$,   (c) $\{y \in \mathbb{R}: y \leqslant -3$ or $y \geqslant -\frac{1}{3}\}$; $x = 0, x = 3, y = 0$; $(-3, -\frac{1}{3}), (1, -3)$,   (d) $\mathbb{R}$; $x = -2, x = 2, y = 0$; none.

30. (a) none,   (b) $(0,0)$ max, $(2,4)$ min,   (c) $(0,0)$ min,   (d) $(3, 1/8)$ max.

31. $\{x \in \mathbb{R}: x \neq -1, 3\}$; $\{y \in \mathbb{R}: y \leqslant -1$ or $y \geqslant \frac{1}{3}\}$; $x = -1, x = 3, y = 1.$

32. (a) max $(1, \frac{1}{2})$, min $(-1, -\frac{1}{2})$; inflexions $(-\sqrt{3}, -\frac{1}{4}\sqrt{3}), (0, 0), (\sqrt{3}, \frac{1}{4}\sqrt{3}).$

33. $\dfrac{3}{3x-2} - \dfrac{1}{2x+3}.$ 34. $\dfrac{1}{x-1} + \dfrac{1}{(x-1)^2} - \dfrac{2}{2x-1}.$

35. $\dfrac{1}{2(x-1)} + \dfrac{1-x}{2(x^2+1)}.$ 36. $\dfrac{1}{3(x+1)} - \dfrac{1}{x-1} + \dfrac{2}{3(x-2)}.$

37. $-\dfrac{1}{2} + \dfrac{3}{2(2x+1)} + \dfrac{2}{3-x}.$ 38. $\dfrac{1}{1-x} - \dfrac{1-x}{1+x+x^2}.$

39. $x - 2 - \dfrac{2}{3(x-1)} + \dfrac{8}{3(x+2)}$.

40. $\dfrac{1}{x-1} + \dfrac{2}{(x-1)^2} - \dfrac{1}{x+1} + \dfrac{3}{(x+1)^2}$.

Exercise 19.1 (pp. 366–368)

1. (a) $2e^{2x}$, (b) $-5e^{-x}$, (c) $3e^{3x+5}$.

2. (a) $6x^2 e^{2x^3}$, (b) $\dfrac{1}{2\sqrt{x}} e^{\sqrt{x}}$, (c) $\dfrac{1}{x^2} e^{-1/x}$.

3. (a) $\cos x\, e^{\sin x}$, (b) $-2\sin 2x\, e^{\cos 2x}$, (c) $4\sec^2 x\, e^{4\tan x}$.

4. (a) $(2x^2 + 1)e^{x^2}$, (b) $(5x + 2)xe^{5x}$, (c) $(\cos x - x\sin x)e^{x\cos x}$.

5. (a) $e^{2x}(2\cos 3x - 3\sin 3x)$, (b) $e^{-x^2}(\cos x - 2x\sin x)$,
   (c) $\tfrac{1}{2}(x + 1)^2(x + 7)e^{x/2}$.

6. (a) $-2e^{4x}(1 - e^{4x})^{-\frac{1}{2}}$, (b) $e^{(x+e^x)}$, (c) $e^x \cos(e^x)$.

7. (a) $e^{2x} - e^{-2x}$, (b) $(2 + e^x)/(1 + e^{-x})^2$, (c) 0.

8. (a) $\tfrac{1}{3}e^{3x} + c$, (b) $-e^{-x} + c$, (c) $e^{x+4} + c$.

9. (a) $3(e^2 - 1)$, (b) $2(e - 1)$, (c) $e^6 - 1$.

10. (a) $\dfrac{1}{x}$, (b) $-\dfrac{1}{x}$, (c) $\dfrac{2}{x} - 1$.　　　12. $y = e(3x - 5)$.　　　13. $e - 1$.

15. $(1, e^{-1})$ max.　　　16. $(-2, -e^{-2})$ min.

17. $(-1, -e^{-\frac{1}{2}})$ min, $(1, e^{-\frac{1}{2}})$ max.　　　18. $(0, 1)$ max, $(1, 0)$ min.

19. $(1, e)$ min.　　　20. $(2k\pi, 1)$ min, $(\{2k + 1\}\pi, e^2)$ max, $k \in \mathbb{Z}$.

21. $4\,\mathrm{m}, -2\,\mathrm{m\ s}^{-2}$.　　　22. $x = -1$, max; $x = 2$, min.

23. $x = \pi/4$, max; $x = 5\pi/4$, min.

24. $\tfrac{1}{2}(e^2 - 3 + 2e^{-1}) \approx 2{\cdot}56$; $\tfrac{1}{4}\pi(e^4 - 3 + 2e^{-2}) \approx 40{\cdot}7$.

Exercise 19.2 (pp. 371–372)

1. (a) $\dfrac{1}{x}$, (b) $\dfrac{1}{x+3}$, (c) $\dfrac{2}{2x-1}$.

2. (a) $\dfrac{3x^2}{x^3 + 4}$, (b) $2\cot 2x$, (c) $\tan x$.

3. (a) $x(2\ln x + 1)$, (b) $(1 - 2\ln x)/x^3$, (c) $1/x\ln x$.

4. (a) $\dfrac{3}{x}$, (b) $\dfrac{2}{4x + 5}$, (c) $-1 - \ln x$.

5. (a) $\sec x$, (b) $\dfrac{4x}{x^2 + 4}$, (c) $(\log_{10} e)/x$.

6. (a) $\dfrac{3x-4}{x(3x-2)}$,   (b) $\dfrac{1}{2x(x+1)}$,   (c) $\dfrac{x}{1-x^2} - \tan x$.

7. (a) $2x$,   (b) $\sec^2 x$,   (c) $\dfrac{2}{x} - 1$.   8. $y = 3x - 6$.   9. $t/(1+t)$.

11. (a) $2p + q + 1$,   (b) p/q,   (c) $1/(p+q)$,   (d) e^{p+q}
12. (a) $t = 0$ or $\ln 2$,   (b) $x = -\ln 2$.
13. (a) none,   (b) none,   (c) $(1,0)$ min.   14. $(1,1)$ min.
17. (a) $3^x \ln 3$,   (b) $5^{2x} 2 \ln 5$,   (c) $\ln 10 \cos x (10^{\sin x})$.

18. (a) $x^x(1 + \ln x)$,   (b) $(2 \ln x) x^{(\ln x - 1)}$,   (c) $(\ln x)^x \left\{ \ln (\ln x) + \dfrac{1}{\ln x} \right\}$.

19. (a) $\dfrac{2(x-2)}{(2x+1)^3}$,   (b) $\dfrac{(6-5x)x^2}{2(1-x)^{3/2}}$,   (c) $\dfrac{4x^2(x-1)e^{4x}}{(x+1)^3}$.

20. (a) $\frac{1}{2}(13 - 10x)\sqrt{\left\{ \dfrac{x+2}{(1-5x)^3} \right\}}$,   (b) $\dfrac{4x}{(x-2)^{2/3}(x+4)^{4/3}}$.

(c) $\dfrac{4 \sin^2 x + 1}{\cos^3 x \sqrt{(\sin 2x)}}$.

Exercise 19.4 (pp. 378–379)

1. (a) $\frac{1}{2} \ln (2x + 7) + c$,   (b) $\frac{1}{5} \ln (5x - 2) + c$.
2. (a) $-\ln (1 - x) + c$,   (b) $\frac{1}{2} \ln (1 - 2x) + c$.
3. (a) $\ln (2 - 3x) + c$,   (b) $-2 \ln (3 - 4x) + c$.
4. (a) $\ln |x + 3| + c$,   (b) $-3 \ln |3 - x| + c$,   (c) $\frac{1}{2} \ln |4x + 5| + c$.
5. (a) $x + \ln |x - 1| + c$,   (b) $x + 2 \ln |x - 4| + c$,   (c) $\frac{1}{2} x + \frac{1}{4} \ln |2x + 1| + c$.
6. (a) $\frac{1}{2} x^2 - \ln |x| + c$,   (b) $x - \ln (1 + x^2) + c$,   (c) $-\frac{1}{2} x^2 - \ln |1 - x| + c$.
7. (a) $-\frac{1}{2} \ln |1 - x^2| + c$,   (b) $\frac{1}{3} \ln |x^3 + 8| + c$,   (c) $\frac{1}{4} \ln |2x^2 + 4x - 1| + c$.
8. (a) $\ln (1 + \sin x) + c$,   (b) $\ln |\sin x| + c$,   (c) $x + \frac{1}{2} \ln |\sec 2x| + c$.
9. (a) $\ln (1 + e^x) + c$,   (b) $\ln |\ln x| + c$,   (c) $2 \ln (1 + \sqrt{x}) + c$.
10. (a) $5 \ln 2$,   (b) $\ln 4$,   (c) $\ln 3$.   11. $\frac{1}{3} \ln \frac{5}{2}$,   (b) $-\ln 4$,   (c) $2 + \ln \frac{2}{3}$.
12. (a) $\ln 2$,   (b) $\ln 5$,   (c) $\ln \frac{4}{3}$.   13. (a) $0 \cdot 805$,   (b) $1 \cdot 10$.

14. $\dfrac{5(1-x)}{(2x-1)(3-x)}$; $-0 \cdot 167$.   15. $\frac{3}{4} - \ln 2$.   16. $\pi(8 + \ln 3)$.

Exercise 19.5 (p. 380)

1. (a) $2 \cosh 2x$,   (b) $3 \sinh 3x$,   (c) $2 \sinh x \cosh x$,   (d) $\dfrac{\sinh x}{2\sqrt{(\cosh x)}}$.

2. (a) $\cosh x + c$,   (b) $\frac{1}{2} \sinh 2x + c$,   (c) $\ln (\cosh x) + c$.
3. (a) $\operatorname{sech}^2 x$,   (b) $-\operatorname{cosech}^2 x$,   (c) $-\operatorname{sech} x \tanh x$,   (d) $-\operatorname{cosech} x \coth x$.
5. (a) 0 or $\ln 5$,   (b) $-\ln 2$.

Exercise 19.6 (pp. 380–382)

1. (a) $e^{3x}(3x + 1)$,   (b) $e^{2x}\left(\dfrac{1}{x} + 2\ln 4x\right)$,   (c) $a^x \ln a$.

2. (a) $\dfrac{1}{x}\cos(\ln x)$,   (b) $\dfrac{1}{x} - x - 2x\ln x$,   (c) $\operatorname{cosec} x$.

3. (a) $\dfrac{8}{(x-3)(3x-1)}$,   (b) $2\sec x$,   (c) $\dfrac{3 - 4x^2}{1 - x^2}$.

4. (a) $(\ln 2, 4)$ min,   (b) $(0, 0)$ inflexion, $(3, 27e^{-3})$ max.
5. $x = e$, max.   6. $24/7$
9. $(-1, -2\sqrt{e})$ min, $(4, 18e^{-2})$ max.
10. (a) $\ln 3$,   (b) $\frac{1}{2}\ln 6$,   (c) $\frac{3}{2}\ln 3$.
11. (a) $\frac{1}{3}x - \frac{1}{9}\ln|3x + 1| + c$,   (b) $\ln|x| + \dfrac{2}{x^2} + c$,

    (c) $2x - \ln(x^2 + x + 1) + c$.
12. $\frac{1}{2}\ln(1 + x) - \frac{1}{2}\ln(1 - x) - x$; 0.   14. $2xe^{2x}$; $59\cdot 5$.

16. $\frac{5}{6} + 2\ln 2$.   17. $2 - \dfrac{2}{e}$; $2\pi\left(1 - \dfrac{1}{e^2}\right)$.

18. $(2, 3)$, $(3, 0)$; $y + 3x = \pm 6\sqrt{2}$.
19. $(-1, -\frac{1}{2})$ min, $(1, \frac{1}{2})$ max; $\frac{1}{2}\ln(1 + a^2)$.
20. Inflexion at $(-\{\ln b\}/c, a/2b)$.
21. Asymptote $x = 6$; $(4, 1)$ max, $(8, 9)$ min; $\frac{15}{2} - 8\ln 2$.
22. $\frac{1}{2}\pi(e^{2h} + 8e^h + 8h - 9)$; $50/\{\pi(e^{1\cdot 5} + 2)^2\} \approx 0\cdot 379$.

Exercise 20.1 (pp. 386–387)

1. $\dfrac{3}{2x^2} - \dfrac{1}{x} + c$.   2. $\frac{1}{7}x^7 - \frac{1}{2}x^4 + x + c$.

3. $\frac{2}{5}x^{5/2} + \frac{2}{3}x^{3/2} + c$.   4. $\frac{1}{3}\sin 3x + c$.   5. $\frac{1}{4}e^{(4x-3)} + c$.

6. $\frac{1}{2}\cos(1 - 2x) + c$.   7. $-\frac{1}{5}(1 - x)^5 + c$.   8. $-\dfrac{1}{x + 4} + c$.

9. $-\dfrac{1}{4(2x - 5)^2} + c$.   10. $\frac{1}{2}\ln|2x - 5| + c$.   11. $\frac{1}{5}\tan 5x + c$.

12. $2\ln|\sin\frac{1}{2}x| + c$.   13. $\frac{1}{2}x - \frac{1}{4}\sin 2x + c$.
14. $\frac{1}{4}\cos 2x - \frac{1}{8}\cos 4x + c$.   15. $-x - \cot x + c$.
16. $-\frac{1}{3}\cos^3 x + c$.   17. $\sec x + c$.   18. $\frac{1}{3}\cos^3 x - \cos x + c$.
19. $x - \ln|x + 2| + c$.   20. $x + \frac{1}{2}x^2 + \ln|x - 1| + c$.
21. $\frac{1}{2}x^2 - 3\ln(x^2 + 5) + c$.   22. $\frac{2}{3}\sqrt{(5x + 3)} + c$.
23. $\frac{1}{4}\ln(1 + x^4) + c$.   24. $\frac{1}{16}(1 + x^4)^4 + c$.   25. $e - 1$.

26. $40\frac{1}{2}$.   27. 3/16.   28. $-2/21$.   29. $(\pi + 2)/24$.   30. 2/15.
31. 3/2.   32. 1/4.   33. $2 - \frac{1}{2}\pi$.   34. $\ln 2$.   35. 2.
36. $\frac{1}{2}\ln(4/3)$.   38. $\sec x; \frac{1}{2}\ln 3$.   39. $\tan\frac{1}{2}x + c$.   40. $3\pi/8$.

Exercise 20.2 (pp. 389–391)

1. $\ln\left|\dfrac{x-1}{x+2}\right| + c$.   2. $\frac{1}{2}\ln\left|\dfrac{1+x}{1-x}\right| + c$.   3. $\frac{1}{3}\ln\left|\dfrac{x-3}{x}\right| + c$.

4. $\frac{1}{2}\ln|x^2 - 4| + c$.   5. $\ln|(x-3)^3(x+1)| + c$.

6. $\ln|(x-2)(x-3)| + c$.   7. $\ln|(x+3)^2(x+1)| + c$.

8. $\frac{1}{2}\ln\left|\dfrac{x^2}{2x-1}\right| + c$.   9. $\ln\left|\dfrac{(x-1)^3}{x-4}\right| + c$.   10. $\frac{1}{2}\ln\left|\dfrac{1+x}{1-x}\right| - x + c$.

11. $\frac{1}{2}\ln|x^2 - 4x - 8| + c$.   12. $\frac{1}{2}x^2 + 2\ln|x^2 - 4| + c$.

13. $\ln|(x+1)(x-2)| + \dfrac{1}{x+1} + c$.   14. $3\ln\left|\dfrac{x-1}{x}\right| + \dfrac{2}{x} + c$.

15. $\ln|x+3| + \dfrac{3}{x+3} + c$.   16. $\ln\left|\dfrac{x^2+1}{x+1}\right| + c$.

17. $\frac{1}{2}\ln\dfrac{(x-1)^2}{x^2+1} + c$.   18. $\frac{1}{4}\ln\dfrac{x^2+3}{x^2+5} + c$.

19. $\frac{1}{2}\ln(2x+1)^2(x^2+2) + c$.   20. $x + \ln\dfrac{x^2+x+1}{(x-1)^2} + c$.

21. $\ln\frac{32}{27}$.   22. $\ln\frac{12}{7}$.   23. $\ln 6$.   24. $\frac{3}{2}\ln\frac{9}{8}$.   25. $\frac{1}{3}\ln\frac{27}{2}$.
26. $\ln\frac{4}{3}$.   27. $\ln\frac{9}{10}$.   28. $2 + \ln\frac{5}{9}$.   29. $\frac{1}{2} + \ln\frac{3}{4}$.
30. $\frac{3}{2} + \ln\frac{8}{3}$.   31. $\frac{13}{2} + \ln\frac{512}{3}$.   32. $11 + 2\ln\frac{6}{5}$.
33. $\frac{1}{2}\ln\frac{40}{17}$.   34. $1 + \ln\frac{5}{2}$.   35. $\ln 2$.   36. $\ln\frac{12}{7}$.

37. (a) $\ln\left(\dfrac{x-1}{x+3}\right) + c$,   (b) $\ln\left(\dfrac{1-x}{x+3}\right) + c$,   (c) $\ln\left(\dfrac{x-1}{x+3}\right) + c$.

38. (a) $\frac{1}{2}\ln\dfrac{(x+1)^2}{2x-3} + c$,   (b) $\frac{1}{2}\ln\dfrac{(x+1)^2}{3-2x} + c$.

Exercise 20.3 (pp. 395–397)

1. $\frac{1}{12}(3x-2)^4 + c$.   2. $-\frac{1}{10}(1-2x)^5 + c$.
3. $-\frac{1}{42}(1-x)^6(1+6x) + c$.   4. $\frac{1}{6}(x^3-1)^4 + c$.   5. $\frac{1}{3}\tan^3 x + c$.
6. $-\frac{1}{6}\cos^6 x + c$.   7. $\frac{1}{3}(x^2+4)^{3/2} + c$.

8. $-\frac{2}{15}(1 - x)^{3/2}(2 + 3x) + c.$ 9. $\frac{1}{3}(x - 1)\sqrt{(2x + 1)} + c.$

10. $\ln(1 + e^x) + c.$ 11. $\sin\theta - \frac{1}{3}\sin^3\theta + c.$

12. $\frac{1}{5}\cos^5\theta - \frac{1}{3}\cos^3\theta + c.$ 13. $\frac{1}{2}\sec\theta + c.$ 14. $2\tan(\sqrt{x}) + c.$

15. $12/5.$ 16. $16/105.$ 17. $\ln 2.$ 18. $\dfrac{e - 1}{2(e + 1)}.$ 19. $\pi/2.$

20. $\pi/18.$ 21. $4/5.$ 22. $\frac{1}{24}(2\pi + 3\sqrt{3}).$ 23. $\frac{1}{3}\ln 2.$

24. $\frac{1}{4}\ln 3.$ 25. $\frac{1}{120}(2x + 3)^5(10x - 3) + c.$

26. $\frac{1}{40}(x^2 - 1)^4(4x^2 + 1) + c.$ 27. $\frac{2}{9}(1 + 3x)^{3/2} + c.$

28. $\frac{2}{3}(x - 6)\sqrt{(x + 3)} + c.$ 29. $\dfrac{1}{3(1 - x^3)} + c.$ 30. $-\dfrac{x}{(x - 1)^2} + c.$

31. $\frac{1}{2}e^{x^2} + c.$ 32. $2\sqrt{(\ln x)} + c.$ 33. $\frac{1}{4}\ln\left|\dfrac{2 + e^x}{2 - e^x}\right| + c.$

34. $6.$ 35. $9.$ 36. $9\pi/4.$ 37. $\sqrt{3}.$ 38. $\frac{1}{6}(4\pi + 3\sqrt{3}).$

39. $\ln(4/3).$ 40. $23\frac{1}{3}.$ 41. $8; 5\pi.$ 42. $3\pi.$ 44. $\frac{1}{2}\pi.$

Exercise 20.4 (p. 400)

1. $\sin x - x\cos x + c.$ 2. $2x\sin\frac{1}{2}x + 4\cos\frac{1}{2}x + c.$

3. $-e^{-x}(x + 1) + c.$ 4. $\frac{1}{4}x^2(2\ln 2x - 1) + c.$

5. $\frac{1}{4}e^{2x}(2x - 1) + c.$ 6. $x\tan x + \ln(\cos x) + c.$

7. $\frac{1}{8}\sin 2x - \frac{1}{4}x\cos 2x + c.$ 8. $x\tan x + \ln(\cos x) - \frac{1}{2}x^2 + c.$

9. $\frac{1}{4}x^2 + \frac{1}{4}x\sin 2x + \frac{1}{8}\cos 2x + c.$ 10. $(x^2 - 2)\sin x + 2x\cos x + c.$

11. $e^x(x^3 - 3x^2 + 6x - 6) + c.$ 12. $\frac{1}{16}x^4(4\ln x - 1) + c.$

13. $\frac{1}{2}x^2(\ln x)^2 - \frac{1}{2}x^2\ln x + \frac{1}{4}x^2 + c.$ 14. $(x - 1)\ln(x - 1) - x + c.$

15. $-\frac{1}{2}e^{-x}(\sin x + \cos x) + c.$ 16. $-2.$ 17. $2/e.$ 18. $\pi/9.$

19. $1.$ 20. $\frac{1}{4}\pi^2.$ 21. $\frac{8}{3}\ln 2 - \frac{7}{9}.$ 22. $10e^{-2} - 17e^{-3}.$

23. $\frac{1}{4} - \frac{3}{4}e^{-2}.$ 24. $\pi - 2.$ 25. $\frac{1}{2}(e^\pi + 1).$ 26. $\frac{5}{4}e^4 - \frac{1}{4}e^2.$

27. $\frac{1}{2}e^2.$ 28. $\frac{1}{30}(x + 1)^5(5x - 1) + c.$

29. (a) $\frac{2}{15}(x - 1)^{3/2}(3x + 2) + c,$ (b) $-\dfrac{(x + 1)}{(x + 2)^2} + c.$

Exercise 20.5 (pp. 403–404)

1. $\sin^{-1}\dfrac{x}{4} + c.$ 2. $\frac{1}{5}\tan^{-1}\dfrac{x}{5} + c.$ 3. $\frac{1}{2}\sin^{-1}2x + c.$

4. $\frac{1}{2}\ln(x^2 + 1) + \tan^{-1}x + c.$ 5. $\frac{1}{5}\sin^{-1}\dfrac{5x}{2} + c.$

6. $\frac{1}{6}\tan^{-1}\frac{3x}{2} + c.$ 7 $\ln|x + 1| - \tan^{-1}x + c.$

8. $\ln\left(\frac{x^2 + 1}{(1 - x)^2}\right) + 2\tan^{-1}x + c.$ 9. $\ln\left(\frac{x^2 + 9}{x^2}\right) + 2\tan^{-1}\frac{x}{3} + c.$

10. $3\ln(x^2 + 4) - \ln|x + 2| - 4\tan^{-1}\frac{x}{2} + c.$ 11. $\frac{1}{2}\tan^{-1}\frac{(x + 1)}{2} + c.$

12. $\sin^{-1}\frac{(x - 2)}{3} + c.$ 13. $\pi/18.$ 14. $\pi/2.$ 15. $\pi/8.$

16. $\pi/2.$ 17. $\ln 2 + \pi/2.$ 18. $\pi/4.$ 19. $\pi/4.$
20. $\frac{1}{2}\ln(1 + e^{2x}) + \tan^{-1}(e^x) + c.$ 21. $\tan^{-1}(e^x) + c.$
22. $\frac{1}{2}\sin^{-1}x + \frac{1}{2}x\sqrt{(1 - x^2)} + c.$ 23. $\sin^{-1}x + \sqrt{(1 - x^2)} + c.$

24. $\ln(x^2 - 2x + 10) + \frac{2}{3}\tan^{-1}\frac{(x - 1)}{3} + c.$ 25. $\frac{1}{2}\tan^{-1}(x^2 + 1) + c.$

26. $-\sin^{-1}\left(\frac{1}{x}\right) + c.$ 27. (a) $-0\cdot123$, (b) $0\cdot545.$

Exercise 20.6 (pp. 407–408)

1. (a) 2/5, (b) 0, (c) π, (d) $\sqrt{3}$, (e) 0, (f) 0.   2.   0.
3. (a) -2, (b) 4, (c) 4.   4. (a) $-1\frac{1}{2}$, (b) $1\frac{1}{2}$, (c) $2\frac{1}{2}$.
5. (a) 0, (b) 8/3.   7. $e - 1.$ 8. $\frac{2}{3}(2 - \sqrt{2}).$
9. $I = \frac{1}{2}\pi, J = 2(e - 1).$ 10. (a) 2, (b) 1, (c) π.

Exercise 20.7 (pp. 408–412)

1. $2 - \frac{1}{2}\ln 3.$ 2. $\ln 2 - 1.$ 3. $\frac{1}{4}\ln\frac{9}{5}.$ 4.   2.

5. $1 + \ln\frac{8}{3}.$ 6. $\frac{64\sqrt{2}}{21}.$ 7.   8/3.   8. $\pi.$ 9.   7/6.

10. $\frac{1}{2}(1 - \ln 2).$ 11. 1/24.   12. $\ln 2.$ 13. $\ln(4/3).$ 14. $\pi/16.$

15. 1/(ln 2).   16. $\frac{1}{5}\ln\left(\frac{x - 3}{x + 2}\right) - \frac{1}{x - 3} + c.$ 18. $\pi/12.$

19. $(\pi - 2)/4.$ 20. $(\pi + 2)/8.$ 21. $\frac{1}{2}\ln 3.$
23. $(\frac{1}{4}, \frac{8}{3})$ min; $\frac{3}{2} - \ln 4.$ 24. $(-4, \frac{4}{3})$ max; $2\ln 3.$

25. $\frac{2}{x - 1} - \frac{x}{x^2 + 1}; 1\cdot04, -0\cdot23.$

27. (i) $a^2 + b^2$, (ii) $2\log_{10} 2 - \log_{10} e$, (iii) $(2\pi + 3\sqrt{3})/48.$
28. $y = x - a, x + y = 5a; 8a^2/3.$
29. $-3\sin t \cos t; y + 3x\sin t_1 \cos t_1 = 3\sin t_1 - 2\sin^3 t_1.$
31. $\frac{1}{2}x^2 \sin 2x + \frac{1}{2}x\cos 2x - \frac{1}{4}\sin 2x + c; \pi; \pi^2(2\pi^2 - 3)/12; \pi^4/6.$

32. $\dfrac{1}{x+1} + \dfrac{x+2}{x^2+3}$; $\ln(\sqrt{2}+\sqrt{6}) + \dfrac{\pi}{2\sqrt{3}}$; $\dfrac{1}{\sqrt{3}}\ln(\sqrt{2}+\sqrt{6}) + \dfrac{\pi}{6}$.

33. $p = 2,\ q = 1$; $\dfrac{1}{4}\pi$; $\ln 2$; $\pi + \ln 2$.

34. (a) $\dfrac{1-t^2}{1+t^2}$ (b) $\dfrac{1}{1-t} + \dfrac{1}{1+t} + \dfrac{8}{1+9t^2}$.

35. (a) $x(\log_e x - 1) + c$; $x\{(\log_e x)^2 - 2\log_e x + 2\} + c$,   (b) $\pi(e-2)$.

36. (i) $\frac{1}{2}\pi - 1$,   (ii) $\frac{1}{2}(1 - e^{-2})$.   37. π.

38. $\dfrac{a^2}{12}(4\pi - 3\sqrt{3})$; $\dfrac{5\pi a^3}{24}$.

39. (i) $\pi(2\ln 2 - 1)$,   (ii) $\frac{1}{2}\pi - 1$.

40. $\frac{22}{15}a^2$, $\frac{7}{12}\pi a^3$.   41. $\frac{16}{3}$, $\dfrac{64\pi}{15}$.

42. $x = \dfrac{\pi}{4}, \dfrac{9\pi}{4}$: max, $x = \dfrac{5\pi}{4}, \dfrac{13\pi}{4}$: min; $\frac{1}{2}(1 + e^{-\pi})$; $\frac{1}{2}e^{-2\pi}(1 + e^{-\pi})$.

Exercise 21.1 (pp. 416–417)

1. $\mathbf{a} - \mathbf{b} + \mathbf{c}$.   2. $\mathbf{a} - 2\mathbf{b} + 2\mathbf{c}$.   3. $60°$.   4. 7, $\sqrt{19}$.
5.   (a) $s = -2, t = 6$,   (b) $s = 6/5, t = 3/5$; $s = -2, t = -1$.
6.   (a) 9,   (b) -1.   7.   (a) $\frac{3}{8}\mathbf{a} + \frac{5}{8}\mathbf{b}$,   (b) $-\frac{1}{2}\mathbf{a} + \frac{3}{2}\mathbf{b}$,   (c) $2\mathbf{a} - \mathbf{b}$.
8.   (a) $\mathbf{i} + 2\mathbf{j} - \mathbf{k}$,   (b) $-7\mathbf{i} - 2\mathbf{j} - 5\mathbf{k}$.
9. $2\mathbf{i} - 5\mathbf{j} + 3\mathbf{k}$, $7\mathbf{i} - 2\mathbf{k}$; $(4, -3, 1)$, $(-1, -8, 6)$.
10. P is a vertex of parallelogram $ABCP$; Q divides AC internally in the ratio $4:3$; R divides BC externally in the ratio $2:3$.
11.   When produced BA and CD meet a point Q such that $BQ:AQ = 7:4$ and $CQ:DQ = 5:2$.
12. $\mathbf{r} = 3\mathbf{q} - 2\mathbf{p}$; $3:2$.

Exercise 21.2 (pp. 422–423)

1.   (a) $\mathbf{r} = (1 + 3\lambda)\mathbf{i} + 2\mathbf{j} - (1 + \lambda)\mathbf{k}$,   (b) $\mathbf{r} = (\lambda + 4)\mathbf{i} - 3\lambda\mathbf{j} + 3(\lambda - 1)\mathbf{k}$.
2.   (a) $\mathbf{r} = 2(1 - 2\lambda)\mathbf{i} + (4\lambda - 3)\mathbf{j} + \mathbf{k}$,   (b) $\mathbf{r} = (1 + 2\lambda)\mathbf{i} + (5 - 6\lambda)\mathbf{j} + 2\lambda\mathbf{k}$,
    (c) $\mathbf{r} = 5\lambda\mathbf{i} + (6 - 13\lambda)\mathbf{j} + 2(5\lambda - 4)\mathbf{k}$,   (d) $\mathbf{r} = 5\lambda\mathbf{i} - 2\lambda\mathbf{j} + 3\lambda\mathbf{k}$.
3. $\mathbf{r} = (1 - \lambda)\mathbf{a} + \frac{1}{3}\lambda\mathbf{b} + \frac{2}{3}\lambda\mathbf{c}$, $\mathbf{r} = -\mu\mathbf{a} + (1 - \mu)\mathbf{b} + 2\mu\mathbf{c}$; $-\frac{1}{2}\mathbf{a} + \frac{1}{2}\mathbf{b} + \mathbf{c}$.
4. $\frac{1}{2}\mathbf{a}$, $\frac{1}{3}\mathbf{a} + \mathbf{b}$, $\frac{1}{3}\mathbf{a} + \frac{2}{3}\mathbf{b}$.   5. $\frac{3}{2}\mathbf{a}$.   6. $1:3$.
7.   (a) Intersect at $2\mathbf{i} - 3\mathbf{j} + 3\mathbf{k}$,   (b) skew,   (c) parallel,
    (d) intersect at $6\mathbf{i} + 13\mathbf{j} - 4\mathbf{k}$.
8.   (a) A, B,   (b) B,   (c) C,   (d) A, B, C.

9.　(a) $\mathbf{r} = (\lambda + 1)\mathbf{i} + (3\lambda - \mu - 2)\mathbf{j} + 2\mu\mathbf{k}$,
　　(b) $\mathbf{r} = (2\lambda - \mu)\mathbf{i} + (2\mu - \lambda)\mathbf{j} - 7\mu\mathbf{k}$,
　　(c) $\mathbf{r} = (\mu + 3)\mathbf{i} + (\lambda + \mu + 1)\mathbf{j} + (\mu - 1)\mathbf{k}$.
10.　$\mathbf{r} = (\lambda + 5\mu)\mathbf{i} + (2\mu - 3\lambda)\mathbf{j} + (2 - \lambda - 2\mu)\mathbf{k}$.
11.　$-\mathbf{i} + 3\mathbf{k}, \mathbf{j}; \mathbf{r} = (2 - \lambda)\mathbf{i} + (5 + \mu)\mathbf{j} + 3\lambda\mathbf{k}$.
12.　$\mathbf{r} = (2t + 1)\mathbf{i} + (2s - t)\mathbf{j} - (2 + s - 3t)\mathbf{k}; (5, 0, 3)$.
14.　$[r(1 - p)\mathbf{c} + p(r - 1)\mathbf{a}]/(r - p), [p(1 - q)\mathbf{a} + q(p - 1)\mathbf{b}]/(p - q)$.

Exercise 21.3 (pp. 427–429)

1.　(a) $p^2 + 2\mathbf{p}.\mathbf{q} + q^2$,　(b) $p^2 - q^2$,　(c) $2\mathbf{p}.\mathbf{r}$,　(d) $p^2 - 2\mathbf{p}.\mathbf{q} + q^2$.
2.　(a) x^2,　(b) $2x^2 - 3y^2$.　　3.　81, 49; 9, 7.　　4.　13, 9.　　8.　$-3/4$.
9.　$3\mathbf{a} - 2\mathbf{b}$.　　14.　(a) 68·3°,　(b) 60°,　(c) 90°,　(d) 35·3°.
15.　(a) 1/3,　(b) 5/11.　　16.　(a) 3,　(b) 2,　(c) 1,　(d) -1.　　17.　65/7, 7/9.
18.　(a) $4\mathbf{i} - 3\mathbf{j}$,　(b) $2\mathbf{i} + 5\mathbf{j}$,　(c) $3\mathbf{i} - 2\mathbf{j}$.
19.　$\angle A = 90°$, $\angle B = 36·9°$, $\angle O = 53·1°$; 30 sq. units.
20.　11/21, $8\sqrt{5}$ sq. units.　　21.　$5\mathbf{i} + 2\mathbf{k}$.
22.　(a) $(2, -1, 1)$,　(b) 70·5°.
23.　$\mathbf{i} - \mathbf{j}, \mathbf{j} + \mathbf{k}; 60°$.　　24.　$-11, -7; 7; 7/57$.

Exercise 21.4 (pp. 434–436)

1.　$-2\mathbf{i} - 2\mathbf{j} + \mathbf{k}$; 3 units.　　2.　$\mathbf{i} - \mathbf{k}$; 9 sq. units.
3.　$3\mathbf{i} - \mathbf{j} + 4\mathbf{k}; 6\mathbf{i} - 2\mathbf{j} + 8\mathbf{k}$.　　4.　$5\mathbf{i} - \mathbf{j} + 6\mathbf{k}$; 13 units.
5.　(a) $\mathbf{r}.(4\mathbf{i} - \mathbf{k}) = 3$,　(b) $\mathbf{r}.(\mathbf{i} - \mathbf{j} - 2\mathbf{k}) = 1$.
6.　(a) $\mathbf{r}.\mathbf{k} = 1$,　(b) $\mathbf{r}.(3\mathbf{i} + 4\mathbf{j} - 2\mathbf{k}) = 0$.
7.　(a) 5,　(b) 3,　(c) 4,　(d) 0.
8.　$2\mathbf{i} - 5\mathbf{j} - \mathbf{k}, \mathbf{r}.(2\mathbf{i} - 5\mathbf{j} - \mathbf{k}) = 7$.　　9.　$\mathbf{r}.(\mathbf{i} + 3\mathbf{j} - 2\mathbf{k}) = 1$.
10.　$\mathbf{r}.(\mathbf{j} - 2\mathbf{k}) = -8$.　　11.　(a) 60°,　(b) 48·2°,　(c) 70·5°.
12.　(a) 11/18,　(b) 5/6,　(c) 6/7.　　13.　$-\mathbf{i} - 2\mathbf{j} - 3\mathbf{k}, 2\mathbf{i} - 2\mathbf{j} + 3\mathbf{k}$.
14.　$\mathbf{r} = (3\lambda + 5)\mathbf{i} - (4\lambda + 3)\mathbf{j} + (\lambda + 4)\mathbf{k}; 2\mathbf{i} + \mathbf{j} + 3\mathbf{k}$.

15.　(a) $\dfrac{x - 1}{2} = \dfrac{y + 2}{3} = \dfrac{z - 1}{4}$,　(b) $\dfrac{x}{1} = \dfrac{y - 2}{-1} = \dfrac{z - 3}{2}$,

　　(c) $\dfrac{x - 2}{5} = \dfrac{y + 3}{-6} = \dfrac{z - 1}{3}$,　(d) $\dfrac{x - 5}{1} = \dfrac{y}{3} = \dfrac{z + 4}{0}$

16.　(a) $2x - 3y + z - 5 = 0$,　(b) $3x + y - 5z - 9 = 0$.
17.　$5x + y + z - 6 = 0$.　　18.　$2x - y + 5z - 3 = 0$.
19.　$\mathbf{i} - 3\mathbf{j} + 2\mathbf{k}$; (a) $\mathbf{r}.(\mathbf{i} - 3\mathbf{j} + 2\mathbf{k}) = -5$, (b) $x - 3y + 2z + 5 = 0$.
20.　$3x + y - 4z - 1 = 0$.　　21.　(a) 70·5°,　(b) 65·9°,　(c) 28·5°.
22.　(a) Plane through O perpendicular to OA,
　　(b) Plane through A perpendicular to OA,
　　(c) Sphere with centre A, radius 1 unit,
　　(d) Plane through O perpendicular to AB,
　　(e) Sphere with diameter OA,
　　(f) Sphere with diameter AB.

Exercise 21.5 (pp. 436–438)

1. $\mathbf{b} - \mathbf{a}, \frac{1}{2}(\mathbf{a} + \mathbf{c}), \mathbf{a} - \mathbf{b} + \mathbf{c}; 2\mathbf{k}, 2\mathbf{i} + 2\mathbf{k}, 2\mathbf{i} + 2\mathbf{j} + 2\mathbf{k}, \mathbf{i} + \mathbf{j} + 2\mathbf{k}, 2\mathbf{j} + 2\mathbf{k}; (2\sqrt{2})/3$

2. $\frac{1}{2}(\mathbf{a} + \mathbf{b}), \frac{1}{2}(\mathbf{b} + \mathbf{c}), \frac{1}{2}(\mathbf{c} + \mathbf{d}), \frac{1}{2}(\mathbf{d} + \mathbf{a}), \frac{1}{2}(\mathbf{a} + \mathbf{c}), \frac{1}{2}(\mathbf{b} + \mathbf{d}); (\mathbf{i} + \mathbf{j})/\sqrt{2}.$

3. Mid-point of XC, where X divides AB in ratio $1:2; \frac{1}{3}\mathbf{a} + \frac{2}{3}(\frac{1}{4}\mathbf{b} + \frac{3}{4}\mathbf{c});$
    R divides AY in ratio $2:1$, where Y divides BC in ratio $3:1$.

4. $\{(1 + \lambda)\mathbf{a} + \mathbf{b} + \lambda\mathbf{c}\}/2(1 + \lambda), \{\lambda\mathbf{a} + (1 + \lambda)\mathbf{b} + \mathbf{c}\}/2(1 + \lambda),$
    $\{\mathbf{a} + \lambda\mathbf{b} + (1 + \lambda)\mathbf{c}\}/2(1 + \lambda); \frac{1}{2}(1 + \sqrt{5}).$

6. $3\mathbf{i} + 2\mathbf{j} + 4\mathbf{k}; \mathbf{r} = 3\mathbf{i} + s(2\mathbf{i} + 5\mathbf{j} + 4\mathbf{k}) + t(\mathbf{j} + 2\mathbf{k}).$

7. $\mathbf{r} = (1 - \lambda)\mathbf{i} + (6\lambda + 3)\mathbf{j} + (4\lambda + 2)\mathbf{k}.$ 9. $70.5°.$

11. $\frac{1}{3}(\mathbf{a} + \mathbf{b} + \mathbf{c}).$ 12. $\lambda:\mu = 1:6; \mathbf{r} = (1 + t)\mathbf{a} + 6t\mathbf{b}; -12\mathbf{i} - 6\mathbf{j} + 6\mathbf{k}.$

13. (i) $\mathbf{r} = (1 + \lambda + \mu)\mathbf{i} - 2\lambda\mathbf{j} - 3\mu\mathbf{k}$ or $\mathbf{r}.(6\mathbf{i} + 3\mathbf{j} + 2\mathbf{k}) = 6,$
     (ii) $\mathbf{r} = \lambda(6\mathbf{i} + 3\mathbf{j} + 2\mathbf{k}),$ (iii) $6(6\mathbf{i} + 3\mathbf{j} + 2\mathbf{k})/49.$

14. (i) $(1, -2, 0), (4, 4, -3),$ (ii) $90°, 90°,$
     (iii) $x - y - z - 3 = 0, x + z = 1,$ (iv) $90°.$

15. $(p - \mathbf{a}.\mathbf{n})/(\mathbf{b}.\mathbf{n}); (2\frac{1}{3}, 2\frac{1}{3}, 2\frac{2}{3}).$

16. $-1, 1; \mathbf{i} + 5\mathbf{j} - \mathbf{k}, -3\mathbf{i} + 3\mathbf{j} + \mathbf{k}; 2\sqrt{6}.$

17. (i) $-\mathbf{i} + \mathbf{j} + 3\mathbf{k},$ (ii) $3\mathbf{j} - \mathbf{k},$ (iii) $55°,$ (iv) $35°.$

Exercise 22.1 (pp. 442–444)

1. (a) $n(n + 2),$ (b) $\frac{1}{6}n(n - 1)(2n + 5),$ (c) $2^{n+1} - 2,$
    (d) $\frac{1}{12}n(n + 1)(n + 2)(3n + 1),$ (e) $\frac{3}{2}(1 - 3^{-n}),$
    (f) $\frac{1}{4}(n + 4)^2(n + 5)^2 - 100.$

2. (a) $\dfrac{n}{2(n + 2)},$ (b) $\dfrac{3}{4} - \dfrac{1}{2(n + 1)} - \dfrac{1}{2(n + 2)} = \dfrac{n(3n + 5)}{4(n + 1)(n + 2)},$

    (c) $\frac{1}{12} - \dfrac{1}{2(n + 2)} + \dfrac{1}{2(n + 3)}.$

3. (a) (i) $0,$ (ii) $1,$ (b) (i) $-n,$ (ii) $n + 1.$ 4. $\frac{1}{3}n(n + 1)(n + 2)$

7. $\frac{1}{6}n(n + 1)(2n + 1)(3n^2 + 3n - 1).$ 8. $(n + 1)! - 1.$

9. (a) $\frac{2}{3}n(n + 1),$ (b) $\frac{1}{6}n(n + 1)(38n + 1).$

10. (a) $n^2,$ (b) $\frac{1}{3}n(2n - 1)(2n + 1).$

11. (a) $352\,800,$ (b) $56\,953,$ (c) $\frac{1}{4}n^2(3n + 1)(5n + 3),$·   (d) $-n^2(4n + 3).$

12. $r(r + 3); \frac{1}{3}n(n + 1)(n + 5).$

13. $(3r - 1)^2; \frac{1}{2}n(6n^2 + 3n - 1).$

14. $2r(2r - 1); \frac{1}{3}n(n + 1)(4n - 1).$

15. $r(r + 1)(r + 4); \frac{1}{12}n(n + 1)(n + 2)(3n + 17).$

16. $\dfrac{1}{r(r + 3)}; \dfrac{11}{18} - \dfrac{1}{3}\left(\dfrac{1}{n + 1} + \dfrac{1}{n + 2} + \dfrac{1}{n + 3}\right).$

17. $\dfrac{1}{(2r - 1)(2r + 1)}; \dfrac{n}{2n + 1}.$

18. $\dfrac{1}{(2r - 1)(2r + 1)(2r + 3)}; \dfrac{1}{12} - \dfrac{1}{8(2n + 1)} + \dfrac{1}{8(2n + 3)}.$

19. $\dfrac{r}{(r+1)(r+2)(r+3)}; \dfrac{1}{4} + \dfrac{1}{2(n+2)} - \dfrac{3}{2(n+3)}.$

20. $\dfrac{x^{n+1}-1}{x-1}; \dfrac{nx^{n+1}-(n+1)x^n+1}{(x-1)^2}.$

21. $\dfrac{nx^{n+2}-(n+1)x^{n+1}+x}{(1-x)^2}.$

22. $\{1 - a - (2n+3)(-a)^{n+1} + (2n+1)(-a)^{n+2}\}/(1+a)^2.$

Exercise 22.2 (p. 446)

1. $1 - \frac{1}{2}x^2 + \frac{1}{24}x^4,$ 2. $x + \frac{1}{3}x^3.$ 3. $1 + \frac{1}{2}x^2 + \frac{5}{24}x^4.$
4. $-\frac{1}{2}x^2 - \frac{1}{12}x^4.$ 5. $x^2 - \frac{1}{3}x^4.$ 6. $x - \frac{1}{2}x^2 + \frac{1}{6}x^3 - \frac{1}{12}x^4.$
7. $x - \frac{1}{3}x^3.$ 8. $1 + x + \frac{1}{2}x^2 - \frac{1}{8}x^4.$ 9. $x + \frac{1}{6}x^3.$
10. $x + x^2 + \frac{1}{3}x^3 - \frac{1}{30}x^5 - \frac{1}{90}x^6.$

Exercise 22.3 (pp. 450–452)

1. $1 - 3x + 6x^2 - 10x^3.$ 2. $1 + x - \frac{1}{2}x^2 + \frac{1}{2}x^3.$
3. $\frac{1}{8} - \frac{3}{64}x + \frac{15}{1024}x^2 - \frac{35}{8192}x^3.$ 4. $1 + 4x + 8x^2 + 16x^3.$
5. $\frac{1}{4} - \frac{1}{2}x + \frac{7}{16}x^2 - \frac{5}{16}x^3.$ 6. $1 + 2x^2 + 8x^3.$ 7. $1 - x + x^3.$
8. $1 - \frac{1}{2}x + \frac{11}{8}x^2 - \frac{29}{16}x^3.$ 9. $1 + \frac{1}{3}x + \frac{8}{9}x^2 - \frac{49}{81}x^3,$
10. $1 - x + \frac{1}{2}x^2, |x| < 1.$ 11. $2 + \frac{25}{12}x + \frac{1175}{288}x^2, |x| < \frac{1}{3}.$
12. $1 + \frac{1}{2}x^2, |x| < \frac{1}{5}.$ 13. $\frac{1}{3} - \frac{2}{9}x + \frac{7}{27}x^2, |x| < 1$
14. $1 - 3x + 9x^2, |x| < \frac{1}{2}.$ 15. $1 + \frac{5}{2}x + \frac{43}{8}x^2, |x| < \frac{1}{2}.$
16. $3 + x + 11x^2 + 25x^3 + 83x^4, |x| < \frac{1}{3}.$
17. $\frac{4}{3}x + \frac{8}{9}x^2 + \frac{28}{27}x^3 + \frac{80}{81}x^4 + \frac{244}{243}x^5, |x| < 1.$
18. $1 + 2x + x^2 + x^4 + 2x^5, |x| < 1.$
19. $4 - x + 12x^2 - 11x^3 + 38x^4, |x| < \frac{1}{2}.$
20. $2 - 2x + 2x^4 - 2x^5 + 2x^8, |x| < 1.$
21. $-1 + x + \frac{7}{4}x^2 + \frac{1}{2}x^3 - \frac{3}{16}x^4, |x| < \sqrt{2}.$
22. $3 + 3x + 9x^2; \{(-1)^r + 2^{r+1}\}x^r.$
23. $4x - 8x^2 + 28x^3; \{1 - (-3)^r\}x^r.$
24. $2 - \frac{3}{2}x + \frac{17}{4}x^2; \{(-2)^r + 2^{-r}\}x^r.$
25. $1 + \frac{1}{2}x - \frac{3}{8}x^2 + \frac{7}{16}x^3; |x| < \frac{1}{2};$ (a) 1·0885, (b) 1·019 428.
26. $(a+b) + 2(1-a+b)x + (-4-2a+3b)x^2 + 4(-1-a+b)x^3; 13, -8.$
27. $n = 6, a = \frac{1}{2}.$ 28. $a = 3, b = 1; 70/13.$

Exercise 22.4 (pp. 455–457)

1. (a) $1 - x + \frac{1}{2}x^2; \dfrac{(-1)^r x^r}{r!}$, (b) $1 + 3x + \frac{9}{2}x^2; \dfrac{3^r x^r}{r!}$,

   (c) $1 + x^2 + \frac{1}{2}x^4; \dfrac{x^{2r}}{r!}$, (d) $e + ex + \frac{1}{2}ex^2; \dfrac{ex^r}{r!}$.

2. (a) $1 + 4x + 6x^2 + \frac{16}{3}x^3$, (b) $1 - 3x + \frac{7}{2}x^2 - \frac{13}{6}x^3$,
   (c) $1 - x + \frac{3}{2}x^2 - \frac{7}{6}x^3$.
3. $2 \cdot 7183; 0 \cdot 3679$.
4. (a) $3x - \frac{9}{2}x^2 + 9x^3; -\frac{1}{3} < x \leqslant \frac{1}{3}$. (b) $-\frac{1}{2}x - \frac{1}{8}x^2 - \frac{1}{24}x^3; -2 \leqslant x < 2$.
   (c) $\ln 2 + \frac{1}{3}x - \frac{1}{18}x^2; -3 < x \leqslant 3$. (d) $1 - \dfrac{x}{e} - \dfrac{x^2}{2e^2}; -e \leqslant x < e$.

5. (a) $x - \frac{3}{2}x^2 + \frac{1}{3}x^3 + \frac{1}{4}x^4$, (b) $x - \frac{5}{2}x^2 + \frac{7}{3}x^3 - \frac{17}{4}x^4$,
   (c) $-4x + 3x^2 - \frac{34}{3}x^3 + \frac{63}{2}x^4$. 6. $1 \cdot 0986$.
7. (a) $(1 - r)/r!$, (b) $(4 + 5r - 3r^2)2^{r-2}/r!$, (c) $(4r^2 + 1)/2^r r!$.
8. (a) $x + \frac{1}{2}x^2$, (b) $4 - 4x + 3x^2$, (c) $1 + \frac{15}{2}x + \frac{193}{8}x^2$, (d) $2x$,
   (e) $1 + 2x + \frac{5}{2}x^2$, (f) $2 + x + \frac{11}{6}x^2$.
9. $0 \cdot 6931$. 10. $a = 2, n = -2$. 11. $a = \frac{1}{2}, b = 2; 31/170$.

Exercise 22.5 (p. 458)

1. (a) $0 \cdot 2955$, (b) $0 \cdot 9211$, (c) $-0 \cdot 4161$, (d) $0 \cdot 8415$.
2. (a) $3x - \frac{9}{2}x^3 + \frac{81}{40}x^5$, (b) $1 - 2x^2 + \frac{2}{3}x^4$, (c) $x - \frac{1}{2}x^2 + \frac{1}{6}x^3$,
   (d) $e - \dfrac{e}{2}x^2 + \dfrac{e}{6}x^4$, (e) $1 + \frac{1}{6}x^2 + \frac{7}{360}x^4$, (f) $x + \frac{1}{3}x^3 + \frac{2}{15}x^5$.
3. (a) $x + x^2 - \frac{2}{3}x^3 - \frac{1}{6}x^4$, (b) $2x - 2x^2 + \frac{4}{3}x^3$, (c) $\frac{4}{3}x^4$,
   (d) $1 + 2x + x^2 - \frac{2}{3}x^3 - x^4$.

Exercise 22.6 (pp. 458–460)

1. (a) $\frac{1}{3}n(n^2 - 1)$, (b) $\frac{1}{3}(n + 1)(4n^2 + 14n + 9)$, (c) $\dfrac{n + 1}{n(2n + 1)}$,

   (d) $\frac{3}{4} - \dfrac{1}{2n} - \dfrac{1}{2(n + 1)}$.

2. (a) $\frac{1}{12}n(n + 1)(n + 2)(3n + 5)$, (b) $n(n + 1)(2n^2 + 2n - 1)$.

3. $\frac{1}{6}n^2(n + 1)^2(n - 1)$. 4. $\dfrac{1 - (n + 1)x^{2n} + nx^{2n+2}}{(1 - x^2)^2}$

5. $(x + 1)(x + 2)(x + 3); \dfrac{1}{x + 1} + \dfrac{2}{x + 2} - \dfrac{3}{x + 3}$.

6. (a) $2^{n+1} - 2 + n^2$,   (b) $a = -2, b = -1$; 73/74.

7. $1 + \dfrac{1}{2x^2} - \dfrac{1}{8x^4}, 1 - \dfrac{1}{2x^2} - \dfrac{1}{8x^4}$.

8. $2 - \frac{1}{4}x - \frac{1}{64}x^2$; $2 + \frac{7}{4}x + \frac{175}{64}x^2$, $|x| < \frac{1}{2}$.   9. $2 + x - \frac{3}{2}x^3$.

10. (a) $3x - 3x^2 + 9x^3$, $\{1 - (-2)^r\}x^r$, $|x| < \frac{1}{2}$,

    (b) $\frac{1}{6}x + \frac{5}{36}x^2 + \frac{19}{216}x^3$, $\left(\dfrac{1}{2^r} - \dfrac{1}{3^r}\right)x^r$, $|x| < 2$,

    (c) $1 + 5x + 18x^2$, $\frac{1}{2}(5 \cdot 3^r - 2^{r+1} - 1)x^r$, $|x| < \frac{1}{3}$.

11. (a) $1 - 2x - x^2 + 2x^3 + \frac{3}{2}x^4$; $|x| < 1/\sqrt{2}$,

    (b) $1 + 4x + 14x^2 + 40x^3 + 104x^4$; $|x| < \frac{1}{2}$,

    (c) $3 + 6x + 6x^2 + 12x^3 + 36x^4$; $|x| < \frac{1}{2}$.

12. (a) $x + \frac{5}{24}x^3 - \frac{1}{8}x^4$; for $|x| < 1$; $a = -\frac{1}{4}$,

    (b) $1 - \frac{1}{2}x + \frac{3}{8}x^2 - \frac{5}{16}x^3$, $\dfrac{1 \cdot 3 \cdot 5 \ldots (2r-1)}{2^r r!}(-1)^r x^r$; 0·099 504.

13. (a) (i) $(0, 1)$,   (ii) $(0, 1)$,   (iii) $(1, 0)$,   (iv) $(0, 0)$;

    (b) $7x + \frac{1}{2}x^2 + \frac{43}{3}x^3 + \frac{49}{4}x^4$, $-\frac{1}{3} \leqslant x < \frac{1}{3}$; $\{(-2)^{n+1} + 3^n\}x^n/n$.

14. $1 + x + x^2 + \frac{1}{3}x^3$; 0·287.

15. (i) $x - \dfrac{x^2}{2} + \dfrac{x^3}{3} - \dfrac{x^4}{4} + \ldots + (-1)^{n+1}\dfrac{x^n}{n} + \ldots$;   (ii) 0·6931; 1/3, 23/60.

16. $p^2 - 2, p^3 - 3p$; $-px - \frac{1}{2}(p^2 - 2)x^2 - \frac{1}{3}(p^3 - 3p)x^3$.

17. $1, \sqrt{3}, 2$.

Exercise 23.1 (pp. 466–468)

1. 0·697.   2.   5·731.   3.   45·992.   4.   4·154.   5.   0·144.
6. 0·825.   7.   Greater.   8.   Greater.   9.   Greater.
10. Less.   11. Greater.   12. Less.   13. 0·8358.   14. 0·4783.
15. 0·6807.   16. 0·8945.   17. 0·2763.   18. 3·2413.
19. $1 + 12x^2 + 66x^4 + 220x^6 + 495x^8$; 1·7655; 1·9253.
20. 0·0711; 0·0715.
21. (a) 10·075,   (b) 9·99.   22. (a) $7·175\,\text{m s}^{-1}$,   (b) $11·85\,\text{m s}^{-1}$; 131 m.
23. (a) 422·5 J.   (b) 423 J.   24. 0·7444.   25. 1·4241.
26. 1·68.   27. 0·524.

Exercise 23.2 (pp. 474–475)

1. 2·7, $-0·7$.   2.   0·7.   3. $-2·1$.   4. $-0·6, 1, 1·6$.
5. $-1·8, -0·4, 1·2$.   6.   0·8.   7. $0, \pm 1·9$.   8. $-3·6, -2·1, 1·3$.
9. 1·1.   10. 1, 4·2.   11. One.   12. Two.   13. Three.
14. Five.   15. One; $-3, -2$.   16. One; 1, 2.
17. Three; $-4, -3$; 1, 2; 2, 3.   18. Three; $-3, -2$; $-1, 0$; 1, 2.
19. One; 1, 2.   20. One; 1, 2.   21. Two; $-3, -2$; 1, 2.

22. One; 2, 3.　　23. 3·2.　　24. $-0·8, 1·6$.　　25. $-3, 1; 1·1$.
26. 2·2.　　27. $-5·2, -0·6, 2·9$.　　28. $-0·2, 0·6, 2·0$.　　29. $-4·1$.
30. 1·8, 4·5.　　31. $-1·3, 1·9, 4·0$.
32. (a) $-1·75, 0·43, 1·32$,　(b) $-1·6, 0·7, 1·1$.
33. (a) $-0·1$,　(b) 0·25,　(c) 0·4,　(d) 0·2.

Exercise 23.3 (pp. 478–479)

1. 1·20.　　2. $-1·11$.　　3. $-1·52$.　　4. 2·39.　　5. 1·56.
6. 0·79.　　7. $-1·90$.　　8. 1·17.　　9. 2·803.　　10. 1·650.
11. $-0·830$.　　12. $-1·834$.　　13. 1·278.　　14. 2·219.　　15. 0·453.
16. 3·6; 3·6913.　　17. Two; 3·98, $-1·06$.
18. 2, $a: = 2, h: = 0·01, g(x): = e^x - 2; 1·68$.

Exercise 23.4 (pp. 484–486)

1. (a) 2·24, (b) 1·26, (c) 0·79, 3·87.　　2. (a) 1·414, (b) 3·162, (c) 3·606.
3. 1·71.　　4. 0·769.　　5. 1·821.　　6. $-3·794$.
7. 0·1926; for $x_0 = -6$ the sequence diverges, for $x_0 = -5$ the sequence converges to the positive root.
8. 1; 1·260, 1·312.　　9. 1·732.
10. 1·087 using $x_{n+1} = (4 - \frac{5}{2}x_n)^{1/3}$, $x_{n+1} = \dfrac{8}{2x_n^2 + 5}$ or Newton's method.

11. 2·618; decision box should ensure maximum error of 0·1.　　12. 0·7.

Exercise 23.5 (pp. 486–490)

1. 3·69, 6·71.　　2. 4, 3; (a) 4·826, (b) 4·8224.　　3. 0·4778; 0·4783.
4. 0·410.　　5. (i) 2·09, (ii) $-1·53, 0·26, 1·27; 0·5$.
6. (i) two, (ii) $m < -\frac{1}{2}$.　　7. $(0, 0), (2, 4e^{-2})$.　　8. $q < 0$.
9. 2·4; underestimate.　　10. Three; 1·43, larger.　　11. (ii) output "2, 3".
12. (a) 2·208, (b) 2·208.　　13. 1, 3; $-4, 0; a < -4$ or $a > 0$; 4·1.
14. 3·43; 3·75; 15.　　15. $(x - 2)(x - 3)(x^2 + x + 2); 3·065$.
16. (a) 0·818, (b) 0·810.　　17. 0·74.　　18. 0·5, 0·73.
19. 1·2.　　20. 0·77.　　21. $x = (3x - 1)^{1/3}; 1·53$.

Exercise 24.1 (pp. 494–495)

3. (a) and (d).　　4. 2, -1.　　5. 1, 0, 2.　　6. $\dfrac{dy}{dx} = 3x^2$.

7. $x\dfrac{dy}{dx} = y + x^2$.   8. $x\dfrac{dy}{dx} + y = 0$.   9. $\dfrac{dy}{dx} + y = 0$.

10. $x + y\dfrac{dy}{dx} = 0$.   11. $2x\dfrac{dy}{dx} = y$.   12. $x\dfrac{dy}{dx} = 2x - y$.

13. $x\dfrac{dy}{dx} = 2y + x^2$.   14. $2\dfrac{dy}{dx} + y\tan x = 0$.

15. $x\ln x\dfrac{dy}{dx} = y\ln y$.   16. $\dfrac{d^2y}{dx^2} + y = 0$.

17. $\dfrac{d^2y}{dx^2} - 2\dfrac{dy}{dx} - 3y = 0$.   18. $3\dfrac{dy}{dx}\left(\dfrac{d^2y}{dx^2}\right) + y\dfrac{d^3y}{dx^3} = 0$.

19. $\dfrac{d^3y}{dx^3} - 2\dfrac{d^2y}{dx^2} + \dfrac{dy}{dx} = 0$.

Exercise 24.2 (pp. 499–501)

1. $y = x^3 + x + c$.   2. $y = 2\sin\frac{1}{2}x + c$.   3. $y = \frac{1}{2}x^2 + \ln|x| + c$.
4. $y = x + \ln(x - 1)^2 + c$.   5. $y = \cos x + \frac{1}{3}x^3 + Ax + B$.

6. $y = e^{-x} - e^x + Ax + B$.   7. $y = \dfrac{1}{2x + k}$.   8. $y = \tan^{-1}(x + k)$.

9. $y = \ln|x + k|$.   10. $y = (c - x)^{-1/3}$.   11. $y = \frac{1}{3}(x + 1)^3 - 9$.
12. $y = 1 + \sqrt{(2x + 3)}$.   13. $y = x\sin x + \cos x + 1$.
14. $y = \ln\frac{1}{2}(1 + x^2)$.   15. $y = \frac{1}{4}(x - \sin 2x)$.
16. $y = 2\ln x + x^2 - 4x + 3$.   17. $y = 3e^{-2x}$.   18. $y = 1 - e^x$.
19. $y = \tan(x + \frac{1}{4}\pi)$.   20. $y = (3 + e^x)/(3 - e^x)$.   21. $y = x/(1 + kx)$.
22. $y = kx + x\sin x$.   23. $y = kx^2 - x$.   24. $y = x - e^{1-x} + 2$.

25. $xe^y\dfrac{dy}{dx} + e^y; y = \ln\left(x - \dfrac{2}{x}\right)$.

Exercise 24.3 (pp. 504–506)

1. $y = (x^2 - x + c)^{1/3}$.   2. $y = 1/(c - 3x^2)$.   3. $y = -\ln(\cos x + c)$.
4. $y = \ln(e^x + c)$.   5. $y = \sin^{-1}(\frac{1}{2}x^2 + c)$.   6. $y = \tan^{-1}(3x + c)$.
7. $y = Ax$.   8. $y = A/(1 - x)$.   9. $y = A(x^2 + 1)^2$.
10. $y = A(x - 1)/(x + 1)$.   11. $y = x/(1 - 2x)$.   12. $y = 5e^{-x^2}$.
13. $y = 2\sec x$.   14. $y = \frac{1}{2}\ln(x^2 + 1)$.   15. $y = 2e^{x^2} - 1$.
16. $y = xe^{x-1}$.   17. $y = \sin^{-1}(1 + x^3)$.   18. $y = \sin^{-1}(x - 1)$.
19. $y = 1/(1 - 2x^2)$.   20. $y = (x - 1)/(x + 1)$.   21. $y = Ae^{-x}/(1 - x)$.
22. $y = Ae^x(x - 1)/(x + 1)$.   23. $y = \tan(e^x + c)$.   24. $y = \ln(1 + Ae^{x^2})$.
25. $y = e^{-x}\sqrt{(2x + 1)}$.   26. $y = \sqrt{\{(\ln x)^2 + 9\}}$.
27. $x^2 - y^2 - 2xy + 2x + 2y = A$.
28. $x^2(x^2 - y^2) = A$.

Exercise 24.4 (pp. 507–509)

1. $x^2 + y^2 = 5.$ 2. $y = 1/x^2.$

3. $\dfrac{dC}{dt} = kC; C = C_0 e^{kt}; t = \dfrac{1}{k}\ln\frac{3}{2}.$ 4. $\dfrac{d\theta}{dt} = -k\theta.$

5. $(1 + \sqrt{2})t.$ 6. $\dfrac{dx}{dt} = -kx;$ 93 days; 320 mg.   7.   40 min.

8. $x = 100(1 + e^{-t/10});$ 137 litres; 6 min 56 sec.   9. $30\ln 2$ min., $100e^{-1}$ kg.

10.   2·99.   11. $t = \dfrac{\ln 3}{V\beta}; m = \dfrac{V}{\alpha(1 + 3e^{-V\beta t})}.$

Exercise 24.5 (pp. 514–515)

1. $y = A\cos 4x + B\sin 4x.$ 2. $y = A\cos\frac{\sqrt{7}}{2}x + B\sin\frac{\sqrt{7}}{2}x.$
3. $y = 2 + A\cos 3x + B\sin 3x.$ 4. $y = 1 + A\cos\sqrt{10}x + B\sin\sqrt{10}x.$
5. $y = Ae^{6x} + Be^{-6x}.$ 6. $y = Ae^{2\sqrt{2}x} + Be^{-2\sqrt{2}x}.$
7. $y = -\frac{1}{27} + Ae^{\sqrt{3}x} + Be^{-\sqrt{3}x}.$ 8. $y = \frac{1}{4} + Ae^{2x} + Be^{-2x}.$
9. $y = 4\cos 2x - 3\sin 2x.$ 10. $y = 3e^{4x} + 7e^{-4x}.$ 11. $y = 6\cos\frac{1}{6}x.$
12. $y = 4\sin\frac{4}{3}x - 5\cos\frac{4}{3}x.$ 13. $y = -2e^{5x/2} - 7e^{-5x/2}.$
14. $y = 4e^{-2\sqrt{3}x}.$ 15. $y = -\frac{4}{7} + 3e^{7x/3} + 6e^{-7x/3}.$
16. $y = \frac{8}{5} + 4\cos\frac{5}{2}x + 9\sin\frac{5}{2}x.$ 17. $y = 2 + \sin\sqrt{3}x.$
18. $y = -3 + e^{9x/4} + e^{-9x/4}.$ 19. $y = -3 + \sqrt{2}e^{3\sqrt{2}x}.$
20. $y = \frac{1}{2} - 4\sqrt{3}\cos 2\sqrt{3}x - 3\sqrt{3}\sin 2\sqrt{3}x.$

Exercise 24.6 (pp. 515–519)

1. $\left(\dfrac{dy}{dx}\right)^2 - 4x\dfrac{dy}{dx} + 4y = 0.$

2. $(2x + 1)\dfrac{d^2y}{dx^2} - 2\dfrac{dy}{dx} - (2x + 3)y = 0.$

3. $y = x^2; y = x^2 + 2x.$
4.   (a) $\ln\frac{1}{3}(3 - 7u) = 7(t - 5),$ (b) $3(y + 18) = (x^2 + 9)^{3/2}.$
5.   (a) $2x^3 + 11x^2 + 20x = 37 - 2t,$ (b) $y = \{\frac{1}{2}(5e^{x+1} - 3)\}^{1/2}.$

6. $y = 36e^{-t/6} + 27;$ 11 minutes; 27 degrees.   7. $y = \sin x + \dfrac{\cos x - 1}{1 + x}.$

8.   (a) $x^2 - 4y^2 = 4;$ $x - y\sqrt{3} = 1.$
9.   (a) $\tan y = 1 - \cos x,$ (b) $y = \ln\frac{1}{2}(1 + e^{2x}).$
10.   (i) $y = e^{-x}(1 + x)^2,$ (ii) $y^2 = 2x.$

12. $y = \dfrac{2x}{x^2 + cx + 1}$; (a) $y = \dfrac{2x}{x^2 + 1}$, (b) $y = \dfrac{2x}{x^2 + x + 1}$,

(c) $y = \dfrac{2x}{(x + 1)^2}$.

13. $\dfrac{dy}{dx} = \dfrac{y}{x}$, $y = 2x$; $\dfrac{dx}{dt} = -2x^3$, $x = \dfrac{1}{\sqrt{(4t + 1)}}$.

14. (a) $y\dfrac{d^2y}{dx^2} + \left(\dfrac{dy}{dx}\right)^2 = 0$.

15. (i) (a) $y = A + \ln[\ln(1/x)]$,   (b) $y = A + \ln(\ln x)$,   (iii) $y = x$, $y = 2 - x$.

16. $20°$, $53\tfrac{3}{4}°$.   17. (a) $x = 2 + \dfrac{1}{12}\ln\left(\dfrac{5(3y - 2)}{3y + 2}\right)$,   (b) $\dfrac{dp}{dt} = kp$.

18. (a) $y = \tfrac{1}{3}(5e^{3x-6} - 2)$,   (b) $\dfrac{dm}{dt} = -km$; $75\cdot98\%$.

19. $\dfrac{dP}{dt} = kP(N - P)$, $P = N/(1 + Ae^{-Nkt})$; $N = 400\,000$; N is the limiting size of P.

20. $\dfrac{dh}{dt} = -\lambda$, $\pi h\dfrac{dh}{dt} = -(Ck + \pi\lambda h)$.

21. (i) $\dfrac{dQ}{dt} = -kQ$; $Q = Q_0 e^{-kt}$; $Q = 2\cdot5 \times 10^{-4}$,   (ii) $y = 3e^{5x} + e^{-5x}$.

22. $y = 2 - 4\sin 3x$; -2, $\tfrac{2}{3}n\pi + \tfrac{1}{18}\pi$, $\tfrac{2}{3}n\pi + \tfrac{5}{18}\pi$.

23. (i) $(y + 1)e^{-y} = (1 - x)e^x$,   (ii) $y = 4 - 2\sin 2x$; $\tfrac{1}{2}r\pi$, r an integer.

24. (i) $y = Ae^x/(1 + x)$,   (ii) $y = \tfrac{1}{2}(1 - \cos 2x - \sin 2x)$.

25. $y = \tfrac{1}{2} + A\cos(2x^2) + B\sin(2x^2)$; $y = -\tfrac{1}{2} + Ae^{2x^2} + Be^{-2x^2}$.

Exercise 25.1 (pp. 524–525)

1. (a) 1/7,   (b) 1/8,   (c) 21/13,   (d) 7/4,   (e) 15/8,   (f) 3/4.
2. (a) (5,0),   (b) (−2, −2),   (c) (2, −2),   (d) $(-\tfrac{1}{2}, 1\tfrac{1}{4})$.
3. (a) (12, −5),   (b) (6, −19),   (c) (−4, −1),   (d) $(7, -8\tfrac{1}{2})$.
4. (a) 1,   (b) 2,   (c) $\sqrt{2}$,   (d) $\sqrt{13}$,   (e) 9,   (f) $2\sqrt{10}$.
5. (a) 6,   (b) 24,   (c) 18,   (d) $11\tfrac{1}{2}$,   (e) 0,   (f) $36\tfrac{1}{2}$.
6. (a) $2x + y - 1 = 0$, $x - 2y - 2 = 0$.   (b) $x + y - 1 = 0$, $x - y - 1 = 0$.
    (c) $x = -\tfrac{1}{3}$, $y = \tfrac{1}{3}$.   (d) $2x - y + 4 = 0$, $x + 2y - 13 = 0$.
7. $45°, 45°, 90°$.   8. $45°, 26\cdot6°, 108\cdot4°$.   9. $(-3/7, 12/7)$.
10. $(5\tfrac{5}{18}, 3\tfrac{1}{2})$.   11. 3.   12. $31\cdot0°$.   13. (2, 3).
14. $(-\tfrac{1}{2}, -\tfrac{1}{2})$.   15. (i) (6, 7),   (ii) 16/15,   (iii) $8\sqrt{2}$,   (iv) 80.

Exercise 25.2 (pp. 527–528)

4. $x^2 + y^2 - 6x - 2y - 10 = 0$, $(5, 5)$; $x^2 + y^2 - 6x - 2y - 70 = 0$, $(-1, -7)$.

5. $(11/5, 13/5)$.

6. $x^2 + y^2 - 2x - 2y - 23 = 0$, $x^2 + y^2 - 18x - 14y + 105 = 0$, $4x + 3y = 32$,
$3x - 4y + 26 = 0$, $3x - 4y = 24$.

7. $x^2 + y^2 - 6x + 10y - 16 = 0$, $x^2 + y^2 + 12x - 14y - 40 = 0$;
$3x - 4y = 4, 10$

8. $4x - 3y = 3$.

9. $x^2 + y^2 - 6x + 4y - 12 = 0$; $x^2 + y^2 + 14x - 6y - 42 = 0$.

12. (a) $2x - 2y - 1 = 0$,   (b) $x^2 + y^2 - 2y - 1 = 0$.

13. (a) $x^2 + y^2 + x - 4y + 1 = 0$,   (b) $x^2 + y^2 - 3y = 0$,
(c) $x^2 + y^2 + 4x - 7y + 4 = 0$.

14. (a) $x^2 + y^2 + x - 4y - 9 = 0$,   (b) $5x^2 + 5y^2 + 23x - 29y = 0$,
(c) $2x^2 + 2y^2 - 7y - 23 = 0$.

15. $x + 1 = 0$, $x + 2\sqrt{6}y = 11 - 2\sqrt{6}$, $x - 2\sqrt{6}y = 11 + 2\sqrt{6}$.

Exercise 25.3 (pp. 532–534)

1. (a) $(3t^2, 6t)$,   (b) $(3t, 3/t)$,   (c) (t^2, t^3),   (d) $(5t/2, 5/2t)$,   (e) $(4t^2, 4t^3)$,
(f) $(5t^2/2, 5t)$.

2. (a) $(3\cos\theta, 2\sin\theta)$,   (b) $(3\cos\theta, 3\sin\theta)$,   (c) $(\sqrt{5}\cos\theta, \sin\theta)$,
(d) $(\cos\theta, \frac{2}{3}\sin\theta)$,   (e) $(\cos\theta, 3\sin\theta)$,   (f) $(5\cos\theta, 1 + 5\sin\theta)$.

3. $x + t^2y = 8t$; $ty = t^3x + 4 - 4t^4$.   4. $x + 4y = 4, 2y = 8x - 15$.

5. $x + 2\sqrt{3}y = 4$, $4\sqrt{3}x - 2y = 3\sqrt{3}$.

7. $4x + y = 4c$ at $(\frac{1}{2}c, 2c)$, $4x + y + 4c = 0$ at $(-\frac{1}{2}c, -2c)$.

9. $x = t, y = \dfrac{3}{2t} - \dfrac{3t^3}{2}$.

10. $x + pqy = a(p + q)$, $x + p^2y = 2ap$; $\left(\dfrac{2apq}{p + q}, \dfrac{2a}{p + q}\right)$.   14. $xy = 2c^2$.

15. $2y = 3tx - at^3$; $\dfrac{at^2}{4}, -\dfrac{at^3}{8}$; $t = 0$.

16. $(3\{p^2 + pq + q^2\}, \frac{9}{2}pq\{p + q\})$; $9y^2 = 12x - 16$.

18. $\dfrac{x^2}{a^2} + \dfrac{y^2}{b^2} = 2$.   19. $x\sin\theta + y = 2\tan\theta$; $x^2 - y^2 = 4$.

20. (a) $d^2 \sin^2\theta$,   (b) $-1, 3/2$.

Exercise 25.4 (pp. 538–539)

1. (a) $4/5$; $(\pm 4, 0)$; $x = \pm 25/4$,   (b) $3/5$; $(\pm 3/2, 0)$; $x = \pm 25/6$,
(c) $\frac{1}{2}\sqrt{3}$; $(\pm\sqrt{3}, 0)$; $x = \pm(4\sqrt{3})/3$,   (d) $2/3$; $(\pm 2, 0)$; $x = \pm 9/2$,
(e) $\frac{1}{3}\sqrt{5}$; $(0, \pm\sqrt{5})$; $y = \pm(9\sqrt{5})/5$,   (f) $\frac{1}{2}\sqrt{3}$; $(0, \pm\frac{1}{2}\sqrt{3})$; $y = \pm\frac{2}{3}\sqrt{3}$.

2. (a) $5/4; (\pm 5, 0); x = \pm 16/5; y = \pm\frac{3}{4}x$, (b) $\sqrt{2}; (\pm 2\sqrt{2}, 0); x = \pm\sqrt{2}; y = \pm x$,
    (c) $\frac{1}{2}\sqrt{5}; (\pm\sqrt{5}, 0); x = \pm 4/\sqrt{5}; y = \pm\frac{1}{2}x$.

3. (a) $\frac{1}{2}\sqrt{3}$, (b) $4/5$, (c) $\frac{1}{3}\sqrt{5}$, (d) $4/5$.

4. (a) $\dfrac{x^2}{16} + \dfrac{y^2}{12} = 1$, (b) $\dfrac{x^2}{225} + \dfrac{y^2}{144} = 1$.

5. $5x^2 + 9y^2 - 40x - 18y + 44 = 0$.

6. (a) $x = 3, y = 0$,   (b) $2y = x + 4, 2x + y + 3 = 0$,
    (c) $9x + 4y = 20, 8x - 18y = 7$,   (d) $2x + y + 12 = 0, 2y = x + 1$.

7. (a) $4xx_1 + 9yy_1 = 36$, (b) $\dfrac{xx_1}{a^2} + \dfrac{yy_1}{b^2} = 1$, (c) $\dfrac{xx_1}{3} - \dfrac{yy_1}{2} = 1$.

8. $2xy + 2kx + 2ky = 7k^2$.

11. (i) $2ax - 2by = a^2 - b^2$; (ii) $(0, -b), \left(\dfrac{3\sqrt{3}}{5}b, \dfrac{4}{5}b\right)$.

12. $a^2 = 2c^2$.

Exercise 25.5 (pp. 540–543)

1. 7.
2. $x - 2y + 9 = 0, x + 3y = 16y; x^2 + y^2 - 2x - 10y + 1 = 0$,
    $x^2 + y^2 - 7x - 144 = 0$.
3. $\frac{1}{5}|a + 4|; a = 1, 3x + 4y = 7$.
4. $(5, 5), \sqrt{10}; 3m^2 - 10m + 3 = 0; y = \frac{1}{3}x, y = 3x$;
    (i) $53\cdot1°$, (ii) $x^2 + y^2 + 2x - 14y + 40 = 0$
5. $2x + y + 4 = 0, (2, -8), (-4, 4); 108$.   6. $2, 5; 3/10, \pm2/5$.
7. $(0, 8), 4\sqrt{2}; (9, -1), 5\sqrt{2}; (4, 4); 167°$.   8. $-1, 5; 3/4; 0, -8/9$.
9. (i) $3x - 4y = 9$, (ii) $(-1, -3), (\frac{23}{25}, -\frac{39}{25}), 2x^2 + 2y^2 + x + 8y + 5 = 0$.

10. $(8, 2); 16/3$.   12. $\left(ct + \dfrac{c}{t}, ct + \dfrac{c}{t}\right)$.   13. $-4c^2/a^2; 1/2; 2:3$.

14. $\left(\dfrac{8}{9}, \dfrac{16\sqrt{2}}{27}\right), \left(\dfrac{2}{9}, -\dfrac{2\sqrt{2}}{27}\right)$.   15. $8\frac{2}{3}$.

16. $x\cos t + y\sin t = 2\sin t\cos t; 3\pi/8$.
17. (a) $ay + bx = ab\sqrt{2}$, (b) $(ax - by)\sqrt{2} = a^2 - b^2; \frac{1}{4}\pi ab, \pi ab$.
18. $0°, 60°; (2, 0), (1, 3/2)$.

19. $bx\sec\theta + ay\cosec\theta = ab; \dfrac{x^2}{a^2} + \dfrac{y^2}{b^2} = \left(\dfrac{ab}{a^2 - b^2}\right)^2$.

20. $t_1t_2 + t_2t_3 + t_3t_1 = 0; -2t$.

Exercise 26.1 (pp. 546–548)

1. (a) $5i$ (b) $i\sqrt{5}$,   (c) $3 - 4i$,   (d) $2 - 3\sqrt{2}i$.
2. (a) ± 2,   (b) $\pm 2i$,   (c) $\pm i\sqrt{2}$,   (d) $\pm\frac{3}{2}i$,   (e) 0, $\pm i\sqrt{3}$,   (f) ± 1, $\pm i$.
3. (a) $1 \pm i$,   (b) $3 \pm i$,   (c) $2 \pm 3i$,   (d) $\frac{1}{2} \pm i$,   (e) $\frac{1}{4}(-3 \pm i\sqrt{7})$,   (f) $\frac{1}{2}(1 \pm i\sqrt{3})$.
4. (a) $3 - 5i$,   (b) $4 + 7i$,   (c) $-3i$,   (d) -4,   (e) $-1 - i$.
5. (a) $7 + 9i, 3 + 7i$,   (b) $3 - i, 1 + 7i$,   (c) $8 - 4i, -2 + 2i$,
    (d) $2 + 7i, -4 - 3i$.
6. (a) $3 + 11i$,   (b) $7 - 9i$,   (c) $4 - 7i$,   (d) 25,   (e) $-21 - 20i$,   (f) $-2 - 2i$
7. (a) $-i$,   (b) i,   (c) 1 (d) -1,   (e) $-i$,   (f) i.

8. (a) $-1 + 2i$,   (b) $\frac{1}{5} + \frac{3}{5}i$,   (c) $\frac{5}{2} + \frac{1}{2}i$,   (d) $\frac{1}{2} - \dfrac{\sqrt{3}}{2}i$,   (e) $-\frac{1}{2}i$,   (f) $\frac{4}{25} - \frac{3}{25}i$.

9. (a) $\frac{4}{13}$,   (b) $\frac{7}{25} + \frac{1}{25}i$,   (c) 6.
10. (a) $a = -1, b = 1$,   (b) $a = 2, b = \frac{1}{2}$.
11. (a) $\pm(2 - i)$,   (b) $\pm(1 + i)$,   (c) $\pm(3 + i)$,   (d) $\pm(5 - 2i)$.
12. (a) $-4, 5$,   (b) $2, 10$,   (c) $0, 16$,   (d) $-6, 34$.
13. (a) $(x + i)(x - i)$,   (b) $(x + 5i)(x - 5i)$,
    (c) $(3x + 2i)(3x - 2i)$,   (d) $(x + 1 + 2i)(x + 1 - 2i)$,
    (e) $(x + 3 + 2i)(x + 3 - 2i)$,   (f) $(2x - 3 + 4i)(2x - 3 - 4i)$.
14. $0, 0; 1, 0; -\frac{1}{2}, \frac{1}{2}\sqrt{3}; -\frac{1}{2}, -\frac{1}{2}\sqrt{3}$.   15. $x = 4, y = -3$.
16. $2 - i, 2 + 3i$.   17. $32 + 47i, 32 - 47i; 53, 61$.
18. $-5 - 4i, 1 + 7i; -3, -1$.
19. (a) $0, \pm 1$,   (b) $\pm(1 + \sqrt{2}), \pm(1 - \sqrt{2})$.   20. $\pm(3 + 2i), 2 + 4i, -1 + 2i$.

Exercise 26.2 (pp. 550–552)

5. -2.   6. $3 - i, -3$.   7. $1 - i, -2; 4$.   8. $2 + 3i, -1; -3, 9$.

9. $-i, \frac{1}{2}(-1 \pm \sqrt{5})$.   10. $-1 - i, 2 \pm i$.   11. $-\frac{1}{2} \pm \dfrac{\sqrt{3}}{2}i$.

12. $\alpha, \alpha\omega, \alpha\omega^2$; (a) $3, -\frac{3}{2} \pm \dfrac{3\sqrt{3}}{2}i$,   (b) $-2, 1 \pm i\sqrt{3}$,

    (c) $-i, \dfrac{\sqrt{3}}{2} + \frac{1}{2}, -\dfrac{\sqrt{3}}{2} + \frac{1}{2}i$.

13. (a) $2, -1 \pm i\sqrt{3}$,   (b) $-1, \frac{1}{2} \pm i\dfrac{\sqrt{3}}{2}$,   (c) $0, -\frac{3}{2} \pm i\dfrac{\sqrt{3}}{2}$.

14. (a) 0,   (b) -1,   (c) -1.   15. (a) $-\omega$,   (b) $1 - \omega$,   (c) $\omega - 1$.
16. $a^3 + b^3 + c^3 - 3abc$.   17. $9z^3 - 12z^2 + 6z - 1$.   18. $-1, -1$.

Exercise 26.3 (pp. 555–556)

1. (a) $3 + 2i$,   (b) $-2 + 4i$,   (c) $5i$,   (d) $1 - 2i$,   (e) -2.

2.   (a) 5,   (b) $\sqrt{29}$,   (c) 3,   (d) $\sqrt{2}$,   (e) 4.
3. $-2 - i, 2 - i, -2 + i, -1 + 2i, 1 - 2i.$ 4. $2i, -2 + 2i, \frac{1}{2} - \frac{1}{2}i.$
5. $6 + 8i, i.$ 6.   (a) $\pm i$,   (b) $\pm(1 - i)$,   (c) $\pm(2 + i)$,   (d) $\pm(4 + i)$.
8.   (a) $k(1 + 2i), k \geqslant 0$,   (b) $k(1 + 2i), -1 \leqslant k \leqslant 0$,   (c) $k(1 + 2i), k \leqslant -1$.

10.   (a) 5,   (b) $\sqrt{85}$,   (c) $\sqrt{13}$.   12. $\frac{4}{3} + \frac{2\sqrt{2}}{3}i, \frac{2}{3} + \frac{4\sqrt{2}}{3}i.$

Exercise 26.4 (pp. 561–562)

1.   (a) 2, $\pi/6$,   (b) $\sqrt{2}, -\pi/4$,   (c) 4, $\pi/2$,   (d) 3, π.
2.   (a) 5, -0.927,   (b) $\sqrt{5}, 2.678$,   (c) $\sqrt{10}, -1.893$,   (d) $\sqrt{34}, -0.540$.
3.   (a) 5, $\pi/6$,   (b) $1/2, -\pi/3$,   (c) $1/\sqrt{2}, \pi/4$,   (d) $\sqrt{2}, 3\pi/4$.
4.   (a) 5, $\pi/3$,   (b) 1, $-\pi/2$,   (c) 1, $-2\pi/3$,   (d) 2, $-3\pi/4$.
5.   (a) $2\sqrt{3}\{\cos(-\pi/3) + i\sin(-\pi/3)\}$,   (b) $8\{\cos 0 + i\sin 0\}$,
     (c) $2\sqrt{2}\{\cos(-3\pi/4) + i\sin(-3\pi/4)\}$,   (d) $1\{\cos(-\pi/2) + i\sin(-\pi/2)\}$
6.   (a) $r, \theta - \pi$,   (b) $r, \theta + \frac{1}{2}\pi$,   (c) $r^2, 2\theta$,   (d) 1, 2θ.

7.   (a) -1,   (b) $-\dfrac{\sqrt{3}}{2} + \frac{1}{2}i$,   (c) $-\dfrac{1}{\sqrt{2}} - \dfrac{1}{\sqrt{2}}i$,   (d) $-\frac{1}{2} + \dfrac{\sqrt{3}}{2}i$,

     (e) $-i$,   (f) $\frac{1}{2} + \dfrac{\sqrt{3}}{2}i$.

8.   (a) 10, $\pi/2$; 2, $\pi/3$; 20, $5\pi/6$; 5, $\pi/6$,
     (b) 4, $5\pi/6$; $\sqrt{2}, -\pi/4$; $4\sqrt{2}, 7\pi/12$; $2\sqrt{2}, -11\pi/12$.
9. $\sec\theta, \theta$.
10. $2\sin\frac{1}{2}\theta, \frac{1}{2}(\theta - \pi)$; $2\sin\frac{1}{2}\theta, \frac{1}{2}(\theta + \pi)$; $\frac{1}{2}\csc\frac{1}{2}\theta, \frac{1}{2}(\pi - \theta)$; $\frac{1}{2}\csc\frac{1}{2}\theta, \frac{1}{2}(\theta - \pi)$.
11.   2, $\pi/3$; 2, $\pi/2$.   12. $\pm\pi/2$.
13.   (a) $\frac{1}{13} + \frac{5}{13}i, 1.37; 2.75, \frac{1}{13}$,   (b) $|z|^2 : 1$.

Exercise 26.5 (pp. 568–570)

12. $x^2 + y^2 + 4x = 0$.   13. $x^2 + y^2 - 9x - y + 16 = 0$.   14. $x = 2$.
15. $5x + 3y = 14$.   16. $2x^2 + 2y^2 + 25x + 75 = 0$.
17. $5x^2 + 5y^2 - 26x + 8y + 1 = 0$.   18. $x^2 + y^2 = 25$, excluding $(-5, 0)$.
19. $x^2 + y^2 - 2x + 2y = 0$, excluding $(2, 0)$.   20. $5x - 2y + 6 = 0$.
21. $xy = 1$.   22. $x^2 - y^2 = 1$.   23. $x(x^2 + y^2 - 1) = 0$, excluding $(0, 0)$.
24. $y(x^2 + y^2 - 9) = 0$, excluding $(0, 0)$.   36.   (a) 9,   (b) 3,   (c) 3,   (d) 4.
37. $5\sqrt{2} + 3, 5\sqrt{2} - 3$.   38.   24, 2.   39. $x^2 + y^2 + 10x + 16 = 0$.
40.   (i) $1 \pm i\sqrt{5}$,   (ii) $1 + i$.

Exercise 26.6 (pp. 573–574)

1.   (a) 1,   (b) $-i$,   (c) $\frac{1}{2} - \dfrac{\sqrt{3}}{2}i$,   (d) $-\frac{1}{2} + \dfrac{\sqrt{3}}{2}i$.

2. $2\left(\cos\dfrac{\pi}{6} + i\sin\dfrac{\pi}{6}\right)$; $512 - 512\sqrt{3}i$, $-\dfrac{\sqrt{3}}{256} + \dfrac{1}{256}i$.

3. $\sqrt{2}\left(\cos\dfrac{3\pi}{4} + i\sin\dfrac{3\pi}{4}\right)$; 256, $-\frac{1}{8}i$.   4.   (a) 1,   (b) -1.

5. $4\cos^3\theta - 3\cos\theta$, $3\sin\theta - 4\sin^3\theta$, $\dfrac{3\tan\theta - \tan^3\theta}{1 - 3\tan^2\theta}$.

6. $16\sin^5\theta - 20\sin^3\theta + 5\sin\theta$, $1 - 12\sin^2\theta + 16\sin^4\theta$.
8. $32\cos^6\theta - 48\cos^4\theta + 18\cos^2\theta - 1$, $32\cos^5\theta - 32\cos^3\theta + 6\cos\theta$,

$$\dfrac{6\tan\theta - 20\tan^3\theta + 6\tan^5\theta}{1 - 15\tan^2\theta + 15\tan^4\theta - \tan^6\theta}.$$

9.   (a) $\frac{1}{16}(\cos 5\theta + 5\cos 3\theta + 10\cos\theta)$,
     (b) $\frac{1}{64}(\cos 7\theta + 7\cos 5\theta + 21\cos 3\theta + 35\cos\theta)$,
     (c) $\frac{1}{16}(2\cos\theta - \cos 3\theta - \cos 5\theta)$.
10. (a) $\frac{1}{4}(3\sin\theta - \sin 3\theta)$,   (b) $\frac{1}{64}(35\sin\theta - 21\sin 3\theta + 7\sin 5\theta - \sin 7\theta)$,
     (c) $\frac{1}{64}(3\sin\theta + 3\sin 3\theta - \sin 5\theta - \sin 7\theta)$.
12. (a) $3\pi/8$,   (b) $\pi/32$.

Exercise 26.7 (pp. 574–579)

1. $\dfrac{x}{x^2 + y^2} - \dfrac{y}{x^2 + y^2}i$.   2. $3, 1; -3, -1$.   3. $1 + 2i; 5\sqrt{2}; -2, -1$.

4.   (i) $\pm(1 - 3i)$,   (ii) $2 - 2i$, $1 + i$.
5.   Sum of squares of diagonals of a parallelogram = sum of squares of sides.

6. $\pm 1, \pm i, \pm\dfrac{1}{\sqrt{2}}(1 - i)$, $-\dfrac{1}{\sqrt{2}}(1 + i)$.

7.   (i) $-1 + i\sqrt{3}, 2, 2\pi/3; \dfrac{\sqrt{3}}{2} + \frac{1}{2}i, 1, \pi/6$,

     (ii) $1 \pm 2i$; (a) $p^2 = q - 4$, (b) $2p = q + 5$.
8.   (a) $-3\sqrt{3} + 5i; 2\sqrt{13}, 2\cdot 38$ rad,   (b) $5, -20$.
9.   (i) $-1 - i, 3\pi/4$,   (ii) $2 - i, 2; -10$.

10. (b) $-1, \frac{1}{2} \pm \dfrac{\sqrt{3}}{2}i$,   (c) $-1 - 3i, \frac{1}{2}(1 - 3\sqrt{3}) + \frac{1}{2}(3 + \sqrt{3})i$,

     $\frac{1}{2}(1 + 3\sqrt{3}) + \frac{1}{2}(3 - \sqrt{3})i$.

11. $-\frac{1}{2} \pm \dfrac{\sqrt{3}}{2}i; 1 \pm i\sqrt{3}, \frac{5}{2} \pm \dfrac{\sqrt{3}}{2}i; 28$.

12. (ii) $x^3 - 3abx + a^3 + b^3$; $-\sqrt[3]{2} - \sqrt[3]{4}, -\omega\sqrt[3]{2} - \omega^2\sqrt[3]{4}, -\omega^2\sqrt[3]{2} - \omega\sqrt[3]{4}$.
13. (i) $\pm(3 - 2i)$,   (ii) $3 \pm i\sqrt{3}$.   14. (i) (a) $7/5, -4/5$;   (b) $2 \pm i$.
15. (i) $1 - i, -1 \pm 2i$,   (ii) $\frac{1}{2}(3 + i\sqrt{3}); \pi/6, 2\pi/3$.

16. (i) 2, 32; $\pi/3$, $-\pi/3$; $-16\sqrt{3}$, (ii) $2 + 3i$.   17. (i) -1, (ii) $1 + 2i$, $2\sqrt{5}$.
18. (i) $\sqrt{2}$, $-\pi/4$; $\frac{1}{2} + \frac{1}{2}i$, $8i$.   20. (i) $2 - i$, $3 - 4i$; $(2, -1)$.
21. (ii) $3x^2 + 3y^2 + 10x + 3 = 0$.   22. (i) $x = 1$, $y = 2$ or $x = -1$, $y = -2$.
23. (i) (a) 13, $-23°$, (b) 1, $90°$;   (ii) 12;   (iii) $|z + 1 + i| \geqslant 4$.
24. $2\sin\theta$; $\frac{1}{2}\operatorname{cosec}\theta$, $-\theta$; $y = -\frac{1}{2}$.   25. $2\sqrt{2} - 2$.

26. $2\cos\frac{1}{2}\theta$, $\frac{1}{2}\theta$; $\left[2\cos\left(\dfrac{\theta}{2}\right)\right]^n\cos\left(\dfrac{n\theta}{2}\right) + i\left[2\cos\left(\dfrac{\theta}{2}\right)\right]^n\sin\left(\dfrac{n\theta}{2}\right)$.

Index